Pitt Series in Nature and Natural History

Marcia Bonta, Editor

Publication Chairman
Winston J. Wayne
Delmarva Ornithological Society

Editorial Consultant
Howard P. Brokaw
Delmarva Ornithological Society

Technical Editor
Stephen J. Stedman
Tennessee Technological University

Art Consultant
Nancy C. Willis

Graphics Consultant
Martha B. W. Olson

Scientific Reader
Chandler S. Robbins
U.S. Geological Survey, Biological Resources Division

Sponsoring Organizations
Delmarva Ornithological Society
Delaware Museum of Natural History
Delaware Nature Society
Department of Natural Resources and Environmental Control

Birds of Delaware

Gene K. Hess

Delaware Museum of Natural History

Richard L. West

Delaware Museum of Natural History

Maurice V. Barnhill III

Department of Physics and Astronomy
University of Delaware

Lorraine M. Fleming

Delaware Nature Society

University of Pittsburgh Press

Published by the University of Pittsburgh Press, Pittsburgh, Pa. 15261

Copyright © 2000, Delmarva Ornithological Society

Manufactured in the United States of America

Printed on acid-free paper

10 9 8 7 6 5 4 3 2 1

Library of Congress Cataloging-in-Publication Data

Birds of Delaware / Gene K. Hess . . . [et al.].

p.   cm. — (Pitt series in nature and natural history)

Includes bibliographical references (p.) and index.

ISBN 0-8229-4069-8 (alk paper)

1. Birds—Delaware. I. Hess, Gene K., 1955– . II. Series.

QL684.D3B57   1999

598'.09751—dc21   97-51395

CIP

A CIP catalog record for this book is available from the British Library.

Contents

List of Figures, Maps, and Tables   vii

Foreword   ix
   Howard P. Brokaw

Acknowledgments   xi

List of Abbreviations   xvii

Chapter 1. Delaware Habitats   3

Geology and Landforms   3

Soils   3

Climate   4

Wetlands   5

Aquatic Environments   7

The Delaware Estuary and Inland Bays   7

Beach and Duneland   8

Forests   8

Agricultural Land   11

Chapter 2. Conservation of Delaware Birds   12

Declining Species   12

Extirpated Breeding Species   12

Rare and Threatened Breeding Species   12

Other Species with Low Breeding Populations   12

Breeding Species of Management Concern   12

Other Declining Breeding Species   13

Migrants and Winter Visitors of Management Concern   13

Increasing Species   13

Habitat Degradation and Loss   14

The Future of Bird Conservation in Delaware   19

Chapter 3. Early Bird Records and the Growth of Ornithology in Delaware   21
   Gregory A. Inskip

The Earliest Records   21

The Eighteenth Century   22

Progress Toward Systematic Ornithology in Delaware   23

The Twentieth Century   24

Essay: History of Breeding Bird Atlases   26
   Chandler S. Robbins

Chapter 4. Introduction to the Delaware Breeding Bird Atlas   27

Objectives   27

Atlas Organization   27

Methods   27

Relative Abundance Study   32

Atlas Results   32

Changes in Delaware Breeding Avifauna   35

Chapter 5. Introduction to the Species Accounts   37

The State List   37

Nomenclature and Arrangement   37

Sources   37

Definitions of Terms   41

Species Accounts   44

Essay: Pelagic Birding   52
   Maurice V. Barnhill III

Essay: Pea Patch Island: A Siege of Herons (and Egrets and Ibises)   69
   Charles R. Vickers

Essay: Snow Geese   99
   Winston J. Wayne

Essay: Canada Goose Management   105
   Norman G. Wilder

Essay: Delaware's Coastal Impoundments and Their Birds   133
   William H. Meredith

Essay: Hawk Migration in Delaware: Timing, Magnitude, and Ecology   162
   Robert W. Russell

Essay: Birds and the Law   185
   H. Lloyd Alexander

Essay: Spring Shorebirds on Delaware Bay   233
   Howard P. Brokaw

Essay: Forest Fragmentation and Forest Birds   431
   Roland R. Roth

Essay: Blackbird Roosts in Delaware   523
   John T. Linehan

Essay: Irruptive Northern Visitors to Delaware   543
   Gregory A. Inskip

Appendices

A. Common and Scientific Names of Animals and Plants   563

B. The Breeding Bird Atlas and Relative Abundance Study Grid   565

C. Relative Abundance Study   566

D. Breeding Dates and Clutch Sizes   567

E. Breeding Bird Survey   569

F. Breeding Bird Census   570

G. May Counts (Delaware Spring Roundup)   571

H. Christmas Bird Counts   573

I. Trend Analysis of Delaware Bird Populations   574

J. Estimates of State Populations of Breeding Birds
    Richard L. West   579

Observers and Sources   583

Literature Cited   603

Sources of Illustrations   630

Addendum   630

Index   631

List of Figures, Maps, and Tables

Figures

Figure 4.1 Portion of Field Card 31

Figure 4.2 Progress of the Atlas Project 32

Figure 5.1 Delaware Bird-banding Records in U.S. Fish and Wildlife Service Computer Files (except Starlings and Blackbirds) 38

Figure 5.2 Seasonal Bar Graph Key 41

Figure G.1 Effective Effort and Party-Hours 571

Figure G.2 Eastern Wood-Pewee, Annual Trend 571

Figure G.3 Eastern Wood-Pewee, May Trend 572

Figure G.4 Carolina Wren Populations by Three Methods 572

Figure G.5 House Sparrow Trends by Three Methods 572

Maps

Map 1.1 Generalized Geological Map of Delaware 3

Map 1.2 Delaware General Soil Map 4

Map 1.3 Delaware Major Wetland Complexes and Deepwater Habitats 5

Map 1.4 Delaware General Forest Cover Types 9

Map 4.1 U.S. Geological Survey Quadrangle Names 28

Map 4.2 Delaware Road Maps:
(a) New Castle County, (b) Kent County,
(c) Sussex County 29

Map 4.3 Species Richness: Atlas Blocks 33

Map 4.4 Species Richness: Atlas Quadrangles 33

Map 4.5 Relative Species Richness: Relative Abundance Study Blocks 34

Map 4.6 Relative Species Richness: Relative Abundance Study Quadrangles 34

Map 5.1 Breeding Bird Survey Regions 39

Map B.1 Portions of Delaware Not Separately Reported in the Atlas Project or the Relative Abundance Study 565

Tables

Table 1.1 Delaware Timberland Forest Groups and Types 9

Table 4.1 Breeding Evidence Criteria 28

Table 4.2 Widely Reported Breeding Species 32

Table 5.1 Delmarva Ornithological Society Weekly Surveys 40

Table A.1 Names of Animals 563

Table A.2 Names of Plants 563

Table B.1 Portions of Eastern Delaware Not Separately Reported in the Breeding Bird Atlas Project 563

Table B.2 Atlas Blocks Not Separately Reported in the Relative Abundance Study 563

Table F.1 List of Delaware Breeding Bird Census Sites 570

Table G.1 Species Selected for Indexing 571

Table I.1 Avian Population Trends in Delaware, 1966–91 574

Table J.1 Delaware Breeding Species, 1983–87, and Their Estimated Populations 579

Unnumbered figures, maps, and tables also appear in individual essays.

Foreword

There is probably no better way to gain a sense of Delaware's outdoor riches than by birding its forests and fields, its marshes and shores. This state is a wonderful place for birds, and the pursuit of them will ultimately and inexorably carry the local adventurer into all the state's special terrains at all seasons of the year.

Although Delaware is small in area, it is large in birdlife. Migrants from the Neotropics pass through in the spring, some stopping here to breed; northern breeders come by in the fall, some staying for the winter; our loyal full-time residents are, of course, with us throughout the year; and occasionally there are the exciting appearances of accidental species from the American West, from the Canadian far north, and even from Europe.

But set aside for a moment the fascination of dedicated birders with their avocation. Birds are of interest to thousands of others in the state—people with backyards, with feeders, and with bird houses, and visitors to the countryside, the state parks, the wildlife refuges, and the beaches and bays. Birds are also important to all of those who understand that birds serve as a critical indicator of environmental health.

This book began as simply a report of the five-year Breeding Bird Atlas Project conducted throughout the state from 1983 through 1987. The committee formed to plan the publication soon realized, however, that here was an opportunity for a more comprehensive work, and that an expanded scope would be feasible for a state as small as ours. The committee decided to produce an account of not just breeders but of all occurrences of bird species in Delaware. In fact, the authors have reached back into the early colonial period to bring forward obscure and hitherto unpublished information on changes in Delaware birds.

Anyone interested in Delaware birds should enjoy this book. It is, primarily, a reference work, not for the identification of our birds, but for their numbers and frequency, for their breeding and seasonality, for their population trends, for their habitats, for maps of their distribution, and for graphs of their past history. And, beyond Delaware, it is an essential reference for anyone doing population studies on bird species in the Mid-Atlantic region. But there is reading of a casual kind as well—essays on bird topics of special interest for Delaware, chapters on the state's natural features, and discussions of ornithological history and of conservation.

This book should also be a valuable resource for wildlife managers and land managers. It defines, quantitatively and geographically, just where we stand today, thus supplying a scientifically valid base against which to measure change and evaluate future plans and results. And because birds can legitimately serve not only as a useful and easily detectable tool for measuring the natural environment and its health, but also as an understandable and sympathetic symbol for nature, the results of these measurements can have implications for conservation that go far beyond the birds themselves.

The *Birds of Delaware* is a monument to voluntarism. The work of preparation was financed by contributions from individuals and by the four sponsoring organizations—Delmarva Ornithological Society, Delaware Nature Society, Delaware Museum of Natural History, and Delaware Department of Natural Resources and Environmental Control. It evolved from the dedication of the four authors and of many other people—all of whom worked for the love of it—putting in thousands of hours of fieldwork and thousands of hours with pen and computer.

I hope this book will persuade you, if you are not already a birder, to give that avocation a try. If you do try, you just might become converted—and then you, too, will experience the joys and intellectual challenges of birding.

Howard P. Brokaw

Acknowledgments

The authors acknowledge with deep appreciation the hundreds of individuals who contributed in some way to *Birds of Delaware*—to the information it contains and to its production.

The *Birds of Delaware* Publication Committee deserves special commendation for providing constant guidance and encouragement from 1984 through publication. Those who have served over the years are: Chairman Winston J. Wayne, Howard P. Brokaw, Barbara H. Butler, Lloyd L. Falk, Lorraine M. Fleming, Lisa Gelvin-Innvaer, Gene K. Hess, David M. Niles, Michael E. Riska, Janis Thomas, Richard L. West, and Norman G. Wilder. Equally important in bringing the project to fruition were the efforts of the Fund Development Group: Howard P. Brokaw, Lorraine M. Fleming, Joan Priest, Michael E. Riska, Winston J. Wayne, Richard L. West, and Norman G. Wilder.

The manuscript could not have been completed without the interest and generosity of the contributors to the *Birds of Delaware* Publication Fund.

Benefactors

Mrs. Lammot duPont Copeland
Delaware Department of Natural Resources and
    Environmental Control
Crawford H. Greenewalt

Patrons

David A. Cutler
Donald G. Hunton
National Audubon Society
AstraZeneca, formerly ICI Americas, Inc.

Donors

Howard P. and Mary T. Brokaw
Mrs. Henry B. duPont
Alan B. and Yvonne Palmer
Winston J. Wayne

Sponsors

Peter H. and Karen Flint
Sheila S. Foster
Rick and Shirley B. Rickenbaugh
Richard L. West
Barbara A. Wolf

Supporters

Maurice V. Barnhill III
Dorcas W. Beatty

Doris J. Boller
Barbara H. Butler
Charles A. Butler
Judith W. Charles
Herbert S. and Elizabeth Cutler
Mrs. Robert N. Downs
Maurice L. Ernsberger
Richard A. and Lorraine M. Fleming
Robert B. and Lucile Flint
William H., Jr., and Nancy G. Frederick
Karin Grosz
Gene K. Hess
Wayne E. Johnson
Lois Ann Kinckiner
Brian R. Marshall
Ruth L. Miller
Joyce Clark Newman
Edith duPont Pearson
John A. Pié
Carroll F. and Lynn Poole
J. Grier Ralston, Jr.
Chandler S. Robbins
Robert G. Rufe
Charles E. Sample
Edward P. Strickland
Tri-State Bird Rescue and Research, Inc.
Anthony W. White
Norman G. Wilder
Flora D. Woessner
Joan W. Zerbe

Contributors

Edward L. Altemus
Mervil A. Anthony
Donald R. Baer
Edwin and Elsie Bailey
H. Franklin Baker
David N. Ball
Douglas G. and Karen Batt
Donald G. Bayard
Paul E. and Susan Beach
Max S. Bell, Jr.
C. Eugene Bennett
Herbert and Yvonne Blades
Gov. and Mrs. J. Caleb Boggs
Dorothy Borcherdt
James P. Brennan
William A. Brokaw

Robert F. Brown
Armistead Browning
Frank C. Buhl
Henry T. Bush, Jr.
Agnes A. Cadot
Mrs. A. Leslie Calloway
Judge and Mrs. Andrew T. Christie
Joel D. Citron
Albert E. and June Conway
Edward E. Crawford
Barbara L. Davison
Sally D. Decker
Alvan Donnan
Paul G. DuMont
Elizabeth Dyer
Fred W. and Sandra Eckfeldt
Andrew P. Ednie
Katherine L. Esterly
Lloyd L. Falk
Beverly W. Finch
Ronald M. Finch
Louis J. Finger
William A. Fintel
John and Lynne Frink
Clarence W. Gault
Douglas M. Gay
Lila M. Gierasch
Frank B. Gill
Garry G. Greenstein
Helen V. Griffith
Joseph E. III and Margaret M. Hagan
Frances L. Hamilton
George S. Harrington
Paul N. Harris
Julian W. Hill
Harry and Eilene C. Hurst
Cynthia K. Hoagland
H. Gilbert and Elizabeth Ingersoll
Gregory A. and Betty Inskip
Robert C. Irons
Ruth E. Jardine
Naomi L. Jefferson
Curtis O. Johnson
Thomas W. Keesee, Jr.
Philip K. Klabunde
Richard N. Knowles
Philip B. Kraus
Robert W. and Juanita Krebs
Bertha V. Lasher
Greta B. Layton
Jay G. and Christine Lehman

Beatrice B. Linton
Meta C. Little
June D. MacArtor
Elizabeth Madeira
Victor J. Mankin
Carl S. Marvel
Albert S. Matlack
Henry Matthews
Lucien G. and Jean Maury
Margaret V. McCann
Sallie C. McCoy
Ellice, Jr., and Rosa McDonald
Blaine C. McKusick
Rita L. McWhorter
James K. Meritt
Edgar R. Miller, Jr.
Dorothy P. Miller
John C. Miller
Walter E. Mochel
F. M. Mooberry
John H. Moorhouse
Gerda B. Mortenson
Huldah J. B. Moss
Joan B. Nacman
David M. Niles
Rudolph and Virginia R. Nyhoff
George F. O'Shea
Joseph L. and Dorothy T. Parker
E. Kathryn Pennypacker
Barbara M. Peoples
Roger Tory Peterson
James F. and Jean Pfeffer
Bruce S. and Lydia Phalen
William Poole
Theodore H. and Dorothy S. Projector
Thalia C. Putney
Dennis C. Quinn
Maynard S. Raasch
Michael E. Riska
Eldon M. Robinson
Charles S. and Doris M. Ross
Mrs. Donald P. Ross
William D. and Sophie E. Ross
Roland R. Roth
Mary West Ryon
Charles A. and Susan Salkin
Jane H. Scott
Phoebe G. Sipple
Gwynne P. Smith
Evan C. and Diane Speck
Stanley B. and Esther Speck

Martha F. Steel

Halsey B. Stevenson

William G. Stoopes, Jr.

Richard and Dale H. Stratton

Joe Swertinski

Robert W. Thomen

Philip J. Vanderhorst

Philip M. Walters

John and Mary H. Watkins

Karl H. Weber

David T. Weesner

Anita Edge Weisbrod

Franklin H. West

Martha Whitcraft

Gerald M. Whitman

Claudia P. Wilds

J. Robert and Ruth W. Woodward

Karen Zeitler

M. Ralph Browning (USNM); Greg Butcher, Cornell University; Lloyd Kiff (WFVZ); Mary Le Croy (AMNH); Kenneth C. Parkes, Carnegie Museum; James Van Remsen (LSU); Mark Robbins, Academy of Natural Sciences of Philadelphia; Roland Roth, University of Delaware; and Chris Wood (UWBM) made their collections available to the authors and provided information from collections in their care.

Connie Alexander, Don Baer, Jody Baker, Doris Boller, Francis Cramer, Louise Hastings, Bud Holden, Elizabeth Hulbert, Janet Jewett, Harry Keller, Carolyn Ostapchenko, Roy Pierson, Carroll Poole, Elizabeth Roszel, and Harry West gave invaluable assistance in manuscript preparation. Yvonne Blades, Richard Fleming, Suzanne Quinn, and Winston Wayne worked with citations. Yvonne Blades compiled U.S. Fish and Wildlife Service waterfowl banding data, drafted the banding and recovery maps, and assisted the project in several other ways. Michael McGrath provided strong initial direction in digitizing atlas maps. Lloyd L. Falk performed literature searches; Darwin Palmer shared Lattinoken Club newsletters; Walter J. Angulo, Fran James, and John Sauer provided statistical support; C. M. West gave computer support; George Reynard provided a recording of a young Barn Owl; and Ellen Kusik, Lloyd Simmons of the Delaware Forest Service, and DNREC provided temporary living quarters that greatly aided completion of the Atlas project. L. Ellen Rendle and Constance J. Cooper of the Historical Society of Delaware were helpful in tracing Delaware's ornithological history.

Important information and essential data were obtained through the outstanding cooperation of Chandler S. Robbins, Danny Bystrak, Sam Droege, and Bruce Peterjohn of the U.S. Fish and Wildlife Service Patuxent Research Center and the Breeding Bird Atlas Project coordinators in nearby states: Eirik A.T. Blom, Maryland; Dan Brauning, Pennsylvania; Dorothy Hughes, New Jersey; and Sue Ridd, Virginia. The Natural History Society of Delaware contributed archival manuscript material.

For their contribution of valuable data for the species accounts, the authors recognize the organizers and fieldworkers of: Weekly Censuses; Christmas Bird Counts, especially Winston J. Wayne; May Counts, especially Robert G. Rufe; Breeding Bird Surveys, especially John T. Linehan; and Breeding Bird Censuses, especially John T. Linehan and Robert Jones. The authors also express appreciation for the use of data from banding stations, obtained from Albert E. Conway, Norman E. Holgersen, Richard Knowles, and W. C. Russell, and especially from John T. Linehan's Operation Recovery; Hawk Watch Data, especially that of James Oliver; and study results and project reports shared by DNREC and National Wildlife Refuge personnel in Delaware. The authors thank all compilers and contributors of field notes and all editors of the *Delmarva Ornithologist,* especially John T. Linehan and L. L. Falk. Delaware data from the Neotropical Songbird Coastal Corridor Study were very useful in the species accounts; the authors acknowledge the hundreds of dedicated birders who contributed to the study and the sponsors of the study: The Nature Conservancy, National Oceanographic and Atmospheric Administration, Virginia Department of Conservation and Recreation, Maryland Nongame and Urban Wildlife Program, New Jersey Endangered and Nongame Species Program, Delaware Natural Heritage Program, and Cape May Bird Observatory.

Seal T. Brooks, Kathleen Herbert, John C. Miller, David M. Niles, Grace Prest, Allan R. Stickley, Jr., Winston J. Wayne, and others maintained and contributed accumulated personal field notes, which supplemented those of the authors. The authors also thank the numerous individuals who filled out nest record cards in either the Cornell program or its Delaware counterpart, and we express appreciation to the many property owners on whose lands data were collected for their interest and cooperation.

James C. Bednarz, Paul F. Burns, Duncan S. Evered, Lisa A. Gelvin-Innvaer, John P. Hubbard, John T. Linehan, Brooke Meanley, Dorothy P. Miller, Bruce Peterjohn, Ken Reynolds, Mark Robbins, Roland R. Roth, David Rothstein, Stephen J. Stedman, Thomas Whittendale, Jochen Wiese, Claudia Wilds, and an anonymous reader were extremely helpful as technical readers for the species accounts. Yvonne Blades, Howard P. Brokaw, Joan Brown, Marjorie Crofts, Franklin Daiber, Edward Daino, Donald Eggen, Richard Fleming, Lisa Gelvin-Innvaer, Kyle Gulbronson, Richard Hall, Marianne Hardesty, Holger Harvey, Lyle Jones, Timothy Kaden, George Kent, Frank Kuncir, Susan Laporte, Linda Lyon, Michael McGrath, Robert McKim, Judy McKinney-Cherry, William Moyer, Thomas Pickett, Anthony Pratt, Edward Ratledge, David Saveikas, David Shields, Tracy Skrabal, Robert Tjaden, Leslie Trew, and Charles R. Vickers read text or provided technical information for the "Delaware Habitats" and "Conservation of Delaware Birds" chapters; and Howard Brokaw and Frances Hamilton Oates gave strong editorial direction to the conservation chapter. Trevor Lloyd-Evans of Manomet Observatory provided substantial information for the irruptive northern visitors essay. Gregory A. Inskip, Esq., handled all legal matters for *Birds of Delaware,* an invaluable contribution.

In particular the authors are grateful for the contributions of the essayists whose bylined works are distributed throughout the species accounts and introductory chapters and for use of original pen-and-ink drawings by Margaretta B. Brokaw, Joyce E. Stark, Rob Stine, Elizabeth Traynor, and Nancy C. Willis. Other illustrations in the species accounts are reprinted with permission: R. I. Brasher illustrations from *Birds of America,* 1917, T. Gilbert Pearson, Editor, The University Society, Inc., and 1936, Doubleday & Co., Inc., and Garden City Publishing Co., Inc.; illustrations from *Birds of Massachusetts and Other New England States,* three volumes, Edward Howe Forbush, 1925, Massachusetts Department of Agriculture; Margaretta B. Brokaw drawings from Philadelphia Wildfowl Exposition, 1979, Academy of Natural Sciences of Philadelphia and Academy of Natural Sciences Wildfowl Art Expo, 1981, and *Delaware's Outstanding Natural Areas and Their Preservation,* Lorraine M. Fleming, 1978, Delaware Nature Education Society; illustrations from *Pennsylvania Birds, An Annotated List,* Earl L. Poole, 1964, Delaware Valley Ornithological Club; illustrations from *Bird Studies at Old Cape May,* Volumes 1 and 2, Witmer Stone, 1937, Delaware Valley Ornithological Club, reprinted by Dover Publications, Inc.; illustrations from *Birds in Our Lives,* Alfred Stefferud, Editor, 1966, U.S. Department of the Interior, Bureau of Sportsfisheries and Wildlife, U.S. Government Printing Office; illustrations from *A History of North American Birds,* S. F. Baird, T. M. Brewer, and R. Ridgway, 1875, *Land Birds,* Volumes 1, 2, and 3, and *The Water Birds of North America,* Volumes 1 and 2, 1884, Little Brown & Co.; T. M. Shortt drawings from *The Ducks, Geese, and Swans of North America,* Francis H. Kortwright, 1943, Wildlife Management Institute; and illustrations from the first and second editions of *A Guide to Bird Finding East of the Mississippi,* Olin Sewall Pettingill, Jr., 1951 and 1977, Oxford University Press, and the 1953 and 1981 editions of *A Guide to Bird Finding West of the Mississippi,* Olin Sewall Pettingill Jr., Oxford University Press.

Cover art for this book was created by Nancy C. Willis. The loan of photographs of the Black-necked Stilt by Mervil Anthony, James Woodward, and Andrew Ednie to assist the artist is appreciated.

Grateful recognition is due the Delaware Breeding Bird Atlas Project Committee: Richard L. West, State Coordinator; Regional Coordinators Douglas G. and Karen M. Batt, Doris J. Boller, David T. Weesner, David P. Wolanski, George F. O'Shea, William Frech, Gene K. Hess, and Andrew P. Ednie; and Kathleen Gordon, Newsletter Editor; and the organizations sponsoring the Atlas project—Delaware Museum of Natural History, Delaware Nature Society, Delmarva Ornithological Society, Department of Natural Resources and Environmental Control, Delaware Audubon Society, Tri-State Bird Rescue and Research, Inc., U.S. Fish and Wildlife Service (Wildlife Refuges), University of Delaware Department of Entomology and Applied Ecology, and Natural History Society of Delaware. The Atlas fieldworkers and others, who contributed a vast body of breeding bird data, are noted below with deep appreciation. Those with an asterisk after their names made particularly significant contributions.

M. J. Addy, Melvin Alfree, Hale Allen, Karen Angulo, Dan Anstine, M. L. Atchison,* John Auld, Aycoth, Edwin and Elsie Bailey, Katherine Bailey, Jennie Baldwin, David Ball, M. V. Barnhill,* Eric Barthel, D. G. and Karen Batt,* Gary I. Bayne, J. C. Bennett, James H. Bennett, Craig Berman, Herbert and Yvonne Blades,* B. E. Blust, D. J. Boller,* G. M. Bond, Dan Brauning, J. D. Brighton, Sr.,* Edward Brittan, Murray Brockman, H. P. and M. T. Brokaw,* W. A. and Pat Brokaw,* R. F. Brown,* Alta Buckingham, J. G. Buckley, F. C. Buhl,* Bessie Burdziak, Burket, Paul Burns, C. A. Butler, Danny Bystrak, H. M. and Agnes Cadot, Alice Campbell, Mary Carey, Terry Carmine, D. I. Carroll, C. Chalfant, Mae Clark, J. F. Cleary, Jr., Tim Coffin, Randall V. Cole, James L. Coleman,* P. F. Collins, Joe and Mary Cregg, D. A. Cutler, Paul D. Daly, Barbara L. Davison,* Deanna Dawson, Marti De Chene, Sally Decker, Gwen Delaney, David Detweiler, Mrs. Detweiler, Richard Donham, Richard S. Du Pont, Jack Dukes, Elizabeth Dyer,* A. P. Ednie,* J. Ennis, Brad, Susan, Matt, Jason and Dan Fager,* L. L. Falk,* W. A. and S. W. Fintel,* Betty Fleming, Lorraine Fleming, Anthony Florio, Focht, W. W. Frech,* Betsy Frey, John and Lynne Frink, Judy Fullhart, Rob Gano, Lila Gierasch, Nancy Goggin, Jeff Gordon, M. K. Gordon, Fritz Gottfried, C. H. Greenewalt, G. G. Greenstein, H. V. Griffith,* Karin Grosz,* Haines, Karen Hall, W. Hanna, H. H. Harvey, R. W. Hendrickson, Lynn Herman, G. K. Hess,* Armas Hill, Jean Hitchens, Claude Hoffman, Wayne Holden, N. E. Holgersen,* Virgil Holmes, S. P. Homsey, Joe Hughes, R. C. Irons, L. S. Jaco, F. and M. Jahn, F. L. Jalot, Jr., J. P. Janowski,* Chere Jarrell, Clark Jeschke,* Bill Jones, John Judge, Jan Kalb, Joe Kaznica, R. J. Keene,* Ralph E. Kelly, Robert Ketcham, Don Knoll, Virginia Larason, Bertha Lasher, David and Donna Laux, J. A. Leath, Jay Lehman,* Edward Liehr, J. T. and Betty Linehan,* Meta Little,* George Long, Greg Loper, R. E. Magnan,* Hank and Lloyd Maier,* Jimmi Mallory, Bruce Marine, Alan and Mary Marsh, T. J. and S. A. Marshall, Cathy Martin, Peter Martin, Laura Marvel, Virginia Mast, A. S. and E. F. Matlack, Sean McCandless, McHugh, John McKibben, Rob McKim, B. C. McKusick, Mickey McLaughlin, R. L. McWhorter, Robert Meadows, Lee Meinersmann, W. H. Meredith, Bob and Cindy Miller, Charles and Dorothy Miller, D. P. Miller,* D. R. Miller,* Ruth Miller,* Charles Moore, Jim Moore, B. J. Morgan,* Frank Muller, Janice Munyan, Bill Murphy, Carmen Nelson, D. M. Niles,* Dave Nuttall, E. J. O'Donnell, Jim O'Neill, G. F. O'Shea,* Martha W. Olson, D. B. Palmer, R. A. Parkinson, J. W. Patterson,* J. T.

Paul, Charles A. Pelizza,* Margo Perkins, Carl Perry, Jean Pfeffer, Phillips, J. A. Pié, Chris Popetti, Helen Preiss, G. A. Prest, Cathy Price, Proud, Amelia Quillen, D. C. Quinn,* J. Greir Ralston, Jr., Jane Rawlins, George and Mary Jac Reed, D. M. Reese, Jr., Jan Reese, Jack Rigby, Tom Riley, Karen Robb, S. Rohwer, Audrey Rosenblatt, E. Ross, Roland Roth,* Mary Ann Rubin, R. G. Rufe, J. W. Russell, R. W. Russell,* Ralph Salter, Marc Samonisky, Charles E. Sample,* David E. Saveikis, W. P. Schaefer, W. H. Schneider, Dave Sharp, D. T. Shock, Lloyd Simmons, Walter Simpson, Jana L. Skolnicki, Frank Smith, Carl Solberg, E. B. Speck,* Eric Speck, Evan Speck, S. B. Speck,* Lee Spence, David and Deanne Stevens, Elizabeth Stoner, P. Edward Strickland, Mike Swartz, Joe Swertinski,* Kay Tebbens, Janis E. Thomas,* Tri-State Bird Rescue and Research, Inc.,* P. Vanderhorst, R. D. Walker, Irmadel Ward, Roberta Ward, W. J. Wayne,* Tom Webb, David T. Weesner,* Douglas Wenny, R. L. West,* Paul W. Western, Barbara Wethe, A. W. White, J. F. White, Jr.,* Thomas Whittendale, Edward and Ethel Wilson, David P. Wolanski,* Fred Wolff, Loretta Woods, W. W. and K. I. Zeitler,* and Joan Zerbe.

Finally, the authors wish to thank their family members who gave patient, steadfast support through the long process of this book's production.

List of Abbreviations

AFB	Air Force base		*n*	number (of a sample)
AMNH	American Museum of Natural History, New York		n.d.	no date
			NA	natural area
Anon.	anonymous		NOAA	National Oceanographic and Aeronautical Administration
ANSP	Academy of Natural Sciences, Philadelphia			
AOU	American Ornithologists' Union		NORAC	North American Ornithological Atlas Committee
BBC	Breeding Bird Census			
BBS	Breeding Bird Survey		NWR	National Wildlife Refuge
ca.	circa		*p* < .05	significance level (probability of occurring by chance)
CA	Conservation Area			
CBC	Christmas Bird Count		PCBs	polychlorinated biphenyls
C&D Canal	Chesapeake and Delaware Canal		pers. comm.	personal communication
CM	Carnegie Museum of Natural History, Pittsburgh		pers. obs.	personal observation
			ppt	parts per thousand
Co.	County		Rd.	Road
comp.	compiler		Rt.	Route
DAS	Delaware Audubon Society		SF	State Forest
DMNH	Delaware Museum of Natural History, Greenville		SP	State Park
			sq mi	square mile
DNHI	Delaware Natural Heritage Inventory		TSBR	Tri-State Bird Rescue and Research, Inc.
DNREC	Delaware Department of Natural Resources and Environmental Control		UF	University of Florida
			UDEL	University of Delaware (Department of Entomology and Applied Ecology)
DNS	Delaware Nature Society			
DOS	Delmarva Ornithological Society		unpub.	unpublished
DVOC	Delaware Valley Ornithological Club		USFWS	U.S. Fish and Wildlife Service (usually referring to the research branch at Patuxent Research Center, which became the National Biological Service, and was then transferred to the U.S. Geological Survey).
E	east			
ed.	editor(s)			
EPA	Environmental Protection Agency			
ft	foot, feet			
ha	hectare = 2.5 acres		USNM	National Museum of Natural History, Washington, D.C.
in.	inch			
km, k	kilometer(s)		UWBM	University of Washington, Burke Museum, Seattle
LSU	Louisiana State University, Baton Rouge			
m	meter(s)		v.	volume
mi	mile(s)		WA	Wildlife Area (wildlife management area)
min	minute(s)		WFVZ	Western Foundation for Vertebrate Zoology, Los Angeles

Despite Delaware's small size of about 1.3 million acres, the state possesses remarkable diversity of habitats, flora, and fauna—the result of both geography and geology. Delaware lies along the Mid-Atlantic seaboard at 39° north latitude, at the biological interface for the ranges of northern and southern species—for example, the Northern Harrier and Swamp Sparrow from the north and the Brown-headed Nuthatch and Summer Tanager from the south. Past geological events in the state have created two distinct physiographic provinces—the northernmost 5% being in the Appalachian Piedmont Province and the remainder in the Atlantic Coastal Plain Province. Avian diversity also derives from the state's location on an ocean, on a large estuary, and its placement along a major migration route, the Atlantic Flyway.

Geology and Landforms

Appalachian mountain building episodes between 500 and 200 million years ago formed the severely metamorphosed schists and gneisses and the igneous gabbros and pegmatites of the Piedmont (Thompson 1976), now characterized by rolling hills and steeply incised stream valleys. A fall zone, or fall line, occurs at the junction of the Piedmont and Coastal Plain Provinces, which is also an ecological transition area (see map 1.1); the alignment of state Rt. 2 roughly delineates the zone.

The deposition of the unconsolidated sediments of the Coastal Plain, which began some 150–120 million years ago as eroded water-borne sands, silts, and clays, was followed by marine sediment deposited in periods of alternating sea encroachment and retreat. The sequence of marine depositions was continuous until about 45 million years ago, and several marine incursions occurred about 15 million years ago. In association with the advance and retreat of continental glaciers and their dramatic effects on sea level, all of this sediment was then capped by fluvial sands and gravels during the Pleistocene epoch, starting about 1.8 million years ago. These sediments form a wedge over bedrock from a few feet thick in the north to more than 10,000 feet at Fenwick Island (Pickett 1976). In the past 10,000 years, rising sea level has filled coastal valleys with sediment, forming extensive tidal marshes.

Coastal Plain streams meander broadly in shallow channels, and the landscape is generally flat, with elevations ranging from sea level to about 125 feet. The highest point in Delaware, 448 feet above sea level, is located in the Piedmont north of Wilmington near the Pennsylvania state line.

Soils

The state's soils are classified primarily into four soil orders: Ultisols (well-developed, usually acidic mineral soils), Histosols (organic soils), Inceptisols (mineral soils in early development), and Entisols (mineral soils forming in recent geologic materials). They are grouped into 21 associations by location, drainage characteristics, and parent material (Lyle Jones, DNREC, pers. comm.). (See map 1.2.) The Piedmont soils are derived from highly weathered micaceous schist, gneiss, and gabbroic rocks and are older, better developed, and more eroded than those of the Coastal Plain. They tend to be deep, except on steep slopes, well drained, fairly fertile, and to have good water retention properties. The gently sloping soils of the

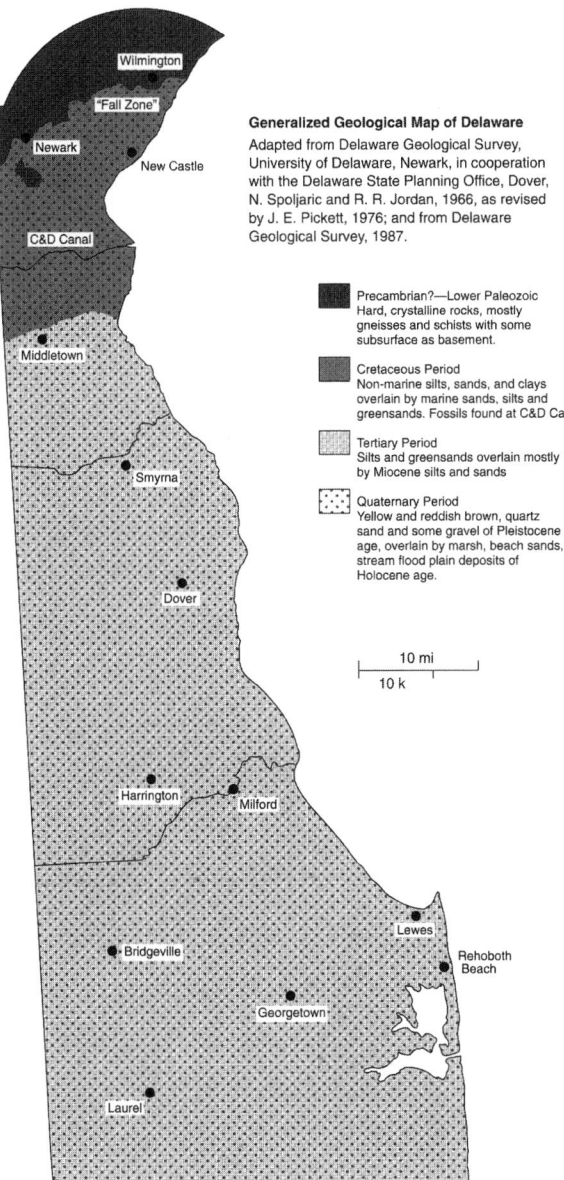

Generalized Geological Map of Delaware
Adapted from Delaware Geological Survey, University of Delaware, Newark, in cooperation with the Delaware State Planning Office, Dover, N. Spoljaric and R. R. Jordan, 1966, as revised by J. E. Pickett, 1976; and from Delaware Geological Survey, 1987.

Precambrian?—Lower Paleozoic
Hard, crystalline rocks, mostly gneisses and schists with some subsurface as basement.

Cretaceous Period
Non-marine silts, sands, and clays overlain by marine sands, silts and greensands. Fossils found at C&D Canal.

Tertiary Period
Silts and greensands overlain mostly by Miocene silts and sands

Quaternary Period
Yellow and reddish brown, quartz sand and some gravel of Pleistocene age, overlain by marsh, beach sands, stream flood plain deposits of Holocene age.

10 mi
10 k

Map 1.1

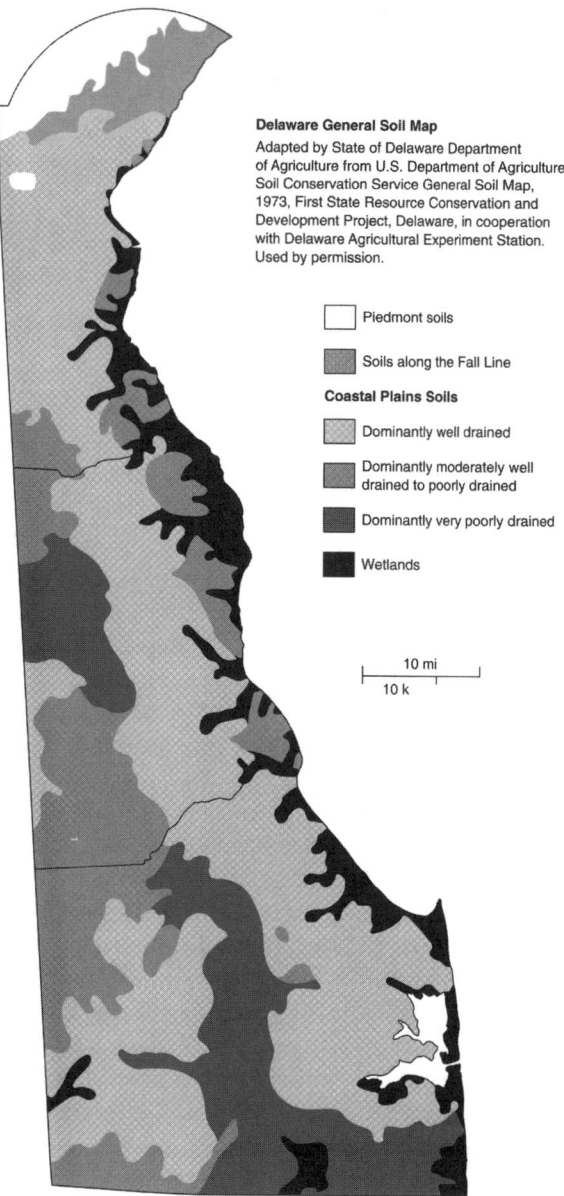

Delaware General Soil Map
Adapted by State of Delaware Department of Agriculture from U.S. Department of Agriculture Soil Conservation Service General Soil Map, 1973, First State Resource Conservation and Development Project, Delaware, in cooperation with Delaware Agricultural Experiment Station. Used by permission.

☐ Piedmont soils

▨ Soils along the Fall Line

Coastal Plains Soils

▨ Dominantly well drained

▨ Dominantly moderately well drained to poorly drained

■ Dominantly very poorly drained

■ Wetlands

10 mi
10 k

Map 1.2

fall zone include those formed on old alluvium of stream terraces and severely disturbed urban associations.

Coastal Plain soils vary widely in the proportions of sands, silts, and clays they contain and in their location relative to the water table (Matthews and Lavoie 1970). Predominantly sandy soils may be either excessively drained and dry or poorly drained when the water table is high. Soils with high amounts of clays and silts have a tendency to be wet because water cannot percolate through them (Matthews and Ireland 1971; Ireland and Matthews 1974; U.S. Soil Conservation Service 1973). The mineral and organic materials in tidal and freshwater marshes comprise three associations of very poorly drained soils rimming the coastline from Wilmington to Fenwick Island, surrounding the Inland Bays and the confluence of

Broad Creek and Nanticoke River, and forming the core of the Great Cypress Swamp. An ancient beach ridge capped by low dunes and consisting of deep coarse sandy soils occurs in the Nanticoke River–Broad Creek vicinity. Wet, weakly developed soils occur along most watercourse floodplains in the state (Lyle Jones, DNREC, pers. comm.). The remaining soils in all three counties are classed as dominantly moderately well drained to poorly drained.

There is little information to enable a direct correlation between soils and Delaware birds' habitat use. An exception is the Vesper Sparrow, associated with cultivated fields, specifically in locations of well-drained, sandy soil.

Climate

In the state's generally mild, modified continental climate, periods of sustained hot or cold temperatures are typically brief since extremes are moderated by the Delaware Bay, the Atlantic Ocean, and nearby Chesapeake Bay (Paulson et al. 1991). Mean annual temperatures are 55–58°F; the average temperature difference from New Castle County to Sussex County is about +6.8°F in January and +1.6°F in July. Annual precipitation, averaging 44–45 inches, is distributed throughout the year. October and November, commonly the driest months, average 2.5–3.0 inches. Heaviest average rainfall is slightly over 5 inches per month in July and August. Average yearly precipitation, however, is fairly even throughout the state, with 41.3 inches cited for New Castle, 44.9 for Wilmington, 44.4 for Dover and Bridgeville–Greenwood, 43.7 for Georgetown, and 45.1 for Lewes (Talley 1989).

The growing season ranges from 180 to 188 days. New Castle County experiences the greatest average snowfall; Wilmington's average is 21.4 inches, compared with 16 inches for Sussex County. The first frost occurs between early October and mid-November, and the last freeze occurs from late March to early May.

Delaware's weather, influenced primarily by the migration of systems from the west, is variable, with regular sequences of alternating fair and cloudy-rainy or snowy days. Air masses affecting the area change frequently in spring and fall and are either warm, moist maritime tropical air from the Atlantic Ocean or Gulf of Mexico, dominant in summer, or cold, dry continental polar masses from Canada or the Midwest, dominant in winter. Occasional maritime polar air masses from the North Atlantic blanket the state in a flow around a low-pressure area moving up the Atlantic coast. The Bermuda High, or subtropical Atlantic high-pressure cell, when present, has a major effect on Delaware's summer weather patterns.

Average wind velocity varies from 7.4 mph in August to 11.2 mph in March, and seasonal variations in speed and direction are the norm. Summer winds are commonly from the west and southwest, shifting to predominantly northwest and west-northwest in winter. Calm conditions prevail less than 10% of the year.

Wetlands

Soils, hydrology, salinity regime, and climatic conditions are primary determinants of indigenous vegetation communities. Approximately 17%, or 216,000 acres, of Delaware is wetlands (Tiner and Finn 1986), as defined by the presence of a tidal or nontidal water regime, hydric soils, and hydrophytes. Ninety-eight percent of the state's wetlands occur in the Coastal Plain. Included in the total acreage but not shown on the accompanying map (map 1.3) are marine beaches and bars and riverine and lacustrine wetlands, about 4% of the total.

About one-third of the wetlands are estuarine, or coastal, wetlands subject to diurnal tides; salinities vary from 0.5 to 30 parts per thousand (ppt). More than half of tidal wetlands, an estimated 44,000 acres, was ditched in a grid or parallel pattern for mosquito control by the Civilian Conservation Corps in the 1930s (Whitman and Cole 1986). The coastal wetlands fall into three classes—estuarine emergent, estuarine scrub-shrub, and intertidal flats (Tiner 1985).

The estuarine emergent wetland types in Delaware (Daiber et al. 1976) include: (1) cordgrass marsh—brackish to strongly saline (5–30 ppt), inundated by the daily tides and dominated by saltmarsh cordgrass with salt hay, spike grass, big cordgrass, and high tide and groundsel bushes on higher sites; (2) salt hay marsh—at slightly higher elevation and inundated by the lunar tides (salinity 5–30 ppt), with salt hay, or saltmeadow cordgrass, and spike grass the dominant species associated with saltmarsh cordgrass, big cordgrass, high tide and groundsel bushes; (3) phragmites—fresh to slightly brackish waters (< 5 ppt), almost exclusively this grass; (4) transition marsh—low salinity (0.5–5 ppt), with a diverse plant association, possibly including saltmarsh cordgrass, big cordgrass, phragmites, rose mallow, three-square, cattails, wild rice, arrow-arum, pickerel weed, and tide marsh water hemp; and (5) arrow-arum or pickerel weed marsh—fresh water (< 0.5 ppt), dominated by those two species in association with wild rice, rose mallow, and arrowhead. A small proportion of the latter type is classified in the National Wetlands Inventory as riverine tidal wetlands.

Higher-salinity estuarine emergent wetlands are used by the Gadwall, Northern Harrier, Clapper Rail, Herring Gull, and Boat-tailed Grackle all year; Blue-winged Teal, Sora, and Laughing Gull in the summer; and Snow Goose and Short-eared Owl in the winter. The Saltmarsh Sharp-tailed Sparrow nests exclusively in saltmarsh cordgrass; the Seaside Sparrow and Black Rail use salt hay marsh with upland edges of hightide and groundsel bushes, also the former habitat of the Henslow's Sparrow. The state's most prominent saltmarsh nester, the Willet, uses both saltmarsh cordgrass and salt hay marsh; Ospreys nest on structures in saltmarshes along the Inland Bays. Brackish to fresh tidal marshes are characterized by the Swamp Sparrow and Virginia Rail year-round and by breeding Least Bittern, Sedge Wren (rare), and King Rail and in winter by the Northern Pintail, Common Snipe, and American Coot. The American Bittern, American Black Duck, and Ring-necked Pheasant are associated with both salt and brackish marshes, as

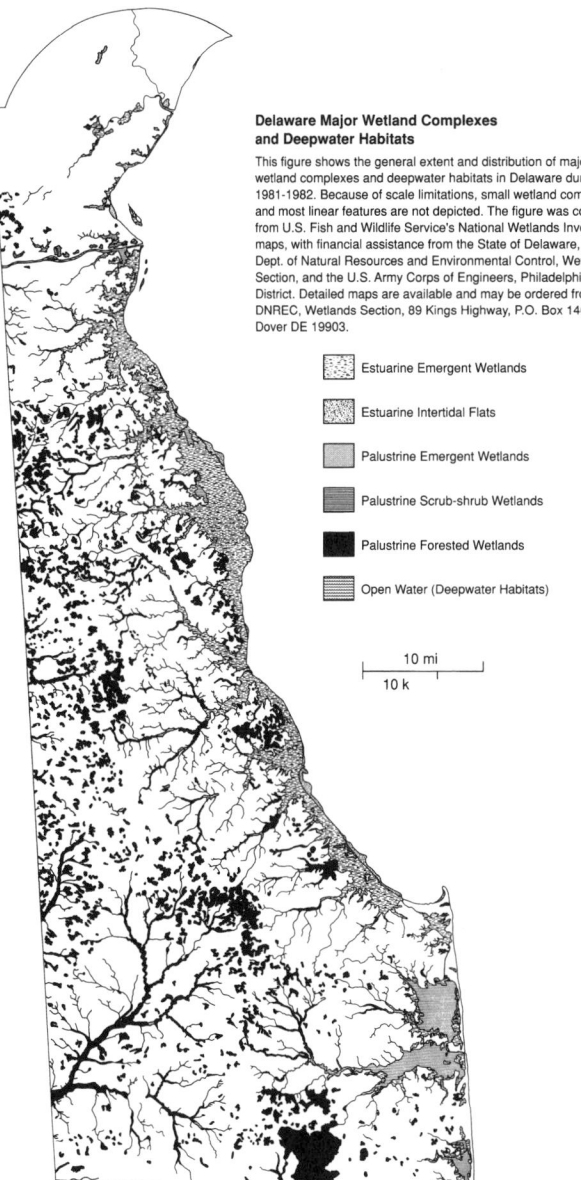

Delaware Major Wetland Complexes and Deepwater Habitats

This figure shows the general extent and distribution of major wetland complexes and deepwater habitats in Delaware during 1981-1982. Because of scale limitations, small wetland complexes and most linear features are not depicted. The figure was compiled from U.S. Fish and Wildlife Service's National Wetlands Inventory maps, with financial assistance from the State of Delaware, Dept. of Natural Resources and Environmental Control, Wetlands Section, and the U.S. Army Corps of Engineers, Philadelphia District. Detailed maps are available and may be ordered from DNREC, Wetlands Section, 89 Kings Highway, P.O. Box 1401, Dover DE 19903.

⬚ Estuarine Emergent Wetlands

⬚ Estuarine Intertidal Flats

⬚ Palustrine Emergent Wetlands

⬚ Palustrine Scrub-shrub Wetlands

⬛ Palustrine Forested Wetlands

⬚ Open Water (Deepwater Habitats)

10 mi

10 k

Map 1.3

are the Rough-legged Hawk and Savannah Sparrow in the winter. While phragmites marsh is generally regarded as having low value for all wildlife, including birds, it is used by several species (see chapter 3, "Conservation"). On Pea Patch Island, phragmites provides nest substrate for the Snowy Egret, Little Blue Heron, Tricolored Heron, Cattle Egret, and Glossy Ibis (see "Pea Patch Island" essay). Woods with mature trees adjacent to tidal brackish wetlands or saltmarsh are nesting habitat for the Great Blue Heron, Great Egret, and Fish Crow, and their edges for the Eastern Kingbird.

By definition riverine wetlands have only nonpersistent vegetation and occur mainly below the mean high-tide mark on mudflats in tidal rivers and in stream channels and their fringes in nontidal rivers. Lacustrine wetlands also contain nonpersistent emergent vegetation or aquatic bed plants, such as fragrant water lily, duckweed, bladderworts, and pondweeds. They develop in the shallow water and shorelines around lakes, ponds, and reservoirs. Riverine and lacustrine wetlands are minor components of Delaware's wetlands, totaling less than 800 acres (Tiner 1985).

Estuarine scrub-shrub wetlands, at the elevation limits of tidal influence, are dominated by high tide and grounsel bushes, often in association with wax myrtle and bayberry. These wetlands represent only 1% of the estuarine category. Brackish and freshwater scrub-shrub wetlands provide nesting grounds for the Willow Flycatcher, Yellow Warbler, Common Yellowthroat, and Red-winged Blackbird.

The intertidal flats of the Delaware Estuary and Inland Bays typically are not vegetated but are habitats for a variety of edaphic algae and burrowing crustaceans and are an important feeding ground for many higher life forms (DNREC 1987). Approximately 8,900 acres, they constitute just under 10% of the estuarine wetlands. At the time of horseshoe crab spawning, mudflats along the Delaware Bay shoreline become a critical staging area for hundreds of thousands of spring migrant shorebirds, particularly the Red Knot, Ruddy Turnstone, Semipalmated Sandpiper, and Sanderling (see "Spring Shorebirds" essay). These flats are visited by lesser numbers of Black-bellied and Semipalmated plovers, yellow legs, Willets, Dunlin, Short-billed Dowitcher, White-rumped and Pectoral sandpipers, and Wilson's Phalarope. Also the Wimbrel, Hudsonian and Marbled godwits, and Western Sandpiper feed on salty flats.

The inland palustrine wetlands, wholly fresh water, occur along watercourses above the limits of tidal influence or in seasonally or permanently flooded locations, accounting for about 68% of the state's wetlands. Of the three major classes—forested, emergent, and scrub-shrub—90% are palustrine forested wetlands, or wooded swamps. They are grouped by woody vegetation and by the extent and duration of saturation or inundation.

Tree associations in seasonally flooded locations include the elm-ash–red maple group, often with black gum, box elder, and other moist site species; the loblolly pine–shortleaf pine group, with sweetgum, pond pine, black gum, green ash, and red maple; and the oak–gum–cypress group, the most common, with some swamps consisting predominantly of red maple. Other species in the latter group are Atlantic white cedar, comparatively scarce but found along some waterways in southern Delaware, and a bald cypress–water tupelo (swamp black gum) combination—a rare remnant in southern Sussex County. The Prothonotary Warbler is locally common in the state's cypress swamps.

In palustrine forested tidal situations, such as the upper reaches of the Nanticoke and Murderkill Rivers, deciduous species dominate with green ash, black gum, and red maple (the most abundant), often accompanied by sweetbay magnolia and black willow; loblolly pine and Atlantic white cedar may also be present (Tiner 1985, 1987b). In deep, permanently

flooded wetlands bald cypress historically dominated; today it is limited largely to portions of the James Branch watershed (Fleming 1978). Ten forest cover types were identified in a study of selected bottomland forests aimed at better silvicultural management (Willis 1988).

The state's most abundant forested wetlands are temporarily flooded and therefore most vulnerable to human disturbance or destruction. Such places support a diversity of tree species that varies with the location and soils; common canopy species may include red maple, sweetgum, loblolly pine, white ash, green ash, box elder, sycamore, willow oak, and swamp white oak.

Forested wetlands are important habitat for a number of resident and migrant species, typically the American Black Duck, American Woodcock, Red-shouldered Hawk, and Barred Owl all year; the Yellow-rumped Warbler and a few Winter Wrens in winter; the Wood Duck, Yellow-billed Cuckoo, Whip-poor-will, Acadian Flycatcher, Blue-gray Gnatcatcher, Prothonotary Warbler, Louisiana Waterthrush, and Kentucky Warbler in summer; and during migration periods Gray-cheeked, Swainson's, and Hermit thrushes, Northern Parula, and Nashville, Connecticut, and Canada warblers. Species favoring wooded floodplains for breeding habitat in Delaware are the Broad-winged Hawk, Ruby-throated Hummingbird, Veery, Yellow-throated and Warbling vireos, Cerulean Warbler (localized), and American Redstart.

Palustrine emergent wetlands, freshwater marshes, may be either tidal—lying along the upper reaches of waterways, usually above the mean high-water mark—or nontidal, the nontidal being about four times more common. In tidal situations common plants may include rose mallow, beggar ticks, smartweeds, and cattails. Nontidal freshwater marshes typically are dominated by grasses, sedges, and a variety of herbaceous species, including cattails, spatterdock, arrow-arum, pickerel weed, water willow, burreed, soft rush, and sometimes rarer plants, such as pitcher plants, swamp pink, pipeworts, and orchids (Tiner 1987b). Plant composition is determined in part by whether flooding is semipermanent or seasonal. These marshes represent about 10% of the state's nontidal wetlands (David Saveikis, DNREC, pers. comm.). Freshwater marshes along the Delaware River are nesting habitat of the Marsh Wren and Red-winged Blackbird.

The least abundant class, the palustrine scrub-shrub wetland, is exemplified by Delmarva bays, centripetally drained depressions that are perennially or seasonally water filled. These bays, also termed whale wallows or Carolina bays, are concentrated in a band running diagonally from southeastern New Castle County to northwestern Kent County; they are also scattered throughout the Coastal Plain, particularly where clay-rich soils occur. Buttonbush, typically surrounded by sedge and grass species (C. Ronald Vickers, DNREC, pers. comm.), is predominant in the center of the bay; perimeter species usually include sweet pepperbush, red maple, sweet gum, sweetbay magnolia, highbush blueberry, deerberry, and black gum (Fleming 1978). Characteristically, these bays are sites of high biological diversity and homes of rare plants and amphibians (Vickers 1988; White 1988).

Scrub-shrub wetlands also occur upstream along some tidal waterways, such as Cedar Creek and the Murderkill River. Here the mixture of prominent woody plants may include wax myrtle, evergreen bayberry, buttonbush, hazel alder, seaside alder, sweet pepperbush, winterberry, sweetbay magnolia, silky dogwood, and southern arrowwood (Tiner 1985; Fleming 1978).

Aquatic Environments

Approximately one-third of the state lies in the Chesapeake Bay drainage area and the remainder in the Delaware River Basin and Atlantic Ocean drainage. Delaware's 843 miles of perennial streams and rivers form 41 drainage basins and sub-basins and differ distinctively according to location. Piedmont streams, exclusively fresh water, normally have beds composed of cobbles, in a few cases boulders, with some sands and gravels. Fish and food organisms, primarily bottom-dwelling arthropods and some mollusks, live in pools and riffles. These streams have a steeper gradient and swifter flow than Coastal Plain waterways; however, in estuarine creeks powerful currents are generated by tidal flow.

In Delaware's tidal streams salinity varies seasonally and with distance from the ocean. Bottom composition is usually mud and clay, with some areas of gravel or sand. Faunal species present differ according to salinity; in general, more crustaceans are found in brackish tidal waters than in tidal fresh waters (Martin 1974). More than 1,000 acres of fresh waterways have been classified as deepwater habitats (water depth 6.6 feet or greater), including about 850 acres of tidally influenced rivers (Tiner 1985). Commonly associated with tidal creeks in winter are the Green-winged Teal and Hooded and Common mergansers. The Belted Kingfisher can be found all year along both inland and coastal watercourses and the Ring-billed Gull along larger rivers. Migrating Solitary and Spotted sandpipers feed along banks or shallow margins of streams; and the Northern Rough-winged Swallow inhabits banks and ditches.

Many small Coastal Plain streams, mainly in the western half of the state and along the southern Delaware–Maryland state line, have been channelized to assist wetland drainage for agricultural purposes. Currently more than 2,000 miles of channels in Delaware are managed by some 248 tax ditches, political subdivisions that have maintenance taxing authority. Privately maintained drainage ditches may extend another 2,000 miles (Richard Smith, DNREC, pers. comm.). The channels revert to functioning ecological systems over time if not maintained, a condition that exists now in some watersheds. It has been estimated that 12.5% of the state's palustrine forested wetlands, mainly in Kent and Sussex Counties, have been drained by channelizing and ditching since 1955 (Tiner 1985).

Other deepwater habitats, 235,000–275,000 acres (Tiner 1985; Tiner and Finn 1986), comprise freshwater ponds and lakes, reservoirs, and the salt waters of the Delaware Bay and the Inland Bays—Rehoboth, Indian River, and Little Assawoman Bays, separated from the Atlantic Ocean by a coastal barrier. The ponds and lakes amount to about 4,500 acres, the Inland Bays to about 28,800 acres, and the Delaware Estuary the remainder.

The state's lakes and ponds are twentieth-century survivors of 130 historic millponds, many more than 250 years old, and are distributed somewhat equally among the three counties. Of the 60 ponds that are five acres or larger, 30 are publicly owned; the number of smaller, privately owned ponds is unknown. Submerged aquatic vegetation in publicly managed ponds consists of a number of indigenous species and some exotic weeds. Plants that may occur include pondweed, duckweed, bladderworts, fragrant water-lily, watershield, floating-heart, naiad, water starwort, water milfoil, coontail, and hydrilla (Martin and Miller 1986). All ponds are subject to seasonal algal blooms.

The list of birds using the state's ponds, impoundments, and open water areas in marshes includes most of the shorebirds that also feed on mudflats. All year long Pied-billed Grebes, Mute Swans, some nonmigratory Canada Geese, Mallards, Gadwalls, and Ring-billed and Herring gulls may be found in ponds with shoreline or submerged vegetation. In winter Common Loons, Tundra Swans, Snow Geese, Green-winged Teal, Northern Pintails, Northern Shovelers, Canvasbacks, Ring-necked Ducks, Lesser Scaup, Common Goldeneyes, Bufflehead, and Hooded and Common mergansers are found on inland or impounded waters that are not iced over; in the summer the Wood Duck and Blue-winged Teal breed and feed in these waters. Migrating Greater and Lesser yellowlegs are visitors to shallow impoundments, American Avocets use both fresh and saltwater impoundments, and Black-necked Stilts nest and feed in association with brackish pools.

The Delaware Estuary and Inland Bays

Salinity in the Delaware Estuary varies with the inflow of fresh water but is generally 28–30 ppt at the mouth, decreasing to zero at Philadelphia. Salinities in the lower river transitional zone—from the Pennsylvania–Delaware state line to the beginning of the Delaware Bay at Liston Point, about 3.5 river miles north of the New Castle–Kent county line—have ranged from near zero to 15.9 ppt and recently have averaged just under 1 ppt; the average for the upper portion of the bay is about 8.4 ppt (Marino et al. 1991). The nearshore bottom sediments are mud in the Delaware River and sandy mud and muddy sand for most of the 48 miles of the bay (Biggs and Church 1983). Sandy deposits of varying widths line the perimeter from Bombay Hook southward; and from Bowers Beach to Lewes these washover barriers are composed of Pleistocene sands and gravels derived from the highlands immediately landward of the coastal marshes.

The Delaware Bay, which has a drainage area of approximately 4,800 square miles, is an ancient drowned river valley (NOAA 1990). With an average depth of 21 feet, the bay has a natural 55-foot-deep channel extending 12 miles upstream from the mouth; the remainder of the shipping channel is maintained at 40 feet below mean low water by dredging.

Brackish portions of the Delaware River and the bay are wintering grounds for many waterfowl, including the Brant, Canvasback, Redhead, Greater and Lesser scaups, Oldsquaw, all three scoters, Common Goldeneye, Red-breasted Merganser, Ruddy Duck, and in some years a few Common and King eiders. The Double-crested Cormorant is now found there all year.

The Inland Bays, draining a 300-square-mile area, are relatively shallow, with an average depth of four feet, and have a combined volume of four billion cubic feet. Bottom sediments consist of fine to medium sand, with varying proportions of silt, clay, mud, and silt-clay mixtures. Salinity ranges from 14 to 17 ppt. In Little Assawoman Bay turbidity is significantly higher and subsurface algae populations much lower than in Rehoboth or Indian River Bays (Anderson 1991; Tinsman 1991).

Despite past severe pollution of the upper estuary, Delaware Bay water quality is now rated as good. Its ecological system is generally healthy, although there is concern about degradation of nearshore areas. In the Inland Bays systems, however, the quality is declining progressively because of: insufficient flushing through the single ocean outlet at Indian River Inlet, the degradation of local groundwaters discharging to the bays, and extensive sediment and other pollutants in storm water runoff. Although once present, submerged aquatic vegetation is now absent from both the Delaware Bay and the Inland Bays because of suspended sediments that make the waters opaque (DNREC 1987; DNREC, NJDEP, and PADER 1988; Sullivan et al. 1991). The absence of submerged vegetation markedly reduces the value of these areas for waterfowl, wading birds, and other birds that feed directly on the plants or associated animal life. Nevertheless, Red-throated and Common loons, the Horned Grebe, Double-crested Cormorant, Snow Goose, American Black Duck, and a number of species of diving ducks may be present there in winter. Forster's Terns nest at Rehoboth Bay, Black Skimmers and Ospreys feed in the Inland Bays in summer, and Gull-billed and Black terns use the area during migration.

Beach and Duneland

Beach and duneland habitats compose the barriers and headlands along the Delaware Bay, the 25 miles of Delaware's Atlantic coastline, and the beaches on the Inland Bays and their tributaries. In all situations the foreshore is usually unvegetated, the backshore may have scattered vegetation, and the foredune supports established vegetation to varying degrees. Plants on a Delaware Bay back beach include some mix of the following: American beach grass, salt hay, sea rocket, seaside goldenrod, poison ivy, wild black cherry, American holly, bayberry, and winged sumac. Where secondary dunes or back-barrier flats have developed, associated vegetation may include beach plum, eastern red cedar, greenbrier, and sand blackberry.

During the past 2,000 years the prevailing longshore currents have produced a notable dynamic landform, Cape Henlopen, at the mouth of Delaware Bay (Kraft 1971; Kraft and Caulk 1973). Of marked interest are the biotic communities of its beaches, stable and walking dunes, bogs, and tidal marshes (Fleming 1978). When protected from incompatible human usage, beaches at the tip of the cape are suitable sites for colonial beach nesters: Piping Plovers, Common and Least terns, and Black Skimmers. These birds also nest on barrier beaches along the Atlantic Ocean.

Delaware's ocean beaches are characterized by a steep profile and high-energy wave impacts. In many locations the beaches are maintained by structures such as snow fences and groins and by sand nourishment. Many dunes have been manipulated to raise their height and stabilized with plantings of American beach grass, thereby diminishing their value for beach nesting birds and other wildlife, though recent dune management has been more sensitive to natural processes and vegetative cover (Anthony Pratt, DNREC, pers. comm.). Common Nighthawks nest on these dunes, and their vegetation provides cover for wintering Savannah Sparrows and Snow Buntings. Other plant species occurring on coastal dunes include beach heather, cocklebur, seaside beardgrass, beach plum, bayberry, and, often stunted, blackjack oaks and loblolly or Virginia pines. Maritime forests are established in a few dune hollows with such species as wild black cherry, blackjack oak, sassafras, American holly, eastern red cedar, evergreen bayberry, highbush blueberry, and, rarely, cranberry. Interdunal swales, uncommon in Delaware, are frequently sites of rare plants.

Delaware Rt. 1 traverses the length of the coastal barrier–Inland Bay system, thus thwarting the natural landward migration of the barrier. More than 2,400 acres of marine and estuarine beaches and bars were identified by the National Wetlands Inventory (Tiner 1985). Ring-billed, Herring, and Great Black-backed gulls are found on the barrier beaches all year. American Oystercatchers, Laughing Gulls, Caspian and Royal terns, and occasionally Gull-billed and Sandwich terns are there in summer, and Sanderlings, Dunlins, and Bonaparte's Gulls in winter. Purple Sandpipers may be seen on coastal jetties and groins in winter.

Forests

About 389,500 acres, approximately 31.5% of the state, is in forest cover in several stages from early reversion to old growth (Frieswyk and DiGiovanni 1989). Some 376,400 acres, about 97% of the whole, are classified as timberland; the remaining acres are noncommercial forest land. In an analysis of land use changes from 1974 to 1984 by photointerpretation, Mackenzie (1989) identified about 364,800 acres as forest—55% deciduous, 18% coniferous, and 27% mixed (see map 1.4). The 36,900 acres of brushland, included in the Frieswyk and DiGiovanni U.S. Forest Service statistics, were not classified as forest by Mackenzie.

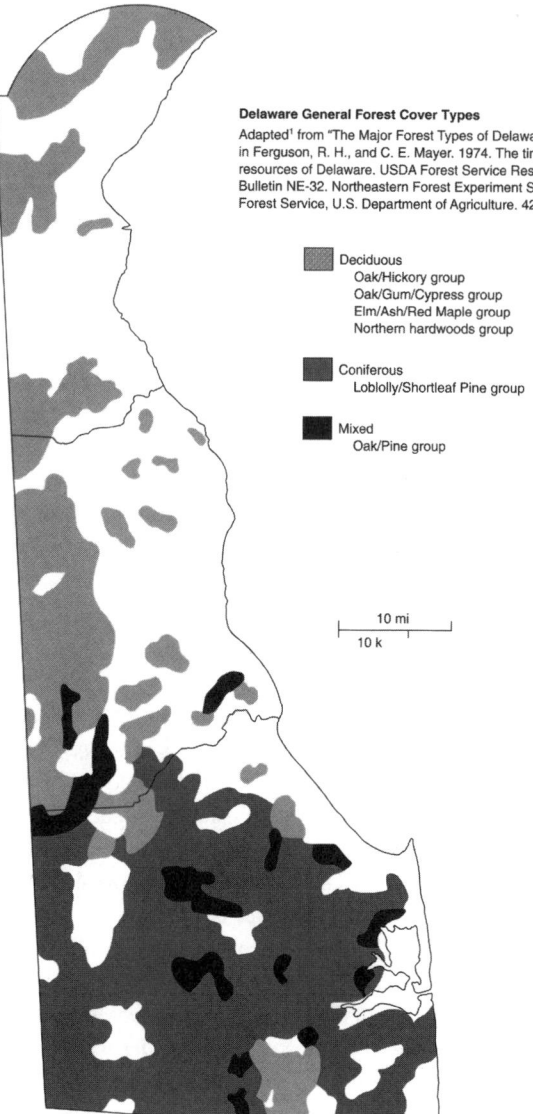

Delaware General Forest Cover Types

Adapted[1] from "The Major Forest Types of Delaware" map in Ferguson, R. H., and C. E. Mayer. 1974. The timber resources of Delaware. USDA Forest Service Resource Bulletin NE-32. Northeastern Forest Experiment Station. Forest Service, U.S. Department of Agriculture. 42 pp.

Deciduous
Oak/Hickory group
Oak/Gum/Cypress group
Elm/Ash/Red Maple group
Northern hardwoods group

Coniferous
Loblolly/Shortleaf Pine group

Mixed
Oak/Pine group

10 mi
10 k

Map 1.4

Brushland, particularly young shrubby deciduous growth, is important habitat for many birds. On Pea Patch Island it is the preferred nesting substrate of the Snowy Egret, Little Blue Heron, Cattle Egret, and Glossy Ibis. Upland scrub is used by the Carolina Wren, Gray Catbird, Cedar Waxwing, Northern Cardinal, Eastern Towhee, and American Goldfinch, and (where moist) by the American Woodcock throughout the year; in summer by the Black-billed Cuckoo (rare), Brown Thrasher, White-eyed Vireo, Yellow-breasted Chat, and Chipping Sparrow; and in winter by the American Tree Sparrow, Dark-eyed Junco, and (where moist) Yellow-rumped Warbler, Fox Sparrow, and Swamp Sparrow.

The U.S. Forest Service recognizes six forest groups consisting of 20 forest types in Delaware. (See table 1.1.) The most abundant group, oak–hickory, comprises 41.7% of the timberland. It occurs primarily in northern and southwestern New Castle County and parts of western Kent County and is locally abundant in northern Sussex County. The group is represented by eight forest types with the dominant species being one or more oaks (northern red, white, black, scarlet, chestnut, post, and/or southern red) or yellow-poplar (tuliptree), accompanied by American beech, white ash, red maple, and pignut and mockernut hickories. On low moist sites they are accompanied by sweetgum with flowering dogwood, sassafras, and a great diversity of other tree species as possible understory occupants. More than half of the total forests classified as oak–hickory group are the mixed central hardwood type. Most oak–hickory forest types occur principally on well-drained upland sites, ridges, and flats, but some are found on moist slopes and flats. Oak–hickory types and northern hardwoods types constitute the bulk of old growth in the state, now only about 1% of the total forested area, located mainly in the Brandywine Creek valley (Fleming 1978).

Table 1.1 Delaware Timberland Forest Groups and Types
(13,100 acres of noncommercial forest land not included)

Group	Type	Approx. percentage in Delaware
Deciduous		
Oak–hickory		
	white oak	6.2
	northern red oak	1.7
	yellow-poplar–white oak–northern red oak	0.8
	sweetgum–yellow-poplar (tuliptree)	4.0
	yellow-poplar	1.6
	scarlet oak	3.9
	red maple–central hardwoods	1.5
	mixed central hardwoods	22.0
	TOTAL	41.7
Northern hardwoods		
	black cherry	1.8
	mixed northern hardwoods	0.8
	TOTAL	2.6
Oak–gum–cypress		
	swamp chestnut oak–cherrybark oak	1.3
	sweetgum–nuttall oak–willow oak	9.9
	sweetbay–swamp tupelo–red maple	4.2
	TOTAL	15.4
Elm–ash–red maple		
	black ash–American elm–red maple	0.6
	red maple (lowland)	1.3
	American elm–green ash	0.8
	TOTAL	2.7
Mixed		
Oak–pine		
	Virginia pine–oak	4.2
	loblolly pine–hardwood	11.8
	TOTAL	16.0
Coniferous		
Loblolly–shortleaf		
	loblolly pine	19.9
	Virginia pine	1.6
	TOTAL	21.5

Source: Adapted from Frieswyk and DiGiovanni 1989.

The northern hardwoods group's two forest types represent only 2.6% of the state's forests. Northern hardwoods are characteristically found at higher elevations or latitudes and are largely confined to the Piedmont. American beech, black cherry, and mixed northern hardwoods variously predominate on fertile, moist, well-drained upland sites. Sugar maple, yellow birch, and white pine—either dominant or associate species in other northern states—may once have been native to Delaware but now are reintroductions.

The Yellow-bellied Sapsucker, Brown Creeper, Rusty Blackbird (wet areas only), and Purple Finch (now uncommon) winter in Delaware's deciduous woodlands; and the White-breasted Nuthatch is present all year in the northern part of the state. Summer residents—the Veery, Wood Thrush, Red-eyed Vireo, Worm-eating Warbler, Ovenbird, and Kentucky and (rarely) Hooded warblers, and Summer Tanager (in southern Delaware)—and migrants, such as the Ruby-crowned Kinglet; Least Flycatcher; Blue-headed and Philadelphia vireos; Tennessee, Cape May, Black-throated Blue, and Black-throated Green warblers; and Rose-breasted Grosbeak, depend mainly on the oak–hickory group.

The forested wetlands constitute about 35% of the total forests. The oak–gum–cypress group, 15.4%, is described in the preceding wetlands section. These wooded swamps occur from southern New Castle County southward in Delaware, particularly in alluvial soils along inland waterways and other very moist sites. Also on freshwater streamsides are the elm–ash–red maple group types, a total of 2.7%. The remainder of the forested wetlands are mainly in the loblolly–shortleaf pine group, described hereafter. (Delaware's forested wetlands are discussed in the "Wetlands" section of this chapter.)

The 16% of forests in the oak–pine group are prominently scattered in southern Kent and Sussex counties on soils that are excessively to moderately drained. This group usually occurs in stands 50% or more in upland hardwood species, mainly oaks, with abundant Virginia, loblolly, or shortleaf pine, or eastern red cedar, and commonly sweetgum, black gum, red maple, hickory, and tuliptree, depending upon the dryness of the site. Of the two types in the group, loblolly pine–hardwood is predominant in Delaware and is found mainly in harvestable aged stands (Frieswyk and DiGiovanni 1989).

No bird species are known to use mixed forests exclusively, although in Delaware many are found in both deciduous and mixed woodlands; for example, those occurring throughout the year are the Great Horned Owl, the scarce Red-headed Woodpecker in association with old dead trees, the Red-bellied and Downy woodpeckers, Pileated Woodpecker in large tracts with large trees, and Brown-headed Cowbird at edges. Summering species include the Broad-winged Hawk (uncommon); Yellow-billed Cuckoo in edges and understory; Whip-poor-will, Ruby-throated Hummingbird, Eastern Wood-Pewee, Great Crested Flycatcher, Scarlet Tanager in larger tracts; and Baltimore Oriole in open woods.

The loblolly–shortleaf pine group includes the 21.5% of forests dominated by either or both of these species or by Virginia pine (scrub pine), pond pine, pitch pine, or eastern red cedar, in association with oaks, sweetgum, red maple, black gum, or the other pines. Shortleaf pine is comparatively rare in Delaware, occurring only in the southernmost parts of the state close to the Maryland border. This group is found on a broad range of soils, from moderately well drained to wet, primarily in Sussex County. Old-growth loblolly pine is limited to a few specimen trees and neglected remnants; one small stand and a few scattered trees in the Inland Bays area are the sites of the state's breeding Brown-headed Nuthatches. Delaware's coniferous woodlands provide important roosting habitat for the Barn Owl all year and for a few Long-eared Owls in winter; other winter residents are the Red-breasted Nuthatch, Pine Siskin, and occasionally the Red Crossbill. The Prairie Warbler and Chipping Sparrow nest in scrub growth and open areas; the Pine Warbler is found in pines of both coniferous and mixed forests the year round. The Cooper's Hawk is found in both coniferous and mixed woods all year and the Chuck-will's-widow nests in brushy areas.

Red-shouldered and Red-tailed hawks, Hairy Woodpecker, Northern Flicker, Blue Jay, Carolina Chickadee, Tufted Titmouse, and, at edges, Carolina Wren can be found in all types of woodlands throughout the year. In summer, general woods dwellers include the Eastern Phoebe in open woods, House Wren in edges, Blue-gray Gnatcatcher in moist brushy woods, and, rarely, Black-and-white Warbler in moist, mature woods. Migrating Blackburnian, Bay-breasted, and Black poll warblers use various woodland types.

An analysis of all Delaware forests, indigenous and planted, completed in 1989 by the Forestry Section (Delaware Department of Agriculture, unpub.) presented a new classification consisting of eight forest groups and 48 types. When published, it will be a comprehensive reference on Delaware tree associations.

The extensive fragmentation of habitats that ensues with agricultural and urban–suburban development inevitably reduces both plant and animal diversity. For example, forest fragments may be so narrow that they are entirely edge, thereby diminishing or eliminating all species requiring forest interior (Robbins et al. 1989). (See "Forest Fragmentation" essay.)

Nevertheless, the fragmented woods of uplands and stream corridors, in combination with landscape plantings and food supplement from a large number of bird feeders, make suburbia acceptable habitat for individuals and populations of some 45 of Delaware's birds. Resident or partially migrant species that occur in suburbs include the American Kestrel, Rock Dove, Mourning Dove, Eastern Screech-Owl, Great Horned Owl, Killdeer, Downy Woodpecker, Northern Flicker, Blue Jay, American Crow, Fish Crow, Carolina Chickadee, Tufted Titmouse, Carolina Wren, Eastern Bluebird, American Robin, Gray Catbird, Northern Mockingbird, Cedar Waxwing, European Starling, Northern Cardinal, Song Sparrow, American

Goldfinch, Common Grackle, House Finch, and House Sparrow. In suitable suburban locations other species can be found in summer: Chimney Swift, Ruby-throated Hummingbird, Eastern Wood-Pewee, Eastern Phoebe, Great Crested Flycatcher, Purple Martin, House Wren, Wood Thrush, Brown Thrasher, Warbling Vireo, and Orchard and Baltimore orioles. In winter the Black-capped Chickadee, White-crowned Sparrow, Purple Finch, Pine Siskin, and Evening Grosbeak may be seen sporadically, and the White-throated Sparrow and Dark-eyed Junco regularly.

Agricultural Land

The *1987 Census of Agriculture* (U.S. Bureau of the Census 1989) reports that about 608,250 acres, or 49%, of the state's land area is in agricultural uses, excluding forestry; about 82% of the total is cropland, 3% pastureland, and the remainder devoted to confined feed lots and other farm uses. On farms, the buildings, cultivated lands, fallow fields, hedgerows, ponds, and woodlots provide significant habitat for many bird species. Exotics such as multiflora rose, autumn olive, oriental bittersweet, and Kudzu vine, previously planted for game food and cover, have proliferated and aggressively displaced native plants, and they are now recognized as pest species in need of rigorous control.

Nearly all of the species adapted to suburbia also frequent farms. Many others are common to elements of the farm; for example, hedgerows harbor the Ring-necked Pheasant, Northern Bobwhite, and Eastern Towhee all year; White-eyed Vireo, Blue Grosbeak, and Indigo Bunting in summer; and Fox Sparrow and the now rare Loggerhead Shrike in winter. Tundra Swans, Snow and Canada geese, and huge blackbird flocks forage in cultivated fields for grain in winter, and Cattle Egrets and Laughing Gulls forage for invertebrates in summer. Black and Turkey vultures and Red-tailed Hawks are associated with woodlots and open areas. Woods edges attract migrating Canada and Palm warblers, wintering American Tree Sparrows, breeding Eastern Kingbirds, and, in southern Delaware, resident Wild Turkeys. The Barn Owl and Barn Swallow use farm buildings, and the Turkey Vulture and American Kestrel nest in abandoned buildings. Brewer's Blackbird is a rare winter visitor to cattle feedlots. Grassy fields with wet spots harbor several shorebird species, including Killdeer, migrant American Golden-Plover, migrant and summering Black-bellied Plover, and (rarely) Upland Sandpiper, migrant and lingering Lesser Yellowlegs, and in winter Common Snipe and American Pipit. Old pasture or long grass is ideal nesting habitat for the Field and Grasshopper sparrows, Eastern Meadowlark, and where cavities are available, Tree Swallow and Eastern Bluebird. Open fields are visited by migrating blackbird flocks (occasionally with a Yellow-headed Blackbird) and in winter by the Horned Lark and, rarely, Snow Bunting and Lapland Longspur.

Declining Species

Many Delaware birds are in trouble. A look at the species accounts demonstrates that fact. Four species that previously were regular breeders have been extirpated from the state, and 11 others were not found nesting during 1983–94 and thus may be extirpated. The populations of an additional 24 breeding species are so small—fewer than 20 pairs—that they are threatened with extirpation. Beyond that, 21 breeding birds and 16 migrants and winter visitors are of management concern because they show low or declining populations or their habitats have severely deteriorated. An additional 17 breeders that are declining, though not expected to become threatened in the near future, nevertheless deserve investigation of reasons for the declines. Altogether, 93 species of Delaware birds are in trouble.

The cause for all this? In part, Delaware bird populations are affected by conditions that have arisen outside the state of Delaware—to the south, at the winter homes of our migrants and summer residents, or to the north, in the breeding areas of our winter visitors. But changing conditions in Delaware itself are to a greater or lesser extent responsible for the declining fortunes of many of the troubled species in the state. This is, of course, entirely true for those nonmigratory birds that reside here year-round; it is true in varying degrees for our part-time visitors, and particularly for the summer residents that breed here. Threats to bird populations in Delaware are primarily the result of human activities that have affected the birds' habitats.

The lists that follow show the species of concern by category. Details on the status of the individual species are provided by the species accounts, and a discussion of the statistical analysis of population trends is found in appendix I.

Extirpated Breeding Species

Previous regularly breeding birds not found breeding during 1983–94, considered extirpated:
Ruffed Grouse
Wild Turkey (now reintroduced)
Savannah Sparrow
Henslow's Sparrow
Previous rare or irregularly breeding birds not found breeding during 1983–94, with date of last nesting record (some may have bred regularly):
Northern Shoveler, 1965
American Wigeon, 1962
Ruddy Duck, 1979
Sora, 1973
Purple Gallinule, 1975
Spotted Sandpiper, 1880
Long-eared Owl, 1937
Short-eared Owl, 1938
Least Flycatcher, 1976
Loggerhead Shrike, 1924
Swainson's Warbler, 1957

Rare and Threatened Breeding Species

Species with fewer than 20 breeding pairs, potentially subject to extirpation:
Pied-billed Grebe
American Bittern
Tricolored Heron
Yellow-crowned Night-Heron
Green-winged Teal
Hooded Merganser
Bald Eagle
Northern Harrier
Cooper's Hawk
Broad-winged Hawk
Peregrine Falcon
Upland Sandpiper
Piping Plover
Gull-billed Tern
Black Skimmer
Cliff Swallow
Brown Creeper
Sedge Wren
Chestnut-sided Warbler
Yellow-throated Warbler (sycamore population)
Cerulean Warbler
Hooded Warbler
Rose-breasted Grosbeak

Other Species with Low Breeding Populations

Strong colonists not in need of management assistance:
Double-crested Cormorant
Mute Swan
Herring Gull
Great Black-backed Gull

Breeding Species of Management Concern

Of management concern because of low or declining populations or deterioration of habitat:
Least Bittern
Gadwall
American Black Duck

Blue-winged Teal
Red-shouldered Hawk
Black Rail
King Rail
Forster's Tern
Common Tern
Least Tern
Barn Owl
Barred Owl
Common Nighthawk
Yellow-throated Vireo
Brown-headed Nuthatch
Veery
Blue-winged Warbler
Northern Parula
American Redstart
Vesper Sparrow
Saltmarsh Sharp-tailed Sparrow

Other Declining Breeding Species

Declining but still relatively numerous:
Green Heron
American Kestrel
Ring-necked Pheasant
Northern Bobwhite
American Woodcock
Whip-poor-will
Chimney Swift
Northern Flicker
Acadian Flycatcher
Brown Thrasher
Black-and-white Warbler
Eastern Towhee
Field Sparrow
Grasshopper Sparrow
Eastern Meadowlark
American Goldfinch
House Sparrow

Migrants and Winter Visitors of Management Concern

Based on observational data contained in this book; independent of Delaware Division of Fish and Wildlife and U.S. Fish and Wildlife Service work:
Canada Goose
Gadwall
American Wigeon
Northern Shoveler
Northern Pintail
Canvasback
Ring-necked Duck
Greater Scaup

Surf Scoter
Black Scoter
Common Goldeneye
Common Merganser
Red-breasted Merganser
Ruddy Duck
Sora
American Coot

Data in this book show that during the twentieth century 15 of Delaware's breeding birds with now strong populations either became reestablished after earlier extirpation caused by human persecution or became established through natural extension of their ranges. In addition, the Wild Turkey, extirpated in the nineteenth century, has been successfully reintroduced. This book also shows that the populations of 22 additional species of breeding birds increased during the 1966–91 period—largely because of human-induced habitat change.

Increasing Species

Relatively Recent Breeding Species

Reestablished or newly established through range extension in the twentieth century:
Double-crested Cormorant
Great Egret
Snowy Egret
Cattle Egret
Glossy Ibis
Black Vulture
American Oystercatcher
Black-necked Stilt
Laughing Gull
Herring Gull
Great Black-backed Gull
Chuck-will's-widow
Red-bellied Woodpecker
Horned Lark
Boat-tailed Grackle

Other Increasing Breeding Species

Increased during the period 1966–91:
Great Blue Heron
Mallard
Osprey
Red-tailed Hawk
Willet
Yellow-billed Cuckoo
Pileated Woodpecker
Eastern Wood-Pewee
Eastern Phoebe
Purple Martin
Northern Rough-winged Swallow
Red-eyed Vireo

Fish Crow
Blue-gray Gnatcatcher
Eastern Bluebird
Wood Thrush
American Robin
Northern Mockingbird
Yellow Warbler
Blue Grosbeak
Indigo Bunting
Orchard Oriole

Habitat Degradation and Loss

Delawareans who want a healthy natural environment—demonstrated and rewarded by a rich diversity of bird life—must help in planning human life and work in the state. Because habitat change is the primary factor within the state that affects bird populations, this chapter examines what has been happening to the various Delaware habitats important to birds and ways to maintain and improve the critical habitats that are under stress.

The paper on which this chapter is based, "Delaware Birds and Conservation Issues" by Lorraine M. Fleming, is available from the Delaware Nature Society.

Planning for Human Population Growth

Behind the deterioration and losses of natural habitats lie inadequacies in dealing with human population growth in the state. For lack of proper land-use planning or controls, unnecessary destruction and degradation have taken place in all types of bird habitats.

Suburban New Castle County experienced explosive population expansion after 1940, growing by 428% in 50 years. Drastic conversions of land took place to accommodate 266,000 more people, with farmland and other open space being taken over for roads and for residential and commercial development. Populations in the two southern counties, relatively stable for 100 years before 1950, have increased markedly: Kent County's by 193% and Sussex County's by 85%.

The growth continues. From 1980 to 1990 the total Delaware population increased by 12%—more than 18% faster than the national average—to 665,000. New Castle County grew by 11%, to 442,000; Kent County by 13%, to 110,000; and Sussex County by 15.5%, to 113,000. By early 1994 the state's population had reached 700,000.

Farmlands and Grasslands

The farmland and grassland birds whose populations show significant declines in Delaware between 1966 and 1991 include the American Kestrel, Grasshopper Sparrow, Vesper Sparrow, Field Sparrow, and Eastern Meadowlark. Also declining are two species that inhabit the brushy hedgerows of rural areas: Eastern Towhee and Northern Bobwhite. This decline in populations is influenced by both loss of farmland and changes in farming practices.

Conversion of agricultural lands to residential and commer-cial developments, occurring at a rapid rate since the middle of the twentieth century, permanently reduces available habitat for several bird species. Total land in farms declined 37%, from approximately 904,000 acres in 1950 to 570,000 acres in 1990. Pasture fields declined precipitously—by 85%, from 100,000 acres in 1950 to 15,000 acres in 1987. Those parts of Delaware where population and development pressures (and the loss of farmland) have been greatest include northern New Castle County, the Middletown-Odessa area, the Dover-Smyrna area, and coastal Sussex County, including the Inland Bays watershed.

Since 1968, owners of farmlands have had the option of placing them in a preferential property tax program under the Farmland Assessment Act. Lands in this program are taxed at the lowest rate available while they remain in agricultural use; if the lands are later converted to a nonagricultural use, penalties and rollback taxes may be imposed. In practice, however, this program has provided little incentive to keep land in agricultural use.

Part of the rollback taxes can be used in a voluntary program created by the 1991 Delaware Agricultural Lands Preservation Act. The act allows farmers to place their lands in agricultural districts of at least 200 contiguous acres, and as of 1998 more than 100,000 acres of land were enrolled in the program. In 1995–98 $40 million was appropriated to begin purchasing the development rights to lands in agricultural districts to ensure permanent preservation for agricultural use. Additional appropriations will be needed to continue this program.

Popularity of no-till crop management has risen sharply in the last two decades. In no-till farming, herbicides are used to "burn down" unwanted vegetation so that crops can be planted. When such herbicide application is carried out at the beginning of the nesting period, cover and foraging areas are destroyed, reducing the nesting success for some grassland birds. Grub problems associated with no-till, however, have recently led farmers to try minimum-tillage practices using less herbicide, which may pose less risk to the birds.

It is possible that farmland and grassland birds can be helped by increasing the use of grass filter strips between crop fields to combat soil erosion, trap nutrients, and prevent pesticide runoff, but trials with this technique should be monitored to ensure that predator corridors are not inadvertently created. Mowing of the strips should be delayed until July to avoid interference with nesting. To protect grassland nesters, the staffs of the Delaware Nongame and Endangered Species Program, the three county conservation districts, and the Soil Conservation Service should work together in educating farmers to adjust mowing and herbicide application schedules.

Since 1987 several hundred acres of Delaware farmland have been taken out of production for specified periods of time under the federal Conservation Reserve Program (CRP). Early-stage vegetation reversion helps the American Kestrel, and later stages help the Prairie Warbler and Field Sparrow. Additional acres in the CRP would aid these birds.

The brushy hedgerows that have vanished from large areas of the state provided valuable habitat for many birds, including the Eastern Towhee and Northern Bobwhite. Hedgerows should be reestablished in rural areas, taking care to avoid the use of invasive exotic plants.

Except for the Mourning Dove and Snow Goose, all game birds in Delaware declined between 1966 and 1991. The U.S. Fish and Wildlife Service sets hunting seasons and bag limits for migratory game birds, but the state has conservation responsibility for nonmigratory game birds and can impose even stricter limits for the migratory birds. The Delaware Division of Fish and Wildlife needs to react quickly to pronounced reductions in a species' numbers, as it did for the Canada Goose and is now doing for the Northern Bobwhite.

Forests

Continuing forest losses, forest fragmentation, and selective logging throughout Delaware have reduced populations of many migrants and forest interior breeding birds (see "Forest Fragmentation" essay). Among the breeding birds most drastically affected are the ground-nesting Whip-poor-will, which requires large contiguous forests of oak and pine at the scrubby pole stage; the Black-and-white Warbler, which nests in similar woodlands; the Cerulean Warbler, which nests in large wooded floodplain areas with some old trees; the Brown-headed Nuthatch, which requires mature pines; the Red-headed Woodpecker, which needs stands of large, old trees; and the Eastern Towhee, which along with several other species has been hit by increased Brown-headed Cowbird parasitism associated with the additional forest edges created by fragmentation.

The mature and old-growth northern hardwood and oak-hickory forests of Piedmont stream corridors found in the White Clay, Red Clay, and Brandywine Valleys provide not only nesting habitat for many Delaware birds but also important feeding areas for spring and fall migrants, particularly warblers. The Cerulean Warbler, declining throughout its breeding range in the United States, is now limited in Delaware to the Piedmont valleys of the White Clay and Brandywine Creeks. This warbler and other deep-woods birds can be permanently protected by taking into public ownership additional lands in the White Clay Creek Preserve/State Park–Middle Run Natural Area (now more than 3,500 acres in Delaware and Pennsylvania), by allowing more acreage to revert to mature forest, and by preserving and connecting substantial acreage in both private and public ownership in the Brandywine and Red Clay stream valleys. As a vital part of this effort, increasingly rare and highly marketable old oak trees must be protected, not selectively removed under the guise of forest improvement. Removal of mature oak trees has had a catastrophic effect on such once-wonderful migratory sites as the Alapocas Woods.

Migrant birds, particularly in the fall, use the woods along the Delaware River and south along the coast more intensively than those in the interior, so special attention should be paid to maintaining their integrity.

Similarly in Sussex County, the high value of mature pines for saw timber threatens the old growth pine forest required by the Brown-headed Nuthatch, which is now confined to a small area and could be wiped out in Delaware if timbering occurs there.

The Red-headed Woodpecker is now too scarce in Delaware to be monitored by statistical sampling. This woodpecker's initial decline may have been a result of competition for nesting holes from the European Starling, especially in cities and suburbs. In recent years, the threat has come from the clearing of forested wetlands with large trees and the clear-cutting of uplands for conversion to agriculture and housing, particularly in Sussex County, which have destroyed nearly all the state's remaining Red-headed Woodpecker colonies. To help this and other forest birds, statewide regulations on timber cutting are sorely needed, requiring that large dead trees be left standing for wildlife use in both wetlands and uplands.

To reduce predation and cowbird nest parasitism along forest edges, government and private conservancy programs aimed at reconnecting fragmented habitats into larger contiguous forests should receive budgetary priority and public support. Examples are the Greenspace Plan and the Greenways, Natural Areas Preservation, and rare-plant protection programs. To promote forest stewardship on private lands, landowner education is essential; this is one of the goals of the Delaware Forest Stewardship Committee.

Mackenzie's analysis (1989) of Delaware land use changes from 1974 to 1984 indicated a 6.9% decrease in forest cover, exclusive of brushland. He found a net decline of 7,500 acres (3.6%) in deciduous forest, 11,800 acres (15.4%) in coniferous forest, and 7,600 acres (7.1%) in mixed deciduous-coniferous forest. The lost forest acreage was converted to brushland, agriculture, and residential use. The greatest losses by far for all three forest categories were in Sussex County.

Current laws provide modest encouragement for retention and increase of forest habitats. These laws include the Delaware Farmland Assessment Act of 1968; a special provision for a 30-year tax exemption for forest plantations; a New Castle County ordinance that limits the harvest of trees in floodplains; and the Delaware Seed Tree Law of 1989, requiring reforestation whenever tracts of ten acres or more are timbered. Additional state and local laws, regulations, and policies are needed to promote forestry practices that favor the full range of Delaware forest birds by encouraging some woodlands to reach an old growth state.

Wetlands

At the time of European settlement, more than one-third of Delaware's area was freshwater and saltwater wetlands, now reduced to one-sixth, or some 216,000 acres. In recent decades, 1,400 acres of wetlands were lost each year, mainly in freshwater wetlands. Forested wetlands decreased in area by 17% between 1955 and 1981, with all classes of palustrine (inland) wetlands diminishing by 21%. Most wetlands were lost to agricultural drainage, channelization, forest clear-cutting, and urban development. There is some indication, however, that losses have slowed considerably in the 1990s.

The disappearance of inland freshwater wetlands may have contributed to the elimination of Henslow's Sparrow as a Delaware breeding bird by greatly diminishing its prime habitat—broom sedge fields and wet meadows. The American Woodcock, inhabitant of young wet woods, is declining because of drainage and conversion of forested wetlands; and breeding populations of the King Rail and American Bittern have fallen significantly with the loss of freshwater marshes.

The breeding status of the Red-shouldered Hawk and Barred Owl in Delaware is unclear, but suitable breeding habitat for both species has been severely reduced by cutting timber and draining forested wetlands. Both birds are forest interior nesters and prefer mature bottomland woods with a relatively open understory.

Although there is no state law to protect freshwater wetlands, other efforts at protection are underway. New Castle County, for example, has mandated the mapping of wetlands on development sites in an effort to avoid their destruction. The federal wetlands protection program, administered by the U.S. Army Corps of Engineers and overseen by the Environmental Protection Agency (EPA), requires a permit to fill more than one acre of wetlands. However, this program has been far more effective in Delaware as a second layer of protection for tidal wetlands than as a preventive measure against conversion of inland freshwater wetlands.

In tidal wetlands, Delaware's extensive cordgrass marshes should provide a home for sizable populations of the American Bittern, Saltmarsh Sharp-tailed Sparrow, Black Rail, Northern Harrier, and Short-eared Owl. But because of a variety of human activities, the marshes no longer accommodate the numbers of birds they once did. Now all these species are scarce, and the American Bittern, Black Rail, Northern Harrier, and Short-eared Owl are among the U.S. Fish and Wildlife Service's 20 migratory "birds of management concern in the Northeast." The Sedge Wren, denizen of the inner margins of tidal wetlands, is nearly gone from Delaware. Human disturbance, particularly at marsh edges, has encouraged the growth of phragmites, which chokes out the native cordgrasses and other valuable wetland plants. Marsh nesters suffer from other habitat-altering activities, such as open marsh water management for mosquito control and water-level manipulations to increase duck production. The state Division of Fish and Wildlife should require all efforts to control plant and insect pests on wetlands to take into account critical periods in the life cycles of all marsh nesters. On public lands the agency should allow only those wildlife management strategies that have proved beneficial to these birds.

Since 1973 the Delaware Wetlands Act has protected tidal wetlands from most destructive activities, yet many coastal marsh breeding birds still seem to be losing ground. Virginia and King rails are hard-to-find game birds monitored only through the number killed. Since few kills are reported, game managers assume lack of hunter interest and give low priority to management for the rails. Prohibiting the hunting of rails in impoundments would help protect them without eliminating the sport altogether. Pied-billed Grebe reproduction has suffered from management practices of the past 20 years on coastal marsh impoundments. Records show that this grebe thrives only in impoundments that have been recently flooded. Initially thought to be desirable wildlife habitat, impoundments have turned out to attract predators, recreational visitors, and unproductive exotic vegetation. New state impoundment management programs to restore vegetation useful to birds should be extended to all coastal marsh impoundments (see "Coastal Impoundments" essay).

The importance for tidal wetlands of maintaining and enforcing the 1971 Delaware Coastal Zone Act cannot be overstated. Protection afforded by this act and the 1973 Wetlands Act slowed losses of estuarine wetlands from an estimated average of 444 acres in 1954 to about 20 acres in 1973 and less thereafter. The Coastal Zone Act has served well to prevent location of new heavy industry and bulk-transfer facilities along the coastline, to limit expansion of nonconforming uses, and to discourage pollution from manufacturing. The quality of the tidal wetlands that remain has nevertheless been diminished. Ditching for mosquito control and disposal of dredge spoil have been degrading factors, but far more inhibiting to waterfowl, wading birds, and shorebirds on coastal marshes has been the rampant spread of phragmites. At the same time in the state's freshwater marshes, an invasive exotic plant, purple loosestrife (Lythrum salicaria), is rapidly replacing native plants.

Mechanical and chemical controls have been only modestly effective in checking the spread of phragmites and purple loosestrife. For phragmites, an expensive state program of herbicide spraying is beginning to show some results. For loosestrife, recent research indicates good prospects for biological control using three European insects, but introduction of the insects demands the utmost caution.

Most losses of wetlands result from residential, industrial, and commercial developments, including marinas and roads. Other losses of wetlands proceed from natural causes, such as erosion from storms and the continuing rise in relative sea level. Direct wave action during storms has eroded the northern Delaware Bay shoreline marshes by 13–20 feet per year. The central and southern shorelines with sandy barrier beaches have eroded at 7–10 feet per year, diminishing both spawning areas for horseshoe crab and breeding and resting areas for spring migrant shorebirds. Marsh sediment accretion and the formation of new wetlands would keep pace with natural loss from erosion and rising sea level, but landward migration of marshes is almost totally thwarted by adjacent development.

Atlantic Ocean and Delaware Bay Beaches

Because of intense recreational use of the state's 25 miles of ocean beach during the nesting season, the Least Tern, Piping

Plover, Common Tern, Black Skimmer, and Common Nighthawk have declined precipitously. Site protection, public education, and media attention have resulted in a marked increase in Least Tern nesting success and may rescue the nationally endangered Piping Plover. Similar attention should be given to the Common Tern, Black Skimmer, and Common Nighthawk, with nest areas located and stringently protected under the Delaware Nongame and Endangered Species Program to obviate heroic measures in the future.

"Saving beaches" from the natural eroding action of storms and the rising sea level has destroyed natural habitats while encouraging incompatible and ultimately ephemeral human construction and recreational uses. Public works projects aimed at beach protection have included building jetties to stabilize inlets, building bulkheads and sea walls to "harden" the shoreline, installing groins to interrupt sediment transport, planting American beach grass to stabilize foredunes, and large-scale pumping of sand. Given the ongoing, ultimately irresistible geological processes, however, such methods can be effective only in the short term. (For the potential effects of rising relative sea level and global warming, see "Spring Shorebirds" essay.)

The Delaware Estuary and the Inland Bays

Since the nineteenth century the Delaware River has been identified as one of the world's most polluted streams, but in the last 30 years it has improved dramatically because of the reduction or elimination of industrial discharges and the upgrading of municipal wastewater treatment plants. Even so, the minimum 24-hour average standards for dissolved oxygen—critical to aquatic life—are not consistently met at the Pennsylvania–Delaware state line and the Delaware Memorial Bridge, and occasional lapses also occur in the upper Delaware Bay. There are also high levels of nutrients in the river, primarily from storm-water runoff. The nutrients do not cause extensive algal blooms, however, probably because of high turbidity from suspended sediments.

Chemical contaminants, including polychlorinated biphenyls (PCBs), pesticides, and heavy metals—frequently bound to sediments—continue to enter the river, disperse, and cycle through living organisms. Water samples from the Delaware Memorial Bridge area have shown both acute and chronic toxicity. Although a 1991 analysis of sediments collected from Artificial Island to Trenton showed that amounts of most metals had decreased during the previous decade, high levels of copper, lead, zinc, cadmium, and chromium were still present. Metal complexes tend to be toxic and nondegradable; the free ions are biologically reactive and may be taken up by aquatic organisms, with sublethal effects. The effects of heavy metals on the estuary's ecological system are not fully understood, nor are those of chronic small, shipping-related oil spills.

Dredging to aid shipping in the Delaware River began early in the nineteenth century. By the 1880s the U.S. Army Corps of Engineers had dredged a shipping channel 35 feet deep from Philadelphia to the mouth of Delaware Bay; in 1944 the depth was increased to 40 feet. The Corps of Engineers now plans a 5-year project to deepen and maintain the channel at 45 feet so as to accommodate larger vessels and reduce barging and lightering. The plan raises serious concerns, including the resuspension of toxic substances from bottom sediments and the potential for enormous cargo spills.

Response by the U.S. Coast Guard, the U.S. Army Corps of Engineers, and the EPA to a major oil or chemical spill in the Delaware estuary is coordinated by the Coast Guard Captain of the Port of Philadelphia and may involve as many as 11 federal and three state agencies, all members of a Multi-Agency Emergency Response Team. The Delaware River and Bay Cooperative, a nonprofit consortium financed by petroleum-related industries within the estuary, is an associate member of the team. Response capability has increased substantially since the 1989 *Presidente Rivera* oil spill. In the event of a spill Tri-State Bird Rescue and Research, located near Newark, initiates a wildlife rehabilitation operation for oiled birds in cooperation with the U.S. Fish and Wildlife Service.

Water quality is routinely monitored in only 29% of the Delaware Bay, and Delaware authorities have been forced to restrict shellfishing because of high near-shore bacterial counts. A total of 171 of the bay's 782 square miles nevertheless meets federal fishable and swimmable standards, and the general health of the bay's living system is surprisingly good considering the unresolved upstream water quality problems and the loss or alteration of habitat to dredging and installation of bulkheads and jetties. Nevertheless, there is a danger to the health of herons, Osprey, Bald Eagle, and other fish-eating birds from the high levels of toxic substances found in fish tissue from the bay, including PCBs and metabolites of DDT.

Phytoplankton, the basis of the bay's food chain, is apparently increasing, but submerged aquatic vegetation has been largely absent from the system for more than 100 years, the last record of any occurrence being 1929. Dabbling ducks that once fed in the river and bay by the tens of thousands are few there today.

The health of the Inland Bays continues to deteriorate from human impact on this system, a watershed that encompasses 300 square miles, from Lewes to the Maryland line and to the west of Millsboro. Population has grown by more than 40% in the watershed during the 1970–90 period, reaching 28,000 permanent and 56,000 seasonal residents. The attendant residential and commercial development has drastically reduced open space and disrupted natural communities; and along with changes in farming practices it has degraded ground waters and caused sharp increases in sediment, nutrient, and bacterial contamination of the bays' waters.

Although the quality of the ocean waters on Delaware's coast meets standards for all designated uses, the Inland Bays' water quality is not adequate for either recreational uses, agricultural and industrial water supply, or support of aquatic life.

The Delaware Geological Survey estimates an extremely high discharge of 1,056–2,640 lb per day of nitrates to Rehoboth and Indian River Bays, primarily from fertilizers and malfunctioning septic systems. The resulting algal blooms are largely to blame for increased summer turbidity. The dredging of marina basins and the bulkheading of one-third of the approximately 120 miles of Inland Bays' shoreline have further diminished habitat and water quality.

Nine of Delaware's wintering diving ducks are losing ground: Ring-necked Duck, Canvasback, Greater Scaup, Common Goldeneye, Black Scoter, Surf Scoter, Common Merganser, Red-breasted Merganser, and Ruddy Duck. Stressed from overshooting by hunters, all nine have also experienced serious declines in reproduction in recent years because of drought and harsh, protracted winters in their wetland breeding areas, which lie in the north-central United States and Canada and in Canada's Maritime Provinces. Their Delaware environment is degraded by severely diminished water quality in the Inland Bays, parts of Delaware Bay, and many of the state's streams and ponds.

Although these nine ducks formerly wintered in large numbers on fresh, brackish, and saltwater bodies throughout Sussex County, they are now found in only a few places, where water quality is still good, and never in large numbers. If these ducks are to winter in Delaware successfully, even in reduced numbers, the state must tighten and enforce surface water quality standards and work quickly to alleviate runoff pollution. Discharges of treated wastewater to streams should be eliminated wherever possible, using land disposal for the treated water instead. In addition, we must follow the Comprehensive Conservation and Management Plans developed for the Delaware and Inland Bays estuaries under the EPA's National Estuary Program.

Ponds and Streams

Of the 742 miles of streams covered by the 1994 Delaware Watershed Assessment Report, 27% fail to meet the federal fish, aquatic life, and wildlife use standards, and 93% fall short of swimming standards. Only 13% of the stream miles fully support the state's designated uses, 15% support them partially, and fully 72% do not support them at all. Contributing to the streams' poor condition are industrial and municipal discharges, affecting 280 miles; malfunctioning septic systems, 253 miles; agricultural activities, 709 miles; and runoff from urban, construction, landfill, and hazardous waste sites, 524 miles. Furthermore, streamside wetlands destruction, floodplain disruption, and general lack of sensitive management in urban areas have severely stressed aquatic systems in many stream segments.

A recent study of 47 of Delaware's 60 ponds of five acres or more found that all 47 are eutrophic or severely eutrophic—that is, overloaded with nutrients that often produce a choking growth of algae and other aquatic plants. This overload has

rendered the ponds unsuitable for ducks and other waterbirds. Of 2,800 acres of ponds assessed, only 25% fully support their designated uses, 37% either partially support the uses or are considered threatened, and 38% do not support them at all. The principal causes of pond-water degradation are storm sewer overflow, septic tank malfunction, and urban and agricultural runoff that contains nutrients, bacteria, organic chemicals, and toxic substances.

Chemical Pollution

Birds, like other animal and plant life, adapted over millions of years to an imperceptibly slow change in the natural composition of the earth's atmosphere. Today, human activities are causing changes at a (perhaps literally) breathtaking rate. The few studies of air pollutants' toll on birds have shown not only direct mortality, but also tissue accumulation of airborne cadmium, fluoride, lead, and mercury, which may have sublethal effects, such as physiological stress, that lower survival rates. Problems continue even after heavy metals settle out of the atmosphere or are removed by rain, snow, and fog. Plants and soil life wane and water bodies are contaminated.

Although the effects of ozone on vegetation and wildlife in Delaware are not well documented, it is known that high levels of ozone affect plant growth and reproduction. Numerous examples of foliage and root damage in trees and farm crops have been noted in the state, and ozone has been rated as the air pollutant most harmful to regional forests, habitat of many of Delaware's birds.

Acid rain is not currently regarded as a problem in the state. The pH of rainfall, influenced by sources in the Midwest, averages about 4.3, varies from 3.1 to 5.6, and is usually most acid in the summer. Reports from 30 of Delaware's ponds showed only one, Trap Pond, with an average pH below 5.0.

Widespread use of DDT on farms and marshes from the 1950s into the 1970s is a persisting specter in the 1990s, despite severe limitations placed on its use in 1972 and a complete ban by the EPA since January 1, 1973. DDT is still found in surface and ground waters, although it is far less common today than its metabolites DDE and DDD. These long-lasting compounds accumulate in aquatic food chains, working their way up the chains to raptors, wading birds, and other carnivorous and piscivorous species. Although species that declined drastically in the 1960s because of DDT have made a pronounced recovery, current evidence indicates that DDE is causing eggshell thinning among Ospreys and other raptors, particularly near Delaware Bay. In addition, the DDT analogs methoxyclor and dicofol have been shown to cause cross-generational abnormalities in sexual development among American Kestrel.

The sensitivity of birds to PCBs, also found in the Delaware estuary, apparently varies. Wildlife studies in the Great Lakes Basin have shown that organochlorides there, including PCBs, disrupt reproduction in the Double-crested Cormorant, Black-crowned Night-Heron, Bald Eagle, Osprey, Herring Gull, Ring-billed Gull, Forster's Tern, Common Tern, and Caspian Tern. The EPA in 1979 prohibited the manufacture, processing, and distribution of PCBs. Other organochlorides, insecticides once commonly used but now banned or severely restricted in the United States, are aldrin, chlordane, dieldrin, endrin, heptachlor, kepone, mirex, and toxaphene.

The role of organochlorides has been largely filled by organophosphate insecticides, which persist in water, soil, foliage, invertebrates, and birds for a few hours to several weeks. Organophosphates work by inhibiting enzymes and disrupting nerve function. Their documented effects on birds range from direct mortality to anorexia, hypothermia, depressed nestling growth, and possibly increased vulnerability to predation. Currently, many common organophosphate insecticides, such as Parathion, have been severely restricted by the EPA, and bans on their use are being sought.

Since its development in 1970 the granular formulation of carbofuran, an insecticide used on potatoes, corn, and other row crops, has been responsible for countless bird deaths in Delaware and elsewhere. Seed-eating birds have died from direct ingestion, and other birds have died as a result of consuming poisoned prey. In 1991 the EPA reached agreement with the manufacturer to remove its granular, carbofuran-containing product, Furadan, from the market in several stages, though restrictions on the liquid form of carbofuran have yet to be addressed.

In the early 1990s the state annually sprayed thousands of acres of Delaware's public and private forests with diflubenzuron, Dimilin, a chitin inhibitor, to suppress gypsy moth caterpillars. This insecticide, which persists on foliage, is applied at a time when many insect-eating birds are feeding nestlings. Although there has been no short-term reduction in bird abundance in diflubenzuron-treated areas, recent studies indicate indirect adverse effects on nine nesting forest birds in the form of reduced insect availability and lowered fat reserves.

There is in fact scant hope of eradicating the gypsy moth, which exhibits distinct population cycles. Attempting to control it chemically, except around residences, is futile in the long term. One alternative for controlling the moths is the biological agent *Bacillus thuringiensis* (BT), currently used by the state near water and in other environmentally sensitive areas. Recent research, however, has shown that BT may also have harmful effects on birds. The most promising treatment, an insecticide that contains a gypsy moth virus, is available commercially.

Contact herbicides commonly used over broad areas in no-till farming or to control weeds such as phragmites are generally less harmful to vertebrates than are insecticides. Roundup and other formulations of glyphosate apparently have few, if any, direct effects on birds.

The Future of Bird Conservation in Delaware

A successful program to sustain and improve bird diversity and abundance in the state must have four essential elements: monitoring and research, protection and legislation, restoration of habitats, and education and publicity.

Monitoring and Research

This book provides a good baseline of knowledge about the status of birds in the state; that knowledge must be kept up-to-date if we are to recognize and respond promptly to both threats and successes. Fortunately we have the framework for monitoring and research, which can function well if given effective support. That framework consists of the state and federal professionals, university scientists, and skilled volunteers involved in such work as the state's Nongame and Endangered Species Program, the Delaware Natural Heritage Program, Partners in Flight, the Breeding Bird Survey, the tri-state Gap Analysis Project, and the Christmas and May bird counts. The program must include monitoring and research not only on the birds themselves and their habitats but also on such key elements of their livelihood as horseshoe crabs in Delaware Bay.

Protection and Legislation

The Piping Plover nearly disappeared from Delaware before vigorous protection was mounted against destructive human activities. The state finally stepped in with strong measures, and the bird may yet be saved as a breeder here. Delaware needs a strong endangered species law similar to those in many other states. There should be a state policy to increase diversity by protecting birds that are at the limits of their breeding or wintering range here and also potential Delaware residents now classified as threatened or endangered in neighboring states. Species that do not breed in Delaware now but might be encouraged to do so include the Brown Pelican, Spotted Sandpiper, Short-eared Owl, Loggerhead Shrike, Swainson's Warbler, Henslow's Sparrow, and Dickcissel.

The nationally outstanding example of legislative protection in Delaware was, of course, the pioneering Coastal Zone Act of 1971, which led the way for similar legislation by a number of other states. It has been under attack many times since its passage, and conservationists must continue to rally to its support. Eternal vigilance is the price of conservation.

The state Natural Areas Preservation System Act of 1978 declared a policy of preserving areas of unusual natural significance, created an Office of Nature Preserves in DNREC's Division of Parks and Recreation, established an Inventory of Natural Areas qualified to become Nature Preserves, and set up a citizen Natural Areas Advisory Council. Currently 19 Nature Preserves protect more than 2,100 acres of diverse bird habitats. Beginning in 1983 the Nongame Wildlife, Endangered Species, Natural Areas Preservation Fund Act gave citizens the chance to donate money, either directly or when filing their state income tax return, to the work of the Office of Nature Preserves and the Office of Nongame and Endangered Wildlife; annual contributions have been running at only $55,000. The Delaware Land Protection Act of 1990 established a state Open Space Council to set priorities for state purchases, and a companion Open Space Bond bill created a funding mechanism to yield about $7 million a year. More than 6,400 acres were protected in the 4 years of the program. In 1995–98 $40 million was appropriated from the 21st Century Fund for additional land purchases. Other recent legislation of note includes the Horseshoe Crab Protection Act, assigning DNREC to regulate harvest of horseshoe crabs in the bay—the food supply for the hundreds of thousands of spring shorebird migrants.

There are excellent examples of nonlegislative protective steps taken in the state in recent years:

• The 1986 dedication by the governors of Delaware and New Jersey of Delaware Bay as the first Hemispheric Reserve in the Western Hemisphere Shorebird Reserve Network.

• The 1992 designation for protection by the Ramsar Convention of 143,850 acres of Delaware estuary lands (64,272 acres in our state).

• The designation in 1994 by the National Oceanic and Atmospheric Administration of about 4,000 acres of state-nominated lands along the St. Jones River and Blackbird Creek as the Delaware National Estuarine Research Reserve System.

Add to this the valuable land protection programs being carried out or promoted by nongovernment organizations in the state—the Delaware Nature Society, Delaware Wild Lands, The Nature Conservancy, the Brandywine Conservancy, the Christina Conservancy, the Nanticoke Watershed Conservancy, The Woodlawn Trustees, the Coalition for Natural Stream Valleys, the Delaware Audubon Society, the Red Clay Valley Association, the Sierra Club Delaware Chapter, the United Auto Workers Community Action Program Council, the Agricultural Lands Foundation, and others.

Of paramount importance to the long-term protection of bird habitats—and hence bird abundance and diversity—in Delaware is intelligent land use planning in each of our three counties. We need plans that protect and connect the crucial elements of the land's natural resources and that direct residential, commercial, and highway development to the ecologically least-sensitive areas. The poor planning, weak zoning and subdivision ordinances, and lax enforcement of the past, still prevalent in some cases, have taken a heavy toll of high-quality bird habitats in all of the state's counties and municipalities. Using the sophisticated inventory and mapping capabilities of Geographic Information Systems, planners now have an opportunity to create comprehensive development plans of unprecedented caliber. Once created, these plans must be followed, enforced through strong legal tools, and updated regularly.

Restoration of Habitats

Although restoration is difficult and expensive—the better course being to prevent damage in the first place—degraded ecosystems can sometimes be restored, and it often proves worthwhile to do so. Recently, techniques for restoring salt-marsh cordgrass plant communities have become predictably successful. Now there is considerable interest in creating or restoring freshwater wetlands.

Research has begun on restoring hardwood forests. The ability to accelerate the development of climax vegetation would be a superlative aid to preserving birds and other wildlife.

Restoring and protecting natural vegetation buffers along streams and ponds will greatly slow storm water runoff, thereby allowing absorption and slow release of waters that carry excess nutrients, sediments, and a host of water pollutants from farms, urban and industrial developments, roadways, and shopping centers. Efforts by regulatory agencies to control nonpoint sources of pollution should be stepped up now that the majority of discharges from industrial and municipal point sources are under reduction schedules through a federal-state permit program.

Habitat creation projects are also a possibility—for example, building dredge spoil islands as nesting sites for Spotted Sandpiper and other species that require isolated open ground.

Education and Publicity

Broad public support is needed if we are to achieve and maintain strong legislation, good research and management programs, and public and private habitat protection. It is essential that the citizens of the state be educated in the critical importance of ecosystem preservation, not only for the pleasure but also for the health, both physical and economic, of future generations of Delawareans.

A good deal of this task is currently being carried by private organizations, such as the Delaware Nature Society, the Delaware Audubon Society, and the several conservancies. A broader reach is needed, one that can be filled only by the school system. As a part of inculcating the principles of good citizenship, ecology and conservation must be taught as part of the regular school curriculum.

If conservation is to succeed in Delaware, we need the sort of education and publicity that have in recent years transformed our image of a hawk from that of a scoundrel to that of a useful and picturesque member of the ecological community.

CHAPTER 3

Early Bird Records and the Growth of Ornithology in Delaware

Gregory A. Inskip

Delaware's ornithological record extends back to the seventeenth century, and the folk knowledge from which that record grew is older still. In the strict sense ornithology emerged in Delaware only after the pioneering work done elsewhere by Alexander Wilson and John James Audubon enabled students to look for and recognize the variety of species in the state. By the late nineteenth century systematic study of Delaware birds was underway. Participation has been growing ever since.

The Earliest Records

The first Delaware bird record is a place name. In 1631 the Dutch established a settlement at Lewes and named it *Swanendael* (or *Zwaanendael,* Valley of the Swans), apparently for swans seen wintering or passing through on migration (see DeVries in Jameson 1909, 214, 226). No further observations were forthcoming from this settlement, which was annihilated in less than a year by a native group (DeVries in Myers 1912).[1]

The American "backwoods" pioneer culture, including its animal lore and plant lore, was shaped by the more peaceful interaction of the Lenni-Lenape, or Delaware Indians, and the colonists of New Sweden (Jordan and Kaups 1989). Seventeenth-century explorers and settlers recognized many Delaware birds as similar to those they had left behind in Europe, and they talked about others with the Lenape.

Lenape youths, like those of other American Indian tribes, sought a vision of a personal guardian spirit, often in the form of an eagle, mountain lion, or bear. European settlers, being Christians, did not share this religious belief, but they bought swans, geese, ducks, grouse, pigeons, turkeys, and woven turkey feather quilts from the Lenape (Lindestrom 1925). Campanius Holm's Lenape-Swedish lexicon (1702, 164–65; 1834, 149) gives Lenape terms for loons, swans, Canada Goose, Snow Goose, ducks (and duck hunting), Sandhill Crane, Common Moorhen, crows and thrushes or blackbirds.

From July to October 1634, the English sea captain Thomas Yong sailed up the Delaware Bay and River as far as the Falls at what is now Trenton, New Jersey. Yong hunted "covies" of "partriches" (Northern Bobwhite) and saw "wild hawkes" chasing the same birds. He remarked on the abundance and variety of other species: "There are infinit number of wild pidgeons, blackbirds, Turkeys, Swans, wild geese, ducks, Teales, widgins, brants, herons, cranes etc. of which there is so great abundance, as that the Rivers and creekes are covered with them in winter" (Myers 1912, 48). (This is perhaps a somewhat exaggerated account intended to impress the expedition's sponsor.)

Similar lists were left by Peter Lindestrom, an engineer in New Sweden in 1654 and 1655 (Lindestrom 1925, 187); by William Penn in 1683 (Myers 1912, 229), by Gabriel Thomas in 1698 (ibid., 321); and by Thomas Campanius Holm in 1702, based largely on the observations of his grandfather Johannes from 1642 to 1648. Together they record an avifauna of seventeenth-century Delaware (and adjoining parts of Pennsylvania and New Jersey) that was richer than it is today, yet a recognizably Delaware avifauna all the same:

Loon sp.	Thomas: "Divers"; Campanius Holm: in Swedish, *Lomars,* "Loom."
Great Blue Heron	Yong and Governor Johan Rising: "herons" in fall or winter.
Swan sp.	All observers, probably referring to both Tundra and Trumpeter swans.
Canada Goose	All observers list geese, usually generically. The "gray" geese that Governor Rising reported arriving in the region from mid-September to mid-October probably were Canadas (Campanius Holm 1702, 31; 1834, 41). Penn also reported "gray" geese.
Brant	Yong, Penn, and Thomas list "brant" alongside one or two other kinds of "goose" (Myers 1912, 48, 229, 321).
Lesser Snow Goose (Blue morph)	Governor Rising, quoted in Campanius Holm (1702, 31; 1834, 41), stated that "white-headed" *(hwithufdade)* geese passed northward through the region in late March, just ahead of the "white pied" *(hwitbrokote)* geese (Greater Snow Geese?). He distinguished both of these from the "gray" (Canada) geese seen in the fall.
Greater Snow Goose	The "white" geese listed by Penn and Campanius Holm (1702, 165; 1834, 149) were presumably of this race.
American Black Duck	Yong distinguished ducks from wigeon and teal and undoubtedly referred to this species, among others.
Green-winged Teal	Yong: "Teales" in winter.

American Wigeon	Yong.
Turkey Vulture	Lindestrom: "vultures."
Bald Eagle	Lindestrom, Thomas, and Campanius Holm: "eagles."
Cooper's Hawk	Yong: "wild hawkes" observed chasing "partriches" across the Delaware River.
Hawk sp.	Lindestrom: "hawks."
Falcon sp.	Campanius Holm: *"falkar."*
Ruffed Grouse	Penn and Thomas: "pheasants"; Lindestrom: "hazel" and "wood grouse."
Greater Prairie-Chicken	Penn and Thomas: "Heath-birds."
Northern Bobwhite	Yong, Penn, and Thomas: "partriches" or "partridges"; Lindestrom and Campanius Holm: "quail."
Wild Turkey	All observers.
Sandhill Crane	"Cranes" listed in addition to "herons" by Yong and Campanius Holm.
Common Moorhen	Campanius Holm.
Curlew sp.	Penn and Thomas, probably referring to both Whimbrel and Long-billed Curlew, but may also have included Willet and godwits.
Sandpiper sp.	Penn and Thomas; "snipe"; Campanius Holm: "snippor"; perhaps including common snipe but probably also referring to dowitchers, knots, and other shorebirds.
Sanderling	Campanius Holm (1702, 31): *"strandlo-pare."*
Tern sp. or Wilson's Storm-Petrel	Lindestrom (1925, 187, n. 18): "sea-swallows" *(sioswalor)* listed among the "fish" of New Sweden.
Passenger Pigeon	All observers.
Mourning Dove	Campanius Holm: "Turtle-Doves."
Carolina Parakeet (?)	Campanius Holm: "Parrots" (Swedish: *Papegojor*).
Cuckoo sp. (?)	Lindestrom.
Ruby-throated Hummingbird	Campanius Holm.
Common Raven (?)	Campanius Holm's Lenape lexicon (1702:165) includes the simple word *Ahas* and two compound forms, *Manunckus Ahas* and *Tzackamaeaes Ahas*. Campanius Holm translated *Ahas* as "crow" *(krakan)* and *Manunckus Ahas* as "raven" *(korpen)* or "crow."
American Crow	Campanius Holm.
Northern Mockingbird	Thomas.
Thrush sp. (?)	Campanius Holm: in Swedish, *Trast,* possibly mistaking blackbirds (icterids) for thrushes.
Blackbird	Yong and Thomas, probably referring to both Red-winged Blackbird and Common Grackle
American Goldfinch	Lindestrom, Campanius Holm; "goldfinches."
Pine Siskin	Lindestrom: "siskins."

The Eighteenth Century

In the eighteenth century Delaware's ornithological record grew at a slower pace than it had during the burst of exploration and settlement in the seventeenth century. Birds were a sidelight to geography rather than a subject to be investigated in their own right. Two exceptions are the all-too-brief Delaware accounts by two Swedes, Andreas Hesselius and Peter Kalm.

Hesselius, the rector of Holy Trinity (Old Swedes) Church during 1711–24, lived in Wilmington on the Christina River. His journal (Hesselius 1947) mentions the following Delaware species: Turkey Vulture, Bald Eagle, Ruffed Grouse, Wild Turkey, Passenger Pigeon, Mourning Dove, Ruby-throated Hummingbird, Eastern Phoebe, and American Crow. Hesselius records several observations of bird behavior, including Ruffed Grouse drumming and Bald Eagles swooping in to steal waterfowl downed by gunners.

A botanist and a student of Carl von Linnaeus, Kalm was an acute observer of the natural world. He sailed from England to America in 1748 and apparently saw Wilson's Storm-Petrels and shearwaters (possibly Sooty, Greater, and Cory's) in Delaware waters (Kalm 1937, 13).[2] Kalm made a short trip to Wilmington, but most of his observations in the Delaware Valley were made around Philadelphia and Swedesboro, New Jersey. Nevertheless, his conversations with "old Swedes and Englishmen born in America" doubtless conveyed some information about Delaware birds, particularly aquatic ones, since at the latitude of Swedesboro, the Delaware–New Jersey boundary is the high-water mark of the Delaware River on the New Jersey side. Kalm was told that since the late seventeenth century there had been a pervasive decline in regional populations of geese, ducks, Sandhill Crane, Wild Turkey, Northern Bobwhite, and Ruffed Grouse (Kalm 1937, 152–53). Kalm blamed the decline on relentless shooting, deforestation, and unregulated plunder of nests. Foreshadowing today's suburbia, Kalm noted that two animal species had profited by European settlement: grackles and squirrels.

One area that remained wilderness through the eighteenth century, the Great Cypress Swamp astride Delaware's southern border with Maryland, was described in a 1782 letter to Thomas McKean, a prominent patriot, from a citizen of Delaware, identified as John Jones by Herman (1992). The letter was published anonymously in Philadelphia in 1797 in the

American Universal Magazine, then edited and republished in *Delaware History* by Frank Morton Jones (1949). This primarily botanical account is our first record of American Robins (wintering in the swamp and feeding on the abundant berries there) and Great Horned Owls (one of which was shot after depredations on domestic pigs, turkeys, and geese).

Geography and History of America by Christopher Daniel Ebeling, published in Germany in 1799, contains a brief note on Delaware birds (Ebeling 1883, 42). According to Ebeling, the "landbirds that have a permanent home in this state are not numerous," though he noted "many water and swamp birds." The permanent residents listed by Ebeling were Ruffed Grouse ("Pennsylvania pheasant"), Northern Bobwhite ("Maryland" and "Virginian" "partridges"), and Loggerhead Shrike ("butcher-bird"). Of the "multitudes of birds of passage" in Delaware, Ebeling listed "giant lark" (Eastern Meadowlark?), "snow lark" (Horned Lark or Snow Bunting?), "red-breasted fieldfare" (American Robin), "corn-thief" (Common Grackle and Red-winged Blackbird; see Kalm 1937, 248), and Passenger Pigeon.

In another geography, Joseph Scott (1807, 28, 169) provided a list of Maryland and Delaware birds that included several not previously recorded in this area: Northern Gannet, "plovers," American Woodcock, Whip-poor-will, woodpeckers, and Northern Cardinal ("red birds").

Progress Toward Systematic Ornithology in Delaware

From the mid-eighteenth through the mid-nineteenth century, a few men laid the intellectual groundwork for the systematic study of American birds, with much of this work conducted in nearby Pennsylvania. William Bartram compiled a lengthy bird list that stands as "the beginning of Pennsylvania ornithology" (Fingerhood 1992a, 35). Bartram befriended and encouraged Alexander Wilson, a young Scottish immigrant (Cantwell 1961) who went on to write the monumental *American Ornithology* (1808–14). The other pioneering giant of American ornithology, John James Audubon, also did a substantial part of his work in Pennsylvania.

Wilson first arrived in America at New Castle on July 14, 1794, and on his walk to Philadelphia observed many birds and collected a Red-headed Woodpecker (Cantwell 1961). Among the Delaware references in Wilson's *American Ornithology* are Greater Snow Goose, American Crow, Northern Mockingbird, and, at the mouth of Delaware Bay, Ruddy Turnstone. The geese appeared in February and March, "about and below Reedy Island, particularly near Old Duck Creek, in the state of Delaware. They feed on the roots of the reeds, tearing them up from the marshes like hogs" (Wilson and Bonaparte, 1859–60, 3:66). Of Northern Mockingbirds, Wilson observed, "In the country round Wilmington and New Castle, they are very numerous, from whence they are frequently brought here [Philadelphia] for sale" as caged songbirds (ibid., 2:23). Of the crows, Wilson stated, "The most noted Crow roost

with which I am acquainted is near Newcastle, on an island in the Delaware. It is there known by the name of the Pea Patch" (ibid., 1:123). Wilson reported that crows roosting in the reeds once drowned by thousands in a storm, but that "the disaster . . . seems long ago to have been repaired, for they now congregate on the Pea Patch in as immense multitudes as ever." Delaware farmers, angry at depredations on corn, had banded together "to kill or banish the Crows from their roost on the Pea Patch." Wilson made what he expected would be a futile economic argument on the crows' behalf (ibid., 1:124).[3]

Thomas Nuttall likewise referred to the Pea Patch Island crow roost in his *Manual of Ornithology* (1832) and added his 1829 observations of one on Reedy Island. Nuttall traveled in Delaware in 1809, visiting Duck Creek, Lewes, Cape Henlopen, the Great Cypress Swamp, and the Nanticoke River (McDowell 1989). His objectives were primarily botanical, but he mentioned some birds, including Whip-poor-wills that kept him awake at night.

Delawareans were not immune to the early nineteenth-century impulse toward scientific exploration of the natural world. The Delaware Academy of Science, which was organized in 1827 and persisted for 33 years, included the study of birds and other animals within its purview. "The lecture courses covered a wide range of subjects, from phrenology to the evils of novel reading, but apparently they contributed very little to a knowledge of local natural history" (Jones 1950, 15). Delaware bird study remained largely invisible in the published record of the nineteenth century (Conway 1972a), although Turnbull's (1869) and Krider's (1879) observations include some from Delaware. John Cassin also explored Delaware and, near Wilmington, collected the state's first Prothonotary Warbler specimen (Turnbull 1869).

By the late nineteenth century a few ornithologists were making serious observations of Delaware birds and their behavior. The journal of Walter Danforth Bush (1851–1904), on file at the Historical Society of Delaware, lists the Delaware birds he observed and collected from 1879 to 1881,[4] including a variety of wood warblers and other small passerines that had escaped notice here in the seventeenth and eighteenth centuries. Bush noted migration dates of blackbirds; dispersal of their winter flocks; local wintering of Eastern Bluebirds; nesting data on the Least Tern, Yellow-billed Cuckoo, Eastern Bluebird, and Yellow-breasted Chat; and brood parasitism on the latter by the Brown-headed Cowbird. Bush's collection and personal communications contributed substantially to the groundbreaking work of Charles J. Pennock, as reflected in Pennock's unpublished notebooks on file at the Historical Society of Delaware.

Pennock (1857–1935) was active in a variety of business and civic affairs, but his first love was ornithology (see brief biographies in Conway 1972a, and Palmer 1954). A native of Kennett Square, he owned a farm near Odessa, made extended observations there and in Sussex County, and did more than any other to place Delaware ornithology on a firm footing.

In collaboration with Samuel N. Rhoads, a fellow member of the Delaware Valley Ornithological Club (DVOC) and the American Ornithologists Union, Pennock compiled the first comprehensive list for the state (Rhoads and Pennock 1905; supplemented by Pennock 1908). He published 13 articles about Delaware birds and presented a number of papers to the DVOC that were abstracted in its journal *Cassinia*. In 1904 he was appointed state ornithologist, the only person in Delaware known to have held that position.

Rhoads, a wide-ranging ornithologist and mammalogist (Palmer et al. 1954), did most of his work in other states, but he collected a number of Delaware specimens now at the Academy of Natural Sciences in Philadelphia.

The Twentieth Century

In his later years Pennock corresponded with Herman H. Hanson, the state chemist, and a young ornithologist, J. H. Buckalew (1912–92) of Milford. Hanson, who lived in Dover, gave us our first modern view of Kent County bird life. His notebook of observations from the 1920s through the early 1940s (on file at the Delaware Museum of Natural History) is a major compilation, cited many times in this book. Hanson's correspondents included R. E. Dickey of Christiana, Buckalew, and J. Herholdt, first refuge manager at Bombay Hook NWR. Buckalew had started observing, banding, and collecting birds as a high school student in Milford in the late 1920s, adding greatly to Delaware ornithology. He ultimately became refuge manager at Chincoteague NWR and in that position continued to report on birds on the Delmarva Peninsula into the 1950s.

W. C. Newton prepared a list of Delaware vertebrates as a master's thesis (1916) essentially recapitulating Rhoads and Pennock's 1905 bird list. E. M. Barry published lists of state birds in 1939 and 1942, partly based on the collected records of the Society of Natural History of Delaware. After Barry's list, none appeared until that of Linehan and Jones in 1971.

In Delaware, as in the nation at large, the twentieth century has been marked by the growth of recreational birding and by larger collaborative efforts among birders.[5] Christmas Bird Counts (CBCs) are one measure of the movement. Pennock and Rhoads conducted the first Delaware CBC on December 28, 1907, at Lewes. Other early CBCs were run at Arden (1922); Delaware City (1927, 1931, 1932); Montchanin (1930); Middletown and Odessa to the Delaware River (1932); Townsend, Odessa, and Port Penn (1933); and Rehoboth Beach and Indian River (1937). CBCs are now conducted annually at Wilmington (since 1965), Middletown (1931, 1938, 1944, 1946–48, 1951–58, 1960, and annually since 1966), Bombay Hook (1939–43 and annually since 1945), Cape Henlopen–Prime Hook (since 1964), Rehoboth (1939–41, and annually since 1953), and Seaford–Nanticoke (since 1983). At least one CBC has been conducted in Delaware every year since 1937 (see Falk 1972a, 1987).

In the era of Bush and Pennock, Delawareans began organizing to foster the study of birds. The Society of Natural History of Delaware was established on October 29, 1891, with William M. Canby as president and Walter D. Bush as vice president (*Every Evening,* 1894, 192–93). The society's emphasis appears to have been primarily botanical, entomological, and mineralogical, but it conducted ornithological programs as well, including lectures by Bush and field trips led by Pennock (Jones 1950, 18), and later weekly studies of the birds of Hoopes Reservoir and Churchmans Marsh. Members of the society were actively birding into the 1950s (Brooks 1973).

A letter to Hanson mentions a Dover Bird Club, but no details are known to us. In the late 1940s a group of chemists, the "Speed Marvel Bird Watching Association," began making organized trips whenever Carl S. Marvel, the eminent University of Illinois polymer chemist and an avid birder, was in town. Most of the members of this informal group went on to become members of the Delmarva Ornithological Society. The Lattoniken Club was organized on May 7, 1955, and survived to late April 1960. The Newark Bird Club was formed in the late 1940s, had about a dozen members, and kept minutes of its meetings. Funds of this club were used to publish the Linehan and Jones list of 1971.

In 1962 Seal T. Brooks circulated a questionnaire to birders he knew, including members of the foregoing groups, proposing the formation of a wider society for the study of Delaware birds. The results were encouraging, and the Delmarva Ornithological Society was established in February 1963 (Brooks 1973; Wayne 1983). On June 13, 1983, the Sussex Bird Club was formed by a group of 16 birders from Sussex County. Both organizations meet regularly and conduct field trips. The Delmarva Ornithological Society publishes articles and records of note in the *Delmarva Ornithologist,* an early issue of which (1965, 2:26) anticipated the preparation of this book.

The Delaware Museum of Natural History maintains a growing collection of research specimens of Delaware birds. The museum, the Delaware Nature Society, and the state Division of Parks and Recreation present a variety of programs to educate the public about birds and other wildlife.

Among hunters and birders alike, deeper acquaintance with birds and other wildlife usually leads to a desire to secure their future from overexploitation and habitat destruction. The first Delaware Audubon Society was organized on April 7, 1900, at the home of Mrs. William S. Hilles, Wilmington, for the purpose of "protection of birds and the discouraging of their use in wearing apparel and for the purposes of ornament" (*Bird Lore,* 2:95–96).[6] By and large, the effort to protect egrets, terns, and other birds from direct persecution has been successful. Other groups now are taking up the challenge of securing enough habitat for species that cannot adapt to environments severely altered by development. (See "Conservation of Delaware Birds.")

The "pidgeons" and heath birds of the seventeenth-century authors are gone, but the quail, hawks, and eagles are hanging on. We have brought back the turkeys, we still have some of the abundant wild geese and other waterfowl that Yong saw, and we know far more than he did about our shorebirds and woodland songbirds. Let awareness be the first step to keeping them all.

Notes

1. One of the founders, David DeVries, was abroad at the time and so was spared to leave us a record of the colony, as well as a lucid narrative of the history and natural history of New Netherland to the north.

2. Kalm saw storm-petrels "from the Channel to the shores of America. . . . They look like swallows and like them sometimes skim on the water" (Kalm 1937, 13). On the American side of the Atlantic, they would have been mostly Wilson's Storm-Petrels. Kalm also saw shearwaters "everywhere" from the Channel to the "American coasts" (ibid.). Although Kalm listed the shearwaters as one species, his description suggests that he saw three. Some, like a "dark gray seagull," were Sooty Shearwaters. Another kind had a "brown back and commonly a white ring around its neck, and has a peculiar slow way of flying." The brown-backed shearwaters with a white "ring" around the neck were Greater Shearwaters. Those without the neck ring probably were Cory's Shearwaters. Kalm's ship made its American landfall by running aground on a sandbar on the Maryland coast on September 13. Once free, it sailed north up the coast, around Cape Henlopen, and on into Delaware Bay. Kalm had several hours to make observations in Delaware waters, where he may have seen all four of the foregoing pelagic species.

3. To belabor the obvious, the crows have endured. Although the roost has shifted over the years (Stone 1937, 2:724), wintering American and Fish crows still roost on or near Pea Patch Island to this day. In late afternoon in any of the past several winters, I have seen small flocks flying on a bearing toward Delaware City from points as scattered as Churchmans Marsh, White Clay Creek State Park near Newark, St. Georges, and Middletown. Shortly after sunrise in winter, groups of crows can be seen flying across Rts. 13, 896, and 301 on westward courses away from the Delaware River.

4. During the nineteenth and early twentieth centuries, many other students collected birds and eggs in Delaware, documenting range changes, clutch-completion dates, and even the occurrence of species. Known from their extant collections or from their publications are W. L. Abbott, W. L. Bailey, R. D. Benson, F. L. Burns, J. D. Carter, C. Cottam, W. B. Crispin, S. T. Danforth, E. J. Darlington, A. J. Duvall, A. B. Eastman, J. T. Emlen, R. Erskine, A. C. Gardner, G. W. Gill, G. Hensel, B. C. Hiatt, W. E. Hughs, E. M. Kenworthy, P. Knappen, D. N. McCadden, R. C. McClanahan, R. F. Miller, G. S. Morris, W. C. Newton, W. Palmer, F. Regener, W. Robinson, L. W. Saylor, A. R. Smith, H. M. Smith, G. L. Stevens, W. Stone, E. T. Stuart, G. M. Sutton, H. S. Swarth, J. W. Tatum, S. Trotter, and C. Wrench.

5. In Delaware, as elsewhere, the publication in 1934 of Roger Tory Peterson's *A Field Guide to the Birds* did much to popularize the study of birds in the field.

6. The modern Delaware Audubon Society, a chapter of the National Audubon Society, was established in 1976 and conducts various environmental advocacy and nature study activities.

History of Breeding Bird Atlases

Chandler S. Robbins

Breeding bird atlases are a relatively new birding adventure—compared with the Christmas Bird Count (CBC), approaching its hundredth anniversary, and the Breeding Bird Survey, now aged 33. Along with the venerable CBC and the survey, which attract thousands of participants each year, atlases provide an opportunity for birders at all levels of expertise to contribute to an important scientific and conservation effort.

Grid-based atlases originated in England, where the first natural history atlas, the *Atlas of British Flora* (Perring and Walters), was published in 1962. It was produced by the Botanical Society of the British Isles before the start of either of the two major bird monitoring programs, the British Common Birds Census and the North American Breeding Bird Survey. Using the ten-kilometer National Grid, 1,500 botanists searched atlas blocks in Great Britain and Ireland over a ten-year period, mapping the distribution of about 2,000 plant species.

While the British Trust for Ornithology (BTO) debated the feasibility of a bird atlas for the entire country, the West Midland Bird Club conducted an atlas project in three counties in 1966–68, based on the ten-kilometer National Grid. The result was the *Atlas of Breeding Birds of the West Midlands* (Lord and Munns 1970). As fieldwork in the West Midlands neared completion, the BTO and the Irish Wildbird Conservancy initiated a five-year atlas for the whole of Britain and Ireland using the ten-kilometer grid. Despite early predictions that adequate data could not be accumulated for more than 25% of the blocks in Scotland and Ireland and more than 50% of those in Wales, the project was an overwhelming success. During the five-year period 1968–72, each of the 3,862 ten-kilometer blocks was visited; four years later the monumental *Atlas of Breeding Birds in Britain and Ireland* (Sharrock 1976) was published. It included a series of plastic overlay maps showing climatological and botanical features. This atlas set the standard and style for many others to follow: a drawing of each species, appropriate text adjacent to a distribution map, a statistical summary, and pertinent references. It also included extensive data on bird populations and habitat from BTO files and scientific literature.

The immense popularity of the British atlas program spread rapidly to Western Europe. In 1971 a European Ornithological Atlas Committee was formed to standardize methodology among the countries, and in 1976 delegates from 18 countries attended a committee meeting in Szymbark, Poland. In Europe, atlases were published for France and Denmark in 1976, the Netherlands in 1979, Switzerland in 1980, West Germany in 1977 and 1982, Finland in 1983, Czechoslovakia in 1987, Belgium in 1988, and Hungary. Detailed regional atlases include those for London and more than a dozen counties in England; West Berlin; and one or more regions in Spain, Portugal, Italy, Switzerland, and Poland. In Africa, atlases were published for Natal Province of South Africa in 1980 and for the Sudan in 1987. Australia joined the list in 1984 and New Zealand in 1985.

In North America, Vermont produced the first state breeding bird atlas (Laughlin and Kibbe 1985), followed by atlases for Ontario (Cadman et al. 1987), Maine (Adamus 1988), New York (Andrle and Carroll 1988), Ohio (Peterjohn and Rice 1991), Michigan (Brewer et al. 1991), Alberta (Semenchuk 1992), the Maritime Provinces (Erskine 1992), Rhode Island (Enser 1992), Pennsylvania (Brauning 1992) and Maryland/DC (Robbins 1996). Massachusetts was the first in the United States to initiate atlas fieldwork, but its book has not yet been published. Atlas fieldwork is complete or nearing completion for most states east of the Mississippi River, for the other Canadian provinces, and for several western states.

The North American Ornithological Atlas Committee (NORAC) was formed to provide guidelines for breeding bird atlasing standards in the Americas and to serve as a means of regular communication between the states and provinces involved in atlases. The committee consists of one representative from each of the states and provinces that are conducting or planning a breeding bird atlas, a representative of each participating county in California, representatives of the fish and wildlife services in the United States and Canada, individuals most involved in atlasing in the Americas, and editors of the various atlas volumes. Its officers are chair, Sarah B. Laughlin, Birds of Vermont Museum; vice chair, Chandler S. Robbins, National Biological Service; and secretary, Sue Ridd, Virginia Breeding Bird Atlas Project. Its steering committee includes Mike Cadman, Biology Department, University of Waterloo; Hugh Kingery, Colorado Atlas Project; James R. Travis, Albuquerque, New Mexico; and, John Zimmerman, Division of Biology, Kansas State University.

CHAPTER 4

Introduction to the Delaware Breeding Bird Atlas

The maps showing the distribution of birds breeding in Delaware are the product of the Delaware Breeding Bird Atlas Project. This project, Delaware's largest ornithological undertaking, lasted from 1983 through 1987 and involved more than 100 volunteer observers. It had the support of the natural history organizations in the state and the cooperation of many landowners. The information from the state Atlas project, which most states publish as separate volumes, is included in *Birds of Delaware* in the "Breeding" section of the species accounts.

Objectives

The objectives of the Delaware Breeding Bird Atlas Project were

• to determine the distribution of all bird species breeding within Delaware during the period 1983–87;

• to publish a permanent record of the data collected;

• to provide information for environmental and resource management by identifying sensitive species and habitats, supplying a database against which subsequent change could be measured, and contributing to a rationale for land-use planning.

Atlas Organization

The Delaware Breeding Bird Atlas Project was initiated in 1982 at a meeting called by Doris Boller, then president of the Delmarva Ornithological Society, who invited representatives of natural history and conservation organizations. The consensus was to proceed with the project; the following organizations lent their support and their names:

Delaware Department of Natural Resources and Environmental Control (DNREC)

Delmarva Ornithological Society (DOS)

Delaware Nature Society (DNS)

Delaware Museum of Natural History (DMNH)

Delaware Audubon Society (DAS)

Tri-State Bird Rescue and Research, Inc. (TSBR)

U. S. Fish and Wildlife Service (Wildlife Refuges)

University of Delaware, Department of Entomology and Applied Ecology

Society of Natural History of Delaware

Doris Boller recruited R. L. West to coordinate the project, and a steering committee formed from members of the sponsoring organizations included M. L. Ernsberger, L. L. Falk, John Frink, Kathleen Gordon, G. K. Hess, D. M. Niles, Darwin Palmer, and Joanne Patterson. The DOS treasurer served as treasurer for the project, and DOS served as the parent organization. Annual donations for an annual operating budget of $1,000 were received from DNREC, DOS, DAS, TSBR, and individuals. Kathleen Gordon edited the Atlas newsletter.

The expense of the fieldwork was borne by those doing the work. The state was divided into six equal regions; and the following served as regional coordinators during the project: D. and K. Batt, D. J. Boller, A. P. Ednie, W. W. Frech, G. K. Hess, G. F. O'Shea, D. T. Weesner, and D. P. Wolanski.

Data entry, verification, and feedback were performed by the project coordinator using BASIC computer programs custom written by C. M. West. During the verification process some questionable reports were eliminated, the rationale being that a conservative course was desirable even if a few valid records were lost in the process.

Methods

The Atlas technique has evolved from that developed by the *Atlas of Breeding Birds of Britain and Ireland* (Sharrock 1976). (See "History of Breeding Bird Atlases" essay.) Protocol for this technique, codified in *Proceedings of the Northeastern Breeding Bird Atlas Conference* (Laughlin 1982), was used in the Delaware project with the modifications discussed later.

There are two essential components of the Atlas technique: a statewide grid and breeding codes.

Grid

The grid used was based on the U.S. Geological Survey topographic maps, 7.5-minute quadrangle series. Each quadrangle was divided into six equal blocks, each 25 square kilometers (9.6 square miles). These blocks served as the basic sampling unit of the Atlas survey. Problems with surveying fractional blocks along the state border (almost half the blocks) were resolved as follows:

• The 41 fractional blocks along the Delaware–Maryland border were studied entirely by either the Maryland or the Delaware Atlas project, as mutually agreed.

• Four blocks mostly in Delaware but extending into Pennsylvania were studied in their entirety by Delaware, and four blocks lying mostly in Pennsylvania were not studied by Delaware.

• No New Jersey territory was included in the two blocks that extended across the Delaware River into that state.

• Some data from 15 blocks of less than 2 sq km of land that border the Atlantic Ocean or the Delaware River or Bay were reported in an adjacent block (see appendix B for details).

The small exchanges of area with adjacent states, made to accommodate the grid, had no significant effect on the results. Map 4.1 shows the 222 blocks, 50 quadrangles, and quadrangle names. The Delaware road map shows in more detail the locations of the blocks (Maps 4.2a, 4.2b, and 4.2c).

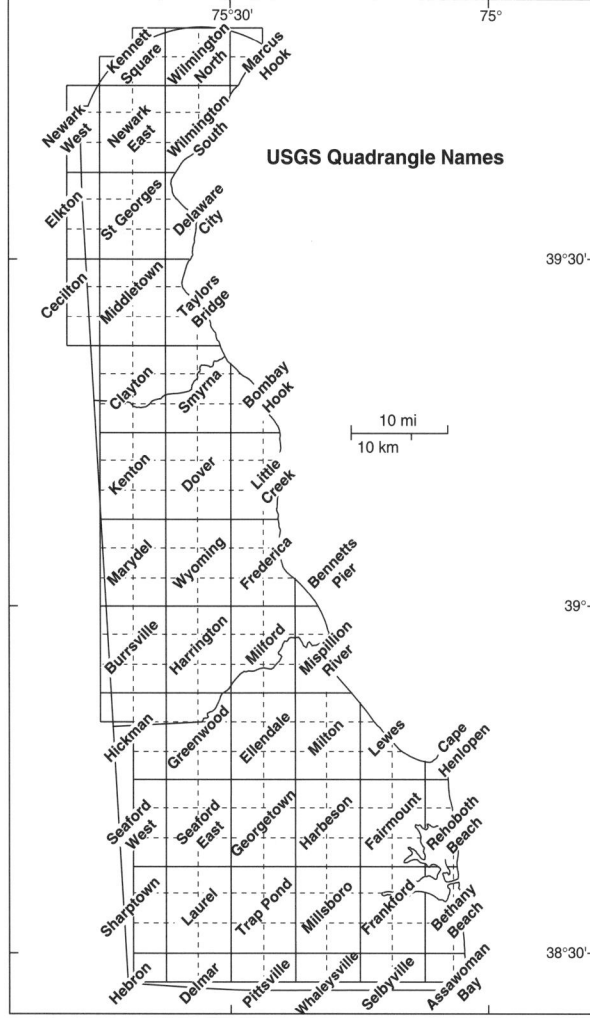

USGS Quadrangle Names

Map 4.1

Safe Dates

To avoid recording migrating or dispersing birds as breeders, the Delaware study used the "safe dates" concept developed by the Maryland Breeding Bird Atlas Project (Bystrak and Klimkiewicz 1982). For each species the safe dates were set to begin after most individuals of that species have completed their spring migration and continue until the species begins to disperse from its breeding grounds. Safe dates for nonmigratory birds were set according to their breeding season, thereby excluding dispersing young birds. Safe dates for individual species are printed on the breeding distribution maps in the species accounts.

Breeding Codes

A system of breeding codes was used to convert a variety of behavior observations into a set of three levels of evidence of breeding—confirmed, probable, and possible. The field card had columns for each level of breeding evidence and a column for observations not associated with breeding. The sizes of the dots on the breeding distribution maps reflect the highest level of breeding evidence found for each species in each block. The dot size does not refer to abundance but only to the breeding evidence.

The breeding codes are listed in table 4.1. They were taken from those recommended by the Panel on Code Standardization (Robbins 1981) with these exceptions:

• *Pair* is defined as dimorphic pair. Other pairs were recorded as possible breeders.

• All codes denoting possible breeding, and codes for pair and territory, required observation of a species within its Safe dates.

• For colonial breeders—some of the herons, egrets, and ibises; gulls and some terns; and Bank Swallow—only codes of confirmed breeding apply.

• For the Turkey Vulture and Least Tern, only the codes for confirmed and probable breeding are used.

Table 4.1. Breeding Evidence Criteria

Observed

X   Species (male or female) observed during the breeding season. Colonial birds, birds flying overhead, birds seen in unlikely breeding habitat, or birds seen outside their Safe dates. Records were not entered on breeding distribution maps.

Possible

O   Species (male or female) observed in suitable nesting habitat during its Safe dates.
S   Singing male detected in suitable nesting habitat during its Safe dates.
P   Pair (sexes not distinguished) observed in suitable nesting habitat during its Safe dates.

Probable

P   Dimorphic pair observed in suitable nesting habitat during its Safe dates.
T   Permanent territory presumed from observing defense. Fighting, chasing, or singing from the same location on days at least a week apart—during its Safe dates.
C   Courtship behavior or copulation. Courtship feeding and displays; not used for waterfowl.
N   Visiting probable nest site. A bird's consistent flights into a thicket, for example; use with caution for repeated visits when no other breeding evidence is observed.
A   Agitated behavior or anxiety calls from adults. Agitated response to pishing or tape recordings not included.
B   Nest building by wrens or excavation of holes by woodpeckers.
D   Distraction display or injury feigning. Less than a strong display.

Confirmed

DD   Distraction display. Appearance of being life threatening.
NB   Nest-building by all but woodpeckers and wrens. Carrying sticks, without a nest, might be just courtship behavior.
PE   Physiological evidence of breeding (for banders). Highly vascularized incubation patch or egg in oviduct, based on bird in hand.
UN   Used nest or egg shells found.* Generally acceptable only after examination by an expert.
FL   Recently fledged young of altricial species incapable of sustained flight* or downy young of precocial species restricted to natal area by dependence on adults or limited mobility. Birds that have obviously left the nest quite recently.
ON   Occupied nest. Adults entering or leaving a cavity nest or those too high to examine; also sitting birds that may be brooding young rather than incubating.
AY   Attending young.* Adult carrying fecal sac or food for young, or feeding recently fledged young; not terns or Osprey, which some times carry food long distances.
NE   Nest with eggs,* usually identified by seeing the adult. Contents of nest must be determined.
NY   Nest with young seen or heard.* Observers warned not to approach nests.

Note: *Presence of cowbird egg or young was confirmation of both cowbird and host species.

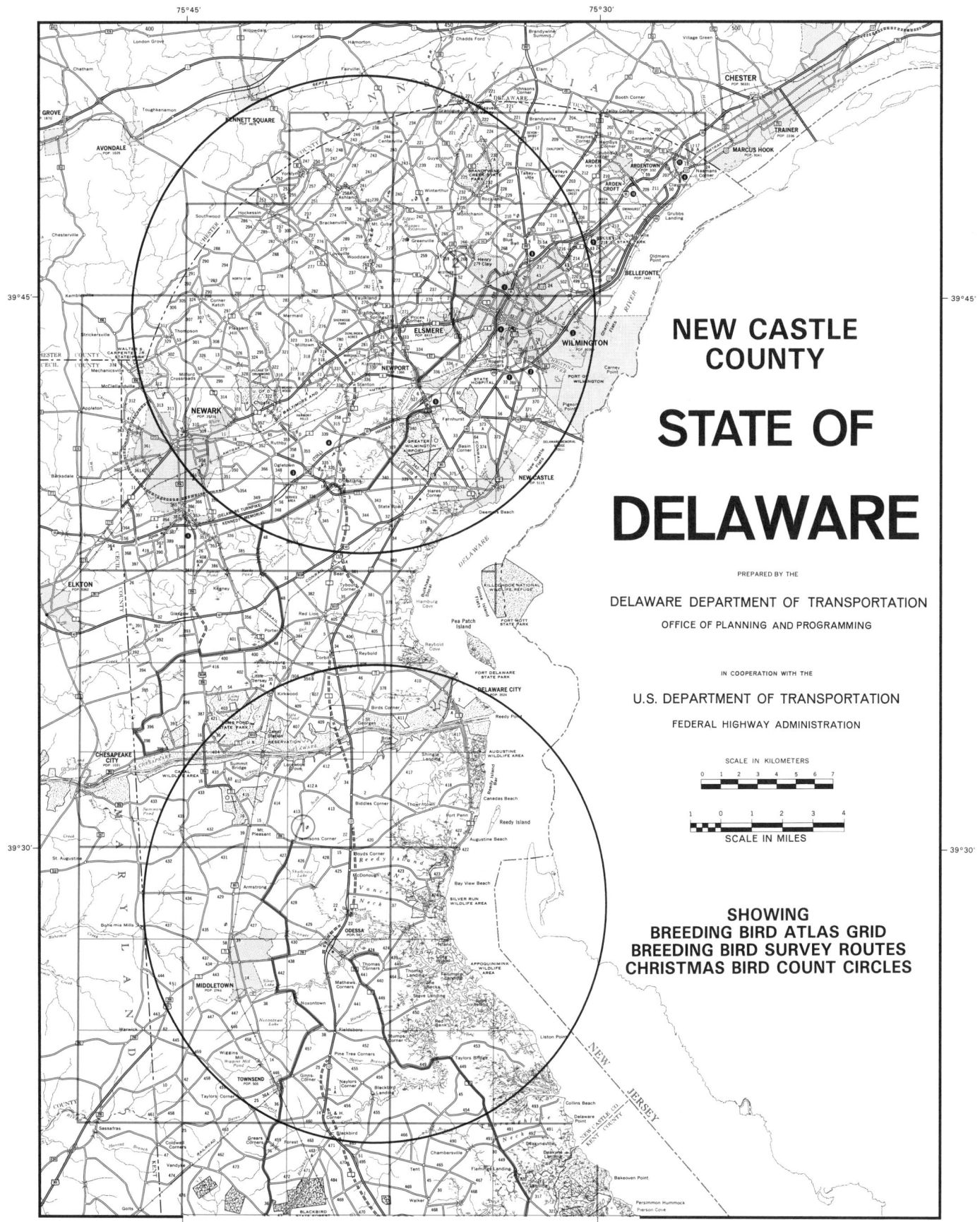

NEW CASTLE
COUNTY

STATE OF

DELAWARE

PREPARED BY THE

DELAWARE DEPARTMENT OF TRANSPORTATION

OFFICE OF PLANNING AND PROGRAMMING

IN COOPERATION WITH THE

U.S. DEPARTMENT OF TRANSPORTATION

FEDERAL HIGHWAY ADMINISTRATION

SCALE IN KILOMETERS

SCALE IN MILES

SHOWING
BREEDING BIRD ATLAS GRID
BREEDING BIRD SURVEY ROUTES
CHRISTMAS BIRD COUNT CIRCLES

Map 4.2a Delaware Department of Transportation, Contract Administration, P.O. Box 778, Dover, DE 19903. $2.00/map.

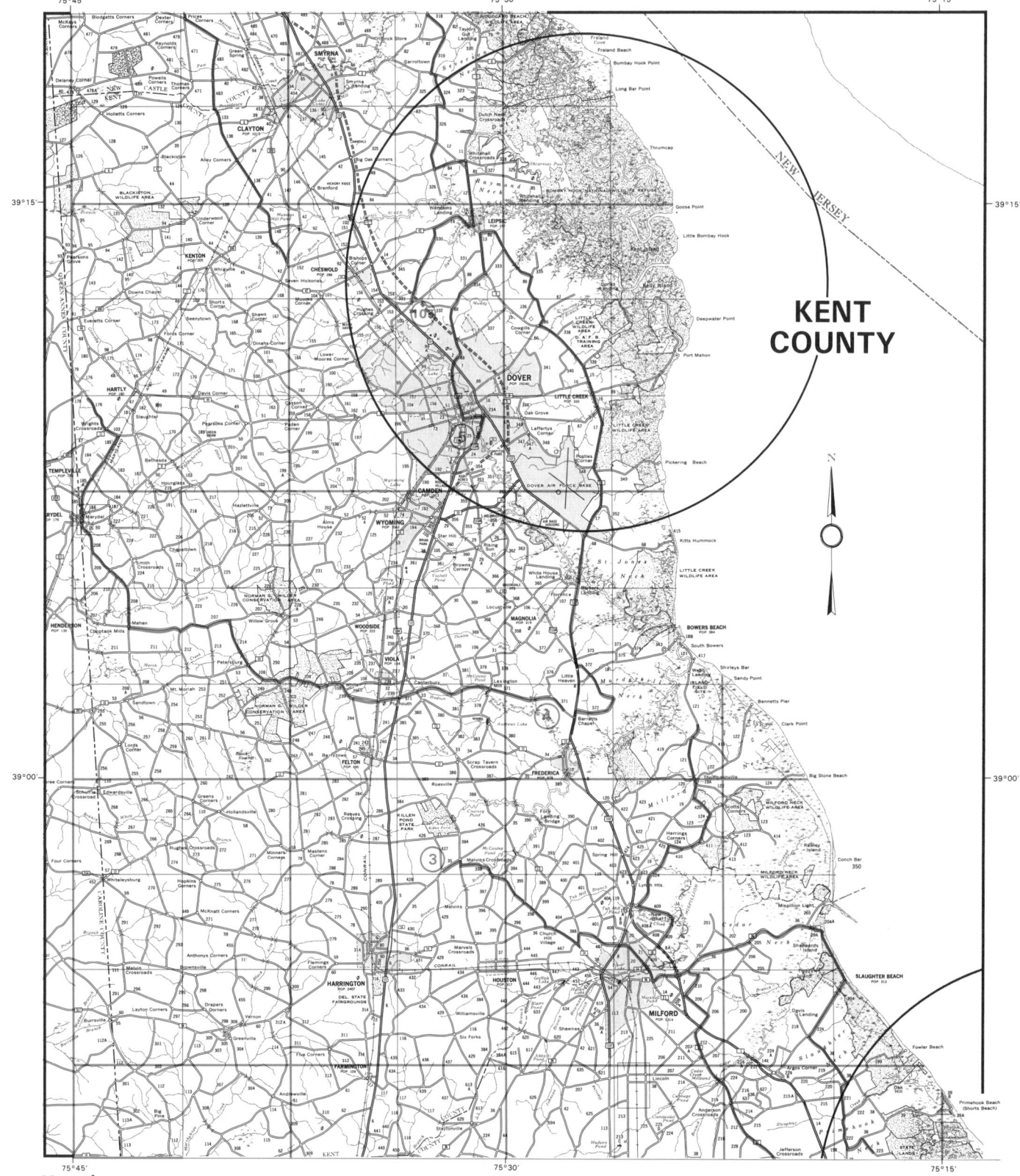

Map 4.2b

Date of Observations

Field cards (usually one per block per year; more where observers worked independently) requested the date of observation of confirmed breeding (fig. 4.1). The dated observations of nests with eggs and nests with young provided a portion of the data used for construction of the clutch-completion graphs in the species accounts. In some instances the dated observations identified errors in interpretation or reporting. For example, a Cedar Waxwing reported to be feeding fledged young on 30 May was obviously engaged in courtship feeding (which

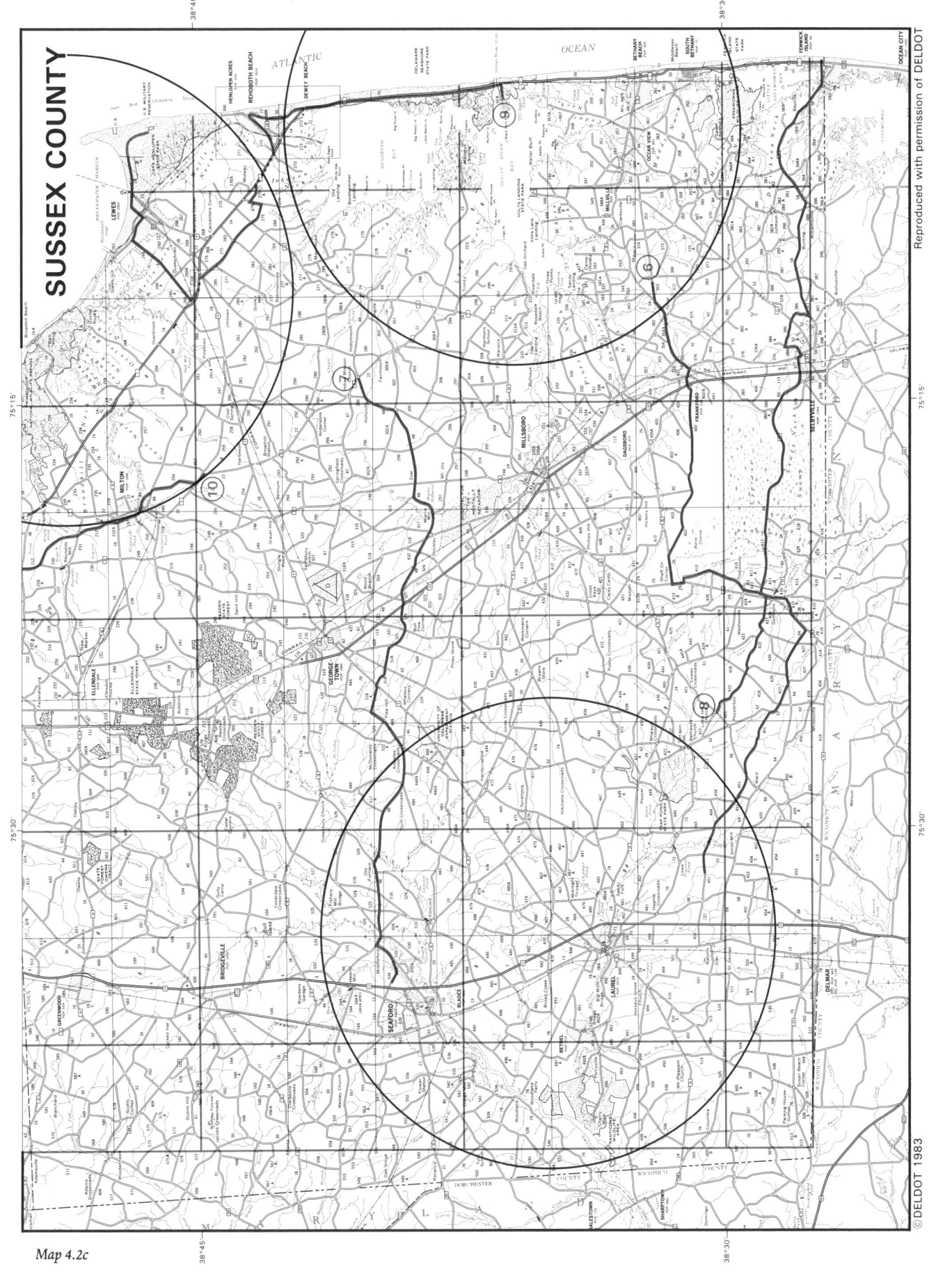

Map 4.2c

NAME	OB	PO	PR	CO Date
Sparrow, Sharp-tailed				
" , Seaside		P		
" , Song				NE 5/31
" , Swamp				
Blackbird, Red-winged			P	
Meadowlark, Eastern		S	T	5/31, 6/8
Grackle, Boat-tailed				
" , Common				AY 6/8
Cowbird, Brown-headed			C	
Oriole, Orchard		S		6/8
" , Northern				
Finch, House		O		
Goldfinch, American	X			
Sparrow, House				NB 5/31
other				

Fig. 4.1 Sample Field Card

begins in late winter in this species). In this case the observer was informed of courtship feeding in waxwings and asked to keep looking for breeding evidence the next year. Without the dated observation, courtship feeding could not have been separated from feeding young, which usually occurs in July. The dates of breeding observations would have been even more useful for determining breeding chronology had some codes been further broken down to distinguish the nesting stage; the much used "attending young" code does not differentiate between feeding young in the nest and feeding fledglings.

Fieldwork

The fieldwork was conducted by volunteers who selected or were assigned specific blocks. Professionals shared observations made during the course of their work—an important addition to the data, providing a number of confirmations for difficult species (such as vultures and rails). An experienced observer visited each block to conduct a 15-stop relative abundance study. The regular field work was supplemented by block-busting (intensive one-day studies) conducted by DOS members on Memorial Day weekends and individually by R. L. West, R. W. Russell, J. G. Lehman, and others. Progress in the field work was enhanced each year by providing computer generated reports of the status of each block and maps showing the emerging distribution of the species. Beginning 20 June 1987, the last summer of the survey, the plotted data were reviewed, and a number of gaps on the breeding distribution maps were filled by revisiting blocks to locate common species that had not yet been identified in them.

Relative Abundance Study

Concurrent with the last three years of the Atlas project (1985–87) a small group of observers experienced in making point counts conducted the relative abundance study. Fifteen three-minute morning stops were made from late May to early July in each of 216 Atlas blocks (totaling 3,280 stops). A list of the species identified, but not their numbers, was recorded at each stop. The number of stops (frequency) at which each

species was encountered in each block was plotted on a Delaware map to indicate its relative abundance throughout the state; 87 of these relative abundance maps are printed next to the breeding distribution maps in the species accounts to show where a species is most likely to be found and how commonly. This survey also added some new species to the blocks and served as a starting point for rapidly surveying blocks that had not yet been covered. (See appendix C for details.)

Along Delaware's eastern edge, two Atlas blocks were eliminated from the relative abundance study because they had too little land area for the required 15 stops at half-mile intervals. In three other cases, two or three blocks were combined to provide land sufficient for the 15 stops. The colored areas on the relative abundance maps of combined blocks are larger than the others. (See the Willet species account for an example and appendix B for details.)

Atlas Results

Progress and Completeness of the Project

The number of new records averaged more than 3,500 per year for the first four years (fig. 4.2), beginning in the first year with records of the more common species in blocks near observers' homes. The experience of the observers grew to match the difficulty of finding scarcer species, and enthusiasm took them farther afield. The fifth year of the project had more effort but resulted in far fewer new records (1,700) as work focused on filling in missing species, especially those more difficult to find. The point of diminishing returns had been reached; had the project continued for an additional year at the same level of effort, fewer than 500 new observations, or 3% of the five-year total, would have been recorded.

One measure of completeness of the study is that 43 species were found in more than 91% of the blocks, 18 in 99% of the blocks. These species are listed in table 4.2.

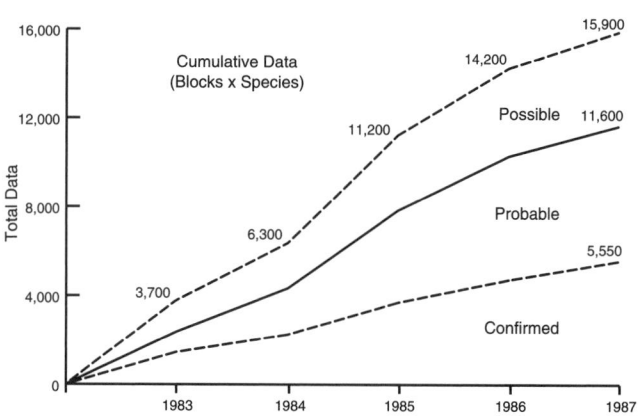

Fig. 4.2 Progress of the Atlas Project

Table 4.2. Widely Reported Breeding Species Found in Greater than 91% of the Atlas Blocks

	Percentage of Blocks
Most frequently reported species	
Red-winged Blackbird	100
Common Yellowthroat	99.5
Game species	
Northern Bobwhite	99.1
Mourning Dove	99.1
Nocturnal species	
Great Horned Owl	95.5
Eastern Screech-Owl	95.0
Species wintering in the tropics	
Barn Swallow	99.1
White-eyed Vireo	99.1
Gray Catbird	98.6
Red-eyed Vireo	98.2
Wood Thrush	97.3
Indigo Bunting	97.3
Eastern Wood-Pewee	95.9
Ruby-throated Hummingbird	95.5
Blue Grosbeak	95.0
Great Crested Flycatcher	94.6
Eastern Kingbird	91.9
Scarlet Tanager	91.4
Chimney Swift	91.4
Orchard Oriole	91.4
Introduced species	
European Starling	99.1
House Sparrow	98.6
Rock Dove	93.7

The other 20 include residents and short-distance migrants.

Killdeer	Northern Mockingbird
Red-bellied Woodpecker	Brown Thrasher
Downy Woodpecker	Northern Cardinal
Northern Flicker	Eastern Towhee
Blue Jay	Chipping Sparrow
American Crow	Field Sparrow
Carolina Chickadee	Song Sparrow
Tufted Titmouse	Common Grackle
Carolina Wren	Brown-headed Cowbird
American Robin	American Goldfinch

Each year the quality of breeding evidence was upgraded, reaching the final level of 35% confirmed, 38% probable, and 27% possible. The number of records upgraded is a reflection of the quality of the fieldwork.

Species Richness

The Atlas project and relative abundance study provide indicators of species richness in Delaware. Maps 4.3 and 4.4 present, for each block and quadrangle, the number of species for which breeding evidence was obtained; the averages are 71 species per block, and 80 species per quadrangle in which four or more blocks lay within Delaware.

Maps 4.5 and 4.6 present, for each block and quadrangle, the number of species found in the relative abundance study; the averages are 46 species per block and 70 species per quadrangle in which four or more blocks lay within Delaware. Although the number of species found are much lower than those from the Atlas project, the effort was identical for each block (15 three-minute stops); the results thus give a controlled indication of the relative species richness in various parts of the state. The common species, important determinants of species diversity, are the ones found in the relative abundance study. The 15-stop sample for each block is small, so high or low numbers for groups of blocks, rather than individual blocks, are better indicators of species richness.

Number of Breeding Species

During the Atlas project 160 species were identified as breeding (appendix J). Of these, 153 were confirmed as breeding, 5 (American Bittern, Black Rail, American Coot, Loggerhead Shrike, and Northern Parula) were listed as probable breeders, and the remaining 2 (Spotted Sandpiper and Short-eared Owl) as possible breeders.

The Breeding Bird Atlas project added six new species to the list of birds breeding in Delaware. A pair of Peregrine Falcons began breeding on the Delaware Memorial Bridge in 1987—in response to the Peregrine Fund program to reestablish this species in the East. (This species probably did not previously breed in Delaware, where there are no attractive cliff nesting sites.) On Rehoboth Bay islands, searches led by William Fintel discovered nesting Forster's Terns in 1985. This species had been expanding northward since protection of terns began at the turn of the century—85 years before their establishment (or reestablishment) in Delaware. A Great Black-backed Gull nest was discovered by West in the course of a DNREC-sponsored shorebird census trip to Slaughter Beach in 1986. The Upland Sandpiper was first recognized as a breeding species at the New Castle County Airport in 1987 by L. L. Falk—an observation subsequently supported by the discovery of a nest in 1992. Wild Turkeys were successfully reintroduced into Delaware by DNREC during the 1980s. Flightless young Red-breasted Mergansers were reported from the Inland Bays; interpretation as breeding must be cautioned by the lack of a nest record from the Mid-Atlantic region.

Additions to Delaware breeders have continued beyond the Atlas project. In 1988 a Rose-breasted Grosbeak nest was found near Newark by R. R. Roth. This species will probably not become a regular breeder so far south. Double-crested Cormorants reported breeding on structures in the Delaware Bay in the 1990s will very likely become common, competing with herons and egrets. Cliff Swallows were found breeding on a concrete bridge east of Odessa on 9 May 1993 by A. P. Ednie—more satisfactory breeding evidence than a 1984 nest from near Townsend that could not be clearly assigned to that species.

Of the 163 species listed as breeding since 1983, additional breeding evidence in Delaware is needed for the following:

Double-crested Cormorant	Insufficient published details
Green-winged Teal	No published nest record
Red-breasted Merganser	No Mid-Atlantic nest record

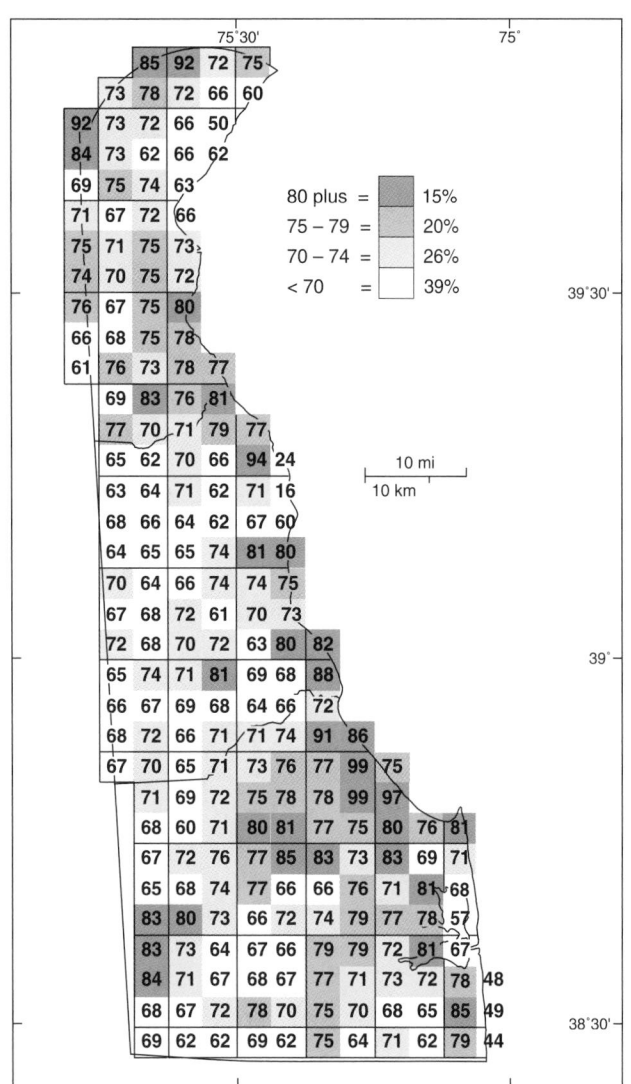

Map 4.3. Atlas Blocks

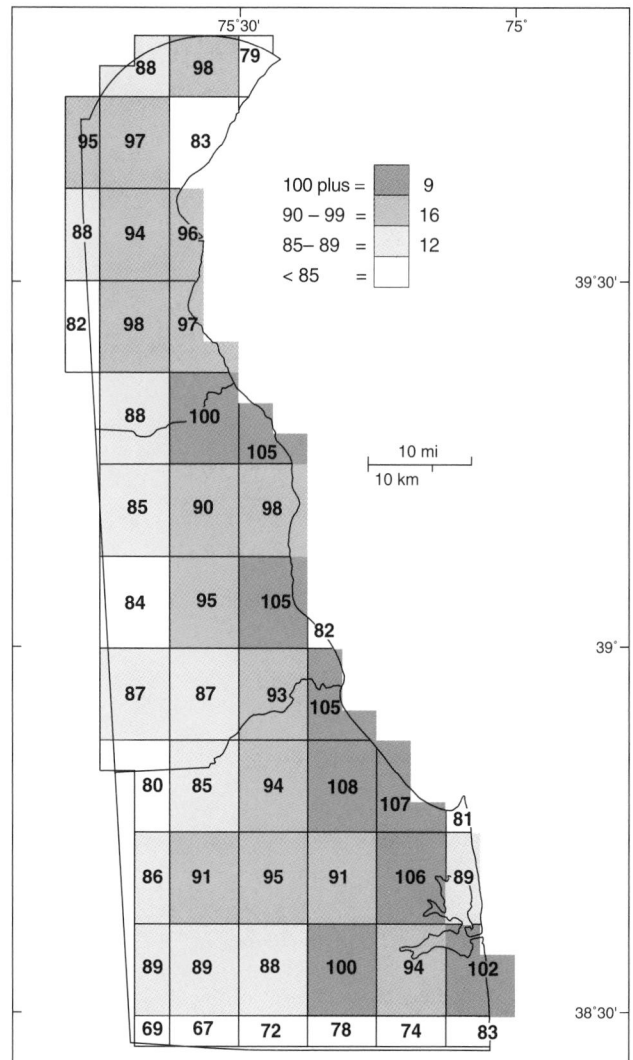

Map 4.4. Atlas Quadrangles

Spotted Sandpiper	No breeding details since 1880
Upland Sandpiper	No published nest record
Short-eared Owl	No nest record since 1938
Brown Creeper	No nest record
Loggerhead Shrike	No nest record since 1924

Thirteen additional species that formerly bred at least once in Delaware were not found during the Atlas project:

Occasional (extralimital) breeders

Northern Shoveler	American Wigeon
Ruddy Duck	Sora
Purple Gallinule	Gull-billed Tern
Black Tern	Least Flycatcher

Former (extirpated) breeders

Ruffed Grouse	Long-eared Owl
Swainson's Warbler	Savannah Sparrow
Henslow's Sparrow	

Other species may have bred in Delaware at some point but no longer do so: Greater Prairie Chicken (Heath Hen), Wilson's Plover, American Avocet, Carolina Parakeet, Red-cockaded Woodpecker, Royal Tern, Dickcissel. Also the Northern Pintail, Red-breasted Nut-hatch, and Golden-crowned Kinglet have displayed some breeding behavior in Delaware, but breeding, if it occurred, was not proved (see species accounts). The 160 species reported during the Breeding Bird Atlas project are listed in appendix J.

Changes in Delaware Breeding Avifauna

The Atlas results and other recent reports indicate the following changes in the status of breeding species; some of them are long-term changes and others occurred in a matter of decades. Landscape alterations from changing farming practices (fewer pastures, woodlots, and hedgerows; more drainage) and forestry practices (clear cutting, then natural regeneration and pine plantations) have surely been the biggest cause of change. Bird protection laws, conservation practices, and the banning of DDT have led to the restoration of some species, but these gains are being offset by the impact on other

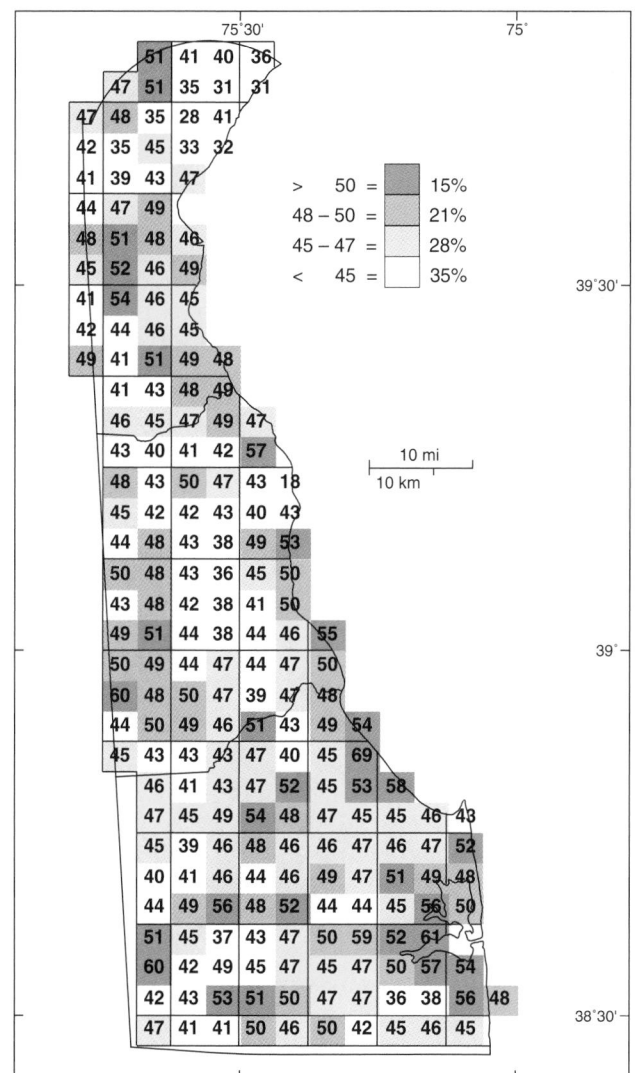

Map 4.5. Relative Abundance Study Blocks

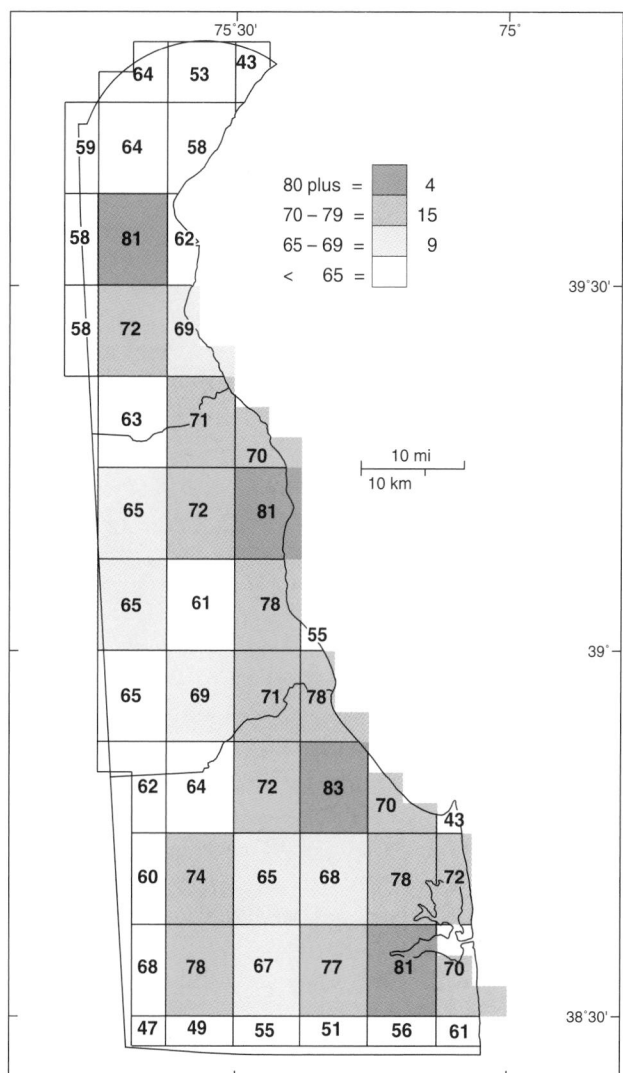

Map 4.6. Quadrangles

species of human population growth, suburban sprawl, and the proliferation of vacation homes.

The following are examples of changes in avian population:

Double-crested Cormorants, once a species of concern, possibly the result of DDT toxicity, were reported breeding in Delaware in 1991.

Great Egrets and Snowy Egrets, formerly extirpated by plume hunters, have become reestablished in this century.

Cattle Egrets have extended their range into Delaware (from Africa); and Tricolored Herons, Yellow-crowned Night-Herons, and Glossy Ibises may never have bred in Delaware before the twentieth century.

Mute Swans were introduced as a breeding species from Europe, and the Canada Goose and Mallard were introduced as local breeders.

Breeding ducks, including the Wood Duck, which had extremely low populations in the early twentieth century because of unrestricted hunting, have since increased in numbers.

Some ducks that have extralimital breeding records in Delaware

do not breed here now: Northern Shoveler, American Wigeon (possibly a result of introductions in the East), Ruddy Duck, possibly Red-breasted Merganser, and Northern Pintail.

Gadwalls and Blue-winged Teals began breeding in Delaware in the late 1930s, possibly the result of unknown introductions and the formation of wildlife impoundments.

Hooded Mergansers, cavity nesters first recorded breeding here in 1980 in a Wood Duck box, possibly bred here in primeval swamps.

Black Vultures expanded their range northward in the twentieth century, probably encouraged by the clearing of the land.

Bald Eagles, reduced to a single unsuccessful breeding pair by the late 1960s under the accumulation of DDT, increased to 5 successful nests by 1992. The Northern Harrier, which showed a similar pattern, was much less studied.

Cooper's Hawks, possibly extirpated at one time, have come back to breed now in low numbers.

Red-tailed and Broad-winged hawks increased during the twentieth century.

Peregrine Falcons were introduced into Delaware and began breeding here in 1987.

Purple Gallinules were extralimital breeders in the 1970s.

Ring-necked Pheasants were introduced as a game bird at the beginning of the twentieth century.

All shorebirds suffered severe population declines into the twentieth century from over hunting by market hunters and sportsmen, but most have now recovered. The Killdeer and Willet again breed here in numbers, and the Piping Plover, American Oystercatcher, and Black-necked Stilt have returned. The Spotted and Upland Sandpiper may only be extralimital breeders. The American Avocet again breeds in the East and summers in Delaware. The Wilson's Plover increased to breed again in New Jersey and Maryland, but its breeding range is now receding southward. The American Woodcock, reduced to low numbers and partly recovered, is now being reduced again by habitat losses.

Gulls and terns were extirpated by the early twentieth century by market egg collectors, plume hunters, and sportsmen. The Laughing Gull, Common Tern, Forster's Tern, Least Tern, and Black Skimmer returned as regular breeders, but the terns and skimmer are again decreasing.

Herring Gulls and Great Black-backed Gulls have expanded their range southward to include Delaware, pursuing the offal of civilization.

Gull-billed Terns and possibly Black Terns have bred here occasionally since the 1950s.

Royal Terns, possible former breeders in Delaware, once bred regularly in the region.

Rock Doves were introduced.

Mourning Doves have greatly increased in summer and winter, the result of habitat alteration and hunting regulation.

Long-eared Owls, formerly occasional breeders, no longer breed here.

Chuck-will's-widows extended their breeding range north into Delaware, encouraged by deforestation.

Chimney Swifts surely increased in numbers when European settlement provided chimneys for dry, secure nest sites.

Red-headed Woodpeckers dropped to the status of rare breeders during the twentieth century, probably reflecting a loss of large stubs and the introduction of starlings.

Red-bellied Woodpeckers have extended their range northward into Delaware since the 1920s, becoming a common breeder.

Pileated Woodpeckers have recovered from the brink of extirpation earlier this century, no longer being shot for food.

Willow Flycatchers have extended their breeding range eastward as the eastern forests were cleared, as have (Prairie) Horned Larks and Cliff Swallows.

Eastern Phoebes have become much more common by taking advantage of nest sites in buildings and under bridges; they were formerly restricted to breeding in rocky crevices.

The swallows have generally benefited from clearing of forests.

Bank Swallows may not previously have bred in Delaware, which lacks large natural sand banks. Tree Swallows probably had a more northern range. If the Barn Swallow previously bred in Delaware, its numbers were much lower because it was dependent on natural forest openings and natural nest sites. Cliff Swallows began breeding in Delaware, probably for the first time, in 1993 under a modern bridge on Rt. 9. Only Purple Martins would have bred here in numbers before European settlement, using cavities in dead trees along coastal marshes for small colonies and gourds provided by Native Americans.

Brown Creepers began breeding in deep woods, probably a reestablishment of its precolonial range.

Sedge Wrens have virtually vanished, probably the result of habitat changes along marsh edges.

Veeries have colonized northern New Castle County; they probably bred here when a continuous canopy provided a cooler microclimate.

Northern Mockingbirds and Northern Cardinals have become much more common, examples of range expansion by species well adapted to suburban habitats.

Loggerhead Shrikes once bred in Delaware, but never more than casually.

European Starlings were introduced.

Many warblers and other insectivores have shown an increase since institution of the Breeding Bird Survey in 1966. These increases may reflect a delayed rebound since DDT was banned.

Blue-winged Warblers became established from a more western range in the nineteenth century.

Northern Parulas became very scarce, probably following removal of damp mature forests in the eighteenth and nineteenth centuries.

Chestnut-sided and Cerulean warblers' ranges expanded into Delaware in the 1960s.

Hooded Warblers' range expanded into Delaware from the south in the 1920s.

Summer Tanagers have expanded substantially in southern Delaware in the twentieth century, probably a result of habitat alteration.

Rose-breasted Grosbeaks' breeding range expanded into Delaware from the north in 1988, though they may previously have bred here in deep forest.

Blue Grosbeaks greatly increased in number in Delaware in the twentieth century.

Savannah Sparrows, which bred on the dunes south of Rehoboth Beach as recently as the 1930s, were the first beach nesters to be extirpated after migratory birds were protected.

Boat-tailed Grackles' range expanded into Delaware from the south in the twentieth century.

House Finches were introduced into the East in the mid-twentieth century.

House Sparrows were introduced.

CHAPTER 5

Introduction to the Species Accounts

In describing the material included in the species accounts we also provide the information needed to interpret them. Details on how we analyzed and interpreted the data are given in the appendices.

The State List

Criteria for a species' inclusion on an "official" state list of birds vary among states. In early regional works the official list usually included only those species represented by a specimen taken in the area. A museum specimen is indisputable evidence of a species occurrence and has the unique advantage of allowing an examination of the bird at any time. Although such a strict criterion is the ideal, collecting is not always feasible. Other less satisfactory forms of documentation must thus be accepted.

Today, field identification knowledge has advanced far beyond what it was 20 or 30 years ago—cameras and film have improved and so have the skills of photographers. Although a photograph shows only a single aspect of a bird at a given moment under one set of light conditions, many species are sufficiently distinctive that a photograph can provide acceptable documentation. Satisfactory photographs of such species are accepted as evidence of occurrence in Delaware.

In the absence of a specimen or recognizable photograph, no single approach to evaluating sight records of rarities or unseasonable occurrences is necessarily better than another. Any report of a rarity with a substantive description made in the field was evaluated, the evidence outlined, and an opinion expressed. Any unpublished report that lacked details (e.g., no written description available) was not considered for inclusion in this work. If a report was published without details, and no details were available to us, we have mentioned the report, noting the lack of details. In some cases we express an opinion. The names of species lacking adequate supporting documentation are placed in brackets. In so doing, we are not implying that any given observation is unreliable, but that the bracketed species must be treated differently from those for which we have a specimen, recognizable photograph, or adequate documentation. We thus prefer to call these species uncorroborated, rather than hypothetical.

A few species that occur annually or nearly so but lack adequate documentation are nevertheless accepted as occurring in Delaware. We hope that these species will be photographed or specimens obtained.

We have attached particular meaning to the words *report* and *record*. A record of the sighting of a species has been relatively well authenticated and has survived the scrutiny of the authors, whereas a report has not. Of course, there is no fixed dividing line between these terms, and certainly many reports are correct. This distinction is primarily made in reference to migration dates or unusual numbers reported.

Nomenclature and Arrangement

The nomenclature and sequence of families and species follows the seventh edition of the *Check-list of North American Birds* (AOU 1998).

Sources

We are fortunate to have access to many data sources that supplement the published literature. We undoubtedly overlooked some, however, and for a few we were unable to obtain access.

Specimens

Specimens, the foundation of ornithology, are accessible evidence of past records. Such documentation is essential to any well-grounded assessment of an avifauna and is the base that gives sight records their veracity. Specimen data were obtained from museums designated as follows:

AMNH American Museum of Natural History, New York
ANSP Academy of Natural Sciences, Philadelphia
CM Carnegie Museum of Natural History, Pittsburgh
DMNH Delaware Museum of Natural History, Greenville
LSU Louisiana State University, Baton Rouge
UDEL University of Delaware, Newark
UF University of Florida, Gainesville
USNM National Museum of Natural History, Washington, D.C.
UWBM University of Washington, Burke Museum, Seattle
WFVZ Western Foundation for Vertebrate Zoology, Los Angeles

Banding Data

The U.S. Fish and Wildlife Service (USFWS) allows capture of birds, under permit, for identification by means of a uniquely numbered band placed on the leg of the bird. Such banding studies are an important part of wildfowl management for hunting. Bands are also issued and band numbers recorded by the USFWS Bird Banding Laboratory for many volunteer and professional activities and for a cooperative fall banding operation that bands birds along migration corridors. In Delaware a fall migration banding station located at Red Lion Creek east of Rt. 9 and later located near Newark was operated in the 1960s under a permit held by J. T. Linehan; many other banding studies have been conducted in the state. The USFWS provided us with their computerized banding records through 1990.

The banding information in the text and on the banding

recoveries maps for waterfowl were derived from birds banded in Delaware and recovered either outside the state or later in Delaware and from birds recovered in Delaware that were banded elsewhere. Maps for waterfowl were constructed from bands returned mostly by hunters. Usually the waterfowl were banded as chicks on the breeding grounds or as migrants netted on wildlife refuges. Banding recoveries maps for starlings and blackbirds were constructed from birds banded in Delaware and later shot or found dead.

Early and late dates are supported, when possible, with banding information, which may be more reliable than routine sight records.

Banding bar graphs use the number of the target species banded divided by the total number of all birds banded (excluding blackbirds and starlings) during the same five-day period (as a substitute for the number of net-hours). A more accurate analysis divides the number of birds banded by the number of net-hours spent capturing the birds, but net-hours are available for only a small portion of birds banded in Delaware. Dividing the number of the target species banded by the total number of birds banded provides some adjustment for differences in banding effort. The graphs produced with this adjustment are easier to interpret than those produced without it. A graph of total birds banded each five-day period is given in fig. 5.1. These graphs were used for selected species as a supplement to the migration analyses derived from the regular field observations.

Nest Record Data

Delaware data used for the analysis of the breeding season came mainly from these sources:

Cornell nest records. The North American Nest-Record Card Program housed at Cornell University, Ithaca, New York.

Nest records. The Delmarva Ornithological Society's Nest Record Card program, housed at DMNH.

Egg records (often followed by a museum's specimen number). Records of egg collections, or the egg collector's notes, housed at several museums.

Atlas notes. Dated records of nests with eggs or young submitted during the Delaware Breeding Bird Atlas Project.

Fledgling records. Records of young birds received at Tri-State Bird Rescue and Research, Inc., Newark, Del.

H. H. Hanson's notes. Measurements and notes taken by H. H. Hanson as he prepared a Delaware nest collection, notes filed at DMNH.

J. H. Buckalew's notes. Especially his nest-searching notebook. He recorded the contents of thousands of nests he found on the Delmarva Peninsula, notes filed at DMNH.

Data from these sources were used to present the following information:

Clutch-completion bar graphs. Prepared from the nest record data by estimating clutch-completion dates (appendix D) and summarizing the results graphically by thirds of a month.

Extreme egg dates. The earliest and latest dates reported in the nest record data for viable eggs.

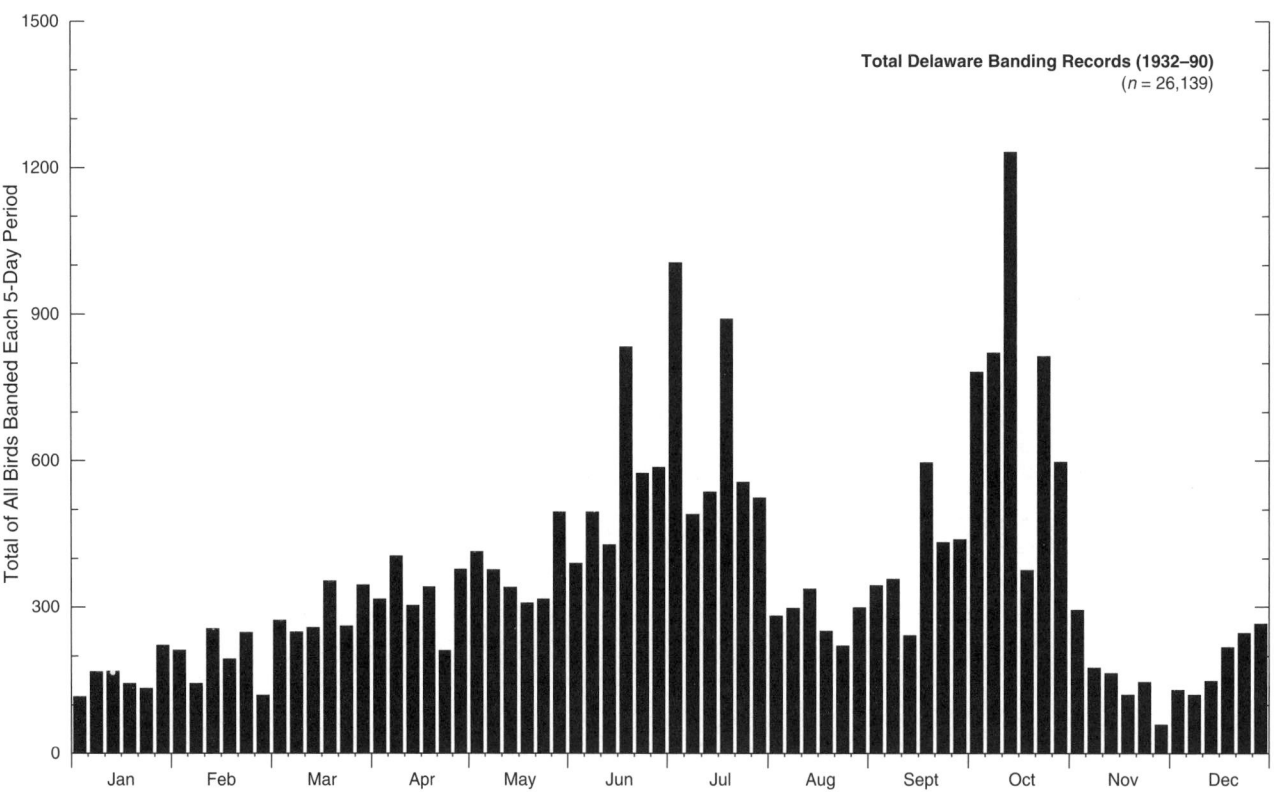

Fig. 5.1

Clutch size and range. Estimates using complete clutches if known.

Nest descriptions, situations, and some of the habitats. Extracted from the various nest record sources.

Breeding Bird Survey

The Breeding Bird Survey (BBS), sponsored by the USFWS and the Canadian Wildlife Service across the continent each June, follows 24.5-mi long routes, recording the birds identified at 50 3-minute stops located 0.5 miles apart on each route once each year (appendix E). About 3,000 routes are surveyed annually in North America. Each of the 10 Delaware routes (maps 4.2a, b, and c) was surveyed about 20 times during 1966–90, and in all some 200,000 individuals were identified and counted. USFWS analyses of Delaware population trends derived from these surveys, provided by the Office of Migratory Bird Management, were useful, particularly the ten-year analysis for 1981–90 and the 25-year analysis for 1966–90. The results of the latter are tabulated in appendix I.

BBS trends referred to in this book are *significant* ($p < .05$) increases or decreases as determined by the USFWS analyses. Occasionally, deduced trends of lower certainty are stated, always in cautious terms, such as an "increasing tendency." The magnitude of a trend, though always less well known than its direction, is sometimes presented.

Only 10 BBS routes fall within Delaware, so trends deduced from them are based on only a marginal amount of data and are most reliable for species occurring on all routes. Trends in the East are compared with trends in Delaware. For some Atlantic coast species, such as the Willet, trends for the Upper Coastal Plain are more meaningful for Delaware than East trends and more reliable than trends based only on scant Delaware data. (Map 5.1 shows what is meant by "Upper Coastal Plain" and "East," and appendices E and I discuss BBS trends.)

Birds per route (the number of birds of a single species observed on a 50-stop BBS route), when averaged over a number of years and over the routes in a state or region, provides a population index useful for comparing population densities among states and regions and for generating relative population density maps.

Breeding Bird Census

The Breeding Bird Census (BBC), started by the National Audubon Society in 1937, is most useful for determining the species composition and density of birds in particular habitat types. It is conducted by experienced observers who, after plotting the location of singing males and of other bird interactions during eight or more census trips, construct maps of territories of individual males. Usually applied to homogeneous habitats of 15–40 acres (6–16 ha), such mapping has been used in Delaware primarily on woodlots. The technique is laborious but provides a good measure of the breeding territory sizes of common species and the composition of avian communities (appendix F). Pairs per 100 ha is the standard method of report-

Map 5.1. Breeding Bird Survey Regions

ing population densities. Pairs per 100 acres, approximately pairs per 40 ha, used to be standard in the United States. Densities were rounded to one or two significant figures after conversion to hectares.

Delaware Spring Roundups (May Counts)

The Delmarva Ornithological Society conducts a statewide, one-day May Count (appendix G) during the first two weeks of May. The state is divided into six areas, and observers record numbers and species of birds found in each area and the number of party-hours spent (Rufe 1985). Statewide effort increased from about 180 party-hours in the early 1970s to about 360 party-hours in the late 1980s. The results are published in the *Delmarva Ornithologist*.

High and low May Counts refer to the highest and lowest numbers of individuals of a species reported statewide on these multiparty events over the years. The date as well as the year is often stated for migrants, because counts of migrants taken in early May differ from those in mid-May.

May Count trends were derived by analyzing the results for the period 1969–91 to obtain an average annual rate of change that could be compared with the rates of change on the Breeding Bird Survey (West 1992). (See appendices G and I.)

Christmas Bird Counts

A Christmas Bird Count (CBC) is a winter survey taken on a single calendar day within a 15-mi-diameter circle (see Maps 4.2a, b, and c for circle locations, and appendix H for descriptions of them). Counts are held during the period starting approximately one week before Christmas Day and ending one week after. Groups of observers tend to provide consistent coverage of each count circle. The results are published annually by the National Audubon Society. A CBC is designated by the year in which the CBC period begins (e.g., a January 1987 Cape Henlopen-Prime Hook CBC is referred to as Cape Henlopen 1986).

We analyzed the 1966–89 results for the Wilmington, Middletown, Bombay Hook, Cape Henlopen–Prime Hook, and Rehoboth count circles for changes in numbers of birds present. The sixth Delaware count, the Seaford–Nanticoke CBC, has been conducted too few years to be included in the analyses. In the species accounts in this book, field data are provided in the following ways:

Tables

Tables summarize the species occurrence, the range of number found, and the median number in each of the five CBC circles for the 24-year period analyzed. CBC highs are numbers of birds, not birds per party-hour.

Bar graphs

Bar graphs compare the species' average abundance, in birds per party-hour in the five areas, from north to south. The left-hand bar gives the state average, which is marked with the 95% confidence limits of this average. This is our best estimate of the "state CBC abundance," in terms of birds per party-hour, for those species that show no trend. For those species having graphs of significant trends, the value of the trend line in 1989 should be used instead of the state average given in the left-hand bar.

Trend graphs

Trend graphs show the direction and rate of change if a significant change was detected in the number of birds per party-hour on the five CBCs. A line shows the constant annual rate of change that best fits the CBC results; this rate is stated in the caption (e.g., decreasing at about 3.8% per year). There can be large relative errors in the rate stated, and it should be used with caution. For the year 1989, an error range shows the 95% confidence interval for the indicated state CBC abundance in terms of birds per party-hour. The 1989 figures provide our most current indices of species that have undergone population changes. They may be used for comparison with other states or with future results. Peaks and low points in the population of some species that do not show a linear trend are graphed. Several other graphs show changes in species that are not trends. Among the wintering species that did not show a statistically significant long-term trend, some, like the Red-bellied Woodpecker, showed so little change that no

change was detected with reasonable certainty; some, like the Pine Siskin, had any long-term trend disguised by the years of eruption; and some had such a high year-to-year variation that no statistically significant trend could be detected, even though a fairly distinct trend might be suspected. High variability might be caused by the degree of coldness of the winter, year-to-year differences in fieldwork, and, no doubt, many other factors. We compared the CBC trends to the USFWS trend analysis of the BBS in Delaware for the same time period (see appendix I).

Delmarva Ornithological Society Records

The Delmarva Ornithological Society (DOS) conducted weekly surveys at the sites and during the years given in table 5.1.

Table 5.1. Delmarva Ornithological Society Weekly Surveys

Location	Survey Date
Piedmont	
Hoopes Reservoir, Centerville	1943–1945, 1964
Brandywine Creek SP, Tallyeville	1967–1971
Winterthur Museum and Estate, Centerville	1972
White Clay Creek, Newark	Apr 1976–Jun 1978
Ashland Nature Center, Yorklyn	Sep 1978–Sep 1979
Mt. Cuba, Yorklyn	Nov 1988–Dec 1990
Burrows Run, Centerville	Mar 1991–Jul 1992
Coastal Plain	
Churchmans Marsh, Stanton	Jan 1965–Jan 1966, 1980
Dragon Run Marsh, Delaware City	Mar 1973–Dec 1975
Bombay Hook NWR, Smyrna	Jun 1981–May 1983
Little Creek WA, Dover	1964

Records from the 1983–87 Delaware Breeding Bird Atlas Project (see chapter 4) were used to produce the breeding distribution maps. On these maps the size of the dot indicates the quality of breeding evidence observed, the extent of the dots indicates the breeding distribution.

Concurrent with the Atlas project, an indication of relative abundance was obtained for breeding species; the numbers in the relative abundance maps indicate the number of three-minute stops where each species was detected (out of 15 stops made in each ten-square-mile study block). These numbers can be compared among groups of blocks for a single species, but comparison between species is unwarranted (see chapter 4 and appendix C). On some relative abundance maps there are shaded blocks without any numbers; these indicate that the results from an unnumbered block were combined with those of an adjacent block for reporting purposes (see appendix B).

The DOS solicits random observations from their members and asks for reports at each meeting. These are filed, reviewed, and some are published in seasonal reports in the *Delmarva Ornithologist*.

Data from Individuals

Several individuals made their personal records available to us. William W. Frech provided much needed systematic data from coastal Sussex County covering 1977–89. John C. Miller abstracted significant reports from his files. Douglas and Karen

Batt, Lloyd L. Falk, William A. Fintel, David M. Niles, Grace A. Prest, Alan R. Stickley, Winston J. Wayne, and heirs of Seal T. Brooks, John H. Buckalew, H. H. Hanson, and Kathleen Herbert made their files available to us, greatly supplementing those of the authors. C. J. Pennock's notebooks (1890s–1930s) were made available to us by the Historical Society of Delaware, and a compilation of Delmarva Peninsula bird records through the 1930s was made available to us by the Society of Natural History of Delaware.

Tri-State Bird Rescue and Research, Inc.

Nationally known for their efforts to rehabilitate birds contaminated by oil spills, TSBR has achieved local recognition for rehabilitating injured and orphaned birds. Their carefully maintained records have provided much data on breeding locations to the Atlas project and nest chronology data for the nest-records program. In 1988 TSBR conducted a weekly, year-long survey on the Middle Run Natural Area, contributing additional data to the authors.

Agency Records

Recent reports of the Delaware Department of Natural Resources and Environmental Control (DNREC) were searched. Heronry, shorebird, Bald Eagle, Least Tern, and Piping Plover data supplied by DNREC personnel were especially helpful. Many Pittman-Robertson Act reports filed by DNREC contained useful information.

The Delaware Natural Heritage Inventory (DNHI) provided data on selected species to supplement publicly available information.

The daily records and annual and narrative reports of Bombay Hook NWR and Prime Hook NWR were supplied to us.

Manomet Bird Observatory made available its Delaware data obtained on the International Shorebird Survey and studies of Delaware heronries.

J. Wiese made available his 1975–78 study of the Pea Patch Island heronry sponsored by Delmarva Power and Light.

The National Wildlife Federation Raptor Information Center made available for citation the information on Bald Eagle found in their annual reports.

The Delaware portion of the 1991 Neotropical Migratory Songbird Coastal Corridor Study sponsored by the National Oceanic and Atmospheric Association, USFWS, USFWS Foundation, and The Nature Conservancy was made available to us. This study provided over 2,000 fall migration records.

The Cornell Laboratory of Ornithology provided us with a printout of the Colonial Waterbird Registry.

The Patuxent Wildlife Research Center made available its bird distribution and migration files.

Definition of Terms

The species accounts use certain terms that have a particular meaning specific to this book, and they are defined as follows.

Frequency of Occurrence

Regular. A species that normally occurs in the state every year. When the frequency of a species is not stated, it is assumed to be regular.

Occasional. A species that does not occur in the state every year but occurs more or less regularly in the region and is expected to occur again in the state.

Casual. A species that has occurred a few times in the state or region and may occur again.

Accidental. A species that has occurred at least once in Delaware but is unlikely to occur again.

Seasonal Occurrence

Resident. A species found in Delaware throughout the year; breeds or may breed in the state (e.g., Northern Cardinal).

Occurs all year. A species found in Delaware throughout the year but not known to breed in Delaware (e.g., Lesser Yellowlegs).

Summer resident. A species found throughout the summer and known or thought to breed in Delaware but normally not present throughout the year (e.g., Scarlet Tanager).

Summer visitor. A species found in the summer but not thought to breed (e.g., Ruff).

Winter visitor. A species that spends all or part of its winter in the state (e.g., Dark-eyed Junco).

Migrant. A species whose individuals pass through the state between breeding and wintering grounds (e.g., Blackburnian Warbler).

Terms Describing Populations

The terms *abundant, common, fairly common, uncommon,* and *rare* describe how many individuals of a species can usually be found in one day's work by a competent observer in suitable season and working in a variety of habitats. The band widths in the seasonal bar graphs (see fig. 5.2, "Seasonal Bar Graph Key") and the terms in the text correspond to average abundances reported during the 1963–89 period. The difference between "uncommon" and "rare" lies in how frequently a species is encountered. If a species does not usually occur annually, or during a certain period, and usually only 1–3 individuals are found when it does occur, it is considered "rare." A broken line indicates irregular occurrence at the beginning and end of a migration or in a few cases the entire period of occurrence.

The term *local* is used to describe a species that is found in

Seasonal Bar Graph Key

Abundant: more than 100*

Common: 11–100

Fairly common: 4–10

Uncommon or Rare: 1–3

Irregular

Isolated observations

*Number seen in a field day.

Fig. 5.2.

only a few localities despite the presence of seemingly acceptable habitat elsewhere in the state or a species that occurs in a habitat that is only found in one or a few localities within the state (e.g., Cerulean Warbler).

Data Summary

The seasonal graph that introduces each species account is based on the DOS surveys, adjusted CBC data, published data, and data from individuals for the period 1963–89. Each bar graph was made by using a computer program to summarize and plot the abundance by weekly intervals. After initial smoothing by the program, we examined the graphs for unexpected results. When unexpected results were detected, detailed information in our database was examined and, if needed, the bar graph was changed.

Migration dates are based on the same data as the seasonal bar graph plus specimens and banding data. The three or four earliest and latest acceptable records for spring and fall migration are tabulated.

Red-throated Loon (Gavia stellata)

Regular; winter resident; fairly common to common. Expected mid-October through early May.

J	F	M	A	M	J	J	A	S	O	N	D

HABITAT: Saltwater; coastal bays, offshore waters.

SPRING: Peak northward movement takes place during March. In most years the majority leave by 5–10 May, though a few stragglers may be present into early summer. High counts are

13 Mar 1966	280	Prime Hook NWR [RusW3]
27 Mar 1971	600	Cape Henlopen [Carl12]
22 Apr 1973	375	Cape Henlopen [DuPG2]

SUMMER: Red-throated Loons are seldom present past mid-May. Late records include 1 along the coast during 2–19 June 1981 [Frec1] and 1 in Rehoboth Bay on 13 June 1982 [Barn15]. Such birds summering inshore are probably unfit individuals incapable of migrating to Arctic breeding grounds.

FALL: In most years Red-throated Loons arrive during 15–20 October, though occasionally they arrive in fair numbers as early as 1–15 October. An unusually early report of 6 at Cape Henlopen on 4 August 1960 [Davi17], if correct, undoubtedly refers to birds summering offshore rather than to early southward migrants (Paxton et al. 1979). An early (or summering)

Red-throated Loon arrived at Cape Henlopen on 12 September 1969 [DuPG13] and another at Assawoman WA on 20 September 1980 [Edni39]. Peak migration occurs during the latter half of November, slightly later than the 5–18 November peak recorded at Manomet Point, Mass. (Powers and Cherry 1983). The high count is 600 birds per hr passing Rehoboth Beach on 14 November 1985 [Frec1].

1966–89 CBC Summary

Christmas Bird Count	Years Found	Range of No. Found	Median
Wilmington			
Middletown	2	1–2	
Bombay Hook	15	1–19	1
Cape Henlopen	24	2–295	42
Rehoboth	24	1–194	41
STATEWIDE (low in 1980, high in 1982)	24	5–466	100

WINTER: Numbers of Red-throated Loons present in late December are so variable that no CBC trend can be determined. They are most often found on the Cape Henlopen and Rehoboth CBCs. The high count is 1,000 at Rehoboth Beach on 15 December 1946 [Tous1], considerably higher than the more recent multiparty high counts of 295 and 294 birds, respectively, reported on the 1966 Cape Henlopen and 1982 Rehoboth CBCs. On a statewide basis, Red-throated Loons have been reported in greater numbers than Common Loons on CBCs. Falk's (1975) 6-year summary of loon CBC data from the Mid-Atlantic region also indicates that Red-throated Loons are more abundant than Common Loons in Delaware Bay. Red-throated Loons are so rarely reported in New Castle County at any season that occurrences there should be documented.

SPECIMENS: 6; DMNH, USNM.

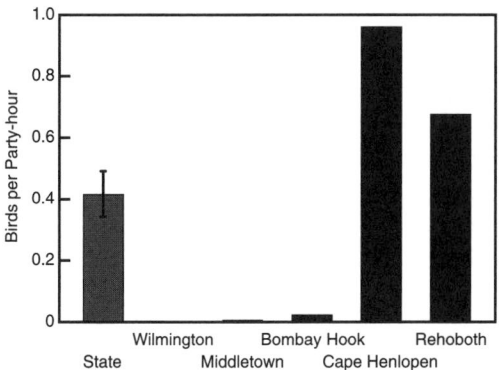

CBC Geographic Distribution; Average of 4 Count Areas

Common Loon (*Gavia immer*)

Regular; winter resident; uncommon to fairly common. Expected early October through late May, but a few may summer offshore.

HABITAT: Coastal bays, offshore waters; reservoirs (in migration). Haney (1990) notes that Common Loons in the South Atlantic Bight (Cape Hatteras, North Carolina, to Cape Canaveral, Florida) prefer waters up to 30 ft (9 m) deep and avoid highly turbid waters within 3–9 mi (5–15 km) of shore.

SPRING: Migration takes place during 1–10 April to 20–25 May. Most leave by the end of May, but a few may summer. High counts are

29 Apr 1967	30	Delaware R., New Castle to Bombay Hook [Marv1]
18 May 1986	15	on a pelagic trip [Rufe8]
25 May 1975	21	Prime Hook NWR [BroW10]

Common Loons, in contrast to Red-throated Loons, are often observed migrating overland in small numbers through New Castle County in spring. Small numbers of overland migrants occur in the Mid-Atlantic region (Boyle et al. 1979; Kerlinger 1982).

SUMMER: Occasionally, 1 or 2 remain through summer on saltwater, presumably first- or second-year birds or individuals incapable of making the northward migration. Five of 7 birds recovered along the ocean coast, June–August, were in worn basic (winter) plumage (DMNH 78308, 78309, 78312, 78313, 78314), while the other 2 were in worn basic plumage with scattered alternate (breeding) body feathers (DMNH 76650, 78310). One from the Susquehanna River, Maryland, had nearly finished its molt into alternate plumage (DMNH 78311). Although first- and second-year birds are known to summer in saltwater farther north (Godfrey 1962, 33), individuals summering in the Mid-Atlantic region are rarely encountered on pelagic trips (Rowlett 1980b) [Barn1].

FALL: Typical first arrival is 5–10 October, but in some years the first few arrive during September. Migration probably ends in late November. High counts are

15 Oct 1988	30	Rehoboth Bay [Swer1]
25 Oct 1983	25	Cape Henlopen [Frec40]
17 Nov 1974	120	Indian River Inlet [DuPG36]

Common Loons are occasionally seen in New Castle County at Dragon Run and Hoopes Reservoir and over White Clay Creek. Over land, the migrating birds are about one-tenth as common in fall as in spring. Kerlinger (1982) suggests that in fall loons fly downwind to the Atlantic coast before heading south, whereas variable spring winds may allow loons to migrate northward along ridges.

1966–89 CBC Summary

Christmas Bird Count	Years Found	Range of No. Found	Median
Wilmington	4	1–2	
Middletown	2	1–3	
Bombay Hook	22	1–7	1
Cape Henlopen	17	1–6	1
Rehoboth	23	1–26	10
STATEWIDE *(low in 1976, high in 1987)*	24	2–34	14

WINTER: The irregular numbers of Common Loons found on CBCs show no long-term trend, but they sharply decreased during 1986–89. They are most abundant on the Rehoboth CBC. High counts are 220 on the 1959 Rehoboth CBC and 300 at Cape Henlopen on 29 January 1955 [Abbo8]. Although Common Loons are less common than Red-throated Loons on Delaware CBCs, they are much more common offshore over the continental shelf (Rowlett 1980). Haney (1990) observed that they also avoided turbid, near-shore waters.

SPECIMENS: 12; DMNH.

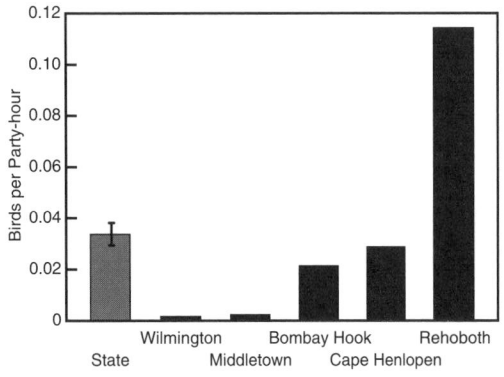

CBC Geographic Distribution

Pied-billed Grebe *(Podilymbus podiceps)*

Resident; uncommon. Peak migration occurs in March and probably October. Winter populations apparently declining.

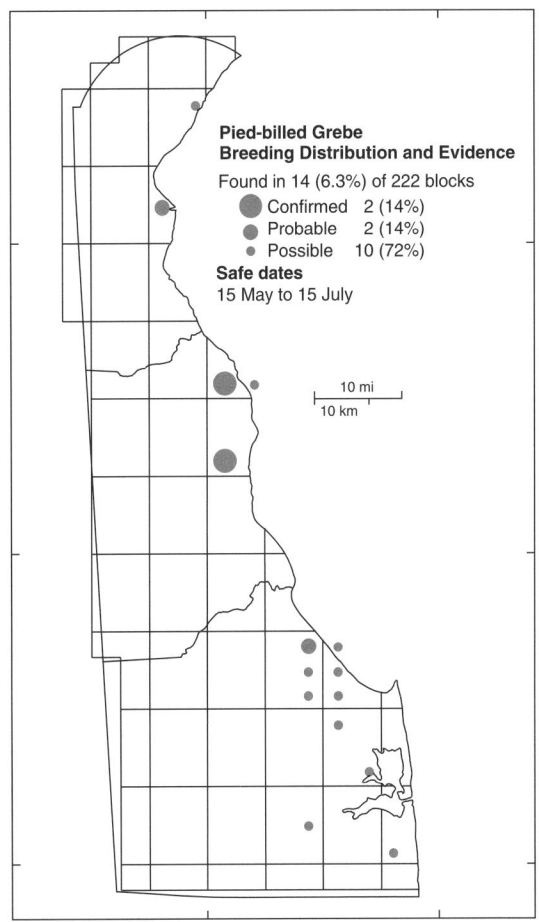

**Pied-billed Grebe
Breeding Distribution and Evidence**

Found in 14 (6.3%) of 222 blocks
● Confirmed   2 (14%)
● Probable   2 (14%)
• Possible   10 (72%)
Safe dates
15 May to 15 July

10 mi
10 km

HABITAT: Breeding: Ponds (as small as 2 ha) with shore and emergent vegetation, marshes with areas of open water and marsh inlets (D. Rothstein, DNHI, pers. comm.); also impoundments with emergent vegetation interspersed with open water greater than 25 cm deep (summarized in Gibbs and Melvin 1992c); reported breeding in Delaware tidal marshes (Miller 1942). Nonbreeding: Also more open situations and coastal areas.

SPRING: Migration may begin in late February or early March and clearly peaks through most of March; it probably ends by mid-April. High counts of 20–26 have been recorded from the last half of March.

BREEDING: After the last migrants leave Delaware and breeding birds become secretive around their nests; this small grebe is difficult to find. During the breeding season it is most often found in weedy fresh-to-brackish impoundments around Delaware City, Bombay Hook NWR, and Prime Hook NWR, but it can be found anywhere in the eastern part of the state. It will accept the most insignificant of ponds provided there is sufficient depth for diving.

Atlas. Breeding was confirmed twice during the Atlas period: a chick picked up just east of Dover [SPCA1]; and striped young observed at Finis Pool, Bombay Hook NWR (notes), on 21 June 1987. During 1990–92 adults, possibly breeding adults, were located within the Safe Date period in a number of Sussex County sites where none were found during the Atlas project: Silver Lake, Red Mill, Haven, Waples, Marshall, Diamond, and Burton ponds (D. Rothstein, DNHI, pers. comm.). These records suggest that this species breeds more widely than shown on the distribution map.

Nesting. Pied-billed Grebes typically breed in ponds with emergent grasses and other vegetation interspersed with patches of open water deeper than 25 cm (Fredrickson and Reid 1986, 75), such as Finis Pool and some Delaware millponds. The nest is composed of a mass of decaying vegeta-

tion in shallows as far as 15 m from open water (D. Rothstein, DNHI, pers. comm.). They do not usually breed in tidal salt-marshes, but Herholdt (Miller 1942) reported 5 nests in cord-grass at Bombay Hook NWR during April 1941, and Meredith [MerW2] reported a bird sitting on an empty nest in the tidal portion of Bombay Hook NWR during July 1983. Miller (1942) suggested it would accept saltmarsh habitat as long as tidal fluctuations did not tear the nest from its moorings. Miller also noted that 2-ft tidal fluctuations in the Richmond, Pa., marshes were acceptable. Lesser (1964, 1965) reported extensive breeding in an impoundment at Little Creek WA, with brood counts of 16 and 12 in 1961 and 1962, respectively, and June population peaks of 40 and 28. No grebes were observed there during a follow-up weekly survey in the summer of 1964 (Stickley 1967), and the species has not been reported breeding there since. Extensive breeding in new brackish impoundments in Louisiana (Chabreck 1963) resembles that at Little Creek WA.

Estimated clutch-completion dates for 4 nests and 4 broods are 16 May–9 July; 6 of the 8 are 22 June–9 July. These data do not include the 5 nests reported for April 1941, for which details are lacking. Thus the peak egg-laying period appears to be the last third of June. Egg dates range from 10 May to 21 July [Buck3], extending later than the Maryland egg dates of 17 May–5 June (Robbins 1996; Robbins and Bystrak 1977), so the Delaware observations may include renesting attempts (Forbes et al. 1989).

Trends. Analysis of May Count data indicates an almost 7% average annual decline. The BBS technique does not satisfactorily monitor this species. The relatively few BBS routes on which Pied-billed Grebe occurred in the northeastern states found low numbers (0.04 birds per route) (Gibbs and Melvin 1992c).

Breeding population. The instances of possible breeding reported during the Atlas project usually involve single sightings, which may either represent wandering nonbreeding birds or indicate this grebe's elusiveness. Based on the presence of grebes in 18 blocks during the Atlas project, usually not more than 1 pair per block, the Delaware breeding population is probably in the range of 10–100 pairs.

Conservation. This grebe's sharp decline (see "Trends") and low population suggest that it is threatened with extirpation as a Delaware breeding bird. It was extirpated in Rhode Island after the 1950s. It is listed as an Endangered breeding species in New Jersey, Endangered in New Hampshire and Connecticut, and is proposed as a Species in Need of Conservation in Maryland (Gibbs and Melvin 1992c). Gibbs and Melvin call for standardized monitoring procedures, as well as preservation and creation of relatively large wetlands with an interspersion of dense, robust emergents, submergent vegetation, and open water. They point out that the grebe's preferred habitat represents a particular stage in wetland succession requiring periodic management intervention. In Delaware, posting of some weedy parts of millponds to prevent nest disturbance by fishermen may be required.

FALL: The migration period may be during September and October, but observations are too few to give a clear indication. The number of reports increases during the first week of October and is sustained into the winter. Stewart and Robbins (1958) give the normal period in Maryland as 10–20 August to 1–10 December, peaking from 10 September to 10 November. The seasonal high count is 64 at Little Creek WA on 13 September 1961 (Lesser 1964).

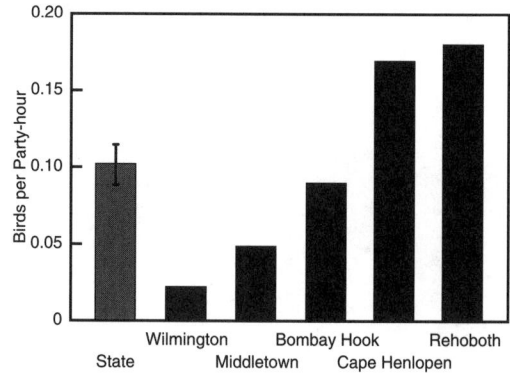

CBC Geographic Distribution

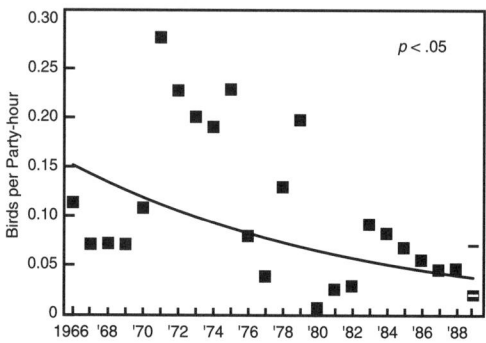

CBC Trend; May be Autocorrelated

WINTER: Pied-billed Grebes have declined on CBCs. This indicator species should be closely monitored in winter as a means of indirectly monitoring its breeding population, as well as the general productivity of fresh wetlands in the Northeast. The seasonal high count is 62 on the 1975 Rehoboth CBC.

SPECIMENS: 8; DMNH, CM, UDEL, USNM.

1966–89 CBC Summary

Christmas Bird Count	Years Found	Range of No. Found	Median
Wilmington	19	1–15	1
Middletown	14	1–24	1
Bombay Hook	23	1–30	3
Cape Henlopen	21	1–47	7
Rehoboth	22	4–62	14
STATEWIDE	24	2–119	33
(decreasing; low in 1980, high in 1971)			

Horned Grebe (*Podiceps auritus*)

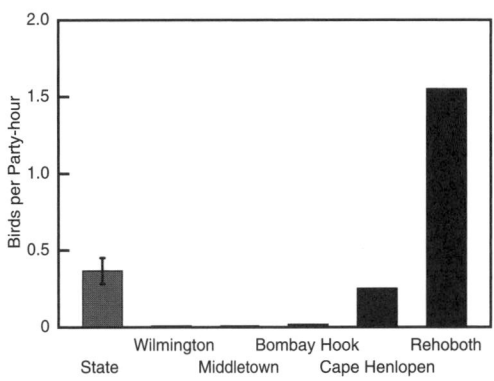

CBC Geographic Distribution

Regular; winter resident; uncommon to fairly common. Expected early November to early May. Winter population decreasing at 6% per year.

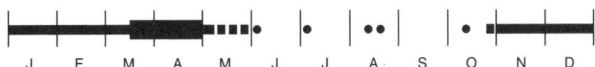

HABITAT: Salt, brackish, and fresh waters; most numerous on coastal marshes and bays, and occasional on inland lakes and reservoirs.

SPRING: Migration may begin 1–10 March. Peak migration occurs from mid-March to late April. Most leave by 1–7 May, though a few can sometimes be found as late as the first week of June. High counts are

11 Mar 1972	160	Rehoboth Beach [Holg12]
20 Mar 1980	200	Rehoboth Beach [Frec1]
8 Apr 1983	150	Cape Henlopen [Frec1]

SUMMER: Because this species breeds in the northern prairies, breeding is not suggested in any of the following instances:

5–11 Jun 1977	1	Bombay Hook NWR (notes)
3, 14 Jun 1972	1	Bombay Hook NWR, breeding plumage [Bonh1]
1 Jul 1972	2	Little Creek WA [Holg56]
17 Aug 1979	2	Port Mahon [Pure11]
19, 21 Aug 1985	1	Roosevelt Inlet, Lewes [Frec45]

FALL: The first birds sometimes arrive during the last third of October, but usually first arrival is 1–5 November. The earliest recorded arrival was 1 at Cape Henlopen on 13 October 1989 [Frec1]. Two were collected on 28 October 1904 near Millsboro (ANSP 48147, ANSP 48148). High counts are 32 at Rehoboth Beach on 14 November 1979 [Frec1] and 52 at Cape Henlopen on 17 November 1983 [Frec40].

1966–89 CBC Summary

Christmas Bird Count	Years Found	Range of No. Found	Median
Wilmington	5	1–6	
Middletown	3	2–5	
Bombay Hook	20	1–6	1
Cape Henlopen	22	1–62	12
Rehoboth	24	9–1,008	73
STATEWIDE	24	11–1,030	97
(decreasing; low in 1981, high in 1966)			

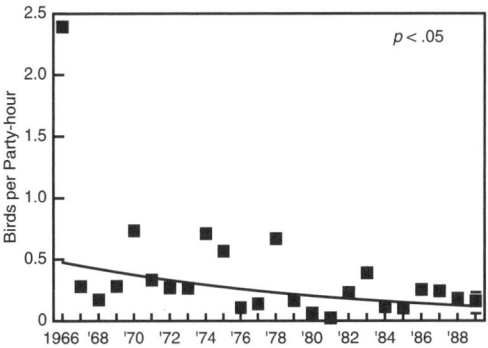

CBC Trend; Decreasing at 6% per Year

WINTER: This species' status should be monitored carefully because its CBC numbers for the 1980s appear to be lower than those for the 1970s. It is most numerous on the Rehoboth CBC.

SPECIMENS: 16; DMNH, ANSP, USNM.

Red-necked Grebe (*Podiceps grisegena*)

Occasional (37 years, 1912–94); winter visitor; usually rare. Should be looked for from November through March along the coast and on inland lakes and reservoirs.

HABITAT: Inland lakes and reservoirs in migration; coastal bays and open ocean in winter.

REMARKS: Red-necked Grebes winter regularly, at least in small numbers, along the Atlantic coast from the Bay of Fundy to Florida (AOU 1983) and are, therefore, to be expected in Delaware. About 65% of Delaware records date from December through February, with early and late dates of

6 Nov 1986	1	Cape Henlopen [Frec54]
16 Nov 1986	1	Cape Henlopen [Frec50]
3 May 1912	1	Rehoboth Beach [Penn2]

11 May 1972	1	Lewes [McNe1]
17 May 1994	1	Indian River Bay [RusJ5]

Although most reports cite only 1 or 2 birds, there are 2 reports of 4 each: Rehoboth Beach on 14 March 1948 [Davi24] and Indian River Inlet on 4 February 1987 [Frec48]. Most birds are found on saltwater, but some spring migrants were seen on Kent or New Castle County impoundments or at Hoopes Reservoir, as in these examples:

12 Mar 1962	1	Little Creek WA (Lesser 1964)
13 Mar 1994	19	Bombay Hook NWR [Jann1]
3 Apr 1984	2	Hoopes Reservoir [Batt6]

An unprecedented invasion brought large numbers to Delaware during 3 January–17 May 1994. Particularly outstanding were 25 found by Frech on Lewes area ponds and 65 seen by Campbell in Indian River Bay (Lantz 1994).

1966–89 CBC Summary

Christmas Bird Count	Years Found	Range of No. Found
Wilmington		
Middletown		
Bombay Hook	1	1
Cape Henlopen	3	1–2
Rehoboth	7	1–2
STATEWIDE (high in 1982)	9	1–3

SPECIMEN: USNM 422169, Indian River Inlet, 18 February 1934.

Eared Grebe (*Podiceps nigricollis*)

Casual (13 years, 1953–95).

DOCUMENTATION: Photograph (M. E. Gustafson, AB 46: 241).

REMARKS: The Eared Grebe is a western bird, wintering casually in eastern North America (AOU 1983). It was recorded at Bombay Hook on 6 October 1981 [SutC1] and on 26–27 November 1971 [Abbo18]; descriptive notes, not available to us, apparently accompanied both reports. We have convincing notes from Frech of a bird seen in Roosevelt Inlet on 13 December 1978 [Frec24] and another seen from the Henlopen fishing pier on 5 March 1979 [Frec4]. One was sighted on 4 January 1992 at Cape Henlopen SP [Gust1].

Additional individuals, for which documentation is not available, have been reported at plausible locations and dates:

13 Nov 1992	1	Cape Henlopen SP [Frec55]
29 Nov and 6 Dec 1953	1	Bombay Hook [Gold1]
20 Dec 1991	1	Indian River Inlet [Gust4]

31 Dec 1972	1	Cape Henlopen [Beac9]		16 Mar 1968	1	Bombay Hook NWR [Brez1]
11 Jan 1995	1	Cape Henlopen [Dyke8]		3–5 Apr 1984	1	in alternate plumage
17 Feb 1991	1	Fenwick Island [Barn22]				Hoopes Reservoir [SpeE10]
20 Feb 1994	1	Rehoboth Beach [Edni12]		13 Apr 1990	1	Indian River Inlet [Jan06]

[Western Grebe *(Aechmophorus occidentalis)*]

[Clark's Grebe *(A. clarkii)*]

Casual (5 years, 1948–93).

DOCUMENTATION: Notes, convincing as to genus but less definite as to species.

REMARKS: Both Western and Clark's grebes are western birds found very rarely on the East Coast (AOU 1983). Until recently they were considered color morphs of a single species but are now regarded as separate species. Field identification requires moderate care. The first "Western" Grebe reported in Delaware was found on 25 November 1948 at Indian River Inlet and described by Hake (1949). Another bird was found on 28 March 1965 at Cape Henlopen [PerD1]. In May 1965 a bird, presumably the same individual, was found dead at the same location [JohA1], but the specimen was not preserved. A wintering grebe was seen repeatedly in the Cape Henlopen area between 10 February and 30 April 1972 (Wilds 1972) [Conw13; DuPA7; Falk5; Well2]. Wilds (1972) provides a description adequate to determine that this 1972 individual was a first-year bird. All

these birds were observed prior to the split of the former Western Grebe into Western and Clark's grebes (AOU 1985), and none provides sufficient details to indicate which of the 2 species was present.

A grebe well seen on 26 November 1988 at Indian River Inlet was probably a Clark's Grebe (Hess 1989a). Its eye was clearly surrounded by the white cheek. The age of the bird was not determined, and it should be noted that the extent of white or dark on the cheeks is a more reliable field mark in adults than in immatures. The notes leave no doubt that the bird was either a Western or Clark's grebe, and we consider it likely that the identification as Clark's Grebe is correct.

Pelagic Birding

Maurice V. Barnhill III

The search for pelagic species offers one of the few ways that birding, a rather tame sport (as we know it in North America), perhaps approaches adventure. At first glance it seems like an easy form of birding. A few leaders arrange for a boat, take you to the exact spot where there are likely to be birds, and even point in the direction of your target. There are no trees or bushes in your way, and the noise made by your companions will not drown out the calls of pelagic birds that make few audible sounds at sea.

In reality, pelagic birding is not that simple. The ocean is almost never flat, so the boat deck is almost never level. Finding birds through binoculars when the "ground" is moving is challenging. Moreover, since many species either sit on the water or fly low over the surface, they may actually be hidden by waves more than three-quarters of the time. Even the lack of trees is ultimately a problem; there are no landmarks to use in pointing out the birds spotted. Add to all these matters the fact that pelagic species in our region are most abundant during winter, when the air and water are cold, the wind usually moderately high, and the waves always a problem, and you have an activity that is definitely for the hardy. And I have not even mentioned seasickness.

Identification of pelagic species is a new skill for birders who have not previously been to sea. The best land birders seem to have the most trouble, for they are used to their instinctive identifications being correct, but at sea they are beginners again. Some pelagic species are small (storm-petrels, phalaropes, some alcids), they often sit on the water where they are hard to see, and many have no clearly visible distinctive characters. Beginners should carefully watch common species, noting the shape and especially the flight characteristics. Many pelagic species can be identified at considerable distances solely by their manner of flight. Notice the speed and depth of the wing-beats, the stiffness or floppiness of the wings, whether the bird beats its wings constantly or uses a flap-glide pattern, whether the body travels in a straight line or moves up and down, and whether the flight direction continually varies.

In addition, there are some well-known pitfalls in using field guide characteristics too literally. For instance, the forked tail of the Leach's Storm-Petrel is seldom seen and the rump of the Cory's Shearwater is not always dark. The Leach's Storm-Petrel is most easily identified by its deep, nighthawk-like wing-beats. Cory's and Greater shearwaters are best distinguished not by looking for the Greater's white rump but by checking for the Cory's yellow bill and the Greater's dark cap.

Even the common species are not well documented in Delaware waters. It is therefore important to keep in mind which species are relatively distinctive and which can be confused. There are 4 groups of problem species: storm-petrels, shearwaters, jaegers and skuas, and alcids.

There are three species of likely storm-petrels. Wilson's is common, Leach's is rare, and Band-rumped is casual at best. Distinctions among the species are moderately difficult at sea, so reports of Leach's and Band-rumped storm-petrels need to be carefully documented.

Five shearwaters and the Northern Fulmar occur in Delaware waters. The fulmar is rather gull-like and quite distinctive, and sight records of the species are usually reliable. The Cory's and Greater shearwaters are similar and are easily distinguished only at moderate to close range. Sight reports of these two should note the field marks used and how closely the bird was approached. The Sooty Shearwater is distinctive even at a great distance. The remaining two—Audubon's and Manx shearwaters—are similar to each other, so sight reports of both must be accompanied by extensive documentation if they are to be accepted.

There are five species of jaegers and skuas possible here. The difficulty of their identification is notorious. About two-thirds of the jaegers seen at sea in the Mid-Atlantic region are reliably identifiable. The best observers occasionally disagree about the identifiability of some jaegers, and no observer is immune to error. In an incident off the coast of Maryland, when three experienced observers in separate parts of a boat saw five jaegers flying in a line, they simultaneously and independently called the first two Parasitics and the final three Pomarines. Although the independent identifications would seem to have established at least the consistency of the identification criteria, the observers thereupon spent more than ten minutes discussing *why* they agreed on the identifications.

Among the more likely alcids, the Dovekie, because of its small size, is seldom misidentified. The white cheek of the Atlantic Puffin makes it reasonably easy to identify when it is moderately close, so notes should at least mention the distance to the observed bird. Common Murres and Thick-billed Murres can be mistaken for Atlantic Puffins, especially in flight at a considerable distance. The species are not easy to distinguish from each other, so reports of either should be documented at least to the point of describing the circumstances of the observation.

Along the Mid-Atlantic coast, one goes out looking *for*, not *at*, pelagic species. Large numbers are unusual and generally far offshore. The first peak of pelagic activity is usually at an ocean depth of 30 fathoms (180 ft), 25–35 miles offshore; and the most reliable activity occurs at the eastern edge of the continental shelf. The western edges of deepwater canyons, at 80–100 miles from Delaware docks, usually have the most birds.

There are no firm data from our region on the reasons for these distribution patterns, but we can infer very plausible explanations for them. No truly pelagic species is a breeder here, so only food distribution and high winds affect the local occurrence patterns of pelagic species. The area around 30-fathom depths includes some of the best fishing grounds in the Mid-Atlantic region, and the fish attract pelagic birds. Farther out, at the edge of the continental shelf, currents cause upwelling of water from the depths, bringing nutrients to the surface that nourish organisms taken as food by birds. The species composition of the fish and microscopic organisms changes with the increased depth at the canyons on the edge of the shelf, thus attracting a different set of birds. When commercial fishing fleets are working in the canyons (except during the summer), they are usually surrounded by immense flocks of wintering and migrating gulls. In migration the gulls are accompanied by jaegers and Northern Gannets, and in winter by gannets and occasional skuas. At these times, the distribution of individuals suggests that discarded material from fishing boats provides the majority of the available food for surface feeders.

Off the coast of Delaware the Gulf Stream is too far offshore for one-day trips. However, the stream regularly sheds vortices, large circling masses of water that drift westward into inshore waters. The vortices may be recognized from boats by the presence of small amounts of *Sargassum* and on occasion by the presence of flying fish. Vortex-ring locations based on satellite infrared data are now regularly given in marine forecasts. Although I have not made a careful statistical analysis, my records from Ocean City, Maryland, trips show a tendency of warm-water avian species to occur in vortices, whereas cold-water species avoid them. Of the warm-water species found in the region—Black-capped Petrel, Bridled Tern, Audubon's Shearwater, White-faced Storm-Petrel, and Band-rumped Storm-Petrel—all but the first have been recorded in Delaware waters.

In view of the distances involved and the difficulty of locating birds on any given day, it is not surprising that there have been few productive pelagic birding trips in Delaware waters (see accompanying table). Richard Rowlett, Ron Naveen, and Gene Scarpulla ran a long series of one-day cruises out of Ocean City, Maryland. Most of our knowledge of pelagic birds in the region comes from those trips, but few of them, unfortunately, have been made in Delaware waters. Edward Strickland earlier ran a series of relatively nearshore trips out of Indian River Inlet, and much of what we know about Delaware comes from those trips. Even in Maryland, our knowledge of the occurrence of pelagic species is roughly what our knowledge of hawk migration would be if birders had visited mountains, usually in bad weather, approximately once a month for ten years. A summary of the trips led by Strickland has been published (Strickland 1987), as has the earlier part of the data coming from the Ocean City trips (Rowlett 1980). Additional information about the occurrence of pelagic species in Delaware waters from 1978 to 1980 is found in Powers (1983).

In the following accounts of pelagic species, we record all birds occurring in coastal waters between a northern boundary line, drawn due east from the point in Delaware Bay where the "middle of the shipping lane" crosses the line between Cape Henlopen and Cape May, and a southern boundary line, drawn due east from the intersection of the Maryland–Delaware boundary with the coastline. Thus Delaware oceanic waters extend from approximately 38°50'N to 38°27'4"N, from Broadkill Beach to Fenwick Island—a strip of ocean 26.3 statute miles (23 nautical miles) wide. In addition, pelagic birds in the Delaware part of Delaware Bay are reported. In view of the small amount of data from Delaware, we frequently mention the status in the Mid-Atlantic region in the species accounts. By this region we mean specifically waters off Delaware and the Delmarva Peninsula; and we have relied heavily on Rowlett (1980) and our own data from trips out of Ocean City, Maryland, for this information.

To demonstrate the limitations in our experience we tabulate here the month and day of the 33 known trips into the Atlantic off Delaware. A repeated day means that trips occurred on that date in more than one year, and the 11–15 August entry was a single five-day trip. Given the spotty coverage, this table should be consulted before concluding that the absence of a report means the absence of a pelagic species from Delaware at any particular time of the year.

Known Pelagic Trips in Delaware Waters

Month	1st	2nd	3rd	4th
		Quarter of Month		
Jan				
Feb		9, 10		
Mar		9	17	
Apr				
May		14	18, 22	24, 25, 27
Jun				27, 29, 29
Jul	3	11, 12	18, 20, 21 29, 31	
Aug	6	11–15		24, 26, 26, 27, 27, 29
Sep			21	
Oct		10		
Nov			23	29
Dec				

[Yellow-nosed Albatross *(Thalassarche chlororhynchos)*]

DOCUMENTATION: Sight record.

REMARKS: Wayne (1989) observed 2 albatrosses at close range in misty weather on 1 January 1989. The birds, described as appearing to have all-white underwings, were reported as Yellow-nosed Albatrosses. Because of a heavy fog, neither the dark wing margins and dark wing tips nor the black tail could be seen. Apparently no other birds were visible at the same time. The identification of the birds as albatrosses seems reliable, but the poor viewing conditions probably did not allow a distinction between the two plausible species (McDaniel 1973). The more likely species, Yellow-nosed Albatross, has a narrow dark margin on the underwings. The less likely Black-browed Albatross *(T. melanophris)* has a broad dark margin on the front of the underwings and a moderately narrow dark margin on the rear of the underwings. Both have dark wing tips. Given the description of the underwings as all white, the dark markings on the wings could not be used to distinguish the two species.

Northern Fulmar *(Fulmarus glacialis)*

Presumably regular; uncommon; winter visitor. Expected between September and March or perhaps as late as May.

DOCUMENTATION: Brief notes. Discarded carcass.

HABITAT: Pelagic.

REMARKS: Of the 2 Delaware records available, the first is of a bird that had been dead for "a few days" at Dewey Beach on 29 November 1952 (Broun 1953). No description was given, but a misidentification by Broun of a bird of this species in the hand is extremely unlikely. To the best of our knowledge, the specimen was not preserved. The second report cites observations by many experienced observers on 25 May 1991 on a DOS pelagic trip off Cape Henlopen [Barn43]. No description is available.

The Northern Fulmar breeds in the arctic and winters in small numbers offshore along the northern Atlantic coast (AOU 1983). Before 1973 this species was virtually unknown in Mid-Atlantic waters (Rowlett 1980b), but after that year it was found regularly there, mostly near fishing fleets, in time becoming an uncommon winter visitor, more common in migration. In March 1977, at the end of the observations reported by Rowlett, the United States began enforcing a 200-mi (322-km) territorial fishing limit. Since that date the Northern Fulmar has been rare but regular in the Mid-Atlantic region (Barnhill, pers. obs.). Sibley (1993) lists 8 records off Cape May County between 1977 and 1989. It is likely that the status off Delaware is similar to that in the rest of the region. The paucity of Delaware records of Northern Fulmars in part reflects the infrequency of winter boat trips into Delaware waters, as fulmars are almost never seen from land other than near their nesting colonies.

Cory's Shearwater (*Calonectris diomedea*)

Regular; summer visitor; common. Expected late May to mid-October.

DOCUMENTATION: Multiple sight records.

HABITAT: Pelagic.

OCCURRENCE: The Cory's Shearwater breeds in the eastern Atlantic (AOU 1983) in June and July and occurs off Delaware as a summer visitor. Palmer (1962,159) states that its age at first breeding is unknown, but birds dispersed over the central Atlantic in midsummer and concentrated off New England in August through November are probably prebreeders. The species was not found in Delaware until 9 July 1962, when several hundred were seen with 1 Greater Shearwater on a pelagic trip between Cape May and Rehoboth Beach [Rosc2]. The normal occurrence dates in the Mid-Atlantic region are late May to mid-October (Rowlett 1980b). A Delaware report in early May 1973 (Scott and Cutler 1973b), outside this range and undocumented, should be discounted. The next earliest report is 3 seen offshore on 25 May 1991 [Hess1; Barn1], slightly earlier than Rowlett's earliest. The next earliest is 1 on 27 May 1989, 45 mi offshore [Buhl1]. The latest record is 12 seen offshore from Indian River Inlet on 19 October 1969 [Wayn69], the same day as Rowlett's latest regional record (19 October 1974). Given the small number of trips offshore from Delaware (see "Pelagic Birding" essay) Delaware data alone cannot supply detail of seasonal changes in the abundance of Cory's Shearwater; the highest counted number recorded in the state is 130, seen by Rowlett 93 mi east of Rehoboth Beach on 14 August 1975 during a research cruise [Rowl18].

There are sufficient observations to establish the occurrence of the species in the state despite the lack of conventional documentation, but a photograph or even a written description of a bird seen in Delaware waters would be welcomed. As mentioned in the essay, the only serious identification problem is the separation of distant Cory's and Greater shearwaters, so our confidence in the occurrence of both in Delaware is enhanced by the fact that the 2 have been seen on the same seagoing trip at least 7 times (Barnhill, Fintel, Hess, Rowlett, and others).

Greater Shearwater (*Puffinus gravis*)

Regular; summer visitor; fairly common. Expected mid-May to early December.

DOCUMENTATION: Multiple sight records.

HABITAT: Pelagic.

OCCURRENCE: The Greater Shearwater was first found in Delaware on 9 July 1962; seen with Cory's Shearwaters on a pelagic trip between Cape May and Rehoboth Beach [Rosc2]. The normal dates of its occurrence in the Mid-Atlantic region are mid-May to early December (Rowlett 1980b), a period that brackets the Delaware range of dates—from 25 May 1991 [Barn44] to 29 November 1991 [Camp1]. The species is clearly acceptable for the state list based on multiple sight records off the Delaware coast and regular occurrence in the region, but photographic documentation would be welcomed. The only serious potential source of misidentification is Cory's Shearwater; as mentioned in the account of that species, Cory's and Greater shearwaters have been seen on the same trip at least 7 times.

REMARKS: The Greater Shearwater breeds in the southern hemisphere and winters in the Mid-Atlantic region during our summer and fall (AOU 1983). The Greater and Sooty shearwaters and the Wilson's Storm-Petrel are the only southern hemisphere breeders regularly present off the Delaware coast.

Sooty Shearwater *(Puffinus griseus)*

Regular; summer visitor; fairly common. Expected May through September.

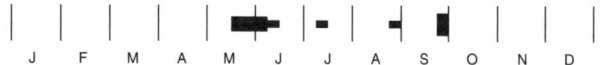

J F M A M J J A S O N D

HABITAT: Pelagic.

OCCURRENCE: The Sooty Shearwater breeds in the southern hemisphere and winters, at least in part, in the North Atlantic. Most of the wintering birds appear to stay north of our region (Powers 1983), but the Delaware records range from 18 May [Barn11] to 13 July, "badly decomposed" [Buck11] without an obvious gap. An additional report on 6 May (Scott and Cutler 1973b) is not documented and thus cannot establish an early arrival date. Although Rowlett (1980b) gives its dates of normal occurrence as late April to mid-June in the Maryland–Delaware region, Delaware records indicate that the species frequently lingers much later. In addition to the 13 July date cited, the latest dates are

27 Aug 1988	1	5 mi offshore [Fint10]
29 Aug 1970	1	offshore [Stri4]
24 Sep 1965	30	Lewes ferry [JohH1]

Sooty Shearwaters are seen from land along the Delaware coast much more frequently than any other shearwater, especially during times of strong easterly winds in May.

The first 2 Delaware specimens of the Sooty Shearwater were found dead on the beach about 2 mi north of the Maryland line on 5 June 1959 (Post 1960). Buckalew had picked up a Sooty Shearwater carcass on 13 July 1932 near the site of the Old Cape Henlopen lighthouse, but the specimen was too badly decomposed to preserve (Buckalew 1950, in Post 1960).

SPECIMENS: DMNH 78192, Dewey Beach, 5 June 1992; AMNH 6434 and AMNH 6435, near Bethany Beach, 5 June 1959; USNM 556949, Rehoboth Beach, 19 June 1982.

Manx Shearwater *(Puffinus puffinus)*

Presumably regular; uncommon; migrant.

DOCUMENTATION: Photographs (J. Bazuin, DMNH 136–38).

HABITAT: Pelagic.

REMARKS: The Manx Shearwater breeds north of Delaware and winters at sea (AOU 1983). It is expected during spring and fall migration and possibly during winter; the May and June birds are thought to be prebreeders less than 4 years old (Post 1967). Confusion of Manx and Audubon's shearwaters is a significant field identification problem, as mentioned in the essay "Pelagic Birding." The Manx is characteristic of colder water than the Audubon's and is expected to have a different seasonal distribution. Barnhill's experience in the Mid-Atlantic region indicates that Manx is considerably more common inshore than is Audubon's, but observations at distances beyond 100 mi (170 km) from shore show that the 2 species may be nearly equally abundant far offshore. Sibley (1993) quotes more records of Audubon's than Manx near and offshore from Cape May. Five Delaware pelagic records are available:

18 May 1986	1	[Barn16]
17 Jun 1981	1	[Kane1]
31 Aug 1981	1	photographed [Bazu1]
23 Nov 1991	3	[Barn1]
29 Nov 1991	8	(Campbell 1992)

The 17 June record is outside Rowlett's range of Mid-Atlantic dates: 23 April–1 June in the spring and 8 August–6 December in the fall. Except for the photograph of the 31 August 1981 bird, none of these reports are documented.

[Audubon's Shearwater *(Puffinus lherminieri)*]

Presumably occasional; summer visitor; rare. To be looked for primarily in late summer.

DOCUMENTATION: Unsupported sight records, uncorroborated but very probable. Reports for 5 occurrences have been published, and descriptive notes for 1 of them are available.

HABITAT: Pelagic.

REMARKS: The Audubon's Shearwater breeds in the Caribbean and farther south, occurring in summer along the Atlantic coast (AOU 1983). It is more common south of Delaware and Maryland, becoming quite common in the waters off North Carolina and southern Virginia. Inshore the Manx Shearwater usually outnumbers Audubon's [Barn1]. However, Audubon's occurs regularly in the general region in warm-water eddies and the Gulf Stream (Rowlett 1980b; Post 1967); Barnhill [Barn1]. In fact, a series of summer surveys off Delaware in Gulf Stream waters encountered Audubon's Shearwaters but no Manx (Powers 1983). There are 5 Delaware reports, all on plausible dates:

21 Jul 1974	9	160 mi offshore [Vaug1]
21 Jul 1980	1	Indian River Inlet [Gord7]
15 Aug 1975	4	38°41'N 73°34'W [Rowl18]
26 Aug 1967	1	offshore [Stri4]
25 Sep 1965	1	Lewes ferry [JohH1]

Although the 21 July 1980 record is supported by descriptive notes, in view of Lee's (1988) discussion of the identification of small shearwaters, we believe that it will be difficult to write convincing notes on isolated Audubon's or Manx shearwaters even though experienced observers can quite accurately distinguish the 2 species. A specimen or clear photograph is needed.

Wilson's Storm-Petrel *(Oceanites oceanicus)*

Regular; summer visitor; common to abundant. Expected mid-May to mid-September.

J F M A M J J A S O N D

DOCUMENTATION: Multiple sight records.

HABITAT: Ocean and bay waters, rare within sight of land.

REMARKS: The Wilson's Storm-Petrel, a southern hemisphere breeder that spends its winter off our coast during our summer, is the characteristic storm-petrel of Delaware's offshore waters. In season, it is seldom missed on boat trips and is sometimes the only pelagic species seen. In Maryland waters during May and September, migrating Wilson's Storm-Petrels occur in flocks of a thousand or more, most often along the edge of the continental shelf (Barnhill, pers. obs.). In summer Wilson's is present in smaller numbers, more dispersed. The species was found regularly, usually represented by 1 or 2 individuals, on the New Jersey side of the Delaware River and Bay during surveys conducted from 12 June to 4 September 1986. Larger, perhaps uncharacteristic, numbers (15–144) were seen on 12 June, and 7 and 9 July (Barber 1987). The status on the Delaware side may be similar if the requisite food source is available. The possibility that substantial numbers of Wilson's Storm-Petrels may be present in Delaware Bay in early summer is intriguing and needs investigation.

Of historical interest is Krider's (1879: 79) remark that he "found this bird on one occasion in the Delaware Bay, near Lewistown, Delaware."

White-faced Storm-Petrel (*Pelagodroma marina*)

Casual (1972 and 1984).

DOCUMENTATION: Photographs (H. Morrin; Barnhill and DuMont 1973).

HABITAT: Pelagic.

OCCURRENCE: There are 2 records: 26 August 1972, about 20 mi (30 km) east of the Delaware coast at 38°45'N 74°40'W [Barn27], and 15 August 1984, during a cruise that was part of the Manomet Bird Observatory Guest Observer Program, about 130 mi (200 km) east of Delaware at 38°29'N 72°42'W (pers. comm.) [Ever2]. A photograph of the 1972 bird by H. Morrin clearly shows the features of the species (Barnhill and

DuMont 1973, DMNH 1–4). The August Delaware records are consistent with a pattern of occurrence off the East Coast of the United States from late August to early October (Viet and Petersen 1993).

This species breeds widely in subtropical Atlantic and Pacific waters, including the Cape Verde Islands and the Salvages (near the Canary Islands).

Leach's Storm-Petrel (*Oceanodroma leucorhoa*)

Regular; migrant; rare. Expected late April to mid-August.

HABITAT: Pelagic.

OCCURRENCE: Two records by an experienced observer are available. A specimen was obtained about 80 mi (130 km) east of Delaware on 11 August 1975 [Rowl17] on a research cruise sponsored by the Marine Science Consortium. Rowlett [Rowl19] reported 8 Leach's 160 mi (420 km) east of Delaware on 18 July 1979 at 38°48'N 70°13'W. A Delaware City report (AFN 10: 13) lacks the details necessary to support so surprising a location. Rowlett (1980b, 18) considers the species present in

the Mid-Atlantic region "late April to mid-August" and "probably present in fall with perhaps a few stragglers in winter, especially in deeper waters." More recent observations (Barnhill, pers. obs.) indicate that it is at best extremely rare except in migration, as is likely for a species that breeds along the coast from northern New England north and winters primarily south of the Mid-Atlantic region. Birds reported from Delaware waters on 24 August 1968 and 26 August 1967 [Stri4] are slightly later than the period suggested by Rowlett. The species is almost never seen from land in the Mid-Atlantic region, making its exact status difficult to determine. Since the species is rather difficult to identify (see "Pelagic Birding" essay), all reports should be carefully scrutinized.

SPECIMEN: USNM 567673, 38°45'N 73°34'W, 11 August 1975.

Band-rumped Storm-Petrel *(Oceanodroma castro)*

Casual (1975, 1979, 1984).

HABITAT: Pelagic.

OCCURRENCE: There are 3 records, 100–260 mi (160–420 km) east of Delaware:

18 Jul 1979	1	38°48'N 70°13'W	[Rowl6]
14 Aug 1975	1	38°41'N 73°13'W	[Rowl5]
Aug 1984	4	38°55'N 72°21'W	[Ever1]

The 1975 record refers to a specimen from a Marine Science Consortium cruise; the 4 birds in the 1984 record were seen on a cruise that was part of the Manomet Bird Observatory Guest Observer Program. Because identifying this species is difficult, its status is not well known. Band-rumped Storm-Petrels are now seen regularly in North Carolina waters, usually with flocks of Wilson's Storm-Petrels, and may be more common in the Mid-Atlantic region than is indicated by the small number of records. According to Haney (1985), in the South Atlantic Bight (east of southeastern United States) the Band-rumped Storm-Petrel occurs primarily beyond the continental shelf in upwelling caused either by topography or Gulf Stream eddies. At the sites where Band-rumps were seen, Wilson's and Leach's storm-petrels were present but in below-average numbers. Observers seeking this species in the Mid-Atlantic should look in warm water associated with Gulf Stream eddies. Storm-petrels with long wings and shallow wing-beats, appearing to fly like a shearwater, are especially worth pursuing. Sight identifications of this species must be documented with unusual care and in comparison with Wilson's or Leach's storm-petrel or both.

SPECIMEN: USNM 567674, 38°41'N 73°13'W, 14 Aug 1975.

Northern Gannet *(Morus bassanus)*

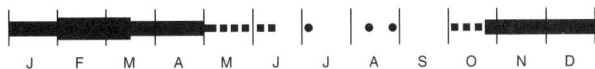

Regular; winter resident; fairly common to common. Expected from late October, rarely earlier, to late April and sporadically into early summer.

J	F	M	A	M	J	J	A	S	O	N	D

HABITAT: Offshore and pelagic.

SPRING: Last departure is usually late April to early May, but a few persist into late May and June. The latest specimen was found at Indian River Inlet on 15 May 1988 (DMNH 77112). Peak numbers usually occur from early February to mid-March, but the late high count of 300 was obtained on 27 March 1949 between Indian River Inlet and Ocean City, Maryland [Robb1]. More recent high counts include

5 Feb 1975	200	off Rehoboth Beach [Rowl16]
14 Mar 1985	150	Cape Henlopen [Frec1]
15 Mar 1985	100	Cape Henlopen [Frec1]

SUMMER: Gannets rarely remain into July and August, but 1–3 birds (age not reported) have been seen from Cape Henlopen SP south to Bethany Beach by various observers. Gannets do not return to their colonies until their third year and do not defend territories until their fourth; they have a mostly light plumage by their third year (Nelson 1978). Because prebreeders arrive at their colonies later in spring and leave earlier in summer (Cramp 1977), gannets seen off Delaware in summer are probably prebreeders from Canadian maritime colonies. Summer records include

10 Jun 1982	1	Lewes [Barn10]
2 Jul 1979	1	Cape Henlopen [Frec25]
12 Aug 1974	1	45 mi east of Cape Henlopen [Rowl14]

The dots for August on the seasonal bar graph are supported by several records.

FALL: First arrival is usually late October. Earlier records:

5 Oct 1987	1 adult	Dewey Beach (DMNH 77173)
11 Oct 1982	1 adult	Bethany Beach (DMNH 72944)
17 Oct 1975	1 immature	Centerville (DMNH 54800, Grantham 1977)

Migration probably continues into early December. Counts of 50–200 birds are fairly common throughout November [Frec1].

1966–89 CBC Summary

Christmas Bird Count	Years Found	Range of No. Found	Median
Wilmington			
Middletown			
Bombay Hook			
Cape Henlopen	5	1–16	
Rehoboth	17	1–152	2
STATEWIDE (increasing; high in 1983)	17	1–158	3

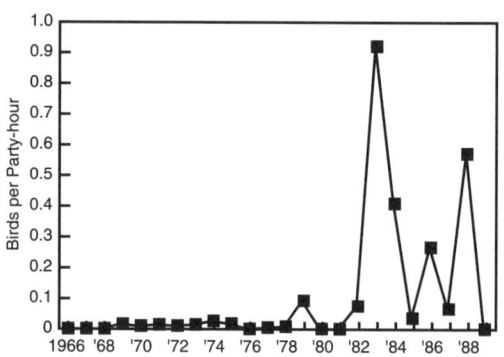

CBC Data

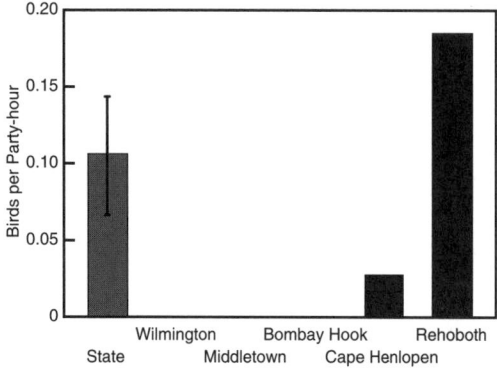

CBC Geographic Distribution; Average of 2 Count Areas

WINTER: Analysis of CBC data suggests an increase in numbers, which may be partly the result of an increase in sea-watching hours by CBC participants (hours not recorded). It is reported only on the Cape Henlopen and Rehoboth CBCs, most commonly on the latter. High CBC reports, all on the Rehoboth count, are 100 in 1988, 152 in 1983, and 250 in 1956. Other seasonal highs are

6 Dec 1982	200	Rehoboth Beach [Frec1]
10 Dec 1983	200	Cape Henlopen [Fint1]
5 Feb 1975	200	Rehoboth Beach [Rowl16]
24 Feb 1990	2,500	Cape Henlopen [Frec18]

SPECIMENS: 10; DMNH.

American White Pelican *(Pelecanus erythrorhynchos)*

Occasional (6 years, 1946–93); rare.

DOCUMENTATION: Notes. Photograph, A. Brady, not seen by the authors.

OCCURRENCE: The American White Pelican breeds west of the Mississippi, with a normal wintering range no closer than Florida (AOU 1983). Delaware's records come from the general vicinity of Bombay Hook NWR and Little Creek WA. This pelican was first recorded in Delaware on 8 December 1946 at Bombay Hook [Robe1]. Single birds have since occurred in the state:

30 Nov–1 Dec 1983	Port Mahon [Wayn22]
3 Dec 1983	Bombay Hook NWR [Fogl1; Edni43]
17 Aug 1985	Bombay Hook NWR (Hess 1986)
1 Jul 1989	Port Mahon [Shoc7]
25 Jul 1989	Bombay Hook, photograph [BraA1]
8 Aug 1989	Little Creek WA [Holg28]
21 May 1990	Bombay Hook NWR [Vand3]
12 Apr 1993	Cape Henlopen [Gelv1]

REMARKS: Because the species is unmistakable to reasonably careful observers, its occurrence in the state is unarguable. The records of the 4 dates from fall and early winter may represent birds straying through Delaware on their way to the winter range in Florida. Some strays remain through the winter in the mid-Atlantic region, as there are records of wintering birds in Chincoteague NWR, Virginia, and a record of a bird on 6 January, 1986, at Cape May (K. Seager, tabulated in Sibley 1993).

Brown Pelican *(Pelecanus occidentalis)*

Formerly casual, now regular; summer visitor; rare to uncommon. Expected mid-May through mid-August. Three records of 1 or 2 in 1934, 1978, and 1981; present annually in small numbers during 1982–93.

HABITAT: Bay and ocean coast. Along the ocean, seldom more than a few hundred meters from shore.

OCCURRENCE: Brown Pelicans usually arrive about mid-May and remain until mid-August, occasionally into September. One seen along coastal Sussex County on 28 February 1984 was unusually early [Atch6]. A late flock of 12 was seen flying from Cape May, New Jersey, into Cape Henlopen on 15 October 1983 [Fint9].

REMARKS: There are only 2 reports prior to the general population crash caused by chlorinated pesticides. The first Brown Pelican reported in Delaware was seen at Rehoboth Bay on 30 May 1934 (Tatum 1934). Barry (1942) listed it as "cas[ual], Records at Rehoboth, Woodland Beach." Post contamination and prior to 1982, the status of the Brown Pelican in Delaware was casual, but its status abruptly changed:

| 4 Jul 1978 | 2 | Rehoboth Beach [AbbF1] |
| 21 Jan 1981 | 1 | Millsboro (inland!) (Photograph published in *The Whale,* a local newspaper.) |

In 1982 there were 7 reports, including a high count:

| 30 Jul 1982 | 40 | Indian River Inlet [SchE1] |

In 1983, 12 reports, including:

| 24 Jun 1983 | 52 | Delaware Bay [Barn48] |

In 1984, 12 reports, including a high count:

| 14 Jun 1984 | 26 | Bethany Beach [Gamb1] |

Since 1984 the number of reports has declined, possibly because observers no longer consider the species remarkable. The number of individuals sighted on any given day may have declined somewhat from a peak in 1983, but a high of 47 was reported at Indian River on 8 May 1993 [Cutl15]. A sighting impressively far up Delaware Bay involved 1 opposite Delaware City on 13 June 1987 [RusR2]. The increase in the number of observations of Brown Pelicans occurred at a time when breeding colonies from North Carolina southward were recovering. Brown Pelicans began nesting in Maryland in 1987 (Robbins 1996), but no breeding has yet been noted in Delaware. Evidence of the establishment of a breeding colony in Delaware should be sought.

SPECIMEN: DMNH 78315, Fenwick Island, 23 August 1992.

Great Cormorant *(Phalacrocorax carbo)*

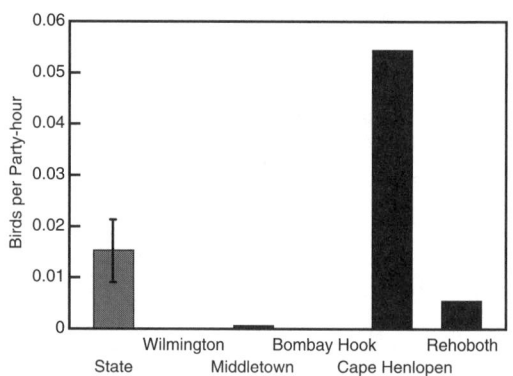

CBC Geographic Distribution; Average of 3 Count Areas

Regular; winter resident; uncommon. Expected mid-October to mid-April, primarily at Cape Henlopen.

HABITAT: Jetties; bays and coastal marshes.

SPRING: Migration probably begins about 10–15 February and ends by 10–15 April. Relatively high numbers from early February through early April may represent staging of southern birds for migration as well as actual northward movement. High counts are 40 on 25 March 1972 [Rowl2] and on 16 March 1991 [Camp15], both at Cape Henlopen SP. Fewer than 10 are usually seen.

SUMMER: Stragglers remain into late spring and occasionally into summer:

8 May 1971	3	Lewes [BucP1]
17 May 1973	2	Cape Henlopen SP [Bowl1]
13 Jun 1968	1	Lewes [BucF1]
Summer 1988	1	Cape Henlopen SP, most of the summer [Frec1]

FALL: The usual first arrival is 20–30 October, but Great Cormorants have arrived earlier in 8 years. The earliest reports are

24 Sep 1984	1	Henlopen Fish Pier [Frec1]
3 Oct 1989	1	Henlopen Fish Pier [Frec1]
7 Oct 1987	1	Henlopen Fish Pier [Frec1]
9 Oct 1965	1	Cape Henlopen [Herb1]
10 Oct 1970	8	Indian River Inlet [Carl13]

A high count of 22 was obtained on 26 November 1972 at Cape Henlopen SP [Rowl12]. As in the spring, fewer than 10 are usually sighted.

WINTER: No CBC trend is apparent; the high winter count of 18 was made at Cape Henlopen on the CBCs of 31 December 1978 and 28 December 1986. This species is found most often on the Cape Henlopen CBC, but it strayed north to the Middletown CBC on 29 December 1974 and to Reedy Point on 5 January 1974 [BroW3].

1966–89 CBC Summary

Christmas Bird Count	Years Found	Range of No. Found	Median
Wilmington			
Middletown	1	1	
Bombay Hook			
Cape Henlopen	16	1–18	1
Rehoboth		6	1–5
STATEWIDE (high in 1978 and 1986)	18	1–18	2

REMARKS: Barry (1942) stated there was no Delaware record of the Great Cormorant; it probably began wintering at Cape Henlopen while the cape was still under military control. The first Delaware report came from the cape on 2 March 1963 [Bake2], signaling the southward expansion of its winter range. The species also expanded its breeding range southward to Maine in 1983 and to Massachusetts in 1984 (Viet and Petersen 1993), and it substantially increased its breeding population in Canada (Godfrey 1986).

SPECIMENS: DMNH 72429, Cape Henlopen, 24 October 1981; UDEL 43-68, Delaware River below Wilmington, no date available.

Double-crested Cormorant *(Phalacrocorax auritus)*

Occurs all year; common to abundant. Peak numbers noted in April and October. Winter population increasing at 11% per year.

HABITAT: Along Delaware River and Bay and associated estuaries and impoundments, inland bays, occasionally large lakes, reservoirs.

SPRING: Migration begins about 25 February–1 March and continues to 1–5 June. The peak is from 25–30 March to 1–5 May. During migration, counts of hundreds and occasionally thousands are not unusual:

13 Apr 1985   5,000   Indian River [Frec1]

2 May 1991   3,000   Roosevelt Inlet (D. Rothstein, pers. comm.)

SUMMER: Although this species occurs commonly in the summer (typically not more than 10–20 birds per day) it was not found breeding before or during the Atlas project. The first known summer observation was 8 birds on 5 July 1937 at the Assawoman Bay marshes (McClanahan 1938). The next published record describes 40 along the Delaware River during the summer of 1964 [Conw7]. Since 1969 this species has increased about 10% annually on the May Count, probably corresponding to similar increases in late migrants and summering birds. Russell observed large numbers on Reedy Island in 1987 and speculated that they may begin to breed there [RusR2]. H. H. Harvey reported large numbers in the vicinity of the heronry on Augustine Creek during late spring of 1990 (pers. comm.).

The presence of large numbers of cormorants near the Pea Patch Island and Augustine Creek heronries represents a competitive threat to the colonial herons breeding there. The Dou-

ble-crested Cormorant is also a colonial breeder. In New York state it moved into a mixed colony and built up a population exceeding a thousand pairs in a few years. The resulting guano killed a large number of the trees and bushes used as nesting substrate, and when continued breeding broke down the dead bushes, nests had to be placed on the ground (Arbib 1988a). If the cormorants begin to nest on Pea Patch Island, some of the breeding herons are likely to be displaced.

BREEDING: Three Double-crested Cormorant nests were spotted on channel markers in the Delaware River east of Slaughter Beach during the summer of 1990 but "apparently in New Jersey waters" [Edni10]. On 27 July 1991 5 Double-crested Cormorants were observed, using a Questar telescope, sitting on nests on a navigation structure in the Delaware River far to the southeast of Port Mahon Rd.; they may have been on the New Jersey side of the channel (W. H. Howe, USFWS, pers. comm.). Nests unquestionably in Delaware were reported in 1991 on pilings at Port Mahon; no date was given [Cutl14]. Breeding also began in Maryland during 1990 (Robbins 1996).

FALL: Migration begins about 15–20 September and continues through early December, with peaks throughout October. As in spring, migration flights can number in the thousands of birds. One such flight observed at Cape Henlopen SP on 20 October 1983 was estimated at 6,000 birds [Frec1].

WINTER: Double-crested Cormorants have increased significantly on CBCs, corresponding to the rapid increase in their Canadian breeding populations (Price and Weseloh 1986; Ver-

1966–89 CBC Summary

Christmas Bird Count	Years Found	Range of No. Found	Median
Wilmington	7	1–4	
Middletown	12	1–27	
Bombay Hook	15	1–4	1
Cape Henlopen	24	1–39	11
Rehoboth	24	1–600	5
STATEWIDE	24	2–633	23
(increasing; low in 1969, high in 1984)			

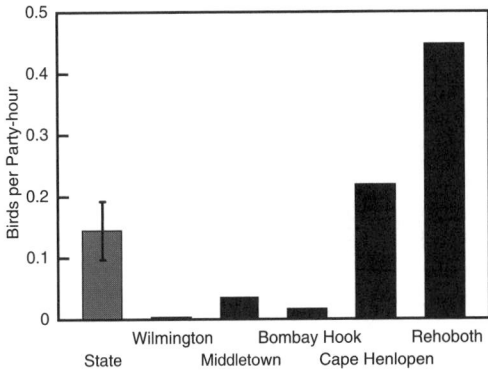

CBC Geographic Distribution

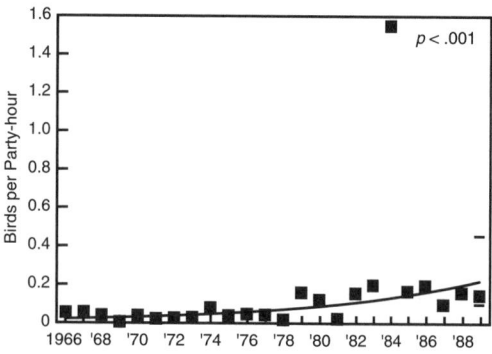

CBC Trend; Increasing at 11% per Year

meer and Rankin 1984). They are most abundant on the Cape Henlopen and Rehoboth CBCs; the 600 reported on the 1984 Rehoboth CBC comprise almost half of the total number reported on Delaware CBCs through 1989. This species is now more common in summer than in winter; non-CBC winter highs are

2 Dec 1984	12	Lewes [Frec44]
9 Dec 1978	10	Lewes [Frec1]
17 Dec 1983	13	Indian River Inlet [Barn42]

SPECIMENS: 8; DMNH, USNM.

Anhinga *(Anhinga anhinga)*

Accidental (1995).

DOCUMENTATION: Written notes.

REMARKS: An individual of this species was seen on 23 April 1995 at the Nanticoke WA by a DOS field trip led by Ednie [Edni32]. The bird was seen overhead moving directly south with very little flapping. We have notes from Ednie mentioning, among other things, the length of the tail ("even longer than the length of the neck") and the long, straight wings. One observer noted a long, narrow yellow patch that appeared to be a yellow bill.

This species occurs regularly as far north as North Carolina and sporadically to Virginia, Maryland, and New Jersey (AOU 1983, Sibley 1993). Its eventual occurrence in Delaware was expected, and the notes on this record are convincing.

Magnificent Frigatebird *(Fregata magnificens)*

Casual (1954, 1969, 1980).

DOCUMENTATION: Published notes (remote possibility of a different frigatebird species).

REMARKS: This species breeds north to the Florida Keys and ranges at sea to North Carolina and casually north to New England and Nova Scotia (AOU 1983). There have been 3 acceptable reports from Cape May County, New Jersey (Sibley 1993). There are also 3 Delaware reports: 1 captured at Lewes on 11 January 1954 and transported to Florida by car [Ulme1]; 1 seen on 22 June 1969 from the Cape May–Lewes ferry just outside the outer jetty (Meritt 1969) [Bloo1]; and 1 pursued along the coast from Maryland into southern Delaware on 28 April 1980 [Rowl7]. Frigatebirds are distinctive, and there seems very little doubt that these birds were frigatebirds. The 1969 bird was described (Meritt 1969), and the 1954 record was observed in the hand by highly competent observers. The 1980 bird was photographed, but we have not seen the photographs. There is a remote chance that a frigatebird species other than *magnificens* was the subject in 1 or more of these reports, although no regional records of such other species exist.

American Bittern (*Botaurus lentiginosus*)

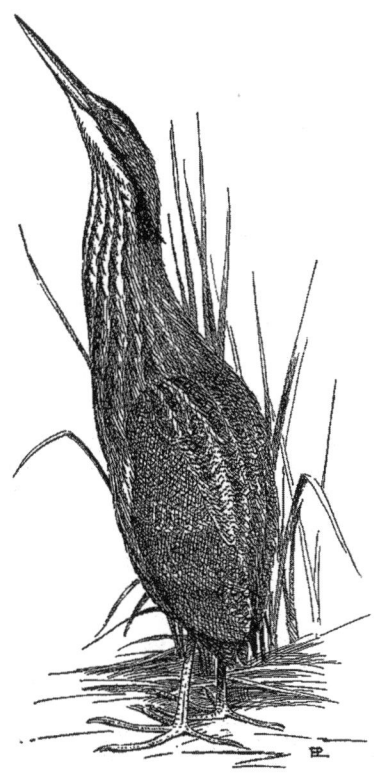

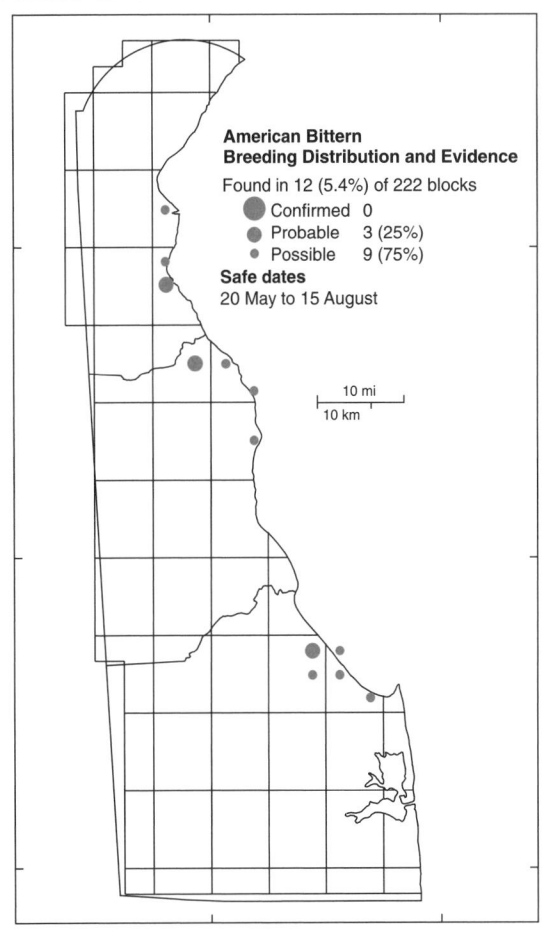

**American Bittern
Breeding Distribution and Evidence**

Found in 12 (5.4%) of 222 blocks

- Confirmed 0
- Probable 3 (25%)
- Possible 9 (75%)

Safe dates
20 May to 15 August

10 mi
10 km

Resident; rare to uncommon. Rare breeding bird. Winter population decreasing at 5% per year.

J F M A M J J A S O N D

HABITAT: Usually unimpounded brackish tidal marshes during breeding. Over most of its range it breeds in freshwater wetlands with tall emergent vegetation, so the usual Delaware breeding habitat is the least important breeding habitat throughout much of its range (Gibbs, Melvin, and Reid 1992); formerly bred in a freshwater marsh west of Harrington; occasionally uses upland marshy fields during migration; early winter sightings are close to tidal guts, which may be most resistant to freezing. Prefers habitat of wetlands dominated by narrow-leaved cattail, Olney three-square, needlerush, and switchgrass.

SPRING: The number of times the American Bittern is reported increases during April, suggesting onset of migration, but additional studies are needed to establish its migration period. Stewart and Robbins (1958) give the normal migration period in Maryland as 10–20 March to 5–15 May, with the peak 25 March to 25 April. Gibbs, Melvin, and Reid (1992) suggest this bittern may be nonmigratory in the milder southern parts of its range, which includes the Delmarva Peninsula. The high count is 5 birds at Bombay Hook NWR on 22 May 1983 [Bayn4].

BREEDING: This rare species often remains well camouflaged within the cover of cattails and reeds. Pennock recorded

it twice in fresh marshes during its breeding season: 8 May 1909 on the Nanticoke River below Concord and 14 May 1927 at a freshwater pond near Rehoboth Beach [Penn1]. Upland marsh areas that harbored bitterns in the 1930s [Hans1] have been drained. The remaining Delaware population appears restricted to the brackish tidal marshes along the Delaware River, with the highest concentration probably in Prime Hook NWR.

Atlas. Breeding was not confirmed during the Atlas project. The most substantive Atlas reports describe a courting pair in the brackish marshes near Taylors Gut in April 1984 and regular sightings at Prime Hook NWR. Two Atlas sightings are anomalous: 1 on 25 May 1984 near the end of Angola Neck was the only report from the Inland Bays, and 1 in 1983 in the White Clay Creek valley was the only report from the Piedmont. These reports probably do not represent breeding pairs. The distribution map may underrepresent this cryptic species. For example, 1 was seen 8 May 1993 behind Big Stone Beach (West, pers. obs.), an area where none was reported during the Atlas project.

Nesting. Nest records:

13 May 1990	4 eggs	Little Creek WA [Camp3]
14 May 1927	2 eggs	near Rehoboth Beach [Penn1]

17 May 1935	3 nests	
	(5 eggs each)	near Harrington [Hans1]
20 May 1934	3 eggs	near Dover [Hans 1].

In 1935 Hanson found the 3 nests in an upland marsh 2 mi west of Harrington. He described the site as a swampy pond in a woods with water 1 or 2 ft deep and with a heavy growth of grass, reeds, and low bushes. The nests, placed in bushes about 1 ft above the water, were constructed of marsh grass and were rather bulky and flat-topped, having an inside diameter of about 7 in. This group of 3 nests suggests that small breeding colonies can form, but most nesting is solitary. One clutch in this group was hatching 17 May, and another was well advanced, suggesting clutch completion in late April [Hans 1]. Estimated clutch-completion dates extend from 15 April to 6 May ($n = 6$).

Breeding population. Refuge personnel estimate the population of bitterns in Prime Hook NWR to be about 10 individuals [Prim1]. This and the 8 breeding season records during the Atlas period outside Prime Hook NWR support a state population estimate of 5–50 pairs. The loud spring call of this species, nicknamed "thunder pumper" and "stake-driver," is rarely heard in Delaware, good evidence that its population here is genuinely small. Males within a range of about 500 m often respond to each other's pumping call in early spring (Gibbs, Melvin, and Reid 1992).

Conservation. Continued protection of estuarine brackish marshes is necessary if the American Bittern is to be retained as a breeding bird in its last remaining breeding locations. It was listed as a migratory nongame bird of management concern in 1982 and 1987 by the USFWS (1987). It is listed as Threatened in New Jersey and Pennsylvania and a Species of Special Concern in Maryland (Gibbs and Melvin 1992a). It was Blue-Listed during 1976–86 (Tate 1986).

FALL: Few data are available for this period, but 1 seen in Brandywine Park on 10 October 1912 was surely a migrant [Penn 1]. Most observations cite 1–2 birds. Stewart and Robbins (1958) give the normal migration period in Maryland as 1–10 September to 1–10 November, with a peak from 20 September to 20 October.

1966–89 CBC Summary

Christmas Bird Count	Years Found	Range of No. Found	Median
Wilmington	3	1	
Middletown	5	1–2	
Bombay Hook	19	1–7	1
Cape Henlopen	17	1–8	1
Rehoboth	16	1–4	1
STATEWIDE	24	1–14	4

(decreasing; low in 1985 and 1987, high in 1970)

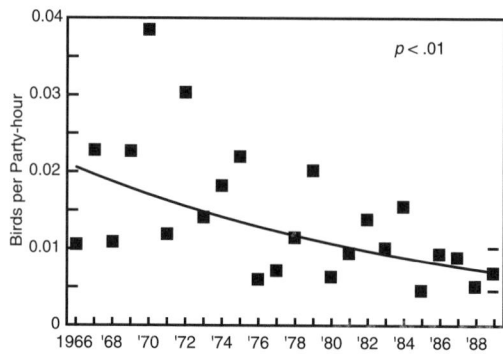

CBC Trend; Decreasing at 5% per Year

WINTER: This species needs continued monitoring because it shows a significant downward CBC trend. The CBC data provide the most effective method for measuring its trend, but it is not known whether wintering birds are the same ones that breed in Delaware.

SPECIMENS: 7; DMNH, ANSP, USNM.

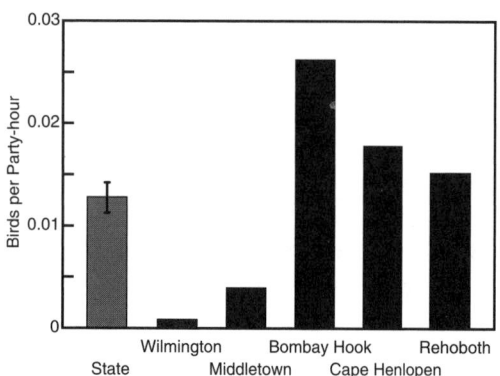

CBC Geographic Distribution

Least Bittern *(Ixobrychus exilis)*

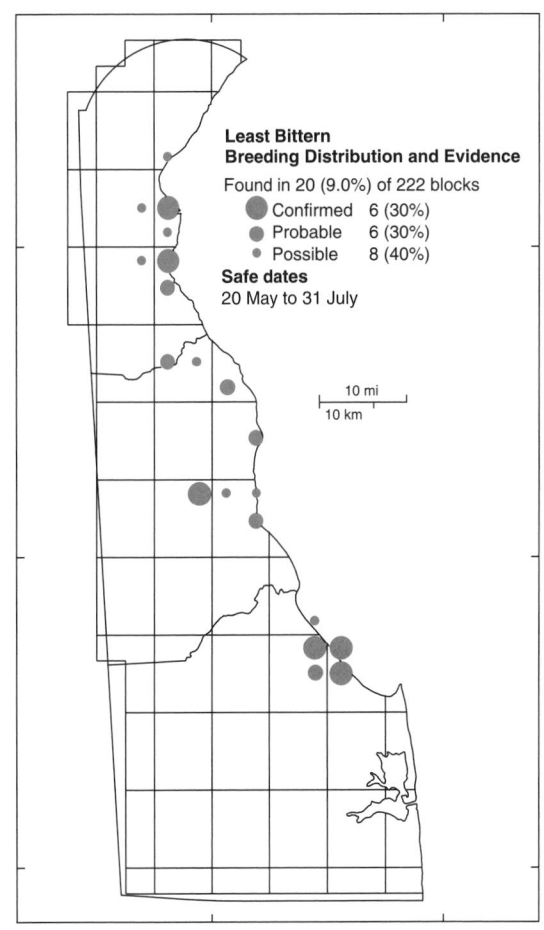

Least Bittern
Breeding Distribution and Evidence
Found in 20 (9.0%) of 222 blocks
- Confirmed 6 (30%)
- Probable 6 (30%)
- Possible 8 (40%)

Safe dates
20 May to 31 July

10 mi
10 km

Regular; summer resident; uncommon to fairly common. Expected early May, rarely earlier, to early September, rarely to late September.

J F M A M J J A S O N D

HABITAT: Estuarine marsh, especially narrow-leaved cattail marsh for breeding; occurs at other times in various marsh types, as well as in scrub-shrub swamps. Frequents the open water side of a stand of reeds, not the shallower side, toward land. Formerly nested in wild rice and cattails but now found nesting in the phragmites stands that dominate most fresh and brackish marshes. Tall vegetation in dense stands above deep water is given as a generalized habitat (Gibbs, Reid, and Melvin 1992; Frederick et al. 1990), but these authors do not list phragmites as a breeding habitat. Nests in fresh and brackish marshes up to at least 7 ppt, the salinity at Taylors Gut (sea water is 32–35 ppt) (Meanley 1985, 31).

SPRING: Least Bitterns begin arriving in mid-April, but because of the difficulty in detecting them, no clear migration period is discernible. Stewart and Robbins (1958) note that peak numbers occur in Maryland from 5 May to 1 September. A high count of 10 was obtained at Cape Henlopen SP 13 May 1972 [Wayn42]. As with American Bittern, more information is needed to determine the species' migration periods and numbers in Delaware.

BREEDING: The Least Bittern breeds primarily from Delaware City south to Prime Hook NWR in estuarine marshes and impoundments.

Atlas. Although it usually stays hidden in reeds, a Least Bittern can be detected by its dovelike call and is seen occasionally as it flies from one feeding site to another. Searching by boat is the most productive survey method. During the Atlas period, it was located along the Delaware River in marshes from Army Creek to Prime Hook NWR, and once farther south in White Creek, just west of Fenwick Island. Atlas workers did not find

the Least Bittern in southern Delaware areas where it had been observed in summer in prior years: Gordon Pond, Dewey Beach, Fenwick Island, and Assawoman WA. The general lack of Atlas reports suggests that it has withdrawn from most of Delaware south of Cape Henlopen. It was not reported from Milford Neck, presumably because of inadequate coverage; it has bred there in the past, and suitable habitat remains. Detection improves when a recorded playback of its call is used (Swift et al. 1988). Breeding was confirmed 6 times during the Atlas period: clutches in 3 Prime Hook NWR blocks [O'Sh1] and in 1 block west of Delaware City [Nile2], and fledged young in 2 blocks.

Nesting. In 1923 Hanson (notes) found a nest supported by wild rice about 18 in. above the marsh water level. It was a frail platform of coarse grass, 7 in. across and almost flat.

The peak estimated clutch-completion period is mid- to late May (*n* = 7). Extreme egg dates are 14 May and 1 July. Weller (1961) surmised from bimodal nest initiation dates that the Least Bittern is double-brooded in Iowa; no data are available for marked birds. No Delaware population has been studied for double broods, and no late nesting has been reported.

Trends. It has declined on the May Count at an average rate of about 6% annually. It has not been encountered on any Delaware BBS route.

Breeding population. Past reports indicate 55 pairs breeding at Little Creek WA in 1962 (Lesser 1964), 15 at Dragon Run in 1974 [DOS1], and 50 in Prime Hook NWR in 1975 and 1977 [Prim1]. The present population of Least Bittern is probably 100–1,000 pairs; it was reported in 21 blocks and may average 10 pairs per block where it occurs. Its presence was probably undetected in some blocks along the Delaware River.

Conservation. The Least Bittern was listed as a migratory nongame bird of management concern in 1982 and 1987 by the USFWS (1987). It is listed as Threatened in Pennsylvania, declining in New Jersey, and as a Species of Special Concern in Maryland (Gibbs and Melvin 1992b). Perhaps the conversion of phragmites marshes back to cattail and wild rice will help maintain its population in Delaware. One such improved impounded marsh east of Taylors Bridge supports breeding Least Bitterns.

FALL: As in the spring, no clear migration period is discernible. Most depart by 7 September. Late reports:

21 Sep 1899	1	near Odessa (ANSP 66221)
24 Sep 1988	1	near Delaware City (DMNH 77811)
27 Sep 1975	1	Dragon Run [West2]
3 Oct 1961	1	Little Creek WA (Lesser 1964)

On 6 September 1975 a high count of 6 was obtained at Dragon Run [Stri5].

WINTER: Two undocumented December reports have been published:

17 Dec 1967	1	Bombay Hook NWR [Levy1]
19 Dec 1971	1	Lewes [BroW25]

Its winter range is described as lying south of areas with prolonged frost; south along the Atlantic Coastal Plain from Maryland and Virginia (Gibbs, Reid, and Melvin 1992). An occasional December record in Delaware is consistent.

SPECIMENS: 9; USNM, ANSP, DMNH. Egg records: DMNH.

Pea Patch Island: A Siege of Herons (and Egrets and Ibises)

Charles R. Vickers

The story goes that Pea Patch Island sprouted from a sand-bar in the middle of the Delaware River more than 200 years ago when a boatload of peas sank in the shallows. The peas sprouted and grew and trapped silt and sand, thereby changing the sandbar into an island. During the early part of the twentieth century the north end of the now 287-acre island was filled in by dumping gravel spoil dredged from the Delaware River.

Most people know of Pea Patch Island, one mile northeast of Delaware City, as the home of historic Fort Delaware. The fort was built after the War of 1812, used as a prison during the Civil War, and garrisoned during the Spanish-American War, World War I, and World War II. The island was declared surplus by the military in 1943 and became Fort Delaware State Park in 1951. Thousands of visitors seek out the island every year to learn the history of the fort. For birders, however, the main interest is the northern part of the island, the site of the largest heronry on the East Coast from Maine to Virginia. This heronry is a critical component of the Delaware Estuary ecosystem.

During the late 1950s and early 1960s a small heronry at Kill-cohook NWR, nearby in New Jersey, shrank in size, although the species and number of colonial waders as a whole were on the rise in the Delaware–New Jersey area. It is thought that birds that left Killcohook established the heronry on Pea Patch. The island heronry now numbers several thousand nesting pairs representing nine species: Cattle Egret, Snowy Egret, Glossy Ibis, Little Blue Heron, Great Egret, Black-crowned Night-Heron, Great Blue Heron, Yellow-crowned Night-Heron, and Tricolored Heron.

Although most birds are solitary nesters, some species of seabirds and waterbirds nest colonially thereby gaining the security of collective alerts and defense against predators. As in the case of Pea Patch, colonies are often located on islands, which provide freedom from most mammalian predators. The Pea Patch colony has grown and prospered in the Delaware Estuary, which contains 200,000 acres of tidal marsh feeding habitat.

In 1964 the first documented account of the heronry noted 900 pairs of 7 species of colonial waders, and it included new state breeding records for Cattle Egret and Glossy Ibis (Cutler 1965). In 1968 1,940 nests were counted. Through the 1970s the heronry grew in size, with numbers for individual species fluctuating, and two new species, Yellow-crowned Night-Heron and Tricolored Heron, were added to the list of breeders. In 1977 a survey of all known heronries from Maine to Virginia showed that Pea Patch harbored the most nesting pairs—topping 7,000. The next largest, at Stone Harbor, New Jersey, had just over 2,600. The count at Pea Patch in 1989 exceeded 12,000 nests, a number paralleled in 1993 during the most recent field-work.

Accurate counting of birds on Pea Patch Island is difficult because of their large numbers and the inaccessibility of the phragmites marsh, which is used extensively as nest substrate. Although sampling methods differ among researchers, preventing a precise quantitative comparison, estimates of the number of nests and nesting pairs are useful for interpreting trends and for gauging relative numbers (see accompanying table).

Along with the gains made in total nesting pairs, there were major changes in species composition during the period

Wading Birds Nesting on Pea Patch Island

Year	Total	Cattle Egret	Snowy Egret	Glossy Ibis	Little Blue Heron	Great Egret	Black-crowned Night-Heron	Great Blue Heron	Yellow-crowned Night-Heron	Tricolored Heron
Number of nesting pairs [1]										
1975	7,095	4,500	250	1,500	200	175	400	20	20	20
1976	7,059	4,500	900	600	400	175	400	4	40	40
1977	6,937	3,900	1,000	650	550	250	500	2	40	45
1978	5,727	3,000	1,000	550	300	225	550	2	35	65
Number of nests [2]										
1985	6,600	5,535	234	18	414	183	18	198	0	0
1986	5,652	3,932	543	275	549	169	67	58	41	18
1987	6,893	5,181	372	150	597	338	50	133	6	66
1989	12,144	9,783	158	236	900	639	1	727	0	0
Number of breeding pairs [3]										
1993	12,109	4,642	2,456	2,100	1,327	603	519	389	43	30

1. Weise 1979.   2. DNREC 1991.   3. Parsons 1993.

1964–93. Most conspicuous is the growing proportion of Cattle Egrets. Having increased from 100–150 pairs in 1964 to an average of 6,000 in recent years, they accounted in 1993 for nearly 40% of the colony's population. After previous wide variations, Snowy Egrets and Glossy Ibises showed a marked resurgence in 1993, exceeding 2,000 pairs each. Little Blue Herons and Great Egrets have kept pace with the growth of the heronry, at 10% and 5% of the total, respectively, throughout the period. Black-crowned Night-Herons, after declining drastically in the 1980s, recovered in 1993 to their former level of 500 pairs. Great Blue Herons, which almost disappeared during the 1970s, have subsequently risen to an average of 300–400 pairs. Yellow-crowned Night-Herons and Tricolored Herons have remained scarce.

The trends over the 30-year period reflect changes on Pea Patch Island itself as well as regional influences. The surge in the number of Cattle Egrets in Delaware mirrored the bird's general population gains across the United States. The appearance of Yellow-crowned Night-Herons and Tricolored Herons followed a northward range extension of these two species in the 1970s. Year-to-year population changes in total numbers may to some extent result from weather patterns; severe winters have been followed by lower total numbers, and mild winters have tended to precede increased populations. Loss of nesting substrate and nest-site competition influence numbers. Other smaller heronries in the region have shown declines in numbers that may have contributed to the population increase at Pea Patch. The loss of nearby feeding sites through conversion of wetlands and development of agricultural fields may have affected fledging success and resulted in an overall decline in some species' numbers. New research is directed at interpreting regional data for several heronies and at standardizing data collection. The goal is better interpretation of the changes in species composition and abundance.

The birds nesting on Pea Patch are migratory, spending winters in the Carolinas and farther south, although some individual Great Blue Herons, and to a lesser extent Great Egrets, stay in Delaware through the winter. By mid-March migrant Great Blue Herons, Great Egrets, and Yellow-crowned Night-Herons return and begin nest site selection in the mixed hardwoods of red maple, sweet gum, and tupelo. Black-crowned Night-Herons and Glossy Ibis show up in late March to early April and nest in smaller hardwoods and the phragmites marsh. By mid-April Cattle Egrets, Little Blue Herons, and Tricolored Herons return and choose sites in the highbush black blueberry and common elderberry shrub layer and in the phragmites marsh. Snowy Egrets also arrive at this time and tend to nest in the phragmites.

Pair formation in herons and egrets is initiated through a series of courtship displays by the male, involving stretching, bowing, and bill snapping. The female repeatedly attempts and eventually succeeds in landing on a male's rudimentary defended nest. Pair bonding takes place through mutual nest building and recognition of a mate's call; in a multiple-nest area such as Pea Patch, call recognition greatly aids in locating the correct nest. Both sexes incubate eggs and brood young. Typically, two to five eggs are laid; incubation begins with the first egg, resulting in variously aged young in a nest. Brood size is adjusted to food availability through starvation of the last hatched and thus least competitive nestling.

Despite the relative safety of Pea Patch Island, outside influences and other inhabitants of the island do pose many threats to the birds, their nesting sites, and their feeding areas. The weather can directly and indirectly affect individual survival, nesting success, and food supply. Although mammalian predators are few, avian predators are numerous. American and Fish crows eat eggs and nestlings. Great Horned Owls, island residents, prey on both nestlings and adults; and Black-crowned Night-Herons eat other herons' nestlings. Any human intrusion into the heronry during nesting season causes nestlings to move out of the nest; in many cases, physically unable to return to the nest, they die.

Contaminated food is another threat. In 1976, Snowy Egrets and Tricolored Herons ate mummichogs infected with a parasitic nematode that caused peritonitis and killed many young birds. The heronry is located within easy flying distance of many chemical, oil-refining, and other industrial plants, as well as a nuclear power plant, raising the possibility of contamination of food by heavy metals, radionuclides, and other toxics.

Every day approximately 30 million gal of crude oil are carried by tanker through the Delaware estuary to refineries upstream of Pea Patch Island. A major oil spill would affect the heronry in several ways. Crude oil kills marine organisms that are at the base of the food chain. It can also directly kill many of the waders' prey items, such as fish, crustacea, amphibians, reptiles, and aquatic invertebrates. And when the birds themselves become contaminated by contact with oiled marsh vegetation and attempt to clean their feathers, they ingest oil. The result is a breakdown of the gastrointestinal tract lining, inability to absorb nutrients, and eventual starvation. Further, when oiled-coated adult birds return to the nest, the contaminant is passed on to the young, which in turn ingest oil when preening.

The loss of feeding sites is stressing the heronry. Upland foraging areas for Cattle Egrets and Glossy Ibises, formerly agricultural or open lands, are being developed for housing and highways. When such foraging sites near the heronry are lost, the birds must fly farther for food and spend more time away from their nests.

The ultimate factor in determining the size of the Pea Patch Island heronry may be the quality of trees, shrubs, and marshland available for nest sites. During the 1970s a buildup on the ground of large amounts of nitrogenous excrement from the nesting and roosting of thousands of birds killed off the shrub layer in many parts of the heronry. The regrowth consisted of plants less suitable for supporting nests, and a high incidence of nest collapse and failure occurred when the herons used some of the weaker shrubs. As a result, many of the waders started nesting in the phragmites marsh; the 1993 survey found that more than 80% of all nests were located in the phragmites.

What does the future hold for the Pea Patch Island heronry? How are some of these threats to its continued existence being addressed? In May 1988 the heronry was dedicated as a State Nature Preserve, the highest level of protection for conservation lands in Delaware. The management plan for the preserve stringently limits public access and land use; the heronry may be observed only from a platform on the south end of the island. The state has devised an oil spill response plan that contains detailed protection measures for the heronry and its occupants. Public and private conservation agencies have undertaken land protection efforts on major tributaries and upland buffers along the Delaware estuary to preserve permanently the colonial waders' feeding sites. Fieldwork is continuing on measurement of bird abundance and productivity, and toxicological studies are underway.

The Pea Patch Island heronry is a dynamic scene during the spring and summer, with birds flying to and from the island; nestlings and fledglings of various ages hopping around; and the squawking, hissing, and croaking of a multitude of long-legged birds. From a scientific perspective the heronry affords excellent opportunities for research on population changes, predator-prey relationships, and nest site selection, for example. With vigilant monitoring and protection, the siege of herons, egrets, and ibises will remain a unique part of Delaware's natural heritage.

Great Blue Heron *(Ardea herodias)*

Resident; common. Most numerous February–March to late October.

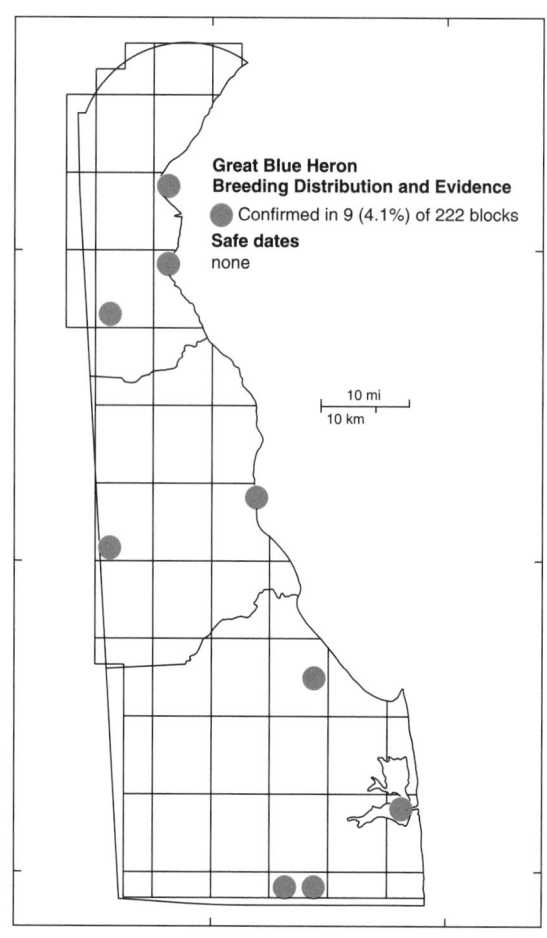

Great Blue Heron
Breeding Distribution and Evidence
● Confirmed in 9 (4.1%) of 222 blocks
Safe dates
none

HABITAT: Feeds primarily on fish in impoundments, marshes, ponds, lakes, and streams; breeds in wooded floodplains, swampy forests near streams, or deciduous or pine woods near marshes.

SPRING: This cold-tolerant heron arrives in February or early March, depending on weather conditions. The end of migration is not clear but is probably mid- to late April. High counts reported in spring are at heronries:

12 Mar 1988	165	3 Sussex heronries [Wayn70]
21 Mar 1986	150	Prime Hook NWR [Frec1]

Historic high counts:

10 Apr 1925	200	Delaware City [Pott3]
2 May 1928	200	Delaware City [Hans1]

Recent daily observations away from heronries typically total fewer than 50–60 birds per day.

BREEDING: The Great Blue Heron is the most widely known of its family in Delaware, and almost any farm boy can tell of seeing a "crane" or "stork" feeding on the farm. Breeding, however, is mainly concentrated in colonies, from which the herons disperse to feed. A large Great Blue Heron colony is located at Augustine Marsh on the Armstrong property. The large mixed heronry on Pea Patch Island includes varying numbers of Great Blue Herons. A third major heronry for Great Blues is located near Milford.

Atlas. Other smaller heronries, containing only Great Blue Herons, were located during the Atlas project. The breeding status of this species is indicated by its known colonies:

Heronry Counts for Great Blue Heron
(1983–87 Atlas reports)

Location	Size range in pairs
NEW CASTLE COUNTY	
Pea Patch Island	20–200 (high?)
Augustine Creek	100–200
Townsend	1 (1985 only)
KENT COUNTY	
Sandtown	4–20
Bombay Hook	1 (1985 only)
SUSSEX COUNTY	
Ellendale	(not located)
Prime Hook	80–100
Burton Island	20
Gumboro	10
Near Cypress Swamp	40(?)
Near Millsboro	(not located)
TOTAL IN DELAWARE	200–600

Erwin (1979) estimated that 174 pairs bred in Delaware in 1977. Andrews (1990), using DNREC data, estimated that 497 pairs bred in the 3 largest sites in the state in 1985. Parsons and McColpin (1994) counted 389 nests on Pea Patch Island and 69

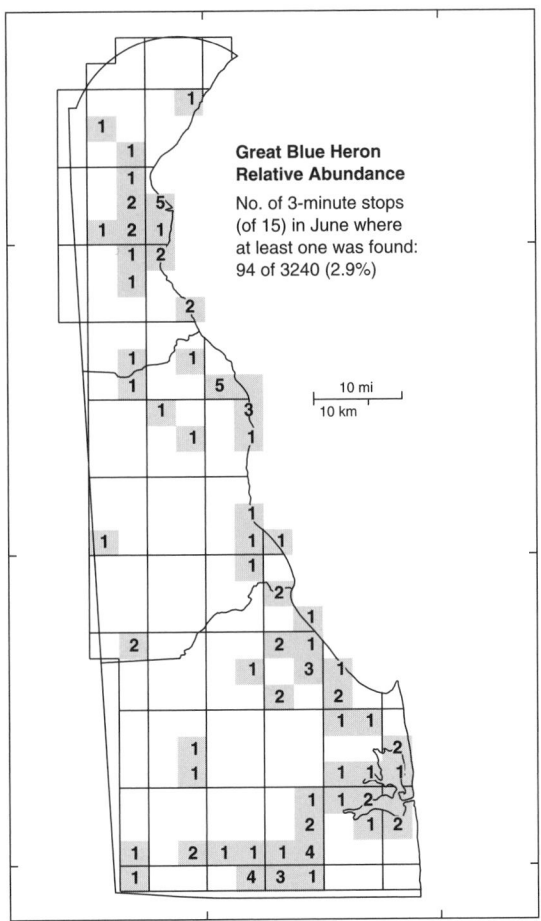

Great Blue Heron Relative Abundance

No. of 3-minute stops (of 15) in June where at least one was found: 94 of 3240 (2.9%)

nests on Augustine Creek in 1993. The following winter, state biologists detected two new colonies south of Augustine Creek and more recently a mixed colony was found in Sussex County (L. Gelvin-Innvaer, pers. comm.). In Maine, the size and location of colonies were best explained by the distribution of foraging habitats (Gibbs 1991), where there is a limited availability of suitable colony sites. Other studies also suggest that available food is a critical limiting factor in this heron's breeding population (Butler 1992).

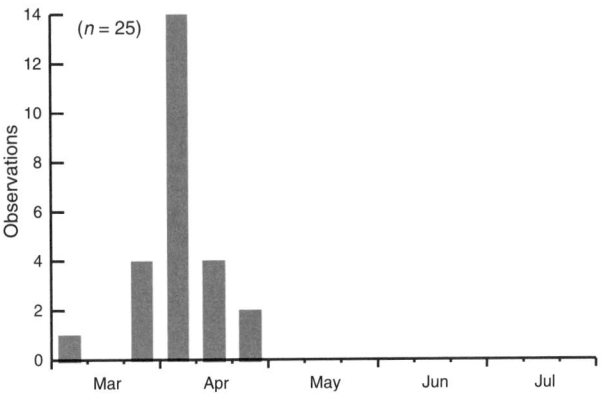

Estimated Clutch-Completion Dates

Nesting. Most birds arrive at heronries by mid-March to begin territory establishment, courtship, and nest building. Great Blue Herons typically pick the tallest trees for their rather flimsy stick nests. Nests at the Pea Patch Island heronry were all higher than 5 m (Wiese 1978), and those observed along Augustine Creek were estimated at 60–90 ft (20–30 m) [Abbo2]. Solitary nesting and nests on the ground are rare; 2 solitary ground nests on small islands were reported during the Atlas project: 1 at Bombay Hook NWR [West3] and 1 in a small farm pond near Townsend [Dyer2]. Three additional sites with single pairs breeding were found in 1991–92 (D. Rothstein, DNHI, pers. comm.). Colonial nests are constructed in oak and other hardwoods except for those in the Prime Hook heronry and a heronry reported near Gumboro, where the substrate is pine [O'Sh2; Edni4]. A composite description of nests at the Delaware City heronry is a 3- or 4-ft platform of coarse sticks interlaid and slightly lined with finer sticks, vines, or grass.

The peak egg-laying period is probably the first third of April. Extreme dates of eggs collected in Delaware are 9 April and 10 May, but eggs are to be expected both earlier and later than those dates (Robbins and Bystrak 1977). Clutch-size distribution from a 1-day visit to the Delaware City heronry on 4 April 1939 was 5 eggs (in 24 nests), 4 eggs (5 nests), 3 eggs (3 nests); average was 4.7. Few, if any, incomplete clutches were included, since no 2- or 1-egg clutches were recorded [Buck1]. One Delaware clutch contained 6 eggs (WFVZ [Crispin and Darlington] egg data) out of 49 sets described.

History. Miller (1943) reported 2 historic Delaware breeding colonies. The one near the New Castle pumping station on Nonesuch Creek, between Newport and New Castle, persisted from at least 1892 to at least 1912 (Clark 1938). Another colony existed until 1938 near Delaware City on the Higgins farm, south of Dragon Run and north of the Chesapeake and Delaware Canal. Said to be over 100 years old in 1907 (Clark 1938), it had 35 active nests in 1912 (Bent 1926) and about 200 nests in 1927 (Hanson notes) and was subject to regular egg collecting and intermittent lumbering (Stone 1937). During 1935–37 the colony moved to the Morrow farm just west of River Rd. on the south side of the canal at Scotts Run, staying there until at least 1944. It then moved to the Armstrong farm, where it is now protected (Hoff 1973).

In 1963 H. S. Peters noted a thriving colony of Great Blue Herons and Great Egrets on the north end of Pea Patch Island during an Audubon Society flight over the island in search of an eagle's nest [PeHS1]. The Pea Patch Island colony was first publicly reported in 1964 by Cutler and Cutler [Cutl33]. (See "A Siege of Herons" essay.)

The heronry near Milton, which consists of Great Blue Herons only, may have moved there across Rt. 14, now Rt. 1 (Erwin 1979).

Conservation. The 2 major heronries containing Great Blue Herons—on Pea Patch Island and in the private Armstrong Wildlife Preserve owned by Delaware Wild Lands—are protected by Nature Preserve status. However, the heronries at Prime Hook and Sandtown are in unprotected private woods containing valuable timber, so preservation agreements with the owners of those properties are desirable. Colonial breeders, more than other species, are subject to major breeding failures resulting from human disturbance, inadequate or contaminated food in the nearby area, and predators. The Pea Patch Island and Augustine Creek heronries both showed high reproductive success in 1993, although egg shells in the latter were abnormally thin (Parsons and McColpin 1994).

FALL: Postbreeding movement and fall migration begin gradually, 15–20 July, and finish in late October. After that, only a few hardy birds attempt to winter. High counts:

15 Aug 1972	85	Bombay Hook NWR [Holg73]
30 Aug 1970	625	Bombay Hook NWR [Brez3]
27 Sep 1981	55	Bombay Hook NWR [Edni34]
30 Nov 1974	48	Dragon Run [BroH1]
7 Dec 1988	37	Cape Henlopen SP [Holg1]

Typical counts are similar to those obtained during spring migration.

1966–89 CBC Summary

Christmas Bird Count	Years Found	Range of No. Found	Median
Wilmington	24	1–26	6
Middletown	24	3–49	17
Bombay Hook	24	13–128	62
Cape Henlopen	24	4–61	21
Rehoboth	24	33–126	56
Statewide	24	91–290	187
(low in 1989, high in 1988)			

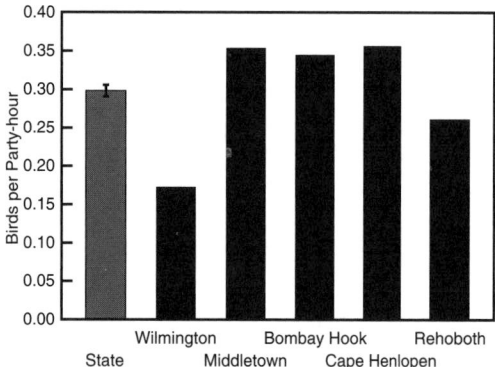

CBC Geographic Distribution

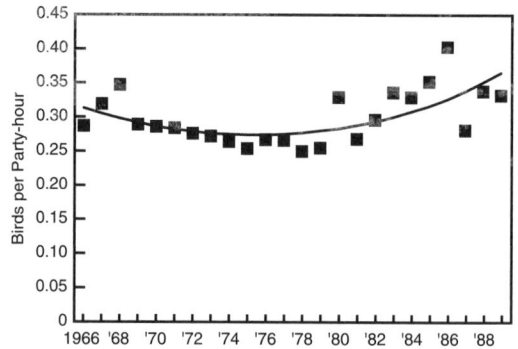

CBC Trend

DMNH 63492, DMNH 71362). The number of wintering birds appears to be increasing, but they may have declined in the 1970s, perhaps resulting from severe winters, such as in 1976–77 (Buckley et al. 1977).

SPECIMENS: 19; DMNH, USNM. Egg records: CM, DMNH, LSU, WFVZ.

WINTER: This heron is usually present until ponds and streams freeze. Occasionally one that lingers perhaps because of injury or weakness, is frozen in a pond (DMNH 63045,

Great Egret *(Ardea alba)*

Regular; summer resident; fairly common to common. Expected mid-March to early November; may be present earlier or later, more or less regularly, depending on weather conditions. Returned as a breeding bird during the 1960s.

HABITAT: Feeds primarily on fish in impoundments, marshes, ponds, and streams; breeds on wooded islands or dense deciduous or pine scrub near saltmarshes.

SPRING: First arrival is mid-March. Migration appears to end by late March. High counts:

17 Mar 1974	35	Dragon Run [West21]
29 Mar 1985	30	Cape Henlopen SP [Frec1]
28 Apr 1974	37	Dragon Run [BroW7]

BREEDING: The Great Egret breeds mainly on Pea Patch Island; a second, small mixed heronry including this species was recently discovered in Sussex County (Rothstein and Gelvin-Innvaer 1992).

The Great Egrets breeding on Pea Patch Island feed in both Delaware and New Jersey. During nesting about one-third of the population feeds in the Delaware River marshes near the Chesapeake and Delaware Canal and in the Christina River marshes. After the young fledge larger numbers appear farther south in the Delaware River marshes, including those at Bombay Hook NWR and Little Creek WA.

Atlas. During the Atlas project the Great Egret was found breeding only on Pea Patch Island, arriving there by mid-March (Wiese 1978; Thomas 1989b). The relative abundance map suggests its dispersal pattern from Pea Patch Island in June. Those seen in southern Delaware in the 1980s are deduced to have come north from Maryland heronries because no nesting egrets were found in southern Delaware during the Atlas project.

Nesting. The Great Egret selects the highest available nest

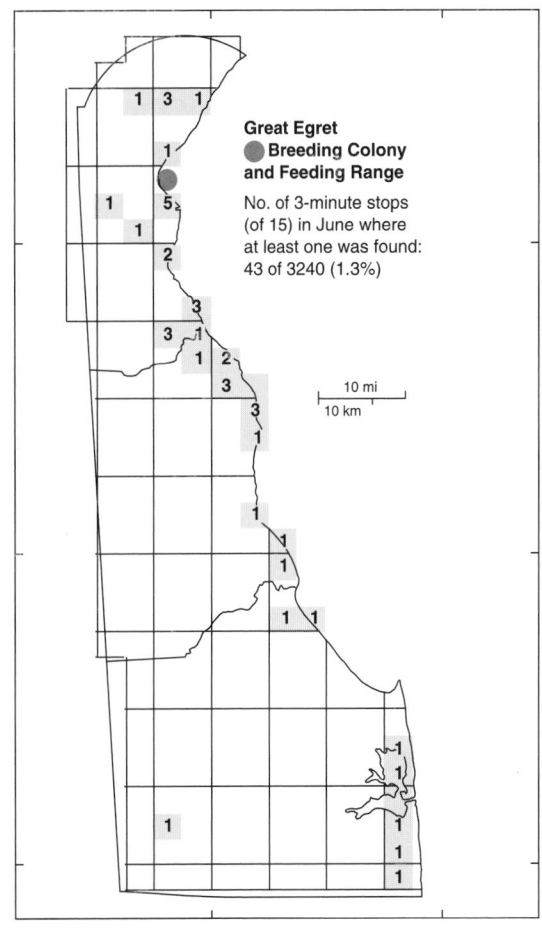

Great Egret
● Breeding Colony
and Feeding Range

No. of 3-minute stops
(of 15) in June where
at least one was found:
43 of 3240 (1.3%)

10 mi
10 km

sites in hardwoods (e.g., red maple and black gum) and places its nest more than 5 m above ground (Wiese 1978), although ground nesting occurs rarely (Salzman 1985).

History. The recovery of the Great Egret after its decimation by plume hunters can be traced by these observations:

6 Jul 1902	1	east of Odessa [Penn1]
1 Jul 1906	3	near Stanton ("Mr. Hensel said they may breed near Churchman's Bridge") [Penn1]
5 Aug 1908	28	near Concord (A. D. Pool)[Penn1]
25 Sep 1929	20	near Delaware City [Penn2]
8 Aug 1930	2	Milford Heronry [Buck3]
May 1932	nest with young	Milford (Buckalew 1933)
Sep 1935	over 100	Wilmington Marsh [Hans1]
1939	"summer resident"	(Barry 1939)
18 Apr 1941		Bombay Hook NWR [MayR1]
mid-Apr– Oct 1961	abundant summer resident	Little Creek WA (Lesser 1964)

By the early 1960s a heronry at Killcohook, New Jersey, was declining (Linehan 1974 *in* Wiese 1976, 9) while another was forming at Pea Patch Island. Breeding after 1932 was not reported until 1963 [PeHS1] and 1964 [Cutl33] on Pea Patch Island.

Breeding population. Estimated numbers averaged 200 nests during 1985–87 and have since increased to about 600 (Parsons 1993).

Conservation. If the recently established second breeding site can be protected, continued breeding in Delaware will be more secure. Delaware lacks potential new, undisturbed breeding sites, with tall trees, in the coastal zone.

FALL: Postbreeding movement begins 15–20 June. By 5–10 November most have departed, leaving behind only a few hardy birds; even these leave by the end of December. High counts:

19 Jun 1962	106	Little Creek WA (Lesser 1965)
2 Aug 1961	941	Little Creek WA (Lesser 1964)
30 Aug 1970	650	Bombay Hook NWR [Brez3]

1966–89 CBC Summary

Christmas Bird Count	Years Found	Range of No. Found	Median
Wilmington	1	1	
Middletown	2	2	
Bombay Hook	13	1–28	1
Cape Henlopen	7	1–3	
Rehoboth	5	1–6	
STATEWIDE (high in 1970)	19	1–28	3

WINTER: This species was first reported in winter on 22 December 1936 (Cottam 1937). Although it has occurred on CBCs in 19 of 24 years, 42% of the total Great Egrets reported on CBCs came in 3 years from Bombay Hook: 28 in 1970, 14 in 1972, and 15 in 1973. The remaining counts reported fewer than 10 birds each. The only 4 post-CBC January reports were single birds in Kent and Sussex counties. February reports:

5 Feb 1952	2	New Castle [Quic1]13
Jan–9 Feb 1953	1	Middletown [Pell2]
20–23 Feb 1986	1	Red Mill Pond [Frec46]

SPECIMENS: 8; DMNH.

Snowy Egret *(Egretta thula)*

Regular; summer resident; common. Expected mid-March through October, becoming less numerous through early winter.

HABITAT: Feeds primarily on fish in impoundments, marshes, and streams; breeds in dense deciduous scrub and in phragmites on Pea Patch Island.

SPRING: The first Snowy Egrets usually arrive about 15–20 March. Earlier reports are 8 seen on 2 March 1977 at Bombay Hook NWR and Delaware City [Lehm21], and 1 on 6 March 1989 at Hoopes Reservoir [SpeE9]. The high count is 100 at Delaware Seashore SP on 23 March 1982 [Frec1]. Typical reports involve up to 10–15 birds.

BREEDING: This egret was once on the verge of extirpation in eastern North America because it was shot to collect its beautiful plumes. However, by 1977 the Snowy Egret had become the most numerous of the herons and egrets breeding in the Northeast, with an estimated population of 10,000 pairs north of North Carolina (Erwin 1979), and in 1984–85 it was still among the most numerous (Andrews 1990). In 1989 Maine was its northernmost breeding site (Drennan and Bowman 1993).

Atlas. During the Atlas project the Snowy Egret bred only on Pea Patch Island. In spring and summer it feeds in nearby tidal marshes or impoundments in the marshes. As the young

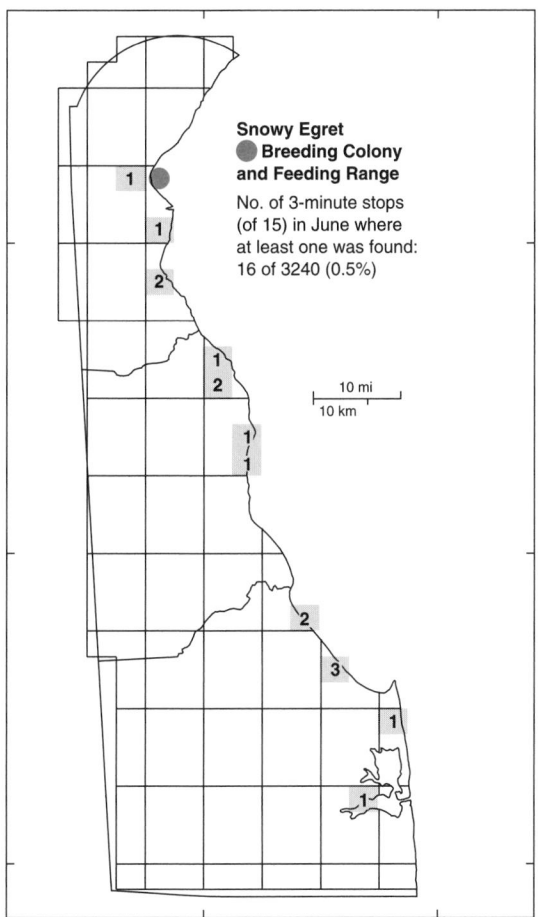

Snowy Egret
● Breeding Colony
and Feeding Range

No. of 3-minute stops
(of 15) in June where
at least one was found:
16 of 3240 (0.5%)

The major cause of fledging failure on Pea Patch Island in 1976 was a nematode *(Eustrongylides ignotus)* infestation of nestlings transmitted in mummichogs, a principal food (Wiese 1977). Other causes were starvation, predation, and nest collapse. Avian predators included Fish Crow, Great Horned Owl, and night-herons (Wiese 1979).

History. Stone (1937) considered the Snowy Egret rare or accidental in New Jersey and considered the Great Egret and the immature Little Blue Heron to be the two common white herons.

Trends. The Snowy Egret population declined sharply to about 300 pairs in the late 1980s, but has since recovered to about 2,500 pairs in 1993 (Parsons 1993). The decline may have resulted from the nematode infestation.

Breeding population. The average estimated breeding population at Pea Patch Island was 380 pairs during 1985–87 (Thomas 1989b).

FALL: First dispersal movements begin 10–15 July. Peak numbers occur from 25 July to 5 August with migration continuing throughout October. Most leave by 30 October to 5 November. High counts:

17 Jul 1971	1,000	Port Mahon [Lawr2]
1 Aug 1970	1,000	Little Creek WA [Holg48]
2 Sep 1986	500	Cape Henlopen SP [Frec1]
7 Sep 1961	885	Little Creek WA (Lesser 1964)

1966–89 CBC Summary

Christmas Bird Count	Years Found	Range of No. Found
Wilmington		
Middletown		
Bombay Hook	5	1–2
Cape Henlopen	1	1
Rehoboth	3	1–9
STATEWIDE (high in 1969)	11	1–2

WINTER: Few Snowy Egrets remain in Delaware between November and mid-March. One or 2 birds were found on each of 9 CBCs. A bird observed at Bombay Hook NWR on 19 January 1974 [Holg83] is the only one reported lingering after the CBCs.

SPECIMENS: DMNH 71824, Delaware City, 6 May 1981; DMNH 71145, Delaware City, 17 May 1980; DMNH 71207, Delaware City, 21 May 1980; DMNH 78193, New Castle, Penn Acres, 30 September 1991.

fledge, the population builds up along the Delaware coastal marshes until several hundred can sometimes be seen in some of the marshes from Delaware City south to the Maryland state line.

A small number now breed in a mixed colony in Sussex County (Rothstein and Gelvin-Innvaer 1992).

Nesting. The Pea Patch Island colony originally nested in blueberry shrubs, small black gums, and elderberry bushes partly supported by dead bushes. As the shrubs died from overuse and the colony increased in size, competition for nest sites became more severe. The species now nests also in stands of phragmites (Wiese 1976–79). Snowy Egrets also nest in phragmites on Long Island (Sazman 1985) and on the ground in Maine (Drennen and Bowman 1993).

Poor nesting success in the shrubs on Pea Patch Island was reported by Wiese as follows:

Reproductive Success

	1975	1976	1977	1978
No. of clutches monitored	25	96	58	106
Eggs per complete clutch	3.5	3.5	3.0	3.6
Hatching success rate[1]	92%	91%	91%	94%
Fledging success rate[2]	35%	21%	24%	71%
Nesting success rate[3]	29%	15%	21%	57%

1. Omitting nests and eggs destroyed prior to hatching.
2. Number fledged divided by number hatched.
3. Number fledged divided by total number of eggs laid; causes of loss include nest collapse and predation.

Little Blue Heron *(Egretta caerulea)*

Regular; summer resident; uncommon. Expected late March or early April to late October, occasionally to early winter.

| J | F | M | A | M | J | J | A | S | O | N | D |

HABITAT: Feeds in marshes, impoundments, and streams on crustaceans, amphibians, insects, and small fish; breeds on Pea Patch Island in dense deciduous scrub and phragmites.

SPRING: Extreme arrival dates are in the last half of March, but the usual first arrival is 1–5 April. Earliest arrival records are

23 Mar 1984	1	Lums Pond SP [Wees1]
24 Mar 1990	1	Dragon Run [Camp1]
26 Mar 1989	1	Lewes Beach [Frec1]
27 Mar 1976	"a few"	Dragon Run [Barn25]

A historical high count was 100 pairs at a heronry near Milford on 10 April 1930 [Hans1]. A high count away from a heronry is 46 at Dragon Run on 28 April 1974 [BroW1]. Typical daily counts away from its breeding sites total 10–20.

BREEDING: The Little Blue Heron forages in marshes close to Pea Patch Island during nesting. After the young fledge, it frequents the impounded tidal marshes along the Delaware coast, usually in small groups.

Atlas. The only place the species bred in Delaware during the Atlas period was Pea Patch Island, where it averaged about 520 pairs. It colonized that heronry after Great Blue Herons and Great Egrets became established.

Nesting. The Little Blue Heron nests colonially, primarily in shrubs and saplings—such as blueberry, black gum, and elderberry—and in phragmites, as do other small herons on Pea Patch Island (Wiese 1979, 95).

A 1933 nest found near Milford was described as 22 ft up in a 35-ft white cedar, placed beside a trunk 4 in. thick, loosely made of sticks and twigs, slightly saucered and 15 in. across. It was one of a colony of 50 Little Blue nests and 75 Black-crowned Night-Heron nests in a white cedar–red maple swamp in Sussex County near Milford. On 13 May nearly all nests of both species contained young (LSU 73), indicating that most clutches were completed by 20 April. Extreme egg dates reported are 24 April 1936 [Buck1] to 29 May 1934 (WFVZ egg data).

Nesting success on Pea Patch Island was reported by Wiese (1976–79) as follows:

Reproductive Success

	1975	1976	1977	1978
No. of clutches monitored	11	29	29	15
Eggs per complete clutch	3.3	3.8	3.5	3.6
Hatching success rate [1]	84%	92%	95%	96%
Fledging success rate [2]	53%	78%	68%	87%
Nesting success rate [3]	47%	69%	53%	72%

1. Omitting nests and eggs destroyed prior to hatching.
2. Number fledged divided by number hatched.
3. Number fledged divided by total number of eggs laid; causes of loss include nest collapse and predation.

Parsons, using a slightly different calculation, reported 2.2–2.3 nestlings surviving per nest in 1993, comparable with Wiese's data.

Buckalew (notes), based on 493 nests in Delaware from 1929 to 1939, recorded an average of 3.7 eggs per nest (range 1–6, mode = 4). Only 1 egg was found in 51 of the nests, and 2 eggs in 43 nests; most of these were probably incomplete clutches. In his 3 May 1937 observations, average clutch size of 50 nests at Cedar Beach is the highest recorded and probably represents the clutch size potential of this species. The average clutch was 4.36 ± 0.84, with this distribution: 6 eggs (in 4 nests), 5 eggs (17 nests), 4 (23), 3 (5), and 2 eggs in 1 nest. This 1937 average clutch is considerably higher than the 3.3–3.8 found by Wiese in the 1970s and a little higher than the 4.1–4.2 reported by Parsons for 1993. Buckalew seems to have recorded the contents of every nest he found on a given visit, but Wiese counted only complete clutches from which 1 or more eggs hatched.

History. Little Blue Herons were first reported in Delaware as follows:

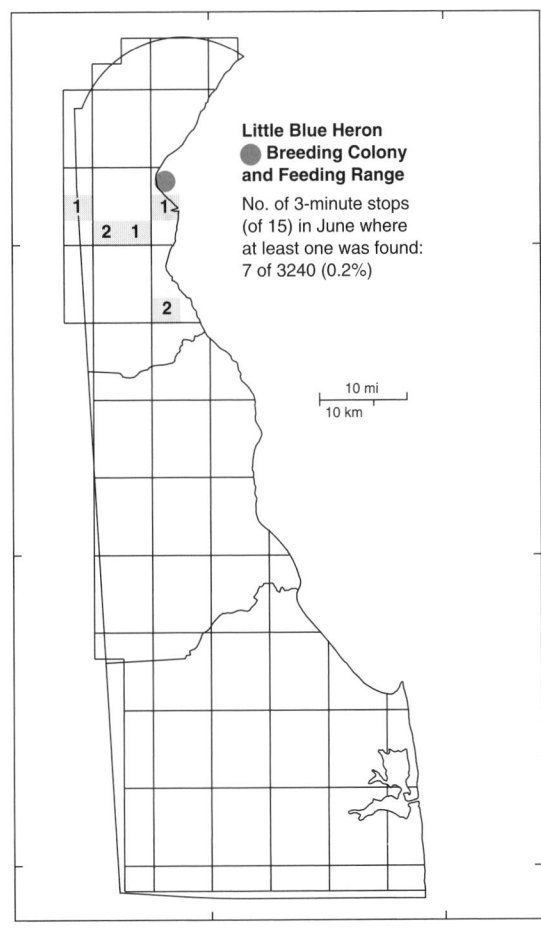

Little Blue Heron
● **Breeding Colony and Feeding Range**

No. of 3-minute stops (of 15) in June where at least one was found: 7 of 3240 (0.2%)

10 mi
10 km

FALL: Typically, the majority of Little Blues leave by 15–20 October, and all but the occasional lingering bird are gone by the last week of October. Postbreeding season high counts:

16 Aug 1970	325	Little Creek WA [DuPG32]
10 Sep 1961	120	Fenwick Island (probably Assawoman WA) [Davi19]
18 Oct 1967	218	Bombay Hook NWR [Holg41]

Typical daily counts are 10–30.

WINTER: This species has occurred on 3 CBCs:

15 Dec 1974	1	Bombay Hook CBC
23 Dec 1978	2	Middletown CBC
26 Dec 1982	1	Middletown CBC

Rarely, 1 or 2 individuals linger beyond the CBC period. Holgersen [Holg67] reported 2 at Bombay Hook NWR on 31 January 1972, and Carrick [Carr14] reported an immature at Bethany Beach on 4 February 1967.

SPECIMENS: USNM 421824, Milford, 30 April 1932; USNM 422162, Cedar Beach, 3 August 1932. Egg records: LSU, WFVZ.

25 Sep 1920	9	south of Delaware City [Penn 1]
1 Sep 1923	1	Millsboro [Hans1]
14 May 1927	2	near Rehoboth Beach [Penn1]
12–13 May 1928	7	near Rehoboth Beach [Penn1]

Breeding began in the same decade; Buckalew found a heronry with at least 200 Little Blue Heron nests and some Black-crowned Night-Heron nests just south of Milford on 25 July 1929 [Hans1]. In 1930 the colony, which moved a small distance [Penn1], contained about 100 pairs of Little Blues and 50 pairs of Black-crowned Night-Herons (Pennock 1930). In 1932 this colony was believed to be the most northerly one still flourishing [Gill2], and it was still active in 1934 (Stone 1937). In 1935 Stone, with R. T. Peterson and J. K. Potter, visited a heronry that contained Little Blues "some distance below Camden [Delaware]"; he revisited it in 1936. Stone (1937) noted that this species was not usually seen before 12 July at Cape May, New Jersey.

Breeding population. Breeding population was about 500 pairs during the Atlas period and about 1,300 in 1993 (Parsons 1993). This one colony gives Delaware the largest state population north of the Carolinas (Rogers and Smith 1995).

Tricolored Heron *(Egretta tricolor)*

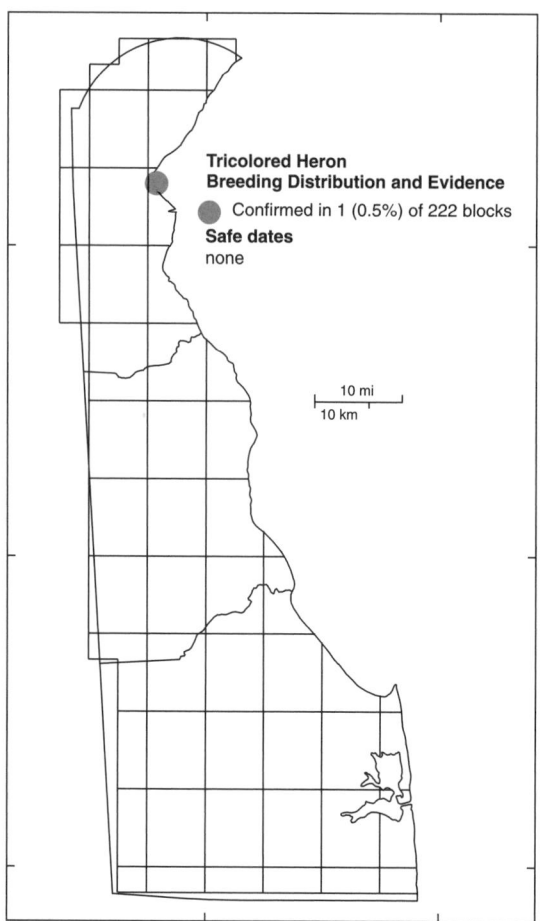

Tricolored Heron
Breeding Distribution and Evidence

Confirmed in 1 (0.5%) of 222 blocks

Safe dates
none

10 mi
10 km

Regular; summer resident; uncommon. Expected mid-April through October and sporadically later.

J F M A M J J A S O N D

HABITAT: Feeds primarily on fish in marshes, tidal ditches, and impoundments; breeds in dense deciduous scrub on Pea Patch Island.

SPRING: The usual period of arrival is 15–20 April. It is difficult to distinguish an early arrival from a wintering individual, but the report of 2 at Indian River Inlet on 1 April 1988 [Frec1] is probably the earliest reliable spring record. There are few spring records, especially when compared with the number of fall records. Typical counts for this period are 1–4 birds.

BREEDING: The Tricolored (formerly Louisiana) Heron breeds in low numbers, on Pea Patch Island only. It can be most easily observed feeding on fish in the upper Delaware tidal marshes or from Prime Hook southward. Those seen in southern Delaware probably come from nearby Maryland heronries.

Atlas. This colonial species was an uncommon breeder during the Atlas period. It was so rarely seen in Delaware marshes that breeding was suspected only from prior knowledge of nesting in the Pea Patch Island heronry.

Nesting. Most small herons will accept secondary nest sites in phragmites, but the Tricolored Heron was not observed to do so at Pea Patch Island (Wiese 1979).

Nesting success on Pea Patch Island was reported by Wiese (1977–79) in the following table:

Reproductive Success

	1976	1977	1978
No. of clutches monitored	4	5	4
Eggs per complete clutch	3.5	3.2	3.1
Hatching success rate[1]	100%	85%	100%
Fledging success rate[2]	14%	18%	78%
Nesting success rate[3]	14%	14%	54%

1. Omitting nests and eggs destroyed prior to hatching.
2. Number fledged divided by number hatched.
3. Number fledged divided by total number of eggs laid; causes of loss include nest collapse and predation.

The low success rate in 1976 and 1977 is the result of a nematode infestation that affected piscivorous herons (see Snowy Egret).

History. The Tricolored Heron is a relative newcomer to Delaware. Hanson (notes) reports, "One individual bird seen by Herbert Buckalew and John Herholdt at the bird refuge south of Woodland Beach, 16 August 1937. Identification positive." Buckalew secured a specimen at Indian River Inlet 4 days later (USNM 422166). These records are the first of the species in Delaware. The next published report mentions 1 at Bombay Hook NWR on 21 July 1953 [Spri2]. By this date, observations of Tricolored Herons were not particularly unusual, as the species was seen regularly in the Mid-Atlantic region. The timing of its establishment as a breeding bird on Pea Patch Island lies obscured in a trail of partial observations and cryptic reports. The first report that strongly suggests breeding describes two Tricolored Herons at the Pea Patch Island "roost" on 20 May 1967 [Pres6]. The roost was actually an established mixed heronry. Linehan (in Wiese 1976) reported 4 pairs of nesting Tricolored Herons at Pea Patch Island in 1973 and 200 pairs in 1974; the latter number is the highest estimate of a Delaware breeding population. In 1975 Akers and Wiebolt (AN 31: 31) reported 100 pairs at Pea Patch Island on 29 May, and Wiese (1976) estimated 20 pairs bred there based on his 1975 4-month study (Wiese 1976, 1979).

Breeding population. Numbers of breeding pairs fluctuate; 0, 18, 66, and 28 pairs were estimated for 1985, 1986, 1987, and 1988, respectively (Thomas 1989b). This fluctuation is partly related to extrapolation from a small sample, but competition with other species for suitable nest sites may adversely affect this species in some years. A 1993 study estimated 30 pairs (Parsons 1993), not significantly different from the 1980s data.

FALL: Postbreeding movement begins about 15–20 July and peaks about 10–15 August to 10–15 September. Typically, most individuals leave by late October. However, this heron appears more hardy than the other small herons and egrets, and some lingerers depart only when freezing temperatures occur regularly. High counts:

16 Aug 1970	85	Little Creek WA [DuPG32]
30 Aug 1970	35	Bombay Hook NWR [Brez4]
13 Sep 1961	40	Little Creek WA (Lesser 1964)

Typical high counts are in the 20s, and most observers report fewer than 10 birds.

1966–89 CBC Summary

Christmas Bird Count	Years Found	Range of No. Found
Wilmington		
Middletown	1	5
Bombay Hook	3	1–2
Cape Henlopen	1	1
Rehoboth	9	1–2
STATEWIDE (high in 1978)	11	1–6

WINTER: This species has occurred on 14 CBCs, in numbers from 1 to 5. It has been found most frequently (9 times) on the Rehoboth CBC. About 2 dozen records exist for January through mid-April.

REMARKS: Stone (1937) considered this species to be accidental in the region in the first part of the twentieth century, consistent with the lack of Delaware records before 1937.

SPECIMENS: USNM 422166, Indian River Inlet, 20 August 1937; DMNH 862, Sussex Co., 14 September 1958.

Reddish Egret *(Egretta rufescens)*

Casual (1991 and 1993).

DOCUMENTATION: Photograph (C. D. Campbell, DMNH 404).

REMARKS: The first state record pertains to an individual photographed (Campbell 1991b) [Edni11] at Port Mahon on 2 July 1991 and seen sporadically during the following week [Camp14]. Photographs by both Campbell and Ednie, on file at DMNH, clearly reveal the shaggy appearance, the red neck contrasting with the blue back, and the thick bicolored bill. An immature lingered at Little Creek WA 29 July to 22 August 1993 (Campbell 1994) [Cutl16].

The closest Reddish Egret population, in coastal peninsular Florida, begins breeding as early as December. After breeding, some disperse northward along the Florida coasts and stray casually north to Virginia (AOU 1983; Stevenson and Anderson 1994). In May 1991 Reddish Egrets were recorded north to Jamaica Bay, New York [WalS1], and Wellfleet Bay Wildlife Sanctuary, Massachusetts [Hale1]. The Delaware records fit this pattern of postbreeding dispersal of individuals breeding in winter.

Cattle Egret (*Bubulcus ibis*)

Regular; summer resident; common to abundant. Expected mid-
March through October and sporadically thereafter.

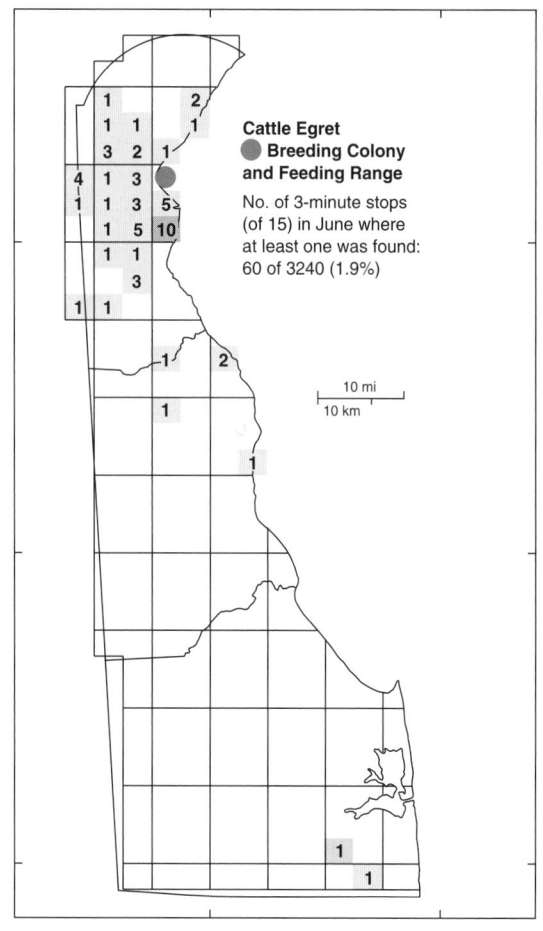

Cattle Egret
● Breeding Colony
and Feeding Range

No. of 3-minute stops
(of 15) in June where
at least one was found:
60 of 3240 (1.9%)

10 mi
10 km

HABITAT: Primarily a terrestrial forager, feeding on insects
stirred up by livestock in upland pastures, following plows, and
scavenging at landfills; nests in dense deciduous scrub and
phragmites on Pea Patch Island.

SPRING: First arrival is about 15–20 March. Typical migration counts involve up to 200 birds. Individual birds have been
reported surviving into the winter months, so early spring
arrivals can be recognized only by their multiple numbers. The
earliest are

27 Feb 1981	15	Arundel [RusR4]
2 Mar 1977	8	Bombay Hook NWR [Lehm21]
15 Mar 1973	10	Leipsic [Holg17]

High counts are all from the Dragon Run survey, which
observed large numbers feeding in the fields and passing overhead on foraging flights from the Pea Patch Island heronry:

7 Apr 1974	360	[BroW7]
20 Apr 1974	265	[Wayn25]
28 Apr 1974	220	[BroW19]
3 May 1975	502	[Citr5]

During migration the species occurs throughout the state
and in spring is often found on fields that are being plowed.

BREEDING: This heron, Delaware's most numerous, is also
the most recent addition to the waders breeding in North
America. African in origin, it spread naturally to the New
World and has rapidly increased in numbers. During the breeding season it is often found in fields in New Castle County and
in the county landfill. It occurs only sporadically in eastern

Kent County. The few that occur in southeastern Sussex County presumably come from Maryland heronries, but there may
be some small, undetected rookeries nearby. Congregations of
100 or so are often found in eastern Delaware after the young
fledge.

Atlas. The mixed heronry on Pea Patch Island is the only
known breeding site in Delaware.

Nesting. Cattle Egrets typically nest on blueberry, elderberry,
maple, and southern arrowwood shrubs on Pea Patch Island,
but they have also moved into the phragmites marsh, starting
in 1978. In 1975 121 pairs began nesting (or renesting) on Pea
Patch Island in late July (Wiese 1976). The clutch size distribution between early and late clutches was:

	5 eggs	4 eggs	3 eggs	2 eggs	1 egg
Early nests	4 (1%)	75 (29%)	159 (61%)	24 (9%)	
Late nests		2 (2%)	55 (45%)	59 (49%)	5 (4%)

Average clutch size, early nesters = 3.22 ± 0.62 STD (*n* = 262), late nesters =
2.45 ± 0.60 (*n* = 121), the latter lower than the usual range of 3–4. (Telfair 1994)

In 1978 late-nesting Cattle Egrets did not fledge young until
October (Wiese 1979), suggesting clutch-completion dates
ranging from April to August.

Nesting success on Pea Patch Island was reported by Wiese (1976–79) as follows:

Reproductive Success

	1975	1976	1977	1978
No. of clutches monitored[1]	76	101	137	155
Eggs per complete clutch	3.2	2.8	2.7	2.8
Hatching success rate[2]	94%	92%	83%	89%
Fledging success rate[3]	47%	49%	42%	75%
Nesting success rate[4]	43%	40%	29%	61%

1. Nests sampled along transects in the more accessible portion of the colony; excludes late-breeding pairs and those breeding in phragmites.
2. Omitting nests and eggs destroyed prior to hatching.
3. Number fledged divided by number hatched.
4. Number fledged divided by total number of eggs laid; causes of loss include nest collapse and predation.

Parsons, studying nests in both shrubs and phragmites, found that most measures of Cattle Egret reproductive success were higher in the marsh than in upland habitat in 1993. Predation losses were less in the marsh.

History. The Cattle Egret was first recorded breeding in the United States in Florida during May 1953 (Crosby 1972). The first recorded occurrence of Cattle Egret in Delaware was 1 near Leipsic on 13 May 1954 and another (or the same) individual 2 days later at Bombay Hook NWR [Spri3; Heac1]. Five subsequent reports cited 1 or 2 birds each. On 9 April 1962 150 were found at St. Georges [Bro05]. Lesser noted only 1 at Little Creek WA in 1961 but saw numbers up to 59 there from 17 April to 20 August 1962 (Lesser 1964). The Cattle Egret may have started breeding in Delaware in 1962. Two years later it was discovered breeding on Pea Patch Island (Cutler 1965).

Breeding population. Its population on Pea Patch Island during the Atlas period averaged about 5,000 pairs (Thomas 1989b) and was about the same in 1993 (Parsons 1993).

FALL: Postbreeding movement probably begins in early July and usually ends, except for stragglers, about 20–25 October. Peak numbers occur throughout September. High counts:

9 Sep 1973	455	Dragon Run, census [Beac13]
15 Sep 1973	420	Dragon Run, census [SpSB22]
22 Sep 1973	364	Dragon Run, census [SpSB13]
24 Sep 1973	950	Bombay Hook NWR [Holg21]

As in the spring, typical counts range up to 200.

WINTER: This species occurred on the 1978 Bombay Hook and Wilmington CBCs and on the 1987 Middletown CBC. Seven additional reports of 1 or 2 birds pertain to the winter period.

SPECIMENS: 9; DMNH.

Green Heron *(Butorides virescens)*

Regular; summer resident; uncommon to fairly common. Expected mid-April (rarely earlier) to early October and sporadically thereafter.

HABITAT: Feeds in various water-edge or shallow-water habitats; breeds along wooded streams and ponds and along the edge of tidal marshes bordered with brush or woods.

SPRING: First arrival is usually 10–20 April. Early reports:

6 Mar 1982	2	Bombay Hook NWR [SpSB13]
5 Apr 1977	1	Port Mahon [Pure8]
7 Apr 1974	2	Dragon Run [BroW7]

The first of these reports is exceptionally early, suggesting either birds that overwintered or a mistaken report. A high count of 16 came from Cape Henlopen SP 5 May 1984 [Edni40]. Typical daily counts total fewer than 10 birds.

BREEDING: This little heron is not generally a colonial breeder in Delaware. The lone exception is a report of 6 nests in wax myrtle shrubs along a ditch south of Dewey Beach on 7 May 1983 (Ednie, photograph, DMNH). This assemblage may have been a response to abundant food, but in other states this species sometimes breeds in colonies (Davis and Kushlan 1994).

Atlas. During the Atlas period only 17 confirmations were registered, surprisingly few for a species that was located in 172 blocks and that often places its nest in a small tree in a relatively open situation. It was most often confirmed by finding the nest. Six of the confirmations referred to "fledged" young—perhaps meaning simply young that were out of the nest and scrambling around the branches. Young fly to feeding grounds with parents when 25 days old (Davis and Kushlan 1994). The general lack of reports from central Sussex County probably reflects this heron's inconspicuousness as well as its reduced presence in the parts of this county that lie on watershed boundaries and thus have little permanent water.

Nesting. Nests found in Delaware have been placed in deciduous trees (sassafras, myrtle, beach plum, and willow oak) and in cedars. One nest, 20 ft up in a small willow oak, was "a slight platform of sticks through which the eggs could be seen from below. Nest about 10 in. across and very flat" [Hans1]. The extrapolated clutch-completion period is 26 April to 7 June,

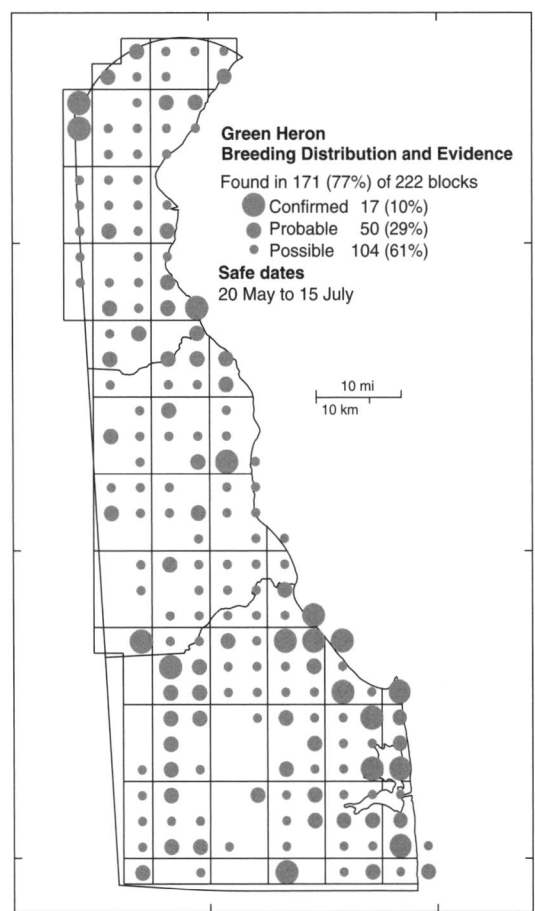

**Green Heron
Breeding Distribution and Evidence**

Found in 171 (77%) of 222 blocks

● Confirmed 17 (10%)
● Probable 50 (29%)
• Possible 104 (61%)

Safe dates
20 May to 15 July

10 mi
10 km

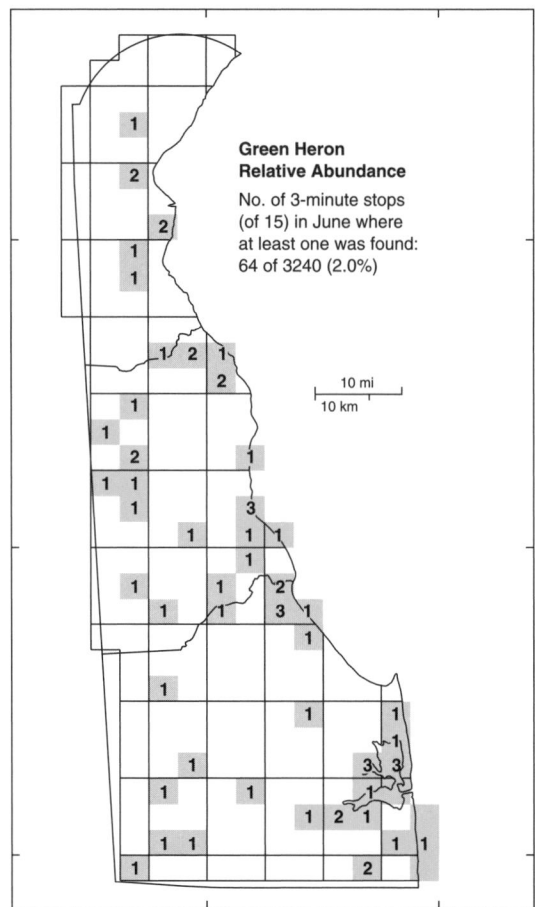

**Green Heron
Relative Abundance**

No. of 3-minute stops
(of 15) in June where
at least one was found:
64 of 3240 (2.0%)

10 mi
10 km

with most completed during 27 April to 15 May ($n = 14$). Extreme egg dates are 4 May (DMNH 26402) to 8 June; a late nestling was reported on 25 July [Hans1]. In Maryland, eggs have been found through the end of July (Robbins and Bystrak 1977). Clutch sizes reported in Delaware were 2–5 eggs ($n = 21$); 12 were 4 eggs, and 1 was 5 [Buck1]; some of those with fewer than 4 eggs may represent incomplete clutches.

Trends. May Count data indicate that the population is declining at an average rate of 2% per year. Recent dry summers and marsh-draining activities may account for some of this decline.

Breeding population. Although this heron breeds throughout

the state near water, the relative abundance study data suggest that it is about 5 times more common within 1 mi of tidewater than it is farther inland. During dispersal, after the young have fledged, concentrations (but not flocks) of more than 20 sometimes occur, and there is 1 report of 150 in a mixed group of herons going to roost in the Bombay Hook–Little Creek area on 30 August 1970 [Brez4]. Because this heron was not hunted for plumes, it has never been scarce in the state.

FALL: Most birds depart by about 5 October. Typical high counts total fewer than 15 birds.

1966–89 CBC Summary

Christmas Bird Count	Years Found	Range of No. Found
Wilmington	2	1
Middletown	3	1
Bombay Hook	2	1
Cape Henlopen	3	1–2
Rehoboth	3	1–2
STATEWIDE (high in 1970 and 1977)	9	1–3

WINTER: One or 2 individuals have occurred on 14 CBCs. Other winter reports are

10 Dec 1977	1	White Clay Creek [MiDP12]
11 Dec 1974	1	Prime Hook NWR (notes)
1 Jan 1980	1	Bombay Hook NWR (injured) [Gord11]

SPECIMENS: 10; DMNH, UDEL, USNM. Egg records: DMNH, WFVZ.

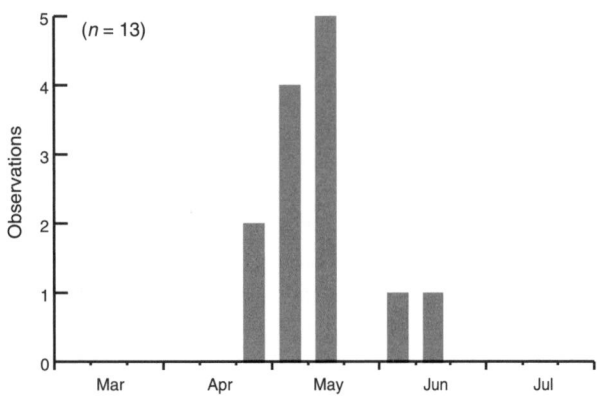

($n = 13$)

Observations

Mar Apr May Jun Jul

Estimated Clutch-Completion Dates

Black-crowned Night-Heron *(Nycticorax nycticorax)*

Resident; fairly common to common. Expected commonly mid-April (occasionally earlier) to mid-November and less commonly through the winter. Winter numbers apparently decreasing after a high in the mid-1970s.

HABITAT: Feeds in various water-edge or shallow-water habitats; breeds on Pea Patch Island in dense stands of young or scrubby trees and in phragmites.

SPRING: First arrival is variable, occasionally as early as late March. High counts are

30 Mar 1984	24	Cape Henlopen SP [Frec1]
4 Apr 1982	35	Bombay Hook NWR [Edni34]
10 Apr 1982	43	Bombay Hook NWR [Kell4]

A report of historical interest cited 100 at Bombay Hook NWR 8 April 1956 [Davi8].

BREEDING: This colonial breeder seems too widely dispersed in Delaware to be restricted to the single colony at Pea Patch Island.

Atlas. There may be an undetected breeding site in eastern Sussex County near the Lewes-Rehoboth Canal because roosts persist there late into the spring, and Black-crowns are regularly seen foraging in the area, suggestive of nearby breeding. Another breeding site may exist in southeastern Sussex County.

Nesting. Hanson (notes) recorded that Black-crowns were nesting in 1929 in old cedar trees. He described a nest made of sticks, 15 in. across and 1 in. deep, which was better constructed than those of the Little Blue Heron. In 1933 Black-crowns were nesting near Milford in a white cedar–red maple swamp (R. F. Miller, LSU 73). A nest he found in 1935 was 3 in. thick and 12 in. in diameter, situated 30 ft up in a thick holly tree. In 1975 the species nested in shrubs and blueberry bushes on Pea Patch Island, but in 1976 most nests were found in phragmites because blueberry bushes had died or collapsed under the pressure of nesting. In 1977 and 1978 nesting occurred only in phragmites (Wiese 1979), and during the Atlas period about 50 pairs nested in the reeds (Thomas 1989b).

Nesting success on Pea Patch Island was reported by Wiese (1976) as follows:

Reproductive Success

	1975
No. of clutches monitored	15
Eggs per complete clutch	2.9
Hatching success rate [1]	88%
Fledging success rate [2]	62%
Nesting success rate [3]	46%

1. Omitting nests and eggs destroyed prior to hatching.
2. Number fledged divided by number hatched.
3. Number fledged divided by total number of eggs laid; causes of loss include nest collapse and predation.

In Wiese's sample of 15 nests, 1 clutch was taken by a predator prior to hatching, and 1 clutch of nestlings disappeared following hatching. Wiese ascribed the loss of 4 nestlings to starvation of smaller siblings. He lists the Black-crowned Night-Heron as the primary predator of other wader nestlings under 3 weeks old.

On 13 May 1933 nearly all (of 75) nests contained young, indicating that most clutches were completed by 20 April (R. F. Miller, LSU 73). Extreme egg dates are 24 April 1936 [Buck1] to 8 June 1957 (DMNH 3098), but surely the dates extend into early or mid-April.

On 28 April 1935 a colony "chiefly with complete clutches" had the following distribution of clutch sizes: 5 eggs (in 2 nests), 4 (16 nests), 3 (9), 2 (8), and 1 (4) (mean = 3.1; n = 39) (Miller and Reinman, LSU 111). Buckalew examined the contents of 790 nests with eggs during 1929–40. An undetermined number of nests had incomplete clutches, but the data showed a strong mode of 4 eggs per clutch (64%), and 12 nests (1.5%) had 5 eggs. A 5 May 1935 visit to a Cedar Beach heronry indicated a high average clutch size, probably reflecting few incomplete clutches: 5 eggs (in 1 nest), 4 (139 nests), 3 (16), and 2 (1) (mean = 3.9, n = 157) [Buck1]. These data from the 1930s show considerably larger clutch sizes than the 2.9 average that Wiese found on Pea Patch Island in 1975.

History. This heron is a long-established breeder in

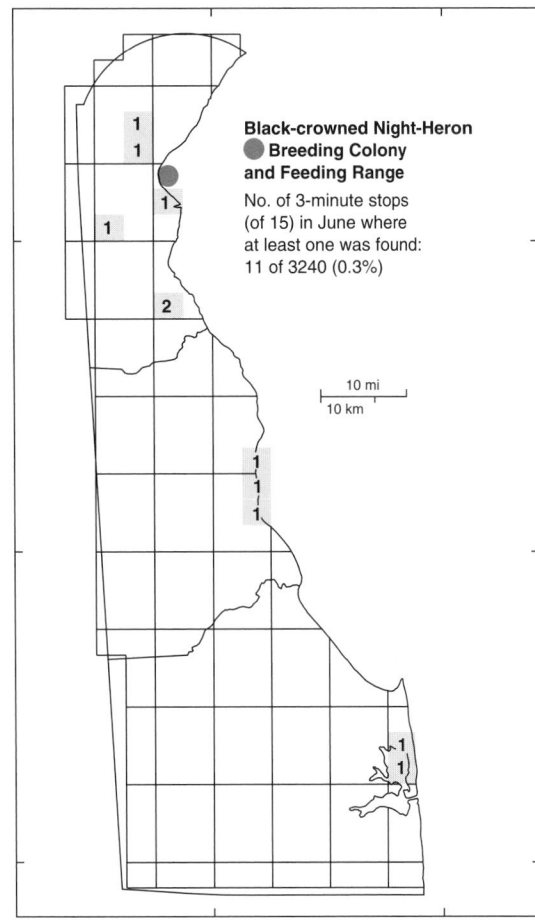

Black-crowned Night-Heron
● Breeding Colony
and Feeding Range

No. of 3-minute stops
(of 15) in June where
at least one was found:
11 of 3240 (0.3%)

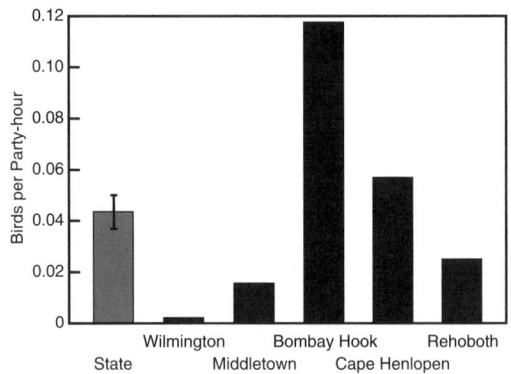

CBC Geographic Distribution

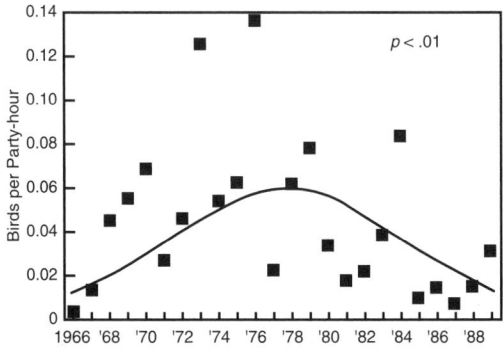

CBC Trend

Delaware. Pennock (notes) saw 1 on 30 May 1901 at River Farm, found it abundant 26 August 1905 at Delaware City, and listed it as a summer resident (Rhoads and Pennock 1905). Buckalew (notes) found 60 nests near Milford in 1929, 157 nests at Cedar Beach in 1935, 202 nests there in 1937, and 48 nests at Little Creek in 1939. Hanson (notes) writes of some 200 or more nests in a heronry in Little Creek in 1938. Fifty immatures were seen in the Christina Marshes 9 August 1935 (J Hill, SNHD).

Trends. The known breeding population in Delaware declined 95% between 1977 and 1985; the population in the East declined more than 20% during the same period (Andrews 1990). An estimated 519 pairs were breeding on Pea Patch Island in 1993 (Parsons 1993) suggesting a full recovery to the 1970s level.

Conservation. The decline in breeding population in the 1980s and the recent recovery is puzzling. The population should be monitored for a repeat in this decline, and the causes should be sought. It has been an established breeding bird in Delaware at least since the 1920s.

FALL: Postbreeding movement probably begins in July. Most depart by 25 November to 5 December. High counts are

3 Jul 1982	54	Bombay Hook NWR [Patt7]
4 Aug 1971	100	Bombay Hook NWR [Holg8]
22 Aug 1961	450	Little Creek WA (Lesser 1964)

WINTER: In many years a few individuals remain until mid- or late January, and in some years 1 or 2 may be present from late January through late March. The 2 winter specimens are from Indian River Bay on 1 January 1977 (DMNH 59607) and Wilmington on 4 February 1981 (DMNH 71375). This species has declined in numbers after peaking in the late 1970s. One possible reason for this pattern is that winter roosts inside the CBC circles were abandoned. Winter records in Delaware and banding recoveries throughout winter indicate that some birds have a limited migration or are sedentary (Davis 1993).

1966–89 CBC Summary

Christmas Bird Count	Years Found	Range of No. Found	Median
Wilmington	1	8	
Middletown	12	1–11	
Bombay Hook	24	1–28	5
Cape Henlopen	17	1–17	2
Rehoboth	15	1–16	1
STATEWIDE	24	1–59	12
(decreasing; low in 1966, high in 1976)			

SPECIMENS: 8; DMNH, USNM. Egg records: LSU.

Yellow-crowned Night-Heron (*Nyctanassa violacea*)

Regular; summer resident; uncommon. Expected late April to early October and sporadically thereafter.

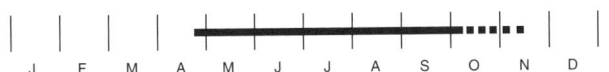

HABITAT: Feeds in various water-edge or shallow-water habitats; breeds in dense stands of young or scrubby trees near saltmarshes. On Pea Patch Island it nests apart from other herons, using taller trees than the scrubby growth used by the other small herons.

SPRING: First arrival is usually 25–30 April, noticeably later than other herons and egrets. Earlier reports are

3 Apr 1949	1	Bombay Hook NWR [Kram6]
8 Apr 1956	2	Bombay Hook NWR [Davi8]
9 Apr 1970	"present"	Bombay Hook NWR [Holg45]

Typically, only 2 or 3 individuals are reported; at Delaware City 8 birds were found on 20 May 1975 [Line7]. Watching morning and evening flights to and from Pea Patch Island remains the best way of observing this nocturnal species.

BREEDING: This is an uncommon bird in Delaware and the least common of the breeding herons.

Atlas. There were few reports elsewhere than Pea Patch Island during the Atlas period except 1–2 at Bombay Hook NWR from 9 June to 3 July 1987, suggesting that most of the small population may feed primarily on the New Jersey side of the river or along the inaccessible river shore. Usually fewer than 10 pairs breed on Pea Patch Island. About 40 pairs were estimated breeding in 1975–78, 1989, and 1993, but during the Atlas project in the mid-1980s probably only a few pairs bred (Wiese 1976–79; Thomas 1989b; Parsons 1993).

Nesting. Wiese (1977, 131) reported, "All Yellow-crowned Night-Heron nests were located in tall hardwoods along the

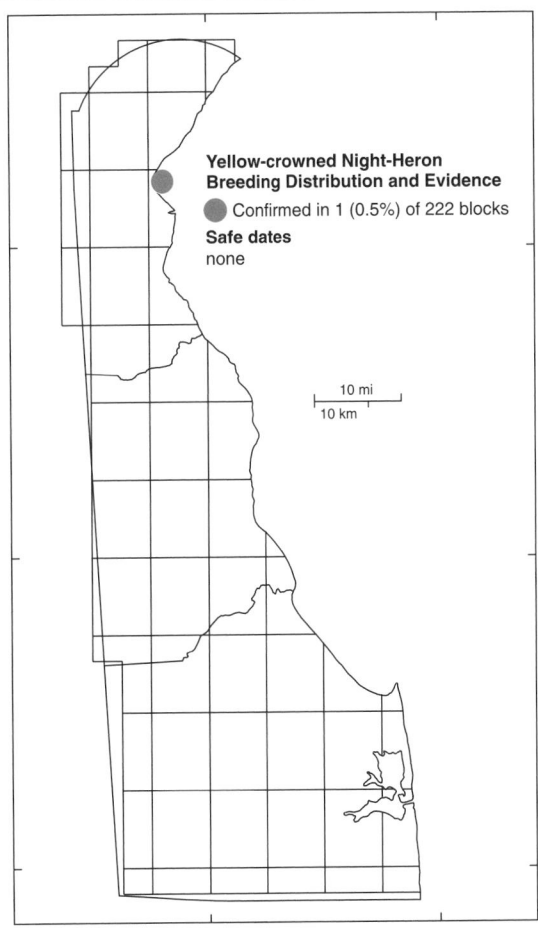

Yellow-crowned Night-Heron Breeding Distribution and Evidence
● Confirmed in 1 (0.5%) of 222 blocks
Safe dates
none

southern and eastern hardwood zone several meters above ground." In 1977 it began nesting in phragmites, in addition to 30 pairs nesting in hardwoods (Wiese 1978, 139). Its nesting was again limited to hardwoods away from the rest of the colony in 1987.

History. The first report of this night-heron in Delaware, 1 collected near Wilmington in August 1879 (UDEL 412-70), probably refers to a bird dispersing after breeding farther south.

Buckalew (notes) recorded 5 May 1935 that he found a Yellow-crowned Night-Heron nest with 3 eggs in a colony of 157 Black-crown nests at Cedar Beach. He had by then 6 years' experience with night-herons, but the eggs of the 2 species are indistinguishable, so this record is subject to question. Hanson (notes) recorded in 1938: "While occasional [Yellow-crowned Night-Herons] have been seen in company of Black-crowned, it was not until the summer of 1938 that a nest was found and identified with certainty. This year in a colony of perhaps 200 [Black-crowned Night-Heron] nests about 3 mi east of Dover Herbert Buckalew found a nest containing young birds." The downy young of the 2 night-herons are identifiable (Harrison 1978), and Buckalew had the experience to do so. The next breeding report in Delaware was a nesting pair at Bombay

Hook in 1957 (Oring 1958). The species was first reported on Pea Patch Island in 1967 [(Pres6] and again in 1975 [Line7].

It is not clear whether this night-heron is a new breeding bird in our region or merely reestablished (Watts 1995). Although Bent (1926) indicated no breeding on the Atlantic coast north of South Carolina, northward range extension (or reclamation) had probably begun by that date. A young heron collected in New Jersey just after the turn of the twentieth century grew to maturity in the Bronx Zoo, where it was identified as a Yellow-crown by William Beebe (Cruikshank 1942); probable breeding was first reported in New Jersey in 1926 (Potter 1926) and confirmed in 1927 from coastal Cape May County when two nests were found (Stone 1937, 1: 156). In Massachusetts, breeding was first deduced in 1891 and confirmed at Ipswich in 1928 (Townsend 1929; Griscom and Snyder 1955 in Veit and Petersen 1992). Several nests were found in southeastern Pennsylvania around the turn of the century, but not another until 20 April 1946 (Schutsky 1992). Four nests were found on Long Island in 1938, the first record in New York (Cruikshank 1942). Both Allen (1962b, 491) and Erwin (1979) either discounted or overlooked these breeding reports, giving the impression that breeding in the Northeast began only in the 1950s.

FALL: Last departure is usually early October. Late reports are

24 Oct 1978	1	Gibbs Pond, Lewes [Frec1]
4 Nov 1972	1	Cape Henlopen SP [Mudd1]
12 Nov 1966	2	Assawoman WA [DuPG10]

The highest counts are 6 at Woodland Beach on 4 October 1964 [LesC2] and 6 at Lewes on 5–6 September 1978 [Frec1]. As in the spring, typical daily totals are 1 or 2 birds.

WINTER: One Yellow-crowned Night-Heron was reported on the 1977 Middletown CBC.

SPECIMENS: DMNH 78194, Sussex Co., Rd. 402, W. Frankford, 20 August 1990; UDEL 412–70, Wilmington, August 1879.

White Ibis (*Eudocimus albus*)

Irruptive (14 years, 1962 to 1993), in late summer and fall.

J F M A M J J A S O N D

DOCUMENTATION: Photographs D. T. Schoch (DMNH 429–34).

REMARKS: The White Ibis, now common north at least to North Carolina, has occurred in Delaware in small numbers in late summer and fall during a few scattered years: 1962, 1965, 1968, 1970–72, 1977, 1979, 1980, 1984, 1988, 1989, 1992, and 1993. Almost all individuals were immature. The species has occurred from Thousand Acre Marsh [Pure9] south to Prime Hook NWR [Holg39] and once at Indian River Inlet [Gord9]. The first White Ibis recorded in Delaware was an immature present during 9–17 August 1962 at Little Creek WA [Spri4]; it was generally solitary, showing little inclination to associate with nearby Glossy Ibis (Lesser 1964). During the 1977 season 1 was at Bombay Hook NWR on 24 July [Pure9]; a week later an exceptional 12 were seen there [Abbo19], part of a widespread invasion of the Northeast.

In most years of occurrence the White Ibis is recorded from mid-July to mid-September. Early spring records include

24 Mar 1988	2	Prime Hook NWR [Frec1]
24–26 Apr 1979	1	near Lewes [Frec4]
13 May 1984	1	Little Creek WA [DuPG6]

Late fall reports, from Bombay Hook NWR, include 1 on 17 October 1968 [Holg33] and 2 during 23–25 October 1970 [Holg4].

Glossy Ibis (*Plegadis falcinellus*)

Regular; summer resident; common. Expected mid-March (sometimes earlier) to mid-September and sporadically through early winter.

J F M A M J J A S O N D

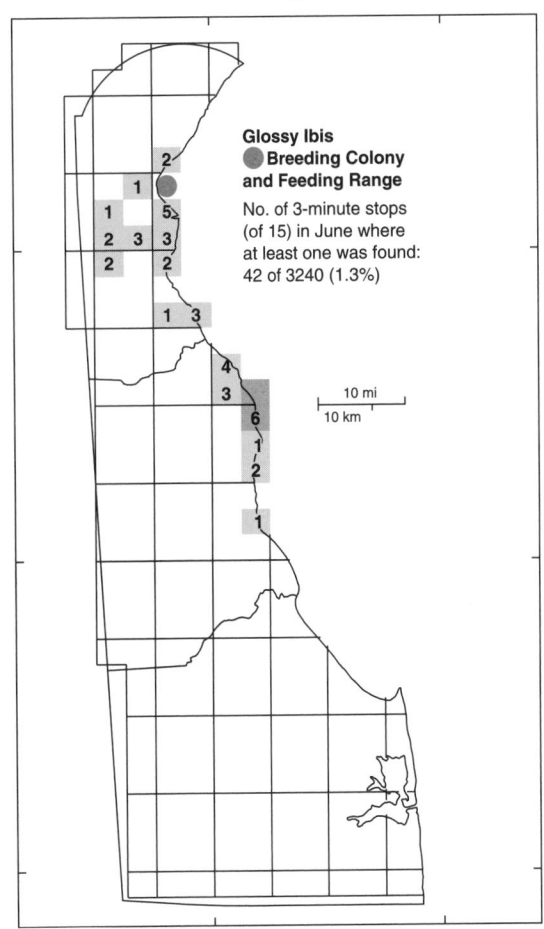

Glossy Ibis
⬤ **Breeding Colony and Feeding Range**

No. of 3-minute stops (of 15) in June where at least one was found: 42 of 3240 (1.3%)

10 mi
10 km

HABITAT: Feeds in mud flats, wet pastures, and plowed fields; breeds in dense stands of young or scrubby trees near saltmarshes or in phragmites.

SPRING: First arrival is usually 10–15 March, but arrivals prior to 10 March have been reported in 5 years. The earliest are

22 Feb 1977	5	Prime Hook NWR [Prim1]
28 Feb 1971	2	Bombay Hook NWR [Hol103]
1 Mar 1975	2	near Smyrna [Lehm11]
2 Mar 1972	12	Little Creek WA [Holg69]

High counts are

5 Apr 1972	800	Bombay Hook NWR [MiJC1]
8 Apr 1986	120	along Rt. 9 [SpSB1]
18 Apr 1972	300	Little Creek WA [HilJ1]

Typical counts total 30–100 birds.

BREEDING: Pea Patch Island continues to be the only Glossy Ibis breeding site.

Nesting. Nesting success on Pea Patch Island was reported by Wiese (1976–77) as follows:

Reproductive Success

	1975	1976
No. of clutches monitored	20	22
Eggs per complete clutch	3.4	3.1
Hatching success rate[1]	88%	57%
Fledging success rate[2]	62%	70%
Nesting success rate[3]	46%	40%

1. Omitting nests and eggs destroyed prior to hatching.

2. Number fledged divided by number hatched.

3. Number fledged divided by total number of eggs laid; causes of loss include nest collapse and predation.

These Glossy Ibis studies were discontinued because the birds stopped nesting in shrubs, which had been killed by guano deposits, and started nesting in phragmites, where breeding was less easily observed (Wiese 1978). In 1986 some were again nesting in shrubs (Thomas, nest record).

History. A Glossy Ibis found in Wilmington Marsh on 27 May 1927 sparked sufficient interest to produce three parallel notes in *The Auk* (Bailey; Hiatt and Emlen; Stone and Erskine; all 1927). Stone said it was the first encounter in the Philadelphia area since 1866. Krider (1879, 60) perhaps overstates its earlier abundance in recalling, "This bird is often shot in September, on the marshes of the Delaware River. When shooting rail I have often seen as many as four killed in a day." Records subsequent to 1927, all of fewer than 10 birds, are

9, 23 Apr 1939	Delaware City [Kram2; Cadb1]
9 May 1942	Bethany Beach [Cadb2]
3, 10 May 1947	Bombay Hook [BarI2; Mann1]
1 Jun 1947	2 of 5 were collected
	Fowlers Beach (Buckalew 1949, USNM 421924 and 421925)
5 May 1957	Delaware City [Abbo6]

By 1959 Glossy Ibis had become sufficiently regular in the Mid-Atlantic region to cease being noteworthy, and by the early 1960s they were present in numbers up to 200–300.

Trends. This species was first reported nesting in 1964 on Pea Patch Island, where Cutler (1965) noted "25 with nests and young." A peak breeding population of 1,500 pairs was reached in 1975 (Wiese 1976); the reported population declined about 80% during the next decade. A 1993 survey, however, estimated its population at 2,100, the highest yet (Parsons 1993).

Breeding population. DNREC estimated the Pea Patch Island population at 275 breeding pairs in 1986 and 236 pairs in 1989 (Thomas 1989b). The population was probably understated because counting the numbers breeding in the phragmites was impossible.

Glossy Ibis are most easily observed feeding in wet fields, marshes, and impoundments from Delaware City to Little Creek WA. In late summer, flocks of more than 100 may be seen almost anywhere near the tidal marshes as young fledge and postbreeding dispersal begins.

FALL: Postbreeding dispersal probably begins in July and usually ends by 10–15 September. Peak numbers occur from 1–10 July to 5–10 September. High counts are

10 Jul 1989	800	Port Mahon [Shoc3]
25 Jul 1981	513	Bombay Hook NWR [Falk8]
6 Aug 1972	1,000	Little Creek WA [DuPG35]

Typical counts are similar in number to spring counts.

WINTER: This species has occurred on 7 CBCs. Twenty-nine were counted in 1971, 2 in 1978, 2 in 1979, 1 in 1982, and 5 in 1984. The few January records include

2 Jan 1980	1	Little Creek WA [RusR9]
20 Jan 1980	1	Little Creek WA [Gord11]
26–31 Jan 1974	2	Prime Hook NWR [Hol101]

BANDING: A Glossy Ibis banded in Delaware in May 1969 was recovered that October in Cuba. One banded in New York in August 1966 was recovered in Delaware on 3 January 1967.

SPECIMENS: USNM 421924 and USNM 421925, both Fowlers Beach, 1 June 1947; DMNH 76548, Pea Patch Island, 20 June (1980s).

White-faced Ibis *(Plegadis chihi)*

Casual (1982, 1991, 1993).

DOCUMENTATION: Published notes.

REMARKS: White-faced Ibis breed in North America east to southern Idaho and Alabama and occur, at least casually, along the East Coast as far north as New York (AOU 1983). The published notes on the 20 March 1982 record (Russel 1983) mention crucial field marks, including the color of face and eyes. A series of reports was made in the spring and summer of 1991 [Gill1; O'BM3]; we have entirely satisfactory notes from Gill. A White-faced Ibis found on 28 May 1993 at Bombay Hook NWR was present to 25 June [PeBG1].

Wood Stork *(Mycteria americana)*

Accidental (1973).

DOCUMENTATION: Banding recovery.

REMARKS: A Wood Stork banded in Florida on 22 May 1972 was recovered at Gordon Pond, Cape Henlopen SP, during the first 10 days of January 1973 [Usfw3].

This is probably not this species' first recorded appearance in Delaware. Pennock included it on a circa 1935 list of "275 Birds Found at Rehoboth Beach," but details are lacking.

This rather spectacular southern species' postbreeding dispersal pattern frequently brings it north to South Carolina, and it has occurred as a vagrant along the Atlantic coast as far north as Maine and New Brunswick (Allen 1962). There are a number of records for New Jersey, New York, and Pennsylvania (Leck 1984). The Delaware record is thus not surprising.

Black Vulture (*Coragyps atratus*)

Resident; uncommon to fairly common. Migrates February–March and mid-September–October. Numbers increasing at about 10% per year. Became part of Delaware avifauna during the twentieth century.

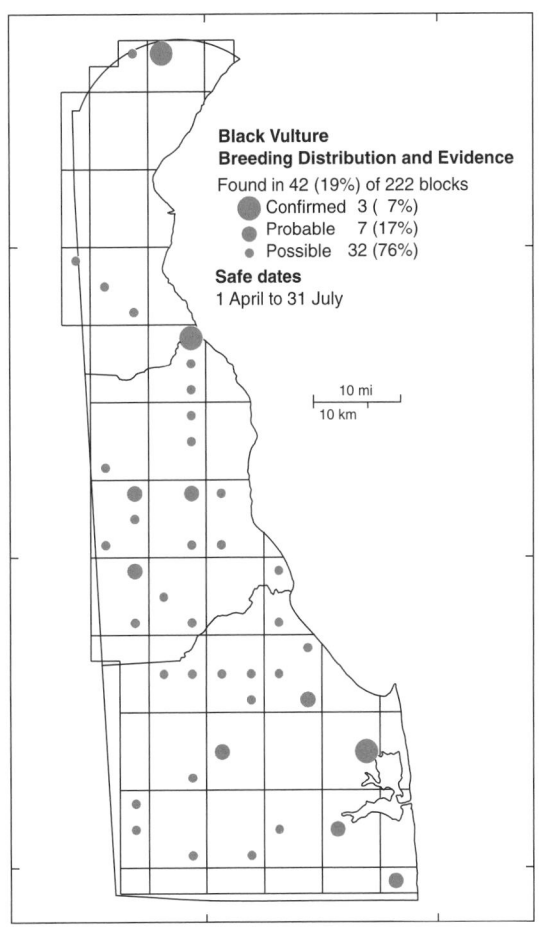

Black Vulture
Breeding Distribution and Evidence
Found in 42 (19%) of 222 blocks
● Confirmed 3 (7%)
● Probable   7 (17%)
• Possible 32 (76%)
Safe dates
1 April to 31 July

10 mi
10 km

HABITAT: Agricultural and other open habitats. Cattle feed-lots and chicken farms. Woods away from human habitation usually necessary for nesting.

REMARKS: This species is considered a resident throughout much of its range. However, Delaware is near the northeast edge of its range, so some migratory movement is expected. This movement probably involves individuals breeding north of Delaware where range expansion is taking place (Peterson 1980, map 177).

SPRING: February through March appears to be the main period of movement. High counts, all from Sussex County, are

9 Feb 1983	30	Milton [Frec10]
24 Feb 1984	35	along Rt. 88 [Frec1]
9 Mar 1985	40	during hawk survey (Hess 1987)

The last report may reflect local birds rather than migrants.

BREEDING: It appears to be more common in Sussex and western Kent Counties than elsewhere, based on analysis of a hawk survey. In these areas one might see more than 30, where-as along the coast and in New Castle County one might find only 6–12 during a 25–30 mi hawk survey in spring (Hess 1987).

Atlas. During the Atlas project 5 nests with eggs were found in 3 locations. Black Vultures have a home range of about

15,000 ha—equivalent to about 6 Atlas blocks (Coleman and Fraser 1989)—so Atlas observers were cautioned not to report them as possibly nesting if birds were seen flying overhead. Given the relatively large home range of Black Vultures, assess-ing the true breeding distribution in Delaware is difficult. Its general distribution from the Chesapeake and Delaware Canal southward is probably correct.

Nesting. Dyke noted a pair from 2 May 1959 through July at Assawoman WA and thought they were probably nesting [Dyke9], but it was not until 17 September 1966 that he found a very late nest with 2 young with "natal" down at that site [Dyke13]. This species was also found nesting in a cave near the Brandywine River, with eggs noted on 22 March 1983, and 25 April and 2 July 1984 [Wayn4]; in a vacant building on Angola Neck on 7 April 1987 [Spen1]; and in a collapsed and overgrown building in the woods north of the Smyrna River on 12 April 1987 [BrRF1]. Eggs are laid without any nest preparation. This species is single brooded, but renesting attempts extend its already long breeding season.

History. This vulture is a newcomer to Delaware as a result of its general northward expansion in the East. Krider (1879, 2) reminisced that he had "never seen it farther north than North

Carolina." The first Delaware report mentions 1 near Cedar Creek on 26 April 1932 [Buck3]. Subsequent records include 1 from Wilmington in 1934 [Ersk1] and March 1940 [Anne1], 2 near Delaware City in 1940 [Rigb3], and 1 in April 1941 [Mack1]. It was counted on the Bombay Hook CBC in December 1941, 1945, and 1946 and reported there from 10 November 1946 (numerous observers, Potter 1947) to November 1947 [Mann2]. By the 1950s reports were regular.

Trends. May Count data indicate a 12% average annual increase (1969–91), a more pronounced increase than shown by CBC data. This increase is not reflected in the results of the BBS, which does not adequately sample this species.

Breeding population. The best estimate of Black Vulture population in Delaware can be derived from roadside hawk surveys conducted during 1984–86 (Hess 1987). Extrapolation from this study suggests a state population of about 60 pairs (extrapolation method follows Pennock 1914). The ratio of Black to Turkey vultures is about 3: 100. On 9 May 1980 O'Shea reported a high count of 54 individuals at Prime Hook NWR (notes), undoubtedly representing a high percentage of the breeding population drawn to a food source.

FALL: High numbers are reported from 15–20 September through 25–30 October. Some movement probably continues into November. High counts are

10 Oct 1987	60	Milford [SpSB13]
20 Oct 1985	59	central Sussex County hawk count [West 24]
6 Nov 1982	50	Prime Hook NWR (notes)

These counts may include some migrants.

1966–89 CBC Summary

Christmas Bird Count	Years Found	Range of No. Found	Median
Wilmington	9	1–13	
Middletown	14	1–12	1
Bombay Hook	21	1–73	2
Cape Henlopen	18	1–25	3
Rehoboth	23	1–164	7
STATEWIDE	24	3–175	23

(increasing; low in 1967, high in 1988)

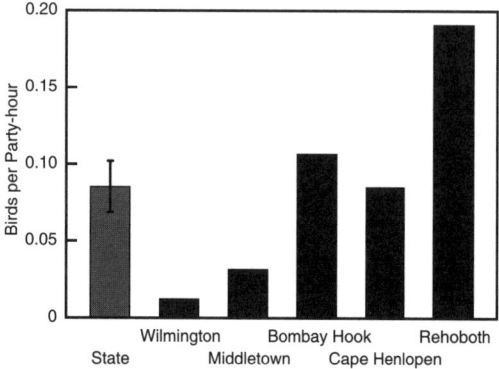

CBC Geographic Distribution

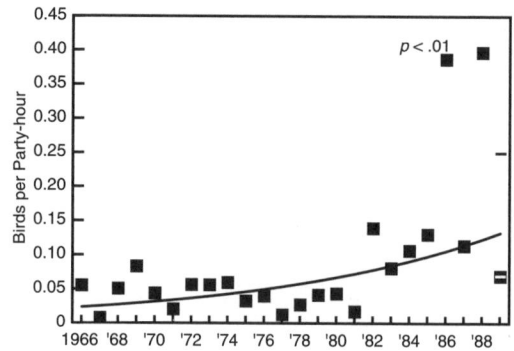

CBC Trend; Increasing at 8% per Year

WINTER: This species has shown a significant increase over 24 years of CBCs. High counts also show a gradual population increase:

Nov 1954	17	Bombay Hook NWR [MiJC1]
Jan 1960	20	Fenwick Island [Davi13]
Jan 1970	44	near Milton [Carl10]

High counts on the Piedmont:

| January 1986 | 26 | Winterthur [Wayn12] |

This vulture is most commonly found on the Kent and Sussex County CBCs.

SPECIMEN: DMNH 76171, 2.5 mi (4 km) W Port Penn, 16 March 1985.

Turkey Vulture *(Cathartes aura)*

Resident; common to abundant. Migrates March–April and September–November.

HABITAT: Farm country with woodlots; abandoned buildings sometimes used for breeding; natural, cave-like sites.

SPRING: An increase in numbers during March and early April indicates that the primary period of migration probably occurs then. This is supported by Jackson (1988b, 32), who notes that in south-central Wisconsin it arrives during the last week of March and further states that "there is much movement in middle U. S. latitudes from mid-Mar. through Apr. (a

peak usually the last week in Mar.)." Although no peaks were found, roadside hawk survey data reflected higher numbers of birds in spring and fall than in winter (Hess 1987). High counts, all from that survey, are 252 on 23 February 1985, 193 on 1 March 1986, and 213 on 17 March 1984. Typical daily counts are in the range 15–50.

BREEDING: This species forages widely in Delaware but is least common over developed areas near Wilmington, over marshes, or above Fenwick Island.

Atlas. Atlas workers reported Turkey Vultures in almost every block, and it surely breeds over a wide range. All "possible" reports were deleted from the distribution map because this wide-ranging species can travel the width of Delaware during a normal day's foraging. The resulting distribution map should still be interpreted with caution since not enough confirmed data supports any conclusions other than the widespread distribution of Turkey Vultures. Average home range for 11 Turkey Vultures tracked for 3 months in summer in Maryland and Pennsylvania was 27,000 ha (105 sq mi or about 11 Atlas blocks), but 2 breeding vultures had a smaller average home range of 7,000 ha (Coleman and Fraser 1989).

Nesting. Data from 11 Delaware nest records show that nests

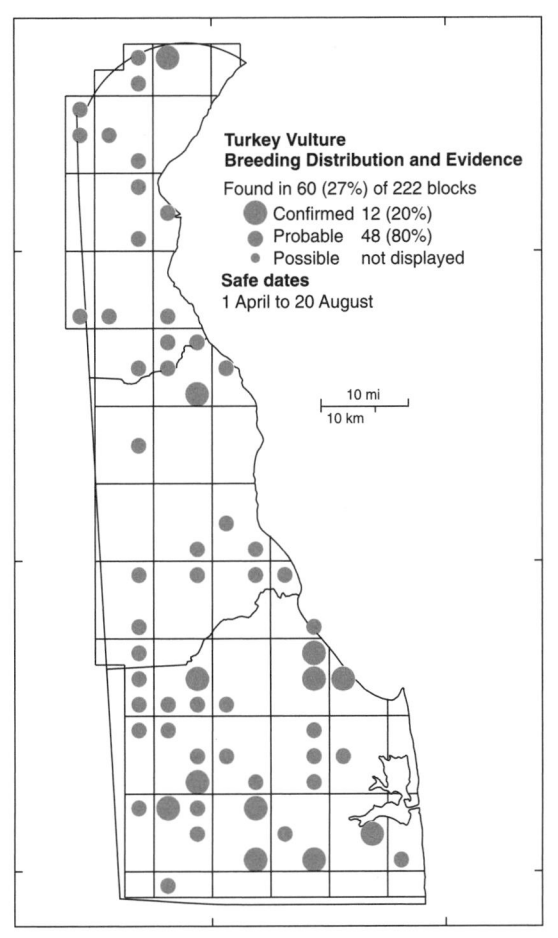

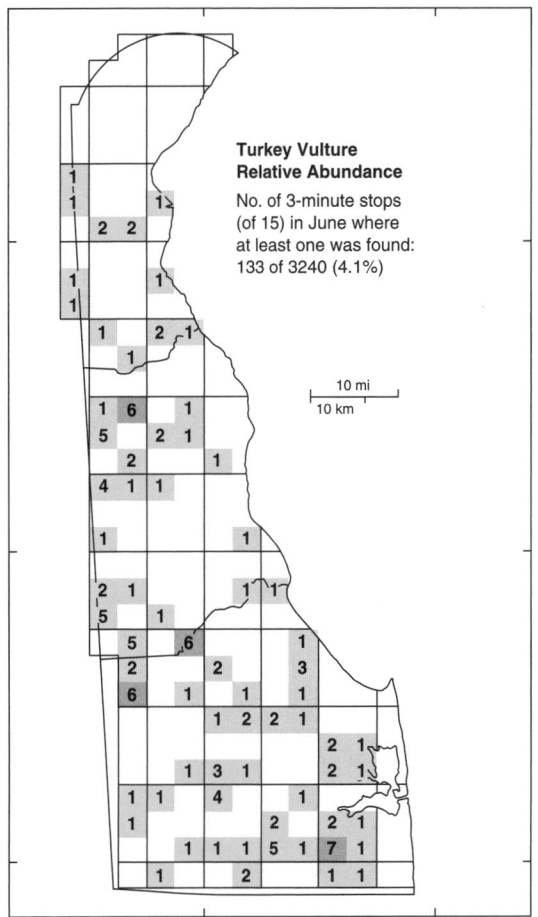

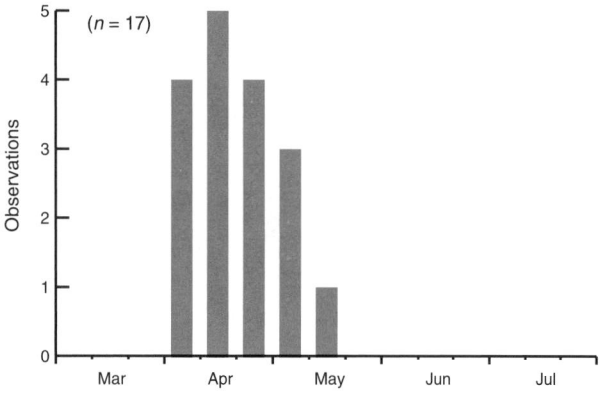

Estimated Clutch-Completion Dates

are often on the ground near a log, stump, or treefall and hidden by brush and vines. Nests were also found in a cave and under a rock in New Castle County and in an old shed on Prime Hook NWR. Several Atlas reports of probable breeding referred to vultures flushed from the tangled windrows made from trees removed where drainage ditches had been dug, and since the conclusion of the Atlas project, we have received an undated report of a nest found in one such windrow. There are about 2,000 mi (3,200 km) of these ditches in Delaware, half having windrows.

Most clutches are completed in April. Extreme egg dates are 9 April 1939, 2 eggs [Buck1]; and 27 May 1893, incubation started (WFVZ egg data). Downy young on 24 May 1960 [Dyke13] must have come from a clutch started in early April. Clutch size is 2.

History. "I shot a . . . large bird of prey, very much like a turkey. It had a head like a turkey; yet the wattle is not so big. It is such a stinking bird, since it feeds on dead bodies, that one cannot very well handle it." Thus in the journal of Reverend Hesselius for 1712 (Hesselius 1947) we read that the Turkey Vulture was known in New Castle County in colonial times and is not a newcomer like the Black Vulture. He goes on to describe a home remedy using its fat to give "incredible relief if rubbed in for dry aches." Krider (1879, 1) wrote "I have found it breeding in . . . Delaware."

Trends. Pennock (1914) counted vultures year-round from trains, searching one-half mi (0.8 km) on either side of the tracks, and saw 2.5 vultures per mi (4 per km) in Delaware during 500 mi (800 km) of travel. In a somewhat similar 1983–86 hawk survey (Hess 1987) 1.1 Turkey Vultures per mi (1.8 per km) were counted, searching one-quarter mi on either side of roads (during 5,000 mi, or 8,000 km of travel) during April. The small change in observed population density, in view of the imprecision of the studies, cannot be used as evidence of a decline, but it does suggest that the population has not changed by as much as an order of magnitude during the 75-year interval. Also, our trend analyses do not suggest a significant population change since the 1960s.

Breeding population. Hess's data indicate a visible population of about 1 pair per sq mi (0.4 per sq km) in April during the

breeding season—at least 2,000 pairs for the state. The highest number seen on a day during the breeding season was 374 during the 1984 May Count.

FALL: Migration probably takes place from September through November. Jackson (1988b, 33) notes that some birds leave Canada as early as August, and that movement is generally noticeable throughout the United States from early September into November. High counts, all from the hawk survey (Hess 1987), are 263 on 15 September 1984, 324 on 8 October 1983, and 388 on 15 October 1983. A migratory peak is evident in November from observations at hawk watches. (See "Hawk Migration" essay.) Typical daily counts range from 20 to 80.

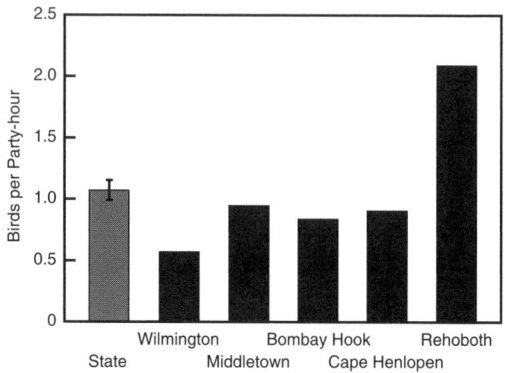

CBC Geographic Distribution

1966–89 CBC Summary

Christmas Bird Count	Years Found	Range of No. Found	Median
Wilmington	24	18–308	71
Middletown	22	2–176	49
Bombay Hook	23	3–149	47
Cape Henlopen	23	1–138	65
Rehoboth	24	40–412	177
STATEWIDE (low in 1980, high in 1987)	24	156–913	458

WINTER: The number of Turkey Vultures reported on CBCs has varied irregularly over a five-fold range, but no long-term trend is apparent. This species is more abundant on the Rehoboth CBC than on the other counts for the 24-year period analyzed. The Seaford CBC for the 1983–89 period resulted in observations of 6 birds per party-hour, noticeably more than the Rehoboth CBC but similar to the nearby Denton, Maryland, CBC average of 5.5 per party-hour (Falk 1984). Jackson (1988b, 31), describing its continental range, similarly observed that "there are notable winter densities between Del. and the Chesapeake Bay." High winter roost counts are 250 near Burtons Pond (located near a dump, a likely food source), Sussex County, on 28 December 1979 [Gord4] and 147 at Winterthur on 22 January 1972 [SpSB14].

SPECIMENS: 9; DMNH. Egg records: DMNH, LSU, WFVZ.

Fulvous Whistling-Duck *(Dendrocygna bicolor)*

HABITAT: Coastal impoundments and ponds.

REMARKS: This species wanders irregularly. The North American population breeds in the rice belt of southeast Texas and southwest Louisiana and along the coastal lowlands of Mexico. Small breeding colonies persist in California and Florida. Most winter in Mexico (Bellrose 1976). McCartney (1963, in Bellrose 1976, 76) notes that starting in 1955 a series of invasions took place along the Atlantic coast. The species was first recorded in Delaware when 2 were noted at Bombay Hook NWR on 6 August 1963 [Hard1]. Since then it has been present in 1964–68, 1972–75, 1979, 1981, 1984, 1990, and 1992, and in every month except January. The duration of stay varies from 1 or 2 days to 3 or 4 months. It is usually found in numbers fewer than 10, but as many as 25 have been present:

25 Jun 1965	25	Bombay Hook NWR [Hard8]
13 Apr–18 May 1974	24	Prime Hook NWR [Hol106; Rowl20]

The species has been recorded most often at Bombay Hook NWR but has also been noted at Delaware City, Little Creek WA, Prime Hook NWR, Rehoboth Beach, and a few other places along the coast.

SPECIMEN: UDEL 5-65, Little Creek WA, 27 December 1964.

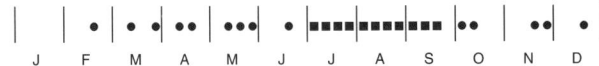

Irruptive (15 years, 1963–92), most reports July through September.

J F M A M J J A S O N D

[Pink-footed Goose *(Anser brachyrhynchus)*]

Possible escape; adequate documentation of identification.

REMARKS: The only record describes a single bird at Bombay Hook NWR from 1 November 1953 to 21 January 1954 [Cutl17]. The published notes (Cutler 1955b) are convincing as to identification. Since the Pink-footed Goose breeds in Greenland and Iceland (AOU 1983), wild birds could logically occur in eastern North America. There is no evidence as to whether this particular bird was an escaped captive.

Greater White-fronted Goose *(Anser albifrons)*

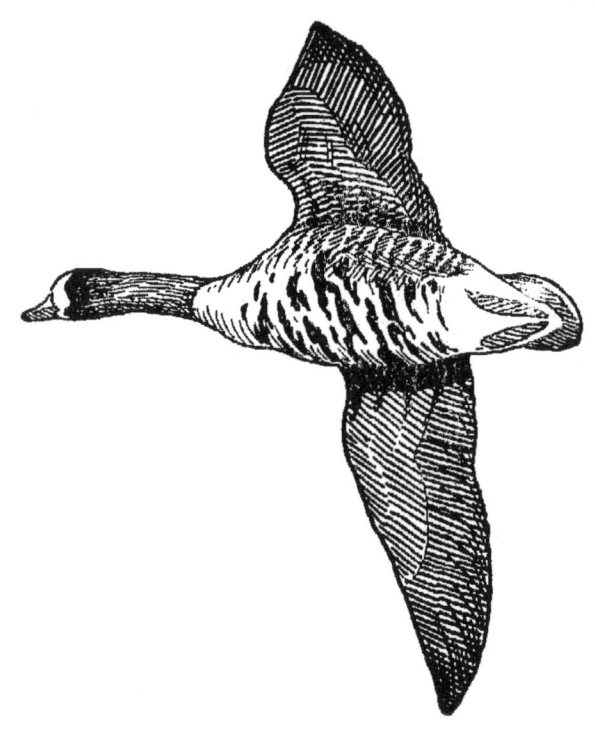

Occasional (29 years, 1956–91); migrant and winter visitor; rare.

J F M A M J J A S O N D

HABITAT: Coastal impoundments and fields, deep ponds.

SPRING: Wintering birds usually leave by 5 March to 16 April. The latest bird reported was 1 at Bombay Hook NWR 20 May 1965 [Hard6].

FALL: One or 2 birds generally appear between the last week of October and the first week in January. An exception is 2 birds seen occasionally at Bombay Hook NWR from 25 August 1973 until 23 December [Hol100]; the unusual arrival date and the sedentary nature of this pair suggest they were escapes. An exceptionally early flock of 9 present in a field near Leipsic on 24 September 1985 and around Bombay Hook NWR thereafter had orange bills characteristic of the Greenland race *(A. a. flavirostris)* [Insk1]; this population begins departing its breeding ground in August, and a storm-assisted flight direct from Greenland may account for the early arrival of this flock. The next earliest (and more usual) arrival date is 20 October 1989 [Holg14].

WINTER: This species, usually as a single bird, has occurred on 9 CBCs and during the count week of 3 others. The few instances of possible wintering birds all come from Bombay Hook NWR. One was banded at Silver Lake, Rehoboth Beach, on 18 January 1967 [Hals1].

1966–89 CBC Summary

Christmas Bird Count	Years Found	Range of No. Found
Wilmington		
Middletown		
Bombay Hook	8	1–3
Cape Henlopen		
Rehoboth	1	1
STATEWIDE (high in 1982)	9	1–3

REMARKS: Most Delaware reports are of pink-billed birds, probably from the population of *A. a. frontalis* that migrates via the Central Flyway to the Gulf Coast.

A Greater White-fronted Goose report from Woodland Beach 19 December 1961 was described as the third state record [Less11], but we have located only 1 previous report—1 on the 26 Dec 1956 Bombay Hook CBC.

SPECIMEN: DMNH 68276, 3 mi (5 km) NW Middletown, 7 November 1979.

[Lesser White-fronted Goose *(Anser erythropus)*]

Probable escape.

REMARKS: The Lesser White-fronted Goose breeds from Scandinavia to eastern Siberia and winters west to western Europe, so an occurrence in North America would most plausibly involve a bird that overshot its winter range during fall migration. The AOU Check-list lists records in North Dakota, Pennsylvania, and Delaware and notes the possibility of some or all of the birds being escapes (AOU 1983, 1993, 1995). The Delaware bird was shot in Bombay Hook NWR on 21 December 1972 and photographed (National Photoduplicate File 171.3-1Ca and 1Cb) [Holg16]. The small number of records in North America strongly suggests that the bird escaped from captivity.

Snow Goose (*Chen caerulescens*)

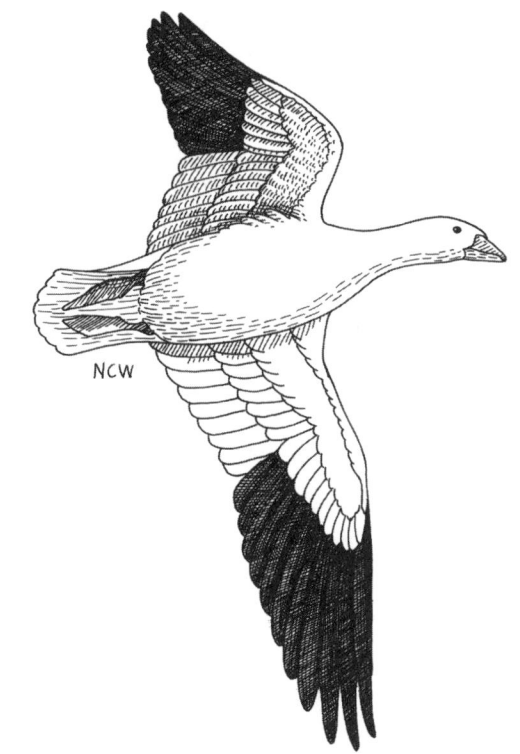

NCW

Regular; winter visitor; common to very abundant. Expected early October to early April, but in some years it migrates earlier or later. Occasionally summers, but without suggestion of breeding. Winter populations increasing at 33% per year, a rate that obviously cannot continue.

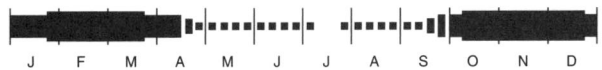

| J | F | M | A | M | J | J | A | S | O | N | D |

HABITAT: Saltwater cordgrass marshes, impoundments, bays, and upland fields.

HISTORY: Alexander Wilson wrote in 1814 that "this species . . . arrives in the river Delaware from the north, early in November, sometimes in considerable flocks, and is extremely noisy, their notes being shriller and more squeaking than those of the Canada, or common Wild Goose. On their first arrival they make but a short stay, proceeding, as the depth of winter approaches, farther to the south; but from the middle of February until the breaking up of ice in March, they are frequently most numerous along both shores of the Delaware, about and below Reedy Island, particularly near Old Duck Creek, in the state of Delaware. They feed on the roots of the reeds there, tearing them up from the marshes like hogs" (Wilson and Bonaparte 1859–60, 3: 66). The Snow Goose population dropped as a result of uncontrolled hunting in the nineteenth century, but began a slow recovery after protection started. In a 1934 survey "several reports were received of a comparatively small number of Snow Geese observed feeding on the salt-

marsh meadows . . . in November" south of Rehoboth Beach (Cottam 1935). No Blue Geese were seen that year, but one had been captured on the Indian River in the late fall of 1930. (See "Snow Geese" essay for recovery since 1936.)

SPRING: The February peak noted by Wilson is characteristic as southern flocks move north. The highest February count is 100,000 birds at Bombay Hook NWR on 27 February 1982 [Barn59]. The high March count is 27,000 birds at Bombay Hook NWR 16 March 1980 [Keel1]. By 20–30 March many birds have left, and flocks are noticeably smaller. The last flocks usually depart by 10–20 April.

SUMMER: The occasional summering birds usually are crippled individuals. No reports of breeding exist. A published report of 25 in July (Barnhill 1977) is rejected; it may have referred to domestic fowl.

FALL: A few may arrive in September; Snow Goose arrival is expected about 1–10 October. The earliest arriving groups reported are

25 Aug 1991	5	Bombay Hook NWR [Barn54]
6 Sep 1983	100	Bombay Hook NWR [Hess9]
9 Sep 1989	6	Bombay Hook NWR [Barn49]

The numbers build quickly, and within a few weeks the sky and marshes are filled with Snow Geese. (See "Snow Geese" essay for high counts.)

1966–89 CBC Summary

Christmas Bird Count	Years Found	Range of No. Found	Median
Wilmington	8	1–25	
Middletown	17	1–16,002	12
Bombay Hook	24	68–65,504	6,758
Cape Henlopen	21	1–63,006	1,023
Rehoboth	23	5–8,135	253
STATEWIDE	24	81–138,467	10,449
(increasing; low in 1968, high in 1988)			

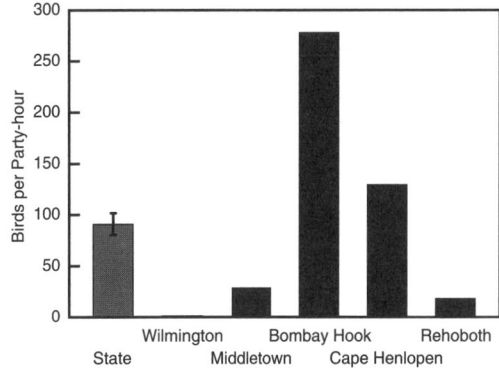

CBC Geographic Distribution; Average of 4 Count Areas

WINTER: CBC data reflect a significant increase in numbers. The CBC trend graph shows an exponential growth for the ear-

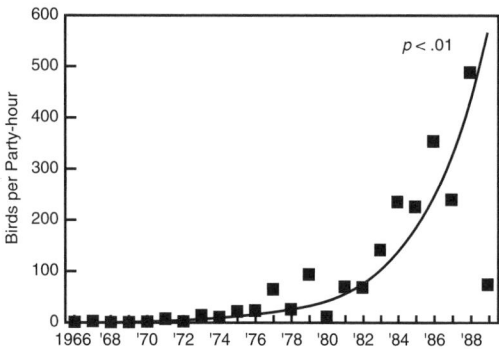

CBC Trend; Increasing at 33% per Year

ly winter population of Snow Goose, though such growth cannot continue unabated.

The annual average October–January Snow Goose population, as determined by DNREC monthly aerial surveys, is similar to CBC data, showing continued growth through 1991 (see "Snow Geese" essay). This goose is found abundantly on the Bombay Hook CBC.

REMARKS: There are two subspecies of Snow Geese. One, called "Lesser Snow Goose," is relatively small and has two color morphs (with intermediates), one all-white and one dark, the latter known as the "Blue Goose." This subspecies winters primarily in the West and Midwest and is uncommon in Delaware. The larger subspecies, known as the "Greater Snow Goose," winters abundantly in our area; its dark morph is extremely rare (Palmer 1976, 2: 128–29).

Snow Goose migration and wintering movements have changed. From the first half of the nineteenth century, even into the 1970s, there was a midwinter hiatus when the Snow Goose population was all found south of the Delaware Bay. But from the late 1970s on, concurrent with the expansion of its migratory population here, large numbers have remained in the Delaware Valley throughout the winter. Stone (1937), referring to "Greater Snow Goose," notes that the birds on first arrival stayed a short time but that large flocks were sometimes present at least until mid-December before proceeding south. Then, in February, the geese returned to Delaware Bay. Bellrose (1976), also referring to "Greater Snow Goose," states that it left its North Carolina and Virginia wintering grounds about mid-February (occasionally delaying into March) and remained in the Delaware Bay into April. With regard to fall movements he notes that the vanguard arrived in Delaware Bay in late September and the majority during the third week of November. Our data show large numbers present from mid-October through the third week of December, followed by a 5-week midwinter period of lower (but still substantial) numbers. In February numbers build again. A period of decreasing numbers follows as the birds move north.

BANDING: Delaware recoveries of "Greater Snow Geese" include 20 banded on their breeding grounds on the high arctic islands of northeastern Canada; 28 banded on the St. Lawrence River east of Quebec City, the major stopping place on its migration corridor; and 4 banded in North Carolina.

SPECIMENS: 14; DMNH, ANSP, UDEL, USNM.

Snow Geese

Winston J. Wayne

For a view of Nature at her richest, the Snow Geese at Bombay Hook have been compared to the Sandhill Cranes along the Platte River in Nebraska and the Greater Flamingos on Great Inagua Island in the Bahamas (Wiley 1992). The huge flocks of Snows pitching in or flushing from fields or ponds with loud, high-pitched honking, and the procession of long strings of wavies in the sky make a thrilling spectacle.

Snow Geese have been reported in Delaware during the wintering season since the 1600s (Penn 1683), but systematic counts of their numbers did not begin until 1937, when the Bombay Hook NWR came into being. The refuge provided a sanctuary for the geese, which fed primarily in the tidal marshes and roosted on open water. Dikes and freshwater impoundments built in the late 1930s and early 1940s by the Civilian Conservation Corps increased the area of open water for roosting and eventually produced freshwater marsh plants for feeding.

The accompanying table and figure show the highest counts of Snow Geese recorded in Delaware by season for the years 1936–93. The data show that from 1936 through 1979, the high counts of Snow Geese in the fall were variable but never exceeded 12,000. The winter high counts were generally lower,

and several winters saw no Snow Geese because of snow cover and freezing, which prevented feeding and forced them farther south. Except for 1936–42 the spring high counts were also generally lower than those of the fall, lacking any geese in many years.

In the period 1943–48 Snow Geese were exceptionally sparse in Delaware. The number in the only refuge then available to them, Bombay Hook, was greatly reduced because of rocket testing and gunnery practice by military planes in 1944. Snow Geese also wintered across the Delaware Bay in the marshes around Fortesque, New Jersey, which became a haven for geese disturbed at Bombay Hook. In late March 1946, when a military plane flushed the Fortesque flock, a well-known photograph was taken of the geese in flight over the bay; when they were counted on an enlargement, it revealed 13,944 individual birds (Bombay Hook NWR 1946).

In March 1980, 27,000 Snow Geese were counted, marking the beginning of the dramatic increase in Delaware during the 1980s and 1990s. Unusually high counts include 100,000 in February 1982; 93,800 in January 1990; 148,000 in November 1992; and 166,200 in December 1993.

In 1937–65, the earlier years of systematic Snow Goose

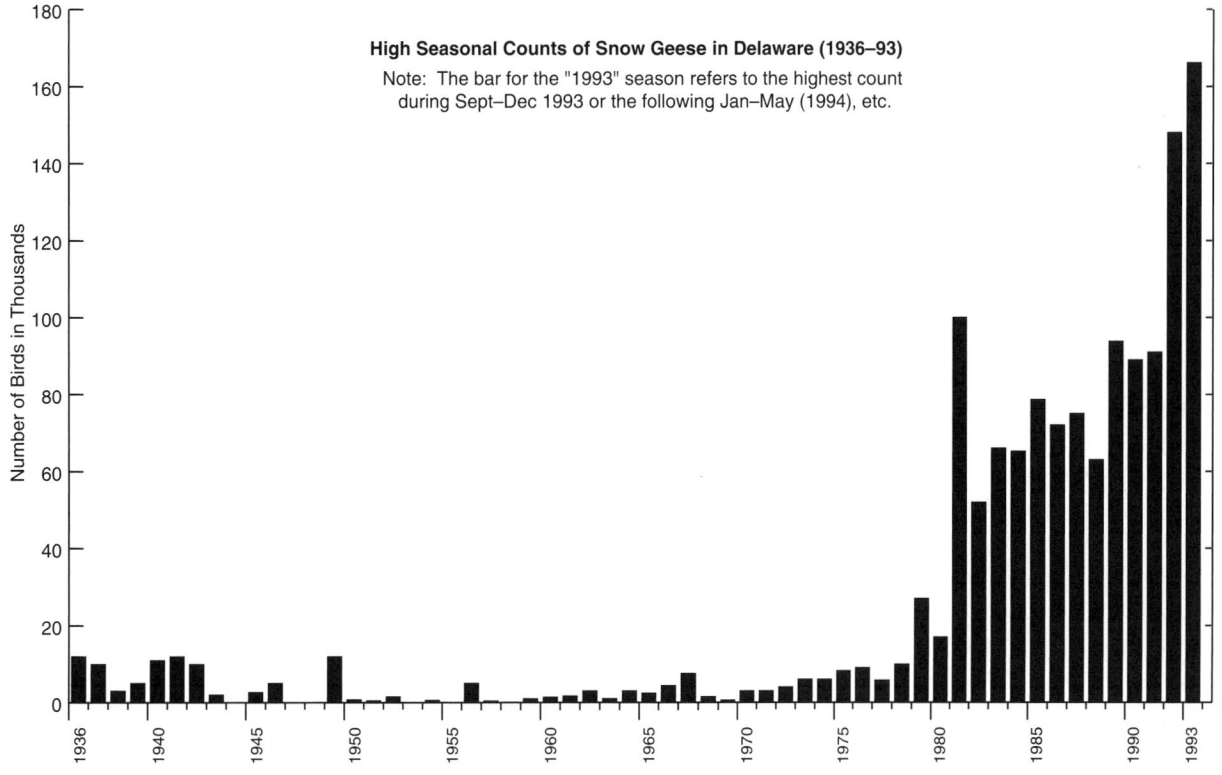

High Seasonal Counts of Snow Geese in Delaware (1936–93)
Note: The bar for the "1993" season refers to the highest count during Sept–Dec 1993 or the following Jan–May (1994), etc.

High Counts of Snow Geese in Delaware, 1936–93

Year	Fall	Winter	Spring	Year	Fall	Winter	Spring
1936	3,000		12,000	1965	2,400		
1937	1,700		10,000	1966	4,350	106	
1938	3,000	700	1,000	1967	7,500	100	1,500
1939	5,000		20	1968	1,500	100	350
1940	11,000		2,000	1969	600		10
1941	12,000	18		1970	3,000	120	800
1942	10,000		10,000	1971	3,000	3,000	1,600
1943	2,000			1972	4,000	85	17
1944	75			1973	6,000	200	360
1945	2,660			1974	6,000	3,400	
1946	5,000			1975	8,300	5,100	
1947	4			1976	9,100	8,000	260
1948	6			1977	5,760	4,000	225
1949	12,000	8,000	300	1978	10,000	6,200	2,680
1950	750			1979	10,000	10,000	27,000
1951	500		1	1980	16,500	17,500	2,250
1952	15	1,000	1,500	1981	36,200	100,000	50,500
1953	10	50	5	1982	52,000	30,000	20,000
1954	600	3	3	1983	66,000	14,700	1,000
1955	12		1	1984	65,200	40,000	20,000
1956	5,000	5,000		1985	78,600	45,000	20,000
1957	440	80		1986	72,000	30,000	30,000
1958	5	130		1987	75,000	40,000	10
1959	1,000	400		1988	53,000	63,000	6,000
1960	1,400		6	1989	86,200	93,800	15,000
1961	1,700	78	8	1990	89,000	25,700	
1962	3,000	3	16	1991	91,000	45,300	900
1963	1,000		10	1992	148,000	64,200	
1964	3,000	150	50	1993	166,200	70,800	

Sources: The data are from various published and personal bird notes, Bombay Hook NWR Narrative Reports (1938–91), Christmas Bird Counts (1939–92), Delaware Division of Fish and Wildlife Count Summaries (1950–69; 1974–93), Prime Hook NWR Narrative Reports (1970–90), and a Delmarva Ornithological Sociey census of Bombay Hook NWR (1981–83).

Note: "1989" includes the fall of 1989 and the following winter and spring of 1990. A blank space means no data, usually because of the absence of geese. The seasonal data for each year cover the fall months (September–December), the contiguous winter (January–February), and the spring season (March–May) of the following year.

counting, reports came almost exclusively from Bombay Hook NWR and the surrounding area. Beginning in 1965, however, there were reports of small numbers of Snow Geese in the Prime Hook–Rehoboth Beach area. In 1975 reports also started to show up from the Assawoman WA region and the vicinity of Wilmington. These additional data came from observations at Prime Hook NWR and from the more systematic coverage provided by aerial counts made by the Delaware Division of Fish and Wildlife. Peak counts in the Prime Hook–Rehoboth Beach area ranged from 500 to 5,000 through 1979, and as high as 67,300 through the 1980s and as late as 1993. During the 1980–92 period the aerial surveys showed peak counts ranging from 950 to 15,000 in the Assawoman WA region and as high as 19,000 in the Seaford area (DNREC 1974–93).

Although aerial surveys by the Division of Fish and Wildlife began in 1950, only the totals for the state as a whole were reported through 1968, and during the following five years no aerial counts were made. Resuming in 1974 and continuing to the present, aerial counts have been reported from 11 sections

along the eastern two-thirds of the state, from Wilmington in the north to Fenwick Island in the south. Whittendale describes these surveys, which are made from a small plane at an altitude of about 100 feet. The surveys must be made at first light, before the Snow Geese leave their roosting areas and break up into separate flocks. Many leave Delaware to feed in New Jersey, Maryland, and as far south as Virginia. Later in the day they return to their Delaware roosting areas (T. W. Whittendale, Jr., DNREC, pers. comm.).

The total winter Snow Goose population in eastern North America has grown in recent years, after several highly successful nesting seasons in the High Arctic (E. F. Smith, DNREC, pers. comm.). The geese winter throughout much of the Mid-Atlantic region, from New Jersey to as far south as North Carolina. In January surveys for the years 1984–91, the total count in the East ranges from 100,000 to as high as 276,000 in 1992. Spring surveys taken in the St. Lawrence River, Quebec, staging area show even higher counts: 355,900 in 1991, 434,500 in 1992, and 421,000 in 1993 (USFWS 1993).

The population of Snow Geese has grown dramatically since 1980, and the state has gotten more than its expected share of the increased population. Availability of good habitat may be part of the reason. Since the establishment in 1937 of Bombay Hook NWR (now 15,122 acres), an additional 20,000 acres of publicly owned feeding and roosting areas have been provided by the establishment of Woodland Beach WA (1953), Little Creek WA (1957), Prime Hook NWR (1963), and the Harvey Tract (1979). The construction of many ponds and open emergent wetlands on farms and changes in agricultural practices have also created additional opportunities for roosting and feeding by Snow Geese. The upgraded habitat has apparently made Delaware more attractive as a wintering area for a growing influx from the north.

Snow Geese are opportunistic feeders, a characteristic noted in Delaware in some detail over the years (Bombay Hook NWR 1938–91). In the early years of Bombay Hook NWR they fed mainly in the tidal marshes on the green shoots, roots, and tubers of cordgrass. However, over time they began to feed on most of the tidal and freshwater marsh plants, including bulrushes, cordgrasses, cattails, and sedges. In 1962 Snow Geese accompanied Canada Geese into the upland grain fields, first exploiting waste corn and young wheat, eventually also turning to rye, buckwheat, ladino clover, and grasses. In the 1980s they began feeding on undigested corn in manure spread on cattle farms.

In 1982, when population peaked in March at 50,500 Snow Geese in Bombay Hook NWR, intensive feeding by the geese on cordgrass turned 500 acres of tidal marsh into mudflats and open water. Cordgrass continued to revegetate, and many Snow Geese also fed in upland fields. Nevertheless, by 1987 more than 1,000 acres of refuge marsh had been converted to mudflats, which are subject to erosion by tidal movement.

In an attempt to disrupt such destructive feeding by dispersing the geese, the damaged areas were opened to Snow Goose hunting in 1983, and a special, early Snow Goose hunt was tried in the fall of 1987. Success was limited, as the geese returned when hunting stopped. Continued use of special hunting arrangements in following years, however, did move many of the geese from Bombay Hook NWR to Prime Hook NWR, where they did most of their intensive feeding not in the saltmarsh but in large freshwater impoundments. Here the destruction of perennial plants such as cattail apparently enhances the growth of more desirable annual marsh plants (Smith, pers. comm.). In contrast, the large impoundments in Little Creek WA are brackish because of flushing with tidal water, the predominant plant is cordgrass, and heavy feeding by the Snow Geese results in mudflats and open water (W. R. Whitman, DNREC, pers. comm.).

In 1985 Snow Geese were poisoned by ingestion of lead shot during feeding at Bombay Hook, where 300 dead geese were recovered that year and 600 in 1986. Fortunately, this has not been a continuing problem (Smith, pers. comm.).

As noted in the species account, nearly all of the Snow Geese visiting Delaware are the Greater subspecies *(A. c. atlantica)*, which breeds in a small section of Greenland and on several arctic islands in the extreme northeastern part of Canada. They migrate and winter along the eastern edge of North America as far south as North Carolina. The blue color morph of this subspecies is rare. The Lesser Snow Goose *(A. c. caerulescens)* nests on Baffin Island, at several locations along the west side of Hudson Bay, and in northwestern North America and Siberia, well south of the Greater Snow Goose breeding area. A small portion of these Lesser Snow Geese migrates across western New York and central Pennsylvania to the Atlantic coast as far south as North Carolina (Bellrose 1976). An unusually high count of 400 of the blue morph was reported in Delaware in 1980. This suggests that some Lesser Snow Geese may occasionally be stopping in Delaware on the eastern leg of their fall migration.

Ross's Goose, a smaller look-alike of the Snow Goose, has been reported in Delaware with increasing regularity over the past ten years. In an exciting new dimension to Snow Goose watching, birders search, with surprising success, for the small Ross's Geese on the fringes of large flocks of feeding or roosting Snow Geese.

The goal of the U.S. Fish and Wildlife Service and the Delaware Division of Fish and Wildlife is to maintain as large a population of wintering Snow Geese in Delaware as the habitat will sustain. The means to this end are adjustment of harvest levels and proper management of wildlife areas. The agencies are seeking to balance the greatest number of Snow Geese for hunting and wildlife viewing with the least damage to the habitat (Smith, pers. comm.).

Ross's Goose *(Chen rossii)*

Occasional (11 years, 1981–93), but may eventually be determined to be regular; migrant or winter visitor; rare.

DOCUMENTATION: Photographs (R. Augustine, AB 36: 158).

REMARKS: The Ross's Goose is a western species that has recently been noted in very small numbers associating with wintering Snow Geese at many locations in the East. The first one reported in Delaware was at Bombay Hook NWR on 28 October 1981 [Abbo17]. A photograph of 1 at Bombay Hook NWR on 14 November 1981 was published [Augu1], and we have additional excellent photographs of 1 seen near Bombay Hook on 14 October 1993 (Jeffrey A. Gordon, photographs at DMNH 435–37). Subsequent observations suggest that Ross's Geese occur primarily with Snow Geese, in the ratio of 1 Ross's Goose for every 20,000 Snow Geese. Field identifications should be made with care to exclude the possibility of Snow Goose x Ross's Goose hybrids (Perry 1988). Extreme dates reported in Delaware are

10 Oct 1989	1	Bombay Hook NWR [Holg89]
12 Oct 1982	1	Bombay Hook NWR [Gord13]
28 Mar 1987	4	near Kitts Hummock [Perr1]
31 Mar 1989	2	Bombay Hook NWR [Barn55]

Canada Goose *(Branta canadensis)*

Resident; fairly common to very abundant. Most abundant October to mid-March. Winter populations declined at about 10% per year during 1979–89. Breeding population is descended from captive stock bred in Delaware.

| J | F | M | A | M | J | J | A | S | O | N | D |

HABITAT: Open water and fields in winter, sheltered ponds and streams in summer.

SPRING: Usually the large winter flocks leave by 10–30 March, with last departure 5–15 May. High counts are

27 Mar 1965	45,000	SE New Castle and NE Kent counties [Abbo15]
27 Mar 1965	20,000	Bombay Hook NWR [MiJC2]
15 Apr 1965	10,000	Bombay Hook NWR [Faus1]

BREEDING: The state breeding population is concentrated on ponds and along creeks in the Piedmont. South of the Piedmont Canada Geese are much less common, and flocks are smaller. In Sussex County most are in the ponds of the Nanticoke drainage, but a few breed in saltmarshes of the Inland Bays.

Atlas. Breeding was readily established during the Atlas project by observing goslings or by local residents speaking of goslings.

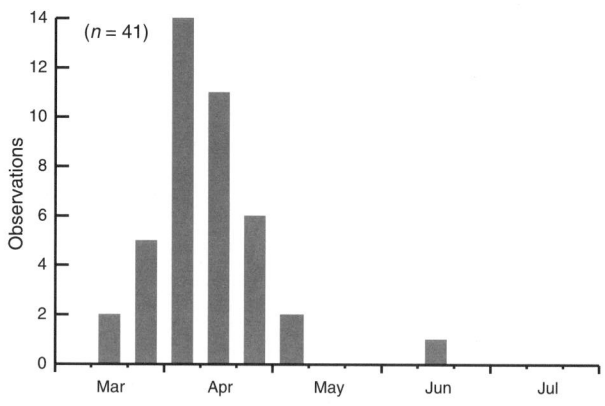

Estimated Clutch-Completion Dates

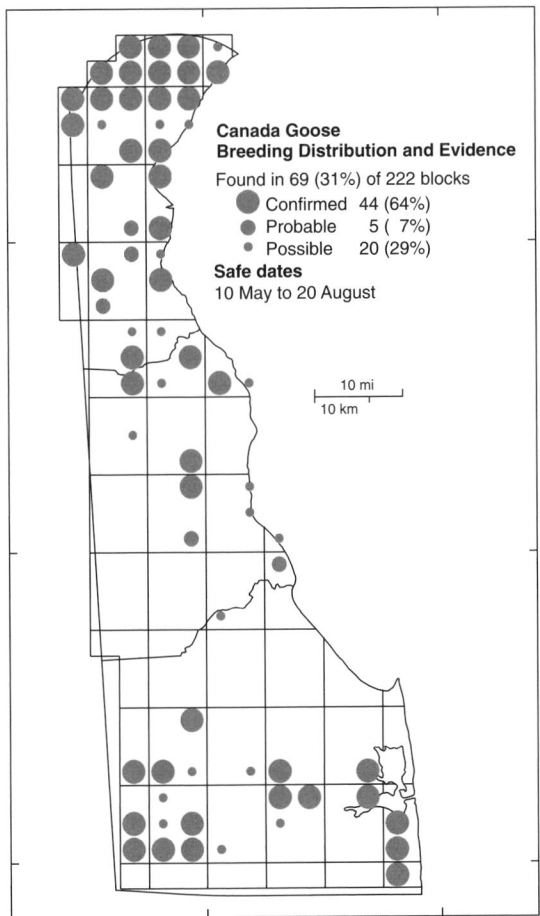

**Canada Goose
Breeding Distribution and Evidence**

Found in 69 (31%) of 222 blocks

● Confirmed 44 (64%)
● Probable 5 (7%)
• Possible 20 (29%)

Safe dates
10 May to 20 August

10 mi
10 km

Nesting. Nests, usually placed on the ground, are constructed of straw, lined with down and feathers.

The extrapolated clutch-completion period is 17 March to 12 June, with a peak in early to mid-April. Early egg dates are 5 April 1983 (adult on nest) [Jahn1]; and 6 April 1957 (slight incubation; DMNH 2483); the late date is 11 May 1983 [Patt1]. One distinctly late brood of "8 very small goslings" was observed on Hoopes Reservoir on 12 July 1982 [SpeE3]. Clutch sizes are 6 eggs (4 nests) and 5 (2 nests); 8 goslings have been reported three times.

History. The Canada Geese that breed in Delaware belong to a feral population of introduced birds, which are not migratory but move in search of food, shelter, or open water. Pennock reported a nest 20 May 1907 near Ocean View [Penn4], and Buckalew (notes) found nests near Milford in 1935 and 1938. Pinioned or wounded birds were the source of flocks established on the ponds of prosperous Piedmont farms. One such flock was introduced in 1938 at Whitely Farms north of Newark by S. Hallock du Pont. These flocks have generally grown and spread, and occasionally estates have had to reduce their populations to manageable numbers. An early flock established by Thomas Rowan in Kent County at Taylors Bridge was used to decoy flocks of migrating geese that had been bypassing Delaware. This ploy was immediately successful; he attracted a flock of wild geese in 1949 (du Pont 1963). The next year

this technique was used successfully at Bombay Hook NWR, and breeding began there in 1964 [Hard7]. Alexander Wilson observed such decoying by hunters in the Delaware valley about 1800 (Wilson and Bonaparte 1859–60).

Trends. The May Count, conducted after most of the migratory geese have gone north, indicates an average annual 4% decline in the population of this species in Delaware (1969–90), counter to the 5% annual increase in the Upper Coastal Plain [Usfw1]. This difference may reflect the efforts to control goose populations in northern Delaware while more southern states are seeking to establish flocks.

Breeding population. Breeding Canada Geese spread out along creeks or at farm ponds instead of forming flocks. As soon as the goslings hatch and become mobile, territoriality dissolves, and flocks reform. The total of 239 reported at Winterthur 5 August 1972 [ThoR3] is the high summer count.

There are probably only a few hundred breeding pairs in Delaware (DNREC estimate, pers. comm., 1993) and a few hundred nonbreeding summer residents.

FALL: In late August and early September small flocks of presumably resident birds are present. The first migrants arrive 20–30 September. Peak fall levels are reached by early October. A count of 77,500 was made at Bombay Hook NWR on 18 October 1981 [Kell4]. The highest state aerial count was 183,000 in October 1980, and the mean October population for the years 1973–88 was 123,000. The state aerial counts show that the population drops from its October peak to 40% of that level during November through January (DNREC 1974–93).

1966–89 CBC Summary

Christmas Bird Count	Years Found	Range of No. Found	Median
Wilmington	24	1,825–17,716	7,392
Middletown	24	1,644–27,850	8,791
Bombay Hook	24	2,436–53,414	29,536
Cape Henlopen	23	995–13,950	6,072
Rehoboth	24	1,121–8068	3,093
STATEWIDE	24	13,463–90,459	56,022
(decreasing; low in 1989, high in 1985)			

WINTER: Feral flocks are enlarged in winter by wild birds that return in family groups after breeding on traditional grounds to the north. (See also "Canada Goose Management" essay.) The first regular wintering flocks in recent times appeared in 1949 at Taylors Bridge, where a domestic flock was used to hold them (Beck 1988).

DNREC records show an increase in winter population from 3,000 in the mid-1950s to 10,000 in 1959. Their aerial counts for November, December, and January from 1973 to 1988 show a clear reduction in the winter population from a peak in the late 1970s. A wildlife management project was initiated in 1983 by the USFWS, Delaware, and 7 other states in the region. This project neck-banded and tracked more than 50,000 geese, using also the established techniques of leg banding, wing surveys, and aerial surveys. The general findings of these studies strongly support the following conclusions:

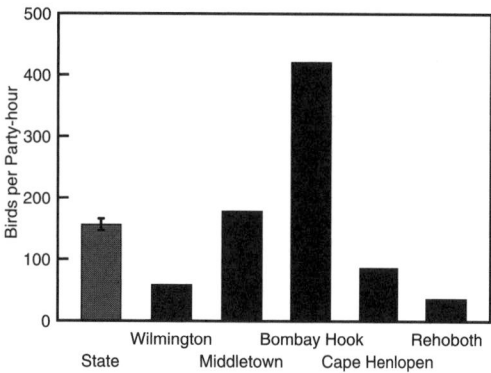

CBC Geographic Distribution

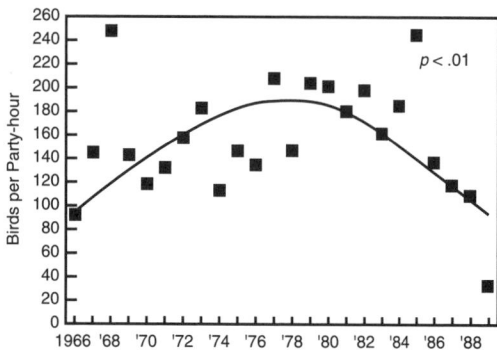

CBC Trend; Autocorrelation may Invalidate the Significance Test

1. The population of Canada Geese wintering in Delaware and Maryland is declining significantly.

2. The decline in the Delmarva Canada Goose flock is caused primarily by excessive hunting within the region.

3. Canada Geese are not "shifting" from Del-Mar-Va to another region.

4. Canada Geese have a strong fidelity to return to Del-Mar-Va as a wintering site (Alexander 1989).

Canada Goose hunting was reduced by lowering the daily bag to 2 birds and shortening the season to 70 days in 1988, down from 4 birds per day during a 90-day season for the previous 10 years.

Analysis of CBC data supports the findings of DNREC: the Canada Goose population has been declining during the past 10 years, currently at the rate of about 10% per year. Canada Geese are found most commonly on the Bombay Hook and Middleton CBCs. Seasonal non-CBC highs are

5 Dec 1987	10,000	Bombay Hook NWR [Barn54]
31 Jan 1982	20,000	Prime Hook NWR (notes)
6 Feb 1983	16,000	Bombay Hook NWR [Bayn3]

BANDING: Recoveries include 2,759 geese banded in Delaware and an additional 2,173 geese banded outside the state and recovered here. (See banding recovery map.)

REMARKS: The birds wintering on the Delmarva Peninsula come primarily from two populations: (1) the North Atlantic contingent, which breeds from "the Labrador Peninsula east of the height of land from Hopes Advance Bay to the north shore

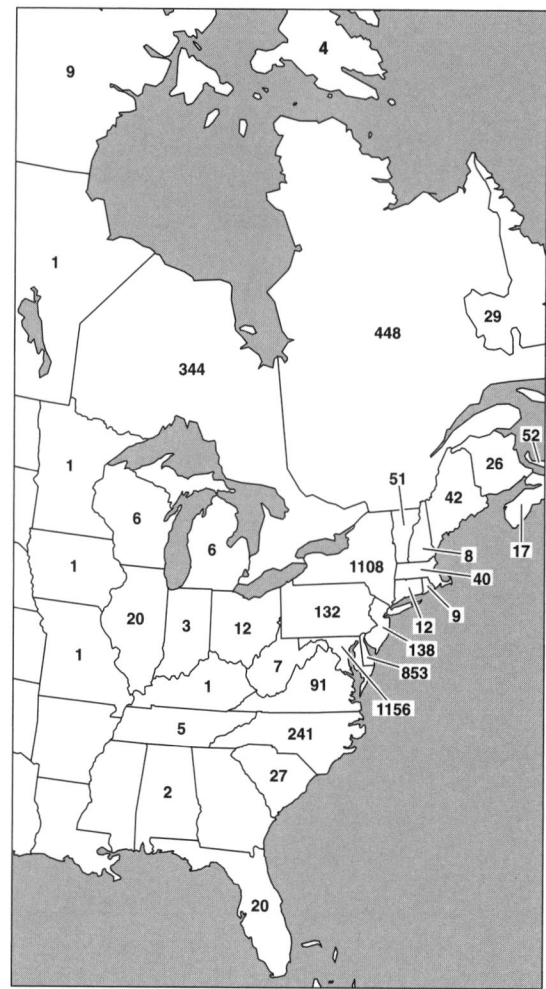

Total Canada Geese Either Banded or Recovered in Delaware, or Both

of the St. Lawrence . . . includ[ing] Newfoundland" (Todd 1963), and which winters south to New York, New Jersey, and Pea Island, North Carolina; (2) the Mid-Atlantic, which breeds primarily "in the tundra zone of the Ungava Peninsula, Quebec" (Addy and Heyland 1968, in Bellrose 1976, 144) and now south into Maine, and which winters in New England and central and western New York south to coastal Virginia and the Carolinas. Bellrose (1976) notes that an unknown number of North Atlantic birds winter on the Delmarva Peninsula, and that 537,000 Mid-Atlantic birds wintered there during 1970–75. He also notes that the primary wintering site for the Mid-Atlantic birds was Lake Mattamuskeet, North Carolina, during 1948–52; in 1953 a portion moved to Maryland. In 1965 North Carolina lost more birds to the Delmarva Peninsula. Bellrose's data indicate that 80% of the Mid-Atlantic population wintered on the Delmarva Peninsula during 1970–75.

Buckalew (notes) found a "Hutchin's Goose" (B.c. hutchinsii) at Fowlers Beach on 27 March 1948; Cutler reported one at Bombay Hook NWR (notes); Pennock's notes list one shot near Rehoboth Beach November 1874.

SPECIMENS: 24; DMNH, ANSP, UDEL, USNM.

Canada Goose Management

Norman G. Wilder

The spectacular rise in the number of Canada Geese in Delaware in the 1950s, 1960s, and 1970s came late in this species' long history here. Throughout the 1600s European visitors to Delaware Bay described the Canada Goose. Because these geese bred in the arctic regions and wintered as far south as the Gulf of Mexico, the birds recorded may have been either migrants or overwintering flocks.

Other than such scattered early records, little is known about the occurrence of this species in Delaware before the twentieth century. William Baxter, a noted hunter throughout Delaware in the early 1900s, barely mentions Canada Geese in his hunting log. Oral history indicates that there was sporadic goose hunting in the Indian River Bay area in the 1920s. In the 1930s, possibly earlier, a flock of about a thousand geese started to winter in and around Silver Lake at Rehoboth Beach, as did a flock of about a hundred birds at Fleetwood Pond near Concord. Both of these areas served as refuges where the geese were protected from hunting and other harassment. On the Whitely Farms north of Newark a breeding flock of captured birds was introduced in 1938 by S. Hallock du Pont. Their progeny appeared to enter the annual migration and to return to their natal site to breed.

In the 1930s most geese of the Atlantic Flyway were still wintering south of Maryland, but migration to the Gulf of Mexico was greatly reduced. The largest wintering flocks were in eastern North Carolina. From the 1920s through the 1940s the Lake Mattamuskeet area was known as the goose hunting capital of the world. Its winters were relatively mild, a federal refuge served as a haven for the birds, the lake was a source of fresh water, and the residue of crops harvested on surrounding farms provided ample food.

By the 1960s great Canada Goose concentrations at Mattamuskeet had become a thing of the past, because most geese could find all they needed for overwintering without flying as far as North Carolina. The eastern shore of Maryland became the major wintering ground of geese on the Atlantic Flyway. These population shifts were thought to be related to changes in land use that affected goose feeding, combined with possible overshooting at Mattamuskeet.

Before 1950 Canada Geese all but ignored Delaware, both as a resting area during migration and as a place to overwinter. Their absence was puzzling, since corn production here was high, and harvesting with corn pickers left substantial residue for wildlife. Thomas Rowan, a farmer who had moved to Taylors Bridge in southern New Castle County from the Eastern Shore of Maryland, observed geese flying high over his Delaware farm in the spring and fall but never landing there. Knowing from his Maryland experiences that flying geese could be decoyed by others on the ground, Rowan constructed a shallow freshwater pond in the middle of his largest cornfield and pinioned live geese there during the migration periods. His strategy was immediately successful. In the spring of 1950 Canada Geese landed on Rowan's farm and fed for a few days before continuing north to breed. The next fall geese were again attracted, and by the following year were wintering on his and surrounding farms. The combination of ample food, decoys, fresh water, and a degree of protection from human harassment had done the trick.

Rowan's simple technique was soon widely duplicated in Delaware, and a gradual buildup of geese followed. In the early 1960s aerial surveys conducted by the state showed 25,000 Canada Geese overwintering in Delaware, and the number doubled by the late 1960s and tripled by the late 1970s, with even more geese in occasional years. The increase was expedited by two factors: farmers could obtain assistance in pond building from the state Fish and Game Commission, and a system of federal, state, and private refuges was created as havens for geese.

It became apparent that geese could be hunted quite heavily without driving them away if adequate refuges with open water areas were established a few miles apart. By 1960 Delaware sustained throughout the fall, winter, and early spring large flocks of geese from Claymont to Fenwick Island, concentrated at unhunted resting areas at or near Whitely Farms, Hoopes Reservoir, Winterthur, the Appoquinimink-Blackbird marshes, Woodland Beach, Bombay Hook, Little Creek, Kitts Hummock, the Lewes marshes, Rehoboth Bay, Indian River Bay, and Little Assawoman Bay. Owners of lands surrounding these areas built hundreds of shallow ponds to attract geese, and some rented hunting privileges at fees above $2,000 per blind per season. Delaware goose hunting became a multimillion dollar business that attracted resident and nonresident hunters in unprecedented numbers. Hunting seasons were extended and bag limits were raised, reflecting what appeared to be an increasing number of geese in the Atlantic Flyway.

This fortunate combination of circumstances, from the hunters' standpoint, was too good to last. In the 1980s the number of overwintering geese in Delaware began to decline, leveling off at 30,000–40,000 in the late 1980s and early 1990s.

Data from studies in Delaware and elsewhere showed quite plainly that the number of geese killed by hunters had begun to reduce the production of goslings on the breeding grounds to a serious extent. Scientists had determined that a goose flock must have an annual survival rate of about 76% to maintain a stable population, and the survival rate for geese wintering in Delaware had declined from 82% in the 1960s to 64% in the late 1980s. More Canada Geese were being shot on Delaware cornfields in the winter than were being added to the population on Canadian nesting grounds in the summer. On Canada's Ungava Peninsula, the great goose breeding area, nesting success had been poor for nearly a decade. Reproductive success varies with the weather, and adverse conditions such as heavy snow cover in late spring had contributed to below-average hatching rates.

At the same time, states north of Delaware were instituting management techniques to hold geese that otherwise might have migrated farther south. On top of all this, new, more efficient models of corn pickers were leaving less residue for wildlife.

To stem the decline, the state reduced hunting pressure on Canada Geese by means of shorter seasons, lower bag limits, and establishment of additional refuges. These measures are certainly steps in the right direction, but it is too soon to determine their effect on the future of Delaware's wintering Canada Goose population.

Brant *(Branta bernicla)*

Regular; winter resident; common to abundant. Expected mid-October to early May.

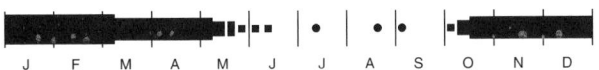

| J | F | M | A | M | J | J | A | S | O | N | D |

HABITAT: Shallow saltwater bays with eel grass or sea-lettuce.

SPRING: Bellrose (1976) gives a Chesapeake Bay migration period of 20 February–10 April, and a Brigantine NWR, New Jersey, period of late March to late April. Migration in Delaware probably begins mid- to late February or early March. The usual last departure is 10–20 May:

19 May 1989	35	Cape Henlopen SP [Frec1]
20 May 1980	8	Savages Ditch [Frec1]
20 May 1990	69	Sussex County [Barn54]

High counts in the Lewes area include 2,000 on 4 March 1980 and 5,000 on 5 and 7 March 1980 [Frec1], but after 1980 the spring counts are noticeably lower than those for winter.

SUMMER: Records include 1 (probably unfit) at Cape Henlopen on 9 July 1982 [Frec1] and puzzling reports of 13 on Rehoboth Bay on 13 June [Barn34] and 6 there on 17 August 1968 [Even1].

FALL: The usual first arrival is 10–15 October, when the birds begin to be reported regularly. The first 3 of these early records may pertain to summering birds:

4 Sep 1981	1	Roosevelt Inlet, Lewes [Frec1]
13 Sep 1970	6	Cape Henlopen SP [DuPG18]
6 Oct 1984	1	Cape Henlopen SP [Frec1]
11 Oct 1979	24	Cape Henlopen SP [Frec26]

The high count is 2000 at Indian River Inlet 8 November 1982 [Frec1].

1966–89 CBC Summary

Christmas Bird Count	Years Found	Range of No. Found	Median
Wilmington			
Middletown	4	1–250	
Bombay Hook	17	1–64	4
Cape Henlopen	21	1–864	55
Rehoboth	24	500–7,561	1,873
STATEWIDE *(low in 1978, high in 1973)*	24	678–7,762	2,121

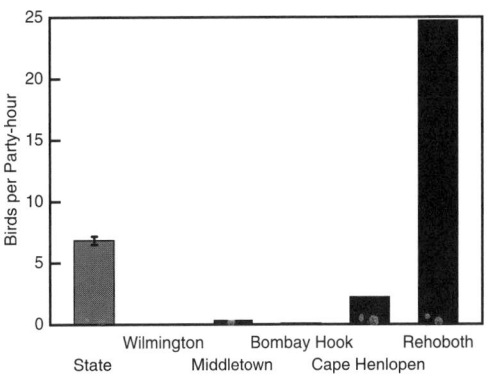

CBC Geographic Distribution; Average of 4 Count Areas

WINTER: A peak occurs from January to early March as southern birds move north. Sample high counts during this period are

24 Jan 1970	1,800	along the coast [Holg44]
Jan, Feb 1980	up to 6,000	Sussex County coast [Frec1]
20 Feb 1982	5,000	Sussex County coast [Frec1]
5 Feb 1984	3,000	Sussex County coast [Frec1]
27 Jan 1985	2,000	Sussex County coast [Frec1]

Bellrose (1976) notes that 3,500 birds winter on the Delaware Bay—a reasonable estimate, although we do not have baywide data.

Analyses of CBC data show no long-term trend; the numbers present vary greatly from year to year. The Brant is found most commonly on the Rehoboth and Cape Henlopen CBCs.

BANDING: Delaware recoveries include 7 banded in wintering areas (4 on Long Island, 3 on coastal New Jersey) and 73 banded on breeding grounds (69 on Southhampton Island at the upper part of Hudson Bay and 4 on islands farther north).

SPECIMENS: 12; DMNH, USNM.

Barnacle Goose *(Branta leucopsis)*

Casual (7 years, 1965–86), late fall and winter.

DOCUMENTATION: Convincing notes.

REMARKS: This Eurasian goose has been recorded 7 times in Delaware, all at Bombay Hook NWR. Published field notes that are convincing as to identification document occurrences on 13 November–26 December 1973 and 1–26 January 1980 (Holgersen 1974; Barnhill and Gordon 1979) [Pero1]. Other occurrences, all of single birds at Bombay Hook NWR, are

13 Nov 1965	[Paul1]
25 Nov 1967	[Higm1]
14 Dec 1982 to 2 Jan 1983	[SmiP1]
5–6 Feb 1986	[CutH2]
20 Feb 1982	[Cutl6]

Barnacle Geese breed in eastern Greenland and normally winter in Europe (AOU 1983). Whether North American records of Barnacle Geese concern wild birds or escapes remains undetermined and controversial. Since they occur in Greenland, straying to North America is plausible. Barnacle Goose is the most frequently recorded exotic goose on the East Coast but is not similarly represented in captivity. We therefore infer that most of these records are likely to refer to wild birds. To our knowledge no special effort has been made to determine whether any of these birds were escapes.

Mute Swan *(Cygnus olor)*

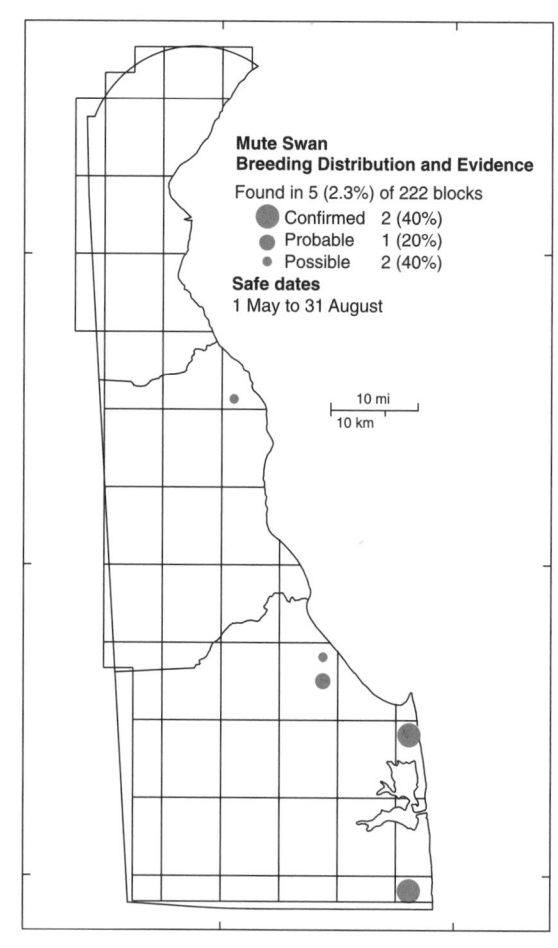

Mute Swan
Breeding Distribution and Evidence
Found in 5 (2.3%) of 222 blocks
● Confirmed   2 (40%)
● Probable   1 (20%)
• Possible   2 (40%)
Safe dates
1 May to 31 August

10 mi
10 km

Resident; locally uncommon to fairly common. Introduced.

DOCUMENTATION: Sight and nest records.

HABITAT: Fresh ponds and impoundments. Sheltered bays and estuaries, especially during freezes.

BREEDING: The Mute Swan was most numerous in Delaware in the 1970s and occurred in all 3 counties.

Atlas. During the Atlas project it was most often seen at Assawoman WA or at Gordon Pond WA in Cape Henlopen SP. Cygnets were found in those 2 blocks. Birds usually begin breeding in their third to fifth year (Palmer 1976, 2: 43), so some reports may refer to nonbreeders.

Nesting. The Mute Swan builds a large nest of stems and straw, usually mounded up on an islet in a coastal impoundment. Young a week or two old have been noted 7 and 29 May, and a female was incubating 25 May.

History. This species was introduced from Europe as a decorative bird. It first became established on Long Island, New York, beginning in 1912 (Bull 1974). In Delaware feral Mute Swans were first reported on 22 August 1954 near Rehoboth Beach [Terb1], and feral nesting was first reported on 3 July 1965 when 1 gray and 5 white cygnets were seen at Assawoman WA [King1]. Maximum counts are

30 Dec 1972	69	Rehoboth CBC
29 Sep 1973	77	Assawoman WA [Holg57]
11 May 1974	42	May Count (Barnhill 1975)

The population level then plunged; none was found on any Delaware CBC in 1982. Numbers remained low during the 1980s, reaching a peak of 14 reported at Broadkill Beach on 10 May 1989 [Frec1]. More than 10 were seen along the Delaware coast on 16 July 1991 [Barn1].

Breeding population. Though the population in Delaware has fluctuated, fewer than 5 breeding pairs were present during most of the 1980s.

Conservation. These beautiful exotics from Eurasia give pleasure when seen in a park, garden, or farm pond. However, if the owner allows them or their progeny to escape, they may degrade impoundments managed for wild ducks. When feeding, they uproot much aquatic vegetation, and there is speculation that these swans "eat out" ponds and otherwise render them less useful for other waterfowl (Reese 1975; Palmer 1976, 2: 46). This view has been somewhat rebutted by a study in Connecticut that concluded that Mute Swans feed on different vegetation and at different water depth than native waterfowl (O'Brien and Askins 1985), but this opinion has not been accepted by the game management community.

The Mute Swan is not endangered in Delaware but represents a small introduced population of a robust and widespread species.

1966–89 CBC Summary

Christmas Bird Count	Years Found	Range of No. Found	Median
Wilmington			
Middletown			
Bombay Hook	14	1–36	1
Cape Henlopen	6	1–9	
Rehoboth	17	2–69	9
STATEWIDE	22	1–93	11
(zero in 1982 and 1989, high in 1972)			

WINTER: Analyses of CBC data show irregular numbers.

[Trumpeter Swan *(Cygnus buccinator)*]

---

with Gregory A. Inskip

Formerly present in the region, but no acceptable Delaware records.

DOCUMENTATION: Unsatisfactory published notes.

REMARKS: The Trumpeter Swan was formerly a winter resident along the Atlantic coast. Some authorities have mapped its distribution as extending from New Jersey to North Carolina, including Delaware (Banko 1960, 26; Bellrose 1976, 89). In 1709, Lawson (1967, 150) found both "trumpeter" and "hooper" (Tundra) swans wintering in early eighteenth-century coastal North Carolina. Bones of both species (1 individual each) were found in a seventeenth-century Susquehannock Indian midden at Washington Boro, Lancaster County, Pennsylvania (Guilday, Parmalee, and Tanner 1962, 61). Banko (1960, 20) stated that there are "enough acceptable records" to establish the Trumpeter Swan's occurrence as a transient or winter resident in Maryland, Virginia, and North Carolina during the last half of the nineteenth century.

"Reliable sportsmen" told Turnbull (1869, 45) that they had "shot it on the Chesapeake, as also Delaware Bay," though by the mid-nineteenth century it was a "rare straggler" at best. A Trumpeter Swan was reported in Lincoln, Delaware, on 9 November 1886 (Cooke 1906, in Pennock 1908b, 284). A similar report (of the same bird?) concerns 1 shot out of a flock of 12–15 at Slaughter Beach Marsh on 8 November 1889 by Stevens, of Lincoln, Delaware; published measurements are so garbled that the species cannot be distinguished (Stevens 1890). The AOU Check-list (3d ed., 1910) included this species as accidental in Delaware (possibly on the basis of the Lincoln report), but the sixth edition does not include Delaware in its former range (AOU 1983). Bellrose (1976) simply states that it wintered "on Chesapeake Bay and Currituck Sound" in the East.

The Trumpeter Swan was extirpated in the East as a result of heavy exploitation for food and skins on both its inland breeding grounds and coastal wintering grounds (Palmer 1976, 2: 60). Restoration efforts in the eastern part of its breeding range (Hindeman 1985; Nichols 1990; Lumsden 1991; Mitchell 1994) may result in its wintering again along the Mid-Atlantic coast.

Tundra Swan (*Cygnus columbianus*)

Regular; winter resident; fairly common to common. Expected early November to late March. The winter population is apparently decreasing after peaking in the early 1980s.

HABITAT: Coastal impoundments and millponds, grain fields, Delaware River.

SPRING: Last departure is usually 20–25 March. Last reports of flocks include

24 Mar 1978	50	near Blackbird and 50 near Smyrna [Patt4]
31 Mar 1975	50	Little Creek WA [Pure1]
12 Apr 1975	65	Dragon Run [Dyer1]

Swans in Chesapeake Bay leave from early March to early April, with the peak about mid-March (Bellrose 1976; Stewart and Robbins 1958). Typical counts involve fewer than 20 birds. Peak counts take place 15–20 January to 15–20 February. High counts include

3–20 Jan 1983	3,000	near Middletown [Usfw5]
26 Jan 1974	900	Killens Pond SP [Holg84]
6 Feb 1973	1,500	near Bowers Beach [Pure3]

SUMMER: The Tundra Swan nests on arctic tundra from Alaska east to Baffin Island and the northwest coast of Quebec. One or 2 birds are occasionally reported in Delaware from May through September. Some of these may be sick or injured birds or Mute Swans that have been misidentified.

FALL: Bellrose (1976) states that Chesapeake Bay swans pass Minnesota, Wisconsin, and Michigan mainly during 5–15 November. Thus the absence of early fall records in Delaware is expected. First arrival may be 1–10 November but more often is 15–30 November. Early fall arrivals are obscured by a few summering individuals, but the following flocks were probably migrants:

10 Oct 1987	10	Little Creek WA [Barn60]
21 Oct 1980	7	Cape Henlopen SP [Frec34]
27 Oct 1962	6	Woodland Beach [Less17]

A flock of 44 reported on 12 September 1966 should have been reported as Mute Swans [Lake8], and 6 reported on 23 August 1973 [Pure15] may have been similarly confused.

High counts include

3 Nov 1971	398	Bombay Hook NWR [Holg11]
16 Nov 1969	1,100	Bombay Hook NWR [Holg42]
27 Nov 1983	400	Bowers Beach [Edni18]

Typical counts total 50 birds.

1966–89 CBC Summary

Christmas Bird Count	Years Found	Range of No. Found	Median
Wilmington	5	1–27	
Middletown	20	4–1,593	111
Bombay Hook	22	1–558	22
Cape Henlopen	12	2–79	
Rehoboth	19	2–70	7
STATEWIDE	23	6–1,995	238
(decreasing; zero in 1968, high in 1979)			

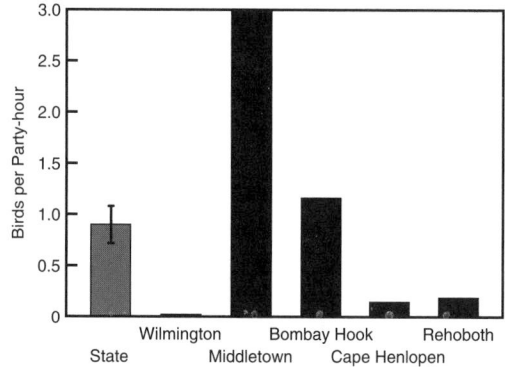

CBC Geographic Distribution

WINTER: Bellrose (1976) notes that 40,000 winter on Chesapeake Bay, making it the most important wintering site in the Atlantic Flyway. He also indicates that fewer than 100 birds winter in Delaware and New Jersey. However, for the period December–February there are at least 36 Delaware observations of flocks totaling 100 or more birds. For example, during 3–20 January 1983 the USFWS survey recorded 3,000 swans statewide [Usfw5]. Holgersen [Holg78] noted thousands feeding in fields in the western third of the state during January and February 1973. On 6 February 1973 1,500 were reported from Bowers Beach [Pure3]. Also of note are 1,593 recorded on the 1979 Middletown CBC. The average number present in the state for the winter period is slightly greater than 100. Based on 1-day counts, with no sustained counts from a single area, it is

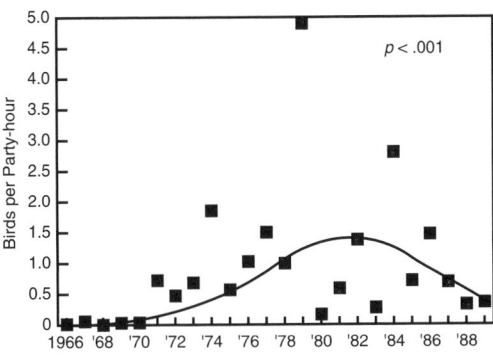

p < .001

CBC Trend

Analyses of CBC data indicate an upward trend that peaked in the early 1980s, followed by a downward trend. Tundra Swans are abundant on the Seaford CBC, averaging more than 900 birds during 1983–89. Along the Delaware River they are found most commonly on the Middletown and Bombay Hook CBCs.

BANDING: Delaware recoveries of swans banded out of state include 9 banded on wintering areas (6 near Chesapeake Bay, 3 on coastal North Carolina) and 2 banded along the migration corridor (Michigan 1, Ohio 1).

SPECIMENS: UDEL 438-72, near Odessa, 2 February 1972; DMNH 76555, Seaford, 12 March 1987; UDEL 112-67, Bombay Hook, December 1966; DMNH 52566, Bombay Hook, early 1970s.

not possible to determine how many birds are wintering and how many are foraging visitors.

Wood Duck *(Aix sponsa)*

Regular; summer resident; fairly common. Expected late February to mid-November, increasingly scarce thereafter.

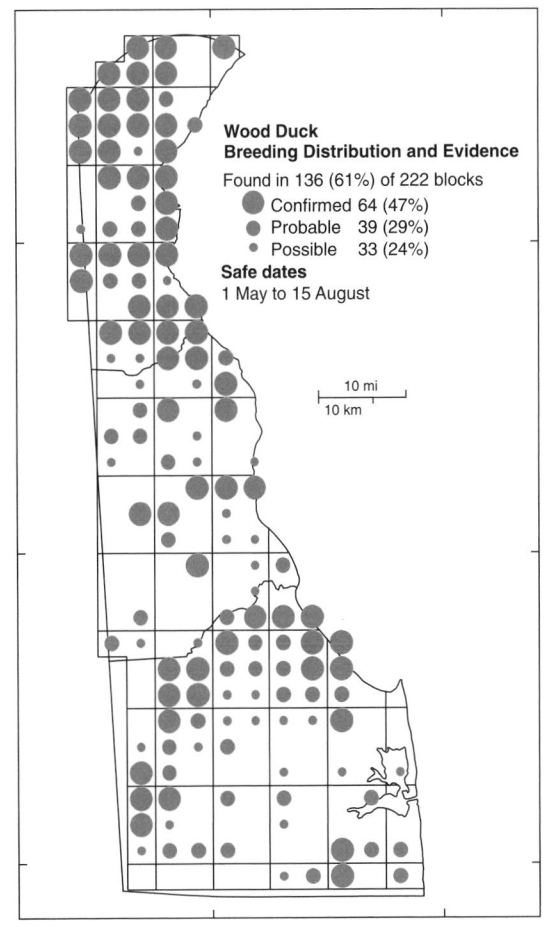

**Wood Duck
Breeding Distribution and Evidence**
Found in 136 (61%) of 222 blocks
● Confirmed 64 (47%)
● Probable 39 (29%)
· Possible 33 (24%)
Safe dates
1 May to 15 August

10 mi
10 km

HABITAT: Wooded wetlands and ponds. Typically breeds near water and trees with cavities. Not found in saltmarshes, but present in a wooded impoundment in Assawoman WA, in the fresh Finis impoundment in Bombay Hook NWR, and above the dam in Dragon Run—all areas that were once tidal marshes.

SPRING: First arrival is usually 20 February–1 March. Bellrose (1976) indicates that the migration period for the Mid-Atlantic region occurs during February. The few data available indicate that migration in Delaware is just beginning in Febru-

ary. Early counts of more than 3 birds (less likely to include overwintering birds) are

7 Feb 1991	4	Greenville [BroH1]
13 Feb 1932	4	Smalleys Dam [Hans1]
14 Feb 1990	5	Bombay Hook NWR [Holg2]

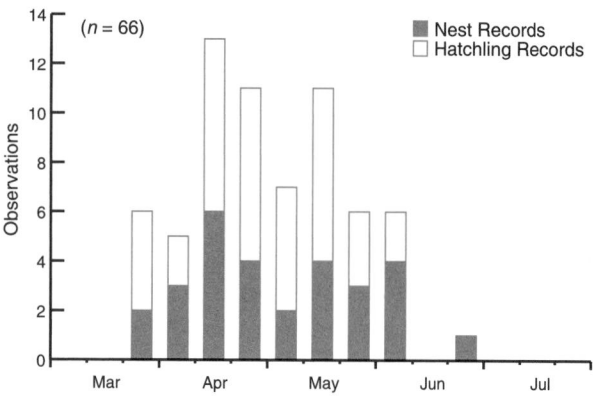

Estimated Clutch-Completion Dates

High counts are

2 Mar 1975	30	Dragon Run [SpSB1]
13 Mar 1965	25	Churchmans Marsh [Klab10]
22 Mar 1975	74	Dragon Run [Wayn2]

BREEDING: This is perhaps our most numerous and certainly most beautiful breeding duck. Delaware has many wooded wetlands and streams ideal for the production of Wood Ducks, and nesting occurs in all parts of the state.

Atlas. The Atlas results show Wood Ducks breeding in 61% of the blocks. It may have been unrecorded in perhaps another 10% in blocks because of the difficulty of obtaining access to wooded areas of farms. It was most easily confirmed by seeing or being told of ducklings with adults.

Nesting. The Wood Duck nests in cavities in trees and readily accepts nest boxes. Down is added as a lining over the natural litter in the cavity.

In Delaware the extrapolated clutch-completion period extends from late March to early June, with 1 late-June record; most were completed mid-April to mid-May. One exceptionally late brood of "seven young Wood Ducks swimming with their parents" on 4 August 1982 [SpeE3] is perhaps late enough to be a second brood. The same is true of Eastman's (1915) report of "several broods of little ones" during the latter part of July. Rogers and Hanson (1967) observed banded Wood Ducks incubating second clutches in Missouri and summarized similar reports from several other states including Maryland. They conclude that "second broods apparently occur regularly among Wood Ducks but are too few to be a significant production factor. However, the fact that they occur shows that these birds are extremely persistent renesters with the urge to renest extending well into the brood rearing period in some instances." About 10% are double brooded in the southeast (Hepp and Bellrose 1995). Clutch sizes reported in Delaware range from 9 to 13 (*n* = 4).

History. Partly as a result of springtime hunting, the Wood Duck was in serious decline in much of its range earlier in the twentieth century, and ornithologists and conservationists were so alarmed by the virtual disappearance of this duck that

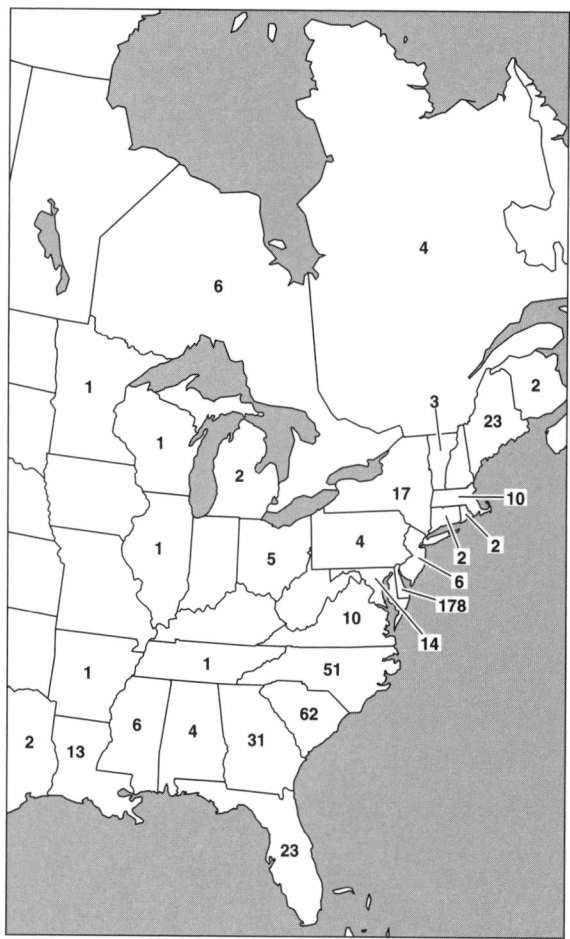

Total Wood Ducks Either Banded or Recovered in Delaware, or Both

they voiced fears of extinction (Bellrose 1976). Wood Ducks bred near Delaware City in 1903 [Penn1], and an adult and 6 young were seen near Medford Mills 3 July 1904 [Cart1]. They were still present in 1908 near Rehoboth Beach, where Pennock (notes) saw 3 on 27 May and heard from the landowner that 100 or 200 appeared there almost every evening. Eastman (1915) wrote that "they were fast relegating to the rare list in many sections" but went on to describe their regular summer occurrence on a millpond near Wilmington.

Wood Ducks were given complete protection from 1918 to 1941, and the population recovered remarkably as a result of this protection and new habitat management programs.

Trends. The Wood Duck has clearly recovered from low numbers earlier in the twentieth century. Its population increased in the East and Upper Coastal Plain for 1966–90 [Usfw1]. The Delaware BBS for the same period encountered too few Wood Ducks for reliable analysis. Delaware May Count data, based on an average sample of 80 birds per year, show an average annual increase of 2% for 1969–91.

Breeding population. Wood Ducks are very difficult to survey by traditional ground or air methods of the wildlife biologist (Bellrose 1976). Sutherland (1971), using indirect methods, estimated the Delaware 1965 population at 2,500 pairs (in Bellrose 1976). The Atlas results are consistent with this estimate and the estimated population trend.

Conservation. NWR personnel and many citizens have set up nest boxes, which Wood Ducks readily accept.

Much obviously productive forested wetland has been destroyed as the water table in Sussex County has been lowered by means of the tax ditch system. This drainage converts wooded wetland to agricultural fields.

FALL: Bellrose (1976) indicates that migration in the Mid-Atlantic region occurs from October to early December. Our data show that most birds leave by the last half of November. High counts at Dragon Run are 140 on 21 September 1975, 126 on 6 October 1974, and 101 on 2 November 1974 [Wayn2].

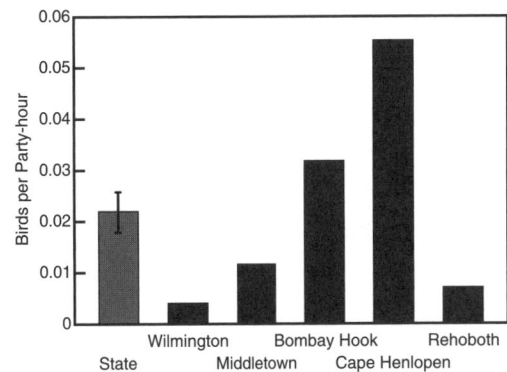

CBC Geographic Distribution

1966–89 CBC Summary

Christmas Bird Count	Years Found	Range of No. Found	Median
Wilmington	7	1–4	
Middletown	9	1–6	
Bombay Hook	24	1–7	2
Cape Henlopen	17	1–45	1
Rehoboth	7	1–5	
STATEWIDE (low in 1966, high in 1979)	24	2–48	6

WINTER: Winter levels are reached by late November and are sustained until late December or early January. Few reports are available from mid-January to the end of February. The CBC trend analysis shows an increasing tendency parallel to May Count results. This trend is partly obscured by a 1979 high count 6 times greater than the average number of birds per hour. The Wood Duck is found most commonly on the Cape Henlopen and Bombay Hook CBCs. Seasonal non-CBC highs are

6 Dec 1975	8	Dragon Run [Beac2]
17 Dec 1981	25	Prime Hook NWR (notes)
20 Feb 1983	12	Bombay Hook NWR [Hess21]
24 Feb 1974	9	Dragon Run [Citr1]

BANDING: Recoveries include 406 banded in Delaware and 91 banded elsewhere. These data indicate that the main wintering areas for Wood Ducks breeding in or passing through Delaware are North and South Carolina, Georgia, and Florida, with fewer birds moving west through the Gulf states.

SPECIMENS: 19; DMNH, USNM. Egg records: WFVZ.

Gadwall *(Anas strepera)*

Resident; uncommon (breeding season) to fairly common (migration, winter). Migrates primarily during October–November and March–April. A disjunct breeding population, first recorded in 1939, is now established in Delaware and the East.

HABITAT: Ponds, lakes, impoundments, brackish ponds; nesting primarily in tidal marshes associated with impoundments.

SPRING: Bellrose (1976) notes that Gadwalls start to leave winter areas in February, with most gone by late April. This migration pattern is reflected in Delaware by an increase in reports beginning the last week of February and lasting through the first half of April. Some high counts are

22 Feb 1967	1,200	Little Creek WA [Line14]
4 Apr 1964	630	Little Creek WA [LesC4]
15 Apr 1971	600	Bombay Hook NWR [Holg7]

Daily counts are often in the range of 50–100.

BREEDING: Small numbers frequent impoundments and marshes in Kent and Sussex Counties.

Atlas. Gadwalls were found mostly from Bombay Hook NWR to Prime Hook NWR and in smaller numbers south to Assawoman WA. Confirmations, including 7 broods and 4 nests, were made primarily by wildlife biologists.

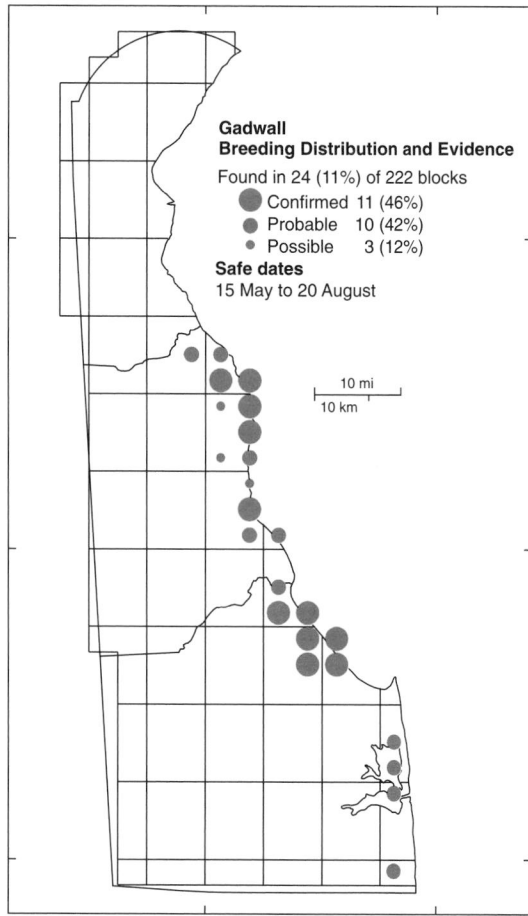

Gadwall
Breeding Distribution and Evidence
Found in 24 (11%) of 222 blocks
● Confirmed 11 (46%)
● Probable 10 (42%)
· Possible 3 (12%)
Safe dates
15 May to 20 August

10 mi
10 km

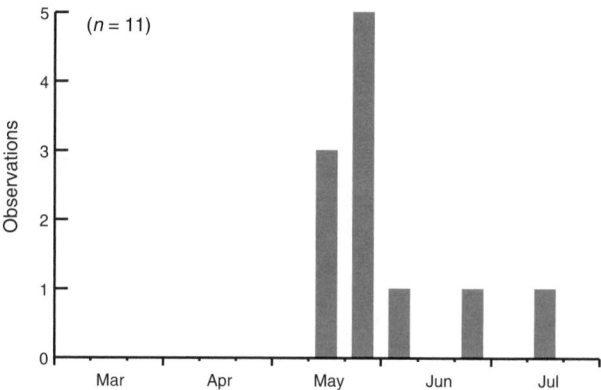

Estimated Clutch-Completion Dates

Nesting. Most nests were found in brackish tidal marshes, though one was in an upland field containing blackberry and Canada thistle. Henny and Holgersen (1974) state that *Spartina patens–Spartina alterniflora* marshes are ideal nesting areas for Gadwall. Griffith (1946) noted that in the 1940s the nests at Bombay Hook were built in saltmarshes and contrasted that placement with the Gadwall's nests on the prairie, which are built on dry ground "never near water" (Kortwright 1942).

Clutch completion peaks in late May, but replacement clutches extend the season. Extreme egg dates are 1 June 1983 [MerW1] and 8 eggs on 25 July 1988 [Peli1], both at Bombay Hook NWR. Early broods of 8 and 11 were observed 13 June 1965 [Hard9], indicating clutches completed by mid-May.

History. The Gadwall, mainly a bird of the northern prairies, became established as a breeding bird in Delaware and along the East Coast beginning in 1939. Wilson (1859–60) stated that he was unaware of where it bred. Rhoads and Pennock (1905) did not include it for any season in their early Delaware bird list, although Krider (1879, 73) remarked "not common in Delaware. They winter in Virginia." Hanson (notes) records its being shot in winter by J. N. DeHaven at Rehoboth Beach from 1874 to 1877; by Dr. Spencer Trotter near Rehoboth Beach on 12 December 1912; and by Buckalew, who obtained a pair at Fowler Beach on 15 March 1935. It was equally scarce in southern New Jersey (Stone 1937).

Its early breeding history at Bombay Hook NWR is as follows: female with 7 3-day old chicks on 24 June 1939; pair but no brood in 1940; 9 pairs and 6 broods on Raymond Pool, Bombay Hook NWR in 1941; 30 pairs on 8 April and 8 broods in 1942; at least 20 young in 1943, but military use interfered with observation that year; 4 broods in 1945 (Griffith 1946). Breeding has probably occurred every year since. An increase in breeding was reported when the impoundment was built at Little Creek WA: 1 brood in 1960 (Tindall 1961), 25 broods in 1962 (Lesser 1964), and 2 broods in 1965 [Hard9]. Whittendale reported 173 young were produced in 1962, 272 in 1969, 307 in 1970, 648 in 1971, and 310 in 1972 at Little Creek WA (Henny and Holgersen 1974). Similar breeding population increases occurred in the Atlantic Flyway from Massachusetts to South Carolina. Henny and Holgersen attribute this establishment and increase in breeding to the creation of a number of federal and state impoundments in former saltmarshes but suggest that this process was accelerated by transplant activities at some refuges in neighboring states.

Trends. The May Count, taken after the spring migration, shows an average annual decline of 5% for the period 1969–91.

Breeding population. During the Atlas period it was found sparingly in 24 blocks, and the state breeding population was probably below 100 pairs. In 1971 (a year of high breeding success), 2,800 breeding pairs were estimated in the Atlantic Flyway, including 300 at Bombay Hook NWR (Henny and Holgersen 1974).

FALL: Bellrose (1976) notes that those wintering in Chesapeake Bay arrive by the end of October, whereas those wintering in South Carolina and south arrive in numbers in early November. Our data reveal an increase in reports in mid-October and increased numbers about 5 November to 5 December. Some high counts are

15 Sep 1972	1,500	Bombay Hook NWR [Holg75]
27 Sep 1972	1,500	Bombay Hook NWR [Holg13]
27 Oct 1974	1,000	Dragon Run [SpSB1]
10 Nov 1946	1,000	Bombay Hook NWR [Pott1]

Typical daily counts run 75–200.

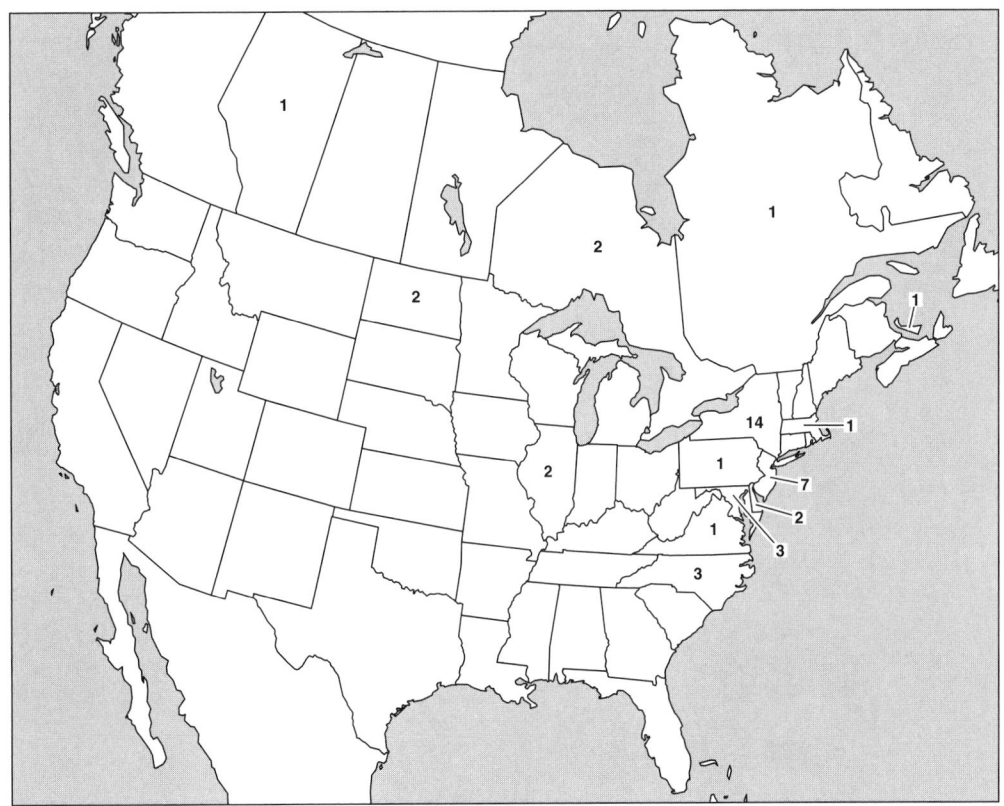

Total Gadwalls Either Banded or Recovered in Delaware, or Both

1966–89 CBC Summary

Christmas Bird Count	Years Found	Range of No. Found	Median
Wilmington	3	1–2	
Middletown	10	1–26	
Bombay Hook	24	1–1,517	107
Cape Henlopen	17	1–245	7
Rehoboth	20	1–145	20
STATEWIDE (low in 1968, high in 1971)	24	2–1,617	190

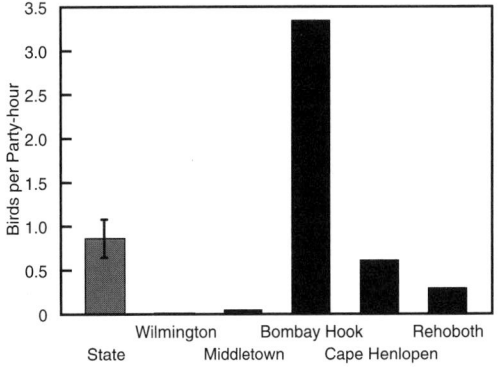

CBC Geographic Distribution

WINTER: The CBC data reflect a considerable fluctuation in early winter numbers with no long-term trend. It is most abundant on the Bombay Hook CBC. Bellrose (1976) states that about 1,000 winter in the Chesapeake Bay area and few north of there, but his figures do not fully reflect the recent establishment of an eastern breeding population. Non-CBC highs are

29 Jan 1955	500	Bombay Hook NWR [Abbo8]
9 Feb 1975	110	Dragon Run [BroW21]
12 Feb 1989	50	Island Farm, Prime Hook NWR [Frec1]

Typical winter reports do not exceed 10–15 birds.

BANDING: Banding recoveries in Delaware include individuals banded as flightless young in Maryland, New York, New Jersey, Massachusetts, Ontario, Prince Edward Island, North Carolina, and North Dakota. Recoveries include 7 birds banded in Delaware and 34 banded elsewhere. This suggests that about 80% of our fall and winter Gadwalls have been birds produced from the newly established Atlantic Flyway population, and

that fluctuation in its numbers is influenced by East Coast conditions.

SPECIMENS: USNM 421915, Milton, 15 March 1932; DMNH 72856, 72852, Abbotts Pond, SW of Milford, 7 December 1980.

Eurasian Wigeon (*Anas penelope*)

Occasional (36 years, 1928–93); migrant; rare.

DOCUMENTATION: Notes.

HABITAT: Fresh and brackish ponds and impoundments.

REMARKS: This species usually occurs from October to April, but stragglers continue until June. A pair summered from 24 June to 30 July 1960 at Bombay Hook NWR [JonW1]. It attempted to winter at Assawoman WA in the 1960s and occurred on 7 Rehoboth CBCs. Early arrival dates are

27 Oct 1991	1	Little Creek WA [PeBG2]
17 Oct 1976	1	Little Creek WA [Hurl1]
17 Oct 1982	4	Bombay Hook NWR [Palm1]

Typically, only 1 or 2 are present in association with American Wigeon. They usually remain a few days, rarely a month. Banded Eurasian Wigeons from Iceland, its nearest known breeding site, have been recorded in Canada and the United States, and probably most vagrants to eastern North America are from Iceland (Cramp 1977, 475).

This species was not listed for Delaware by Rhoads and Pennock (1905), so the observation of 1 at Delaware City on 17 March 1928 [Hiat1] appears to be Delaware's first record. It was recorded 4 times in the 1930s and once in 1940.

American Wigeon (*Anas americana*)

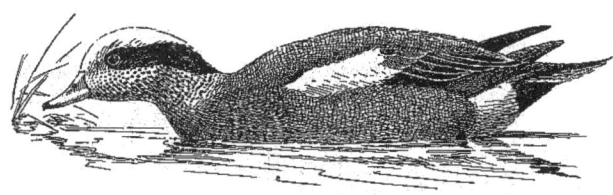

Regular; fairly common (winter visitor) to common (migrant). Expected early September to mid-April. Sporadic and rare breeder. Winter numbers declining from a peak in the mid-1970s.

HABITAT: Brackish and fresh ponds and impoundments.

SPRING: Birds wintering in the south begin to arrive at staging areas in early March, peak the first half of April, and then decline abruptly (Bellrose 1976). In Delaware numbers of American Wigeon begin to increase 20–30 January; high numbers are usually present from 5–10 March to 10–15 April—the following February high count is unusually early. Some high counts are

22 Feb 1967	7,500	Little Creek WA [Line14]
9 Mar 1963	2,000	Little Creek WA [Davi21]
4 Apr 1964	5,000	Little Creek WA [LesC4]

Typical daily counts total about 150 birds. Occurrence after mid-April is sporadic; flocks reported in May include

4 May 1929	4	Delaware City [Wort1]
5 May 1973	22	Little Creek WA [John8]
5 May 1991	6	Little Creek WA [Camp1]

BREEDING: The only published Delaware breeding record for American Wigeon describes a brood of 6 young at Assawoman WA on 12 August 1962 [Kofe1]. A pair also spent the summer of 1964 there, but no breeding was observed [Dyke12]. At least 1 breeding pair was present at Little Creek WA in the early 1970s (K. Reynolds, DNREC, pers. comm.)

Its principal breeding range is the prairies of northwestern North America. It became a very rare and local breeder on the East Coast about 1960.

History. George Ord, in his edition of Wilson's *American Ornithology,* relates that "a few breed annually in the neighborhood of Duck Creek, in the state of Delaware. An acquaintance brought me thence, in the month of June, an egg, which had been taken from a nest situated in a cluster of alders. The nest contained eleven eggs" (Wilson and Bonaparte [1859–60], ed. by George Ord). Stone (1937) suggests the egg must have come from an American Black Duck nest.

FALL: Bellrose (1976) states that the first birds arrive at their winter quarters in late September or early October, with a steady increase through the fall. In Delaware the first arrival is usually 1–10 September, with these earliest arrivals recorded:

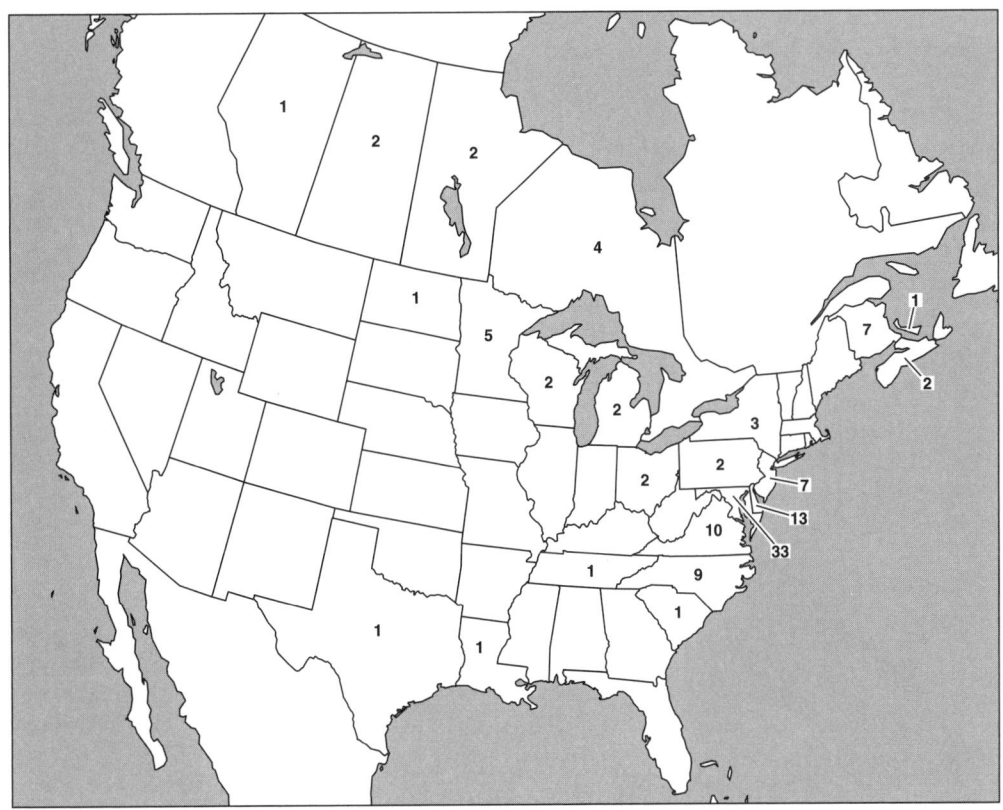

Total American Wigeon Either Banded or Recovered in Delaware, or Both

3 Sep 1989	6	Broadkill Beach [Frec1]
4 Sep 1957	4	Thousand Acre Marsh [Orin1]
4 Sep 1965	1	Churchmans Marsh [Broo27]

High numbers are quickly reached and maintained through November. Some high counts are

17 Oct 1982	355	Bombay Hook NWR [Wayn25]
20 Oct 1971	1,500	Bombay Hook NWR [Holg54]
28 Nov 1953	350	Rehoboth Beach [Davi5]

Typical daily counts total 50–100 birds.

1966–89 CBC Summary

Christmas Bird Count	Years Found	Range of No. Found	Median
Wilmington	7	1–9	
Middletown	16	1–250	3
Bombay Hook	24	1–3,152	97
Cape Henlopen	18	2–130	2
Rehoboth	22	2–300	37
STATEWIDE	24	18–3,176	187
(decreasing; low in 1986, high in 1977)			

WINTER: The CBC data suggest a downward trend after a peak in the mid-1970s. During the late 1960s and early 1970s many Chesapeake Bay birds shifted their wintering grounds to Currituck Sound, North Carolina (Bellrose 1976). No doubt many Delaware birds did likewise. On the Atlantic Coast most American Wigeons winter in South and North Carolina and Florida, with smaller numbers wintering north along the coast

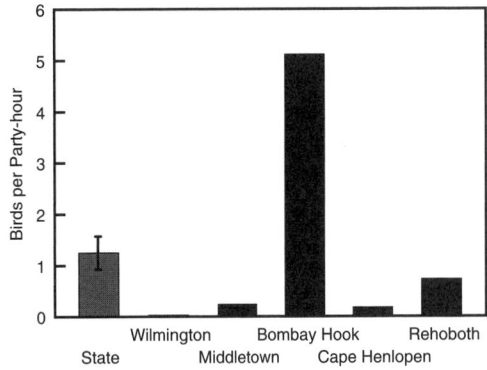

CBC Geographic Distribution

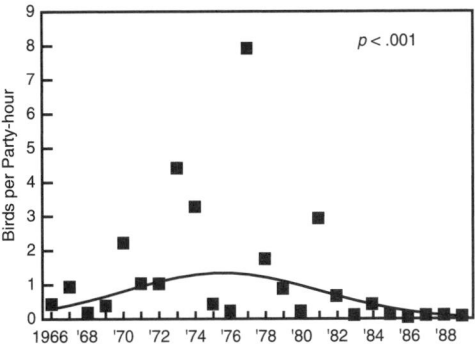

CBC Trend

as far as Connecticut (Bellrose 1976). They are most numerous on the Bombay Hook CBC. High non-CBC reports are

21 Dec 1978	231	Prime Hook NWR (notes)
29 Dec 1952	125	Rehoboth Beach [Davi3]
24 Jan 1952	180	Rehoboth Beach [Davi1]

Typically, few are present from mid-December to mid-January.

BANDING: Recoveries include 83 birds banded in Delaware and 29 banded as flightless young in New Brunswick, Nova Scotia, Prince Edward Island, North Dakota, Alberta, and Saskatchewan.

SPECIMENS: USNM 422170, Milton, 1 February 1932; USNM 421859, Milton, 5 December 1931.

American Black Duck *(Anas rubripes)*

Resident; fairly common to common. Winter population apparently declining.

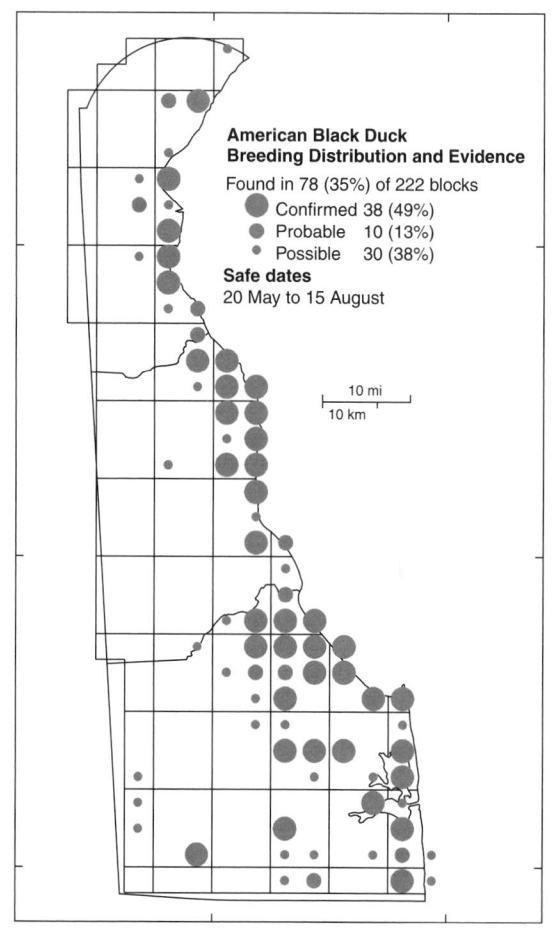

American Black Duck
Breeding Distribution and Evidence
Found in 78 (35%) of 222 blocks
● Confirmed 38 (49%)
● Probable 10 (13%)
• Possible 30 (38%)
Safe dates
20 May to 15 August

10 mi
10 km

HABITAT: Breeding: fresh to salt tidal (estuarine) marshes, palustrine wooded wetlands. Wintering: nearly all kinds of marshes, ponds, streams, occasionally open bays.

SPRING: Migration begins mid-February to early March and continues through late April. A historic high count was 500 at Delaware City on 10 April 1926 [Emle1]. The next reports of comparable numbers made were on 28 March 1964, when 344 were observed at Little Creek WA [StiA4], and on 3 March 1971, when 475 were recorded at Prime Hook NWR (notes).

BREEDING: The American Black Duck breeds primarily in the Delaware River and Bay marshes, but some breed in the Atlantic coastal marshes, the Nanticoke drainage, and in other wet woods on the Coastal Plain.

Nesting. A nest along Indian River was described as "among round grass [*Juncus*] on the side of river backwash. Nest made up of small stems and down, also oak leaves" (WFVZ egg data). Nest locations extend from tidal marshes to wooded swamp.

Extrapolated clutch-completion dates suggest peak breeding activity from the last few days of April through mid-May. Extreme dates are 13 eggs found on 5 April 1938 at Bombay Hook NWR [Buck1] and 10 eggs being incubated on 27 June 1988 at Bombay Hook NWR [Peli1]. Another duck incubated a

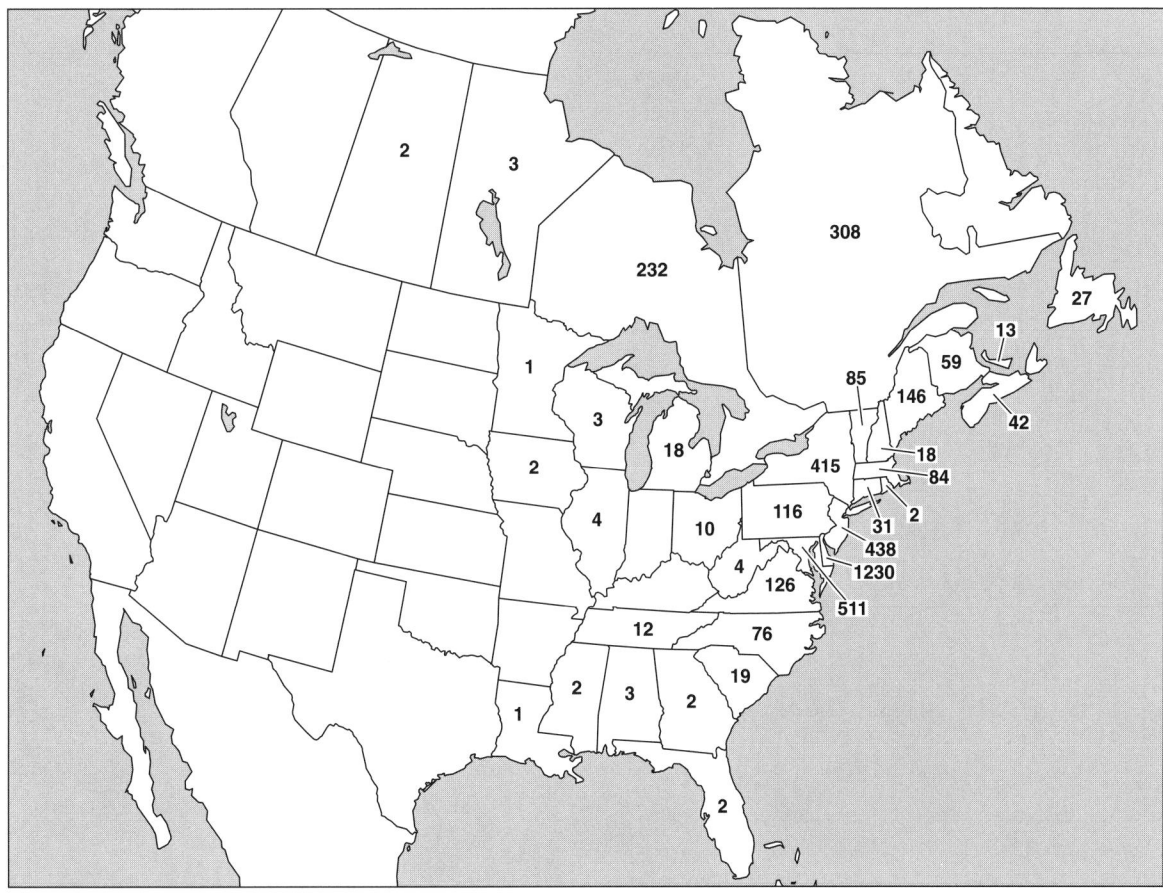

Total American Black Ducks Either Banded or Recovered in Delaware, or Both

clutch that decreased from 5 eggs on 5 July to 2 eggs, on 26 July 1968 [Jame1]. The earliest brood, estimated at 3 days old, was found on 7 April 1971 at Indian River [Mich1]. The most common clutch size was 8 (20%), most clutches had 5 to 10 eggs (82%), and only 5 clutches had 11–13 (4%, $n = 113$). The range given in Bent (1932), "6 to 12 eggs in a set, usually 8 or 10," must be modified for Delaware to 5–10 eggs usual, occasionally up to 13. Delaware mean clutch size, after eliminating presumably incomplete clutches of fewer than 5 eggs, is 7.6, lower than the 9–10 found in Maryland, Quebec, Maine, and Vermont (Palmer 1976).

Trends. The American Black Duck breeding population has declined from the peak numbers at some locations. Lesser (1964) reported for the 1962–63 seasons that 50–60 broods were produced annually at Little Creek WA, but only one-tenth of those numbers are produced there now. Seventy nests were found on Bombay Hook NWR in 1938 [Buck1], but a recent refuge effort found only one-tenth as many [Atla1]. These declines from high nesting densities are characteristic of new impoundments in their first few years. Delaware BBS data suggest an increasing tendency during 1966–90.

Breeding population. Delaware is one of the strongholds for breeding American Black Ducks. Although numbers have declined from their high point in some of the impoundments,

large numbers of birds still breed on private land in areas such as Milford Neck. A high of 273 was reported on the 1988 May Count. More than 200 congregate on Fresh Pond in July (West, pers. obs.). Fifteen were reported in the Great Marsh study area on 21 May 1987, when incubation would have been at its peak [DNRE1]. In suitably managed wetlands, populations may reach 30 pairs per sq mi (10 pairs per sq km); the much higher numbers found in several studies reported by Kirby (1988) are exceptional.

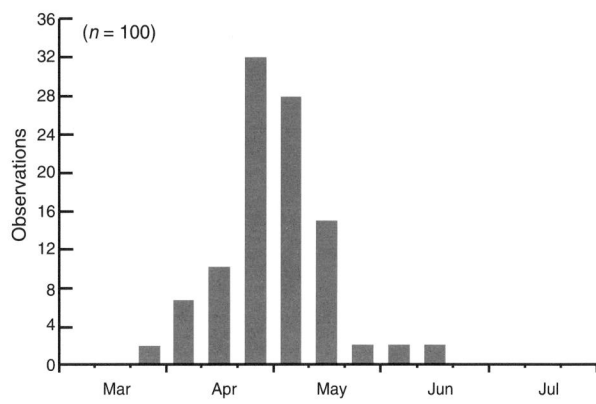

Estimated Clutch-Completion Dates

Conservation. Delaware's coastal zone law, maintenance of healthy marshlands, and limitations on hunting pressure are good conservation measures for a summer population in the face of a widespread decline in the Atlantic Flyway (Hartman 1992). However, draining and timbering of upland nontidal wetlands continue to remove some habitat.

There is increasing hybridization with Mallards. In 1978 9% of American Black Ducks reported shot in Delaware were Black x Mallard hybrids (Voelzer et al. 1982). The 10-year average for 1971–80 was 4% (Carney et al. 1983). This influx of Mallard genes will continue to mongrelize the American Black Duck population. In Delaware it is not unknown for hunting farms to buy 100 or even 500 Mallard ducklings to stock their coastal marshes. This will inevitably lead to further hybridization pressure in the traditional breeding grounds of American Black Ducks. Current records show Mallards breeding in the saltmarshes, once the stronghold of the American Black Duck.

FALL: Migration usually begins 10–20 September, but migrants are not numerous until 1–10 October. High counts are

13 Sep 1961	887	Little Creek WA (Lesser 1965)
21 Oct 1980	1,186	Prime Hook NWR [Prim1]
22 Oct 1986	1,872	Bombay Hook NWR [Wees1]

Typical counts, by birders who do not have access to much of the marshes, total fewer than 100 birds. State aerial surveys in 1989 showed an early-winter peak of the southward migration: 5,000–7,000 in October, 7,000 in November, 15,000–20,000 in December, and 8,000 in January (DNREC 1989).

1966–89 CBC Summary

Christmas Bird Count	Years Found	Range of No. Found	Median
Wilmington	24	21–499	117
Middletown	24	63–6,118	276
Bombay Hook	24	978–9,724	3,185
Cape Henlopen	24	140–1,611	400
Rehoboth	24	349–1,953	903
STATEWIDE	24	2,239–13,892	6,300
(decreasing; low in 1989, high in 1974)			

WINTER: This species has significantly decreased in numbers on CBCs. Its trend line suggests an annual decrease of about 4%. It is reported most abundantly on the Bombay Hook CBC. Seasonal non-CBC highs are

1 Jan 1978	100	Rehoboth Beach [Frec1]
11 Jan 1964	600	Little Creek WA [Broo11]
9 Feb 1964	1,330	Little Creek WA [Broo11]

BANDING: Recoveries include 2,548 banded in Delaware and 1,503 banded elsewhere. Distribution of recovery or banding sites corresponds to much of the American Black Duck's range. Also recovered were 75 Black x Mallard hybrids banded in Delaware and 32 banded elsewhere.

REMARKS: Stone (1937) observed, "The Black Duck is the common wild duck of Cape May. Present throughout the year, it is the only duck to be found regularly in the summertime. . . .

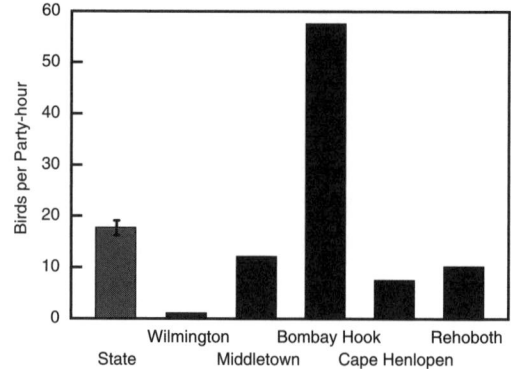

CBC Geographic Distribution

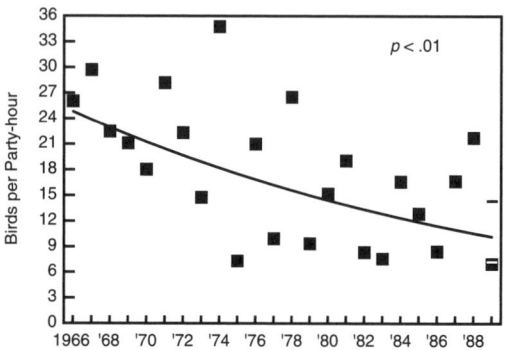

CBC Trend; Autocorrelation may Invalidate the Significance Test

In winter the Black Ducks increase in numbers augmented as they are by migrants from farther north and great flocks gather on the sounds." Writing about Mallards, he notes that they are "not nearly so common as in years gone by" and "that a gunner who today gets a pair in a season's shooting is doing remarkably well." Stone reports high counts of American Black Ducks seen on the Delaware River from Fort Mott in 1935 (mainly in the Delaware part of the river): 6 October, 10,000; 3 November, 20,000; 1 December, 70,000. Ten thousand Black Ducks were also recorded from the same place on 6 October 1929 and 1 December 1934 (Stone 1937, citing Julian Potter).

Today a quite different scenario prevails: Mallards are at least as common as, or even more common than, American Black Ducks, which may be declining. In Stone's time the only breeding Mallards were a few semiwild birds probably derived from domestic stock.

SPECIMENS: UDEL 25-65, Milford, 7 December 1965; DMNH 77198, Assawoman Bay, near Fenwick Island, 17 December 1988; DMNH 76843, Rehoboth Bay, December 1985. Egg records: DMNH, WFVZ.

Mallard (*Anas platyrhynchos*)

Resident; fairly common (summer) to common (winter). Migration from late February to early May and from mid-September to early December.

| J | F | M | A | M | J | J | A | S | O | N | D |

HABITAT: Breeding: ponds, streams, or ditches bordered with marsh vegetation; emergent wetlands. Nonbreeding: ponds and impoundments.

SPRING: Migration probably begins in late February or early March. Most leave by 20–30 March, and migration ends about 5–10 May, as much as 3 weeks later than the migration of the American Black Duck. A high count of 850 occurred on 3 March 1974 at Dragon Run [Beac2]. Typical daily counts total 25–50 birds.

BREEDING: An introduced population, fully wild and feral Mallards now breed throughout Delaware.

Atlas. Mallards were reported in 170 (77%) Atlas blocks. Many blocks where it was not reported are along watershed divides, such as between the Nanticoke and the Indian River. Questioning local residents in one of these blocks produced 3 reports of Mallard breeding evidence, but their occurrence was so infrequent, in ditches so difficult to reach, that the initial Atlas effort missed them. Within blocks where breeding was reported, it was usually confined to ponds, fresh marshes, creeks, and ditches, though some bred in saltmarshes.

Nesting. Mallards typically hide their nests in fairly open grassy areas near freshwater streams, ponds, and marshes. They also breed in brackish cordgrass marshes exemplified by nests located at Little Creek WA on 21 May 1977 [Nile2], Prime Hook NWR on 5 June 1980 [O'Sh2], and Bombay Hook NWR on 10 June 1987 [Peli1]. In contrast, another was found on pine needles under a pine on 1 May 1983 [Patt1]. Ground nesting is the rule, but 1 nest was in a tree at the Wilcastle Center, Wilmington [Adam1]. The nest is usually in a hollow, lined with grass and down.

The estimated clutch-completion dates extend from late March to mid-June. Extreme egg dates are 5 eggs on 2 April 1935 [Buck1] to 9 eggs with incubation already begun on 25 June 1934 [Hans1]. The earliest hatchlings recorded include 7 "downy young" seen on 28 April 1977 [Hess4] and a brood of downy chicks, weighing up to 34 g each (about 2 days old), brought to Tri-State Bird Rescue on 25 April 1989 (TSBR 89–0190). Clutch size distribution (*n* = 18) is

4 nests	11 eggs each
2 nests each	5, 9, or 12 eggs per nest
1 nest each	3, 6, 7, 10, 13, 14, 15, or 19 eggs per nest

History. The Mallard population has surely benefited from the activities of humans. In the first place, Mallards are easily semidomesticated, an ideal choice for stocking farm ponds and marshes. Second, clearing land for farming created a prairie-like habitat for eastward extension of the original breeding range and for the establishment of feral populations. The third

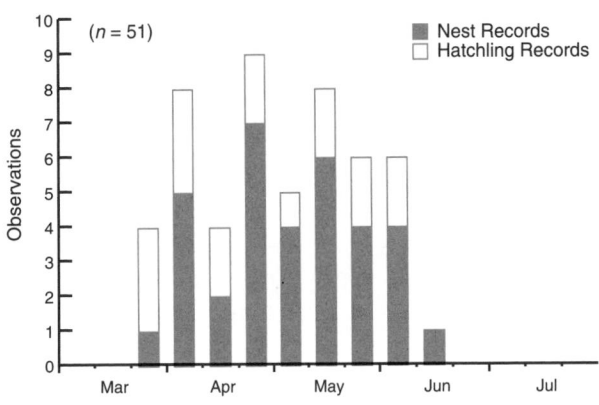

Estimated Clutch-Completion Dates

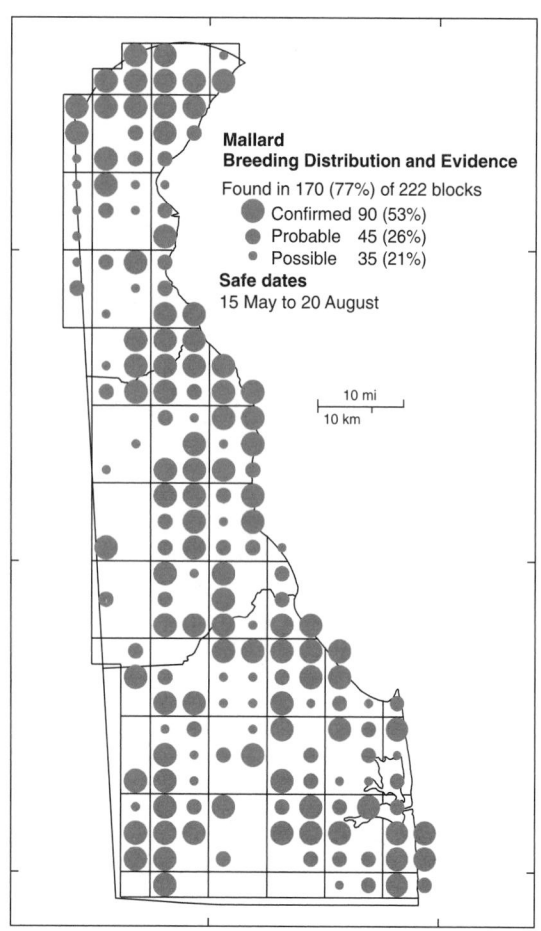

Mallard
Breeding Distribution and Evidence

Found in 170 (77%) of 222 blocks

● Confirmed 90 (53%)
● Probable 45 (26%)
· Possible 35 (21%)

Safe dates
15 May to 20 August

10 mi
10 km

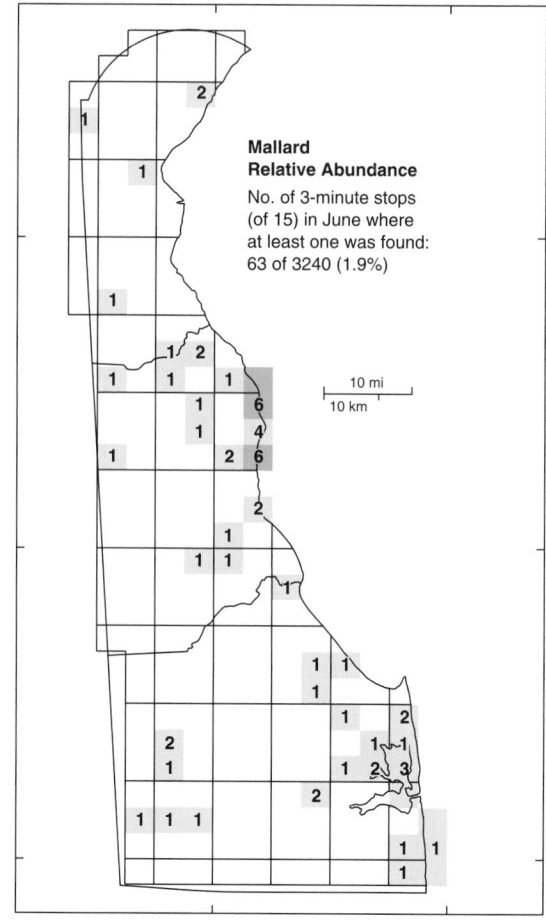

Mallard
Relative Abundance

No. of 3-minute stops
(of 15) in June where
at least one was found:
63 of 3240 (1.9%)

10 mi
10 km

edition of the AOU Check-list (1910) states that Mallards bred rarely south to northern Maryland, and Rhoads and Pennock (1905) listed it as only a winter resident in Delaware. Hanson (notes) first recorded feral breeding on 18 April 1934 when a Mallard nest with 15 eggs was present on Dr. Sipple's pier at Silver Lake, Dover, a bird sanctuary. He also wrote the following note: "June 24, 1934, a Mallard with 14 eggs beside the porch of the High Tide Tea House in Rehoboth; the duck was so tame it would eat from the hand." The next year Buckalew (notes) located 5 feral nests near Milford. Stewart (1962), speaking of waterfowl in the upper Chesapeake region, including part of Delaware, notes that "a few scattered pairs of birds breed in the region during the summer months. The breeding birds probably are derived from game-farm stock."

Trends. Mallards increased on the May Count and the Delaware BBS at an average rate of about 4% per year during 1966–90 [Usfw3]. Stocking programs have probably aided this increase, but changes in the land from woods to open farmland have had great influence.

Breeding population. Some areas had a high density of Mallards where heavy stocking occurred during the Atlas project, but there is no information on any permanent increase in the breeding population. Bellrose (1976) estimates that 20,000 pairs breed in the Chesapeake and western Mid-Atlantic area.

FALL: First arrival is about 15–20 September. Mallards become common in early October, and their migration is probably finished by early or mid-December. High counts include

2 Oct 1986	1,510	Bombay Hook NWR [Wees1]
2 Nov 1974	3,250	Dragon Run [Edni1]

Typical daily counts total 100–200 birds. Bellrose (1976) points to a peak during late November and early December.

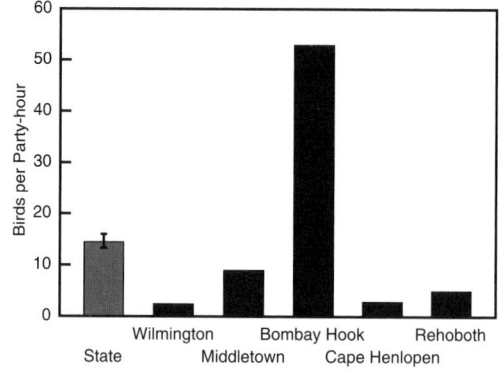

CBC Geographic Distribution

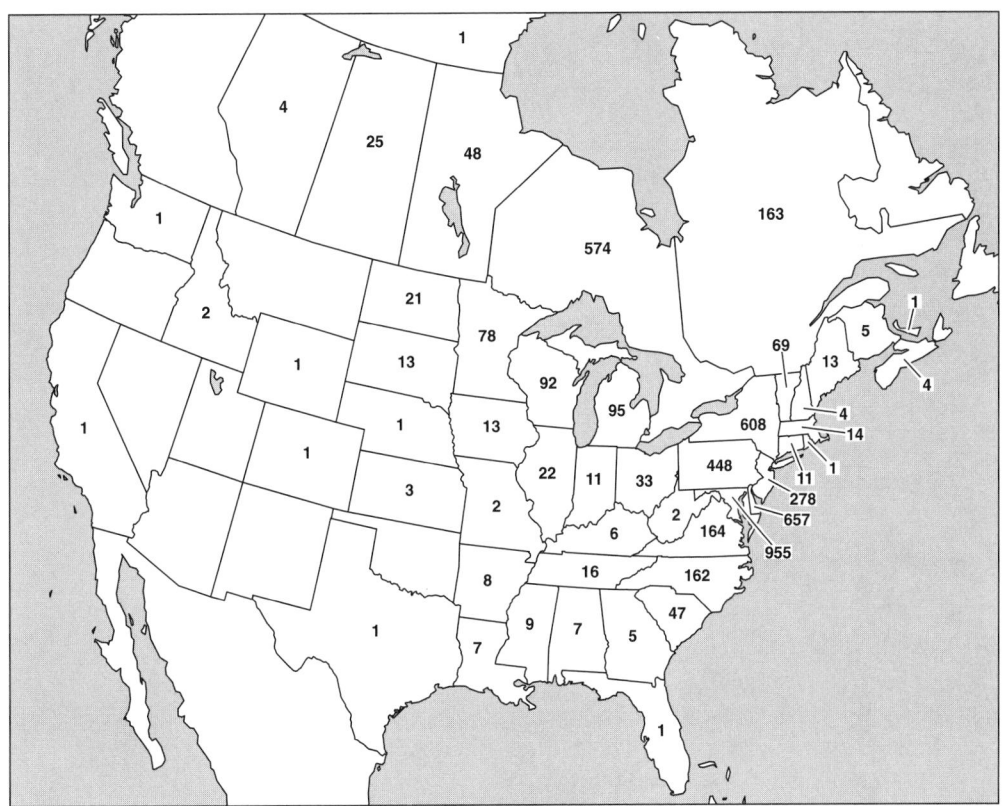

Total Mallards Either Banded or Recovered in Delaware, or Both

BANDING: Recoveries include 2,516 birds banded in Delaware and 2,191 banded elsewhere. Forty-one states, 8 provinces, and the Northwest Territories are represented, attesting to the widespread distribution of Delaware Mallards in North America.

SPECIMENS: 12; DMNH, UDEL.

1966–89 CBC Summary

Christmas Bird Count	Years Found	Range of No. Found	Median
Wilmington	24	114–1,250	253
Middletown	24	34–3,202	316
Bombay Hook	24	482–9,000	3,221
Cape Henlopen	24	15–1,329	131
Rehoboth	24	119–1,220	465
STATEWIDE (low in 1967, high in 1973)	24	2,351–11,142	5,210

WINTER: The CBC data show high year-to-year variation and no significant trend. Like the American Black Duck, the Mallard is found most abundantly on the Bombay Hook CBC. Bellrose (1976) estimated the Chesapeake Bay region wintering population at 40,000. Seasonal non-CBC highs, all by Holgersen at Bombay Hook NWR, are

27 Dec 1972	6,000	[Holg78]
31 Dec 1973	5,000	[Holg84]
10 Jan 1973	12,000	[Holg78]
10 Feb 1972	15,000	[Holg70]

Blue-winged Teal *(Anas discors)*

Regular; summer resident; fairly common (spring migrant) to common (fall migrant). Expected early March to late October.

HABITAT: Breeds in short-growth, tidal cordgrass marshes and impoundments, sometimes with tall cordgrass, switchgrass, and groundsel bush; also cattail marsh, Delmarva Bay. At other seasons uses tidal marsh, ponds, impoundments.

SPRING: Bellrose (1976) notes a spring peak late March to early April. These early reports of more than 2 birds signal the beginning of spring migration:

2 Mar 1975	10	Dragon Run [SpSB34]
6 Mar 1965	7	Little Creek WA [Broo29]
12 Mar 1964	12	Assawoman WA [Davi22]

The migration peak occurs in early April, shown by an increased frequency of reports and these high counts:

6 Apr 1962	1,580	Little Creek WA (Lesser 1965)
10 Apr 1961	2,000	Little Creek WA (Lesser 1965)
25 Apr 1943	500	Bombay Hook NWR [Cutl26]

Typical daily counts tally fewer than 50 birds.

BREEDING: The best place to see this duck in summer is along weedy edges of freshwater impoundments in the wildlife refuges. Lesser (1964) reported an astonishing 50–75 brood count annually at Little Creek WA during 1961–62 and said it was the most numerous breeding duck there. ("Brood count" was the sum of the broods observed on each weekly count during the summer.) It remained so through the mid-1970s with more than 100 broods reported annually. By the late 1970s degradation of the marsh impoundments by salinity resulted in declining production, and in 1989 only 5 broods were reported (K. Reynolds, DNREC, pers. comm.).

Atlas. The breeding distribution in Delaware during the Atlas period shows some extension over these earlier reports, but the Blue-winged Teal is no longer as common as reported by Lesser at Little Creek WA in the 1960s (Lesser 1965), or as at Bombay Hook NWR in 1938 when Buckalew (notes) found 33 nests. Atlas workers reported breeding on ponds south of Cape Henlopen, inland in small creeks west from Prime Hook, along

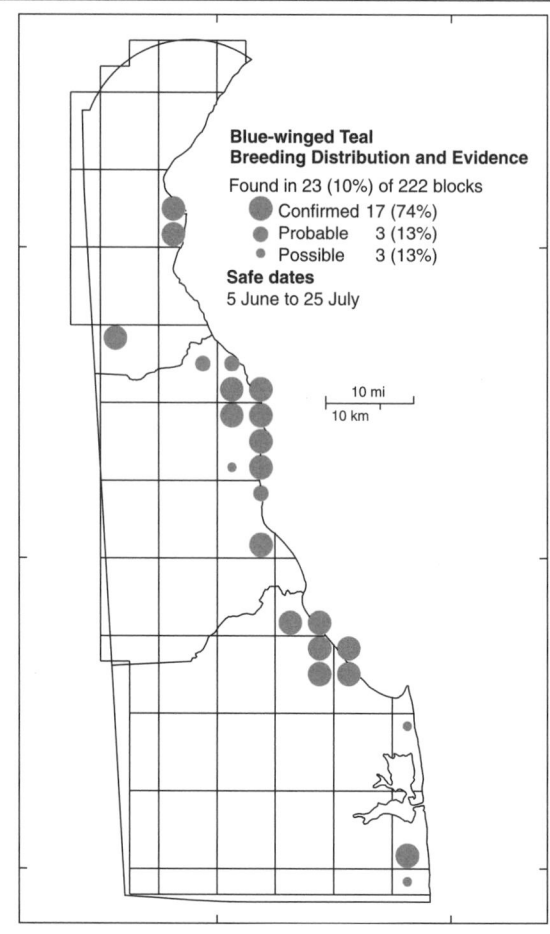

Blue-winged Teal
Breeding Distribution and Evidence

Found in 23 (10%) of 222 blocks
● Confirmed 17 (74%)
● Probable 3 (13%)
· Possible 3 (13%)
Safe dates
5 June to 25 July

10 mi
10 km

the wildlife impoundments in Kent County, and an adult with young in a Delmarva Bay near Blackbird in early July 1984 [Hess3].

Nesting. The favored nest site is dense grassy vegetation along dikes of tidal impoundments. In 1935 Miller found a clutch in a nest "built on dry ground . . . well hidden at edge of large cattail marsh . . . at bottom of a low grass-weed covered bank. Composed of grasses and down entirely, about 10 inches across and 3 inches deep" (LSU 234).

Clutch completion peaks in the first third of May. Extreme egg dates are 1 May 1982, a "female sitting on nest, male nearby" at Bombay Hook NWR [Boll2]; and 25 June 1987, nest with 11 eggs at Bombay Hook NWR [Peli1]. After eliminating clutches of fewer than 8 as presumably incomplete, clutch size ranged from 8 to 12, once 13 (n = 42). Clutches most commonly had 10 or 11 eggs (55%) and averaged 10.1 eggs—slightly smaller than given by Palmer (1976).

History. Delaware is part of the breeding range of a reestablished (or new?) Eastern population of this essentially northern prairie duck. Neither Wilson (1859–60) nor Audubon (1843) describes a Mid-Atlantic breeding population in the early 1800s. Early breeding records for the East come from Long Island

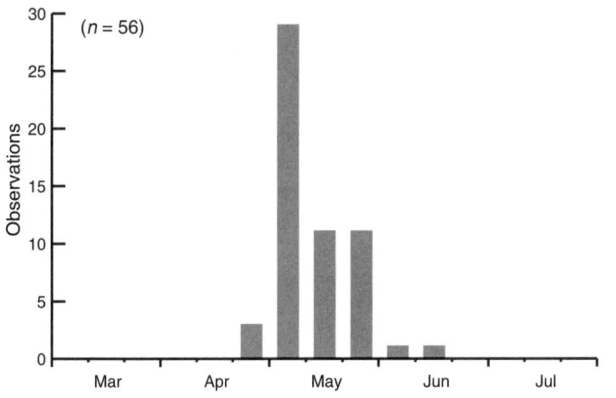

(*n* = 56)

Estimated Clutch-Completion Dates

(Giraud 1844, in Bull 1964, 128). Phillips (1923) called it a rare breeder in the eastern United States and gave additional breeding records for the Atlantic seaboard in Rhode Island (in Howe and Sturtevant 1899) and Elliot's Isle, Maryland (undated).

In Delaware, the Blue-winged Teal was listed only as a win- ter resident in 1904 (Rhoads and Pennock 1905). Breeding began at least by the 1930s in all 3 counties, with records from Broadkill Beach on 11 May 1933 (Buckalew 1934), 30 May 1934 [McMu1], and 10 May 1935 [Hans1]. Miller [anon19] reported a nest with 11 eggs near Delaware City on 19 May 1935. Her- holdt reported a number of flocks of young on and around Kent Island, Bombay Hook NWR, on 24 June 1937 [Hans1]. There are records of nests and eggs from Sussex County col- lected on 20 May 1934 and 16 May 1935 (DMNH mount 339), and of a juvenile at Bombay Hook NWR on 23 July 1937 (USNM 340609). Stone (1937), in view of these records and others, stated that Blue-winged Teal "have of late years re- sumed nesting in Maryland, Delaware, and New Jersey," but "resumed" may just be a presumption of previous nesting, as he offers no information about previous breeding.

Trends. The May Count, taken a month after the migration peak, shows an average annual decline in the breeding popula- tion of 8% during 1969–91.

Breeding population. Bellrose (1976) says it is not abundant

Total Blue-winged Teal Either Banded or Recovered in Delaware, or Both

along the Atlantic seaboard, but he goes on to estimate a breeding population of 10,000–25,000. Delaware's contribution to this figure is quite small. It was reported in 23 blocks but was nowhere common; the total state population undoubtedly falls below 200 pairs.

FALL: Bellrose (1976) shows a peak from the first week of September to the last week of October, whereas Robbins and Bystrak (1977) note high numbers for Maryland from the second week of September through the second week of October. Our data show a slightly different pattern. Migrants arrive during 25–30 August and high numbers continue until 5–10 October. Frech recorded a peak of 500 on 23 September 1978 at Assawoman WA [Frec1]. Daily counts are typically about 50–100 birds.

WINTER: Most Blue-winged Teal winter in the Caribbean region, but this species has occurred on 14 Delaware CBCs in numbers ranging from 1 to 9. Occasional midwinter reports involve 1 or 2 individuals along the coast.

1966–89 CBC Summary

Christmas Bird Count	*Years Found*	*Range of No. Found*
Wilmington		
Middletown	1	8
Bombay Hook	7	2–7
Cape Henlopen		
Rehoboth	6	1–9
STATEWIDE (high in 1967 and 1969)	11	1–9

BANDING: Recoveries include 90 birds banded in Delaware and 24 banded elsewhere. Recovery sites of Delaware-banded birds include Surinam and Guyana (8), Cuba (7), Dominican Republic (7), Puerto Rico (5), Trinidad (3), Venezuela (2), Panama (1), and Colombia (1).

SPECIMENS: DMNH 76417, Dover, 22 April 1986; USNM 421842, Fowler Beach, 29 April 1932; DMNH 75070, 2.8 mi (4.5 km) W, 2.8 mi S Townsend, last week of August 1983. Egg records: DMNH, LSU.

Cinnamon Teal (*Anas cyanoptera*)

Accidental (1993).

DOCUMENTATION: Notes by several experienced observers.

OCCURRENCE: A male Cinnamon Teal in breeding plumage was seen at Shorts Beach on 27 February 1993 under favorable conditions by Short, Swertinski, and others [Shor6]. Although it departed before being photographed, the distinctive plumage of this species leaves no room to doubt the correctness of its identification by these observers. This western relative of the Blue-winged Teal occurs casually "in eastern North America from . . . New York and New Jersey south to the Gulf coast" (AOU 1983). However, it has not been definitely established that this individual was of wild origin.

Northern Shoveler (*Anas clypeata*)

Regular; fairly common (winter visitor) to abundant (migrant). Expected late September to late April. Breeding episodes in the 1930s and 1960s.

HABITAT: Ponds, lakes, brackish ponds; breeding especially in newly constructed impoundments.

SPRING: Bellrose (1976) notes that although some birds leave the wintering range in February, most do not depart before March or April. Delaware data reflect the same pattern. Migration usually begins 15–20 March and ends 20–25 April. High counts, all associated with sites where they bred, are

22 Feb 1967	3,800	Little Creek WA [Line14]
21 Mar 1970	3,100	Little Creek WA [DuPG31]
25 Apr 1943	900	Bombay Hook NWR [Cutl26]

Counts of 100–200 are not unusual.

BREEDING: Except for the breeding episodes in the 1930s and 1960s (see "Nesting"), the Northern Shoveler is a rare straggler in late spring and summer. A few remained at Bombay Hook NWR on 4 June 1971 [Holg52]. Five lingering shovelers were out of expected habitat at Oyster Rock Rd., Sussex County, on 31 May 1989 [Frec1].

Atlas. No breeding was reported during the Atlas period.

Nesting. This species bred in Bombay Hook NWR during 1937–42. Herholdt found 8 broods totaling 33 young on Raymond Pool in 1937 (1 juvenile collected, USNM 340609). Buckalew [Buck1] found 18 nests on the saltmarsh in 1938; 7 of these, found between 12 and 27 May, held clutches of 9–11 (mean = 10.3). Dates for first clutches at Bombay Hook are early April to early May (Sowls 1976, 512). Studies conducted on Bombay Hook NWR in 1938 showed that the Northern Shoveler built its nest on the saltmarsh, mostly in patches of dead cordgrass, the live and dead stems of which constituted protective covering. All nests were near tidal guts, except 1, which was approximately 30 yd from Delaware Bay (Griffith 1946). This adaptability by an essentially freshwater duck from the western prairies is remarkable. In 1939, 31 nests were found, including 1 with eggs hatching on 30 May (Griffith 1946). In 1940, the peak year, 44 nests were found. Nesting continued in 1941–42, with 250 young produced in 1942. At this time records became incomplete because of military activity on part of Bombay Hook NWR (Buckalew notes; Griffith 1946) [Hans2].

No post–Word War II report of nesting at Bombay Hook is known, so shovelers must have been much reduced. The only other reports of breeding are from Little Creek WA during 1961–65. Three broods were observed in these impoundments in 1961, and a brood count of 20 was made in 1962 (Lesser 1964). ("Brood count" was the sum of the broods observed on each weekly count during the summer.) The last breeding reported were broods of 1 and 2 seen on 26 June 1965 [LesC3]. Occasional extralimital breeding is not uncommon among ducks. The common element between the records in the 1930s and those in the 1960s is the establishment of new, productive impoundments in saltmarsh.

FALL: The usual first arrival is 25 September to 1 October, although in some years small flocks arrive as much as 3 weeks earlier [Barn1]. Early arrival of larger flocks has been recorded twice:

9 Sep 1986	190	Bombay Hook NWR [Wees1]
12 Sep 1982	155	Bombay Hook NWR [RusR1]

Much of the migration takes place during the first 3 weeks of October. High counts include

6 Oct 1991	200	Bombay Hook NWR [Litt1]
26 Oct 1948	500	Bombay Hook NWR [McLa1]
11 Nov 1986	790	Bombay Hook NWR [Wees1]

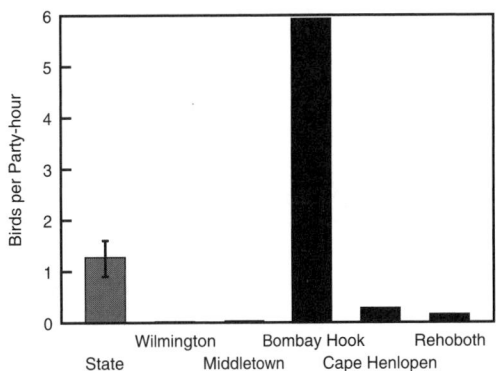

CBC Geographic Distribution

1966–89 CBC Summary

Christmas Bird Count	Years Found	Range of No. Found	Median
Wilmington	1	8	
Middletown	7	1–5	
Bombay Hook	23	1–2,234	150
Cape Henlopen	12	1–230	
Rehoboth	20	1–100	9
STATEWIDE (low in 1980, high in 1971)	24	2–2,480	211

WINTER: Its abundance has exceeded 2 birds per party hour on CBCs during only 3 CBC periods (1970, 1971, 1987). It is most numerous on the Bombay Hook CBC. Non-CBC highs are

2 Dec 1986	255	Bombay Hook NWR [Wees1]
9 Feb 1964	460	Little Creek WA [Broo24]

Typical reports are of fewer than 50 birds.

BANDING: In the East it winters along the Atlantic coast from Long Island to Florida, the West Indies, and Cuba (Bellrose 1976). Northern Shovelers banded in Delaware were recovered in Saskatchewan, Wisconsin, New Jersey, and North and South Carolina (1 each). Recovered in Delaware were individuals banded in New York (2), Minnesota, Ontario, and New Brunswick.

SPECIMENS: USNM 340609, Bombay Hook NWR, 23 July 1937; DMNH 76254, DMNH 76264, DMNH 76274, Little Creek WA, 5 November 1985.

[White-cheeked Pintail *(Anas bahamensis)*]

Probable escape (1967).

REMARKS: The White-cheeked Pintail is a sedentary resident of the West Indies and South America. Delaware's single report was made on 25 October 1967 at Assawoman WA [Coff1]. Although this report is mentioned in the sixth AOU *Check-list* (1983) and the species occurs casually in Florida and has been recorded in a scattering of eastern locations, the bird seen at Assawoman WA may well have escaped from captivity. Documentation for the sighting is apparently unavailable.

Northern Pintail (*Anas acuta*)

Regular; winter visitor; common. Accidental breeder. Expected mid-September to mid-April, sporadically earlier and later. Winter numbers apparently declining after a peak in the mid-1970s.

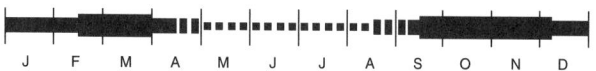

HABITAT: Ponds, lakes, impoundments, brackish marsh.

SPRING: In the middle latitudes numbers peak mid- to late March and rapidly decline by early April (Bellrose 1976). The Delaware peak migration period runs from 10–20 February to 25–30 March. Most leave by 10–15 April, although a few occasionally summer. A flock stayed exceptionally late on Churchmans Marsh in 1964—100 on 17 April and 15 on 1 May—and 5 summered at least until 3 July (West and Klabunde 1977). Other late dates for flocks are

17 Apr 1982	18	Bombay Hook NWR [Edni48]
18 Apr 1964	29	Little Creek WA [LesC7]
5 May 1973	7	Little Creek WA [John8]

Representative peak counts are

1 Mar 1972	12,000	Bombay Hook NWR [Holg70]
2 Mar 1930	10,000	Delaware City [Weyl2]
10 Apr 1961	15,000	Little Creek (Lesser 1964)

Since 1972 the number of spring migrants has decreased, and typical daily counts are 500 or fewer.

SUMMER: Hanson (notes) records a report indirectly from Joseph Watson, game warden, "that pintail ducks were breeding this spring (1930) at Prime Hook." There are no subsequent reports until a female was flushed at Little Creek WA in 1961; the bird's feigning "actions almost certainly indicated that a brood was present" (Lesser 1964).

A summering bird was reported during the Atlas period in Rehoboth Bay [Frec1], and a pair was noted on 12 June 1990 at Bombay Hook NWR (notes).

Northern Pintails breed occasionally in the Mid-Atlantic states, and breeding pintails were reported during the New York, Vermont, and Pennsylvania Breeding Bird Atlas projects (Eaton 1988c; Ellis and Ellison 1985) and in Pennsylvania (Fingerhood 1992). However, the species' principal breeding range in North America is the western prairies of Canada southeast into Montana and the Dakotas (Bellrose 1976).

FALL: Bellrose (1976) notes that in the "New Jersey–Chesapeake Bay" region this species arrives 2 to 3 weeks earlier than at points south, and that "significant numbers are not present until mid-October and peak numbers until late November." Our data show first arrival about 10–15 September and high numbers from mid-September to late November or early December. A high count of 5,000 was obtained on 15 October 1970 at Bombay Hook NWR [Holg5]. Typical counts report up to several hundred birds.

1966–89 CBC Summary

Christmas Bird Count	Years Found	Range of No. Found	Median
Wilmington	6	1–6	
Middletown	20	1–153	12
Bombay Hook	24	1–5,611	944
Cape Henlopen	24	1–331	39
Rehoboth	24	2–514	35
STATEWIDE	24	81–5,681	1,182

(decreasing; low in 1968, high in 1975)

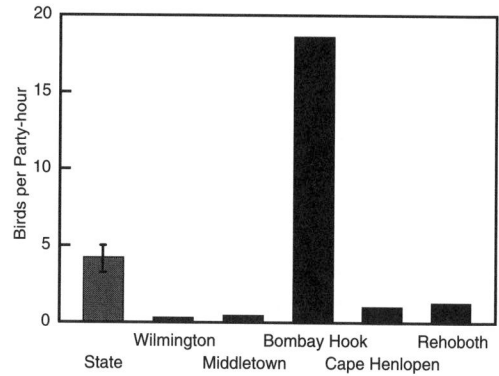

CBC Geographic Distribution

WINTER: The numbers of Northern Pintails reported on Delaware CBCs changed between 1966 and 1989, peaking in the late 1970s and then declining. The breeding population in North America is down 55% from its 1955–88 average (1989 USFWS data), a decline reflected in recent CBC data for Delaware. Northern Pintails are seldom reported in large numbers on counts other than Bombay Hook. Winter non-CBC highs are

2 Dec 1986	1,920	Bombay Hook NWR [Wees1]
19 Jan 1972	2,000	Bombay Hook NWR [Holg70]
31 Jan 1970	2,500	Little Creek WA [Holg44]
22 Feb 1967	7,600	Little Creek WA [Line14]
25 Feb 1970	8,500	Bombay Hook NWR [Holg44]

The increased numbers of the late February reports signal the onset of spring migration; usually fewer than 200 birds are found.

BANDING: Records include recoveries of 165 individuals banded in Delaware and 158 recoveries in Delaware of birds

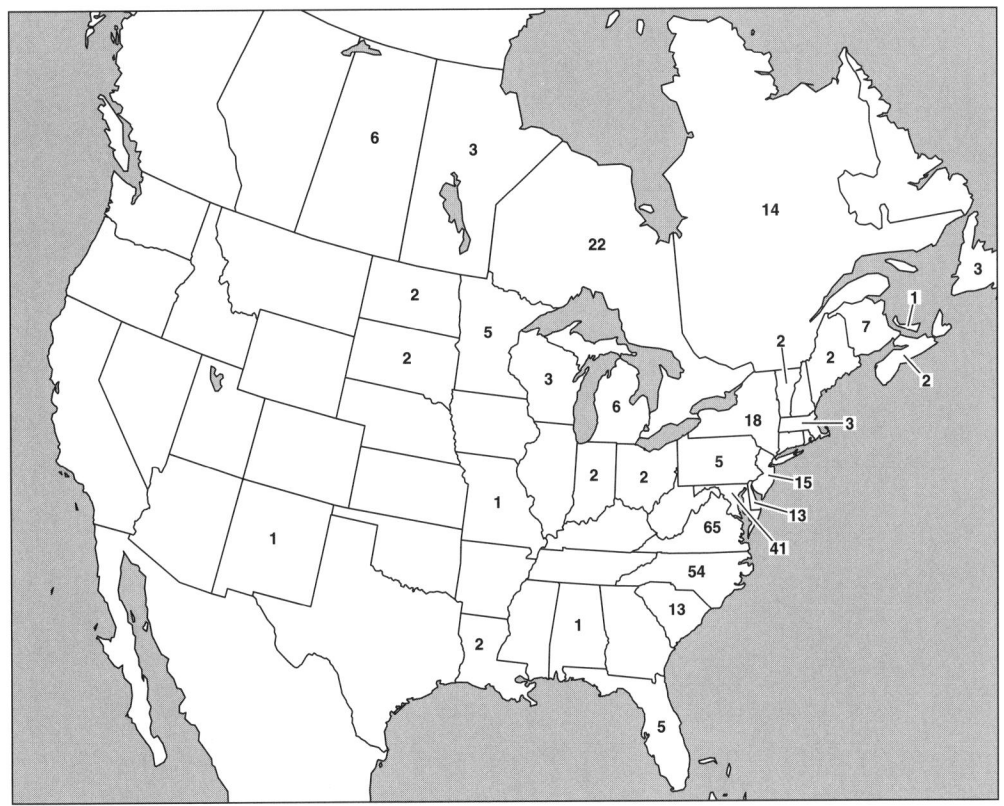

Total Northern Pintails Either Banded or Recovered in Delaware, or Both

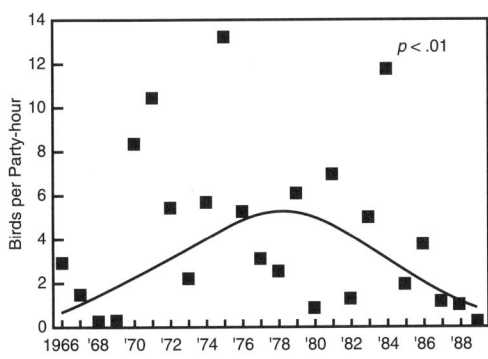

CBC Trend

banded out of state. The Banding map indicates that Northern Pintails seen in Delaware as fall migrants or winter visitors come from the western prairies and from breeding populations in Quebec, Ontario, Newfoundland, the Maritimes, and possibly the northeastern states. In the Atlantic Flyway the chief wintering areas are the Carolinas, Florida, the West Indies, and Cuba (Bellrose 1976).

SPECIMENS: USNM 421793, Milton, 1 February 1932; USNM 421860, Milton, 30 November 1934; ANSP 170840, Rehoboth Beach, 30 December 1912.

Garganey (*Anas querquedula*)

Accidental (1976).

DOCUMENTATION: Notes (DMNH).

REMARKS: A male was recorded at Bombay Hook NWR 24 April–12 May 1976 [Finc1]. Notes made under difficult conditions by DuMont on 24 April and under good observing conditions by Barnhill the next day detail all relevant marks. The dark chestnut head and prominent eye stripe were clearly distinguishable [DuPG1].

The AOU (1983) lists the species as accidental in continental North America, but cautions that some of the vagrant records, "particularly those in eastern North America, may pertain to escaped individuals." Nonetheless, Ryan (1976) stated that the Delaware record "is apparently legitimate" as "no one is breeding Garganey in the United States, and the last importation was several years ago. These birds did not fare well, and very few are left—none in the area in question." The Garganey is a long-distance migrant wintering in the northern tropics of Africa and Asia and breeding in northern Europe and Siberia, so it is physiologically capable of making long-distance flights. It is no more than accidental in Iceland (Cramp et al., eds., 1977, 530), and Godfrey (1986) lists 7 accidental occurrences in Canada, all in May or June, as if they were wandering migrants; the species occurred once each in New Brunswick and Quebec.

Green-winged Teal (*Anas crecca*)

Regular; migrant and winter visitor; fairly common to common. Expected early September to early May. Summers occasionally; breeds sporadically.

HABITAT: Ponds, impoundments, tidal creeks and ponds.

SPRING: The numbers of Green-winged Teal increase from 1–10 March through 15–20 April as southern birds arrive. Unusually early were 30 seen 7 February 1938 at Delaware City [WriM1]. Most depart by 1–5 May. The high migration count is 1,500 at Prime Hook NWR on 19 March 1973 [Holg78]. Bellrose (1976) notes that southern birds begin moving north in early February, and his graphs show peaks in the Mid-Atlantic region during February and April.

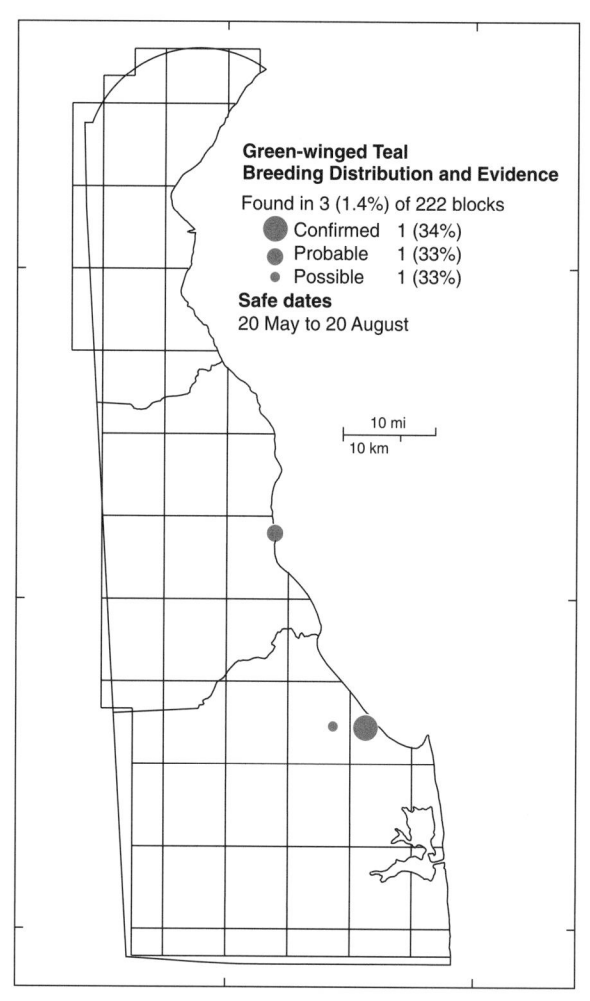

Green-winged Teal
Breeding Distribution and Evidence

Found in 3 (1.4%) of 222 blocks

● Confirmed 1 (34%)
● Probable 1 (33%)
· Possible 1 (33%)

Safe dates
20 May to 20 August

10 mi
10 km

BREEDING: The first reported summer bird was at Bombay Hook NWR on 1 August 1958 (Oring 1958). A female with young was found at Little Creek WA on 21 September 1961; 6

broods in 1962 (Lesser 1964); and a female with 10 young on 28 June 1980 [Barn1]. It was found in numbers up to 6 during the summer of 1971 at Prime Hook NWR (notes) and found through the 1981 summer at Bombay Hook NWR [DOS1].

A single confirmation was registered during the Atlas period: a female with 9 young reported from Prime Hook NWR on 1 August 1983 [O'Sh4]. Other Atlas reports, all from Bombay Hook NWR, are 1 "still present" on 1 June 1985 [Wayn23]; 1 on 27 June 1986 [Hess11]; and 1 on 11 June 1987 [Quin2].

The summer population is usually fewer than 10; sometimes none are reported. Delaware is far outside this teal's principal, mainly Canadian, breeding range, so the occasional flocks of 10–100 that appear in July and August are puzzling. Examples are

6 Jul 1975	18	Little Creek WA and Bombay Hook NWR [Lehm17]
18 Jul 1981	57	Bombay Hook NWR [Patt8]
31 Jul 1965	90	Little Creek WA [PylR7]
12 Aug 1962	25	Little Creek WA [Davi20]
27 Aug 1989	75	Prime Hook NWR [Frec1]

FALL: The first migrants may arrive during 25–30 August but are more likely during 1–10 September; by mid-September, peak autumnal levels are reached. A high count of 3,000 occurred on 27 September 1972 at Bombay Hook NWR [Holg75]. Bellrose (1976) shows a peak period for the Mid-Atlantic region during November.

1966–89 CBC Summary

Christmas Bird Count	Years Found	Range of No. Found	Median
Wilmington	4	1–3	
Middletown	12	1–13	
Bombay Hook	24	2–4,156	139
Cape Henlopen	22	1–925	83
Rehoboth	21	1–40	6
STATEWIDE (low in 1985, high in 1984)	24	14–4,381	394

WINTER: The number of birds present declines in late fall and early winter. The 1984 Bombay Hook CBC count of 4,156 is the highest winter number. Bellrose (1976) states, "The Atlantic Flyway winters about 77,000 . . . , Delaware 1,200," a reasonable estimate, particularly for early winter. Seasonal highs at single locations are

2 Dec 1986	1,000	Bombay Hook NWR [Wees1]
4 Dec 1976	1,270	Prime Hook NWR (notes)
18 Feb 1984	600	Prime Hook NWR (notes)

The CBC data show no trend and irregular numbers. The Green-winged Teal is found most commonly on the Bombay Hook and Cape Henlopen CBCs.

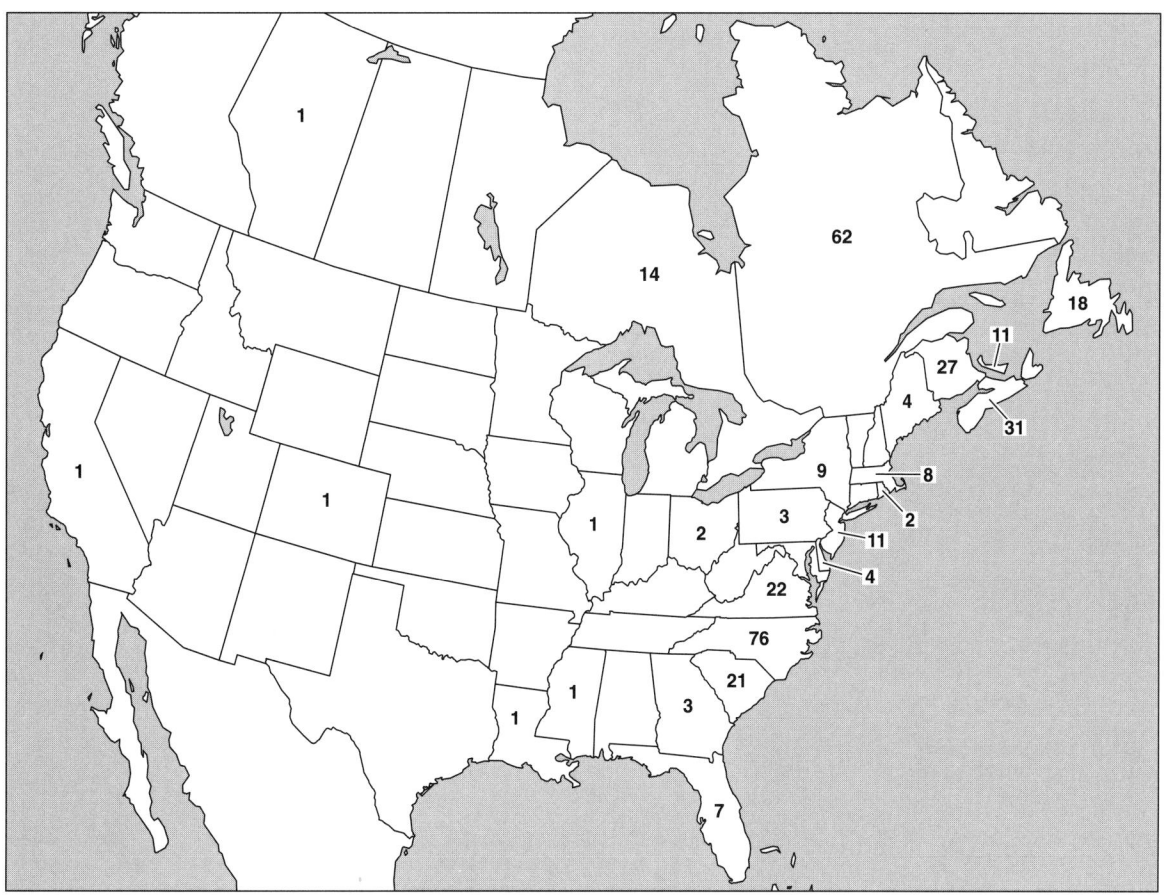

Total Green-winged Teal Either Banded or Recovered in Delaware, or Both

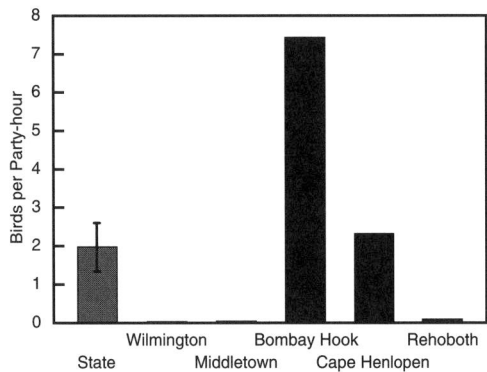

CBC Geographic Distribution; Average of 4 Count Areas

BANDING: Recoveries include 15 banded in Delaware and 329 banded elsewhere and recovered in Delaware. The banding recovery map indicates that most of the Green-winged Teal passing through Delaware stay within the Atlantic Flyway, from the breeding range in eastern Canada to the wintering areas in Virginia and in North and South Carolina. Two aberrant records exist: an individual banded at Prime Hook NWR 21 September 1977 was shot in California in January 1980; another, banded in Colorado in September 1980, was shot the following year in Delaware.

REMARKS: The breeding-plumaged drake of the Eurasian race, *A. c. crecca,* can be distinguished from the North American race, *A. c. carolinensis.* Many observers have ceased to distinguish or to report the two since the forms were lumped into a single species. The first reported Eurasian form in Delaware was at Rehoboth Beach on 29 December 1951 [GolT1]. It has since been recorded at least 11 times through 3 March 1990 [Holg31; Camp1]. Extreme dates of occurrence are 28 November 1953 [WriJ2] and 4 April 1963 [StiA4].

SPECIMENS: 9; DMNH, ANSP, UDEL, USNM.

Delaware's Coastal Impoundments and Their Birds

William H. Meredith

Tidal wetlands have a long history of being managed to augment their natural productivity. Impoundments have been used to create, restore, or improve waterbird habitat for nesting, brood rearing, migratory resting, and wintering, as well as for saltmarsh mosquito control, muskrat production, fish and shellfish nursery habitat, aquaculture, hunting, fishing, crabbing, and bird watching. During past centuries marshes have been impounded along the Atlantic Coast from the Canadian Maritime Provinces to South Carolina and Georgia for other purposes, including salt hay production, and rice cultivation. Except for rice growing, impoundment has been the strategy for excluding all tidal flooding. Impounded wetlands help to compensate for habitat lost to urban encroachment, landfills, inlet stabilization, draining for mosquito control, and other destructive activities.

Delaware's first European settlers began impounding marshes in the seventeenth century, chiefly for agricultural purposes. In recent years Delaware tidal impoundments were constructed primarily to provide habitats for waterbirds and other wildlife and to control breeding of saltmarsh mosquitoes. In developed areas along the Delaware River in New Castle County, impoundments now function to keep many residential, commercial, and industrial properties from being flooded by the river. Impounding Delaware marshes to improve waterfowl habitat and hunting dates back about a century, whereas impounding for mosquito control has been done only during the last 40 years, both using controlled floodings of the impounded areas.

Impoundments purposefully alter the frequency and duration of tidal flooding, thus controlling surface inundation, surface exposure, and water depth, which affect salinity and plant composition within the impounded area. Water supply to an impoundment comes from tidal flooding, rainfall, and freshwater runoff out of upland areas. Large impoundments that are properly managed have water control structures and seasonal management plans.

Low-level coastal impoundments have low levees with crests that can be overtopped by spring tides or storm tides, making water levels, salinity, and vegetation patterns more difficult to manage. High-level impoundments, surrounded by high levees, are usually managed by manipulating water control structures or by pumping water. They are more costly to build and maintain than low-level impoundments but allow better control. Most federal, state, and large private impoundments are the high-level type.

Coastal Impoundments in Delaware

More than 10,000 of Delaware's approximately 90,000 acres of tidal wetlands are impounded marsh, on federal, state, and private lands (DNREC 1994). Individual impoundments vary in size from privately owned units of only a few acres to state and federal units of several hundred acres.

State-owned impounded coastal wetlands are managed by the Division of Fish and Wildlife of the DNREC. The Little Creek WA has a major impoundment of 730 acres divided into three units, including the Port Mahon impoundment of about 500 acres. Three impoundments in the Ted Harvey Conservation Area near Kitts Hummock range from 45 to 430 acres. Other state-owned impoundments include 250 acres in the Augustine WA near Port Penn, the 100-acre Gordon Pond below Cape Henlopen SP, and six impoundments ranging from 25 to 75 acres in Assawoman WA. Most of the state-owned, high-level impoundments east of Dover and in the Assawoman area were built from the mid-1950s through the early 1960s to control saltmarsh mosquito breeding and improve waterfowl habitat. All provide valuable waterbird habitat.

There are more than 70 privately owned impoundments in the state. Some 20 range from 15 to 250 acres each, totaling more than 2,500 acres (W. R. Whitman, DNREC, pers. comm.). There are a few large private impoundments ranging up to 1,000 acres each; of the other, smaller ones, about two-thirds cover fewer than one acre and most of the others less than five acres (Hardin 1987).

About half of Delaware's impounded wetland acreage is on federal lands managed by the USFWS. Built primarily for migratory waterfowl, there are 4 large impoundments totaling 1,135 acres on Bombay Hook NWR—Raymond Pool (built in 1939), Finis Pool (1944), Shearness Pool (1956), and Bear Swamp (1961). Some 4,000 acres of impounded marsh areas on Prime Hook NWR were created or restored between 1981 and 1988 for waterfowl habitat improvement and phragmites suppression.

Beginning in the early 1950s, a rapid incursion of phragmites (*Phragmites australis*) struck many of Delaware's wetlands. Today dense, monotypic stands cover some 10,000 acres of coastal marshes. The most extensive and robust stands are found in the New Castle County marshes—Army Creek, Red Lion Creek, Thousand Acre, Augustine Creek, lower Appoquinimink River, and Blackbird Creek marshes are examples. Phragmites drastically lowers the wildlife habitat value of a wetland by usurping space and displacing food sources for waterfowl, wading birds, shorebirds, and other marsh dwellers. Reasons for its swift spread remain speculative but are often related to manmade disturbance of the marsh.

In the mid-1980s the Delaware Division of Fish and Wildlife began a cost-sharing program with private landowners to control phragmites by means of herbicide applications and prescribed burns. Experience indicates that two years of such treatments followed by persistent water management with spot herbicide spraying can control, though not eradicate, phragmites. This program is a moderately expensive course of action for the long term, but an ultimate solution to this serious problem is elusive.

Impoundment Management— Problems and Practices

Marsh impoundment is an ambitious approach to habitat improvement, requiring careful planning and a long-term commitment to active management. Only monitoring and timely manipulation of water exchanges and water levels can create and maintain the desired habitat conditions; otherwise, the impoundment becomes progressively dysfunctional beginning three to four years after filling.

Impounded marshes kept too wet for too long, or at the wrong time of year, lose desirable emergent vegetation, leaving an open water body—a poor wildlife habitat. This occurred earlier in some of the Bombay Hook impoundments. To correct the problem, water-level management began in the 1980s at Shearness and Raymond pools. It involved partially drawing down the impoundments in summer and allowing them to refill in the fall from rain and upland runoff or from controlled influx of brackish tidal water. This approach has reestablished the natural emergent plant species valuable to waterbirds.

When saline or brackish water is pumped to fill impoundment pools and water loss is limited to evaporation, emergent vegetation declines as salts concentrate in the soils. Some impoundments in the Little Creek WA and the Ted Harvey Conservation Area suffered from this problem in the 1970s. In both areas the loss of vegetation for waterfowl nesting and brood rearing severely reduced waterfowl production from that of the first years following impoundment completions, when lush stands of emergent vegetation were present. At the 730-acre impoundment completed in the early 1960s at Little Creek, for example, more than 200 broods per year of dabbling ducks were produced in the first few years, averaging 2.4 young per acre of impounded habitat (Lesser 1965); production then tapered off to fewer than a dozen broods per year.

To solve this problem, tidal water control structures that permit changes in water level coordinated with tidal stages were installed at Little Creek in the late 1980s. The resulting increase in water circulation hastened salt leaching from the soil and led to substantial restoration of emergent vegetation. After three years, some 40% of the Little Creek impoundment was covered by saltmarsh cordgrass, an environment that

should gradually bring the ducks back. The Ted Harvey Conservation Area impoundments were fitted with similar control structures in 1990 and 1991.

Habitat improvement goals and practices must be carefully balanced. Low levels of impoundment water detract from the bird habitat and encourage phragmites growth; however, water-level manipulations to relieve dryness and promote emergent plant growth in Shearness Pool at Bombay Hook in the late 1980s inadvertently promoted mosquito production.

The long-term water management strategy at state-owned impoundments intends to provide full-pool habitat for migrating and wintering waterfowl and to accommodate hunting in the autumn. The strategy will maximize tidal flushing in the late winter and early spring, then stabilize the water at lower levels in late spring and summer, while still allowing frequent tidal changes. This will improve habitat for waterfowl nesting and brood rearing from mid-April to late July and will provide foraging areas for migrant shorebirds in late summer. On an experimental basis, water levels also will be adjusted to curtail mosquito production and excessive phragmites growth. Such a water management strategy will better integrate impounded wetlands with the open estuary, thereby increasing tidal exchanges for fish passage and for nutrient exchange, while creating better fish nursery habitat.

Bird Habitats and Use

In many locations impoundments offer a closely juxtaposed mosaic of wetland communities and hence varied bird habitats. Plant assemblages of cordgrasses, three-squares, rushes, cattails, smartweeds, and mallows, interspersed with shallow pools, create an ideal blend of open water and emergent vegetation in equal proportions. Within the shallow pools, benthic mat algae, widgeongrass, and other submerged aquatic vegetation, along with associated invertebrates, offer good feeding areas for dabbling ducks. If cover for brood protection is available nearby, such areas are excellent for rearing young waterfowl. Small killifishes and other aquatic organisms in the pools provide ready forage for herons, egrets, and Glossy Ibis. Exposed mud surfaces along the pool edges harbor worms, mollusks, insect larvae, and other invertebrates for probing shorebirds. Grasses and shrubs on impoundment dikes or on islands in pools are good nesting sites for songbirds such as Marsh Wrens, Yellow Warblers, Common Yellowthroats, and Song Sparrows. A recent study (Epstein and Joyner 1987) showed that properly managed brackish impoundments have significantly greater and more diversified avian use than unimpounded marshes.

Waterfowl concentrations on impoundments during spring and fall migrations are truly spectacular at times. Feeding and resting geese, swans, dabblers, and diving ducks are abundant and readily observed at full-pool levels. Sandpipers, plovers, dowitchers, yellowlegs, Dunlin, Sanderling, Ruddy Turnstone, Red Knot, American Avocet, and rarer species such as phalaropes and godwits feed on mudflats or in shallow waters, with peak abundance in May and August.

Delaware's coastal impoundments are valuable nesting and brood-rearing habitat for American Black Duck, Mallard, Gadwall, Blue-winged Teal, and Canada Goose. When impounded wetlands grade into wooded upland, prime breeding habitat for Wood Ducks is created. Grassy impoundment edges are nesting areas for Pied-billed Grebe, American and Least bitterns, King and Virginia rails, and Common Moorhen. Willet, Killdeer, Black-necked Stilt, Sedge Wren, and Boat-tailed Grackle also nest in association with impoundments.

Several species of herons and egrets, as well as Glossy Ibis, use impoundments intensively for foraging. Fish-eating birds that feed by aerial approach, including Osprey, Belted Kingfisher, Black Skimmer, and several species of terns, find shallow impoundment waters productive. Several gulls satisfy their omnivorous appetites by feeding on or near impoundments. Swallows on the wing consume numerous insects, such as midges and gnats, that periodically emerge from impounded wetlands.

Proliferation of the Snow Goose in Delaware in recent years presents another marsh management problem. Since Snow Goose foraging can strip emergent vegetation from large expanses of marshland, the species has been particularly detrimental to impoundments in the process of vegetative restoration. Special hunting seasons and the use of harassment techniques to disperse the geese and curtail grazing have had only limited success.

The diverse management practices applied in Delaware's coastal wetlands must be kept from working at cross-purposes. Control of mosquitoes and phragmites in impoundments must be balanced with habitat management goals, and the improvement, restoration, and creation of high-quality waterbird habitats must consider the needs of estuarine aquatic organisms. Such coordination is a goal of the Delaware Division of Fish and Wildlife's ongoing Integrated Marsh Management Program.

Canvasback (*Aythya valisineria*)

Regular; migrant and winter visitor; fairly common to common; local. Expected late October to mid-April and sporadically thereafter. Winter numbers decreasing at 4% per year.

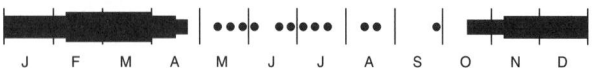

HABITAT: Estuaries with submerged aquatic vegetation, inland lakes, and ponds.

REMARKS: This species was rare at the beginning of the twentieth century. Cooke (1906) lamented "the great flocks that formerly covered Chesapeake Bay are of the past, but a few still winter on the coast of the Carolinas." Rhoads and Pennock (1905) could find but one Delaware record to cite: "one shot by H. C. Webb, near Odessa, March 22, 1903." Stone (1937) said there was a record of 2 at Delaware City on 10 April 1925, but it had "become so scarce that its shooting was stopped in 1936." In the 1930s Canvasbacks began appearing on Silver Lake, Rehoboth Beach, increasing to 250 there on 31 March 1946 [Cutl27].

SPRING: From the 1950s to the 1980s counts of 500–1,000 were not unusual during February and March. Some high counts from that period are

18 Feb 1956	1,000	Silver Lake, Rehoboth Beach [Davi7]
6 Mar 1977	3,000	Cape Henlopen [Lehm30]
7 Mar 1984	3,000	Silver Lake, Rehoboth Beach [Frec1]
31 Mar 1963	1,500	Little Creek WA [Davi21]

Bellrose (1976), describing the migration pattern, notes that Canvasbacks begin to leave winter quarters in early February, with consequent increases in numbers at mid-migration points followed by sharp declines in the last half of April. The pattern in Delaware is similar, except that the first major decrease in numbers occurs at the end of March. Latest flocks recorded are

13 Apr 1978	25	Silver Lake, Rehoboth Beach [Frec1]
13 Apr 1981	8	Silver Lake, Rehoboth Beach [Frec1]
13 Apr 1986	8	Silver Lake, Rehoboth Beach [Frec1]
16 Apr 1979	35	Silver Lake, Rehoboth Beach [Frec1]

SUMMER: Occasionally a bird will attempt to summer; 2 found at Bombay Hook NWR on 22 July 1969 are exceptional [Abbo10].

FALL: This species arrives later than most ducks; before the first of November there are few observations. A bird seen on 25 September 1965 at Assawoman WA [Lake3] may have summered locally. Early records are

10 Oct 1932	1	Milford (USNM 421918)
20 Oct 1980	1	Silver Lake, Rehoboth Beach [Frec34]
22 Oct 1986	20	Bombay Hook NWR [Wees6]

Frech [Frec1] recorded a high of 2,000 at Silver Lake, Rehoboth Beach, on 18 November 1980. Typical November numbers reach several hundred.

1966–89 CBC Summary

Christmas Bird Count	Years Found	Range of No. Found	Median
Wilmington	10	1–36	
Middletown	19	1–402	45
Bombay Hook	24	2–1,006	25
Cape Henlopen	10	1–29	
Rehoboth	24	128–2,925	828
STATEWIDE	24	361–2,927	915
(decreasing; low in 1986, high in 1967)			

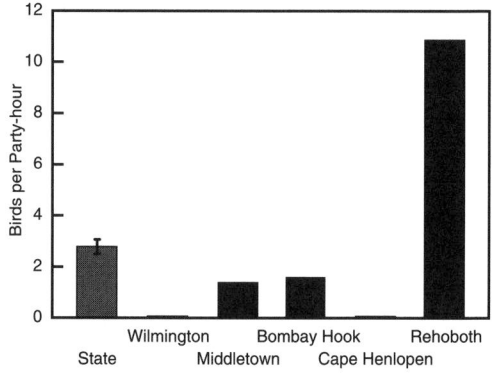

CBC Geographic Distribution

WINTER: Bellrose (1976) notes that of the approximately 145,000 birds wintering on the Atlantic Flyway, about 2,300 are found in Delaware (data for 1960–71). Our records indicate that this is a reasonable estimate for those years and through the winter of 1984. Maximum numbers reported ranged as high as 3,000 found on 1 March 1984; average wintering numbers were in the 500–800 range. However, records since then indicate a decrease in the numbers of birds wintering in Delaware. Since 1984 a maximum of 1,000 were reported in 1985 and 1986, 150 in 1987, and 400 in 1989 [Frec1]. At the same time average numbers have declined to the 50–200 range. In all periods the number of reports is approximately the same. This change is also reflected in the significant decline in CBC numbers (not included in the preceding numbers).

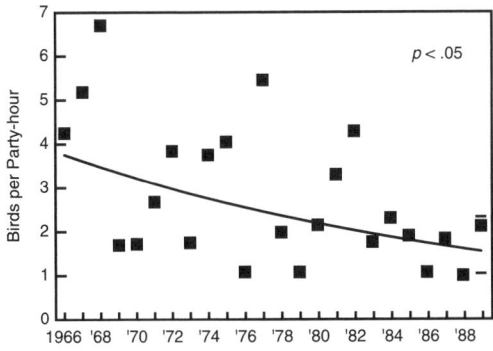

CBC Trend; Decreasing at 4% per Year

Currently, the Canvasback can be found in low numbers in Rehoboth Beach at either Spring Lake or Silver Lake. It is most numerous on the Rehoboth CBC and substantially less so on the Middletown and Bombay Hook CBCs.

BANDING: Of 600 recoveries of birds banded in Delaware, 594 were banded during 1954–68. Birds banded in Delaware were recovered at such widespread sites as Alaska (2), California (4), Arizona (1), and Mexico (1), as well as many from Maryland (262). Recovered in Delaware were 103 birds banded elsewhere, including 66 banded in Maryland. These results suggest there is easy interchange between the large population wintering on the Chesapeake Bay and the Delaware population. These wintering birds come primarily from the main breeding grounds in the Dakotas and western Canada, but a few breed as far away as Alaska.

SPECIMENS: USNM 421856, Milton, 17 January 1934; USNM 421918, Milford, 10 October 1932.

Total Canvasbacks Either Banded or Recovered in Delaware, or Both

Redhead *(Aythya americana)*

Regular; winter visitor; rare to uncommon. Expected sporadically, mid-November to late March.

DOCUMENTATION: Multiple sight and banding records.

HABITAT: Brackish estuarine waters with plentiful aquatic plant growth.

SPRING: Redheads are seldom present after 15–20 March. Bellrose (1976) notes that by mid-March the wintering range is deserted. The latest flocks recorded are

| 3 Apr 1948 | 20 | Silver Lake, Rehoboth Beach [Lowe1] |
| 4 Apr 1978 | 6 | Burton Pond [Frec1] |

May records of stragglers include

5 May 1973	1	Pickering Beach [Rich4]
14 May 1972	2	Little Creek WA [Cutl2]
17 May 1984	1	Little Creek WA [Cutl9]

Usually fewer than 5 are found, but an astounding count of 135 was made on 6 March 1977 at Cape Henlopen [Lehm30]. The next highest count is 17 at Silver Lake, Rehoboth Beach, on 7 March 1982 [Frec1].

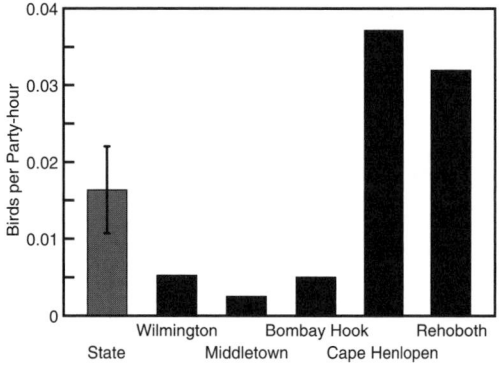

CBC Geographic Distribution

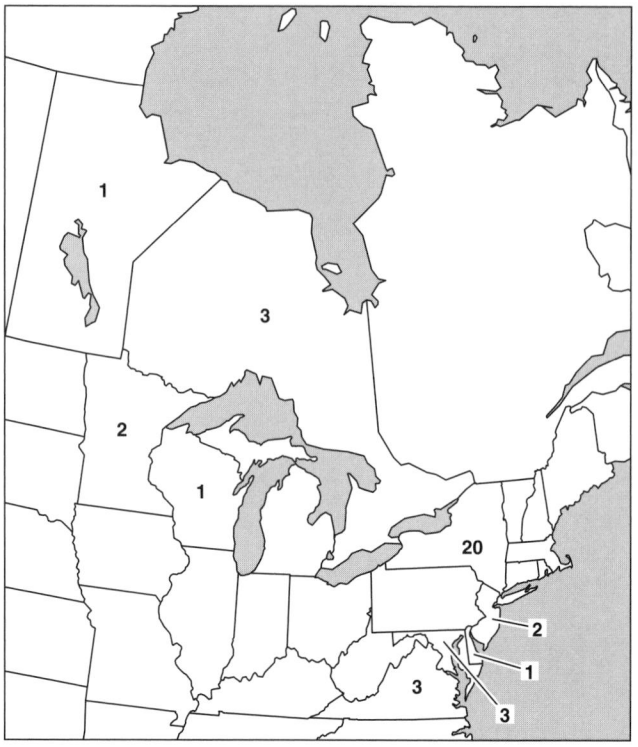

Total Redheads Either Banded or Recovered in Delaware, or Both

FALL: This species is so scarce during most of the fall that the first arrival frequently is not found until 15–30 November, but in some years migrants arrive in October:

12 Oct 1971	10	Bombay Hook NWR [Holg67]
18 Oct 1964	1	Hoopes Reservoir, Wilmington [Nixd2]
30 Oct 1928	1	shot at Kitts Hummock [Hans1]
31 Oct 1972	7	Lewes [Keit1]

High counts include

2 Nov 1952	10	Rehoboth Beach [anon3]
10 Nov 1961	10	Bombay Hook NWR [anon10]
17 Nov 1972	60	Bombay Hook NWR [Holg13]

Unusually early for a migrant, a bird found on 8 August 1964 at Assawoman WA [Dyke6] may have summered locally.

WINTER: Most Redheads winter along the coast of the Gulf of Mexico; about 10% winter along the Atlantic coast, chiefly on Chesapeake Bay (Bellrose 1976), and sparsely in Delaware. Bellrose (1976) notes that they suffer from high annual mortality rates among both adults and young; consequently, their status is so precarious that they have been afforded special protection. The CBC data do not show a trend; the 25 Redheads found on the 22 December 1985 Cape Henlopen count dominate the CBC analyses of this otherwise rare wintering duck. More Redheads are found on the Cape Henlopen and Rehoboth CBCs than on the others.

1966–89 CBC Summary

Christmas Bird Count	Years Found	Range of No. Found	Median
Wilmington	5	2–6	
Middletown	1		4
Bombay Hook	7	1–2	
Cape Henlopen	9	1–25	
Rehoboth	17	1–8	2
STATEWIDE	21	1–28	5
(zero in 1968, 1981, and 1984; high in 1985)			

BANDING: Delaware-banded birds were recovered in Ontario (3), New York (2), Virginia (2), Delaware, Maryland, New Jersey, Minnesota, and Manitoba (1 each). The 24 recoveries in Delaware include Redheads banded in New York (18), Maryland (2), and one each in New Jersey, Virginia, Minnesota, and Wisconsin.

REMARKS: Two immatures collected by Pennock (notes) at Indian River Inlet on 28 October 1904 are not extant.

Ring-necked Duck *(Aythya collaris)*

Regular; fairly common to common migrant and uncommon winter visitor. Expected late October to mid-April. Winter numbers decreasing at 7% per year.

HABITAT: Mostly freshwater ponds and deep impoundments; occasionally brackish or fresh estuarine waters.

HISTORY: The Ring-necked Duck was not included on the first Delaware list (Rhoads and Pennock 1905). Emlen and other DVOC members saw this species regularly at Delaware City, beginning with 29 present on 28 March 1928 [Emle2]; and Buckalew shot 1 (of 4) on 16 November 1931 at Griffith Pond, Milford [Hans1]. Wilcox Brown (1934a) saw 5 on 4 March 1933 and a peak of 25 on 16 March 1933 on the recently completed Hoopes Reservoir.

SPRING: Peak migration is during March, and most leave by 10–15 April. Later reports are

21 Apr 1992	6	Bombay Hook NWR [Anth1]
26 Apr 1987	5	Silver Lake, Rehoboth Beach [Frec1]
30 Apr 1958	1	Sussex County (DMNH 849)

Stragglers stay into May. Falk and Speck recorded a high of 175 at Thousand Acre Marsh on 19 March 1984 [Falk18]. Typical counts for this elusive species total fewer than 50 birds.

FALL: First arrival may be as early as 15–25 October but is usually 25 October to 1 November. Peak numbers occur from then until 1–10 December. Early reports include

19 Sep 1971	2	Brandywine Creek SP [Edni1]
23 Sep 1986	2	Bombay Hook NWR [Wees6]

Some peak counts, all in Sussex County near Lewes, are

6, 17 Nov 1972	60	Red Mill Pond [Holg75]
17 Nov 1980	50	Gravel Hill [Frec1]
3 Dec 1983	125	Gravel Hill [Frec1]

Observers usually find 15–20 birds.

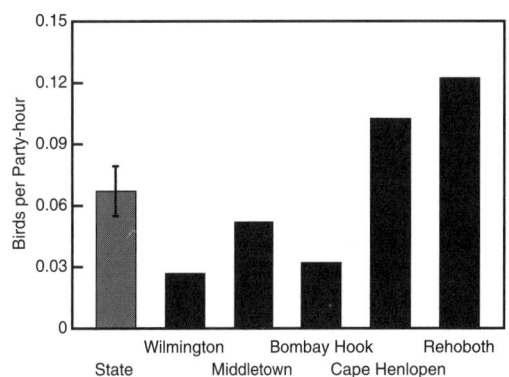

CBC Geographic Distribution

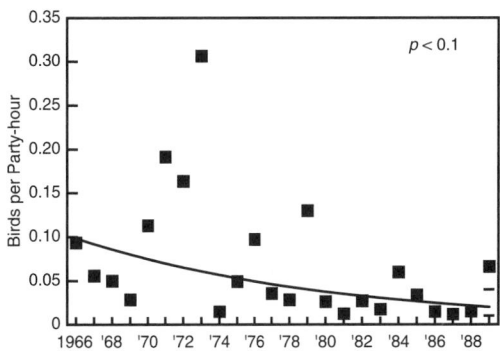

CBC Trend; Decreasing at 7% per Year

WINTER: About 45% of Ring-necked Ducks winter in the Atlantic Flyway, mainly in South Carolina and Florida (Bellrose

1976). The CBC data show a decreasing trend. Bellrose (1976) notes that from 1955 to 1974 its numbers declined in the Atlantic Flyway, increased in the Mississippi Flyway, and remained the same elsewhere. On coastal counts more Ring-necked Ducks are found on the Rehoboth and Cape Henlopen CBCs than on the 3 to the north. In contrast, western Sussex County millponds, in the Chesapeake drainage, are more attractive to Ring-necked Ducks than millponds elsewhere in Delaware; the Seaford CBC averaged 360 birds per year (7 birds per party-hour for 1983–89). High non-CBC reports are

10 Dec 1986	550	Chipman Pond, Laurel [Frec1]
23 Dec 1983	103	Gravel Hill [Frec1]
21 Dec 1979–16 Jan 1980	100	Gravel Hill [Frec1]

1966–89 CBC Summary

Christmas Bird Count	Years Found	Range of No. Found	Median
Wilmington	11	1–32	
Middletown	12	1–26	
Bombay Hook	23	1–10	2
Cape Henlopen	17	1–60	3
Rehoboth	14	1–71	2
STATEWIDE (low in 1987, high in 1973)	24	4–119	15

Total Ring-necked Ducks Either Banded or Recovered in Delaware, or Both

BANDING: A total of 60 bands have been recovered, 39 of birds banded in Delaware and 21 of those banded out of state. Delaware-banded birds were recovered in North Carolina (13), Delaware (8), Ontario (5), Maryland (4), Virginia (3), Maine (2), and 1 each in Florida, Pennsylvania, Minnesota, and New Brunswick. Recoveries were recorded in Delaware of individuals banded in North Carolina (11), Maryland (3), Nova Scotia (2), and 1 each from Pennsylvania, Virginia, West Virginia, Minnesota, and Quebec. These banding results, and analysis of migration patterns by Mendall (1976), are consistent with fall migrants and those few wintering birds in the Delaware Valley arriving via the Atlantic Flyway from northeastern breeding grounds. Some fall migrants from more western breeding grounds cross from the Great Lakes to wintering grounds in the Chesapeake drainage and southward. Spring migrants pass through the Delaware Valley going to either breeding ground.

SPECIMENS: UDEL 30-66, Wilmington, 19 January 1966; DMNH 849, Sussex Co., 30 April 1958.

Greater Scaup *(Aythya marila)*

| J | F | M | A | M | J | J | A | S | O | N | D |

Regular; winter resident; fairly common to common. Expected mid-October to mid-April. Winter numbers declining at 11% per year.

DOCUMENTATION: Multiple sight and banding records.

HABITAT: Salt and brackish bays and estuaries (Delaware Bay and the Inland Bays), rarely lakes, ponds, reservoirs (e.g., Hoopes Reservoir).

REMARKS: No doubt, because of difficulty in distinguishing this species from the next, most reports simply refer to "scaup species." For this reason a single seasonal bar graph for the 2 scaup species is presented. There is some justification for this presentation, as Bellrose (1976) found that the chronology of passage of Greater Scaups "appears to coincide with that of Lesser Scaups."

SPRING: In Maryland the normal migration period is 1–10 March to 10–20 May with a peak 15 March to 20 April (Stewart and Robbins 1958). The situation in Delaware is probably similar, with these reports marking spring migration:

6 Mar 1982	85	Bombay Hook NWR [SpSB13]
12 Mar 1988	50	Broadkill Beach [Wayn72]
16 Mar 1968	1,000	Prime Hook NWR [Carr15]
16 Mar 1991	200 +	Lewes Harbor [Camp15]
11 Apr 1992	30	Little Creek WA [Hess16]

SUMMER: A few undocumented reports from May through September are attributed to this species. Stragglers in May are reasonable, but undocumented summer reports are not accepted. In North America Greater Scaups breed in Alaska and the western Canadian subarctic (Bellrose 1976).

FALL: In Maryland the normal migration period is 1–10 October to 1–10 December (Stewart and Robbins 1958). Six flocks of 2,000 to 10,000 have been noted along Delaware Bay between 18 October and 7 November. Two high counts are 5,000–10,000 at Pickering Beach on 23 October 1965 [Wayn16] and 8,000 at Kitts Hummock on 7 November 1983 [Edni53].

Undocumented reports before 5 October (Lesser 1964) may refer to Lesser Scaup (Bellrose 1976, 338; Robbins and Bystrak 1977).

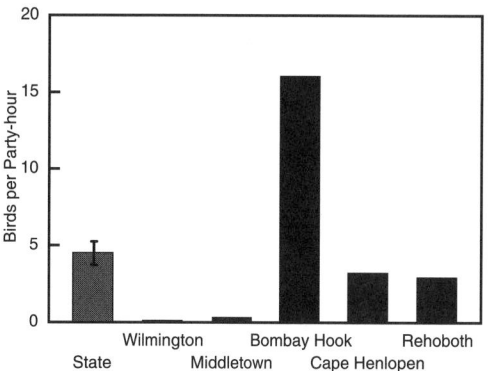

CBC Geographic Distribution

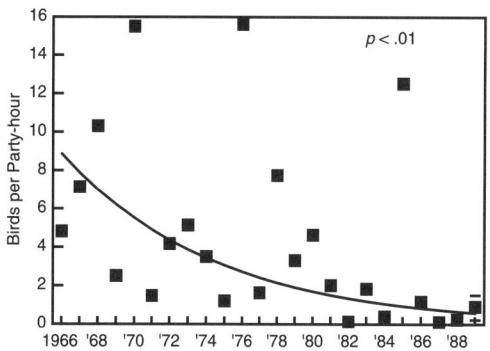

CBC Trend; Decreasing at 11% per Year

1966–89 CBC Summary

Christmas Bird Count	Years Found	Range of No. Found	Median
Wilmington	11	1–51	
Middletown	14	1–329	2
Bombay Hook	24	7–5,451	318
Cape Henlopen	22	5–2,044	47
Rehoboth	23	1–1,406	138
STATEWIDE	24	38–6,031	1,244
(decreasing; low in 1987, high in 1970)			

WINTER: The CBC data show a significant downward trend. Greater Scaups are reported most commonly on the Bombay Hook CBC. Bellrose (1976) notes that most Atlantic Flyway birds winter in the region around Long Island, New York, and New Jersey, declining sharply south of Chesapeake Bay.

BANDING: Two birds banded in Delaware were recovered, 1 in the Bahamas, the other in North Carolina. Recoveries in Delaware of individuals banded elsewhere include birds from New Jersey (4), New York (3), Maryland (1), and Virginia (1).

Lesser Scaup (*Aythya affinis*)

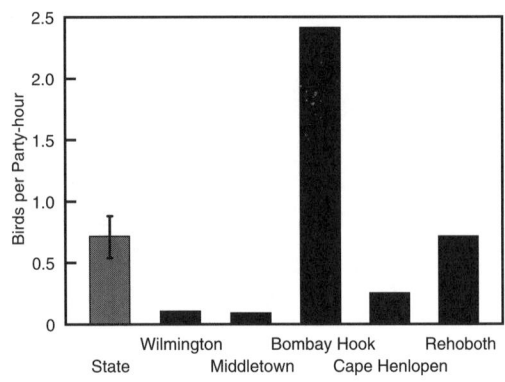

CBC Geographic Distribution

Regular; migrant and winter resident; fairly common to common. Expected mid-October to late April.

HABITAT: Bays, estuaries (salt and brackish), ponds, lakes, reservoirs.

SPRING: The normal migration period in Maryland is identical to Greater Scaup (Stewart and Robbins 1958), and the same is likely true in Delaware, where the spring migration is punctuated with these counts:

5 Mar 1985	100	Little Creek WA [Edni56]
16 Mar 1968	1,000	Assawoman WA [Carr15]
20 Mar 1982	205	Bombay Hook NWR [RusR18]
9 Apr 1989	150	Wilmington Sewage Treatment Plant [Edni44]
19 Apr 1986	>1,000	Kent and Sussex Counties [Barn1]

SUMMER: Several undocumented reports of stragglers in May, as well as one found 6 June 1961 at Little Creek WA (Lesser 1964), are attributed to this species.

FALL: The normal migration period in Maryland is 25 September–5 October to 15–25 December with a peak 10 November–10 December (Stewart and Robbins 1958). The same is likely true in Delaware. The only report exceeding a few birds mentions 500–1,000 observed at Kitts Hummock on 22 October 1983 [Batt4]. DNREC aerial counts suggest it is common in Delaware Bay between Kitts Hummock and Bowers Beach.

WINTER: In contrast to data collected about the more common Greater Scaup, the CBC data do not show a decline for this species. It is most commonly reported on the Bombay Hook CBC. Bellrose (1976) observes that "The largest number of Lesser Scaups wintering in the Atlantic Flyway, like many people, select Florida." An estimated 285,000 winter there, and 95,000 winter from Long Island, New York, to North Carolina, about two-thirds on Chesapeake Bay. Lesser Scaups are not expected to winter in large numbers in Delaware, so the following reports are notable:

17 Dec 1988	223	wintered, Wilmington [Whit3]
18 Jan 1982	500	Indian River Inlet [Frec36]

1966–89 CBC Summary

Christmas Bird Count	Years Found	Range of No. Found	Median
Wilmington	13	1–223	1
Middletown	11	1–72	
Bombay Hook	23	1–1,150	43
Cape Henlopen	15	1–92	1
Rehoboth	21	1–750	15
STATEWIDE (low in 1980, high in 1973)	24	4–1,165	147

BANDING: The 47 banding records of Lesser Scaup include 20 recoveries of birds banded in Delaware and 27 recoveries in Delaware of individuals banded out of state. These banding results support the migration pattern given by Bellrose (1976): Lesser Scaup migrate from northwestern breeding areas through the Great Lakes to the Mid-Atlantic coast south from Long Island. They proceed south along the Atlantic coast, some going as far south as Florida and crossing over to the Gulf coast.

Lesser Scaup either banded or recovered in Delaware were found in Northwest Territories (1), Manitoba (2), Ontario (1), Minnesota (3), Wisconsin (1), Michigan (1), Ohio (1), New York (3), New Jersey (7), Delaware (2), Maryland (10), Virginia (3), North Carolina (8), South Carolina (1), Florida (2), Alabama (1).

REMARKS: See remarks under Greater Scaup.

SPECIMENS: DMNH 63017, near Claymont, February 1974; ANSP 84665, Smyrna, 16 October 1927; DMNH 76492, Little Creek WA, 5 November 1985; DMNH 72078, 1 mi (1. 6 km) west of Pickering Beach, 27 December 1981.

King Eider *(Somateria spectabilis)*

Occasional (21 years, 1966–91); winter visitor; uncommon.

DOCUMENTATION: Photograph (R. F. Ringler, A.B. 36:77).

HABITAT: Delaware Bay, ocean; especially inlets.

WINTER: Although this species occurs most frequently during winter, it has been found every month of the year. Birds were found between mid-April and mid-September, indicating stragglers or summering birds, in 8 of the 21 summers from 1971 to 1991. Usually, 1–3 birds are seen. One or 2 individuals have occurred on 5 Cape Henlopen and Rehoboth CBCs, including an immature male at Broadkill Beach on 23 December 1966 for the first state report [Carr19]. A photograph of a male at Indian River Inlet on 7 February 1982 was published [Ring1]. Like the Common Eider this species is most often found at Cape Henlopen and Indian River Inlet.

Birds (one of which was present through the summer) have been reported in September in 3 years, but the earliest true migrants are probably

| 18 Oct 1969 | 1 | Indian River Inlet [Wayn14] |
| 29 Oct 1989 | 4 | Cape Henlopen [Fint5] |

No single birds have been seen before December. The highest counts are

6 Feb 1971	10	Cape Henlopen [Carl14]
8 Feb 1970	9	Indian River Inlet [ThoR2]
22 Mar 1986	10	Indian River Inlet [Frec1]

Although all high counts are after the first of the year, about 45% of King Eiders arrive before year end. The 1986 flock dwindled to 2 stragglers by 5 April [Frec1], signaling the last of the migration. A bird reported at Cape Henlopen on 8 April 1972 may also have been a northward migrant, but those reported later in the spring appear to be stragglers, some known to summer.

REMARKS: The earliest mention of this species in Delaware was made by Rhoads and Pennock (1905): "Two eiders recorded by Mr. Woolman were presumably [King Eiders]." A 1967 report of a mixed flock of 100 Common and King eiders has been excluded from this account (see Common Eider account). King and Common eiders associate in winter, and some birds should be recorded simply as "eiders" because some immatures and females of the two species are difficult to distinguish.

Common Eider *(Somateria mollissima)*

Occasional (33 years, 1940–91), winter visitor; rare to uncommon.

DOCUMENTATION: Photograph (M. G. Jahn DMNH 459), banding record.

HABITAT: Delaware Bay, ocean; especially near jetties.

REMARKS: The nearest population, breeding from Labrador southward, was reduced to one known breeding station in 1907 but has since doubled in numbers repeatedly to about 20,000 nesting pairs in 1970. More recently 15,000 pairs were breeding in New Brunswick and Nova Scotia alone (Erskine 1992). With this increase it extended its breeding range southward to Maine by 1969 (Palmer 1976), and breeding was successfully established in Massachusetts in 1973–75 (Viet and Petersen 1993). Concurrent with this increase, its status in Delaware has changed. First recorded in Delaware on 4 December 1940 [MayR1], it was also reported on the Rehoboth CBC that year. The first specimen examined was shot by a hunter in "Hundred [Thousand?] Acre Marsh near the mouth of the Delaware River, New Castle County" on 16 October 1944 (Cottam 1945). Since 1970 this species has been found every year but 2, most often at Cape Henlopen or Indian River Inlet.

SPRING: There are a few reports of this species, beginning in late January. During March–May it has been reported in only 7 years (1966–83), with never more than 1 seen.

SUMMER: A straggler is occasionally found from May through September [Brez2; RusR1; Fint6]; stragglers have also been reported farther south, from the Virginia part of the Delmarva Peninsula (Kain 1987).

FALL: The earliest arrival date, 30 September 1983 and 1986 [Frec41; Fint2], has been attributed to possibly summering birds. There are no more records until 12 October when birds begin to be found regularly. Highest numbers found are

mid-Oct 1966	8	(not a 1-day count) coast [RusW7]
28 Nov 1959	7	Indian River Inlet [MiJC1]
8 Dec 1962	8	Indian River Inlet [Davi22]

WINTER: This species has occurred on 7 Cape Henlopen and Rehoboth CBCs in numbers ranging from 1 to 5. A report of a mixed flock of 100 Common and King eiders on 22 January 1967 at Pickering Beach (Faust 1968) cannot be accepted without corroboration because the number and the location away from jetties are both unusual.

BANDING: The only recovery involves a female banded in Maine on 3 July 1970 and shot on the Delaware River during December 1980.

Harlequin Duck (Histrionicus histrionicus)

Occasional (21 years, 1938–91); winter visitor; uncommon.

|■■■·■|■■■■·|■■■ | |·■■| | | | | |·| |■■■|
| J | F | M | A | M | J | J | A | S | O | N | D |

DOCUMENTATION: Photograph (C. D. Campbell, DMNH 367).

HABITAT: Ocean, especially around jetties and breakwaters.

WINTER: The first published report of this species in Delaware described 1 at Indian River Inlet on 31 March 1938 [HilJ2]; it has been reported in more than half the years since 1959. The earliest arrivals occur in November:

| 1 Nov 1969 | 2 | immatures [Carl9] |
| 5 Nov 1989 | 1 female | [Fint12] |

The next earliest arrivals are not until 15 December, when they begin arriving more frequently. One or 2 individuals have occurred on 5 Rehoboth CBCs. High counts, all of 3 birds at Indian River Inlet, were made on 27 December 1988 [Frec1], 31 December 1983 to 2 January 1984 [Fint1; Frec1], and 22 January 1977 [Barn19]. The following May reports probably represent late migrants:

5 May 1940	1	Rehoboth Beach [HilJ3]
7 May 1977	2	Indian River Inlet [MooJ2]
10 May 1970	2	Cape Henlopen [Cutl24]
17 May 1983	2	Cape Henlopen [Reim2]

This species occurs with about the same frequency as King Eider and, like the eider, is usually found at Cape Henlopen or Indian River Inlet.

[Labrador Duck (Camptorhynchus labradorius)]

Gregory A. Inskip

Extinct. Formerly present in the region, but no specific Delaware records.

REMARKS: This duck was probably an uncommon winter resident off the Atlantic coast and in Delaware Bay until its extinction about 1875 (Greenway 1967, 173–74). In 1869 George Boardman wrote that the Labrador Duck had been "a common bird all along our coast, from Delaware to Labrador"

(Rowley 1877, 207). Audubon stated that it wintered from the Maritimes to Chesapeake Bay, and that it sometimes ascended the Delaware River "at least as far as Philadelphia" (Rowley 1877, 209–10; Audubon 1843, VI:329). Bent commented that the species was probably always uncommon and succumbed to persecution on its breeding ground on the southeast Labrador coast (1925, 67).

Wilson (1859–60) commented that "It is called by some gunners the Sand Shoal Duck, from its habit of frequenting sand bars. Its principle food appears to be shellfish, which it procures by diving. The flesh is dry, and partakes considerably of the nature of its food. It is only seen here during winter; most commonly early in the month of March a few are observed in our market [Philadelphia]."

Surf Scoter *(Melanitta perspicillata)*

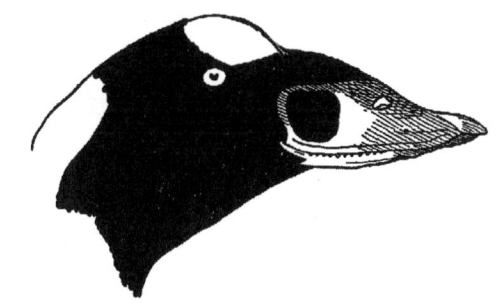

Regular; migrant and winter resident; fairly common. Expected early October to late April and sporadically thereafter.

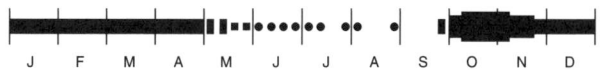

J F M A M J J A S O N D

HABITAT: Near shore along the Atlantic coastline, also in bays and estuaries.

SPRING: The last departure is usually 25–30 April, with stragglers present into May. Late records of flocks include

25 Apr 1980	10	Cape Henlopen [Frec1]
2 May 1985	15	Rehoboth Beach [Frec1]
17 May 1983	6	Cape Henlopen [Frec1]

In some years 1 or 2 stragglers are present as late as August. Although the data do not show a clear peak in numbers during migration, the number of reports received increases during April. Stewart and Robbins (1958), writing about Maryland, note the normal migration period is 10–20 February to 5–15 May, with the peak occurring 25 February to 25 April. Some high Delaware counts are

18 Mar 1985	100	Rehoboth Beach [Frec1]
9 Apr 1983	50	Cape Henlopen [Frec1]
11 Apr 1979	1,000	Rehoboth Beach [Frec1]

Most reports are of fewer than 15 birds.

The first record for this species in Delaware involves a partly eaten bird found on the beach south of Rehoboth Beach on 3 May 1912 by Pennock (notes).

FALL: Flocks of Surf Scoters usually arrive 1–5 October; the occasional earlier ones may have summered south of the breeding range:

29 Aug 1965	12	Lewes [Mulh1]
30 Aug 1964	14	Cape Henlopen [PylR4]
2 Oct 1982	50	Indian River Inlet [Frec1]
3 Oct 1988	400	Slaughter Beach [Edni60]

They are usually more common during the fall migration than during winter or spring, as evidenced by an observation of 8,000 on 24 October 1980 at Cape Henlopen [Frec1]. The peak migration period is similar to that of Black Scoter but slightly longer. Migration counts of nearly 1,000 are not unusual.

1966–89 CBC Summary

Christmas Bird Count	Years Found	Range of No. Found	Median
Wilmington			
Middletown			
Bombay Hook	14	1–14	1
Cape Henlopen	23	1–1,459	46
Rehoboth	23	3–342	42
STATEWIDE (low in 1986, high in 1969)	24	4–1,574	143

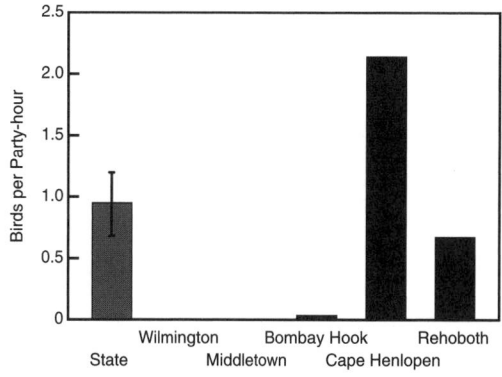

CBC Geographic Distribution; Average of 3 Count Areas

WINTER: The Surf Scoter is most abundant on the Cape Henlopen CBC and has never been recorded on the Middletown or Wilmington CBCs. High counts include 200 at Cape Henlopen on 4 January 1979 and 500 at Rehoboth Beach on 25 January 1982 [both Frec1]. Typically, only a few are reported. The first published report of this species in Delaware is 40 found on the Rehoboth CBC on 19 December 1939.

SPECIMENS: UDEL 473-73, Mispillion Light, 17 October 1971; DMNH 77585, Bethany Beach, 24 October 1988; DMNH 680, Sussex Co., 30 December 1956.

White-winged Scoter *(Melanitta fusca)*

Regular; migrant and winter resident; uncommon to fairly common. Expected mid-October to early April.

J F M A M J J A S O N D

HABITAT: Near shore along the Atlantic coastline, also in bays and estuaries.

SPRING: Most leave before mid-April; the last reports of more than 2 birds are

6 Apr 1930	large raft	Delaware Bay [Pott7]
9 Apr 1983	4	Cape Henlopen [Frec1]
11 Apr 1980	34	Cape Henlopen [Frec1]
12 Apr 1978	4	Cape Henlopen [Frec1]

Stragglers remain through April and occasionally into May, with the last straggler reported on 25 May 1978 at Cape Henlopen [Frec1]. Peak numbers are present from 20 February [Barn1] through 11 April [Frec1]. Most observers report fewer than 10 birds.

SUMMER: The center of abundance of summering pre-breeders (on the Atlantic side) is in the Gulf of St. Lawrence and adjacent waters of Newfoundland and southern Labrador (Palmer 1976). It may be these birds that begin to arrive in Delaware waters in August and September:

12-22 Aug 1985	1	Cape Henlopen [Frec1]
23 Aug 1965	4	Fenwick Island [PylR6]
22 Sep 1989	1	Cape Henlopen [Frec1]

FALL: Most White-winged Scoters arrive after mid-October. Their numbers remain fairly constant until 5–10 December when the lower winter level is reached. The high counts include an undetermined proportion of a mixed flight of 1,400 White-winged and Surf scoters that passed Fowler Beach in a hour on 18 October 1971 [Holg54]. Other high counts are

| 30 Oct 1981 | 200 | Cape Henlopen and Rehoboth Beach [Frec1] |
| 1 Nov 1983 | 200 | Cape Henlopen [Frec1] |

Typical counts involve fewer than 30–40 birds.

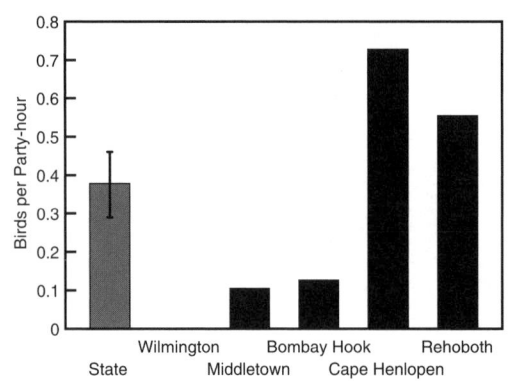

CBC Geographic Distribution; Average of 4 Count Areas

WINTER: The White-winged Scoter is the least common of the 3 scoters on the CBCs. Most are found on the Cape Henlopen and Rehoboth CBCs. It is present in low numbers during most of the winter and then increases in February when migration begins. The highest counts (during this low period) are

9 Dec 1980	25	Delaware Seashore SP [Frec1]
18 Dec 1982	14	Cape Henlopen [Frec1]
4 Jan 1980	12	Delaware Seashore SP [Frec1]

Although this species was reported to be in Delaware in the early twentieth century (Rhoads and Pennock 1905; Pennock 1908a), the first dated reference to this species notes 2 taken at Fowler Beach on 14 December 1931 [Buck3].

SPECIMEN: UDEL 440-73, Mispillion Light, 16 October 1972.

1966–89 CBC Summary

Christmas Bird Count	Years Found	Range of No. Found	Median
Wilmington			
Middletown	4	4–150	
Bombay Hook	16	1–175	1
Cape Henlopen	20	3–530	20
Rehoboth	24	1–371	23
STATEWIDE *(low in 1986, high in 1975)*	24	2–559	51

Black Scoter *(Melanitta nigra)*

Regular; common migrant and fairly common winter resident. Expected mid-September, occasionally earlier, to mid-May and sporadically thereafter.

HABITAT: Near shore along the Atlantic coastline, also in bays and estuaries.

SPRING: Most individuals depart by 15 April, the remainder within a month. Although our data do not show a clear peak in numbers, an increase in the frequency of reports occurs 1–20 April. High counts are

9 Apr 1979	100	Indian River Inlet [Frec1]
11 Apr 1979	1,000	Rehoboth Beach [Frec1]
25 Apr 1982	75	Rehoboth Beach [Frec1]

Most reports total fewer than 50 birds. In some years a few nonbreeding individuals summer; a summer high of 11 males was reported at Cape Henlopen on 27 July 1968 [Wayn27].

FALL: Individuals present in late August or September may be early arrivals or summering birds. These earliest flocks may be prebreeders that summered south of the breeding grounds (Palmer 1976):

24 Aug 1990	6	Cape Henlopen [Edni1]
7 Sep 1974	8	Indian River Inlet [Lehm1]
18 Sep 1981	27	Cape Henlopen [Frec1]

The main migration takes place from 25–30 September to 10–15 November, with the peak occurring during October. Some high counts are

4 Oct 1977	1,500	Cape Henlopen [Frec1]
9 Oct 1977	2,000	Rehoboth Beach [Frec1]
4 Nov 1988	1,000	Cape Henlopen [Frec1]

During migration, counts of 200 or more birds flying down the coast are not unusual. Buckalew (notes) collected a male at Fenwick Island on 6 November 1933 (not extant).

WINTER: Although the Black Scoter was included in the first Delaware list (Rhoads and Pennock 1905), the first published record notes 4 on the Rehoboth Beach CBC on 22 December 1937. It is about twice as common on the Cape Henlopen CBC as on the Rehoboth CBC, but numbers reported on CBCs are highly variable. The high non-CBC count is 75 at

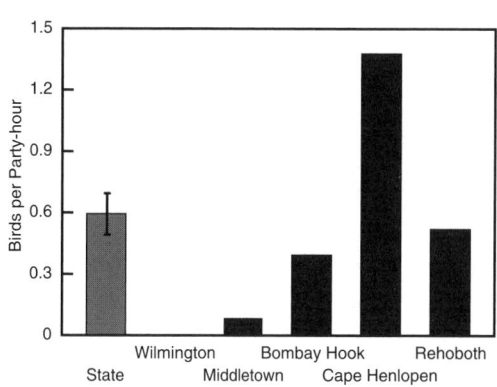

CBC Geographic Distribution; Average of 4 Count Areas

Cape Henlopen on 3 December 1983 [Frec1], though, typically, fewer than 25 birds are reported.

1966–89 CBC Summary

Christmas Bird Count	Years Found	Range of No. Found	Median
Wilmington			
Middletown	6	2–50	
Bombay Hook	21	1–230	7
Cape Henlopen	24	1–491	44
Rehoboth	21	6–182	41
STATEWIDE (low in 1986, high in 1977)	24	2–591	135

SPECIMENS: DMNH 850, Sussex Co., 15 February 1958; DMNH 77687, Indian River Inlet, 4 October 1987; UDEL 439-73, and UDEL 441-73, Mispillion Light, 16 October 1972.

Oldsquaw *(Clangula hyemalis)*

Regular; winter resident; fairly common to common. Expected late October to mid-April.

| J | F | M | A | M | J | J | A | S | O | N | D |

HABITAT: Usually saltwater bays and estuaries, sometimes on the ocean, rarely as far upriver as Wilmington, on Hoopes Reservoir during migration.

SPRING: Most leave by mid-April, when the last flocks seen were

8 Apr 1989	12	Indian River Inlet [Frec1]
10 Apr 1986	5	Indian River Inlet [Frec1]
13 Apr 1978	75	Indian River Inlet [Frec1]

Single stragglers remain through May, and once until 30 June 1974 at Cape Henlopen [Wayn47].

FALL: It usually arrives from late October to mid-November and does not become common until December. The earliest reports include 1 on 17 October at Cape Henlopen and 3 on 21 October 1983 at Rehoboth Beach [both Frec1]. A report of 30 at Cape Henlopen on 25 October 1984 represents the high count [Frec1]. Typical reports total 5–10 birds.

WINTER: Although the first published dated report for this species resulted from 24 found on the Rehoboth CBC on 19 December 1939, Pennock saw a mounted Delaware specimen in 1903 (Rhoads and Pennock 1905), and Barry stated they could be found at "Lewes, Rehoboth Bay, and Indian Bay" (Barry 1939).

January to early March is the peak period, with high counts of 300 on 18 January 1982 [Frec36] and 1,000 on 14 February 1981 [Frec1], both at Indian River Inlet. Typical counts total fewer than 100 birds. This species' CBC data suggest its population has been stable since 1966, but it has greatly recovered since the early 1900s. Large flocks, sometimes found on the upper Delaware Bay and Delaware River, have been reported on the Bombay Hook and Middletown CBCs.

1966–89 CBC Summary

Christmas Bird Count	Years Found	Range of No. Found	Median
Wilmington	3	1–16	
Middletown	10	1–102	
Bombay Hook	23	1–973	6
Cape Henlopen	24	1–49	13
Rehoboth	24	5–216	87
STATEWIDE *(low in 1968, high in 1972)*	24	30–1,093	109

SPECIMENS: USNM 482028, 2 mi (3.2 km) S Dover, 29 November 1964; DMNH 57880, Claymont, 23 December 1975.

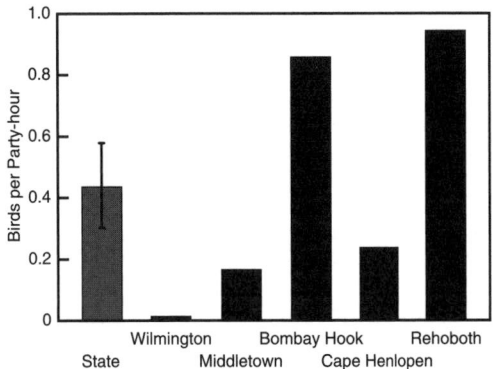

CBC Geographic Distribution

Bufflehead *(Bucephala albeola)*

Regular; migrant and winter resident; fairly common to common.
Expected late October to mid-May.

J	F	M	A	M	J	J	A	S	O	N	D

HABITAT: Salt and brackish bays and estuaries, inland lakes and reservoirs.

SPRING: Many birds wintering leave 15–20 March, but occasional migrating flocks pass through later. Examples of late high counts are

| 11–14 Apr 1980 | 150 | Cape Henlopen [Frec1] |
| 13 Apr 1985 | 100 | Holts Landing SP [Frec1] |

Typical April counts range up to 50 birds. The last small flocks remain into mid-May:

10 May 1978	8	Delaware Seashore SP [Frec1]
14 May 1972	16	Indian River Inlet [Cutl2]
16 May 1970	4	Indian River Inlet [DuPG15]

Stragglers remained past May in only 3 years.

FALL: This is a late-arriving species. Occasionally a few birds arrive in late October, with these the earliest:

20 Oct 1978	3	Gibbs Pond, Lewes [Frec1]
22 Oct 1985	2	Rehoboth Beach [Frec1]
23 Oct 1980	4	Cape Henlopen [Frec34]

Reports increase in early November, and numbers build during mid-winter. Some unusually high counts are

30 Oct 1988	100	Indian River Inlet [Frec1]
9 Nov 1985	350	Cape Henlopen [Frec1]
25 Nov 1984	100	Lewes [Frec1]

Typically, about 25 birds are reported.

WINTER: Except for high counts in 1966, 1970, and 1987, the state CBCs have averaged between 1 and 3 birds per party-hour and show no trend. It is most numerous on the Rehoboth CBC. Peak numbers occur from 10–15 January to 15–20 March. Some high counts are

18 Jan 1982	500	Indian River Inlet [Frec36]
3 Feb 1981	500	Lewes [Frec1]
2 Mar 1986	500	Dewey Beach [Frec1]

1966–89 CBC Summary

Christmas Bird Count	Years Found	Range of No. Found	Median
Wilmington	5	1–8	
Middletown	17	1–39	3
Bombay Hook	24	7–132	55
Cape Henlopen	24	18–229	96
Rehoboth	24	322–3,346	708
STATEWIDE	24	390–3,645	906
(low in 1968, high in 1970)			

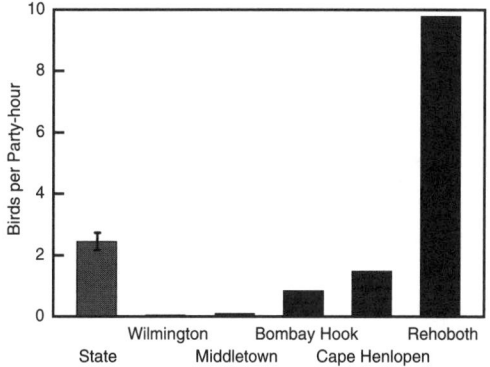

CBC Geographic Distribution

BANDING: Six Buffleheads banded elsewhere have been recovered in Delaware—3 from their breeding grounds in Alberta and 3 from wintering areas in New York (2) and Maryland (1).

SPECIMENS: DMNH 76477, Little Creek WA, 5 November 1985.

Common Goldeneye *(Bucephala clangula)*

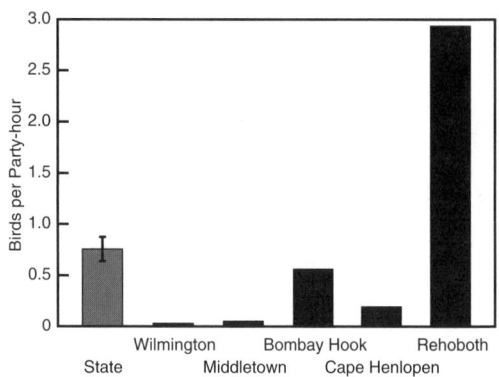

CBC Geographic Distribution

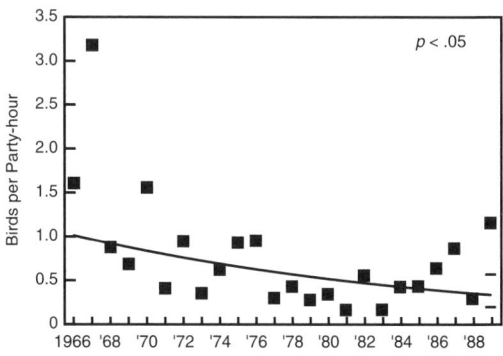

CBC Trend; Decreasing at 5% per Year

Regular; winter resident; uncommon to fairly common; expected early December to late March. Winter numbers decreasing at 5% per year.

HABITAT: Salt and brackish bays and estuaries; inland lakes and reservoirs.

SPRING: No migration peak is apparent. Most leave by late March, but the following small flocks remained into April:

1 Apr 1984	4	Dewey Beach [Frec1]
2 Apr 1989	7	Delaware Seashore SP [Frec1]
13 Apr 1983	13	Delaware Seashore SP [Frec1]

One straggler remained until 2 June 1983 [Frec1], and another, found on 16 August 1953 at Indian River Inlet [DuPA1], is 2 months too early for a fall migrant. High counts are

7 Mar 1936	50	Delaware City (DVOC, in Stone
	---	1937, 177)
9 Mar 1963	600	Little Creek WA [Davi22]
16 Mar 1986	25	Indian River Inlet [Frec1]

Typical counts total fewer than 30 birds.

FALL: Fall reports are few, most involving 1–4 birds. In most years Common Goldeneyes do not begin arriving until early December and do not become numerous until later in the month. Earlier arrivals have occurred in 10 years, with the following earliest:

17 Oct 1981	24	Indian River Inlet [Frec1]
30 Oct 1985	1	Bombay Hook NWR [Wayn58]
8 Nov 1986	1	Delaware Seashore SP [Frec1]
13 Nov 1971	1	Brandywine Creek SP [Wayn67]

Others have noted that immature and female goldeneyes tend to arrive earlier than males and may reach their wintering grounds in late October (Bellrose 1976).

WINTER: This species shows a long-term decline of about 5% per year on CBCs. It is much more common on the Rehoboth CBC than on others. High counts are

2, 24 Jan 1984	30	Indian River Inlet [Frec1]
6 Jan 1985	75	along the coast [Barn54]
18, 28 Jan 1982	100	Indian River Inlet [Frec37]

Fewer than 15 birds are usually reported.

1966–89 CBC Summary

Christmas Bird Count	Years Found	Range of No. Found	Median
Wilmington	1	1–25	1
Middletown	16	1–11	3
Bombay Hook	24	2–245	14
Cape Henlopen	21	3–54	10
Rehoboth	24	37–1,770	162
STATEWIDE	24	67–1,783	249
(decreasing; low in 1983, high in 1967)			

SPECIMENS: USNM 421857, Indian River Inlet, 2 February 1949; DMNH 76743, Brandywine River at Smith Bridge, 13 July 1987; DMNH 53957, Bombay Hook NWR, 1970s.

[Barrow's Goldeneye *(Bucephala islandica)*]

ROB STINE

Accidental (1989).

DOCUMENTATION: Notes.

REMARKS: There are only 2 reports of Barrow's Goldeneye occurring in Delaware, 1 unsatisfactory and 1 involving a good description of a female. Hanson (notes) describes an immature male and female shot 16 November 1929 on Marshall Pond, Milford. The wings of these birds, as described by Hanson, are consistent with Barrow's Goldeneye, but Carney (1964, in Bellrose 1976) states that the wings of the females and immatures of the 2 species are indistinguishable even in the hand. Moreover, the length of the body and wing of the female were too long for Barrow's, being more consistent with Common Goldeneye. The measurements of the male were consistent with either species. The white facial spot of the male was just beginning to appear, and at that stage the shape of the spot is frequently misleading. We do not consider this occurrence proven.

A second record was described in the following terms: "most unusual was a well-described female at Indian River Inlet," from 7–9 January 1989 [Holg27]. The notes are good, but the difficulties of identifying females remain (Carney 1964, in Bellrose 1976).

Hooded Merganser *(Lophodytes cucullatus)*

Regular; migrant and winter resident; uncommon to fairly common. Expected late October to mid-April. Occasionally breeds.

HABITAT: Inland lakes, ponds, reservoirs; also tidal marsh creeks and ponds, and sheltered bays.

SPRING: Migration probably takes place 20–25 February to 5–10 April, with the peak 10–25 March. Reports of late groups of birds include

12 Apr 1989	4	Prime Hook NWR [Frec1]
18 Apr 1964	9	Little Creek WA [LesC7]
8 May 1971	4	Little Creek WA [John3]

Singles and pairs remain into the summer. High counts are

9 Mar 1963	60	Little Creek WA [anon13]
6 Apr 1962	44	Little Creek WA (Lesser 1965)

Typically fewer than 10 birds are found in a day.

BREEDING: The Hooded Merganser, a cavity nester, breeds casually south to Florida (Stevenson and Anderson 1994). Breeding was first recorded in Delaware when a nest with 12 eggs was found on 11 April 1980 in a Wood Duck box over open water at Prime Hook NWR [O'Sh2]. Hooded Merganser eggs were found again in a Wood Duck box at Prime Hook in 1986 [O'Sh1]. Other summer observations include a pair on 4 June and a female on 16 July 1973 at Bombay Hook NWR [Holg81], and a juvenile on 12 June 1991 in Dover (DMNH 77657).

FALL: Arrival is usually 25 October to 5 November. A bird seen 10 September 1971 [Holg54] should be regarded as a local bird, and a published arrival on 4 October [Wees6] was actually on 4 November [Wees1]. Earliest migrants are probably

18, 24 Oct 1985	1–2	Little Creek WA [Wayn2]
21 Oct 1990	1	Rehoboth Bay [Shor4]
26 Oct 1991	3	Bombay Hook NWR [Barn1]
27 Oct 1990	2	Bombay Hook NWR [Edni1]

Ten reported on 30 October 1985 at Bombay Hook NWR [Wayn64] were surely migrants. High counts, all at Bombay Hook NWR, are 30 on 15 November 1981 [Wees9], 110 on 28 November 1953 [WriJ2], and 42 on 2 December 1986 [Wees1]. Most reports involve fewer than 10 birds.

Christmas Bird Count	Years Found	Range of No. Found	Median
Wilmington	9	1–6	
Middletown	1	1	
Bombay Hook	24	2–199	15
Cape Henlopen	16	2–30	3
Rehoboth	22	1–52	10
STATEWIDE (low in 1980, high in 1986)	24	9–219	37

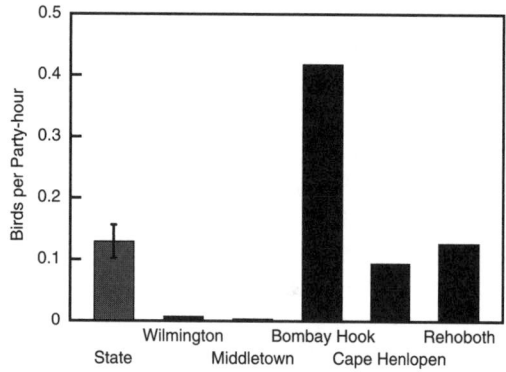

CBC Geographic Distribution

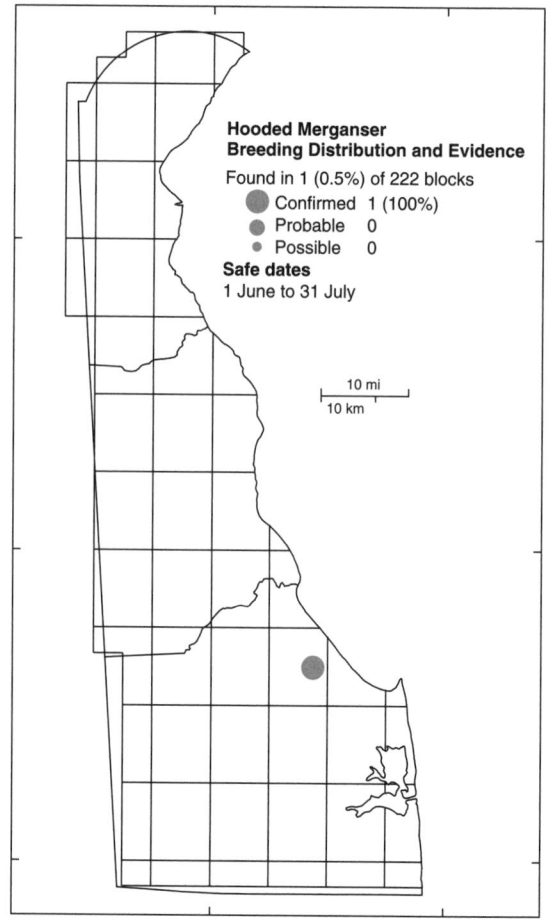

Hooded Merganser
Breeding Distribution and Evidence
Found in 1 (0.5%) of 222 blocks
● Confirmed 1 (100%)
● Probable 0
● Possible 0
Safe dates
1 June to 31 July

10 mi
10 km

WINTER: This species does not show a CBC trend, but high numbers reported in 1984 and 1986 give some promise of an increase. It is reported in highest numbers on the Bombay Hook CBC. The high counts are

5 Jan 1975	42	Assawoman WA [DuPG28]
9 Feb 1964	12	Little Creek WA [Broo24]
19 Feb 1987	17	Rehoboth Beach [Frec1]

SPECIMENS: DMNH 847 and DMNH 848, Sussex Co., 15 May 1958; DMNH 77657, Dover, 12 June 1991; DMNH 77078 and DMNH 77095, Prime Hook NWR, 28 December 1987.

Common Merganser *(Mergus merganser)*

Regular; fairly common to common migrant and usually rare winter resident. Expected mid-November to mid-April, with stragglers present thereafter.

DOCUMENTATION: Multiple sight records.

HABITAT: Freshwater reservoirs, ponds, and impoundments. Seldom in saltwater.

SPRING: Migrants appear rather abruptly on 1–5 February, and their numbers peak through 25–30 March. The last small flocks are

17 Apr 1965	5	Churchmans Marsh [Klab6]
17 Apr 1983	4	Bombay Hook NWR [DOS1]
18 Apr 1964	3	Hoopes 1964 (Falk 1971)

Stragglers may remain until late May, as indicated by 1 on 26 May 1976 at Ashland [Dyer3]. High counts, all at Bombay Hook NWR, include 220 on 5 February 1984 [Wees5], 1,000 on 6 February 1983 [Bayn4], and 464 on 20 February 1983 [Hess17]. Counts of a few to 40–50 birds are typical.

FALL: Fall reports are few. The Common Merganser occurs more commonly in late winter and spring. Migration takes place 10–20 November to 5–10 December, and thereafter the species is scarce until spring migration. All early reports are from Bombay Hook NWR: 1 on 18 October 1981 [Kell7], 14 on 22 October 1986 [Wees5], and 6 on 30 October 1985 [Wayn2]. High counts are 25 at Bombay Hook NWR on 15 November 1981 and 49 there on 5 December 1982 [Patt7].

1966–89 CBC Summary

Christmas Bird Count	Years Found	Range of No. Found	Median
Wilmington	20	1–171	7
Middletown	14	1–107	2
Bombay Hook	24	2–456	115
Cape Henlopen	8	1–13	
Rehoboth	17	1–51	2
STATEWIDE (low in 1969, high in 1974)	24	17–486	141

WINTER: This species' numbers appear to be declining after peaking in the late 1970s. It is much more abundant in Shearness Pool on the Bombay Hook CBC than on the coastal counts, where a few are sometimes found at Red Mill Pond or Silver Lake. It is usually uncommon until February, when its numbers begin to increase again, but timing is influenced by ice on freshwater. In 1974 300 were present by 25 January [Holg60], and in 1980 and 1990 it remained common throughout January. In 1945 a weekly survey at Hoopes Reservoir showed the species declining sharply during the first 2 weeks of January and becoming common again by mid-February.

REMARKS: Delaware specimens collected on 30 November 1931 and 20 January 1935 [Buck1] may not be extant.

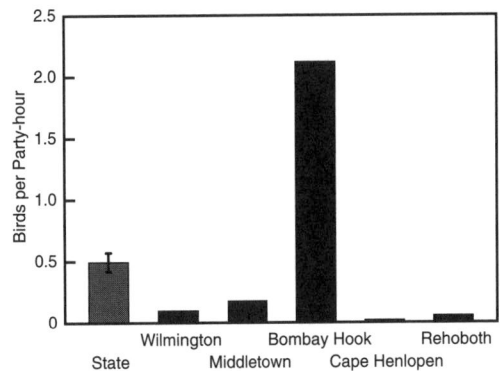

CBC Geographic Distribution

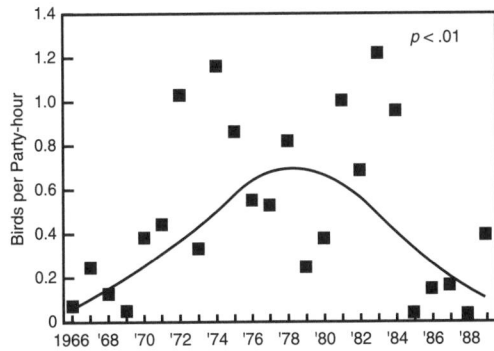

CBC Trend

Red-breasted Merganser (Mergus serrator)

Regular; migrant and winter resident; fairly common to common. Expected late October to mid-May, with a few sometimes lingering into summer. May occasionally breed, but no nest found. Winter numbers decreasing at 7% per year.

HABITAT: Saltwater bays and estuaries, ocean; rarely inland freshwater.

SPRING: Migration usually begins 20–25 February. High counts include 150 on 3 March 1985 and 200 on 10 March 1985, both at Indian River Inlet [Frec1]. Often fewer than 25 birds are found. Although most leave by mid-April, small flocks remain into May in some years:

19 May 1982	5	Cape Henlopen [Frec1]
21 May 1989	8	Sussex County [Barn54]
22 May 1991	15	Sussex County [Barn23]

One or 2 stragglers may remain later, and some birds summer.

SUMMER: Palmer (1976, 2:470) states that "Prebreeding (yearling) Red-breasted Mergansers sometimes remain far south of their breeding range into, even throughout, summer; most such occurrences are on brackish and salt water." Accordingly, most of the summering birds in Delaware are yearlings.

Atlas. Possible young were seen in the Inland Bays during 4 Atlas years. On 12 June 1983 an adult was noted in Indian River

Bay with 2 flightless birds, which were distinctly smaller than the adult, as they jumped from the bank and swam away [Barn32]. On 25 June 1984 Frech [Frec1] saw 2 birds that were possibly young of the year. On 14 June 1986 Fintel and Frech [Frec47] found 2 groups in Rehoboth Bay, an adult male and an adult female with 2 flightless young, and a pair with a flightless young (DMNH print collection, Fintel); its malar stripe is not conspicuously visible in the photograph but is suggested. On 21 June 1987 a flightless young bird was observed at Indian River Inlet [Frec1]. To sum up, these reports refer to clearly seen adult Red-breasted Mergansers with smaller birds made on repeated occasions by reliable observers who interpreted what they saw as breeding evidence (rather than yearling birds in molt).

Atlantic coast breeding, disjunct from the species' more northern breeding range, is indicated by the AOU Check-list (1983): "casually south along the Atlantic coast to New York (Long Island)." Breeding evidence for Long Island is summarized by Sibley (1988b) and Bull (1974), and for Massachusetts by Viet and Petersen (1993) and Phillips (1926). Leck (1984) says the Red-breasted Merganser was reported as a breeding bird from Barnegat Bay, New Jersey, in 1937 and 1950, and there was a spate of reports from the Carolinas in the 1960s and 1970s (Burton, in Sprunt and Chamberlain 1970, 592; Parnell 1967; Teulings 1970, 1972, 1974). No doubt some of these breeding records are correct, but none from Massachusetts southward mentions the finding of an actual nest.

FALL: The first migrants usually arrive during 25–30 October, with flocks of 4 arriving earlier at Cape Henlopen on 10 October 1980, 20 October 1985, and 23 October 1983 [Frec1]. An earlier single bird, seen on 7 October 1980 [Frec1], may have summered locally. High counts are 350 along the Delaware coast on 12 November 1955 [Sutt2], 50 at Rehoboth Beach on 14 November 1985, and 50 at Cape Henlopen on 16 November 1988 [Frec1]. Typical counts report 25 birds.

1966–89 CBC Summary

Christmas Bird Count	Years Found	Range of No. Found	Median
Wilmington	8	1–5	
Middletown	5	1–3	
Bombay Hook	21	1–25	5
Cape Henlopen	24	2–130	33
Rehoboth	24	6–587	140
STATEWIDE	24	19–690	186
(decreasing; low in 1981, high in 1967)			

WINTER: This species' CBC data show a downward trend. Red-breasted Mergansers are most numerous on the Rehoboth and Cape Henlopen CBCs and are seldom found on the Wilmington and Middletown CBCs. High counts are 100 at Lewes on 1 January 1985 and 100 at Cape Henlopen on 25 January 1983 [Frec1].

SPECIMENS: USNM 353626, Delaware City, 26 April 1926; DMNH 77339, Rehoboth Beach, 21 May 1988; DMNH 76510, Little Creek WA, 5 November 1985; DMNH 76844, Rehoboth Bay, December 1985.

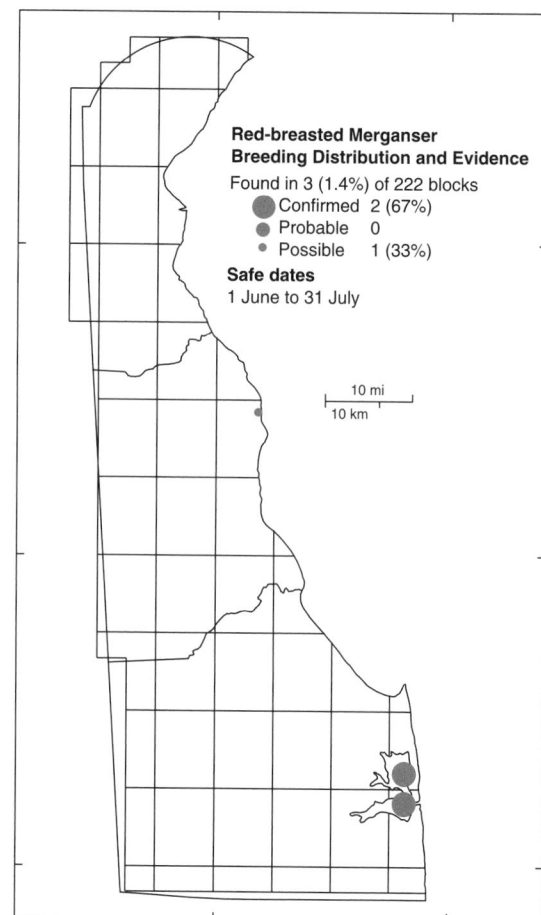

Red-breasted Merganser
Breeding Distribution and Evidence
Found in 3 (1.4%) of 222 blocks
● Confirmed   2 (67%)
● Probable   0
· Possible   1 (33%)
Safe dates
1 June to 31 July

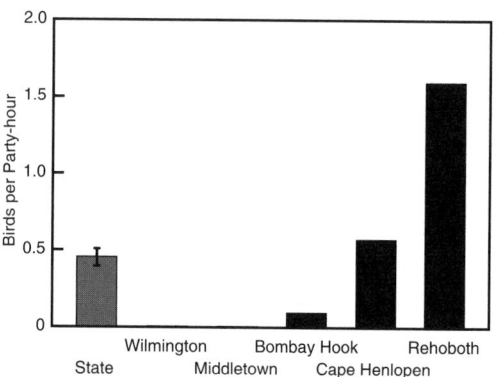

CBC Geographic Distribution

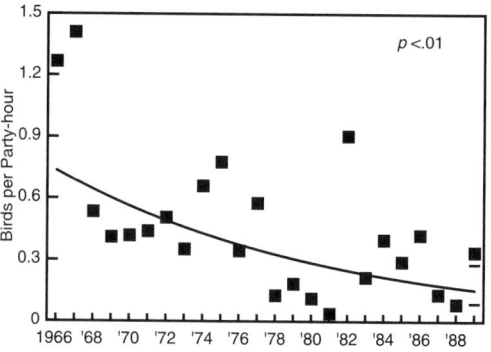

CBC Trend; Decreasing at 7% per Year

Ruddy Duck (*Oxyura jamaicensis*)

Regular; migrant and winter resident; fairly common; expected early October to mid-April, with lingering birds present thereafter. Occasionally, a few have bred. Historically, most numerous on the Wilmington CBC but has become much less so since the mid-1970s.

J F M A M J J A S O N D

HABITAT: Freshwater ponds and impoundments. Also, especially in mid-winter, bays and estuaries with plentiful aquatic plants or mollusks. Formerly large numbers on the Delaware River.

SPRING: Locally wintering birds leave during February, perhaps when ponds freeze over; in March they are supplemented by birds presumably wintering south of Delaware. Virtually all depart by 10–15 April. One was at Silver Lake, Rehoboth Beach, 20 April 1957 (DMNH 650). Bellrose (1976) notes that a gradual exodus begins in February and continues to the end of April. An exceptional count of 1,800 was made at Port Mahon on 15 April 1972 [Rich2]. The next highest reports are from Bombay Hook NWR during late March and early April 1982 when 100–200 birds were observed [Bayn2]. Typically, fewer than 50 birds are found.

BREEDING: In some years Ruddy Ducks are still reported in late spring and summer, but no evidence of breeding has been reported since 1979.

Atlas. Three Ruddy Ducks in nonbreeding plumage were seen on 2 July 1985 at Little Creek WA [Hess10], but they were not entered as a breeding record for the Atlas. Six at Great Marsh, Lewes, on 8 July 1987 were not believed to be breeding [DNRE1].

History. Three broods of Ruddy Ducks found at Little Creek WA during August 1961 probably constitute the first authentic breeding records. Lesser's report states that "in 1961 two to ten birds were observed in courtship throughout the breeding season. On August 28 the first two broods, totaling eight ducklings, were found, and at least one other brood was raised that year. In 1962 16 birds were observed in courtship until June 12

after which numbers started to decrease. By July 9 all had apparently departed, probably because of the rapid fall in water level" (1964, 27) [Less10]. Seventeen years later, 9 adults, including a female with 4 ducklings, were seen at Little Creek WA on 7 July 1979 [Abbo5].

FALL: First arrival is 1–10 October. These earlier fall dates should probably be associated with summering birds:

8 Sep 1974	1	Bombay Hook NWR [Lehm1]
11 Sep 1960	4	Fenwick Island (probably Assawoman WA) [Davi17]
12 Sep 1981	1	Assawoman WA [Frec1]

A peak of 2,500 was recorded 8 November 1966 along the Delaware River [Carr13]. Other high counts are

26 Oct 1948	500	Bombay Hook NWR [McLa1]
28 Nov 1953	400	Rehoboth Beach [anon5]
22 Nov 1981	300	Bombay Hook NWR [Ross1]

1966–89 CBC Summary

Christmas Bird Count	Years Found	Range of No. Found	Median
Wilmington	21	1–3,231	53
Middletown	16	1–773	2
Bombay Hook	23	3–1,688	113
Cape Henlopen	17	1–90	4
Rehoboth	24	6–1,060	245
STATEWIDE (low in 1980, high in 1973)	24	13–4,373	758

WINTER: Although this species does not show a statistically significant trend, we present the CBC data because obvious changes have occurred. The data suggest a decrease in the population, but the irregular or perhaps cyclic nature of its occurrence makes interpretation difficult. At one time this species could be found in large rafts (2,000–3,000 birds) on the Delaware River off Wilmington (Wilmington CBC reports). In 11 years starting in 1967 a total of 18,766 Ruddy Ducks were counted on the Wilmington CBC; the count in the following 11 years was only 37.

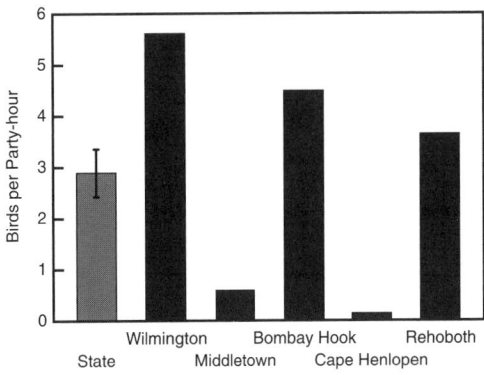

CBC Geographic Distribution

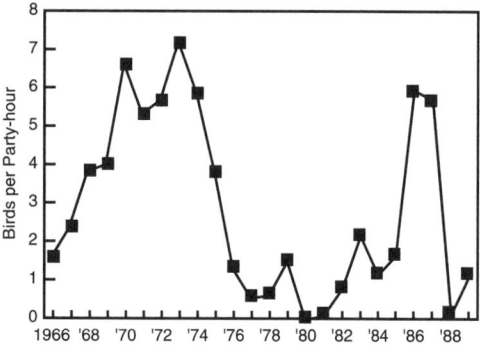

CBC Data

REMARKS: This species should be listed as threatened in Delaware because (1) its wintering population level has drastically fallen over the past 25 years; (2) its favorite resting place was on the Delaware River; (3) many Ruddy Ducks have been killed by oil spills, a continuing threat; and (4) the threatened designation would indicate concern for the species to the public and to the shipping industry, as well as to the courts.

SPECIMENS: 14; DMNH, ANSP, USNM.

Osprey (Pandion haliaetus)

Regular; summer resident; fairly common to common in the Inland Bays and in migration. Expected mid-March to late October and sporadically into early winter.

HABITAT: Open waters for fishing, including ocean, bays, ponds, and lakes. Nests on manmade structures, snags, or trees near a food source. Not breeding along Delaware Bay as was once common.

SPRING: Hanson (notes) recorded arrival dates during 1924–46 wherever first seen from St. Georges south to Milford. Arrivals were 15 March (early) and 21 March (median); more recently, an earlier Kent County arrival was on 8 March 1974 at Bombay Hook NWR [Lieh3]. Early Sussex County records, all of single birds, are

2 Mar 1984	Mispillion Inlet [FinS1]
3 Mar 1974	Assawoman WA [DuPG24]
5 Mar 1991	Lewes [Gros1]

Exceptional for New Castle County was an early migrant at Burrows Run on 3 March 1992 [SpSB24]. High counts in March are

16 Mar 1989	4	Cape Henlopen SP [Frec1]
26 Mar 1983	8	Delaware Seashore SP [Frec1]
29 Mar 1992	10	Indian River Inlet [Samp1]

Band recoveries (Poole and Agler 1987) and nest record data strongly suggest that breeding Ospreys are present by late March and early April, implying that early spring Ospreys are overlooked or underreported. Thus, although we lack the needed reports, the seasonal bar graph should probably show the same abundance level in April as shown in May.

BREEDING: The highest concentration of nests is in the southeast corner of Rehoboth Bay where 14 could be seen from Savages Ditch in 1979 [Jahn6]; 41 nests were active in Rehoboth Bay in 1989 (Gelvin-Innvaer 1992b). Ospreys are common around the Inland Bays and uncommon breeders elsewhere in the state.

Atlas. During the Atlas period the Osprey began regaining its range up the Delaware River, with 3 nests north of the Chesapeake and Delaware Canal particularly notable. The possible and probable reports may come from birds foraging many miles from their nests. The high number of confirmed records around the Inland Bays comes from data in DNREC reports.

Nesting. Currently, nests are most commonly built on duck blinds on marsh islands or on the rubble left when blinds collapse. In the 1930s, however, most nests described by egg collectors were placed in trees or snags in marshes or fields. A few nests were reported in living trees, such as black gum, partly dead oak, and live cedar. The nest is made from sticks and

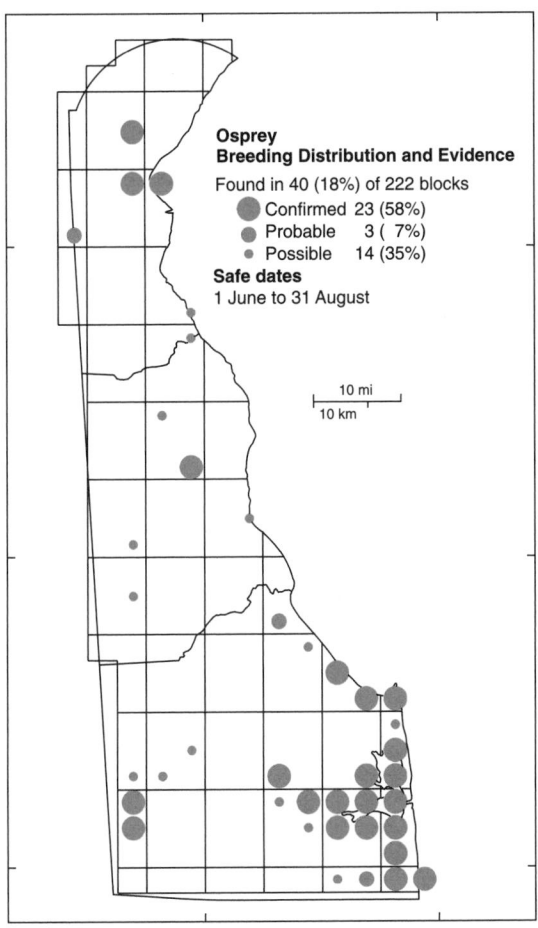

Osprey
Breeding Distribution and Evidence

Found in 40 (18%) of 222 blocks

● Confirmed 23 (58%)
● Probable 3 (7%)
• Possible 14 (35%)

Safe dates
1 June to 31 August

10 mi
10 km

History. Until the introduction of DDT, the Osprey was a common bird in Delaware. In 1923 it was reported as very common along the coast and river shore [Hans1]. Hanson continued to report its presence in Kent County until 1945 without making any further comment concerning its abundance. In a bird list issued in 1939 (Barry) the Osprey was described as "abundant over any salt water area. From many highways the nests can be seen with their characteristic brush-pile appearance in the tops of tall trees." Barry further commented in 1942 that "Over 90 nests were located in Kent County, the majority of which were east of Highway 113."

No further reports were made concerning this species until 17 years later, by which time it had become very scarce in Kent County. Scott and Potter (1959) reported that Ospreys were reduced in numbers along the Delaware Bay in New Jersey and suggested that loss of nest sites was the cause. Three nests were reported in Bombay Hook NWR and 1 at Woodland Beach WA in 1964, and 1 at Woodland Beach WA in 1966. One nest each was reported at Little Creek WA and Woodland Beach WA in 1968. The last nest reported in Kent County was at Bombay Hook NWR in 1972 [MiJC3]. Although these nest records are fragmentary, they seem to occur at a time when nests would have been reported if they existed. This withdrawal from Kent County was given scant attention because a small concentration remained in the Inland Bays.

By the 1970s the crash in Osprey population had become a national concern. This last concentration in the Inland Bays, where there was disturbance from fishing and recreational use, became a concern to the Delaware Game and Fish Commission, which initiated a monitoring and banding program. In 1971, in addition to the 22 nests producing young found on the Inland Bays, 3 other nests produced young; also, 27 nests produced eggs but no young [Todd1]. Nests reported from the Inland Bays that produced at least 1 young increased from 22 in 1970 and 1971 to 27 in 1974 (Todd 1977). These were the years of lowest productivity. DDT, which was found to disrupt breeding by causing eggshell thinning, was banned from large-scale use in 1972. Subsequent monitoring of the Inland Bays showed a general increase in the number of young produced in that region (Whittendale 1983–84; Gelvin-Innvaer 1992b). (See the following Osprey productivity table.)

Trends. May Count data indicate that the Osprey population increased an average of 7% annually from 1969 to 1991, an increase in agreement with regional BBS data; the Delaware BBS inadequately samples its population.

Breeding population. The present breeding population in the area surveyed in the Inland Bays is about 60 pairs, with perhaps 20 additional pairs breeding in other areas of the state.

Conservation. Recovery should not be considered complete until many more nests are established along Delaware Bay. This range reestablishment is particularly needed because human population, summer activity, and pollution may continue to increase around the Inland Bays. The Osprey's absence from the Kent County tidal marshes, where "90 pairs" once nested, is

increases in size with each year's use; it is lined with grass, salt hay, corn husks, and similar materials.

The extrapolated clutch-completion period was calculated from pre-1940 egg-collection data. Data collected by DNREC biologists in the 1960s were excluded, because the timing of their nest visits biases the clutch-completion calculation. Extreme egg dates are 2 eggs on 2 April 1932 [Buck3, in Hans1] and 2 half-incubated eggs on 23 June 1901 (WFVZ egg data). The size distribution for 81 pre-1940 clutches was 3 nests with 4 eggs, 67 with 3, 10 with 2, and 1 with 1; some clutches may be incomplete.

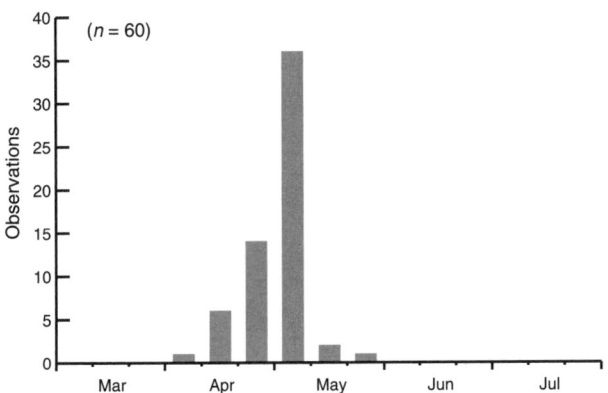

Estimated Clutch-Completion Dates

a clear signal of a lingering environmental problem in Delaware Bay. The DNREC has been encouraging the building of nest platforms, and some of these have been used by Ospreys.

Osprey Productivity: Nesting Activity of Delaware's Lower Bays

Rehoboth and Indian River Bays

	1970	1971	1972	1973	1974	1975	1976
Active nests	22	22	21	26	27	25	26
Fledglings per nest				1.4	1.7	1.3	
Young banded	22	22	18	30	36	25	44

Rehoboth, Indian River, and Little Assawoman Bays

	1977	1978	1979	1980	1981	1982	1983	1984
Active nests	—	37	54	56	52	47	56	50
Eggs	—	82	126	124	134	105	121	69
Survived to banding age	24	36	46	55	75	57	76	49

Rehoboth, Indian River, and Little Assawoman Bays

	1985	1986	1987	1988	1989	1990	1991	1992
Active nests	43	45	45	37[1]	64	43	44	55
Eggs	95	97						
Survived to banding age	69	41	68	46[1]	72[1]	46	78	59

SOURCES: Whittendale 1983–84; Gelvin-Innvaer 1992b.
NOTES: In 1992 there were also 11 active sites in the Nanticoke River drainage and 3 in New Castle County.
1. Little Assawoman Bay was not completely checked in 1988–89.

FALL: Kennedy (1973) reported that juvenile birds from Maryland and Virginia began southward movement at the end of August, and by 15 September most had left the United States. Delaware birds also begin migrating by late August. Allen and Peterson (1936) note that peak migration at Cape May, New Jersey, occurs during the middle 2 weeks of September. An increase in reports away from the breeding grounds and hawk watch data show the arrival of northern birds beginning in mid- to late August and lasting through 15–20 October. A 1978–84 hawk watch at Carpenter SP reported Ospreys from 3 September to 17 October, with a broad peak in late September [Oliv1] (see also "Hawk Migration" essay). A 1976 Newark hawk watch recorded 12 Ospreys migrating from 9 September to 10 October 1976 [Edni15]. The highest reports are counts of 18 on 24 September and 17 on 30 September 1966 at Brandywine Creek SP (Mohr 1967). Virtually all pass through by the end of October, after which reports of more than 1 or 2 are unusual.

WINTER: One bird was seen on each of 6 CBCs (Middletown 1951, 1971; Rehoboth 1975; Wilmington 1985; Seaford 1985, 1987). Additional December reports are

10–11 Dec 1985	1	Hoopes Reservoir, Wilmington [SpeE15]
12 Dec 1979	1	near Dover [Pure2]
13 Dec 1951	1	near Smyrna [Kron1]

SPECIMENS: 9; DMNH, USNM. Egg records: DMNH, LSU, WFVZ.

Swallow-tailed Kite (*Elanoides forficatus*)

DOCUMENTATION: Photograph (K. Grim, DMNH 129).

REMARKS: This southeastern kite has been found 7 times since 1977 from Greenville south to Indian River Inlet. These records occur only in May, and hence there is no suggestion of breeding. The species' Delaware occurrence is documented by a photograph (DMNH 129) of 1 of 2 birds flying over Bombay Hook NWR on 17 May 1981 and by separate sets of convincing notes by Ednie, Moorhouse, and Niles of a bird seen on 7 May 1977 (Ednie 1977). The remaining birds, for which we have little or no descriptions, occurred

4 May 1993	1	Greenville [SpeE16]
11 May 1979	1	Cape Henlopen SP [PetB1]
24 May 1987	1	Angola Neck, Sussex County, brief notes [McWh1]
27 May 1982	1	Lewes [Frec57]
31 May 1983	1	Delaware Bay, near Brandywine Light (Fintel 1984)

Casual (7 years, 1977–92); spring; rare.

Mississippi Kite *(Ictinia mississippiensis)*

Casual (1982, 1984, 1992, and 1993).

J	F	M	A	M	J	J	A	S	O	N	D

DOCUMENTATION: Convincing notes.

REMARKS: There are 5 published sight records:

9 May 1992	1	Bombay Hook NWR [Gust2]
18 May 1993	1	Big Stone Beach [HilA4]
26 May 1984	1	near Harrington [West25]
6 Jun 1982	1	Lewes [Maur1]
20 Jun 1982	1	near Bethany Beach [Beza1]

The Harrington bird was briefly but adequately described. The description of the adult at Bombay Hook NWR is meticulous and convincing, noting in particular the short outermost primary [PeBG3]. This species is a regular vagrant near Cape May, New Jersey, so its casual occurrence in Delaware is expected.

Bald Eagle *(Haliaeetus leucocephalus)*

Resident; rare. Migrants are reported in spring and fall. Winter population augmented by nonresidents. Winter numbers are increasing after a low in the 1970s.

J	F	M	A	M	J	J	A	S	O	N	D

HABITAT: Tidal waters, inland lakes, ponds, and streams; needs solitude for nesting.

BREEDING: Bald Eagles currently breed in all 3 counties. It is most easily observed at Bombay Hook NWR, where breeding cycle begins in December.

Atlas. During the Atlas period 4 pairs bred, and 4 additional reports suggested potential new breeding sites. The distribution map is supplemented by one including historical sites (Abbott 1982; Tyrrell 1943; DNREC files). The active sites change, but the eagles tend to use the same group of sites where food and habitat are suitable (Abbott 1978).

Nesting. One Delaware nest was described as a huge mass of large and small sticks, lined with grass, corn husks, and a few feathers (Gardner, DMNH 28684). Nests are 45–80 ft above ground, often in living trees—deciduous in Kent and New Castle Counties and coniferous for all but 1 in Sussex County.

Extreme egg dates are 18 February 1971 and 16 March 1935 ($n = 10$); eggs being incubated as late as 28 April 1965 were not viable.

Bald Eagles usually lay clutches of 2 or 3 eggs. Darlington (1912a) reported a clutch of 4 from Delaware on 9 March 1911 and believed it was unprecedented. Abbott (1978), using data from the Chesapeake Bay region (including Delaware), gave the following ratio for the 1930s: 2 eggs, 51%; 3 eggs, 39%; 1

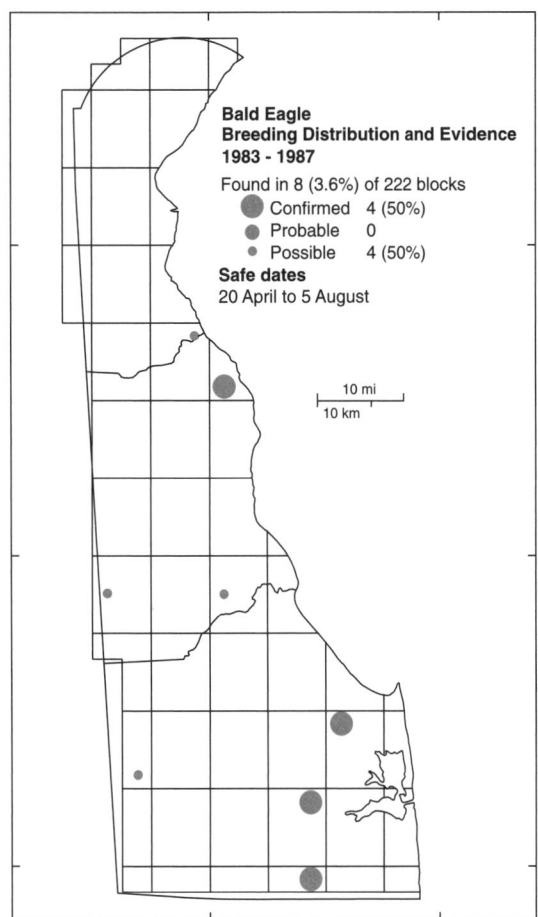

Bald Eagle
Breeding Distribution and Evidence
1983 - 1987

Found in 8 (3.6%) of 222 blocks
● Confirmed 4 (50%)
● Probable 0
· Possible 4 (50%)
Safe dates
20 April to 5 August

10 mi
10 km

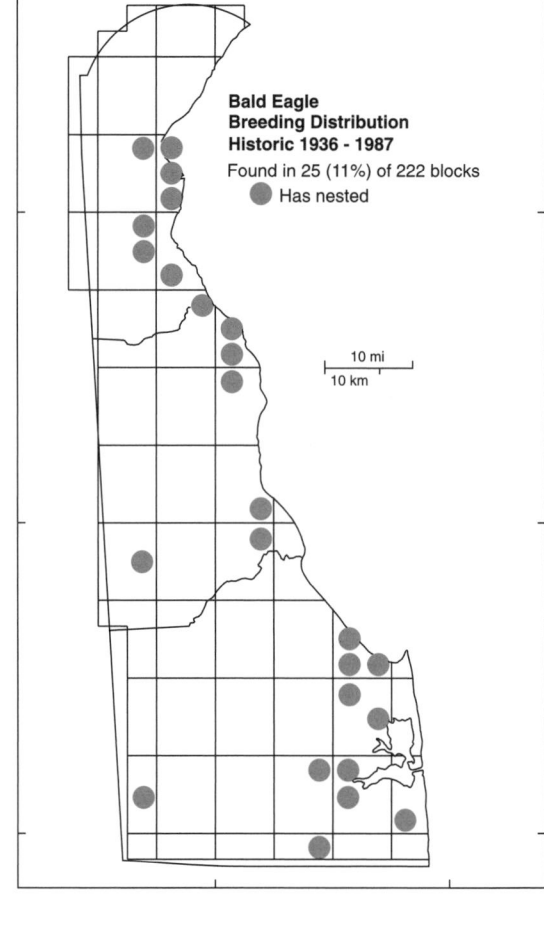

Bald Eagle
Breeding Distribution
Historic 1936 - 1987

Found in 25 (11%) of 222 blocks
● Has nested

10 mi
10 km

egg, 8%; and 4 eggs, 2% (2 pairs). He further found that clutch size decreased in the 1940s and particularly in the 1950s and 1960s but has since increased.

History and trends. "I shot a white-headed eagle. . . . [Its] look is grim, otherwise it is not very destructive, but when it may come upon some waterfowl, such as are shot by the common people, it comes forward and hovers about boldly, in order to secure its share." From these remarks by Reverend Hesselius made on 12 July 1712 one can surmise he was commenting on a common bird. Krider (1879, 15) reminisced that "The Bald Eagle is very plenty along the coast of Virginia, Delaware, and New Jersey."

References to eagles in Delaware in the early 1900s indicate that it was persecuted then. These references mostly discuss collecting the eggs, which were highly prized and could be traded for other scarce eggs. Stone (1919) also pointed out that Bald Eagles "have a habit of making off with wounded ducks in shooting season, and the farmers, with their usual antipathy to all birds of prey, make a practice of chopping down the eagle tree or of shooting the old birds, so that another of Delaware's ornithological attractions is threatened with extinction."

The first survey of breeding Bald Eagles in Delaware, made in 1936 by W. Bryant Tyrrell for the National Association of Audubon Societies, located 4 active nests, each of which fledged 2. Tyrrell visited 3 other nests and heard of an eighth.

He reported that oologists were doing considerable damage in Delaware, exemplified by Darlington's willingness to pay $5 for every nest shown him. Duck hunters also contributed to the species' population decline.

Broley's (1947, 1958) studies in Florida showed a decrease in nesting success from 72% for 1941–46 to 14% in 1957, with a dismal 7 young produced from 43 occupied nests—0.6 young per nest. He was the first to suggest DDT as the cause.

In the 1960s Bald Eagle productivity in Delaware was almost nil, although there were plenty of nesting attempts. Before the early 1960s, there were 12 active sites: 4 in New Castle County, 3 in Kent, and 5 in Sussex (Abbott 1978). During the 1960s 11 sites were active at one time or another, but never more than 3 were active in any given year. Even in the 1970s, when production was improving but breeding pairs were scarce, 2 additional sites were active, but most of the 1960s sites were not.

Insecticide pollution was still a problem in 1977. A nonviable egg collected at Bombay Hook NWR had a high degree of thinning and contained lethal levels of DDE, dieldrin, and PCBs. The level of DDE was the highest for any Bald Eagle egg analyzed at the Patuxent Wildlife Research Center (Wiemeyer 1977). In the last 30 years at Bombay Hook NWR, where the most consistent attempts to breed have occurred, young have been successfully fledged in only 8 years: 1970, 1976, 1979, 1983, 1984, 1987 (2 fledged), 1988, and 1992.

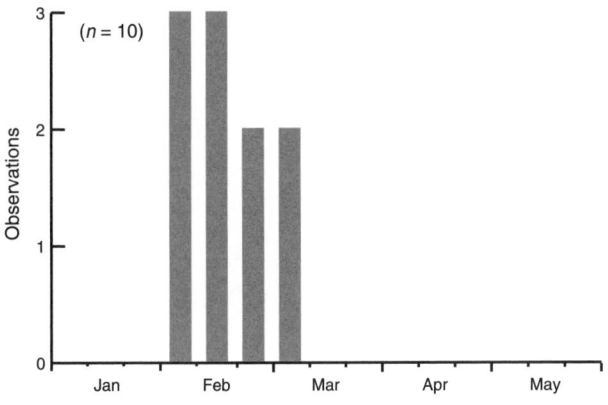

(n = 10)

Estimated Clutch-Completion Dates

Bald Eagle Nest Success, 1936–92

Year	Active nests	Successful nests[1]	Fledged young	Unhatched eggs	Productivity[2]
1992	6	5	7	0	1.2
1991	7	4	8	0	1.1
1990	6	4	7	0	1.2
1988	6	4	5	1	0.83
1987	4	2	4	0	1.0
1986	2[3]	2	5	1	2.5
1985	2	2	2[4]	1	1.0
1984	3	2	2[4]	0	0.67
1983	4	3	4	1	1.0
1982	4	2	3	1	0.75
1981	4	2	3	0	0.75
1980	2	1	2	0	1.0
1979	2	2	2	0	1.0
1978	3	0	0	0	0
1977	2	1	1	—	0.5
1975	1	0	0	—	0
1970	2	1	1	—	0.5
1964–68	3	0	0	—	0
1962	1	—	—	—	0
1941[5]	3	3?	8?	—	2.7
1940[5]	3	3?	5?	—	1.7
1939[5]	3?	3?	6–8?	—	2.7?
1938[5]	4	4?	8?	—	2.0
1936[5]	4	4	8	—	2.0

Sources: Abbott 1985; Gelvin-Innvaer 1992c; Potter 1938-1941; Thomas 1989d; Tyrrell 1936.

    1. Young raised to fledging.

    2. Young per active nest.

    3. One new nest located late in season after 1–2 young fledged, not included in table.

    4. One additional young found dead, not included in table.

    5. Southern Delaware probably not covered.

Conservation. The Bald Eagle, our national bird, is listed as Threatened. It is still protected by the Bald Eagle Protection Act (16 USC 668–668c), which stipulates a first-offense fine of $5,000 and criminal fines of up to $20,000. The Delaware fine for disturbing a Bald Eagle at its nest is not more than $500, together with costs, or imprisonment for 50 days, or both. One Delaware nest failed in 1992 following human disturbance (Gelvin-Innvaer, pers. comm.). The Bald Eagle has sufficiently recovered from the pesticide poisoning problem that the USFWS removed it from the Endangered list.

Some of the 12 most recent nest sites still appear suitable for eagles, but at least 1 in New Castle County has been rendered unacceptable by encroaching subdivision development.

MIGRATION: A few migrants pass through the Piedmont in both spring and fall; for example,

14 May 1992	1	Burrows Run, near Centerville [SpeE11]
16 May 1987	1	White Clay Creek [Barn43]
9 Sep 1987	1	near Centerville [Flin1]
14 Oct 1975	1	Newark [Edni52]

1966–89 CBC Summary

Christmas Bird Count	Years Found	Range of No. Found	Median
Wilmington	1	1	
Middletown	6	1	
Bombay Hook	24	1–6	3
Cape Henlopen	6	1–2	
Rehoboth	11	1–3	
STATEWIDE (increasing; high in 1986)	24	2–9	4

WINTER: The Bald Eagle appears to be increasing after a decline ending in the 1970s (see CBC trend graph). Reports of more than 2 birds at known breeding sites suggest additional overwintering individuals.

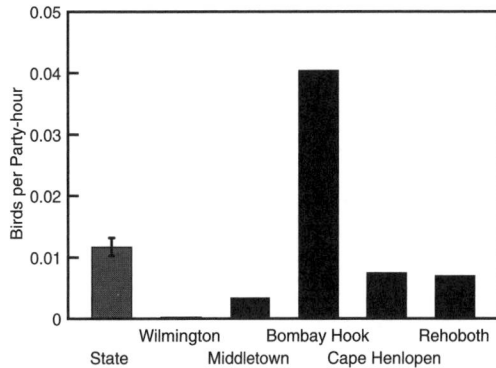

CBC Geographic Distribution

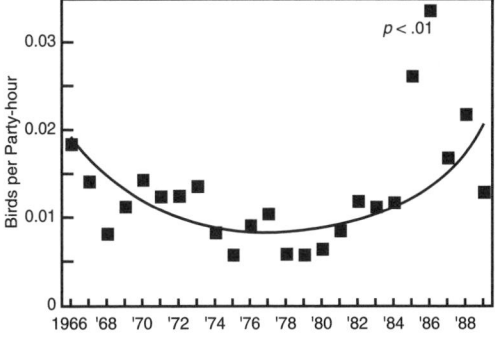

CBC Trend

SPECIMENS: ANSP 88351 (no locality given), 19 December 1929; USNM 309369, Delaware City, 25 December 1900. Egg records: DMNH, LSU, WFVZ.

Hawk Migration in Delaware: Timing, Magnitude, and Ecology

Robert W. Russell

Few people have studied hawk migrations through Delaware, perhaps because of a misconception that most hawks migrate along mountain ranges. The comparative lack of interest in Delaware is puzzling in view of the state's location—midway between Cape May and the Kittatinny Ridges, two areas of national repute for the study of migrating raptors.

Migration of hawks occurs over a broad front throughout Delaware during both autumn and spring. The visible migration, however, is concentrated in the extreme northern part of the state and along the Atlantic coast. In northern Delaware, good sites for observing migrant hawks include Walter S. Carpenter, Jr. SP (usually the best), Brandywine Creek SP, the Winterthur Museum grounds, the Delcastle Recreation Area, hilltops in the vicinity of the Ashland Nature Center at Hockessin, and occasionally apartment rooftops in downtown Wilmington. In southern Delaware, sizable numbers of hawks may be seen occasionally anywhere along the coast, but flights tend to be less predictable.

Northern Delaware Migrations

Autumn

Autumn is the best time for observing large flights of hawks in northern Delaware. The season may be roughly divided into three periods defined by the relative numbers of the most abundant species: Broad-winged Hawks dominate through September, Sharp-shinned Hawks are the most abundant during the first three weeks of October, and Red-tailed Hawks are most numerous thereafter (see Relative Abundance graph).

James K. Oliver logged more than 300 hours of observation at Carpenter SP from 1978 to 1984 (unpub.) and showed that up to 90% of a season's migrant Broad-winged Hawks may pass during one or two days of spectacular flights. For example, more than 2,500 were counted over Arundel in one hour on 18 September 1980 (pers. obs.). (Interestingly, these large Broad-winged Hawk flights are often accompanied by equally impressive evening flights of Common Nighthawks.)

Large numbers of the other two common buteos, Red-tailed and Red-shouldered hawks, move through northern Delaware from late October into December. In fact, cold fronts and winds from the north or northwest can bring small migratory movements of these two species until almost Christmas.

Accipiters (mostly Sharp-shinned Hawks), Ospreys, and American Kestrels peak during late September and early October (see Seasonal Timing graphs), and high daily counts of these species tend to coincide. My observations and Oliver's

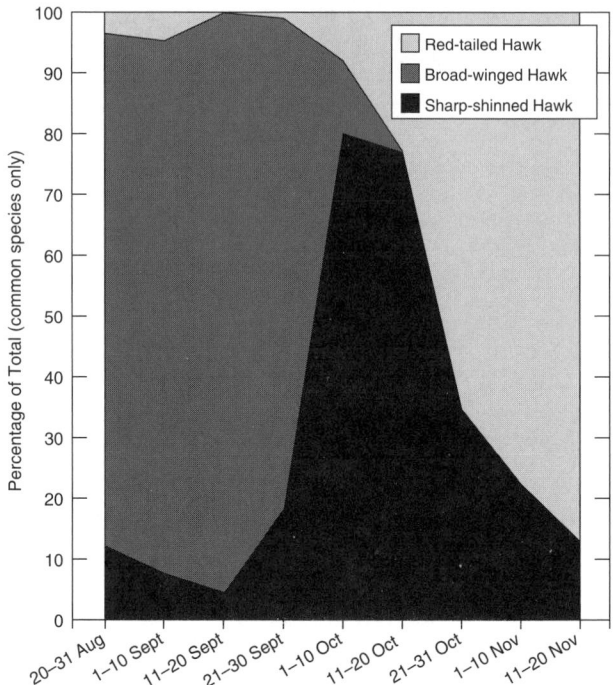

Relative Abundance of Three Common Migrant Hawks at Carpenter SP

data suggest a ratio of one Cooper's Hawk to every 15 Sharp-shins.

Passage of Northern Harriers is nearly uniform from August into December. Substantial numbers of Turkey Vultures also occur throughout the period; many are probably locals, but a migratory peak is evident in November (see Seasonal Timing graphs). Black Vultures are regular in low numbers, also peaking in November. Merlins (October), Golden Eagles (late October to November), and Bald Eagles (late August to early October) are occasional. Northern Goshawks, Peregrine Falcons, and Rough-legged Hawks are the rarest migrants.

In northern Delaware, large visible flights of hawks occur in the vicinity of the fall line (the topographic boundary between the Piedmont Plateau and the Atlantic Coastal Plain), especially after cold fronts and associated northwesterly winds. Average hawk counts at Carpenter SP, a fall line site, exceeded 50 birds per hour over the course of seven years of autumnal study. This figure, favorably comparable with most of the better known hawk-watching spots in the United States is biased upward by more coverage on peak migration days.

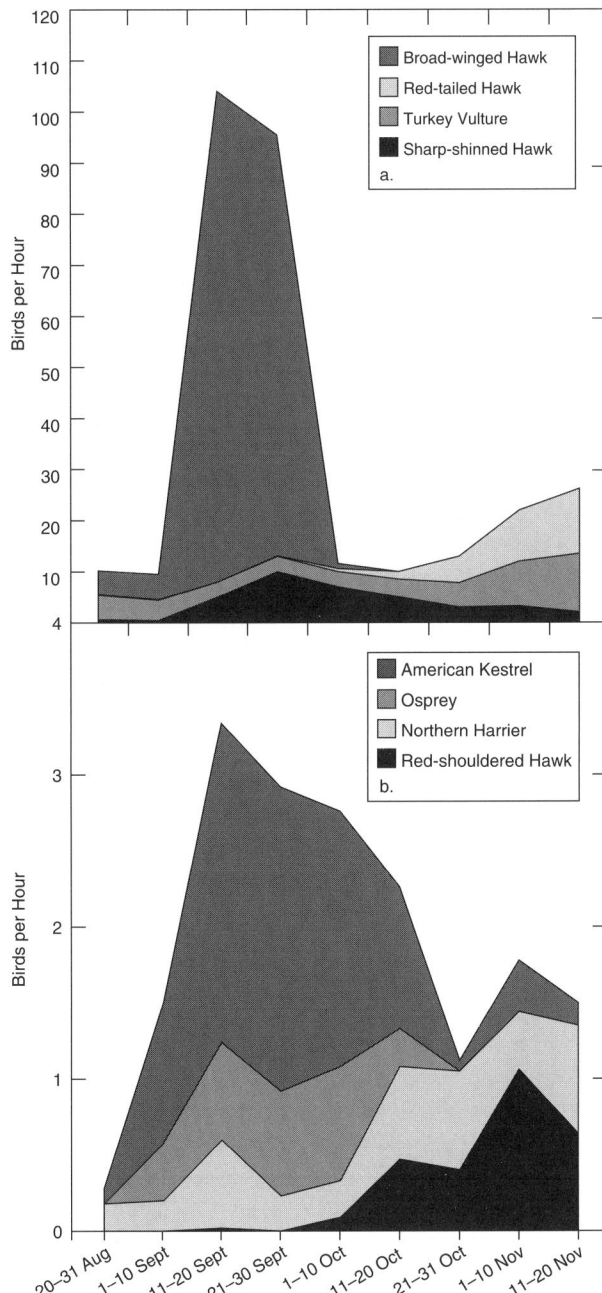

Seasonal Timing of Migration at Carpenter SP

Large migratory flights often occur along leading lines (i.e., geographic features such as mountain ranges and shorelines that cause migrating birds to reorient). The large hawk flights along the fall line in Delaware suggest that this feature is acting as a leading line, diverting and concentrating broad-front migrants at the edge of the Coastal Plain. This diversion along the fall line probably results from the geographical configuration of the Delmarva Peninsula. Over the Piedmont, migratory movements of hawks are generally oriented to the southsouthwest. Birds that enter Delaware on that course and then travel down the peninsula will encounter the Chesapeake Bay, a major water barrier. Because thermals are scarce over the

water during the day, water crossings require strong powered flight, which is energetically costly for species adapted to a soaring mode of migration. Water crossings also present major safety risks, including the potential for being pushed out to sea by unpredictable winds and the potential for attack by gulls and other hawks (MacRae 1985). Migrant hawks that reorient their flight from the south-southwest toward the west along the fall line can pass around the bay and need not cross it.

Several predictions can be derived from the hypothesis that migrant hawks reorient along the fall line to avoid crossing Chesapeake Bay. First, species least inclined to fly over water should be rarest on the peninsula. Accordingly, Broad-winged Hawks seem to be particularly scarce migrants on the Coastal Plain, in marked contrast to the large numbers passing through the northernmost part of the state. Second, if water crossings do in fact impose significant costs on migrant raptors, then the costs should be reflected in different age ratios of migrants over the Piedmont and over the Coastal Plain. Immatures on their first migration that purposely or inadvertently proceed into the Coastal Plain probably experience higher mortality from unsuccessful attempts to cross water barriers. Furthermore, those individuals that choose not to attempt water crossings and instead turn back northward to retrace a route around the barrier incur stiff penalties of time and energy and then may be inclined to explore alternative routes in subsequent years. The pool of birds remaining for the following migration should therefore consist largely of individuals that either followed more inland routes the first year or learned that coastal routes are likely to lead to water barriers. Thus most migrants observed south of the fall line should be immatures, and adults should be much more common along the fall line and to the north and west. This prediction can be tested if observers in Delaware systematically record the ages of any raptors they observe during fall migration.

Visible flights of hawks near the fall line have been much larger following the passage of cold fronts. This fact suggests that the northern Delaware flights may be augmented by migrants that reorient along the fall line after being displaced, or caused to drift, by the strong northwesterly winds that typically accompany cold fronts. Previous workers have often invoked wind drift to explain large hawk flights along leading lines when winds are from the northwest (e.g., Allen and Peterson 1936; Mueller and Berger 1967). Although wind drift should not be discounted as a possible reason for the appearance of large flights over northern Delaware (especially the Broad-wing flights), there is a plausible alternative explanation. Murray (1964) proposed and Kerlinger and Gauthreaux (1984) partially confirmed that large numbers of Sharp-shinned Hawks are seen at Cape May in northwest winds not because of wind drift but because the birds descend to low altitudes when they encounter Delaware Bay in such conditions. Similar numbers of birds are apparently aloft on other days as well but are less likely to be noticed because they fly at higher altitudes, often exceeding 500 meters (Kerlinger and Gauthreaux 1984).

A similar explanation might account for the patterns observed in northern Delaware if hawks descend in altitude on encountering the edge of the Coastal Plain. More study is needed.

Spring

Spring flights in northern Delaware feature buteos, with Red-shouldered Hawks often outnumbering Red-tailed Hawks as they begin to pass through in early March. Red-shouldered Hawks peak in mid-March and wane rapidly thereafter. The more protracted Red-tailed Hawk migration continues into April, when the Broad-winged Hawk flights begin. Broad-wing flights peak about the third week in April and usually end by the beginning of May. Substantial buteo flights are often accompanied by large numbers of migrating Turkey Vultures. Spring patterns of abundance and timing for the other species are poorly known.

In contrast to autumn movements, few large hawk flights have been documented in northern Delaware in spring, and no major concentration points have yet been discovered. Little is known about geographic patterns of hawk migration in spring.

Coastal Migrations

Autumn

Autumn migration along Delaware's Atlantic coast is unpredictable but can be impressive at times. American Kestrels are commonly seen along the coast, sometimes flying in from the bay or ocean. Merlins can be quite common between mid-September and late October. Peregrine Falcons, however, are scarce along the Delaware coast, in marked contrast to their abundance at Cape May.

Numbers of accipiters are especially unpredictable; on many days few birds are evident, but large flights are not unusual. Small numbers of Northern Harriers and somewhat larger numbers of Ospreys occur, but migrant buteos and vultures are notably rare along the coast in autumn.

Data from 54 hours of observation on 14 days between 10 September and 18 October 1981 (P. F. Burns and A. L. Zayatz, unpub. data) suggest that Cape Henlopen SP may be a good vantage point for hawk watching at that time of year. Raptor sightings averaged 14 birds per hour flying southwest, primarily Sharp-shinned Hawks (7.6 per hour) and American Kestrels (3.1), with lesser numbers of Ospreys (1.6), Merlins (0.5), and several other species. Although this study was too brief for a detailed analysis of the factors responsible for flights, it suggested several interesting conclusions. First, flights of Sharp-shinned Hawks and American Kestrels usually did not coincide. Flights of Sharp-shins typically occurred when winds were light (4–7 mph), and they were rarely seen at all when wind speed exceeded 11 mph, whereas kestrel flights occurred in winds of up to 18 mph. Second, striking and consistent differences between the behavior of these two species occurred during periods of major flights. Sharp-shins were usually observed flying at high altitudes, from about 30 meters up to the limit of

unaided vision. In contrast, kestrels usually flew no higher than 30 meters and often even below eye level.

Although the data reported here indicate that moderate-sized hawk flights sometimes occur at Cape Henlopen, my studies (unpublished) and those of Kerlinger (1989) on the orientation of American Kestrels and Sharp-shinned Hawks departing Cape May Point suggested that landfall in Delaware for these species may frequently be northwest of Cape Henlopen. Autumn concentrations of migrant hawks have seldom been reported, however, along the western shore of Delaware Bay; whether the birds quickly disperse inland on arrival (perhaps in search of prey) or promptly follow the coastline south is not known.

Patterns of relative abundance of different hawk species in coastal Delaware during autumn may reflect in part interspecific differences in water-crossing behavior. Sharp-shinned Hawks, American Kestrels, and Merlins are plentiful, whereas buteos and vultures are comparatively rare along Delaware's ocean coast. This pattern corresponds well to data on water-crossing tendencies reported by Kerlinger (1981), based on a study at Cape May Point. He found that most Sharp-shinned Hawks (81%), Merlins (74%), and American Kestrels (68%) undertook bay crossings. In contrast, fewer than half of the Broad-winged Hawks and Turkey Vultures attempted to cross, and virtually all that did so eventually turned back and returned to Cape May. On the other hand, Peregrine Falcons, which are common at Cape May, never hesitated to cross the bay, yet this species is seldom seen along the Delaware coast. This anomaly suggests that the destination of Peregrines departing from Cape May might be south of Delaware—perhaps the coast of Maryland or Virginia.

Water-crossing behavior of raptors is still incompletely understood, however, and researchers using different techniques at various times have obtained divergent results. In a detailed telemetry study at Cape May Point, Holthuijzen and Oosterhuis (1985) found, in contrast to Kerlinger's observations, that only one radio-marked Sharp-shinned Hawk out of a sample of 43 birds (2%) flew directly across the bay, arriving at Cape Henlopen about 30 minutes later; the remainder of the birds eventually flew north along the eastern shore of Delaware Bay. In a more visual study in 1992, I obtained results intermediate between those of Kerlinger (1981) and those of Holthuijzen and Oosterhuis (1985): 38% of migrant Sharp-shinned Hawks and 31% of American Kestrels initiated water crossings from Cape May Point toward the Delaware coast and maintained their course until they were out of aided visual range. Some of these inconsistencies may be attributable to differences in prevailing weather patterns among the different studies, because migrants are more reluctant to cross bodies of water with strong lateral winds (Kerlinger 1989). However, detailed studies on the Delaware side of the bay will be necessary before the reasons for these disparate results can be fully resolved.

Spring

Few data are available on spring hawk flights along the Delaware coast. Flights at Cape Henlopen may be comparable in magnitude and composition to those recorded at Sandy Hook, New Jersey (see Bouton and Sutton [1987] for a summary of nine years of spring hawk counts at that site). Based on my casual observations, conducted mostly in Delaware Seashore SP, Sharp-shinned Hawks and American Kestrels are the most abundant species; Ospreys and Merlins are less numerous but may be common on some days. Northern Harriers, Cooper's Hawks, and Turkey Vultures are sometimes seen. Small buteo flights presumably occur but have rarely been noticed.

Species-specific timing along the Delaware coast in spring is not well documented. American Kestrels, Ospreys, and Northern Harriers probably peak in early April, but several large flights of kestrels have been noted in late March. Most other species reach peak numbers during late April or the first week in May, except Red-tailed and Red-shouldered hawks, which probably peak in March. Flights continue through at least the second week of May, with stragglers occurring throughout the month and, rarely, into June.

The flight path of migrant hawks along Delaware's coast in spring is also a matter of speculation. Flights of American Kestrels, Sharp-shinned Hawks, and Cooper's Hawks have been observed moving north along the bayshore at Broadkill Beach, but these species have also been seen heading directly over the water from points south of Cape Henlopen. Whether or not birds choose to cross Delaware Bay may be determined by a combination of local winds and the physiological condition of the birds.

In summary, hawk migrations occur throughout Delaware in both spring and autumn, but are concentrated over the extreme northern part of the state during autumn and along the Atlantic coast during both spring and autumn. Important physiographic features influencing these movements include the fall line, Delaware Bay, and Chesapeake Bay. Many aspects of Delaware's hawk migrations remain undescribed or poorly known, and detailed studies of the Delaware flights will be essential for unraveling the complex dynamics of hawk migration in the Mid-Atlantic region.

Northern Harrier *(Circus cyaneus)*

Resident; fairly common to common migrant and winter visitor, rare breeder. Most numerous mid-October through February.

HABITAT: Saltmarshes most commonly, grain fields, and meadows. Breeding largely confined to cordgrass marshes and adjacent fields. Observed in summer near Delaware City, where the marshes are too fresh for cordgrass.

SPRING: Bildstein (1988, 265) notes that there is movement from March into April in the southern United States and to mid-May in northern states. Although the number of birds present decreases at the end of February, the number of reports does not decrease until 20–25 May, suggesting that wintering birds leave about the end of February, and more southerly migrants continue to pass through into May. In Delaware there are few reports and few birds in June and July. The highest counts, possibly aggregates of migrant and wintering birds, are

16 Mar 1973	30	Bombay Hook NWR [Holg79]
28 Mar 1982	12	Bombay Hook NWR [Bayn1]
10 Apr 1980	11	Prime Hook NWR (notes)

Typically fewer than 4 birds are reported on a spring day.

BREEDING: Marsh Hawk, its former name, is appropriate in Delaware, for it hunts and breeds close to the marshes along the Delaware River.

Atlas. The Atlas project reported this species in 21 blocks, from Dragon Run on 1 and 8 July 1983 [Nile5] to Indian River Inlet on 12 June 1983 [Frec1] with 3 confirmations. At both Flemings Landing [BrRF2] and Little Creek [RusR2] males were observed bringing food to females. A nest with eggs hatching was found east of Dover Air Force Base (Thomas 1987b).

Bombay Hook NWR personnel have reported regularly summering harriers at the refuge, and nests were reported there on 10 June 1988 and 8 June 1989 [Peli1].

After the Atlas project researchers recognized that this

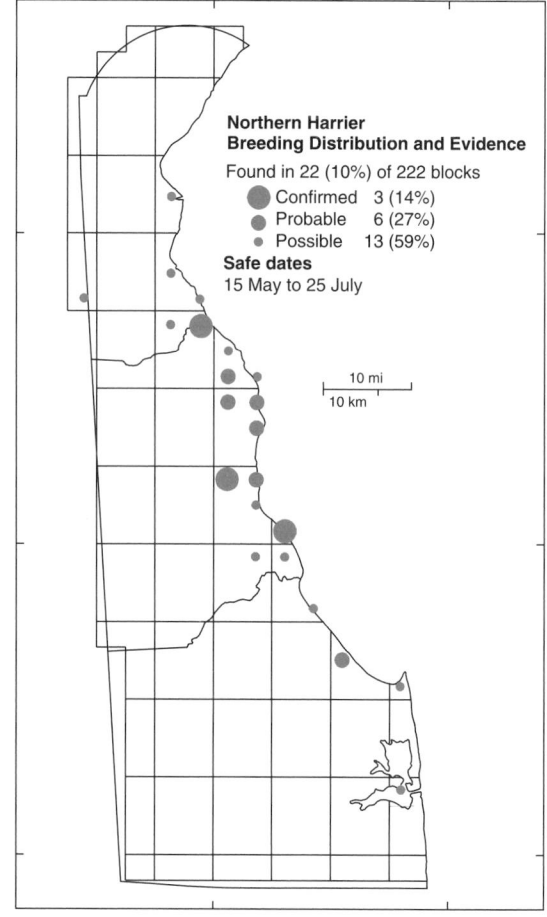

Northern Harrier
Breeding Distribution and Evidence

Found in 22 (10%) of 222 blocks

● Confirmed 3 (14%)
● Probable   6 (27%)
● Possible   13 (59%)

Safe dates
15 May to 25 July

10 mi
10 km

species needed to receive special study in Delaware, as it had in New Jersey (Dunne 1984) and New York (England 1985). Rothstein partly met this need in 1991 by locating 10 nests at 6 distinct sites along the bay marshes from Kent County south to Cape Henlopen. Two sites had polygynous males with 3 females (Rothstein 1991b).

Nesting. On 11 June 1986 a nest with eggs and young was found by West as the second young was hatching; 3 remaining eggs failed to hatch. A presumed male in subadult brownish plumage brought food to the brooding female. The nest was in a winter barley field near a tidal ditch, and it was unintentionally destroyed by farm machinery before the young fledged (Thomas 1987b). Hanson (notes) describes a nest of grass stems built directly on the ground on an island in a marsh near Slaughter Beach. Rothstein (1991b) reports that cordgrass marshes are preferred, but 1 pair nested in poison ivy surrounded by phragmites. A nest at Bombay Hook NWR was a loose cup of straw placed on a mound of straw in phragmites (P. Daly, in 1989 Bombay Hook NWR narrative report).

Extreme egg dates are 4 eggs on 9 May 1938 [Buck1] and eggs hatching 11 June 1986 [West4]. Clutch-completion dates extend from late April through May, probably peaking in early May (n = 18). The latest nest contained 5 eggs on 8 June and 5-week-old young on 11 July 1989 (P. Daly 1989, Bombay Hook NWR narrative report). Clutches ranged from 6 to 2 with mode of 5 (n = 16); some or all of the clutches of 2 may have been incomplete.

History. More Northern Harriers seen in Delaware in summer are brown (i.e., first-year males, and females) than gray. This leads to questions as to how regularly the species breeds here or whether our birds are usually just first-year nonbreeding birds. Compilations since 1905 (Rhoads and Pennock 1905) have listed it as resident. Harriers certainly bred here in the past: Hanson (notes) reports 3 nests found in 1932–33, and Buckalew (notes) corroborates these and adds another 10 harrier nests located by Buckalew and Civilian Conservation Corps workers in 1938 and 1939. After 40 years in which no breeding was reported though birds were present, Russell reported a male passing food to a female on 11 May 1980 at Little Creek WA [RusR3].

Trends. The Northern Harrier declined significantly in the Northeast (including Delaware) from 1965 to 1980 (Robbins et al. 1986). Tate (1986), in the Blue List, reported its numbers down or greatly down almost everywhere. On the contrary, the Delaware May Count, taken after the main migration, indicates its numbers increased during 1969–91, and this finding is supported by the BBS for the Mid-Atlantic coast, 1966–90 [Usfw3]. The coastal population from Virginia north to New Jersey or Long Island seems stable or increasing as long as its coastal habitat remains constant (Serrentino and England 1989), whereas changing agricultural practices are adversely affecting the inland population—and those of many other grassland species.

Conservation. The harrier has been on the Blue List since the list began (Arbib 1971) and is being monitored by many northeastern states. It is Endangered in New Jersey but not listed in Pennsylvania or Maryland (Serrentino 1992).

Harriers tend to return to their breeding site if breeding is successful (M. England, pers. comm.), so careful protection of breeding attempts should pay off in terms of a stable breeding population.

FALL: Bildstein (1988) notes that some young of the year are on the move by August and birds at the northern edge of the breeding range disperse by early September and continue migrating until late November. In Delaware there is an increase in the number of reports beginning 30 July to 5 August. One at Brandywine Creek SP on 9 August 1969 [Broo15], 2 at Carpenter SP on 24 August 1984 [Oliv1], and 2 there on 29 August 1987 [Barn13] were clearly migrants since they were seen away from their usual Delaware habitat. Migration probably continues into December. An increase in numbers begins 10–15 September, reflecting both the increase in numbers seen at hawk watches (see "Hawk Migration" essay) and the buildup of winter visitors along the marshes. Bildstein (1988) also notes that

high numbers may be expected from mid-September to the end of October. The highest counts include

20 Sep 1981	10	Bombay Hook NWR [Broo22]
27 Sep 1981	9	Bombay Hook NWR [Edni45]
18 Oct 1986	10	Bombay Hook NWR [Edni65]
17 Oct 1985	15	along Rt. 9 [Wayn64]

Usually 6 or fewer birds are seen in a day.

1966–89 CBC Summary

Christmas Bird Count	Years Found	Range of No. Found	Median
Wilmington	24	2–11	7
Middletown	24	7–79	47
Bombay Hook	24	31–155	64
Cape Henlopen	24	12–58	29
Rehoboth	24	2–28	14
STATEWIDE *(low in 1983, high in 1975)*	24	90–290	164

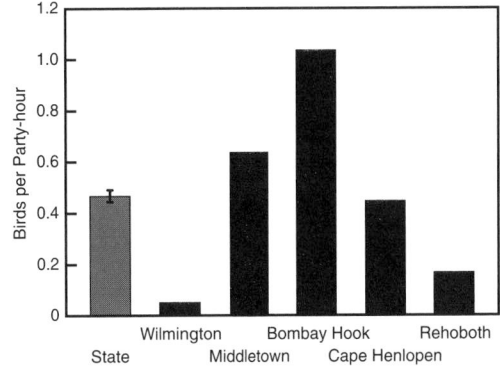

CBC Geographic Distribution

WINTER: No CBC trend is apparent. CBCs, which cover about 70% of Delaware's coastline, have reported between 90 and 290 (CBC table), about 10 times the summer population. This species is more common in the river marshes north of Cape Henlopen than around the Inland Bays (CBC distribution figure).

SPECIMENS: 9; DMNH, UDEL, USNM.

Sharp-shinned Hawk (*Accipiter striatus*)

Regular; common migrant and fairly common winter resident. Expected late August to early May. Winter numbers increasing at 11% per year.

HABITAT: Wooded, brushy areas.

SPRING: Migration is not particularly apparent but probably takes place from 15–20 April to 1–7 May. Palmer (1988, 4:313) notes that "In the lat. of Pa. and Md., some movement is noted by very early Mar., most pass in last 3 weeks of Apr., and movement ceases around May 10." High counts are

4 Apr 1978	11	St. Georges Chapel, Sussex Co. [Frec1]
27 Apr 1985	6	Cape Henlopen SP [Frec1]
5 May 1986	12	Cape Henlopen SP [Frec1]

Typical daily totals are 1–4 birds.

SUMMER: Rhoads and Pennock (1905) list this bird as resident in Delaware, a designation extended by Barry (1939), who said it was "fairly numerous summer and fall." There are still occasional summer sight records of this hawk in Delaware by experienced observers, but breeding has been neither suggested nor expected. There are no summer specimens, no breeding records were found when Linehan prepared a list of breeding birds (1967a), and there are no subsequent breeding records. In the Mid-Atlantic states it breeds mainly in mountainous areas and only casually elsewhere. Observers, therefore, should be sure of their identification before reporting summer birds. Formerly, however, it bred in nearby Pennsylvania. Warren (1890), for example, lists 3 birds taken during breeding season for a short time in 1880—on 30 May in Delaware County and on 2 and 3 June in Chester County.

From limited evidence, 2 opposing speculations arise:

1. Sharp-shinned Hawks have never (significantly) bred in Delaware, or else we would have a specimen, nest record, or satisfactory report, and the statements saying it has bred here were based on misidentification of male Cooper's Hawks or on its occurrence during migration or in Pennsylvania, or

2. Sharp-shinned Hawks formerly bred in Delaware but were extirpated by a combination of deforestation and farmers intent on protecting poultry.

Supporting the possibility of extirpation is this quotation from a letter to *The Auk* (Carey 1926): "Since 1922, and probably earlier, a farmer in Delaware has been trapping Hawks wholesale. During the fall and winter of 1922–1923, up to January 20, he had captured 35, and as many as six in one day. His methods were widely advertised in the press and his farm visited by many admirers who have doubtless used his methods." Nuttall (in Warren 1890) states that "In thinly settled districts, this hawk seems to abound, and proves extremely destructive to young chickens, a single bird having been known regularly to come every day until he had carried away between twenty and thirty."

FALL: First arrivals are observed in the last half of August.

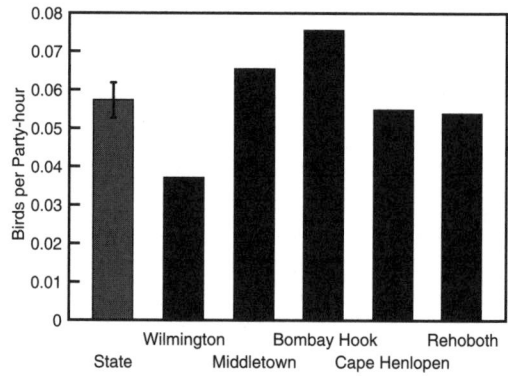

CBC Geographic Distribution

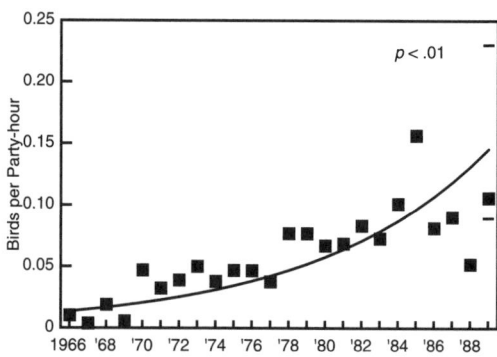

CBC Trend; Increasing at 11% per Year

Migration continues from then to 25–30 October. Some high counts along the coast are

17 Sep 1980	35	Rehoboth Beach [Frec1]
27 Sep 1980	35	Cape Henlopen SP [Frec34]
2 Oct 1983	39	Cape Henlopen SP [Frec1]
26 Oct 1983	45	Cape Henlopen SP [Frec1]

Some high counts at Carpenter SP by Oliver (notes) are 23 September 1983 (87), 24 September 1983 (133), and 29 October 1983 (56).

1966–89 CBC Summary

Christmas Bird Count	Years Found	Range of No. Found	Median
Wilmington	22	1–15	6
Middletown	20	1–11	5
Bombay Hook	21	1–15	4
Cape Henlopen	21	1–9	4
Rehoboth	23	1–12	5
STATEWIDE	24	1–57	23
(increasing; low in 1967, high in 1985)			

WINTER: This raptor is fairly evenly distributed among CBC areas. It has shown a significant increase in numbers, probably because of protective laws. Also, these birds were adversely affected by DDT, and restriction of its use has allowed them to recover. Sharp-shinned Hawks frequently hunt wintering birds at backyard feeders. Understandably, many people do not like to see their songbirds fly away or be caught when a Sharp-shinned Hawk takes up residence; however, this is the natural way of life for these birds.

SPECIMENS: 28; DMNH, UDEL, USNM.

Cooper's Hawk *(Accipiter cooperii)*

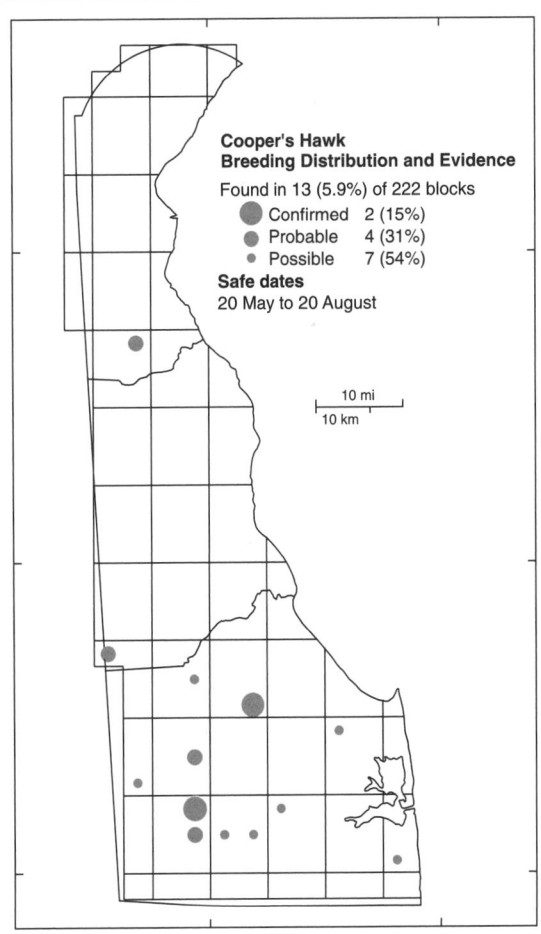

**Cooper's Hawk
Breeding Distribution and Evidence**

Found in 13 (5.9%) of 222 blocks
● Confirmed   2 (15%)
● Probable   4 (31%)
· Possible   7 (54%)
Safe dates
20 May to 20 August

10 mi
10 km

Resident; uncommon migrant and winter visitor, rare breeder. Migration probably occurs February–April and September–early December, but more data are needed to determine migration periods. Winter numbers apparently increasing.

J F M A M J J A S O N D

HABITAT: Wooded, brushy areas. Nests reported in both pine and holly. The only known breeding territory in New Castle County was located in planted pines at Blackbird SF; pine and pine–deciduous forests generally predominate where it nests in Sussex County.

SPRING: The migration period is not apparent in the seasonal bar graph because virtually all reports mention single birds. Based on the frequency of reports most wintering birds probably depart in March. A slight increase in the frequency of reports during the last 2 weeks of April is probably best interpreted as an increased obviousness of breeding birds in courtship and while establishing territories, but some late migrants may be involved. Stewart and Robbins (1958) give the Maryland migration period as 1–10 March to 5–15 May, with the peak during 5–30 April.

BREEDING: The Cooper's Hawk is a rarely reported, discreet breeder, primarily in Sussex County. April and May reports of this hawk from White Clay Creek in the late 1970s and from Burrows Run in the early 1990s are suggestive of undetected breeding in New Castle County.

Atlas. There had been no breeding reports or even carefully documented summer reports of Cooper's Hawks for 50 years until Paul Burns, DNREC, reported to the Atlas project that he had been following a small population of Cooper's Hawks in Sussex County. During the Atlas period he reported 3 nests, and he and others reported summer records from 8 other blocks, including 1 each in southern Kent and southern New Castle Counties. The New Castle County pair was reported for several summers at Blackbird SF.

Nesting. Hanson (notes) described a nest with 3 eggs found on 27 April 1929 about 40 ft above ground in a pine in woods on the south bank of Moores Mill Creek, near Dover: "The nest was built of sticks and lined with a little bark and a few pine needles. It was about 18 inches outside diameter and 12 inches deep. The inside was about 7 ½ inches across with a definite hollow for the eggs." On 27 April 1931 Buckalew found a nest with 5 eggs 30 ft above ground in a holly near Lincoln [Buck8]. The latest egg date is 15 May 1930 near Slaughter Beach [Buck1]. Most clutches were probably completed in the last third of April. Clutch size ranged from 3 to 5 (median 4); some clutches may have been incomplete (n = 9).

History. The farmer who shot or trapped "chicken hawks" at every opportunity was the enemy of this raptor and its smaller congener, the Sharp-shinned Hawk. The farmer's practice was an economic necessity in the days of open chicken coops as this hawk catches poultry-sized birds with ease, and such shooting and trapping was fully supported by society for many years. Cooper's Hawks are now protected in Delaware under state and federal laws. After persecution by farmers, the Cooper's Hawk was dealt a second blow in the East by widespread use of DDT (Bednarz et al. 1990). Presumably, this raptor suffered by consuming songbirds that had ingested DDT-contaminated invertebrate prey.

Until the 1980s the only breeding records for Cooper's Hawk in Delaware were a nest found by Dicky and Hanson near Dover in 1929 and 8 nests in Kent and Sussex Counties located by Buckalew during 1930–35 [Buck8; Hans1].

Breeding population. The total Delaware population of perhaps 10–20 pairs is buttressed by a larger population in the adjacent counties of Maryland.

Conservation. This bird has been on the Blue List since 1971.

It should be carefully protected. The Delmarva population may be particularly jeopardized because of its peninsular isolation from the rest of this species' population.

FALL: Rosenfield (1988) notes fall migration extends from late August through early November, peaking at many hawk lookouts from mid-September through mid-October. The Delaware data do not reflect the period of migration. However, there are a few reports beginning mid-September and more in October and November, signaling the arrival of wintering birds. All reports refer to 1–3 birds.

1966–89 CBC Summary

Christmas Bird Count	Years Found	Range of No. Found	Median
Wilmington	15	1–4	1
Middletown	14	1–4	1
Bombay Hook	20	1–4	1
Cape Henlopen	11	1–3	
Rehoboth	15	1–7	1
STATEWIDE	24	1–17	6

(increasing; low in 1968 and 1980, high in 1989)

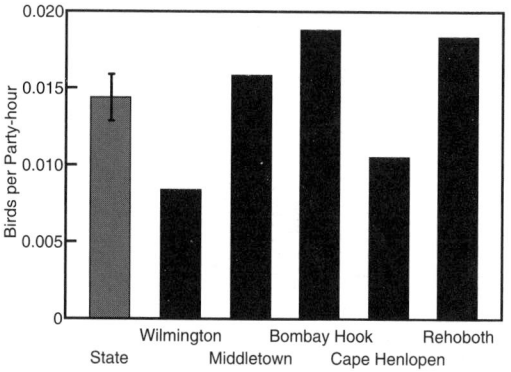

CBC Geographic Distribution

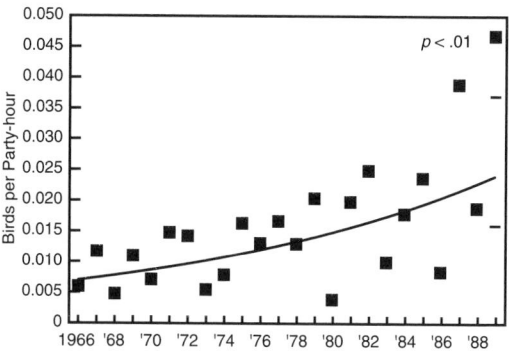

CBC Trend; Autocorrelation may Invalidate the Significance Test

WINTER: This species has shown a significant increase in numbers, though it is much less abundant than the Sharp-shinned Hawk. As outlined in the breeding section, a decline in persecution may be responsible for its recent increase.

SPECIMENS: 7; DMNH, USNM.

Northern Goshawk (*Accipiter gentilis*)

Occasional (19 years during 1935–92); fall migrant and winter visitor; rare.

J F M A M J J A S O N D

DOCUMENTATION: One banding recovery and convincing notes (DMNH).

REMARKS: This largest and most northerly of the accipiters is found regularly in modest numbers along the Pennsylvania migration routes but is seldom seen in migration away from mountain ridges. It winters occasionally in small numbers throughout the Mid-Atlantic region. It has been reported on 5 Delaware CBCs. Most of the available records range from 18 October 1981 [Burn1] to 27 March 1965 [Klab1]. Records from 8 November to 15 March include these having convincing descriptions:

8 Nov 1981	2	near White Clay Creek [Insk2]
15 Nov 1975	1	along White Clay Creek [Edni1]
9, 29 Jan 1982	1	Seaford [Fint1]
4 Feb 1982	1	near Hoopes Reservoir [SpeE4]
15 Mar 1981	1	Bombay Hook NWR [Grim2]

A bird banded at Cape May, New Jersey, on 25 October 1973 was found dead near Indian River Inlet on 23 November 1973 [Usfw3]. A goshawk seen at Hoopes Reservoir 16 February 1964 apparently overwintered in the area; the Specks had 1 at their feeder near Hoopes Reservoir several times [SpSB4]. This species also visited the Sample's feeder in Sherwood Park 1 February 1987 and Miller's feeder a few miles away near Newark on 24 February that winter [MiDP7; Samp4].

In view of the scarcity of March records for this species (only 1 documented), judgment must be withheld on April records that lack contemporaneous documentation. Endorsement of brief but otherwise satisfactory notes on 1 seen 27 June 1966 at Little Creek must be withheld because of the unlikely date and atypically open habitat (Linehan 1967c). Similarly, Hoopes Reservoir records for 29 May and 12 June 1943

[Hoff4] must be treated with caution. The closest to Delaware this species breeds is in the forested Appalachian Mountain section of Pennsylvania (Bednarz and Kimmel 1992) and the New Jersey Highlands section (Speiser and Bosakowski 1984). Many nonbreeding goshawks were encountered in the New Jersey study. There is a concentration of late winter records near Hoopes Reservoir, where the habitat is perhaps suitable. Similarly, April 1992 sightings at nearby Burrows Run, although reasonable, should be supported with contemporaneous notes, as there are no documented April reports in Delaware.

Five of the 7 goshawks reported in Delaware during the 1970s were seen during the 1972–73 invasion years (Mueller et al. 1977). The large increase in goshawk reports in Delaware during the 1980s, not accompanied by an increase in reports at Hawk Mountain (Bednarz 1990), may derive partly from misidentifications. Goshawks should be reported only after careful field study and note taking, and should never be identified by size alone.

Red-shouldered Hawk *(Buteo lineatus)*

Resident; uncommon. Migration probably occurs March–April and October–November, but more observations are needed.

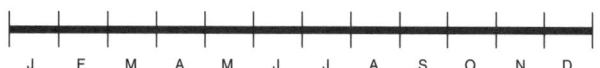

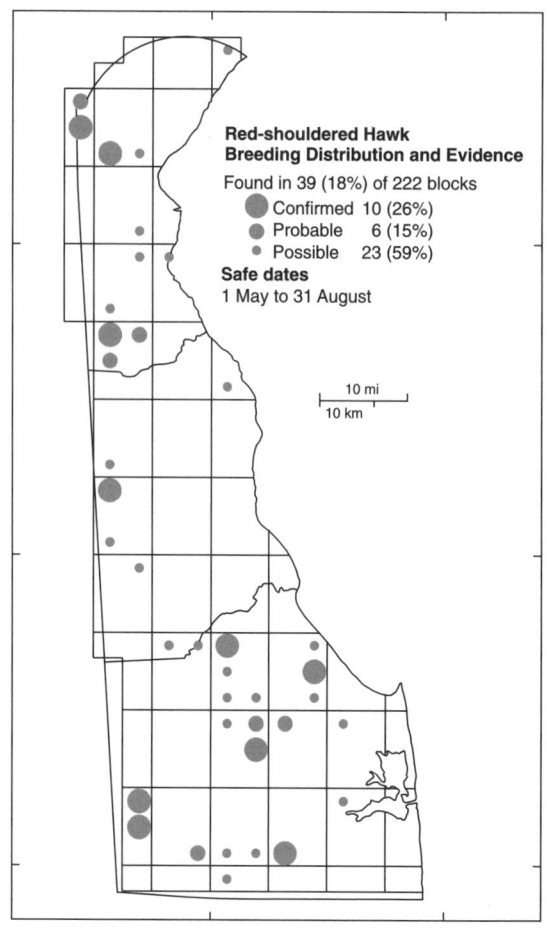

**Red-shouldered Hawk
Breeding Distribution and Evidence**
Found in 39 (18%) of 222 blocks
Confirmed 10 (26%)
Probable   6 (15%)
Possible   23 (59%)
Safe dates
1 May to 31 August

10 mi
10 km

HABITAT: Mature lowland forest with a stream or open water and clearings nearby. Nests primarily in deciduous trees, but mixed forest used at Assawoman WA and pine forest at Phillips Landing on the Nanticoke River.

SPRING: Migration probably occurs during March and April. Stewart and Robbins (1958) give the Maryland migration period as 15–25 February to 10–20 April, with a peak from 1 March to 5 April. The only reports of more than a few birds are

| 13 Mar 1982 | 60 | Arundel, New Castle Co. [RusR6] |
| 23 Apr 1983 | 8 | Carpenter SP [Oliv1] |

BREEDING: Found throughout Delaware in relatively low numbers wherever its habitat remains, the Red-shoulder is more common in inland swamp remnants.

Atlas. These birds have relatively small woodland breeding ranges of somewhat less than a square mile (Stewart 1949). This hawk is harder to detect than the Red-tailed Hawk. They may have been missed by some Atlas workers, because most Atlas work was done after the leaves were on the trees and after the March–April courtship period. Places where they probably were missed are Assawoman WA, where it has bred before, and Cedar Swamp, where it is known to breed at least on the Maryland side. Six confirmations came from finding nests, 4 from young on territory.

Nesting. Two nest descriptions exist from earlier in the twentieth century. On 14 April 1931 Dicky, Buckalew, and Hanson found a nest with 3 eggs 45 ft above ground in a cedar in a swamp near Milford. On 29 April of that year Dicky and Hanson (notes) found a nest near the St. Jones River, south of Dover: "35 feet up in a large oak tree, well saddled in a crotch of four limbs. The nest was about 18 inches across outside and 10 inches inside. The opening was about 2 inches deep. It was built mostly of sticks but contained some dried grass intermixed and was lined with green pine needles and twigs, one laurel twig and down. There was some down on the outside seen from the ground." It contained 1 egg and 2 newly hatched young. Nests have also been reported from White Clay Creek (35 ft up in a sugar maple), the Choptank drainage (40 ft up in a maple, 9 April 1927—first known breeding record), Phillips Landing (50 ft up in a pine), and Cedar Swamp 2 mi northeast of Gumboro (55 ft up in a large American beech). A just-fledged young was found on 29 May 1966 in Assawoman WA. The Red-shoulder is reported as regular at Prime Hook NWR by O'Shea, but it should be expected in coastal areas only around wet woodlands.

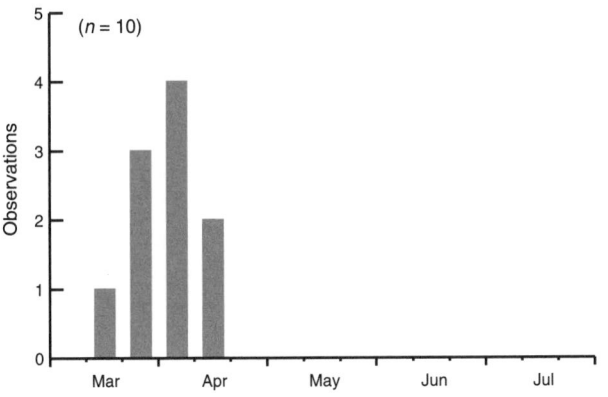

Estimated Clutch-Completion Dates

Extrapolated clutch-completion dates appear to peak in early April. Egg dates fall in the narrow range of 1–29 April, but based on Maryland egg dates (Robbins and Bystrak 1977) egg-laying probably begins in early March. Clutch size is 3 (*n* = 6).

History and trends. This bird, once common in the northeastern forests, is declining as its forest habitat decreases (e.g., for New Jersey Coastal Plain, see Sutton and Sutton 1986). After much of the eastern forests were cleared, and continuing until the mid-1900s, its numbers were further reduced by shooting and trapping. Its status was reported as "common winter visitor and rare resident" (Barry 1939). We have no satisfactory means of monitoring its population in Delaware except by monitoring loss of habitat. The BBS provides an inadequate sample, and the May Count results probably reflect a focused effort to find at least 1 of its kind. Similar studies have not been able to detect a trend in the Northeast based on BBS or CBC data (Peterson and Crocoll 1992). In contrast, other raptors—Bald Eagle, Osprey, Sharp-shinned Hawk, and Red-tailed Hawk—have shown strong increases in Delaware according to data from Delaware counts.

Breeding abundance. Based on its being recorded in 33 Atlas blocks, its state population is estimated at about 50 pairs, with considerable allowance for error. A relative abundance study in 1985–87 recorded only one-sixth as many Red-shouldered as Red-tailed hawks in June, but this study was done in early morning hours when neither species tends to be obvious. The May Count from 1969 to 1991 recorded a similar 1:6 ratio. The roadside hawk census of 1984–86 shows a ratio of 1:15 for March and April, but this survey, more so than others, was probably biased toward the more obvious Red-tailed Hawk.

Conservation. Tax ditches, channelization of streams, and lack of protection of fresh wetland and streamside forests have led to habitat loss. Mature forests, particularly in wetland areas, have decreased. As the wet deciduous woods have declined, so, probably, have Red-shouldered Hawks. As the wet woods have declined, the drier, more open habitat preferred by Great Horned Owls and Red-tailed Hawks has increased and so have the numbers of these 2 species. Both adult and young Red-shouldered Hawks fall prey to Great Horned Owls (Brown and

Amadon 1968). Both the owl and Red-tails dominate Red-shoulders in the choice of nest sites in Michigan (Craighead and Craighead 1956, 225). More study of this scarce raptor should be undertaken to define its status and needs in Delaware before its habitat is further reduced. On the Blue List since 1972 (Tate 1986), it is also listed as Endangered in New Jersey, Threatened in New York, and as a migratory nongame bird of management concern by the USFWS (Peterson and Crocoll 1992).

FALL: The migration period is probably similar to that of Red-tailed Hawk, with migration peaking in late October to mid-November (see "Hawk Migration" essay). Stewart and Robbins (1958) give a more extended Maryland migration period of 10–20 September to 20–30 November with the peak 20 September to 15 November. High counts include

22 Oct 1974	5	White Clay Creek [Lehm1]
3 Nov 1984	14	Carpenter SP [Oliv1]
3 Nov 1972	7	Brandywine Creek SP [Phal3]
16 Nov 1980	7	Carpenter SP [Oliv1]

A report of 17 at Brandywine Creek SP on 16 September 1973 probably refers to Broad-winged Hawk [RobT2].

1966–89 CBC Summary

Christmas Bird Count	Years Found	Range of No. Found	Median
Wilmington	23	1–5	2
Middletown	14	1–4	1
Bombay Hook	24	1–6	2
Cape Henlopen	16	1–4	1
Rehoboth	17	1–9	1
STATEWIDE	24	4–16	7
(low in 1967 and 1984, high in 1966)			

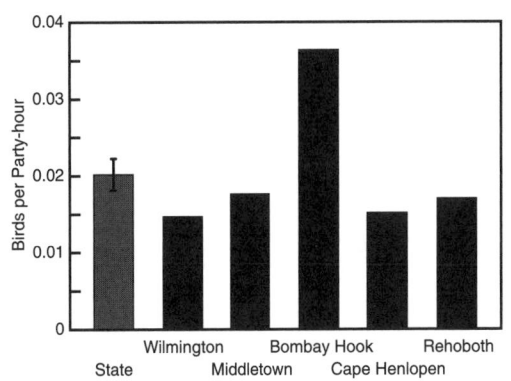

CBC Geographic Distribution

WINTER: No CBC trend is apparent, and the numbers counted have fluctuated 4-fold. Aside from the CBCs, the high counts are

6 Dec 1981	3	Bombay Hook NWR [Edni50]
13 Feb 1977	6	Prime Hook NWR (notes)
12 Jan 1985	3	on the hawk survey [SpSB29]

Red-shouldered Hawks were little reported on the hawk survey perhaps in part because of a low population and because its preferred woodland habitat is difficult to survey from roadsides (Hess 1987). The Seaford CBC for 1983–89 reported 50% more birds per party-hour than did the Bombay Hook CBC for those years. The Red-shoulder is substantially less common than the Red-tailed Hawk on Delaware CBCs by the ratio of 7:158.

SPECIMENS: 7; DMNH, ANSP, USNM. Egg records: DMNH.

Broad-winged Hawk (*Buteo platypterus*)

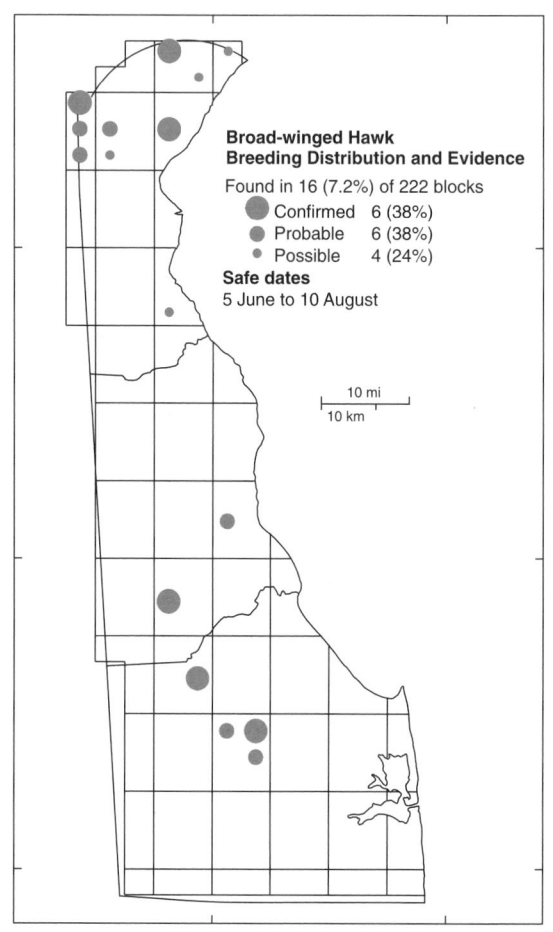

Regular; local, rare breeder, abundant migrant. Expected mid-April through September.

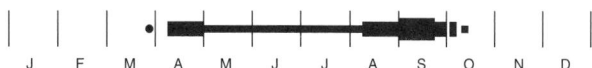

| | | | | | | | | | | | |
|J|F|M|A|M|J|J|A|S|O|N|D|

HABITAT: Mature hardwoods with an open understory along streams with adjacent small fields in the Piedmont. Mixed deciduous–pine woods typical of the Coastal Plain in 2 sections of Redden State Forest and at Trap Pond.

SPRING: First arrival is 10–15 April; migration ends by the beginning of May. The few late March reports all lack documentation. Any report prior to 10 April should be carefully documented. High counts, all from the Newark area, are

17 Apr 1983	2	[Oliv1]
18–23 Apr 1981	75	[RusR5]
23 Apr 1983	14	[Oliv1]
24 Apr 1989	24	[RusJ1]

BREEDING: Although numbers of Broad-wings migrate across the Piedmont, few stay to breed, the best known breeding area being along White Clay Creek.

Atlas. Atlas workers found it in about half the eligible Piedmont blocks with creek valleys. A smaller population is thinly scattered over the Delmarva Peninsula, with Atlas records from 2 sections of Redden SF. One confirmation referred to an immature bird salvaged on 7 August 1983 at Harrington (DMNH 75033). The other confirmed Atlas reports from southern Delaware referred to newly fledged young begging for food. No nests have been reported south of the Chesapeake and Delaware Canal. However, before the Atlas project, Moorhouse reported a Broad-winged Hawk carrying nesting material on the north side of Trap Pond SP on 13 May 1978 [MooJ1].

Nesting. One Delaware nest was at least 60 ft above ground in a black oak near the shore of Smalleys Pond. It was "about 8 inches across, built of sticks including one or two twigs having green leaves. It was lined with pieces of [oak] bark, some of them at least 1 inch by 3 inches. The inside of the nest was not more than 5 inches across and a scant 2 inches deep" [Hans1].

This nest location was unusually high and the nest unusually small. The typical Broad-winged Hawk nest is summarized by Mosher (1988, 10) from various studies of over 500 nests: "the nest generally is 25–40 feet up (range 8–70) in the first crotch of a moderate- to large-sized tree and in the bottom ⅓ of the forest canopy." Peck and James (1983) state that nests range from small to bulky platforms and give outside diameters for 3 as 12–24 in. Hanson's nest may be the smallest Broad-wing nest on record, but there is little doubt that the identification and measurements are correct.

Estimated clutch-completion dates in Delaware, based on 3 observations, fall in the first two-thirds of May.

History. The first known Delaware record for the Broad-winged Hawk was made on 28 June 1900 at Townsend (Burns 1911). Rhoads and Pennock (1905) listed it as "resident," possibly because of confusion in winter with immature Red-shoulders. The first known nest, containing 3 eggs, was found at Smalleys Dam on 10 May 1933 [Hans1].

Breeding population. The overall state population is estimated at 10–20 pairs. It was reported from only 16 blocks, and was found in some of the well-studied Piedmont blocks during only 1 year. Five or 6 pairs nested north of the Chesapeake and Delaware Canal.

Conservation. The entire Delaware population is threatened by suburban development and loss of habitat, quite contrary to Mosher and Palmer's (1988, 5:32) optimistic speculation that "today, the Broadwing may be at least as numerous as it was before Caucasian settlement. Decline in agriculture in much of the Broadwing's continental range and consequent growth of discontinuous woodlands has created much suitable habitat . . . [A] combination of factors bodes well for the future of the Broadwing."

As land development continues, northern Delaware may be able to retain several pairs in the creek valleys for a few years, but the necessary combination of quiet mature woods, water, and small fields will continue to diminish. More information is needed on Coastal Plain pairs. If these birds are part of a remnant Delmarva breeding population, management of hardwood forest stands becomes important. Drainage ditching, channelization of freshwater streams, and reforestation with monoculture pine will only hasten extirpation of this population of Broad-winged Hawks.

FALL: The first large flocks usually arrive 1–10 September, peak migration occurs 10–30 September, and virtually all have gone through by 1–7 October (see, for example, "Hawk Migration" essay). Any report thereafter should be carefully documented. Although no notes are available, the following are probably bona fide late migrants:

8 Oct 1983	4	Carpenter SP [Oliv1]
12 Oct 1980	1	Carpenter SP [Oliv1]
14 Oct 1984	1	Carpenter SP [Oliv1]

Eleven other reports from later in October through December lack details to support such late dates.

Reports of early migration are scarce, with the following being the earliest flocks reported:

23 Aug 1983	10	Carpenter SP [Oliv1]
20 Aug 1984	16	Carpenter SP [Oliv1]
24 Aug 1984	19	Carpenter SP [Oliv1]

Some high counts, all from the Newark area, are

20 Sep 1984	1,843	[Oliv1]
17 Sep 1984	2,173	[Oliv1]
18 Sep 1980	2,500	[RusR12]

Virtually all migrants pass through the Piedmont. Hagar (1988, 23) states that "no records at all for Cape Henlopen. . . . substantial numbers of passage Broadwings are seen on the mainland side of the Delaware R. n. of Cape May at Port Penn, Del." We are aware of a few unpublished records from Sussex County but do not have clear evidence that the birds crossed Delaware Bay from Cape May. See Hagar (1988, 12–25) for a full and fascinating account of Broad-winged Hawk migration.

WINTER: This species has been reported on 5 CBCs. If these reports are correct, the birds were substantially north of the generally accepted Broad-winged Hawk wintering range. These and future winter observations should be treated with extreme caution. Observers of winter hawks should notice, record, and report all details that distinguish the birds they see as immature Broad-winged Hawks and not immature Red-shouldered or Cooper's Hawks. Immature Broad-winged Hawks are more likely to be in North America in early winter than are adults, based on Florida data (Tabb 1973). An immature Broad-winged Hawk was brought to Tri-State Bird Rescue (TSBR 92-37) on 21 January 1992. The specimen's (DMNH 77885) identity has been confirmed at the USNM.

SPECIMENS: 7; DMNH.

Red-tailed Hawk (*Buteo jamaicensis*)

Resident; fairly common. Migration probably occurs March–April and September–December.

HABITAT: Farms with woodlots and pastures. Nest placed in either deciduous tree (tulip tree, oak) or pine. Wide tolerance for forest type. Fields or open areas necessary for hunting, often done from an exposed perch.

SPRING: No clear period of migration is apparent, even though winter populations are higher than spring populations (Hess 1987). Spring hawk watches are needed to establish the migration period. Stewart and Robbins (1958) cite the migration period in Maryland as 10–20 February to 10–20 April, with the peak from 25 February to 1 April.

BREEDING: This is the common large hawk in Delaware. The relative abundance study shows it to be more common in Sussex County than in the northern half of the state, probably a result of more forest–field edge in the south. A highly interesting spectacle is the bold feasting of several Red-tails on exposed, possibly injured, rodents in fields where harvesting of winter wheat is in progress (West pers. obs.).

Atlas. This was an easy species to find. Most confirmations were based on fledged young, which are easy to locate when begging for food during the week or two after they leave the nest. Twenty-five confirmations were based on finding the nest or observing nest building.

Nesting. The nests reported have ranged from 30 ft up in a

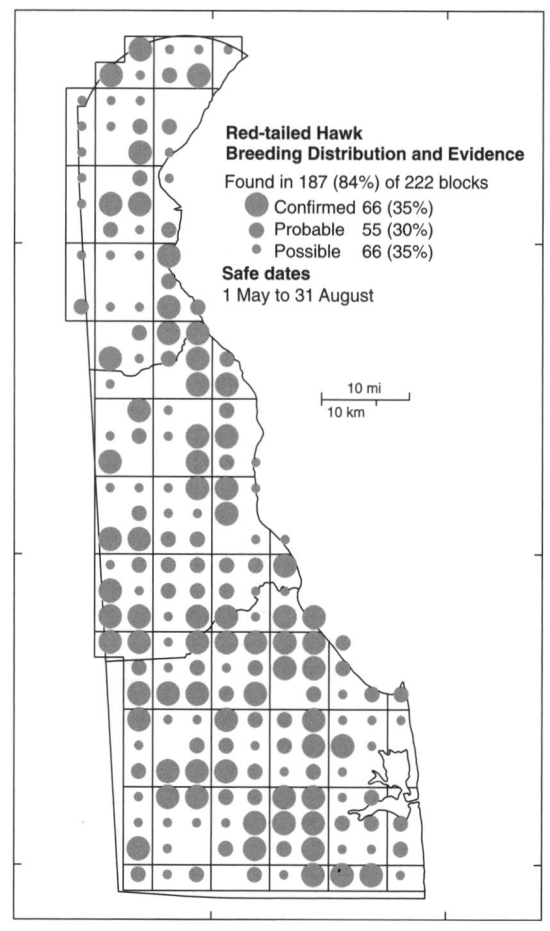

Red-tailed Hawk
Breeding Distribution and Evidence
Found in 187 (84%) of 222 blocks
● Confirmed 66 (35%)
● Probable 55 (30%)
· Possible 66 (35%)
Safe dates
1 May to 31 August

10 mi
10 km

pine to 90 ft up in the triple crotch of a tulip tree. The nest is frequently placed next to the trunk in a crotch.

Buckalew (notes) recorded nests with 2 eggs on 12 April and 17 April. Adults have been reported in "incubation position" from 8 April [Smit1] to 27 May [Frec3]. A downy young was visible on 6 June, and just fledged young were reported on 5 July. These clutches were probably all completed in April.

History. Settlement and clearing of land for agriculture led to an increase in the habitat preferred by Red-tailed Hawks. No doubt shooting and trapping in the past prevented this species from reaching maximum breeding density. In 1904 the State Board of Agriculture published a leaflet describing the Red-tailed Hawk's diet as being 90% rodents, other mammals, and insects more or less harmful to farmers (Pennock 1904b). Comparing that diet to the Cooper's Hawk's diet, the leaflet concluded that "A comparison of these figures shows ample grounds for a more extended study of these large hawks and should stop their indiscriminate slaughter."

We surmise that the slaughter continued and was fairly complete. Red-tailed Hawks are absent from the published and unpublished Delaware notes of Pennock, the collections of Bush (1880s) and Gardner (1920s), and the early CBCs. Hanson

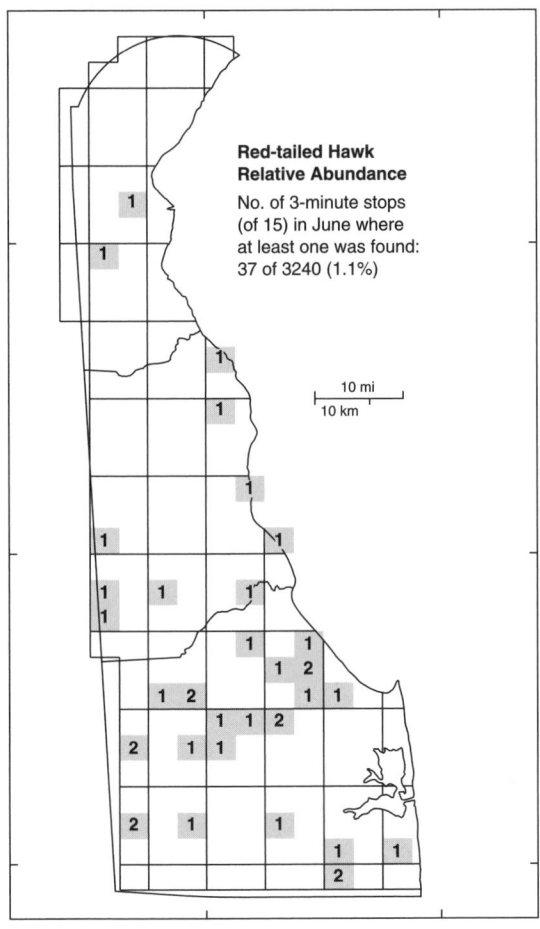

Red-tailed Hawk
Relative Abundance

No. of 3-minute stops
(of 15) in June where
at least one was found:
37 of 3240 (1.1%)

er densities in cropland (Rothfels and Lein 1982). Home range is usually less than 2 sq mi (5 sq km) (Palmer 1988, 5:116). Atlas survey results show 184 blocks occupied. The species was probably missed in another 10–15 blocks, and about one-fifth of the well-covered blocks were known to contain more than 1 pair. Thus estimated total population is about 240 pairs or 1 pair per 7 sq mi of upland habitat (1 pair per 18 sq km). Establishing the actual breeding density requires further study.

FALL: Migration occurs September to early December, peaking in November (see "Hawk Migration" essay). Stewart and Robbins (1958) give the migration period in Maryland as 5–15 September to 1–10 December, with the peak 10 October to 15 November. The high counts, all from Carpenter SP, are 113 on 29 October 1983, 78 on 13 November 1982, and 51 on 13 November 1983 [Oliv1].

1966–89 CBC Summary

Christmas Bird Count	Years Found	Range of No. Found	Median
Wilmington	24	10–64	40
Middletown	24	9–57	37
Bombay Hook	24	21–63	37
Cape Henlopen	24	3–35	15
Rehoboth	24	8–37	22
STATEWIDE	24	115–192	158
(increasing; low in 1967, high in 1986)			

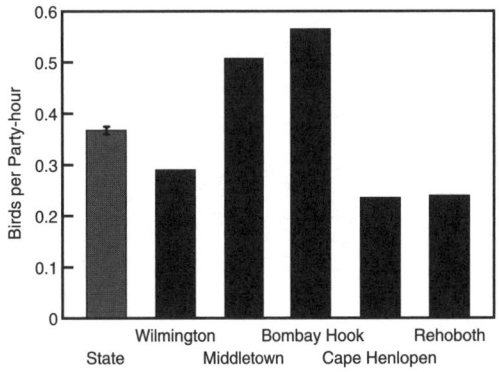

CBC Geographic Distribution

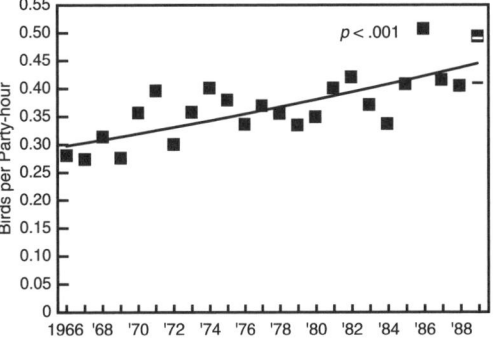

CBC Trend; Increasing at 2% per Year

(notes) records this hawk once at Smalleys Dam in February 1932 and once near Delaware City on 19 February 1937. Although Hanson was collecting nests and eggs of Delaware species, he never found a Red-tail nest. Buckalew knew this hawk in the 1930s but first found a nest in 1938. Presumably the Red-tail was so frequently shot that it was infrequently observed. Barry (1939) reported Red-tailed Hawk numbers declining.

Red-tails have been regularly reported in winter since the Middletown CBC of 26 December 1938. Breeding season reports remained unusual—another nest at Bombay Hook NWR on 12 April 1939 [Buck1], a bird observed on 24 May 1958 at Bombay Hook NWR (Brooks et al. 1955, 31), and an adult seen on nest at Taylors Bridge on 28 March 1965 [Abbo2]. Starting with regular census work in 1965, this hawk has been reported regularly and fairly commonly through the breeding season.

Trends. Analysis of May Count data indicates it increased at an average annual rate of 5% (1969–91), consistent with other indicators of its trend. This probably reflects recovery after low numbers in the first half of the twentieth century.

Breeding population. A number of studies from California to New York report breeding densities of Red-tailed Hawks averaging about 1 pair per 2.2 sq mi (1 pair per 5.7 sq km) with low-

WINTER: This species has shown a significant increase in numbers. The Seaford CBC for 1983–89 reported numbers of birds per hour similar to those on the Middletown and Bombay Hook CBCs. High non-CBC reports are 9 at Bombay Hook NWR on 5 December 1982 (Bombay Hook census) and 15 at Dragon Run on 4 January 1975 [Mars1]. The 1983–86 hawk survey recorded a maximum of 19 on 23 February 1985 (Hess 1987).

A 1983–86 hawk survey appears to indicate that there were about twice as many Red-tailed Hawks in Delaware during January–February as during the breeding season, but the species is much easier to see in winter (Hess 1987). A 35% increase over 20 years in the winter population probably reflects an increase in resident birds at our latitude (Palmer 1988, 5:110). An immature Red-tailed Hawk banded on 8 November 1966 at Lehigh Furnace Gap, Pennsylvania, was retrapped by W. A. Clark on 8 February 1969 at Flemings Landing, showing at least 1 instance of an adult winter visitor in Delaware (Holt and Frock 1980).

SPECIMENS: 18; DMNH, ANSP, UDEL, USNM.

Rough-legged Hawk *(Buteo lagopus)*

Regular; winter resident; uncommon. Expected mid-November through March. Winter numbers declining at 3% per year.

HABITAT: Marsh. Tends to use open habitat more or less neglected by other buteos (Mindell 1988, 161–62).

SPRING: The Rough-legged Hawk does not show a migration peak in Delaware; instead the departure of wintering birds is marked by a sharp decline (about 50%) in the number of reports during March, and after the first week of April there are few reports. This corresponds well with Mindell (1988, 165) who states that at the southern wintering limits some movement takes place in February and much occurs during March and early April. The latest published observation that can reasonably be accepted without notes is 1 seen on 3 April 1965 at Churchmans Marsh [SpSB7]. Later published records, without notes but by qualified observers, are

17 Apr 1954	1	Smyrna [Hewi1]
20 Apr 1962	1	Taylors Bridge [Schw2]
28 Apr 1965	1	Bombay Hook NWR [Abbo9]

A May 1972 report (DuMont and DuMont 1972a) lacks sufficient documentation to support such a late date. High counts are 9 near Smyrna on 17 February 1974 [Lehm22] and 4 at Broadkill Beach on 12 March 1978 [Frec1].

FALL: Mindell (1988, 165) notes that many "do not leave breeding range until around mid-Sept.–Oct." Consequently, the near absence of reports in Delaware before mid-November is expected. The 3 published September reports lack the documentation needed for such an unexpected date (DuMont and DuMont 1970a; Pyle 1969; Ednie 1985). Rough-legs begin arriving in October:

24 Oct 1965	1	Bombay Hook NWR [Lake4]
25 Oct 1981	2	Bombay Hook NWR [RusJ6]
25 Oct 1981	2	Broadkill Beach [Frec1]

A sharp increase in the number of reports takes place during the middle 2 weeks of November, and this level of reporting remains fairly constant to the end of February. High counts of 4 come from Bombay Hook NWR on 8 November 1981 [Bayn4] and from Prime Hook NWR (notes) on 10 November 1978 and 19 November 1983.

1966–89 CBC Summary

Christmas Bird Count	Years Found	Range of No. Found	Median
Wilmington	9	1–4	
Middletown	19	1–8	1
Bombay Hook	24	2–27	11
Cape Henlopen	22	1–15	4
Rehoboth	8	1–5	
STATEWIDE *(decreasing; low in 1988, high in 1970)*	24	6–41	22

WINTER: Palmer (1988, 5:163) states that in the East Rough-legged Hawks principally occur from Cape Cod to the Chesapeake Bay region, thus placing Delaware at the southeast periphery of the winter range. The species is declining signifi-

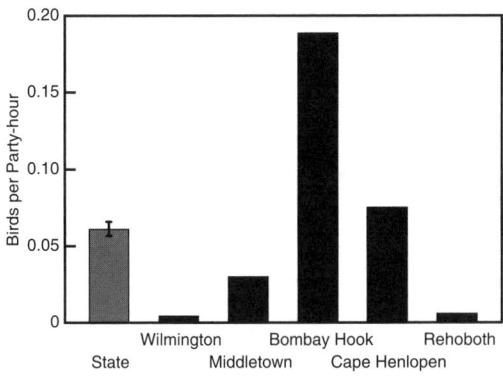

CBC Geographic Distribution

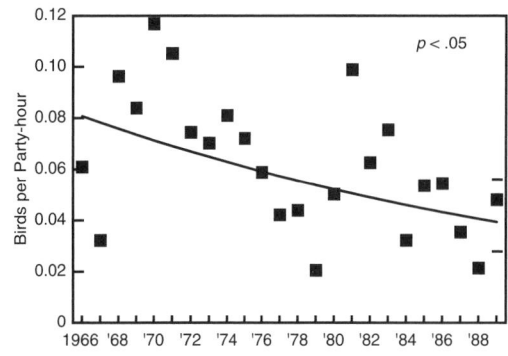

CBC Trend; Decreasing at 3% per Year

cantly on Delaware CBCs and becoming increasingly uncommon. Typically, it is reported in ones and twos. It is more abundant on the Bombay Hook and Cape Henlopen CBCs than on the others.

REMARKS: An "American Rough-legged Hawk" is listed in *Catalogue of the Birds in the British Museum* (1874, I:198):

"♂ var. sk., Delaware USA, E. Doubleday, Esq. (P.)." Another was collected on 7 February 1902 by Earle Lyman and mounted by Geo. Hensel, Stanton [Lyma1].

SPECIMENS: DMNH 18370, N Little Creek, 11 November 1925; USNM 311746, Delaware City, 28 November 1899.

Golden Eagle *(Aquila chrysaetos)*

Most reports have been from November through January. Millsap and Vana (1984) discuss winter records in the East. Spring and fall transients are rare. Individuals reported in March 1987, August 1971, October 1974, and October 1991 lack the documentation needed for such unusual dates (Boyle et al. 1987; DuMont and DuMont 1971b, 1975b; Ednie 1992).

Occasional (22 years during 1954–91); migrant and winter visitor; rare.

J F M A M J J A S O N D

DOCUMENTATION: Sight records, notes.

WINTER: One or 2 birds have been recorded in about 20 winters since the first report of 1 at Woodland Beach WA on 7 November 1954 [MiJC6]. Golden Eagles have been recorded elsewhere in the region, so the species' presence in Delaware is expected.

American Kestrel (*Falco sparverius*)

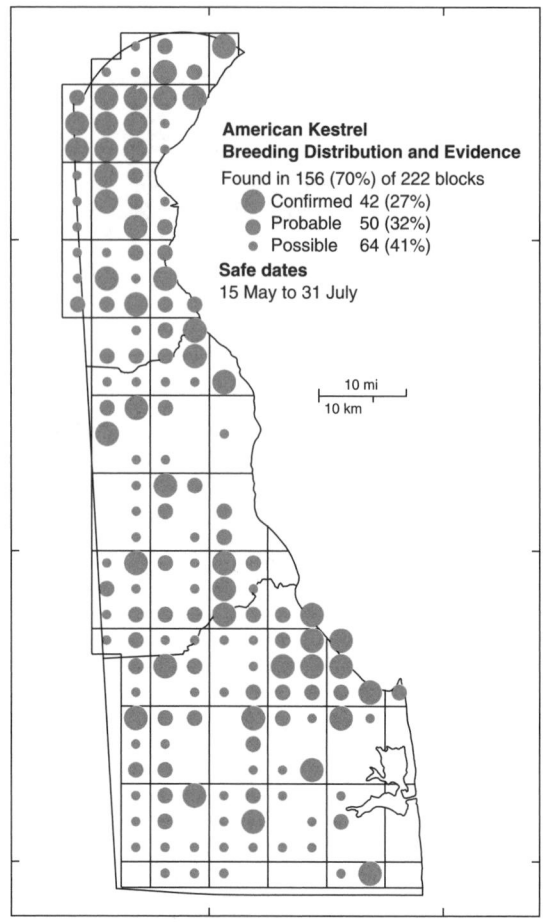

American Kestrel
Breeding Distribution and Evidence
Found in 156 (70%) of 222 blocks
● Confirmed 42 (27%)
● Probable 50 (32%)
● Possible 64 (41%)
Safe dates
15 May to 31 July

10 mi
10 km

Resident; uncommon to fairly common. Migration occurs mid-February to mid-April and late August to late October. Summer and winter numbers decreasing.

J F M A M J J A S O N D

HABITAT: Open agricultural areas with high perches. A farm and open suburban bird, attracted to edges of open fields and to utility lines.

SPRING: Migration appears to take place from 15–20 February through at least 10–15 April, continuing into early May in some years. Stewart and Robbins (1958) give the migration period as 1–10 March to 1–10 May in Maryland. Banding data provide additional evidence of migration: larger than normal numbers of kestrels were banded in 1–5 February, 6–10 and 11–15 March, comprising about 10–12% of all birds banded in each 5-day period (Usfw2]. Evidence of migration after mid-April, at least in some years, may be found in the following reports:

25 Apr 1984	35	Cape Henlopen SP [Frec1]
1 May 1982	60	Prime Hook NWR (notes)
1 May 1988	10	the Lewes area [Frec1]

Some high counts, all from Cape Henlopen SP, are 50 on 23 March 1984, 60 on 9 April 1983, and 50 on 13 April 1987 [Frec1]. On 29 March 1983 at Cape Henlopen SP, Magnan observed "literally, hundreds of kestrels sailing around the park, and perched on buildings, telephone wires, and in the low shrubs and trees. In many spots, three or four would be perched side by side" [MagR1]. Typical daily counts are 1–10, with higher numbers usually found close to the Delaware Bay.

BREEDING: American Kestrels are evenly, but rather sparsely, distributed across the state. They were found at only 0.8% of

the stops in the Relative Abundance study, and were easier to find in farm country than in other habitats.

Atlas. This species was probably missed in some blocks as suggested by the irregular pattern in the distribution map. A single pair in a 10-sq-mi block would be difficult to find if it were nesting away from roads. The most frequent confirmation method was finding the dependent young, which form conspicuous groups for a week or two as they wait for food to be brought by their parents. Nests were found in 18 blocks.

Nesting. The American Kestrel lays its eggs in cavities, such as those made by flickers, without adding nest material. It will also nest inside farm buildings and in nest boxes. During the Atlas period nests were reported in ventilation ducts at the Delaware Park race track and the Du Pont Experimental Station. It adapts to nesting in suburbs.

Most clutches are completed in late April to early May. Extreme egg dates, with one exception, extend from 1 to 19 May. Early nestlings were reported on 3 May 1974 [MiJC3], and the latest young was an 82 g nestling brought to Tri-State Bird Rescue on 24 July (TSBR 89-1116). We have 1 report of eggs found on 17 July [O'Sh2], which, if viable, would be late enough to represent a second clutch. Second clutches have

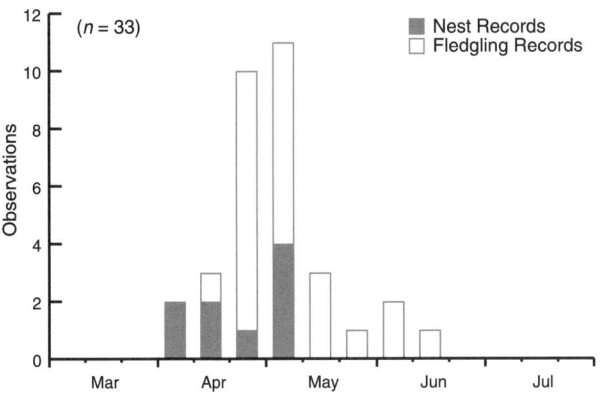

Estimated Clutch-Completion Dates

FALL: Migration takes place 20 August to 20 October, peaking from mid-September to mid-October (see "Hawk Migration" essay). Bird (1988, 264) notes that at the latitude of New Jersey "there are large numbers of migrant Kestrels . . . about the 3d week in Sept., and most have passed by Oct. 10." Some high counts are

4 Oct 1981	35	Cape Henlopen SP [Frec1]
10 Oct 1981	33	Cape Henlopen SP [Frec1]
16 Oct 1979	31	Cape Henlopen SP [Frec1]
20 Oct 1979	25	Prime Hook NWR (notes)

been reported from Virginia (Bird 1988, 278) and documented for Missouri (Toland 1985) and southward. Heinzelman and Nagy (1968) report a late egg date of 4 July in southeastern Pennsylvania. A 101 g fledgling was brought to Tri-State Bird Rescue from Calvert County, Maryland, on 24 August (TSBR 90-1173), late enough to have come from a second brood. Delaware may be within the northern limits of double broods for this species.

Trends. Widespread deforestation and land development have fostered a continent-wide population increase of this remarkably adaptive raptor (Bird 1988, 259). However, its population in Delaware has been decreasing at an average annual rate of about 4% according to May Count data (1969–91), a startling contrast to the increasing Red-tail population. Decreasing numbers found on the CBCs may also partly reflect a decrease in breeding kestrels as the adults are largely resident at the latitude of Delaware (Bird 1988, 264). The BBS does not adequately monitor this species in Delaware because the sample is too small. Fuller et al. (1987) suggest, based on 1966–79 BBS data, that only in Illinois and Arkansas have kestrels declined, and that generally American Kestrel numbers are stable or increasing along BBS routes. In Delaware kestrels have declined significantly through 1991.

Breeding population. Kestrels were reported in 153 blocks. If allowances for misses and multiple pairs per block are made, the state population is probably 200–500 pairs. Cade (1982) estimated its population at our latitude as averaging 2 pair per 2 sq mi, which for Delaware would mean about 1,000 pairs.

Conservation. Perhaps a nest box program would increase the kestrel population in Delaware. Hamerstrom (1973) found in a Wisconsin study area that natural cavities produced only 3 kestrel broods in 20 years, while young were reared successfully from boxes 51 times in 5 years. Kestrel boxes should not be placed too close to bluebird boxes, because kestrels sometimes take nestlings and small birds. The kestrel population was probably less seriously affected than some other raptor populations by accumulation of DDT in the food chain, but DDT and other insecticides kill large insects, an important part of its food supply.

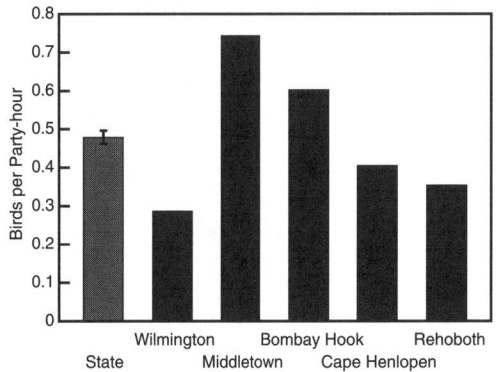

CBC Geographic Distribution

1966–89 CBC Summary

Christmas Bird Count	Years Found	Range of No. Found	Median
Wilmington	24	10–77	44
Middletown	24	20–91	52
Bombay Hook	24	14–97	36
Cape Henlopen	24	14–62	26
Rehoboth	24	10–68	37
STATEWIDE	24	86–289	194
(decreasing; low in 1989, high in 1979)			

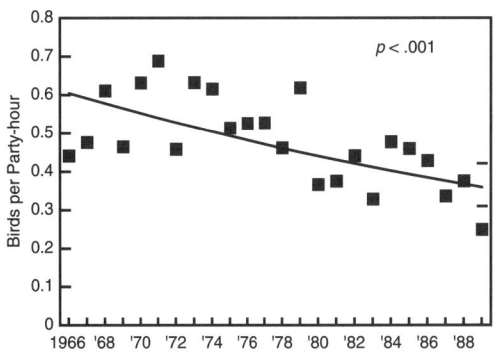

CBC Trend; Decreasing at 2% per Year

WINTER: This species has declined significantly on CBCs, though some indication of an upward trend was noticeable in the early 1970s. It has been about equally numerous on all CBCs.

SPECIMENS: 34; DMNH, UDEL, USNM.

Merlin *(Falco columbarius)*

Regular; migrant and winter visitor; rare. Expected mid-September to mid-May.

| | | | | | | | | | | | |
|J|F|M|A|M|J|J|A|S|O|N|D|

HABITAT: Often found along the coast, but may occur anywhere.

SPRING: A migration period from 20 April to 15 May is suggested by a peak in the frequency of reports. Clark (1985, in Palmer 1988, 5:302) states that at Cape May Point Merlins "do not appear in numbers until after Apr. 20, and most have passed by May 5." Virtually all Delaware reports are of single birds. One remarkable observation comes from two parties at Cape Henlopen on 24 April 1988, when a stiff north wind was blowing. For about 3 hours an estimated 24 Merlins per hour streamed by the rather awestruck observers [Whit6]. Late reports are:

19 May 1991	1	Bombay Hook NWR [MacG1]
22 May 1983	1	Bombay Hook NWR [Bayn5]
28 May 1979	1	Cape Henlopen SP [Frec1]

SUMMER: An 1882 breeding record for Merlin (nest and male reported collected but not extant) is not considered reliable because it is was 6 weeks too early, 400 mi too southerly, and not considered unusual by the reporter (Gibson 1883). The reporter regarded Merlins as resident on the Delmarva Peninsula, but his contemporaries, Rhoads and Pennock (1905), subsequently listed them as winter residents. The fifth AOU Check-list (1957) listed them as breeding south to northern New York, New Hampshire (probably), and Maine, but records in these states were rejected by Bull (1964) and others, and northern Ontario is the southeasternmost breeding location given in the sixth AOU Check-list (1983). Recently they were again reported breeding in northern New York (Paxton et al. 1993).

FALL: Onset of fall migration, shown in the seasonal bar graph, is supported in Delaware with a specimen from Milford on 7 September 1932 (USNM 421839). This agrees well with Palmer (1988, 5:302), who states that migration begins late in August, and "In the lat. of cent. Calif. across to the Chesapeake Bay, there is much movement by the 2d week in Sept., diminishing rapidly in the latter ½ of Oct." Likewise, Stewart and Robbins (1958) give the migration period as 20–30 August to 1–10 November in Maryland. In Delaware more reports occur during 15–20 September through 15–20 October than during the rest of the fall period. Other early fall arrivals are

22 Aug 1989	1	Bombay Hook NWR [Wayn25]
27 Aug 1989	1	Bombay Hook NWR [Holg1]
30 Aug 1982	1	Cape Henlopen SP [Frec1]

These reports come from sites with shorebirds, an important food for migrating Merlins. One to 3 birds are usually reported.

1966–89 CBC Summary

Christmas Bird Count	Years Found	Range of No. Found	Median
Wilmington	3	1	
Middletown	6	1	
Bombay Hook	11	1	
Cape Henlopen	7	1–2	
Rehoboth	8	1–3	
STATEWIDE	21	1–5	1
(zero in 1973, 1975, and 1979; high in 1971)			

WINTER: Because Delaware is on the northern edge of the Merlin's wintering range, predictably few are seen during winter. No CBC trend is apparent from the small number of records.

REMARKS: Pennock (notes) recorded 3 shot: 21 January 1899, River Farm; 26 September 1908, 3 mi south of Rehoboth; and 24 April 1913, near Henlopen Lighthouse (ANSP 66123).

SPECIMENS: 8; ANSP, DMNH, UDEL, USNM.

Peregrine Falcon (*Falco peregrinus*)

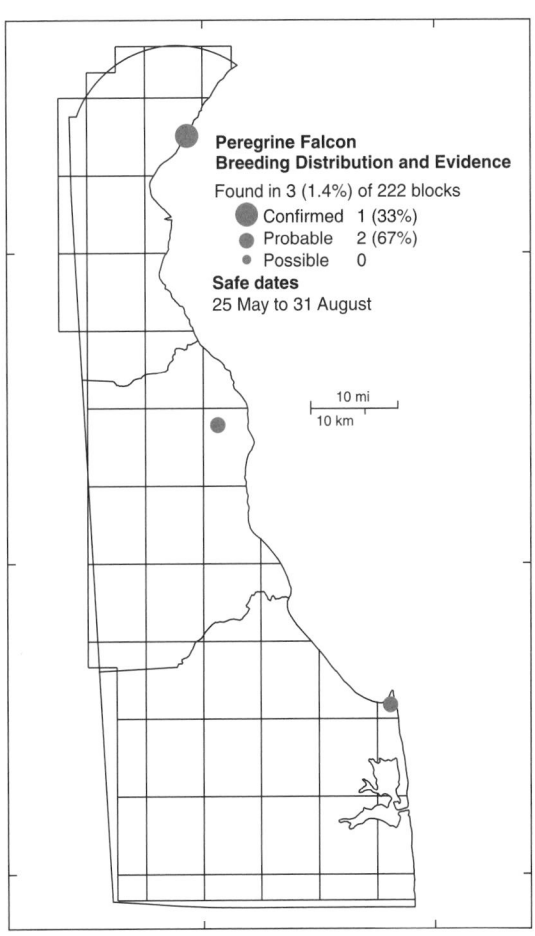

Peregrine Falcon
Breeding Distribution and Evidence
Found in 3 (1.4%) of 222 blocks
● Confirmed   1 (33%)
● Probable   2 (67%)
• Possible   0
Safe dates
25 May to 31 August

10 mi
10 km

Regular; rare migrant and winter visitor, rare introduced breeder. Migration occurs April–May and September–October.

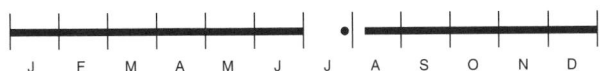

J F M A M J J A S O N D

HABITAT: Along ocean and bay beaches and adjacent marshes.

SPRING: Onset of the migration period is indicated by an increase in frequency of this bird; the data reveal peak numbers of records from 1 April to 10–15 May. Hunt and Ward (1988) found Peregrines staging at Padre Island, Texas, in April. Palmer (1988, 5:346) notes that before they were extirpated, eastern birds "were present and active at aeries by Feb. or early Mar."

BREEDING: These magnificent birds, federally listed as Endangered, were not known to breed in Delaware before 1987 (AOU 1957; Friedmann 1950), although the entire Delmarva Peninsula is included in a generalized map of their historic range (Palmer 1988, 5:341). Breeding Peregrines were extirpated in the eastern United States and much of eastern Canada by 1964 as a result of DDE (a breakdown product of DDT) poisoning; this toxic substance became concentrated in the food chain and caused lethal thinning of eggshells. Initial restocking programs (with noneastern birds) resulted in 3 breeding pairs in New Jersey, as well as 1 pair each in Maryland, Maine, and southern Quebec. Many younger and nonbreeding birds were in the wild by the beginning of the 1980s (Cade 1982). Stocking efforts in Delaware in 1981 were disrupted because of interference by Great Horned Owls, and it is not known whether the released birds survived (Burns 1982). Nonetheless, Peregrines have become established in Delaware.

Atlas. On 11 June 1982 a Peregrine was noted flying over and sitting on the Delaware Memorial Bridge [GarR1]. By 1986 3 potential nest sites attracted birds in Delaware: a pair at a nest box on the Delaware Memorial Bridge, 1 or 2 birds at a secluded tower in the marshes at Bombay Hook NWR, and usually just 1 at a nest box on a beacon at Cape Henlopen [Gilr1]. In 1987 a nest with 3 chicks was confirmed under the Delaware Memorial Bridge. The fledging success of the chicks is not known, but the pair returned to the same location in 1988 (DNREC 1988), and breeding has continued each year since. In 1992 2 female chicks fledged, 1 surviving a fall into the Delaware River. Peregrines continue to be seen around Bombay Hook NWR and Cape Henlopen SP, but no resident pairs are established at either site. Beginning in 1991 a pair began frequenting high-rise buildings in Wilmington, but they did not breed in 1991 or 1992 (Gelvin-Innvaer, DNREC files, pers. comm.).

Nesting: In Pennsylvania, and probably Delaware, introduced Peregrines appear to have adopted a life-history similar to the extirpated eastern population. Breeding pairs are permanent residents near nest sites. Nesting begins in March long before migratory populations pass through. Eggs appear to be laid in March or April, and the young fledge in late May or June. So far, no introduced bird has nested in a natural cliff aerie (Brauning 1992a).

Conservation: Delaware birds are not genetically derived from the native subspecies of Peregrine Falcon, which "became extinct or nearly so over much of its range during the 1940s to 1970s." (White 1988). While introduction of this species as a breeding bird has popular support, it was perhaps an unnecessary distraction from more valid conservation programs.

FALL: An increase in reports during 20 September to 15 October points to the migration period. Ward et al. (1988) report the migration period at Assateague Island, Maryland–Virginia, as 21 September to 18 October. Virtually all Delaware reports involve 1 or 2 birds.

1966–89 CBC Summary

Christmas Bird Count	Years Found	Range of No. Found
Wilmington	1	1
Middletown	4	1
Bombay Hook	6	1–2
Cape Henlopen	6	1–2
Rehoboth	2	1–2
STATEWIDE	13	1–3
(high in 1983, 1987, and 1989)		

WINTER: One or 2 birds have been reported on 18 CBCs during 1939–65, and on 19 more during the 1966–89 CBC analysis period. One wintered at the Cape Henlopen lighthouse in 1986–87 [Frec1].

REMARKS: Pennock (notes) prepared a skin of 1 shot by H. C. Webb 2 mi east of Odessa on 4 November 1899.

SPECIMEN: USNM 421914, Indian River Inlet, (no date on tag).

Gyrfalcon *(Falco rusticolus)*

Accidental (1974).

DOCUMENTATION: Published notes.

REMARKS: The Gyrfalcon has been seen once in Delaware, on 11 November 1974 over the Brandywine Country Club Golf Course by J. Grier Ralston, Jr. [Rals1]. His notes are satisfactory, including the "silver white" color of a gray-phase bird, the large size in direct comparison with a crow, the long narrow tail, and the slow wingbeats. In view of its occasional occurrence in Pennsylvania and New Jersey, the Gyrfalcon should be looked for during the winter.

Birds and the Law

H. Lloyd Alexander

Protection of birds under law has a long history. The Old Testament makes early reference to the concept of bird conservation in the laws of Deuteronomy (22:6), which give protection to adult female birds during the nesting season. In America a legal tradition of protecting birds was handed down from the English. The nobility in England enacted stringent laws to protect game for their exclusive use. When the United States became an independent nation, however, sovereign rights to wildlife were transferred to the people as a public trust, thereby separating wildlife from property ownership.

During the colonial period, settlers hunted in Delaware for subsistence; later hunting became commercial and now is solely for recreation. The first conservation laws were local measures prompted by sport hunters who saw their recreational resource declining dramatically because of the wholesale slaughter of wildlife throughout the nation in the late eighteenth century.

Delaware's first state wildlife protection laws, passed in 1859, placed restrictions on hunting. Twenty years later the General Assembly chartered the Delaware Game Protective Association to help pass additional wildlife laws, including the establishment in 1893 of hunting seasons for all wildlife. The state legislature initiated wildlife management in 1911 by creating the Delaware Game and Fish Commission, which evolved into today's Division of Fish and Wildlife within the Department of Natural Resources and Environmental Control.

Bird protection became a national issue with passage of the Weeks-McClean Act of 1913. This law placed migratory birds under the federal government's protection, but it left a gap in authority. A framework for protection of birds on the North American continent was created in 1916 under a treaty signed with Great Britain, acting for Canada; protection was implemented by the Migratory Bird Treaty Act of 1918. Although originally aimed primarily at protecting birds as a food source and as predators on crop insect pests, the provisions of the treaty established the basic authority for migratory bird protection still in effect today; these provisions include no killing of nongame species, limited seasons for migratory gamebirds, prohibitions on commercial taking of wildlife, and limitations on methods of taking.

Hunting Seasons and Regulations

Since the late nineteenth century, as concepts of hunting regulation have changed, the Delaware General Assembly has regulated hunting seasons and hunting methods by law. Conservation law is contained in Title 7 of the Delaware Code.

Chapter 1 of the code defines the powers of the Division of Fish and Wildlife. Section 102 empowers the division to protect and manage all wild birds, and Section 105 enables license fee collection and participation in federal aid programs for bird conservation.

The federal Pittman-Robertson Act of 1927 has been the primary source of funds for a wide variety of projects benefiting Delaware bird populations along with other wildlife. Under its provisions, states that carry out wildlife conservation are eligible to receive a share of the revenue generated by a 10% tax on firearms and ammunition if states match the funds by means of hunting license fees. Part of the 38,900 acres of land in the state's system of wildlife areas was purchased through this program, and it provides most of the funds for land management. Areas managed include upland habitats and wetlands that benefit nongame species, such as shorebirds, wading birds, and songbirds. Pittman-Robertson money also helps to support research and inventory work, such as Osprey and Bald Eagle studies and the construction of observation blinds and other public facilities for birders, hunters, and tourists.

General Protection of Birds

The authority for protection of Delaware's birds is derived from a combination of state and federal laws, since nonmigratory gamebirds are not covered by federal law. Under Section 101 of Title 7 of the Delaware Code, all wild birds in the state are classified as "protected wildlife" and regulated by the Division of Fish and Wildlife, which can also initiate research and management projects, such as introduction of the Peregrine Falcon and reintroduction of the Wild Turkey. Section 702 defines the gamebirds that may be hunted; Section 741 gives complete protection to all birds except gamebirds and exotic species; Section 742 protects bird nests; and Section 747 separately addresses the protection of Bald Eagles and their nests.

In the past wildlife laws focused on protection of individual animals and lacked provisions for population management or habitat protection. In recent decades federal laws, such as the Fish and Wildlife Coordination Act of 1934, as amended in 1946 and 1958, and the National Environmental Policy Act of 1969, have incorporated broader concepts of wildlife management. They require both state and federal wildlife agencies to comment on the environmental effects of proposed federally assisted projects. In fact, bird populations must now be considered in any use of federal funds or issuance of permits under federal programs.

New programs developed in the 1980s recognized the values of ecosystems. Delaware Bay was designated as the first Hemispheric Reserve in the Western Hemisphere Shorebird Reserve Network, thereby emphasizing the international value of the bay for migrating shorebirds. The wetlands of the Delaware Estuary were designated Wetlands of International Importance under the Ramsar Convention in 1992.

An agreement signed in May 1991 by seven federal agencies, including the U.S. Fish and Wildlife Service, created a Neotropical Migrant Initiative, aimed at conserving migratory birds that breed in North America and winter south of the United States. The Delaware Nongame and Endangered Species and Delaware Natural Heritage programs are participating in an inventory of Neotropical migrant species that use habitats within the state.

The North American Wetlands Conservation Act of 1989 authorized up to $15 million a year to protect and restore major U.S. wetland systems identified as critical under the North American Waterfowl Management Plan, an international agreement to increase declining waterfowl populations by preserving their habitats. Projects are conducted as partnerships of federal, state, and private organizations. In 1992 the program matched private donations, enabling The Nature Conservancy to acquire a 2,200-acre tract on Milford Neck, intended for protection of critical coastal habitat for migrating shorebirds and waterfowl and nesting Black Ducks.

Nongame and Endangered Species

In 1971 the Delaware General Assembly enacted a law to protect both domestic and foreign endangered species and explicitly mandated the Division of Fish and Wildlife to manage species other than those taken by sport hunting. As part of Chapter 6 of Title 7, the state prohibits transportation, importation, possession, or sale of any endangered species within the state.

The federal Endangered Species Act of 1973 gave the U.S. Fish and Wildlife Service an expanded role in protecting endangered species by regulating a wide range of activities that affect plants or animals designated as endangered or threatened. The legislation provides for funding to assist the states to manage such species better. Delaware has used these federal funds to protect Bald Eagle nesting, to experiment with introduction of Peregrine Falcons, and to institute Piping Plover recovery work.

Commercialization has been a primary cause of decline in many bird populations; as species become rare, their value to collectors increases markedly. Hence the interstate movement of endangered or rare birds is a factor of major concern in any strategy for their conservation. The federal Lacey Act, passed in 1900 and amended in 1960 and 1981, forbids the interstate transport, sale, receipt, acquisition, or purchase of any plant or animal taken contrary to state, federal, tribal, or foreign laws. Federal assistance in law enforcement is given to state and foreign governments. The act is a vital tool in preventing the commercial sale and transport of wild birds.

Recognizing a gap in funding for protecting state wildlife species not commonly trapped, killed, captured, or consumed for sport or profit, several local conservation groups banded together. They promoted the Nongame Wildlife, Endangered Species, Natural Areas Preservation Fund Act of 1983, now part of Chapter 2 of Title 7 of the Delaware Code. The law states that "it is in the best interest of the State to preserve and enhance the diversity and abundance of nongame fish and wildlife, and to protect the habitat and natural areas harboring rare and vanishing species of fish, wildlife, plants, and areas of unusual scientific significance or having unusual importance to the survival of Delaware's native fish, wildlife, and plants in their natural environments. Rare and endangered species are a public trust in need of active, protective management, and it is in the broad public interest to preserve and enhance such species." While largely dependent upon voluntary contributions from the state income tax checkoff set up by the law, the Nongame and Endangered Species Program has been able to protect several threatened or endangered species.

The basis in law for protection of wild birds through the centuries, from the laws of Deuteronomy to contemporary international treaties and complex statutes, is a response to direct threats from human activities. Preservation of bird diversity in Delaware demands conservation laws that are continually refined and strengthened.

Ring-necked Pheasant *(Phasianus colchicus)*

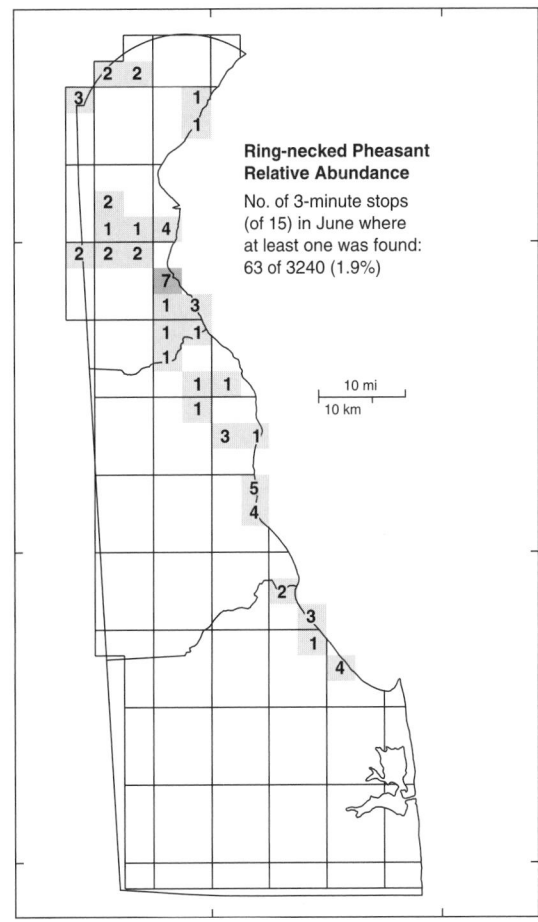

**Ring-necked Pheasant
Relative Abundance**

No. of 3-minute stops
(of 15) in June where
at least one was found:
63 of 3240 (1.9%)

10 mi
10 km

Resident; fairly common; introduced. Population decreasing at about 7% per year.

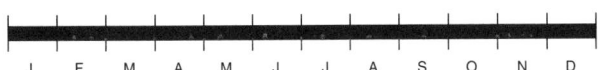

| J | F | M | A | M | J | J | A | S | O | N | D |

HABITAT: Hedgerows, edges of fields and tidal marshes, farms.

BREEDING: The Ring-necked Pheasant is most numerous in the undeveloped portion of the Piedmont and near Odessa and

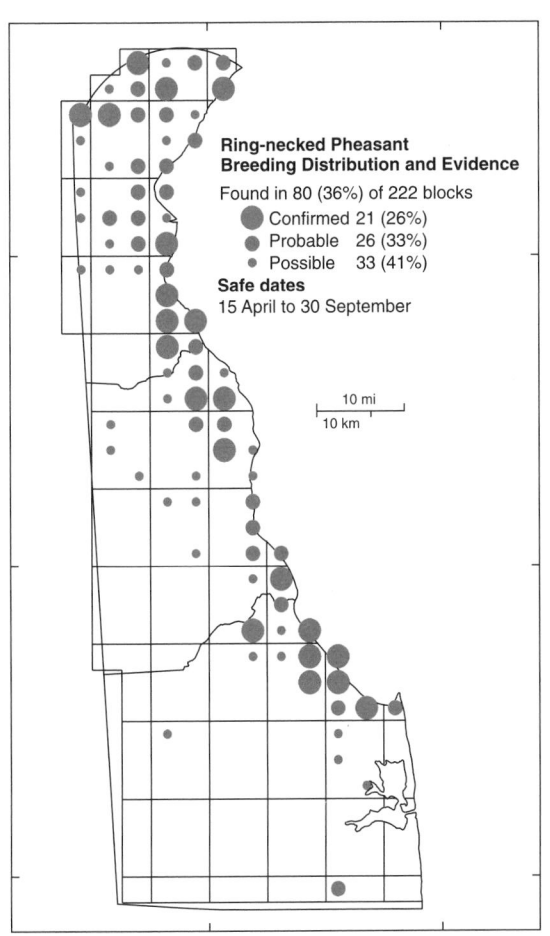

**Ring-necked Pheasant
Breeding Distribution and Evidence**

Found in 80 (36%) of 222 blocks

- Confirmed 21 (26%)
- Probable 26 (33%)
- Possible 33 (41%)

Safe dates
15 April to 30 September

10 mi
10 km

less common south adjacent to the river and bay marshes to Cape Henlopen. It was formerly seen regularly around suburban areas in New Castle County but considerably diminished in numbers there during the 1980s.

Atlas. Continued private releases have led to an exaggeration of the pheasant's range shown on the distribution map. For example, several hundred birds were released near Selbyville, and those that survived were recorded in an adjacent block containing a large wooded area for safe refuge. Other isolated records may also be from recently released stock. Delaware represents the southern extreme of the Atlantic seaboard range (Johnsgard 1975).

Nesting. A nest found in the White Clay Creek valley was described as deep, made of grass, lined with down, and placed on the ground under a 4-ft Virginia pine. It contained 13 eggs that hatched between 15 and 30 April 1978 [Jahn1]. The breeding season must be quite long because a female and 4 young, 2–3 weeks old, were seen in Prime Hook NWR on 12 August 1980 [O'Sh2].

History. A 1908 reference to this imported game species by the state ornithologist states that "Several pairs were purchased and distributed over the state, a few years ago, by the Delaware

Game Protective Association, but it is believed they have not survived" (Pennock 1908b). There is a single report of a male seen north of St. Georges on 18 June 1926 [Dick1]. They were not reported on early CBCs from northern Delaware but were reported on the nearby West Chester counts starting 27 December 1933. Barry (1939) includes a special section on pheasants in his Delaware list, stating that this species has adapted to American soil and frequents the high lands, rolling country, and marshes of northern Delaware. It was first reported on the Bombay Hook CBC on 29 December 1940. It was reported regularly on the Hoopes Reservoir survey in 1943 [Hoff4]. The "distribution and relative abundance map" published from a 1953–55 state survey showed the birds doing well north of the Chesapeake and Delaware Canal and less well in a band southward in tidewater marsh vegetation (Game and Fish 1954; McGinness 1956). The pheasant population continued to increase and reached a peak in the 1960s. The last year for release and hunt management was 1975, when 1,143 pheasants were released and 827 were taken during the special season (DNREC 1976).

A total of 2,014 Green Pheasants, a Japanese form formerly regarded as a separate species (AOU 1983; National Geographic 1983), were released at 10 sites in Delaware between 1973 and 1980, but the introduction was not successful (Whittendale 1976; DNREC 1983).

Trends. May Count data for this species show an average annual decline of about 6%. BBS and CBC data support this finding, with the 3 methods giving an average decline of about 7%—an overall reduction from 1966 to 1991 of over 80%. These figures correlate well with the hunter harvests, estimated at 6,000 for the 1975–76 season, decreasing to 1,000 for the 1986–87 season (DNREC 1988).

Breeding population. Based on its being found in 80 of 222 blocks, its having been heard at 63 stops in the relative abundance study, and an estimated take of 1,000, its population in the late 1980s was probably in the range of 500–5,000 breeding females. The lower figure represents an average of 12 per block where it was reported.

Conservation. This attractive bird was introduced for hunting and paid for by hunting taxes, but it has captured the hearts of many other people who also enjoy the outdoors. At some point the hunting pressure should be curtailed to allow the population to recover.

1966–89 CBC Summary

Christmas Bird Count	Years Found	Range of No. Found	Median
Wilmington	24	2–108	22
Middletown	24	2–32	8
Bombay Hook	24	1–29	4
Cape Henlopen	11	1–3	
Rehoboth	4	1	
STATEWIDE	24	10–145	41

(decreasing; low in 1987 and 1989, high in 1969)

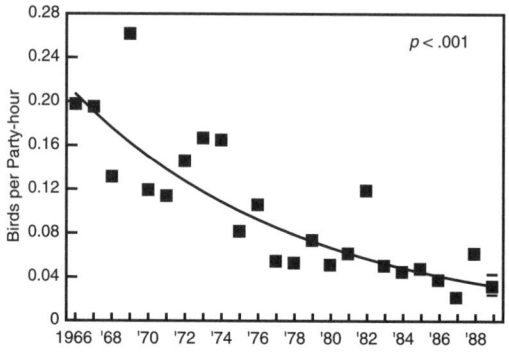

CBC Trend; Decreasing at 8% per Year

WINTER: This species has shown a significant decline in winter numbers of about 8% per year (see "Trends"). It is less common on CBCs in southern Delaware.

SPECIMENS: 6; DMNH, UDEL.

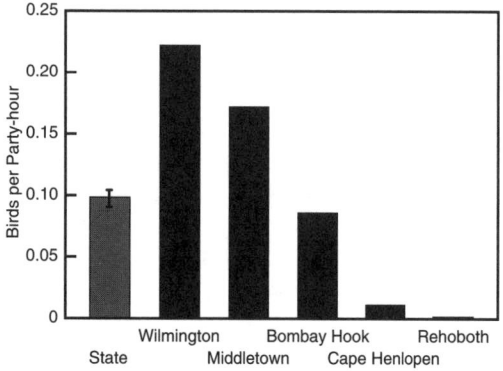

CBC Geographic Distribution

[Ruffed Grouse *(Bonasa umbellus)*]

Gregory A. Inskip

Extirpated; reintroduction unsuccessful.

DOCUMENTATION: Historical reports only.

REMARKS: The Ruffed Grouse was a permanent resident of northern Delaware woodlands in colonial times, persisting until late in the nineteenth century (Hesselius 1947 [1712], 89–90, including remarks of Dr. F. M. Jones, fn. 70). Hesselius shot 1 (probably near Wilmington) on 14 August 1712. He noted the drumming behavior of the species.

Rhoads and Pennock (1905) remarked that this bird was for-merly not uncommon in the northern hill country. One was shot in the fall of 1902 in Pennsylvania within a mile of Delaware. Pennock (1908b) further elaborates by noting that "The old residents of northern New Castle County tell me that up to about 1865 or 1870 they were 'rather common' in suit-able localities—Ashland, Mt. Cuba, and on the rough, rocky, wooded hill slopes of the Brandywine and Red Clay Creeks." The last record in a hunter's bag was in the 1880s. A report in the 1970s from New Castle County should be attributed to a Ring-necked Pheasant flushing from the nest.

Attempts have been made to reestablish the Ruffed Grouse. Between 1969 and 1976, 76 birds were released in the Nanti-coke WA. Surveys in 1975 revealed 7 drumming locations and 1 brood of 4 (Whittendale for DNREC, 1975). The population was not self-sustaining, and the last one recorded was a road kill in 1979.

The Ruffed Grouse still occurs in southeastern Pennsylva-nia, for example, in the Middle Creek WMA in northern Lan-caster County. In nearby Maryland it has occurred in Cecil County and even the Pocomoke Swamp in Worcester County (Stewart and Robbins 1958). Although the latter record indi-cates that the Ruffed Grouse might be able to survive in Coastal Plain habitats, a reintroduction of the species would be more likely to succeed in the Piedmont region.

[Greater Prairie-Chicken *(Tympanuchus cupido)*]

Gregory A. Inskip

Eastern population extinct; formerly present in the region, but no spe-cific Delaware records.

DOCUMENTATION: None.

HABITAT: Fire-created prairies or blueberry barrens, associ-ated with sandy soils (Aldrich 1963, 537).

REMARKS: The extinct eastern population of the Greater Prairie Chicken, called the Heath Hen, probably was a perma-nent resident in parts of Delaware. It occurred in coastal areas from Massachusetts (perhaps Maine) south to Maryland or Vir-ginia (and perhaps the Carolinas) (AOU 1983; Bent 1932, 266; Greenway 1967, 190). Johnsgard (1973) includes the entire Del-marva Peninsula as the southern end of its range. Aldrich (1963, 537) includes only the northern portion of the peninsu-la, including most of Delaware. Inclusion of Delaware within its range probably stems from Samuel Cabot's 1855 report that it occurred in Delaware (*Proc. Bos. Soc. Nat. Hist.* 5:154).

In a letter dated 1683 to the Committee of the Free Society of Traders, William Penn described the wildlife and other attributes of Pennsylvania, which then included Delaware. Of "Fowl of the Land," Penn listed "Phesants, Heath-Birds, Pid-geons, and Partridges in abundance" (Myers 1912, 229). "Phe-sants, Heath-birds . . . and Partridges" probably means Ruffed Grouse, Heath Hens, and Northern Bobwhite, though colonial usage was not consistent. In any event, Penn probably referred to all 3 species because he used 3 words to designate "fowl" other than turkeys and pigeons.

C. S. Wescott told George Bird Grinnell that this species for-merly occurred, "according to tradition—in Maryland and

Delaware, on the shores of the Chesapeake Bay and on the Peninsula of Maryland and Virginia" (Stewart and Robbins 1958, quoting Grinnell 1910). A specimen (now destroyed) was collected from Maryland near Washington, D.C., and another was collected from Lancaster County, Pennsylvania (Stewart and Robbins 1958; Greenway 1967,195). The Heath Hen was shot out early in most areas, confined after 1835 to Martha's Vineyard (AOU 1983; see also Bent 1932, 266, 269) and last reported there in 1932 (AOU 1983; Greenway 1967, 191).

Wild Turkey *(Meleagris gallopavo)*

with Gregory A. Inskip

Resident, recently reestablished.

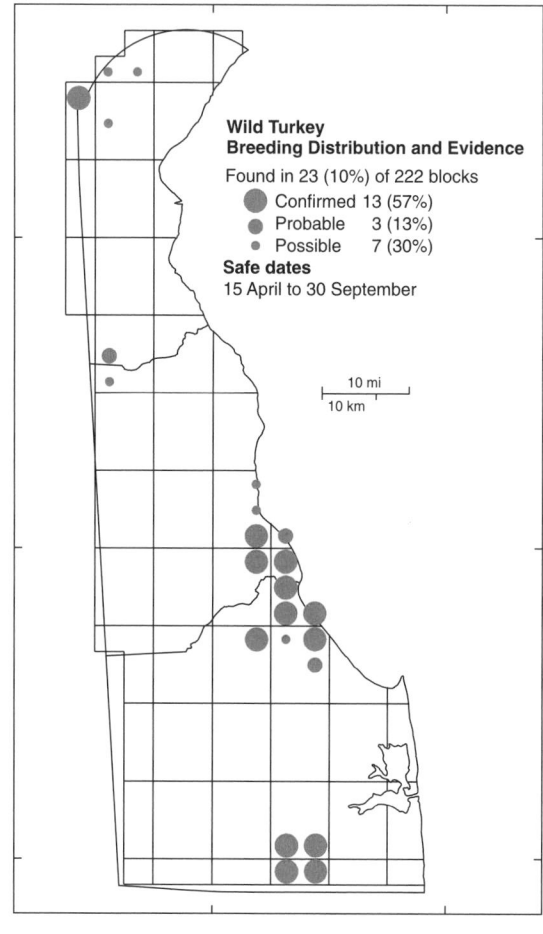

Wild Turkey
Breeding Distribution and Evidence
Found in 23 (10%) of 222 blocks
● Confirmed 13 (57%)
● Probable 3 (13%)
• Possible 7 (30%)
Safe dates
15 April to 30 September

10 mi
10 km

DOCUMENTATION: Multiple sight records. Ninety-three harvested in 1991.

HABITAT: Optimally, a mixture of about 50% forest and 50% open areas (such as pasture, crops, old fields).

Turkeys have adapted to relatively small woodlots in Delaware (K. Reynolds, DNREC, pers. comm.). Formerly "extensive forest" might have been given as the species' habitat, since this was its last refuge before it was extirpated.

REMARKS: Introduced and spreading from Milford Neck and Burnt Swamp.

Atlas. Its introduction was contemporaneous with the Atlas project, and reports show its expansion. Confirmations usually involved hens with poults.

Nesting. A nest with 9 eggs was reported on Milford Neck in 1984, and broods with small poults were found on 25 May 1984, and 22 May, 25 May, and 1 June 1987. Average brood size in 1987 was 9.5 (Reynolds 1984, 1987).

History. The Lenape Indians snared the Wild Turkey for food and wove garments out of its feathers (Johnson 1917, 280–81). Apparently, the Lenape also invented the turkey shoot:

"He who is sachem has a turkey placed very high in the air, whose entrails are removed and [the body] filled again with their money. And the one who then can shoot it down, he receives the money." (Lindestrom 1925 [1691], 215).

The Wild Turkey was a permanent resident in colonial times. It was reported from the Delaware Valley by William Penn (1683) in a letter to the Society of Traders in England: "Of fowl of the land, there is the turkey (forty or fifty pounds weight), which is very great." Turkeys were subsequently reported in Delaware in the 30 September 1712 entry of Reverend Hesselius' journal. He noted that it was "found in great numbers in the autumn." Significantly, he also described how to shoot them all at their night roost. Schorger (1966) estimated the pre-Columbian turkey population in Delaware at 10,000, or 5 per sq mi. Uncontrolled hunting, particularly by market hunters, extirpated it from Delaware, probably in the early nineteenth century (Hesselius 1947 [1712], 90, including Dr. Frank M. Jones' remarks, fn. 73), though habitat destruction may have contributed to its demise.

An attempted reestablishment of game-farm raised birds in the 1960s at Bombay Hook NWR proved unsuccessful (A. Florio, pers. comm.). In 1981, 54 game-farm raised birds were released in Burnt Swamp, Sussex County. This release was also unsuccessful—a common result with birds raised by humans.

In 1984, 14 wild-trapped turkeys were released in Burnt Swamp and 22 on Milford Neck. Breeding was detected that year, and after 5 breeding seasons the population reached 350 birds in 150 sq mi of habitat. The Milford Neck population, in particular, has expanded, with sightings reported from Prime Hook NWR north at least to Little Creek WA. The distribution map reflects the releases in Kent and Sussex counties. Turkeys seen in northwestern Kent County in 1987 are, no doubt, from releases made in Maryland's Millington WA (Reynolds 1987). Turkeys reported in northwestern New Castle County must be from nearby releases in Pennsylvania in the upper White Clay Creek valley. A limited hunting season was opened in April 1991, when 93 gobblers were harvested (Reynolds 1992a).

Breeding population. The turkey population was estimated at 800–1,000 birds in 1992 (Reynolds 1992b) and at nearly 1,000 birds in 1993 (DNREC 1993, 16). An ultimate state population of 3,000–5,000 birds may be possible (Reynolds 1988). Turkeys will have to be protected from disturbance to reach this population level, since any type of human activity disturbs them, particularly incubating hens (Wright and Speake 1965; Williams et al. 1971).

WINTER: This species was reported on 2 Bombay Hook CBCs after its release there. Since its most recent reintroduction it has been recorded on 1 Bombay Hook and 3 Cape Henlopen CBCs.

Northern Bobwhite (*Colinus virginianus*)

Resident; common. Winter population decreasing at 7% per year.

HABITAT: Hedgerows, wood margins, brushy fields in agricultural areas.

BREEDING: The relative abundance data show it was equally common in all 3 counties south of the Chesapeake and Delaware Canal but only one-fourth as common in the northernmost 10% of the state.

Atlas. The distribution map shows the bobwhite's presence in every block in the state except 2 in Bombay Hook NWR that are entirely covered with tidal marshes. Bobwhites were easily detected by call; 90% of the confirmed reports were the result of finding broods.

Nesting. A typical nest is placed in an old field and made and roofed over with grass. The nest's inside diameter is about 5 in., with the entrance on the side [Hans1]. An atypical situation—a hollow in swampy woods—was recorded by Rhoads and Norris (WFVZ egg data).

Extreme egg dates are 24 May 1924 (with only 5 eggs, so incomplete) and 1 September 1932, a nest of 16 eggs [both Hans1]. On 13 May 1982 a pair was seen with 5 young [SpeE3], which must have come from a clutch completed in late April. Parents with 3 young not over several weeks old were seen at Bombay Hook NWR on 2 October 1953 [Spri1]. Reported clutches vary from 15 to 18 eggs.

HISTORY: The Northern Bobwhite has always been common in the Delaware Valley. Dutch captain Cornelis Hendricksen, the first documented Delaware Bay explorer, reported seeing partridges (bobwhite) in 1616. Bobwhite abundance along the lower Delaware River in 1634 was described by English explorer Thomas Yong as "so great as can hardly be believed, wee took at one time 48 partriches together. . . . I myself sprang in two hours 5 or 6 covies in walking of a mile" (Jackson 1967). It is the one gamebird that has fared well with the arrival of Europeans because clearing and planted grain pro-

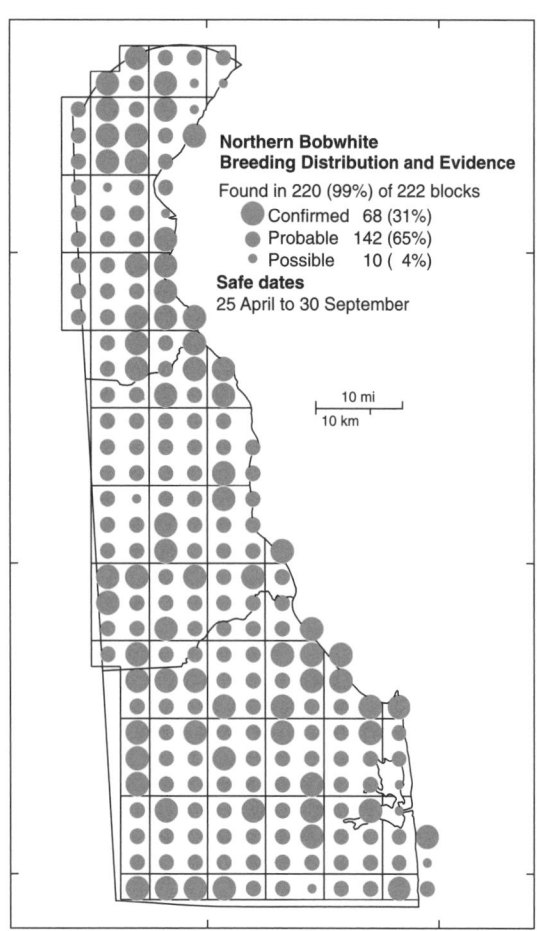

Northern Bobwhite
Breeding Distribution and Evidence
Found in 220 (99%) of 222 blocks
⬤ Confirmed 68 (31%)
⬤ Probable 142 (65%)
• Possible 10 (4%)
Safe dates
25 April to 30 September

10 mi
10 km

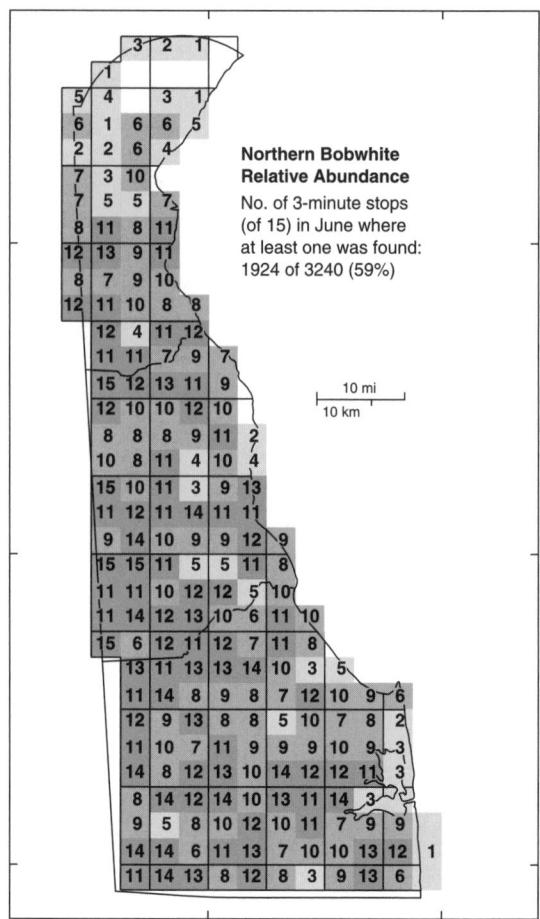

Northern Bobwhite
Relative Abundance
No. of 3-minute stops
(of 15) in June where
at least one was found:
1924 of 3240 (59%)

10 mi
10 km

vide ideal habitat. It was regarded as "quite common" in the 1920s [Hans1].

In 1937 the legislature provided for statewide hunting and fishing licenses, specifying 25% of the income to be spent for restocking bobwhite. Although the status of bobwhite was noted as good in Kent and Sussex counties, 2,000 birds were restocked (Findlay 1938).

Trends. The various monitoring schemes agree that the bobwhite population has irregularly declined since the 1970s. The CBCs and hunting harvest estimates agree on about a 70% decline from an early 1970s peak to a late 1980s low. May Count data also reflect a pronounced decline during this period but at only about half the rate noted from the CBC data. The BBS data show that the Delaware bobwhite population density changed from being among the highest of any state in the 1970s (Robbins et al. 1986) to being in a sharp decline during the 1980s [Usfw1]. This is particularly notable because population changes of common birds are hard to detect using the BBS technique (Robbins et al. 1986, 9). The factors that caused this long-term decline are not completely understood, but deep winter snow and wet springs can cause short-term population declines (Rosene 1969).

Breeding population. The relative abundance study found bobwhites at 60% of the stops.

If a density of 1 nest per 20 acres of suitable habitat (Johnsgard 1973) is usual, the 600,000 acres of Delaware farmland (Brooks 1992) could support 30,000 nesting females, but the population probably fell well below that level during the decline. Late summer population in the 1960s, 1970s, and 1980s (at least before the population decline) would have been considerably higher, sufficient to support the average annual hunting harvest of about 40,000 birds per year (Rosene 1969; DNREC 1988; Reynolds 1992).

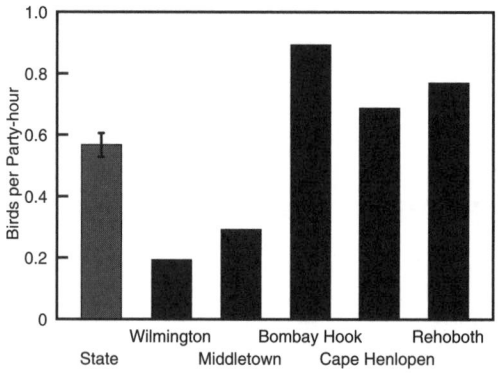

CBC Geographic Distribution

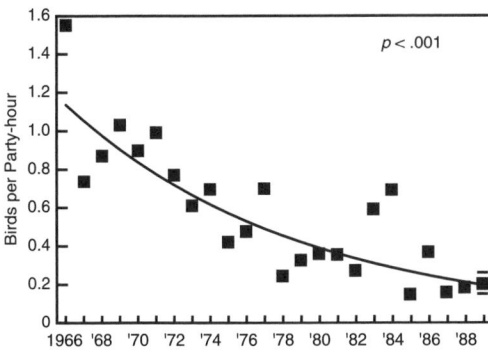

CBC Trend; Decreasing at 7% per Year

1966–89 CBC Summary

Christmas Bird Count	Years Found	Range of No. Found	Median
Wilmington	21	1–92	27
Middletown	22	1–66	17
Bombay Hook	24	1–265	50
Cape Henlopen	24	1–209	40
Rehoboth	24	8–204	72
STATEWIDE	24	57–650	225
(decreasing; low in 1985, high in 1966)			

WINTER: This species has shown a significant decline in winter numbers (see "Trends"). In contrast to Ring-necked Pheasant, it becomes progressively more common in the CBC circles southward.

SPECIMENS: 17; DMNH, CM, USNM. Egg records: DMNH, WFVZ.

Yellow Rail *(Coturnicops noveboracensis)*

Regular; migrant; seldom detected. To be looked for during May, September, and October.

HABITAT: Fresh and brackish tidal marsh, grassy fields.

REMARKS: Before 1989 the Yellow Rail was thought to be of casual occurrence in Delaware. At that time there were only 7 records, including reports in May, September, and October, and 1 additional report without details for 11 February 1938 (Buckalew notes, in Holgersen 1971a). Since 1989 spring observations have been more frequent.

SPRING: In the spring of 1989 there were at least 5 reports of 1 to 3 birds at Little Creek WA, starting on 15 May and extending to at least 21 May [RusW8]. In 1990 1–2 Yellow Rails were found at Bombay Hook NWR on 9–11 May, and 4–5 at Little Creek WA on 12–17 May (Shoch 1990) [Camp12]. In 1991 the first report came from Port Mahon on 30 April, and 1 or 2

birds were present for at least a week [Shor3]. Thus in these 3 years this rail was regularly present during part of May. Shoch (1990) has surmised this sudden increase of records is a reflection of observational effort rather than change of status.

FALL: Knowledge of the fall migration comes from these few records:

16 Sep 1972	1	flushed at Woodland Beach WA [Wert1]
24 Sep 1971	1	banded at Bombay Hook NWR (Holgersen 1971b)
26 Sep 1908	1	Rehoboth Beach (ANSP 66229)
26 Oct 1968	1	near Bombay Hook NWR (USNM 532271)

H. Cottman captured the 1971 bird (preceding) by hand in a grassy field that he was mowing. He reported that the previous September he had also observed single Yellow Rails on at least 2 occasions while he mowed grass near the edges of corn fields (Holgersen 1971b). The 1908 specimen came from 5–6 mi south of Rehoboth Beach [Penn1]. The 1968 specimen, reported to have been picked up at the Bombay Hook NWR information booth, was actually found dead on the road about 1 mi west of the refuge entrance in an area of agricultural fields on 20 or 26 October 1968 (USNM 532271, Holgersen 1971b). Anderson (1977:67) notes that average departure from southern Canada and the northern United States occurs during late September and early October, consistent with the dates of fall Delaware records.

SPECIMENS: ANSP 66229, Rehoboth Beach, 26 September 1908; USNM 532271, Bombay Hook, 26 October 1968.

Black Rail (*Laterallus jamaicensis*)

Regular; summer resident; uncommon. Expected May through early October. In tidal marshes from Bombay Hook NWR to Broadkill Beach.

HABITAT: Salt hay, three-square (Todd 1977). In Delaware, salt hay marshes. Dense mats of dead grass, providing cover and nest material. Soil inundated with surface water only during spring tides, but saturated or wet. Exceptionally, a more upland site including low shrubs bordering the saltmarsh (Rothstein 1991a).

SPRING: The earliest reports are usually from the first week of May, but this rail was detected earlier in 1991:

| 13 Apr 1991 | 1 | Broadkill Beach marsh [Shor2] |
| 27 Apr 1991 | 12 | Port Mahon Road [HilA5] |

Robbins and Bystrak (1977) indicate this species arrives in mid-April in Maryland.

BREEDING: This tiny rail, described as a feathered mouse by Alexander Sprunt, Jr., is seldom found by the naturalist because of its scarcity and its habit of staying hidden. It occurs in the marshes of Kent and Sussex counties and is most frequently reported from Port Mahon Rd. and Broadkill Beach Rd., where public access is available. In some recent years it has been difficult to locate along Broadkill Beach Rd. in Prime Hook NWR. This area has undergone salinity changes because a channel was deepened, and it has been sprayed with herbicide and burned in a phragmites control program; these factors may have contributed to this species' scarcity in some years.

Atlas. All Atlas reports are based on hearing the call. The Black Rail was reported from 5 blocks in areas where it was already known to occur but may have been present in other areas.

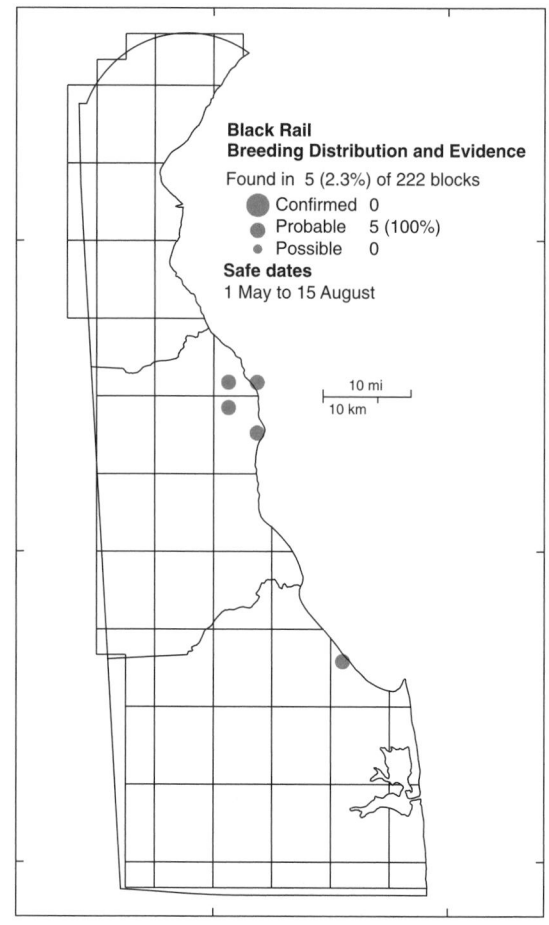

In 1988, after the conclusion of the Atlas project, it was located in 2 new areas: near Thompsonville [HilA2] and the southwest corner of Dragon Run on 16 May [Perr3; Armi1]. The bird reported at the latter site was probably a migrant, because it is the only one reported from this well-monitored location, and the habitat appears unsuitable.

In an informal survey conducted in 1991 south of Dover, Black Rail sites were identified in 5 marshes between Pickering Beach Rd. and Broadkill Beach Rd. (Rothstein 1991a).

A survey conducted in 1992 determined that the Black Rail was not present in significant numbers in the breeding season north of Bombay Hook NWR but possibly occurred at Broadway Meadows just south of the Smyrna River. Fifty sites with potentially suitable habitat were sampled (Maier 1993).

Nesting. The first nest was located in 1938 [Herh1] A nest with a fledgling was found at Bombay Hook NWR on 15 July 1939 [Kram3]. The usual Black Rail nest, placed on the ground, is a deep cup of grasses, with overhanging grasses and stems pulled together to form a canopy (Harrison 1978).

History. Presumably, the Black Rail was known to some of the rail hunters of the nineteenth century, but it would have escaped the notice of most because of its small size and reluctance to fly. At one time it was included among game birds, along with other rails, but there has not been an open season on the Black Rail in the United States in recent years (Todd 1977).

This difficult-to-find bird was not included in the earliest published Delaware bird lists or notes (Rhoads and Pennock 1905). The first definite identification was recorded by Hanson (notes) as follows: "I had previously been of the opinion that I had seen glimpses of the Little Black Rail on our marshes but the first positive identification occurred June 16, 1933. I was on the marsh about a mile south of Dewey Beach between the bay and the new road to the inlet. Coming suddenly upon a small open space in the marsh grass I saw a bird on the bare black mud. It was crouched and motionless for probably a half minute and not more than four feet distant. The dark color and the white markings on the back were plainly seen. It was apparently about five inches long. It flew but a short distance and settled in the marsh grass." It was included in a typescript list for Rehoboth Beach (Pennock 1935). Buckalew banded 6 on 25 and 31 May 1938 (Refuge Reports, in Patuxent Bird Distribution and Migration Files). Based on this sighting and perhaps other sightings, it was included in Barry's *Delaware Birds* (1939) as a migrant and summer resident. Except for the earlier mentioned Hanson's Dewey Beach report, and a 1964 report from one-half mi south of Indian River Inlet (Sundell 1968), reports prior to 1988 had all come from Little Creek WA and Bombay Hook and Prime Hook NWRs, where it has been fairly regularly recorded for the past 25 years.

Breeding population. Its population status is largely unknown in Delaware and elsewhere. A rough population estimate, calculated from the Atlas results by assuming an average of 10 pairs per block, is 50 pairs for the state. Since it has subsequently been found at additional sites, 10–100 pairs should serve as a preliminary estimate.

Conservation. Some techniques used to see this elusive bird are invasive and damaging to breeding. Activities that require either entering its nesting grounds or persistently using a tape recorder are not recommended. Todd (1977) points out that a number of workers have commented on the inclination of California Black Rails to desert their nests when disturbed and suggests that it is unwise to encourage unsupervised visits to Black Rail breeding sites. The best chance to see this bird without disturbing it is to watch from a public road during an exceptionally high tide on a spring morning. Note that the young of other rail species are black and can be confused with adult Black Rails.

The New York Atlas reported its population as only 1 bird (Carroll 1988a). The Black Rail is listed as Threatened in New Jersey and "in need of conservation" in Maryland (Davidson 1992). It is listed as a migratory nongame bird of management concern in the United States (USFWS 1987) and proposed as a candidate for listing as a federally Endangered or Threatened species (USFWS 1991). Todd (1977) recommended that states initiate habitat assessment and population estimation, and that Black Rail habitat be protected from human disturbance. Davidson (1992) recommended that "states in the Northeast, especially Delaware. . . , need to conduct intensive surveys to more accurately determine population levels and trends."

FALL: The fall migration is poorly documented and little known for Delaware. There are only 4 records after mid-July:

14 Aug 1965	1	Little Creek WA [Kram4]
9 Sep 1962	1	Little Creek WA [Sche1]
14 Sep 1972	1	Prime Hook NWR (notes)
6 Oct 1988	1	west of Red Mill Pond (DMNH 77659)

The Black Rail is thought to migrate from early September through mid-October in Maryland (Stewart and Robbins 1958).

SPECIMEN: DMNH 77659, along Rd. 260, ca. 3 mi SW Milton, 6 October 1988.

Clapper Rail (*Rallus longirostris*)

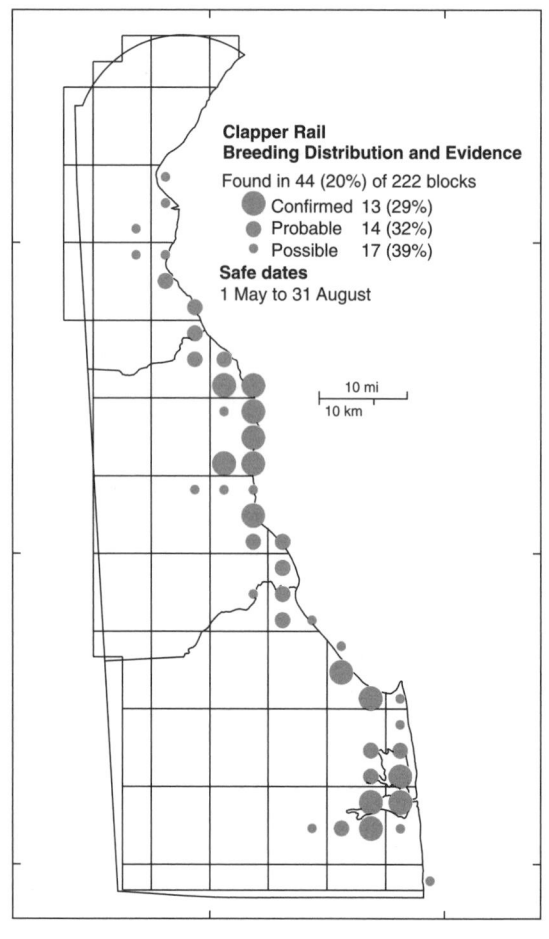

Regular; summer resident (absent only during the coldest months of winter); uncommon to fairly common. Expected mid-March to early January, depending on weather conditions.

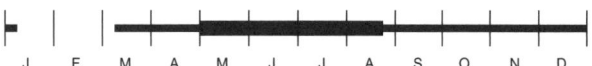

HABITAT: Salt and brackish tidal marshes, with salinity as low as 6 ppt (Meanley and Weatherby 1962). It typically lives and nests in the saltier areas along tidal guts that contain predominantly tall saltmarsh cordgrass, saltmarsh bullrush, and big cordgrass, but it will intermingle with King Rails in less saline regions containing short saltmarsh cordgrass and high tide bush. Needlerush is also a component of its habitat in Delaware.

SPRING: The first spring reports are from mid-March, but despite the lack of late winter reports it is possible that some individuals are present year-round, particularly in those years with mild winters. Early arrivals are

20 Mar 1983	1	Bombay Hook NWR [Hess2]
4 Apr 1982	1	Bombay Hook NWR [Edni1]
11 Apr 1992	1	Little Creek WA [Hess16]

The peak starting the first of May probably reflects increased rail vocalization and observer effort more than increased migration, which should be completed by then. As noted by Meanley (1985), "little is known about the spring migration of the Clapper Rail, and it can be deduced, mainly by noting an increase in calling activity in the marsh, that there must have been some movement of populations along the coast."

BREEDING: During the Atlas project Clapper Rails were found in salt to brackish marshes from Assawoman WA up the Delaware River as far as Pea Patch Island. There is no confirmed breeding Atlas record for New Castle County, but it is reasonable that breeding Clapper Rails have extended northward along with the intrusion of the salt line of the Delaware River, which now extends to Wilmington in some months. It is common enough in Delaware to remain a game bird with an open season, although few hunters seek it (Mangold 1977, tab. 3-6). We have no information about its area of greatest abundance or about its population stability.

Atlas. Atlas workers recorded it in 42 blocks, and it may have been missed in as many as 10 blocks of brackish habitat. Some of the more inland sites may have had King Rails also or intergrades. The Clapper Rail was also undoubtedly present in several inaccessible blocks on Delaware Bay that were not surveyed because they contained less than 1 sq km (0.4 sq mi) of

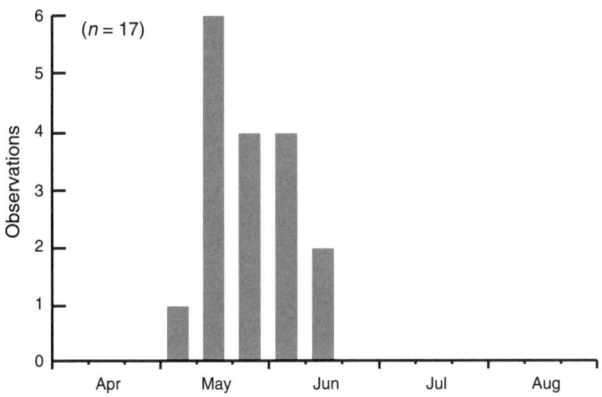

Estimated Clutch-Completion Dates

land. Nests with eggs were reported twice; other confirmations were the result of observing young.

Nesting. Extrapolated clutch-completion dates for 17 clutches range from early May to mid-June, with most falling in mid-May to early June. Extreme egg dates are 6 May 1938 [Buck13] to 14 June 1986 [ThoJ2]. Complete clutches contained 9–12 eggs. Fourteen broods of downy young have been reported from 15 June 1986 [Rufe2] to 15 August, indicating a much longer season. Although observed brood size averaged only 6 (range 1–10), this should be regarded as a minimum because the entire brood is not always seen. Clapper Rails are sometimes double-brooded in New Jersey (Schmidt and McLaine 1951) and South Carolina (Blandin 1963) and probably are here also. In the South Carolina study 13 of 29 marked birds renested, and 7 produced 2 successful broods. Near Cobb Island, in the Virginia portion of the Delmarva Peninsula, 16 Clapper Rail nests with eggs were found on 23 July 1971 [Byrd2]; the late date is consistent with second broods.

History. Clapper Rails are not now nearly as common as when described by Audubon (1840) for the New Jersey marshes. He reported that it was not uncommon for egg collectors to collect 100 dozen in a day, and 1 or 2 birds would be met every 8 or 10 steps. Likewise, Cooke (1914) reported that about 10,000 Clapper Rails were shot near Atlantic City, New Jersey, in September 1886. Because the days of egging and unregulated hunting are long past, and because the Clapper Rail is no longer a popular game bird, it might have been expected to regain its former numbers. Its failure to do so may be the result of loss or impairment of habitat.

Breeding population. A Bombay Hook NWR survey in the summer of 1979 estimated the refuge population at 400, including young [GarM1], and a similar number was reported at Prime Hook NWR (notes) in August of the same year. The highest May Count figure is 212 in 1975 (Rufe 1986). On 5 May 1984 30 were found at Indian River Inlet (Ednie 1985). Mangold (1977) lists densities of 3.2 breeding birds per ha in New Jersey and 8.4 per ha in Virginia in prime habitat, suggesting that either the Clapper Rail population in Delaware is considerably higher than our counts indicate, or our marshes are less productive than those in neighboring states for this species.

Conservation. Fiddler crabs are highly susceptible to some insecticides, and their loss limits the rail populations. Raccoons, known to be predators of Clapper Rails elsewhere, destroy only a few nests and are probably of minor importance in limiting rail populations in Delaware marshes where Clapper Rails breed (Meanley 1965, 1985).

In New Jersey 206 of 1,226 (17%) Clapper Rails killed in the 1950 hunting season beginning 1 September were young birds still unable to fly (Schmidt and McLain in Meanley 1985:79). If the season opened later, a higher proportion of the young would survive to breed.

FALL: Migration probably begins during 20–25 August and continues through the early winter, with a peak perhaps during late September and early October. The reported numbers of this inconspicuous species do not increase much during the fall migration, but migrants begin appearing in places where Clapper Rails do not breed. For example, Clapper Rails were recorded 6 times from 25 August [Gran4] to 22 December [Citr6] on a 1973–75 survey of the Dragon Run impoundment, a freshwater marsh where they were never recorded during the breeding season. The northernmost Delaware specimen (UDEL 524-75) was collected on 29 August 1975 at New Castle, north of its Delaware breeding range and so presumably was a migrant. An injured rail was picked up in urban Brandywine Hundred 20 September 1975 (Conway 1976). According to Meanley (1985, 81) migration in the Mid-Atlantic region apparently begins during late August and September.

1966–89 CBC Summary

Christmas Bird Count	Years Found	Range of No. Found	Median
Wilmington Middletown	7	1–8	
Bombay Hook	23	1–20	2
Cape Henlopen	18	1–27	1
Rehoboth	21	1–45	2
STATEWIDE (zero in 1989, high in 1974)	23	1–73	9

WINTER: Meanley (1985, 81), basing his comments on CBC data and band recoveries, notes that few Clapper Rails winter in the northern part of the species range (Connecticut and Long Island), and that the largest concentrations can be found along the coast from South Carolina to Florida. He also notes that in mild winters large numbers can be found in Virginia and North Carolina. Banding studies conducted in New Jersey and at Chincoteague, Virginia, indicate that the Mid-Atlantic population winters predominantly in South Carolina and Georgia. The CBC data demonstrate that some rails stay in Delaware into early winter. However, the only times that Clapper Rail CBC totals exceeded 9 (range 11–45) were on 11 counts from 1971 to 1975; these higher counts were the result of a unusually large amount of time spent searching marshes (unsuccessfully) for Le Conte's Sparrows (D. N. Phalen, pers. comm.).

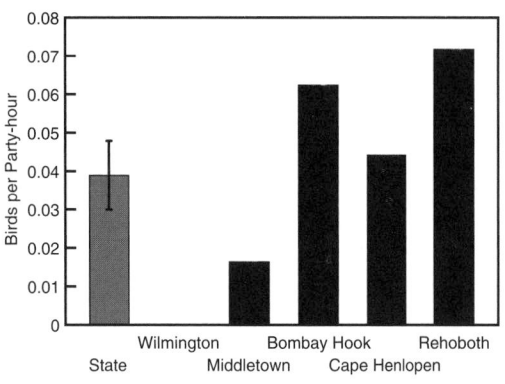

CBC Geographic Distribution; Average of 4 Count Areas

bers were down by two-thirds (Ferrigno, in Meanley 1985), and since then numbers on Delaware CBCs have been much reduced. The only post-CBC winter record noted 3 trapped at Bombay Hook NWR in a muskrat trap during February 1966 [Hard5], but if this species is usually silent in cold weather, small numbers may go undetected. Mangold (1977) states that the northern Clapper Rail occasionally attempts to winter in New Jersey, usually with poor success. Both he and Meanley regard the Delaware population as migratory (Meanley 1985). It is found in highest numbers on the 3 southern CBCs, reflecting the amount of appropriate habitat available in the count circles.

REMARKS: See "Remarks" under King Rail for a discussion of the relationship between these 2 species.

SPECIMENS: 24; DMNH, ANSP, UDEL, USNM.

A severe freeze in the winter of 1976–77 extended down the coast into the south Atlantic wintering range of the Clapper Rail. During the following breeding season in New Jersey num-

King Rail *(Rallus elegans)*

Regular; summer resident (absent only during the coldest months of winter); uncommon to fairly common; expected March through January, depending on weather conditions.

HABITAT: Fresh and brackish marshes with salinity up to 7 ppt (sea strength is 32–35 ppt) (Meanley and Weatherby 1962). Found in the wetter portions of fresh-brackish transitional marshes associated with cattail, rush, and pickerel weed (Rothstein 1991a).

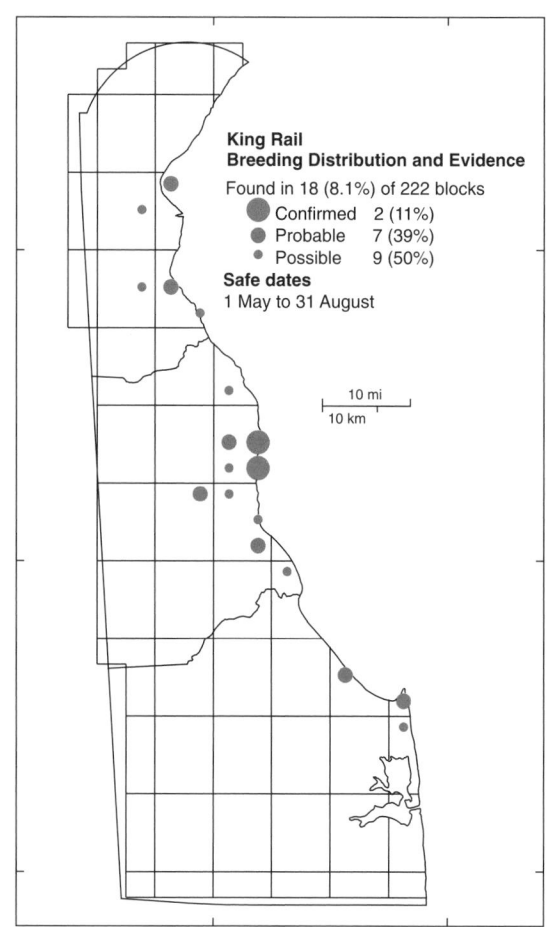

King Rail
Breeding Distribution and Evidence
Found in 18 (8.1%) of 222 blocks
● Confirmed   2 (11%)
● Probable   7 (39%)
• Possible   9 (50%)
Safe dates
1 May to 31 August

10 mi
10 km

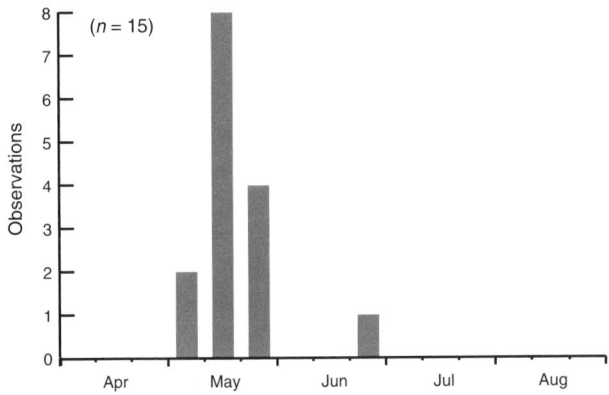

Observations

(n = 15)

Apr   May   Jun   Jul   Aug

Estimated Clutch-Completion Dates

King and Clapper rails intermix to some extent in the brackish marshes near Taylors Gut in northeastern Kent County (see "Remarks"). The habitat there is 50% saltmeadow cordgrass, 15% saltmarsh cordgrass, and 25% Olney's three-square. High-tide salinity measured there was 3.7 ppt (Meanley 1965, 1985). Two miles upstream at Flemings Landing only King Rails are found (Meanley and Wetherby 1962).

SPRING: No clear peak is present. Usually the first birds return in late February or early March. The May Count registered none or 1 in 4 years and as many as 25 in 1975.

BREEDING: King Rails are found during breeding season from Wilmington Marsh (16 May 1986) [MiJC1] to the Inland Bays (26 June 1980) [Frec1] and Assawoman WA (19 May 1990) [Camp15]. They are found in tidal marshes and impoundments built in such marshes.

Atlas. During the Atlas project King Rails were reported from a marsh north of Red Lion Creek south to Gordon Pond WA. However, there are large areas of marshes where they probably breed but were not located. Also it was difficult for Atlas workers to distinguish King from Clapper rails because of their overlapping call notes (Meanley 1985) and because they are difficult to see.

Since the end of the Atlas project King Rails have been found along the Smyrna, Murderkill, Mispillion, and Broadkill rivers, and in Deep Creek, north of Broadkill Beach Rd. (Rothstein 1991a). In 1991 a King Rail pair was observed at Assawoman WA on 8 June, and a lone bird was seen at the Ted Harvey CA, Logan Tract on 25 May [Camp2]. These represent sites where the species was not detected during the Atlas project.

Nesting. Hanson recorded nesting in a millpond near Milford as follows: "On May 21, 1929 Mr. Dicky and I in company with Mr. Herbert Buckalew visited the marsh on the west shore of Marshall Pond [S. Milford] where Mr. Buckalew had found two nests. The first one was out in the marsh about 25 feet from the edge in a bunch of sedges. The nest was built entirely of sedges, was twelve inches across outside and four inches deep, the bottom being at the water level. The hollow was 7 inches across and a half inch deep. It contained twelve eggs. The sec-

ond nest was in a similar situation near a little island but was two inches smaller in diameter. It contained only 8 eggs, but Mr. Buckalew said there had been ten a few days previous and as this was an older nest hatching may have commenced." Rothstein (1991a) found 12 nests, situated 7–10 in. over surface water, containing clutches of 7–13 eggs (average was 9.6).

Egg dates reported in Delaware extend from a "few days before" 21 May [Buck3] (10 eggs) to 3 June 1928 [Cart2], corresponding to the peak of first nests. Downy young with adults observed in early August (Meanley 1969, 54) must have come from a clutch completed in late June or July. Second broods are not known, but the long nesting season in the South suggests that some females have 2 broods (Meanley 1992). The closely related Clapper Rail sometimes has 2 broods.

History. The first documented occurrence of King Rail in Delaware resulted from 1 collected near Odessa on 10 December 1898 (ANSP 66196). It probably was regularly present in the Wilmington markets in the days when market hunting was common, because it is flushed when Soras are hunted (Meanley 1975, 9).

Breeding population. Some evidence indicates that the numbers of this species are down, as it is no longer easy to locate at Dragon Run, where it was recorded 63 times during the 1973–75 survey. In 1986 Barnhill failed to locate it either there, at Prime Hook NWR, or at Gordon Pond WA, but did find it near Odessa. Rothstein's (1991a) field work adds a number of new sites and the possibility of higher numbers. At present, the state breeding population should be estimated at 100–1,000 pairs.

Conservation. If the King Rail is as sparse as the Atlas results indicate, then steps should be taken to protect it. Rail hunting in fresh or brackish marshes should be limited to small rails to protect this species.

FALL: Migration is probably protracted, beginning 20–25 August and continuing into early winter. Meanley (1969, 13; 1992, 2) notes that at Patuxent NWR, Maryland, most breeding King Rails had left by late September. He also states that "Winter records for the Middle Atlantic and North Central States suggest the possibility of permanent residency by some individuals." He goes on to cite 3 band recoveries in Maryland that support his suggestion. Our data also suggest that at least a few are present through most of some winters.

1966–89 CBC Summary

Christmas Bird Count	Years Found	Range of No. Found	Median
Wilmington	1	2	
Middletown	8	1–8	
Bombay Hook	13	1–9	1
Cape Henlopen	4	2–5	
Rehoboth	9	1–13	
STATEWIDE (high in 1973)	18	1–25	1

WINTER: In 1975 it was found regularly during January and February (5 on 22 February) [SpSB43], suggesting that some successfully wintered in Dragon Run. CBC numbers are so variable depending on weather conditions before and during the counts that no long-term trend can be detected. As noted in the Clapper Rail account, D. Phalen actively searched the marshes during 1973–75 and thus undoubtedly accounted for high numbers of marsh species during that period.

REMARKS: The King Rail is treated as a Clapper Rail subspecies by Mayr and Short (1970) and by Ripley (1977), but most ornithologists (AOU 1983) treat the 2 as distinct species. They occur together in the brackish marshes along the Delaware River and elsewhere along the Atlantic and Gulf coasts. Meanley (1962) collected viable eggs attributed to a King x Clapper Rail pair at Taylors Gut, and specimens collected between Flemings Landing and Woodland Beach WA show a wide variation from typical King to typical Clapper plumage (Meanley 1965, 1985; 5 such specimens are at the USNM). Over much of these species' ranges the King Rail is strictly a freshwater marsh bird and the Clapper Rail a saltmarsh bird.

Analysis of mitochondrial DNA did not satisfactorily resolve the species–subspecies debate. The genetic distance between these two rails is more than the distance shown between Cinnamon and Blue-winged teals or Snow and Ross's geese, but less than that shown within populations of Red-winged Blackbirds or Yellow-rumped Warblers (Avise and Zink 1988).

King Rails include more plant food in their diet than do Clapper Rails. For example, in a Louisiana study plant food comprised 21 percent of their annual diet. A King Rail collected at Taylors Gut in late September had its gizzard full of wax myrtle seeds. Those that winter in this locality feed on seeds of aquatic plants or even cultivated grain gleaned from stubble fields when crustaceans and other animal life are scarce. However, crustaceans (e.g., red-jointed fiddler crab at Taylors Gut) are a principal food of King Rails as with Clapper Rails (Meanley 1965, 1985).

SPECIMENS: 12; USNM, ANSP, DMNH. Egg records: DMNH.

Virginia Rail (*Rallus limicola*)

Resident; uncommon to fairly common. Absent only during February in colder years.

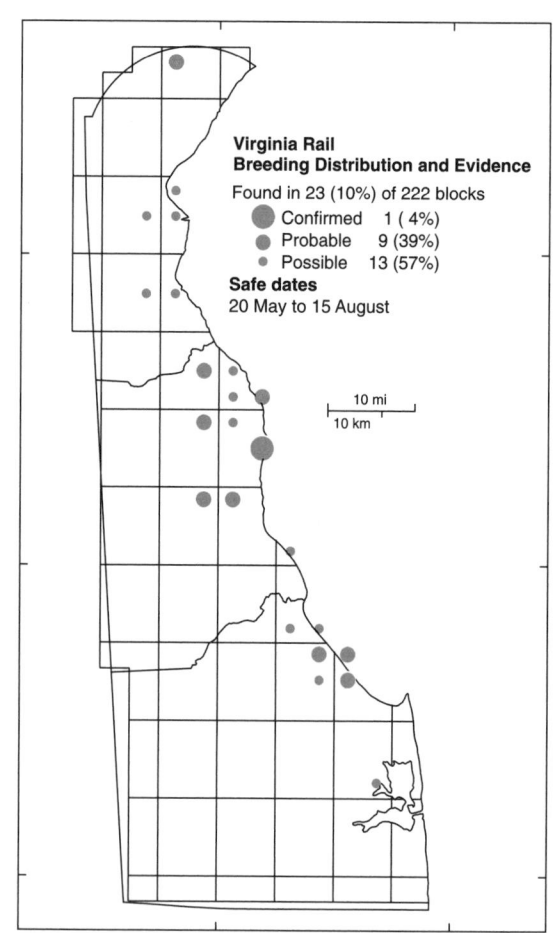

HABITAT: Breeds in fresh and brackish marshes and on the drier, fresher edges of transition marshes in reeds near shrubs. Winters in brackish marshes, more salty than where it breeds, and sporadically in a fresh marsh kept open by a spring.

SPRING: Our knowledge of this secretive species is limited, for the most part, to hearing its call at night. It is probably more common than shown by the seasonal bar graph, which represents actual reports. Migrants usually begin arriving in early April at our latitude (Zimmerman 1977, 46–56; Townsend, in

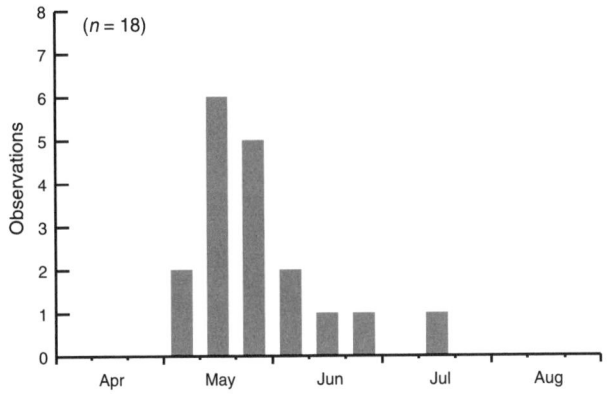

Estimated Clutch-Completion Dates

Bent 1926). Early arrivals may be confused with wintering birds, but 3 reported by Boller on 26 March 1988 at Dragon Run [Boll4], where they had not been heard during late winter, may be the earliest arrivals reported in Delaware. The May peak shown in the seasonal bar graph may reflect an influx of summering birds, increased calling activity as they set up territories, increased observer effort, or some combination of these. Intense calling activity continues at least through the first half of June (Maier 1993).

BREEDING: Adults with young have been seen in Brandywine Creek SP [BroH5], and the species breeds along the Delaware River and Bay marshes south to Prime Hook NWR (notes), where it is common.

Atlas. During the Atlas period the Virginia Rail was found in 24 blocks. It was found in 10 additional blocks during the course of a 1992 rail survey along the inland edges of saltmarshes (Maier 1993). It probably occurs in another 10 or 20 blocks. Both the Atlas work and historical records suggest that its breeding is primarily limited to the marshes on the Delaware River and Bay. The Virginia Rail should be looked for in small numbers at the edges of tidal marshes of the Inland Bays since it was found in a few locations on the Atlantic side of the Delmarva Peninsula in Maryland and Virginia (Robbins 1996; Ridd 1988).

Nesting. Hanson (notes) describes a nest he found on the south bank of the Christina River just below the brickyard: "On June 13, 1928, [we] found a nest containing five eggs. The nest was in a tussock of marsh grass built over an old blackbird or sparrow nest and raised just above the level of the marsh, which was very wet. About 50 feet from the river." The nest was 6 in. across and 1.5 in. deep above the old nest, and was shallow and saucer shaped. Rothstein (1991a) found Virginia Rails nesting on the drier, shrubby edges of brackish marshes up tidal streams from Delaware Bay.

Extrapolated clutch-completion dates peak in mid-May. Extreme egg dates extend from 11 May, 9 fresh eggs (DMNH 28694), to 19 July (Pennock 1908c). Clutch size in Delaware is 6–11, assuming 1 clutch of 5 was incomplete.

History. The first available records mention 2 collected on 22 and 24 September 1879 on Townsends Marsh (UDEL 282-68

and UDEL 372-68). Pennock (1908c), in correcting a claim that it was rare in the Delaware Valley, gives the first nest record and status: "This bird breeds not uncommonly in the extensive marshes along the Delaware River and its tributaries to at least 25 miles south of Wilmington, Del. I have a set of 11 eggs collected near Odessa, Del., July 19, 1903, and I have seen the bird in the nesting season near Rehoboth."

Breeding population. The Virginia Rail is quite common in its preferred habitat, and at some locations 10 were within earshot during a 1992 survey of Kent and New Castle county marshes (Maier 1993). On that basis its population is placed in the 1,000–10,000 pair range, perhaps too low given the 20,000 ha of Delaware wetlands.

Conservation. This bird was probably shot occasionally by hunters seeking the tastier Sora or larger rails. It is not an important game species (Zimmerman 1977).

FALL: Migration probably occurs during September and October (Zimmerman 1977).

1966–89 CBC Summary

Christmas Bird Count	Years Found	Range of No. Found	Median
Wilmington	15	1–8	1
Middletown	20	1–10	1
Bombay Hook	20	1–9	2
Cape Henlopen	13	1–13	1
Rehoboth	9	1–12	
STATEWIDE	24	1–42	6
(low in 1982, high in 1973)			

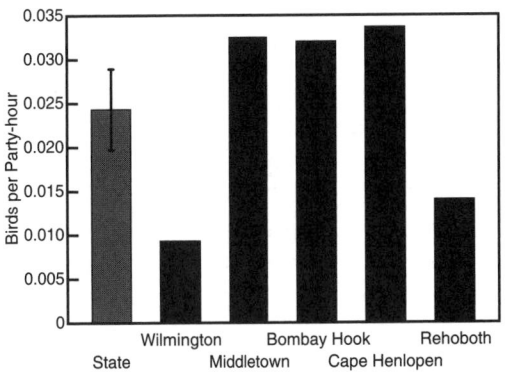

CBC Geographic Distribution

WINTER: Although a few individuals have occurred on many CBCs, and there are a handful of January and February records, it is likely that most move south when the marshes begin to freeze. One rail overwintered at a spring in Brandywine Creek SP. Two were seen on 1 and 5 January 1969 [Broo9] and subsequently 1 on 11 and 25 January and 1 March 1970. The next winter 1 was seen on 27 December 1970, 17, 24, and 31 January, 8 February, and 4 April 1971 (DOS notes). On cold but sunny days it searched for food along the open edges where sunshine had somewhat thawed the soil.

SPECIMENS: 12; DMNH, UDEL, USNM. Egg records: DMNH.

Sora (*Porzana carolina*)

ROD STINE

Regular migrant; occasional summer resident; uncommon. Expected mid-April to mid-May, sporadically through the breeding season, and in September, rarely early winter.

J F M A M J J A S O N D

HABITAT: Various kinds of fresh and brackish marsh, rarely saltmarsh.

SPRING: Migration occurs mostly during 15 April to 15 May. The earliest reports may refer to wintering birds:

15 Mar 1986	1	Wilmington (DMNH 76406)
28 Mar 1975	1	Dragon Run [John7]
4 Apr 1980	1	Little Creek WA (DMNH 69310)

Peak numbers are reported during the first 2 weeks of May. High counts are 15 at Broadkill Beach on 4 May 1967 [Armi8] and 35 at Little Creek WA on 10 May 1962 [Less15]. Usually only 1 or 2 birds are reported.

BREEDING: Delaware is south of the Sora's principal range, but Stewart and Robbins (1958) describe this species as a rare and local breeder in the tidewater area of the Chesapeake, and there are some breeding records in southeastern Pennsylvania (Reid 1992b). Rhoads and Pennock (1905) state that "a few are said to stay [in Delaware] and breed." Some may have bred here before nineteenth-century egging and market hunting reduced its numbers.

Breeding in Delaware was not proven until 14 August 1973. An adult Sora with a brood of 5 chicks was observed in a freshwater impoundment at Bombay Hook NWR. Holgersen (1974) judged the chicks were no more than 1 week old. They were feeding on a narrow mud flat between open water and dense vegetation. The chicks picked most of their own food from the ground but occasionally took food morsels from the adult's bill.

Other summer reports are suggestive of breeding: On 23 July 1962 2 Soras were seen at Little Creek WA (Lesser 1964); and throughout the 1978 summer a Sora was observed at Bombay Hook NWR [RusJ3].

Atlas. None was found during the Atlas project.

FALL: The first few birds appear in July, making it difficult to distinguish migrants from newly discovered summering birds. These may be early migrants:

5 July 1961	1	Little Creek WA (Lesser 1964)
6 July 1991	1	Augustine WA [Camp5]
9 July 1991	1	Thousand Acre Marsh [Edni30]
23 July 1962	2	Little Creek WA [Less12]

Migration begins to build in August; Lesser (1964) reported a peak number of 8 on 23 August 1963 at Little Creek. At Delaware City the bulk of the migration occurs about 1 September [Reyb1]. The main migration probably continues through the third week of September. The last fall birds were

23 Sep 1962	1	Little Creek WA [Less8]
25 Sep 1983	1	Lewes [Frec1]
10 Oct 1961	1	Little Creek WA (Lesser 1964)

Although there is only 1 October report and none in November, a few early winter reports suggest that Soras should be looked for throughout fall.

HISTORY: Cooke (1914) states that the Sora formerly existed in immense numbers in the marshes of the Atlantic states where it had been a favorite object of pursuit by hunters and a highly prized table delicacy. He goes on to say that 2 men shot 1,235 of these 15–16 September 1881 on a marsh near the mouth of the James River, Virginia, and that as many as 3,000 have been shot in a single day on a marsh of 500 acres. They were likewise once a popular gamebird in Delaware; Pennock (notes) recalls shooting 103 in 1 tide on a marsh 2 mi down river from Odessa and seeing many more after he had used all his shells. Eighty were shot by "one gun."

1966–89 CBC Summary

Christmas Bird Count	Years Found	Range of No. Found
Wilmington		
Middletown		
Bombay Hook	1	1
Cape Henlopen	3	1–2
Rehoboth		
STATEWIDE (high in 1972)	4	1–2

WINTER: Of 5 CBC occurrences since 1940, the 3 January 1971 bird on the Cape Henlopen count provides our latest winter record. These few additional records complete the winter portfolio of this species:

6 Dec 1963	1	Bombay Hook NWR, released from a muskrat trap [Hard2]
16 Dec 1975	1	Woodland Beach WA (DMNH 37644)
22 Dec 1966	1	Newport Marsh [Carr7]

SPECIMENS: 6; DMNH, UDEL.

Purple Gallinule *(Porphyrula martinica)*

Irruptive (8 years, 1948–90); rare breeder. Occurs most often mid-May to mid-September.

DOCUMENTATION: Photographs of bird and nest (W. A. Brokaw, DMNH 7–9).

HABITAT: Permanent freshwater impoundments with luxuriant growth of cattail, water lily, and spatterdock.

SPRING: Earliest dates recorded are

18 Apr 1976	1	Dragon Run [DuPG29]
29 Apr 1950	1	Wilmington Marsh [Wayn1]
1 May 1948	1	Wilmington Marsh [KraE1]

During migration it has occurred rarely in almost all of the northeastern United States and southeastern Canada (Holliman 1977).

BREEDING: From 18 May to 21 September 1974, 1–3 Purple Gallinules were observed by W. A. Brokaw and many others in the cattails of Dragon Run (Anthony, photograph, 19 May 1974, DMNH 460, and DOS notes). Displays were observed on 18 May and 18 July, and young were seen on 3 occasions in late summer (Brokaw 1975).

Purple Gallinules returned to Dragon Run in 1975 and were seen there regularly from 18 May to 10 August [m.ob1]. Three or 4 exhibited nesting behavior on 31 May [Lehm33]. W. A. Brokaw found a nest with 4 eggs there on 22 June (photographs DMNH 7–9). Also in 1975 at Finis Pool, Bombay Hook NWR, a different pair with 3 young was seen on 24 July (Putman 1977), with supporting sightings on 10 July (pair with young) [MiJC8], and 3, 5, and 8 August [Rowl21]. This species was reported the next year on 18 April, again at Dragon Run [DuPG29], but did not stay to breed.

These breeding records so far north are unusual; the DuMonts [DuPA9] say there are no recent breeding records for Maryland or Virginia. Stewart and Robbins (1958) give only 5 occurrences for Maryland 1845–1953. In contrast, Eaton (1910) relates that Mr. Nicholas Pike states that it was formerly plentiful on Long Island (see Dutcher, 1893).

Atlas. No reports were submitted during the Atlas period.

FALL: Latest dates of observations are

10 Aug 1975	1	Dragon Run [SpSB23]
21 Sep 1974	1	Dragon Run (Brokaw 1975)
17 Oct 1961	1	Little Creek WA [Less18]

History. The First AOU Check-list (1885, 143) reported that it occurred "casually northward to Maine, New York, Wisconsin, etc." Pennock (1935) included the Purple Gallinule on his typescript list of birds seen at Rehoboth Beach based on 1 reported there on 15 May 1915 by Mrs. Wright [Penn1]. Three previous Delaware records come from the cattails of Wilmington Marsh: 1 in 1937 (Goldstein, in Brokaw 1975); 1 on 1, 2, and 9 May 1948 [KraE1]; and 1 on 29 April 1950 [Wayn25]. One was observed at close range at Little Creek WA on 17 October 1961 [Less18].

Common Moorhen *(Gallinula chloropus)*

Regular; summer resident; fairly common. Expected early April to early October and sporadically thereafter.

HABITAT: Impounded brackish marshes, occasionally on inland waters. Nests commonly found in phragmites.

SPRING: The first birds arrive 1–10 April. It is hard to tell if reports in March refer to early migrants or individuals that wintered:

2 Mar 1985	1	along the coast [Barn1]
3 Mar 1974	1	Dragon Run [Beac6]
25 Mar 1984	1	Delaware City [Wayn1]

Later migrants include 1 perched 8 ft high in a crotch of a tree on Iron Hill on 4 May 1965 [Faus1], and 1 seen at Trap Pond SP, far from any breeding location, on 2 May 1981 [Barn1]. Some high counts are

28 Apr 1973	22	Dragon Run [SpSB30]
28 Apr 1974	38	Dragon Run [BroW19]
21 May 1939	47	Delaware City to Port Penn [Cadb3]

BREEDING: It breeds principally in impounded marshes along the Delaware River and Bay from Newport south to Prime Hook NWR.

Atlas. During the Atlas period it was found down the Delaware River from Wilmington Marsh to the St. Jones River and at Prime Hook NWR. The most inland record was on Garrison Lake in the low-lying Leipsic River basin. A nest with eggs was found on 1 July 1983 near Delaware City [Nile2]; the other confirmations were made by seeing young.

Nesting. A nest, found on 29 May 1926, was described by Hanson (notes): "a nest containing eight eggs on [the] marsh near Leipsic. The nest was oval in shape, 7″x 10″ outside and 4″

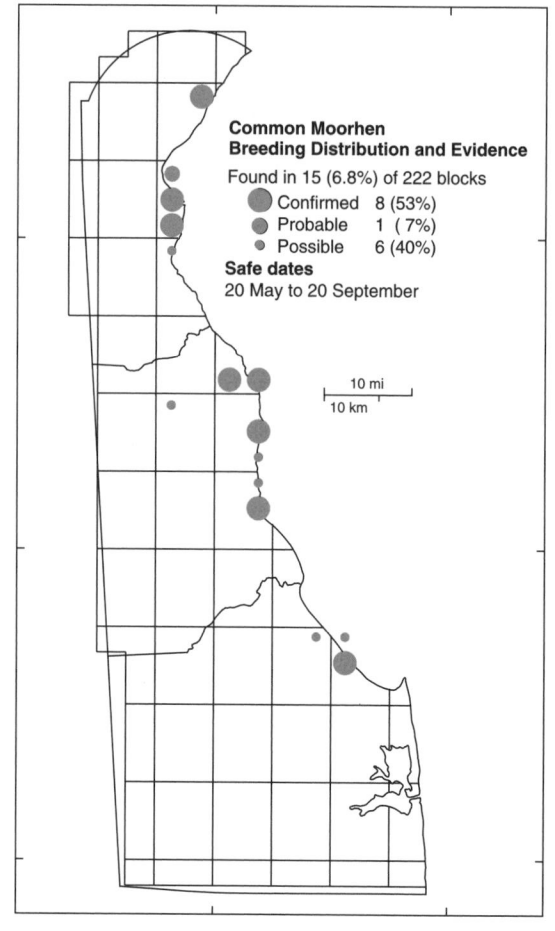

Common Moorhen
Breeding Distribution and Evidence
Found in 15 (6.8%) of 222 blocks
● Confirmed 8 (53%)
● Probable 1 (7%)
• Possible 6 (40%)
Safe dates
20 May to 20 September

x 7″ inside. It was rather flat, built of rushes, and was about 10″ from the mud flat, which at high tide is covered with water and must have been at that time within a few inches of the water."

The extrapolated clutch-completion dates for 20 clutches fall between early May and mid-June; 14 of these were from 17 to 26 May. Miller, in a similar calculation, figured a clutch-completion date of 7–16 May for 7 clutches from the Philadelphia region (Miller 1946). Dependent young have been noted from 30 May [Buck1] and 4 June [Gill1] to 21 August [West26]. According to Miller (1946), Common Moorhens are double- and probably triple-brooded in the Delaware Valley.

History. The first published breeding record is Pennock's report of an adult with 4 very small young near Odessa 2 July 1902 (Rhoads and Pennock 1905). It was less common in the Delaware Valley region during the nineteenth century than during the first half of the twentieth century; the first breeding records for Philadelphia and Delaware Counties, Pennsylvania, were in 1904 and 1916, respectively (Miller 1946). Pennock, on 6 June 1925, observed a courting pair in Wilmington Marsh, which he later described (Bent 1926, 346–47).

Trends. Numbers breeding in Delaware appear to have

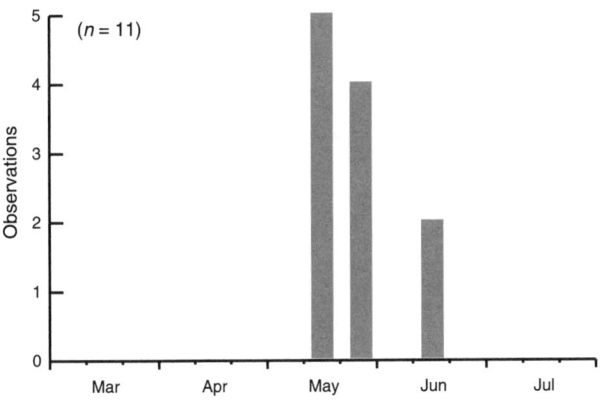

Estimated Clutch-Completion Dates

increased in the twentieth century. Only 1 or 2 birds or families were reported until 22 were found at Delaware City on 21 August 1927 [McDo1]. Cadbury (in Miller 1946) saw 47 in the same vicinity on 21 May 1939. The highest aggregations noted were 80 on a 100-acre fresh pond in Bombay Hook NWR in August 1946 (Spinner, in Miller 1946) and 79 at Dragon Run on 6 September 1975 [Stri1]. Barry (1939) listed them as abundant, nesting throughout Delaware marshes.

There are few reports from Sussex County. Pennock (1935) designates it as a summer bird on his list of birds at Rehoboth Beach. It was found once in both 1958 and 1959 during weekly surveys of a new impoundment at Assawoman WA (Tindall 1961) and also reported there on 30 May 1960 [Davi16]. Starting in 1971 it was reported regularly at Prime Hook NWR (notes).

Common Moorhens were common on a 1961–62 survey of the newly built impoundments at Little Creek WA, with many broods reported and a peak count of 45 occurring 26 September 1961 (Lesser 1964, 1965), but it was not summering there in 1964 (Stickley 1967). It was common on the impoundment during the 1965 Churchmans Marsh survey (West and Klabunde 1977), with a peak of 20 on 4 July but was not found there on the follow-up 1980 survey of the same area after the dike was breached (Hess 1983). It was common on the 1973–75 Dragon Run survey, with an early summer peak of 20 on 9 June 1974 and regular on the 1981–83 Bombay Hook survey, with a peak summer number of 5 on 7 June 1981 [DOS1].

It has never been reported on an inland mill pond or from the Piedmont portion of Delaware during the breeding season. On the May Count, the only annual survey that monitors its numbers, the Common Moorhen has not shown a significant change in numbers.

Breeding population. It was found in 16 blocks, always in small numbers. Its state population is probably under 50 pairs, fewer than reported in the early 1960s.

Conservation. As a gamebird it presents little challenge or reward, so is little hunted. Its current breeding status in Delaware is mainly, if not entirely, dependent on the provision of suitable habitat in impoundments built in tidal marshes.

FALL: The onset of fall migration is difficult to detect, but flocks of breeding birds and young decrease in September, and most are gone by the end of October. High counts are

| 21 Sep 1975 | 105 | Dragon Run [Wayn25] |
| 26 Sep 1961 | 45 | Little Creek WA (Lesser 1964) |

Late dates for flocks are

14 Oct 1989	5	Broadkill Beach [Frec1]
27 Oct 1974	12	Dragon Run [Wayn38]
28 Oct 1989	6	Thousand Acre Marsh [Edni26]

The latest specimen was taken from Delaware City on 21 October 1971 (UDEL 450-73). A few birds sometimes linger into winter. Stewart and Robbins (1958) give a migration period of 22 September to 22 November in Maryland.

WINTER: This species has been found 6 times on CBCs. The bird seen on the 1966 Wilmington CBC was unable to fly and took refuge in a culvert under Rt. 13 when approached (West, pers. obs.). Late wintering birds include 1 at Dragon Run 24 November, 7 December, and 11 January 1975 [Rich1]; and 1 at Bombay Hook NWR 27 November, 26 December 1971, and 10 February 1972 [Holg70].

SPECIMENS: 7; DMNH, ANSP, UDEL, USNM.

American Coot *(Fulica americana)*

Regular; winter visitor; uncommon to abundant. Expected mid-October, occasionally earlier, to late April, occasionally thereafter, but sporadic and rare into summer and early fall. Winter population apparently declining. Sharply declining May population since an influx in 1961.

HABITAT: Brackish estuaries, ponds in brackish marshes, inland lakes and ponds.

SPRING: Migration begins about 25 February and continues through 25–30 April. Peak banding occurred 11–15 February to 16–20 March [Usfw3]. Some monthly high counts, all from Little Creek WA, are

27 Feb 1975	40	[Pure1]
28 Mar 1964	122	[anon16]
17 Apr 1961	800	(Lesser 1965)

BREEDING: Breeding is sporadic in Delaware, which is outside the species' northern plains population center.

Atlas. The only Atlas period records were observations of 1 or 2 several times on Dragon Run and a single summer observation at Bombay Hook NWR.

Nesting. No nests have been reported in Delaware. Flightless young have been reported from 8 July [Edni4] to 15 August [Usfw2].

History. Pennock and Rhoads (1905) comment that it "possibly breeds rarely," perhaps based on an April 1884 specimen taken by Bush [Penn1]. Two were seen on 11 June 1928 in Wilmington Marsh, suggesting breeding [Livi1], but this species was listed only as an abundant migrant by Barry (1939). Not until early July 1948 was breeding in Delaware proven by observation of a brood of very young coots attended by adults at Bombay Hook NWR [BroC1].

Trends. An outbreak of breeding in Delaware and adjoining regions took place in 1961. Young birds were banded at Little Creek WA 15 August 1961 and 23 July 1962 (USFWS, unpub.

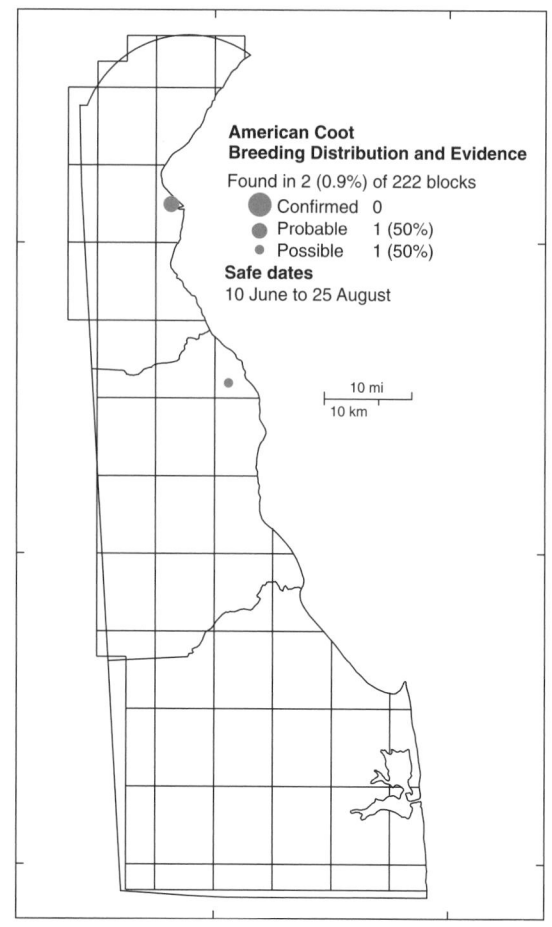

data). Dyke reported that a few pairs spent the 1961 summer at Assawoman WA and probably bred [Dyke3]. Lesser reported 9 breeding pairs on 20 June at the impoundments in Little Creek WA [Less9] and later reported brood counts of 24 for 1961 and 19 for 1962 (Lesser 1964, 1965). ("Brood count," as used by Lesser, was the sum of the broods observed on each weekly count during the summer.) No broods were reported on the 1964 Little Creek survey (Stickley 1967).

Coots were observed in the impoundments along the Delaware River each summer from 1969 to 1973 [Wayn1]. Broods of 3 and 4 were found on the Chesapeake and Delaware Canal spoils pond south of Dragon Run on 21 July 1974 [Lehm3] and seen again on 27 July [Falk3]. On 8 July 1978 an immature flightless young with 2 adults were seen in Dragon Run [Edni4].

After the 1961 outbreak, its May population declined irregularly but steeply, according to May Count data (1969–91).

Breeding population. The state population is currently under 10 pairs; perhaps none breed in most years.

Remarks. Lesser's 1961–62 brood figures are apparently the basis for Florio's communication that "recently about 20 pairs nested annually" in Delaware (Fredrickson 1977, 131); this probably represents a liberal estimate made during a sporadic nesting peak. Likewise, the published (Fredrickson 1977, 134) 204 sq mi of Delaware habitat suitable for nesting, migrating, and wintering (10% of the state) does not take into account that in Delaware coots are almost entirely confined to impounded marshlands or fresh water (less than 1% of the state).

FALL: Sometimes small flocks of coots arrive in September, but typically first arrival is 10–15 October. Peak numbers occur 20–30 November. Some high counts are

29 Oct 1972	800	Bombay Hook NWR [Holg76]
18 Nov 1971	1,400	Bombay Hook NWR [Holg68]
24 Nov 1974	2,165	Dragon Run [Phal1]

According to Fredrickson (1977, 139), the Delaware harvest of coots was estimated to be 3,000 in the 1971–72 season, and hunters' interest was said to be "nil." For comparison, the 1971–72 U.S. harvest was estimated at 800,000, with another 300,000 crippled.

1966–89 CBC Summary

Christmas Bird Count	Years Found	Range of No. Found	Median
Wilmington	8	1–29	
Middletown	17	1–2,002	5
Bombay Hook	23	1–3,104	71
Cape Henlopen	18	1–443	5
Rehoboth	23	1–1,754	57
STATEWIDE	24	6–5,607	335
(decreasing; low in 1981, high in 1972)			

WINTER: Numbers vary widely from year to year, with highest numbers in December 1971 and 1972, and a secondary

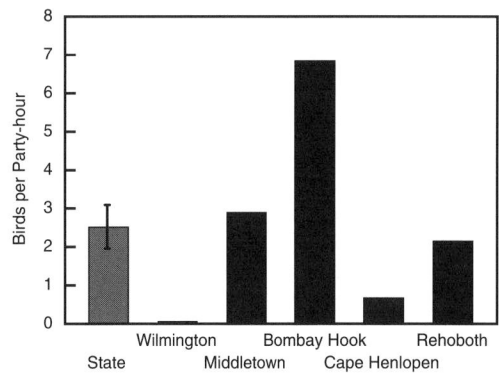

CBC Geographic Distribution

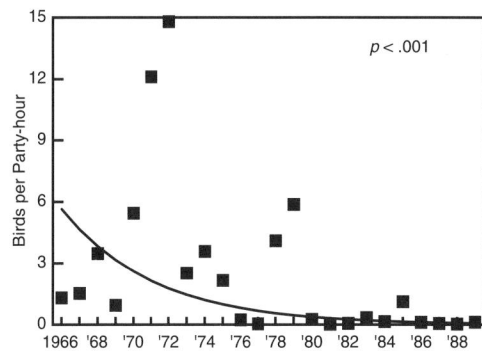

CBC Trend; May be Autocorrelated

high in 1978 and 1979. Beginning in December 1980, numbers have been very low.

SPECIMENS: 9; DMNH, UDEL, USNM.

Sandhill Crane (*Grus canadensis*)

with Gregory A. Inskip

Casual (6 years, 1969–91).

DOCUMENTATION: Photograph (W. A. Fintel, DMNH 332).
REMARKS: Migratory Sandhill Cranes breed in the western United States east to Michigan, Canada, and Siberia north to the Arctic and, in North America, winter from the southwestern United States south into Mexico and east to Florida and southern Georgia (AOU 1983). Delaware records probably result from birds moving north in the wrong direction from their winter range or birds straying north of their intended wintering sites. Cooke (1914) suggests that in colonial days cranes were not an uncommon migrant from New York and southern New England southward. Records include

18 Oct 1969–Apr 1970	Bombay Hook NWR [Hol02]
27 Mar 1976	Bellevue SP near Wilmington (Conway 1976)
3 May 1986	Prime Hook NWR [Fint13]
18, 31 Dec 1987	Woodland Beach WA [ThoJ3]
30 Nov 1991	Prime Hook NWR [Fint16]

Field notes for the 1969 (Barnhill) and 1976 (Conway) birds are on file at the DMNH, as are photographs of the 1986 bird (Fintel). The possibility of some of these birds being escapes from Patuxent Research Center has not been checked.

HISTORY: Although now very rare, the Sandhill Crane was once a regular and numerous winter visitor and transient in the Delaware River and Bay and indeed from Newark Bay, New Jersey, in the north (Jameson 1909, 221) through the Chesapeake Bay (Smith 1907 [1606], 1:57) to coastal North Carolina in the south (Lawson 1967 [1709], 149–50).

In 1634 an English captain, Thomas Yong, sailed from Virginia into Delaware Bay and described the winter birdlife: "there are infinit number of wild pidgeons, black birds, Turkeyes, Swans, wild geese, ducks, Teales, widgins, brants, *herons, cranes, etc.,* of which there is so great aboundance, as that the Rivers and creekes are covered with them in winter" (Myers 1912, 48, emphasis added). The italicized words suggest that Yong (like Captain Smith) knew the difference between a crane and a heron—and that both occurred in winter in the marshes of Delaware Bay.

In February 1749 Peter Kalm saw flocks of Sandhill Cranes ("*Ardea Canadensis*") passing north and sometimes stopping at Swedesboro, New Jersey, just across the Delaware River from northern Delaware (Kalm 1937, 1:247). Kalm was told by a "Swede above ninety years old" that in his youth (i.e., about 1675) "Cranes at that time came hither by hundreds in the spring; at present there are very few" (Kalm 1937, 1:152–53).

Skeletal remains of a Sandhill Crane were found at the seventeenth-century Susquehannock Indian site at Washington Boro, Lancaster County, Pennsylvania, on the lower Susquehanna River (Guilday et al. 1962, 62).

[Whooping Crane *(Grus americana)*]

Gregory A. Inskip

Formerly present in the region, but no Delaware records.

REMARKS: The Whooping Crane wintered on the Atlantic coast within the historical period. Allen (1952, 2) mapped the distribution as consisting of 2 disjunct areas—coastal New Jersey north to the mouth of the Hudson River, and coastal South Carolina and Georgia. However, evidence is available indicating that the coastal distribution of this always scarce bird was more continuous. Allen (1952, 508) notes possible records from coastal North Carolina, and it apparently occurred in Virginia and Maryland as well. Captain John Smith explored Chesapeake Bay in 1606 and described its winter bird life as follows: "In Winter there are great plentie of Swans, *Cranes, gray and white with blacke wings, Herons,* Geese, Brants, Ducke, Wigeon, Dotterell, Oxeies, Parrats, and Pigeons" (Smith 1907 [1606],

1:57, emphasis added). The italicized passage indicates that Smith probably saw Sandhill Cranes, Whooping Cranes, and Great Blue Herons, and that he did not mistake one species for another.

New Jersey records include "white and gray cranes" noted in Newark Bay in 1642 by David De Vries (Jameson 1909, 221) and 3 Whooping Cranes seen by Turnbull (1869, 43) at Beesley's Point near Ocean City. Perhaps more significant for Delaware is Wilson's observation (Wilson and Bonaparte 1859–60, 1:312; Stone 1937) that "A few [Whooping Cranes] sometimes make their appearance in the marshes of Cape May in December, particularly on and near Egg Island." Birds arriving at Cape May in the fall often proceed across the Bay to Delaware.

Northern Lapwing *(Vanellus vanellus)*

Accidental (1953).

DOCUMENTATION: Brief published notes.

REMARKS: A Northern Lapwing found 14 March 1953 by Price and Miller (Price et al. 1955) "feeding on a slight grassy ridge" in a large wet field at Bombay Hook NWR was approached to within about 30 ft. The published notes mention only that "As the throat was white it evidently was still in winter plumage." This observation was corroborated the next day by D. A. Cutler who located the bird in the same field, watched it feed at close range, saw it flush, and heard "its characteristic call" (Bagg 1967). Cutler's unpublished notes mention the crest, a white and black tail, chestnut undertail coverts, and many confirming marks. The description is completely convincing. Possibly the same individual was seen and described by different observers on 8 March 1953 about 15 mi away in New Jersey (Price et al. 1955).

Black-bellied Plover (*Pluvialis squatarola*)

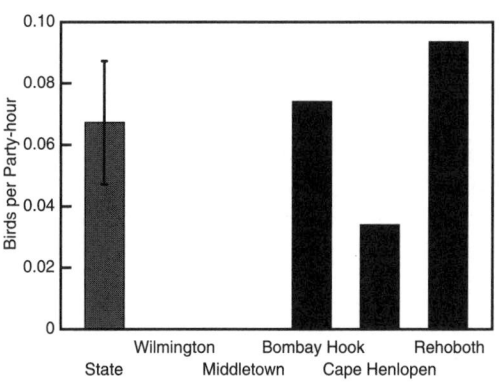

CBC Geographic Distribution; Average of 3 Count Areas

Regular; migrant; fairly common to common. Most expected from early April to early June and mid-August through the Christmas Counts in early January; sporadic in winter and summer.

HABITAT: Sandy beaches subject to tidal inundation, intertidal mud flats, fields, and pastures, especially near salt or brackish water.

SPRING: The migration is from about 1 April to 31 May, although a few birds are present in late winter and early spring. The peak is usually 10–31 May. High counts include

4 May 1993	935	Bombay Hook NWR [Samp3]
20 May 1989	300	Prime Hook NWR [Frec1]
25 May 1993	450	Woodland Beach WA [SpSB31]
28 May 1989	3,000	Bombay Hook NWR [Holg1]

These unusually late flocks were reported:

5 Jun 1988	30	Broadkill Beach [Frec1]
7 Jun 1981	11	Prime Hook NWR (notes)
18 Jun 1989	30	Little Creek WA [Holg1]

SUMMER: In most years a few nonbreeding birds, usually fewer than 12, are found in summer. They may represent incomplete migration of first-year birds or unfit birds.

FALL: Migration is from about 5 August to 15 November. The peak usually occurs from 15 August to 10 September. Counts during this peak period include

15 Aug 1985	53	Cape Henlopen SP [Frec1]
21 Aug 1972	60	Bombay Hook NWR [Holg76]
6 Sep 1986	100	Bombay Hook NWR [Barn42]

Numbers decline after this period until only a few are present to linger into winter.

WINTER: This species was first recorded in winter at Rehoboth Bay on 22 December 1936 (Cottam 1937). It occurs on the Bombay Hook and Rehoboth CBCs every year in fairly low numbers. Its numbers are highly variable, probably in response to the varying coldness of the December weather. As the weather becomes more severe and the birds die or move south, the number of reports declines sharply. A few linger some years in Sussex County:

17 Jan 1987	36	Rt. 24 at Angola, in stubble [Frec1]
30 Jan 1988	12	Delaware Seashore SP [Frec1]
23 Feb 1985	10	Delware Seashore SP [Frec1]

1966–89 CBC Summary

Christmas Bird Count	Years Found	Range of No. Found	Median
Wilmington			
Middletown			
Bombay Hook	20	1–37	2
Cape Henlopen	10	1–9	
Rehoboth	23	1–29	9
STATEWIDE (low in 1976, high in 1973)	24	2–50	14

REMARKS: This plover gradually recovered from nineteenth-century market hunting and was first recorded in Delaware 16 and 17 October 1923 when 1 of 10 or 12 at Kitts Hummock was shot by Ralph Wilson. Another was shot there by Wilson on 12 November that year and given to Hanson (notes).

SPECIMENS: 9; DMNH, ANSP, USNM.

European Golden-Plover *(Pluvialis apricaria)*

Accidental (1989).

DOCUMENTATION: Super-8mm movie, numerous written descriptions.

REMARKS: The European Golden-Plover, a Eurasian species, occurs regularly in migration in Greenland and casually in Newfoundland (AOU 1983; AOU 1995). A major incursion into Newfoundland occurred during April and May of 1988, with single birds also present during August in Newfoundland and during October in Nova Scotia [MacT1]. The species is quite similar in appearance to the American Golden-Plover, which presents a major identification problem.

A bird found on 25 July 1989 in Shearness Pool at Bombay Hook NWR constitutes the single Delaware record of European Golden-Plover. Apparently first seen by Robert Hilton, William S. Clark, Daphne Gemmill, and perhaps others [Hilt1], it was viewed by many other observers on 25 July and especially during the next 2 days. There were no observations of this bird after 27 July. A golden-plover seen at the same location 23 July [Shoc1], if an American Golden-Plover, would have been an early and isolated record. That bird was not considered unusual in appearance at the time but in retrospect may have been the same bird seen on the 25th.

On 26 July Hart Rufe shot film of the bird using a Super-8mm camera attached to a Questar telescope. The film was later copied to videotape, and copies of the videotape were circulated. Written descriptions, most based directly on notes taken in the field, were made available by numerous observers, many of whom provided copies of original field notes (on file, DMNH). The overwhelming, but not universal, opinion of the field observers is that the bird was a European Golden-Plover (Norman Holgersen, in particular, dissenting). Observers familiar with the Pacific Golden-Plover *(P. fulva)* described this bird as bulky and thick-necked rather than slim like *fulva*. Those who had the best views described the underwings as being quite white generally with light gray margins. The breast was quite black without white flecks, and the sides and flanks showed a broad white stripe. The undertail was white. Those people familiar with the European Golden-Plover who have seen the videotape have supported the identification of the taped bird as this species. In view of the color of the underwings, the shape, and numerous supporting field marks, the identification of this bird as a European Golden-Plover seems quite reasonable.

American Golden-Plover *(Pluvialis dominica)*

Regular; migrant; uncommon to fairly common. Expected April to mid-May and early August to early November, sporadically through the summer.

HABITAT: Cultivated fields, short-grass pastures, mud flats, and beaches.

SPRING: This species migrates primarily through the middle of North America in spring and casually to both coasts (AOU 1983). As expected, few spring records exist for Delaware, the majority of reports occurring from 1 April to 15 May. Earlier reports are

16 Mar 1974	1	Bombay Hook NWR [Holg22]
24 Mar 1973	3	near Smyrna and Bombay Hook NWR [Holg79; BroW24]
28 Mar 1971	1	near Smyrna [BrMa1]

The highest count is

14 Apr 1973	37	Bombay Hook NWR [Holg99]

In the course of his 1928–37 study, Urner never recorded this species during spring along the New Jersey coast (Urner and Storer 1949). Likewise, Stone (1937) reports no spring records. The dearth of records reflects a much lower population in the first half of the twentieth century as a result of near extinction from hunting; it is now found in spring at Cape May (Sibley 1993). The first Delaware report was from Delaware City 12 May 1928 [Hiat3].

SUMMER: A few nonbreeding birds will summer occasionally. Late reports include

25 May 1975	1	Prime Hook NWR [BroW5]
12 Jun 1971	1	Little Creek WA [Holg9]
30 Jun–18 Jul 1988	2	Broadkill Beach [Frec15]

There are July reports of single birds in 6 additional years.

FALL: American Golden-Plovers migrate primarily over the Atlantic Ocean in fall (AOU 1983), but from time to time come to shore. They are reported roughly twice as often during fall as during spring, with about twice as many birds reported per observation. First arrival is usually 7–15 August, but the earliest flocks reported are

30 Jul 1984	4	Cape Henlopen SP [FinS2]
4 Aug 1929	5	Kitts Hummock (Bender 1931)
7 Aug 1965	4	Cape Henlopen SP [Lake2]

Peak migration lasts from about 15 September to 15 October. The high count is 180 near Smyrna on 5 October 1970 [Holg5]. Last departure is usually 1–10 November. Later reports are

13 Nov 1970	10	Bombay Hook NWR [Holg50]
15 Nov 1969	2	Bombay Hook NWR [Holg37]
18 Nov 1973	1	Bombay Hook NWR [Holg59]

The last bird was a straggler from a large flock.

SPECIMEN: ANSP 66254; Rehoboth Beach, 28 September 1908.

Wilson's Plover *(Charadrius wilsonia)*

Casual (1937 and 1985); summer visitor; rare.

DOCUMENTATION: Published notes.

HABITAT: Favors breeding habitat consisting of sand dunes and other barren or nearly barren situations, usually close to salt or brackish water; open areas on sandy islands and the higher, drier portions of sandy beaches (Johnsgard 1981). Feeds on quiet sand and mud flats.

SUMMER: It was twice recorded in Delaware during 1985—the only recent records. On 8 May 1 was found at Gravel Hill near a gravel pit (Brokaw and Wayne 1985). The inland location is unexpected, since there are few inland spring records in nearby states. On 26 July another was seen in a suitable spot on Indian River Bay at Haven Rd. [Barn35]. Both records are acceptable but do not represent breeding.

History. Wilson's Plover may have been a summer resident in southern Delaware during the mid-twentieth century. It was listed by Pennock (1935) and Barry (1939, 1942) as a summer resident, but the only supporting report is Twining's report of Wilson's Plover at Indian River on 25 August 1937 [Twin1]. Leck (1984) wrote that it regularly breeds "as far north as Delaware," but the mention of Delaware must be based on reports not now available.

Wilson's Plover has apparently disappeared from part of its former Mid-Atlantic range, although Johnsgard (1981) describes it as still common enough that it has not appeared on the Blue List. Since Delaware is situated near the northern edge of its breeding range, details of its past status are necessary in understanding its current status. It was first recognized as a species by Wilson, who collected 3 on 13 May 1813 on the shore of Cape Island (Cape May, New Jersey). He painted it but died before describing it. It was described by George Ord, who brought out Volume 9 of Wilson's *American Ornithology* in 1814, after Wilson's death. One of the birds collected was a female with an egg in the oviduct, confirming breeding there. Ord said it was rare there but added later that he and T. R. Peal found it "pretty common" in May near Brigantine (about 1820) (Wilson and Bonaparte 1859–60). Audubon (1839) said it was found as far east as Long Island, where it was considered rare. W. H. Baird collected 2 at Cape May in June 1843 but complained that gunners were very numerous (Stone 1937); after that Stone lists only 3 New Jersey records, all in the 1930s.

The AOU Check-list (1983) states that it breeds "from southern NJ south," but the last recorded breeding in New Jersey was at Holgate in the early to mid-1960s (Leck 1984). The current anchor of its northern breeding range is the Atlantic coastal islands off the Virginia portion of the Delmarva Peninsula where some 50 pairs breed with regularity. Intermittent breeding has occurred on the Maryland portion of Assateague Island, but the northernmost regular breeding location is now Wallops Island, Virginia [Vaug2]. It has never been found breeding north of Holgate, New Jersey, but during spring migration it continues to appear north of its breeding range in most years, sometimes to Nova Scotia and occasionally away from the Atlantic beaches, such as at Sandy Point SP northeast of Annapolis, Maryland, on the Chesapeake Bay.

Conservation. It is listed as Threatened in Maryland and Virginia—a recognition of its withdrawal from the northern part of its range.

Semipalmated Plover (*Charadrius semipalmatus*)

ROB STINE

Regular; migrant; fairly common; also a rare summer visitor in some years. Expected late April to early June and mid-July to early November, sporadically outside those periods.

J F M A M J J A S O N D

HABITAT: Mud flats, wet sand flats, flat open margins of ponds and lakes.

SPRING: Reports in March are unusual:

23 Mar 1980	2	Red Mill Pond [Frec1]
24 Mar 1990	1	Sussex County [Barn1]
31 Mar 1983	1	Cape Henlopen SP [Frec1]

A few also arrive during the first half of April some years. The earliest flock was composed of 14 that arrived on 14 April 1973 at Dragon Run [BroW15], but first arrival is usually 25–30 April. The main migration is 5–25 May, and virtually all birds have left by 5 June. A report of 4,300 at Little Creek WA on 19 May 1974 (Scott and Cutler 1974b) was probably an overestimate. High counts include

11 May 1963	500 (peak)	Little Creek WA (Lesser 1964)
11 May 1993	800	Bombay Hook NWR [Atch4]
15 May 1993	1,476	Ted Harvey CA [Camp13]
27 May 1993	525	Little Creek WA [MurW2]

See also "Spring Shorebirds" essay for high numbers.

SUMMER: In some years a few nonbreeding individuals summer.

FALL: Beginning about mid-July the few summering birds are joined by the vanguard from the breeding range. Migration continues to 1–10 November. Peak numbers usually occur from 5 August to 7 September. The high counts include

29 Jul 1987	200	Bombay Hook NWR [Holg1]
12 Aug 1962	400	Little Creek WA [Sche1]
17 Aug 1986	1,000	Kent and Sussex counties [Barn1]
21 Aug 1981	230	Bombay Hook NWR [SpSB39]

WINTER: Usually most birds leave well before winter's arrival, but 1 or 2 have been recorded on 7 CBCs during the 1966–89 analysis period. Twelve were found in 1990 on the Bombay Hook CBC and 5 on the Cape Henlopen CBC. The latest record in winter involves 1 at Bombay Hook NWR on 8 January 1974 [Holg85], 16 days after it had been counted on the CBC.

1966–89 CBC Summary

Christmas Bird Count	Years Found	Range of No. Found
Wilmington		
Middletown		
Bombay Hook	3	1–2
Cape Henlopen	3	1
Rehoboth	1	2
STATEWIDE	7	1–2
(two in 1973, 1974, and 1982)		

SPECIMENS: DMNH 7634*3 and DMNH 76344, 0.3 mi (0.5 km) N Pickering Beach, 22 May 1986; USNM 412253, Fowler Beach, 15 August 1932; ANSP 66243, Rehoboth Beach, 26 September 1908.

Piping Plover (*Charadrius melodus*)

Regular; summer resident; local. Expected early March through August, sporadic into winter. Atlantic coast population federally Threatened; listed as Endangered by 5 northeastern states, including New Jersey and Maryland.

HABITAT: Sand beaches, especially those favored by Least Tern colonies. Nests on sand dunes with shells and pebbles; also mud flats, wet fields during migration.

SPRING: First arrival is usually 1–10 March, with these the earliest noted:

3 Mar 1973	2	Cape Henlopen SP [Hann2]
4 Mar 1972	2	Cape Henlopen SP [Barn5]
7 Mar 1970	3	Cape Henlopen SP [Hahn1]

During the 1980s the earliest recorded arrival is 11 March 1981 [Frec1].

BREEDING: Piping Plovers have bred in the past from Cape Henlopen to Fenwick Island, but few are left.

Atlas. During the Atlas period it was so scarce that breeding was detected in only 3 locations. It was probably not missed as a breeding bird in any blocks.

Nesting. The nest, located in the open in drier sand, is a shallow depression, sometimes lined with bits of shell. Estimated clutch-completion dates range from 30 April to 12 June (*n* = 15), shorter than the 26 April to 23 July reported for Long Island (Wilcox 1959). Later clutches are probably replacement clutches (Palmer 1967) rather than second broods. These later clutches have a lower fledging success in Delaware (Rothstein, DNHI, pers. comm.).

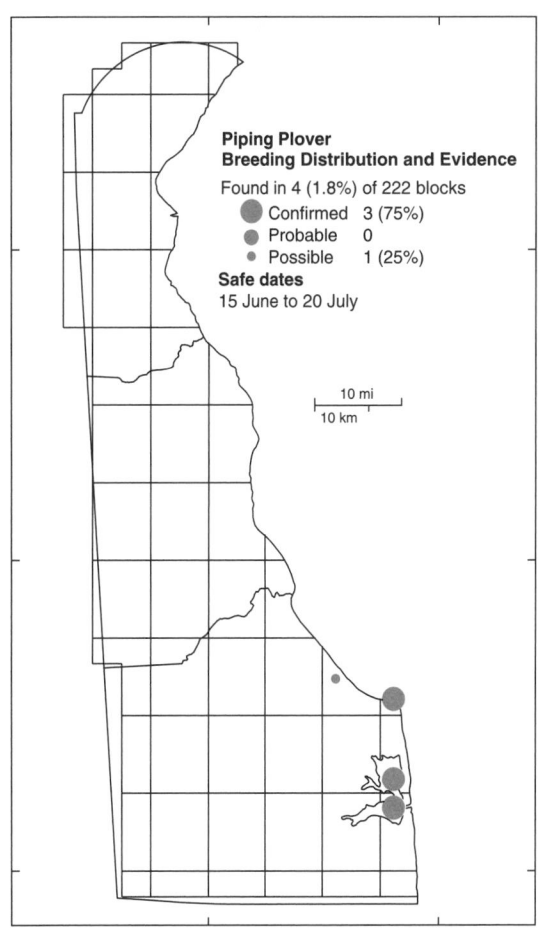

Piping Plover
Breeding Distribution and Evidence
Found in 4 (1.8%) of 222 blocks
● Confirmed 3 (75%)
● Probable 0
· Possible 1 (25%)
Safe dates
15 June to 20 July

History and trends. The population of this beach-nesting species was greatly reduced around 1900 by uncontrolled shooting (Tyler 1929), but it was included on the first Delaware list (Rhoads and Pennock 1905). It partly recovered but is in trouble again, this time from conflict with humans on the sand beaches and dunes that it requires for breeding. Palmer (1967) summed up its decline on the East Coast, saying that "the Piping Plover population was greatly reduced by 1900, with many beaches unoccupied by any nesting birds; now the bird is common, though there are still fairly undisturbed potential nesting areas in northern part of its range where this fine bird is notable for its scarcity or absence." The May Counts for 1969–91 show a downward trend in its population (*p* < .1) at an average annual rate of 5%—a two-thirds decline in 22 years starting from an already small number.

Breeding population. Cairns and McLaren (1980) estimated the East Coast population as 910 pairs at most, including a 1978 estimate of nearly 40 pairs in Delaware [Line9]. A 1980 Delaware Audubon Society census resulted in the location of only 42 individuals, and since then the population has fallen sharply to 1–4 breeding pairs.

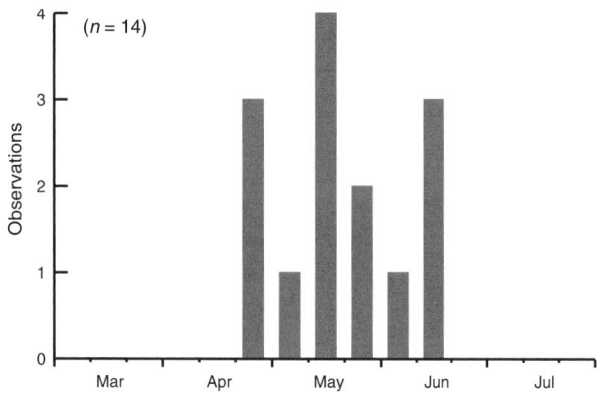

Estimated Clutch-Completion Dates

In 1988 the population was closely monitored. Three nests were found: 1 was abandoned, and the chicks from the others did not reach flight stage. These chicks, unlike Least Tern chicks, which are fed fish, must feed in the intertidal zone outside the protected nest areas, and so are more vulnerable to human disturbance (Thomas 1988c). This means, for example, the 0.25-oz (8 g) chicks have to safely cross beach-buggy tracks (a sizable barrier) and avoid joggers and fishermen with dogs.

In 1989 4 nests were found: 1 was lost to grackle predation (Thomas 1989c), and the other 3 produced 8 chicks and fledged 7. Predator exclosures (snow fencing), temporary wardens, and educational efforts led by J. Thomas (DNREC) helped with this improvement [Edni9].

The best recent year was 1990: 4 successful pairs fledged 10 chicks. State protection continued, and beaches were closed from the dunes to the surf in the nesting areas.

In 1991 2 successful pairs each fledged 4 young at Cape Henlopen SP and Delaware Seashore SP, but adults of 2 other pairs at the latter location were killed by cats in spite of the use of exclosures.

In 1992 breeding was disrupted. A pair was reported to have renested at Cape Henlopen SP, producing 3 chicks, and fledging 2 (Gelvin-Innvaer 1992a).

In 1993, 2 pairs nested on Cape Henlopen: 1 pair raised 1 chick on a second nesting; the other pair failed (Gelvin-Innvaer 1993).

Conservation. If Piping Plovers have a future in Delaware, it will only be on public lands with government protection. Experienced volunteers are needed for monitoring the beaches prior to egg-laying and recognizing courtship. The section of beach used should then be closed. Piping Plovers have been seen on Beach Plum Island during migration, where they might find the needed isolation to raise young if they could be induced to nest there. Avoidance of human disturbance is most important, but possible predators include feral cat, red fox, Fish Crow, Great Horned Owl, grackles, gulls, and hognose snake.

"There can be little question that this species is declining throughout its range and now is in rather serious trouble. It has

been on the Audubon Society's 'Blue List' since the inception of that list in 1971" (Johnsgard 1981). The East Coast population was federally listed as Threatened by the *Federal Register* entry 50733 on 11 December 1985. It is listed as Endangered by neighboring states.

FALL: The last individuals are usually gone by the end of August, but later ones have been found from September to November in 7 years. Included is 1 on 7 September 1986 at Pickering Beach, the only Kent County record [Nile8].

WINTER: This species does, or did, occasionally attempt to winter in ones and twos. It was reported on the Rehoboth CBCs on 1 January 1956 and 1958. It was also found in winter at Cape Henlopen on 5 January 1974 [Barn28] and on 10 January and 8 February 1976 [Barn6]. Six found at Broadkill Beach on 31 December 1978 [Barn47], both at an unusual site and numerous for the season, were carefully studied and Semipalmateds in basic (winter) plumage eliminated [Line2].

SPECIMEN: USNM 422244, Dewey Beach, 20 August 1932.

Killdeer *(Charadrius vociferus)*

Resident; uncommon to fairly common.

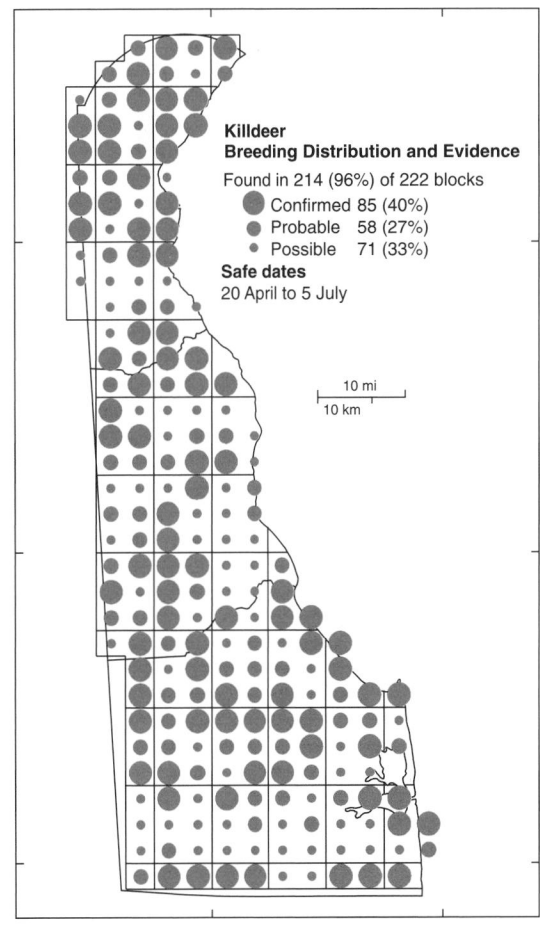

Killdeer
Breeding Distribution and Evidence
Found in 214 (96%) of 222 blocks
● Confirmed 85 (40%)
● Probable 58 (27%)
· Possible 71 (33%)
Safe dates
20 April to 5 July

10 mi
10 km

HABITAT: Upland fields, bare ground, gravel, short-grass turf, roof tops. During migration and winter in fields, near farm ponds, mudflats and shallow impoundments, on bay-shores.

SPRING: Migration begins 20–25 February. Peak numbers occur 10–25 March. High counts are

19 Mar 1978	75	Prime Hook NWR [Frec1]
20 Mar 1983	25	Bombay Hook NWR [Wayn41]
26 Mar 1972	34	Winterthur [Falk9]

BREEDING: The Killdeer, or "killdee," is known to every farmer, who finds it scurrying away from him and breeding in fields throughout the state. It is certainly one of the most numerous North American shorebirds, and its capacity for exploiting agricultural habitats and tolerating the close proximity of humans results in a very favorable conservation outlook (Johnsgard 1981). The relative abundance study reveals that it is least common in New Castle County, with a population density ratio of 3:5:8 in New Castle, Sussex, and Kent counties, respectively. It is particularly common in southwestern Kent County (3 times the state average), which has many fields and relatively well-drained soil.

Atlas. Atlas workers had little difficulty locating this bird, although it was absent from most of the horse farms, where the grass may be too lush for it to find the required bare spots for nesting or where it perhaps cannot find sufficient grubs for food. Beetles and other insects make up 80% of its diet (McAtee, in Bent 1929, 209). The most frequent method of confirmation was by finding chicks after being alerted to their presence by vocal parents.

Nesting. The Killdeer has shown a remarkable tolerance for humans by nesting on flat gravel roofs and many disturbed habitats. For example, a nest with 4 eggs was found on 5 June 1988 in a scrape on a hump of gravel on the roof of the 3-story Delaware Museum of Natural History. Killdeer are also suspected of breeding on roofs at Winterthur, the Wilmington Country Club, and the Concord Mall Shopping Center. The graveled transformer yards of the power company are also favored breeding areas, though access to these areas to locate nests was usually difficult. A Killdeer was reported performing a broken-wing distraction display along a little-used graveled railroad track south of Bridgeville. Other nest sites in human surroundings were located in Silver Lake Cemetery, by the Louviers Building, on the hospital grounds in Dover, on the grounds of Gunning-Bedford School, and frequently on old gravel roads.

The extrapolated clutch-completion dates extend from late March to late June, with 51% occurring in May. The earliest hatched young were banded on 20 April 1930 [Buck3; Hans1]. Extreme egg dates are 6 April (twice) to 7 July [Lyma2]. Clutch-size distribution for 28 clutches was 4 (22 times), 3 (5 times), and 2 (1 time) (Cornell and DOS nest records); clutches of fewer than 4 may be incomplete. Double broods have been report-

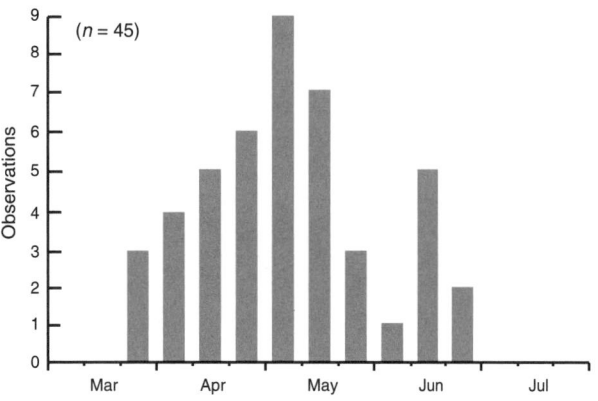

Estimated Clutch-Completion Dates

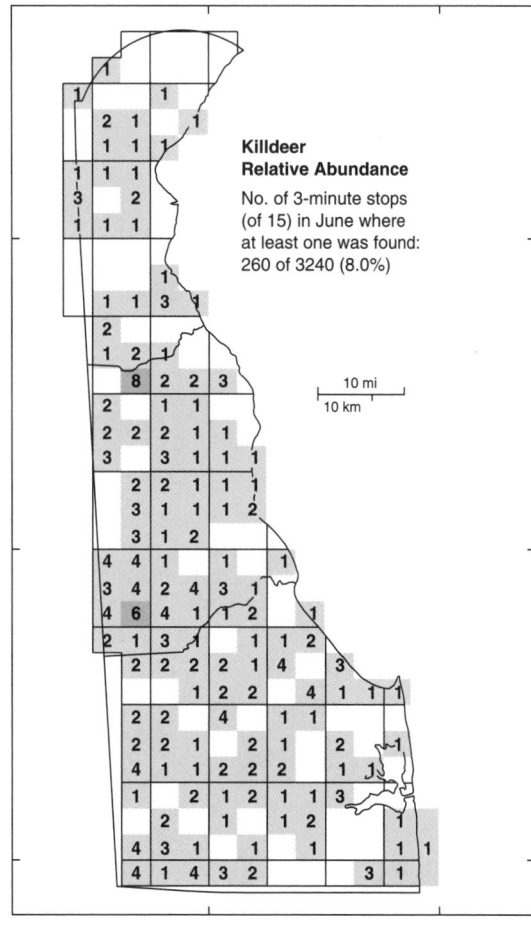

**Killdeer
Relative Abundance**

No. of 3-minute stops
(of 15) in June where
at least one was found:
260 of 3240 (8.0%)

10 mi
10 km

was reported as very rare in New York (Eaton 1910) and rare in the Philadelphia region around 1900 (Miller 1949).

Trends. It is more common today, and BBS data show that its population has increased in the East during 1966–90 [Usfw3] (Robbins, Bystrak, and Geissler 1986). The Delaware data do not show a significant trend.

Breeding population. Killdeers breeding in Minnesota on open fields and asphalt areas had average densities of about 31 pairs per 100 ha (31 in 245 acres), whereas those on planted fields had a density of about 15 pairs per 100 ha (2 in 35 acres) (Mace 1971). Nol and Lambert (1984) calculated similar densities of 13–19 pairs per 100 ha on a sandy lakefront in southern Ontario.

FALL: No migration period is clearly delimited. High numbers are observed from July through mid-December. Stewart and Robbins (1958) give the migration period as 5–15 July to 5–15 December in Maryland, with the peak from 20 August to 25 November.

1966–89 CBC Summary

Christmas Bird Count	Years Found	Range of No. Found	Median
Wilmington	24	1–100	13
Middletown	20	1–191	5
Bombay Hook	24	1–502	15
Cape Henlopen	23	1–194	8
Rehoboth	23	2–150	38
STATEWIDE *(low in 1982, high in 1971)*	24	15–823	103

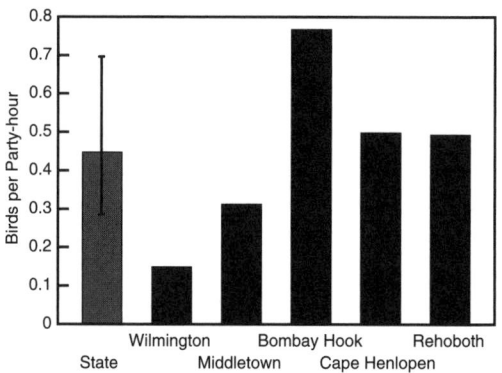

CBC Geographic Distribution

ed in Delaware [Hans1], and the extended breeding season suggests double broods are common.

History. The Killdeer must have benefited from clearing the land for farming, which has substantially increased its habitat. This plover does not form the large predictable aggregations necessary for market hunting and so escaped to some extent the decimation in the nineteenth century. However, Forbush (1925) reports that it had become practically extinct in New England at the beginning of the twentieth century. Similarly, it

WINTER: Numbers of birds decline during the coldest part of winter, from mid-December to the end of February. At that time, as the weather becomes milder, spring migration begins. No CBC trend is apparent because its numbers are so variable, perhaps in response to the weather; 5 of the 6 years in which it was most abundant were 1971–75. It is most abundant on the Bombay Hook CBC.

SPECIMENS: 7; DMNH, CM, UDEL, ANSP.

American Oystercatcher (*Haematopus palliatus*)

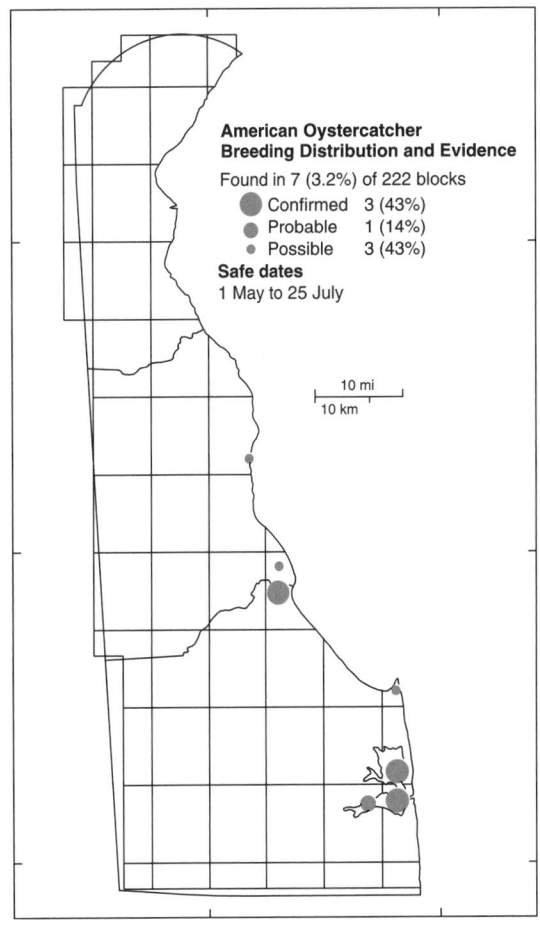

Regular; summer resident; uncommon. Expected late February through August and sporadically thereafter into winter (January records in 6 years). Reestablished as a breeding bird in Delaware during the 1960s.

DOCUMENTATION: Photograph (R. L. West, DMNH 251).

HABITAT: Sandy, shell-strewn beaches. Nests usually on sand, even sandy patches on saltmarsh islands in Rehoboth Bay.

SPRING: First arrival is from about 18 February to 7 March, but the earliest ones may have wintered locally. Numbers of birds remain low (usually fewer than 5) until June.

BREEDING: The first dated observations of this species in Delaware occurred at Indian River Inlet on 11 August 1962 [Davi20] and 11 May 1963 on the first DOS May Count [Wayn1], but it was probably present there beginning in the 1950s. It was seen fairly regularly at Indian River Inlet in the 1960s (e.g., Brooks 1965; Rufe 1987). Its first nest was discovered on a small spoils island there on 22 June 1968 [Wayn5]. It breeds in Sussex County from the Mispillion River south to Indian River Bay and is also found in summer in Kent County.

Atlas. During the Atlas period it was found primarily in Rehoboth Bay, where about 20 adults were seen on 12 June 1983. A nest was found at the mouth of the Mispillion River, much farther up Delaware Bay than any other nest, but perhaps the birds fed on the oyster beds in the creeks emptying into the Delaware River Bay south from Woodland Beach WA. The Atlas reports of probable or possible breeding could refer to prebreeding birds, because females do not usually breed until their fourth year. Prebreeders tend to keep by themselves in groups, the 2-year-olds exhibiting some display behavior and even excavating "nest" sites (Palmer 1967). If the oystercatcher can successfully adapt to breeding in saltmarshes, the outlook for it is fairly good.

Nesting. The first nests found in Delaware were scrapes in hard sand, but several have been reported since on saltmarsh islands in Rehoboth Bay. Breeding sites on the marsh islands have been along the wrack line and close to shore. The mean estimated clutch-completion date is 23 May (5 nests, 3 broods; range 7 May to 10 June). Extreme egg dates are 17 May 1986 [West4] and 29 June 1968 [Wayn5]. In the Carolinas and Georgia, fresh clutches appear from April to early May, later ones probably being replacement nests (Palmer 1967). The earliest egg date for Maryland is 9 April in Worcester County (Stewart and Robbins 1958), so April clutches may be possible in Delaware.

Clutch size on the inland bay islands has averaged 2.4 eggs. Nesting success in this possibly suboptimal habitat is unknown (D. Rothstein, DNHI, pers. comm.).

History. This striking shorebird has become reestablished in the Northeast. Post and Raynor (1964) summarize the breeding history in our area as follows: "The American Oystercatcher formerly bred on the Atlantic coast as far north as Labrador (Audubon 1835). Although this report has been questioned (Bent 1929), other records (Baird, Brewer, and Ridgway 1884) document its former occurrence as far north as New England.

During the mid-nineteenth century this species disappeared from the northern part of its range, and by 1910 Virginia was listed as the northernmost breeding limit (AOU 1910). For several decades this limit remained static but in 1939 the first recent Maryland breeding record was obtained (Stewart and Robbins 1958). In the early 1940s the species increased on the beaches of southern New Jersey and in 1947 the first nest was found (Kramer 1948)." This bird was unknown in Delaware at the beginning of the twentieth century (Rhoads and Pennock 1905), and Pennock (1908b) reported the only known nineteenth-century record, a bird shot in the early summer of 1862 at or near Port Penn. It appears as casual on manuscript Delaware lists maintained by Hanson and by Pennock in the early 1930s, presumably on the basis of this 1862 record (Hanson 1932; Pennock ca. 1935). During the 1880–1930 period it was recorded on the New Jersey coast about 10 times (Stone 1937). By 1980 it bred as far north as southern Massachusetts and extended its range to Boston Harbor in 1988 [Perk1]

Trends. Oystercatchers reported on the May Counts increased from an average of 2 in the 1970s to 10 in the 1980s, indicating a distinct increase in numbers.

Breeding population. The Delaware summer population is probably in the range of 10–50 birds (not all breeding), numbers that compare reasonably with over 200 estimated in New York (Lent 1988).

Conservation. Lent (1988) suggests that 2 possible reasons for the increase in oystercatchers in New York are the elimination of market hunting and an increase in bivalves as a result of decreased pollution. The need for large expanses of relatively undisturbed shore and flats must be an important factor in the distribution of this bird, yet even with increased human use of the seashore the oystercatcher seems to be reoccupying certain areas in eastern North America from which it was driven or shot out (Palmer 1967).

FALL: After late August this species is erratically present at a low level (usually fewer than 5) until early winter.

WINTER: Few winter records exist; most notable is the report of a small group (up to 7 birds) present at Indian River Inlet until the end of December in 1988 [Frec1].

Black-necked Stilt *(Himantopus mexicanus)*

Regular; summer resident; fairly common. Expected early April to mid-September.

J F M A M J J A S O N D

DOCUMENTATION: Photograph (A. P. Ednie, DMNH 59).
HABITAT: Wet mud flats (fresh and salt), tidal shore edges. Typically breeds along the grassy shorelines of shallow fresh-

water or brackish pools having extensive areas of mudflats (Johnsgard 1981). In Delaware, nests in impoundments.

SPRING: In most years the first birds arrive 10–15 April. Early arrivals are

17 Mar 1991	25	Bombay Hook NWR [Edni1]
19 Mar 1972	6	Little Creek WA [Abbo3]
29 Mar 1975	1	Port Mahon [Pure1]

BREEDING: This species breeds at Bombay Hook NWR and Little Creek WA, and in 1989 it bred at Prime Hook NWR [Frec3]. It has also been present at the Delaware City marshes and Kitts Hummock for short periods.

Atlas. The distribution map reflects its presence in various blocks in Bombay Hook NWR and Little Creek WA during the Atlas project. The 3 confirmations were made by locating nests with eggs. Its summer range extended from Woodland Beach WA [Wayn6] to Prime Hook NWR in 1993.

Breeding. Almost all nests reported in Delaware have been placed on small islands in shallow, managed impoundments of former tidal marshes. An exception is a nest found in a tidal brackish marsh at Bombay Hook NWR [MerW2]. The Black-necked Stilt's nest is frequently described as a shallow scrape, but Delaware nests have often been on built-up platforms of miscellaneous vegetation up to 6 in high, sometimes built in response to rising water as described in Bent (1927).

The estimated clutch-completion dates based on 15 nests with eggs and 4 with young range from 12 May to 24 June. The

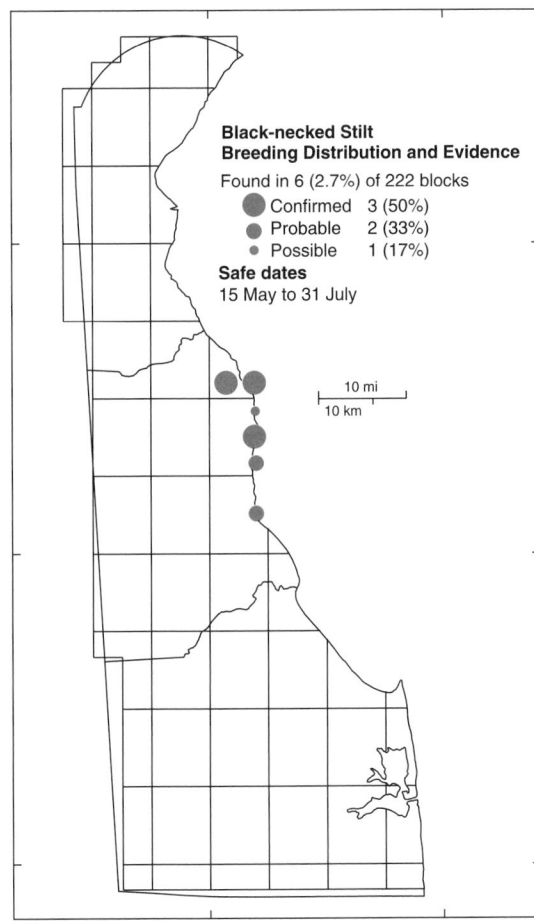

**Black-necked Stilt
Breeding Distribution and Evidence**

Found in 6 (2.7%) of 222 blocks

● Confirmed 3 (50%)
● Probable 2 (33%)
• Possible 1 (17%)

Safe dates
15 May to 31 July

10 mi
10 km

6, and 7 (which may involve some of the same clutches, since only 1 of his 6 clutches was reported to be viable). These large clutch sizes warrant more study.

History. In the nineteenth century the Black-necked Stilt may have nested in Delaware since it nested east and north to coastal New Jersey. Shooting extirpated it from the East, and the stilt has never reoccupied parts of its former breeding range (Palmer 1967). Two Black-necks observed at the Little Creek WA impoundments on 24 May 1962, establishing the first record in the state (Lesser 1964), were encouraging. Before then the birds had expanded their breeding range in 1956 to the outer banks of North Carolina from strongholds in South Carolina and southward. The Little Creek WA impoundments were new and very productive. Since the stilts returned every year in increasing numbers, breeding was suspected. On 20 June 1964 6 pairs were present [StiA7], and 2 groups of adults with young were reported on 26 July [PylR8]. Stilts began breeding in the Port Mahon impoundment of Little Creek WA in 1969; Carlson [Carl8] reported a pair with 3 flightless young there on 5 July 1969, but the first nest was not found until 1970 when Holgersen (1971a) found 1 with 3 eggs on 15 May 1970. On 27 May he found 4 more nests with eggs and during the season observed another 5 nests from a distance. His was not the only confirmation. Samson and Longcore (1971) found 6 nests on 24 June after heavy rains the preceding week. Interestingly, 1 nest had 6 viable eggs laid over 7 spoiled ones. Both observers noticed the stilts building up their nests to avoid flooding—by 24 June the nests were 6 in. high. In 1971 at least 23 chicks in 9 broods were also observed at the Port Mahon impoundment [Holg65]. Stilts were observed in Bombay Hook NWR beginning in 1974. Bombay Hook NWR is presently a breeding stronghold for the species, with 16 nests and 87 birds reported on 3 July 1987 [Holg1]. That year there were also 14 adults and 7 nests at Little Creek [Holg1]. In 1989 stilts started breeding at a third site, Prime Hook NWR [Aull1]. In 1991 Holgersen had the highest count ever at Bombay Hook NWR—92 birds on 3 and 24 May, with 37 nests in Shearness Pool and 13 in Bear Swamp [Holg98]. Nesting success in Delaware has apparently affected its status in the East, since it is now regularly seen in nearby states. It bred at Chincoteague, Virginia, in 1971 and 1975, appeared to be breeding at Deal Island, Maryland, in 1985 (where it has been a regular breeder since 1987 [Robbins 1996]), and was discovered breeding in the sewage ponds in Philadelphia on 12 June 1989 [MiJC4].

Breeding population. The state population estimate during the Atlas project was 20–30 pairs, based primarily on Holgersen's studies. Its numbers have since increased to 50–100 pairs.

FALL: Last departure is usually 10–15 September. Late records include

19 Sep 1964	1	Little Creek WA [Free1]
19 Sep 1970	1	Little Creek WA [Holg6]
22 Sep 1967	1	Bombay Hook NWR [Bake1]
1 Oct 1990	1 juvenile	Bombay Hook NWR [Holg94]

later clutches are assumed to be renestings. Extreme egg dates are 15 May 1970 (Holgersen 1971a) and 29 June 1990 [Bomb2]. The latest breeding is implied by a downy young observed on 27 July 1974 [Edni4].

The clutch size generally reported is 3 to (rarely) 5. Cramp (1983) dismisses larger clutches by the closely related Black-winged Stilt as probably the result of egg-laying by 2 females. Holgersen's (1971a) report of 5 nests with 2, 4, 8, 8, and 8 eggs is astonishing, and Samson and Longcore (1971) corroborate by reporting clutches at the same site 27 days later of 3, 4, 5, 6,

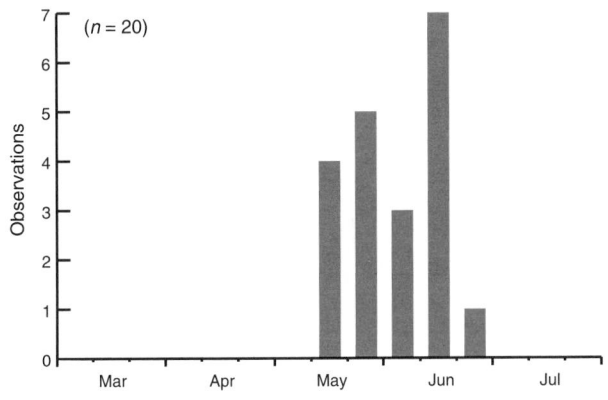

Estimated Clutch-Completion Dates

American Avocet (*Recurvirostra americana*)

Regular; migrant and summer visitor; locally fairly common to common. Expected late February to early December, sporadically into early winter.

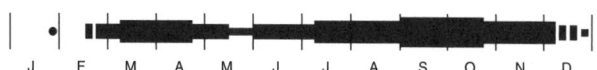

| J | F | M | A | M | J | J | A | S | O | N | D |

DOCUMENTATION: Photographs (G. K. Hess, DMNH 28–29).

HABITAT: Shallow muddy borders and bottoms of both fresh and salt ponds.

HISTORY: In about 1810 Wilson found a nest of this species on 20 May in the Cape May, New Jersey, marshes. He noted its behavior, described the nest and eggs, and stated that avocets arrived in Cape May in late April and departed in early October (Wilson and Bonaparte 1859–60). Apparently, Wilson's is the only known early East Coast nest record. Delaware is not mentioned in any of the early accounts, but the species probably occurred here. Palmer (1967) states that "In former times of unrestricted gunning the Avocet, like the Stilt, was eliminated from its easterly breeding range (bred locally north to Long Island). Maybe the Avocet will reoccupy part of this area, as summering nonbreeders now are regular in small numbers in s. New Jersey." This hope is beginning to be realized. DuMont (1957), stimulated by observing 17 birds at Brigantine NWR, New Jersey, summarized the approximately 20 available records from East Coast national wildlife refuges. The earliest known Delaware record derives from 3 birds collected (specimens not extant) at Fowler Beach on 5 October 1933 by Buckalew [Buck3]. Herholdt reported 2 avocets on 24 September 1937 and 1 on 16 October 1939 at Bombay Hook NWR [Herh3]. One or 2 birds were present during the fall of 1947 [m.ob5; BarI1]. Since 1949 it has been recorded almost annually. All reports through 1960 were from the fall. Spring records occurred in 1961, when the first April and May sighting was made [Holg66], and in 1964, when the first June record was established [Lawr5]. Winter records began to occur in 1965 with the first December records on the 15th (Holgersen 1972) and 25th [MurF1]. It was not until 1963 that the species was regularly recorded in numbers greater than 10.

Avocets first began to breed in the East again in North Carolina in 1968 (AOU 1983) and first bred in Virginia in 1991 (Armistead 1991). Although no nest of this striking bird has been found in Delaware, eventually it may breed here.

SPRING: First arrival is about 20 February to 5 March, with these the earliest arrival dates:

18 Feb 1986	5	Bombay Hook NWR [Char1]
22 Feb 1971	1	Bombay Hook NWR [Hol109]
25 Feb 1974	3	Bombay Hook NWR [Wees1]

Numbers peak from 25–30 March to 20–30 April. High counts, all from Bombay Hook NWR, are 65 on 26 March 1982 [MiJC1], 110 on 4 April 1982 [Edni50], and 130 on 10 April 1982 [Kell1].

SUMMER: A few nonbreeding avocets are present throughout the summer.

FALL: Numbers are high from 12–20 July through 20–27 November. Sample high counts include

28 Jul 1979	132	Bombay Hook NWR [Lawr4]
24 Sep 1990	441	Bombay Hook NWR [Holg1]
3 Oct 1982	300	Little Creek WA [Batt1]
18 Oct 1981	394	Bombay Hook NWR [Kell7]

Generally most avocets leave by 1–7 December.

WINTER: Reports from the second week of December to early March are few. The few December records no doubt represent lingering fall migrants. The first avocet for the Wilmington CBC was found on 15 December 1990 near the Port of Wilmington [Whit1]. Two birds present at Bombay Hook NWR on 29 January 1969 probably represent a very late departure, because 17 were present there on 5 December 1968 [Holg36]. Similarly, several seen at the refuge on 14 January 1992 [Barn1] may be the same birds found on the 15 December 1991 Bombay Hook CBC. The late February records probably represent very early arrivals.

Greater Yellowlegs *(Tringa melanoleuca)*

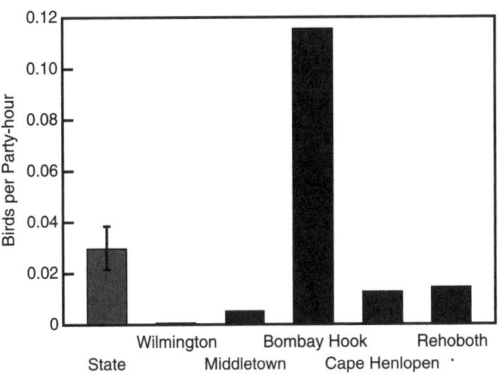

CBC Geographic Distribution

Regular; migrant; common to abundant. Expected mid-March through December, sporadically thereafter and uncommon in mid-summer. Winter numbers increasing.

HABITAT: Often found wading belly deep in shallow flats in marshes and impoundments.

SPRING: This is one of the earliest arriving shorebirds. The presence of a few wintering individuals makes it difficult to pinpoint the onset of migration, but these small flocks are probably the first migrants reported:

3 Mar 1929	4	Delaware City [Weyl1]
6 Mar 1982	4	Bombay Hook NWR [RusJ11]
6 Mar 1983	8	Bombay Hook NWR [SpSB13]

Usual arrival is about 10–15 March. Most birds leave by 25 May to 1 June. High counts include

21 Mar 1976	25	Bombay Hook NWR [Lehm19]
11 Apr 1992	455	Little Creek WA [Edni49]
24 Apr 1993	870	Little Creek WA [MurW2]
14 May 1926	200	Woodland Beach [Hans1]

SUMMER: A few nonbreeding birds usually remain between migrations—early June through early July. Example highs are 20 on 22 June 1986 at Bowers Beach [Lehm2] and 6 on 3 July 1986 at Prime Hook NWR [Frec1].

FALL: First arrival is 7–15 July. Most flocks leave 1–7 December. Typical high counts are

25 Jul 1964	400	Little Creek WA [StiA5]
8 Aug 1975	500	Bombay Hook NWR [DuPG5]
6 Sep 1970	725	Bombay Hook NWR [Carl15]
26 Sep 1982	505	Bombay Hook NWR [Wayn25]

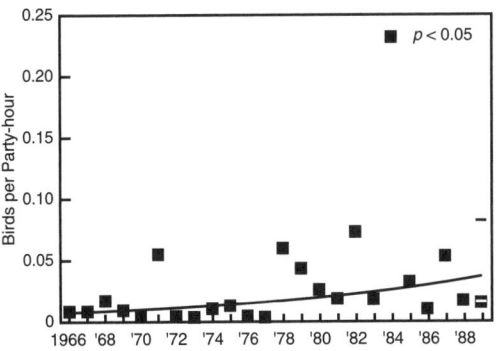

CBC Trend; Increasing at 7% per Year

1966–89 CBC Summary

Christmas Bird Count	Years Found	Range of No. Found	Median
Wilmington	1	1	
Middletown	2	1–7	
Bombay Hook	19	1–56	3
Cape Henlopen	7	1–5	
Rehoboth	14	1–5	1
STATEWIDE (increasing; high in 1984)	24	1–69	5

WINTER: In most years a few stay until the end of December; stragglers are rarely present from January to early March. The species has increased on CBCs at about 7% per year. It is most abundant on the Bombay Hook CBC.

SPECIMENS: 7; ANSP, DMNH, UDEL.

Lesser Yellowlegs (*Tringa flavipes*)

24 Jul 1966	1,500	Little Creek WA [RusW5]
8 Aug 1975	2,500	Bombay Hook NWR [DuPG5]
30 Aug 1985	1,000	Bombay Hook NWR [MiJC1]
14 Sep 1962	3,500	Little Creek WA [Less14]

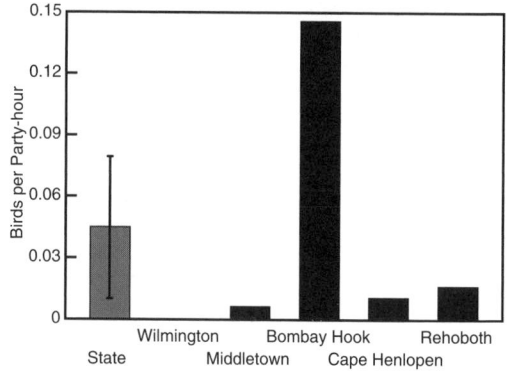

CBC Geographic Distribution; Average of 4 Count Areas

Regular; migrant; common to abundant. Expected mid-March through December, sporadically thereafter and in early summer.

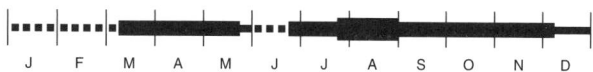

HABITAT: Shallow flats in marshes, impoundments, rain pools on farmland or meadows. Prefers areas more sheltered than those frequented by Greater Yellowlegs.

SPRING: The pattern is similar to that of Greater Yellowlegs. Small numbers of winter birds are joined in March by migrants; these are among the first:

11 Mar 1974	12	Bombay Hook NWR [Holg85]
12 Mar 1993	50	Bombay Hook NWR [Hess1]
14 Mar 1980	8	Red Mill Pond [Frec1]

Peak numbers occur during late April and early May, including

25 Apr 1971	250	Lewes area [Crea1]
2 May 1984	100	Sussex County coast [Frec1]
6 May 1984	200	Sussex County coast [Frec1]

Even higher numbers have been reported on the DNREC 1993 shorebird survey. Stone (1937) rarely noted this species in spring at Cape May, New Jersey. Claudia Wilds (1990) also reports this species rare in spring south of Delaware on the Delmarva Peninsula. The observations of spring birds in Delaware are significant and corroborate similar recent observations at Cape May (Sibley 1993).

SUMMER: A few nonbreeding birds usually remain between migrations—late May through late June.

FALL: This species peaks for a longer period (late July through September) than Greater Yellowlegs (August). Some high counts are

1966–89 CBC Summary

Christmas Bird Count	Years Found	Range of No. Found	Median
Wilmington			
Middletown	3	1–8	
Bombay Hook	22	1–81	3
Cape Henlopen	7	1–7	
Rehoboth	8	1–19	
STATEWIDE *(zero in 1989, high in 1984)*	23	1–86	5

WINTER: In most years a few birds stay to the end of December, showing a CBC pattern and abundance similar to the Greater Yellowlegs. Few are present from January to early March. No CBC trend is apparent, but numbers were much higher in 1984 and 1987 than in any of the other years during 1966–89. Like the Greater Yellowlegs, it is most often found on the Bombay Hook CBC.

SPECIMENS: 6; DMNH, USNM.

Solitary Sandpiper *(Tringa solitaria)*

Regular; migrant; uncommon. Expected late April through mid-May and early August to late September, rarely through June and July.

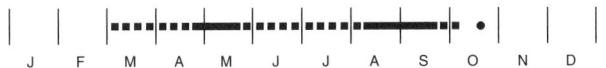

J F M A M J J A S O N D

HABITAT: Feeds along mud banks of freshwater streams, lakes, and pools.

SPRING: A few birds occur earlier in April, but the main migration is from about 25 April to 20 May. The earliest reports are

6 Apr 1986	1	west of Dover [Swer3]
11 Apr 1992	1	Bombay Hook NWR [DNRE2]
15 Apr 1978 and 1980	1	near Red Mill Pond [Frec1]

One extraordinary report mentions 150 in southern Delaware on 7 May 1983 [Cutl7]. Typical high counts are 8 on 11 May 1983, 12 on 17 May 1983, and 12 on 5 May 1984, all in the Lewes area [Frec1]. Usually no more than 6 are found at a time. The end of spring migration tapers off with only 3 reports in late May:

26 May 1986	2	Prime Hook NWR [Frec1]
30 May 1961	1	Little Creek WA (Lesser 1964)
31 May 1986	1	Woodland Beach WA [Frin1]

SUMMER: Records of June stragglers include

5 Jun 1971	2	Brandywine Creek SP [Wayn2]
7 Jun 1981	1	Bombay Hook NWR [Kell9]
16, 19 Jun 1986	1	near Dover [SpSB26]
25 Jun 1989	1	Prime Hook NWR [Frec1]

July has 19 records, typically single birds.

FALL: The main migration is from about 7 August through 20 September. Usually no more than 3 are found at a time, making the Solitary Sandpiper slightly less common than during spring. High counts are

29 Aug 1957	6	Bombay Hook NWR [anon6]
10 Sep 1989	8	Lewes [Frec1]
12 Sep 1982	6	Prime Hook NWR [Frec1]

Late reports include

2 Oct 1978	1	Assawoman WA [Frec1]
4 Oct 1991	1	White Clay Creek [MiDP1]
6, 16 Oct 1987	1	Prime Hook NWR [Frec1]

REMARKS: An 1880 specimen, Delaware's first record, was unknown to Pennock, so the Solitary Sandpiper was not included on early Delaware lists. Possibly the next reliable record of this species was made on 17 August 1937 at Bombay Hook NWR by Buckalew and Herholdt [Hans1]. It was included on Barry's (1939) list of birds of Delaware.

SPECIMENS: UDEL 240-68, Wilmington, Delamore Place, 27 April 1880; DMNH 705, Sussex Co., 25 May 1957.

Willet *(Catoptrophorus semipalmatus)*

Regular; summer resident and migrant; common and locally abundant along bayshores in Kent and Sussex counties. Expected early April to late September, sporadically into early winter. Reestablished as a breeding bird in Delaware after extirpation in the nineteenth century.

J F M A M J J A S O N D

HABITAT: Tidal saltmarsh, bay and ocean shores, mud flats, and sand bars. Reaches its ecological limit near Bombay Hook where the Delaware River salinity range is 5–10 ppt in times of high flow to 15–20 ppt in times of low flow (seawater is > 30

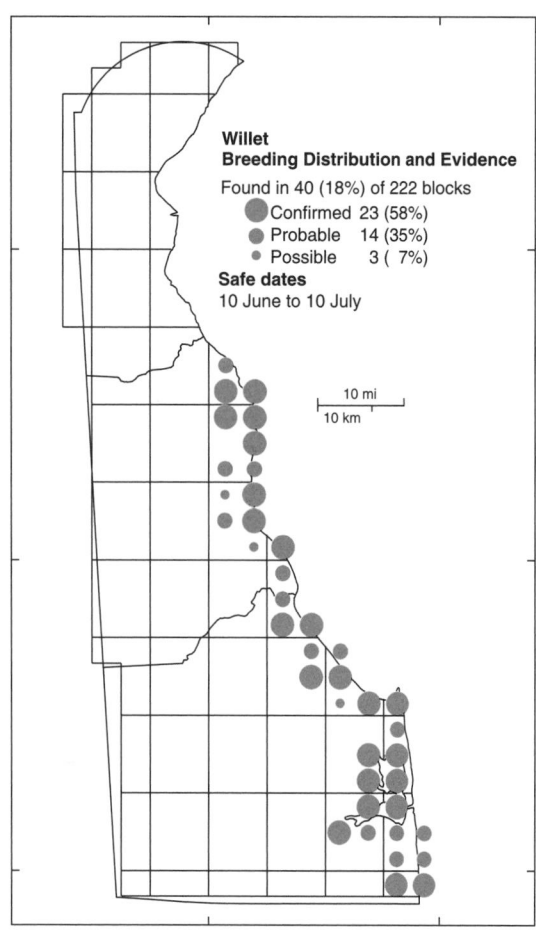

Willet
Breeding Distribution and Evidence

Found in 40 (18%) of 222 blocks

● Confirmed 23 (58%)
● Probable 14 (35%)
• Possible 3 (7%)

Safe dates
10 June to 10 July

10 mi
10 km

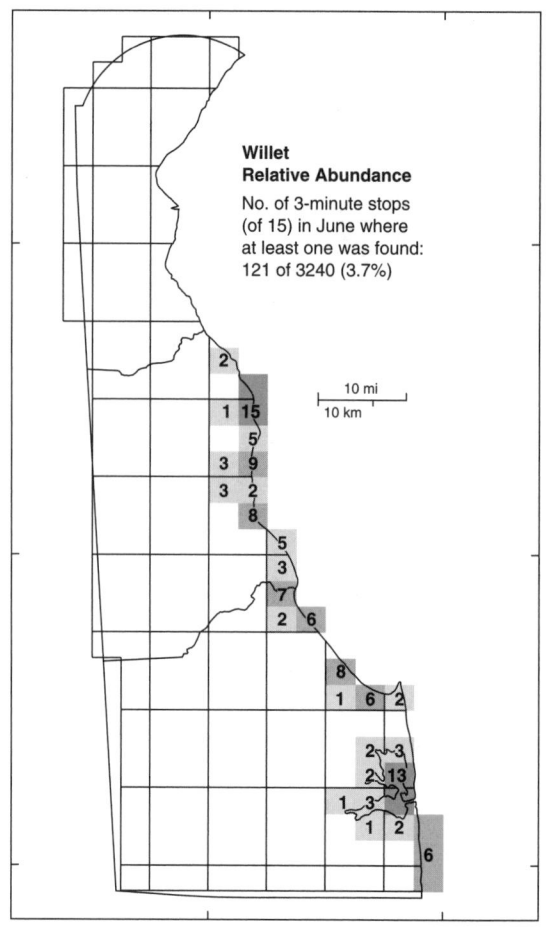

Willet
Relative Abundance

No. of 3-minute stops
(of 15) in June where
at least one was found:
121 of 3240 (3.7%)

10 mi
10 km

ppt). Typically nests in or along edges of saltmarshes vegetated with saltmarsh cordgrass or salt meadow cordgrass.

SPRING: Migration usually begins 1–7 April, but the earliest arrivals are

9 Mar 1988	1	Great Marsh, Lewes [DNRE1]
16 Mar 1990	1	Bombay Hook NWR [Wayn64]
20 Mar 1983	1	Bombay Hook NWR [Hess2]

Peak numbers are present from mid-April through early July. Typical high numbers during migration are

11 Apr 1959	255	Assawoman WA [Dyke2]
2 May 1985	200	Rehoboth Beach [Frec1]
23, 30 May 1986	350	Bombay Hook NWR (Thomas 1986)

BREEDING: Although the Willet is our most obvious shore-bird in the tidal saltmarshes south from Bombay Hook NWR, no records exist for sites north from Woodland Beach WA.

Atlas. This noisy species was easily found in saltmarshes and common enough that 16 of 22 confirmations resulted from finding the nest. One confirmation stemmed from a distraction display; young were reported 5 times.

Nesting. The nest is usually a distinct cup of grasses placed on the ground in vegetation in a dry place of an otherwise wet marsh. Spoil piles in a ditched marsh were selectively used for nest sites in 1 New Jersey area because they provided a drier

location (Burger and Shisler 1978). In Delaware many nest on marsh islands along Delaware Bay and in the Inland Bays. A few nest among grasses in dunes (Rothstein, DNHI, pers. comm.).

Estimated clutch-completion dates range from 26 April to 27 June; 80% are from 11 May to 10 June. Extreme egg dates are 7 May [Nile2] and 1 July [SpSB2]; earliest date for young is 31 May [Rals3]. Delaware's median clutch-completion date is 23 May, 18 days later than that calculated from Tompkins' data for northern Georgia, and 6 days later than that from Howe's data for Wallops Island, Virginia. Of 59 clutches, 47 had 4 eggs, and 12 had 3 (some of which may not have been complete). An adult was flushed from a clutch of 2 on 1 July [SpSB2]—not counted in the preceding data.

History. Wilson (1808–14) said it bred in great numbers in New York, New Jersey, Delaware, and Maryland. It formerly nested along the East Coast north to Nova Scotia. Hunting and egging pressure divided the population, leaving one in Nova Scotia and another extending north to New Jersey (Peterson 1988c). After 1889 and until recently nesting records in New Jersey were only along Delaware Bay. During that time it was scarce in Delaware as well. Bush (notes) found a few Willets at Indian River on 27 August 1880, but the species was not listed by Rhoads and Pennock (1905). It was first noted near

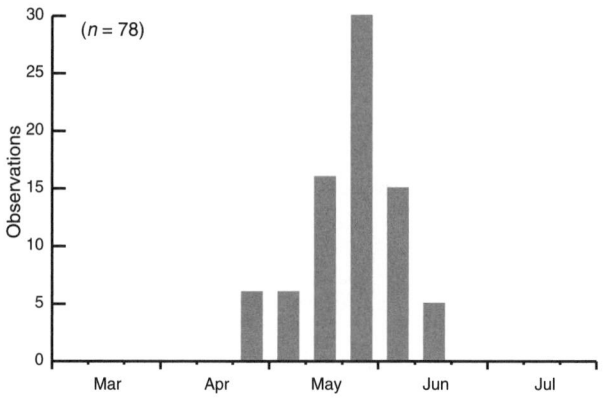

Estimated Clutch-Completion Dates

Rehoboth Beach on 7 September 1928 and at Indian River Inlet on 17 and 18 August 1934 [Hans1]. Pennock (1935) listed it as casual at Rehoboth Beach. These fall records may represent fall migrants of the western population, some of which migrate south along the East Coast and which were seen even at the low point of the eastern population. Urner recorded its date of principal migration on the New Jersey coast (1928–37) as 2 August to 8 September (Urner and Storer 1949). A Willet collected at Cedar Beach on 13 May 1934 (USNM 421816) is the first indication of its return to Delaware in the breeding season (if it was ever fully extirpated). Willets were rediscovered breeding in the Kent County marshes on 1 June 1937. Herholdt reported the species was common on the marshes there, and the next year Buckalew found several nests, including 1 clutch of eggs he collected and brought to Hanson (notes). It had similarly been rediscovered breeding across the Delaware River at Fortesque in 1930 where, in 1932, an old resident said it had been there as long as he could remember (Stone 1937).

Trends. The May Count results for 1969–91 show that this species has increased an average of 4% per year. The count is taken during the late part of the migration (first half of May), so the observed increase may reflect changes outside of Delaware.

Breeding population. Estimation of Willet numbers in Delaware is difficult, and East Coast density estimates have varied from a guess of about 0.01 per ha averaged over all the saltmarshes of Georgia (Tompkins 1965) to 1 nest per ha in a New Jersey study site (Burger and Shisler 1978) to 5–25 nests per ha in a site picked for study at the southern end of Wallops Island, Virginia (Howe 1982). The cause of this variation is the tendency of Willets to breed semicolonially in suitable habitat. An estimate for Delaware, based on its presence in 40 Atlas blocks and Tompkins' guess of 0.01 per ha (2–3 pairs per square mi, i.e., about 25 pairs per block), is about 300–3,000 pairs. A similar estimate could be justified based on its being recorded at 121 stops of the relative abundance study. These estimates are conservative and based on land surveys. Fintel (1985), in summing up 4 years of boat surveys, said that probably more than

200 pairs bred in Rehoboth Bay marshes. This area lies in four 10-sq-mi (25-sq-km) Atlas blocks, so the breeding density averaged more than 50 pairs per block. Howe's 105-ha study site on Wallops Island averaged 79 nests and may be similar to parts of the Rehoboth Bay marshes.

FALL: By 25–30 September most Willets have left; a few sometimes linger to early winter. The late fall and winter birds are likely to be from the western population, since adults of the breeding population begin migration in midsummer.

WINTER: Willets disappear before year-end, with these last reports:

19 Dec 1982	1	Bombay Hook CBC
23 Dec 1979	2	Bombay Hook CBC
4, 10, 24 Dec 1983	1 (2 on 24th)	Bombay Hook NWR [Barn1; Batt5]

One (or 2?), reported "at Bombay Hook to at least Feb. 6 was the first attempt to overwinter since 1976" (Boyle et al. 1983), represents our only midwinter record [Fogl3].

REMARKS: There are two populations of Willets. The western population *(C. s. inornatus)* breeds inland in the prairies and migrates in the fall partly via the East Coast to its more southern maritime wintering range. Our breeding population *(C. s. semipalmatus)* is confined to the Atlantic and Gulf saltmarshes.

SPECIMENS: 11; DMNH, USNM.

Spotted Sandpiper (*Actitis macularia*)

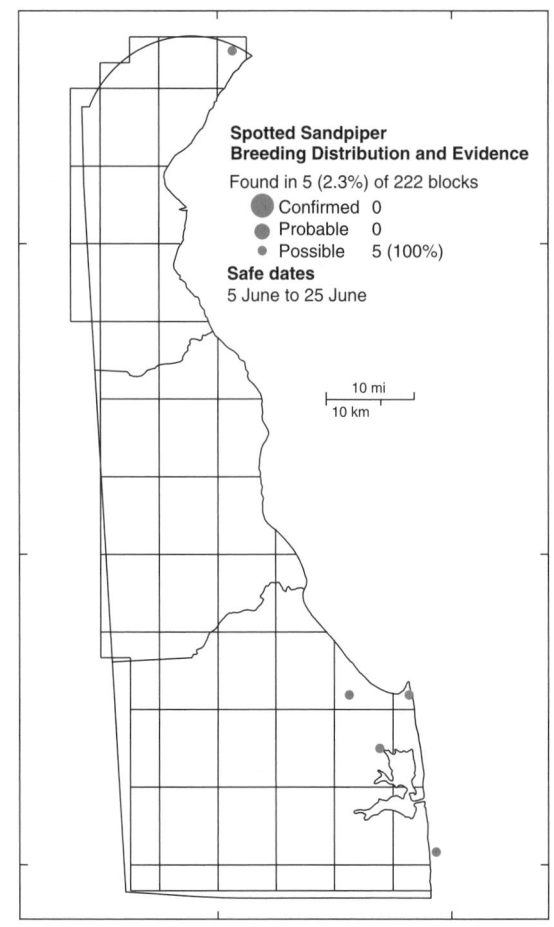

Spotted Sandpiper
Breeding Distribution and Evidence
Found in 5 (2.3%) of 222 blocks
- Confirmed 0
- Probable 0
- Possible 5 (100%)
Safe dates
5 June to 25 June

10 mi
10 km

Regular; migrant; uncommon. Expected late April to mid-September, with few during June. Possibly still a rare breeding species.

HABITAT: Shallow-water shorelines along streams, ponds, impoundments. Breeds in sheltered grassy areas usually near water. Occurred as a breeder in a brickyard by the Christina River.

SPRING: First arrival is 20–27 April. Peak migration occurs throughout May. Earlier arrivals include

7 Apr 1974	1	Dragon Run [BroW7]
11 Apr 1978	1	Prime Hook NWR (notes)
13 Apr 1980	1	Rehoboth Beach [Frec1]

Some high counts include

7 May 1983	23	Bombay Hook NWR [Patt7]
12 May 1968	30	Little Creek WA [DuPA3]
22 May 1983	26	Bombay Hook NWR [Bayn1]

The annual statewide May survey reports about 68 per year, including a high of 184 on 5 May 1984 (Rufe 1987).

BREEDING: The few summer records represent mainly migrants or nonbreeding birds. In 1990–91 breeding evidence was observed in the Brandywine, White Clay, and Red Clay creek valleys; in 1 instance a pair was seen from a boat at the confluence of Red Clay and White Clay creeks on 28 June 1991, apparently with a nest beside a stump—contents not seen (Rothstein, DNHI, pers. comm.).

Atlas. During the Atlas period downy young were observed on 2 July 1983 in the Claymont SW block on the New Jersey bank of the Delaware River [Frey1]; this nearby record was not counted for the Delaware Atlas even though part of the block lies in Delaware. The lower Delaware observations most likely represent nonbreeding birds. The brief range of safe dates eliminated most observations from consideration, but there

may be no truly safe dates, because northward migration is protracted in some years. For example, during the 1992 DNREC shorebird survey all Spotted Sandpipers seen were before 27 May except for 4 on 2 June. In contrast, 13 were seen after 28 May 1993, including 5 in the second week of June during the 1993 shorebird survey. At Chincoteague NWR, where Spotteds do not breed, they have been recorded in the second and third weeks of June (Wilds 1990).

Nesting. Since Spotted Sandpipers may once again breed in Delaware, it seems advisable to present the following nest information from general works. "Nest usually among grasses, sometimes under bush or log. Sometimes several nests on a small islet if ground cover suitably low. Nest is a mere depression in ground litter with almost nothing added, or a thin but definite cup of grasses or weeds. Often remote from water" (Palmer 1967). "Rarely found near the ocean. . . . This is certainly the most widespread and probably most abundant North American scolopacid, and it is thus not of concern from a conservation standpoint" (Johnsgard 1981).

History. Our most definite nesting record is also our earliest record for this species. Bush recorded in his collecting notebook that he cornered 2 downy young, about a week or 10 days old, on 22 June 1880 (specimens at DMNH). Dyke, in response to a request for breeding records, wrote that he had found nests and young in Assawoman WA but gave no dates [Dyke13]. This latter report fits well with others obtained earlier in the twentieth century. Stewart and Robbins (1958) write that it was a fairly common breeding bird in the tidewater areas of the eastern shore section of Maryland and uncommon elsewhere. They cite a nearby Worcester County, Maryland, record of downy young 9 July 1949. Likewise, Stone (1937) describes the Spotted Sandpiper as "the most generally distributed breeding shore bird of Cape May" with the exception of Killdeer. He goes on to describe nests in the sand hills and flats immediately back of the dunes where a scant growth of dune grass offers them sufficient cover.

In Delaware, authors from Rhoads and Pennock (1905) to Barry (1942) and Peterson (1980, range map) list this species as a summer resident. Linehan (1967) was the first to point out the lack of a nest record. Certainly Hanson, who was collecting nests in the 1930s of every breeding species in Delaware, was looking for it, but he was unable to find any during his 13 years of active collecting.

Robbins (1996) lists 10 blocks with probable breeding evidence on the Delmarva Peninsula, but only 1 confirmed breeding. In Virginia there have been no Coastal Plain breeding records for at least the last 50 years (Kain 1987; Ridd 1989).

Conservation. Special conservation attention should be given to this species as a potential Delaware breeding bird.

FALL: The migration period is from 5–10 July to 15–20 September and tends to overlap with the breeding period. Early records include

26 Jun 1965	3	Churchmans Marsh [WarM4]
26 Jun 1984	1	southwest of Porter, New Castle County [West5]
27 Jun 1964	4	Little Creek WA [Line12]
1 Jul 1989	1	Prime Hook NWR [Frec1]

The late records are

17 Oct 1987	1	Gravel Hill, Sussex County [Frec1]
18 Oct 1971	"last"	Prime Hook NWR [Holg68]
26 Oct 1981	1	Roosevelt Inlet, Lewes [Frec1]

A late November 1974 [Guar1] report lacks the documentation needed to support a late date.

SPECIMENS: DMNH mount, Wilmington, Delamore Place, 27 April 1880; USNM 422270, Sussex Co., Oyster Rocks Road, 22 May 1948; DMNH 75611, 0.6 mi (1 km) N Kitts Hummock, 2 August 1984; DMNH 76205, and DMNH 76206, 0.3 mi (0.5 km) N of Pickering Beach, 28 August 1985.

Upland Sandpiper *(Bartramia longicauda)*

Regular; rare spring migrant; fairly common to common summer visitor and fall migrant. Expected mid-April to mid-May and, more commonly, late June to early September. Occasionally breeds.

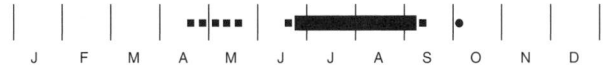

J F M A M J J A S O N D

HABITAT: Short grasslands such as airports, sod farms, pastures. The horse pastures of western Kent County appear ideal for this species, but they do not support it, Killdeer, or Eastern Meadowlark, presumably because sufficient food is lacking.

SPRING: Small numbers (1–3) are sometimes reported during April and May. The earliest reports are

5 Apr 1959	1	Augustine Beach [HurB1]
8 Apr 1991	1	Greater Wilmington Airport (Campbell 1992)
16 Apr 1970	1	Bombay Hook NWR [Abbo11]

Upland Sandpipers have been reported on only 3 May Counts (1969–92).

BREEDING: The best places in Delaware to look for breeders and migrants of this species are airports, particularly the Wilmington Airport. The Dover Air Base and adjacent fields near Bombay Hook NWR are also good places to monitor.

Atlas. Upland Sandpipers were first reported at the Wilmington Airport on 6 August 1972 [Conw8]. In 1986 Falk began studying the population there, noting the first arrival of 29 on 15 July. Continuing this study in 1987, he found that 22 were already present on 26 June when he made his first visit. He found an adult shepherding 2 half-sized, clear-breasted young on his fifth visit on 1 July. This breeding report is the first for the state and the only Atlas report (Falk 1988).

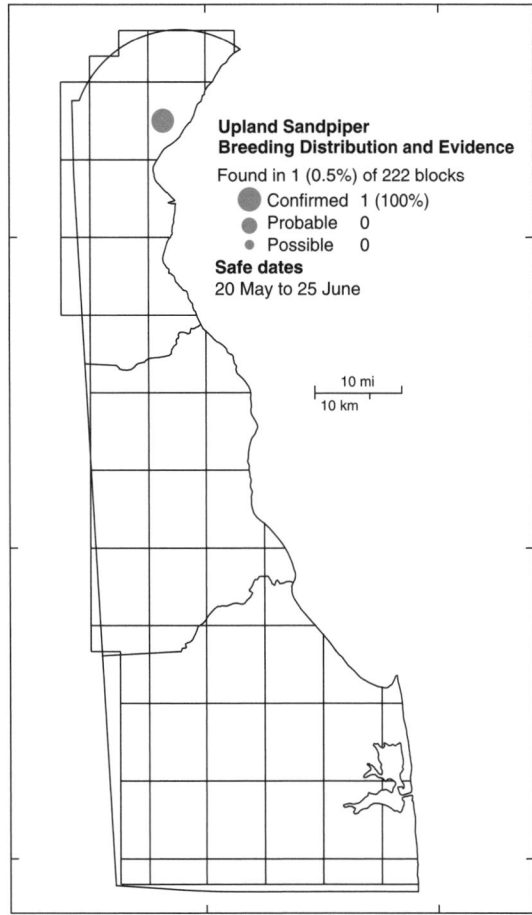

Upland Sandpiper
Breeding Distribution and Evidence

Found in 1 (0.5%) of 222 blocks

● Confirmed 1 (100%)
● Probable 0
● Possible 0

Safe dates
20 May to 25 June

10 mi
10 km

In 1988 and again in 1989, this species did not appear until July. Even with the late June records of 1987, there is no published report of Upland Sandpipers falling between 17 May and 18 June.

In 1992 a nest with eggs was located in Sussex County (R. Keene and D. Rothstein, DNHI, pers. comm.), and an adult with young was found in eastern Kent County (D. Rothstein, DNHI, pers. comm.).

Nesting. The nest is usually well hidden, frequently by vegetation that overhangs and hides it from above (Johnsgard 1981). It is placed in a shallow depression 4–5 inches in diameter and nearly 3 inches deep, and lined with small bits of dried grass. Clutch size is usually 4 eggs. Egg dates for Pennsylvania and New Jersey are 6 May to 11 June (*n* = 15) (Bent 1929).

History. "Formerly its summer domain was short prairie and muskeg country, but it extended its range in eastern North America with the transition of the landscape from forest to agriculture. Soon afterward, in the 1880s and early 1890s, perhaps in part for lack of Passenger Pigeons to shoot, market hunters depleted its numbers severely. Confronted thereafter with unfavorable agricultural practices such as mowing, and grazing of livestock, as well as continued shooting on winter range, this handsome sandpiper became very scarce. It has nev-

er regained its former numbers. It shows some signs now of at least tolerating technological culture, occurring in season on various airports along with Killdeer and Horned Lark" (Palmer 1967). Since Palmer made these comments, the Upland Sandpiper's breeding range in the Northeast and in our immediate region has continued to shrink (Boyle et al. 1980).

Starting with the first list in 1905 (Rhoads and Pennock), the Upland Sandpiper has been listed as a summer resident in Delaware, but translating that status into breeding status has been difficult because spring and fall migrations occur so close together. Linehan properly left it off his list of Delaware breeding birds (1967) because no breeding records were available.

Conservation. From 24 June to 3 July 1991 Upland Sandpipers were reported as very early migrants at Queen Anne, Easton, and Pocomoke City, Maryland, all on the Delmarva Peninsula (Armistead 1991). These reports, along with the Delaware breeding records, suggest a small breeding population on the peninsula. Its protection should be a matter of priority, since this species is listed as Endangered in 6 northeastern states, including Maryland and New Jersey, and as Threatened in 3 others (Carter 1992). The establishment of mowing regimes that will allow successful breeding at airports is particularly important.

FALL: Southward migration begins about 1 July, with occasional (nonbreeding?) birds reported earlier. Most individuals depart by 5–10 September. The best place to see Upland Sandpipers in recent years has been the Wilmington Airport where totals of 68 and 67 were found on 23 August 1967 and 18 July 1968, respectively (Falk 1988). Late records include

12 Sep 1979	2	Rt. 9, Kent County [Conw9]
12 Sep 1985	1	near Red Mill Pond [Frec1]
2 Oct 1979	6	Centerville [RusR8]

SPECIMEN: ANSP 66236 (no location given), 14 August 1898.

[Eskimo Curlew (*Numenius borealis*)]

Gregory A. Inskip

Formerly present in the region; no Delaware records.

REMARKS: This nearly extinct curlew probably occurred on occasion as a fall transient in Delaware. In the fall it usually migrated offshore from Labrador to South America. Some were blown back to land by gales, and there may have been a minor route from Hudson's Bay across the Great Lakes to the Atlantic Coast (Bent 1929, 132). The Eskimo Curlew returned north in the spring through the prairies west of the Mississippi River (Bent 1929, 127). Turnbull (1869, 33) said that it was "rather rare" on the New Jersey coast, "appearing in May, and again in September." Overshooting brought it to the brink of extinction by the beginning of the twentieth century (Bent 1929, 127). Weston and Williams (1965) noted 5 Atlantic coast records since 1929 from Long Island to South Carolina. One bird, probably an Eskimo Curlew, was seen at Cape May, New Jersey, on 20 September 1959 by Lovett E. Williams, Jr.

Whimbrel (*Numenius phaeopus*)

Regular; migrant; uncommon to fairly common; expected mid-April through May and mid-July to mid-October.

HABITAT: Saltmarsh with short vegetation, beaches, and mud flats. Tends to follow the tideline rather than wading. Often concentrates in areas with large numbers of fiddler crabs.

SPRING: First arrival is 10–15 April, with birds present through the end of May. First flocks are

| 13 Apr 1982 | 5 | Oyster Rocks Rd., Sussex Co. [Frec1] |
| 14 Apr 1980 | 14 | Rehoboth Beach [Frec28] |

The only report before this period describes 1 at Little Creek WA improbably early in March 1978 (Barnhill 1979). Typical counts report up to 6 birds. High counts are

22 Apr 1966	25	Bethany Beach [Armi3]
23 May 1968	38	Bombay Hook NWR [Holg32]
25 May 1970	32	Bombay Hook NWR [Holg38]

Urner and Storer (1949) note that the Whimbrel was increasing in numbers (maximum = 500 in 1935 and 1938) in New Jersey. Cook (1946) notes at Brigantine NWR that up to about 1,000 birds used the refuge in 1942, 600 in 1943, and 3,000 in 1945; at Chincoteague NWR an estimated 500 went through during April 1945. Unfortunately, Delaware lacks records from the same period; thus we cannot determine whether numbers have declined or if Delaware's low numbers result from the state's lying at the edge of the Whimbrel's migration route.

SUMMER: No records of summering are known.

FALL: Although the fall migration is shown as being continuous at a low level, the available records suggest it may be bimodal and essentially discontinuous. Whimbrels first occur during July followed by few reports in August and early September (34 records from 8 July to 1 September). The second, smaller, influx is during mid-September to late October (17 records from 17 September to 25 October). There are no records 2–16 September. Wilds (1990) comments that at Chincoteague southbound birds "begin to arrive the first week of July and are most common the second half of the month. Numbers decline steadily in August and September; October sightings are rare."

A remarkable 200 were recorded on 27 July 1958 on Fenwick Island [anon7]. Other high counts are

12 Jul 1959	76	Fenwick Island [anon8]
19 Jul 1987	25	Cape Henlopen SP [Frec1]
20 Jul 1975	14	along the coast [Barn30]

All other reports are of fewer than 10 birds.

Cook (1946) noted a daily maximum of 1,500 and an estimated seasonal total of 5,000 at Brigantine in 1943 and an estimated total of 5,500 in 1944. Whimbrels migrate from their "James Bay [breeding] area southeast toward the Atlantic Coast and make [an] overseas flight to South America. A few stop on the Atlantic coast" (Palmer 1967). Only a very few stop in Delaware compared to the numbers stopping in the more exposed marshes of New Jersey and the southern Delmarva peninsula.

WINTER: An individual of the "European race" was discovered at Holts Landing SP on the 22 December 1984 Rehoboth CBC [Phal8], and "exceptional field notes" were provided (Ringler and Wilds 1985). It was present through 6 January 1985 [Frec13].

SPECIMEN: DMNH 40021, 7 mi (11 km) S Dewey Beach, 16 April 1974.

[Long-billed Curlew *(Numenius americanus)*]

Gregory A. Inskip

Formerly common in the region; no Delaware records.

REMARKS: The Long-billed Curlew was a common transient visitor to the New Jersey saltmarshes in May and September in Wilson's time and until the mid-nineteenth century, when it was extirpated from the region by gunners (Stone 1937, 1:414–15; Turnbull 1869, 32; Wilson and Bonaparte 1859–60, 2:320). It probably occurred in Delaware in the same months. Without providing documentation, Buckalew reported 1 at Rehoboth Beach in April 1929 [Buck3].

Black-tailed Godwit *(Limosa limosa)*

Accidental (1994).

DOCUMENTATION: Photograph (D. Gardner DMNH 468).

REMARKS: A bird of this species in full alternate plumage was seen at Prime Hook NWR from 6 to 15 June 1994 [Frech, NASFN 48:928]. We have notes by Campbell and definitive photographs by Gardner on this individual. According to Paxton et al. (NASFN 48:928) this record is the third "fully confirmed" record for the Hudson–Delaware region. That same season there were 2 records outside the region. A Black-tailed Godwit seen at Wellfleet Bay Wildlife Sanctuary in Massachusetts on 1 June (NASFN 48:925) and another seen on Pea Island, North Carolina, from 23 to 31 July (NASFN 48:935) seem likely to be the same individual in view of the general rarity of the species. In particular, the North Carolina bird was "rapidly changing into basic plumage," consistent with the Delaware bird having been in alternate plumage a month earlier. If these 3 records are all of the same bird, the discovery of the bird at 3 widely separated locations is a clear indication of the density of bird-watchers along the Atlantic coast. The photographs clearly establish the presence of the bird in Delaware.

There is also a 1987 sight report (Paxton et al. 1988) of a bird that was not found again after being seen by the first observers.

Hudsonian Godwit (*Limosa haemastica*)

Regular; migrant; uncommon to fairly common; expected early August to late October, sporadically in July and November.

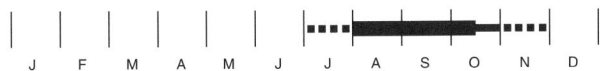

J F M A M J J A S O N D

DOCUMENTATION: Multiple sight records.

HABITAT: Intertidal mud flats, impoundments, beaches, saltmarsh margins.

SPRING: The northward migration passes primarily through the Great Plains. The only spring report is of 3 birds at Little Creek WA in May 1974 (Scott and Cutler 1974b) and lacks the documentation needed to support such an unusual date.

FALL: Usual first arrival is 1–5 August, and migration continues through 25–30 October.

Earliest arrivals are

3-5 Jul 1988	1	Broadkill Beach [Frec1]
13 Jul 1991	1	Bombay Hook NWR (Campbell 1992)
17 Jul 1971	1	Bombay Hook NWR [Carl2]

Late reports, all from Bombay Hook NWR are

18 Nov 1990	1	[HilA1]
21 Nov 1969	1	[Holg43]
28 Nov 1986	1	[Wees7]

Counts of 8–10 are not unusual. High counts are

26 Aug 1983	55	Lewes ferry [WarD8]
30 Sep 1975	22	Dover Air Force Base [WarD3]
18 Oct 1964	32	Bombay Hook NWR [Lake6]

Marbled Godwit (*Limosa fedoa*)

Regular; migrant; uncommon; very rare in spring, expected early August to late September, sporadically to mid-November.

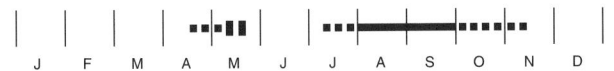

J F M A M J J A S O N D

HABITAT: Intertidal mud flats, impoundments, beaches, saltmarsh margins.

SPRING: The only 4 records, all lacking documentation, follow

23 Apr 1987	2	Great Marsh, Lewes [DNREC,unpub.]
30 Apr 1971	1	Port Mahon [Hann1]
13 May 1988	4	Bombay Hook NWR [Shoc2]
2 May 1985	40	Little Creek WA [Edni7]

These records are noteworthy because in North America this species migrates primarily through the western interior and along the California coast and occurs only casually in the fall along the Atlantic coast (AOU 1983). Urner and Storer (1949) lack spring records in New Jersey. Stewart and Robbins (1958) note that it is casual in spring and cite 3 reports, 2 from the Ocean City, Maryland, area. Given its scarcity in spring, all such reports should be documented.

SUMMER: No records of summering are known.

FALL: First arrival is 1–5 August; migration continues through 15–20 November, with no distinct peaks. Earliest arrivals are

15 Jul 1987	1	Bombay Hook NWR [Holg1]
31 Jul 1974	1	Thousand Acre Marsh, Delaware City [Lehm1]

Late departures, all from Bombay Hook NWR, are

11 Nov 1986   1   [Wees1]
21 Nov 1988   1   [Holg87]
27 Nov 1990   1   [Hol105]

Usually only single birds occur. The highest count involves 5 near Smyrna on 2 September 1971 [Holg63]. Urner and Storer (1949) give 15 August and 9 January as extreme dates for New Jersey.

SPECIMEN: USNM 421888, Indian River Inlet, 21 September 1936.

Spring Shorebirds on Delaware Bay

Howard P. Brokaw

Delaware's share of the resident and migratory bird populations in its region is generally proportional to the small size of the state. In one aspect, however, Delaware, in company with New Jersey, has not only disproportionate importance for bird populations, it has truly international significance. The shores of Delaware Bay in late May and early June are host to huge concentrations of shorebirds. The bay is an essential refueling area—with no adequate alternatives—for several species of shorebirds that migrate from their wintering grounds in Latin America to their breeding grounds in the Arctic. For some species these concentrations represent substantial portions of their Western Hemisphere populations.

These shorebird species have evolved a pattern of living gauged to take advantage of the best of two hemispheres. They spend our winter in the warm climate of the Southern Hemisphere, and breed during our summer in the huge expanse of Arctic tundra, with its long days and heavy flush of insect prey. This pattern, however, requires extensive migratory flights and, along the migration routes, dependable feeding areas to build the fat that fuels those flights.

It turns out that such feeding areas are few and far between. The shorebirds that come to Delaware Bay in the spring typically fly here nonstop from the coast of Surinam or the Bay of Panama—flights of 2,000–3,000 miles at altitudes of 10,000 or more feet requiring three or four days. Once here, they must put on enough fat to power the next nonstop flight of 1,500–2,500 miles to the Arctic and arrive there at the right time with sufficient fat reserves for the early stages of breeding. There simply is no other area along the U. S. East Coast that could support such a task on the requisite schedule.

Delaware Bay can furnish that support because it is the breeding ground for by far the largest concentration of horseshoe crabs, *Limulus polyphemus,* along the Atlantic coast and because the peak of the crabs' spawning coincides with the precise timing needs of the shorebirds. For thousands of years, horseshoe crabs by the millions have deposited their tiny eggs by the billions on the beaches of Delaware Bay. The shorebirds, in turn, have gobbled up the eggs at a rate of as high as 9,000 per bird per day until in about a week and a half to three weeks their weight may increase by 70% or more, and they are fit to resume their journey. In total over the season the shorebirds consume hundreds of tons of eggs (Castro and Myers 1993).

The metabolizable energy of horseshoe crab eggs is low because of the resistance of the egg cuticle to digestion. That problem, however, is more than compensated for by the sheer abundance of the eggs and the rapidity with which they go through the bird's gut. For Sanderlings, less than one-third of the eggs eaten are digested, but the eggs pass through the bird's digestive system in about an hour (Castro et al. 1989).

As long ago as the beginning of the nineteenth century Alexander Wilson observed concentrations of Ruddy Turnstones feeding on horseshoe crab eggs in Delaware Bay in May (Wilson and Bonaparte 1859–60). But it was not until 1981 that an aerial survey, carried out by the Cape May Bird Observatory, began to reveal the true importance of the bay as a spring shorebird migration staging area—the largest one in eastern North America. The surveys continued with three flights in both 1982 and 1983. Then, from 1986 through 1995, in a cooperative program of the Delaware and New Jersey state wildlife divisions, four to six weekly flights per year (depending on the weather) have been made in May and early June covering both shores of the bay, and a continuance of these surveys is planned.

The height of the migration generally occurs between mid-May and early June, with a day's count sometimes reaching 200,000 or more birds, the numbers usually divided about equally between the Delaware and New Jersey shores. Moores Beach, Reeds Beach, and Villas are among the best sites in New Jersey. In Delaware the largest concentrations occur on the bayshore of Bombay Hook National Wildlife Refuge, on the beaches from Port Mahon to Kitts Hummock, at Bowers Beach and South Bowers, and near the mouth of the Mispillion River. Lesser numbers are present at Cape Henlopen.

Over 95% of the shorebirds in the flocks along the bayshore consists of four species—Semipalmated Sandpiper, Ruddy Turnstone, Red Knot, and Sanderling. May 27–28 has been the median peak date for Semipalmated Sandpiper and Ruddy Turnstone, May 24–25 for Red Knot and Sanderling. Smaller numbers of Dunlin and Short-billed Dowitcher and about a dozen other shorebird species are also present, and Laughing Gulls by the thousands likewise participate in the feast. The aerial surveys cannot cover the marshy ponds behind the bayshore. Semipalmated Sandpipers trade back and forth between the beach and the marsh, where they are sometimes present by the tens of thousands. The marshes also harbor substantial numbers of Dunlin and lesser numbers of dowitchers (Kathleen E. Clark, pers. comm.).

Over the period 1982–95 as many as 272,000 **Semipalmated Sandpipers** have been counted in one day on both shores of the bay, with the average high day in a year being 112,000. Since 1988, however, no day count has exceeded 100,000. The actual number moving through is somewhat larger than the high day count because of turnover during the migration period and because some birds are missed on the count, particularly those feeding in the marshes. Most of these birds winter on the mud flats of Surinam, although a few go as far as Peru and Brazil (Stein et al. 1988). They fly nonstop the 2,700 miles from Suriname to Delaware Bay—an astonishing overseas journey, against all the hazards of wind and weather, for a creature weighing about one ounce on arrival. The birds passing through Delaware Bay breed in the low Arctic of Canada from Victoria Island east to northern Labrador. Their return route in autumn lies east of the spring route, with the upper Bay of Fundy serving as a crucial staging area for the overwater flights to South America (Harrington and Morrison 1979).

The annual high day count on **Ruddy Turnstones** during the decade has averaged 70,000 (high of 108,000 in 1989), perhaps three-quarters of the eastern North American population (Harrington et al. 1989). These birds winter from South Carolina to southern South America, mostly on the Atlantic coast, and breed in the mid-Canadian Arctic. Although the frenzied activities of the multitudes of horseshoe crabs result in exposing most of the eggs eaten by the birds, the turnstones provide an additional foraging service for other species. They have the capability, with their sturdy bills, of digging holes in the sand to expose more of the buried crabs' eggs. Since their bills are short, however, they abandon the hole to longer-billed species before the supply from the hole is exhausted.

The principal wintering grounds of the **Red Knots** that migrate through Delaware Bay are in Tierra del Fuego and nearby areas of southern Argentina—10,000 miles from their breeding grounds. During March and April they move north in stages through Brazil, to arrive in May at Delaware Bay (Harrington 1986). It is estimated that about half of the Western Hemisphere Red Knot population passes through the estuary (Morrison and Harrington 1992). As many as 96,000 have been counted in one day on the shores of the bay, with the average high day during the survey period being 48,000. They breed on the central islands of the Canadian low Arctic.

Many of the **Sanderlings** that stage in Delaware Bay come from Brazil, with small numbers from the sandy coasts of Peru and Chile (Myers 1989). Some winter as close as Florida, and, in fact, a few Sanderlings, along with some Ruddy Turnstones, spend the winter at Delaware Bay. They breed in a narrow latitudinal range in the central Canadian high Arctic. In spring, Sanderlings are generally concentrated down toward the mouth of the bay. The maximum daily count, which was at 56,000 in 1982, has dropped steadily to a level of 10,000 in 1993, 1994, and 1995. This decline follows a substantial—perhaps 80%—decrease in East Coast Sanderling populations from 1972 to 1982 (Howe et al. 1989).

In the fall Delaware is not a major migration staging area. Several thousand shorebirds of a broad diversity use the estuary, including such species as American Golden-Plover and Hudsonian Godwit that are rare or absent in the spring. But the fecund horseshoe crabs are gone—there is no powerful attractant in the fall for the vast hordes of birds that visit in the spring.

Because of the key role played by shorebird staging and wintering sites, the Western Hemisphere Shorebird Reserve Network (subsequently renamed Wetlands for the Americas) with 13 countries now participating, was established in 1985 to give international recognition to critically important shorebird habitats and thus promote their conservation. In May 1986 Governors Castle and Kean of Delaware and New Jersey formally issued a joint proclamation dedicating the lower part of the Delaware estuary as the first Hemispheric Reserve in the network. This designation is a public, although not legally binding, commitment to manage the site so as to maintain its importance for migratory shorebirds. A Hemispheric Reserve must meet the criterion of harboring at least 500,000 shorebirds annually or at least 30% of a species' flyway population. With the support of many government agencies as well as private scientific and conservation organizations, 12 additional Hemispheric Reserves have since been established—six each in North America and South America.

A growing threat to shorebirds using Delaware Bay is now coming from human disturbance, which not only causes the birds to waste energy by flushing, but is also likely to displace them, temporarily or permanently, from their optimum feeding areas. Shorebirds are more prone to such displacement by occasional disturbance than are gulls or waterfowl (Burger 1986), and the presence of few birds or none at a site does not mean that larger numbers have not been previously displaced. At its worst, heavy or frequent human disturbance can make an otherwise high quality site unusable. The resultant energy cost to the birds can hinder or even prevent their meeting the tight breeding schedule imposed by the shortness of the Arctic summer. The most serious disturbance is caused by fast movement and noise—dogs, joggers, unattended children. Fishermen, who remain relatively still, and vehicles are less of a problem, but birders, particularly in groups, and even slow walkers often cause the birds to flush. It will probably become necessary to regulate human activity on beaches where there are high shorebird populations during the critical spring weeks; this should include devising means for people to view the birds without disturbing them.

There are other threats. Occupation or destruction of the marshes behind the bay eliminates places the birds require as alternate feeding areas or for roosting during high tides. Further, Delaware Bay is a major site of chemical manufacture and the largest oil transfer port-of-entry on the East Coast of the United States; a major spill of oil or other industrial chemicals during the migration period could be catastrophic for the birds.

More significant, probably, are threats to the horseshoe crab population, which would, perforce, threaten the birds. In the past, heavy harvesting appears to have reduced their populations. During the 1870s over 4 million crabs per year were consumed for fertilizer and animal feed. By the 1920s the annual consumption was down to about 1.5 million and by the 1950s to 100,000 (Shuster and Botton 1985). The population had then been recovering, but has recently been seriously threatened again by a resurgence of harvesting to satisfy a growing market for eel and conch bait. Stricter regulation is sorely needed for hand harvesting from the Delaware and New Jersey beaches and especially for the large numbers being dredged from the bay and from the ocean off the Middle-Atlantic States.

Of major importance for the crabs, however, is the effect of the interglacial rise in sea level relative to the land, which has occurred at a rate of nearly 5 in. per century for the last 2,000 years but has accelerated to 13 in. per century during the last 75 years (John C. Kraft, pers. comm.). In the geological past the barrier beaches and the marshes behind them have accommodated to the rise by migrating landward over the coastal plain—in the case of the Delmarva Peninsula for a distance of 100 miles during the past 14,000 years. If the expected rate of sea level rise continues, the Delaware shore will inexorably maintain its inland march during the geological future.

Recently, human settlement along the bayshore, with its buildings, roads, and boating facilities, has stimulated attempts to prevent this movement. The bayfront beaches are thin and narrow, a result of the limited supply of sand now flowing from the ocean beaches. Sand has been pumped from shoals in the bay to replenish Lewes, Broadkill, and Slaughter beaches, but increasing costs will eventually render this short-lived solution impractical.

Limited attempts have also been made to resist the rise by structural means. Changes in the conformation of beaches caused by jetties, riprap, and seawalls have rendered some stretches unsuitable for horseshoe crab spawning. Such construction is now regulated in both Delaware and New Jersey, but for the near future at least, pressure will continue for hardening the beaches to prevent damage to private property. In Japan one of the Indo-Pacific horseshoe crabs, *Tachypleus tridentatus,* has been reduced to an endangered species through destruction of spawning habitat by extensive diking and polder construction. It will take long-range thinking, accompanied, perhaps, by some innovative engineering, to prevent devastation of the Delaware Bay beaches and consequent loss of the shorebirds (Kraft 1988).

An even more serious threat, to the extent it occurs, would be global warming. This would pose at least two problems. First, because of its relatively greater effect at the higher latitudes, global warming could adversely affect the critical timing relationship between horseshoe crab egg laying and emergence of insects in the Arctic (Lester and Myers 1990). Secondly, any warming would contribute to the rate of sea level rise and thus to the destructive effect on the beaches of the interglacial rise.

Research has barely begun to uncover the salient factors affecting shorebird and horseshoe crab populations on the bayshore. Such research and the indicated conservation actions must be carried out if the bird populations are to survive the human development of the coast. The shorebird species that gather in the spring on Delaware Bay are not rare. Nevertheless they are threatened—by the rarity of their vital migratory refueling sites.

Ruddy Turnstone *(Arenaria interpres)*

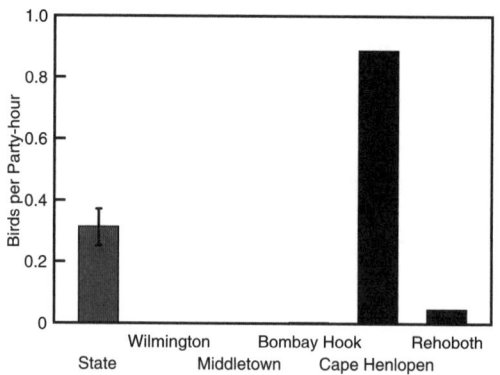

CBC Geographic Distribution; Average of 3 Count Areas

Occurs all year; common to abundant; most abundant mid-May to early June and early November to early December.

HABITAT: Beaches, jetties, tidal flats, and shorelines.

SPRING: During the peak migration period, 10 May–7 June, flocks of 2,000–7,600 are not unusual in any one location along Delaware's shoreline. Some high counts are

22 May 1985	6,000	Port Mahon [Edni1]
28 May 1987	7,590	Mispillion Inlet (Thomas 1987a)
3 Jun 1985	7,000	Cape Henlopen SP [Frec1]

These counts do not represent daily baywide totals, which are much higher and aggregate to an estimated 50% of the North American population (see "Spring Shorebirds" essay).

SUMMER: In some years a few nonbreeding individuals remain from mid-June until the first southbound migrants arrive in late July.

FALL: First arrival is 20–25 July; peak numbers occur from that period until 25–30 August and again from 15–20 October to 1–7 December. High counts are

3 Aug 1984	500	Pickering Beach [Edni19]
28 Aug 1985	150	Pickering Beach [Nile11]
17 Nov 1983	100	Cape Henlopen SP [Frec1]

WINTER: Counts during this period often total a few to a hundred or more birds. Few remain into late winter, but numbers increase as spring and the peak migration approach. No CBC trend is apparent. The Ruddy Turnstone is most often found on the Cape Henlopen CBC.

SPECIMENS: 8; DMNH, USNM.

1966–89 CBC Summary

Christmas Bird Count	Years Found	Range of No. Found	Median
Wilmington			
Middletown			
Bombay Hook	5	1–2	
Cape Henlopen	24	16–187	50
Rehoboth	20	1–22	3
STATEWIDE (low in 1981, high in 1970)	24	17–191	55

Red Knot *(Calidris canutus)*

J. Stark

Regular; migrant; common to very abundant; most abundant late May to early June and late July to mid-August; uncommon and sporadic into early winter.

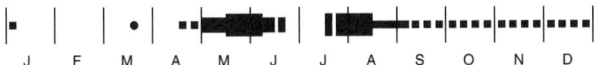

J F M A M J J A S O N D

HABITAT: Sand and mud flats, beaches.

SPRING: Red Knots arrive en masse 1–7 May, reach peak numbers during 20–30 May, and depart by 10–15 June. An unusually early arrival was 1 at Indian River Inlet on 16 March 1975 [Coop3], possibly the same individual present there on 4 and 5 January 1975 [Lehm25]. In a few years first arrival is in the last week of April, but typical examples follow:

3 May 1985	20	Cape Henlopen SP [Wayn2]
4 May 1986	146	Mispillion Light (Thomas 1986)
7 May 1983	100	Bay coast [Barn13]

Examples of high counts are

22 May 1985	8,000	Pickering Beach [Edni57]
24 May 1986	16,000	Mispillion Light (Thomas 1986)

These counts do not represent daily baywide totals, which are much higher (see "Spring Shorebirds" essay).

SUMMER: The only reports between 15 June and 20 July are 5 at Delaware Seashore SP, on 20 June 1981, 2 at Cape Henlopen SP on 20 June 1983 [Frec1], and 20 at Kitts Hummock on 17 July 1985 [Edni22].

FALL: Migration begins 20–25 July and peaks 1–15 August. In most years all depart by 1–5 September, but occasionally a few can be found until early January. One was banded at Little Creek WA on 21 September 1962 [Line5]. An unusual high count involves 1,000 at Pickering Beach on 3 August 1984 [Edni19], but there are few reports of fall migrants, perhaps because most observers are focusing on shorebirds in im-

poundments. A survey that includes the river and bay shore is needed. Examples of high counts are

27 Jul 1974	50	Port Mahon [Lehm32]
27 Jul 1958	30	Assawoman WA [anon7]
30 Oct 1985	100	Kitts Hummock [Wayn60]

REMARKS: Delaware Bay has been recognized as the second largest North American staging area for migrant shorebirds and the largest for Red Knots. The bay, with its spring abundance of horseshoe crab eggs, is a critical staging area for migrating knots. After flying from the coast of Brazil, they rest and feed along the bayshore, preparing for the last leg of their flight to their Arctic breeding range. About one-third to one-half of the North American population uses Delaware Bay in the course of migration (Harrington 1982, 1983). To a lesser extent, the bay is also a staging area during fall, when knots feed on various invertebrates found in the sand and mud. Harrington (1986) presents an excellent overview of Red Knot biology.

SPECIMENS: DMNH 76348, 0.5 mi (0.8 km) N Port Mahon, 5 September 1986; DMNH 76515, DMNH 76516, and DMNH 76546, 0.3 mi (0.5 km) N Pickering Beach, 5 September 1986; DMNH 18379, Kitts Hummock, 18 September 1923.

Sanderling *(Calidris alba)*

Occurs all year (except briefly in summer); common to abundant; spring migration apparently bimodal (March and May); fall migration prolonged, lasting mid-July to mid-December.

| | J | F | M | A | M | J | J | A | S | O | N | D |

HABITAT: Beaches.

SPRING: The spring migration appears to be bimodal. Migration is apparent by late February and peaks occur in March to early April and in late May to mid-June. The early peak may represent staging of birds that wintered along the coast south of Delaware Bay, whereas the later one may represent migration of birds wintering in South America. High counts in the first peak are

14 Mar 1980	300	Indian River Inlet [Frec1]
1 Apr 1982	500	Cape Henlopen SP [Frec1]
7 Apr 1981	200	Bombay Hook NWR [Haas1]

High counts during the second peak are

24 May 1986	2,631	Woodland Beach (Thomas 1986)
28 May 1987	9,310	Woodland Beach WA (Thomas 1987a)
31 May 1986	3,250	Broadkill Beach (Thomas 1986)
3 Jun 1984	2,500	Cape Henlopen SP [Frec1]

Last departures are

13 Jun 1980	50	Cape Henlopen SP [Frec1]
14 Jun 1986	6	Mispillion Light (Thomas 1986)
15 Jun 1982	1,000	Cape Henlopen SP [Frec1]

SUMMER: This species is rarely present mid-June through mid-July (7 reports between 15 June and 15 July) and is not expected to breed away from its high Arctic breeding range.

FALL: First arriving during 15–20 July, it remains common throughout the late summer and fall and does not become less common until 10–15 December. The following high counts were all obtained by Frech (notes) at Cape Henlopen SP: 750 on 7 August 1979; 1,000 on 31 August 1982; and 1,000 on 11 November 1982.

1966–89 CBC Summary

Christmas Bird Count	Years Found	Range of No. Found	Median
Wilmington			
Middletown	1	1	
Bombay Hook	20	1–350	8
Cape Henlopen	24	26–415	102
Rehoboth	24	21–435	173
STATEWIDE	24	84–696	379
(low in 1980, high in 1970)			

WINTER: Flocks of up to 100–200 birds can be seen along the beaches all winter. No CBC trend is apparent. The Sanderling is most often found on the Cape Henlopen and Rehoboth CBCs.

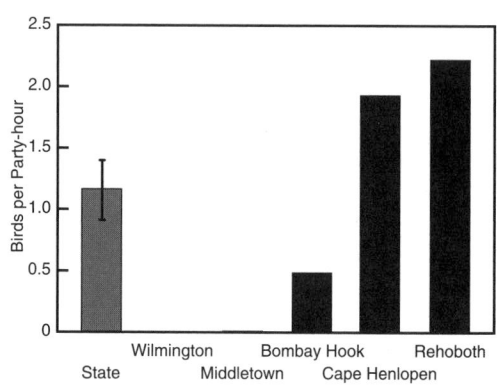

CBC Geographic Distribution; Average of 3 Count Areas

REMARKS: See "Spring Shorebirds" essay for comments regarding the drastic decline in numbers of this species.

SPECIMENS: 14; DMNH, ANSP, CM, USNM.

Semipalmated Sandpiper *(Calidris pusilla)*

Regular; migrant; common to very abundant; expected late April to mid-June and 15 July to October.

| J | F | M | A | M | J | J | A | S | O | N | D |

HABITAT: Wet mud flats on margins of ponds and estuaries; sandy beaches.

SPRING: First arrival is 20–30 April, with peak numbers occurring from 10 May to 5–10 June. Earliest arrivals are

13 Apr 1986	35	Prime Hook NWR [Frec1]
21 Apr 1988	8	Prime Hook NWR [Frec1]
21 Apr 1992	12	Thousand Acre Marsh [SpSB24]

Some high counts are

24 May 1964	75,000	Kitts Hummock [Less19]
19 May 1974	34,000	Little Creek WA [DuPG8]
22 May 1985	15,000	Pickering Beach [Edni57]

These counts do not represent baywide totals, which are much higher (see "Spring Shorebirds" essay).

SUMMER: Phillips (1975) reports that this species is "everywhere scarce or absent between June 9 and July 9, and especially in the period June 18–24 (excluding the highly unlikely reports of Williams, 1938)." However, we have over two dozen reports for 9 June to 9 July, with most numbering fewer than 100 birds. However, the lack of documentation for these reports, in conjunction with Phillips' review, suggests that verification is needed in the form of specimens, photographs, or detailed field notes.

FALL: The migration appears to be bimodal, with the first birds from the Arctic peaking in the last week of July. A second peak occurs during September. Examples of high counts are

27 Jul 1974	8,370	Port Mahon and Bombay Hook NWR [Lehm32]
30 Jul 1989	400	Prime Hook NWR [Frec1]
4 Aug 1974	16,000	Thousand Acre Marsh [Lehm1]
6 Sep 1981	2,020	Bombay Hook NWR [Bayn4]
13 Sep 1981	474	Bombay Hook NWR [Boll6]
23 Sep 1978	500	Assawoman WA [Frec1]

The latest known Delaware specimen is one collected at Indian River Inlet on 23 September 1948 (DMNH 52660). Although we present a seasonal bar graph implying the presence of Semipalmated Sandpipers to the end of October, reports, lacking details, after the first week of October should be considered to refer to unidentified species. Many November and all December reports are probably of Western Sandpipers. Urner and Storer (1949) list 13 July to 30 September as the principal migration period in New Jersey.

WINTER: Considering Phillips' (1975) review and the difficulty of separating Semipalmated and Western sandpipers in basic plumage, all previous December reports are considered likely to represent Western Sandpipers. No reports are available from January through March.

REMARKS: For a discussion of identifying Semipalmated and Western sandpipers see Veit and Jonsson (1984), Phillips (1975), Hayman, Marchant, and Prater (1986), and the references contained therein.

SPECIMENS: 30; DMNH, ANSP, CM, USNM.

Western Sandpiper *(Calidris mauri)*

Regular; migrant; fairly common to common; uncommon and sporadic in spring; expected late July through early winter.

J F M A M J J A S O N D

HABITAT: Mud flats, sandy beaches; typically feeds near or in water, both fresh and salt, rather than on exposed stretches of sand or mud flats.

SPRING: Although this species migrates in small numbers along the Atlantic coast (AOU 1983), its status at this season is poorly known in Delaware Bay. Some reports indicate it is fairly common or even abundant at this time, while others indicate the opposite. Data from elsewhere on the Delmarva Peninsula point to Westerns as rare from early May to mid-July (Wilds 1991). For this reason the bar graph shows the spring status at the lowest abundance level and is dashed to indicate its sporadic and unknown nature. This species occurs more frequently in the fall.

SUMMER: Western Sandpipers appear to be present sporadically in low numbers until the first southbound migrants arrive during mid- to late July.

FALL: The migration appears bimodal, with the first birds (adults, Palmer 1967) arriving between 15–20 July and early August. The second period is much later, October and early November. Examples of high counts are

19 Jul 1975	1,000	Port Mahon [Lehm16]
22 Jul 1990	2,000	Kitts Hummock [Czap2]
8 Aug 1975	2,100	Bombay Hook NWR [DuPG9]
6 Oct 1991	200	Bombay Hook NWR [Litt1]
24 Oct 1982	100	Bombay Hook NWR [SpSB13]

1966–89 CBC Summary

Christmas Bird Count	Years Found	Range of No. Found	Median
Wilmington			
Middletown	1	1	
Bombay Hook	19	1–93	3
Cape Henlopen	3	1–3	
Rehoboth	6	1–3	
STATEWIDE (high in 1974)	20	1–93	4

WINTER: The CBC tabulation is the combination of reports of Western Sandpipers from 28 counts, Semipalmated Sandpipers from 21 counts (see "Winter" account for Semipalmated Sandpiper), and "peep" (most likely Westerns) from 4 counts. In the East, Western Sandpipers winter mostly southward from North Carolina (AOU 1983), so few may be expected to winter along the Delaware Bay shore. From mid-November through most of January the Western Sandpiper may be present in small numbers; its winter status, however, is not clear.

SPECIMENS: 11; DMNH, CM.

Red-necked Stint *(Calidris ruficollis)*

Casual (5 years; 1984–92) in July.

DOCUMENTATION: Photographs (A. P. Ednie, DMNH 278, 279; C. P. Wilds, DMNH 396, 397).

REMARKS: The 4 or 5 Delaware records of Red-necked Stints all come from Little Creek WA and Bombay Hook NWR, and all occurred during late July. The first individual was studied from 22 to 24 July 1984 in the northern impoundment of Little Creek WA near Port Mahon [Coop2; notes from these observers and from Barn43]. In 1986 a Red-necked Stint was reported near the Little Creek WA tower from 25 to 29 July [Pede1]; what was probably a different bird was noted at Bombay Hook NWR on 26 July [Stoc1]. The following year a Red-necked Stint was seen by many observers from 17 to 21 July in Bombay Hook NWR [m.ob2]. Finally, a report with a definitive photograph comes from the Port Mahon impoundments on 29 July 1990 [Coop1] (photograph by R. Augustine at DMNH, print collection). In August 1992 1 was reported as "well described" [Dode1] and 2 unconfirmed reports were submitted in May 1993.

The photographs and multiple records with available descriptions suffice to establish the occurrence of the species in the state.

Its preferred habitat in Delaware is wet, but drying mud in the Little Creek WA impoundments, but 1 was seen feeding on the exposed mud of a tidal creek (Cooper, 1991).

Little Stint (*Calidris minuta*)

Casual (1979, 1982, 1985) in summer.

DOCUMENTATION: Photograph (R. A. Rowlett 1980a).

REMARKS: This European shorebird is very similar to Rufous-necked Stint; in addition, it may be confused, in some plumages, with juvenile Least Sandpipers. All reports involve single birds along the Port Mahon Rd. near Delaware Bay. The first record, on 23 May 1979, is supported by a definitive published photograph and notes (Rowlett 1980a). The second record, from 24 to 30 July 1982, is supported by drawings filed at DMNH [O'BM2]. The last record, on 11 August 1985, is described in the following manner: "We received a careful description of a peep identified as a Little Stint at Port Mahon, Del., Aug. 11 (B and N M[urphy], but without information about molt or age class the record cannot be definitively confirmed" (Paxton et al. 1986).

Least Sandpiper (*Calidris minutilla*)

Regular; migrant; common; expected April-May and July-September.

HABITAT: Sheltered grassy edges of pools in saltmarsh or freshwater lagoons. Generally feeds in low grass rather than on open flats.

SPRING: Least Sandpipers usually arrive 15–20 April. Earliest arrivals are

1 Apr 1989	1	Broadkill Beach [Frec1]
4 Apr 1973	3	Bombay Hook NWR [Holg80]
11 Apr 1992	16	Bombay Hook NWR and Little Creek WA [DNRE2]

Peak numbers occur 5–30 May. Counts of several hundred are typical in May. High counts are

11 May 1963	20,000	Little Creek WA (Lesser 1964)
25 May 1967	10,000	Bombay Hook NWR, Little Creek WA [Abbo7]
30 May 1978	2,000	Cape Henlopen SP [Frec1]

SUMMER: In about half of the years Least Sandpipers are present during June (10 years in the 1970–93 period). Usually fewer than 10 are present.

FALL: The first southbound birds arrive during 1–7 July. Most depart by 15–20 September. Last reports are

24 Oct 1987	7	Bombay Hook NWR [Barn45]
29 Oct 1981	6	Red Mill Pond [Frec1]
1 Nov 1947	40	Bombay Hook NWR [Barl1]

The period of peak abundance lasts from 15–20 July to 20–25 August. Some high counts are

25 Jul 1964	1,500	Little Creek WA [Broo26]
12 Aug 1962	2,500	Little Creek WA [anon11]
30 Sep 1962	150	Little Creek WA [anon11]

WINTER: Rarely are any birds reported beyond the end of September. Since this species winters casually north to Long Island, no known reason explains the lack of November records in Delaware when there are December and January reports (mostly from the Bombay Hook CBC). Most winter reports are of fewer than 10 birds, but the 23 December 1973 Bombay Hook CBC reported 37.

1966–89 CBC Summary

Christmas Bird Count	Years Found	Range of No. Found
Wilmington		
Middletown	1	1
Bombay Hook	9	1–37
Cape Henlopen	1	9
Rehoboth	2	1–4
STATEWIDE (high in 1973)	10	1–47

SPECIMENS: 35; ANSP, DMNH, UDEL, USNM.

White-rumped Sandpiper (*Calidris fuscicollis*)

Regular; migrant; fairly common to common; expected mid-May to mid-June and late July to mid-October.

J F M A M J J A S O N D

HABITAT: Mud flats, marshes, wet fields.

SPRING: First arrival is 10–15 May; the peak occurs during 20–30 May; and most leave by 10–15 June. Earliest arrivals are

25 Apr 1976	1	Port Mahon [Lehm27]
26 Apr 1991	1	Bombay Hook NWR [Holg1]
2 May 1962	1	Little Creek WA (Lesser 1964)

Typically fewer than 10 birds are recorded per trip. High counts include

19 May 1974	145	Little Creek WA [DuPG4]
23 May 1983	100	Slaughter Beach [Wayn11]
6 Jun 1991	200	Bombay Hook NWR [RusR1]

SUMMER: White-rumped Sandpipers are rarely present between 15 June and 18 July (present 5 years in the period 1961–93). Occurrences are

20 Jun 1961	1	Little Creek WA (Lesser 1964)
24 Jun–12 July 1990	1–4	Bombay Hook NWR [Hol104]
27 Jun 1971	1	Cape Henlopen SP [DuPG3]
29 Jun 1987	2	Bombay Hook NWR [Holg1]
9–14 Jul 1991	2–4	Bombay Hook NWR [Camp10]

FALL: First arrival is 20–25 July. Most depart by 10–15 October. Last departures are

13 Nov 1990	1	Bombay Hook NWR [Holg94]
17 Nov 1991	2	Broadkill Beach [Frec56]
18 Nov 1953	1	Bombay Hook NWR [Spri1]

High counts are

11 Sep 1965	100	Delaware City [Carr4]
27 Sep 1987	55	Bombay Hook NWR [Holg25]
30 Sep 1962	100	Little Creek WA and Cape Henlopen SP [anon11]
14 Oct 1953	60	Bombay Hook NWR [Spri1]

WINTER: Because White-rumped Sandpipers winter primarily in South America, winter reports are noteworthy. We have reports of 1–3 birds present in 8 years (1947–91). In at least 2 years (1953, 1988) individuals were known to have been continually present since mid-October. In December, 1 was on the 1965 Rehoboth CBC at Assawoman WA [Dyke7], and 1 was on the 1987 Bombay Hook CBC.

SPECIMENS: DMNH 76342, 0.3 mi (0.5 km) N of Pickering Beach, 22 May 1986; ANSP 66258, no date or locality given.

Baird's Sandpiper (*Calidris bairdii*)

Regular; migrant; rare or accidental in spring, uncommon in fall; to be looked for in late August and September.

J F M A M J J A S O N D

DOCUMENTATION: Multiple sight records.

HABITAT: Mud flats. Tends to feed on the higher parts of the shore or the dry fringes of wetland sites; seldom wades.

SPRING: This species does not normally occur on the Atlantic coast during spring (AOU 1983; Palmer 1967); thus the handful of spring records are of interest. The only report for which notes are available involves 2 birds at Little Creek WA on 10 May 1975 (Richards 1975). A 1974 report mentions only that the bird was "in full breeding plumage," but no details are given (DuMont and DuMont 1975a). Most observations occur in May and include 1 or 2 birds. Urner and Storer (1949) and Stewart and Robbins (1958) mention the lack of spring records for New Jersey and Maryland, respectively. Given the lack of reports from the region and the lack of documentation for all but 1 of the these reports, the Delaware reports should be regarded with the utmost caution, and all future spring reports should be carefully documented.

FALL: Baird's Sandpiper is more likely to occur during the fall migration than the spring migration. Most records occur in August and September. Early arrivals, all of birds at Bombay Hook NWR and lacking notes, are 2 on 12 July 1969 [Carl4], 1

on 19 July 1979 [Abbo4], and 1 on 22 July 1989 [Rufe3]. High counts are

10 Aug 1991	6–8	Bombay Hook NWR [Pulc4]
23 Sep 1978	6	Assawoman WA [Frec1]
6 Oct 1970	6	Bombay Hook NWR [Abbo14]

The single November report mentions 1 bird at Rehoboth Beach 11 November 1978 [Frec1]. Urner and Storer (1949) list 17 August and 7 September as extreme dates in New Jersey.

REMARKS: Because this species occurs in low numbers and because there are no Delaware specimens, all observations, especially those for spring, should be carefully documented.

Pectoral Sandpiper *(Calidris melanotos)*

Regular; migrant; fairly common to common; expected mid-March to mid-May and mid-July to early November.

J F M A M J J A S O N D

HABITAT: Mud flats, margins of still and slowly flowing water with much vegetation, moist grasslands.

SPRING: First arrival is 10–15 March. Most depart by 10–15 May. Two early reports are 2 at Bombay Hook NWR on 23 February 1968 [Carr8] and 1 at Woodland Beach WA exactly 20 years later [Buda1]. Pectoral Sandpiper is an uncommon spring migrant along the Atlantic coast (AOU 1983). Thus a report of 5,000 at Bombay Hook NWR on 16 April 1966 by a reliable observer [Carr5] is truly remarkable. Example high counts are

5 Apr 1981	100	Bombay Hook NWR [MiJC1]
15 Apr 1973	250	along the coast [Rowl13]
12 May 1968	600	Little Creek WA [DuPA3]

Late departures are

22 May 1982	10	Bombay Hook NWR [RusR1]
29 May 1971	3	Little Creek WA [Rowl9]
30 May 1983	few	along the bay coast [Barn23]

SUMMER: This species is rarely present from 1 June to 7 July. Four of the 8 reports during that period involve 1 or 2 birds at Broadkill Beach from 28 June to 4 July 1988 [Frec1]. The remaining reports are also more or less within that range of dates.

FALL: First arrival is 10–15 July. The Pectoral Sandpiper is most often reported from 25 July to 10 October; most leave by 1–7 November. Earliest arrivals are

26 Jun 1962	2	Little Creek WA [Less13]
30 Jun 1989	21	Bombay Hook NWR [Holg1]
3 Jul 1971	1	Bombay Hook NWR [Holg65]

Last departures, all from Bombay Hook NWR, are

21 Nov 1973	1	[Holg58]
22 Nov 1968	2	[Holg34]
27 Nov 1990	1	[Holg95]

High counts are

12 Aug 1962	525	Little Creek WA (Lesser 1965)
26 Sep 1970	750	Bombay Hook NWR [Carl1]
6 Oct 1974	500	Bombay Hook NWR [Even2]

SPECIMENS: 6; CM, ANSP, DMNH, UDEL.

Sharp-tailed Sandpiper *(Calidris acuminata)*

Accidental (1993).

DOCUMENTATION: Photograph (C. Sample, DMNH 461).

REMARKS: The only state record describes an individual in breeding plumage discovered by 3 birders from Chicago at Bear Swamp, Bombay Hook NWR on 8 August 1993 [O'BJ1] and present until 19 August (Campbell 1994). We have prints from Charles Sample and Ken Bass that show the white eye stripe very well and the pattern on the breast adequately. This Asian breeder is recorded rarely in summer and regularly in migration, in western Alaska, and is casual elsewhere in North America, including the northeastern coast (AOU 1983).

Purple Sandpiper *(Calidris maritima)*

Regular; winter visitor; fairly common to common; expected early November to early March; sporadic into spring.

HABITAT: Jetties, breakwaters, and rocky coasts on exposed shores with strong wave action.

SPRING: Purple Sandpipers usually depart by 1–7 March but may be irregularly present through the end of May. Last reports are

24 May 1953	4	Indian River Inlet [anon4]
24 May 1960	4	Indian River Inlet [anon9]
28 May 1984	10	Roosevelt Inlet, Lewes [Fint3]

An exceptional count of 300 was obtained on 9 March 1974 at Indian River Inlet; that same day 150 were counted at Ocean City, Maryland [PylP1].

FALL: Palmer (1967) comments that "In fall there appear to be successive small waves of migrants, in latitude of Maritimes and New England, occasionally beginning as early as late July but with largest flights in Oct." The first birds seldom arrive in Delaware before 1–7 November. Two early reports mention 2 at Lewes on 10 September 1973 [Alex1] and 2 at Indian River Inlet on 24 October 1979 [Frec26]. Reports prior to November should be carefully documented.

1966–89 CBC Summary

Christmas Bird Count	Years Found	Range of No. Found	Median
Wilmington			
Middletown			
Bombay Hook	1	2	
Cape Henlopen	14	2–29	2
Rehoboth	22	5–200	15
STATEWIDE	22	7–200	22
(zero in 1982 and 1984, high in 1976)			

WINTER: Counts of the Purple Sandpiper usually total no more than 20–30. High counts are

27 Nov 1978	100	Indian River Inlet [Frec1]
1 Jan 1977	200	Rehoboth CBC
9 Mar 1974	300	Indian River Inlet [PylP1]

Although no statistically significant CBC trend is apparent, many observers suspect a decline in Purple Sandpiper numbers. Frech (notes), recording numbers of Purple Sandpipers at Indian River Inlet, typically had seasonal highs of 35–50 birds during 1977–85. Since then he has reported 1 high of 20 and the rest 12 or lower. A plot of the CBC data shows a slight downward trend and also reveals a distinct period of higher numbers during 1975–80. This species is most numerous on the Rehoboth CBC.

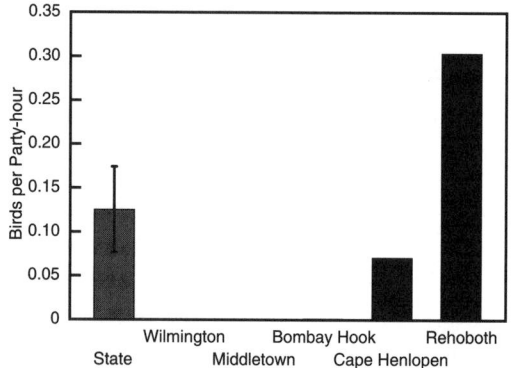

CBC Geographic Distribution; Average of 3 Count Areas

SPECIMENS: USNM 422132, Indian River, 24 February 1951; DMNH 793, Sussex Co., 28 December 1957.

Dunlin *(Calidris alpina)*

Regular; winter visitor; fairly common to abundant; expected late September to early June.

J F M A M J J A S O N D

HABITAT: Feeds on sandy beaches and mud flats at the margins of ponds, bays, and estuaries.

SPRING: Migration begins 20–25 February and continues through 25 May–1 June with the peak during 1 April–25 May. Last departures are

3 Jun 1981	1	Cape Henlopen SP [Frec1]
4 Jun 1962	1	Little Creek WA (Lesser 1964)
8 Jun 1993	4	Bombay Hook NWR and Kitts Hummock [DNRE3]

Examples of high counts, which do not reflect the much higher Bay-wide counts, are

18 Apr 1971	3,000	Bombay Hook NWR [Rowl9]
7 May 1983	8,000	along Delaware Bay [Barn1]
24 May 1986	5,500	Kitts Hummock (Thomas 1986)

SUMMER: This species occurs sporadically from 8 June until late September. We have about two dozen reports in 10 years from 1971 through 1992, some of which may represent early migrants.

FALL: Palmer (1967) comments that "After breeding, adults leave the tundra in late July and through Aug., then apparently linger along the way; then, late for a shorebird, they move rapidly to winter quarters. Their time of passage in conterminous U.S. extends from well along in Sept. through Oct. and even in Nov." First arrival in Delaware is usually 25–30 September. Earliest arrivals are

14 Sep 1991	1	Bombay Hook NWR [Barn54]
20 Sep 1962	1	Little Creek WA (Lesser 1964)
24 Sep 1987	12	Prime Hook NWR [Frec1]

High counts are

24 Oct 1985	1,500	Kitts Hummock [Wayn2]
2 Nov 1983	12,000	Kitts Hummock [Edni54]
8 Nov 1970	5,500	Bombay Hook NWR [anon14]

1966–89 CBC Summary

Christmas Bird Count	Years Found	Range of No. Found	Median
Wilmington Middletown	7	3–140	
Bombay Hook	24	7–8,380	743
Cape Henlopen	24	1–877	103
Rehoboth	24	3–801	203
STATEWIDE	24	176–9,393	1,161
(low in 1989, high in 1984)			

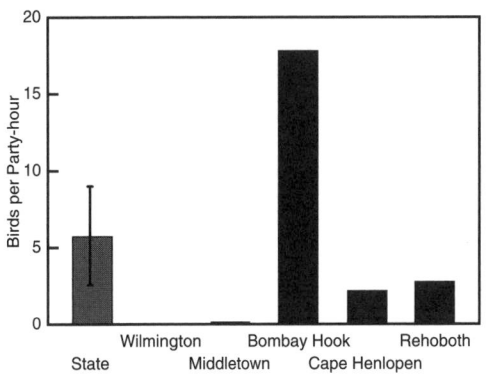

CBC Geographic Distribution; Average of 4 Count Areas

WINTER: Dunlins frequent the shore of Delaware River and Bay all winter. High counts are 8,380 on 16 December 1984, 4,248 on 27 December 1987, and 2,055 on 27 December 1970, all on the Bombay Hook CBC, which reports substantially more Dunlins than do the other coastal CBCs. No CBC trend is apparent.

SPECIMENS: 17; DMNH, USNM.

Curlew Sandpiper *(Calidris ferruginea)*

DOCUMENTATION: Photographs (M. V. Barnhill, DMNH 5–6; D. S. Czaplak, DMNH 398, 399).

HABITAT: Prefers muddy, poorly vegetated fringes, including intertidal mud flats.

OCCURRENCE: The first Delaware record was obtained at Little Creek WA on 20 August 1963 [Dyke5]. The next sighting took place at Bombay Hook NWR 17–20 May 1968 [Holg32] (Linehan 1969b). Since then, except for 1977 and 1978, it has been found annually. Most of the reports occur during the middle 2 weeks of May and the last 2 weeks of July. The length of stay varies from 1 or 2 days to several weeks. The Curlew Sandpiper is most reliably found in Bombay Hook NWR or Little Creek WA.

Regular (23 years, 1963–91); spring and fall visitor; rare; to be looked for in May and mid-July to September.

Stilt Sandpiper *(Calidris himantopus)*

Regular; migrant; fairly common to common; expected in May and early July to mid-September.

DOCUMENTATION: Multiple sight records, banding record.

HABITAT: Wades belly deep at the margins of ponds, bays, estuaries; rarely found on open shores.

SPRING: Most reports are from May, although it is sometimes present during the last 3 weeks of April. Earliest arrivals are

10 Apr 1989	6	Broadkill Beach [Frec1]
11 Apr 1992	2	Little Creek WA [Hess16]

12 Apr 1986	3	Bombay Hook NWR and Little Creek WA [Barn1]

An historic and extraordinarily high count of 100 was made on 30 April 1932 at Delaware City [Debe1]. Recent high counts have been substantially lower:

9 May 1979	15	Lewes area [Frec5]
19 May 1974	13	Little Creek WA [Abbo16]
11 May 1974	12	Cape Henlopen SP [Wayn9]

SUMMER: June reports, all from Bombay Hook NWR, are

13 Jun 1991	1	[Holg92]
15 Jun 1991	1	[Holg92]
23 Jun 1991	9	[Holg92]
27 Jun 1990	1	[Holg91]
29 Jun 1987	1	[Holg24]

FALL: First arrival is usually 1–5 July, with the peak mid-July–mid-August. Most depart by 10–15 September. Reports after mid-October are unusual and should be carefully documented. Earliest reports are

2 Jul 1987	9	Bombay Hook NWR [Holg1]
4 Jul 1972	1	Little Creek WA [Holg74]
6 Jul 1975	70	Bombay Hook NWR [Lehm16]

Some high counts are

28 Jul 1973	475	Little Creek WA [Rowl3]
4 Aug 1974	520	Chesapeake and Delaware Canal [Lehm8]
8 Aug 1975	420	Bombay Hook NWR [DuPG5]

Late records include

2 Nov 1962	1	Little Creek WA (Lesser 1964)
2 Nov 1990	1	Bombay Hook NWR [Holg95]
10 Nov 1968	2	Assawoman WA [Moun1]

WINTER: The only winter records are 1 at Bombay Hook NWR from 10 November to 19 December 1973 [Holg22] and 1 from the 1992 Cape Henlopen CBC [Shor1].

Buff-breasted Sandpiper *(Tryngites subruficollis)*

Nearly regular (11 years, 1968–91); migrant, rare; to be looked for during August and September.

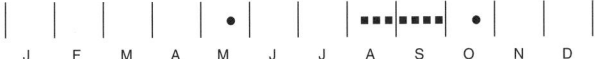

J F M A M J J A S O N D

DOCUMENTATION: Multiple sight records.

HABITAT: Feeds in dry uplands—golf courses, air fields, and baked mud near rivers and other bodies of freshwater. Often found in potato fields.

SPRING: This midcontinent migrant is not expected in spring; thus a report of 1 near St. Georges on 18 May 1968 [Carr9] is noteworthy and should have been documented.

FALL: Although recorded as early as late July, Buff-breasted Sandpipers occur mostly during September; typically, only 1 or 2 birds are noted. In 1970, an extraordinary year in Delaware for this species, various observers reported counts of up to 7 birds from 30 August to 17 October [m.ob4]. Earliest arrivals are

25 Jul 1990	1	Bombay Hook NWR [Hurl2]
8 Aug 1989	2	Bombay Hook NWR [Holg61]
14 Aug 1984	1	Sussex Co., Rt. 88 [Frec1]

Last reports are

20 Sep 1980	2	Assawoman WA [Edni46]
20 Sep 1981	1	Rt. 9, Bellini's sod farm, Kent Co. [Line19]
28 Sep 1968	2	Bombay Hook NWR [Holg60]

Ruff *(Philomachus pugnax)*

ROB STINE

Regular; summer visitor; rare; expected early April to mid-May and early July to early August.

J F M A M J J A S O N D

DOCUMENTATION: Photographs (A. P. Ednie, DMNH 356, 371).

HABITAT: Marshes, moist fields (avoids high grass).

SPRING: First arrival is 1–6 April. Earliest reports are

13 Mar 1981	3	Bombay Hook NWR [Barn39]
17 Mar 1989	1	Rt. 9, Kent Co. [Vand1]
18 Mar 1973	1	near Smyrna [Holg18]

Individuals are regularly present to mid-May and sporadical-ly thereafter. Although only 1 or 2 birds are usually found on any given trip, many reports supported by carefully taken notes reveal that in some years as many as 6–13 different individuals have been present.

SUMMER: Sporadically present mid-May to early July.

FALL: Ruffs occur most frequently during July and early August. In some years individuals may be present into September, and in other years an individual will be found 6–8 weeks after the previous report. Last reports, all from Bombay Hook NWR, are

14 Oct 1969	1	[Atki1]
17 Oct 1991	1	[Gord3]
15 Nov 1989	1	[Holg90]

REMARKS: The Ruff breeds primarily in northern Eurasia and winters from southern Europe, the Persian Gulf, and southeastern China south. In migration it occurs rarely but regularly along the East Coast of North America (AOU 1983).

Short-billed Dowitcher *(Limnodromus griseus)*

Regular; migrant; common to abundant. The seasonal graph combines data for both dowitcher species. Expected April and May and late June to mid-September.

HABITAT: Feeds mostly on intertidal mud flats or impoundments, wading belly deep and probing into the mud. Uses both fresh- and saltwater habitats.

REMARKS: This and the Long-billed Dowitcher *(Limnodromus scolopaceus)* are not easily separable in alternate (breeding) plumage and are virtually inseparable in basic (winter) plumage under normal field conditions. Confounding the issue is the presence in Delaware of 2 subspecies of Short-billed Dowitcher, one of which looks remarkably similar to the Long-billed Dowitcher. Because of the difficulty of separating these forms, there are insufficient reliable data to present substantiated seasonal graphs for each species. Therefore, a single seasonal graph is presented for the 2 species. As will be apparent from these accounts, much remains to be done to work out the details of dowitcher migration in Delaware. For information on identification, the interested reader is referred to Pitelka (1950) and Wilds and Newlon (1983).

SPRING: Urner and Storer (1949) list 29 April–25 May as the principal migration period in New Jersey. Stewart and Robbins (1958) give a migration period of 1–10 April to 25 May–5 June with a peak during 1–25 May in Maryland. Palmer (1967) comments that "In spring, main passage in conterminous U.S. and s. Canada occurs in Apr. and first half of May (peak in latter month)." We have many May reports but comparatively few from March and April.

SUMMER: Some June reports, lacking documentation, have been attributed to this species.

FALL: Urner and Storer (1949) list 6 July–25 August as the principal migration period in New Jersey. Stewart and Robbins (1958) give a migration period of 1–10 July to 10–20 November with a peak from 15 July to 5 September in Maryland. Jehl (1963) presents data from fall migrations in Ocean County, New Jersey, concluding that in *L. g. griseus* and probably in *L. g. hendersoni* there are 3 migration peaks as follows: (1) early July, consisting of females that have bred; (2) late July or early August, consisting of males that have bred; and (3) mid-August to early September, consisting of young of the year.

WINTER: The handful of reports for October–December lack documentation; there are no reports January–March.

SPECIMENS: DMNH 77361, Woodland Beach, 21 August 1988; DMNH 76518, 0.5 mi (0.8 km) N of Pickering Beach, 5 September 1986; DMNH 76547, 0.5 mi (0.8 km) N of Port Mahon, 5 September 1986.

Long-billed Dowitcher *(Limnodromus scolopaceus)*

Regular; migrant; common to abundant. The seasonal graph (see Short-billed Dowitcher) combines data for both dowitcher species. Expected April and May and late June to mid-September.

DOCUMENTATION: Multiple sight records, including many with call notes described.

HABITAT: Prefers grassy margins of shallow freshwater; has much less affinity for saltwater habitats than does the Short-billed Dowitcher.

REMARKS: See remarks under Short-billed Dowitcher.

SPRING: Palmer (1967) comments that the spring migration largely overlaps that of Short-billed Dowitcher. Urner and Storer (1949) mention the lack of spring records in New Jersey. Delaware reports start on 30 March and continue to the end of May.

SUMMER: Some July reports, lacking documentation, have been attributed to this species, but see the comment in the "Fall" section.

FALL: Jehl (1963) concluded from his Ocean County, New Jersey, study that this species "occurs annually in small numbers after the middle of August."

1966–89 CBC Summary

Christmas Bird Count	Years Found	Range of No. Found	Median
Wilmington			
Middletown			
Bombay Hook	13	1–65	1
Cape Henlopen	2	1	
Rehoboth	1	13	
STATEWIDE (high in 1969)	14	1–65	1

WINTER: The CBC tabulation is the combination of reports of "dowitcher species" from 10 CBCs, Longbills from 5 CBCs, and Shortbills from 3 CBCs. A handful of Long-billed Dowitcher reports, all lacking documentation, are available for October–January.

Common Snipe *(Gallinago gallinago)*

Regular; winter visitor; uncommon; expected early September (rarely earlier) to mid-January, sporadically from then to early March and regularly from then to early May.

J F M A M J J A S O N D

HABITAT: Wet spots in fields, along wet ditches, fresh or brackish marsh.

SPRING: Snipe are reported most frequently from about 10 March through 5 May. Tuck (1972, 150–51) notes that "The first large northward movement occurs during late March," and "the main flights into Canada are not until April," with males arriving at least 10 days before females. Late departures are

15 May 1961	1	Little Creek WA (Lesser 1964)
19 May 1987	6	Great Marsh, Lewes [DNRE1]
22 May 1983	4	Bombay Hook NWR [Fogl2]

High counts are

19 Mar 1955	75	Bombay Hook NWR [MiJC1]
23 Mar 1986	50	Milford Neck [Edni61]
15 Apr 1989	50	Broadkill Beach [Frec1]

SUMMER: June reports are well beyond the usual pattern of vagrancy; thus the following reports should be treated with caution:

6 Jun 1953	1	Bombay Hook NWR [WriJ1]
12 Jun 1963	1	Little Creek WA (Lesser 1964)
13 Jun 1991	1	Bombay Hook NWR [Holg92]

FALL: Occasionally a few birds are present beginning 15–30 July and in August, but this species is normally not expected before September. The early record is of a bird that arrived at Little Creek WA on 5 July 1961 (Lesser 1964). Tuck (1972, 264) notes that, though some birds migrate during August, the first significant long-distance movements begin during the latter part of September. Earliest arrivals are

15 Jul 1989	1	Broadkill Beach [Frec1]
18 Jul 1987	1	Bombay Hook NWR [Barn45]
21 Jul 1973	1	Little Creek WA [Holg20]

High counts are

27 Oct 1974	42	Dragon Run [Edni1]
2 Nov 1974	170	Dragon Run [SpSB1]
28 Nov 1972	45	Bombay Hook NWR [Holg76]

Tuck (1972, 266) notes that there is differential migration in fall—females leave before males. "The Atlantic coastal plain and its coastal marshes are important to migrant snipe and have regular wintering populations, but not nearly so substantial as those in subtropical regions farther south" (Tuck 1972, 282–83).

WINTER: The Common Snipe is scarce from mid-January to late February. Aside from some CBC reports, typical counts total fewer than 10–15 birds. No CBC trend is apparent. It is most numerous on the Middletown CBC.

1966–89 CBC Summary

Christmas Bird Count	Years Found	Range of No. Found	Median
Wilmington	18	1–14	2
Middletown	21	1–24	2
Bombay Hook	23	2–180	10
Cape Henlopen	24	1–83	8
Rehoboth	19	1–10	2
STATEWIDE (low in 1989, high in 1974)	24	3–293	32

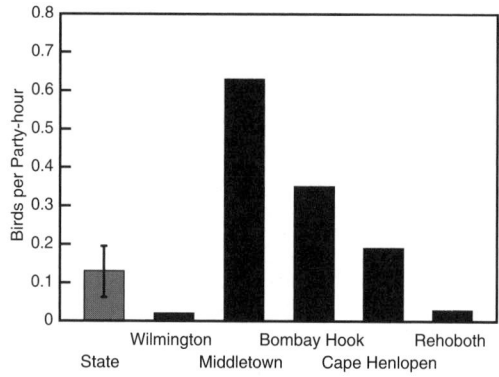

CBC Geographic Distribution

SPECIMENS: 10; DMNH, ANSP, USNM.

American Woodcock *(Scolopax minor)*

Resident; uncommon. Begins breeding in March, with replacement clutches laid through May. Declining in the East and probably in Delaware from habitat loss.

HABITAT: Thickets or dense stands of shrubs and small trees on or adjacent to damp areas. In dense scrub along the upland edge of the Delaware River and Bay marshes (D. Rothstein, DNHI, pers. comm.). Breeds in early successional deciduous growth at the sapling stage with a density of 50,000 stems per acre (125,000 per ha)—too thick to push through comfortably (J. B. Bortner, pers. comm., 1990). Males need an opening of some 10,000 sq m (2.5 acres) for courtship (Kinsley 1982).

SPRING: At Bear, New Castle County, the migration may start as early as 12 February but does not usually begin until the first of March, with the peak about 10 March as measured by the number of singing males (G. Prest, pers. comm.). Sheldon (1967, 101, 103) notes that woodcocks are exceptionally early migrants and that the severity of the January and February weather to a large extent influences the timing of the northward migration. In most years they reach the breeding grounds by the last week of March and the first week of April. Typical reports are of fewer than 6 birds.

BREEDING: Woodcocks breed throughout Delaware in the protection of very dense saplings or other dense scrub.

Atlas. Singing males were not accepted as local breeding evidence until after 10 April in order to reduce the chance of counting a late migrant—about a month after peak activity noted at Bear [Pres1]. This policy made it difficult to locate singing males because courtship flights began to taper off soon after the beginning of the safe dates. In the fifth year of the Atlas project an effort was made to cover each block with a pre-

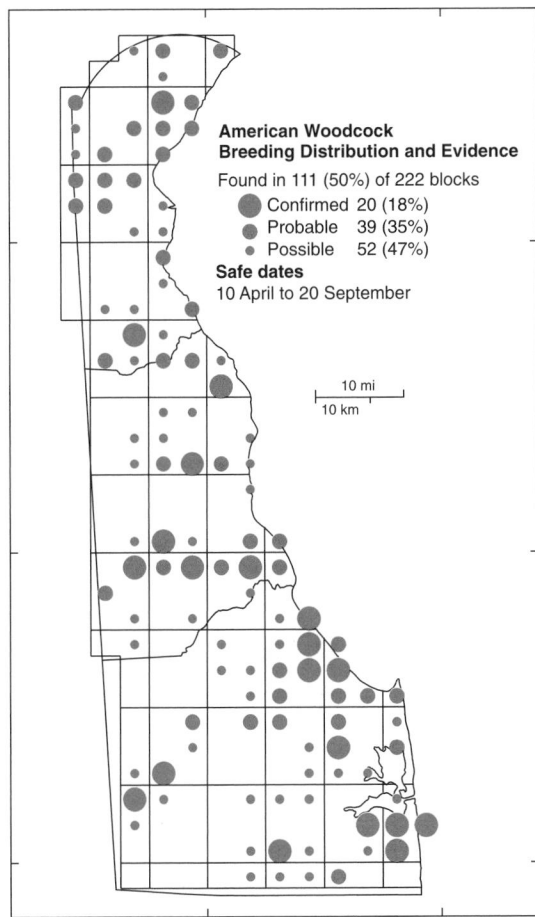

American Woodcock
Breeding Distribution and Evidence

Found in 111 (50%) of 222 blocks
● Confirmed 20 (18%)
● Probable 39 (35%)
· Possible 52 (47%)
Safe dates
10 April to 20 September

10 mi
10 km

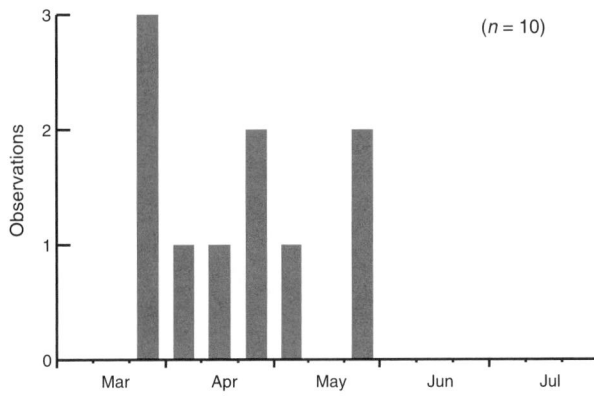

Estimated Clutch-Completion Dates

dawn or dusk woodcock minicount (see "Breeding Population"), but cool, wet weather did not permit all blocks to be checked.

Its occurrence in 50% of blocks is more than anticipated for a state on the southern edge of the principal breeding range (Sheldon 1967). Its distribution in Delaware is difficult to analyze because the shotgun pattern of the distribution map suggests that the survey was not complete. The species appears to be present in more blocks near the river and bay marshes than in those along the Chesapeake-Delaware drainage divide.

Nesting. The woodcock places its nest on the ground in a hollow of dry leaves in drier woodland sites in early succession, low shrubby cover, or tall herbage.

It is hard to determine the onset of breeding. There are winter breeding records in southern states (Whiting and Boggus 1982). Latham (1956) watched early courtship flights of 3 male woodcocks near Petersburg 8 January when the temperature was 25°F, and Prest (notes) heard their *peent* call on 31 December. A female was collected in breeding condition on a male singing ground near Gumboro on 20 February 1973 with the largest follicle 3.5 mm, suggestive of local breeding at a very early date (DMNH 34925).

Estimated clutch-completion dates range from 21 March to 31 May, peak egg-laying is in April, and the 2 late May clutches are probably replacements. Extreme egg dates are 6 April

[Buck1] and 9 June [Flor1]. Early broods were found on 13 April (25-g hatchlings, TSBR 88–160) and 18 April ("just hatched," Stone 1937). Clutches usually have 4 eggs, but 2 clutches of 3 have been reported.

History. Lumsden (1987) wrote that the American Woodcock increased in Ontario after European settlement because of the opening of the forest canopy and the introduction of several European species of earthworms that constitute a major part of its diet. Delaware had a native population of earthworms, changes in the landscape similar to Ontario's must have have favored the woodcock. There are nineteenth-century reports of large migrating flocks at Cape May (Stone 1937), and Delaware probably contributed its share to the Eastern population. By the end of the nineteenth century, its Eastern population had seriously declined from overhunting. Fisher (1901) forecast the woodcock's certain extinction unless prompt action was taken, recommending a short hunting season and bag limits. His 1901 tabulation of hunting seasons shows Delaware as the only state in the Mid-Atlantic or Northeast that still had no closed season on Woodcock. "So great was the decline in Woodcock numbers during the years of practically unrestricted gunning that it was rated a 'vanishing' game bird. With much subsequent protection, it has fared rather well. However, hunting, occasional severe weather on breeding and on winter ranges, and some losses in desirable habitat through man's activities are all factors affecting its numbers. To these must be added long-residual broad-spectrum [insecticides]. . . . Earthworms, the Woodcock's mainstay, concentrate DDT within themselves" (Palmer 1967).

Trends. Population estimates based on singing-ground surveys made between 1963 and 1988 revealed a 2% annual decline in population in the East (Artmann 1975; Bortner 1989). The Delaware May Count shows an average annual decline of 6% (1969–90).

Breeding population. There was such concern for the population of this gamebird that a monitoring program was established. Its protocol required a series of 9 2-min stops at 0.4-mi intervals on a good woodcock road starting 22 min after sundown in favorable weather in late April. Two routes were run in Delaware in 1950–58 (English 1950–56; Chamberlain and Florio 1958). The Golts Rd. route (near Blackbird SF) averaged 0.8 singing grounds per stop; the Wilder WA route averaged 0.5 per stop. No trend was detected.

Randomly selected routes, substituted for the earlier mentioned routes, were run intermittently from 1967 to 1983. Delaware was then dropped from this survey because these random routes had so few birds. The counts averaged 0.06 birds per stop in the years they were run (J. B. Bortner, USFWS, pers. comm., 1990), that is, about 0.5 singing grounds per 100 ha. Singing-grounds surveys do not directly relate to population because

1. a surplus of nonsinging males is ready to use an unoccupied singing ground (Dwyer et al. 1988),
2. males will sing from more than 1 territory, and
3. adult females outnumber adult males (the ratio is 100:63), but the numbers of each sex among first-year birds are equal (Sheldon 1967).

Conservation. Federally supported ditching (tax ditches) and draining of wetlands for row crops made the state less suitable for these birds. Females require very dense young growth to successfully raise young; males require an open field for courtship flights, and both require wetlands for feeding. In 1986 there were 68,000 acres (28,000 ha) of sapling and seedling forests in Delaware, a decrease of 12% since 1972 (Frieswyk and DiGiovanni 1989). Much of the Delaware forest is in suitably damp (poorly drained) areas for woodcock feeding, and is less suited to tilling.

Woodcock harvest by Delaware hunters was reduced more than 60% in the 10 seasons from 1977–78 to 1986–87 to fewer than 1,000 per year. These numbers must be used with caution because hunting pressure probably declined during this time, but they suggest a reduced population of woodcock in late fall (in hunting season, 20 November–3 January). In response to the reduction in population in the East, the USFWS shortened the season and reduced the bag limits, beginning with the 1985–86 season.

FALL: Prest (notes) recorded males *peenting* at Bear on 17, 24, and on 27 November, probably during southward migration. Fall flights appear dependent on weather conditions, so it is difficult to prepare timetables for woodcock migrations even when based on data accumulated for a number of years (Mendall and Aldous 1943). In Canada the migration begins in late September and continues until mid-December, when most birds have reached their wintering grounds (Owen et al. 1977, 152). Banding evidence suggests that birds breeding in New England and adjacent Canada migrate through Delaware and winter in the southern Atlantic states. Stewart and Robbins (1958) list the normal period in Maryland as 1–10 October to 1–10 December and the peak as 25 October–25 November. The time of concentration of heavy flights at Cape May varied from late October to mid-December (Pettingill 1936) and may be taken as a guide for migration in Delaware.

1966–89 CBC Summary

Christmas Bird Count	Years Found	Range of No. Found	Median
Wilmington	10	1–7	
Middletown	8	1–6	
Bombay Hook	22	1–6	1
Cape Henlopen	11	1–7	
Rehoboth	15	1–12	1
STATEWIDE (low in 1984, high in 1988)	24	1–16	6

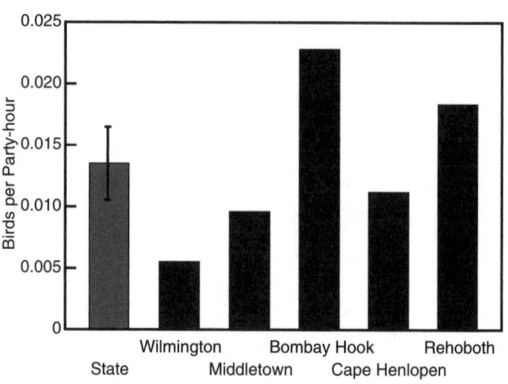

CBC Geographic Distribution

WINTER: No trend is apparent in the variable CBC results, but it is evident that woodcocks winter throughout the state at least during some winters. They are found most commonly on the Bombay Hook and Rehoboth CBCs. Most reports are of single birds.

SPECIMENS: 10; DMNH, UDEL.

Wilson's Phalarope (*Phalaropus tricolor*)

Regular; migrant; uncommon to fairly common; rare in spring; expected early July through September, sporadically into the fall.

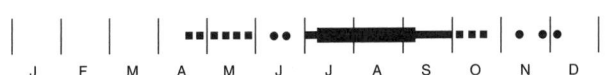

DOCUMENTATION: Multiple sight records.

HABITAT: Large, shallow freshwater ponds or impoundments, mud and sand flats.

MIGRATION: Wilson's Phalaropes are rare in spring; usually only 1 or 2 individuals present for a few days from 15–20 April through May. There are few June reports. Wilson's Phalarope is most numerous from mid-July to early September. First fall arrivals are

1 Jul 1987	1	Little Creek WA [Holg1]
1 Jul 1990	15	Bombay Hook NWR [Edni27]
2 Jul 1989	1	Little Creek WA [Holg1]

As many as 40 have been seen at a single location, eg. at Port Mahon, 8 July 1991 [O'BM1].

The breeding range of Wilson's Phalarope extends farther south than those of the other 2 phalaropes, and, unlike the others, its primary migration route is overland (AOU 1983). Accordingly, the Wilson's Phalarope is essentially never seen at sea off the Mid-Atlantic coast but is frequently seen on land. In Delaware it is most frequently seen in or along the edges of the impoundments at Little Creek WA and Woodland Beach WA and at Bombay Hook NWR. Wilson's Phalarope has also been found near fresh and brackish water at the Marine Terminal and Cherry Island at Wilmington, as well as at Newport, Delaware City, Assawoman WA, and Gordon Pond WA. In addition, several individuals have been observed in rain ponds in Kent and Sussex counties.

Red-necked Phalarope (*Phalaropus lobatus*)

Regular; migrant; uncommon; usually found offshore late April through May and late July to mid-October.

HABITAT: Pelagic waters, large ponds, and impoundments.

MIGRATION: Red-necked Phalaropes migrate through the Mid-Atlantic region in large numbers offshore and in modest numbers over land. Because of the small number of offshore birding trips, most Delaware reports are away from the sea. The Red-necked Phalarope occurs in much the same locations as the Wilson's Phalarope but has been seen more frequently than that species along the Atlantic and lower Delaware Bay coasts. It has been reported from Lewes, Cape Henlopen SP, Rehoboth Beach, and Indian River Inlet. Our only offshore reports are from 11 and 14 August 1975, 73 and 96 mi offshore, respectively [Rowl18].

In the Mid-Atlantic region generally, the species has a broad period of migration in both spring and fall, consistent with the Delaware onshore records (Rowlett 1980b; Barnhill, pers. obs.). As the seasonal graph shows, in most years the period of spring migration in April and May is clearly separated from the period of fall migration in late July through October. Spring reports span

27 Apr 1974	1	Thousand Acre Marsh [Wayn25]
30 May 1990	1	Bombay Hook NWR [Holg93]

In 1991 an individual lingered at Bombay Hook NWR to 2

June [Hol107]. Reports of 15 in early April (DuMont and DuMont 1972b) and in Newark in June (Scott and Cutler 1963) lack the documentation needed for such an unusual date, number, and locality. Fall reports span

25 Jul 1985	1	Bombay Hook NWR [Edni67]
17 Oct 1970	1	Lewes [Wayn15]

Two found in coastal Kent County on 6 July 1991 were early [Barn54].

Red-necked Phalaropes are less numerous than Wilson's, but the comparison is misleading because the majority of Red-necked Phalaropes migrate offshore, virtually undetected.

REMARKS: Because Red-necked and Red phalaropes winter at sea, it is unlikely that they have undergone the hunting pressures experienced by other shorebirds.

SPECIMEN: USNM 422329, Dewey Beach, 30 May 1934.

Red Phalarope *(Phalaropus fulicaria)*

Regular; migrant; rare to uncommon; very rare in spring; expected mid-October to mid-November.

HABITAT: Predominantly pelagic waters; rare along coast.

MIGRATION: On land, Red Phalaropes are the least common of the 3 phalaropes, and this fact alone accounts for the relative scarcity of Delaware reports. Ordinarily, Red Phalaropes are substantially outnumbered by Red-necked Phalaropes offshore.

In the Mid-Atlantic region, the spring migration tends to be brief and concentrated (Barnhill, pers. obs.), in some years occurring within a 1-week period. The fall migration is longer. Onshore reports span 4 April to 21 May and 27 August to 12 November and include 1 report in December.

They have been reported from Bombay Hook NWR, Little Creek WA, Pickering Beach, Prime Hook NWR, Roosevelt Inlet at Lewes, Cape Henlopen SP, Assawoman WA, Delaware Bay (1 report), and offshore in the Atlantic (5 reports).

The Delaware specimen represents a bird picked up dead near Indian River Inlet on 12 November 1977 (Watson 1977; USNM 527826). Although Watson reports it as the second Delaware specimen, we have been unable to locate another.

SPECIMEN: USNM 527826, details earlier.

[Skua *(Catharacta species)*]

Probably rare visitor offshore (4 years, 1967–91).

DOCUMENTATION: Sight reports.

HABITAT: Pelagic, usually well offshore.

REMARKS: Two species of skuas occur off the Mid-Atlantic coast (Rowlett 1980b). The Great Skua *(Catharacta skua)* breeds in the arctic and winters along the Atlantic coast (AOU 1983) as far south as Florida; the South Polar Skua *(Catharacta maccormicki)* breeds on and near Antarctica and occurs in the North Atlantic in small numbers during the northern summer. The 2 species are difficult to separate at sea because of generally difficult viewing conditions and because they seldom approach boats closely. The recognition that South Polar Skuas also occur regularly off the Mid-Atlantic coast came rather recently (see the discussion in Rowlett 1980b), further complicating the evaluation of Delaware records.

Most skuas are sighted near commercial fishing boats, frequently at a distance offshore of more than 30 mi (48 km). Since 1977 the number of such boats has declined greatly, and as a result the number of observations of skuas in the region has also decreased.

OCCURRENCE: The following 5 records of skuas in Del-

aware waters, though made by observers with extensive experience, are not entirely satisfactory because all lack accompanying descriptions:

9 Feb 1975	1	50 mi E of Rehoboth Beach [Rowl8]
10 Feb 1991	2	74°43' W 38°48' N (Campbell 1992)
26 Aug 1967	1	off Lewes [Wayn13]
19 Sep 1970	1	off Indian River Inlet [Wayn7]
12 Oct 1979	1	Rehoboth Beach [Frec1]

Pomarine Jaeger
(*Stercorarius pomarinus*)

Regular, offshore migrants and perhaps winter visitors, uncommon; to be looked for late March to late May and late August to late December.

DOCUMENTATION: Pomarine Jaeger—multiple sight records; Parasitic Jaeger—specimen (DMNH).

HABITAT: Pelagic.

REMARKS: The relative numbers of the 3 jaeger species off-shore the Mid-Atlantic region are unknown. However, knowledgeable observers generally agree that the Parasitic and Pomarine jaegers occur in roughly similar numbers, whereas the Long-tailed Jaeger is substantially less common. We believe that the regional data basically support this judgment, and that the larger number of observations of the Parasitic Jaeger compared to the Pomarine in Delaware is a statistical accident. We find no conclusive evidence of a difference in seasonal pattern between the 2 species. Some evidence suggests that Parasitics average coming closer to shore than do Pomarines (Rowlett 1980b). If so, the fact that many of the Delaware observations of jaegers are from shore or near to shore would help explain the smaller number of Pomarines found.

Rowlett (1980b) gives regional extreme dates of 23 April through 16 May and 11 August through 6 December for the Parasitic Jaeger, compared to 25 March through 29 May and 8

Parasitic Jaeger
(*Stercorarius parasiticus*)

August through 6 December for the Pomarine Jaeger. Delaware records are generally in agreement with this range for the 2 jaegers combined but extend essentially to the end of December.

The specimen of Parasitic Jaeger (DMNH 63415) removes any doubt about its occurrence in Delaware, but no record of Pomarine Jaeger is convincingly documented. However, since records involving more than 17 birds, including some seen at extremely close range, have been reported by expert observers, the occurrence of Pomarine Jaeger is not seriously in doubt.

The Long-tailed Jaeger (*S. longicaudus*) is seldom recorded in this region, and there are no Delaware records. The experience of regional observers with this species is quite limited, and it is therefore possible that the species is being overlooked.

SPECIMEN: Parasitic Jaeger DMNH 63415, Cape Henlopen, 23 December 1965.

Laughing Gull (*Larus atricilla*)

Regular; summer resident; abundant. Expected late March to mid-December, becoming less common late in fall and winter. Breeds colonially on marsh islands in Rehoboth Bay. Reestablished after extirpation in the nineteenth century.

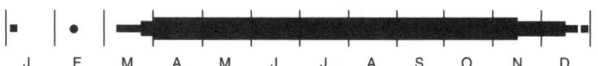

| | | | | | | | | | | | |
|J|F|M|A|M|J|J|A|S|O|N|D|

HABITAT: Maritime, but feeds in fields across the Delmarva Peninsula and in dumps, as well as in the littoral zone. Breeds above high tide line on saltmarsh islands.

SPRING: Typically, the first birds arrive 15–20 March; by 1–5 May most of the breeding and summering population were present in a New Jersey study (Montevecchi et al. 1979). High counts include

14 May 1971	8,000	Pickering Beach [Cutl1]
3 May 1980	5,000	Sussex County [Barn38]
10 May 1986	2,275	from Kitts Hummock to South Bowers [Spen2]

BREEDING: Linehan and Jones (1971) include it in their Delaware bird list as breeding but without supporting information. B. Williams (Colonial Waterbird Registry) reported 120 incubating adults 25 June 1976 on Big Reedy Island. The next year M. A. Byrd (Colonial Waterbird Registry) provided a similar report involving 96 adults. Further confirmation (with more details) came in 1982 when nests, eggs, and young of an estimated 1,000 pairs were found 13 June 1982 in Rehoboth Bay marshes [Barn37] (photograph by Fintel, DMNH 130).

Atlas. During the Atlas project the Rehoboth Bay site was the only confirmed breeding location, but the species was reported regularly throughout the Inland Bays and adjacent farmland, as well as in considerable numbers up the Delaware River to Woodland Beach. Beyond that area it was less abundant. It was also found along the Nanticoke River as far up as Seaford. It is a common plow follower and landfill visitor across the Delmarva Peninsula, and it is regular and abundant enough in the Bombay Hook NWR area for breeding to be suspected though not yet confirmed.

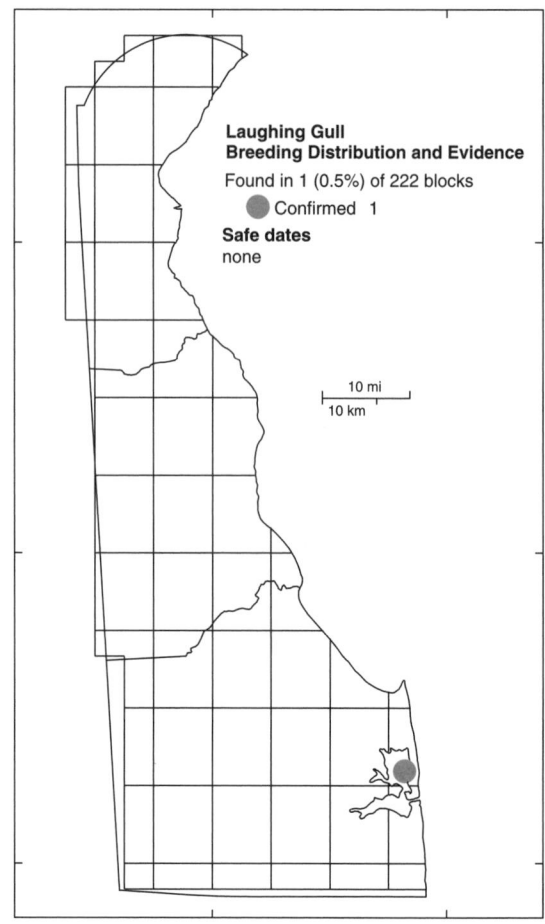

Laughing Gull
Breeding Distribution and Evidence
Found in 1 (0.5%) of 222 blocks
● Confirmed 1
Safe dates
none

10 mi
10 km

Nesting. In Rehoboth Bay it nests on marsh islands subject to tidal action. The nests are depressions in large conical mounds of mud and reeds [Edni4] placed in saltmarsh cordgrass. These mounds sometimes merge in the center of the colonies and sometimes have seaweed and flotsam in their bases. Some nests are placed on the wrack line (D. Rothstein, DNHI, pers. comm.).

Reported egg dates coincide with visits to the colonies and extend from 1–25 June only. Some young were present 9 June 1986 [ThoJ2] and 6 June 1990 and 1992 (D. Rothstein, DNHI, pers. comm.), implying earlier egg dates. Breeding probably extends later in years when storms cause extensive nest failure, as suggested by egg dates extending to 18 July in Maryland (Robbins and Bystrak 1977). Egging was formerly allowed until 4 July on the East Coast (Bent 1907).

History. Although the Laughing Gull is now the common summer gull in Delaware, it did not breed here earlier in the twentieth century. It was probably a common Delaware breeding bird before the nineteenth century, but the view presented by the Delaware records is obscure. It was surely persecuted through the nineteenth century (see Common Tern account). In 1880 Bush (notes), who assembled the best collection of

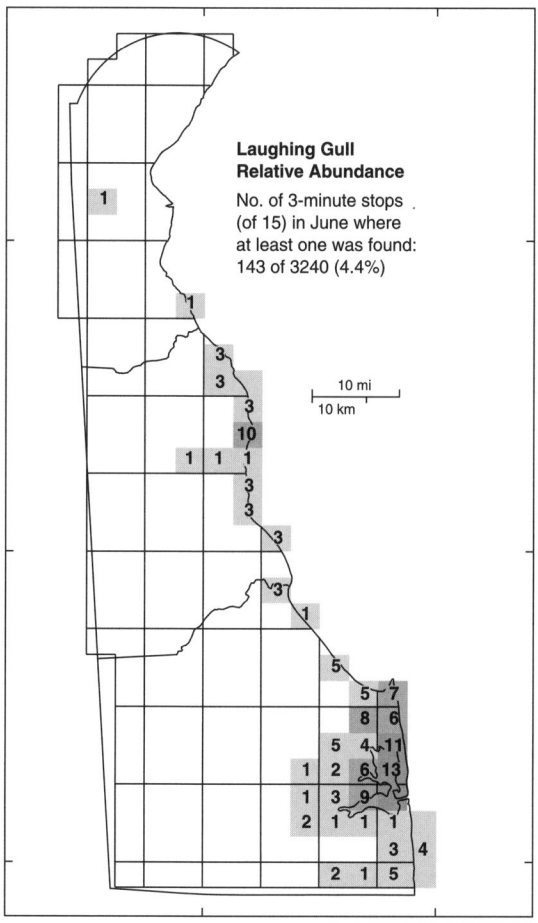

Laughing Gull Relative Abundance

No. of 3-minute stops (of 15) in June where at least one was found: 143 of 3240 (4.4%)

Delaware birds, sailed down to Indian River Inlet from Rehoboth Beach to collect birds. He collected adult and young Least Terns and commented on the presence of Willets and snipe but made no mention of gulls, and he had no gulls in his collection. Rhoads and Pennock (1905) published a Delaware bird list that included 3 species of gulls but not Laughing Gull. Pennock later (1908b) remedied this omission with these comments: "undoubtedly this bird was an abundant summer resident, at least from Lewes down along the coast to Fenwick Light, at the Maryland line, up to the time of extermination of our shore-nesting birds, twenty or more years ago. Many of the younger generation of native gunners do not know this bird at all. . . . I saw two Laughing Gulls May 20, 1907, flying northward at Indian River Inlet." Thus originally abundant in Delaware, Laughing Gulls were extirpated before 1880 and first noted again during 1907. They are again abundant.

Trends. The Laughing Gull has increased throughout its range, including the Mid-Atlantic coast, at an average annual rate exceeding 5% for the period 1966–90 [Usfw1]. The May Count shows a similar upward tendency.

Breeding population. The estimate of the state summer population, including nonbreeding birds, ranged from 2,000 to 10,000 in the 1980s. The higher figure is supported by May Counts of 6,000 on 13 May 1978 and 1989 and 4,000 on 14 May 1988 (Rufe 1987, 1988, and 1989), dates on which most Laugh-

ing Gulls should be on breeding (or summering) grounds (Montevecchi et al. 1979).

Three estimates of the breeding population in Rehoboth Bay were made in 1986. Thomas, with West [West4], estimated 1,000+ pairs on Big Reedy Island, 110+ adults on Little Reedy Island, and 150+ adults on Big Bacon Island, all on 11 June. Three days later Fintel (notes) estimated about 5,000 pairs overall, 3–4 times the numbers he recorded in 1983. Ednie and Skolnicki entered 1 of these colonies on 19 June and located 62 nests with eggs or young [Edni58].

Andrews (1990) estimated the Delaware population at 1,280 nesting pairs in 1985, up from 96 pairs in 1977. Gelvin-Innvaer made a 1991 aerial population estimate of about 2,000 nesting pairs in the east Rehoboth Bay concentration, the largest of several known concentrations of nesting Laughing Gulls in Delaware (Belant and Dolbeer 1993b). Rothstein (DNHI, pers. comm.) estimated the breeding population at 5,000–10,000 pairs in Rehoboth Bay in the early 1990s and suggests that these gulls may displace nesting terns or prey on their chicks.

FALL: By 15–20 October typically only about 100 birds remain, and during November only a few dozen. From then into winter numbers gradually diminish.

WINTER: By mid-December few or no birds are present in Sussex County. It is seldom recorded on CBCs—present on 18% of counts (1966–89)—and is seldom present past the end of December. February reports include single birds in the Rehoboth Beach area on 12 February 1983 [Barn1] and on 22 February 1984 [Frec1].

1966–89 CBC Summary

Christmas Bird Count	Years Found	Range of No. Found	Median
Wilmington			
Middletown	2	1–6	
Bombay Hook			
Cape Henlopen	10	1–21	
Rehoboth	9	1–10	
STATEWIDE (high in 1973)	15	1–22	2

BANDING: Young banded in New Jersey (46), Maryland (8), and Virginia (8) have been recovered in Delaware, demonstrating considerable local interchange. One banded in Massachusetts in August was recovered 2 months later in Delaware [Usfw3]. A Maine-to-Virginia banding analysis found that young Laughing Gulls tended to disperse northward (74%) during August and September; autumn migration was initiated in October. During December and January first-year Northeast Laughing Gulls continued from the Gulf Coast to South and Central America, but many adults remained along the Gulf Coast. Adults returned to their Northeast breeding areas during April–May. In contrast, first-year birds remained on their wintering areas at least through April (Belant and Dolbeer 1993a).

SPECIMENS: 33; DMNH, CM, UDEL.

Franklin's Gull (*Larus pipixcan*)

Casual (1989, 1991, 1992).

DOCUMENTATION: Photograph (D. S. Czaplak, AB 46: 1125).

REMARKS: Franklin's Gull, a bird of western North America, occurs only casually on the Atlantic coast (AOU 1983). Once the distinctive upper-wing pattern of the adult develops, the species is readily identified, but younger birds are easily confused with subadult Laughing Gulls. The Delaware Franklin's Gull records are

9 Jul 1989	1	Port Mahon [Shoc8]
10–15 Sep 1991	1	Bombay Hook NWR [Pulc3] (Campbell 1992)
26 Jul 1992	1	Port Mahon [Czap3]

The 1989 and 1991 records are supported by definitive notes and the 1992 record by an unmistakable photograph (Czaplak, filed at DMNH). The wing pattern on this bird, though not photographed, was observed as the bird flew. The photograph of the 1992 bird clearly establishes the occurrence of the species in Delaware.

Little Gull (*Larus minutus*)

Regular (27 years, 1959–92); winter visitor; rare, but less so in the 1970s. To be looked for from November through May.

J F M A M J J A S O N D

DOCUMENTATION: Photograph (J. A. Gordon, DMNH 77).

HABITAT: Coastal bays, marshes, and beaches.

REMARKS: The Little Gull was first recorded in Delaware on 28 November 1959 at Indian River Inlet [MiJC1]. Since that report, the species has been recorded in all but 6 years through 1992. Most reports are from the vicinity of Little Creek WA–Kitts Hummock or Cape Henlopen–Indian River Inlet, but the species might be found anywhere along the coast. It is most frequently reported in numbers up to about 6, but from late March to early May 1974 (the longest period of continuous presence) 10–15 were regularly reported, and a high of 30 was obtained in mid-April [Conw4]. This species rarely summers in Delaware, but 3 remained through 10 August 1974 from this group [Wayn73] accounting for all but 5 of the birds reported in summer. The earliest winter arrival is 1 on 8 November 1988 at Gordon Pond WA [Holg88].

This European species has recently colonized North America. Though the first North American specimens were apparently taken some time between 1819 and 1822 in northwestern or northcentral Canada (Baillie 1963), Scott (1963) recorded the first observed North American nesting in Ontario. Little Gulls are now seen regularly along the eastern seaboard and in the Great Lakes region, often accompanying Bonaparte's Gulls, and have even been recorded in South America (Blokpoel et al. 1984).

Black-headed Gull (*Larus ridibundus*)

Occasional (27 years, 1956–92); mostly winter visitor.

J F M A M J J A S O N D

DOCUMENTATION: Photographs (A. P. Ednie, DMNH 344, 363).

REMARKS: This species occurs most frequently from November through January, but some migration is observed through May. The only well-described summer record is from 13 June 1985, a bird in breeding plumage [Edni68]. Three birds "apparently molting into winter plumage" on 17 July 1971 (Scott and Cutler 1971) are inadequately described for this plumage and in a season when usually only stragglers are reported, and a report of 1 on 27 August 1967 is not supported with notes (Scott and Cutler 1966). The earliest fall record is a bird in first basic plumage reported on 14 September 1966 at Cape Henlopen that remained into October and was identified by many observers [Lake7]. There are reports from all 3 counties, but over a third of the records are from Indian River Inlet to Cape Henlopen in winter. The first report was a single bird on the 1 January 1956 Rehoboth CBC [Cutl23], the second a bird observed at Indian River Inlet on 28 November 1959 [MiJC1]. The species then went unrecorded until 1964. From then through 1977 it occurred annually, but since 1977 it has occurred sporadically at the Wilmington Wastewater Treatment Plant in the 1989 and 1990 winters.

Bonaparte's Gull (*Larus philadelphia*)

Regular; winter visitor; common. Expected late October to mid-May.

J F M A M J J A S O N D

HABITAT: Ocean, bays, estuaries, and adjacent beaches; during migration, also impoundments and Delaware River.

SPRING: The numbers of birds reported reached a high of 8,000 on 14 March 1980 from Rehoboth Beach to Indian River Inlet [Frec1] and then decrease noticeably during 20–30 March. In April only a few dozen remain and most depart by 15–20 May. As the large winter population near the mouth of the Delaware Bay disappears, spring migration is clearly signaled by the arrival of flocks in Kent County. The first such spring flocks arrived

| 23 Mar 1968 | 300 | Pickering Beach [DuPA6] |
| 24 Mar 1974 | 1,100 | Port Mahan [DuPG25] |

These other flocks help define the migration period:

17 Apr 1961	300 (peak)	Little Creek WA (Lesser 1965)
17 Apr 1965	200	Churchmans Marsh [Klab7]
24 Apr 1966	250	Delaware City [Armi3]
12 May 1984	100	Kitts Hummock [Cutl10]
22 May 1928	several dozen	Kitts Hummock [Hans1]

SUMMER: The few summer records are 1 to 3 nonbreeding birds, all in Kent County. Nonbreeding birds in the East usually summer in coastal areas south to New England and in the interior to the Great Lakes (AOU 1983).

FALL: Although some individuals may arrive in early October, the species is not expected until 25–30 October. Larger numbers appear by late November exemplified by 528 on 17 November 1974 [PylR10] and 2,000 flying north off Cape Henlopen on 22 November 1964 [PylR9]. Frech noted over 1,000 at Indian River Inlet on 15–18 December 1989 and then none for the rest of the winter [Frec19].

1966–89 CBC Summary

Christmas Bird Count	Years Found	Range of No. Found	Median
Wilmington	3	83–275	
Middletown	3	1–4	
Bombay Hook	22	1–350	5
Cape Henlopen	2	2–298	57
Rehoboth	24	7–2,013	205
STATEWIDE (low in 1986, high in 1977)	24	15–2,133	303

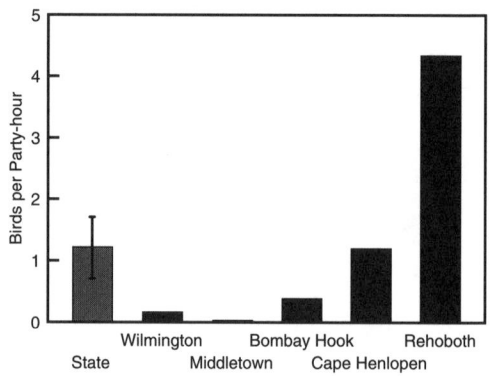

CBC Geographic Distribution

WINTER: Because numbers of birds on CBCs vary noticeably, no trend is apparent. In some winters 2,000–3,000 are present at Indian River Inlet on count day; in others there are few birds. This variation probably reflects daily rather than annual fluctuations and may be related to variations in weather or food supply. Although the species has been found along the Delaware River in New Castle and Kent counties, it is most often found along the lower bay and ocean coast. It is most numerous on the Rehoboth CBC.

SPECIMENS: USNM 422165, Sussex Co., Love Creek, 13 January 1935; USNM 422159, Cedar Beach, 1 April 1932; USNM 421893, Slaughter Beach, 10 April 1932; DMNH 77240, Lewes, 25 November 1988.

Mew Gull (*Larus canus*)

Accidental (1976).

DOCUMENTATION: Photographs (C. P. Wilds, DMNH 79–81).

REMARKS: A single individual seen near Kenton in a large flock of Ring-billed Gulls on 13 April 1978 provides the only record for this small gull [WilC1]. Mew Gulls are considered casual on the Atlantic coast south to Massachusetts in winter, with some sight records farther south (AOU 1983). It is not clear whether the East Coast birds are from the western North American population or the subspecifically distinct population in Europe (Common Gull).

Photographs of the Delaware bird clearly show its small, unmarked bill. The bill was not thinner than those of surrounding Ring-billed Gulls, a finding consistent with measurements made on skins by the observer. Other distinct differences from Ring-billed Gull were a dark eye (on this adult bird) and more white on the outer wing (Wilds notes). Wilds' notes describe the wings as follows: "With wings folded tips appear to be barred evenly black and white—much more white than on any [Ring-billed Gulls]. When flushed, outermost primary showed long white finger above black tip; next one also had extensive white, but less." These distinctions were also confirmed by examination of skins.

Wilds, on reviewing a draft of this account, commented she is "more impressed now with the amount of variation of Ring-billed Gulls," but we think the 1978 photograph and notes remain definitive. No convincing differences in tarsus length or head shape can be seen in the photographs. No one reviewing the slides has ever had any difficulty picking out the bird in question from surrounding Ring-billed Gulls, but nonetheless there seems to be no consistent difference in shape or overall color between this bird and Ring-billed Gulls. We concur with *American Birds* and *Delmarva Ornithologist* editors, who considered the observation reliable.

Ring-billed Gull *(Larus delawarensis)*

Occurs all year; common to abundant. Most numerous mid-September to mid-May. Winter numbers increasing at about 5% per year.

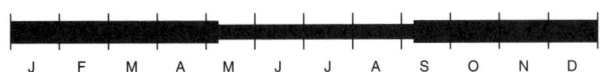

HABITAT: Wide variety, including ocean, bays, beaches, estuaries, inland lakes, reservoirs, and rivers; also landfills, plowed fields, and shopping malls.

HISTORY: Although Audubon called the species the most common gull of the Americas, it did not remain common. Rhoads and Pennock (1905) described it as a "transient visitor, rare in winter" in Delaware. Hanson had no entry for it in the 1920s and 1930s. During that period 2 were collected by Buckalew (notes): 2 February 1933 at Rehoboth Beach and 5 January 1935 at Lewes.

SPRING: The onset of migration is signaled by the appearance of large flocks in plowed fields beginning in late February:

25 Feb 1985	1,600 (early)	Rds. 432 and 435, S oC&Canal [Wayn53]
21 Mar 1986	2,500 (peak)	Rt. 301 and Rd. 457, S of C&D Canal [Wayn53]
28 Mar 1982	1,205 (peak)	Bombay Hook NWR [Bayn4]
17 Apr 1972	800 (peak)	Little Creek WA (Lesser 1965)

Most of the migrants and wintering adults typically depart by 5–10 May, leaving behind nonbreeders and first-year birds. The May Count reported as few as 230 (13 May 1978) and as many as 4,306 (9 May 1987). Most single-party May reports refer to only a few dozen birds.

SUMMER: Some nonbreeding Ring-billed Gulls summer along the Delaware coast, inland bays, and lower river; the Delmarva Peninsula is the southernmost region for significant numbers of summering birds on the East Coast (Ryder 1993,

map). Individuals do not begin to breed until they are 2 or more years old (Ryder 1993, 18). The species reaches fully adult plumage variably at 2–4 years (Ludwig 1974; Blokpoel et al. 1985). The closest breeding areas are located on some of the larger lakes in New York.

Examples of high summer counts include

7 Jun 1975	80	Dragon Run [Wayn2]
20 Jun 1964	165	Little Creek WA [StiA5]
27 Jun 1979	50	Rehoboth Beach [Frec1]

These reports may lead to underestimation of the summer population as indicated by more recent reports of 2,000 and 735 on 13 and 25 June 1986, respectively, at Bombay Hook NWR (Thomas 1986). Typical numbers reported in June are similar to those of mid- or late May, whereas July reports usually involve 10 or fewer. More information is needed on the numbers and ages of summering birds to assess their occurrence in Delaware. For example, Ring-billed Gulls feed at landfills and dumps, yet this is not reported in summer. Thus it remains unclear when population movements take place and which age classes are involved.

FALL: Southward migrants reach the Atlantic coast in August and increase in abundance during fall (Southern 1974); that is, about 5–10 August a few dozen are reported in Delaware. The first reports in the hundreds begin in September with these:

6 Sep 1981	301	Bombay Hook NWR [Bayn4]
11 Sep 1986	100	Edgemore [Edni1]
18 Sep 1965	300	Churchmans Marsh [Klab2]

The arrival dates of juveniles has not been recorded in Delaware, but they usually first arrive in August at Cape May—earliest on 16 June 1982 (Sibley 1993). Banding studies of birds breeding in the Great Lakes basin show that Delaware is on the migration pathway between the summer staging areas in the southern Great Lakes and the primary wintering range in Florida.

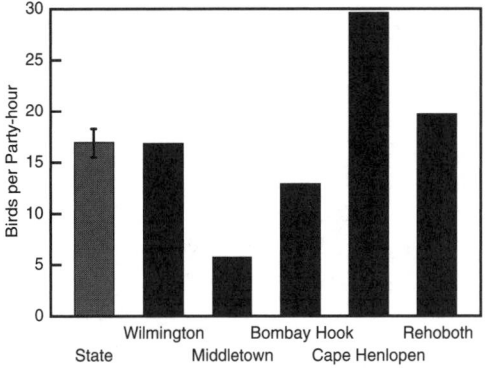

CBC Geographic Distribution

Christmas Bird Count	Years Found	Range of No. Found	Median
Wilmington	24	42–17,222	1,255
Middletown	24	24–2,219	199
Bombay Hook	24	65–1,723	867
Cape Henlopen	24	329–4,652	1,552
Rehoboth	24	568–6,815	1,460
STATEWIDE	24	2,786–21,598	6,045
(increasing; low in 1968, high in 1979)			

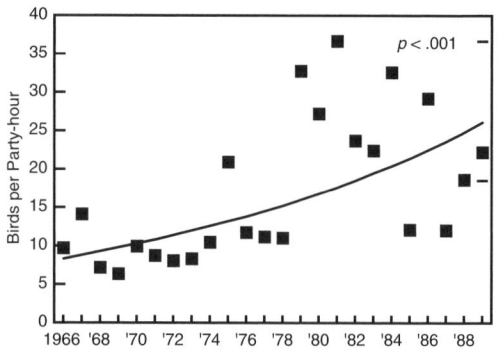

CBC Trend; Increasing at 5% per Year

WINTER: This species has shown an increase in CBC numbers. Large winter counts have been made at garbage-disposal sites on CBCs. The Great Lakes breeding population of Ring-billed Gulls, the source of Delaware birds, increased from about 3,000 pairs in 1930 to 335,000 in 1967 (Ludwig 1974), and this remarkable population increase has continued (Blokpoel and Tessier 1986; Lock 1988).

BANDING: Of 27 Ring-billed Gulls recovered in Delaware, 21 were banded in the Great Lakes region as far west as Michigan, 5 in Quebec, and 1 in Newfoundland.

SPECIMENS: 57; DMNH, USNM.

Herring Gull *(Larus argentatus)*

Resident; fairly common to common. Winter numbers decreasing at 5% per year, but summer population possibly increasing. Breeds only in the Rehoboth Bay marshes in small numbers.

| J | F | M | A | M | J | J | A | S | O | N | D |

HABITAT: Wide variety, including ocean, bays, beaches, estuaries; less commonly lakes and reservoirs; landfills in winter.

SPRING: Migration appears to be obscured by movements to and from food sources. Spring is marked by a decrease in numbers in New Castle County, where the last reports of greater than 100 are

20 Feb 1971	105	Dragon Run [Wayn51]
27 Mar 1965	150	Churchmans Marsh [Klab5]
5 Apr 1980	210	Churchmans Marsh [Kell6]

Similarly, winter numbers at Roosevelt Inlet, Lewes, decreased below 100 after 2 April 1980 [Frec1]. Lesser (1975)

reported a peak count at Little Creek WA of 455 on 5 May 1972, but by that time the gulls are being drawn to the spawning horseshoe crabs. Numbers reported on the May Count range from a few hundred to as many as 3,600. By the end of May noticeably fewer are usually reported, but large local concentrations remain along the bayshore at least into June.

BREEDING: A small breeding population of Herring Gulls inhabits Rehoboth Bay. Linehan and Jones (1971) included the species in their Delaware bird list as breeding but without supporting documentation. B. Williams (Colonial Waterbird Registry) reported 24 adults nesting on 25 June 1976 in a Laughing Gull colony on Big Reedy Island. The next year M. A. Byrd (Colonial Waterbird Registry) made a similar report, with 31 adults present. The breeding colony was present in 1982 [Barn33], and they are still breeding in Rehoboth Bay in about the same numbers as in the early 1990s (D. Rothstein, DNHI, pers. comm.).

Atlas. A small number were found breeding with Laughing Gulls at a single site in the Rehoboth Bay marshes. Only confirmed breeding records were acceptable for the Atlas project. The small breeding population in Delaware may result in predation by this species on some of the smaller beach and marsh nesters such as the terns.

Nesting. The first nest record mentions "about 12 nests" in the Rehoboth Bay saltmarsh about 1 mi south of Dewey Beach on Big Reedy Island on 12 June 1983. One nest was described; it contained 2 eggs and was built on the marsh using grasses [Frec51].

History. The Herring Gull was persecuted by eggers and gunners in the nineteenth century. As a consequence it was

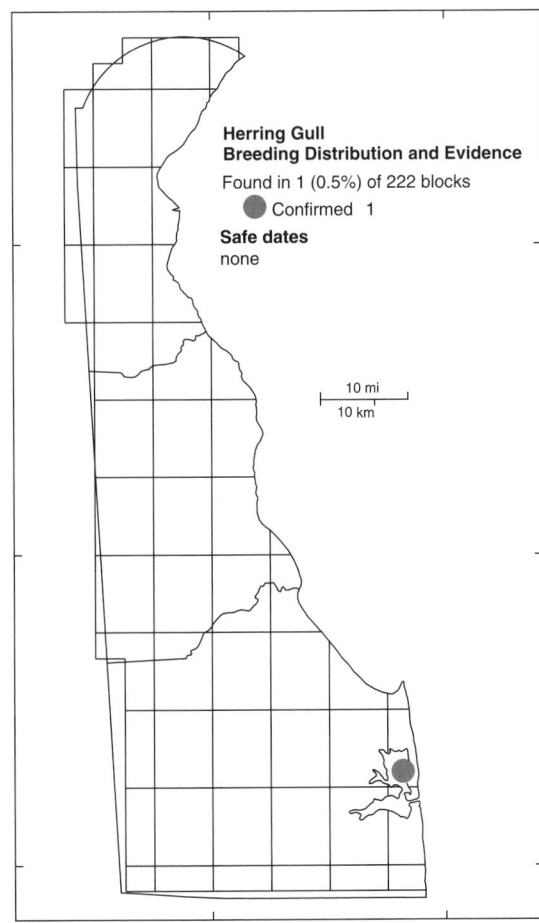

Herring Gull
Breeding Distribution and Evidence
Found in 1 (0.5%) of 222 blocks
● Confirmed 1
Safe dates
none

10 mi
10 km

mi of Delaware's ocean and bay shoreline, and therefore must be in the order of magnitude of 10,000 individuals, including populations at concentration points such as landfills and the sandbars off Bombay Hook NWR. The numbers are subject to huge variation as the summering gulls seek food sources.

FALL: Numbers of birds present in Cape Henlopen SP first reached 100 on 2 September 1977, and larger numbers were frequently reported there beginning 25 September 1977. A pronounced peak of 1,200 was recorded there 17 November 1979 [Frec1]. A peak count of 100 was reached on 6 September on the 1981 Bombay Hook NWR survey. An increase was not seen on the 1965 Churchmans Marsh survey until 150 were counted on 14 November and reached 450 on 28 November [Faus6]. These birds were resting at Churchmans Marsh and could be seen flying to and from the Wilmington landfill. On balance, an increase in numbers in the state usually begins in early October.

1966–89 CBC Summary

Christmas Bird Count	Years Found	Range of No. Found	Median
Wilmington	24	207–12,837	1,431
Middletown	24	31–830	278
Bombay Hook	24	234–5,809	758
Cape Henlopen	24	182–3,085	922
Rehoboth	24	463–10,965	1,376
STATEWIDE	24	1,496–20,400	6,286
(decreasing; low in 1988, high in 1967)			

WINTER: The Herring Gull, like all gulls and terns, suffered from persecution, egg collecting (for food and sport), and shooting for sport. Its numbers began to expand after it was protected, particularly increasing in response to an almost limitless supply of garbage. However, the species' numbers declined during the 1966–89 CBC analysis period. It is most numerous on the Wilmington and Rehoboth CBCs; a new high count of 5,296 was set on the 30 December 1990 Cape Henlopen CBC. The Seaford CBC (1983–89) reports relatively low numbers, similar to the Middletown CBC, not surprising at an inland location.

Comparison of the results of the 1943–45 Hoopes Reservoir

nearly extirpated as a breeding bird from the inland lakes of New York and in 1900 bred only as far south on the coast as Maine (Peterson 1988c). It had extended its breeding range south to Maryland by 1955 (Stewart and Robbins 1958) and now breeds south to South Carolina (AOU 1983). The summer population may have increased along the Mid-Atlantic coast during the 1966–90 period [Usfw1].

Summer population. A breeding population of more than 50 pairs has never been reported. Most Herring Gulls seen in Delaware during summer are immatures, which take 3–7 years to attain breeding condition (Cramp 1983). It is present in all marine habitats and its range penetrates up the Delaware River into Pennsylvania. Most June and July reports are of fewer than 100 birds, but the 1986 DNREC shorebird survey reported 9,000 at Bombay Hook NWR on 13 June (Thomas 1986) and the Bombay Hook NWR staff reported 7,440 on 14 June 1991 [Smit2]. Observations of thousands on sandbars slightly northwest of Bombay Hook NWR have occurred in June [Cutl39]; this site may be a social sleeping ground (Tinbergen 1960, 40). In May and June the gulls feed on overturned horseshoe crabs and their eggs in Kent and Sussex counties and on the New Jersey side of the bay (Sibley 1993). The Delaware summer population might be estimated at about 10 per mi for the almost 100

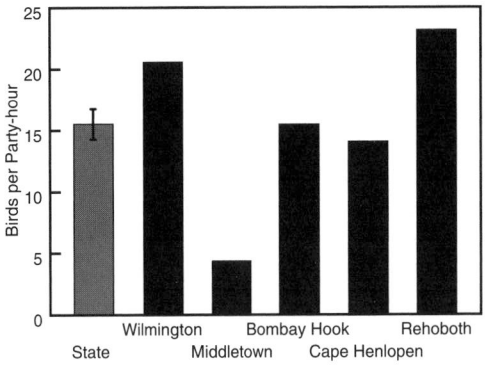

CBC Geographic Distribution

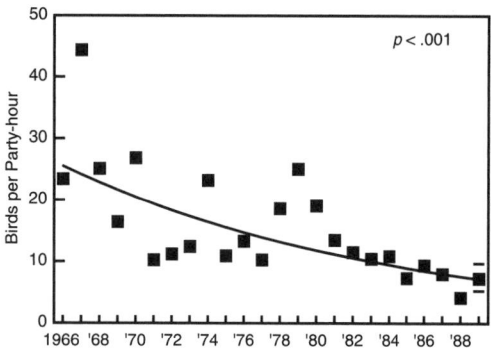

CBC Trend; Decreasing at 5% per Year

survey with the 1964 follow-up survey shows a pronounced increase in Herring Gull winter numbers during that 20-year interval. The Herring Gull occurred 3 times as frequently and in 5 times the numbers in 1964 as in 1943–45. The increase in numbers occurred despite an increase in height and density of the forest canopy at Hoopes Reservoir during the 20-year interval between surveys (Falk 1971), a factor that would tend to decrease the occurrence and observation of gulls.

Herring Gulls winter in large numbers east of Delaware over the continental shelf seaward of the 30-fathom contour (about 40–70 mi offshore) from October to early May (Rowlett 1980b). As many as 20,000 were gathered around fishing vessels 45 and 54 mi southeast of Ocean City, Maryland, 3 December 1977. Similar numbers are to be expected off the Delaware coastline.

BANDING: Of 93 birds recovered in Delaware that were banded in New York, New England, and Eastern Canada, usually as chicks, 69 (74%) were recovered in Delaware from September through December verifying movement southward down the Atlantic coast to Delaware in the fall. All 4 Delaware recoveries of birds banded from the smaller Great Lakes population were made from January through July, suggesting that Great Lakes birds arrive here indirectly.

SPECIMENS: 21; DMNH, UDEL, USNM.

[Thayer's Gull *(Larus thayeri)*]

One sight record.

DOCUMENTATION: Unpublished notes.

REMARKS: An adult seen in Cape Henlopen SP 9 May 1981 constitutes the only report [Barn56], the date given in *American Birds* being a misprint. Unpublished notes from Barnhill provide a detailed comparison of the appearance of the bird with that of Herring Gulls standing beside it. The most relevant points are that the plumage was fully adult, yet the eye was dark; the head was smaller than the heads of Herring Gulls, but the bill was the same size as the Herring Gulls'; there were much reduced white spots in the wing; and the wings had dark gray rather than black tips (not well seen). These notes were reported in *American Birds* as "a plausible description." In the absence of a specimen or diagnostic photograph this species cannot be placed on the Delaware list.

The AOU (1983), in giving Thayer's Gull full species status, added the following caution: Thayer's Gull was formerly regarded as a race of Herring Gull but is now considered a distinct species. Recent field studies indicate that Thayer's Gull and the Kumlien's subspecies of Iceland Gull (once also regarded as a separate species) interbreed in mixed colonies on Baffin Island, but the extent and nature of the interbreeding has not yet been determined (Weber 1981), and Godfrey (1986) lists both Thayer's and Kumlien's gulls as subspecies of Iceland Gull. The status of the complex is still under study (AOU 1993).

Iceland Gull (*Larus glaucoides*)

Regular (25 years, 1962–91); winter visitor; rare. To be looked for along the coast and Delaware River from December to June.

DOCUMENTATION: Photographs (W. A. Fintel, DMNH 329, 330).

HABITAT: Ocean, bays, estuaries, and adjacent beaches. Scavenges at garbage disposal sites.

REMARKS: The first published occurrence of this white-winged gull in Delaware was on 4 June 1962 at Little Creek WA [Less16]. From that time through 1991 it was recorded in every year but 1963, 1973, and 1986–88, and in every month but September. Although birds may remain for an extended period, they are usually sighted only once or twice. The most extended visits were recorded in the Lewes area:

22 Apr–12 Jun 1982	Cape Henlopen [Frec9]
3 Dec–30 May 1983	Lake Gerrar, Rehoboth Beach [Frec12]
11 Dec–10 Mar 1984	Lake Gerrar, Rehoboth Beach [Frec43]

The plumage of the 1984 bird was 1 year more advanced than that of the 1982–83 bird. Although most often found near the coast, Iceland Gulls have been reported in 7 years in New Castle County and 7 years in Kent County. We have excellent photographs of a bird at Port Mahon on 10 May 1991 (C. Campbell, DMNH 366, 403) and of another at the Wilmington Landfill on 21 February 1994 (B. Lantz, DMNH print collection).

This species was listed as casual in Delaware by Barry (1942), presumably based on earlier occurrences for which we have no records.

Lesser Black-backed Gull (*Larus fuscus*)

Occasional (18 years, 1964–93); winter visitor; uncommon. To be looked for from December through March.

DOCUMENTATION: Multiple sight records.

HABITAT: Ocean, bays, estuaries, and adjacent beaches; landfills.

REMARKS: This species was reported much less often than Iceland Gull in the 1960s and 1970s; by the 1980s and into the 1990s the opposite is true. The change, in part, may be the result of observers becoming familiar with this less obvious species, but this increase is paralleled in Massachusetts (Viet and Petersen 1993), where it is more common. After being first recorded during January 1964 [Teel1], it has been noted every year through 1993 except 1966–69, 1971–77, and 1983. It occurs most frequently from December through March, but there are a few records from August through November. The latest spring departure was an adult that stayed at Bombay Hook NWR from 10 March to 4 April 1991 [Camp11]. Three birds were found on a 17 November 1991 pelagic trip [Barn1], but usually only single birds were reported. Most were found along the coast, but there are indications that landfills, if observed more consistently, would in fact produce the majority of records (Shoch 1989).

Glaucous Gull (*Larus hyperboreus*)

Occasional (22 years, 1960–92); winter visitor. Occurs most often in winter or spring.

J F M A M J J A S O N D

DOCUMENTATION: Photographs (D. G. Batt, DMNH 265; J. F. Swertinski, DMNH 364).

HABITAT: Ocean, bays, estuaries, and adjacent beaches. Also at landfills.

REMARKS: The first published occurrence in Delaware of this largest of the circumpolar gulls was on the 2 January 1960 Rehoboth CBC [Cutl20], with additional reports of the species at Indian River Inlet on 13 February and 24 May [Dyke11]. From that time through the end of 1991 this species was recorded, in two-thirds of the years. It occurs most frequently December–March, but a few records have accumulated from spring and mid-summer.

Generally, only one bird is reported. Most occur at Bombay Hook NWR or Cape Henlopen SP, but the species can be found anywhere along the coast and north along the Delaware River to the Wilmington landfill. One was identified at a hog farm near Dagsboro on 22 December 1992 [Whit5]. The earliest fall reports are

14 Nov 1970	1	Indian River Inlet [Gilb1]
25 Nov 1971	1	Cape Henlopen SP [Rowl10]
4 Dec 1983	1	Rehoboth Beach [Frec1]

Great Black-backed Gull (*Larus marinus*)

Occurs all year; common. One nest record (1986). Winter numbers increasing at 2% per year.

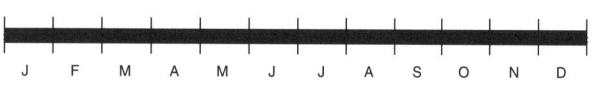

J F M A M J J A S O N D

HABITAT: Ocean, bays, estuaries, and adjacent beaches.

SPRING: No migration period is evident. Higher counts in February and March may reflect the arrival of northern birds seeking to avoid severe weather north of Delaware or may represent staging of birds preparing to migrate to colonies in New England and Canada. Typical reports involve fewer than 100 birds.

BREEDING: The first Delaware nest of this species was found during the Atlas project on the high point of a sandbar near the south Mispillion River jetty. A single egg (DMNH print collection), attended by a pair of gulls, hatched on 7 June 1986 [West4]. Fintel and Frech "suspected one pair nesting" on 21 June 1987 in the Rehoboth Bay marshes [Frec1]. These Delaware records fill a gap in its southward breeding range extension, since it has been reported breeding south to North Carolina (AOU 1983).

Summer population. The statewide summer population of Great Black-backed Gulls is usually fewer than 100 individuals, judging by the field reports on record. High summer reports include 75 at Delaware Seashore SP on 2 and 19 June 1978 and 100 at Cape Henlopen SP on 27 June 1979 [Frec1]. These high numbers illustrate the mobile nature of prebreeders as they opportunistically follow food supplies. Bent (1921) gives the breeding range in his time as south to Nova Scotia and the Bay

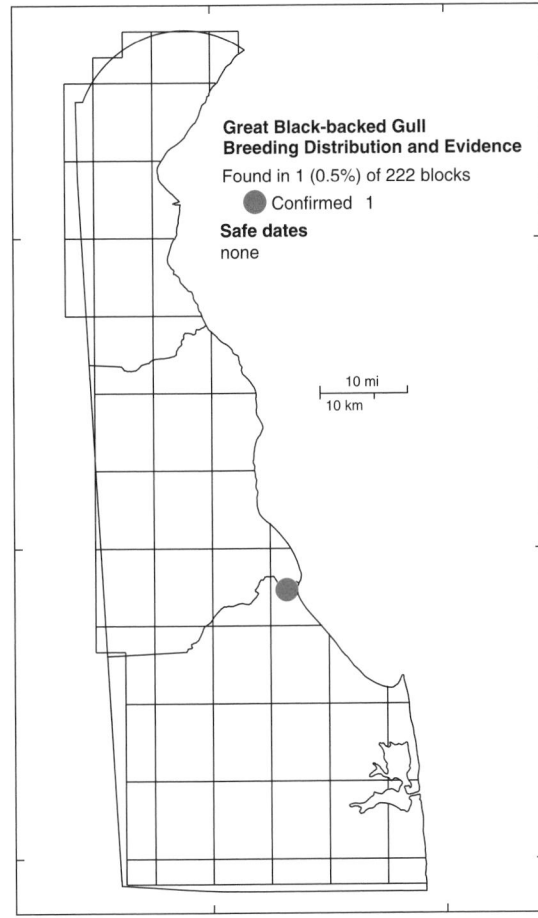

**Great Black-backed Gull
Breeding Distribution and Evidence**

Found in 1 (0.5%) of 222 blocks

⬤ Confirmed 1

Safe dates
none

10 mi
10 km

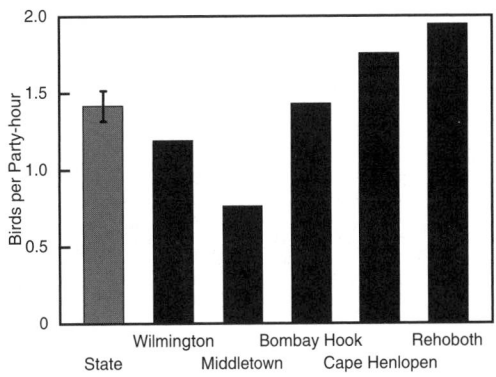

CBC Geographic Distribution

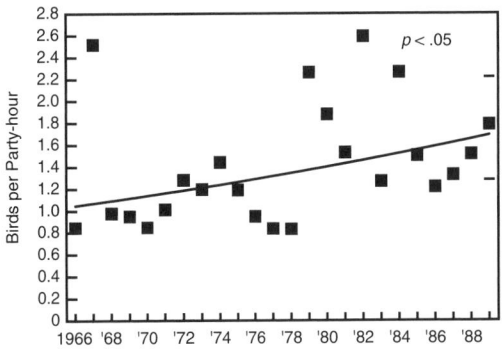

CBC Trend; Increasing at 2% per Year

of Fundy. Like the Herring and Ring-billed gulls, the Great Black-backed has expanded its breeding range southward. It appears to differ from the other species in that there is no indication that this extension is a reclamation of former range; rather it is an historic expansion.

FALL: No clear migration peak is evident. As in spring, numbers vary, but usually fewer than 100 birds are reported.

1966–89 CBC Summary

Christmas Bird Count	Years Found	Range of No. Found	Median
Wilmington	24	10–1,149	89
Middletown	24	4–220	43
Bombay Hook	24	39–484	74
Cape Henlopen	24	41–231	113
Rehoboth	24	65–584	147
STATEWIDE	24	354–1,489	551
(increasing; low in 1968, high in 1979)			

WINTER: The third and fourth editions of the AOU Checklist (1910 and 1931, respectively) state that this species wintered south to the Great Lakes and Delaware Bay (casually to Florida), but the first sightings on record for Delaware are

12 Apr 1931	1	Broadkill Beach [Buck1]
1 Oct 1932	1	Bethany Beach (Knappen, in Cottam 1934)
14 Dec 1933	1	Rehoboth Bay (Cottam 1934)

Buckalew shot 1 during the winter of 1934–35 [Hans1]. Since then the species' range has steadily expanded southward.

CBC data show a gradual but significant increase in Delaware. The high Wilmington numbers probably reflect its presence at the Cherry Island landfill, and other count results suggest it is more common near the ocean.

BANDING: All banded birds (16) recovered in Delaware were banded as chicks from Long Island north to Maine and Quebec. Most (12) were recovered from September through March, but 2 were June recoveries.

SPECIMENS: 13; DMNH.

Black-legged Kittiwake *(Rissa tridactyla)*

Regular offshore, occasional from land, winter visitor, fairly common; expected late October to mid-February.

J F M A M J J A S O N D

HABITAT: Pelagic.

OCCURRENCE: The species is present mid-October–mid-February. The latest reports include 1 at Cape Henlopen SP on 14 March 1963 [Dyke4], 1 at Cape Henlopen SP, and 2 at Indian River Inlet 8 April 1972 [HilC1]. Black-legged Kittiwakes are seldom seen from shore, and when they are sighted, usually only 1 or 2 birds are present. An unusual onshore report involves 35 seen from Cape Henlopen SP on 21 October 1983 [Frec42]. At sea many more birds are present, for example, 102 seen 20 mi (32 km) off Rehoboth Beach on 5 February 1975 and 350 seen 50 mi (81 km) off Rehoboth Beach on 9 February 1975 [Rowl16].

Hanson (notes) first recorded kittiwakes in Delaware: 15 at Indian River Inlet on 9 December 1934, and 2 there on 19 January 1936. Buckalew secured the first specimen there 8 January 1937 (Buckalew 1950).

SPECIMENS: USNM 422179, Indian River Inlet, 8 January 1937; DMNH 35202, Rehoboth Beach, January 1973; DMNH 75538, Indian River Inlet, 18 February 1984; DMNH 73238, Lewes, 25 February 1983.

Sabine's Gull *(Xema sabini)*

Casual (1962, 1983, 1986).

DOCUMENTATION: Photograph (Frech 1984).

REMARKS: Sabine's Gull breeds in the Arctic; it winters rarely in the northern Atlantic and sparingly in the tropical Atlantic (AOU 1983). In the Mid-Atlantic region it is little observed, probably migrating well offshore. The 3 Delaware records involve single birds. The first occurred on 30 September 1962 [Sche2] and the second on 16 May 1983 [Frec53]

(Frech 1984), both at Cape Henlopen SP. The third observation was made 26 October 1986 at the ferry slip near Cape Henlopen [Weis1]. A photograph of the 1983 bird by Fintel was published (Frech 1984), and a copy is at DMNH. The published description mentions black legs, a black bill with a yellow tip, and the "black and white pattern" on the wing, both folded and in flight. The photograph, showing a partial black hood and the small size, satisfactorily supports the identification.

Ivory Gull *(Pagophila eburnea)*

Casual (1969) in winter.

DOCUMENTATION: Published notes.

REMARKS: The Ivory Gull breeds in the far Arctic and is found in winter only casually south of drift ice (AOU 1983), though winter records from as far south as North Carolina have accumulated. A single bird was seen at Cape Henlopen SP on 21 February 1969, the day after a northeasterly storm (Davis

1969). The description is definitive, mentioning black legs, the small, thin, black bill, size, and lack of any dark markings. The appearance was of a "worn" immature or an adult. The species is readily identifiable, and the sighting has been well described in print; therefore, we consider occurrence of the species in Delaware established.

Gull-billed Tern *(Sterna nilotica)*

Regular (at least formerly); migrant; uncommon. Expected early May to early September. Occasional breeder, current breeding status unknown.

HABITAT: Marshes, beaches, and adjacent coastal bays and ocean. Seen over the saltmarshes of Sussex and Kent counties catching insects rather than diving; twice found in New Castle County. A colonial breeder, associating with Common Tern colonies in the Mid-Atlantic coast region.

SPRING: The only reports before May are

23 Apr 1960	1	Fenwick Island [Dyke11]
25 or 26 Apr 1970	1	Indian River Inlet [DVOC2]
26 or 27 Apr 1969	2	Indian River Inlet [DVOC1]

The report of 4 March 1985 at Cape Henlopen should read 4 May [Cutl12]. The species has been reported 4 times on the May Count. Virtually all reports are of 1–3 birds.

BREEDING: It is found occasionally in summer over the salt-marshes, usually from Indian River Inlet north to Bombay Hook NWR. The only accepted reports of more than 4 are

| 7 Jul 1974 | 5 | Little Creek WA [Lehm9] |
| 22 Jul 1959 | 12 | Fenwick Island [Davi12] |

The Fenwick Island report is associated with breeding at Assawoman WA; a published account of 20 on 21 June 1970 at Little Creek WA (DuMont and DuMont 1970b) lacks corroboration.

Atlas. Although never confirmed, this tern was reported during 3 years of the Atlas period. The only dates suggestive of breeding involve a series of observations of 1 and 2 birds on 19 June–8 July 1987 at Bombay Hook NWR [Holg1]. These and others sighted in summer are most likely birds of prebreeding age, because this species takes up a territory only in the fourth year, and begins to breed in the fifth (at least in Europe, Cramp 1985). Gull-billed Terns were also seen at Bombay Hook NWR in 1989 and 1990.

Nesting. Three clutches of 3 eggs each, found on 24 May

1958 on Rehoboth Bay, are the first breeding evidence we have for this species (DMNH 1060, 1061, 13237). The eggs were laid in a hollow on the sand with a few shells around them. That same year Dyke reported adults feeding young at Assawoman WA; 6 young were also noted there on 12 July 1959 [Dyke1]. It returned to Assawoman in 1989 [Shoc6] and 1990, and a nest with 3 eggs was observed there on 7 June 1991 in a cordgrass marsh (D. Rothstein, DNHI, pers. comm.).

History. There appear to be no records of Gull-billed Tern in Delaware predating Hanson's (notes) brief mention of "several observed on the beach north of Rehoboth Sept. 7, 1928." It was on Hanson's 1932 manuscript list of Delaware birds and appeared on Pennock's unpublished list of Rehoboth Beach birds (1935) but was on no other Delaware lists until Linehan's (1967). Springer reported 2 at Bombay Hook NWR on 24 May 1954 [Spri3]. Since then Gull-billed Terns have been identified in Delaware in more than half the years.

This species was discovered by Wilson at Cape May, New Jersey, in 1811, but it was not seen there again until 20 June 1926 when a nest was discovered at Stone Harbor. It has been regular at Cape May since 1954 (Sibley 1993). In support of Hanson's 1928 Delaware observation are two 1928 Maryland observations of this then-accidental species (Stewart and Robbins 1958).

Trends. This species is now a very rare breeder in New York, where only about 5 pairs breed on Long Island (Andrle and Carroll 1987); in southern New Jersey (Sibley 1993); and in Maryland, where only 9 pairs were reported from a single site in 1985 (Robbins 1996; Andrews 1990). In Virginia a 90% decline in the state's breeding population took place 1975–85 (Kain 1987).

Conservation. There is no reason to believe this nearly cosmopolitan tern did not breed here prior to the twentieth century, because its Atlantic coast breeding range extends north to Long Island (AOU 1983). It was placed on the 1987 USFWS list of birds of management concern in the Northeast and is listed as Threatened in Maryland and Virginia (Via and Duffy 1992). It should be listed in Delaware.

FALL: Most birds leave by 10–20 August, though a few are present to early September; any record later than 7 September should be carefully documented. Late reports include

3 Sep 1973	1	Bombay Hook NWR [Lehm1]
7 Sep 1928	several	Rehoboth Beach [Hans1]
30 Sep 1961	3	Port Penn [Broo4]

Although late records are chiefly associated with hurricanes on Long Island (Bull 1974), the surprisingly late September birds (in the preceding list) came during a period of calm weather (National Weather Service data).

SPECIMEN: DMNH 835, Sussex Co., 31 May 1958. Egg records: DMNH.

Caspian Tern *(Sterna caspia)*

Regular; summer visitor; uncommon to fairly common. Expected late April to early November but most numerous from late August to late October.

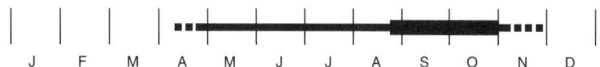

| J | F | M | A | M | J | J | A | S | O | N | D |

HABITAT: Ocean, bays, estuaries and adjacent beaches, especially sand spits. More common inland than the Royal Tern.

SPRING: The first few birds arrive 15–30 April, and the species becomes more common in May. It has been found only 3 times before 15 April, the earliest at the rather unusual location of Lums Pond SP:

11 Apr 1981	1	Lums Pond SP [Barn1]
14 Apr 1972	1	Bombay Hook NWR [Holg72]
14 Apr 1985	1	Prime Hook NWR [Frec1]

Virtually all reports mention 4 or fewer.

SUMMER: This species breeds on 6 continents—but not in Delaware. It breeds at a number of locations on the Great Lakes and locally along the Atlantic coast (Peterson 1980), where the nearest colonies are on the Virginia part of the Delmarva Peninsula (Ridd 1989; Andrews 1990). The small numbers (usually only 1 or 2 per report) found in summer are subadults that migrate more slowly than breeding adults and may not return as far north. This species usually takes 4 years to reach breeding maturity. It is most numerous on sand spits at Cape Henlopen SP and southward but may be found in all 3 counties and as far north as Hoopes Reservoir. A favored New Castle County location is near Delaware City.

FALL: Banding results show that some prebreeders banded as chicks on the Great Lakes appear along the Atlantic coast (including 3 juveniles recovered in Delaware), so Delaware birds should be regarded as part of the Great Lakes population. Some northward postbreeding influx from the small colonies in Virginia may occur as well (Ludwig 1965; Cramp 1985). Migration probably begins in mid-August, most birds leave by 1–5 November, and the last are reported later in the month:

11 Nov 1975	8	Cape Henlopen SP [Lehm1]
23 Nov 1985	1	Cape Henlopen SP [Swer2]
25 Nov 1988	1	Bombay Hook NWR [Barn61]

Reports of 30–40 birds are not unusual in September and early October. Noteworthy, however, are 100 birds resting on a Delaware River sandbar opposite Delaware City on 2 September 1988 and 200 there 8 days later [Gith1].

HISTORY: Early records include 2 Caspian Terns seen by Pennock on 20 May 1920, flying one-quarter mi offshore at Rehoboth Beach [Hans1] and 2 shot by Buckalew—a female at Slaughter Beach on 8 May 1933 (USNM 422178) and an immature male at Rehoboth Beach on 28 September 1933 (USNM 422180). There are 3 published reports in the 1940s. This bird first appeared on a published Delaware list as a casual summer visitor (Barry 1942). Since then it has occurred with increasing regularity, reflecting the gradual increase of terns beginning in the early twentieth century when egg and plume collecting were banned.

SPECIMENS: USNM 422178 and USNM 422180, details earlier.

Royal Tern (*Sterna maxima*)

Regular; summer visitor; fairly common to common. Expected early April through November and sporadically into December.

J F M A M J J A S O N D

HABITAT: Ocean, bays, estuaries and adjacent beaches, rarely up large rivers.

SPRING: First arrival is usually 1–10 April, about 2 weeks earlier than Caspian Tern; March arrivals have been reported in 3 years:

16 Mar 1986	1 (2 on the 30th)	Indian River Inlet [Frec1]
30 Mar 1985	4	Indian River Inlet [Frec1]
31 Mar 1991	2	Fenwick Island (Campbell 1991)

Frech [Frec1] indicate high numbers from 15–20 April to 20–25 May. Some high counts are 75 on 6 April 1985 at Indian River Inlet, 200 on 19 April 1985 at Cape Henlopen SP, and 100 there on 2 May 1982.

SUMMER: This tern is a summer resident but not a breeder. It first appeared on a Delaware list as a "casual summer resident" (Barry 1942). The first dated Delaware record published is Rigby's 28 October 1950 report of 12 at Cape Henlopen [Rigb2]; this report was not attended by any editorial comment to suggest it was unusual, so we conclude it had been seen before but the observations had not been published. That same year the first nests were found in Maryland (Stewart and Robbins 1958). It has been regular in Delaware since at least 1964, when 90 were at Cape Henlopen on 24 October [McLP3].

The species is fairly social, so seeing a group of 5 or more in summer is not unusual. In the period 1 June–25 July numbers observed have exceeded 10 only 5 times—all at Cape Henlopen SP: 14 on 8 June 1981, 12 on 26 June 1982, 12 on 29 June 1983, 12 on 3 July 1987 [Frec1], and 16 on 30 June 1974 [Wayn46].

Royal Terns take four years to reach breeding maturity, so those summering in Delaware are most likely prebreeders. Typically, they breed in large colonies on undisturbed sand islands near good feeding areas. One potential breeding site in Delaware was Sand Island in Indian River Bay, but this spoil island has now disappeared; if reconstructed and protected (first proposed to DNREC by W. A. Fintel, in Thomas 1988), the island would meet the criteria given for Royal Tern nesting (Buckley and Buckley 1972). A large Royal Tern colony exists south of Delaware—3,300–4,600 breeding pairs at Fishermans Island at the tip of the Delmarva Peninsula 1967–84 [BucP2]—and there are several smaller colonies in Virginia and Maryland (Ridd 1989; Robbins 1996).

FALL: Because all large breeding colonies are south of Delaware, the buildup in numbers should be considered a post-breeding influx rather than migration. This influx begins in August, continues into September—for example, 300 were at Cape Henlopen on 18 September 1981 [Frec31]—and ends in November.

WINTER: Virtually all depart by 30 November. The 11 reports in December come from 8 years, with these the latest winter reports:

23 Dec 1984	1	Cape Henlopen CBC [Wayn64]
28 Dec 1966	5	Indian River Inlet [DuPG11]
31 Dec 1978	1	Cape Henlopen CBC [Wayn62]

The CBC observations at Cape Henlopen SP were supported with notes.

REMARKS: Although Royal Terns do go short distances up major rivers (Lowery 1974), any bird sighted north of Delaware Bay should be carefully scrutinized and all field marks checked. First-winter Caspian Terns are sufficiently similar to Royal Terns to cause confusion; Cusa (in Cramp 1985, pl. 3) has prepared an extensive set of illustrations of Caspian Terns, including 1 in this plumage. Some of the New Castle County reports may involve misidentifications. For example, reports of a Royal Tern at Churchmans Marsh 30 August–5 October 1980 (no notes) should probably be ascribed to a first-year Caspian Tern, because a Royal Tern would be unlikely to spend that much time around an inland freshwater marsh. In support of Royal Terns occurring north of Sussex County are 3 accepted records at Tinicum, Pennsylvania (Santner et al. 1992), and a photograph of 1 at Port Mahon (C. Wilds, pers. comm.).

SPECIMENS: DMNH 690, Sussex Co., 25 May 1957; DMNH 714, Sussex Co., 14 August 1957; DMNH 863, Sussex Co., 14 September 1958.

Sandwich Tern *(Sterna sandvicensis)*

Occasional (7 years, 1970–91); summer visitor; uncommon.

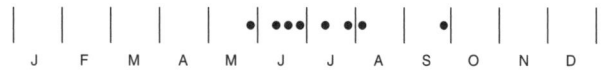

J F M A M J J A S O N D

DOCUMENTATION: Multiple sight records with convincing notes.

HABITAT: Coastal beaches.

REMARKS: This coastal species breeds regularly as far north as North Carolina. The closest known breeding locations are in the Virginia portion of the Delmarva Peninsula (Ridd 1989; Andrews 1990). It is found most frequently in the company of Royal Terns.

The following represent the range of the extreme dates of the 11 Delaware records:

| 25 May 1985 | 2 | Indian River Inlet [RusJ9] |
| 28 Sep 1985 | 9 | Cape Henlopen SP [Edni35] |

The birds observed on 28 September arrived with a hurricane; all occurred along the Atlantic coast, the majority at Cape Henlopen SP. Holgersen's (1970) published notes mention the yellow tip of the bill, the bill shape, and the crested head. We also have brief notes from 3 sightings by Frech, indicating close observation in each case.

HISTORY: One seen at Cape Henlopen 27 June 1970 was claimed to be the first state record [Holg49], but Barry (1942) had already listed it as a casual summer resident. Bent (1921) proposed that it extended its range following European settlement, since it was not known to breed north of Florida in Audubon's time. The first confirmed breeding in 55 years on the Delmarva Peninsula occurred at Fishermans Island, Virginia, in 1967 [BucP3]. It is just as easy to speculate that the large Atlantic coast Royal Tern colonies had already been raided before Audubon's time with sufficient regularity by coastal settlers and fishermen to extirpate this smaller associate of the Royal Tern.

Roseate Tern *(Sterna dougallii)*

Regular; migrant; rare. Found mostly in May.

J F M A M J J A S O N D

DOCUMENTATION: Multiple sight reports.

HABITAT: Pelagic.

SPRING: The Roseate Tern is federally Endangered along the Atlantic coast from Maine to North Carolina (USFWS 1993). Of the multitude of Delaware reports, only a few involving Roseate Terns associating with Common Terns on Cape Henlopen are satisfactorily documented. Given the difficulty of identifying Roseate Terns, we are unwilling to accept any report that is not thoroughly documented in the field. With reservations, we believe Roseate Terns occur regularly during migration, at least offshore, and that they are occasional at Cape Henlopen SP and possibly elsewhere along the coast.

SUMMER: Although a few inland occurrences are documented, it is primarily an offshore migrant. Peterson (1980) notes that it formerly bred from New Jersey to Virginia, but its current eastern North American range extends from Long Island northward into Canada, and a disjunct population (federally Threatened) nests in the Florida Keys. The most recent breeding records from the Delmarva Peninsula date back to 1938 for Maryland (Stewart and Robbins 1958) and to 1927 for Virginia (Kain 1987). No early history for it exists in Delaware. The first report comes from the unlikely location of Delaware City, probably Thousand Acre Marsh, 27 August 1957 (Oring 1958). It was identified on the basis of tail length, but differential wear in August might lead to the wrong conclusion even if based on careful observation. Cramp (1985) regards the Roseate Tern as "at all seasons more thoroughly marine" than any other European tern and "only a vagrant inland anywhere." On the bases of the difficulty of identifying this species and the unlikelihood of location, we reserve judgment on all records away from the immediate ocean coast.

FALL: None of the approximately half dozen reports are documented. The reports span early August to mid-November. Presumably, it occurs regularly as an offshore migrant, although it has not been found on any offshore boat trips in Delaware. Rowlett (1980b) quotes only 1 record from the region, and in Barnhill's experience (pers. obs.) it is almost never seen offshore in the mid-Atlantic in the fall.

Common Tern *(Sterna hirundo)*

Regular; summer resident; fairly common to common. Expected from mid-April to late October and sporadically into early winter. Beach nester with a declining population.

HABITAT: Ocean, bays, and nearby sandy beaches. Breeds on isolated beaches and sometimes on marshy islands.

SPRING: In most years first arrival is not until after mid-April, but early April birds are occasionally seen:

1 Apr 1984	2	Indian River Inlet [Frec1]
4 Apr 1970	5	Bombay Hook NWR [Holg46]
4 Apr 1981	1	Bombay Hook NWR [Barn41]

Arrivals as early as these must be carefully identified to distinguish them from early Forster's Terns. The breeding birds have arrived by 5–10 May. Because typical high counts are 50–100 birds, a report of 2,500 at Cape Henlopen on 16 May 1971 [DuPG22] is remarkable.

BREEDING: This species breeds in colonies varying in location from year to year from Cape Henlopen south to Indian River Inlet. It was reported breeding on 22 July 1967 on fresh spoil pumped from the Chesapeake and Delaware Canal near Delaware City [Carr2]. This is the only breeding report north of Sussex Co.

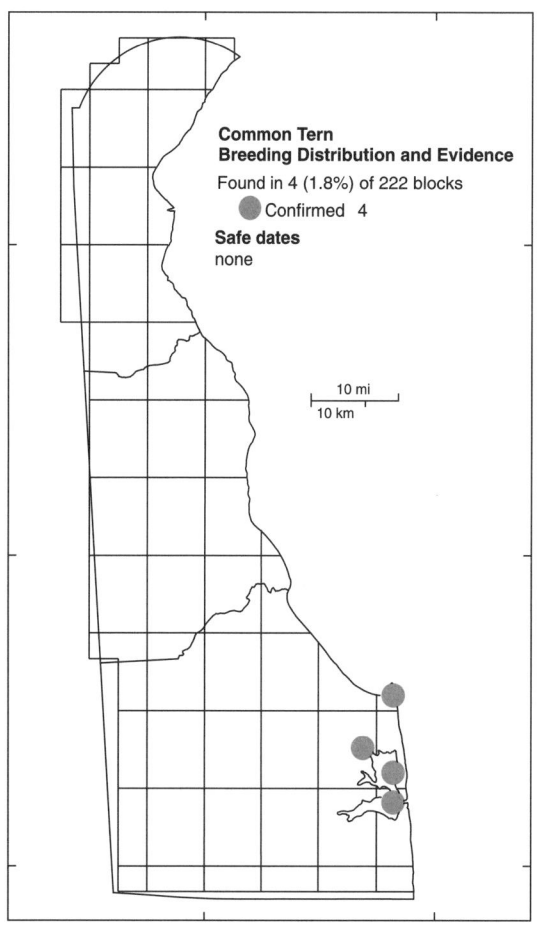

Atlas. During the 1983–87 Atlas period it was reported in 4 blocks by the beach nester study group composed of the Sussex Bird Club, the Delaware Audubon Society, and DNREC. Total population during that period was 200–300 pairs, including nonbreeders. Besides being found from Cape Henlopen to Fenwick Island, where it feeds and breeds, it also ventures up the Delaware River regularly as far as Bombay Hook NWR but is gradually replaced upriver by Forster's Tern as the more abundant species. Because it disperses widely to feed, only confirmed breeding sites are shown on the map.

Nesting. It nests on sand in an isolated spot, such as near the tip of Cape Henlopen or on spoil islands. The eggs are laid in a scrape that is sometimes casually lined with nearby materials. It now also breeds in bay marshes, a habitat usually considered more suited to Forster's Tern. In marshes it places its nest on wrack or live vegetation (D. Rothstein, DNHI, pers. comm., 1992). Two Delaware nests were reported on top of duck blinds [Todd1]. Nests with eggs have been found in Delaware from 17 May to 19 August, but the estimated completion date for over 70% of the reported clutches was during the first 3 weeks of June ($n = 3{,}104$). In many years the peak date is probably affected more by storms, high tides, and disturbance than by the biology of the bird. The timing of census trips strongly affects the estimation of peak clutch-completion dates.

History. This tern, a common nester in the Northern Hemisphere, including the Northeast, was once extirpated as a breeder in Delaware (see "Remarks"). In 1880 when Bush sailed from Rehoboth Beach to Indian River on a collecting trip, he could find only Least Terns. Rhoads and Pennock (1905) describe the Common Tern as a rare summer resident and mention "one seen by Rhoads at Rehoboth June 22, 1903." It had again become a Delaware visitor by 1925, when Hanson reported it as quite common over Indian River Bay 25–30 August. The birds he saw could easily have been postbreeding birds dispersing from colonies in Virginia or New Jersey, since both states had colonies that survived persecution (Bent 1921). The first breeding season report was of 2 at Indian River Inlet on 11 June 1934, but no nest was found [Hans1]. As field work increased, so did records of this species. Two nests with 3 eggs each on Gull Island, Rehoboth Bay, 8 June 1957 (DMNH 1428, 1429) are the first breeding evidence for the state. A report of 2 nests with eggs at Cape Henlopen on 19 August 1963 [PylR2] is the first published record of nesting in Delaware, but the report was made only because of the lateness of the nest. The terns had started nesting there years earlier while Cape Henlopen was under military control; Buckalew banded 100 young there in mid-July 1961, 293 in early July 1962, and 200 in early July 1963 [Usfw3].

Trends. In 1965 regular monitoring and protection of the Cape Henlopen colony was initiated by the DOS (with support of state parks personnel). That year the peak number of nests reported for Cape Henlopen was 103 on 28 June [Wayn29]. Linehan banded 221 young there in late July 1967 [Usfw3]. The highest number of nests reported at Cape Henlopen was 249 in 1968 (Katholi and Linehan 1969); by that time the breeding area had been protected by snow fencing and educational signs. But by 1974 the number of nests had fallen to 135 on the only day they were checked [Wayn1], and Linehan banded only 107 young in late July [Usfw3]. Subsequently, the highest count was 25 pairs nesting on 5 June 1984 [Frec1]. This reduction may well

have been caused by the presence of mammalian predators or by changes in habitat as planted sea oats grew up.

Concurrent with the active colony on Cape Henlopen was a large colony with 1,221 nests found in 1967 by Wayne, West, and Roberts [West23] on Sand Island, a temporary spoil island. This colony declined steadily until the last report of 40 nesting pairs in 1976 (Erwin and Korschgen 1979). We speculate that the most likely reason for decline was storm action on the exposed island. Comprehensive studies in 1976 and 1977 [Barn3; Byrd1; Jahn3; WilB1, in Cornell's Colonial Waterbird Registry] led to the discovery of colonies on Marsh and Bush Islands in Rehoboth Bay in marshy habitat not typical for Common Terns. Fintel et al. (notes) have monitored these islands through 1988, lately as part of a DNREC-coordinated search for beach nesters, and observed an abrupt decline on Bush Island from 300 breeding pairs to 100 pairs in 1987 and 50 pairs in 1988 and little breeding elsewhere (Thomas 1988c). However, at that point the beach-nester program became so focused on the Piping Plover and Least Tern colonies that the Common Tern was not even monitored in 1989, nor were there any plans to do so in 1990. These comprehensive counts, taken at decade intervals, present a clear picture of the declining numbers:

Year	Nests or pairs	Remarks
1957	2	First nesting record this century
1967	1,500	Cape Henlopen and Sand Island
1977	300	On 4 islands plus mainland
1987	100	Mainly Bush Island
1988	50	Only Bush Island
1989	?	No search or report made in 1989 or subsequently

The Delaware population on the May Count decreased at an average annual rate of 9% per year during 1969–91. BBS data for Delaware and the Mid-Atlantic region corroborate this decline, but the sample is small.

Conservation. The Common Tern population has declined in North America since the 1930s (Laughlin 1985) and is listed as Threatened in New York, principally because of serious declines in the upstate population (Peterson 1988a). It is listed as Endangered in New Hampshire and Vermont and is a Species of Special Concern in Maine and Massachusetts (Northeast Nongame Technical Committee 1991). The protection provided by Delaware parks has been inadequate, and this species now needs the protection of a Threatened or Endangered status.

FALL: Most movement takes place 20–30 August through September. Because most birds depart by late-October, any report thereafter should be carefully documented to distinguish this species from the more likely Forster's Tern. Large numbers were first reported in 1955. High counts include

24 Aug 1956	800	Rehoboth Beach [Davi9]
6 Sep 1977	1,000	Cape Henlopen SP [Frec1]
13 Sep 1970	1,250	Cape Henlopen SP [DuPG19]

Typical counts total 100–200 birds. This species has been reported 3 times in December:

6 Dec 1979	1	Rehoboth Beach [Frec6]
12 Dec 1971	3	Indian River Inlet [Barn50]
17 Dec 1977	1	Rehoboth CBC [Barn53]

REMARKS: Common Terns came close to extirpation on the Atlantic coast as a result of a series of human pressures: egg collecting by settlers and fishermen; shooting by sportsmen and collectors; and hunting for the millinery trade. Orders went out from New York milliners for large quantities of Common Terns, Laughing Gulls, Royal Terns, and so on, at ten cents apiece, and the feather merchants themselves stated that the demand for birds exceeded the supply. Chapman, writing in 1899, recounted that 40,000 Common Terns were shot on Cobbs Island, Virginia, alone one summer to supply the fashion market. In 1900 an order was placed in Milford, Delaware, by a New York agent for 20,000 birds to be delivered within 2 months (Anon. 1900b). Reaction to this slaughter resulted in the AOU appointing Witmer Stone chairman of a Committee on Bird Protection, and he administered funds donated to hire wardens to protect every remaining tern colony from Virginia to Maine (Thayer et al. 1900; Anon. 1900a; Anon. 1900b). The Delaware Audubon Society was formed in 1900 (Hilles 1900), and an association of state Audubon societies and others mounted a successful campaign to dissuade women from adorning themselves with the bodies of slaughtered terns. Tern populations recovered nationally as laws protecting them were enacted, enforced, and finally accepted. Now new threats have appeared, such as increased use of recreational boats near nesting beaches and increased presence of dogs, cats, and off-road vehicles roaming these beaches.

SPECIMENS: 9; DMNH, CM, USNM. Egg records: WFVZ.

Arctic Tern (*Sterna paradisaea*)

Occasional (1977, 1978, 1989); migrant; rare; perhaps regular off-shore.

DOCUMENTATION: Definitive field notes.

REMARKS: Records by Jay G. Lehman and others 30 May 1977 [Lehm30] and 27 May 1978 [Lehm6] were made at Cape Henlopen. Lehman wrote detailed notes of both sightings; in addition, Barnhill saw the birds and took notes consistent with those of Lehman. Useful marks noted by Lehman include a bill "blood red to tip" and differing in shape from Common Tern, a meticulously described difference in distribution of white on the face compared to nearby Common Terns, the proper appearance of black on the wings (differing from Common Tern and Roseate Terns, both nearby), the short legs, and dif-ferences in head shape from Common Terns. These notes from a remarkably careful observer, taken in the field, are completely convincing. An additional report describes a bird seen sitting and flying at Indian River Inlet on 2 October 1989 [Fint15].

Arctic Terns occur occasionally in very small numbers offshore in the general region (Barnhill pers. obs.) during spring. The difficulty of identification of the species, the lack of boat trips offshore from Delaware, and the small number of observers who walk to the extreme end of Cape Henlopen make it difficult to determine how frequently this species occurs in Delaware.

Forster's Tern (*Sterna forsteri*)

Regular; summer resident; common. Expected early April to mid-January. Breeds in low numbers at 2 Rehoboth Bay sites only. Has increased on the Mid-Atlantic coast and recolonized Delaware during the twentieth century.

J F M A M J J A S O N D

HABITAT: Saltmarsh and adjacent coastal waters.

SPRING: This species usually arrives 5–10 April and is fairly common by mid-month, a schedule slightly earlier than the one followed by the Common Tern. Earliest arrivals include

29 Mar 1991	1	Port Mahon [Camp19]
2 Apr 1988	1	Broadkill Beach [Frec1]
2 Apr 1989	6	Indian River Inlet [Frec1]

Some high counts are

3 May 1985	50	Cape Henlopen SP [Wayn2]
18 Apr 1988	25	Delaware Seashore SP [Frec1]
24 Apr 1989	35	Broadkill Beach [Frec1]

BREEDING: Adults with juveniles are found north to Delaware City and St. Georges in summer, but nests have only been found in the Rehoboth Bay marshes.

Atlas. The first breeding in Delaware was discovered by the Fintels who found 75 pairs nesting with Common Terns on Marsh Island near the mouth of Love Creek on 9 June 1985 [Fint4]. In June 1986 Fintel and Frech found Forster's Terns in 2 colonies: on Marsh Island and about 124 pairs on Bush Island [ThoJ1]. These are represented by the confirmations shown on the map.

Though Forster's Terns are also consistently found in the Delaware River marshes during June, no nests have been reported from this area. Terns move to good feeding areas as soon as dependent young can fly. There may be some isolated nesting hidden in these marshes, but the possible and probable

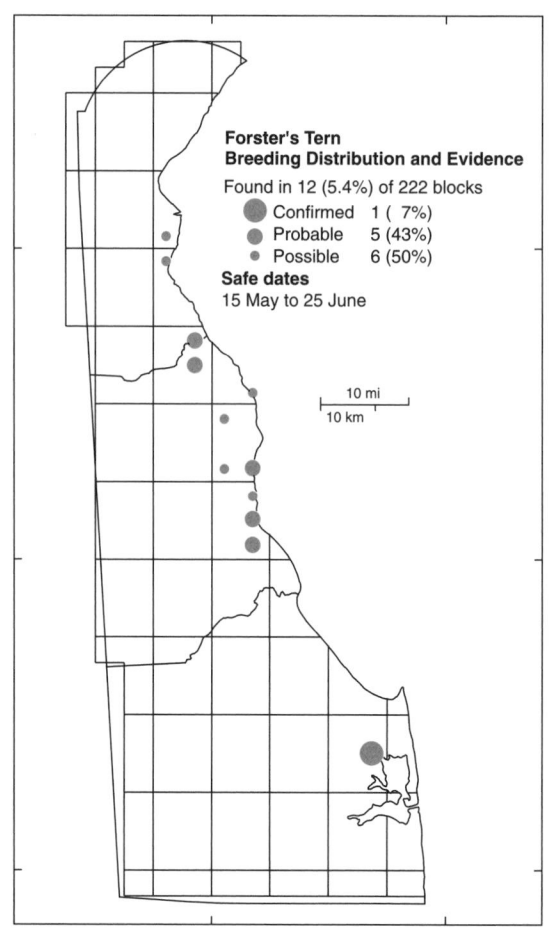

breeding codes indicated on the distribution map are quite speculative because they may arise from movement of dependent young after they fledged. This is the only tern for which we have included locations of probable and possible breeding.

History. The early history of Forster's Tern is confused. Wilson did not recognize it as a species, Nuttall first described it in 1834, and Audubon described the immature as a distinct species. Not until 1862 did Elliot Coues work out all the plumages. Even then the distinction between it and the Common Tern as described by Coues required having the adult bird in hand so that the outermost tail feathers could be examined. Its breeding range probably extended from New Jersey to South Carolina (Connor 1988a), but in the days of unrestrained shooting and collecting its population was surely decimated along with those of other terns. It probably bred in Delaware and was extirpated as a breeding bird before being recognized as a species. Our first records involve 2 shot by Pennock: a female of a territorial pair on a sandbar in Indian River Bay 14 May 1905 (Pennock 1908a,b), and 1 of 5 on the beach one-half mi north of Rehoboth Beach on 28 September 1908 [Hans1]. One was reported at Delaware City on 31 August 1930 [Gill4], and 15 were on the coast on 17 August 1941 [Kram5]. Breeding season records (except for Pennock's) start at least by 1950, when it was regular in the saltmarshes in early May [Wayn1]. Forster's Terns arrived in Little Creek WA in early June 1961 (the year the impoundment was built), reaching a peak of 167 on 28 August and staying until October (Lesser 1964, 1965). Lesser states that they did not breed even though they remained all summer. They continued to be summer residents there, arriving 4 May 1962 (Lesser 1964) and 20 June 1964 (Stickley 1967).

Trends. A 1977 survey of the Atlantic waterbird colonies revealed a breeding population of 2,000 pairs from Brigantine NWR, New Jersey, south to Cape Charles, Virginia, with none breeding in Delaware (Erwin and Korschgen 1979). By 1985 the population had increased to about 5,000 pairs, with 75 in Delaware (Andrews 1990). It also expanded its range into South Carolina (LeGrand 1987) and New York [Zaru1]. The Delaware increase reflected by May Count data averaged 13% per year (1969–91), but this figure probably included migrants to the Great Lakes. The BBS showed a moderate increasing tendency for the Mid-Atlantic coast during 1966–90.

Breeding population. The breeding population is changing rapidly, and currently falls in the range of a few to 200 pairs, plus possibly some pairs in the Delaware River marshes.

Conservation. There is a small Atlantic coast population of this species, limited until recently to southern New Jersey and the southern Delmarva Peninsula. Other populations breed in the Great Lakes basin and prairies, and on the Gulf Coast south into Mexico. The low number of breeding pairs and the breeding concentration in Rehoboth Bay make it potentially subject to sudden extirpation.

FALL: Migration takes place much later than that of the Common Tern. Peak counts of 100–500 birds have been made 10–15 November to 15–20 December (rarely to the end of the month).

WINTER: Except for an occasional individual lingering to the end of the month, most leave by 15–20 January. We are aware of only 2 reports, both undocumented, from February and none from March; therefore, any sighting during that period should be carefully documented.

1966–89 CBC Summary

Christmas Bird Count	Years Found	Range of No. Found	Median
Wilmington			
Middletown			
Bombay Hook	2	1	
Cape Henlopen	10	1–55	
Rehoboth	15	1–455	2
STATEWIDE (increasing; high in 1988)	16	1–479	4

As mentioned in "Breeding," Forster's Tern was extirpated and has begun to reclaim its previous range. This trend appears to be reflected in the recent increase in numbers reported on

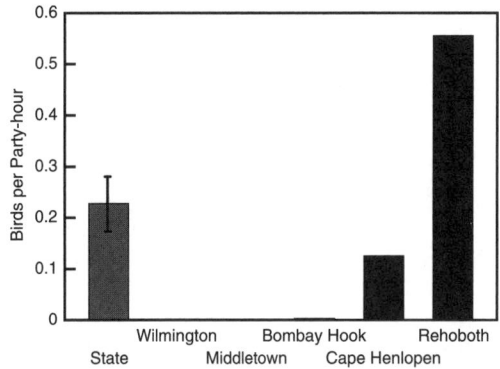

CBC Geographic Distribution; Average of 3 Count Areas

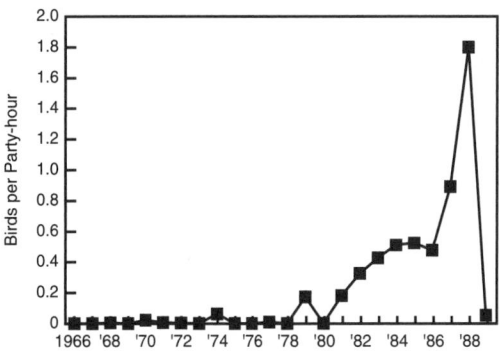

CBC Data

CBCs. The rather rapid increase cannot continue indefinitely and may, in part, be a result of increased observer effort related to searches for Northern Gannets. It is found almost exclusively on the Cape Henlopen and Rehoboth CBCs.

SPECIMENS: 7; DMNH, ANSP, USNM.

Least Tern *(Sterna antillarum)*

Regular; summer resident; locally common to abundant near the Atlantic beaches. Expected late April to early September. Beach nester.

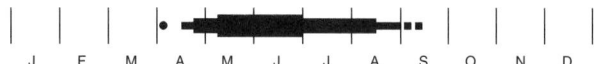

HABITAT: Ocean, bays, estuaries, sandy beaches.

SPRING: This, our smallest tern, typically arrives in modest numbers 20–25 April with most of the breeding population present by 15-20 May. Holgersen's [Holg46] report of 2 birds at Bombay Hook NWR on 4 April 1979, noted as "rather early," is perhaps the earliest published report for the region. In Florida the earliest credible arrival is 17 March, and the earliest specimen, 9 April (Stevenson and Anderson 1994); in Maryland the early date is 12 April (Robbins and Bystrak 1977). A mid-April arrival date attributed to Frech [Frec38] is not in his original notes. Other early reports include

20 Apr 1980	1	Indian River Inlet [Haas3]
22 Apr 1985	1	Delaware Seashore SP [Frec1]
24 Apr 1991	1	Assawoman WA [Edni1]

BREEDING: A federally Endangered species, its principal breeding locations have been close to Indian River Inlet and have been protected by DNREC staff, particularly since the terns seem to harbor breeding Piping Plovers (a federally Threatened species) in their colonies. The Least Tern has nested regularly along the coast from just south of Bethany Beach north to Cape Henlopen and occasionally farther north—to Broadkill Beach in 1971 [Rosc1] and possibly in 1977 [Port1]—and exceptionally near Delaware City—on dredging spoil on 22 July 1967 [Carr1].

Atlas. The colonies tend to shift from area to area over a period of years, so the Atlas results overstate what the distribution would be in any given year. Some isolated nesting of small groups was probably missed. Because it is a colonial breeder that disperses widely to feed, possible breeding—birds merely seen away from breeding sites—is not depicted on the map.

Nesting. Least Tern nests are typically scrapes in white sand

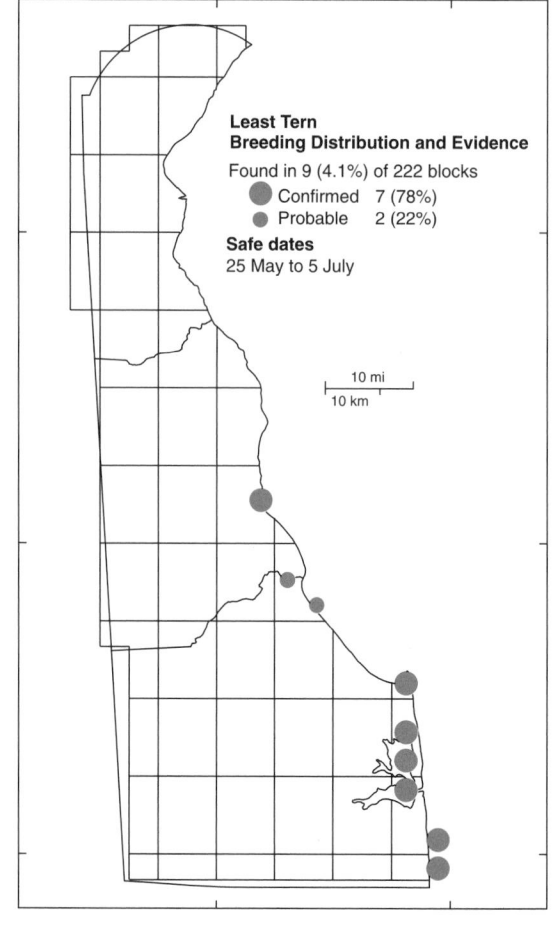

with shells or pebbles, but the species also lays its eggs on cleared sandy construction sites and flat rooftops.

Extreme egg dates range from 15 May [Frec2] to 27 July [Bush1]. The greatest number of nests (152) was found on 26 June 1976 in stages ranging from egg-laying to hatching as follows [Barn24; Wayn26]:

1 egg	21 nests
2 eggs	115 nests
3 eggs	6 nests
4 eggs	1 nest
1 egg, 1 young	9 nests

The number of incomplete clutches is unknown.

History. The first breeding record on file was made 27 July 1880, when Bush (notes) found a great many, including eggs and flightless young, at Indian River Inlet. Although a boat was required to reach the inlet, this colony was not secure from persecution. Pennock found no Least Terns when he visited the inlet on 13 May 1905 and 20 May 1907 (Pennock 1908a). The most recent data that Rhoads and Pennock (1905) could cite were Bush's birds of 25 years earlier, and they described them as "almost exterminated." Pennock (notes) saw a flock of 15 or more near Rehoboth Beach on 11–13 May 1928, the first sign of recovery. On 20 August 1932 Buckalew found the remains of several nests and a number of young birds, most of which could fly. He was able to band 1 about a mile below Dewey Beach. At Indian River Inlet, Hanson (notes) found a group of 3 colonies of more than 100 Least Terns containing 29 nests on 11 June 1934. He added these familiar sounding notes: "With the large increase in visitors to the Inlet for fishing and crabbing the terns moved out. There may have been a few nests in 1935, but in 1936 there were none here although occasional birds were seen. In 1937 they nested [in new locations] along the shore between Dewey Beach and the Inlet." We have no reports for the war years or until members of the public again had access to Cape Henlopen (then Ft. Miles).

We pick up the story of nesting Least Terns in 1956, when a colony with 21 nests was reported within 200 ft of the main laboratory building of the newly constructed Bayside Laboratory at Lewes (Ceglia 1956). Wayne and Speck found 28 nests on Cape Henlopen on 5 June 1965 (Wayne 1965). Breeding met with varying success on Cape Henlopen, and the largest colony there contained 155 nests on 5 June 1972. Factors such as predation by mammals, human disturbance, and changes in habitat as planted grass grew up acted to discourage breeding. Least Terns bred only occasionally at Cape Henlopen during the 1980s as breeding shifted to sites near Indian River Inlet.

Trends. Andrews (1990) recorded an increase from 166 pairs nesting in Delaware in 1977 to 853 in 1985. The May Count shows a slight upward tendency. BBS data for the Mid-Atlantic coast show a strong upward tendency. The Least Tern population has been relatively stable in recent years, helped by protection offered by wardens and signs at the nest sites.

Breeding population. The population of Least Terns was about 900 birds during the 1980s (Thomas 1988c).

Conservation. An effort should be undertaken to reestablish a Least Tern breeding colony on Cape Henlopen, where it can be protected from people and predators more easily than elsewhere. Thomas (1988c) includes Fintel's recommendation for establishing a spoil island for the terns in her annual DNREC report. A platform or an anchored raft might also work but would not accommodate as many pairs.

FALL: The change in abundance shown at the end of June in the seasonal graph probably indicates dispersal from breeding colonies rather than migration. Migration occurs during August as the young become less dependent on the adults. Few Least Terns remain after the end of August; the latest reported are

12 Sep 1978	2	Cape Henlopen SP [Frec26]
8 Oct 1989	1	Indian River Inlet [Camp4]
9 Nov 1968	1	Indian River Inlet [Marv3]

The October record is supported regionally with a 19 October Connecticut specimen (Zeranski and Baptist 1990), but any sighting after mid-September must be treated with caution.

BANDING: Two Least Tern bands have been recovered in Delaware: 1 from Long Island and 1 exactly 20 years old from New Jersey [Usfw3].

SPECIMENS: 6; DMNH, UDEL. Egg records: WFVZ.

Bridled Tern (*Sterna anaethetus*)

Accidental (1993).

DOCUMENTATION: Photograph (L. Larson, DMNH print collection).

REMARKS: This species occurs regularly offshore from the Outer Banks of North Carolina, but is only casual in Maryland waters (Rowlett 1980b). It breeds widely in the Bahamas, and there is a record of breeding on Pelican Shoal, south of Boca Chica Key, Florida (Hoffman 1993). The only Delaware record is an adult found 35 miles east of Indian River Inlet on 22 August 1993. Photographs of this bird show all relevent marks of an adult, leaving no doubt as to the identification.

Sooty Tern (*Sterna fuscata*)

Accidental (1976 and 1979).

REMARKS: This bird of tropical waters has occurred twice in Delaware, each record documented by a specimen. The first occurrence was a bird found dead south of Dewey Beach along the barrier dune on 26 June 1976 (Ednie 1977); this record is noteworthy because it was not associated with a tropical storm. The second bird was found alive, but unable to fly, in downtown Wilmington on 6 September 1979 following the passage of tropical storm *David* the preceding night. The bird was taken to the Delaware Humane Association where it died within 24 hours. Paxton et al. (1980) present a summary of the storm's ornithological effects in our region.

SPECIMENS: DMNH 57882, 2 mi (3 km) S Dewey Beach, 26 June 1976; DMNH 67971, Wilmington, 6 September 1979.

White-winged Tern (*Chlidonias leucopterus*)

Occasional (11 years, 1974–93); summer visitor; local; to be looked for July–September at Little Creek WA.

DOCUMENTATION: Photographs (M. A. Anthony, DMNH 461, 462; D. S. Czaplak, DMNH print collection).

HABITAT: Coastal marshes and impoundments.

REMARKS: The White-winged Tern breeds in marshes from eastern Europe to southeastern Siberia and winters from Africa east to China. It has occurred in Alaska and widely but sparsely in eastern North America (AOU 1983). Some of the Delaware records are

13 Jul–7 Sep 1974	[Marv4; Stod1]
5–28 Jul 1978	[Pure14; Murd1]
summer 1988	[Perr4]
17 Jul–9 Sep 1993	(Campbell 1994)

The 1974 record is supported by published notes (DuMont 1975c, Wayne 1975). The 1978 and 1988 records are supported by published photographs taken by Brady and Mitchell, respectively, although the printed reproduction of the 1978 photograph is not diagnostic. The DuMont notes cover the history of the species' occurrence in North America to 1974 and contain a brief description, quite adequate to identify a species as distinctive as this one in alternate (breeding) plumage. In 1993 at least 2 birds were present, one photographed by B. J. Rose (Campbell 1994).

Nearly all Delaware reports are from the Little Creek WA–Port Mahon marshes. Unlike many vagrants, this species has a tendency to stay in an area for a week or more, providing birders with many opportunities to observe it. Most often a bird arrives in alternate plumage and stays until completing the molt into basic (winter) plumage. No records of juvenile birds are known. The large number of records indicate the unlikelihood that all refer to escaped captives.

The occurrence of this species is perhaps mysterious given that most occurrences in North America have been in the East, not the West (AOU, 1983), yet its range makes movement across the Atlantic seem unlikely. Because the range of the species includes tropical Africa, individuals may be crossing from Africa to Brazil and migrating north in the Americas. A rapid spring migration could be overlooked by observers, with the birds being seen on the more leisurely migration south.

Whiskered Tern (*Chlidonias hybridus*)

Accidental (1993).

DOCUMENTATION: Photograph (B. J. Rose, DMNH print collection).

REMARKS: A Whiskered Tern in alternate plumage discovered and photographed at the Ted Harvey CA, Logan Tract on 19 July 1993 by Rose of Omaha, Nebraska, is the only record in Delaware [Rose1]. It was found by Short and Campbell (1993) the same day and seen by many others during the ensuing month. The first one ever recorded in North America had just been found at Cape May, where it was present from 30 June to 17 July. That bird presumably crossed the Delaware Bay by 19 July and remained probably until 24 August, ranging along the Delaware marshes from the Logan Tract north a few miles to the Pickering Beach end of the Little Creek WA (Campbell 1994). This close relative of the Black Tern breeds in Eurasia, southeast Africa, and southeast Australia (Cramp 1985).

Black Tern (*Chlidonias niger*)

Regular; migrant; uncommon, rare in spring and summer. Expected mostly during August and early September.

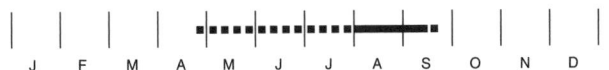

HABITAT: Coastal impoundments, marshes, bays, and estuaries.

SPRING: This tern is not found as a spring migrant every year. When found, early reports are

27 Apr 1974	1	Port Mahon [Wayn25]
27 Apr 1975	1	Little Creek WA [Lehm1]
1 May 1961	5	Little Creek WA (Lesser 1964)

Only 6 reports of more than 6 birds were made in the nearly 50 years of records available:

May 1962	23	Little Creek WA (Lesser 1964)
8 May 1948	30	Bombay Hook NWR [BarI3]

8 May 1966	30	Delaware City [Cutl34]
10 May 1947	30	Bombay Hook NWR [BarI2]
10–20 May 1967	400	along the Delaware River [Cutl22]
12 May 1967	75	Bombay Hook NWR [DuMP1]

SUMMER: Black Terns are occasionally seen in summer after the usual migration dates, a behavior that should be attributed either to late migrants tarrying on the way to breeding grounds (Cramp 1985) or to early fall migrants. The lone breeding report, a nest with 3 eggs found at Bombay Hook NWR on 17 July 1958 by W. R. Jones [Broo1], has no other corroboration. A 1972 summer report from Indian River Inlet was published as a "breeding pair" [Beac3] but no breeding behavior was seen (P. Beach, pers. comm. 1992). This species most frequently breeds on prairie lakes or in other open country situations, but it has bred occasionally near the coast from Maine to Cape May, New Jersey (Novak 1992).

FALL: Black Terns occur most frequently 10–15 August through 5–10 September. Late reports include

20 Sep 1980	1	Indian River Inlet [Frec52]
21 Sep 1961	1	Little Creek WA (Lesser 1964)
23 Sep 1978	1	Assawoman WA [Frec1]
23, 28 Sep 1989	1	Bombay Hook NWR [Holg90]

A November 1990 report (Ednie 1993) is omitted. Only 6 reports of more than 10 birds are known, the 2 highest mentioning 20 at Fenwick Island (probably Assawoman WA) on 26 July 1958 [Davi11] and a remarkable report of "about 100" at Little Creek WA 29 August 1971 [John5].

SPECIMENS: USNM 422330, Slaughter Beach, 26 August 1932; CM 86266, Ocean View, 2 September 1922.

Black Skimmer (*Rynchops niger*)

Regular; summer resident; formerly fairly common. Expected early May (sporadically earlier) to late November. Beach nester needing protection.

HABITAT: Beaches and dunes (breeding); bays, estuaries, and impoundments (feeding).

SPRING: Although Black Skimmers may arrive throughout April, first arrival is usually before 10 May. The full breeding population is present within 1 or 2 weeks thereafter. An unusually early report mentions 17 at Cape Henlopen SP on 21 March 1971 [DuPG23]. Other early arrivals include 2 at Lewes on 4 April 1980, 1 at Oyster Rocks Rd., south of Prime Hook

NWR on 11 April 1983, 1 at Roosevelt Inlet, Lewes, on 14 April 1979, and again on the same date in 1989 [Frec1]. Some high counts at Indian River Inlet total 75 on 13 May 1988, and 50 on 7 May 1985, and 20 on 28 April 1985 [Frec1]. Typical counts involve fewer than 10 birds.

BREEDING: Published records of nesting started in 1965 when the DOS discovered skimmers nesting near Least Terns in Cape Henlopen SP [Wayn28]. Nesting continued there somewhat sporadically, with a high of 81 nests on 24 July 1967 (Linehan 1968a); the last report referred to 2 nests on 11 June 1983 [Jahn10]. A combination of human disturbance, predation by mammals, and habitat change probably caused it to abandon this primary breeding area. As it was being pushed from Cape Henlopen SP, it bred at other locations. Two large colonies near Indian River Inlet contained 100 and 140 adults in 1976, when none bred on Cape Henlopen [Barn3], but the next year only 27 pairs were present in 4 colonies, including 15 adults attempting to nest at Cape Henlopen SP. The colony moved from place to place, including Cedar Island; Delaware Seashore SP near Tower, Conquest, and Keybox roads; and in the vicinity of Indian River Inlet.

Atlas. The distribution map depicts probable and possible breeding in Kent County. These reports most likely refer to pre-breeding birds. Summer reports were submitted for 8 other blocks where breeding was unlikely.

Nesting. This species is a colonial nester, usually associating with terns. It lays its eggs in a scrape in dry sand.

Extreme egg dates range from 26 May [Wayn4] to 3 September—9 nests, 16 eggs, and 56 young on Cape Henlopen (Wayne 1966). Most large colonies were found between 17 June and 6 July, 1 on 24 July. Clutch sizes range from 1 to 6, with the mid-50% containing 3–4 eggs.

History. The Black Skimmer was not hunted commercially for its feathers, but egging, invasion of its colonies, and sport shooting extirpated it from the Northeast. It has now regained much of its prior range. For example, in 1988 2 pairs of Black Skimmers fledged 4 young on Cape Cod, Massachusetts, the northern terminus of its present range [Blod1].

In Delaware, it was not found by Bush (notes) on his 1880 collecting trip to Indian River Inlet, nor by Rhoads and Pennock (1905) or Pennock (1908a) in the early 1900s. Hanson (notes) recorded that Pennock saw it near Rehoboth Beach 11–13 May 1928. Miller [MiJC5] reported 1 in the unexpected location of Edgemoor on 16 June 1932, and the next year Hanson (notes) recorded that Buckalew collected 3 (male, female, and immature) of 12 on Cape Henlopen in September. It was listed as a summer resident, nesting in the Indian River district (Barry 1942). A young bird was banded on 27 June 1954 by Buckalew in the vicinity of Indian River, and the band was later recovered in Maryland [Usfw3]. A nest with 4 eggs was found on Gull Island, Rehoboth Bay, 8 June 1957 (DMNH 2093). It was breeding regularly at Cape Henlopen by the 1960s when Buckalew banded 28, 53, and 41 young in 1961, 1962, and 1963,

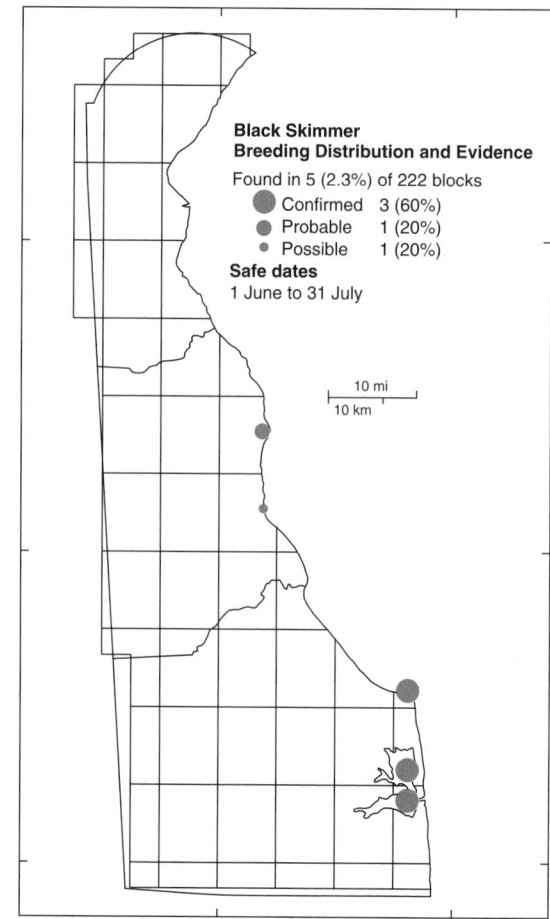

Black Skimmer
Breeding Distribution and Evidence
Found in 5 (2.3%) of 222 blocks
● Confirmed 3 (60%)
● Probable   1 (20%)
· Possible   1 (20%)
Safe dates
1 June to 31 July

10 mi
10 km

respectively [Usfw3]. It was reported breeding on Cape Henlopen, 28 August 1963 [PylR2]; the report was apparently made because the egg date was unusually late, not because breeding on Cape Henlopen was unusual.

Trends. The skimmer population shows a declining tendency on the May Count and on the BBS for Delaware and the Mid-Atlantic region for 1966–91 [Usfw1], but the sample size on the BBS is too small and the numbers on the May Count too variable to be individually useful for reliable trend analysis.

Breeding population. In the 1980s, breeding season adults numbered 50–110 whenever a thorough survey was conducted.

Conservation. This beach nester has been so much disturbed in its breeding habitat that in some years it is still trying to bring off its single clutch as late as September; thus it needs monitoring and protection wherever it breeds. It is listed as Endangered in New Jersey and Threatened in Maryland. As it returned to its historic Mid-Atlantic and Northeast range during the mid-twentieth century, prospects were good that it would remain a Delaware breeder if protected. However, protection from human disturbance was not provided, even on state park land. By 1992 it was rarely seen in Delaware, and no breeding was reported.

FALL: Migration is protracted, probably beginning in late August and early September as the young become independent, peaking late September to mid-October, and extending at least through 10–15 November and in some years to the end of the month. Some high counts are

27 August 1980	500	Bombay Hook NWR [Cut14]
1 October 1983	800	Cape Henlopen SP [Frec1]
20 October 1985	350	Lewes area [Frec1]

WINTER: Black Skimmers have been recorded on 4 CBCs:

1 Jan 1958	2	Rehoboth CBC [Cut19]
2 Jan 1961	7	Indian River Inlet, 1960 Rehoboth CBC [CutH1]
23 Dec 1965	1	Cape Henlopen CBC [Broo23]
28 Dec 1968	2	Rehoboth CBC

One other winter report is 2 seen from Cape Henlopen 13 February 1971 [Davi23].

BANDING: Bands were recovered from young birds banded in Delaware on 27 June 1954, 12 July 1961, 2 on 5 July 1962, 2 on 3 July 1963, and 30 July 1971. Recoveries were from the Mid-Atlantic region except for 1 of the 1963 birds, which was recovered 5.5 years later in Florida [Usfw3]. The banding location, 38°30'N, 75°0'W, corresponds to Indian River Inlet southward to Fenwick Island.

SPECIMENS: USNM 421886, USNM 421895, and USNM 422181, Cape Henlopen, 10 September 1933. Egg records: WFVZ.

Dovekie *(Alle alle)*

Occasional (13 years, 1891–1990); irruptive winter visitor; common offshore in some years.

| J | F | M | A | M | J | J | A | S | O | N | D |

HABITAT: Atlantic offshore waters, occasionally near land.

REMARKS: Like many other alcids, the Dovekie breeds in the Arctic and winters irregularly southward. During winter in the Mid-Atlantic its peak numbers exceed those of any other alcid; it is also seen from shore more frequently than other alcids. It is often present offshore, even in years when there are no records from shore, so caution should be taken about making inferences about its frequency of occurrence in Delaware from the available observations. Since 1960, we have records from only 7 years (1961, 1964, 1968, 1970, 1978, 1983, and 1990), but experience gained on pelagic trips out of Ocean City, Maryland, suggests that Dovekies may be present in our region during as many as half of all winters (Barnhill, pers. obs.). Although there are Delaware records as early as 28 November and as late as 16 March, the species seems to be most frequent in January and February, at least as observed from land.

Voelker reported collecting a Dovekie off Pennsgrove, New Jersey, on the Delaware River (therefore in Delaware) during November 1891 [Voel1]. His record is the first known observation of Dovekie from the state. Inland records include 1 picked up, after a storm, from a woods near the inland location of Greenwood, western Sussex County on 1 January 1932 by W. Hatfield [Hans1]; and 1 seen by Buckalew at Milford on 28 November 1932 (Murphy and Voght 1933), also after a major storm. One was picked up at Milford, another inland location (DMNH 18377).

SPECIMENS: DMNH 18377, Milford, 8 January 1932; DMNH 77394, Cotton Patch, between Indian River Inlet and Bethany Beach, 24 January 1990; ANSP 138501, 2 mi (3 km) W Bethany Beach, 22 February 1940.

[Common Murre *(Uria aalge)*]

Accidental (1993).

HABITAT: Pelagic.

REMARKS: The Common Murre's breeding grounds in North America extend south to Newfoundland and perhaps Nova Scotia, and it winters "primarily offshore in the vicinity of the breeding grounds" (AOU, 1983). Rowlett (1980b) tabulates only 3 records in the region, 1 in February 1976 off Hog Island, Virginia, and 2 in Maryland during the winter of 1976–77. One was reported about 23 mi east of Cape Henlopen on 15 February 1993 [Camp9]. We have notes from Campbell [Camp1] stating that the bird was seen swimming within 50 yards of the boat, after 2 min flushing and flying away. The bird was in alternate (breeding) plumage, and the line between the dark of the throat and the white of the chest was "a shallow, inverted 'V'." This mark distinguishes the Common Murre from the only species likely to be confused with it at so short a range.

Thick-billed Murre *(Uria lomvia)*

Casual (1896, 1969, 1987); winter visitor; rare.

HABITAT: Pelagic.

REMARKS: A specimen was collected at Middletown on 18 December 1896 (ANSP 72793). One was reported from Indian River Inlet on 7 December 1969 [Bord1]. An emaciated male was picked up by John Putre at Bethany Beach on 2 March 1987; it died despite expert care and attempted release (DMNH 76504; Grosz and Hess 1987).

Offshore, Thick-billed Murre is not easily distinguished from the somewhat less rare Razorbill, since both are large alcids with relatively short, thick bills. Experienced observers can distinguish them reliably, but unless the birds are very close it is difficult for an observer to clearly establish the correctness of the identification. Each species is quite rare, even offshore (Barnhill, pers. obs.; Rowlett 1980b). The Thick-billed Murre can also be confused with the even rarer Common Murre.

A substantial series of winter trips offshore would be necessary to establish reliably the frequency of occurrence of the species in Delaware.

SPECIMENS: DMNH 76504, 1 mi (2 km) N Bethany Beach, 1 March 1987; ANSP 72793, Middletown, 18 December 1896.

Razorbill *(Alca torda)*

Occasional offshore (6 years, 1891–1991); winter visitor; rare.

HABITAT: Pelagic.

REMARKS: Specimen records involve a bird picked up in oiled condition on 25 December 1982, which died 3 days later [Frec1] (DMNH 74952). Another was picked up dead on 15 December 1970 [Lake1], but was not preserved. A Razorbill reportedly collected off Pennsgrove, New Jersey, on the Delaware River (therefore in Delaware) in November 1891 [anon18] is not extant in the collection of the Academy of Natural Sciences, Philadelphia (M. Robbins, pers. comm.). Sight records include 1 seen at Rehoboth Beach on 23 January 1932 [Hans1] and another at Indian River Inlet on 17 December 1983 [Barn4]. During the winter of 1990–91, Razorbills were many times seen in numbers of 10–15 per day both from land and from boats a short distance offshore at Cape Henlopen. Many of these observations were at very close range. All the sight records are necessarily of less than ideal reliability.

There are similar numbers of records of Thick-billed Murre and Razorbill from Delaware. Given that the 2 are difficult to distinguish from one another and that observations in Mary-land (Rowlett 1980b; Barnhill, pers. obs.) indicate that Razorbills are in fact substantially more common, the actual relative numbers of the 2 species in the state remain to be determined. Since most Delaware observations are from land and most Razorbills and murres actually stay well offshore, the Delaware observations may not be representative of the actual status of the 2 species.

SPECIMEN: DMNH 74952, Rehoboth Beach, 25 December 1982.

[Atlantic Puffin (*Fratercula arctica*)]

record is undoubtedly correct, but no descriptive notes are available. Another record (Barnhill 1980) is more difficult. It describes a bird seen in flight inshore by a careful and experienced observer, but the outer half of the bill is described as reddish. The cheeks were not described. We are reluctant to accept a record of a bird rare in location that is also described as having an unexpected bill color, regardless of the experience of the observer. Other editors might disagree. Definite placement of Atlantic Puffin on the Delaware list must await further documented records.

Casual (1975 and 1980); winter visitor; rare.

DOCUMENTATION: Sight only.

HABITAT: Primarily offshore, very rare from land.

REMARKS: Atlantic Puffins breed from northern New England north and winter irregularly south along the Atlantic coast, coming farther south than indicated by the sixth edition of the AOU Check-list (Rowlett 1980b). On boat trips they are seldom present close to shore, and Rowlett records no observations in waters shallower than 20 fathoms (120 ft). They are slightly smaller than murres and Razorbills and are readily identified at reasonable distances by size and the medium-gray face. In Barnhill's experience on Maryland trips, alternate (breeding) plumage birds with white cheeks and large, colorful bills are never present in our region. All of his records have been of presumed immatures.

The first Delaware puffin was seen 50 mi off Rehoboth Beach on 5 February 1975 [Rowl15]. Given the observer, the

Rock Dove (*Columba livia*)

Resident; common; introduced. Most numerous around Wilmington and least so in Sussex County. Most breed during March–June.

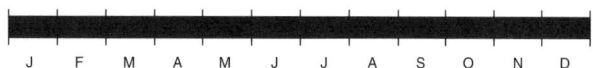

J F M A M J J A S O N D

HABITAT: Agricultural and urban areas where nest ledges are available; fields, park land, and alleys may be used for foraging.

BREEDING: The Rock Dove is common in Wilmington and in some towns and agricultural areas throughout the state. Highway overpasses often have feral colonies breeding on sheltered ledges below them, and these added nesting sites may have led to a population increase. The relative abundance study showed fewer Rock Doves in Sussex County than in the rest of the state—at about half the density of Kent County and a third the density of New Castle County. The lower density in Sussex County results partly from larger areas of woods there, unsuitable for this species.

Atlas. Atlas workers had little difficulty locating farm buildings where Rock Doves bred, but sometimes permission to

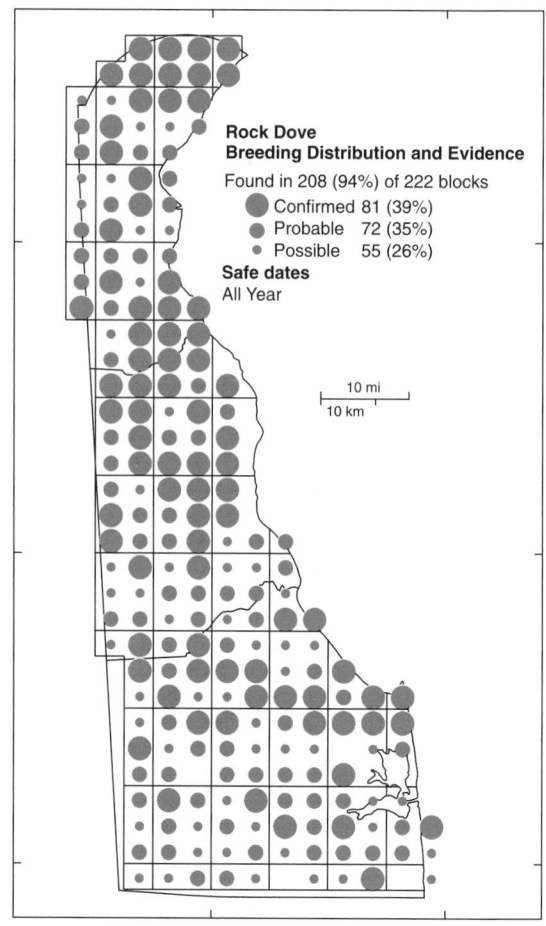

Rock Dove
Breeding Distribution and Evidence
Found in 208 (94%) of 222 blocks
● Confirmed 81 (39%)
● Probable 72 (35%)
· Possible 55 (26%)
Safe dates
All Year

10 mi
10 km

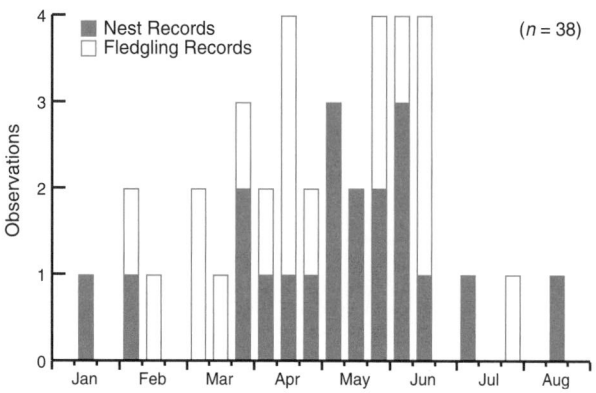

Estimated Clutch-Completion Dates

enter for confirmation was not obtainable. Most confirmations resulted from finding occupied nests. Rock Doves reported in the Atlas project were thought to be feral, but some domestic birds may have been counted by mistake.

This species was difficult to find in some Atlas blocks with good farmland habitat. Some farms, small towns, and building owners eliminate pigeons, thus leaving temporary gaps in the species' distribution.

Nesting. Few records of nesting pigeons are maintained by birders, but Hanson (notes) reports a most unusual nesting: "A large limb was broken from a big elm tree in front of the Ridgely home on the Green, Dover, leaving a hole perhaps 2 ft high and 1 ft wide in the trunk about 15 ft from the ground. In the winter of 1933–1934 a pair of pigeons used this cavity for a nest. During February it was unusually cold, –11 on February 9, and much snow fell. On February 20 there were well grown squabs in the nest." This nesting record is the earliest of the season and one of few tree-nesting reports for North America (Peterson 1986). The nest is usually composed of a thin layer of twigs, straw, and various other objects placed on a protected ledge or loft. Rock Doves usually breed in small colonies.

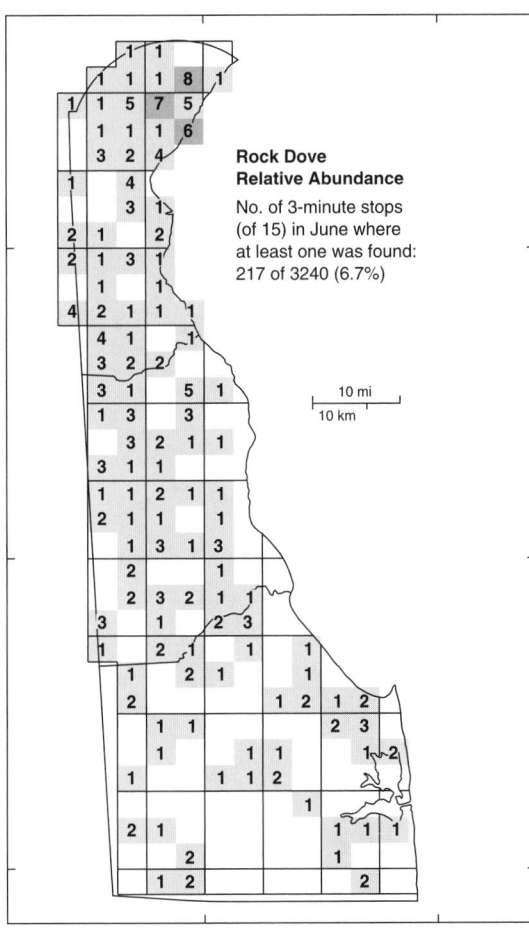

**Rock Dove
Relative Abundance**

No. of 3-minute stops
(of 15) in June where
at least one was found:
217 of 3240 (6.7%)

10 mi
10 km

(Records 3:532, 1933, in Goodwin 1983). Feral Rock Doves derive from domestic pigeons that have strayed, become lost, or been abandoned by their owners (Goodwin 1983).

Trends. The Rock Dove population increased in the East during 1965–79 according to BBS results (Robbins et al. 1986). We have little other evidence for its increase in Delaware other than its presence at new highway bridges; in many populations scarcity of nest sites limits breeders (Johnston 1992).

1974–89 CBC Summary

Christmas Bird Count	Years Found	Range of No. Found	Median
Wilmington	16	202–769	532
Middletown	16	124–486	214
Bombay Hook	16	40–356	181
Cape Henlopen	16	74–394	156
Rehoboth	16	24–353	100
STATEWIDE	16	963–1,715	1,301
(counted 1974–89; low in 1984, high in 1981)			

WINTER: Reports of this species were not accepted on CBCs before 1974. The data taken since then indicate a significant increase in its numbers, perhaps, in part, the result of better record keeping by observers.

SPECIMENS: 16; DMNH.

Delaware clutch-completion dates extend from January through mid-August. This range of dates is consistent with the January–August dates given for Maryland (Robbins and Bystrak 1977). Others have reported that the breeding season is year-round in New York, Pennsylvania, and Maryland (Bull 1974; Dunmore and Davis 1963; Schein 1954). In a Rhode Island study, egg-laying occurred in every month, with about three-quarters of the eggs laid January–July (Preble and Heppner 1981). Delaware records, including records of fledglings, suggest that about three-quarters of the clutches are completed between 21 March and 10 June. The maximum number of broods raised per year by feral birds in the state is unknown, but the long breeding period provides opportunity for multiple broods. More than 6 broods were possible in well-fed captive stock in Texas, where fresh clutches were laid before the previous broods fledged (Burley 1980). Clutch size is 2, sometimes 1 (Burley 1980).

History. This bird, the familiar pigeon of cities and farm yards, was a concomitant of European settlement from the beginning (Schorger 1952; Long 1981). For example, the Council of the Virginia Company sent a letter dated 5 December 1621 to the governor and Council of Virginia stating "Pidgeons" and other commodities were being forwarded, "the preservation and encrease whereof we recommend unto you"

[Ringed Turtle-Dove *(Streptopelia 'risoria')*]

Local; introduced but not established.

HABITAT: Urban areas where introduced and maintained.

REMARKS: The single quotation marks around *'risoria'* follow the practice of Cramp (1985), suggesting that it is not the name of a valid species. This introduced bird has been raised in captivity for so many centuries that its origin is obscure. It appears to be a naturally occurring recessive mutant of the African Collared-Dove *(S. roseogrisea)* (Goodwin 1983; Smith 1987).

OCCURRENCE: A few of these birds began appearing at a feeder in west Wilmington by 1978, and in 1983 3 young came to the feeder with 7 adults [Stri2]. It was recorded there on a 1984 BBS and on the 1982–85 Wilmington CBCs. It stopped appearing after 1987, and its breeding location was never reported. Individual birds were also reported in Newark during 1986 [RusJ1] and in Lewes from 26 June to 4 September 1983 [Frec1]. None of these was regarded as genuinely feral. This species should not be included on a list of Delaware avifauna, because it is not clear that the small 1980s population (about 10 birds) was ever self-sustaining.

SPECIMENS: 6; DMNH.

Mourning Dove *(Zenaida macroura)*

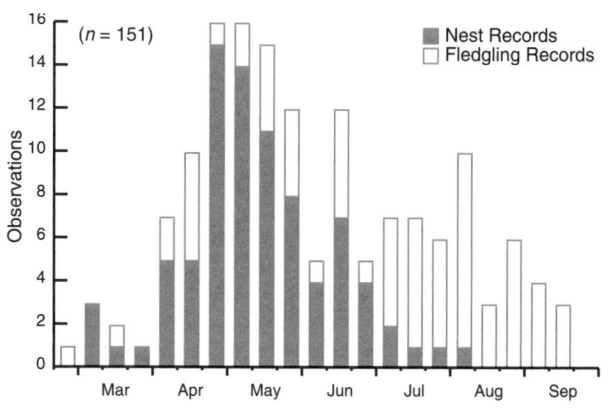

Estimated Clutch-Completion Dates

Resident; common. Part of breeding population migrates, and additional birds arrive in winter. Found throughout the state in summer, particularly in suburban areas. Unusually long breeding season—late February–mid-September. In December more common in eastern Kent and southern New Castle counties than either to the north or south. Winter numbers increasing at 2% per year.

HABITAT: Residential areas, hedgerows, deciduous and mixed wood margins during the breeding season. Agricultural areas in winter.

MIGRATION: In New York and Ohio banding data show that certain individuals are highly migratory and others remain year-round at or near their breeding places (Bull 1974; Peterjohn 1989). Similarly, winter returns of birds banded in Delaware in summer show that 5 stayed in Delaware and 1 each were recovered in Maryland, North Carolina, and Geor-

gia. The Delaware winter population is increased by visitors from the north, indicated by winter recovery of 1 bird banded in New Hampshire, 6 in Massachusetts, 2 in Rhode Island, and 8 in New York [Usfw3].

BREEDING: The Mourning Dove is one of the most numerous birds in both Delaware and the United States. Even though Delaware has very favorable habitat, doves are only about half as numerous here during June as in the states where it reaches its highest abundance: North Carolina and Indiana (Robbins et al. 1986). The relative abundance study shows that during June doves are more common in northern Delaware than southward, about 30% more common in New Castle County than in Sussex County. This trend is a consequence of habitat rather than latitude, as shown by its higher density in suburban areas throughout the state compared to a lower density in the forestry and farming region in central Sussex County.

Atlas. This was an easy species to locate during the Atlas project and was usually confirmed by finding the nest.

Nesting. Egg-laying usually starts in March and extends

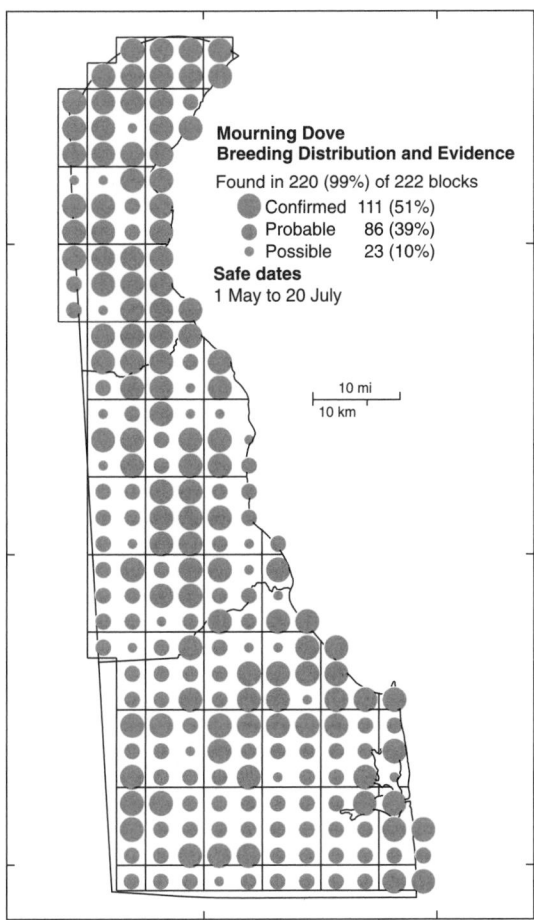

Mourning Dove
Breeding Distribution and Evidence

Found in 220 (99%) of 222 blocks
⬤ Confirmed 111 (51%)
⬤ Probable 86 (39%)
• Possible 23 (10%)

Safe dates
1 May to 20 July

10 mi
10 km

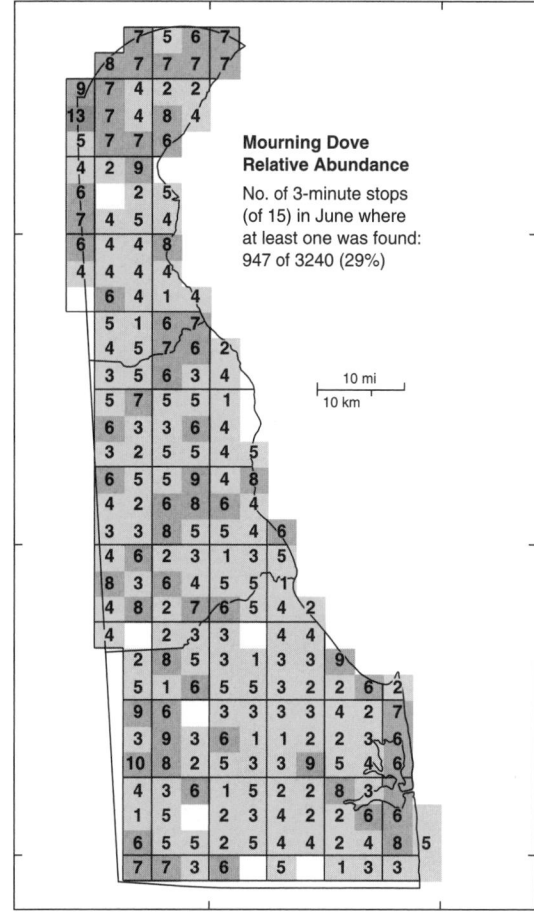

Mourning Dove
Relative Abundance

No. of 3-minute stops
(of 15) in June where
at least one was found:
947 of 3240 (29%)

10 mi
10 km

through mid-September, with a clutch-completion peak occurring in late April and May. With such an extended egg-laying period and a 28–30 day nesting cycle (Westmoreland et al. 1986), it is evident that the number of nests found by observers (who search mostly in late spring) does not correspond to actual nesting activity. Examination of fledgling data at Tri-State Bird Rescue and Research reveals that egg laying extends into the second half of September, with the latest record suggesting clutch completion about 19 September (Baer 1992). The long season and multiple peaks suggest 3 or 4 broods are common in Delaware. Studies in Texas (Swank 1955) and Alabama (Moore and Pearson 1941) report extended breeding seasons and multiple broods. Clutch size is 2 eggs.

History. The Mourning Dove is more common now than before European settlement, presumably because farmland edges and suburbs provide favorable breeding habitats, and harvested grain fields provide fall and winter forage (Hennessee and Van Camp 1963). Three midwinter specimens show it was wintering in Delaware by the end of the nineteenth century (ANSP 26337, ANSP 26341, and ANSP 26342), but it has become more numerous in the latter half of the twentieth century. Year-round hunting pressure may have suppressed its population or its northward spread to Delaware as a common breeding bird. The open hunting season 50 years ago reported-

ly reduced its numbers (Barry 1939), but the current population is withstanding hunting pressure. Similarly, breeding and winter populations have increased during the twentieth century in both New York (Eaton 1988) and Michigan; these increases are ascribed to changes in habitat, food supply, and climate (Brewer and Caldwell, in Brewer et al. 1991, 56, 230).

Trends: According to one source of data, a calling count survey, Mourning Doves declined in the East an average of 1% per year during 1963–73 (Ruos 1974), which might be attributed to trends toward larger fields (Keeler et al. 1967). Since then the population has stabilized or increased slightly (Dolton 1986). Another source, the BBS, shows an upward trend in Delaware and the East during 1966–90 [Usfw4].

Breeding Population: The Mourning Dove is a third more abundant per BBS route in Delaware than in New York during June (Robbins et al. 1986). The New York population has been estimated at approximately 10 million (Decker 1985), so the corresponding estimate for Delaware would be approximately 500,000.

High breeding population densities (males per 100 ha):
55 (6 in 27 acres) in uneven-aged sweet gum–red maple–beech forest (urban woodlot) in New Castle County (Linehan and Burr 1967; 4-year average: 25 per 100 ha).
30 (2.5 in 21 acres) in coastal lowland mixed woods in Sussex County (McLaughlin 1968).

Conservation. Delaware productivity and population support an annual harvest of 15,000 birds each fall, providing recreation and food for 10,000 hunters (Martin 1979). It is a popular quarry for hunters and, with waterfowl and quail hunting, provides the basis for a large industry in Delaware. DNREC, supported by hunting license fees, has long been active in land acquisition and habitat improvement programs for this species.

1966–89 CBC Summary

Christmas Bird Count	Years Found	Range of No. Found	Median
Wilmington	24	132–916	407
Middletown	24	147–1,427	462
Bombay Hook	24	113–1,108	446
Cape Henlopen	24	30–839	138
Rehoboth	24	19–761	207
STATEWIDE	24	893–3,173	1873

(increasing; low in 1969, high in 1977)

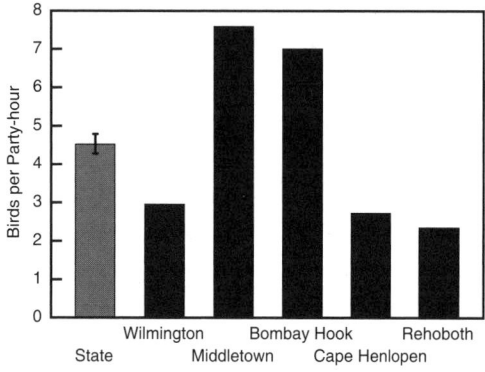

CBC Geographic Distribution

WINTER: It increased significantly on CBCs during 1966–89, and it has generally increased in the Northeast in recent years (K. Parkes, pers. comm., in Root 1988; Laughlin and Kibbe

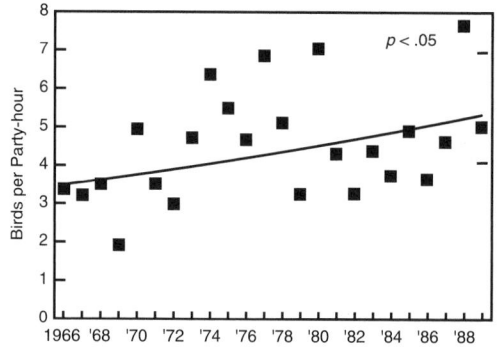

p < .05

CBC Trend; Increasing at 2% per Year

1985). Currently, the Mourning Dove is found in the hundreds on Delaware CBCs, but it was less common earlier in the twentieth century. Pennock (notes) found it interesting enough to record when W. L. Bailey saw "40 together" at Redden on 12 December 1908. For central Delaware Hanson (notes) cites arrival dates in mid-March for the 1920s and in February for 1930 and 1932. He also recorded departure dates in November during those years and mentioned only a few winter observations. This species was found in very low numbers on the Bombay Hook CBCs in the 1930s. Barry (1942) said the winter populations in Kent and New Castle counties were low. Bent (1932) noted that the Mourning Dove occasionally wintered in Maryland and Pennsylvania. Recent CBCs show high numbers on the Middletown and Bombay Hook CBCs. The northern portion of its wintering range now includes southern Ontario (Armstrong and Nokes 1983), Pennsylvania (Keeler et al. 1977), and New York (Root 1988), where it is common at feeders (Eaton 1988).

SPECIMENS: 73; DMNH, ANSP, UDEL, USNM. Egg records: DMNH.

[Passenger Pigeon *(Ectopistes migratorius)*]

Gregory A. Inskip

Extinct. Formerly abundant migrant in the region, but no extant Delaware specimen.

HISTORY: In the seventeenth and eighteenth centuries the Passenger Pigeon was a sometimes abundant transient visitor in Delaware, Pennsylvania, and New Jersey (Myers 1912, 48, 229; Stone 1937; Schorger 1955, 270; Hesselius 1947 [1712], 86–87; Pennock 1908b; Wright 1911, 427–29). Pigeons generally passed northward through the region in March and April and returned south in September and October, but they could be present at any season. Thomas Yong found pigeons to be abundant along Delaware Bay in the winter of 1634 (Myers 1912,

48), and in the beginning of February 1729 a "countless multitude . . . arrived in Pennsylvania and New Jersey" (Stone 1937).

Lindestrom (1925 [1691], 216–17), who was in New Sweden [now Delaware] in 1654–56, stated that Indians killed large numbers of pigeons by cutting their roost trees almost through so that they collapsed when the birds returned to roost. Europeans in turn relentlessly shot, netted, and persecuted pigeons everywhere from their breeding areas in the northern states to their winter range in the South (Townsend, in Bent 1932, 396–401).

Hesselius shot an adult in or near Wilmington on 19 July

1712 (Hesselius 1947 [1712], 86–87). In the words of Dr. Frank M. Jones, one-time president of the Society of Natural History of Delaware, "small flocks were observed here as late as 1872; but since 1914 the Passenger Pigeon as a species has ceased to exist" (Hesselius 1947, 87, fn. 63).

[Common Ground-Dove *(Columbina passerina)*]

No adequately documented record.

DOCUMENTATION: Inconclusive photographs (DMNH 322, 323).

REMARKS: A single individual of this species, which occurs regularly north to North Carolina, was reported from late October 1979 through late January 1980 near Pickering Beach [Pure13]. Although several observers reported the bird, no field notes have survived, nor do the published accounts of this occurrence indicate that satisfactory notes were provided. Photographs, on file at DMNH, are of insufficient quality to permit a judgment for or against the identification.

A Common Ground-Dove was also reported near Bowers Beach in June 1986 [Fage1], but field notes were not taken because the rarity of the bird was not fully appreciated at the time of the sighting.

[Monk Parakeet *(Myiopsitta monachus)*]

Local; introduced but not definitely established.

HABITAT: Urban areas where introduced and maintained; prefers pine trees near water.

REMARKS: A small colony of this noisy and conspicuous parakeet has been present at Silver Lake, Rehoboth Beach, since late 1988 [Frec1]. As many as 16–32 have been reported at feeders in the vicinity of the lake, often feeding on sunflower seeds. Grass seeds are also consumed. Nest building in pine trees and on telephone poles has been observed on 2 streets, but since the species builds nests for use as roosting quarters as well as breeding sites (Forshaw 1973) there is no definite evidence of breeding. Another colony has been reported from the Harrington area [Frec1]. Hubbard (1973, 1974b) and Brooks (1972) mentioned earlier occurrences but did not provide details.

The source of this introduced, South American parakeet is unknown. Because it causes economic damage, it is controlled in many regions.

[Carolina Parakeet *(Conuropsis carolinensis)*]

Gregory A. Inskip

Extinct; no Delaware records, but formerly present in the region.

REMARKS: The Carolina Parakeet enjoyed a wide distribution in the southeastern and central states. Campanius Holm (1720, 30; 1834, 41) listed "parrots" among the birds of New Sweden, but the Carolina Parakeet has not been definitely recorded in Delaware (Hasbrouck 1891, 371; McKinley 1979); Hasbrouck thought it likely the species occurred in Delaware; McKinley thought not. It apparently preferred cypress swamps or river bottoms heavily timbered with sycamore (Greenway 1967, 324–25). Such habitat formerly existed in southern Delaware.

Black-billed Cuckoo *(Coccyzus erythropthalmus)*

Regular; migrant; uncommon; rare, but variable, summer resident and visitor. Expected early May through September, rarely later. Breeding usually confined to brushy areas in the Piedmont. During 1966–90 has generally increased in the East but decreased in the Upper Coastal Plain.

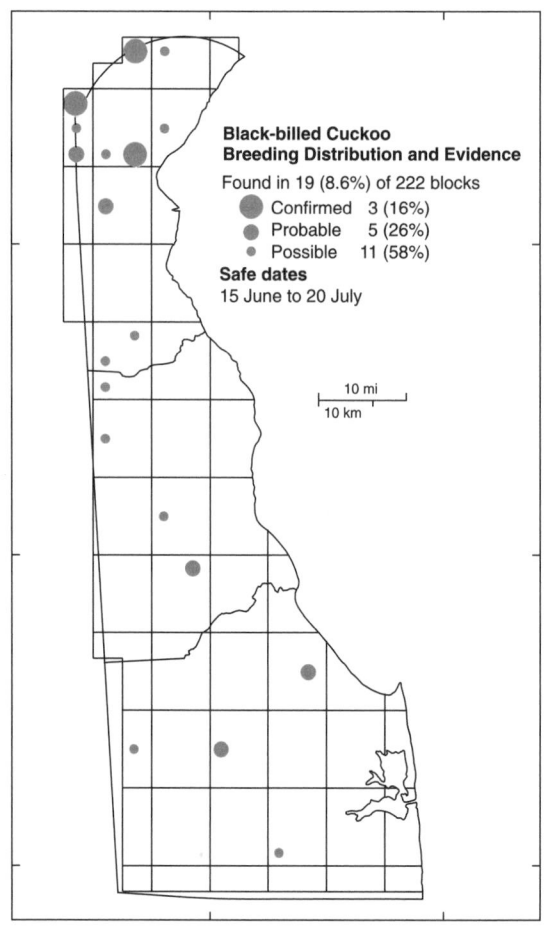

**Black-billed Cuckoo
Breeding Distribution and Evidence**
Found in 19 (8.6%) of 222 blocks
● Confirmed 3 (16%)
● Probable 5 (26%)
• Possible 11 (58%)
Safe dates
15 June to 20 July

10 mi
10 km

HABITAT: Breeds in early succession in brushland stage, such as overgrown pastures, hedgerows, moist thickets, forest edge, and tree farms; any woodland with abundant lepidopteran or other larvae for food during the remainder of its stay.

SPRING: First arrival is 1–5 May, but Stewart and Robbins (1958) list 25 April as the beginning of the normal arrival period in Maryland. The earliest Delaware reports mention

2 May 1981	1	Trap Pond SP [Barn40]
4 May 1974	1	White Clay Creek [Wayn25]
5 May 1973	1	Little Creek WA [John8]
5 May 1980	1	Gordon Pond WA [Frec1]

Most sightings occur 10–20 May. By early to mid-June the number of reports is about half the number for May, and migration is presumably finished. The few reports of multiple birds help define the peak of migration, for example,

9 May 1970	2	Brandywine Creek SP [Broo15]
13 May 1991	4	Nanticoke WA [Camp7]
15 May 1982	2	Bombay Hook NWR [Kell4]
16 May 1982	3	White Clay Creek [Barn46]
17 May 1969	2	Brandywine Creek SP [BroW1]

The May Count averages about 5 birds per count compared with an average of about 32 Yellow-billed Cuckoos per count.

BREEDING: The Black-billed Cuckoo is the more northerly of the 2 Delaware cuckoos, and few breed here. Cuckoos have a nomadic postmigration phase during which good food resources are sought (Hamilton and Hamilton 1965; Sealy 1978, 1985). The Black-billed Cuckoo settles down where food is abundant, and this abundance stimulates egg production (Nolan and Thompson 1975). Early Delaware lists classify this bird as a summer resident (Rhoads and Pennock 1905) or, more precisely, a rare summer resident (Barry 1942). Hanson (notes) saw none during 25 years of residence in the Dover area, but in 1991–92 some evidence for breeding south of the Chesapeake and Delaware Canal was observed in scrubby areas where no insecticides were sprayed (D. Rothstein, DNHI, pers. comm.). This cuckoo is regarded as a similarly rare breeding bird in the Coastal Plain of New Jersey, Maryland, and Virginia (Stone 1937; Stewart and Robbins 1958; Kain 1987).

Atlas. Breeding evidence is difficult to obtain because Black-billed Cuckoos have a compressed breeding cycle: under 3 weeks from nest building to when the last fledgling scrambles from the nest (Spencer 1943), and because this cycle can occur any time from May to August. The only nests for which we have specific records come from the Piedmont, but it was reported to breed in Bombay Hook NWR (Bombay Hook NWR 1972).

During the Atlas project young were reported 3 times:

25 Jun 1987	juvenile, buffy eye ring	Smalleys Pond [Wayn3]
10 Jul 1983	stub-tailed young	near Hoopes Reservoir [SpeE5]
28 Aug 1983	flightless young	near Newark (DMNH 75100).

The observation from near Smalleys Pond and all those made farther south are less indicative of local breeding. The map shows records of birds between 15 June and 20 July, but some seen on the Coastal Plain may be migrants or wandering individuals. Movement away from the nest area in search of food begins when the young can fly, which may be as soon as late June or as late as September (Sealy 1985; Nolan and Thompson 1975). No confirmed observations were reported on the Coastal Plain of the Delmarva Peninsula in Maryland or Virginia Atlas projects (Robbins 1996; Ridd 1989).

Nesting. Nests have been found in the Piedmont 3 times:

4 Jun 1981	1 egg	near Greenville [Nile2]
5 Jul 1981	4 eggs	near Ashland [WilN1]
26 Jul 1919	1 bad egg	Brandywine Creek [Gard1]

These nest records and 3 fledgling records from the Atlas project suggest a clutch-completion range from 24 May to 2 August. Nests were in floodplain scrubby edge: 3 ft high in a low bush, 4 ft high in a multiflora rose, and 5 ft high in a viburnum. D. Rothstein (DNHI, pers. comm.) reports nests in deciduous or coniferous trees, sometimes shrubs, about 6 ft above ground. The nest is a loosely woven cup of twigs lined with finer twigs [Gard1].

Trends. This species' population showed an increasing tendency in the East during 1966–90 and increased significantly in the last 10 years of that period. In contrast, its population significantly declined during this period in the Upper Coastal Plain (includes Delaware), where it is rare [Usfw1].

Delaware BBS data for 1966–87 show a 1:10 ratio in June of Black-billed to Yellow-billed cuckoos recorded. Within this period a peak of 16 Black-bills was found in 1973, 20 times more than the average for 1981–87. It was detected at only 1 stop (of 3,240) in the relative abundance study, compared to 187 stops at which Yellow-bills were detected. These low numbers may reflect a permanent reduction in population, a normal fluctuation, or perhaps observer failure to distinguish accurately between the sometimes similar songs of the 2 cuckoos.

June Abundance Data for Cuckoos Encountered on 3-Min Stops

	Breeding Bird Survey			Relative abundance study
	1973	1966–80	1981–87	1985–87
Black-billed Cuckoo				
Avg. no. per 50 stops	2	0.4	0.1	0.02
Yellow-billed Cuckoo				
Avg. no. per 50 stops	2	3	3	3
Black-billed/Yellow-billed ratio	1:1	1:7	1:23	1:187

NOTE: Actual relative abundance of these species is different from the ratio of the numbers detected because 1 species may be more easily seen or heard than the other, but the trend of this ratio suggests that the Black-billed Cuckoo has become relatively scarcer in June.

Breeding population. Few reports of this species come from the well-studied Piedmont, and fewer still from the Coastal Plain. Thus its current population is estimated at fewer than 10 breeding pairs, but it has been more common in the past, presumably during caterpillar outbreaks.

Conservation. Forest-spraying programs to control tent caterpillars or gypsy moths may disrupt breeding of this species by removing the plentiful food it requires to breed successfully.

FALL: Migration probably occurs during September, but our data do not show a peak. The latest 3 reports are

10 Oct 1988	1	Brandywine Creek SP [Edni63]
12 Oct 1981	1	Delaware Seashore SP [Frec30]
11 Nov 1978	1	Ashland (good notes) [Dyer5]

SPECIMENS: UDEL 314–68, Wilmington, Brandywine Woods, 14 May 1878; DMNH 875, Sussex Co., 15 August 1958; DMNH 859, Sussex Co., 14 September 1958; DMNH 75100, Newark, 28 August 1983.

Yellow-billed Cuckoo (*Coccyzus americanus*)

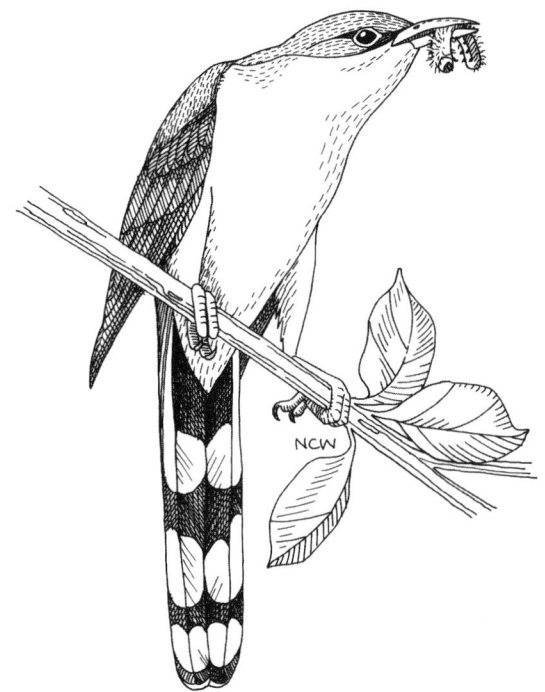

Regular; summer resident; fairly common. Expected early May through mid-September. Most numerous in the western half of the state.

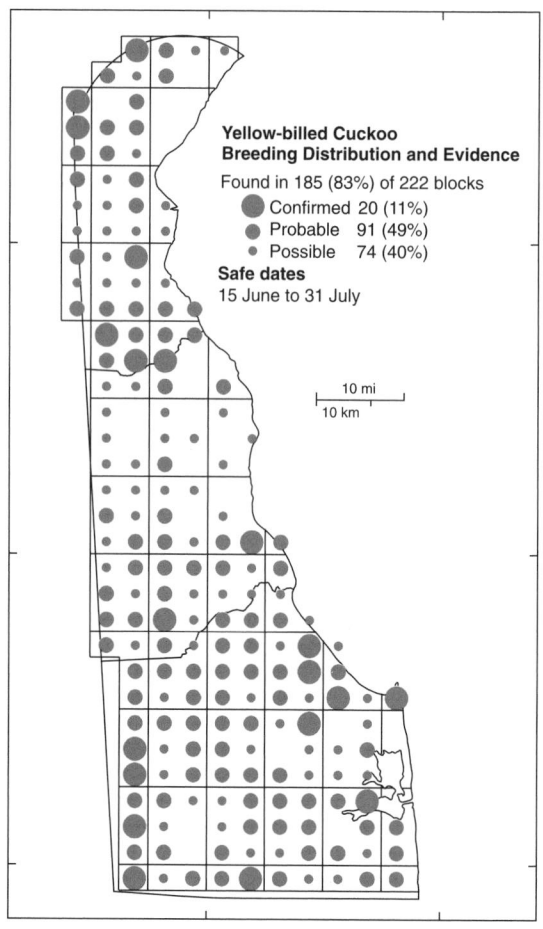

Yellow-billed Cuckoo
Breeding Distribution and Evidence
Found in 185 (83%) of 222 blocks
● Confirmed   20 (11%)
● Probable   91 (49%)
• Possible   74 (40%)
Safe dates
15 June to 31 July

10 mi
10 km

HABITAT: Shrub layer, understory, or edges of open deciduous or mixed woodlands on upland or wetland sites. Like the Black-billed Cuckoo, prefers any woodland with abundant lepidopteran or other arboreal larvae.

SPRING: This secretive species may arrive earlier than the Black-billed Cuckoo. First reports, all of single birds, include

24 Apr 1988	1	coast [Barn54]
27 Apr 1981	1	Five Points [Frec1]
29 Apr 1979	1	Sussex County Rt. 258 [Frec1]
30 Apr 1989	1	Lums Pond SP [Litt5]

It is usually not reported before 1 May. Peak counts are

15 May 1982	16	Bombay Hook NWR [Kell4]
16 May 1970	12	Brandywine Creek SP [WarD9]
3 Jun 1978	11	White Clay Creek [MiDP11]

The 13 May 1979 count totaled 137 birds in 269 party-hours of field work. Although this species is more widespread and more common than the Black-billed Cuckoo, most reports involve only 1 or 2 birds.

BREEDING: The uninitiated may find it hard to believe that a cuckoo is a widespread breeding bird in Delaware, but farmers know the "rain crow" well by its croaking song. The relative abundance study showed that this species is encountered about 3 times as frequently in the western half of the state as in the eastern half.

Atlas. During the Atlas period it was found in 83% of blocks, being present in all except those with heavy urbanization or extensive saltmarshes and barrier beaches. It was difficult for Atlas workers to confirm breeding because this species has a nesting cycle as short as 16 days (Potter 1980); nesting can be initiated anytime during the summer in response to an abundant food supply. Before and after breeding it does not maintain a territory but is more or less nomadic depending on available food (Sealy 1985). Many of the possible and probable records may have resulted from encounters with birds outside their breeding cycles. Had Atlas workers been informed of the problems breeding cuckoos presented and about cuckoo behavior, they could have confirmed them more often, since cuckoos frequently call from their nests, fly directly from their nests, and, when returning, simply work their way out on the limb that holds the nest (Potter 1980). Only 6 confirmations were based on locating a nest; the 14 reports of young could represent encounters close to a food supply after the birds moved away from the nest territory.

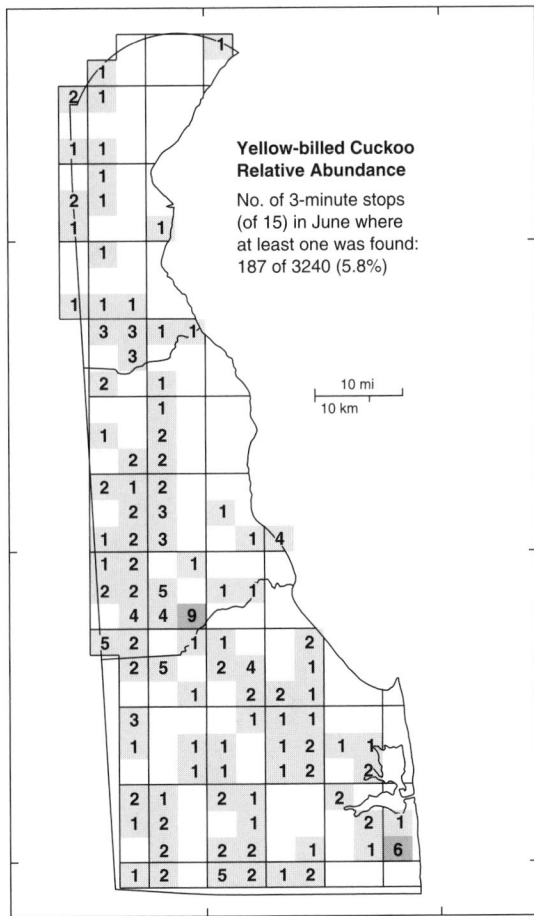

Yellow-billed Cuckoo Relative Abundance

No. of 3-minute stops (of 15) in June where at least one was found: 187 of 3240 (5.8%)

10 mi
10 km

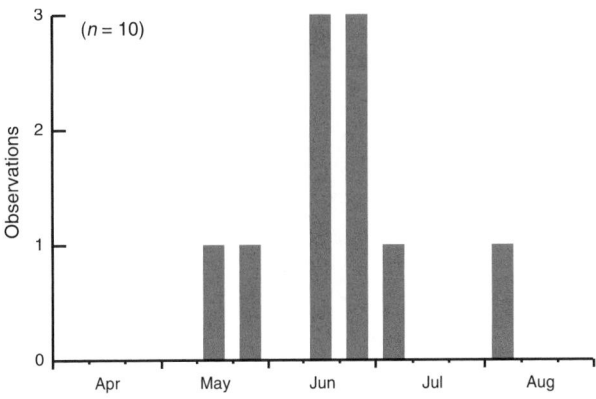

(*n* = 10)

Estimated Clutch-Completion Dates

Nesting. There are 10 nest records of eggs or young, ranging from 2 eggs found on 23 May [Hess4] to nestlings on 23 August [Kenn1]; peak nesting is in late June but probably varies from year to year. The nesting period potentially extends into September based on data from other states. Clutch sizes in Delaware have been 2 or 3 (*n* = 4) but are usually 3 or 4 eggs (Harrison 1978). Hanson (notes) described a nest found on 22 June 6 ft high in a willow oak sapling: "The nest was about 5 inches in outside diameter and was very flat and flimsy. It was constructed of a few sticks, pine needles, and pieces of thin dry bark."

Trends. Although BBS data show an increase in the Yellow-billed Cuckoo population in Delaware and the East during 1965–79, it decreased in the East and possibly in Delaware during 1981–90 [Usfw3] (Robbins et al. 1986).

Breeding population. The Yellow-billed Cuckoo was detected at 187 stops in the June relative abundance study, but this figure may be inflated because some cuckoos are still migrating then. Its population level at a given site is highly variable because it sometimes increases in response to an outbreak of caterpillars.

The following are high breeding population densities (males per 100 ha):

25 (2 in 20 acres) in saltmarsh edge in Assawoman WA (Linehan 1966b)

15 (2 in 35 acres) in uneven-aged mixed hardwood forest

(urban woodlot) in New Castle County (Martin 1973)

Conservation. Its decrease in population in parts of the East was noted on the Blue List (Tate 1986). Because this species winters in South America and requires an ample supply of caterpillars to breed in North America, indiscriminate use of insecticides poses a threat on both continents.

FALL: Most leave by 20–25 September. However, unlike the Black-billed Cuckoo, this species is sometimes present into October (18 sight reports). The 1991 Neotropical migrant study (Mabey et al. 1993) suggests 80% of the fall migrants passed through in August, 14% in September, and 6% in early October (no count was taken in July); nomadic cuckoos may show more year-to-year variation in their fall migration dates than most species. One was banded on 21 October 1966 by Linehan at the University of Delaware woodlot, Newark [Usfw3]. Two November reports are the latest:

1 Nov 1970   1   Bombay Hook NWR [ThoR1]
22 Nov 1976   1   White Clay Creek [Wayn33]

The high count is 20 at Brandywine Creek SP on 21 September 1985 [Nile6]. Typical counts are similar to those in spring.

REMARKS: North American cuckoos do not normally lay eggs in other birds' nests as a breeding strategy as do many Old World cuckoos, but there are occasional reports of it. When they do, the young should fare well as their eggs require a short incubation period and the nestlings mature more quickly than those of many other species. Hanson (notes) found a nest on 1 June 1933 with 5 catbird eggs and 1 Yellow-billed Cuckoo egg near the Red Clay Creek at Stanton.

SPECIMENS: 11; DMNH, USNM.

Barn Owl *(Tyto alba)*

Resident; uncommon. Rare more than 2 mi away from tidal marshes. Resident population presumably increased by migrants during fall. Population increased from the 1950s to the 1980s.

J F M A M J J A S O N D

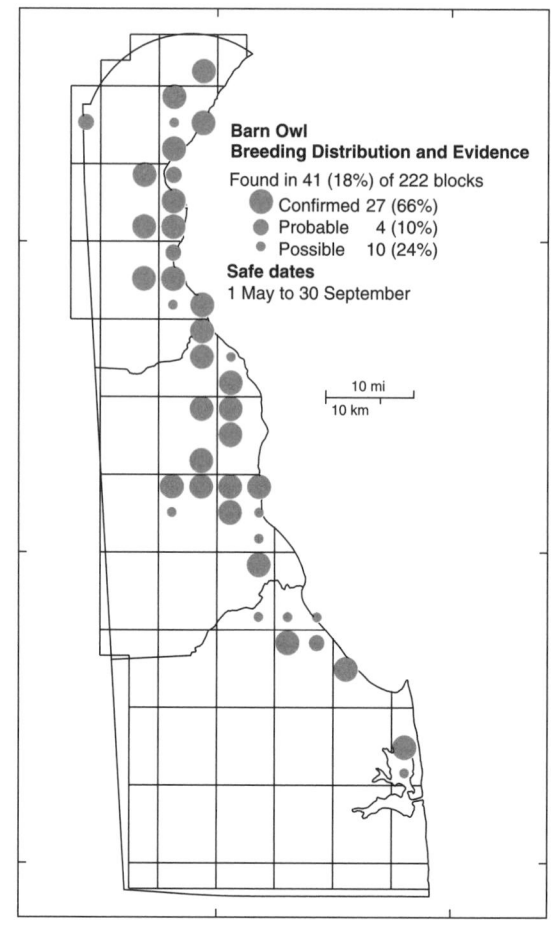

Barn Owl
Breeding Distribution and Evidence
Found in 41 (18%) of 222 blocks
⬤ Confirmed 27 (66%)
● Probable 4 (10%)
• Possible 10 (24%)
Safe dates
1 May to 30 September

10 mi
10 km

HABITAT: Primarily tidal marshes or, rarely, extensive grassy agricultural areas likely to support rodent populations. Breeds in hollow trees or man-made structures; roosts there or in pine groves.

MIGRATION: Stone (1937) reported the Barn Owl as a transient in the fall at Cape May, New Jersey, and a recent study there shows a definite coastal movement in autumn (Russell et al. 1991); these birds no doubt proceed across the bay to Delaware. Duffy and Kerlinger (1992) reported that 90% of Barn Owl captures at Cape May occurred between 6 October and 15 November; 85% of adult captures and 60% of immature captures occurred in October, indicating that adults, on average, migrate a few days earlier. Stewart (1952) concluded, based on banding results, that northern populations are partially migratory. Marti (1992) suggests that dispersing movements of immatures, up to 1,100 mi (1,800 km) (Soucy 1980), may be mistaken for migration. Individuals breeding in Delaware are not thought to migrate, because owls can be found in some barns at any time of year.

BREEDING: The Barn Owl regularly occurs along the marshes of the Delaware River and the Inland Bays, and probably has always occurred in those areas. It is dependent primarily on meadow voles and other rodents inhabiting marshes. Thus a breeding site more than 2 mi from a marsh is a rarity. At such a site the owl requires extensive grassland for foraging. The only inland specimen is 1 from Georgetown on 4 November 1985 (DMNH 76655), a date that may indicate that the bird was a winter visitor. Inland reports come from west of Greenwood on 26 August 1972 [DuPG12] and at a Centerville feeder on 26 January 1980 [Edni6].

Atlas. Atlas observers reported the Barn Owl from 3 inland locations: west of Newark [Edni2], near Woodside [Patt11], and west of Wyoming where a broken egg was found in an Amish barn [Atla1]. The Atlas results confirm its preference for marshes. Additional effort concentrated in blocks near where this species had already been found would probably have produced more records of this nocturnal species. Of the 27 confirmations, 19 resulted from finding the nest, 2 from attending young, and 6 from fledged young.

Nesting. The Barn Owl lays its eggs in a natural or man-made cavity or on a sheltered ledge without adding nesting material. A clutch of 8 eggs was found at Bombay Hook NWR as early as 12 February 1989 [Wees8], and a young bird, captured on Cherry Island Marsh on 19 April 1909, must have come from an egg laid 15–20 February [PooA1]. Other Delaware clutches are

23 Mar 1938	3 eggs	Bombay Hook NWR [Buck1]
28 Apr 1978	6 eggs	Woodland Beach WA [Wees8]
10 May 1987	clutch	Woodland Beach WA [ThoJ1]

Nests with young have been reported from 10 April to 12 July near various marshes. Colvin (1984, 1985a,b) studied Barn Owls for 6 years in the Delaware River marshes of New Jersey, and many of his findings are probably applicable to the marshes just across the river in Delaware. At the beginning of his study about one-third of the nests were placed in man-made structures and two-thirds in cavities in old trees. Though the owls readily accepted nest boxes, provision of nest boxes did not lead to increased population levels, which instead result from abundance of small rodents in saltmarshes or grasslands. The average brood size in New Jersey was 3–4 but ranged up to 7; nests with eggs or young were found there every month except January, but most broods hatched in mid-May. Colvin documented 1 pair that was double-brooded in New Jersey, but most are single-brooded.

History. The Barn Owl has been recorded in Delaware as a resident since Rhoads and Pennock published the first list in 1905. Pennock (1908b) elaborates that it seemed rather abundant near large marshes. It might have been even more common, but, as Witmer Stone (1919) chided about Delaware residents, every Barn or "monkey-faced" owl that showed itself would fall victim to the gun of the farmer. Dicky [Dick1] thought it was rather common in New Castle County in the late 1920s and had several mounts. Hanson (notes) located 4 nests from 1927 to 1933—1 near Kitts Hummock, 2 near Stanton, and 1 in the belfry of the old Presbyterian Church in Christiana.

Breeding population. Colvin (1985) located 107 nest sites in 410 sq mi (1,150 sq km) or 0.26 per sq mi (0.9 per sq km) of New Jersey farm and marsh land during 1980–85, documenting 284 nestings during that period. Nests were principally along the Delaware River marshes near Salem and Bridgeton. A similar density may be expected in suitable Delaware marshes across the river. Colvin (pers. comm. 1993) reports the upland

population has greatly declined with the reduction of dairy farming in New Jersey during the 1980s.

Conservation. It is listed as Threatened or Endangered in some states. Though Blue Listed in 1972–81 and listed as a species of special concern in 1982–86 (Tate 1986), it does not appear to be threatened in the Delaware marshes. Fluctuations in its population may be expected in relation to the natural population cycles of meadow voles. The Barn Owl is able to survive cold weather, though persistent snow cover leads to starvation (Bunn et al. 1982, 170).

1966–89 CBC Summary

Christmas Bird Count	Years Found	Range of No. Found	Median
Wilmington	9	1–3	
Middletown	22	1–8	3
Bombay Hook	24	1–13	3
Cape Henlopen	13	1–3	1
Rehoboth	4	1	
STATEWIDE (low in 1969, high in 1983)	24	3–21	9

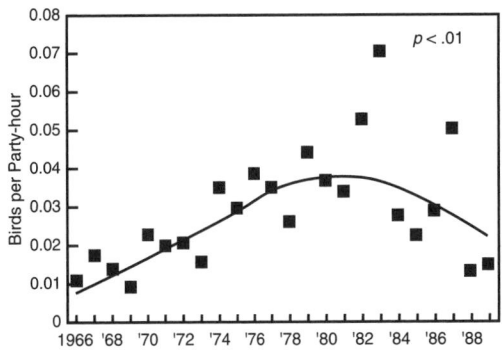

CBC Trend

WINTER: This species showed a significant increase in numbers until the 1980s. A broader analysis of CBCs showed a general increase in Barn Owl populations in the Mid-Atlantic states between the 1950s and 1970s (Stewart 1980). It is most numerous on the Middletown and Bombay Hook CBCs. Usually only 1 or 2 birds are reported. However, at favored roosts more may be present:

| 11 Feb 1978 | 5 | Taylors Bridge [Wayn32] |
| 19 Feb 1983 | 4 | Baxter Tract, Augustine WA [Edni59] |

SPECIMENS: 17; DMNH, UDEL, USNM.

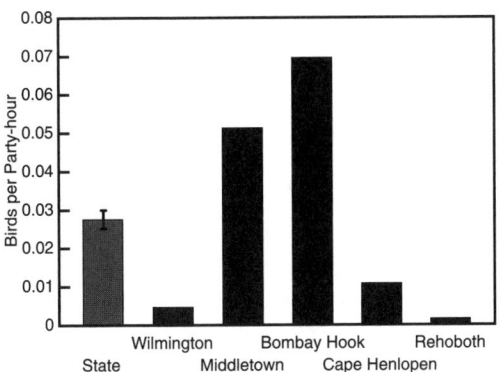

CBC Geographic Distribution

Eastern Screech-Owl *(Otus asio)*

Resident; common; winter numbers increased through the early 1980s.

HABITAT: Associated with edges, running water, wet wood-lands, and open weedy areas, including those in older suburbs (Smith and Gilbert 1984; Ellison 1980). Common in a variety of edge habitats. Adaptable to human-modified habitats such as roadsides, suburban woodlots, cemeteries, parks, and other open spaces of towns.

MIGRATION: Although essentially nonmigratory, this species sometimes exhibits movements in response to severe winter weather and the availability of prey (Gehlbach 1995).

BREEDING: This feathered wildcat is surely the most numerous raptor in Delaware, occupying a wide variety of habitats that provide cavities and mice. Rarely noticed because of its nocturnal habits, it roosts in cavities during the day (Smith et al. 1987).

Atlas. This species could be located by playing a tape record-ing of its call at night at a promising site. This method made it easy to drive from block to block and fill in voids in Atlas cover-age. It probably occurs in the 5 blocks in northern Delaware in which it was not reported, but Atlas workers were understand-ably reluctant to wander through the city and suburbs late at night playing a screech-owl recording in dark corners. Two-thirds of confirmations involved fledged young, which could be distinguished by their off-key calls lacking a tremolo. The young often called as part of a family group.

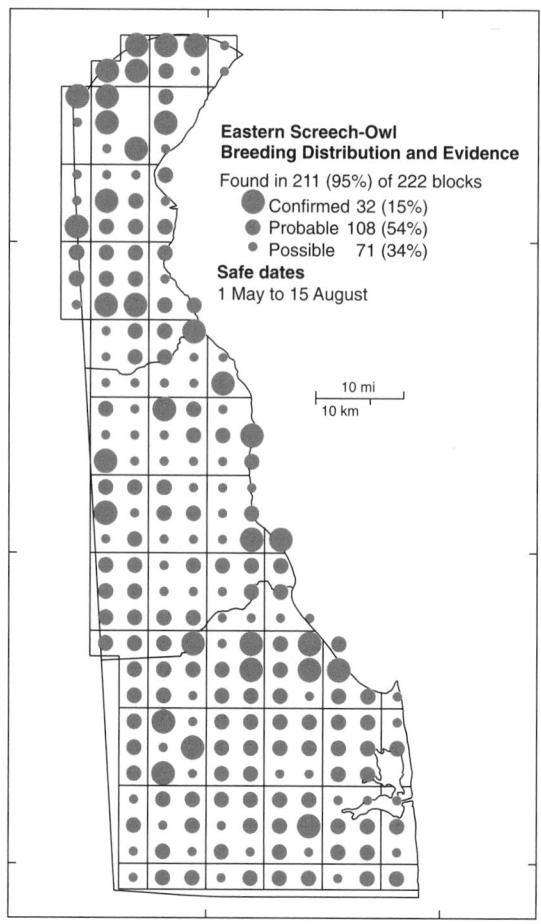

**Eastern Screech-Owl
Breeding Distribution and Evidence**
Found in 211 (95%) of 222 blocks
⬤ Confirmed 32 (15%)
● Probable 108 (54%)
• Possible 71 (34%)
Safe dates
1 May to 15 August

Atlas data were taken until 15 August, but a recent study in Kentucky with radio-tagged juveniles showed that birds fledg-ing between 14 and 27 May dispersed between 8 and 21 July. The average dispersal range was 1 mi, and the maximum dis-persal noted was 10 mi (Belthoff 1987). This early dispersal sug-gests that some late observations reported in Delaware may have involved young dispersed from an adjacent block. Breed-ing has begun by April, so the safe dates should be set from 10 April to 10 July to ensure that only breeding birds are counted. This period is, unfortunately, the time when screech-owls are least responsive to tape-recorded calls (Smith et al. 1987).

Nesting. Eggs are laid in cavities without added nest materi-als. The most common nest situations reported were maple tree cavities [Hans1] and Wood Duck boxes in Prime Hook NWR, for example, 4 in 1980 [O′Sh2]. Six clutches of eggs have been reported, ranging from 13 March 3 eggs [Hans1] to 11 April 5 eggs [O′Sh2]. The estimated peak clutch-completion period based on combined nest records and Tri-State fledgling data is mid-April. Combined data on nests and nestlings (n = 18) suggest that 60% of clutches are completed in April and only 5% in March. Nestlings have been found from 21 May

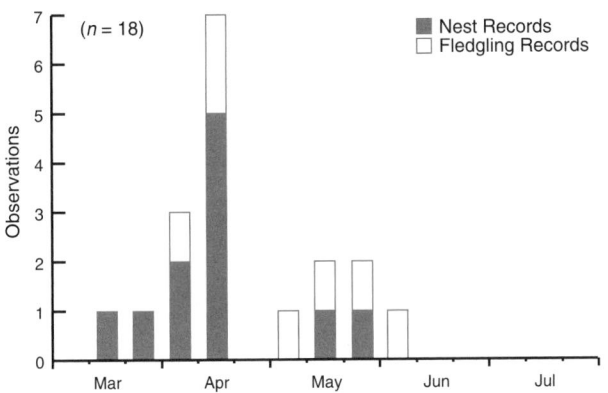

Estimated Clutch-Completion Dates

[Hans1] to 3 July [Bomb1], and a 100-g fledgling, probably less than 4 weeks old, was brought in from Sussex County on 20 July (TSBR 90-973). Clutches were completed a little earlier in Ohio, between 25 March and 15 April (Van Camp and Henny 1975). Females will renest if the first brood is unsuccessful, and clutches completed in May or early June may be the result of such renestings.

Breeding population. A Kentucky study showed an average home range for adults of about 80 acres (32 ha) (Belthoff 1987). In suburban Connecticut home ranges varied with the season, ranging from about 8.8 ha in December to 108 ha in June (Smith and Gilbert 1984). Smith et al. (1987) found screech-owl densities in southern Connecticut and eastern Pennsylvania of 3–4 per sq mi (1.2–1.5 per sq km) in habitat that was three-quarters wooded. A somewhat lower average density in Delaware seems consistent with the field experience resulting from the Atlas project (West, pers. obs), but screech-owls were located at about half the stops made in promising habitat in July. Another indicator of its abundance in Delaware is the 39 found in 12 party-hours of looking for owls on the 15 December 1984 Wilmington CBC, but that was probably fewer than 10% of those that were present in the 175-sq-mi count circle.

Conservation. Surprisingly, the Eastern Screech-Owl was put on the Blue List for 1981 and its population reported down in the Hudson–Delaware Region (Tate 1986). Threats to this species include winter starvation from persistent snow cover and a variety of human-induced hazards such as being struck by vehicles. Persecution by shooting and trapping probably resulted in local decreases earlier in the twentieth century. The owls are protected now, yet even during the Atlas period 1 field observer (West) was playing a screech-owl tape recording when he was suddenly confronted by a very surprised farmer who emerged from behind some rows of corn, shotgun in hand, ready to shoot an owl that had the audacity to call during the day. Low populations were apparent around poultry farms (West, pers. obs), perhaps due to food (rodent) depletion or unintentional secondary poisoning from local rodenticide use (Hegdal and Colvin 1988). Anticoagulant rodenticides are used

inside poultry houses when needed (D. Palmer, Agricultural Extension Services, pers. comm.).

Dispersal. The young become increasingly independent but are tolerated and occasionally fed within their parents' hunting range for most of the summer. Juvenile screech-owls begin to disperse in late summer. All seem to be on the move by August or September (in Texas, Gehlbach 1986). Territorial defense continues through the winter, as evidenced by response to tape recorders, and decreases slightly in March with the onset of incubation (Smith et al. 1987). Some marginal fall and winter territories, such as in cemeteries or suburbs, are vacated in spring.

WINTER: Screech-owls are fairly evenly distributed on

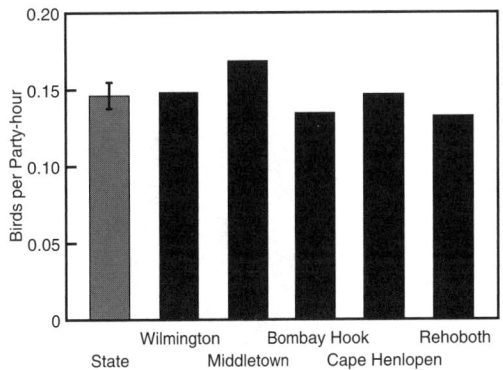

CBC Geographic Distribution

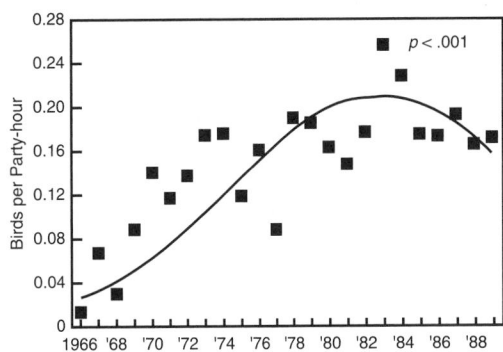

CBC Trend

CBCs. This species has shown a significant change in numbers. After about 15 years of increasing numbers it peaked in the early 1980s. It remains to be seen if it will decline as part of a larger cycle or if the population is stabilizing. The increased use of tape recorders to locate this owl is a complicating factor in assessing its apparent increase before the early 1980s. However, the pattern of screech-owl increase followed by a more recent decrease is also reflected by BBS data, taken without the use of tape recorders, from the East [Usfw3].

1966–89 CBC Summary

Christmas Bird Count	Years Found	Range of No. Found	Median
Wilmington	23	7–39	21
Middletown	24	1–21	12
Bombay Hook	24	1–21	9
Cape Henlopen	23	2–31	9
Rehoboth	24	2–34	10
STATEWIDE (low in 1966, high in 1978)	24	5–102	70

REMARKS: The Eastern Screech Owl has 2 color phases, gray predominates in the north and red in the south (Owen 1963); the gray phase is more cold-tolerant (Mosher and Henney 1976). Owen determined that the Delmarva population was about 37% red phase, consistent with experience gained from specimens received at the DMNH.

SPECIMENS: 44; DMNH, UDEL, USNM.

Great Horned Owl (*Bubo virginianus*)

Resident; common.

| J | F | M | A | M | J | J | A | S | O | N | D |

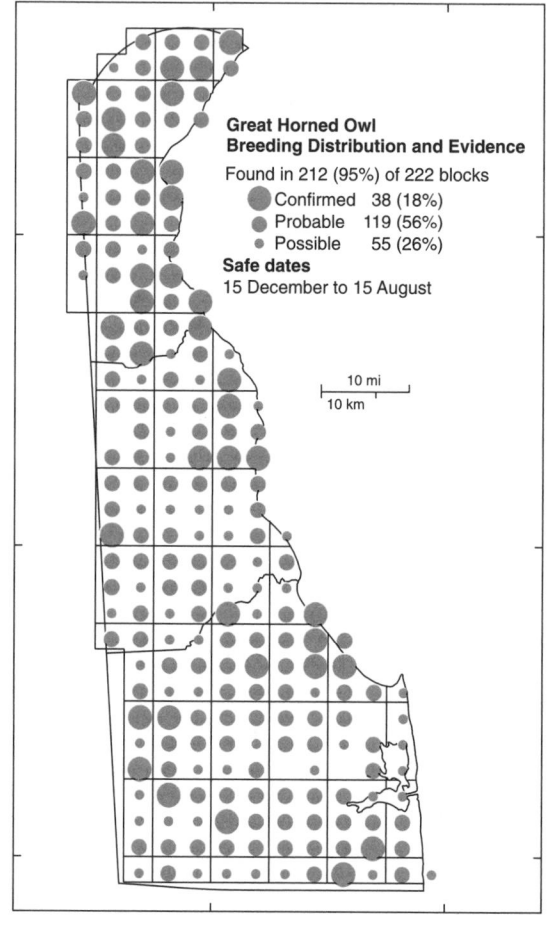

Great Horned Owl
Breeding Distribution and Evidence
Found in 212 (95%) of 222 blocks
● Confirmed 38 (18%)
● Probable 119 (56%)
· Possible 55 (26%)
Safe dates
15 December to 15 August

10 mi
10 km

HABITAT: Woodlots, forests with adjacent fields or marshes.

BREEDING: This owl is now commonly heard hooting from a large variety of woodland edges, including farm woodlots, marsh edges, and even downtown Dover and suburban Wilmington (regularly, for example, in Alapocas Woods and Banning Park). This habitat preference and its attendant association with humans could be a reflection of reduced persecution, since the species was formerly regarded as a deep woods resident (Eaton 1914).

Atlas. Three of the 10 Atlas blocks where this owl was not found lack suitable habitat (i.e., they are marshland with little potential for nest sites), but this owl may have been missed in the other 7 blocks. It was most frequently confirmed by finding young that could not fly well, since they beg distinctively and sometimes sit in the open during the day. In 10 instances a nest was found before young were visible. As the Great Horned Owl does not breed until it is 2 years old (Weller 1965), some "possible" breeding reports from the Atlas project may involve yearling birds.

Nesting. Nests reported were primarily in deciduous trees;

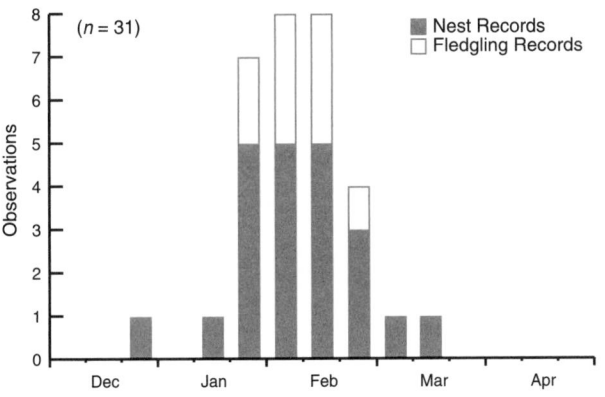

Estimated Clutch-Completion Dates

old nests of Great Blue Herons, Ospreys, and particularly Red-tailed Hawks were used. Great Horned Owls also nest in tree cavities (Harrison 1978), and 3 such nests have been reported in Delaware:

19 Feb 1937	2 eggs	hollow white oak near Dragon Run [Buck3]
20 Feb 1936	2 eggs	same site [Buck3]
7 Mar 1968	3 10-day-old young	banded from a cavity in a sycamore over Red Clay Creek [Crum2]

It is difficult to assess how frequently such hard-to-find sites are used. The first Atlas record for any breeding bird was an unusual ground nest of a Great Horned Owl at Prime Hook NWR found on 1 January 1983 [O'Sh3]. Ground nesting suggests that lack of suitable nest sites may limit this species' population. Data from 22 nest records and 11 fledgling records indicate clutch completion from late December through mid-March, with 87% completed in late January or February. The late date was established by a fledgling estimated at 4–5 weeks old in Alapocas Woods on 25 May [West4]. Horned owls are single-brooded and rarely lay a second clutch, even if the first is destroyed. Clutches are usually 2 eggs (Karalus and Eckert 1973), but 1 of 5 clutches reported in Delaware had 3 eggs [Schm1].

History. In the past many farmers and hunters felt an obligation to shoot this predator on sight. Some had good justification, for it would take unhoused poultry, perhaps making nightly raids on open chicken coops until they were empty, and hunters believed that this large owl competed for their wild game. Persistent persecution suppressed its numbers for many years. In 1919 Witmer Stone, chairman of the AOU conservation committee, wrote in *Delaware Magazine* that "the Great Horned Owl is the only destructive species," a statement that reflects the attitude prevailing at that time, even in the AOU. Austing and Holt (1966, 40) wrote that some hunters "broadcast recordings of hooting owls to draw them in. The hunters wear [head lamps] controlled by gunstock buttons, enabling them to face in the direction of their quarry with gun shouldered, switch on the light, and open fire." These authors also

pointed out that pole traps took advantage of the owl's propensity for sitting on snags, and "some game farms trap as many as 50–75 owls in a single" year in this inhumane way. This number of owls at game farms seem staggering, but the authors point out that "large numbers of rodents also gather at such places." Removal of one cohort of owls would just make room for another to be drawn to the plentiful food.

Trends. Although declining persecution is a factor in the horned owl's population increase, the simultaneous increase in Red-tailed Hawks has probably also benefited the owl, because old Red-tail nests are often used the next year by the owl (Hagar 1957). It has surely increased in the twentieth century because it has become common in areas where it used to be shot. No BBS trend is apparent for Delaware, since the horned owl is encountered infrequently using this census technique; in the East, however, where a larger sample is available, this owl has increased since 1966 [Usfw3].

Breeding population. One index of the Great Horned Owl's present population level is indicated by the CBC maxima, which range from 40 to 56. Since Delaware CBC circles contain 100–150 sq mi (250–400 sq km) of land, the reported population density is about 1 per 2–4 sq mi (5–10 sq km). Just before dawn on late December mornings when owls are especially vocal, it is possible to hear 1 or 2 almost anywhere one stops if the weather is suitable. The same is true at dawn in May, and that is the way the distribution map was filled in. For example, 7 were detected in 5 stops in less than 30 min west of Harrington on 3 May 1985; similarly, 9 were detected in 5 stops west of Dover 8 days later [West3]. Based on these reports, the actual population may average as much as 1 territory per 1 sq mi (3 sq km) in farmland. This density is well within the range of a territory size of one-third to 2 sq mi (1–5 sq km) that Baumgartner (1939) thought could limit its population if its other needs were met (in Kansas). This species successfully bred in a highly urbanized area (in New York), but the investigators found only 4 per 80 sq mi (1 nest per 50 sq km or 4 in 208 sq km) (Minor et al. 1993), one-fourth the minimum density of "probable" breeding found in Wilmington and Brandywine Hundred.

Dispersal. The adults are strictly nonmigratory and maintain

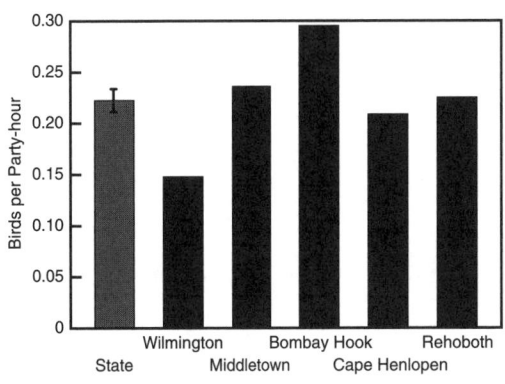

CBC Geographic Distribution

home range year-round. Adults from farther north, or those on marginal territory, tend to remain on their home ranges as long as possible and to leave only when driven by great hunger (Austing and Holt 1966). Young disperse in the fall, about 26 weeks after hatching, and ordinarily establish a territory within 20 mi of where they hatched (Karalus and Eckert 1974). Fewer

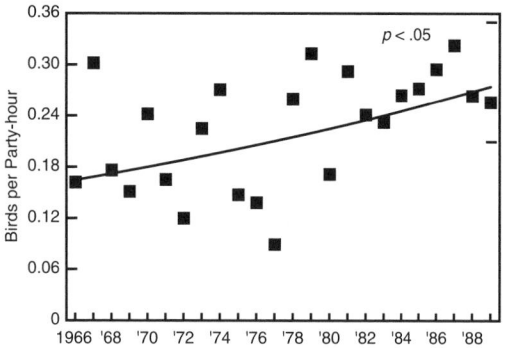

CBC Trend; Increasing at 2% per Year

than 3% have been reported moving more than 50 mi at our latitude (Stewart 1969).

1966–89 CBC Summary

Christmas Bird Count	Years Found	Range of No. Found	Median
Wilmington	24	2–40	20
Middletown	24	1–56	13
Bombay Hook	24	2–46	19
Cape Henlopen	23	1–44	14
Rehoboth	24	1–51	20
STATEWIDE *(increasing; low in 1977, high in 1979)*	24	44–155	99

WINTER: Numbers of Great Horned Owls reported on CBCs have increased significantly on CBCs at about 2% per year, but this increase may be due in part to greater interest in finding owls. The BBS also shows an increase on a significant number of routes in the East during the past 25 years.

SPECIMENS: 30; DMNH, UDEL, USNM. Egg records: DMNH.

Snowy Owl *(Nyctea scandiaca)*

Occasional (16 years during 1926–93, also 1897); winter visitor; rare.

Documentation: Undated specimen from Rehoboth Beach (UDEL 286-69); photograph (J. F. White, DMNH 413).

HABITAT: Open country: marshes, fields, dunes.

REMARKS: This mostly diurnal, circumpolar owl is a moderately frequent, although irruptive, visitor in New Jersey, Pennsylvania, and Maryland, but has been less frequently seen in

Delaware. Contacting the control tower personnel at Dover Air Force Base during flight years might be a useful strategy for locating more owls in Delaware (C. S. Robbins, pers. comm.). The Delmarva Peninsula and Maryland are the normal southern wintering limit for this species in the East (Parmalee 1992), but it is much less common in winter in the Mid-Atlantic region than on the northern Great Plains (Root 1988). Although irruptions were traditionally regarded as a response to a continent-wide crash in lemming populations, dispersion is now thought to be related to local availability of a patchily distributed prey on their wintering grounds and probably within their breeding grounds (Kerlinger and Lein 1988). Additionally, the Snowy Owl is a regular migrant over much of its range, defends wintering territories, and exhibits winter site fidelity (Parmalee 1992).

The earliest report of this owl in Delaware was given at a DVOC meeting: "Mr. Wilde reported a Snowy Owl from Milford, Delaware, taken on October 1, 1897, by Joseph Rogers, of that place" [Wild1]. Other early reports include single birds near Middletown, Laurel, and Delmar during November 1926 and at Bowers Beach in 1930 [Hans1]. Since then arrivals have first been noticed from December through February, and several have stayed into March. Snowy Owls were reported on 9 December 1934 at Rehoboth Beach [Buck6] and about 15 January 1940 (Herholdt) and 12 December 1942 (Gottsoff and Herholdt) at Bombay Hook NWR (Holgersen 1974d). They were also reported in 1954, 1964, 1965, 1975, 1979, and during the winters of 1981–82, 1983–84, 1986–87, and 1992–93. Remarkably, the 1986–87 bird was the first one reported more than twice in the same general location. Seen in the vicinity of Bombay Hook NWR from 3 December [Wayn61] through 4 March [Barn1], it was also elusive until birders discovered favored perches on the tops of 2 farm houses. It was photographed on 30 December 1986 (D. T. Shoch DMNH 463). The most recent records involve a bird discovered on Beach Plum Island, north of Lewes, and photographed on 21 March 1992 (W. A. Fintel, DMNH) and a bird first reported on 22 January 1993 (Campbell and Potrafke 1993) that remained at Cape Henlopen at least to 7 March 1993 [Gust3].

Barred Owl (*Strix varia*)

Resident; uncommon.

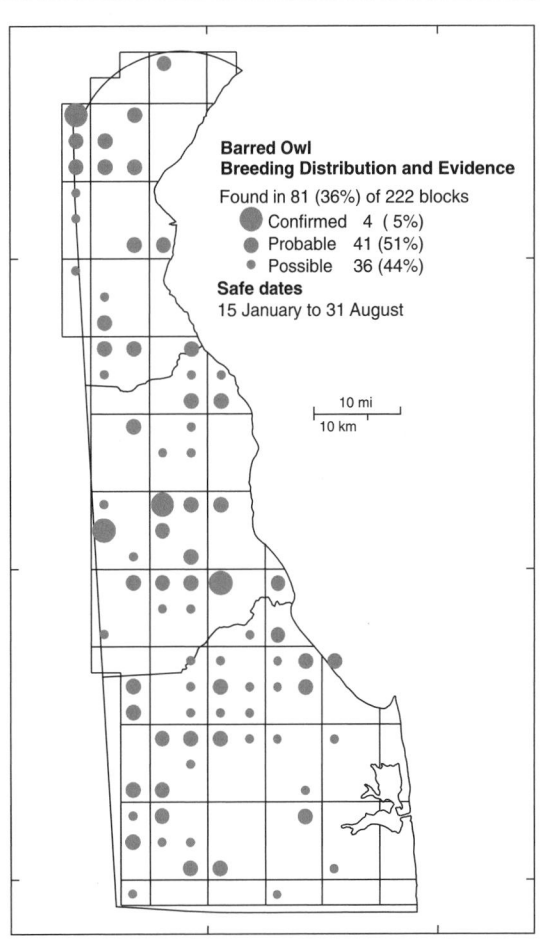

Barred Owl
Breeding Distribution and Evidence
Found in 81 (36%) of 222 blocks
● Confirmed 4 (5%)
● Probable 41 (51%)
· Possible 36 (44%)
Safe dates
15 January to 31 August

10 mi
10 km

HABITAT: Extensive mature deciduous or mixed palustrine forested wetlands. Occasionally roosts in pine groves during winter. On upland sites prefers older growth and open understory.

BREEDING: This owl's patchy distribution reflects its need for mature woods. Pennock considered it quite abundant in the lower part of Delaware (1904b), but habitat changes since then have reduced its numbers.

Atlas. The Barred Owl was more difficult to find than either the Eastern Screech-Owl or Great Horned Owl in those blocks where it was registered, suggesting that it is difficult to detect and nowhere common. This difficulty may partly arise because the adults become quiet during the period when young are in the nest (Weir 1987), and this period corresponds to the period of greatest Atlas activity. Therefore, it may have been missed in some blocks, and its distribution may not be as patchy as Atlas results indicate. A survey done in March would better define its distribution (McGarigal and Fraser 1985). All 4 confirmations resulted from finding noisy, recently fledged young.

Nesting. Tree cavities are its most common nest site, but it sometimes uses old nests of hawks, crows, or squirrels (Karalus and Eckert 1973). The nest hole is about 8 in. in diameter (Evans and Conner 1979), and the preferred nest height is about 30 ft above ground. The following Barred Owl nests with eggs have been reported in Delaware:

| 12 Mar 1929 | 2 eggs (well incubated) | near Camden [Hans1] |
| 19 Mar 1935 | 2 eggs | between Milton and Cedar Beach [Buck3] |

20 Mar 1935	2 eggs	near Milton [Buck3]
26 Mar 1936	1 egg	Milton [Buck1]
31 Mar 1972	2 eggs	Bombay Hook NWR [MiJC3]
3 Apr 1936	3 eggs	Cedar Neck Church [Buck1]

Clutches of 3 eggs are uncommon, those with 4 or 1 rare. It is single-brooded but will replace a lost clutch (Karalus and Eckert 1973).

History and trends. This species has declined over the past 2 centuries as Delaware's wooded swamps have been drained and the land cleared. The numbers are reduced from 1904 when Pennock wrote that it was found quite abundantly in the lower part of the state. These changes have provided habitat more suited to the Great Horned Owl, but both species were frequently killed until the second half of the twentieth century. As the killing dwindled, the dominant Great Horned Owl flourished in the largely open farm country, and the Barred Owl remained in its diminishing wet forests. Partly as a result of habitat alteration, substantially fewer Barred Owls are found in Delaware than in the rest of the Upper Coastal Plain (only 20% as many), whereas 60% more Great Horned Owls are found in Delaware than in the rest of the Upper Coastal Plain (1966–90) [Usfw1].

Breeding population. The Barred Owl is reported one-tenth as often on CBCs as the Great Horned Owl and reported a third to a half as often on the May Count or BBS, but these ratios are biased by how frequently these 2 species call in the various seasons and so do not represent a true ratio of abundance. The statewide high count of Barred Owls on the CBC is 10 and on the May Count 20, so it was unexpected to record it in 81 blocks during the Atlas project, indicating a minimum of 81 pairs.

A high breeding population density given for Maryland is 0.2 pairs per 100 ha (6 pairs in 1,142 acres) in lowland forest along the Patuxent River (Stewart and Robbins 1958). Probably no place in Delaware exists where this density can now be approached. Based on the number of blocks in which it occurs and its reported general scarcity, its population is low, probably in the 100–1,000 pair range.

Conservation. This species should be considered threatened or of special concern in Delaware. More information is needed on its population level and trend because its required habitat is decreasing. The Barred Owl has been listed as Threatened in New Jersey since 1984, with habitat destruction being cited as the principal threat (Sutton 1988); since 1984, surveys have located only 57 pairs, justifying continuation of its Threatened status. The Barred Owl's penchant for old-growth forests—a trait shared by its recently famous relative from the Pacific Northwest, the Spotted Owl—has important management implications. Removal of aged or diseased trees for firewood or thinning purposes can drastically reduce the availability of suitable nesting cavities. Reproduction is rarely successful when pairs are forced to use an old stick nest, exposed to the ele-

ments. Under such circumstances nesting boxes are often readily acceptable alternatives. Habitat fragmentation is a serious threat. Outright preservation of large tracts of mature forest and selective logging practices, in which snags and den trees are left, may be the best way to ensure the future of Barred Owls (Ebbers 1991).

1966–89 CBC Summary

Christmas Bird Count	Years Found	Range of No. Found	Median
Wilmington	21	1–2	1
Middletown	6	1–3	
Bombay Hook	24	1–5	2
Cape Henlopen	10	1–2	
Rehoboth	6	1–2	
STATEWIDE	24	1–10	4

(low in 1968 and 1987, high in 1985)

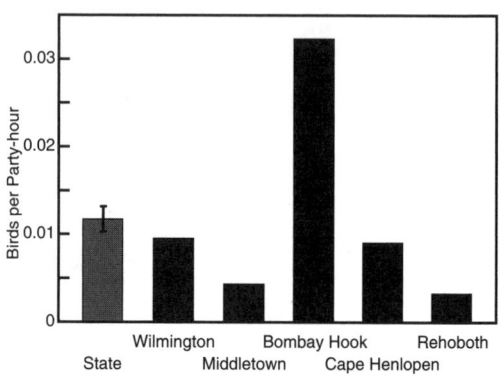

CBC Geographic Distribution

WINTER: In contrast to the Eastern Screech-Owl and Great Horned Owl, this species shows no increasing tendency on the CBCs. It is about equally abundant on all the CBCs except Bombay Hook, where it is reported in substantially higher numbers.

SPECIMENS: 8; DMNH, USNM.

Long-eared Owl *(Asio otus)*

Regular; winter visitor; uncommon. Expected late November to early March, sporadically later. Not reported from Sussex County. Extirpated as a breeding bird; formerly bred irregularly.

HABITAT: Pine stands in the Piedmont and south along the Delaware River and Bay.

SPRING: Karalus and Eckert (1974) note that "the return northward [is] well underway by March." Most reports stop at the end of February, there being only a handful of March records and only 2 old April reports (see "Breeding"). Once communal roost sites are found, this species can be easily monitored for arrival and departure dates.

BREEDING: The only breeding records of this species involve 2 occupied nests found in 1937 in northern Delaware: one with 5 eggs on 25 April and one with 4 young and 1 egg on 4 May [Hiat2]. There may have been prior spring or summer records because Rhoads and Pennock (1905) listed it as resident. This designation may be based on 1 collected on 26 April 1879 just south of Wilmington by Bush (notes). However, Pennock (1904b) more specifically stated that "The Long-eared Owl is found with us throughout the year but more abundantly during the cold months. Occasionally this bird breeds within our limits, generally making use of a deserted crow's nest for such purpose." Egg dates for New Jersey and Pennsylvania range from 14 March to 30 May (Bent 1937). Only 1 other

Delaware record falls between 23 March and 16 November: on 14 September 1941 in central Delaware [Cutl25]. Since this date is earlier than the usual time of winter arrival, the report may be related to local breeding. Today Delaware should be considered south of the species' normal breeding range. A number of years ago Alexander Wetmore commented that it "has decreased greatly over the recorded abundance of 50–60 years ago" (Stewart and Robbins 1958).

FALL: Karalus and Eckert (1974) note that "Normally, all birds of the race [*wilsonianus*—eastern race] that are going to migrate in any given year will have done so by the beginning of December." Thus reports from the last half of November may reflect transients or first arrivals. A lack of records, along with low counts, makes it difficult to determine the migration period for this species.

1966–89 CBC Summary

Christmas Bird Count	Years Found	Range of No. Found
Wilmington	1	4
Middletown	4	1–3
Bombay Hook	3	1–5
Cape Henlopen		
Rehoboth		
STATEWIDE (high in 1981)	8	1–5

WINTER: During 1966–89 the Long-eared Owl has occurred on 8 CBCs (4 times on Middletown, 3 times on Bombay Hook, and once on Wilmington) in numbers ranging from 1 to 5. Some high counts are

24 Dec 1950	6	Bombay Hook CBC
15 Jan 1966	5	south of Hockessin [Know4]
19 Feb 1983	4	Baxter Tract, New Castle County [Edni59]

SPECIMENS: UDEL 376-68, Wilmington, Foley Woods (Richardson Park), 8 February 1880; DMNH 73256, 2 mi (4 km) S Delaware City, 5 March 1983.

Short-eared Owl *(Asio flammeus)*

Regular; winter visitor; uncommon. Expected mid-November through February, sporadically into April or May. Rare summer visitor and possibly extirpated breeder.

HABITAT: Estuarine emergent wetlands and adjacent fields. Formerly also foraged over extensive pasture or other grasslands and still does farther north and west.

SPRING: Our data do not show a migration period; however, it probably takes place late February through March. Most reports are of 1–3 birds.

BREEDING: This owl once bred commonly enough that 6 nests were found in Bombay Hook NWR during 1938. A small, disjunct coastal population extends from Cape Cod to the Virginia side of the Potomac River (Clark 1975; Tate 1992), but it is irregular within its breeding range, dependent on rodent (especially *Microtus*) populations. Accordingly, it may breed in Delaware in years when the food supply is exceptionally abundant. Since 1965 it has been reported 11 times between 18 April and 27 June in the tidal marshes along the Delaware River in all 3 counties. Particularly suggestive of more recent breeding were

8 May 1966	2	Slaughter Beach [DeGa2]
12 May 1966	1	Slaughter Beach [DeGa3]
20 Apr 1969	2	courtship flight, Port Mahon [Robb2]
24 May 1969	1	Port Mahon [Lawr6]

A 1981 Eastern Screech-Owl breeding report was erroneously published as a report of this species [Hess6].

Atlas. A Short-eared Owl was flushed from the marsh at Bombay Hook NWR on 27 June 1986 [Hess22], and another was seen that summer over the marsh at Little Creek WA from the Pickering Beach entrance [Atla1]. Each report was given possible breeding status. Breeding in the Delaware marshes should be expected since it was confirmed to be breeding in Delaware County, Pennsylvania, and Salem County, New Jersey, during the Atlas projects in those states (Brauning, and Hughes, in Tate 1992, 182). It was also observed into June 1991

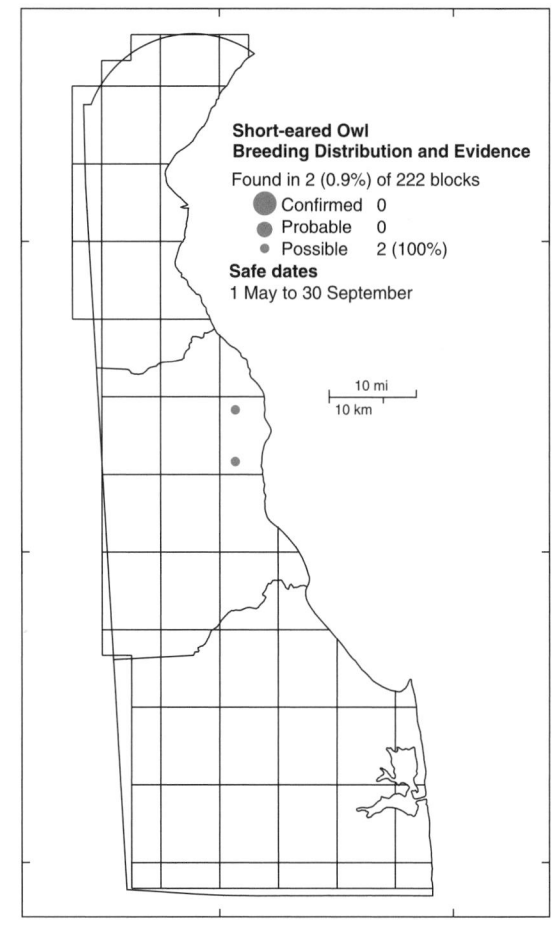

Short-eared Owl
Breeding Distribution and Evidence
Found in 2 (0.9%) of 222 blocks
● Confirmed 0
● Probable 0
• Possible 2 (100%)
Safe dates
1 May to 30 September

10 mi
10 km

and 1992 from Port Mahon Rd. (D. Rothstein, DNHI, pers. comm.), where it was not reported during the Atlas project.

Nesting. The Short-eared Owl was not known to breed in Delaware until "3 eggs, apparently in the first stages of incubation" were found at Bombay Hook NWR on 12 April 1938 by Buckalew [Hans1]. "This nest was in a matted bunch of *S. patens* on Kent Island" [Buck1]. Buckalew further reported a total of 6 nests there on 12, 13, and 23 May, and 14, 15, and 16 June, 1938. The young were banded. From these bandings there were 2 recoveries: 1 found dead on 6 September 1938 at Grand Anse, New Brunswick, and 1 shot on 19 November 1938 at Kemp, Ohio [Buck7]. Egg dates range from 12 April to 23 May [Buck1].

Most often the nest is no more than a slight depression in a little rise of ground, well hidden by surrounding reeds or grasses, and the depression is loosely lined with some dried grasses, weed stalks, and occasionally some feathers from the female's breast. Clutches usually contain 5–7 eggs. It is single-brooded, although occasionally double-brooded in the southern part of its range (Karalus and Eckert 1973).

History. The Short-eared Owl was listed as a winter visitor on all early Delaware lists, so it must have been rare or absent from Delaware in summer earlier in the twentieth century. Ehrlich et al. (1988) report this species as irruptive and nomadic in order to locate areas with high rodent populations, where it then settles and breeds. Such may have been the case at Bombay Hook in 1938. However, it was reportedly more common 50 years ago than now in summer in coastal Virginia (Kain 1987) and New Jersey (Leck 1984).

Conservation. This bird is included in a group of migratory species of management concern in the Northeast and is listed as Endangered in New Jersey and Pennsylvania and is a Species of Special Concern in Maryland (Tate 1992). It should be afforded special protection as a possible breeding bird in Delaware.

FALL: Some early reports of migrants include

1 Sep 1973	2	Bombay Hook NWR [Marv2]
14 Oct 1928	1	near Little Creek [Hans1]
17 Oct 1987	1	South Bowers Beach [Edni1]
19 Oct 1896	1	near Odessa (ANSP 66150)

These records may be of birds that bred nearby. The first fall reports usually occur during November. Typically 1–3 birds are reported.

1966–89 CBC Summary

Christmas Bird Count	Years Found	Range of No. Found	Median
Wilmington	12	1–8	
Middletown	16	1–7	1
Bombay Hook	24	1–18	3
Cape Henlopen	23	1–24	4
Rehoboth	12	1–2	
STATEWIDE (low in 1989, high in 1974)	24	3–39	11

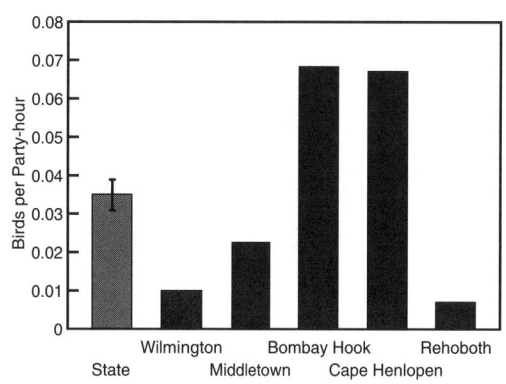

CBC Geographic Distribution

WINTER: No CBC trend is apparent. Some high CBC counts are 22 on the 27 December 1953 Bombay Hook count, 24 on the 22 December 1974 Cape Henlopen count, and 19 on the 31 December 1978 Cape Henlopen count. It is most numerous on the Bombay Hook and Cape Henlopen CBCs. An extraordinary report of 71 found at Port Mahon on 31 December 1967 [Lawr1] is the largest winter roost reported in North America during the twentieth century (Clark 1975), though a larger one was reported in the Netherlands (Cramp 1985). Typical daily counts are 1–3 birds.

SPECIMENS: 7; USNM, ANSP, DMNH, UDEL.

Northern Saw-whet Owl *(Aegolius acadicus)*

Regular; winter visitor; uncommon. Expected December to early March, occasionally earlier or later.

| J | F | M | A | M | J | J | A | S | O | N | D |

HABITAT: Roosts in dense thickets of American holly, catbrier, and pine, or in dense windfalls or other vegetative structures providing a dense spot 1–8 ft up.

SPRING: Usually only 1 bird is found per season, rarely as many as 3, but most observers make little effort to locate additional birds once the first bird is discovered. Two birds were banded on 2 March 1958 and 1 on 24 March 1959 at Pickering Beach by Miller [MiJC7]. The latest reports are

7 Apr 1951	1	Bombay Hook NWR [MiJC1]
10 Apr 1954	1	Pickering Beach Rd. [MiJC1]
3 May 1984	1	Hockessin [Sysa1]

The May report is of a bird on the back deck of a house in Hockessin. The mean banding date during its migration in

New Jersey is the last week of March (the range is early March to mid-April, Holroyd and Woods 1975).

FALL: First fall records are

30 Oct 1989	1	on porch at Ashland [Whit4]
8 Nov 1951	1	Farmington (USNM 422573)
12 Nov 1981	1	Mill Creek valley [RusR1]
25 Nov 1990	1	specimen not saved; Polly Drummond Hill Rd. (Linehan, pers. comm.)

A search through part of *Records of New Jersey Birds* (New Jersey Audubon Society) reveals that in most years the first reports of migrants at Cape May are in November (occasionally in mid- or late October). Holroyd and Woods (1975) note that the mean banding date is the last week in October in New York, New Jersey, and Maryland (range is early September to late November). There is little mist netting in Delaware; more effort might well locate more of these owls in the state in fall.

Peak movements generally occur in the later part of clear nights with west to northwest winds after the passage of a cold front. A full moon and strong, gusty winds tend to suppress migration. Females migrate earlier in the season than males, on average (Cannings 1993).

WINTER: One or 2 individuals of this species have occurred on 19 CBCs from 1951 through 1993 (Wilmington, 3; Middletown, 2; and Bombay Hook NWR, 14). Three birds were banded in 1959 by Miller at Pickering Beach—1 on 3 January and 2 on 21 February [MiJC7]. There are only 4 records from Sussex County:

4 Dec 1965	1	Cape Henlopen [Carl6]
25 Dec 1948	1	Stockley (USNM 421820)
25 Dec 1948	1	specimen, Georgetown (Buckalew 1950)
7 Feb 1947	1	Millsboro (USNM 422312)

In winter, as in spring, the tendency of many observers to "tick off" the first bird and look no further results in failure to record a large winter population when one occurs. We suspect the species is present most years, so additional effort should be made to locate, count, and report as many birds as possible. If feasible, the birds should be monitored until their departure.

1966–89 CBC Summary

Christmas Bird Count	Years Found	Range of No. Found
Wilmington	2	1
Middletown	2	1
Bombay Hook	7	1–2
Cape Henlopen		
Rehoboth		
STATEWIDE (high in 1969)	9	1–2

Saw-whets can be located in winter in Delaware using a tape recording of its call. One responded to a tape recording on the 1989 Middletown CBC, and 2 responded on a survey near Rt. 9 during January 1994 (Winters 1995). Saw-whets are subject to being struck by automobiles; for example, Buckalew collected 4 specimens along Rt. 113 that he presumed had been struck (Buckalew 1950).

REMARKS: This species was on the 1905 Delaware list based on a specimen in Bush's collection taken in January 1879 and a mount taken in Delaware during the 1903–1904 winter (Rhoades and Pennock 1905). Hensel had 3 specimens taken near Stanton, 1 during the 1906–1907 winter, the others earlier (Pennock 1908b).

SPECIMENS: 15; DMNH, UDEL, USNM.

Common Nighthawk *(Chordeiles minor)*

Regular; summer resident; uncommon. Expected early May to late September. Occurs most frequently along the coast in summer; fairly common migrant, feeding over cities and towns; locally common along the Piedmont edge during the fall.

J F M A M J J A S O N D

HABITAT: Open agricultural areas, towns, cities; nests on bare ground in dunes or open woods, fresh burns with open ground, flat gravel roofs.

SPRING: Typically, the first birds arrive 1–10 May. The only April reports are

12 Apr 1990	1	Mt. Cuba [Wayn2]
21 Apr 1992	1	Pike Creek [SpeE11]
26 Apr 1977	1	near Newark [Patt3]

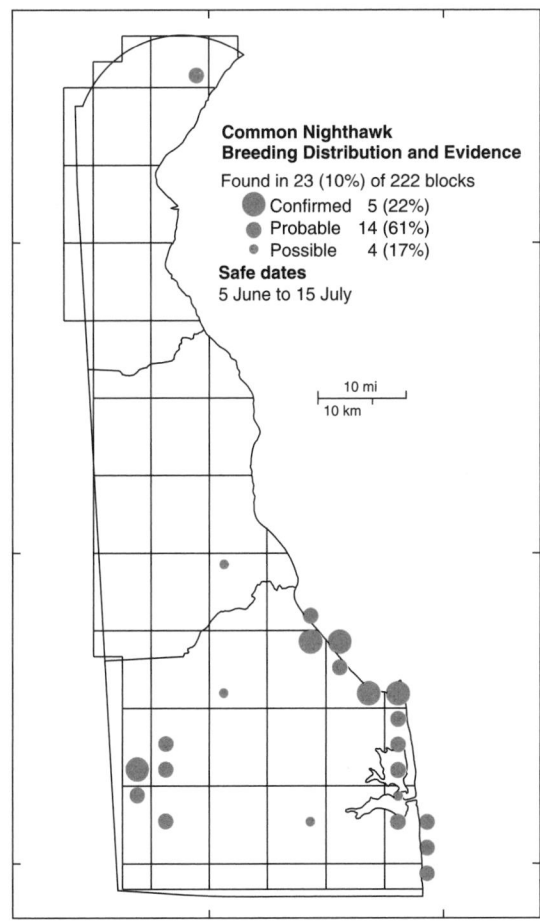

Common Nighthawk
Breeding Distribution and Evidence
Found in 23 (10%) of 222 blocks
● Confirmed 5 (22%)
● Probable 14 (61%)
● Possible 4 (17%)
Safe dates
5 June to 15 July

10 mi
10 km

bare ground, or rooftops. Mengel (1965) gave circumstantial evidence suggesting double-broodedness in Kentucky, and Weller (1958) observed this behavior in Iowa, but there is no evidence of it in Delaware.

History. The first published information on probable breeding in Delaware describes a pair holding a territory in a field near the Indian River Bay at Ocean View on 13 May 1905 (Pennock 1908a). In the 1930s it was reported in the breeding season from Dover but was considered rare [Hans1]. It was also reported there on 2 July 1967 and at Elsmere on 28 June 1967 [McLP1; Pres4].

Trends. BBS data show that its population declined in Delaware and in the East during 1966–90 [Usfw3].

Breeding population. The nighthawk maintains large aerial territories, averaging about 10.4 ha (over Detroit), with a range of 4–23 ha (Armstrong 1965), but when good nest sites are limited, nests may be placed close together (Gross 1940). The population is so low in Delaware that territory size or breeding density is clearly not a factor. Based on its being reported from 23 blocks and the limited habitat in those blocks, the state breeding population of this species may be between 20 and 200 pairs.

Conservation. With so much of the breeding population concentrated in dunes much used for human recreation, this species should be treated with special concern, or it may disappear as a breeding bird. The Maryland atlas listed none along the Atlantic coast (Robbins 1996); and only 3 blocks from the Virginia portion of the Delmarva Peninsula registered this species (Ridd 1989). It also appears to be in trouble as a roof-nesting species in the East. Its numbers were reported down over cities in New York, and it is listed as a Species of Special Concern there (Sibley 1988a). It was on the Blue List during 1975–86 (Tate 1986).

FALL: An increase in abundance beginning in mid-July reflects young recently out of the nest rather than migration. For example, counts at Cape Henlopen SP might increase from 4 to 6 birds (2 or 3 pairs each producing 1 or 2 young) to a total of 6–12 birds [Frec1]. The migration begins about 20 August and continues through September, with an occasional bird in October. The latest specimen is 1 found near Newark on 7 October 1987 (DMNH 77097). Later sight records include

15 Oct 1989	2	Hoopes Reservoir, Wilmington [Edni1]
21 Oct 1979	3	Wilmington [RusR7]
25 Oct 1975	1	Newark [Line10]

Large flights can be seen during September; for example, as many as 1,000 birds were in a single flight north of Newark on 18 September 1980 [RusR13]. Another 1980 report mentions 100 per day during 5–15 September north of Newark [RusR1]. A flight of more than 100 was seen on 12 September 1990 over Alapocas within a half hour; the observer had noted a similar flight exactly a year earlier [Hold1]. Perhaps typical are flights such as 50 over Newark on 21 September 1982 [Litt2] and 90

High counts are

13 May 1973	14	Dragon Run [SpSB1]
15 May 1976	9	White Clay Creek [Lehm29]
18 May 1987	12	Cape Henlopen SP [Frec1]

A statewide high of 18 was recorded on the 14 May 1988 May Count.

BREEDING: This widespread breeding bird has only a patchy breeding distribution in Delaware, with most found in the dunes between Cape Henlopen SP and Fenwick Island.

Atlas. Breeding sites found along Delaware Bay were a good addition to those known along the Atlantic coastal strip. Several other sites were probably associated with roof nesting (Gross 1940): near Seaford and in Delmar (in Delaware but 20 meters south of the boundary of the study). The only Atlas report for Wilmington was over the Brandywine Zoo [Edni2], a surprising scarcity because nighthawks are regularly heard over the city during migration, and there are ample flat roofs for nesting. Perhaps the Atlas survey missed it in some city and town blocks.

Nesting. Eight clutches have been reported from 30 May [Livi2] to 1 July [Frec2], suggesting peak clutch completion in early June. Most of these were along the coast. Two eggs comprise the usual clutch, but 1 clutch on Cape Henlopen on 18 June had 3 eggs [Wayn17]. The eggs are placed directly on sand,

over Wilmington on 28 August 1978 [Nile13]. In migration it is much more abundant along the Piedmont edge than farther south, although formerly (1960s and 1970s) it was not uncommon to see nighthawks perched lengthwise on power lines between Dewey Beach and Indian River Inlet.

SPECIMENS: 11; DMNH.

Chuck-will's-widow *(Caprimulgus carolinensis)*

Regular; fairly common; summer resident beginning in the 1930s; recorded late April through July but probably present into September. Occurs south from Milford Neck in dry open pine and mixed woods. Rare in the western part of the state and north of Dover.

J F M A M J J A S O N D

HABITAT: Oak-pine or open pine woodland, especially brushy open stands of loblolly pine. Drier, more open situations than used by the Whip-poor-will (Mengel 1965). Avoids the wetter portions of the Pocomoke and Nanticoke drainages and northward extension beyond the pine or mixed pine forests.

SPRING: This species' migration is poorly known in Delaware. The earliest spring reports are usually from the first week of May, but a few arrive earlier:

23 Apr 1991	1	Bethany Beach [Edni1]
26 Apr 1991	3	Cape Henlopen SP (Campbell 1992)
28 Apr 1990	1	South Bethany Beach [Jano1]

Probably most arrive the second week of May, but first arrivals should be expected any time after mid-April (Robbins and Bystrak 1977). Most reports are of 1–4 birds. The highest number reported is 12 at Cape Henlopen SP on 18 May 1987 [Frec1]. The highest May Count is 33 in 1984.

BREEDING: This species, a twentieth-century addition from the south to Delaware's avifauna, has become established in Sussex and southern Kent Counties.

Atlas. Atlas results show how broadly it has become established. Once the general pattern emerged in the third year of the project, effort was made to fill in the gaps. This effort was successful on moonlit nights, when singing persists from dusk

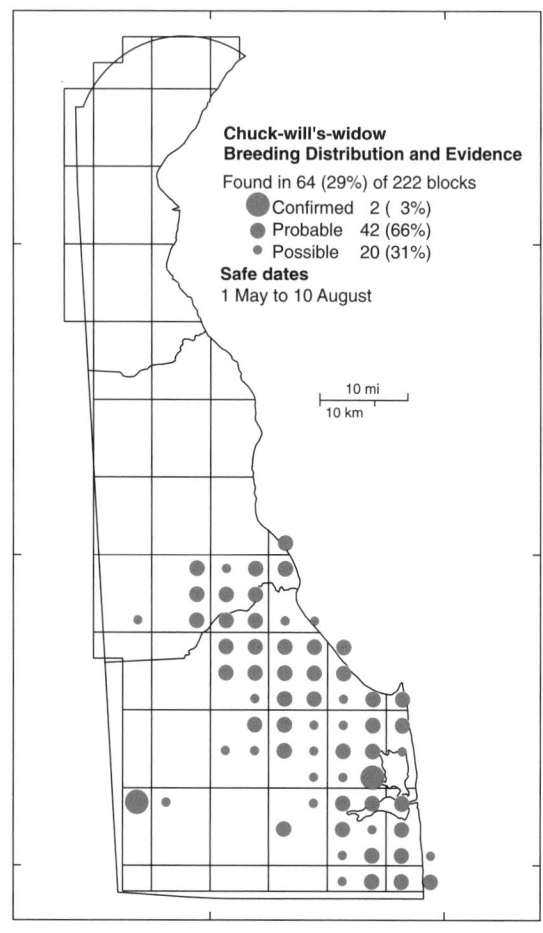

Chuck-will's-widow
Breeding Distribution and Evidence
Found in 64 (29%) of 222 blocks
● Confirmed 2 (3%)
● Probable 42 (66%)
· Possible 20 (31%)
Safe dates
1 May to 10 August

10 mi
10 km

to dawn (Cooper 1981). Several reports, from north of the area shown on the breeding distribution map, probably refer to non-breeding birds:

1 May 1966	1	heard at Bombay Hook NWR [Carr6]
13 May 1988	1	near Rt. 202, north of Wilmington [Cutl13]
21 May 1986	1	near Newark [Atla1]

Nesting. Only 3 nest records have been received:

12 May 1983	eggs	SW of Seaford [MiDP2]
29 May 1977	2 eggs	Angola Neck [Nile2]
29 May 1984	eggs	Angola Neck [West3]

Eggs are placed on needles or leaf litter. Clutches are normally 2 eggs. Egg dates given from Maryland are 10 May–8 July (Robbins and Bystrak 1977). It is single-brooded but will replace as many as 3 lost clutches (Sprunt 1950, 149).

History. The first published Delaware report involves 1 picked up dead near Milford on 13 June 1936 (Buckalew 1950). It was listed as a "summer resident, only in Sussex County," by Barry (1942), suggesting there were local reports not in our files. Three were heard near Milford on 16 May 1954 [MatH1] and 1 was reported near Rehoboth Beach on 16 May 1959 [Davi12]. Stewart and Robbins (1958) published a map that clearly suggested breeding on the lower Delaware coast. Earlier in the twentieth century it was possibly overlooked in Delaware—a nest was found in New Jersey in 1922, and there are 2 records in Philadelphia in 1942 and 1943 (Poole 1964). Draining and clearing the forests created suitable habitat, which allowed this nightjar to expand its breeding range northward (Mengel 1965). It became an established breeder in New Jersey by the mid-1960s, and was first found nesting in New York in 1975 [DavT1]. It now breeds in Ontario (Mills 1987).

Trend. Although it appeared on none of the 10 BBS routes during 1966–83, it was recorded on 3 routes during the next 5 years a total of 13 times. The May Counts show it becoming established, with 12 reported in 1969 and an average of 22 reported for 1981–90.

Breeding population. Atlas reports from 64 blocks and the presence of multiple singing males in many blocks (West pers. obs.) suggest that its population must be between several hundred and a thousand pairs.

FALL: Reports decline in July, with the last songs recorded on 26 July 1986 at twilight near Georgetown [West3]. After singing stops, Chucks may still be located when they utter a "growl" or "croak," somewhat resembling the "chuck" in the song, or when their large eyes are detected as red reflections close to the ground by "jack lighting" with a strong flashlight or with car headlights along country roads (Sprunt 1940; Mengel and Jenkenson 1971). By August they are in full molt, and the almost flightless birds become very inconspicuous (Rohwer 1971), but some still sing intermittently (Hoyt 1953). Reports do not indicate how long in the season this species remains; the latest specimen is 1 collected on 27 July 1960 at Fenwick Island (USNM 431252). At this latitude it normally begins migration in late August and is gone about mid-September (Robbins and Bystrak 1977). Reports of this nocturnal species underrepresent its abundance.

SPECIMENS: Milford, 13 June 1936 (Buckalew 1950, extant?); USNM 431252, Fenwick Island, 27 July 1960.

Whip-poor-will *(Caprimulgus vociferus)*

Regular; summer resident; fairly common. Expected mid-April through (presumably) September. Found throughout Sussex and southern Kent counties. Progressively rarer northward, with only a few migrants recorded in the Piedmont.

| J | F | M | A | M | J | J | A | S | O | N | D |

HABITAT: Mesic mixed or deciduous woodland or scrub with litter. Compared with Chuck-will's-widow habitat: wetter, denser, younger, more deciduous. Accepts a wide variety of habitats throughout its range, including dry pine barrens on Long Island (Bull 1974) or dense young growth (Conner and Adkisson 1975, in Bushman and Therres 1988). Occurs in both habitats in Delaware, for example, open pines on Angola Neck and dense second growth north of Lums Pond. The best syn-

thesis of its needs: open ground and understory for foraging (either within a mature forest or in a field) and dense growth (either early-to-mid-successional growth or edge) for protection of the young. As saturnid moths and other large insects are a major food, the bird is scarce in extensive agricultural areas, near cities, or where pollution or use of insecticides is extensive.

SPRING: This nightjar apparently arrives as much as 10–12 days before the Chuck-will's-widow. The earliest records include

12 Apr 1976	2 singing	Cape Henlopen SP [Nile3]
15 Apr 1990	singing	South Bethany Beach [Jano1]
17 Apr 1941	1	Sussex County [MayR1]

Typical arrival is 20–25 April, and most reports are 1 or 2 birds. High counts are

21 Apr 1974	5	Broadkill Beach Rd. [Edni1]
3 May 1980	6	Prime Hook NWR (notes)
16 May 1981	6	Prime Hook NWR [Frec1]

The highest May Count is 69 reported on 3 May 1980. A specimen taken from Fort Delaware on 4 May 1898 was probably a migrant (USNM 311803).

BREEDING: It is a fairly common nocturnal breeder in the forested areas of southern Delaware. Except for its crepuscular singing, rarely heard outside the breeding season, it is difficult to detect and so seemingly vanishes in late July.

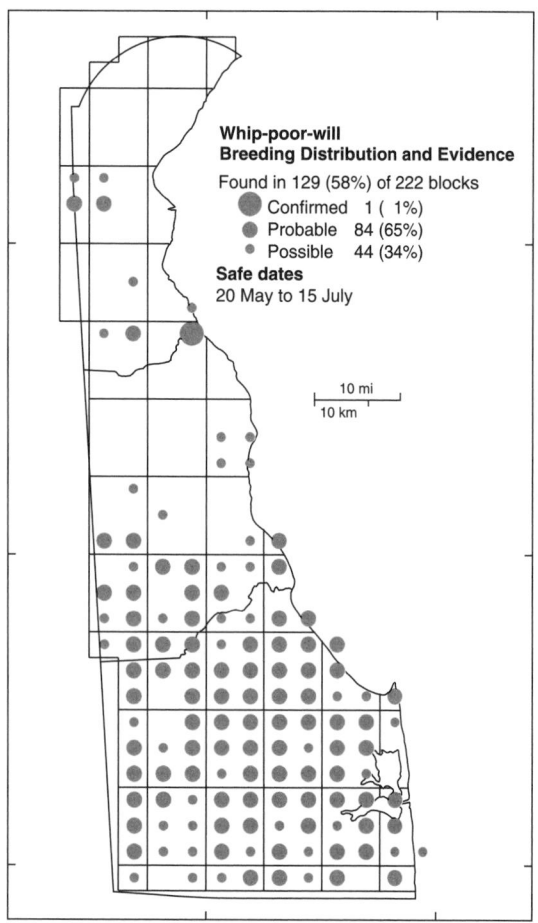

Whip-poor-will
Breeding Distribution and Evidence

Found in 129 (58%) of 222 blocks

● Confirmed   1 (1%)
● Probable   84 (65%)
· Possible   44 (34%)

Safe dates
20 May to 15 July

10 mi
10 km

Atlas. During the Atlas project this species was easy to locate and upgrade to territorial by its singing, which persists throughout moonlit nights during May and June (Mills 1987a). The distribution map displays patchy occurrence in the northern part of Delaware, and its numbers there also decline (West, pers. obs.). This decline is not an indication (as it is with the Chuck-will's-widow) of the northern limit of breeding, for it breeds in most counties in Pennsylvania and northward into Nova Scotia and northern Ontario (Mills 1987). It was confirmed only twice, both times in a block just south of the Smyrna River: a distraction display on 24 June 1984 and a fledged young on 19 July 1986 [BrRF1].

Nesting. We have located only 3 Delaware nest records:

28 May 1935	2 eggs	Griffith Pond, Milford [Buck1]
June 1967	nest with young	Smyrna [Bray3]
6 Jul 1930	2 small young	Thompsonville (Linehan 1968b) [Buck3]

It places its 2 eggs on the ground, usually on leaves, in younger hardwood forests (Harrison 1975). By extrapolation from Maryland data, egg dates should be 24 April–7 July (Robbins and Bystrak 1977).

History. Nuttall wrote Benjamin Barton from Dagsboro in June 1809 that "in the lower part of the State of Delaware, I have found these birds troublesomely abundant in the breeding season, so that the reiterated echoes of 'whip-'whip-poor-will, 'whip-'*peri*-will, issuing from several birds at the same time

occasioned such a confused vociferation as at first to banish sleep" (Nuttall 1916; McDowell 1989). Today it is still noisy, but its mature pine or mixed forest habitat has been reduced to make way for farms.

Trends. The Delaware BBS data (based on only 7 routes) show a significant decline during 1966–90 of about 6% per year, part of a wider, but not so steep, decline in the East [Usfw3].

Breeding population. In some areas of Sussex County the density of calling birds exceeded 3 pairs per sq mi (1 per sq km) during the Atlas period (West, pers. obs.). A high breeding population density (territorial males per 100 ha) given in Maryland is 3.5 (15 in 1,047 acres) in upland forest and brush habitats in Prince Georges County (Stewart and Robbins 1958).

Conservation. It might appear that the Chuck-will's-widow is "pushing" the Whip-poor-will out of southern Delaware, because the former arrived during the twentieth century from the south and the Whip-poor-will is declining. However, the driving force may not be an aggressiveness of the Chuck-will's-widow. Rather, forests have been reduced to woodlots and wet areas drained in much of eastern Sussex County. These land "improvements" have provided habitat for breeding Chuck-will's-widows. In this altered environment Whip-poor-wills no longer find their optimal breeding habitat and so are on the decline. Although interspecific competition may be a factor (Lack 1954, 148), changes in land use must be an underlying cause. Mengel (1965) noticed a similar invasion of Chuck-will's-widows in Kentucky. He further observed at Mammoth Cave NP that when large areas reverted from farmland back to forest since about 1930 Chuck-will's-widows decreased and Whip-poor-wills again became more numerous (Wilson 1950, 22–23).

FALL: As is true for its congener, we have few fall migration data. Observations extending through 26 July were made during the Atlas period [West3]. The following records establish its presence through September:

2 Aug 1924	1	Dover [Hans1]
3 Sep 1931	1	Indian River Bay [Hans1]
5 Sep 1987	1	Newark (DMNH 77127)
11 Sep 1966	1	banded north of Rehoboth Beach [RusW1]
27 Sep 1972	1	Smyrna [Holg76]

More effort should be made to locate and report this bird in August and September. It sings sparingly in September and can also be flushed in hardwoods, located by its *"whit," "whip,"* or sharp *"chuck"* note (similar to the first note of its song), or spotted by the large red reflection of its eyes when spot-lighted (Tyler in Bent 1940). At this latitude, migrant or late-departing birds should be found in reduced numbers through September, with a few remaining into October (Robbins and Bystrak 1977). A fairly hardy species, it winters north to the Carolinas.

SPECIMENS: USNM 311803, Fort Delaware, 4 May 1898; UWBM 36992, Laurel, Nanticoke WA, 23 May 1983; DMNH 77127, Newark, 5 September 1987.

Chimney Swift (*Chaetura pelagica*)

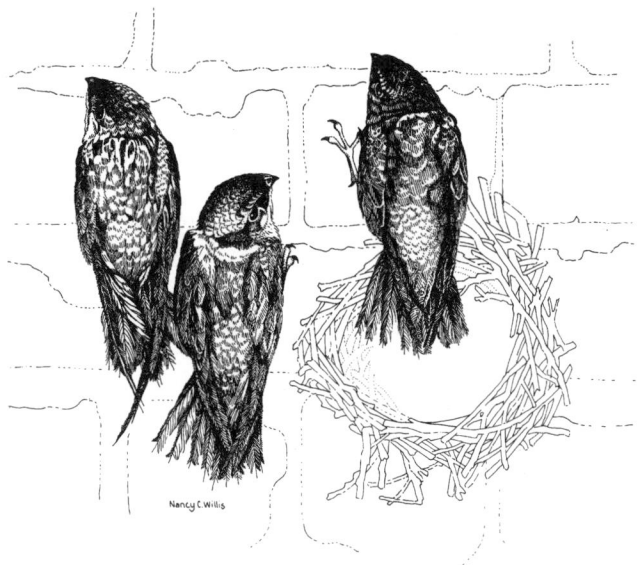

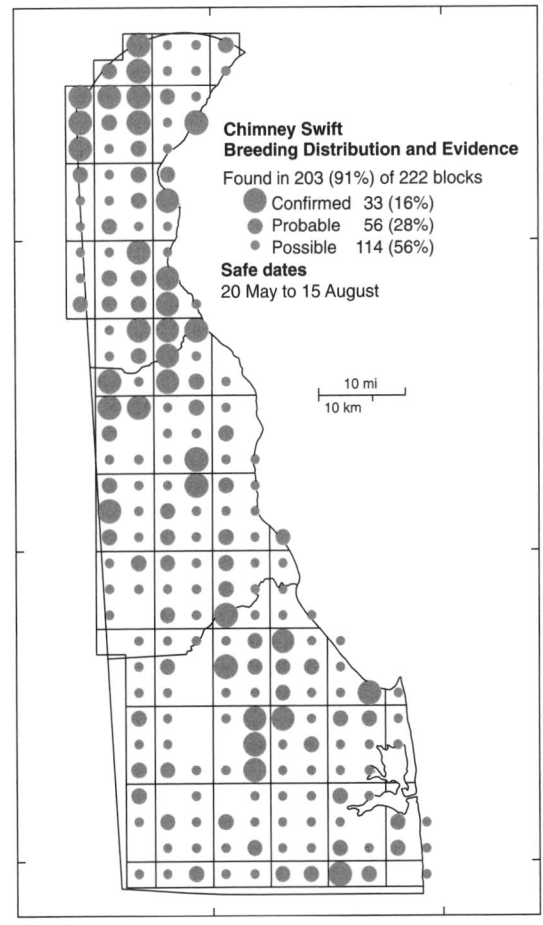

**Chimney Swift
Breeding Distribution and Evidence**

Found in 203 (91%) of 222 blocks

Confirmed   33 (16%)
Probable   56 (28%)
Possible   114 (56%)

Safe dates
20 May to 15 August

10 mi
10 km

Regular; summer resident; fairly common. Expected mid-April through mid-October. Patchily distributed according to breeding site availability. Much more common around towns than in rural areas, but absent from modern subdivisions. Abundant at roost sites during migration, especially in fall.

| J | F | M | A | M | J | J | A | S | O | N | D |

HABITAT: Aerial, often found over cities and towns, and over agricultural areas that are within range of the chimneys or outbuildings needed for nesting and roosting; formerly nested in hollow trees and crevices in cliffs.

SPRING: First arrival is usually mid-April, and the last migrants have departed by 25–30 May. Reports of earlier arrivals include

4 Apr 1981	1	Bombay Hook NWR [Barn13]
7 Apr 1947	1	Dover [Hans1]
8 Apr 1978	1	Broadkill Beach [Frec1]

Undocumented March records cannot be accepted. Peak numbers usually occur 25 April–5 May. Some high counts are

18 Apr 1966	200	Wilmington [Hoff2]
29 Apr 1925	hundreds	Dover [Hans1]
11 May 1974	61	Dragon Run [Conw1]

A high of 581 was recorded on the 14 May 1988 count.

BREEDING: Its distribution within the state is apparent from the map, being generally clustered near cities and towns. The only blocks in which swifts were found during 20% or more of the stops contain an old settlement (i.e., uncapped chimneys): Wilmington, Newport, New Castle, Smyrna, Dover, Lewes, and Seaford.

Atlas. The Atlas results show it to be widespread throughout the state. Those few blocks where it was not recorded lack suitable nest sites. Swifts were hard to find in several other blocks where most of the dwellings were modern, without chimneys. In such blocks the successful Atlas workers would locate a remaining farmhouse and wait for swifts to appear.

When feeding young, the adults regularly forage at least an eighth of a mile from the nest site, and sometimes go a mile or two away, even though they return to the nestlings every half hour (Fischer 1958). There is a substantial nonbreeding population, made up of second-year birds and some older ones (Dexter 1969). These nonbreeding birds and the breeders that are not actually feeding young need not stay close to a nest site. Therefore, the possible observations (56% of the data) are individually open to question, for they may arise from observing wide-ranging feeding forays or roosting nonbreeders. In spite of this possible inexactness of method, the map is well salted with probable and confirmed reports and probably fairly reflects this species' broad breeding distribution in Delaware. Future work should put more emphasis on confirmation of breeding. The easiest way to confirm breeding was simply to ask rural residents if they knew who had swifts in their chim-

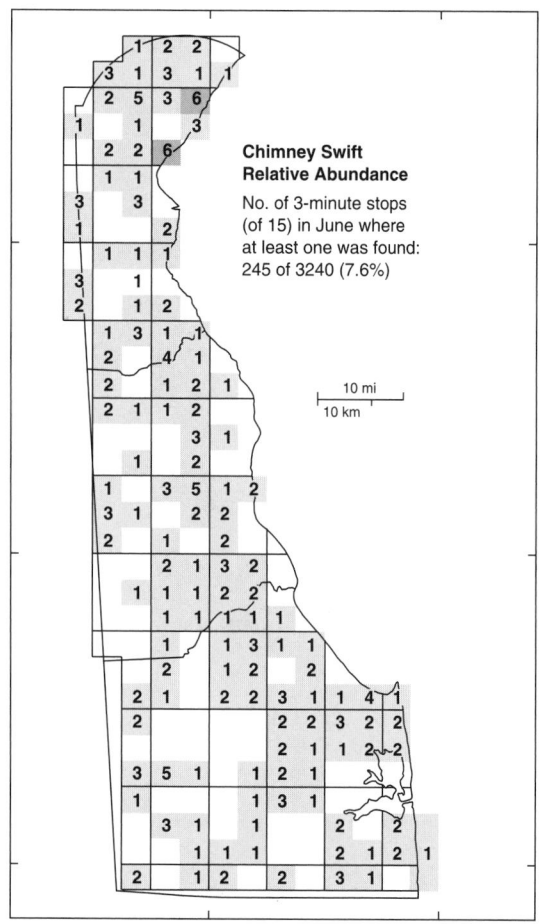

**Chimney Swift
Relative Abundance**

No. of 3-minute stops
(of 15) in June where
at least one was found:
245 of 3240 (7.6%)

10 mi
10 km

neys. The Chimney Swift is a noisy guest whose young beg regularly during the day, so its presence is hard to keep secret.

Nesting. Only 1 pair builds a nest in a given chimney or shaft; 1 or 2 seasonal visitors may share the site and help feed the young (Dexter 1981). Fischer (1958) reported regular breeding in outbuildings in addition to chimneys, and there are still instances in other states of nesting in hollow trees (Turner et al. 1984; Blodgett and Zammuto 1979). Swifts build a half cup of twigs glued to a wall with saliva. While on the wing birds take twigs for nests from dead branches in the tops of trees;

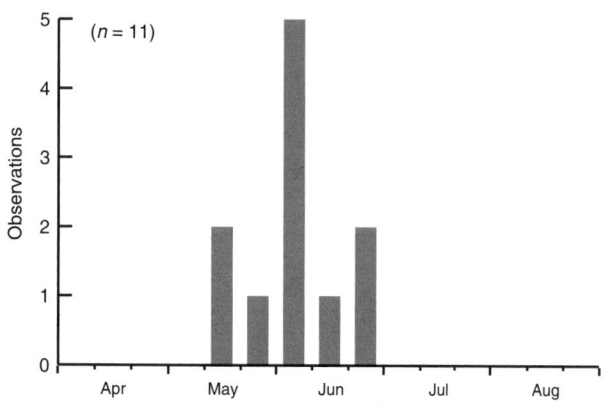

Estimated Clutch-Completion Dates

Hanson (notes) recorded this behavior between 19 May and 24 June, with dates varying from year to year. Delaware egg sets were collected on 30 May, and 8 and 15 June (DMNH 23636, DMNH 23637, DMNH 23638), and 2 on 12 June [Hans1]. They ranged from 2 to 4 eggs, but 3 to 5 eggs are most frequent in New York and Ohio (Fischer 1958). Estimated clutch-completion dates in Delaware range from 21 May to 10 July (TSBR 84-751), with a peak in the first third of June based on these egg sets and 24 reports of fledglings.

History. This species certainly benefited from European settlement, at least as far as suitable nesting habitat is concerned. After being dependent on hollow trees, the swift was suddenly supplied with countless chimneys, exactly the situation it required for nesting—an upright surface within a cavity, protected from the weather (Tyler 1940). In a booklet published by the State Board of Agriculture in 1904, Pennock wrote that the Chimney Swift was an abundant, beneficial bird protected by Delaware law (even in that day!).

Trends. It declined in the East at an average annual rate of 1% during 1966–90 and more sharply, at 7% annually, in Delaware during the same period [Usfw1]. One possible cause for this decline is a reduction in nesting sites (fewer open chimneys and outbuildings). Certainly some new subdivisions in the state are devoid of swifts.

Breeding population. Breeding population is generally limited to 1 breeding pair per suitable chimney.

FALL: After breeding and during migration, swifts form large flocks and roost colonially. Migration begins 10–15 August and continues through 5–10 October. The latest report is of 2 at Bombay Hook NWR on 24 October 1972 [Holg76]. Some high counts are

13 Aug 1981	200	Lewes [Frec1]
20 Sep 1983	1,000	Lewes [Frec1]
6 Oct 1974	113	Dragon Run [BroW1]

Large fall roosts have not been fully described in Delaware, but 1 existed at Hagley Museum in 1959 and 1960 (West, pers. obs.) and another at Townsend Hall, University of Delaware, in the late 1970s (Hess, pers. obs.). Hanson (notes) observed a roost of several hundred at the Academy (now Delaware State University) from 18 September 1932 until 12 October. A roost in an Ardmore, Pennsylvania, chimney contained about 10,000 swifts between 4 and 27 September 1944 (Groskin 1945, photographs by Charles E. Mohr).

SPECIMENS: 10; DMNH, USNM. Egg records: DMNH.

Ruby-throated Hummingbird (*Archilochus colubris*)

Regular; summer resident; common. Not commonly seen except at feeders and in gardens; expected early May through mid-September.

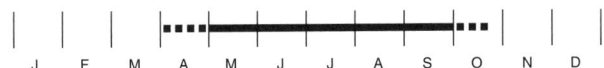

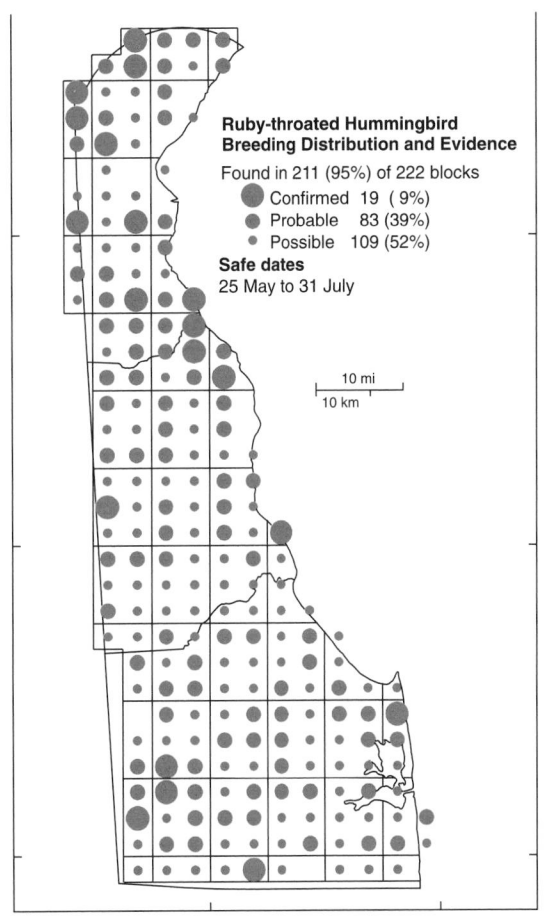

**Ruby-throated Hummingbird
Breeding Distribution and Evidence**
Found in 211 (95%) of 222 blocks
● Confirmed 19 (9%)
● Probable 83 (39%)
● Possible 109 (52%)
Safe dates
25 May to 31 July

10 mi
10 km

HABITAT: Deciduous woods, especially along creeks, hedgerows, wood margins, and edges with brush or small trees where it forages widely for nectar. Found also in mixed woods. Most commonly associated with coniferous forest during fall migration (McCann et al. 1993).

SPRING: Although there are a few April reports, the main migration does not occur until May. Earliest arrivals are

1 Apr 1973	1	Bombay Hook NWR [Reim1]
13 Apr 1971	1	Hoopes Reservoir, Wilmington [CadH1]
16 Apr 1985	1	Rt. 9, Sussex County [Frec1]

Because nearly all reports involve 1 bird, no clear migration peak is discernible; however, about twice as many records are from the first 2 weeks of May as from the second 2 weeks.

BREEDING: It is widely distributed throughout the state except in urban areas and along the Atlantic coast, where its habitat requirements are not met [Usfw1]. It is more common near the marshes in Assawoman WA than in Piedmont woodlots, according to the meager BBC data available.

Atlas. After 4 years of Atlas work fewer than half the blocks had a hummingbird record, and no pattern emerged. Focused searching in the final year—finding a mimosa tree and waiting for a hummingbird to come—quickly filled in most of the voids and demonstrated the statewide occurrence of this species (method from E. Blom, pers. comm.). It might well have been overlooked in some of the 11 blocks where it was not detected.

Nesting. Nests with 2 eggs have been reported on 20 May [Hans1] and 6, 10, 24, and 27 June [Hess4]. Latest nestling reports are

21 Jul 1985	young in nest	Newark [Roth2]
4 Aug 1983	1 young fledged	Pyles Ford Rd. [SpeS1]
29 Aug–9 Sep 1993	2 young in nest	W of Port Penn [Jano2]

The last record, carefully documented, is one of the latest known for the species. Estimated clutch-completion dates range from mid-May to the end of June and to 1 in August with no peak (n = 12). More nest data are needed for Delaware. Females will renest if the first brood fails, and 1 female in Michigan was known to be double-brooded (Nickell 1948). Almost all nests described for Delaware are in deciduous woods, with sycamore and oak preferred, but 1 was seen on a horizontal pine bough in Henlopen Acres (West, pers. obs.). Most interesting, perhaps, is 1 reported on a dead tree in a honeysuckle thicket on a wooded marsh island in Kent County [Schw1]. Hanson (notes) gives this description: "a nest about 12 ft up in a red birch, set on a drooping limb 5/8" in diameter. It was 1 1/2" high at the side and 1 5/8" in diameter. The opening was 3/4" wide and deep. It was made of plant down from ferns held together and fastened to the limb with spider webs and the outside was dotted with bits of lichen."

Trends. It is hard to judge how its population has fared in the past 30 or 300 years, but the profusion of introduced mimosa and escaped trumpet creeper and the provision of feeders and flower gardens are perhaps beneficial to the current population.

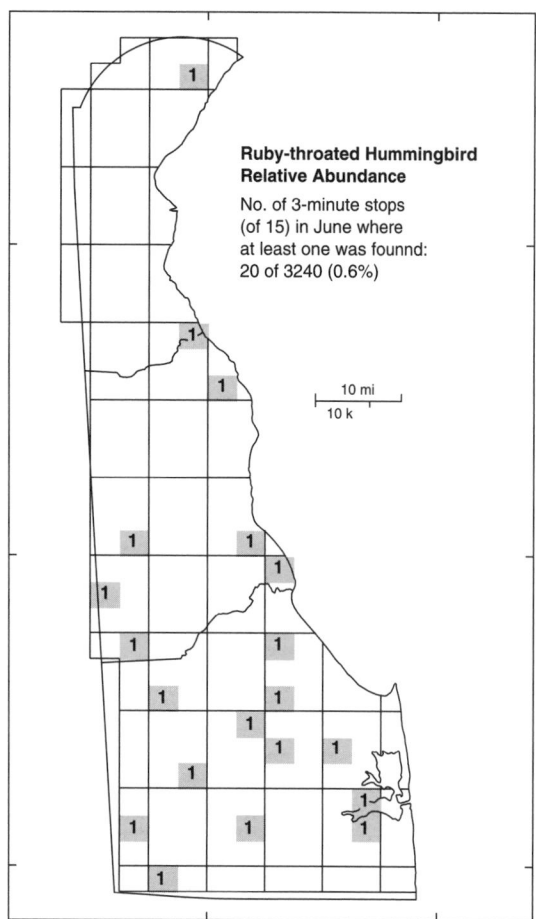

**Ruby-throated Hummingbird
Relative Abundance**

No. of 3-minute stops
(of 15) in June where
at least one was founnd:
20 of 3240 (0.6%)

10 mi
10 k

first half of September. The last report is a bird banded either 26 or 27 October 1965 (Linehan 1965b). Hummingbirds seen after the third week of September should be carefully observed and documented, because after that time the chance of a stray western hummingbird species increases.

REMARKS: A Ruby-throat requires 40% of its weight per day in sugar as nectar. It coevolved with 19 plant species in the East, exchanging cross-fertilization for nectar. Its northward migration correlates with the flowering times of several southern plants, and 9 are in bloom by the time it reaches the Northeast in May (Austin 1975, in Johnsgard 1983). Recently added food sources from mimosa, roadside trumpet creeper, planted flower gardens, and feeders may have a positive effect on survival and brood success. Numerous questions remain about which factors affect its population. We know little about territories except that the male sets up feeding and display territories (Pitelka 1942), but because it is promiscuous the male territory does not coincide with that of a female. In some instances nests are as close as 60 meters (Pickens 1944). The male takes no interest in nesting except copulation. We still do not know what factors restrict its nest site selection, nesting density, and success; nor do we know whether the female somehow knows, when it builds its nest, what next month's food resources and distances to them will be.

SPECIMENS: 13; DMNH, UDEL, UWBM.

Breeding population. The Ruby-throated Hummingbird occurred in 6 of 15 Delaware BBC study areas, never more than 1 per study area and sometimes listed only as a visitor. Its average abundance in these 15 areas was about 2 "pairs" per 100 ha. Average abundance in some Maryland studies in good hummingbird areas was about 15 breeding "pairs" per 100 ha, and the highest number recorded there was 38 per 100 ha in floodplain forest along the Patuxent River (Stewart and Robbins 1958). The BBS shows that its average rate of detection in Delaware (0.26 birds per 50-stop route) is about the same as its average in those regions in the East where it occurs (0.32) but less than found in the rest of the Upper Coastal Plain physiographic region (0.73) [Usfw3].

Conservation. It seems to have disappeared from Wilmington in areas where it was found 30 years ago. It was on the Blue List from 1978 to 1986 based on opinions held by some *American Birds* regional editors that a serious decline has occurred in the Northeast and other areas (Tate 1986). Because no decline has been detected in the East by the more controlled BBS during 1966–90 [Usfw3], the decline reported by Tate may be limited to the larger towns and cities (Sibley 1988c).

FALL: As in the spring, no migration period is evident, but the records suggest the peak period of migration may be the

Rufous Hummingbird *(Selasphorus rufus)*

Casual (1978, 1985, 1991).

REMARKS: A bird found alive but entangled in cockleburs 27 November 1978 in New Castle could not be kept alive and became the first specimen (immature male) as well as the first state record (DMNH 65273; Conway 1978). A second bird was observed and photographed (Fintel, DMNH 326) near Lewes on 28 and 30 November and 1–2 December 1985 (Fintel and Fintel 1986). The published notes state that "There was a distinct orange-rust wash on its side and . . . rufous orange at the base of its tail. This extended partway up the back." A third report describes 1 seen near New Castle on 2 November 1991 and described by Barnhill et al. [Barn17]; photograph by A. Brady, DMNH 405.

The Rufous Hummingbird appears to be the commonest hummingbird in the East in late fall and winter (Conway and Drennen 1979). However, female and immature male Allen's Hummingbirds *(Selasphorus sasin)* are indistinguishable from female and immature Rufous Hummingbirds under field conditions. The amount of detail necessary for a specific identification is impossible to see in the field and questionable even in the best stop-action photographs (Kaufmann 1990:170). Thus, the two records not supported by a specimen might better be regarded as *Selasphorus* species.

SPECIMEN: DMNH 65273, details above.

Belted Kingfisher *(Ceryle alcyon)*

Resident; uncommon. More often found in Sussex County. Becomes more common on the coast after nesting ceases.

HABITAT: Found on edges of streams, ponds, lakes, and tidal areas with clear water harboring fish. Requires an exposed perch to use between forays. Nests in stream banks in the Piedmont and in man-made banks in the Coastal Plain. Moves to tidal waters when inland ponds and streams freeze and when not breeding.

MIGRATION: Presumably, northern breeding birds migrate through Delaware, but no migration period is apparent

because this species is usually reported in ones and twos. Stewart and Robbins (1958) give the normal spring arrival in Maryland as 5–15 March and the normal fall departure as 1–10 November.

BREEDING: The Belted Kingfisher is found along most Piedmont streams but is more patchily distributed on the Coastal Plain where it is dependent on man-made sites for burrows. The relative abundance study, conducted from roadsides, registered it at only 28 stops, 20 of which were in Sussex County, suggesting it is 3 times more abundant there than in the rest of the state.

Atlas. The Atlas results show an irregular distribution. Many blank areas correspond to dry upland areas and upland wetlands that do not have permanent flowing streams. Others probably are areas with no suitable nest sites. Breeding birds might have been found in additional blocks if more streams had been canoed or otherwise carefully examined. Confirmations were equally divided between finding nest burrows and young out of the nest. Reports of young could be misplaced by 1 block, since kingfishers commonly have separate breeding and feeding locations that may be several miles apart.

Nesting. Hamas (1974) comments that this species uses an exposed soil bank devoid of vegetation in which to excavate its nest cavity, and that is our experience in Delaware. Hanson (notes) describes several nests that he excavated that are typical of those described in the literature. One of these was "found in a roadside bank near Thompsonville. The bank was about 5 feet high and the hole 18 inches from the top running back about four feet into the bank. At the end there was a chamber, slightly to one side and about 8 inches in diameter and 4 inches high. Eggs laid on the sand with no lining." This nest had just

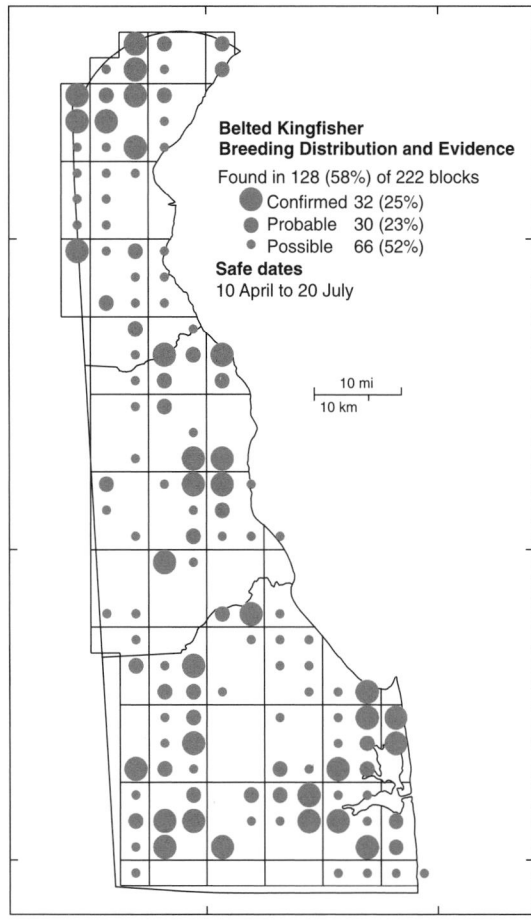

Belted Kingfisher
Breeding Distribution and Evidence

Found in 128 (58%) of 222 blocks
- Confirmed 32 (25%)
- Probable 30 (23%)
- Possible 66 (52%)

Safe dates
10 April to 20 July

10 mi
10 km

Breeding population. Its population appears to be limited by availability of breeding and feeding sites. Natural banks in the Coastal Plain are scarce, particularly near tidal areas, so nest cavities are often found in barrow pits and excavations and may be a mile or more from a stream or pond. It defends about 0.7 mi (1.1 km) of small streams (Davis 1982). Delaware has about 600 mi (1,000 km) of permanent streams, but some will not meet the kingfisher's requirements of being close to a nest site, being clean, having a fishing perch, or being big enough to have fish. These factors limit the population to the range of 100–1,000 pairs.

Conservation. The Stream Watch and Stream Corridors Protection programs will help improve the quality of its food source. Avoiding ditching and channelization and protecting wetlands are important practices in the maintenance of the permanent streams needed by this species.

1966–89 CBC Summary

Christmas Bird Count	Years Found	Range of No. Found	Median
Wilmington	24	4–29	14
Middletown	24	2–18	8
Bombay Hook	24	3–21	11
Cape Henlopen	24	5–27	11
Rehoboth	24	11–56	31
STATEWIDE	24	42–116	79
(low in 1989, high in 1975)			

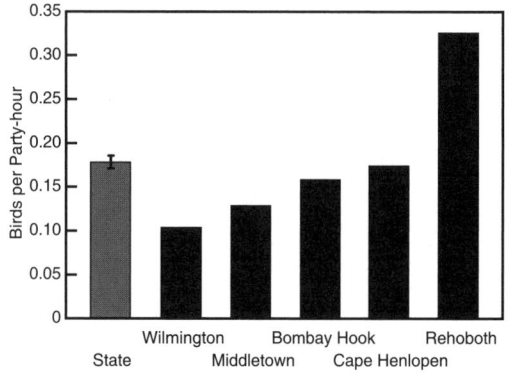

CBC Geographic Distribution

WINTER: No CBC trend is apparent. The kingfisher becomes progressively more common on CBCs in southern Delaware. This increase may be related to slightly warmer temperatures (and thus less ice) or perhaps to more habitat. Most non-CBC reports mention only 1 or 2 birds. Some of the highest counts are

7 Dec 1985	4	Seaford [Frec1]
13 Jan 1985	5	Rehoboth Beach [Edni56]
4 Feb 1978	4	White Clay Creek [MiDP13]

SPECIMENS: 13; DMNH. Egg records: DMNH.

been started on 16 April and had 5 fresh eggs on 15 May 1928. About another he noted that the hole was about 3 in. in diameter, and the tunnel ran slightly upward. Some authors have described typical grooves made in the cavity by the kingfisher's feet (Bailey 1900). Another feature is the presence of a nearby exposed perch where the bird can sit and watch over the cavity (White 1953). In the Coastal Plain nest burrows are found in the walls of gravel and sand pits, along canals, and in other man-made sites rather than in stream banks formed by natural erosion. Delaware egg dates range from 11 to 18 May (DMNH 28711, 28712), and nests with young several days old have been reported from 8 May to 1 June [Hans1]. Estimated clutch-completion dates peak in early May (*n* = 5). A possible late nesting is indicated by kingfisher egg shells found under an active burrow on 7 July 1985 [Cole1].

Trends. Before European settlement clear streams and beaver dams in open climax forests probably provided good feeding habitat for kingfishers, but nest sites may have been scarce. Today's drainage ditches, channelized streams, and millponds provide poorer fishing, but various man-made banks probably provide more nest sites. Its population declined in the East during 1966–90 [Usfw1]; Robbins et al. (1986) detected a specific population reduction as a result of the cold winter of 1976–77 in the East.

Red-headed Woodpecker *(Melanerpes erythrocephalus)*

Resident; rare. Absent in the coldest winters; formerly more common. Breeds locally, primarily in Sussex County.

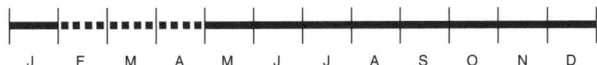

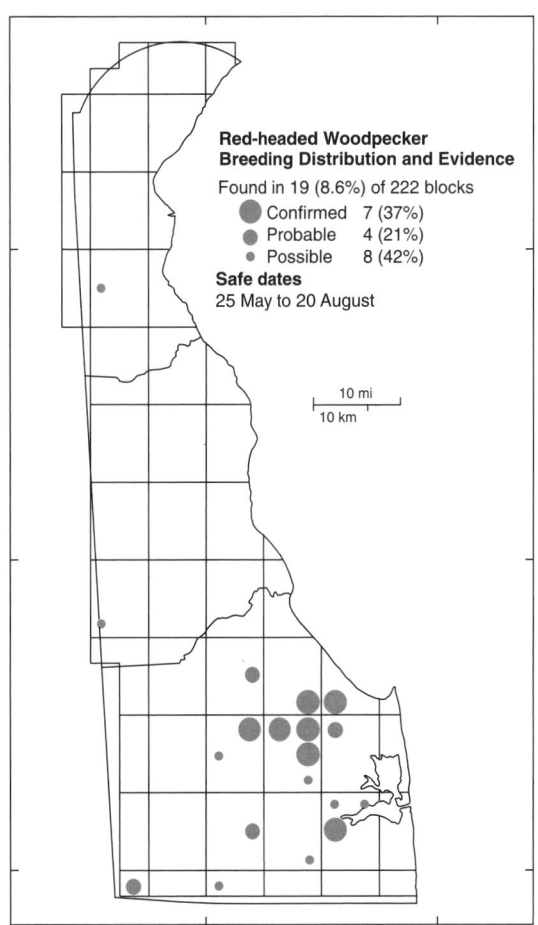

Red-headed Woodpecker
Breeding Distribution and Evidence
Found in 19 (8.6%) of 222 blocks
● Confirmed   7 (37%)
● Probable   4 (21%)
• Possible   8 (42%)
Safe dates
25 May to 20 August

10 mi
10 km

HABITAT: Open areas with many old, dead trees, most commonly remnant trees left when palustrine or lacustrine wetland forests were cut. If too close to towns or farmhouses, starlings sometimes compete successfully for cavities. Has a longer breeding season and can breed after the starling has finished. Red-bellied Woodpeckers do not competitively exclude Red-headed Woodpeckers (Ingold 1989, 1991), so the decline of Red-headed Woodpeckers cannot be ascribed to the increase in Red-bellied Woodpeckers in this century.

MIGRATION: This species' migration is rather irregular. In years and areas of good food supply the birds will overwinter (Bent 1939, 207). When migration does occur, it is usually from the northern one-third of its breeding range (AOU 1983), is in small numbers, and is not usually noticeable (Short 1982), though Graber et al. (1977) note spectacular diurnal fall migrations in Illinois. In Delaware spring migration usually occurs 5–25 May, but an earlier migrant was found in Cape Henlopen SP on 24 April 1979 [Frec1]. Fall migration is diffuse, apparently peaking 15–30 September. Two reports of obvious migrants include an immature at Carpenter SP on 18 September 1982 [Hess8] and another at Brandywine Creek SP on 19 September 1986 [Nile9].

BREEDING: The Red-headed Woodpecker breeds regularly in Sussex County but in decreasing numbers; it breeds sporadically in Kent and New Castle counties.

Atlas. During the Atlas period the only New Castle County

report was one in midsummer 1986 near Middletown [Boll1]. In Kent County 1 was calling on 29 June 1987 near Burrsville [West3]. In Sussex County some pairs inhabited what was left of wet forests, usually reduced to scattered dead trees left from the last timber cut (Pennock 1904b). It was found near the Millsboro power station and nearby residential areas, the headquarters unit of Redden SF and 2 other units, and at a cattle farm west of Red Mill Pond and surrounding woodlots [Frec2].

Nesting. The 4 nest-record cards on file for this species and 7 observations reported during the Atlas project do not provide enough information to construct its nesting chronology in Delaware, since most reports simply state the presence of the birds at a cavity. In Illinois, where it is more common, egg-laying dates extend from 6 May to 7 July (Graber et al. 1977). Clutch size is usually 5. Lost clutches are replaced. Females can be double-brooded (Harrison 1978). Nest sites noted in Delaware were cavities in dead wood, usually old trees without bark, as is usual for this species.

History. The first reference to the Red-headed Woodpecker in Delaware involves 1 shot by Alexander Wilson on 15 July 1794 while he was walking north along the Brandywine Creek on the day after he landed at the Battery, New Castle. He noted there were others in the trees and described it as the most beautiful bird he had ever seen (Cantwell 1961, 84). Pennock (1904b) said it was one of "the two best known woodpeckers" to be found in Delaware. He further (1908) described it as "usually resident throughout the entire state and at times locally abundant. Over at least the lower half it is generally to be seen in suitable localities; the large undrained timbered areas offering attractive feeding grounds for this bird." Pennock acquired some of his information from others; he recorded only the following in his Delaware ledger:

5 Jul 1903	near Granogue
15 May 1905	near Millsboro
6 May 1911	west of New Castle

Hanson (notes) had 2 late May 1923 records in Kent County and found a pair with a fresh cavity on 7 May 1927 at Camp Meeting woods near Camden. Hanson's first Sussex County report mentions 1 seen on 16 July 1931 near Ellendale [Hans1]. Its population may have reached a low in the 1930s, since it was annotated as "no recent records" in 1939 and as "casual visitor" in 1942 by Barry (1939, 1942).

Trends. It is no more common in the late twentieth century than earlier in the century. One was present on a BBC in Brandywine Creek SP in 1966 (West et al., 1967), a June record occurred there in 1967 [Hoff3], and 6 records were accumulated there in 1969, for example, 30 May and 29 June [BroW1; West22]. These are the last known summer records in the Piedmont. The last regular place in Kent County was on Dutch Neck Rd. going into Bombay Hook NWR, where it occurred from 1955 (Brooks et al., 1955) into the 1960s [Wayn1]. It has been declining significantly in the East during 1966–90 [Usfw1].

Breeding population. In the mid-1980s its population was about 10 pairs, but some breeding locations have since disappeared.

Conservation. Red-headed Woodpecker colonies become harder to find each year. In dry years, and with the increasing draining effect of the tax ditches, the few standing trees in wet areas were cut or burned so the land could be used for crops, grazing, or pine plantations. If the Red-headed Woodpecker's extirpation from Delaware is to be avoided, open mature forest and forest remnants with standing dead trees must be preserved. Fortunately, the Sussex County population is buttressed by other colonies on the Delmarva Peninsula (Robbins 1996; Ridd 1989). It is listed as Threatened in New Jersey. It was on the Blue List for 1972 and 1976–81 and was listed as a species of special concern in 1982–86 (Tate 1986).

1966–89 CBC Summary

Christmas Bird Count	Years Found	Range of No. Found	Median
Wilmington	4	1	
Middletown	2	1	
Bombay Hook	8	1–3	
Cape Henlopen	5	1–4	
Rehoboth	10	1–8	
STATEWIDE (high in 1978)	16	1–12	1

WINTER: It is usually present in very small numbers and has been recorded most frequently on the Rehoboth CBC. During 1986–93 it was seen on only 2 CBCs out of the 36 taken: 1 was seen on the 21 December 1991 Rehoboth CBC and 6 on the 29 December 1991 Middletown CBC.

SPECIMENS: 6; DMNH, USNM.

Red-bellied Woodpecker *(Melanerpes carolinus)*

Resident; fairly common. Casual before the twentieth century.

J F M A M J J A S O N D

HABITAT: A wide variety of deciduous and mixed forest and woodlots. Suburbs. Decreased numbers close to the coast.

BREEDING: This woodpecker is, perhaps, our most common, and it is found throughout the state in woods and suburbs. The relative abundance study shows it less common in Sussex County than in the rest of the state.

Atlas. During the Atlas project it was easily found except in marshes and next to the ocean. It was most commonly confirmed by seeing the adult carrying food. In contrast, "nest with young" was reported only 4 times. The young call loudly from the nest, and hearing the call was an easy way to confirm it.

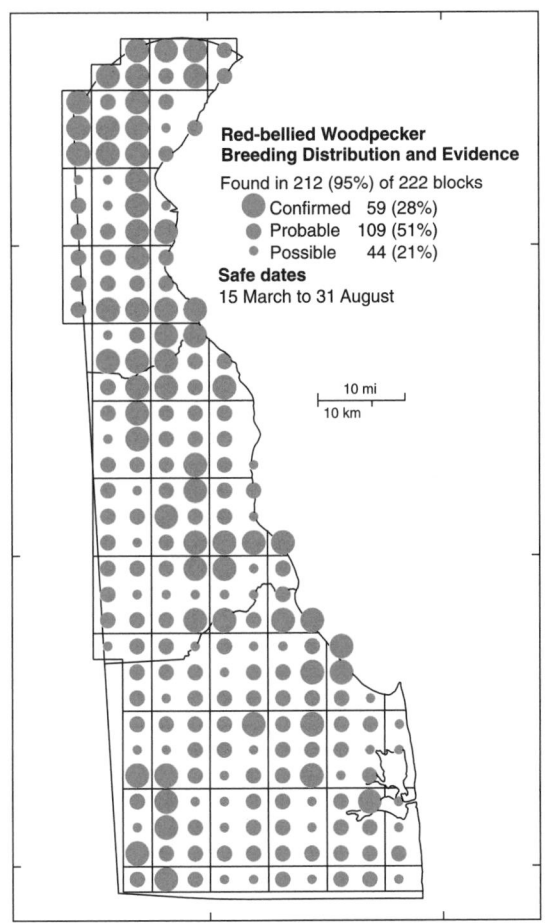

Red-bellied Woodpecker
Breeding Distribution and Evidence

Found in 212 (95%) of 222 blocks

- ● Confirmed   59 (28%)
- ● Probable   109 (51%)
- • Possible   44 (21%)

Safe dates
15 March to 31 August

10 mi
10 km

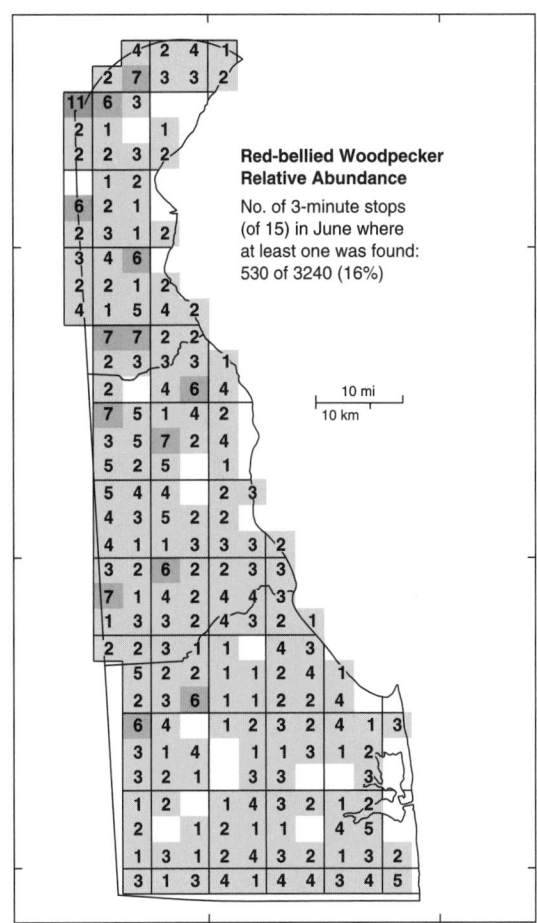

Red-bellied Woodpecker
Relative Abundance

No. of 3-minute stops
(of 15) in June where
at least one was found:
530 of 3240 (16%)

10 mi
10 km

Nesting. Little is known of the Red-bellied Woodpecker's nesting in Delaware because it was not common here when nest and egg collecting were popular, and no modern study involving tree climbing has been conducted. Buckalew (notes) found a nest with 5 young south of Ellendale on 12 May 1935. Wright and Carter collected a nest with 5 eggs from Ellendale on 24 May 1936 (DMNH mount). Clutch completion appears to peak in the first third of May. Nestlings have been reported on 12 May [Buck1] to 16 June [Long1]. It has 2 broods in Mississippi (Ingold 1989), but only 1 farther north in Maryland (Kilham 1961)—and probably in Delaware. It shows a high degree of nest-site fidelity and suffers from nest competition with starlings (Ingold 1989, 1991).

History. This bird extended its breeding range northward to Delaware during the twentieth century. A. K. Fisher wrote of 1 taken in Delaware about 1880 by W. D. Bush [Bush2]. Several were seen near Greenwood in October 1895 [Preb1]. Rhoads (1903) reported finding a Red-bellied Woodpecker on a trip to the Choptank River bottoms near Marydel on 6 June 1903, and it was twice again found at Medford Mills in 1904 [Penn1]. Rhoads and Pennock (1905) designated it a "Summer resident. Found breeding at Marydel. May remain all winter." It must not have been widespread, for Pennock (1904b, 1908a) describes 4 other trips made to southern Delaware in 1903–

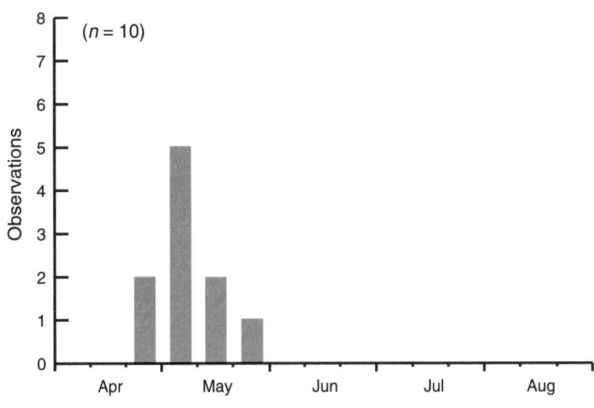

Estimated Clutch-Completion Dates

1905 without reporting any. The AOU Check-list (1910) gives Delaware as the species' northern limit along the East Coast. Pennock shot another at Medford Mills on 26 May 1911 [Penn1]. Hanson gives 9 records in Kent and Sussex counties between 1923 and 1929. His first breeding record involved a pair in a cavity of a dead limb 50 ft high in a gum tree in Camp Meeting woods near Camden in 1927. The adults appeared to be incubating on 28 May and feeding young on 11 June [Hans1]. This species was reported in New Castle County on

29 Apr 1923	Delaware City [Pott2]
8, 9 Mar 1924	Woodland Beach [Cart3]
16 Jun 1929	Wilmington [Clat1]

It was still not common in the 1940s when Barry (1942) reported it as "fairly common in Kent and Sussex as a winter resident." Brooks reported 1 on 16 October 1955 near Churchmans Marsh and said that was as far north as it ranged (Brooks et al. 1955). The Hoopes Reservoir surveys show its dramatic increase from 1 seen on 2 April 1944 (1 on 158 trips, 1943–45) to 77 seen on 52 trips in 1964 (Falk 1971). The range extension has now reached southern Ontario, central New York, Massachusetts (AOU 1983), and northern New England (Nikula 1993).

Trends. The BBSs and the CBCs display a stable population during 1966–90, suggesting its population increase in Delaware had ended by 1966.

Breeding population. Its mean density in Delaware woodland BBCs is 24 males per 100 ha. It occurred on 530 stops in the relative abundance study; it can be heard for 260 yds (240 m) (Whitcomb et al. 1981).

1966–89 CBC Summary

Christmas Bird Count	Years Found	Range of No. Found	Median
Wilmington	24	29–92	66
Middletown	24	6–63	30
Bombay Hook	24	2–105	44
Cape Henlopen	24	3–43	17
Rehoboth	24	14–78	29
STATEWIDE (low in 1968, high in 1970)	24	135–263	198

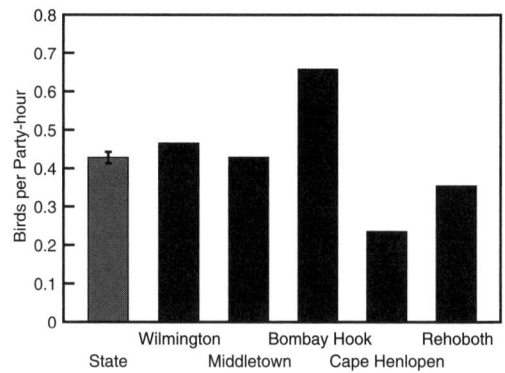

CBC Geographic Distribution

WINTER: This species is about equally common on all CBCs.

REMARKS: The Red-bellied Woodpecker may have occurred in Delaware during the nineteenth century and then withdrawn. Warren (1890) cites several authorities for this species' occurrence in Pennsylvania, starting with Audubon. In southeastern Pennsylvania during the second half of the nineteenth century it was a rare winter visitor (probably dispersed young), and it was "very abundant in the counties west of London," Ontario, until about 1885 (Woodliffe 1987 quoting Macoun and Macoun 1909).

SPECIMENS: 23; DMNH, ANSP, UDEL.

Yellow-bellied Sapsucker *(Sphyrapicus varius)*

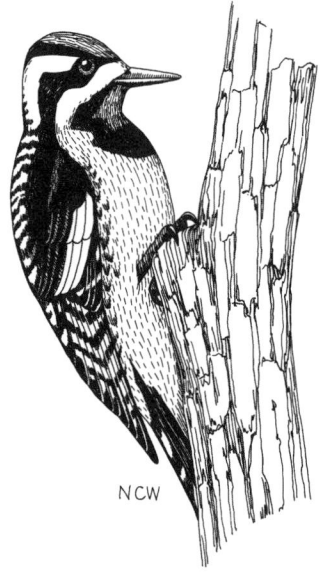

NCW

Regular; migrant and winter visitor; uncommon. Expected late September through mid-April, occasionally later. Rare in winter after December.

HABITAT: Deciduous woods.

SPRING: Short (1982) notes that migration is underway during March, and that birds reach their breeding grounds by late April to late May, with the males often arriving first. In Delaware it is difficult to distinguish early migrants from wintering birds, but perhaps these are the earliest migrants reported in each of the counties:

20 Mar 1983	1	Bombay Hook NWR [Hess14]
24 Mar 1991	1	Delaware City [Hess19]
28 Mar 1982	1	Seaford [Frec1]

Migration peaks in mid-April. All reports involve 1–3 birds.

SUMMER: Reports in early May represent late migrants:

2 May 1965	1	Iron Hill [Faus3]
4 May 1965	1	Alapocas Woods [West1]
4 May 1984	1	Trap Pond [Hess18]

A report of an immature at Bombay Hook NWR on 9 June 1962 (*Cassinia* 46:36) is more likely a mistaken report than a late migrant exhibiting delayed molt. Short (1982) notes that immatures usually complete the postjuvenal molt the following March or April; he also notes that eggs are laid in May and June, and young fledge by late June to July.

FALL: First arrival is after mid-September, with these the earliest:

16 Sep 1983	1	Bombay Hook NWR [Edni64]
17 Sep 1964	2	Rittenhouse Park, Newark [Faus7]
20 Sep 1979	1	Wilmington [Gord10]

Migration peaks from 30 September to 15 October. High counts are 14 on 10 October 1976 and 9 on 16 October 1976, both White Clay Creek [Edni17; Jahn5].

1966–89 CBC Summary

Christmas Bird Count	Years Found	Range of No. Found	Median
Wilmington	21	1–12	2
Middletown	12	1–4	1
Bombay Hook	17	1–10	1
Cape Henlopen	17	1–5	1
Rehoboth	21	1–8	2
STATEWIDE (low in 1966, high in 1985)	24	3–27	9

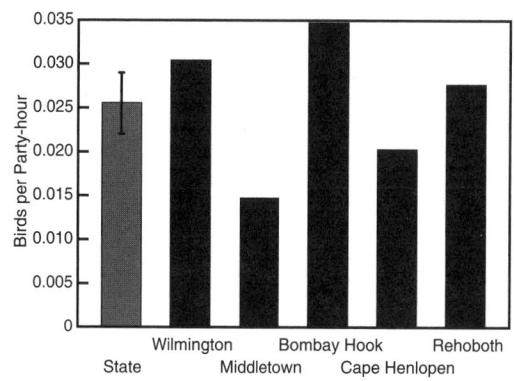

CBC Geographic Distribution

WINTER: This species' numbers are variable on CBCs, which perhaps disguises an upward trend. It is found less frequently as a wintering bird than during migration; it will occasionally come to feeders.

SPECIMENS: 11; DMNH, ANSP, UDEL.

Downy Woodpecker *(Picoides pubescens)*

Resident; fairly common.

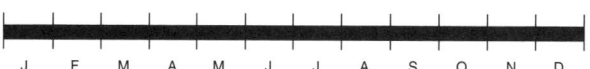

| J | F | M | A | M | J | J | A | S | O | N | D |

HABITAT: Ubiquitous in deciduous and mixed woods, residential areas, and small woodlots. It partitions habitat with Hairy Woodpecker by feeding on smaller limbs of upper and outer parts of trees.

MIGRATION: There is no evidence of either a migratory influx or departure of Downy Woodpeckers in Delaware. However, Short (1982) makes the following remarks: "Migration of Downy Woodpeckers [from the northern edge of its range] along the Atlantic Coast is of regular occurrence. Individuals have been taken as far as 800 mi from where they were banded."

BREEDING: The Downy Woodpecker may well be the most numerous woodpecker in Delaware, but its quieter calls and

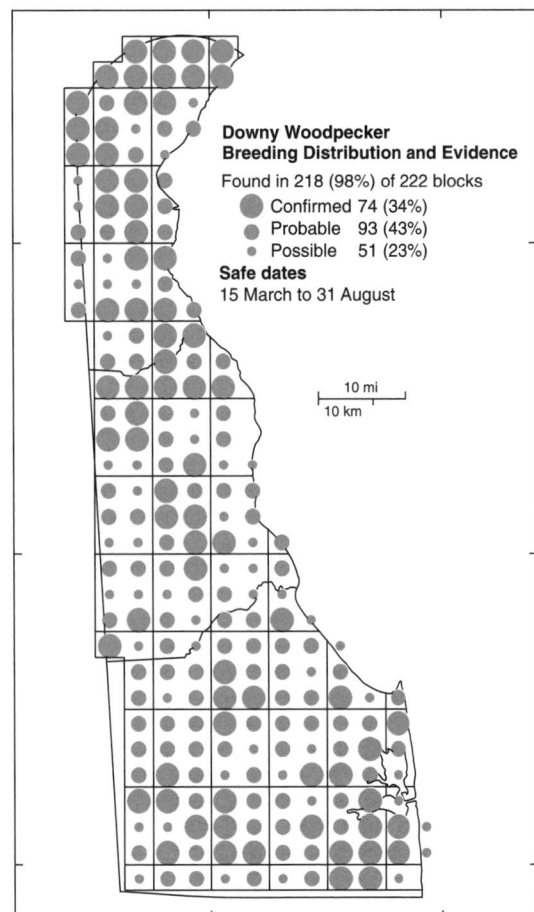

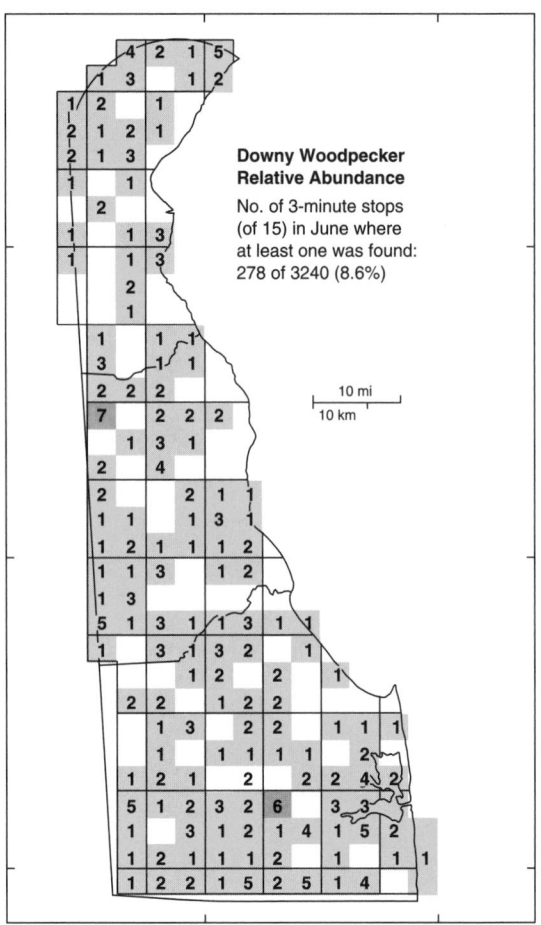

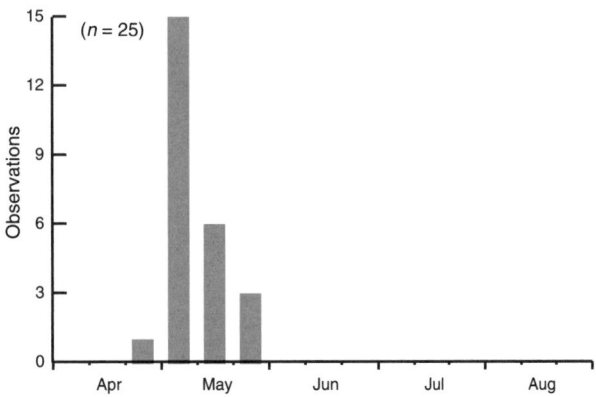

Estimated Clutch-Completion Dates

smaller size make it less noticeable than the Red-bellied Wood-pecker.

Atlas. Both the Atlas study and the relative abundance study show its general distribution, but the latter study shows it is less common near the Delaware River, as well as in marshy or intensively farmed areas without many trees. The most frequent method of confirmation was seeing adults carrying food to young in the nest.

Nesting. In Ontario (Lawrence 1967) and Illinois (Graber et al. 1977) it usually nests in dead wood. For Delaware, in 9 of 15 cases that a nest site was described, it was in dead wood. In the other cases deciduous trees were identified as the sites, but the cavities still may have been placed in dead wood. Its egg dates have not been reported in Delaware, but data from Atlas and other reports indicate that clutch completion peaks strongly in early May, and that females are not double-brooded. Graber et al. (1977) give May as the egg-laying period in northern Illinois but a much earlier 30 March–10 May period for southern Illinois. Clutch size is usually 4–5 (Bent 1939, 57). The young continue to live on their parents' territory after they have become independent, and the adults will drive away young that are not their own (Lawrence 1967).

History. The Downy Woodpecker may have been much less common at the beginning of the twentieth century than now. For example, Pennock (1904b) listed the Red-headed Woodpecker and Northern Flicker as the most common woodpeckers in Delaware then. Furthermore, Pennock (1908a) did not report Downy Woodpeckers on 3 field trips taken to the Indian River country from 1903 to 1905, but he did find them on 2 winter trips to Lewes (Pennock 1904b) [Penn7]. The smaller woodpeckers were known as sapsuckers and were shot by orchard owners, who erroneously thought they were protecting their fruit trees.

Trends. Trend analyses of BBS [Usfw3] and May Count data suggest that the long-term population is fairly stable, though low numbers were recorded in 1976 following an unusually severe winter.

Breeding population. This species is inconspicuous. It maintains a relatively small home range of about 25 acres (10 ha) (Kilham 1983) and tolerates a wide variety of habitats. It was found on 278 of 3,240 stops in the relative abundance study and can be heard from distances up to 100 yds (90 m) (Whitcomb 1981). One indication of its abundance is from BBCs, which show that it is as common as the Red-bellied Woodpecker in Piedmont woodlots, with an average density of about 22 pairs per 100 ha.

1966–89 CBC Summary

Christmas Bird Count	Years Found	Range of No. Found	Median
Wilmington	24	81–181	117
Middletown	24	23–113	49
Bombay Hook	24	16–125	49
Cape Henlopen	24	6–62	31
Rehoboth	24	25–103	51
STATEWIDE (low in 1976, high in 1970)	24	243–434	315

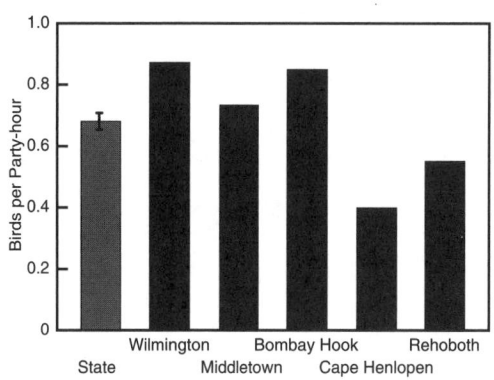

CBC Geographic Distribution

WINTER: It is about equally common on all CBCs, and its population was stable during 1966–89.

REMARKS: The 1882 specimen of Downy Woodpecker in the UDEL collection was probably procured by W. D. Bush. He maintained a collecting notebook during 1878–81 and had not reported seeing one during those dates.

SPECIMENS: 36; DMNH, ANSP, CM, UDEL.

Hairy Woodpecker *(Picoides villosus)*

Resident; uncommon.

HABITAT: Deciduous woods; found in lower numbers in mixed or mature pine woods. Although more common in larger forests in Maryland (Robbins et al. 1989), it selected a wide range of forested habitats in terms of maturity and density in Virginia (Conner and Adkisson 1977), and it must do so in Delaware in order to be so widely distributed.

MIGRATION: None in our area (Short 1982).

BREEDING: This larger version of the Downy is often overlooked because the 2 are so similar. The relative abundance study shows its population level is lower in the open country of southern New Castle County and, surprisingly, in wooded (largely pine) parts of central Sussex County.

Atlas. The Hairy Woodpecker was recorded in 87% of blocks and probably occurred in a higher percentage because it accepts a wide variety of habitat. For example, it was found in coastal pines at Cape Henlopen SP and Bethany Beach during the Atlas period, a habitat unattractive to other woodpeckers. It was usually first found by hearing its penetrating call note, though the bird subsequently needed to be located to be sure it was not an agitated Downy, which can produce a somewhat similar note. It was most frequently confirmed by Atlas workers who saw it feeding young or heard young in the nest.

Nesting. Hanson (notes) describes a nest cavity with vocal young found on 15 May 1925 in a dead limb 25 ft high in a maple tree located in a swamp near Dover. Hairy Woodpeckers

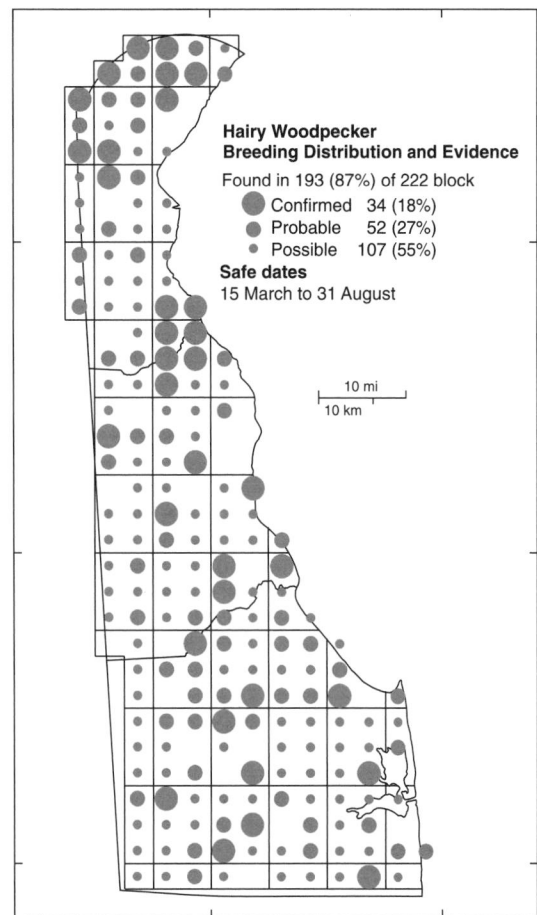

Hairy Woodpecker
Breeding Distribution and Evidence

Found in 193 (87%) of 222 block

● Confirmed 34 (18%)
● Probable 52 (27%)
• Possible 107 (55%)

Safe dates
15 March to 31 August

10 mi
10 km

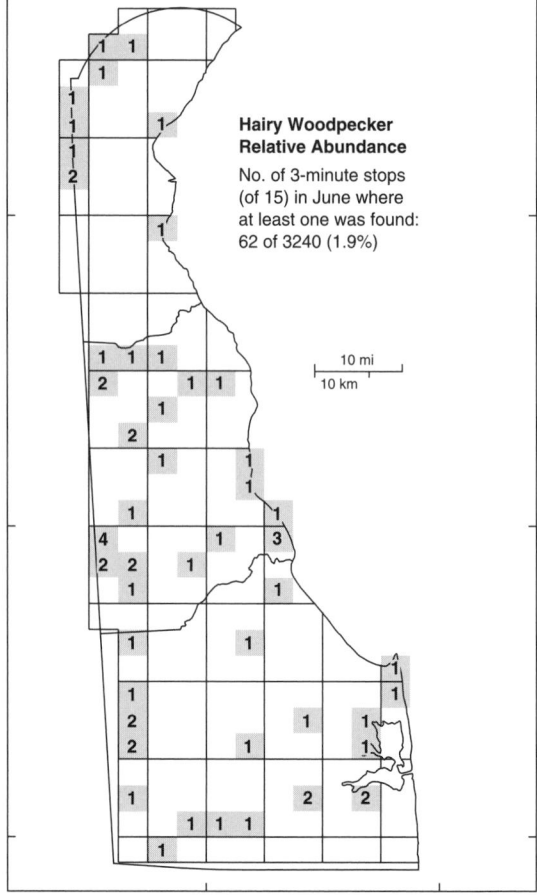

Hairy Woodpecker
Relative Abundance

No. of 3-minute stops
(of 15) in June where
at least one was found:
62 of 3240 (1.9%)

10 mi
10 km

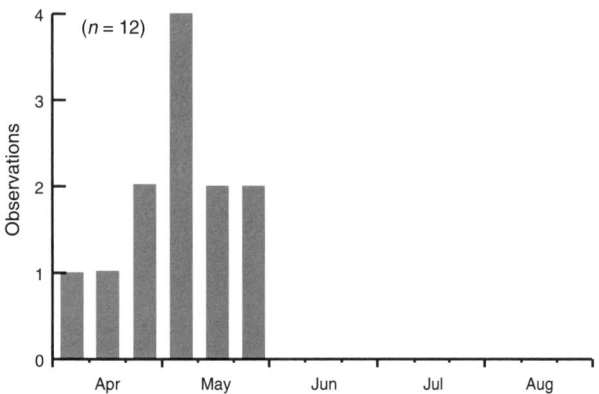

Estimated Clutch-Completion Dates

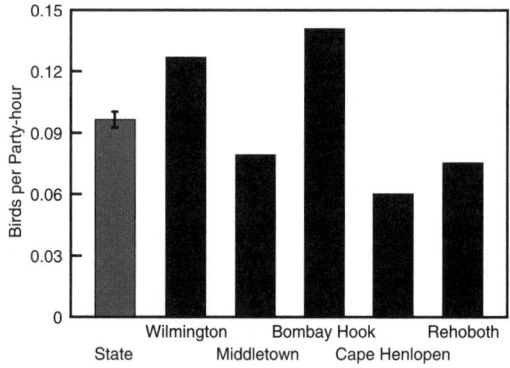

CBC Geographic Distribution

also build nests in living limbs (Lawrence 1967; Graber et al. 1977). Extreme dates for nests with vocal young are 4 May [Hess4] and 29 June [Long1]. This span suggests a longer egg-laying period than that reported for Illinois (20 April–28 May, Graber 1977). Clutch size is usually 4 (Harrison 1978).

Trends. BBS data show it has increased in the East at an average rate of 1% a year since 1966 [Usfw3], but an increase has not been detected in Delaware.

Breeding population. It is less commonly found than the

Downy, as shown by these Hairy to Downy ratios: 0.11:1 on BBSs, 0.15:1 on CBCs, 0.19:1 on May Counts, 0.22:1 on the relative abundance study, and 0.4:1 on BBCs in Piedmont woodland. These differences do not reflect actual changes in populations, but differences of areas sampled, observer differences, and season sampled, all of which affect the relative detectability of the 2 woodpeckers. In round numbers its population may be about 20% of the Downy's. Its territory or home range is larger than that of the Downy Woodpecker but varies with quality of the habitat. Short (1982, 324) suggests 40–50 acres (16–20 ha) of old eastern woodland may be required to support a pair, though defended territories are much smaller.

Conservation. The Hairy Woodpecker is associated with forest interiors and is considered an indicator species of forest fragmentation (Robbins et al. 1989). It was included in the Blue List for 1975–82 and was noted as a species of special concern in 1986 (Tate 1986). Preservation of large tracts of hardwood or mixed forests and woodland corridors is a good conservation practice for this species.

1966–89 CBC Summary

Christmas Bird Count	Years Found	Range of No. Found	Median
Wilmington	24	8–26	17
Middletown	24	2–12	5
Bombay Hook	24	4–22	10
Cape Henlopen	22	1–10	5
Rehoboth	24	1–19	6
STATEWIDE	24	30–68	44
(decreasing; low in 1981, high in 1972)			

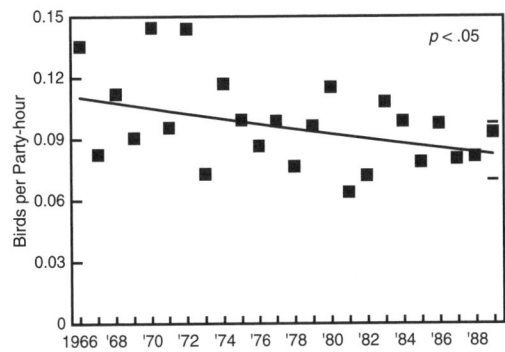

CBC Trend; Autocorrelation may Invalidate the Significance Test

WINTER: The numbers of Hairy Woodpeckers reported on CBCs has gradually decreased during 1966–89. It appears to be most numerous on the Wilmington and Bombay Hook CBCs. Typical reports total 1 or 2 birds; more than 4 or 5 are rarely reported.

SPECIMENS: 11; DMNH.

[Red-cockaded Woodpecker *(Picoides borealis)*]

Gregory A. Inskip

No Delaware records, but formerly present in the region.

REMARKS: This southern woodpecker has bred several times in loblolly pines in Dorchester County, Maryland, near Blackwater NWR (Meanley 1978, 48–50). Less typically, it also bred in a Virginia pine on Assateague Island, Worcester County, Maryland (Meanley 1943, 105). There are isolated nineteenth-century specimens from Hoboken, New Jersey, and near Philadelphia, Pennsylvania, but no Delaware records (Stone 1937). Its range was described as south from New Jersey

by Warren (1890). Gentry (1876–77) comments: "That it is a rare visitor in Eastern Pennsylvania cannot be doubted, as an individual was taken a few years since, and is now deposited with the writer. This specimen was shot in Delaware County, just beyond the southern border of Philadelphia."

Old stands of loblolly pine formerly were more extensive in Sussex County than they are now (Fleming 1978, 265); possibly the Red-cockaded Woodpecker formerly bred there.

Three-toed Woodpecker *(Picoides tridactylus)*

Casual (1968, 1974).

DOCUMENTATION: Photograph (R. L. West DMNH 464), published notes.

REMARKS: The first individual of this species was present from early December 1967 to March 1968. Many observers saw the bird at the Blades' feeder near Hockessin [anon1]; their reports are succinctly discussed by Faust [Faus4]. Controversy occurred among observers at the time as to whether the bird was a Three-toed Woodpecker, an aberrant Hairy Woodpecker, or even a hybrid. The bird was sketched by Crumb and pho-

tographed by Anthony and West. West's photograph (on file at DMNH) supports the identification of this individual as a Three-toed Woodpecker. The darkness of the bird, the back and sides, and especially the shortness of the bill eliminate Hairy Woodpecker as a possibility and make the hypothesis of a hybrid extremely unlikely.

A second bird, also well described, was found in Delaware City on 7 April 1974 (Conway 1974a) [SpSB42]. Among other characters, the notes mention the barred flanks, a white patch on the back ("a smudge rather than horizontal stripes"), and a call note noticeably weaker than the Black-backed Woodpecker, with which the observers were familiar.

The closest breeding location for this species is the New York Adirondacks (Peterson 1988e). The only New York specimen outside its breeding area is 1 from Watertown, and it has also been reliably recorded in winter in western New York (Bull 1974). It has been photographed in Massachusetts and reported in Rhode Island, New Jersey, and Pennsylvania (Veit and Petersen 1993; Leck 1984; Santner et al. 1992).

[Black-backed Woodpecker *(Picoides arcticus)*]

One undocumented report.

DOCUMENTATION: None.

REMARKS: A single bird was reported as being seen "repeatedly at a feeder" in Hockessin during November 1969 (Scott and Cutler 1970) by an observer who had seen the species on the breeding grounds the preceding summer. No description of the bird is available.

Northern Flicker *(Colaptes auratus)*

Resident; common. Also a migrant.

HABITAT: Open situations with dead trees, also open forests.

SPRING: Migration is not as conspicuous in spring as in fall. The number of birds increases 20–30 March, and the peak

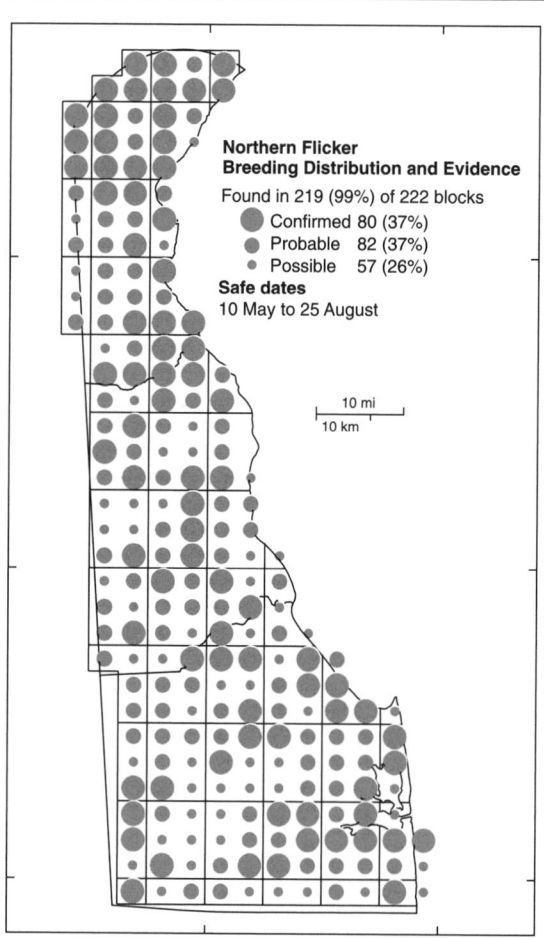

Northern Flicker
Breeding Distribution and Evidence
Found in 219 (99%) of 222 blocks
● Confirmed 80 (37%)
● Probable 82 (37%)
· Possible 57 (26%)
Safe dates
10 May to 25 August

10 mi
10 km

occurs throughout April. The average number of birds reported then is about twice (13 birds per report) that of March or May (5 or 6 birds per report; *n* = 104, 154, and 154 for March,

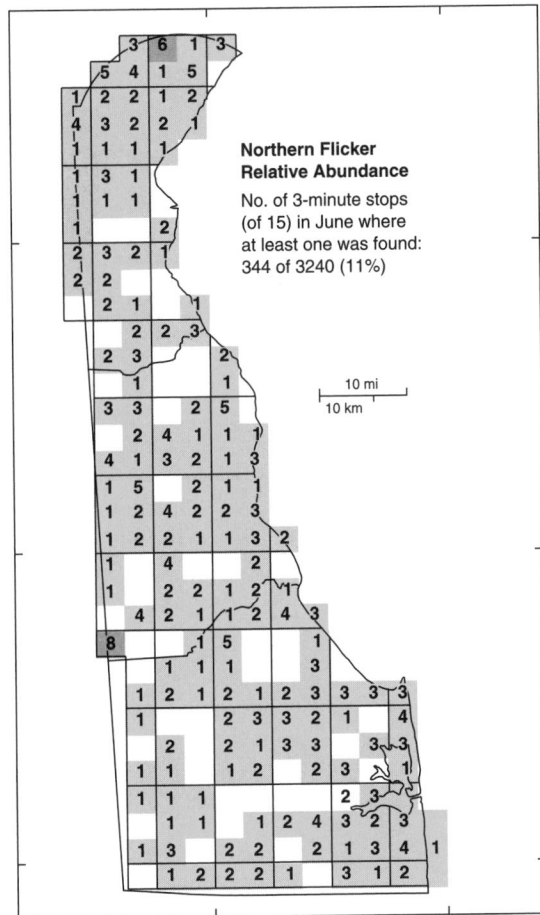

**Northern Flicker
Relative Abundance**

No. of 3-minute stops
(of 15) in June where
at least one was found:
344 of 3240 (11%)

10 mi
10 km

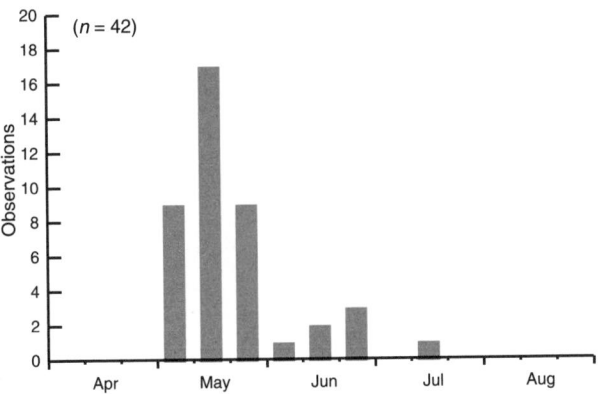

Estimated Clutch-Completion Dates

easy for Atlas workers to locate; 55% of the confirmations were the result of finding the nest. Finding young out of the nest provided 25% of the confirmations, and seeing adults carrying food 20%.

Nesting. Its clutch-completion dates peak strongly in May (83%). Extreme egg dates are 11 May (DMNH 5856) to a rather late 20 July [Brit1] when 2 eggs were found at Bombay Hook NWR. By comparison, Graber et al. (1977) list the Illinois egg-laying dates as 17 April–22 July. Bent (1939) lists this species as double-brooded in the South, and the Delaware late June and July clutches, 6 weeks after the main peak, suggest some instances of second broods. Moore (1995) asserts flickers are single-brooded; they do not regularly produce a second brood in a season, but it may happen occasionally. Clutches in May usually include 6–8 eggs.

Trends. Pennock (1904b) referred to the flicker as one of the best-known woodpeckers in Delaware. It was also abundant in Illinois at that time, but there the population fell 90% by the 1950s (Graber and Graber 1963). It probably also decreased in Delaware during that period. Graber and Graber note that starlings compete with flickers for nest holes and surmise that such competition may be one reason for the flicker's decline in the first half of the twentieth century. BBS data reveal its population has decreased in the East at an average annual rate of 3% during 1966–90. The Delaware May Count data give the same result, but the Delaware BBS did not reveal a significant trend [Usfw3].

Breeding population. The flicker is easier to see than other woodpeckers and can be heard for 260 yds (240 meters) (Whitcomb 1981). Stewart and Robbins (1958) list about 7 per 100 ha as breeding densities in 2 Maryland locations, a figure consistent with our estimate for Delaware. Northern Delaware woodlots averaged a much higher 13–23 pairs per 100 acres (30–60 per 100 ha). Linehan, Jones, and Strehl (1967) reported a high of 16 territories (average of 2 years) in the 35-acre University of Delaware woodlot, Newark (110 per 100 ha) and ascribed this high density to an abundance of standing dead wood and a number of large trees. Longcore, working with Linehan, located and followed the progress of 10 of 13 nests there in 1966 [Long1]. The BBC study by Linehan et al. (1967a) was directed at the productivity of woodlots and was not concerned with how far from the woodlot flickers foraged.

The distribution of flickers is irregular. Dennis (1969) noted a concentration of 19 pairs in 100 acres (47 per 100 ha) of old white pines on Nantucket, Massachusetts, but the average density for the island was only 0.15 pairs per 100 acres (0.4 per 100 ha). Kilham (1983) noted 3 pairs nesting within 70 meters, but he thought their proximity was possible only because the nests were 10 days apart in timing, so the next could be started after the onset of incubation by the earlier pair. Flickers are territorially aggressive in their early breeding season.

Conservation. The continued downward trend in the Northern Flicker population in the East on the BBS since 1966 is widely attributed to loss of nest sites to starlings (e.g., Robbins

April, and May, respectively). Short (1982) reports that "Spring migration is underway in March and continues until late May in the far north."

BREEDING: The relative abundance study shows it is evenly distributed among the 3 counties. It has a distinct tolerance for the suburban sprawl in northern Delaware and is sparse in the young managed forests of Sussex County.

Atlas. Not surprisingly, the flicker was found, and its breeding confirmed, in more blocks than any other woodpecker. Its nests, often placed in dead trees in the open, were relatively

et al. 1986). The large population found by Longcore in a woodlot with ample nest trees shows that leaving dead trees in woodlots, forests, and clearcuts is an important conservation practice (Linehan 1967b).

FALL: The peak migration period occurs from about 15 September to about 5 October, with these high counts recorded from the 3 counties:

27 Sep 1981	33	Bombay Hook NWR [Edni45]
29 Sep 1981	200	Cape Henlopen SP [Frec1]
5 Oct 1991	44	Burrows Run [Wayn64]

Short (1982) notes that in late summer family groups form larger flocks, begin southward movement in late August, and continue migrating through late October or early November. Flicker numbers in Delaware decrease in November, but the low winter level is not reached until December.

1966–89 CBC Summary

Christmas Bird Count	Years Found	Range of No. Found	Median
Wilmington	24	19–97	43
Middletown	24	13–73	29
Bombay Hook	24	28–124	60
Cape Henlopen	24	8–85	36
Rehoboth	24	15–99	66
STATEWIDE (low in 1968, high in 1984)	24	147–394	253

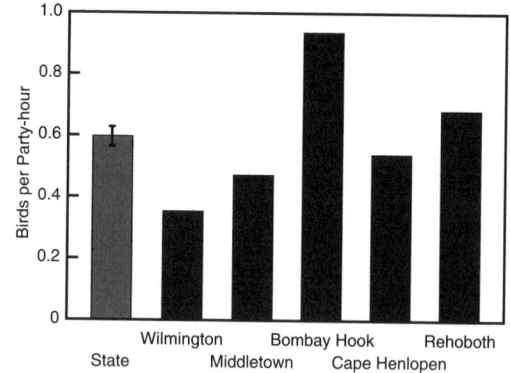

CBC Geographic Distribution

WINTER: Two high counts, possibly of late migrants, are 35 on 2 December 1987 west of Lewes and 100 on 7 December 1985 at Laurel [Fred1]. No CBC trend in the number of wintering flickers is apparent, but a possible increase may be masked by yearly variation. The Seaford CBC for 1983–89 reported high numbers similar to those found on the Bombay Hook CBC.

BANDING: One bird banded in Ocean City, Maryland, on 13 September 1959 was recovered near Dover in early April 1962 [Usfw3].

SPECIMENS: 78; DMNH, CM, UDEL. Egg records: DMNH.

Pileated Woodpecker *(Dryocopus pileatus)*

Resident; uncommon. Found in forested sections, principally in the Chesapeake drainage of the western and southern parts of the state, also in wooded Piedmont valleys. Significantly increased during the twentieth century after having been nearly extirpated.

HABITAT: Large tracts of deciduous or mixed woods with large dead trees. Tracts do not need to be contiguous.

BREEDING: The reemergence of this big woodpecker in

Delaware occurred in the second half of the twentieth century as second-growth woods matured. The small population of Pileated Woodpeckers in the valleys of northern Delaware suggests that the species is tolerant of moderate suburban sprawl and is attracted to the old trees, woodlots, and parks that are preserved. A larger population in the Chesapeake drainage has adapted to second-growth woodland.

Atlas. Atlas records support the range reported by Ednie (1984), consisting of the White Clay Creek valley and extreme southern Delaware, and extend it to new locations. Pileated Woodpeckers were found in good habitat near Smalleys Pond (in northern New Castle County but south of the fall line) by local workmen [MiDP2]. They were found in 3 blocks in southern New Castle County, in Blackbird Forest by Atlas workers, and separately reported by the forester [Benn1]. The report from southeastern Kent County is from Milford Neck WA in June 1986 [Wees2]. One of the 2 reports in southeastern Sussex County came from Assawoman WA by the resident manager [Gano1]. The other was on 30 June 1985 from the upper bridge over Miller Creek where 1 responded to a tape recording [West3]. The Pileated Woodpecker occasionally occurs in northeastern Sussex County (e.g., once on the Cape Henlopen CBC), and it was reported there for the Atlas [Frec1].

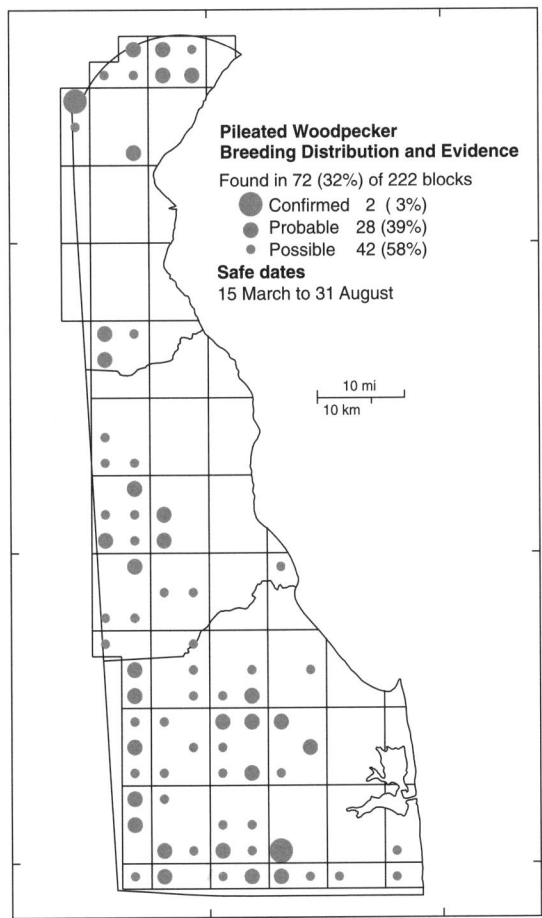

Pileated Woodpecker
Breeding Distribution and Evidence

Found in 72 (32%) of 222 blocks
- ● Confirmed 2 (3%)
- ● Probable 28 (39%)
- • Possible 42 (58%)

Safe dates
15 March to 31 August

10 mi
10 km

United States following land clearing of the early eras, but began a comeback in the 1920s and 1930s, seeming to adapt to second growth woodland and park areas in suburbs—it nested in 1974 on the New Jersey Palisades within sight of Manhattan's skyscrapers!"

Trends. Its range extension continues; 1 was reported in Indian Field in northeast New Castle County on 21 February 1990, so it may have returned to the Naaman Creek valley (Hamilton 1990). May Counts show that it increased in Delaware at about 6% per year since 1969, and BBS data show a 2% per year average increase in the East during 1966–90 [Usfw3].

Breeding population. The Pileated Woodpecker requires large territories, varying with the amount of dead wood available and the time of year. A study in hardwoods in Missouri found that home ranges varied from 0.2 to 0.6 sq mi (53 to 160 ha) and that ample canopy cover and dead wood were good predictors of small territories (Renken and Wiggers 1989). A study in a mixed ponderosa pine forest in Oregon shows that it required about 220 ha (almost a sq mi) home range containing some 45 large dead trees (Bull 1987). Stewart and Robbins (1958) reported 5 in 775 acres (1.6 per 100 ha) of flood-plain forest. Much of the Delaware forest is young and interspersed with fields, so it is unlikely that any Atlas block (2,500 ha) held as many as 10 pairs.

Conservation. Preserving hardwoods along creeks and natural corridors will help this species withstand further suburban development in New Castle County. Fallen trees and standing snags should not be removed, because they harbor insect larvae on which this species feeds.

1966–89 CBC Summary

Christmas Bird Count	Years Found	Range of No. Found	Median
Wilmington	14	1–7	1
Middletown			
Bombay Hook			
Cape Henlopen	1	2	
Rehoboth	4	1	
STATEWIDE (high in 1988)	15	1–7	7

Nesting. Three DOS nest records are on file: 1979, in a dead sycamore by White Clay Creek; 1983, in a dead tuliptree at Carpenter SP; and 1992, in a snag near White Clay Creek [MiDP3]. The eggs are laid in the bottom of a cavity, which usually has an oval opening. They appeared to be incubating about 1 May.

History. The nineteenth-century decline of this species was not entirely a result of clearing the land, though this surely had an effect. There is ample reference to how good this woodpecker tastes; it is about the size of a teal (Stoddard 1969). The earliest reference we have of occurrence in Delaware is from Krider (1879): "This bird is not very abundant in the Eastern and Middle States, but is very plenty in the South. I have shot it in Delaware, New Jersey, and Pennsylvania." Rhoads and Pennock (1905) say it is "still seen rarely throughout lower Delaware where the timber tracts are extensive," based on information garnered from local residents [Penn1]. Hanson's (notes) only reference from the 1920s and 1930s states that "Herbert Buckalew saw one in Ellendale Swamp February 10, 1931. Positive record." No reference is made to it in Barry's 1939 compilation, but in 1942 he described it as "Very rare. Occasional records in Kent and Sussex County."

Hoyt (1957) and Short (1982) describe the scarcity of Pileated Woodpeckers in the early twentieth century as a widespread phenomenon. The latter observed that "It became rare in the

WINTER: The Pileated Woodpecker has been recorded on 19 of the 120 CBCs analyzed. It is much more common on the recently started Seaford–Nanticoke CBC, where highs of 10 were reported in 1984 and 1987, than on other Delaware CBCs. This corresponds to the populations recorded on the nearby CBCs in Maryland (Falk 1978).

SPECIMEN: DMNH 75671, 3 mi (5 km) N Wilmington, 25 August 1984.

Olive-sided Flycatcher (*Contopus cooperi*)

Occasional (16 years, 1964–92); migrant; rare. Most frequently reported from the Piedmont and Bombay Hook NWR during May, August, and September.

DOCUMENTATION: Multiple sight records.

SPRING: The Olive-sided Flycatcher at Bombay Hook NWR on 7 May 1983 [Cutl8] was early for this late-arriving and irregular migrant. The latest date of a Delaware record for this species is 9 June 1973 when 1 was present at Delaware City [Beac11]. This is not unusually late for this species in the Mid-Atlantic region, but the lack of Delaware records between 22 May and 9 June is unexpected and illustrates the rarity and irregularity of this species in spring. All reports mention single birds.

FALL: Although this species occurs from late August into October, most reports refer to occurrences during September; a bird at Bombay Hook NWR on 29–30 August 1970 was erroneously cited as occurring in October [Park1]. Usually only 1 bird is found, but on 4 occasions 2 were reported. Early fall dates are

9 Aug 1969	1	Brandywine Creek SP [Broo31]
19 Aug 1973	1	Brandywine Creek SP [Phal5]

Late dates are

20 Sep 1981	1	Bombay Hook NWR [Kell4]
22 Sep 1979	1	Ashland [Ross2]
6 Oct 1991	1	Coastal Kent County [MagR2]

A series of reports from 28 August to 11 September 1976 suggests an individual remained in the White Clay Valley for 2 weeks [Lehm31].

HISTORY: Pennock listed the Olive-sided Flycatcher as a migrant at Rehoboth Beach in 1935 based on a bird identified by the West Chester Bird Club on 14 May 1927 [Penn1]. Barry (1942) also listed it as a migrant. The next dated Delaware report of this species comes from Hoopes Reservoir on 13 September 1964 [Howk1].

Eastern Wood-Pewee (*Contopus virens*)

Regular; summer resident; fairly common. Expected early May to early October. A widespread breeding bird that is apparently increasing.

HABITAT: Prefers deciduous woods but shows broad habitat acceptance, including wooded suburbs in northern Delaware and mixed woodlands in Sussex County. Likes to feed in high openings and woods margins at subcanopy height (Hespenheide 1971; Johnston 1971b).

SPRING: The first arrival is expected 1–10 May, a full month later than the arrival of Eastern Phoebes. By mid-May wood-pewees are fairly common. Early reports include

16 Apr 1967	1	Hockessin [Broo7]
23 Apr 1966	1	Wilmington area [Carr6]

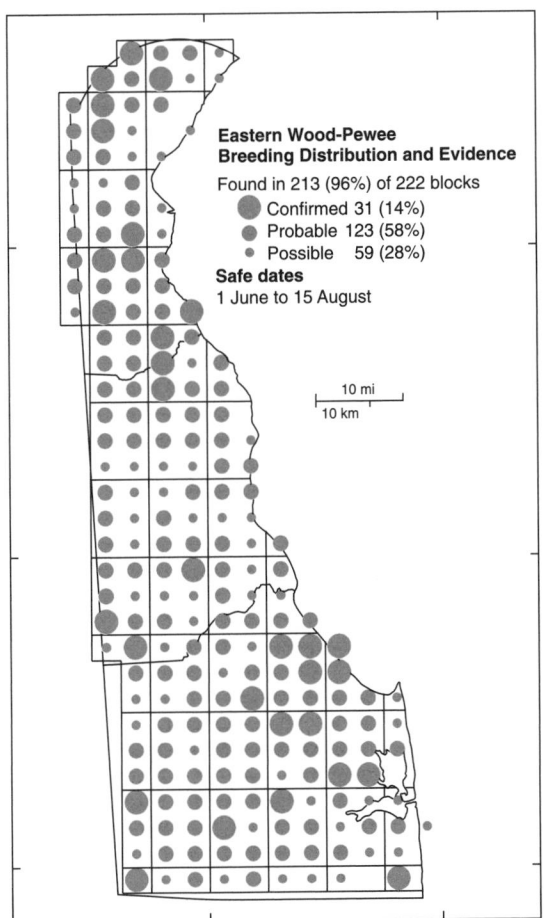

**Eastern Wood-Pewee
Breeding Distribution and Evidence**

Found in 213 (96%) of 222 blocks

● Confirmed 31 (14%)
● Probable 123 (58%)
· Possible 59 (28%)

Safe dates
1 June to 15 August

10 mi
10 km

**Eastern Wood-Pewee
Relative Abundance**

No. of 3-minute stops
(of 15) in June where
at least one was found:
519 of 3240 (16%)

10 mi
10 km

Two high counts from Bombay Hook NWR are 22 on 15 May 1982 [Kell11] and 15 on 22 May 1983 [Bayn4]. Usually only 1–4 birds are found in a day before mid-May; after that, 5–10. The highest statewide May Count is 144 on 14 May 1988, and the lowest 3 on 3 May 1980, reflecting the different stage of the migration for those dates rather than a population fluctuation.

BREEDING: One of our commoner flycatchers, likely to be heard in suburban back yards, the wood-pewee is about half as common in urban Delaware north of the Chesapeake and Delaware Canal as in the rest of the state, and it is more common in Kent County than in pine-forested Sussex County, indicating its preference for deciduous woodlands.

Atlas. During the Atlas project confirmation by locating a nest occurred in only 16 blocks, probably because the nests are well camouflaged and placed so high in trees. Wood-pewees are persistent songsters and were frequently upgraded to territorial on this basis.

Nesting. Hanson (notes) reported a nest with 3 well-incubated eggs on 26 June in a Dover orchard. It straddled a horizontal limb of a pear tree 7 ft above ground and was built of grass and covered with lichens so as to match the limb. It was imperfectly round outside, about 3 in. in diameter and 2 in. high. The inside was 2 in. across and ⅞ in. deep. This nest was unusually low but otherwise typical; most are 15–65 ft above ground (Harrison 1975).

Estimated clutch-completion dates (*n* = 9) range from 27 May [MiDR3] to 7 August; 5 were completed in mid-June. The August date was derived from a series of observations ending with the young about ready to fledge on 5 September [Frec3]. The wood-pewee is single brooded (Ehrlich et al. 1988), so this late date presumably represents renesting after 1 or more failure. Clutch sizes reported in Delaware are 3 or 2 (*n* = 7), but clutches of 4 are possible (Harrison 1978). One nest in Dover had 3 eggs plus 1 cowbird egg on 18 June [Buck1].

Trends. Clearing of dense woods has probably benefited this

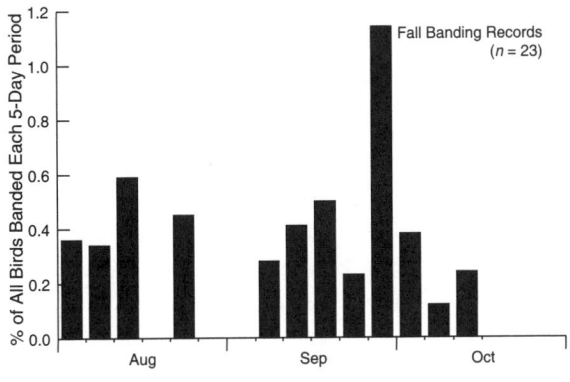

Fall Migration Activity

species by providing edge habitat (Rising 1987). The May Count shows it strongly increasing in Delaware since 1969; consequently, this Neotropical migrant does not appear to be at risk. During 1966–90 its population on the BBS shows a slight but significant average annual decline in the East, but not a significant decline in Delaware [Usfw3]. Some decline might have been expected as a result of urbanization along roadsides during this period.

Breeding population. Breeding population densities in good habitat (males per 100 ha):

33 (3-year average of 3.2 in 24 acres) in coastal lowland mixed woods in Sussex County (Linehan 1969a)

40 (5-year average of 5.4 in 35.6 acres) in uneven-aged mixed hardwoods (Urban woodlot) in New Castle County (Jones 1970)

In ideal habitat it reaches densities of 25–50 pairs per 100 ha in Maryland, West Virginia, and Ontario (Stewart and Robbins 1958; Hall 1983; Speirs 1985; respectively). The Delaware BBSs average 3.7 birds per route, fewer than in Maryland or Pennsylvania, but more than in New Jersey [Usfw3]

FALL: Migration begins in late August, peaks between 25 August and 25 September, and concludes by 1–7 October. Peak numbers of wood-pewees are banded during 25–30 September. Late reports include

12 Oct 1967	2	near Newark [Line15]
13 Oct 1966	1	banded north of Rehoboth Beach [RusW1]
18 Oct 1982	1	Delaware Seashore SP [Wees3]
21 Oct 1978	1	Ashland [Broo18]

Any bird seen after 7 October should be carefully documented to distinguish it from much later departing Eastern Phoebes.

SPECIMENS: DMNH 70378, Delaware City, 17 May 1980; DMNH 74230, Laurel, 23 May 1983; ANSP 79947, Kent Co., Choptank, 27 May 1911; DMNH 35695, Redden SF, 14 July 1971; DMNH 71167, Centerville, 8 September 1980.

Yellow-bellied Flycatcher (*Empidonax flaviventris*)

Occasional (12 years, 1964–89); migrant; rare. Reported mostly in September when identification is difficult and status uncertain.

HABITAT: Deciduous woods.

REMARKS: Specimens were obtained on 26 May 1982 at Centerville (DMNH 72394) and 24 September 1983 near Newark (DMNH 75344). Four records in May, when the species is reasonably identifiable in the field, lack descriptions. Twelve fall banding records are available. Information on in-hand identification of fall flycatchers has been available for many years (e.g., Coues 1903; Mengel 1952); therefore, we accept past *Empidonax* banding records but would prefer records citing the method of identification. Only Knowles noted that a banded bird was identified by using the EBBA Workshop Manual. Linehan's records are accepted because any bird whose identification he doubted was recorded as an unidentified *Empidonax*. Fall sight records have not been accepted because fall birds are extremely difficult to identify in the field. Recently, detailed information on identifying members of this difficult group has become widely available (e.g., Kaufman 1990). As observers become familiar with, and gain skill in using, this information reports should become more reliable and the migration status clarified. Nevertheless, at this time we are reluctant to accept fall *Empidonax* sight records without supporting notes, which in addition to describing visual characteristics should also include a description of any vocalizations. Since no existing sight record is supported by field notes, all are unsatisfactory.

The difficulty in distinguishing the Yellow-bellied from the Acadian Flycatcher and the low number of Yellow-bellied specimens available prevent a complete determination of its status in the state, especially during fall. No seasonal graph has been prepared.

Based on the specimen and fall banding records this species has occurred between 16 August (adult) and 24 September (immature). The first acceptable state record is probably a bird banded 4 September 1964 [StiA6]; the first specimen, 26 May 1982.

SPECIMENS: 2; DMNH 72393, DMNH 75344, details above.

Yellow-bellied Flycatcher Banding Records

Date	Age	Locality	Bander
16 Aug 1965	adult	UDEL woodlot, Newark	J. T. Linehan
27 Aug 1970	immature	UDEL woodlot, Newark	R. E. Jones
1 Sep 1970	immature	UDEL woodlot, Newark	R. E. Jones
1 Sep 1970	unknown	UDEL woodlot, Newark	R. E. Jones
1 Sep 1970	unknown	UDEL woodlot, Newark	R. E. Jones
1 Sep 1970	unknown	UDEL woodlot, Newark	R. E. Jones
4 Sep 1964	immature	Delaware City	J. T. Linehan
4 Sep 1965	unknown	near Hockessin	R. N. Knowles
7 Sep 1967	immature	UDEL woodlot, Newark	J. T. Linehan
11 Sep 1966	immature, sang	near Rehoboth Beach	W. C. Russell
14 Sep 1967	unknown	UDEL woodlot, Newark	J. T. Linehan
24 Sep 1966	immature	near Rehoboth Beach	W. C. Russell

Acadian Flycatcher *(Empidonax virescens)*

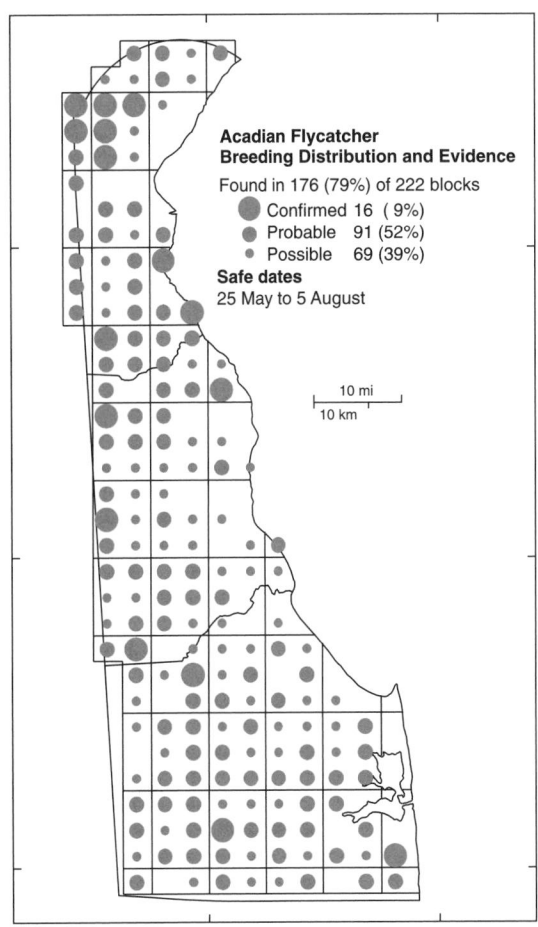

Acadian Flycatcher
Breeding Distribution and Evidence
Found in 176 (79%) of 222 blocks
● Confirmed 16 (9%)
● Probable 91 (52%)
• Possible 69 (39%)
Safe dates
25 May to 5 August

10 mi
10 km

Regular; summer resident; fairly common. Expected early May to mid-September. Widespread but recently declining breeding bird. Almost entirely dependent on wetland forest.

| | | | | | | | | | | | |
|J|F|M|A|M|J|J|A|S|O|N|D|

HABITAT: Mesic deciduous woods with closed canopy, primarily in palustrine wetlands. Feeds in openings beneath a dense canopy, typically provided by streamside growth with open understory above the stream and the adjacent floodplain kept open by periodic flooding.

SPRING: This small flycatcher usually arrives rather abruptly during 1–7 May; however, peak numbers are not reached until about mid-month. It arrives about 1 week earlier than the Willow Flycatcher, the other regularly breeding *Empidonax*. The earliest reports (which should have been documented) are

20 Apr 1976	1	White Clay Creek [Edni14]
22 Apr 1990	1	White Clay Creek [Barn57]
28 Apr 1991	1	Bombay Hook NWR [Hess13]
29 Apr 1989	1	Lums Pond SP [Litt1]

The end of migration cannot be determined clearly from available data but probably falls in late May. Peak counts from White Clay Creek are 28 on 22 May 1976, 27 on 20 May 1978, and 18 on 13 May 1978 [BroH8; Falk11; Dyer7]. The highest May Count is 83 (13 May 1989), and the lowest 11 (5 May 1973 and 4 May 1985).

BREEDING: This forest flycatcher's overall distribution correlates well with the forested parts of the state. The relative abundance study shows its population is about twice as dense in western Kent and Sussex counties as in New Castle County.

Atlas. Acadians can be located during the breeding season by listening along streams for their song. Few nests were found during the Atlas period, but the species was easily upgraded to probably breeding by hearing it sing on territory.

Nesting. It often builds its nest over a wooded stream, but occasionally substitutes a quiet road or path for the stream. Hanson (notes) describes "a nest found June 4, 1927, in deep woods at Pearsons Corner, about fifteen feet from the ground suspended in the fork of a small branch in a small [black] tupelo tree about 4 inches in diameter. The nest was out on the branch about 4 ft. The nest is somewhat irregular in shape and is 4 inches across and 2 inches deep outside, while the opening is 1¾ inches in diameter and one inch deep. It is made of a foundation of tiny sticks or roots, with some plant down, but the most conspicuous part is the oak flowers, or aments, with which the whole nest is both lined inside and covered outside. Many of the aments hang down like a fringe for three to four inches and the whole nest is brown." This nest is fairly typical, but the embellishment varies with the plant materials available.

Estimated clutch-completion dates extend from 21 May to 18 June, with 9 of the 14 dates falling in the last third of May. It

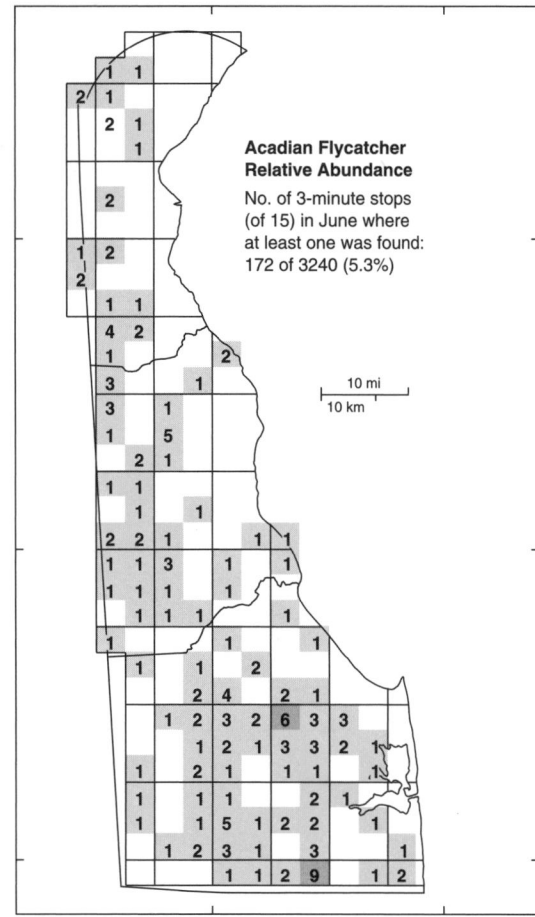

Acadian Flycatcher Relative Abundance

No. of 3-minute stops (of 15) in June where at least one was found: 172 of 3240 (5.3%)

10 mi
10 km

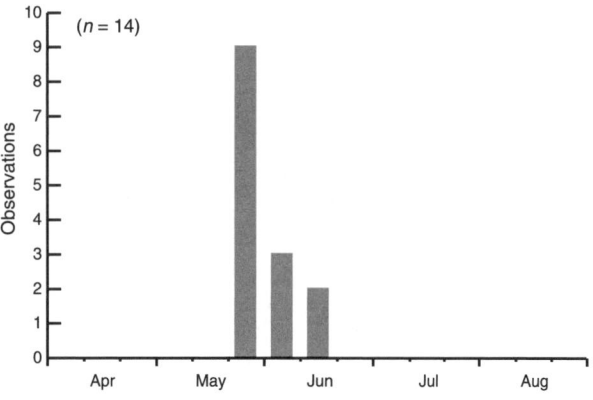

Estimated Clutch-Completion Dates

Breeding population. A high summer count of 49 was reported along White Clay Creek on 3 June 1978 during a survey [SpSB35], and a BBC conducted there in 1970 reported a density of 40 territories per 100 ha (4 in 25 acres) (West 1970). Territory size was small and corresponded well with the average sizes of 1.2 and 1.0 ha observed in Michigan (Walkinshaw 1966a; Mumford 1964).

Conservation. Deforestation, drainage of freshwater swamps, and channelization of streams, mainly in the last 4 decades, have all drastically reduced its habitat. The drainage divides in Sussex County offer examples of wetlands that have been converted to farms where the few remaining streams now flow intermittently in ditches; few Acadian Flycatchers remain in such habitat.

FALL: Migration probably begins mid- or late August. In most years all leave by 10–20 September. The reduction in reported numbers beginning mid-August probably reflects the cessation of singing and the prudent refusal of many observers to identify nonsinging fall *Empidonaces.* Peak reports include

28 Aug 1976	13	White Clay Creek [Lehm34]
12 Sep 1971	9	Brandywine Creek SP [BroW17]
19 Sep 1970	8	Brandywine Creek SP [Beac6]

The latest reports include

22 Sep 1974	1	White Clay Creek [Lehm1]
24 Sep 1977	1	White Clay Creek [SpSB36]
3 Oct 1970	2	Brandywine Creek SP [Ward10]

Lehman's identification on 22 September included hearing its voice; later reports should be carefully documented.

REMARKS: See the Yellow-bellied Flycatcher account for cautions about fall *Empidonax* sight records.

SPECIMENS: 14; DMNH, ANSP, UWBM. Egg records: WFVZ.

may be occasionally double-brooded in Delaware, as in Michigan (Walkinshaw 1966a), but the available records do not show an extended breeding season to support this conclusion. Clutch size is normally 3 (*n* = 9; range 2–4), but 1 brood of 4 was observed on 20 June 1965 [Know2].

Trends. BBS data suggest that it declined sharply in Delaware during the 1980s, in contrast to its generally stable population in the East [Usfw3].

Alder Flycatcher (*Empidonax alnorum*)

Occasional (6 years, 1973–91); migrant; rare.

OCCURRENCE: Eight records range from 17 May to 22 June and may include some misidentifications. A description of vocalizations for the Gordon record [Gord1] states that the Alder Flycatcher song was compared directly to that of a nearby Willow Flycatcher. Three other identifications were based on vocalizations. In addition, 1 heard at Bombay Hook NWR on 25 May 1987 included direct comparison of the song with that of a nearby Willow Flycatcher [Barn58].

Summer reports are perplexing and may involve late migrants and misidentifications. No evidence suggests that this species breeds in Delaware, despite the fact that Barry (1942) listed it as "summer resident." Pennock (notes) recorded the species as "hypothetical" based on a West Chester Bird Club identification of 1 on 14 May 1927 at Rehoboth Beach.

One fall migrant has been reported, without details, and so must be regarded as uncorroborated.

REMARKS: The song of the Alder Flycatcher may be con-fused with a nonburry two-note call of the Acadian Flycatcher. In Delaware there is little opportunity to gain experience with the Alder's songs.

A recent study casts doubt on the technique used to separate Alder and Willow flycatchers in the hand (Seutin 1991), complicating interpretation of the available records. More reports of flycatchers that have been carefully identified by vocalization are clearly needed.

SPECIMEN: DMNH 72436, Centerville, 21 May 1982.

Alder Flycatcher Records

Date	How Identified	Location, Reference
17 May 1980	sight	White Clay Creek [Wayn37]
21 May 1982	specimen	Centerville (DMNH 72436)
24 May 1980	?	Churchmans Marsh [Samp7]
25 May 1987	voice	Bombay Hook NWR [Barn21]
31 May 1980	voice	Bombay Hook NWR [Gord6]
1 Jun 1973	voice	Bombay Hook NWR [Holg82]
15 Jun 1974	?	Dragon Run [Wayn55]
22 Jun 1974	voice	Brandywine Creek SP [Mars2]
24 Aug 1991	?	Brandywine Creek SP (Campbell 1992)

Willow Flycatcher (*Empidonax traillii*)

Regular; uncommon; summer resident. Expected mid-May to late July, probably into September. Twentieth-century addition to state avifauna, invading from the West.

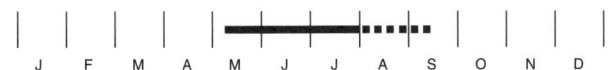

HABITAT: Wet thickets, particularly willow; open areas. Shrub-scrub wetlands. Found typically on the marsh side of the last fields before reaching the river marshes or in willow thickets in untilled depressions and ditches near such fields. Found in open or spoil areas along the Chesapeake and Delaware Canal, and, less commonly, in the Piedmont in open wet scrub.

SPRING: Because this species is seldom recorded before 15 May, any migrant before 10 May should be carefully examined and the report supported with field notes. One reported on 3 May 1980 (in Rufe 1980) is improbably early. More credible early reports include

12 May 1979	1	Ashland [Line20]
14 May 1983	1	Bombay Hook NWR [PieJ1]
14 May 1992	1	Burrows Run [SpeE11]

Migration continues through the first week of June, after which numbers markedly decrease. Peak counts are

15 May 1982	9	Bombay Hook NWR [Kell11]
22 May 1983	5	Bombay Hook NWR [Bayn4])
26 May 1979	8	Ashland [Wayn56]

The Willow Flycatcher was never recorded on the statewide May Count until 12 May 1979; since then it has been found on those counts conducted after 10 May.

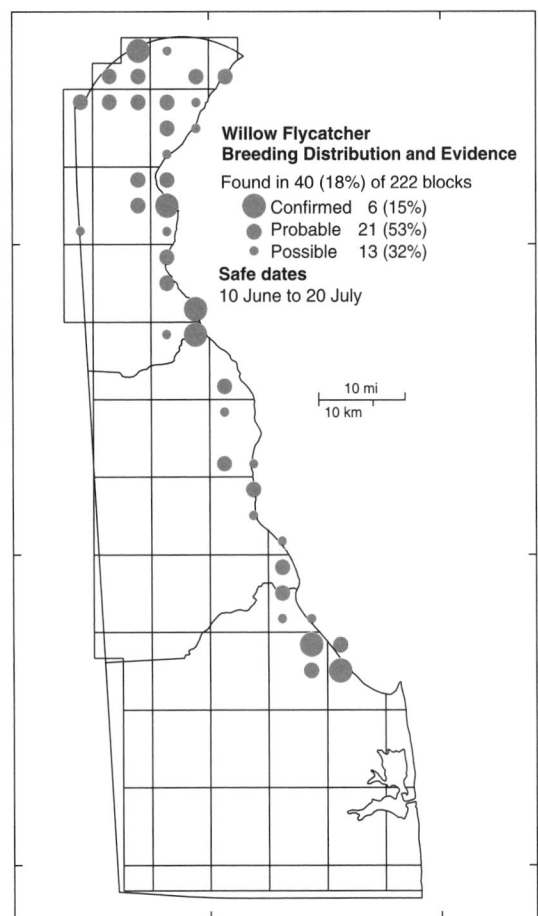

**Willow Flycatcher
Breeding Distribution and Evidence**

Found in 40 (18%) of 222 blocks

● Confirmed 6 (15%)
● Probable 21 (53%)
· Possible 13 (32%)

Safe dates
10 June to 20 July

10 mi
10 km

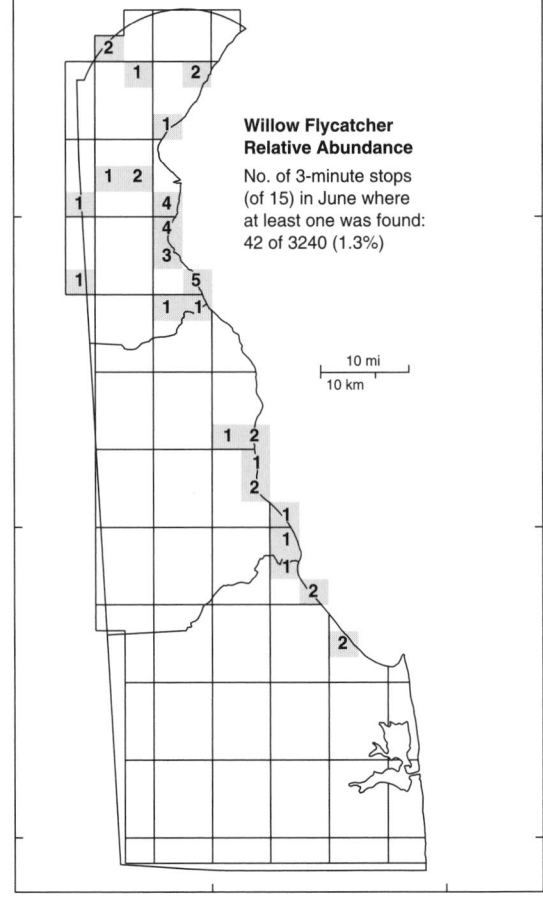

**Willow Flycatcher
Relative Abundance**

No. of 3-minute stops
(of 15) in June where
at least one was found:
42 of 3240 (1.3%)

10 mi
10 km

BREEDING: This flycatcher breeds in the Delaware Piedmont, along the Chesapeake and Delaware Canal, and along the Delaware River south to Prime Hook NWR.

Atlas. The extensive distribution that emerged from the Atlas project was unexpected. The species was probably missed in about 10 riverside and canal blocks because there was insufficient opportunity, once its habitat preferences were known, to arrange access to private marsh and riverfront property. One block near Townsend shows a Willow Flycatcher on the relative abundance map that is not repeated on the distribution map. This bird was found on 28 May 1986 [West3], 3 days before the safe dates and so too early to be recorded as possibly breeding by the Atlas project. Five confirmations resulted from finding the nest, 1 from seeing the adult carrying food.

Nesting. Miller and Linehan observed a Willow Flycatcher (*fitz-bew* song type) building a nest at Thompsons Bridge, White Clay Creek, on 12 June 1972 (Dyer et al. 1993). It was in a brushy floodplain field. The cup was 4 ft above ground in a tangle of rose, grape vine, and green ash. The second attempted nesting was observed 6–27 June 1974 when a pair built a nest at the same location 4 ft above ground in an elderberry, completing it on 12 June [Jahn1]. A pair was reported nesting at Dragon Run on 31 May 1975 [Wayn48] and was subsequently found there on 1, 7, and 14 June [BroW7; Wayn25; Mars3, respectively. Niles [Nile2] reported the first nest with eggs on

22 June 1980 and found the earliest clutch on 14 June 1981 (4 eggs hatched 21 June).

The estimated clutch-completion period (*n* = 8) is 7–24 June (5 were completed 13–17 June). Clutch size is 3 or 4 (*n* = 3). Nests are placed 4–8 ft above ground in locust, elderberry, bayberry, or sumac. The nest is described as compact, resembling that of a goldfinch or Yellow Warbler, and frequently placed in a willow or rose (Abbott 1959; Stein 1963).

History. Willow and Alder flycatchers were long regarded as conspecific. The Willow Flycatcher is a recent arrival, though its date of initial breeding has never been established. Presumably it expanded eastward after forests were cut and favorable habitat provided. In the 1930s 2 song types were recognized, the *fitz-bew* of the Willow Flycatcher and the *wee-bee-o* of the Alder Flycatcher, and it was recognized that birds with the *fitz-bew* song type were spreading eastward out of Ohio at the expense of those with the *wee-bee-o* song type. The *fitz-bew* song type had arrived near Philadelphia and in eastern Maryland by the early 1960s (Stein 1963, 25–27) and bred in the District of Columbia in 1959 (Abbott 1959), so its discovery in Delaware in the 1960s was not unanticipated.

Little mention of this flycatcher group was made in Delaware before the 1960s. Hanson (notes) had no report. Pennock (1935) included "Traill's" Flycatcher (migrant) in a list of 275 birds seen at Rehoboth Beach. Barry (1939) reported

"Alder" as a "recent observation" and later (1942) as a "summer resident." These pre-1960s records must be treated with caution, since the Alder may never have summered in Delaware, and the Willow had not arrived here by the 1940s, though it was then displacing the Alder in upstate New York (Bonney and Burrill 1988).

Only a few records before 1973 clearly apply to this species, but June observations from its present breeding range probably refer to breeding Willow Flycatchers and help trace its arrival in Delaware. Stickley's [StiA1] "singing 'Traill's' Flycatcher at Bombay Hook Refuge, Del." on 9 June 1961 was singing the Willow's song (pers. comm.). Linehan banded 4 "Traill's" Flycatchers near Red Lion Creek in late July 1962, 1 a hatching-year bird [Usfw3]; most likely these were locally breeding Willow Flycatchers (Linehan 1964). "A 'Traill's' Flycatcher [was] found June 3 and 12 [1968] at Lums Pond" [Lehm7]. Linehan (notes) found a "Traill's" Flycatcher at White Clay Creek in early July of 1969 and 1971. Miller and Linehan observed a Willow Flycatcher building a nest at Thompsons Bridge, White Clay Creek, on 12 June 1972, adding that a Willow Flycatcher had responded to a tape recording of the Willow song there in 1970 (Dyer et al. 1973). Several young "Alder" Flycatchers were banded at Red Lion Creek in July 1972 by Paul Schwabe [Schw3]; if local birds, they were likely Willows.

Its presence in summer was regularly reported beginning in 1973, the year the AOU recognized the Willow Flycatcher as a separate species (AOU 1973). Holgersen reported it at Little Creek WA on 17 (or 7) June and 8 July 1973, at Bombay Hook NWR on 23 July 1973 [Holg82], and Lehman reported it in the Piedmont on 16 July 1973 [Lehm12]. *Fitz-bew* song types were reported at Little Creek WA on 19 May and 2 June 1974 [DuPA5], and 1 was apparently holding a territory near Trap Pond SP on 29 June 1974 [Lehm9].

Trends. Its increase was noted in 1982 as follows: "Delaware had 10 pairs where 3–4 were known a few years ago" [Cutl35], and its population continued to increase in the East in the 1980s [Usfw1]. All indicators suggest that it has increased sharply in Delaware since 1973.

Breeding population. The state population exceeds 100 pairs, based on its presence in 40 blocks. Territories average 1–2 acres in Ontario and Michigan (Prescott 1986; Walkinshaw 1966b).

Conservation. Although the declining western population of Willow Flycatcher is cause for concern (Taylor and Littlefield 1986), its expanding eastern and Delaware populations do not require management.

FALL: The fall migration is poorly known, being based on 4 reports from August and 2 from the first week of September. Eight banding records of "Traill's" Flycatcher from 1964 to 1970 occur during 10–30 September (6 are 10–20 September). These are late compared with data from studies farther north where Willows leave their breeding grounds in August; thus at least some records may actually be Alders. Hussell's (1991) banding studies at Long Point Bird Observatory, Ontario, show

the median migration dates for adult Willow and Alder flycatchers to be 8 and 15 August, respectively; for immatures, 23 and 28 August. Thus Willow Flycatchers migrate earlier than Alders, and adults of either species migrate earlier by 2 weeks than immatures.

REMARKS: See the Yellow-bellied Flycatcher account for cautions about fall *Empidonax* sight records and Seutin (1991) for problems in separating Willows and Alders in the hand. The *Empidonax* flycatchers are difficult to identify in the field now and were more so earlier in the twentieth century when binoculars were poorer, recordings unavailable, and ranges and habitat preference not fully understood. Identification in the hand was difficult without a reference collection. In 1973 the AOU recognized the 2 species, Willow Flycatcher and Alder Flycatcher (AOU 1973), and recommended the use of "Traill's Flycatcher" for the superspecies complex. Aldrich (1953) pointed out the differences in nests and nest situations used by the 2 populations. The split is based primarily on research by Stein (1958, 1963). However, a recent study has cast some doubt on Stein's method of in-hand identification (Seutin 1991), leaving room for doubt about the identity of some banded birds. Descriptions of field identifications should include song and calls.

SPECIMENS: UDEL 103-66, Newark, 13 May 1966; DMNH 70380, Delaware City, 21 May 1980; DMNH 72436, Centerville, 25 May 1982; DMNH 65653, Delaware City, 30 May 1979; DMNH 72554, 1.4 mi (2.3 km) W, 1 mi (1.6 km) S Delaware City, 3 June 1982.

Least Flycatcher *(Empidonax minimus)*

Regular, at least formerly (22 years, 1928–91); spring migrant; formerly uncommon and now rare. Probably still a regular fall migrant; uncommon, but current status uncertain. Bred at least once in the Piedmont, but now extirpated as a breeding bird.

HABITAT: Open deciduous woodland.

SPRING: The migration period of this species is not clear. Spring arrival, in years when it is detected, occurs in early May. The lone April report represents a bird singing on 20 April 1967 along White Clay Creek at Thompsons Bridge where the species had nested the previous year [Line13]. One was collected in Wilmington on 11 May 1974 (DMNH 40744). One to 5 have been reported on 11 May Counts during 1973–90. Spring departure remains equally unclear, being obscured by a lack of reports in many years, by individuals present well into June in others, and by at least 1 breeding record.

The numbers of spring migrants may have changed during the twentieth century. It was not included in the list of 231 species by Pennock (1908b). Hanson (notes) lists only an encounter with "One . . . near Camden May 11, 1928." However, Barry (1939) lists it as a fairly numerous migrant as does Conway (1943) for Chester County, Pennsylvania. Furthermore, it seemed common in the early 1970s—12 were reported on 13 May 1972 on the May Count—but it has decreased since then.

BREEDING: The only breeding record of this species is a nest with 4 eggs on 12 May 1966 near White Clay Creek at Thompsons Bridge [Cutl37] in floodplain scrub of a reverting field. Two or more reports through several summers are the only other evidence of breeding. It no longer occurs in Delaware in summer, though it is a rare breeder in southeastern Pennsylvania in the Carolinian life zone (Mulvihill 1992c; Poole 1964).

Atlas. During the Atlas project it was seen on 17 May and 6

June 1986 at Bombay Hook NWR [Barn1]. These observations could be construed as a possible breeding record for the Atlas project, but this bird was not found on subsequent trips, and Least Flycatchers rarely breed southeast of the Pennsylvania mountains (Mulvihill 1992c).

History. The first suggestion of its nesting arises from a series of sightings in 1945 at Hoopes Reservoir: 12 May, 30 May, 16 June, and 29 July. Two were seen on each of the last 2 dates (Hoff in Falk 1971). Least Flycatchers were seen on 3 occasions in May 1964 on White Clay Creek, the last being 4 found by Stickley on 17 May [StiA2]. Two others were seen on 6 June 1964 at Hoopes Reservoir (Falk 1971); the belief at the time was that these birds represented a breeding pair.

Trends. The Least Flycatcher population in the East has decreased an average of 1.6% annually during 1966–90 [Usfw1]. Much of this decline has been in New England and the Adirondacks (Wiedenfeld et al. 1992), locations where our migrants may breed.

Conservation. This flycatcher was included in the Blue List for 1980 (Tate 1981) but is not listed for protection in any northeastern state. The presence of orchards may have encouraged its southward spread earlier in the twentieth century; with unsprayed orchards now a rarity, it has become less common.

Least Flycatcher Breeding Season Reports
(numbers in parentheses indicate number of birds if more than 1)

1944, Hoopes Reservoir, 7, 30 May (2); 8, 27 Aug (2) (Falk 1971)
1945, Hoopes Reservoir, 12, 30 May; 16 Jun (2); 29 July (2) (Falk 1971)
1964, Hoopes Reservoir, 6 Jun (2) (Falk 1971)
1964, White Clay Creek, 3 May [Line16]; 17 May (4) [StiA2], 21 Jun (2) [StiA3]
1966, White Clay Creek, 12 May, nest with 4 eggs [Cutl30]
1967, University Farm, "visitor" during BBC (Linehan et al. 1967)
1968–72, White Clay Creek, early July each year [Line1]
1972, Winterthur, 8, 28 July (Falk 1977)
1976, White Clay Creek, 15, 22, 29 May; 12, 26 Jun; 10, 31 Jul (Speck and Brokaw 1979)
1977, White Clay Creek, 7, 14, 28 May; 4 Jun (Speck and Brokaw 1979)
1981, Bombay Hook NWR, 7 Jun [Edni41]; 15 Jun (B. and F. Haas 1983); 27 Jun [HaaB1]

FALL: The following is a comparison of the distribution of banding records during fall migration from northern Delaware [Line5; Jone2; RusW1] with Frech's (notes) regular survey records from coastal Sussex County:

Period	Banded	Frech
9–15 Aug	1	3
16–23 Aug	1	5
24–31 Aug	0	5
1–7 Sep	5	6
8–14 Sep	9	4
15–22 Sep	10	2
After 23 Sep	2	3
Total no. of records	25	28
Date range	9 Aug–29 Sep	9 Aug–4 Oct

The distribution of the banding data is based on in-hand identifications, but suffers from much reduced effort in August; for example, only 30% as much in August as in September of 1964 and 1967 (Linehan 1964, 1965b, 1969c). Frech's data arises from consistent field effort, but required more difficult field identifications. Frech's results, suggesting peak migration from mid-August to mid-September, is consistent with the migration dates found in Cape May County, New Jersey (Sibley 1993), Maryland (Robbins and Bystrak 1977), and the Northeast (Hus-

sell 1980). Delaware coastal migrants are expected to be hatching-year birds, because the adults take a more inland route and migrate mainly in July (Hussell 1980). Latest reports are

29 Sep 1967	1 immature	University Woodlot [Line5]
3 Oct 1992	1	Cape Henlopen SP [Barn38]
4 Oct 1981	1	Cape Henlopen SP [Frec1]

REMARKS: See the Yellow-bellied Flycatcher account and Kaufman (1990) for cautions about fall *Empidonax* sight records.
SPECIMEN: DMNH 40744, Wilmington, 11 May 1974.

Hammond's Flycatcher *(Empidonax hammondii)*

Accidental (1986).

REMARKS: The single report describes a bird present on the Bombay Hook CBC on 21 December 1986 [RusK1] (Russell 1988). It was relocated about 1 mi south of Woodland Beach on 24 December in poor condition (DMNH 76370) and identified as an immature female by M. B. Robbins.

Since Hammond's Flycatcher is a bird of the montane western United States, this record represents a bird wandering east instead of south during the fall. Two other eastern specimens exist—Ocean City, Maryland, on 9 October 1963 (Gibson

1987); and Lehigh County, Pennsylvania, on 23 December 1966 (Heintzelman 1968). An *Empidonax* flycatcher observed in Norfolk County, Massachusetts, during 19–29 December 1988 was identified as a Hammond's after being captured and videotaped (Veit and Petersen 1993), and another tentatively identified as Hammond's stayed in Monmouth County, New Jersey, during 1–17 December 1983 (Wander and Brady 1984). Two Louisiana specimens may be the only other records east of the Great Plains (Gibson 1987).

SPECIMEN: DMNH 76370, details earlier.

[Gray Flycatcher *(Empidonax wrightii)*]

Accidental (1991).

DOCUMENTATION: Photograph (DMNH).

REMARKS: On 6 December 1991 Frech (notes) found a Gray Flycatcher near the entrance to Ft. Miles in Cape Henlopen SP. It was seen later by W. A. Fintel (notes), W. and N. Murphy and J. Dunn [MurW4], Barnhill (brief notes), and many other observers. It was present on the 22 December Cape Henlopen CBC (J. F. White notes) but was not reported later.

All observers agreed on the slow, "phoebe-like" tail movements, on the size being large for an *Empidonax,* and on the overall light, gray appearance. Frech and Fintel observed the 2-toned bill, with the lower mandible light at the base and dark at the tip. Other observers missed the black tip but noted the dark upper mandible. The chest was gray, slightly striped, and slightly darker along the sides, and Fintel found that the belly was very slightly yellowish in good light. No observer specifically commented on the sharpness of the transition between light and dark on the bill. The *American Birds* report states that it responded to tapes of Gray Flycatcher calls. The photograph confirms the general descriptions but is too small to show the bill color clearly. The bird ranged over a moderately undulating

area of low bushes and stunted pines growing in sand on the edge of the "Great Dune," a few hundred yards from the ocean. The area is somewhat comparable to an arid open conifer breeding habitat of the Gray Flycatcher (AOU 1983).

There can be no question that the bird was an *Empidonax* flycatcher. The movement of the tail supports Gray Flycatcher, and that conclusion is supported by the size and coloration, but the absence of a specific observation of the sharpness of the color change between the base and tip of the lower mandible means that the best field character was not observed.

This vagrant from west of the Rockies was first collected on the East Coast in Littleton, Massachusetts, on 31 October 1969 (Veit and Petersen 1993). Another Gray Flycatcher was netted in Toronto, Ontario, on 11 September 1981, examined in detail in the hand, and photographed (Godfrey 1986).

Eastern Phoebe (*Sayornis phoebe*)

Regular; summer resident; uncommon. Expected mid-March through October and sporadically into early winter. Breeds early, often on man-made structures; appears to be increasing.

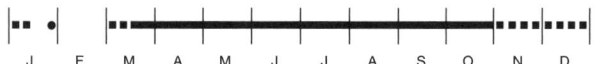

J F M A M J J A S O N D

HABITAT: Open woods; nests primarily under bridges, but also under eaves and in outbuildings.

SPRING: First arrival is usually during mid-March. Hesselius, an early Swedish minister, wrote in his diary, "Anno 1722, February 23" [6 March 1723, new style], "was heard for the first time this year the little bird [phoebe], . . . which of all birds gives the first sign of spring" (Hesselius 1947 [1712], 115). These more recent observations are only slightly earlier:

| 28 Feb 1992 | 2 | Burrows Run [SpeE11] |
| 2 Mar 1991 | 1 | Sandtown [Camp15] |

The end of migration probably occurs in late April. Peak numbers are from late March to early April

27 Mar 1989	10	Cape Henlopen SP [Frec1]
3 Apr 1965	12	Churchmans Marsh [SpSB6]
4 Apr 1964	14	Hoopes Reservoir [Falk19]

BREEDING: This flycatcher is widespread but uncommon. The relative abundance study shows that it is almost half again as abundant in Sussex County as in the upper counties.

Atlas. Although uncommon, it was registered in most blocks, because it frequently puts its nest under a bridge or eaves or in an outbuilding. Persistent searching might have led to its discovery in some of the 37 blocks from which it is missing, since there is no pattern to the blocks where it was missed. It was confirmed frequently, usually by finding the nest.

Nesting. All Delaware reports describe nests on man-made

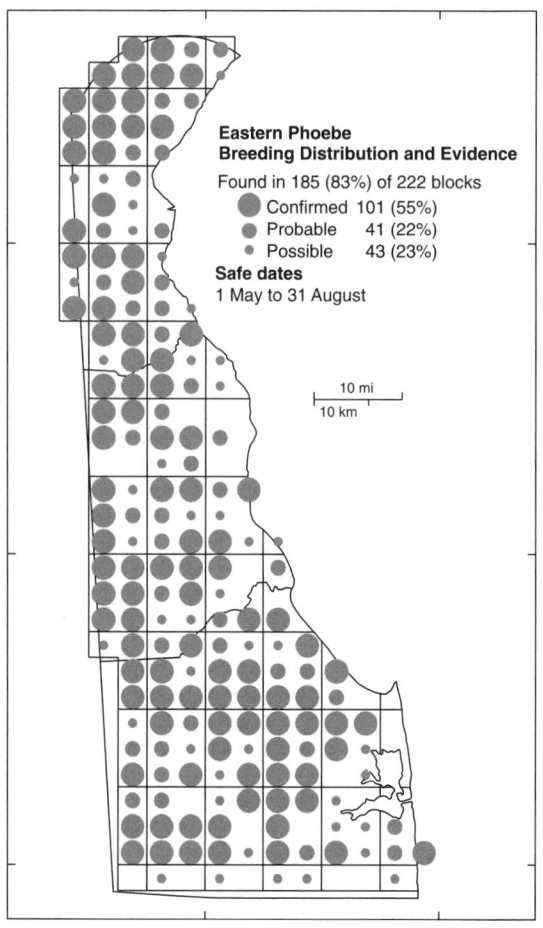

**Eastern Phoebe
Breeding Distribution and Evidence**
Found in 185 (83%) of 222 blocks
● Confirmed 101 (55%)
● Probable 41 (22%)
● Possible 43 (23%)
Safe dates
1 May to 31 August

10 mi
10 km

structures. Its "natural" nest site is a niche on a rocky cliff (Tyler 1942), so it must have been a very rare breeder in early Delaware. Nest sites are within 30 yds (25 m) of a sizable woods. Placement under concrete bridges is preferred. Cowbirds parasitized 33% of the nests in natural locations but only 3% on artificial structures in Indiana (Weeks 1979) and, in contrast, 25% under bridges in Kansas (Klaas 1975). Only 1 pair breeds per site, so the availability of suitable structures for nests limits its population level (Weeks 1979).

Phoebes, like Barn Swallows, build nests of mud and straw in a sheltered place; the phoebe's nest tends to be neater, deeper, lower from the ceiling, and lined with plant fibers rather than feathers.

In Delaware first clutches are completed by mid- to late April, similar to clutch-completion dates in Kansas and Indiana (Klaas 1975; Weeks 1978). Second broods should follow about 45 days later, in late May or early June, whereas nests started earlier in May mainly represent renesting after failure. The 45-day cycle does not allow time for a third brood (Eaton 1988). Although our data show the last Delaware clutches being completed in late June, egg-laying probably continues into July.

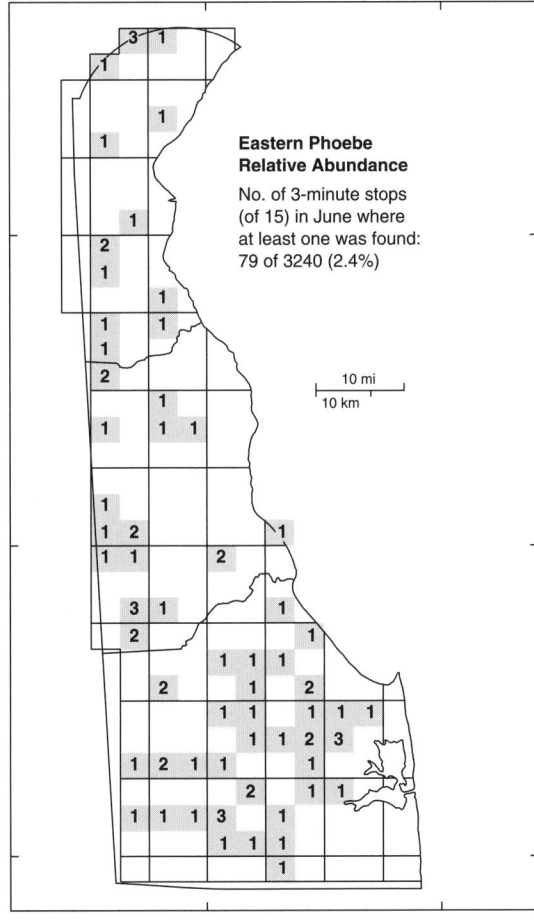

Eastern Phoebe Relative Abundance

No. of 3-minute stops (of 15) in June where at least one was found: 79 of 3240 (2.4%)

10 mi
10 km

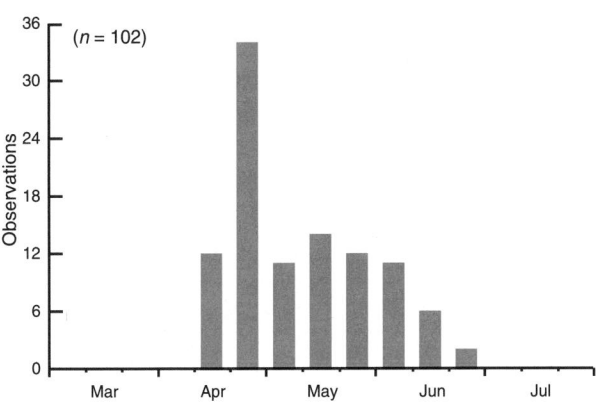

(n = 102)

Estimated Clutch-Completion Dates

Extreme egg dates extend only from 18 April [DeCh1] to 22 June [Hans1], but a female apparently incubating on 7 July suggests a later date [Hess4]. In contrast, extreme egg dates in Maryland are 25 March and 21 July (Robbins and Bystrak 1977), and the egg-laying period observed in a Kansas study extended from 28 March to 5 July (Klaas 1975). Clutch size is usually 5 or 4 (n = 53; range 3–6).

Trends. BBS data reflect an increase in phoebes in the East during the past 10 years at an average annual rate of 5% [Usfw3], indicating recovery from a population crash in the severe winter of 1976–77 in the Southeast (Robbins et al. 1986). This trend is reflected in Delaware; the BBS increasing trend is not statistically significant, but the May Count shows an average annual increase of 4% for 1969–90.

Breeding population. The highest May Count is 65 (1988) and the lowest is 10 (1971). Breeding population densities in good habitat in Maryland (Stewart and Robbins 1958) (males per 100 ha):

18 (6 in 84 acres) in mixed agricultural habitats in Prince George's County (5-year average of 14 per 100 ha)
1.4 (15 in 2,656 acres) in Patuxent NWR, Maryland (2-year average of 1.2 per 100 ha)

Its average density in Delaware is lower than either of these, as suggested by the low May Count numbers and the low numbers on the relative abundance study.

Conservation. The Eastern Phoebe was added to the Blue List in the late 1970s after a hard winter, but weather-related population declines are to be expected. Provision of predator-resistant nest sites under eaves and bridges near woods would augment its population.

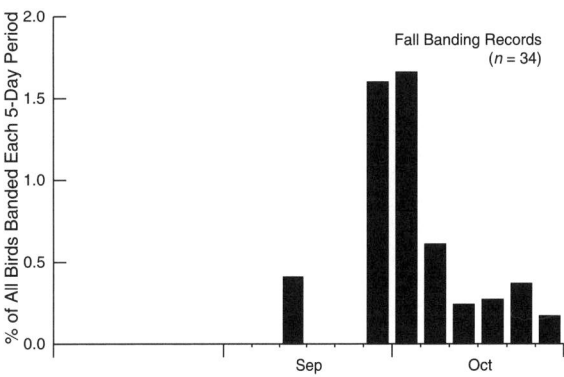

Fall Banding Records
(n = 34)

Fall Migration Activity

FALL: Migration appears to be from 15 September to 25–30 October. The peak banding period occurs from 26–30 September through 6–10 October. In the 1991 Neotropical migrant study (Mabey et al. 1993) phoebes seemed to have a bimodal migration; 29% were identified in the first week in August, then few were seen until October when 60% were found (n = 42). Although most birds leave by the end of October, a few remain into early winter.

1966–89 CBC Summary

Christmas Bird Count	Years Found	Range of No. Found	Median
Wilmington	6	1–3	
Middletown	3	1–2	
Bombay Hook	3	1	
Cape Henlopen	7	1–4	
Rehoboth	7	1–2	
STATEWIDE (high in 1984)	18	1–5	1

WINTER: Phoebes are recorded in low numbers on 1 or 2 CBCs most winters. Few sightings occur after the first week of January, all of single birds:

11 Jan 1989	1	Holts Landing SP [Frec1]
15 Jan 1974	1	Red Mill Pond [Holg86]
21 Jan 1936	1	Milford [Hans1]
27 Jan 1974	1	Bombay Hook NWR [Lieh4]

27 Jan 1991	1	Sherwood Acres, New Castle County [Camp20]
10 Feb 1991	1	Prime Hook NWR [Vand2]

SPECIMENS: DMNH 20768, New Castle Co., Bellevue, 16 June 1971; DMNH 43585, Wilmington, 6 October 1974; ANSP 79954 and ANSP 79957, Newport, 14 October 1911; DMNH 58269, Greenville, 16 October 1975. Egg records: DMNH.

Vermilion Flycatcher *(Pyrocephalus rubinus)*

Accidental (1993).

DOCUMENTATION: Photographs (DMNH 456, 457).

REMARKS: The Vermilion Flycatcher is a western species whose closest breeding locations are in western Oklahoma and central Texas (AOU 1983). It winters on the Gulf Coast through central Florida and casually to southern Florida (AOU 1983). There are breeding populations in South America as far south as Chile (AOU 1983). A spring occurrence in Delaware thus could plausibly be a migrating bird overshooting its North American breeding range or a southern hemisphere bird overshooting its wintering range. The single Delaware occurrence was an adult male on Burtons Island, near Indian River Inlet, from 2 to 5 May 1993 [BarT1] (photograph J. F. Swertinski, DMNH 456, T. Barnekov DMNH 457), each of which unarguably establish the identification.

Great Crested Flycatcher *(Myiarchus crinitus)*

Regular; summer resident; fairly common. Expected late April to mid-September. Widespread cavity nester, occasionally accepting nest boxes.

J F M A M J J A S O N D

HABITAT: Deciduous and mixed woods. Accepts a wide range of open and moderately closed forest situations (Hespenheide 1971).

SPRING: Typically, the first birds arrive from 25 April to 1 May. Migration ends 20–25 May. The earliest reports are

19 Apr 1984	1	near Milton [Frec1]
20 Apr 1927	1	Dover [Hans1]
20 Apr 1972	1	Bombay Hook NWR [Holg55]

The earliest New Castle County report is 1 on 26 April 1970 at White Clay Creek [MiDP1]. Peak counts include

14 May 1983	19	Bombay Hook NWR [PieJ2]
16 May 1964	12	Hoopes Reservoir (Falk 1971)
17 May 1969	17	Brandywine Creek SP [McCT1]

The highest statewide May Count is 174 (14 May 1989) and the lowest 42 (4 May 1971), reflecting different stages of the migration rather than a change in population.

BREEDING: Breeding throughout the state, the Great Crested Flycatcher increases in population density southward from New Castle through Kent to Sussex Counties in the ratio of 1:2.2:3.6, a greater increase than would be expected from increase in forest cover (Frieswyk and DiGiovanni 1988) in the same areas.

Atlas. Since crested flycatchers are noisy around the nest at the beginning of the season, particularly when intruded upon,

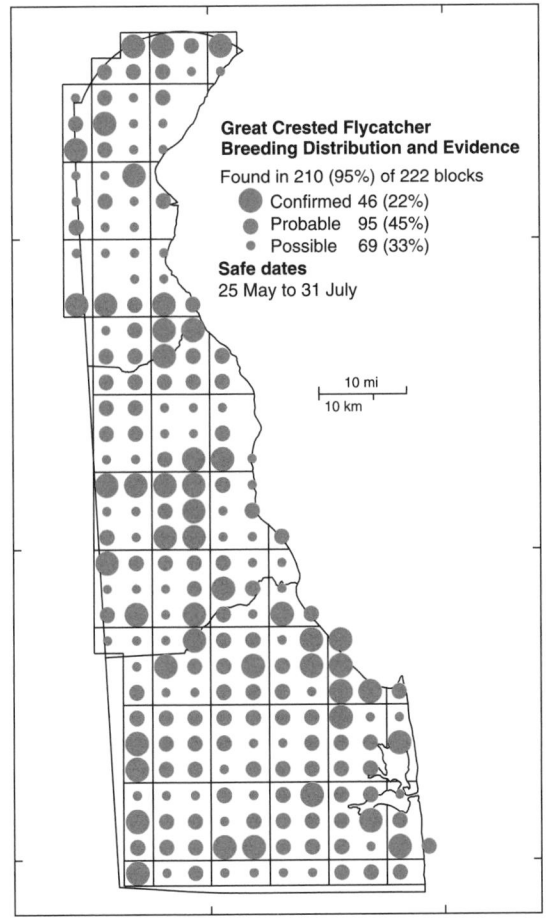

Great Crested Flycatcher
Breeding Distribution and Evidence

Found in 210 (95%) of 222 blocks

● Confirmed 46 (22%)
● Probable 95 (45%)
· Possible 69 (33%)

Safe dates
25 May to 31 July

10 mi
10 km

Great Crested Flycatcher
Relative Abundance

No. of 3-minute stops
(of 15) in June where
at least one was found:
279 of 3240 (8.6%)

10 mi
10 km

it is not surprising that over 80% of Atlas confirmations came from finding nests. However, only 4 of these were specified as nests with eggs.

Nesting. This cavity-nesting flycatcher accepts a wide variety of nest sites, which are often similar to the cavities used by starlings (Stauffer and Best 1982). An Iowa study of Great Crested Flycatcher cavity sites in riparian habitats revealed that cavities average 28 ft up in trees averaging 55 ft in height; cavities were located in limbs or trunks averaging 10 in. in diameter (Stauffer and Best 1982). However, it is not choosy and will accept martin houses and drain pipes, as well as cavities in a variety of living and dead trees. An interesting nest site is recorded in Hanson's notes: "On June 9 [1935] Master Thomas Gordon brought an egg he thought was a snake egg, saying he found it with some dry grass and a snake skin in the bore of an old cannon in front of the Armory in Dover. The egg was one of the Great Crested Flycatcher."

Clutch completion peaks in late May to early June. The subsequent clutches probably represent renestings after failure, since this species is single-brooded in Ontario (Bennett 1987). Clutch size in Delaware is 3–6 (*n* = 6), but clutches of 3 may not be complete (Harrison 1978).

History. Clearing of forests since European settlement began has removed over half its habitat, but no data indicate

whether or not its population density has changed within the remaining wooded areas.

Trends. BBS data show its population in the East has remained stable over the last 24 years but may be slightly declining during the past 10 years [Usfw3], perhaps no faster than the clearing of roadside woods. In Delaware, data from 10 BBS routes suggest the population increased in the 10 years following a 1966–79 decline.

Breeding population. It averages 3–4 pairs per 100 acres in

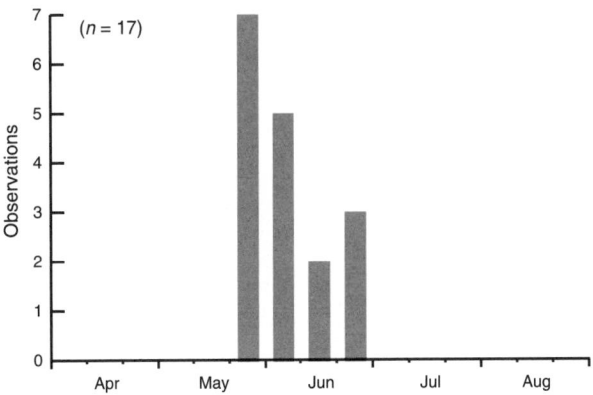

Estimated Clutch-Completion Dates

woodlots in northern Delaware (Martin 1976). A figure of 12 pairs per 100 acres (calculated from Linehan, Jones, and Longcore 1967) includes edges, but the area calculations include only the woodlots themselves. Summarized data for Maryland give a range of 4–8 pairs per 100 acres (Stewart and Robbins 1958).

Conservation. Since it nests in cavities, the number of available cavities could be a limiting factor in its population. Starlings are already entrenched in breeding cavities when Great Crested Flycatchers return from the tropics.

FALL: The onset of migration is not clear but probably begins in early August. In the 1991 Neotropical migrant study (Mabey et al. 1993) Great Crested Flycatchers were most common in the first week in August, most passed through by 8 September, and only 6 stragglers (9%) were found during 14–29

September (*n* = 70). Migration ends 15–20 September, and only a few stragglers remain into October or November. Only 8 Cresteds have been reported after 21 September, the latest being

22 Oct 1972	1	Cape Henlopen SP [Sper1]
1 Nov 1981	1	Bombay Hook NWR [Wayn44]
7 Nov 1991	1	Cape Henlopen SP [Frec1]

Flycatchers seen during October, November, or later should be carefully documented so as to distinguish sightings of this species from those of vagrant western *Myiarchus* flycatchers. See, for example, Murphy (1982) for information on the vagrancy of Ash-throated Flycatcher (*Myiarchus cinerascens*) in the East.

SPECIMENS: 8; DMNH, UWBM. Egg records: DMNH.

Western Kingbird *(Tyrannus verticalis)*

Occasional (18 years, 1912 to 1988).

REMARKS: There are more than 20 records, mostly for occurrences during September to December but with a few during May and June. Pennock collected the first known birds on 31 December 1912 at Rehoboth Beach (ANSP 66031, ANSP 79962), noting on the tags "Three or four individuals in field. Apparently catching some small insects." Other fall records include

	2 Sep 1988	1 early	Cape Henlopen SP [Frec16]
2	4 Oct 1971	8 high	Cape Henlopen SP [Conw12]
	24 Oct 1971	5 high	Fenwick Island [Rowl1]
	1 Dec 1969	1 banded	Bombay Hook NWR [Bomb3]
	17 Dec 1983	1	Seaford CBC
	26 Dec 1949	1	Bombay Hook CBC

Most sightings occur on or close to the Atlantic or Delaware Bay coast. The species winters casually north to South Carolina (AOU 1983).

Spring records range from 1 at Bombay Hook NWR on 7 May 1971 [Buck4] to 1 at Prime Hook NWR on 17 June 1968 (notes).

SPECIMENS: ANSP 66031, ANSP 79962, details earlier.

Eastern Kingbird *(Tyrannus tyrannus)*

Regular; summer resident; fairly common. Expected late April to mid-September. Widespread in open habitat.

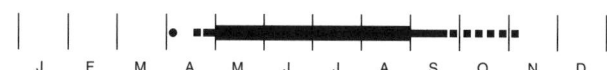

HABITAT: Wood margins, farmsteads, suburbs, roadsides; lone trees in open areas, frequently near water, particularly saltmarshes.

SPRING: The vanguard usually arrives 25–30 April, some even earlier, and the main migration begins the first week of May. The end of migration is probably late May. These reports, lacking details, are the only ones before 19 April:

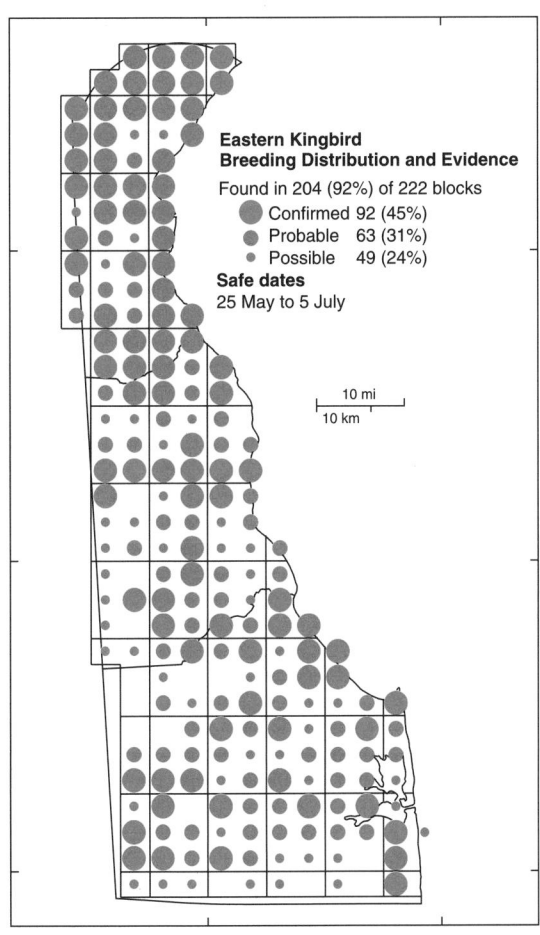

Eastern Kingbird
Breeding Distribution and Evidence

Found in 204 (92%) of 222 blocks

● Confirmed 92 (45%)
● Probable 63 (31%)
● Possible 49 (24%)

Safe dates
25 May to 5 July

10 mi
10 km

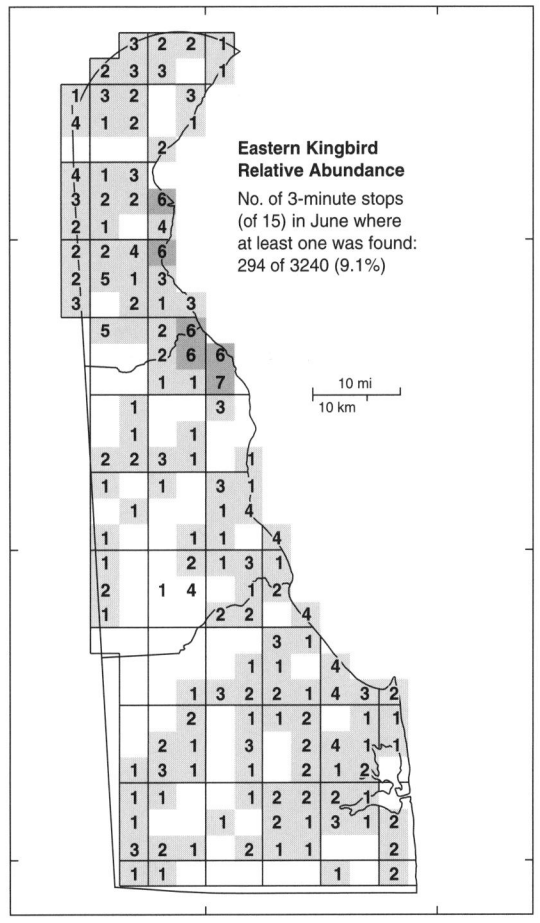

Eastern Kingbird
Relative Abundance

No. of 3-minute stops
(of 15) in June where
at least one was found:
294 of 3240 (9.1%)

10 mi
10 km

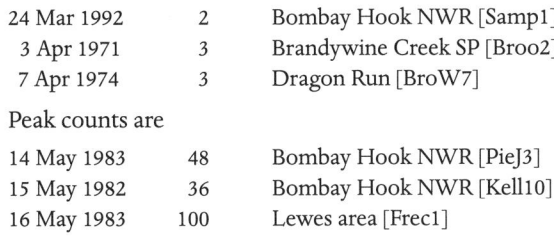

24 Mar 1992	2	Bombay Hook NWR [Samp1]
3 Apr 1971	3	Brandywine Creek SP [Broo2]
7 Apr 1974	3	Dragon Run [BroW7]

Peak counts are

14 May 1983	48	Bombay Hook NWR [PieJ3]
15 May 1982	36	Bombay Hook NWR [Kell10]
16 May 1983	100	Lewes area [Frec1]

The highest May Count is 236 (14 May 1988), and the lowest 46 (5 May 1973).

BREEDING: The Eastern Kingbird is as abundant in New Castle County as in the southern counties, unlike the distribution of the Great Crested Flycatcher. Least numerous in blocks with extensive woods and in the drier areas along the ridge of the peninsula, it is most common near the Delaware River.

Atlas. The Eastern Kingbird was reported in 92% of Atlas blocks but probably breeds in some where not reported. Since migration normally begins by mid-July, reports of possible breeding occurring after 5 July were not included in the data. This diminished the time for field work, so the Sussex County blocks with no reports do not necessarily lack breeding kingbirds. Probable breeding was often indicated by the species' tendency to chase large birds out of the breeding territory.

Since the kingbird nests in trees in the open, with breeding activity easily observed, it was confirmed in almost half the blocks. Most confirmations involved finding the nest; only 14%

of confirmations used the fledged-young code even though feeding of fledglings continues for 3 or more weeks (Morehouse and Brewer 1968).

Nesting. Hanson (notes) describes several kingbird nests that are fairly typical. One was found "with three eggs Aug. 1, 1923, in a sycamore tree on St. Jones Creek. The tree stands at the edge of the water and the nest is on a limb running out over the water and is about 15 ft from the shore and only 2 ft from the water." Another with 4 eggs was "about eight feet from the ground on a horizontal limb of a pear tree beside the road in east Dover" on 12 July 1923. "The nest is four inches deep and five inches across outside and one and three-quarters inches deep and three inches wide inside and is constructed of roots, small stems, and plant fibers, lined with fine rootlets."

Clutch-completion dates are mainly in June; the 2 clutches reported by Hanson represent the latest egg dates. The early egg date is 24 May, 3 eggs [Buck1]. The Eastern Kingbird is normally single-brooded (Blancher and Robertson 1982), so late clutches probably represent renesting after failure. Clutch size in Delaware is 2–4, usually 3 (*n* = 21).

History and trends. This species' population has expanded along with extensive land clearing. BBS data suggest an average downward trend in Delaware of 2% per year during 1966–90 and a slight decline in the East [Usfw3]. Conversely, the May Count shows an increase in Delaware since 1969. This differ-

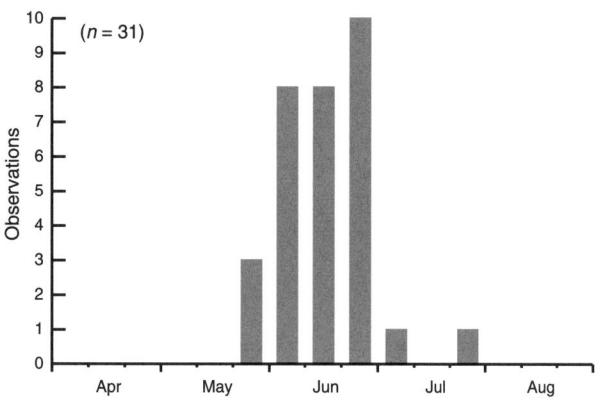

Estimated Clutch-Completion Dates

ence, if correct, can be resolved if the migrants observed on the May Count are part of an increasing population. Kingbirds are, in fact, both common and increasing to the north of us in the St. Lawrence River Plain (Wiedenfeld et al. 1992), and this increasing breeding population might well cause an increase in Delaware migrants.

Breeding population. Breeding population densities (males per 100 ha) in good habitat include:

37 (3 in 20 acres) in saltmarsh edge, Sussex County (Linehan 1966b).

Stewart and Robbins (1958) cite 25 per 100 ha in a suburban

residential area and 7 per 100 ha in mixed agricultural habitats for Maryland. Hall (1983) gives an average of 17 per 100 ha for 3 habitats in West Virginia.

FALL: Migration usually begins 15–25 July, decreases about 1 September, and ends 15–20 September. Peak counts are

27 Aug 1978	60	Prime Hook NWR [Frec1]
5 Sep 1964	14	Hoopes Reservoir (Falk 1971)
6 Sep 1975	13	Dragon Run [Stri5]

More than 100 were observed in a field in southern Delaware in late summer (West, pers. obs.). Stone reported flocks following the coastline at Cape May and crossing the bay toward Delaware: "On several counts I estimated that four hundred Kingbirds passed me within five minutes or about five thousand in an hour." Massed daytime flights occurred with some regularity there, usually between 27 August and 1 September (Stone 1937, 647).

In the 1991 Neotropical migrant study (Mabey et al. 1993) all Eastern Kingbirds passed through during August (*n* = 38). Reports after 30 September should be documented. Credible reports of stragglers include

19 Oct 1981	1	Ashland [Wayn54]
31 Oct 1968	1	Bombay Hook NWR [Holg35]
5 Nov 1977	1	White Clay Creek [Barn20]

SPECIMENS: 14; DMNH, ANSP, CM, USNM. Egg records: DMNH.

[Gray Kingbird *(Tyrannus dominicensis)*]

One report.

DOCUMENTATION: None.

REMARKS: A single individual of this species was reported at Cape Henlopen on 23 May 1968 [Carr10]. Although this species is not now regular north of Florida, it formerly bred north to South Carolina (AOU 1983). It occurs with moderate frequency in North Carolina and is casual north to Massachusetts and perhaps New Brunswick (AOU 1983), so its occurrence in Delaware is plausible. It is relatively easy to identify, but no descriptive notes exist for the report.

Scissor-tailed Flycatcher *(Tyrannus forficatus)*

Casual (6 years, 1968–93).

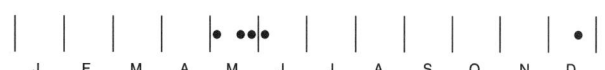

DOCUMENTATION: Photographs (P. McEwan, DMNH print collection; A. P. Ednie, DMNH 458).

REMARKS: The 6 reports are:

| 4 May 1968 | Bombay Hook NWR [WarD12] |
| 17 Dec 1973 | Bombay Hook NWR [Lieh2] |

21–23 May 1988	Bombay Hook NWR [MurW330
May–1 June 1989	Prime Hook NWR [Frec17]
19–20 May 1990	South Bethany Beach (McEwan, photograph at DMNH) [Barn12]
24 July 1993	Bombay Hook NWR [Scar1]

In North America this species breeds east to central Missouri and Arkansas and western Louisiana (AOU 1983). It winters regularly in Florida but is casual to very rare at that season throughout most of the East. It can be confused only with the

Fork-tailed Flycatcher, which is also casual along the Atlantic coast.

The first 2 reports occurred before it was known that the Fork-tailed Flycatcher might occur, and their documentation does not conclusively eliminate the Fork-tailed Flycatcher. The notes for the second of these reports does mention one mark (the expanded end of the tail streamers) indicating that the bird was more likely the Fork-tailed Flycatcher, adverse conditions having prevented observation of further marks. The May 1988 report is supported by convincing notes by Robert Hilton. The 1990 record was of an immature bird whose deeply forked tail was at most a little longer that the length of the body proper. The top of the head was light gray, and there was salmon along the sides deepening to bright rose under the wings at the shoulder [Barn1; Shoc1]. The 1993 observation was reported as an immature, but no notes are available.

Fork-tailed Flycatcher *(Tyrannus savana)*

Casual (1985 and 1989).

DOCUMENTATION: Convincing notes.

REMARKS: The first Delaware sighting occurred on 19 October 1985 near Port Mahon east of Dover (Zerbe 1986). The bird, observed for 20–30 min at short range, had a deeply forked tail and black cap. Though the notes do not mention the bird's size or general coloration, the description of the tail and cap gives credence to the identification. The second sighting took place on 27 September 1989 at Camden, west of Dover [Holg29]. The bird was observed for about 20 min in good light. The notes mention the black cap contrasting with the gray and white below it, the long forked tail, and pure white underparts [Holg1]. Vagrancy along the northeast Atlantic coast is typical of this South American migrant (Monroe and Barron 1980).

Loggerhead Shrike *(Lanius ludovicianus)*

Occasional (50 years, 1924–91); uncommon. Most reported September through April. Probably extirpated as a breeder, but should be looked for.

J F M A M J J A S O N D

HABITAT: Open country with short grass and hedgerows or other perches. Earlier Delaware nesting associated with osage orange.

OCCURRENCE: The Loggerhead Shrike occurs most frequently in winter, especially on CBCs, and least frequently during breeding season. Since its status was summarized by Hess (1980b), 10 individuals of this shrike have been recorded on 8 additional CBCs through 1991. Five of 7 specimens are dated, all from September through December. Banding records are for 21 February 1971 at Lewes [Bays1], 2 September 1967 west of Townsend, and 23 September 1967 at Cape Henlopen SP [Clar1]. Excluding CBC reports, the monthly distribution of records follows:

January	3
February	4
March	5
April	7
May	4
June	1 (including 2 nests by the same pair)
July	2
August	5
September	7
October	4
November	11
December	10

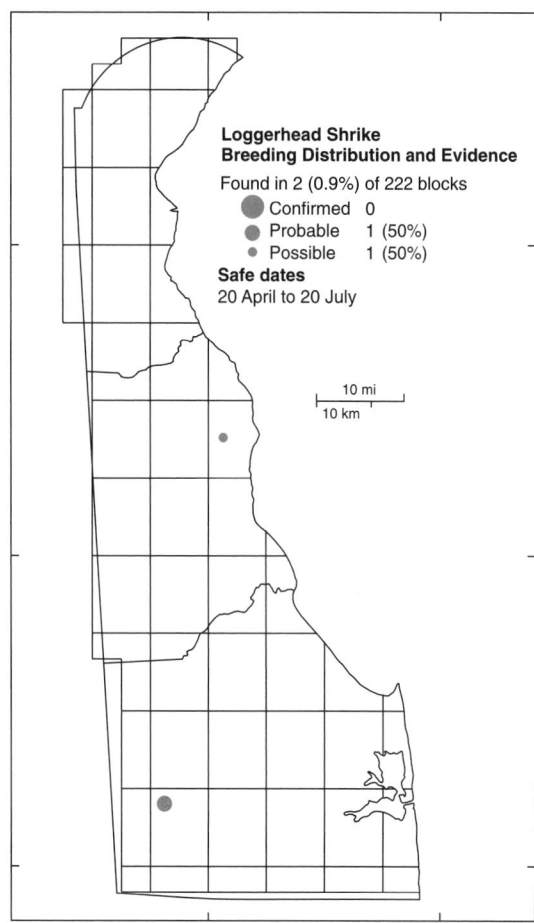

Loggerhead Shrike
Breeding Distribution and Evidence

Found in 2 (0.9%) of 222 blocks
● Confirmed 0
● Probable 1 (50%)
· Possible 1 (50%)
Safe dates
20 April to 20 July

10 mi
10 km

nest records, states that Mr. George Hensel of near Stanton "told [him] that two pairs nested in a hedge by the roadside near Delaware City in 1862." A specimen in Bush's collection was taken in New Castle County in the spring of 1882 [Penn1]. Hanson (notes) found a nest with 4 young in an osage orange hedge near Little Creek on 24 May 1924. Fledged young were nearby on 4 June. "Probably a second nest of the same pair" was found on 19 June.

These are the only Delaware nest records of Loggerhead Shrike, but birds found between 20 April and 20 July (Bystrak and Klimkiewicz 1982) should be regarded as possibly breeding:

7 May 1933	1	Kitts Hummock Rd. [Hans1]
10, 13 May 1986	1	Port Mahon Rd. [Palm2]
31 May 1965	1	Newark [Carr3]
14 (pair), 21, 22 (singing) Jun 1985		
		2.5 mi south of Seaford [Jalo1]

The following July records might be considered as breeding birds:

24 Jul 1965	2	Bombay Hook [Quan1]
24 Jul 1966	1	Milford [Armi4]

Atlas. The 2 breeding season records during the Atlas project were unexpected (10 May and 14 June, preceding). A compilation of Atlas results in the Northeast shows that the probable breeding record near Seaford is the most northeasterly one on the Coastal Plain, though west of the Appalachian Mountains breeding extends north into Ontario.

1966–89 CBC Summary

Christmas Bird Count	Years Found	Range of No. Found	Median
Wilmington	1	1	
Middletown	8	1–6	
Bombay Hook	17	1–5	1
Cape Henlopen	7	1–7	
Rehoboth	10	1–5	
STATEWIDE (high in 1966)	18	1–16	1

Nesting. Hanson described a nest collected on 21 June 1924 from a roadside osage orange: "The nest was built of rather coarse sticks, stems, and roots, and lined with fine rootlets. It measured 7 inches across and 2 inches deep outside, 3½ inches across and 2 inches deep inside."

Conservation. The Loggerhead Shrike is listed as Endangered in 7 northeastern states, as extirpated in 2 others, and as a migratory nongame bird of management concern by the USFWS (Bartgis 1992). It is nearly extirpated in Delaware and should be listed as endangered in Delaware since there are extant, Endangered populations in Maryland and Virginia.

SPECIMENS: 7; ANSP, CM, DMNH, UDEL, USNM.

Multiple reports have occurred in approximately half of the years in which Loggerhead Shrikes have been sighted. One bird wintered near Leipsic in 1985 and another near Broadkill Beach in 1990; but the usual length of stay is only a few days. Typically, just 1 or 2 birds are found, but 10 were present on the 1951 Bombay Hook CBC.

HISTORY: This species was not originally a resident of northeastern North America. Nuttall (1832) gave its range as from North Carolina to Florida. It expanded north and east with the clearing of forests, first occurring in Ontario in 1860 (Cadman 1987), about the same time as Delaware's first occurrence. A general population decrease began in the Northeast as early as the 1930s (Bull 1974) and became increasingly evident by the 1970s (Robbins et al. 1986; Fraser and Luukkonen 1986; Tate 1986). No rigorous Delaware trend analysis can be attempted on this rare and irregular species, but reports of 41 occurrences in the 1960s, 40 in the 1970s, and 12 in the 1980s suggest a decrease. The wintering population along the coast of the Mid-Atlantic states has almost disappeared, probably owing to the decline of the migratory breeding population farther north (Bartgis 1992).

BREEDING: Only 4 nests have been reported in Delaware, none since 1924. Pennock (1908b), reporting his only shrike

Northern Shrike *(Lanius excubitor)*

cating the observer's familiarity with the more expected species. The 6 records are

29 Mar 1909	Yorklyn (ANSP 65909)
23 Jan 1931	Montchanin [BrJW1]
2 Jan 1954	Indian River Inlet [Weir2]
1 Jan 1956	Rehoboth CBC
4 Feb 1978	Cape Henlopen SP [Frec1]
9 Feb–28 Mar 1986	Cape Henlopen SP [Whit7; Barn1]

The Northern Shrike breeds in the Arctic as far south as southern Labrador (AOU 1983) and winters irregularly to middle Pennsylvania, casually to North Carolina. The Delaware records fit this pattern well.

SPECIMEN: ANSP 65909, details earlier.

Casual (6 years, 1909–86), winter visitor.

REMARKS: Early publications indicate that the Northern Shrike may once have been a rare, rather than casual, winter visitor. It is mentioned in 2 early compilations of birds found in Delaware (Barry 1942; Pennock 1935). On the second list the Loggerhead Shrike is also mentioned, as a summer visitor, indi-

White-eyed Vireo *(Vireo griseus)*

ors; also hedgerows and woods margins in agricultural areas.

SPRING: First arrival is usually 15–20 April. Migration usually ends by 20–30 May, with peak numbers in late April and throughout May. Earliest reports:

11 Apr 1983	1	Cape Henlopen SP [Frec1]
12 Apr 1981	1	Prime Hook NWR [Frec1]

High counts along White Clay Creek:

23 Apr 1977	19	[Patt6]
1 May 1976	22	[Barn20]
7 May 1977	54	[Dyer7]
20 May 1978	41	[Falk11]

The highest May Count is 419 (3 May 1980); the lowest 64 (10 May 1969, the first year of the survey).

BREEDING: This southern vireo breeds throughout Delaware, but infrequently attracts notice except by those who recognize its scratchy song. It is common in southern Delaware and the mesophytic woodlands of the Piedmont creek valleys and less common in the Piedmont uplands, where it begins to reach its northern limit. Lower numbers occur in suburbs and near tidal marshes.

Atlas. During the Atlas project it was most frequently con-

Regular; summer resident; fairly common. Expected late April to early October and stragglers later. Most common on the Coastal Plain.

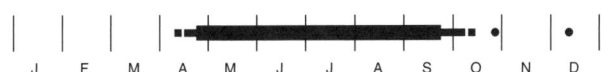

HABITAT: Shrubs or brush in wet or damp areas, usually in open areas but less frequently in shrub layers of woods interi-

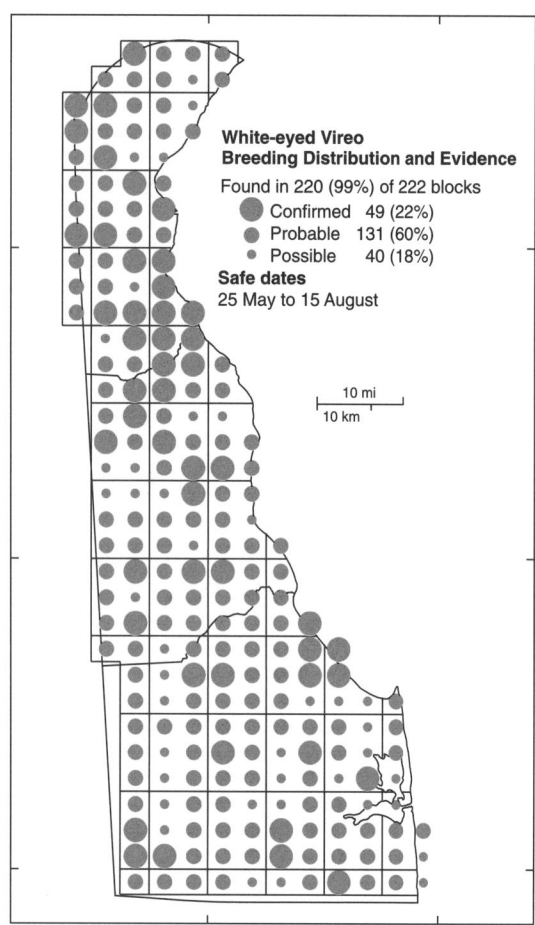

White-eyed Vireo
Breeding Distribution and Evidence

Found in 220 (99%) of 222 blocks

● Confirmed   49 (22%)
● Probable   131 (60%)
• Possible   40 (18%)

Safe dates
25 May to 15 August

10 mi
10 km

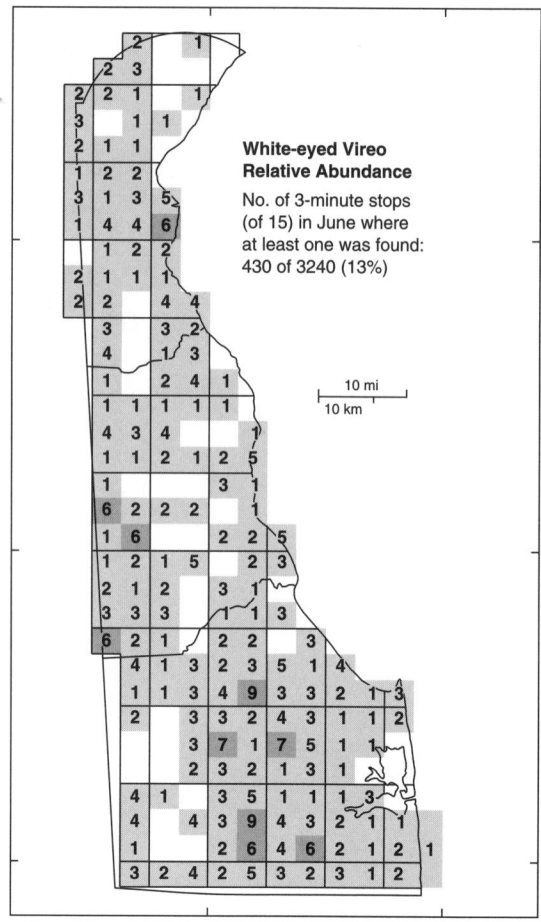

White-eyed Vireo
Relative Abundance

No. of 3-minute stops
(of 15) in June where
at least one was found:
430 of 3240 (13%)

10 mi
10 km

firmed by seeing fledged young or adults feeding young; its well-hidden nest was reported 7 times, and nest-building 3 times.

Nesting. Hanson (notes) collected a nest in a blackberry tangle 2½ ft up in a small American holly bush. The nest, 3 in. across and 4 in. deep, had an oval cup, 1½ by 2 in., and 1½ in. deep. It was carefully woven of shreds of bark and fiber and lined with small pine needles. The outside was trimmed with small white wood chips, small pieces of dead leaves, and bits of green moss fastened with spider web. The whole nest, including the pendants, was rather cone-shaped, with the top edge somewhat drawn in so the widest part of the nest was about an inch below the rim.

Six records of first nestings suggest clutch-completion dates of 14 May–3 June. A "nesting pair" observed on 24 July 1982 [SpeE3] is the latest breeding report. This report and several other July observations of fledglings and adults carrying food suggest renestings or second broods. Robbins and Bystrak (1977) show Maryland egg dates extending from 25 April to 26 July. Mengel (1965) and Graber et al. (1985) remark on the long breeding period in Kentucky and Illinois but cautiously do not conclude that second broods have been produced. Others (Ehrlich et al. 1988; Whitcomb et al. 1981) conclude it is double-brooded, at least in the southern part of its range.

Early-season clutches are 3–4 in Delaware. A recent attempt to develop clutch-size data in Illinois was disrupted by 10 of 12 nests being parasitized by cowbirds (Graber et al. 1985)—a typical problem for all vireos, which is most easily observed in this low-nesting species.

Trends. A scrub and edge specialist, the White-eyed Vireo is more common now than before the land was cleared for agriculture. It has recently expanded its range into New England (Robbins et al. 1986) and in midwestern states such as Minnesota (12 notes in *The Loon,* 1980–91). It has increased at an average rate of 2% per year in Delaware since the 1960s, judging by the May Counts and the BBS [Usfw3].

Breeding population. White-eyed Vireos were detected at 13% of the stops of the relative abundance study—the best available indicator of this vireo's population because its habitat is so patchy. Its actual territory size may be as little as 0.2 ha (Brewer 1955), and breeding densities of up to 100 males per 100 ha were reported in Maryland shrub swamp (Stewart and Robbins 1958).

FALL: Signs of movement begin 15–25 August. Migration peaks during 1–15 September and continues to 25 September–5 October. Stragglers:

17 Nov 1990	1	Assawoman WA [Jano5]
18 Nov 1990	1	Baxter Tract [Camp1]
15 Dec 1984	1	Seaford CBC

High counts, on White Clay Creek:

28 Aug	44	[Patt5]
3 Sep	48	[Barn8]
10 Sep	50	[Dyer4]
11 Sep	39	[Falk7]

In the August–October 1991 Neotropical migrant study (Mabey et al. 1993), 50% of the White-eyed Vireos were recorded during August (*n* = 75) before the residents departed, a peak (16%) was recorded on 7–8 September, and the last 5% in October through the thirteenth.

SPECIMENS: 19; DMNH, ANSP, UDEL, UWBM.

Yellow-throated Vireo (*Vireo flavifrons*)

Regular; summer resident; uncommon. Expected late April to late September. Considerably less common in New Castle County than in the forested portions of southern Delaware. Rare in eastern parts of the state.

HABITAT: Mature floodplain forests; moist, rich upland forests. Highest abundance in mature oak forests (Stewart and Robbins 1958; Reinoehl 1991). An Ontario study revealed how this species and Red-eyed Vireo partition the habitat in a way that may allow their coexistence (James 1976)—Yellow-throated Vireos choose more open canopy than do Red-eyed Vireos (62% closed versus 78%) and feed more in dead parts of the trees (76% versus 14%).

SPRING: First arrival is usually during 25–30 April. Migration continues until 15–20 May, peaking during 1–15 May.

Early arrivals are

17 Apr 1965	1	Redden SF [Broo19]
18 Apr 1964	1	Redden SF [Broo28]
22 Apr 1990	1	Blackbird SF [Hess1]

High counts are

30 Apr 1977	13	White Clay Creek [SpSB16]
13 May 1984	8	White Clay Creek [Hess11]

Usually 15–30 are reported on the May Count.

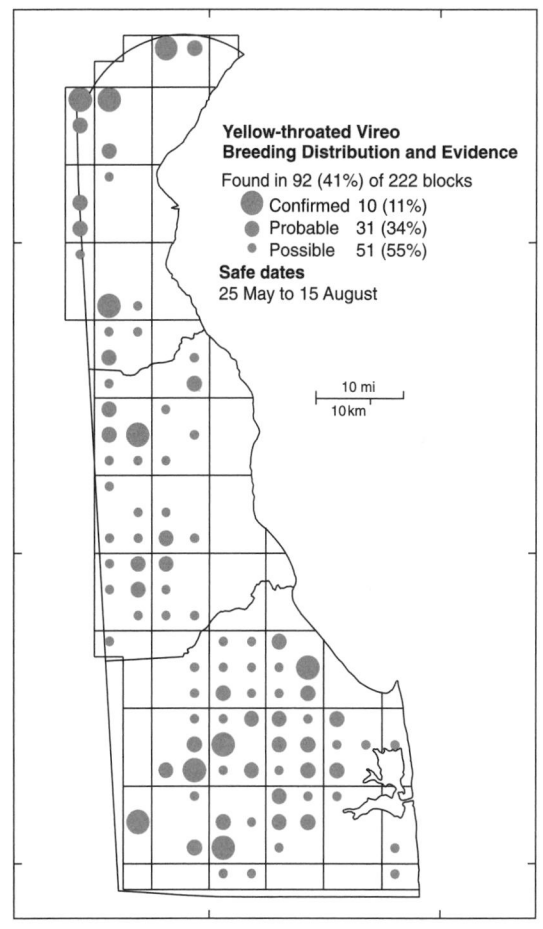

Yellow-throated Vireo
Breeding Distribution and Evidence
Found in 92 (41%) of 222 blocks
● Confirmed 10 (11%)
● Probable 31 (34%)
• Possible 51 (55%)
Safe dates
25 May to 15 August

10 mi
10 km

BREEDING: Before the land was cleared and drained for agriculture, this species was probably common in open mature forest. Today both the distribution map and the relative abundance map for this species show a remarkable correlation with the declining remnants of wet mature forest in the state.

Atlas. This vireo was confirmed most frequently by observing nest building. It was not detected in some well-studied areas in which it has been reported in the past, including White Clay Creek, Middle Run, Hoopes Reservoir, Dragon Run, and Pocomoke Swamp. These failures of detection may reflect real changes in its distribution, but contributing factors may include

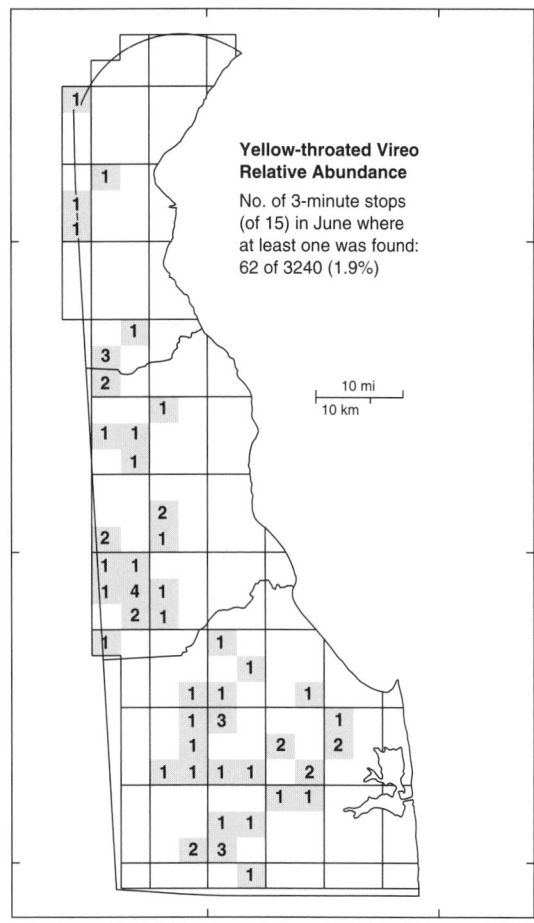

Yellow-throated Vireo
Relative Abundance

No. of 3-minute stops
(of 15) in June where
at least one was found:
62 of 3240 (1.9%)

10 mi
10 km

demonstrated in Wisconsin, 1954–79 (Ambuel and Temple 1982).

Breeding population. This vireo is usually found in lower densities than others: 20 males per 100 ha in a nearby Maryland second-growth swamp (Springer and Stewart 1948c) and an average density of 8–12 males per 100 ha in 4 forest types in Kentucky (Mengel 1965).

Conservation. Smith (1988) pointed out potential problems this species may encounter. It feeds extensively on moth and butterfly larvae in the canopy of mature deciduous woods, making it particularly vulnerable both to chemical and bacteriological measures aimed at controlling gypsy moths; these control measures nonselectively destroy all moth and butterfly larvae, thereby reducing food for the vireo.

In Maryland, Whitcomb et al. (1981, 65) found it more susceptible than many Neotropical migrants to the negative effects of forest fragmentation. In Delaware it did not occur in any of the small woodlots studied by Linehan, Jones, and Longcore (1967) or Jones (1969a,b,c), but it did occur in a larger forest nearby (West 1970).

Eaton (1914) noted the local disappearance of nesting Yellow-throated Vireos following years of high Brown-headed Cowbird parasitism. Such parasitism has increasingly become a hazard for this species since the cowbird's eastward range expansion. In view of the Yellow-throated Vireo's susceptibility to various pressures, its abundance and distribution should be carefully monitored.

FALL: Migration usually begins during 20–25 August and ends by 15–20 September. The highest counts are

27 Aug 1977	5	White Clay Creek [Rufe6]
3 Sep 1984	4	White Clay Creek [SpSB33]

Lingerers include

2 Oct 1977	1	White Clay Creek [West15]
2 Oct 1988	1	Middle Run, Newark [Call1]
3 Oct 1987	1	Cape Henlopen SP [Edni8]

SPECIMENS: ANSP 65951, Rehoboth Beach, 18 May 1906; DMNH 35668 and DMNH 35690, Redden SF, 14 July 1971; ANSP 171957, Wilmington, August 1879.

insufficient coverage and the abrupt decrease in singing of mated males during incubation (James 1984).

Nesting. Although the Yellow-throated Vireo is a regular summer resident, its nest has been reported only infrequently:

4 May 1985	nest building	Nanticoke River [MiDR2]
18 May 1906	egg in oviduct	Rehoboth Beach [Penn1]
20 May 1978	nest building	White Clay Creek [Falk3]
9 Jun 1935	1 young	Milford [Buck10]
19 Jun 1972	2 young	White Clay Creek [MiDP4]
10 Jul 1985	young	Newark [Rubi1]

The 4 May nest was about 30 ft up in open deciduous woods. The 20 May nest was 40 ft up in a sycamore tree. The 19 June nest was 15 ft above ground in a wild black cherry near White Clay Creek; the 2 young were judged by their red mouth linings to be young cowbirds. Estimated clutch-completion dates extend from mid-May to mid-June. Yellow-throated Vireo nests are similar to those of other vireos, though perhaps even more decorated on the sides with bits of lichen and moss and perhaps more secured with spider silk (Bent 1950).

Trends. BBS data during 1966–90 indicate an increase in Yellow-throated Vireos in the East; a possible long-term increase is also shown for Delaware. Perhaps locally more important is a suggestion of a steep decline in Delaware during the 1980s [Usfw1], like the steep significant decline in its population

Blue-headed Vireo *(Vireo solitarius)*

NCW

Regular; migrant; uncommon. Expected late April to early May and mid-September through October, occasionally later.

J F M A M J J A S O N D

HABITAT: Deciduous and coniferous forests.

SPRING: First arrival is usually 15–20 April. Migration usually continues to 5–10 May. Early dates include

| 7 Apr 1973 | 2 | Prime Hook NWR [Wegg1] |
| 14 Apr 1981 | 1 | Assawoman WA [Haas2] |

Highest counts include

26 Apr 1975	4	Redden SF [Lehm1]
29 Apr 1975	3	Greenville [Nile1]
3 May 1975	4	Dragon Run [Citr5]

The latest reports include

| 13 May 1972 | 1 | Bombay Hook NWR [Barn14] |
| 14 May 1977 | 1 | White Clay Creek [Falk11] |

The Blue-headed Vireo was missed on only 3 (of 22) May Counts, which are held after its migration peak. In most years 1–3 birds are reported; highest counts were 10 (10 May 1975 and 8 May 1976) and 9 (12 May 1990, high for so late in May).

FALL: Unlike the compressed spring migration, the fall migration continues for some time as birds trickle through. First arrival is 5–10 September, and migration usually ends by 15–20 October. Earlier reports include

30 Aug 1964	1	Hoopes Reservoir [Falk16]
31 Aug 1991	1	Little Creek WA [Falk4]
3 Sep 1972	1	Winterthur [Gran3]

Peak counts are

| 11 Sep 1976 | 6 | White Clay Creek [Boll5] |
| 18 Oct 1970 | 5 | Brandywine Creek SP [Falk8] |

In the August–October 1991 Neotropical migrant study (Mabey et al. 1993), 50% of the Blue-headed Vireos were recorded during a 13–20 October peak ($n = 32$). The latest reports are

25 Oct 1972	1 banded	University of Delaware woodlot [Line4]
27 Oct 1979	1	Wilmington (DMNH 68131)
5 Nov 1973	1	Bombay Hook NWR [Lawr3]
31 Dec 1981	1	Trap Pond SP [Fint7]

SPECIMENS: ANSP 65955, Hockessin, 15 October 1904; DMNH 68131, Wilmington, 27 October 1979.

Warbling Vireo *(Vireo gilvus)*

Regular; summer resident; rare. Expected early May to early September. Sporadic and local south of New Castle County; no nest located south of Delaware City.

J F M A M J J A S O N D

DOCUMENTATION: Multiple sight records, banding record, nest record.

HABITAT: Open stands of shade trees in residential areas and open canopy floodplain forests. Partial to sycamores. In an Ontario study the Warbling Vireo preferred an average of 34% canopy cover (James 1976).

SPRING: First arrival is usually 1–5 May. Migration is pro–

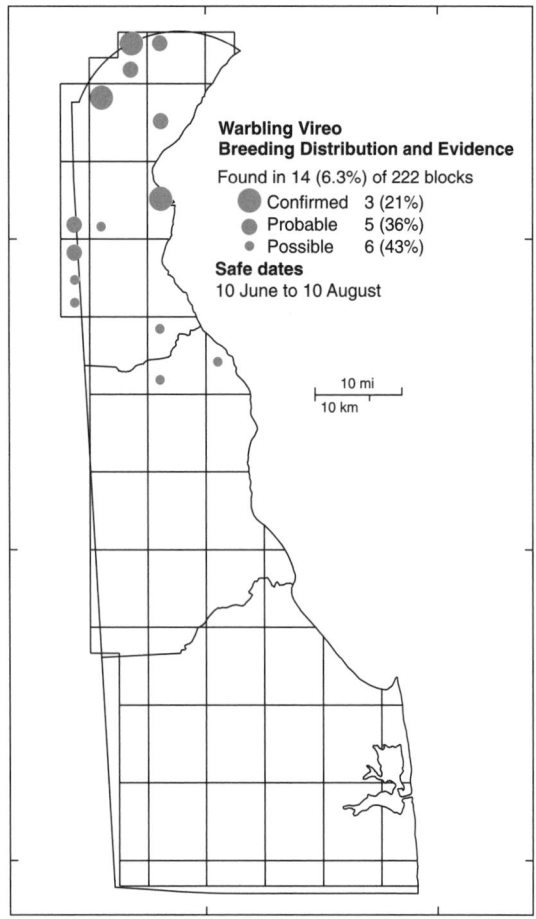

Warbling Vireo
Breeding Distribution and Evidence

Found in 14 (6.3%) of 222 blocks
- Confirmed 3 (21%)
- Probable 5 (36%)
- Possible 6 (43%)

Safe dates
10 June to 10 August

10 mi
10 km

longed, usually continuing to 5–10 June. The earliest arrivals were

24 Apr 1976	1	White Clay Creek [SpSB16]
25 Apr 1992	2	Burrows Run [Wayn64]
27 Apr 1991	3	Burrows Run [Wayn65]

High counts include

7 May 1977	7	White Clay Creek [Dyer7]
8 May 1976	5	White Clay Creek [BroW9]
31 May 1971	7	Brandywine Creek SP [WarD4]

One or 2 birds are the usual numbers reported. It has averaged about 6 per year on the May Counts.

BREEDING: The only regular breeding locations are in the Piedmont valleys, at Delaware City, and near Port Penn.

Atlas. During the Atlas project this vireo was common along Pike Creek and near Ashland along Red Clay Creek. It was found in new locations in the Bohemia and Sassafras basins and a little farther east near Smyrna. The most unexpected location was in a tidal marsh south of Woodland Beach, where 1 sang from an isolated deciduous tree at a remote landing. This tree-top species may have been missed in some blocks if Atlas workers did not recognize its song.

Nesting. Breeding in Delaware was first reported near Milford Crossroads north of Newark, where 4 nests were found in 1968 [WarM1]. Jahn and Lehman reported a Warbling Vireo nest 35 ft up in a sycamore on White Clay Creek near Thomp-

sons Bridge; nest building occurred on 14 May, incubation on 21–24 May, and feeding young in nest on 18 June 1977 [Jahn1; Lehm3]. There were 2 nests with young, 25 and 30 ft above ground in sycamores on the Pike Creek golf course on 18 June 1983 [Patt1]. Nestlings were being fed in an ash in the Red Clay Creek valley during 29 June–6 July 1983 [SpeE13]. A nest was found on the Coastal Plain at the edge of Delaware City, situated at the end of an oak limb; the adult was singing while sitting closely on the nest on 24 May 1987 [Nile2]. Maryland egg dates extend from 24 May to 22 June (Robbins and Bystrak 1977).

Like other vireos, this one builds a pensile basket secured from a fork.

History. It was considered a summer resident by Rhoads and Pennock (1905) and subsequent compilers. Early records include 1 on 6 June 1898 in Wilmington and others were recorded in summer at Granogue, Porter, and Concord [Penn1]. Hanson's only record was of 2 migrants on 2 May 1926 in Dover. Barry's 1939 compilation listed it as a "Summer resident. Not uncommon," which may have reflected its status in Piedmont Delaware but breeding had not been proven.

Warbling Vireos were not recorded in 4 years of censuses around Hoopes Reservoir (1943–45, 1964). Increased field work following formation of DOS in 1963 produced regular summer records on northern Delaware surveys (1969–80).

Trends. The Warbling Vireo is likely more common now than in precolonial times since it requires large deciduous trees in open habitat. Its continental population recorded on the BBS has generally increased during 1966–90 (Wiedenfeld et al. 1992) but has decreased in the East during 1981–90. In Delaware 16 were reported on the BBS from 1967–74; surprisingly, most were from Kent County. None were recorded after 1982 when Barnhill recorded 1 on a Sussex County BBS on 25 June [Usfw3].

Breeding population. It was reported from 14 blocks with some blocks having more than 1 pair, so its breeding population was probably in the 20–200 pair range during the Atlas study.

Conservation. This vireo, which lives in tops of mature trees and feeds on insects, is surely affected adversely by control programs directed at the gypsy moth and other forest pests, especially when used in suburban and other locations of open canopy or isolated shade trees.

FALL: In this season the Warbling Vireo is more inconspicuous than during spring, as shown by few fall reports. The data suggest, however, that it occurs regularly, probably in small numbers, until 10–15 September. One was banded near Red Lion on 15 September 1964 [Line4]. A late report of 1 on 2 October 1966 at Newark [Crum1] is probably acceptable, but all reports of this species after 15 September should be accompanied by field notes distinguishing it from the more common Tennessee Warbler. All reports involve 1 or 2 birds.

Philadelphia Vireo (*Vireo philadelphicus*)

Regular; migrant; rare. Sporadic in spring, expected mid- to late September.

HABITAT: Deciduous forests.

SPRING: This species, seldom noted in spring, has been reported a dozen times from 26 April to 19 May. It migrates primarily west of the Appalachians and occurs casually in the southeastern United States (AOU 1983). Delaware spring reports should be carefully documented. In heavily birded Cape May County, New Jersey, there is only 1 accepted sight record, and no physical evidence of its spring occurrence, even though it is a fairly common fall migrant there (Sibley 1993).

FALL: Philadelphia Vireos are more likely to be found during fall. Virtually all migrants occur between 7 September and 4 October. Four of these rare migrants have been banded:

11 Sep 1970	2	University of Delaware woodlot [Jone2]
18 Sep 1966	1	Rehoboth Beach [RusW1]
4 Oct 1964	1	east of Red Lion [Line5]

Early and late reports include:

26 Aug 1986	1	west of Lewes [Frec1]
31 Aug 1991	1	Little Creek [Falk4]
31 Aug 1991	2	Sussex coast [Atch5]
6 Oct 1986	1	Assawoman WA [Edni23]
10 Oct 1969	1	White Clay Creek [BroW23]

A report later in October seems too late to accept as published (DuMont and DuMont 1970a). The following reports of more than 1 bird are unusual:

15 Sep 1974	3	Newark [Mars1]
29 Sep 1973	3	Dragon Run [RobT1]

In the August–October 1991 Neotropical migrant study (Mabey et al. 1993), 90% of the Philadelphia Vireos were reported from 31 August to 21 September (*n* = 26).

SPECIMENS: DMNH 59239, Newark, 25 September 1976; DMNH 68125, Wilmington, autumn 1975.

Red-eyed Vireo (*Vireo olivaceus*)

Regular; summer resident; fairly common. Expected late April to early October.

HABITAT: Deciduous forests and deciduous stands in mixed forests.

SPRING: First arrival is usually during 25–30 April, the earliest on 21 April 1981 [Haas2]. Migration continues through 25–30 May, peaking 15–25 May. Peak counts are 89 at White Clay Creek on 22 May 1976 [BroH8] and 74 at Prime Hook NWR on 16 May 1982 [Frec1]. The highest May Count is 575 (12 May 1979), the lowest 119 (5 May 1973).

BREEDING: This forest bird, considered to be "by far the commonest woodland bird in the eastern deciduous forest" (Robbins et al. 1986), is found throughout the state. It is most

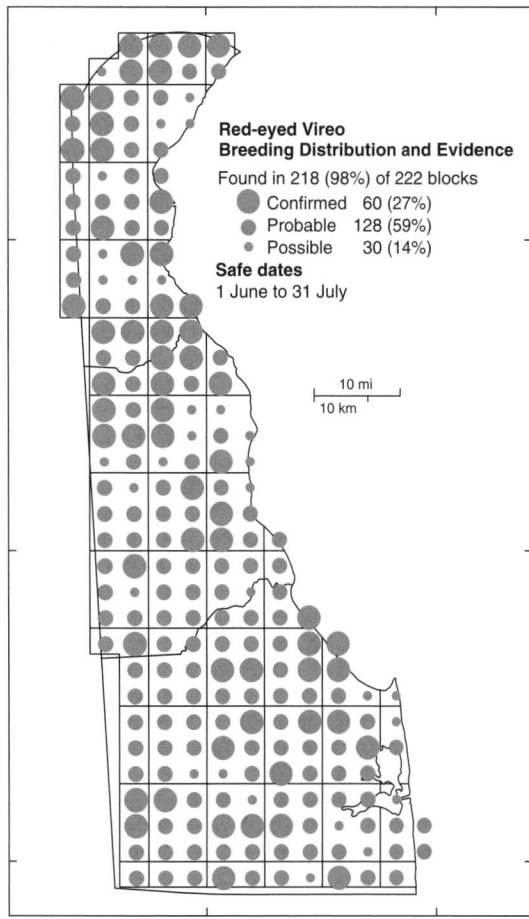

Red-eyed Vireo
Breeding Distribution and Evidence
Found in 218 (98%) of 222 blocks

- Confirmed   60 (27%)
- Probable   128 (59%)
- Possible   30 (14%)

Safe dates
1 June to 31 July

10 mi
10 km

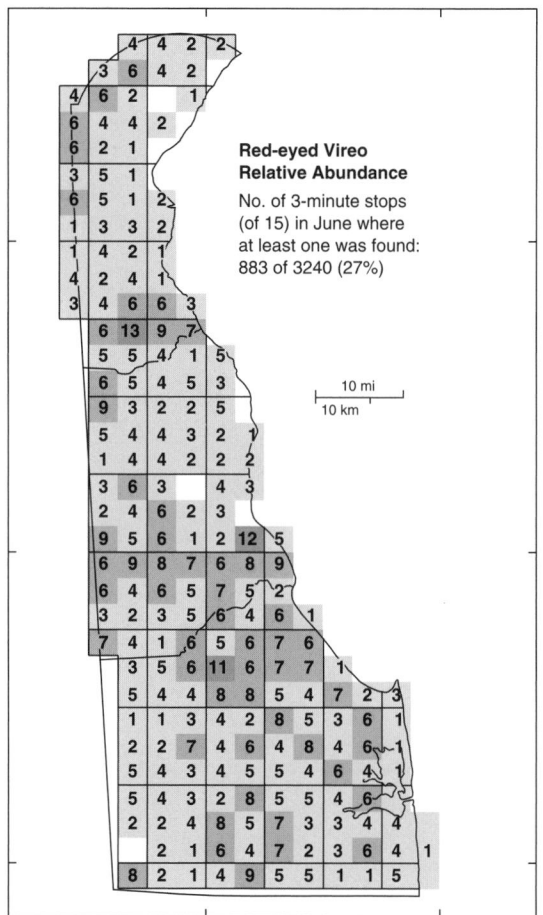

Red-eyed Vireo
Relative Abundance

No. of 3-minute stops
(of 15) in June where
at least one was found:
883 of 3240 (27%)

10 mi
10 km

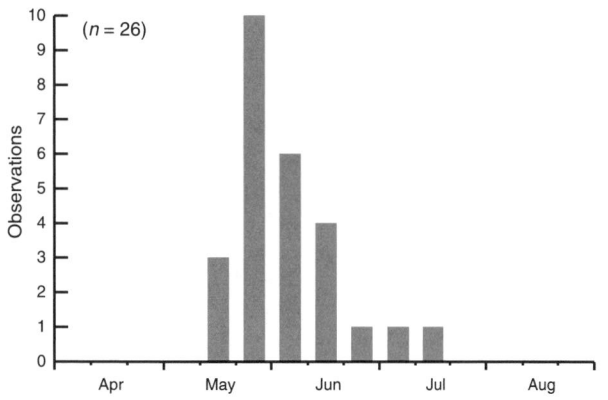

Estimated Clutch-Completion Dates

common along Blackbird Creek in New Castle County, in a belt of forest from the Wilder WA across to Milford Neck in southern Kent County, and in the Ellendale area in northern Sussex County. It is less abundant in the pine forests of Sussex County than in other forested areas.

Nesting. Hanson collected a nest on 11 June 1927. It was suspended 10 ft high in a fork of a slender bush and measured 3¼ in. across and 3 in. deep outside, and 2 in. across and 1¾ in.

deep inside. It was gray, made from plant fibers and down, and lined with a little fine grass.

The earliest egg date reported is 13 May 1985 in Bombay Hook NWR [Edni2]. The latest egg date is 20 July, the latest nestling 3 August [both Holg3]. The July clutch-completion dates, occurring 8 weeks after the peak date, are consistent with second broods but are more likely replacement nestings. No reliable evidence of second broods was found in 2 intensive studies in Ontario (Lawrence 1953) and Michigan (Southern 1958). Furthermore, second broods put a high energy demand on a species that must also undergo a complete molt and migrate to the tropics. Bull (1974) gives 2 examples of second broods (without supporting evidence) in New York, 1 with nestlings on 4 September. Dependent young being feed as late as 12 September is given for Michigan (Kelley 1978; Hull 1991), so late that it could be construed as a second nesting.

Delaware clutch sizes were 2–4, mostly 3 ($n = 12$). Red-eyed Vireos are heavily parasitized by cowbirds, e.g., 72% in a Michigan study (Southern 1958). In Delaware 35% of the nests are parasitized, the highest known rate for any species in the state (Baer 1989). This vireo does not eject cowbird eggs but in Ontario, for example, abandons about one-third of its parasitized nests (Graham 1988), and it probably has a similarly weak defense against parasitism in Delaware.

Trends. In the past 25 years this vireo's population, though fluctuating, has increased at an average rate of 2% per year on the BBS both in Delaware and in the East (Robbins et al. 1986) [Usfw3].

Breeding population. Breeding population densities in good habitat (males per 100 ha):

90 (3-year average of 9.3 in 24 acres) in coastal lowland mixed woods in Sussex County (Linehan 1969a)

60 (5-year average of 8.9 in 35.6 acres) in uneven-aged mixed hardwoods (Urban woodlot) in New Castle County (Jones 1970)

60 (6 in 25 acres) in mixed mesophytic forest in the White Clay Valley in New Castle County (West 1970)

Highest densities reported are

110 (11 in 24 acres) in coastal lowland mixed woods, Assawoman WA, Sussex County (Linehan 1966b)

250 in Maryland (36 in 36 acres) in virgin hardwood forest, Prince Georges County (Stewart and Robbins 1958)

Conservation. Although the Red-eyed Vireo is still common, its population has recently declined, and may continue to do so. It is sensitive to forest fragmentation, being 3 times more likely to occur at a random point in forests over 100 ha than in woodlots of less than 1 ha (Robbins et al. 1989a). So both forest clearing and fragmentation must have reduced the vireo's population since European settlement. Other factors that may adversely affect its future population level are cowbird nest parasitism and such forestry pest control programs as gypsy moth spraying.

FALL: Migration begins in early to mid-August and continues through 5–10 October. The banding graph shows peak

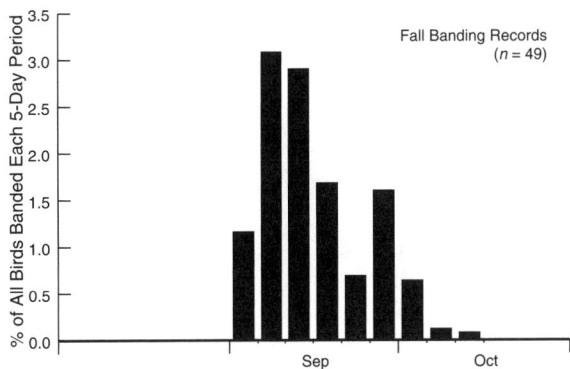

Fall Migration Activity

numbers of Red-eyed Vireos in September. Peak reports from White Clay Creek are 56 on 28 August 1976 [Wayn33] and 50 on 1 September 1987 [Edni65]. The latest records include

7 Oct 1963	1 banded	east of Red Lion [Line4]
14 Oct 1974	1 banded	University of Delaware woodlot [Line4]
26 Oct 1981	1	Cape Henlopen SP [Frec32]

In the August–October 1991 Neotropical migrant study (Mabey et al. 1993), 50% of the Red-eyed Vireos were recorded during a 7–21 September peak (*n* = 961); the last 1% straggled through during 5–13 October [Citr7].

SPECIMENS: 40; DMNH, UDEL. Egg records: DMNH, WFVZ.

[Gray Jay *(Perisoreus canadensis)*]

Escape.

REMARKS: The single published record [Scha1], from October 1965, is now known to refer to an escaped cage bird and should be disregarded.

Blue Jay *(Cyanocitta cristata)*

Resident; fairly common to common.

J F M A M J J A S O N D

HABITAT: Various forest types, wood edges, wooded suburban areas.

SPRING: Migration occurs from 15–25 April to 20–25 May, peaking 25 April–15 May. Peak numbers of Blue Jays are banded in late April and early May. Some high counts are

30 Apr 1972	136	Winterthur [Brow13]
2 May 1970	223	Brandywine Creek SP [SpSB13]
6 May 1980	100	Cape Henlopen SP [Frec1]
9 May 1964	126	Hoopes Reservoir [FalD1]

The highest May Count is 2,388 (4 May 1980); in other years the count was taken later in the month and averaged about 500.

BREEDING: This woodland bird frequents towns and is found in low numbers only in urban, agricultural, or marsh habitat where tree cover is limited. The relative abundance study reveals it to be uniformly abundant statewide.

Atlas. Blue Jays went undetected only in blocks containing the treeless marshes of Kent County and the highly developed barrier beach at Fenwick Island. It was confirmed in half the blocks where detected, high for the Atlas study. Two-thirds of confirmations resulted from finding recently fledged young or observing adults carrying food for young, which are readily located by their persistent begging. After the young fledge, territorial boundaries are abandoned because breeding jays do not defend territories against conspecifics in a different breeding stage (Hardy 1961). This behavior may have compromised Atlas results if movement of a family to another block occurred frequently. This problem is a minimal one, however, because jays are common almost everywhere. This behavior

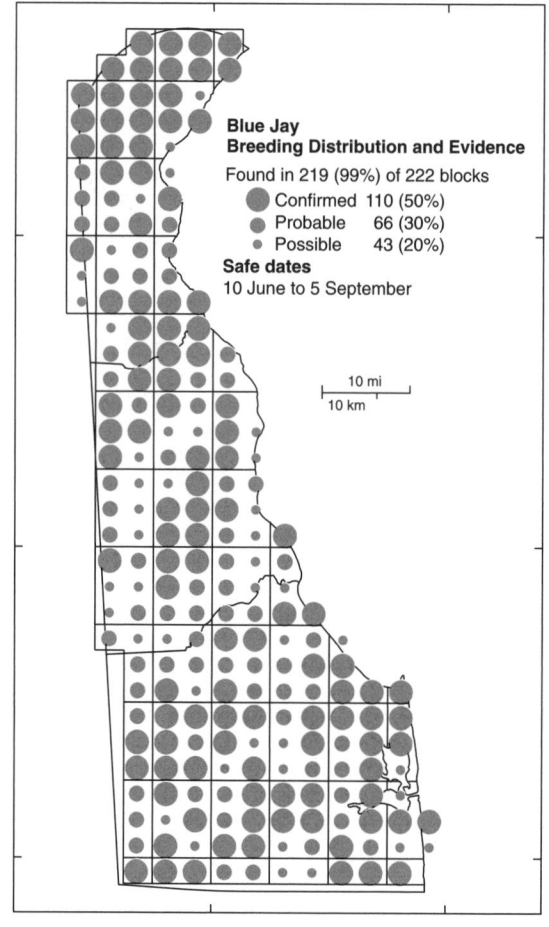

Blue Jay
Breeding Distribution and Evidence
Found in 219 (99%) of 222 blocks
● Confirmed 110 (50%)
● Probable 66 (30%)
· Possible 43 (20%)
Safe dates
10 June to 5 September

10 mi
10 km

may also confuse interpretation of BBC data that assumes territories are held following fledging.

Nesting. Hanson (notes) described 1 nest made of coarse sticks lined with dark rootlets. Interwoven in the sticks were an old rag and several bones, including the skull of a small animal. He also described nests that included grass stalks and straws. Nest heights in Delaware range from 5 ft up in a mountain laurel thicket to 75 ft in the top of an oak. Most nests were in

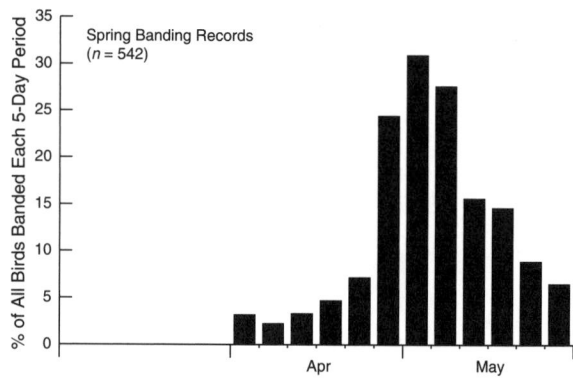

Spring Banding Records
(*n* = 542)

Spring Migration Activity

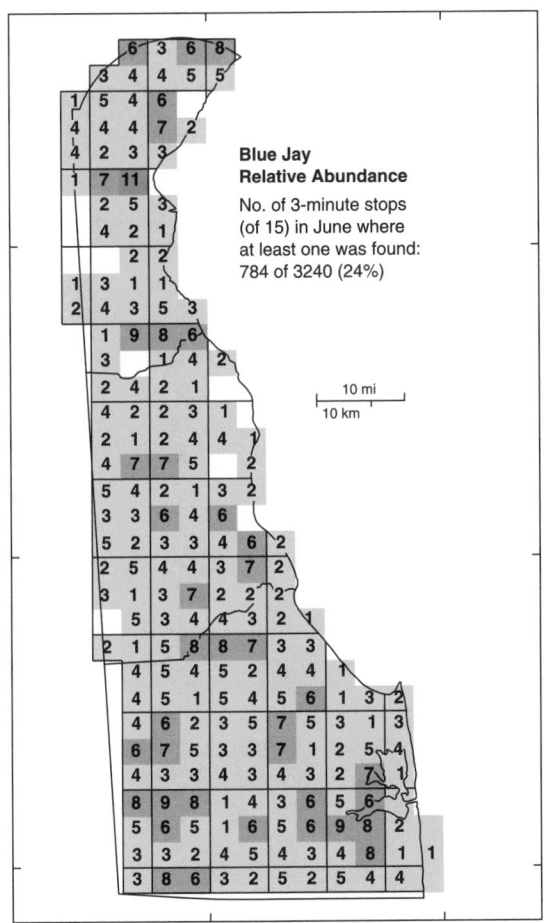

Blue Jay Relative Abundance

No. of 3-minute stops (of 15) in June where at least one was found: 784 of 3240 (24%)

10 mi
10 km

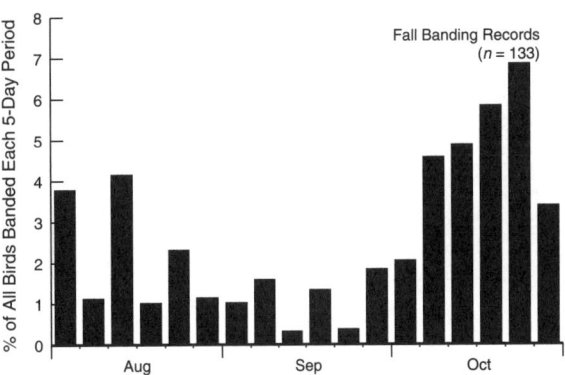

Fall Banding Records
(*n* = 133)

Fall Migration Activity

broad-leaf trees, but Atlantic white cedar, juniper, blue spruce, and pine have also been used.

Clutch completion in Delaware shows a strong peak in May. An early clutch-completion date of late April is estimated from 4 well-developed nestlings found on 25 May [Bray1], and 1 30-g nestling brought to Tri-State Bird Rescue on 13 May came from an even earlier clutch (TSBR 87-216). An unusually late nestling was brought to Tri-State on 28 August 1987, indicating a clutch completed the last week in July (TSBR 87-1107). This nestling may have been from a second brood, since females are double-

brooded in the southern, but not in the northern, part of the range (Laskey 1958; Goodwin 1976).

Trends. The Blue Jay population decreased in the East at an average annual rate of about 2% during 1966–90 according to BBS data, but a corresponding decrease is not evident in the Delaware data [Usfw3]. However, a dramatic increase in Blue Jay population levels since the 1950s and 1960s was ascribed to the increase of suburbs and food supplies in 2 long-term local studies (Hickey and Brittingham 1991; Wilcove 1988) and in a winter study during 1962–71 (Bock and Lepthien 1976a).

Breeding population. BBC studies in woodlots in northern Delaware give densities of 60–70 pairs per 100 ha (25–29 pairs per 100 acres) (Linehan, Jones, Longcore 1967; Martin 1976), in contrast to the representative 12 per 100 ha in Maryland (Stewart and Robbins 1958) or average of 15 per 100 ha in Illinois (Graber et al. 1987). Such urban woodlots harbor many oaks and much edge, both attractive to jays, but they are probably not representative of most Delaware woodland.

Conservation. The success of this species is a conservation problem for other birds, because it preys on nestlings and eggs. Its increase may negatively affect small birds, especially Neotropical migrants (Terborgh 1989, chap. 6).

FALL: The conspicuous diurnal migration of Blue Jays occurs from 5–15 September to 1–10 November, peaking 25 September–20 October. Peak numbers of Blue Jays are banded in October. Some high counts are

1 Oct 1972	650	Winterthur [Broo16]
2 Oct 1966	600	Brandywine Creek SP [Mohr1]
2 Oct 1974	1,000	White Clay Creek [Edni1]

1966–89 CBC Summary

Christmas Bird Count	Years Found	Range of No. Found	Median
Wilmington	24	178–881	387
Middletown	24	51–283	147
Bombay Hook	24	66–507	198
Cape Henlopen	24	26–305	70
Rehoboth	24	35–532	190
STATEWIDE (low in 1968, high in 1982)	24	445–1,877	1,016

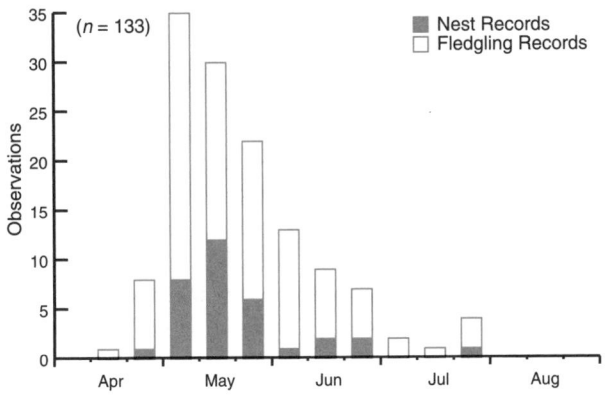

(*n* = 133)

■ Nest Records
□ Fledgling Records

Estimated Clutch-Completion Dates

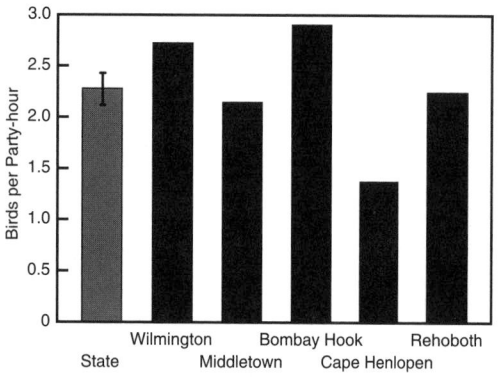

CBC Geographic Distribution

WINTER: Jays are recorded with equal frequency on all

CBCs except the one at Seaford (not illustrated), which records about 60% higher numbers. Some high non-CBC counts are

3 Dec 1977	68	White Clay Creek [Falk21]
17 Dec 1977	89	White Clay Creek [MiDP18]
18 Jan 1964	50	Hoopes Reservoir [PooC1]
6 Feb 1972	46	Winterthur [RobT4]

BANDING: Evidence from birds banded in parts of its range where it is migratory reveals that birds of the year (immature birds) migrate while adults do not (Goodwin 1976). Delaware banding data indicate our birds are largely resident, with most migrants coming from more northern states. The longest distance recoveries were 2 first-year birds banded in Maine and recovered here.

SPECIMENS: 85; DMNH, UDEL, USNM.

[Black-billed Magpie *(Pica pica)*]

Probable escape.

REMARKS: One magpie was reported 23 March 1957 near Wilmington [Rals2]. A misidentification by this observer of so distinctive a bird is implausible, but no documentation is available. In any event the bird probably escaped from captivity after being transported to Delaware.

American Crow *(Corvus brachyrhynchos)*

Resident; common; peak migration mid-March–mid-April and late October through November. Winter numbers apparently declining after reaching a high in the late 1970s.

HABITAT: Agricultural and suburban areas with nearby woodlands. Avoids tidal marshes and the coast but otherwise is fairly evenly distributed throughout the state.

SPRING: Migration probably occurs from early February through April, peaking mid-March–mid-April. Some high counts are

15 Feb 1975	190	Dragon Run [Wayn43]
3 Mar 1974	200	Dragon Run [Beac13]
14 Mar 1964	100	Hoopes Reservoir [Klab8]

BREEDING: The crow was formerly a country bird wary of contact with people because it was often shot. It has adapted to suburban areas, where it is most noticeable early in the day. The relative abundance study shows it to be 40% more common in Sussex and New Castle counties than in Kent County, reflecting its scarcity in the river marshes. It appears to be generally most common in Sussex, western Kent and Piedmont New Castle counties, areas characterized by broken woodland. Our breeding population is probably resident, but northern populations are partly migratory (Goodwin 1976; Stouffer and Caccamise 1991).

Atlas. The American Crow was detected in all but the strict-

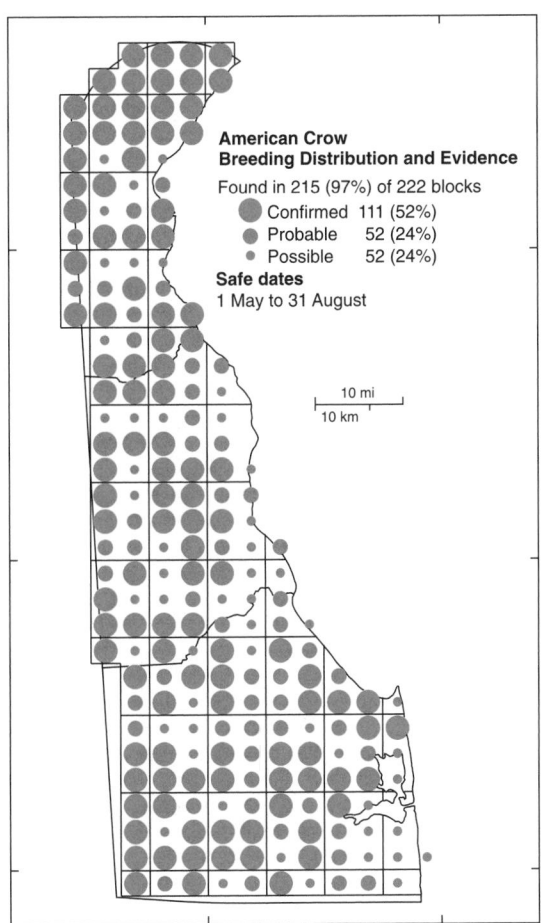

American Crow
Breeding Distribution and Evidence

Found in 215 (97%) of 222 blocks
● Confirmed 111 (52%)
● Probable 52 (24%)
• Possible 52 (24%)
Safe dates
1 May to 31 August

10 mi
10 km

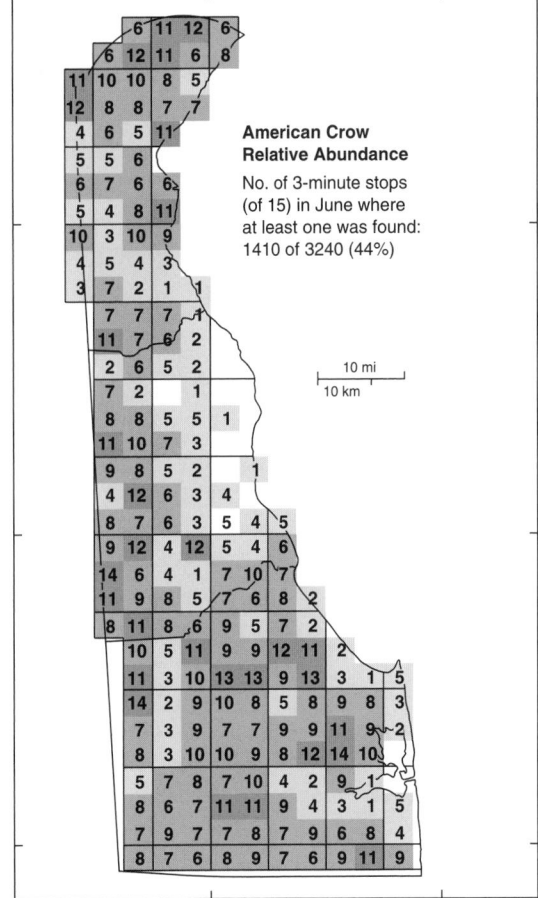

American Crow
Relative Abundance

No. of 3-minute stops
(of 15) in June where
at least one was found:
1410 of 3240 (44%)

10 mi
10 km

ly marsh or maritime blocks where the Fish Crow is more prevalent. Its "possible" breeding near Bethany [West3] is speculative because this species does not usually breed on the immediate coast.

Nesting. Hanson described a fairly typical nest as 13 in. wide by 9 in. deep outside, and 8 in. wide by 5 in. deep inside. It was built of sticks, lined with soft fibrous red cedar bark, and placed somewhat low at 20 ft above ground in a black oak. R. F. Miller described a nest—compactly made of many sticks, bark strips,

and grasses, and lined with bark fibers—32 ft up in the top of an American beech (LSU egg data).

The earliest clutch, found 27 March, contained 3 eggs (LSU egg data) and may not have been complete. An even earlier clutch is implied by 4 young found 4 May. The latest egg date is 9 May when 4 fresh, but cold, eggs were taken (Gardner, DMNH 28700). Clutch size is 3?–6, usually 5 ($n = 30$).

Trends. Delaware BBS results suggest a slight but significant increase in its population in the past 24 years, perhaps the result of a gradual increase following reduced persecution.

Breeding population. The relative abundance study registered American Crows at 1,410 stops. Its active, noisy morning behavior may have led to over-registration because some may have been counted from 2 stops, or some may have been more than a quarter of a mile away from study participants. There is no Delaware data on density of American Crows, but for Maryland Stewart and Robbins (1958) give densities of 0.1 pair per 100 acres (0.2 per 100 ha) for a large tract of farm land and 0.6 per 100 acres (1.5 per 100 ha) for a large tract of mixed forest.

FALL: Migration probably occurs from September through November, peaking in late October and November. A high count is 429 at White Clay Creek on 30 October 1976 [RusJ7].

WINTER: CBC data for the first 15 years of the 1966–89 analysis period indicate an increase, but counts during the last 4

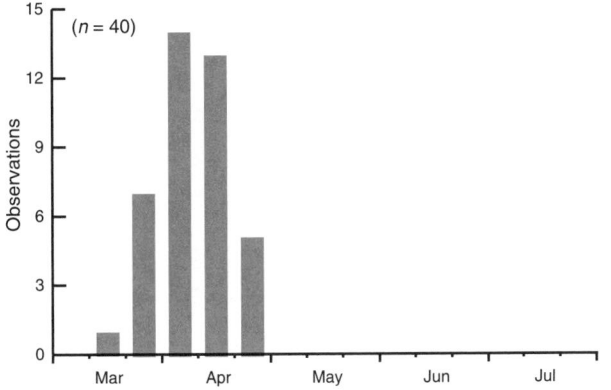

Estimated Clutch-Completion Dates

years have been the lowest of any 4-year period, changing this view. The Middletown and Seaford CBCs report the highest numbers.

1966–89 CBC Summary

Christmas Bird Count	Years Found	Range of No. Found	Median
Wilmington	24	260–878	549
Middletown	24	84–2,820	594
Bombay Hook	24	8–2,441	301
Cape Henlopen	24	33–217	100
Rehoboth	24	49–458	141
STATEWIDE (low in 1989, high in 1984)	24	1307–3,486	1,872

Data for 34 years of Bombay Hook counts show a precipitous reduction of American Crows from close to 10,000 in the early years of the survey to under 50. This reduction to 0.5% of its former numbers suggests abandonment of a roost; such a roost was mentioned by Brooks et al. (Brooks 1955, No. 7), who reported the return by 27 November 1955 of 1,000 crows to the roost in the woods near the wild goose pens at Bombay Hook NWR.

Winter roosting crows in Oklahoma were shown by banding studies to be mainly from Canada (Kalmbach 1939), and a study of a New Jersey roost showed it was composed of birds holding local territories and vagrants surmised to be migrants

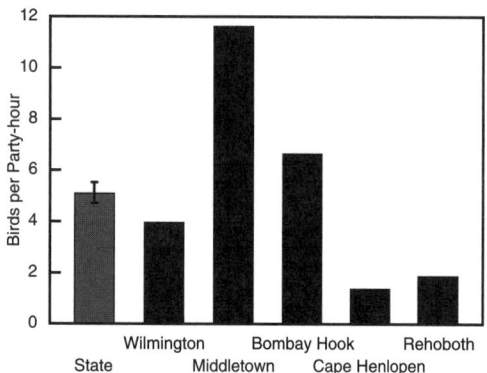

CBC Geographic Distribution

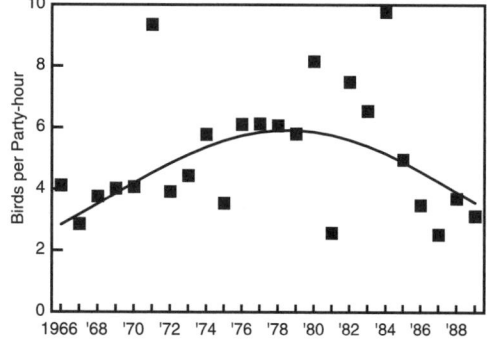

CBC Trend

from farther north and possibly birds dispersed from local natal groups (Stouffer and Caccamise 1991). We have at least one example of crows staying year-round on territory in northern Delaware: 2 crows, each having a few distinct white feathers, maintained residence continuously near Valley View for 3 years [PooE1].

REMARKS: Crow roosts used to be a remarkable feature of the area. Wilson wrote in 1810 that "The most noted Crow roost with which I am acquainted is near Newcastle, on an island in the Delaware. It is there known as the Pea Patch, and it is a low flat alluvial spot, of a few acres, elevated but little above high water mark, and covered with a thick growth of reeds. This appears to be the grand rendezvous, or headquarters, of the greater part of the Crows within forty or fifty miles of the spot. It is entirely destitute of trees, the Crows alighting and nestling among the reeds, which by these means are broken down and matted together. The noise created by those multitudes, both in their evening assembly and reascension in the morning is almost incredible" (Wilson and Bonaparte 1859–60). Nuttall (1832–34) wrote of another crow roost on the Delaware River where "in December, 1829, I had occasion to observe their arrival on Reedy Island, just above the commencement of the bay of that river, in vast numbers; and as the wind wafted any beating vessel towards the shore, they rose in a cloud and filled the air with a clamor. Indeed, their vigilant cawing continued till after dark." The Reedy Island roost was later estimated to contain about 200,000 birds (Kalmbach 1918). Joseph Laup states (in Coggins 1903) "there are winter Crow roosts in the vicinity of Milton. . . . The number of birds is almost innumerable but the best estimation we can give for those which use the Conwell farm would be 2,500 to 3,500. The woodland on this farm comprises about ten acres, most of which is pine and large shrubbery." Other Delaware roosts listed by Coggins were "Pea Patch, Delaware River, deserted 1816 (Rhoads 1886)," and "Reedy Island, Delaware River, deserted at the time the quarantine station was built (since 1886)." A list of crow roosts occupied in 1910–11 included 1,000–3,000 at Milford and an unstated number at Wilmington (Kalmbach 1915). These Delaware roosts seem to be diminished now, even though crows are now less persecuted by farmers. The roosts that they once filled are now filled with starlings, grackles, cowbirds, and Red-winged Blackbirds.

SPECIMENS: 15; DMNH, ANSP, CM. Egg records: DMNH, LSU.

Fish Crow *(Corvus ossifragus)*

Resident; fairly common. Peak migration in March and April, and October and November. Winter numbers apparently declining after a peak in the early 1980s.

HABITAT: Woods, fields, marshes, shore near tidewater; in the interior uses a variety of wooded and urban habitats.

SPRING: Migration probably occurs from February to early May, with peak numbers in March and April. Some high counts are

22 Mar 1975	130	Dragon Run [Wayn52]
11 Apr 1981	60	Lums Pond SP [Barn1]
20 Apr 1974	105	Dragon Run [Wayn49]

BREEDING: Although usually associated with the coast and marshes where the American Crow is less often found, this crow is also distributed inland. For instance, it nests on the University of Delaware campus in Newark and in the Green Acres subdivision north of Wilmington.

Atlas. This crow is difficult to Atlas because it forages at least a half mile from its nest, occasionally causing it to be registered in the wrong block. A higher percentage of confirmations would have decreased this problem, but the species' tendency to approach its nest from above the canopy (Meanley 1981) made the bird harder to see, thereby reducing the observer's chance of associating it with a nest. Probably some identifications were erroneous since young or adult American Crows can make a nasal *caw* that resembles one of the Fish Crow's notes. In spite of these difficulties, the Atlas data document the extent of its distribution in Delaware and provide a better idea of its numbers than was known before.

Nesting. Nest sites described in Delaware include cedar trees in marshes (3), tops of pines (2), a crate in a marsh, and a range light housing near Leipsic. The nests, made of sticks and lined with grass, resemble those of American Crows.

Of 34 nest observations, the earliest nestlings reported were 6 young estimated to be several days old on 1 May [Hans1], suggesting clutch completion about 12 April. This nest was in a

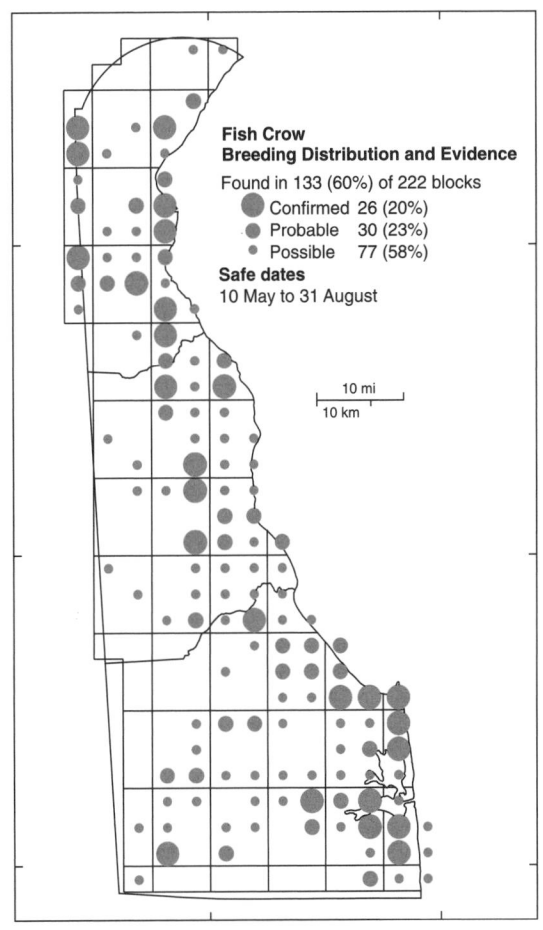

colony with other Fish Crows at Kitts Hummock; all the nests were of similar size, and some contained eggs [Hans1]. Extreme egg dates are 20 April (5 eggs) [Buck1] to 24 June (3 eggs) [Herh2]. Most clutches were completed in early May. The estimated clutch-completion graph is dominated by data from a Slaughter Beach colony of 13 nests with eggs, visited 13 May 1936 [Buck1]; these nests were assumed to be synchronized and completed 9 days earlier. Clutch size was usually 4 or 5.

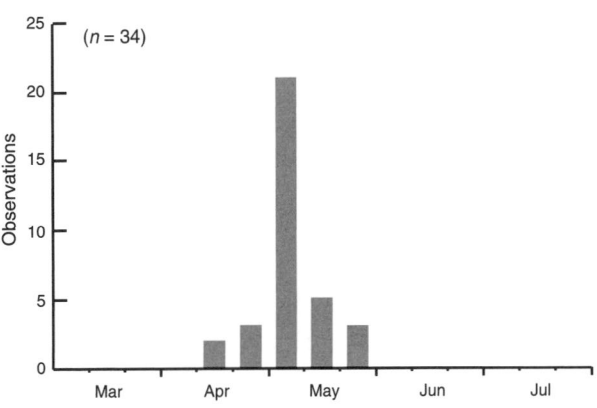

Estimated Clutch-Completion Dates

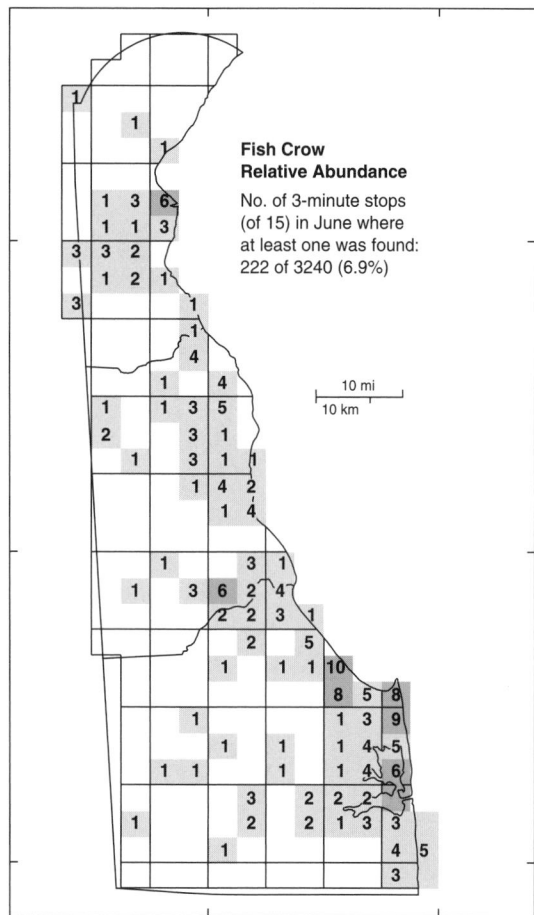

**Fish Crow
Relative Abundance**

No. of 3-minute stops
(of 15) in June where
at least one was found:
222 of 3240 (6.9%)

10 mi
10 km

FALL: Migration probably occurs from late September to early December. A high count is 225 on 12 October 1974 at Dragon Run [Wayn2].

1966–89 CBC Summary

Christmas Bird Count	Years Found	Range of No. Found	Median
Wilmington	23	1–1,178	108
Middletown	23	2–527	41
Bombay Hook	24	1–101	5
Cape Henlopen	8	1–10	
Rehoboth	15	1–14	2
STATEWIDE (low in 1969, high in 1980)	24	12–1,185	318

WINTER: This species has shown an increase in numbers, followed by a recent decline. Most Fish Crows noted on CBCs are reported from the Wilmington and Middletown CBCs. Most of the Wilmington birds have been found at the Cherry Island landfill, where changes in landfill management may have reduced the numbers of birds present.

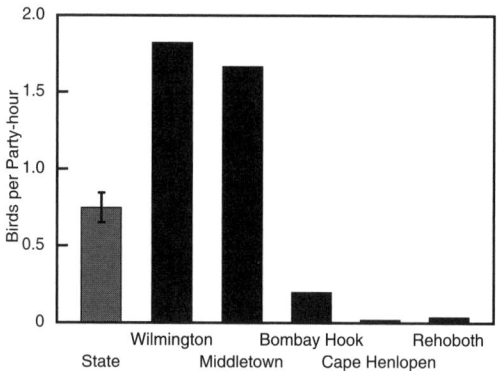

CBC Geographic Distribution

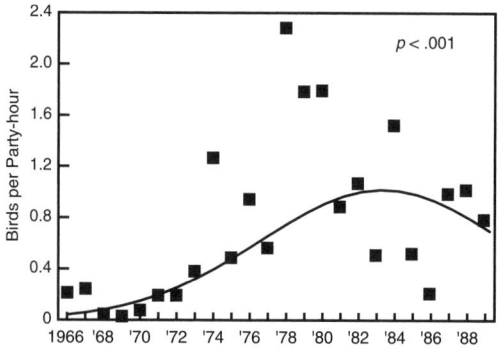

CBC Trend

SPECIMENS: ANSP 66167, Rehoboth Beach, 4 May 1912; DMNH 679, Sussex Co., 25 May 1957; CM 86286, Bethany Beach, 11 September 1922. Egg records: DMNH, WFVZ.

History. This coastal and riverine crow has expanded its range in New York, Pennsylvania, and the Ohio and Shenandoah Valleys during the twentieth century (Bonney 1988a; Poole 1964; Meanley 1981; Peterjohn 1988), but it has been present in Delaware since the earliest accounts. Wilson, writing in about 1810, said he encountered it up the Delaware River at the Schuylkill (Wilson and Bonaparte 1859–60). Krider (1879, 54) reports that "This Crow makes its appearance along the Delaware in Spring, when Shad fishermen commence to haul their nets, to feed on the small fish that are left along the shore. I have found them breeding in New Jersey in May." However, early mention of this species is infrequent, and its numbers in all seasons have clearly increased in recent decades.

Trends. BBS data show an average annual increase in the East of about 3–4% for the 1966–89 period, more than doubling its population. Although the Delaware BBS data is based on a smaller sample, they show a similar tendency [Usfw3], and the May Count data show an annual 3% increase during 1969–90.

Breeding population. The best basis for estimating the Fish Crow's population is its occurrence in 133 Atlas blocks and its presence at 222 stops during the relative abundance study. It is sometimes loosely colonial (Bent 1946) as it is in Newark (Hess pers. obs.).

Common Raven (*Corvus corax*)

Accidental (1994).

DOCUMENTATION: Convincing notes.

HISTORICAL STATUS: During the nineteenth century the raven was a rare permanent resident not only in the mountains of Pennsylvania, where it persists today, but also in the coastal lowlands of New Jersey, for example, Mays Landing, Tuckerton, and Atlantic City (Turnbull 1869, 25; Stone 1937, 720). The remains of 2 ravens were found in the seventeenth-century Susquehannock Native American village at Washington Boro, Pennsylvania, along the lower Susquehanna River (Guilday et al. 1962, 62), and the species at one time was resident in Chester County, Pennsylvania (Burns 1919, 67–68).

The Lenapes, who lived in northern and central Delaware (and New Jersey and eastern Pennsylvania), and the Nanticokes, who lived on the Eastern Shore of Maryland and in southern Delaware, each had separate terms for "crow" and "raven" (Holm 1702, 165; Brinton and Anthony 1888, 14, 160; Speck 1927, 51).

Seventeenth-century colonists found a spectacular wilderness megafauna in Delaware and nearby Pennsylvania, including deer, elk, bear, cougar, and wolf, as well as whales in Delaware Bay (Lindestrom 1925, 185; Myers 1912, 8, 228–29, 321). The raven, an opportunistic scavenger and predator, was probably then a permanent resident in Delaware, feeding on the carcasses of these larger mammals.

REMARKS: Inskip (notes) reported a raven in flight above a group of crows on 2 November 1984 in Wilmington. His description is convincing, citing the "perceptibly but not strikingly wedge-shaped" tail and appropriate distinctions in shape from hawks. The flight behavior of the raven was also convincingly described. This species' range and numbers have dramatically increased in Pennsylvania in recent years, and breeding now occurs within 60–80 mi of Delaware (Mulvihill 1992a), so sightings in Delaware may be expected.

[Sky Lark (*Alauda arvensis*)]

Unsuccessful introduction.

REMARKS: Falk (1972b) presented the known information about the Sky Lark's introduction and its subsequent fate: 2 shipments totaling 42 Sky Larks were introduced in Wilmington in 1853. They were seen on 24 July ascending to the sky, warbling as cheerfully as in England. The birds were subsequently noted at irregular intervals for about 2 years in Delaware and Chester counties, Pennsylvania, and were last seen in West Chester in 1854 [Usda1].

Horned Lark *(Eremophila alpestris)*

Occurs all year; uncommon to fairly common south of the Chesapeake and Delaware Canal; rare north of it. Winter numbers decreasing at 10% per year. The breeding population invaded Delaware from the Great Plains during the twentieth century.

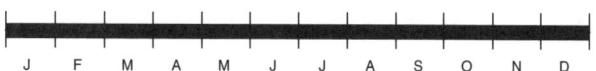

HABITAT: Open fields in agricultural areas; corn stubble.

SPRING: Migration begins early, 5–25 February, and by 10–15 March most visitors have departed. An unusually high number of 1,000 was reported at Cape Henlopen SP on 18 February 1967 [DuPA2]. More typical high counts are

10 Feb 1986	100	Rts. 10 and 42, Kent County [Wayn24]
13 Feb 1982	>100	Kent County [Barn13]
19 Feb 1983	>100	Kent County [Barn13]
17 Mar 1931	180	Blackbird [Hans1]

BREEDING: Not until the start of the BBS in 1966 was the Horned Lark's widespread breeding recognized. In 1967 larks were recorded on all 10 state routes and totaled 91 birds, which remains the high BBS count. Half the population is in the southwest quadrant of the state corresponding to the Nanticoke drainage, a heavily agricultural area. It is also fairly common in agricultural areas in northeastern Kent and southwestern New Castle counties.

Atlas. Nesting is difficult to confirm because adults will leave nests when approached within 100 yards (Pickwell 1931). Of the 31 confirmations, a nest was reported only 3 times.

Nesting. Barry (1942) stated that "Prairie Horned Lark breeds in Delaware," without citing evidence. In 1967 it was again listed as breeding in Delaware without details (Linehan 1967). Consequently, the earliest breeding records result from the finding of 1 egg on 25 March and, separately, 3 eggs on 4 April 1969, both in corn stubble near Leipsic [Holg3].

Estimated clutch-completion dates for the only 3 nests are late March, early April, and early May. It is double-brooded; eggs should be expected into July (Pickwell 1931). Clutch size is usually 4 (Harrison 1978).

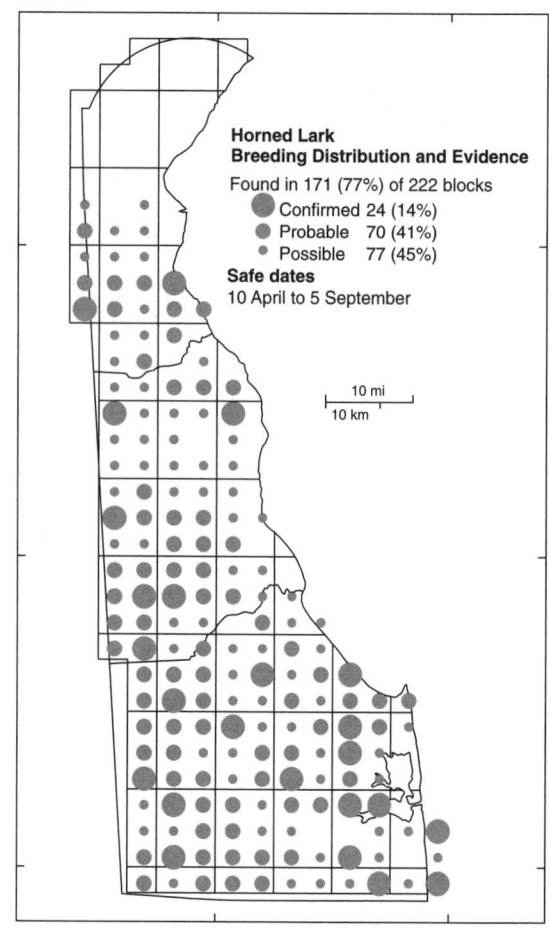

Horned Lark
Breeding Distribution and Evidence
Found in 171 (77%) of 222 blocks
● Confirmed 24 (14%)
● Probable 70 (41%)
· Possible 77 (45%)
Safe dates
10 April to 5 September

10 mi
10 km

Trends. The distribution and relative abundance maps show a void in northern Delaware, though previous records indicate it was found in at least 5 northern locations, including Claymont and Marshallton, where it was banded (see "History"). Linehan and Miller (Dyer et al. 1973) reported its breeding on the Louviers Golf Course before 1973. The Churchmans Marsh surveys recorded 2 on 5 June 1965 and 1 on 19 June. It was not recorded on similar surveys in 1956 or 1980 (Brooks 1957; West and Klabunde 1977; Hess 1983). In the early 1960s it was singing regularly from a field (now built up) near Fairfax (West, pers. obs.). Range extension into northern Delaware was not permanent, and further range contraction should be expected wherever agricultural practices are abandoned. However, its population appears stable in the eastern United States as a whole [Usfw1].

Breeding population. The 1989 May Count found 81, the highest total. Territory size ranges from 0.5 to 5 ha (Beason and Franks 1974).

FALL: The first winter visitors arrive 10–15 November. The end of migration is not clear but may be in early December. High counts are 30 at Prime Hook NWR on 26 October 1980

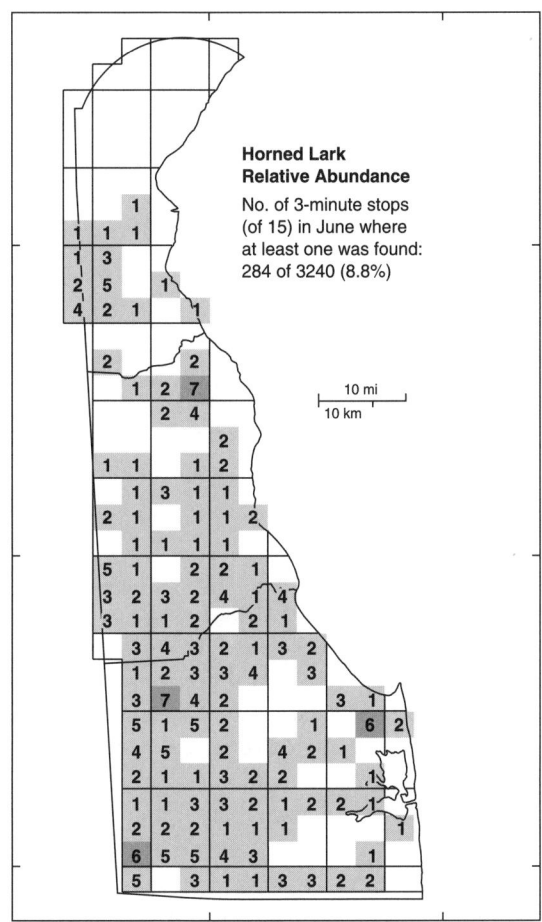

Horned Lark Relative Abundance

No. of 3-minute stops (of 15) in June where at least one was found: 284 of 3240 (8.8%)

10 mi / 10 km

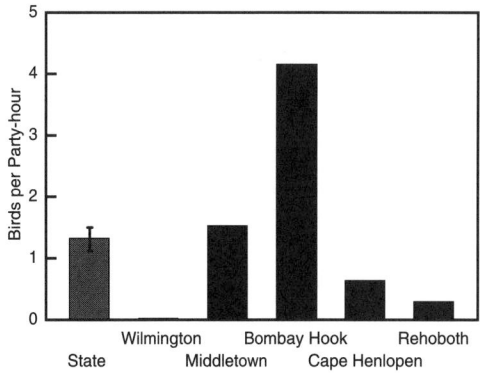

CBC Geographic Distribution

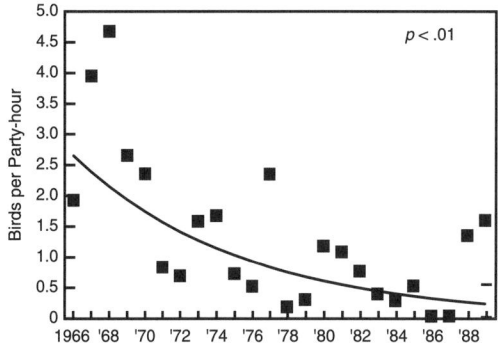

$p < .01$

CBC Trend; Decreasing at 10% per Year

[Frec1] and 50 at Little Creek WA on 15 November 1964 [anon17].

1966–89 CBC Summary

Christmas Bird Count	Years Found	Range of No. Found	Median
Wilmington	6	1–8	
Middletown	16	3–612	15
Bombay Hook	24	6–1,026	169
Cape Henlopen	22	1–168	22
Rehoboth	23	2–109	16
STATEWIDE	24	15–1,434	352

(decreasing; low in 1986 and 1987, high in 1967)

WINTER: Based on CBC numbers, the winter population in Delaware has significantly declined. This trend differs from that of the May Count and the BBS [Usfw3], which monitor the breeding population.

HISTORY: The Horned Lark was only a winter visitor in Delaware until early in the twentieth century. Specimens from 1877, 1907–12, and 1928 were taken between 19 November and 3 March, and all are *E. a. alpestris*, the Northern or Shore Horned Lark (ANSP, DMNH).

The prairie population *(E. a. praticola)* expanded northeastward and southward once forest barriers were removed. One thrust starting in the 1860s carried it through Michigan and Ontario and into New York by the 1880s (Pickwell 1931). It reached Long Island by 1886 (Dutcher 1888). Delaware birds may have come from a second expansion that penetrated the Allegheny Mountains to western Maryland between 1900 and 1910 (Hurley and Franks 1976). Breeding was first reported east of the Alleghenies near Laurel, Maryland, on 23 June 1922 (Swales 1922). Pickwell (1931, 21) reported no evidence of breeding in Delaware or New Jersey, but by 1933 nesting was confirmed in Mt. Holly, New Jersey (Leck 1984).

The first account of the Prairie Horned Lark in Delaware was written by Hanson (notes): "Herbert Buckalew reports shooting one in Feb. 1933 on the shore in Sussex County. It was in company with [Northern] Horned Larks but unfortunately was mangled so badly that a specimen was not saved." The significance of several Prairie Horned Larks observed on 14 May 1933 near Delaware City was not lost on Potter and Stone. Potter noted the birds were "singing and perhaps breeding" [Pott5]. Stone reported that "At Delaware City across the river John Gillespie and others found these birds [Prairie Horned Larks] singing on May 14, 1933, which suggests they nested there as well" (Stone 1937, 688).

Southward expansion continued. Wayne's notes, begun in 1949, show that he found it regularly during the breeding season. It was seen on trips on 1 May 1949 to Bombay Hook and Rehoboth Beach, 8 April 1950 to Indian River Inlet, 18 April 1953 to New Castle and Delaware City, and 17 May 1956 to Bombay Hook NWR [Wayn1].

In 1953 Horned Larks were reported nesting at Norfolk, Virginia, and "J. H. Grey believes it is increasing as a breeding bird on the Lower Peninsula. It was found to be relatively common in mid-June on the Eastern Shore all the way south to Cape Charles" (Scott 1954). Avery banded a Horned Lark near Claymont in July 1956, and Farrand banded 2 at Marshallton on 22 May 1957 [Usfw3].

Not until 25 January 1958 (DMNH 829) and February 1978 and 1985 (DMNH 63487, DMNH 63488, DMNH 76044) were Prairie Horned Larks collected, but on those dates the birds may have been winter visitors or migrants. Thus we have no physical evidence establishing the date of initial Horned Lark breeding in Delaware, although it must have been in the early 1930s.

SPECIMENS: 19; ANSP, DMNH.

Purple Martin (*Progne subis*)

Regular; summer resident; fairly common. Expected early April to early September. Widespread and sharply increasing south of the Chesapeake and Delaware Canal. Subject to starvation in extended cold or rainy weather.

J F M A M J J A S O N D

HABITAT: Open country, near residences providing nesting houses, frequently near water.

SPRING: Although some individuals arrive during 1–7 April, it becomes numerous only after 8–15 April. The end of migration is probably in late May. Undocumented March reports have been received in 6 years, the earliest:

4 Mar 1973	8	Bombay Hook NWR [John9]
10 Mar 1991	1	Ted Harvey CA, Logan Tract [Camp17]
17 Mar 1990	1	Ted Harvey CA, Logan Tract [Litt4]

High counts include

12 Apr 1975	401	Delaware City [Dyer1]
18 Apr 1933	200	Dover [Hans1]
3 May 1980	56	Prime Hook NWR [Frec1]

The highest May Count is 893 (1989), and the lowest is 59 (1974).

BREEDING: The scarcity of Purple Martins in Delaware north of I-95 is difficult to explain, though open fields are becoming increasingly rare, and those who own the fields that remain apparently are not putting up nest boxes. The relative abundance study shows a correlation of martin abundance with coastal areas along the Atlantic Ocean and with inland bays but not with river marshes. In general, its pattern of abundance is subtly different from that of the Horned Lark, although both require open country. The lark requires big dry fields for breeding; the martin needs nest boxes and moist habitat with abundant insect prey. See, for example, in New Castle County where the 2 overlap in only 2 blocks of the distribution map.

Atlas. In the southern part of the state, blocks where martins were unrecorded are wooded and sparsely inhabited. In those blocks Atlas workers presumably checked all roads and houses in open situations without finding maintained martin houses or other evidence of martins.

Nesting. All nest records come from artificial structures. Clutch completion occurs in mid-May for experienced pairs; first-year pairs achieve completion about 2 or 3 weeks later (Morton et al. 1990). Renestings extend the period into late

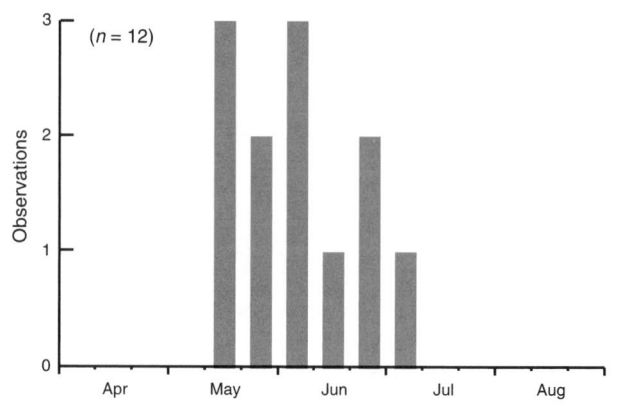

Estimated Clutch-Completion Dates

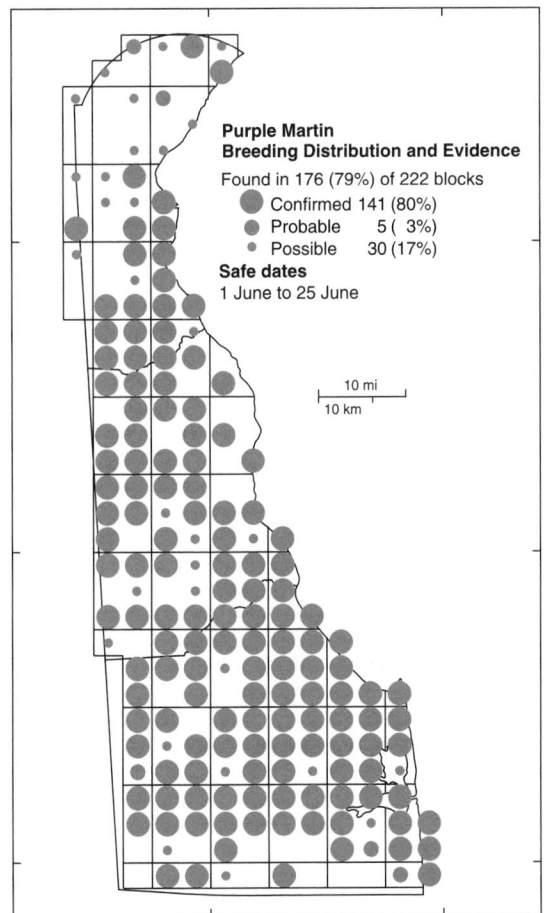

**Purple Martin
Breeding Distribution and Evidence**

Found in 176 (79%) of 222 blocks

● Confirmed 141 (80%)
● Probable 5 (3%)
· Possible 30 (17%)

Safe dates
1 June to 25 June

10 mi
10 km

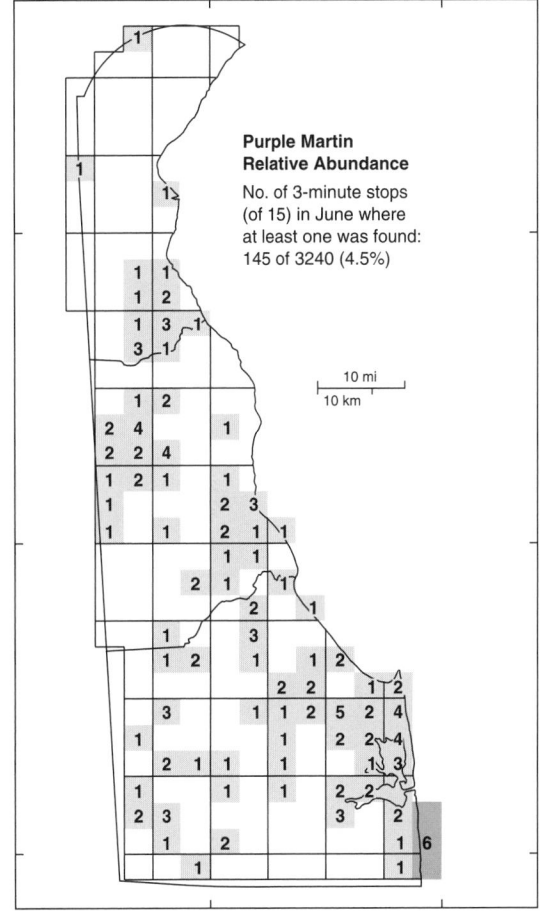

**Purple Martin
Relative Abundance**

No. of 3-minute stops
(of 15) in June where
at least one was found:
145 of 3240 (4.5%)

10 mi
10 km

June. The nest is an accumulation of loose plant material; clutch size is usually 4 or 5 (Harrison 1978).

History. Its natural nesting sites include woodpecker and naturally occurring cavities in dead trees in open areas. Stutchbury (1991) points out that most martin colonies reported at natural sites in the East were small. First the Native Americans (Wilson 1859) and then the Europeans erected gourds or houses for martins. These artificial colonial sites are so readily accepted that it now rarely uses natural sites. By analogy with New York, the Purple Martin population probably declined 30–50% between 1860 and 1910 because introduced House Sparrows and starlings usurped nesting sites (Eaton 1914); Eaton predicted "extirpation within a generation in most localities" if House Sparrows were not kept out of martin houses. His forecast has not been fulfilled, but many people remove House Sparrows from nest houses or put the house up only when martins arrive in the spring.

Trends. Late winter freezes and consequent starvation lead to abrupt population declines. Mayfield (1964) notes the coincidence between a late winter freeze that killed many migrating Purple Martins in Florida in 1958 and a 41% reduction in their population in Toledo, Ohio, but he was careful not to imply causality. The greatest population changes, however, may come from starvation of the nestlings caused by protracted spring rain (Robbins et al. 1986) rather than by late winter

freezes. The eastern population has remained relatively stable over the past 25 years, despite substantial weather-related local fluctuations during that period (Robbins et al. 1986). In the past 10 years martins appear to have increased significantly in Delaware at an annual rate of perhaps 15% [Usfw1]. This increase should probably be regarded as temporary, however, because of the effects of occasional severe weather on its population. An increase in properly erected and maintained martin houses might well increase its overall abundance.

Breeding population. The Delmarva Peninsula has the highest martin density in the Northeast (Hill 1988). There are about 5.8 nests per site in eastern North America (Erskine 1979; Jackson and Tate 1974).

FALL: Purple Martins are one of the earliest departing swallows, with migration beginning in late June or early July and most gone by 1–10 September. High counts are

20 Jul 1977	100	Rehoboth Beach [Frec1]
7 Aug 1984	100	Lewes area [Frec1]
30 Aug 1969	202	Brandywine Creek SP [Wayn25]

Stone (1937) describes a great autumn roost of many starlings, grackles, robins, blackbirds, and 15,000 Purple Martins at Cape May, New Jersey; and late summer flocks of a thousand or more occur in Maryland (Stewart and Robbins 1958). No large flocks have been reported in Delaware.

An October 1970 report of martins (DuMont and Dumont

1971a) seen later than the latest given for Maryland, Pennsylvania, or Cape May, New Jersey, is not accepted because of lack of corroboration. However, it should be possible to find and document stragglers later than Delaware's 3 latest reports, which are for 19 September.

REMARKS: "Mosquitoes appear to be a negligible item in [the Purple Martin's] diet" (Kale 1968). Deer flies are more typical of the insects it eats (Beal 1918).

SPECIMENS: 10; DMNH, CM, UDEL, USNM.

Tree Swallow *(Tachycineta bicolor)*

Regular; summer resident; fairly common to common. Expected mid-March through November and sporadically through the winter. Mostly near Delaware River and Bay, but unevenly spaced. Forms enormous flocks in late summer.

J F M A M J J A S O N D

HABITAT: Open areas, usually near water. Prefers a nest site in a field or over a pond.

SPRING: The first arrival is most often during 10–20 March, but may be earlier some years. It is present in fairly high numbers until 20–25 May, after which only the breeding population remains. Discerning earliest arrival dates is confounded by a few years in which Tree Swallows were found in February; the following may all be unusually early arrivals of birds wintering only slightly to the south:

20 Feb 1988	3	Broadkill Beach Rd. [Buhl2]
21 Feb 1986	4	Oyster Rocks Rd. [Frec1]
2 Mar 1972	25	Bombay Hook NWR [Holg7]
5 Mar 1974	1	Bombay Hook NWR [Holg86]

The peak report is 25,000 birds at Bombay Hook NWR and Little Creek WA on 8 May 1970 [Abbo13]. The highest May Count is 12,918 (11 May 1974), and the lowest is 429 (8 May 1971).

BREEDING: In Delaware the Tree Swallow is close to its southern breeding limit on the Coastal Plain; its numbers are partly maintained by nest boxes. Breeding in Delaware is found in 3 areas: those on the Piedmont nesting primarily in nest boxes, those nesting frequently in nest boxes along the Delaware

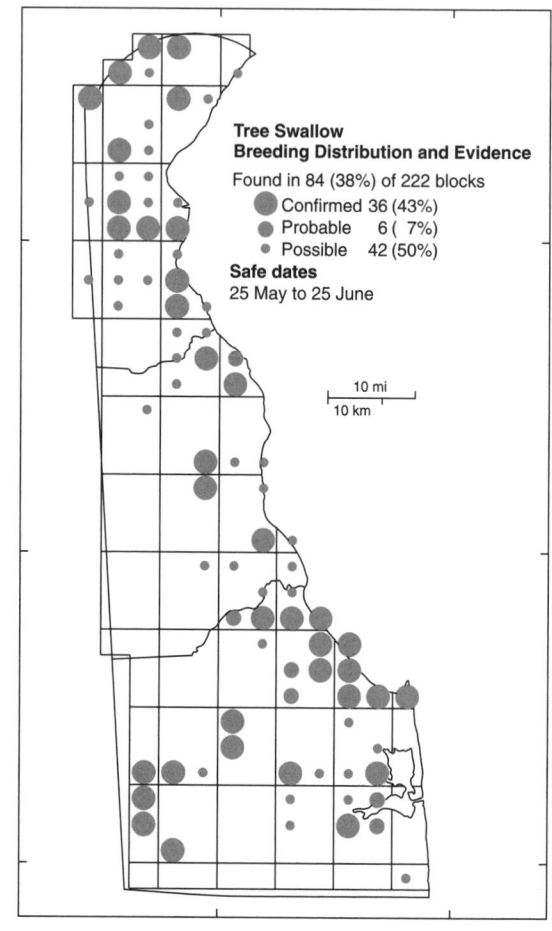

Tree Swallow
Breeding Distribution and Evidence
Found in 84 (38%) of 222 blocks
● Confirmed 36 (43%)
● Probable   6 (7%)
· Possible   42 (50%)
Safe dates
25 May to 25 June

10 mi
10 km

and Indian rivers, and those nesting mainly in dead trees standing in ponds in the interior.

Atlas. Nesting reports from bluebird trails and other nest boxes provided the primary source of confirmations. Tree Swallows also were found breeding in cavities in dead trees standing in large ponds. Of 37 confirmations, 32 involved finding the nest site, and 4 referred to fledged young.

Nesting. Tree Swallows compete with bluebirds and House Wrens for nest sites. One study indicates that Tree Swallows were more successful than the other two species in boxes farther out in fields; if swallows were in boxes more than 20 yds (20 m) from an edge, wrens seldom destroyed their eggs (Rendell and Robertson 1990). Tree Swallows breed either as isolat-

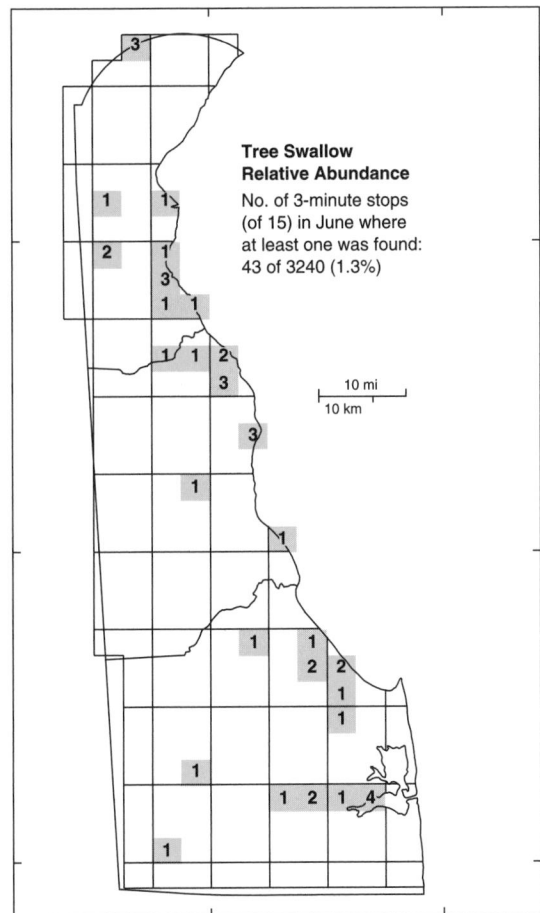

Tree Swallow
Relative Abundance
No. of 3-minute stops
(of 15) in June where
at least one was found:
43 of 3240 (1.3%)

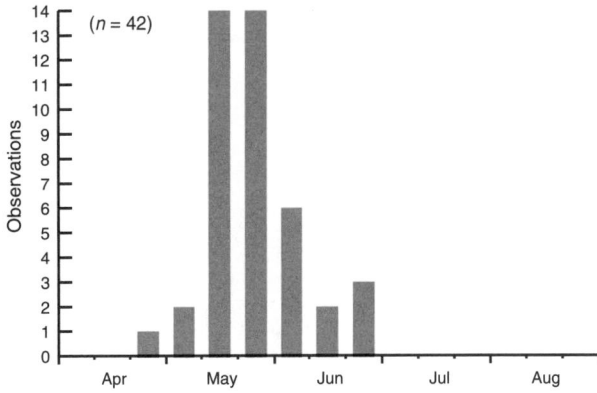

Estimated Clutch-Completion Dates

The highest breeding season count on the Dragon Run survey was 19 on 7 June 1975 [Wayn25]. An unusually high number, 125, was reported at Bombay Hook NWR on 5 June 1982 [Wayn45]. Examples of populations maintained in nest boxes are 11 nests in 1975 at Bombay Hook NWR [Holg3] and a 1980 report of occupied nest boxes at Prime Hook NWR [O'Sh2].

FALL: Fall migration begins 25 June–1 July. During this time numerous flocks of up to 50 birds are often seen perched on utility wires in the countryside. By 15 July enormous flocks gather and move down the river and bay coast. The peak count is 50,000 near Dover AFB on 10 August 1966 [Pres5]. By 20–30 October the large flocks have departed, and after November only occasional small flocks are seen, often high overhead.

1966–89 CBC Summary

Christmas Bird Count	Years Found	Range of No. Found	Median
Wilmington			
Middletown			
Bombay Hook	6	2–47	
Cape Henlopen	12	1–490	
Rehoboth	7	13–382	
STATEWIDE (high in 1966)	13	4–712	6

WINTER: Tree Swallows remain into early winter, a few being found on 1 or 2 CBCs in most years, but they are rarely present from mid-January through February. There are 12 reports from January, of which the most notable involves a flock of 150 feeding on bayberry about one-half mi from Big Stone Beach on 17 January 1975 [Wees1]. Typical January reports include 1–4 birds. A February report of 6 at Broadkill Beach on 12 February 1954 [Davi6] may pertain to wintering birds, and 2 reports later in February are included under spring migration.

SPECIMENS: 15; DMNH, CM, UDEL, USNM. Egg records: DMNH.

ed pairs or in loose colonies, in either case vigorously defending a territory of some 6–8 m around the nest (Robertson and Gibbs 1982).

In Delaware most nest records are from nests found in nest boxes. One nest in a natural cavity had 5 eggs "in a hole in a willow tree standing in the water about 10 feet from the shore in Silver Lake, Dover, May 30 [1927]. Hole 5 feet from the water and about 8 inches deep. It was large enough to get my hand in. . . . The nest contained many feathers" [Hans1]. An exceptional nest site occurred in a telephone pole along Rt. 13 near Delaware State University (Hans1).

Clutch completion is estimated to begin in late April, with a clear peak in mid- to late May. Renestings extend the season into late June. The Tree Swallow is rarely double-brooded in Ohio (Burtt 1989), it may occasionally be double-brooded at Tinicum NWR, Pennsylvania (Stocek 1970), and second broods were suggested by Stone (1937) at Cape May. Clutch size is 3–6, usually 5 (n = 24).

Trends. This species has increased in the East during 1966–90 and may have increased in Delaware. It benefits from the provision of nest boxes when it is in competition with House Wrens for nest sites (Finch 1990), as it is in Delaware.

Breeding population. The highest breeding season count from the Piedmont is 60 on 16 June 1993 at Burrows Run [Wayn25].

Northern Rough-winged Swallow *(Stelgidopteryx serripennis)*

Regular; summer resident; uncommon to fairly common. Expected early April to late August. Nests widely in small colonies or singly. Increasing.

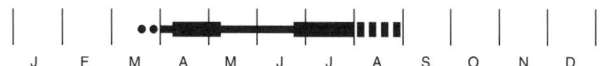

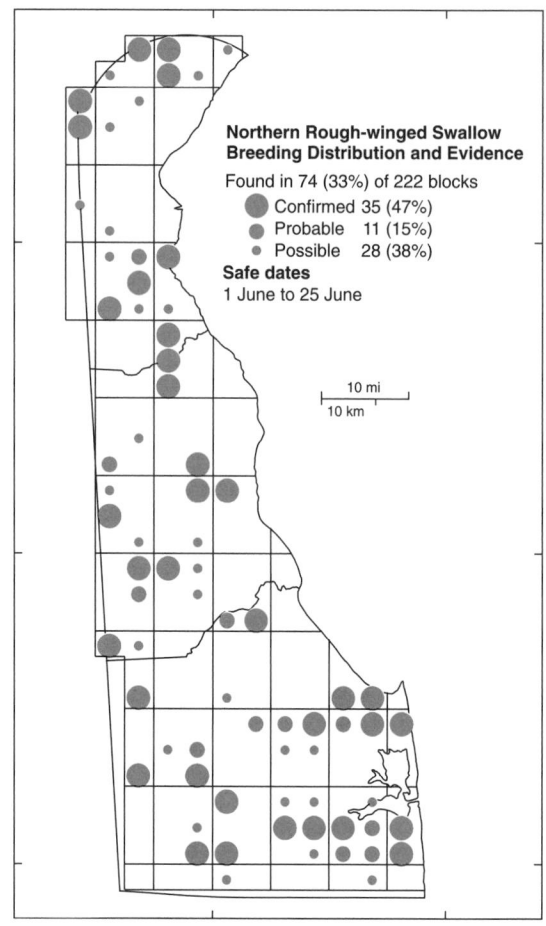

Northern Rough-winged Swallow Breeding Distribution and Evidence

Found in 74 (33%) of 222 blocks

Confirmed 35 (47%)
Probable   11 (15%)
Possible   28 (38%)

Safe dates
1 June to 25 June

10 mi
10 km

HABITAT: Feeds predominantly near open water; places nests in existing burrows, ditches, or drain pipes, or makes nest burrows wherever banks with sandy dirt are available (e.g., sand pits, quarries, and highway embankments even away from water). Nests along tax ditches until erosion and vegetation encroachment make them unsuitable.

SPRING: First arrival is 1–10 April, peak migration occurs 15 April–15 May, and migration probably ends by late May. The earliest reports include

18 Mar 1973	1	Dragon Run [Conw10]
30 Mar 1984	2	Red Mill Pond [Frec1]
31 Mar 1991	6	Trussum Pond SP [Camp18]

Highest counts, both from Dragon Run in 1973, are 50 on 14 April and 42 on 28 April [BroW7]. The highest May Count is 102 (4 May 1985), and the lowest is 13 (7 May 1977).

BREEDING: The Piedmont population must be quite low; a few pairs nest along creeks such as White Clay and Brandywine, particularly in deep crevices of the old stonework associated with mills. The relative abundance study shows that it is less scarce in the southern part of the state but nowhere common. In Kent and Sussex counties it breeds along freshly dug or maintained tax ditches, 1 of the few species to benefit from this program.

Atlas. This species was located by careful searches around ponds, streams, and ditches. It feeds over water more than oth-er swallows (Lunk 1962). As soon as the young fledge, Rough-winged Swallows quit the nesting area and begin migration (Lunk 1962); thus even 25 June may be too late for the end of its safe dates, and some of the possible breeding reports may refer to migrants. The most frequently used confirmation code was "occupied nest."

Nesting. This swallow nests alone or in small colonies (Lunk 1962, 25), frequenting sand banks and creek embankments. Hanson (notes) described a nest at Riverdale in a bank on Indian River Bay: "One nest, 2 feet into the bank, had 7 eggs. . . . At the end of the hole there was a slight enlargement lined with pine needles, May 31, 1924." He described another at Silver Lake, Dover, as 2 feet from the top: "The bank was only about 6 feet high, the hole about 3 inches in diameter and ran into the bank 18 inches, slightly ascending. At the end was a slight enlargement, or chamber, in which was the nest, composed of fine dead grass." We do not know how frequently it digs its own burrow, but it accepts a wide range of natural and artificial nest cavities, such as crevices in old masonry, drain pipes, and used burrows.

Estimated clutch-completion dates start in late April and

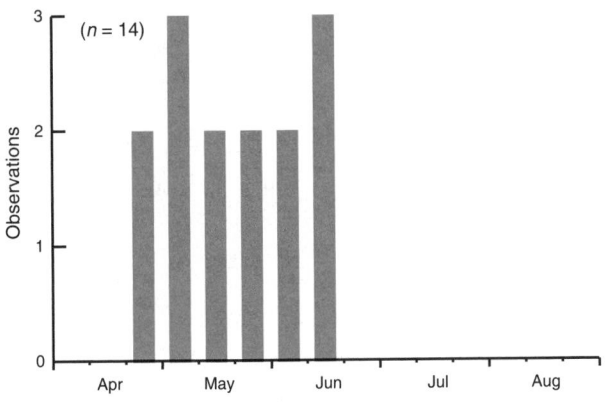

Estimated Clutch-Completion Dates

continue with no obvious peak through mid-June (*n* = 14). The earliest dates come from 2 Trussum Pond SP nests at which young were visible at the mouth of the burrows on 28 May 1977 and from which young fledged before 5 June [Lehm3]. The earliest egg date is 11 May 1957 (a clutch of 6 slightly incubated) from Sussex County (DMNH 9140). The clutch and Lehman's May nestlings are earlier than those usually reported. The latest egg date is 11 June [Edni4], and the latest nest with young 19 July [Atla1]. It is generally single-brooded (Ricklefs 1972). Clutches of 4, 6, and 7 occurred in Delaware; 6 or 7 are the most frequent clutch sizes reported from other states (Lunk 1962; Bent 1942).

Trends. The BBS data indicate a significant increase in the population of Northern Rough-winged Swallows at an average rate of about 3% per year (1966–90). Particularly high numbers were reported in 1982–84 [Usfw3]. The construction of tax ditches may be a factor in this increase.

Conservation. This swallow readily accepts artificial nest sites made from plastic pipe lined with hardware cloth and placed in the banks of gravel pits (Lunk 1962).

FALL: Migration begins in late June or early July. Based on available reports, all leave by 20–30 August, and even some of these few reports may have referred to misidentified birds. Undocumented late reports that may be satisfactory include the following:

22 Aug 1981	5	Bombay Hook NWR [Citr8]
25 Aug 1973	13	Dragon Run [West2]
31 Aug 1974	3	Dragon Run [Phal10]

An October report (Speck and Brokaw 1979) arose from a transcription error, and the only September report lacks documentation (Scott and Cutler 1970). Reports in late August should be made with caution and observations documented as to how the birds were distinguished from young Tree Swallows. Stewart and Robbins (1958) give the normal departure date in Maryland as 5 September and the extreme as 14 September. The peak count is 50 at Broadkill Beach on 24 July 1977 [Frec1].

REMARKS: Krider (1879, 36) reports that he "found it from Delaware to New York."

SPECIMENS: DMNH 676, Sussex Co., 11 May 1957; DMNH 684, Sussex Co., 25 May 1957. Egg records: DMNH.

Bank Swallow *(Riparia riparia)*

Regular; summer resident; locally fairly common. Expected late April to mid-September. Nests in large colonies at only a few sites, primarily sand and gravel quarries.

HABITAT: Areas with open water and large sandy banks.

SPRING: Bank Swallows usually arrive 15–20 April, a little later than other swallow species. Earliest arrivals reported include

31 Mar 1972	1	Bombay Hook NWR [Holg71]
6 Apr 1974	many	Bombay Hook NWR [Wayn2]
9 Apr 1985	1	New Castle Co. [Barn45]

Peak migration occurs 5–15 May, and the last migrants pass through 20–25 May. A migration report of 25,000 in the Bombay Hook NWR–Little Creek WA area 8 May 1970 [Abbo12] was extraordinary, since a few hundred at a time are typical. The highest May Count is 199 (13 May 1989), and the lowest is zero (4 May 1985).

BREEDING: The only colony on public property is located along the Chesapeake and Delaware Canal south of Lums Pond (Faust 1968b). At least four other colonies occur in active sand quarries—near Stanton [MiDP2], near Drawyers Creek [Blad1], and at 2 or more sites along Brown Branch in Kent County [Lehm2, West3]. The Delaware population is near the

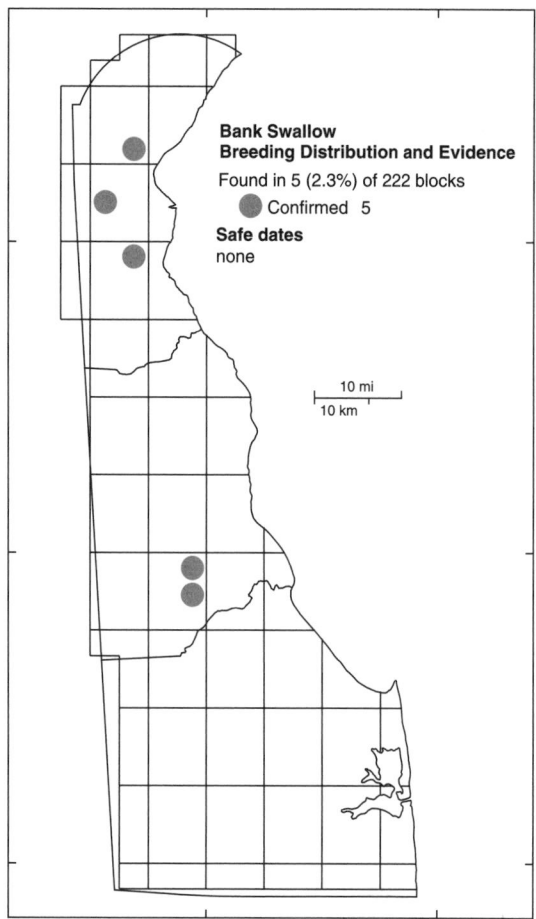

Bank Swallow
Breeding Distribution and Evidence
Found in 5 (2.3%) of 222 blocks
● Confirmed 5
Safe dates
none

10 mi
10 km

cuts, quarries, and canals. The earliest nesting reports are a nest in a railroad bank near Lewes on 7 June 1898 and a large colony nesting in a railroad cut opposite the old Farnhurst railroad station 12–15 July 1905 [Penn1]. One colony is of long standing. On 15 June 1929 Hanson (notes) visited "a colony of Bank Swallows in a gravel bank in Stanton. There were about 50 holes in the bank, most of which, at least, were occupied." Buckalew reported breeding there on 18 June 1930 [Buck8]. Dicky visited the same site in 1931 and reported that the colony at Stanton was larger than ever and that a new colony had been established near the old one in the bank of White Clay Creek [Hans1]. This last colony is the only one reported nesting in natural substrate in Delaware. The species still breeds in a gravel pit near Stanton. It was also breeding along the Lewes and Rehoboth Canal in 1957 (DMNH 9129). The Chesapeake and Delaware Canal site was first reported in 1967 and remains active.

Breeding population. There are about 5 gravel quarries with active colonies, but monitoring them is difficult because the quarries are closed to the public. The population at the Chesapeake and Delaware Canal site was reported to contain 120 active nests in 1967 (Faust 1968), and the others are probably smaller. The state population falls in the range of 100–1,000 pairs.

Conservation. Because of its concentration in a few colonies, all at potentially temporary sites, colonies on public lands should be protected, and quarry owners should be given incentives to maintain colonies on their sites.

FALL: Migration begins in late June and early July. Peak numbers occur from 25 July to 5 September. Few remain after the first week of September. Linehan banded a late one on 7 September 1963 6 mi east of Red Lion [Line5]. High counts are

31 Jul 1981	3,000	Bombay Hook NWR [Grim1]
28 Jul 1979	800–1,000	Cape Henlopen SP [Jahn7]
9 Sep 1962	1,000	Little Creek WA [anon12]

The September report seems high for so late a date, compared with more recent reports. Undocumented late reports, which may include misidentifications, are

3 Oct 1982	2	Bombay Hook NWR [RusJ11]
6 Oct 1974	4	Dragon Run [BroW22]
10 Oct 1987	1	Bombay Hook NWR [Barn60]
11 Oct 1975	2	Dragon Run [Barn1]

SPECIMENS: USNM 355202, Delaware City, 7 May 1926; UDEL 394-68, Bear, 10 May 1968. Egg records: DMNH.

southern limit of its Atlantic Coastal Plain breeding range (Peterson 1980).

Atlas. Several reports were received of Bank Swallows from blocks adjacent to those with colonies. These reports were assumed to be of foraging birds from the breeding colonies and are therefore not plotted on the distribution map. Similarly, during the Churchmans Marsh and Dragon Run surveys Bank Swallows were occasionally reported and in the latter case were about 5 mi from the nearest known colony. With a colonial species, it is proper to report only confirmed breeding colonies, because individuals must often forage far from the colony.

Nesting. The Bank Swallow breeds colonially in large vertical sand banks in open areas. Clutches of 5 and 4 eggs have been found on 23 May [Hans1] and 16 May (DMNH 9129) and a nest and egg on 7 June [Penn1]; nestlings have been reported on 23 May [Hans1], 15 and 23 June [Lehm2], 9 July (Faust 1968), and 12–15 July [Penn1].

Clutches are completed beginning about 7 May, peak in late May, and continue into June. Clutch size in other states is usually 3–6, averaging 5 (Turner and Rose 1989).

History. Since Delaware has no significant natural sand banks, Bank Swallows probably did not nest here until after European settlement and the subsequent creation of railroad

Cliff Swallow *(Petrochelidon pyrrhonota)*

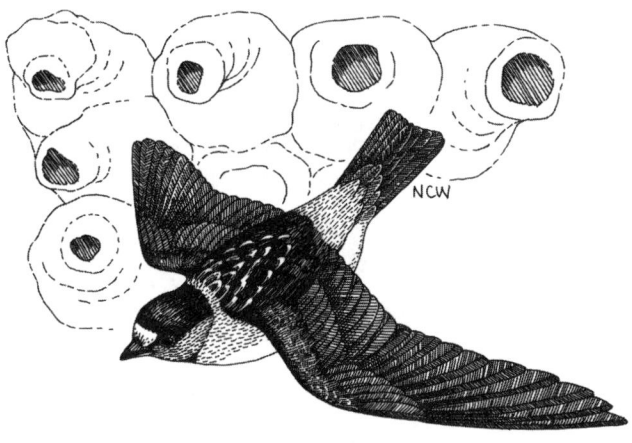

Occasional (18 years, 1966–93); migrant; rare. Most likely in May. Breeding beginning in 1993. Decreased during the twentieth century after becoming common in the East during the nineteenth century.

J F M A M J J A S O N D

DOCUMENTATION: Multiple sight reports, banding record.

MIGRATION: The majority of reports are from spring, with dates ranging from 25 April through 29 May. Earliest reports include

25 Apr 1970	2	Brandywine Creek SP [BroH13]
26 Apr 1971	1	Prime Hook NWR [Holg64]
27 Apr 1992	1	Burrows Run [Wayn64]

Typically, only a few birds are reported, but 100 or more were found on a trip through the state on 17 May 1984 [Cutl11].

The fall migration extends from late July to mid-September, with these extreme dates:

22 Jul 1989	1	Smyrna [Rufe4]
24 Jul 1988	1	Bombay Hook NWR [Shoc1]
5 Sep 1956	1	banded near Red Lion [Line4]
16 Sep 1990	1	near Leipsic [Holg96]

One hundred or more were present near Newark on 6 August 1966 [RusW6], but typically only 1 or 2 birds are reported.

BREEDING: Cliff Swallows were first observed breeding in Delaware on 9 May 1993 when they were found flying in and out of 3 nest structures with 2 entries in each placed on a concrete bridge on Rt. 9 over Appoquinimink Creek. By 1 June, 9 nests were under the bridge, but 6 active nests with 12–14 adults represented peak activity. On 15 June adults were flying back and forth, feeding young (Ednie 1994) [Edni4]. These nests were photographed (Ednie, DMNH 446) [Pulc1].

This swallow may be expected to breed here occasionally, since extralimital breeding such as in Florida (Sykes 1976) is characteristic of the species. Closer to home, it bred near Washington, D.C. in 1958 after a 60-year absence (Booth 1958) and in the Coastal Plain of Virginia near Hopewell 1979–82 (Kain 1987). It regularly breeds in the mountains of neighboring states, but is less common in southeastern Pennsylvania (Schwalbe 1992b). It is now a regular breeder in the Maryland Piedmont and was confirmed in 3 Coastal Plain blocks (Robbins 1996).

History. The Cliff Swallow's historic breeding status in Delaware is uncertain. It did not breed in this area before European settlement and was unknown in the East to Wilson and Audubon. Gross (1942) reports that "as the land of New England was cleared for fields and pastures, and as barns with wide eaves were erected, the Cliff Swallows, finding an abundance of food and sheltered places for their nests, left their primitive environment of isolated cliffs to come in close association with man. Under these new conditions the birds multiplied and spread from place to place where they had not been seen before." This expansion reached southeastern Pennsylvania before a retreat began. Pennock (1887) said it was common and bred in Chester County, Pennsylvania, but he reported in 1902 that the Lenape site, only 5 mi from Delaware, was deserted [Penn3]. Rhoads and Pennock (1905) called it a Delaware summer resident, but Pennock could later give Hanson no localities or records, saying only that it should be in this area. Hanson (notes) never recorded any in the state.

Since Hanson's time, a Cliff Swallow was seen during its breeding season south of Elsmere on 13 June 1971 [Pres4]. A report of a possible nest near Townsend in 1982 is intriguing if not definitive (Hess 1984). Fragments of that nest (DMNH 28793) cannot be distinguished from those of a Barn Swallow's nest because they are too small to discern the original shape.

Conservation. Its range and population in New Jersey have been so reduced that it is listed as Endangered, and nest structures were provided under Delaware River bridges to encourage its breeding (Leck 1984). After declining in the first half of the twentieth century in parts of its range because of the decline of unpainted barns for nest sites, "this trend was reversed with the advent of large dams and superhighway bridges" (Robbins et al. 1986).

Barn Swallow (*Hirundo rustica*)

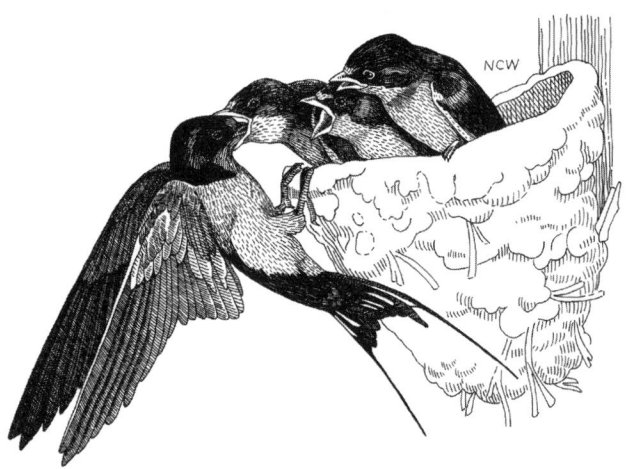

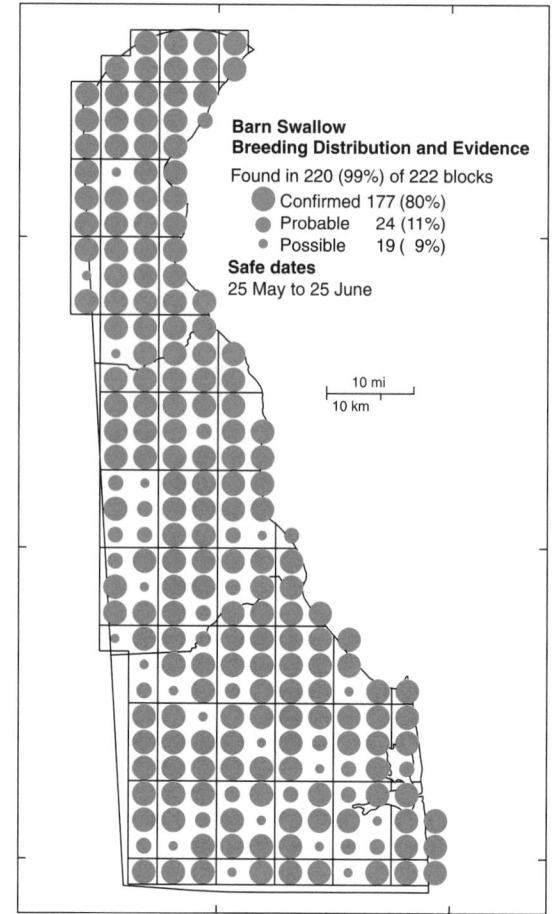

Barn Swallow
Breeding Distribution and Evidence
Found in 220 (99%) of 222 blocks
○ Confirmed 177 (80%)
● Probable 24 (11%)
· Possible 19 (9%)
Safe dates
25 May to 25 June

10 mi
10 km

Regular; summer resident; common. Expected early April through September, with stragglers in October and rarely later. Widespread breeding bird using man-made sites.

HABITAT: Open country with nearby barns, bridges, or other structures providing suitable nesting substrate; needs a source of mud to build its nest.

SPRING: The first arrival is usually 1–7 April, and peak migration is 15 April–20 May. Most migrants leave by 20–25 May. Reports earlier than usual include

25 Mar 1991	4	Lewes [Gros1]
26 Mar 1986	1	Lewes [Frec1]
28 Mar 1992	5	Prime Hook NWR [Samp1]
29 Mar 1929	1	Wilmington [Pott4]

Peak reports are 500 along coastal Sussex County on 17 May 1983 and 1,000 there on 21 May 1983 [Frec1]. The highest May Count is 6,235 (1974), and the lowest is 704 (1975).

BREEDING: This common, cosmopolitan swallow is relatively evenly distributed except in heavily populated areas. The surprising high count in the downtown Wilmington block reflects ideal Barn Swallow conditions—the presence of 3 rivers with attendant open areas, available mud, and nest sites under bridges and wharves.

Atlas. In southern Delaware the Barn Swallow was difficult to find in a few blocks along the ridge of the peninsula where there are only intermittent streams. This was particularly true during summers when dry weather reduced the availability of mud for nest building.

Nesting. All nests reported in Delaware have been on man-made structures. The preferred nest site is a sheltered ledge with a low ceiling (2–20 in above the nest rim) and open areas on 2 sides. The nests are constructed of mud and straw. New nests are placed atop the previous season's nests; one 3-tier nest

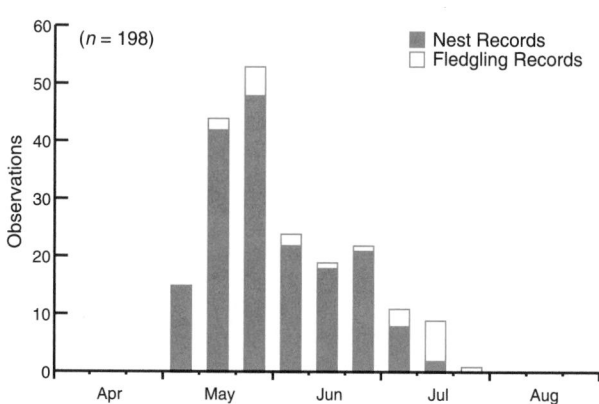

Estimated Clutch-Completion Dates

was 6 in high [Batt2]. The same nest is reused for the second brood.

Clutch completion begins in early May, with first clutches peaking in mid- to late May. The Barn Swallow is regularly double-brooded, which shows as a weak peak in mid-June; this peak is obscured by renestings, which start whenever the first brood is lost. It is occasionally triple-brooded, with breeding extending to August (Turner and Rose 1989). A late nestling

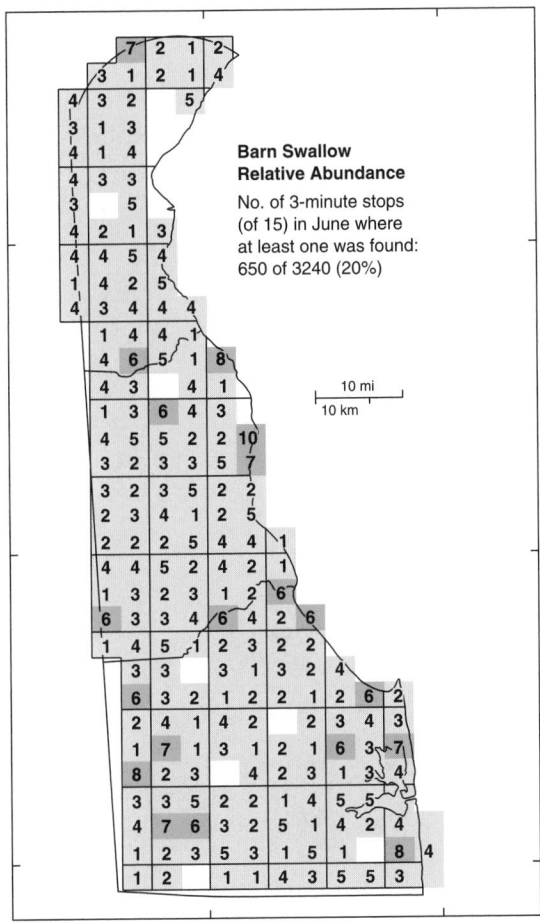

**Barn Swallow
Relative Abundance**

No. of 3-minute stops
(of 15) in June where
at least one was found:
650 of 3240 (20%)

10 mi
10 km

record occurred on 18 August 1980 [Nile2], but no other Delaware data suggest triple-broods. Clutch size is typically 4–5, with 4 more likely in second clutches.

History and trends. Like all the swallows, it benefited from European settlement, gaining fields to forage over and structures in which to build nests. It also increased substantially in abundance and breeding range in the East for the period 1965–

79, an increase attributed to the increase in highway bridges (Robbins et al. 1986). Its population now appears stable but perhaps has declined in Delaware during 1981–90 [Usfw1].

Breeding population. Various DOS weekly surveys showed early June peak counts in the range of 25–50 in areas covering less than a square mile (260 ha) of open land:

Winterthur	51
Hoopes Reservoir	49
Churchmans Marsh	35
Bombay Hook NWR	30
Brandywine Creek SP	29
Dragon Run	24
White Clay Creek	23
Ashland Nature Center	19

Breeding population densities in good habitat (males per 100 ha) were 28 (31 in 275 acres) in mixed agricultural and residential habitats in Prince George's County, Maryland, in 1949 (Stewart and Robbins 1958); those authors also cite 25 per 100 ha in a suburban residential area and 7 per 100 ha in mixed agricultural habitats for Maryland.

FALL: Migrating flocks congregate in late June and early July. By 25 August–10 September the last large flocks have passed through. After the third week of September Barn Swallows are most unusual. Rarely are individuals present during late fall, the 4 reports in November are

4 Nov 1950	3	Bombay Hook NWR [Bald1]
8 Nov 1970	1	Bombay Hook NWR [DuPG19]
13 Nov 1976	1	Bombay Hook NWR [Barn26]
24 Nov 1979	2	Cape Henlopen SP [Frec1].

The peak report is 400 on 28 August 1980 at Cherry Island, Wilmington [Edni1].

WINTER: Single birds were found on the Cape Henlopen CBC in 1979 and 1984, and 2 were recorded on the 1958 Bombay Hook CBC.

SPECIMENS: 15; DMNH, UDEL, USNM. Egg records: DMNH.

Carolina Chickadee *(Poecile carolinensis)*

Resident; fairly common.

J F M A M J J A S O N D

HABITAT: A variety of forest types, wood edges, wooded urban and suburban areas.

BREEDING: The familiar Carolina Chickadee, versatile in habitat use and adaptable to human-modified environments, is found throughout the state. The relative abundance study shows that it is as common in Sussex County as in northern

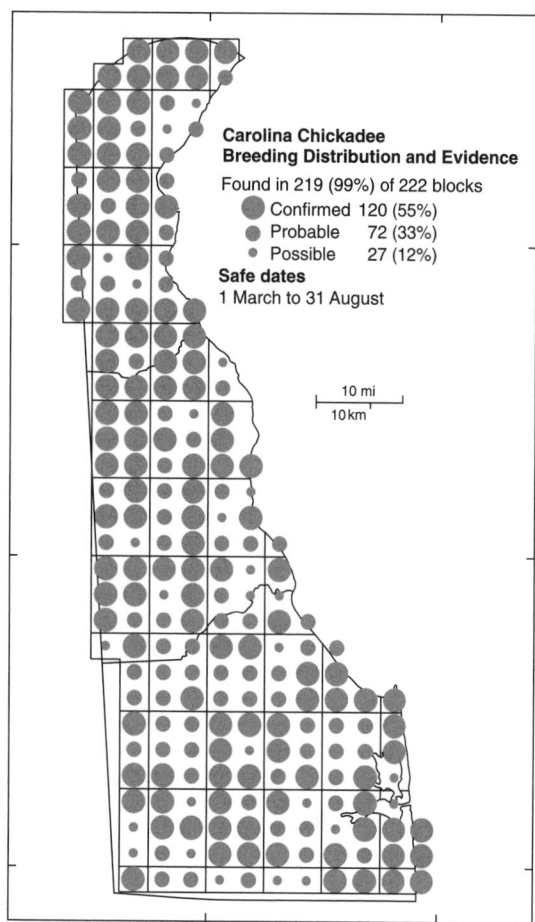

Carolina Chickadee
Breeding Distribution and Evidence

Found in 219 (99%) of 222 blocks
- ● Confirmed 120 (55%)
- ● Probable 72 (33%)
- · Possible 27 (12%)

Safe dates
1 March to 31 August

10 mi
10 km

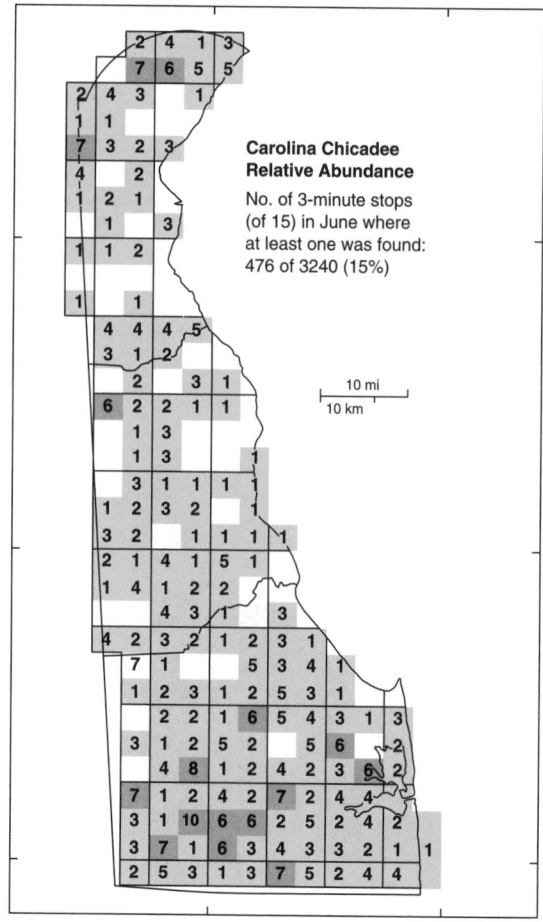

Carolina Chicadee
Relative Abundance

No. of 3-minute stops
(of 15) in June where
at least one was found:
476 of 3240 (15%)

10 mi
10 km

Delaware, but much less common in the farming and marshy areas of Kent and southern New Castle counties.

Atlas. This species was found in all Atlas blocks except 3 dominated by saltmarsh. It was confirmed in over half of the blocks, most often by locating begging young.

Nesting. For breeding it needs only a small woods and a cavity. The cavity can be a pipe (at Camp Arrowhead) or a bluebird box (in Greenville). Hanson (notes) described a typical nest at Moores Mill Pond on 7 May. It was in the end of a dead limb of a black gum next to water. The hole was 2 in. in diameter at the

top, 2¼ in. at the bottom, going down 14 in. The nest "was a beautiful, carefully constructed cup, about 2 inches deep and with the same diameter, made of fine plant fibers and down" (see also Brewer 1961). Carolina Chickadees may pair for life; a pair bond lasting 4½ years was proved (Brackbill 1987).

Extreme egg dates reported are 4 eggs on 26 April [Jahn1] and 5 eggs on 14 June; 10 days later the 14 June nest had a new, empty nest built over the 5 eggs and a wasp nest [Jahn1]. Early nests with young were found in Sussex County on 24 April [DeCh1] and Kent County on 10 May [Hans1]; late nestling dates are 25 June [Lope1] and 24 June [Jahn1]. Carolina Chickadees are normally single-brooded (Dixon 1963) as are most other tits; those clutches completed in June, only a month after the main clutch-completion peak, probably indicate renesting after loss of a clutch or brood.

History. Currently, the Carolina Chickadee ranges northward beyond Philadelphia, Chester and Delaware Counties, Pennsylvania. It overlaps with the Black-capped Chickadee in southern Berks County in a band less than 13 mi (21 km) wide (Gill 1992), south of which Black-capped Chickadees do not breed. This zone of contact has probably not moved much during the twentieth century. For example, Turnbull (1869) regarded the Carolina Chickadee as a southern species found in eastern Pennsylvania, and Rhoads and Pennock (1905) list only the Carolina Chickadee for Delaware.

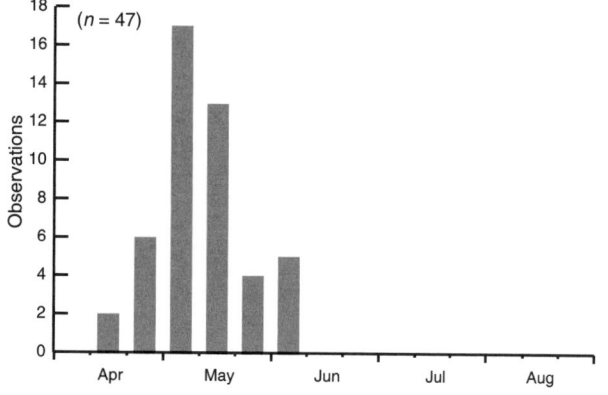

Estimated Clutch-Completion Dates

Trends. The Carolina Chickadee population in Delaware was reduced by 50% following the severe winter of 1976–77, suggesting that severity of winter weather limits its range. Its long-term population (1966–90) is stable, judging from May Counts and the BBSs [Usfw3].

Breeding population. Breeding densities given for deciduous forests in northern Delaware average about 25 pairs per 100 ha, somewhat higher than the 12–22 per 100 ha given for Maryland (Stewart and Robbins 1958). Defended breeding territories average about 2 ha (Dixon 1963).

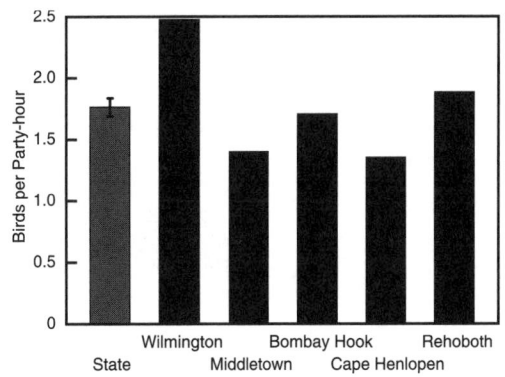

CBC Geographic Distribution

1966–89 CBC Summary

Christmas Bird Count	Years Found	Range of No. Found	Median
Wilmington	24	155–495	354
Middletown	24	43–182	95
Bombay Hook	24	38–224	123
Cape Henlopen	24	13–225	91
Rehoboth	24	64–395	169
STATEWIDE (low in 1967, high in 1982)	24	560–1,259	846

WINTER: The Carolina Chickadee is found about equally often on the coastal CBCs, but the Seaford CBC shows noticeably more birds than the coastal CBCs. No long-term CBC trend is apparent, but the decline following several severe winters in the mid-1970s, especially 1976–77, is noteworthy and corroborates the BBS and May Count results. Since then it has steadily recovered.

BANDING RECORDS: The 115 Delaware banding recoveries reveal that the Carolina Chickadee is sedentary: 107 were recovered in the same 10-min block, 7 in bordering blocks, and 1 in a diagonally adjacent block. The dispersal of the last bird was less than 31 mi (50 km) (Ward 1966). However, Parkes (1966) suggests that this species occasionally disperses north outside of the breeding season and cites 4 recoveries of birds banded near Pittsburgh in support of such dispersal.

SPECIMENS: 90; DMNH, ANSP, UDEL, USNM, UWBM. Egg records: WFVZ.

Black-capped Chickadee *(Poecile atricapillus)*

Occasional; winter visitor; uncommon.

HABITAT: Wood edges, wooded urban and suburban areas.

WINTER: The Black-capped Chickadee is an irruptive winter visitor whose flight years have coincided with other northern species. The species composition of these irruptions and their geographical extent may vary (Bagg 1970). "Robert Ringler, who has analyzed band recoveries of Black-cappeds from the fall and winter on the coastal plain of the Middle Atlantic States, reports (pers. comm.) that these birds are not from the contact zone, nor from the Appalachians, but from southeastern Canada and northeastern United States. Fortunately, these more northerly Black-cappeds should stand out from the local resident Carolinas" (Robbins 1989). Its irruptive nature, and the reluctance of observers to attempt the field identification, have partly obscured its occurrence in Delaware,

but those identifications that have been made are probably largely correct (see "Irruptive Northern Visitors" essay). The separation of typical Black-capped Chickadees from Carolina Chickadees by a careful experienced observer is usually possible in winter when the plumage is fresh (Parkes 1987, Robbins 1989, Kaufman 1990). The problems of identifying birds from the contact zone in southeastern Pennsylvania (Parkes 1987, Robbins 1989) probably do not apply significantly to Delaware, where there are no breeding or reliable summer records.

The 5 specimen records that establish its presence in Delaware span the winter, from 14 September to 26 March. Banding records of carefully measured birds give the following seasonal distribution of 73 birds banded at a Hockessin feeder (Knowles 1965) [Usfw3]:

October	7
November	25
December	20
January	14
February	4
March	3

This data does not mean that the chickadees were more common in early winter, but just that new ones continued to be banded as more arrived or were netted. Three chickadee bands were recovered, 2 from near the banding site and 1 from central New Jersey.

1966–89 CBC Summary

Christmas Bird Count	Years Found	Range of No. Found	Median
Wilmington	15	2–262	5
Middletown	13	2–65	2
Bombay Hook	14	1–6	2
Cape Henlopen	5	1–4	
Rehoboth	4	1–3	
STATEWIDE (high in 1975)	16	2–291	8

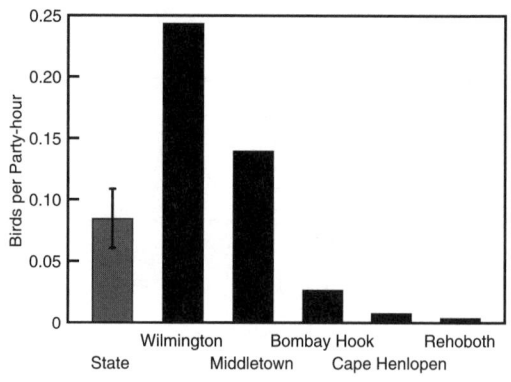

CBC Geographic Distribution

High CBC numbers from the 1960s and 1970s may have been exaggerated by misidentifications, whereas lower numbers more recently may have resulted from failure to properly identify Black-capped Chickadees when they occurred. Observers should be alert for invasion years and practice their identification skills whenever possible. Caution requires that an unidentified chickadee in Delaware be reported as a Carolina, or as an "unidentified chickadee" if a Black-capped Chickadee is suspected but conditions did not allow a more certain identification.

The sharp decline in numbers of Black-capped Chickadees reported from the Wilmington CBC to the southernmost count at Rehoboth does not correlate easily with the idea of a long-distance irruptive species coming from Canada or the New England states. It implies that these long-distance migrants abruptly stopped near the edge of the Piedmont. Increased caution on the Wilmington CBC and increased alertness on the Kent and Sussex county counts are needed to confirm this pattern.

Unusually high numbers were reported on the 1979 Wilmington CBC because the total number of chickadees observed were divided into Black-capped and Carolina chickadees by the 50:50 ratio found at that time at the Hockessin banding station. This procedure may not have been justified, and the totals calculated that year certainly cannot be compared with the ratio obtained by traditional CBC field methods.

REMARKS: Although Black-capped Chickadees can usually be distinguished from Carolina Chickadees by voice and other characteristics (Parkes 1987; Kaufman 1990), Robbins (1989) points out that these characteristics work best when comparing birds well away from the contact zone between the 2 species. Where these chickadees come into contact they may produce hybrids with intermediate vocalizations and morphology (Brewer 1963; Rising 1968; Johnston 1971b; Ward and Ward 1974; Robbins et al. 1986). These 2 chickadees interbreed extensively in the low hills between Boyertown and Kutztown in Berks County, Pennsylvania (Gill 1992), not far north of Delaware; a few probable hybrids have been reported in Delaware.

SPECIMENS: 6; DMNH.

Boreal Chickadee *(Poecile hudsonicus)*

Casual (1954 and 1982), winter visitor.

DOCUMENTATION: Photograph (DMNH 354).

REMARKS: This species was first observed at Bombay Hook NWR on 6 November 1954 [Cutl28]; no documentation is available for this report. A photograph was taken of a bird (DMNH) in Wilmington on 6 April 1982. It was present through 9 April [Gord8].

Tufted Titmouse *(Baeolophus bicolor)*

Resident; common, especially in southwestern Kent County and inland Sussex County.

HABITAT: Deciduous and coniferous forests and woodlots. Wooded suburbs.

BREEDING: The relative abundance study indicates the titmouse is more than twice as common in the southern half of the state as in the north; it avoids marshes and open farmland.

Atlas. Titmice were frequently confirmed by locating adults feeding vocal fledged young; because titmice are secretive near the nest cavity, only 5 nests with young and no nests with eggs were reported.

Nesting. Hanson (notes) described a nest in Camden in a dead stub about 12 ft tall and 1 ft in diameter at the base. The nest hole was 1½ in. in diameter and 4–5 in. deep in the dead wood 1 ft from the top of the stub. A Sussex County nest in a maple cavity was composed of leaves, inner tree bark, and hair, and was lined with the same material, only finer (WFVZ egg data). Rabbit fur, raccoon fur, and pieces of snake skin have also been used. Like the chickadee, the Tufted Titmouse will build in nest boxes (including screech-owl boxes).

The earliest eggs reported were 6 collected on 4 May in Sussex County (for R. W. Jackson, WFVZ egg data), and the latest report of young in the nest was on 26 June 1985 in New Castle County [Zeit2]. Most clutches are completed in early May. Titmice are single-brooded as a rule (Brackbill 1970), but double broods were observed twice in Pennsylvania (Middleton 1949). July nestlings are sometimes reported, for example, on 10 July in Maryland (Stewart and Robbins 1958). Late breeding in Delaware is evident from a 17-g fledgling brought to Tri-State Bird Rescue on 13 July (TSBR 87-826), probably representing a

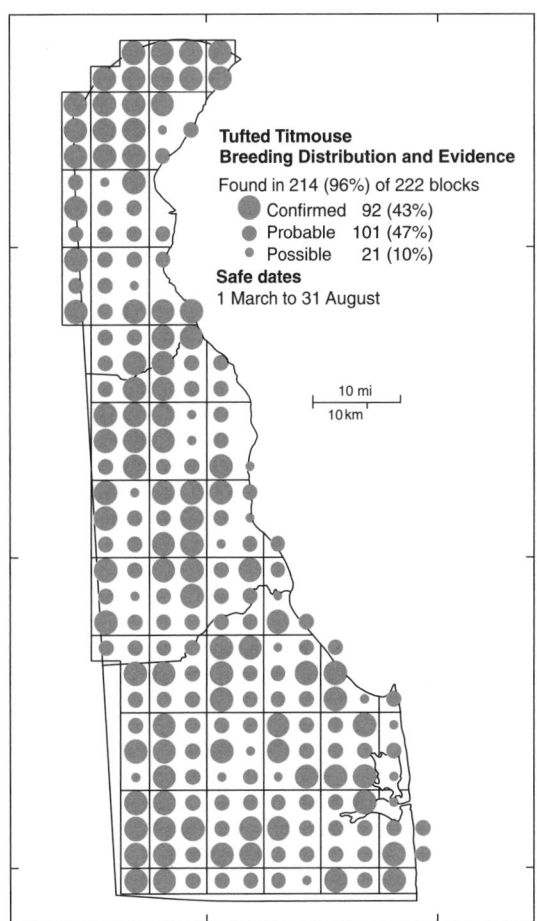

Tufted Titmouse
Breeding Distribution and Evidence
Found in 214 (96%) of 222 blocks
● Confirmed   92 (43%)
● Probable   101 (47%)
· Possible   21 (10%)
Safe dates
1 March to 31 August

10 mi
10 km

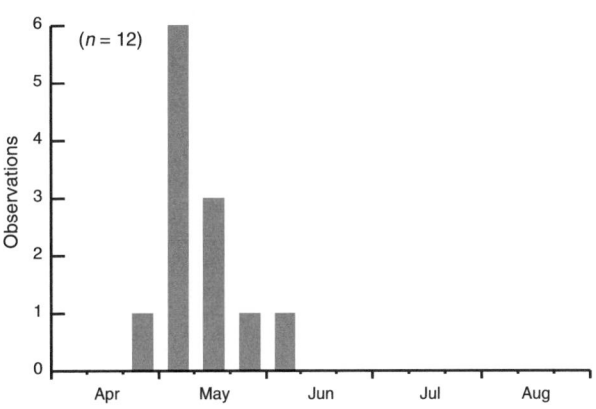

Estimated Clutch-Completion Dates

clutch completed in mid-June. Courtship feeding by a pair renesting in June could easily be confused with feeding young.

History and trends. Titmice invaded New York and New England in the twentieth century, but records show they have always been resident in Delaware. Their northward increase,

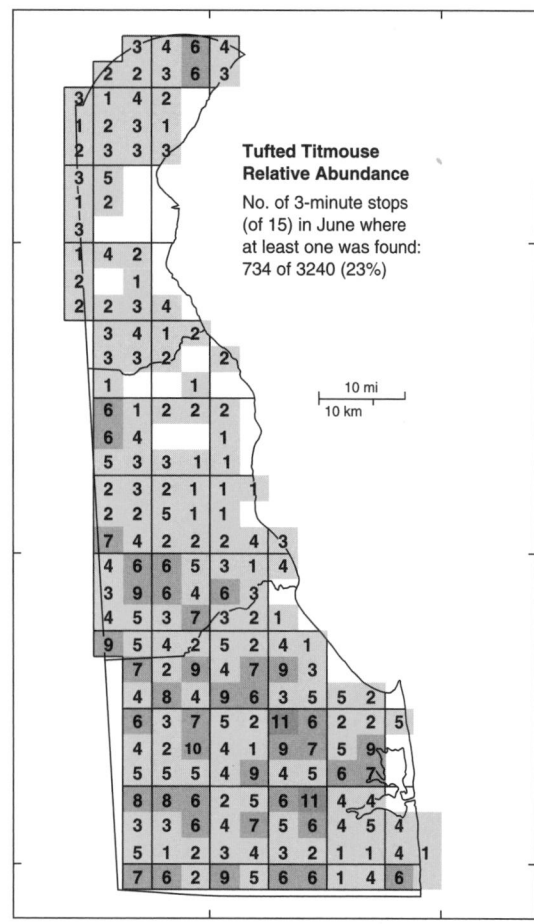

**Tufted Titmouse
Relative Abundance**

No. of 3-minute stops
(of 15) in June where
at least one was found:
734 of 3240 (23%)

10 mi
10 km

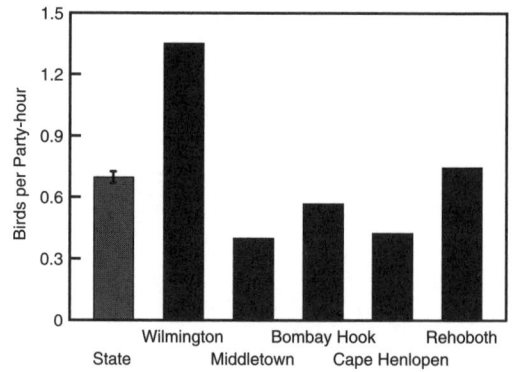

CBC Geographic Distribution

1966–89 CBC Summary

Christmas Bird Count	Years Found	Range of No. Found	Median
Wilmington	24	119–514	182
Middletown	24	7–71	24
Bombay Hook	24	7–109	39
Cape Henlopen	24	4–65	32
Rehoboth	24	17–131	72
STATEWIDE (low in 1977, high in 1974)	24	256–625	353

WINTER: The Tufted Titmouse is equally common on all the coastal CBCs, but the Seaford CBC shows noticeably more. Although no long-term CBC trend is apparent, a decline followed several severe winters in the mid-1970s, especially 1976–77. Since then it has steadily recovered. The high count is 514 on the 1974 Wilmington CBC.

SPECIMENS: 59; DMNH, ANSP, USNM, UWBM. Egg records: WFVZ.

ascribed to warmer winters (Beddall 1963; Meade 1988c), is consistent with sensitivity to severe winters noted in Delaware.

Breeding population. Various measures of titmouse–chickadee relative abundance are shown by these ratios:

0.43:1	CBCs (Seaford CBC, 0.57:1)
0.57:1	year-round counts
0.86:1	May Counts
1.3:1 to 1.6:1	BBC in northern Delaware
1.54:1	relative abundance study
2.2 :1	BBS

Since each species is sedentary (Elder 1985), some differences must result from lower numbers of titmice near the coast and marshes during winter (where the CBC effort is focused), and some from their increased aural detectability during the breeding season when even females sing (Brackbill 1970). Whether it is truly more abundant or just more obvious than the chickadee during the breeding season remains uncertain.

Red-breasted Nuthatch (*Sitta canadensis*)

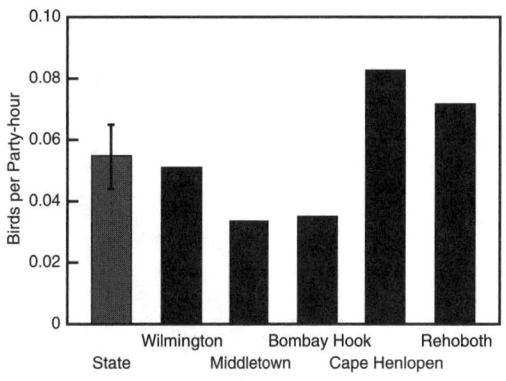

CBC Geographic Distribution

Regular; winter visitor; uncommon. Expected mid-September to late April, and sporadically into May.

J F M A M J J A S O N D

HABITAT: Pine and occasionally deciduous forests. More frequent in deciduous forests during spring and fall than at other seasons.

SPRING: Migration probably begins in March and ends by 25–30 April. The late departure date is confused by stragglers possibly attempting to breed (see "Summer"):

12 May 1965	1	Newark [Faus9]
13 May 1973	1	Dragon Run [SpSB41]
20 May 1984	1	Cape Henlopen SP [Frec1]
24 May 1990	1	Assawoman WA [Edni31]

Some of the highest counts reported are

28 Feb 1981	6	Cape Henlopen SP [Frec29]
21 Mar 1981	5	Cape Henlopen SP [Frec1]
27 Mar 1977	4	White Clay Creek [West9]

SUMMER: The breeding range of this species has expanded southward into New Jersey, Pennsylvania, and Maryland. The closest report describes 3 young raised during 1977 in the Dividing Creek area, New Jersey, 7 mi east of Bombay Hook [Kunk1]. It is an early nester, with egg dates from 30 April to 17 June in New York (Meade 1988b). It becomes relatively quiet during nesting and may be overlooked (Santner 1992a).

The Red-breasted Nuthatch may eventually breed in Delaware. Over a period of a week or 2 in the spring of 1981 a pair excavated 3 cavities with entrances about 2 inches in diameter in a black oak in Brandywine Hills, at the edge of the Piedmont. The limb subsequently broke off, but the pair continued to visit a feeder in the neighborhood throughout the spring (J. Frink, pers. comm.). On 12 and 21 June 1990 1 was seen in Newark [MiDP9]. On 4 July 1992 an immature and a second

bird (calling) were found in Barkley, a suburban area in extreme northern Delaware supporting many spruces and hemlocks. The immature was in the company of chickadees in a clump of white birch [Rydg1].

FALL: First arrival is usually 1–10 September, and migration ceases by 25 October–5 November, peaking during October. Earlier arrivals are

22 Aug 1975	1	Newark [Dyer1]
27–30 Aug 1985	1	Centerville [SpeE14]

Some high counts are

8 Oct 1989	10	Cape Henlopen SP [Frec1]
23 Oct 1965	18	Smith Bridge, Brandywine Creek [SpSB5]
1 Nov 1981	200	Winterthur [RusR10]
12 Nov 1981	150	Mill Creek Valley [RusR10]

1966–89 CBC Summary

Christmas Bird Count	Years Found	Range of No. Found	Median
Wilmington	20	1–43	4
Middletown	16	1–13	1
Bombay Hook	19	1–12	1
Cape Henlopen	15	1–51	2
Rehoboth	17	1–78	2
STATEWIDE (zero in 1979, high in 1975)	23	1–102	21

WINTER: No long-term CBC trend is apparent, but winter numbers are highly variable and correlate with poor boreal cone crops (Bock and Lepthien 1972). The highest CBC reports are 78 on the 1975 Rehoboth CBC, 51 on the 1969 Cape Henlopen CBC, and 43 on the 1981 Wilmington CBC. Some of the higher single-party counts, all from Cape Henlopen SP, are 6 on 8 December 1983, 8 on 4 January 1987 [Frec1], and 20 on 4 January 1975 [Lehm24].

SPECIMENS: ANSP 65864, Lewes, 28 January 1907; DMNH 72239, Centerville, 1 April 1982; ANSP 65866, Odessa, 10 September 1903; DMNH 76288, 1.2 mi (2 km) N Wilmington, 23 October 1985.

White-breasted Nuthatch (*Sitta carolinensis*)

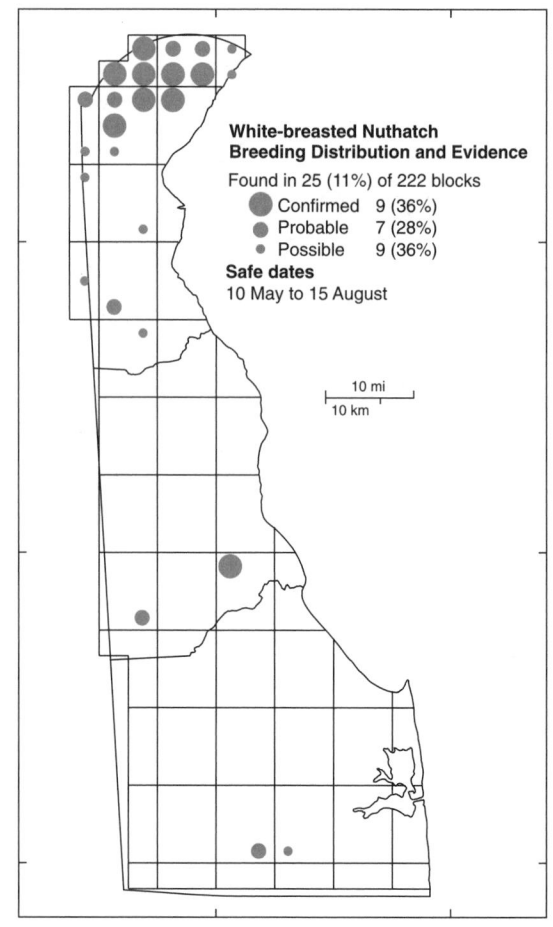

Resident in the Piedmont; uncommon there and rare winter visitor in southern Delaware, October through April.

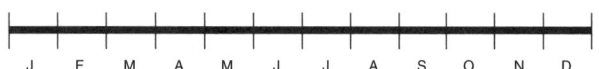

HABITAT: Flood-plain mature forests, moist deciduous upland forests.

MIGRATION: This nuthatch winters in Kent and Sussex counties, where it normally does not breed, from late September or early October until late April. In New Castle County migration is signaled by increased numbers of White-breasted Nuthatches banded in October [Usfw3]. In addition to migration, Stewart and Robbins (1958) note dispersal movements, often as early as the first week of July, into areas within 5–10 mi of the nesting range. Thus the presence of a few individuals a short distance from the Piedmont in mid-summer does not necessarily imply breeding there earlier in the season.

BREEDING: The White-breasted Nuthatch's breeding is almost entirely restricted to the Piedmont. The southern-most Delaware nest was found at Smalleys Dam on 15 April 1931 [Hans1]. Additionally, White-breasted Nuthatches were noted on BBSs south of the Chesapeake and Delaware Canal on 1 June 1970, 2 June 1972 and 1973, and 25 June 1979 [Line5], and a pair was observed near Dover on 29 April 1926 [Hans1].

Atlas. The Atlas results suggest that the White-breasted Nuthatch is a rare breeding bird in coastal Delaware as well as breeding in the Piedmont. It may have been missed in some blocks because it becomes very quiet during the April–June breeding period (Mills 1987b; Kilham 1972). The only down-state Atlas confirmation involved adults "attending young" at Fork Landing Bridge, Kent County, in 1986 [Wees2]. Additional

records that might imply breeding south of the Piedmont are reports on 14 April, 19 May, and 2 June 1973 from Dragon Run [BroW22] and 22 June and 7 July 1986 near Lewes [Edni24] (not included in the distribution map). Field work in the Pocomoke and Nanticoke drainages should produce additional nest records because the Atlas project in nearby Maryland resulted in 6 confirmed and probable records within 6 mi (10 km) of the Delaware line (Robbins 1996).

Nesting. Natural cavities from 15 to 50 ft above ground in deciduous trees have usually been used for nest sites. An exceptional nest site was in a nest box meant for a screech-owl placed only 6 ft above ground on a tulip poplar [Blad2]. Nest material for the only Delaware nest described was very soft and included down and mouse fur [Hans1]. No Delaware clutches are described, but usually comprise 5–9 eggs (Harrison 1978). Clutch completion occurs from the second to fourth week in May, estimated from young first seen from 10 to 24 June [SpeE3; Blad2].

Trends. The White-breasted Nuthatch population in the East increased at a rate of 2% per year during the 1966–90 period [Usfw1]. It is not widespread enough in Delaware to be moni-

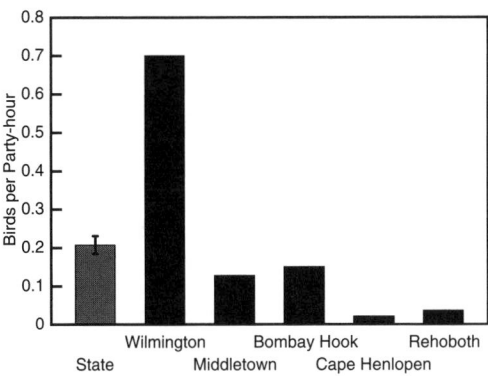

CBC Geographic Distribution

tored by the BBS, but numbers found on the May Counts suggest a decreasing tendency.

Breeding population. Breeding densities reported are 13–14 pairs per 100 ha (250 acres) in Maryland (Stewart and Robbins 1958), but woodlots in northern Delaware rarely have more than 1 pair, or about 7 per 100 ha. These findings are consistent with the birds maintaining year-round territories of about 15 ha (Kilham 1981). They are most common in creek valleys with larger wooded tracts, such as are found at White Clay Creek, Brandywine Creek SP, Alapocas Woods, and around Hoopes Reservoir. Based on the 25 blocks where it was recorded during the Atlas project, the breeding population falls within the

100–1,000 pairs range. High counts for this mainly resident species are 177 on the 1975 Wilmington CBC, 32 on 14 October 1972 on the Winterthur survey [Wayn35], 22 on 5 November 1977 on the White Clay Creek survey [Lehm35], and 18 on 28 November 1970 and 3 July 1971 Brandywine Creek SP surveys [DOS1].

Conservation. Preservation of stands of old trees in the Piedmont is the best conservation measure for this species, which needs old cavities for nesting and roosting. It appears tolerant of suburban development, will come to feeders, and sometimes uses nest boxes.

1966–89 CBC Summary

Christmas Bird Count	Years Found	Range of No. Found	Median
Wilmington	24	52–177	91
Middletown	22	1–35	5
Bombay Hook	24	1–50	7
Cape Henlopen	15	1–13	1
Rehoboth	19	1–9	2
STATEWIDE (low in 1974, high in 1968)	24	56–260	109

WINTER: In winter White-breasted Nuthatches are scarce in Kent and Sussex counties, at least in the coastal areas that are usually visited by observers. Reports are needed from inland areas of Kent and Sussex counties to determine this species' abundance and migration dates.

SPECIMENS: 24; DMNH, UDEL.

Brown-headed Nuthatch *(Sitta pusilla)*

Resident, uncommon. Found only in Sussex County. Population apparently declining.

HABITAT: Open stands of mature loblolly pine, usually near tidewater, with dead branches or dead standing trees.

BREEDING: This nuthatch prefers mature pines in suburban and vacation areas along the Inland Bays.

Nesting. It most frequently nests in dead pine trunks or posts, lays 5–6 eggs, and is rarely double-brooded. Mean clutch initiation for North Carolina was calculated to be 23 April ±16 days (standard deviation) (McNair 1984). Extreme egg dates reported for Maryland are 7 April–7 May (Stewart and Robbins 1958). It usually excavates its own cavity in rotten wood (Bent 1948), but McNair reported 15 nests (out of 309) placed in nest boxes an average of 6 ft above ground.

History. Little change has occurred in this nuthatch's range during historic times. Nuttall did not find it during his 1809 trip

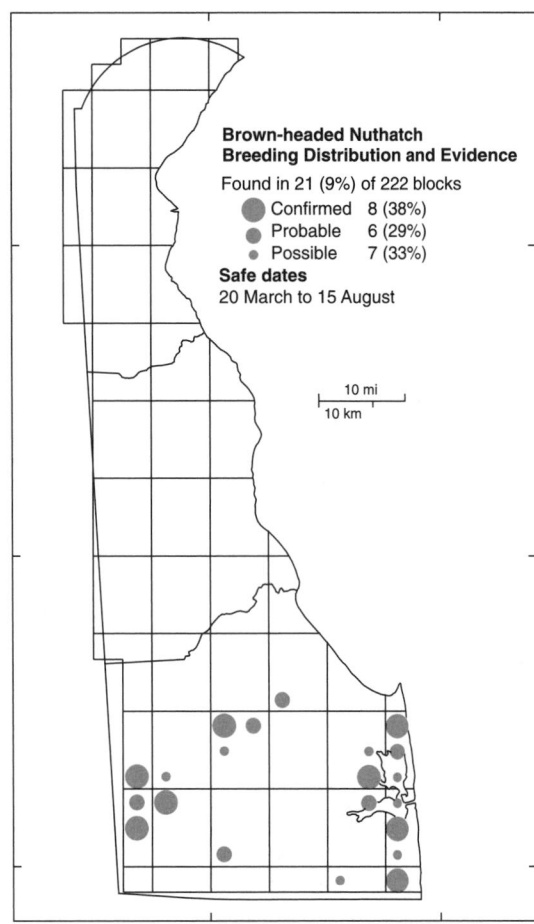

Brown-headed Nuthatch
Breeding Distribution and Evidence

Found in 21 (9%) of 222 blocks

● Confirmed 8 (38%)
● Probable 6 (29%)
· Possible 7 (33%)

Safe dates
20 March to 15 August

10 mi

10 km

Conservation. Forestry management practices should include providing open stands of mature pines, retaining snags, and controlling hardwoods (O'Halloran and Conner 1987). A nest box program may help restore its population.

1966–89 CBC Summary

Christmas Bird Count	Years Found	Range of No. Found	Median
Wilmington			
Middletown			
Bombay Hook			
Cape Henlopen	3	1–8	
Rehoboth	24	3–102	18
STATEWIDE	24	3–103	18

(decreasing; low in 1981, high in 1972)

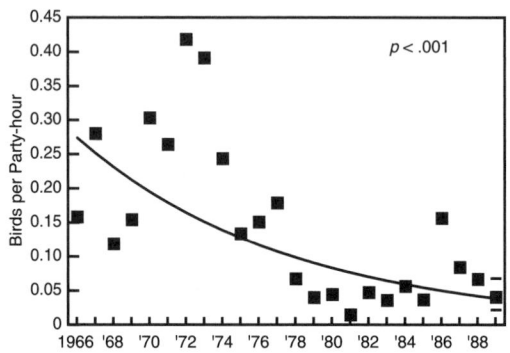

CBC Trend; Autocorrelation may Invalidate the Significance Test

to Lewes, Millsboro, and Dagsboro, but he was then most interested in the botany of the swamps. He later wrote that "it is seldom seen to the north of the State of Virginia" (Nuttall 1832; MacDowell 1989). Turnbull (1869) listed it as "a rare visitant to the lower counties [of Pennsylvania]," probably referring to Delaware. A family group found near Seaford on 18 June 1903 and an individual near Lewes on 5 February 1904 (Pennock 1904a,b; Rhoads and Pennock 1905) were the first definite records for Delaware.

Trends. The May Count results indicate that the Brown-headed Nuthatch declined an average of 5% per year during 1969–91, with high counts of 17 in 1974 and 16 in 1971. This decline is supported by CBC results and by BBS data, which show a decline for the past 24 years, based on a small sample (2 routes). These survey methods collectively indicate that the Brown-headed Nuthatch is declining in Delaware. This is perhaps to be expected at the northern edge of the range of a species that has declined in the East during the past 24 years, [Usfw1].

Breeding population. Although the Brown-headed Nuthatch was found in 21 blocks, the state population is probably less than 100 pairs. In some blocks it disappeared during the 1983–87 Atlas period, and so the population and range are probably reduced from levels suggested by the map.

WINTER: This species is declining at 8% per year on CBCs. High counts on the Rehoboth 1960 CBC of 67 and 102 on the 1972 CBC contrast starkly with the 1980s high count of 16. None have been seen on the Prime Hook count since the 1976 CBC, and none have been found on the Seaford CBC since the 1984 CBC (the first year of that count). A weakness in the trend data is that this species occurs almost exclusively on the Rehoboth CBC, so local changes may affect results.

SPECIMEN: DMNH 637, Sussex Co., 16 March 1957.

Brown Creeper *(Certhia americana)*

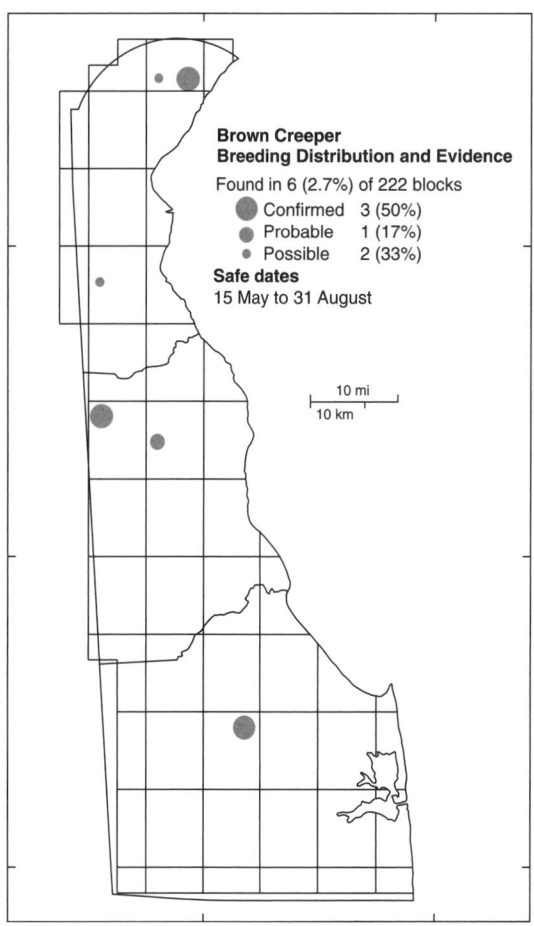

**Brown Creeper
Breeding Distribution and Evidence**
Found in 6 (2.7%) of 222 blocks
● Confirmed 3 (50%)
● Probable 1 (17%)
● Possible 2 (33%)
Safe dates
15 May to 31 August

10 mi
10 km

Regular; winter visitor; uncommon. Expected late September to late April and sporadically thereafter; rare breeder.

J F M A M J J A S O N D

HABITAT: Deciduous and coniferous forests. In Delaware mainly in mature deciduous woods in wet situations, but noted in Redden SF near planted spruce and near Hoopes Reservoir in planted pines.

SPRING: Migration begins 10–20 March and ends in April. Typical reports mention 1–5 birds. The latest banding reports, all from the University of Delaware woodlot, include 1 on 12 April 1970, 3 the next day, 1 on 16 April 1970 [Jone2], and 2 on 19 April 1966 [Line5]. Some of the 8 reports in May refer to birds attempting to breed.

BREEDING: Rather weak evidence suggests occasional breeding in all 3 counties. Before the Atlas project the following 3 summer records suggested breeding. A pair was reported nest building on 6 May 1967 at Trussum Pond SP but a week later could not be found [Broo7]. That same summer a nest with 5 young was found at Patuxent Wildlife Research Center near Laurel, Maryland, the first definite breeding record on the Maryland Coastal Plain (Van Velzen 1967). Two reported at Assawoman WA on 19 June and 9 July 1972 were thought to be breeding, but the report was never confirmed [Conw6]. Single birds were seen on 13 May and 22 July 1973 at Dragon Run [SpSB19].

Atlas. In Redden SF 3 were seen and heard on 7 May 1983

[West6], and on 5 June at the same site an adult and 2 fluffy young were briefly seen [West10]. On 22 May 1983 1 was seen gathering nesting material in Alapocas Woods. After it was joined by another creeper, both flew out of sight and were not relocated [Falk23]. Scott and Cutler commented then that this species had expanded its breeding range southward during the past 20 years to include all of New Jersey and southeastern Pennsylvania (Boyle et al. 1983). Also in 1983 breeding was confirmed in the District of Columbia and on the Maryland western shore in Calvert County [Czap1].

One seen in July 1984 in the pines between Valley Garden Park and Hoopes Reservoir could not subsequently be relocated [Zeit2]. One was near Middletown on 19 May 1985 [Holm1]. On Mudstone Creek just west of Dover 1 responded to a screech-owl tape on 24 July 1985 and was relocated the same way on 17 August [West12]. In Blackiston WA, Kent County, 1 found on 13 June 1986 was calling and flying from trunk to trunk. It was carrying food when it disappeared from view by hitching up a trunk into dense foliage [Edni2].

Subsequent to the Atlas project 1 was noted along White

Clay Creek on 7 May 1989 [Camp1]; another was there on 7 July 1990 [Zeit1]. Brown Creepers were confirmed or probable in 12 blocks in Maryland's lower Eastern Shore (Robbins 1996). There have been several summer records on the Virginia Coastal Plain (Kain 1987) but not on the Delmarva Peninsula portion.

Nesting. Its nest has never been found in Delaware. Based on meager Delaware observations, nest building occurs during 6–22 May, feeding young on 13 June, and fledging as early as 6 June. In Michigan eggs occurred mid-May through June, peaking on 1 June. Nestlings peaked a week later. This species places its nest beneath loose bark on a rotten tree; clutch size was most often 6 (Davis 1978).

Trends. A west Tennessee study describes creepers as expanding southward (Ford 1987), a general phenomenon in the East. In New Hampshire expansion has been ascribed to reforestation (Ellison 1985) and in New York to increased nesting sites brought on by Dutch elm disease (Levine 1988). This species was once common in the Mississippi Lowlands of Missouri (Widmann 1907, in Robbins and Easterla 1991) and may have formerly occurred in Coastal Plain swamps in the East (M. B. Robbins, pers. comm.). Its eventual increase in Delaware is anticipated.

Breeding population. The breeding population during the 1980s was probably fewer than 10 pairs; in most years none is found during breeding season.

FALL: Migration begins 25–30 September, peaks in October, and ends by 10–20 November. These earlier reports may refer to local birds:

| 29 Aug 1985 | 1 | Redden SF [Frec1] |
| 9 Sep 1985 | 1 | Assawoman WA [Frec1] |

Typical reports total 1–5 birds.

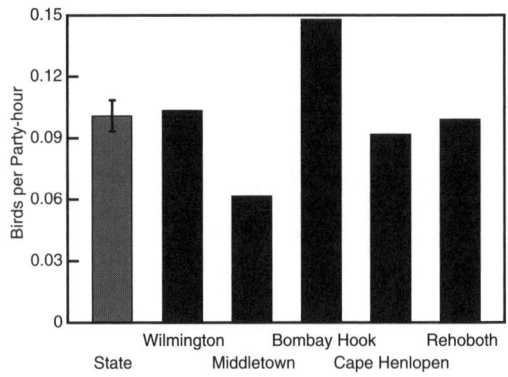

CBC Geographic Distribution

1966–89 CBC Summary

Christmas Bird Count	Years Found	Range of No. Found	Median
Wilmington	24	4–32	14
Middletown	23	1–10	3
Bombay Hook	24	1–26	9
Cape Henlopen	22	1–25	5
Rehoboth	24	1–25	10
STATEWIDE (low in 1966, high in 1982)	24	23–86	41

WINTER: The high CBC report is 32 on the 1982 Wilmington count. Most reports mention 1–3 birds.

SPECIMENS: 14; DMNH, ANSP, UDEL.

Carolina Wren *(Thryothorus ludovicianus)*

Resident; uncommon to fairly common.

| J | F | M | A | M | J | J | A | S | O | N | D |

HABITAT: Wood edges, thickets, wet brushy forests.

BREEDING: The relative abundance study shows that the Carolina Wren has a pattern of increasing abundance toward southern and eastern Delaware, with Milford Neck and the necks behind Fenwick Island having the highest numbers. These areas are also the least snow-covered in the state. This wren's abundance pattern does not correlate with areas containing forest or wetland habitat.

Atlas. The Carolina Wren was found in all blocks except those dominated by saltmarsh. Detection was made easy by this species' tendency to sing loudly and often throughout its

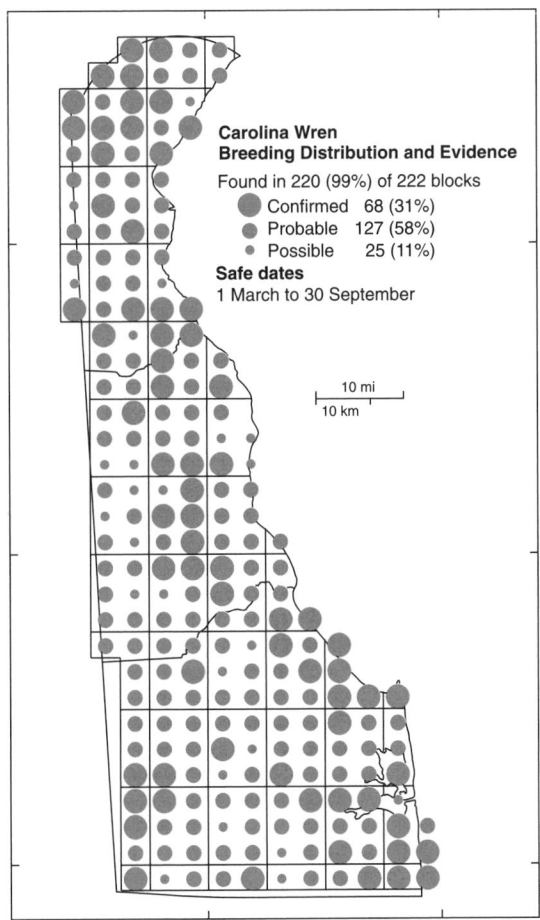

Carolina Wren
Breeding Distribution and Evidence

Found in 220 (99%) of 222 blocks
- Confirmed 68 (31%)
- Probable 127 (58%)
- Possible 25 (11%)

Safe dates
1 March to 30 September

10 mi
10 km

Carolina Wren
Relative Abundance

No. of 3-minute stops
(of 15) in June where
at least one was found:
726 of 3240 (22%)

10 mi
10 km

long breeding season. It was confirmed in 30% of the blocks, about equally by locating either the nest or dependent young. Nests first reported to Atlas workers as "house" wrens frequently belonged to this species.

Nesting. Nests in Delaware are often associated with rural or suburban homesites; for example, 1 nest was placed 6 ft up in a box of cotton on a garage shelf [SpSB2]. This wren nests more frequently, however, in thick undergrowth or some naturally occurring niche or cavity in a tree or bank. The nest is usually domed and placed less than 10 ft above the ground (Harrison 1978).

Clutch completion peaks in early May, with a secondary peak in mid-June, which should be interpreted as a second brood. Third broods are produced in Florida and South Carolina (Sprunt 1954; Sprunt and Chamberlain 1970). Extreme egg dates in Delaware begin on 18 April, when 4 hatched [SpSB2], and extend to 31 August, when a nest with eggs was found in a hanging basket on a porch near the White Clay Creek Preserve [MiDP2].

Trends. At this latitude population changes caused by starvation induced by persistent snow cover are probably more obvious with this species than any other. It has gradually extended its range into the Northeast during the twentieth century (Bent 1948; Beddall 1963) but has probably been a long-time resident in Delaware.

Breeding population. Numbers on BBCs averaged about 12 territorial males per 100 ha in woodlots in northern Delaware during 1972–73 (Martin 1976), but higher counts have been reported: an average for 2 years at 2 small sites of 58 territorial males per 100 ha at Windy Hills (Burr and Jones 1968), and an average for 2 years at 3 sites at Assawoman WA of 33 territorial males per 100 ha (Linehan 1965a,c; McLaughlin 1968). In Maryland densities reported ranged from 14 to 28 territorial males per 100 ha in good years in wooded study areas (Stewart and Robbins 1958). Detection in the relative abundance study was

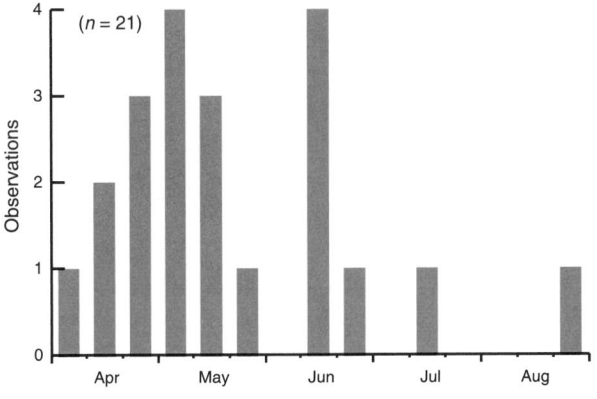

Estimated Clutch-Completion Dates

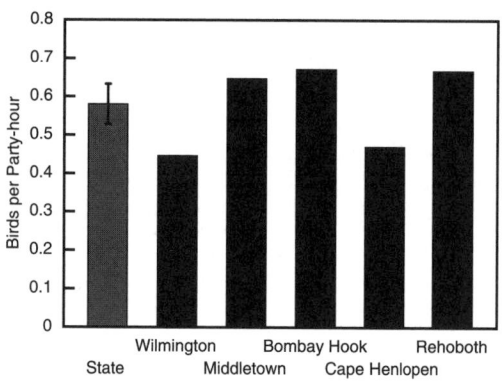

CBC Geographic Distribution

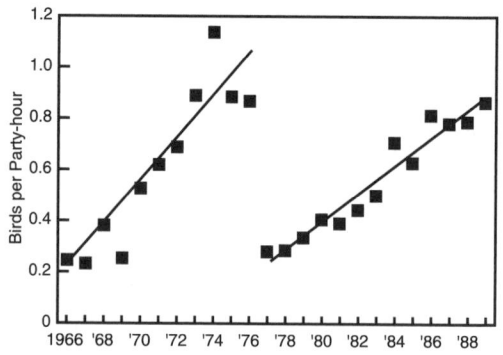

Christmas Bird Count Data

about 0.5 birds per 100 ha, but this technique samples only a fraction of the birds present.

1966–89 CBC Summary

Christmas Bird Count	Years Found	Range of No. Found	Median
Wilmington	24	9–200	50
Middletown	24	7–97	39
Bombay Hook	24	4–97	42
Cape Henlopen	24	4–94	31
Rehoboth	24	27–133	56
STATEWIDE (low in 1967, high in 1974)	24	102–542	233

WINTER: Any assessment of this wren's population must consider its sensitivity to cold weather. The CBC data clearly reveal the drastic reduction of the Carolina Wren population following severe cold during the winter of 1976–77. The 1977 May Count, BBS, and CBC revealed a reduction in numbers of approximately 80% (Appendix G.2). It is currently in a recovery stage, increasing at about 10% per year; presumably, the population will level off unless a severe winter occurs first.

The high CBC count is 200 on the 1975 Wilmington count. High counts other than on CBCs are 13–16 at Dragon Run during the winter of 1974 [DOS1] and 15 at White Clay Creek on 18 December 1976 [Boll5].

SPECIMENS: 31; DMNH, ANSP.

Bewick's Wren *(Thryomanes bewickii)*

Casual (3 years, 1964, 1965, 1966).

REMARKS: The 3 records occurred, oddly enough, in successive years though at different locations. First, an adult bird was banded on 5 April 1964 at Red Mill Pond, Lewes [Pepp1]. A second bird was present on 7 May 1965 near Newark [Ligh1]. The last record involved a bird collected on 24 September 1966 near Gordon Pond WA (Linehan 1966a; UDEL 115-67). This western wren occurs with decreasing abundance east to West Virginia and the mountains of Virginia and Maryland. These records, all near the coast, are particularly noteworthy, since Bewick's Wren is rare on the eastern seaboard.

SPECIMEN: UDEL 115-67, details earlier.

House Wren *(Troglodytes aedon)*

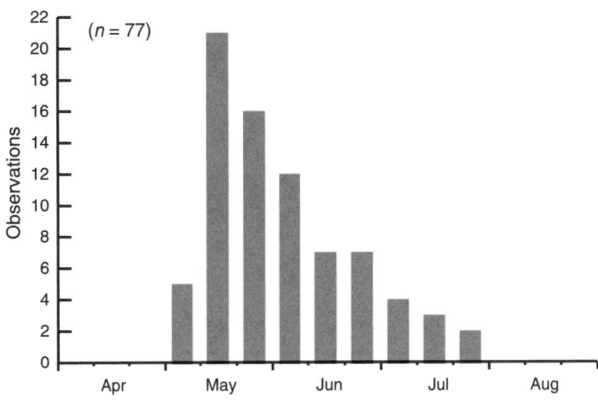

Estimated Clutch-Completion Dates

Regular; summer resident; uncommon to fairly common. Expected mid-April–mid-October and sporadically into winter.

HABITAT: Various edge habitats, including wood edges, hedgerows, and suburban areas. Especially common in swampy borders. Scarce in the woods of central and southern Delaware away from the water but found in villages and scrubby situations with old trees and cut-over areas.

SPRING: First arrival is usually 10–20 April. Migration continues to 10–20 May, peaking 20 April–5 May. The only March reports, 1 on 5 March 1983 at Seaford [Fint8] and 2 on 20 March 1983 at Bombay Hook NWR [Hess14], probably refer to wintering birds. Some high counts are

26 Apr 1964	10	Hoopes Reservoir [Klab4]
1 May 1965	15	Churchmans Marsh [Carr17]
8 May 1982	18	Bombay Hook NWR [Boll4]

BREEDING: In Delaware the House Wren approaches its southern breeding limit on the Coastal Plain (Robbins et al. 1986, 64). The relative abundance study shows it to be 5 times more common north of the Chesapeake and Delaware Canal than in the rest of the state. Farther south it is found mainly near the coast and in towns and villages.

Atlas. It was confirmed in almost half the blocks where found, an occupied nest box being the most frequent means of confirmation.

Nesting. Most nests described in Delaware were in boxes, but Hanson (notes) reported 1 in a maple stub on a creek bank behind Dover School and another in a stub on the bank of a creek above Lebanon.

Estimated clutch completion extends from early May to late July, but extreme egg dates (*n* = 52) are

15 May	5 eggs	Louviers golf course [Jahn1]
22 Jul	2 eggs	Centerville [Wayn4]

Extreme nestling dates are

2 Jun	(fledged 10 Jun)	Walnut Ridge [SpeE2]
31 Aug	(fledged 1 Sep)	Hockessin [Know1]

It is frequently double-brooded (Drilling and Thompson 1991), as suggested by the extended clutch-completion dates.

Males were polygynous 7% of the time in an Illinois study (Kendeigh 1941). Unmated males build multiple nests. In establishing its territory, it destroys nearby nests and eggs of other species, as well as those of other House Wrens (Belles-Isles and Picman 1986).

History and trends. Delawareans have been supplying houses for the House Wren since before 1851, when Montgomery wrote of "boxes for wrens, sheltering whole families" (in Findlay 1938). It comes into towns and suburbs where it finds nest situations around human habitation. Its population has probably increased as a result of European settlement. Its numbers have not shown any significant change for the last 25 years in Delaware but are highly variable (May Count, [Usfw1]). A long-term Ohio study showed marked population low points that correlated with low temperatures in its winter range (Kendeigh 1944). It also showed a general decline in the East following the severe winter of 1976–77 (Robbins et al. 1986), but this decline was not apparent in Delaware.

Breeding population. The House Wren was found 35% as frequently as the Carolina Wren during the relative abundance study, in part because it sings less loudly. It is only about 20% as common here as in Pennsylvania or Maryland, based on BBS data (Robbins et al. 1986). Its population density is highly variable in Delaware, varying from an average of 120 singing males per 100 ha in Assawoman WA on 3 BBC sites studied in the

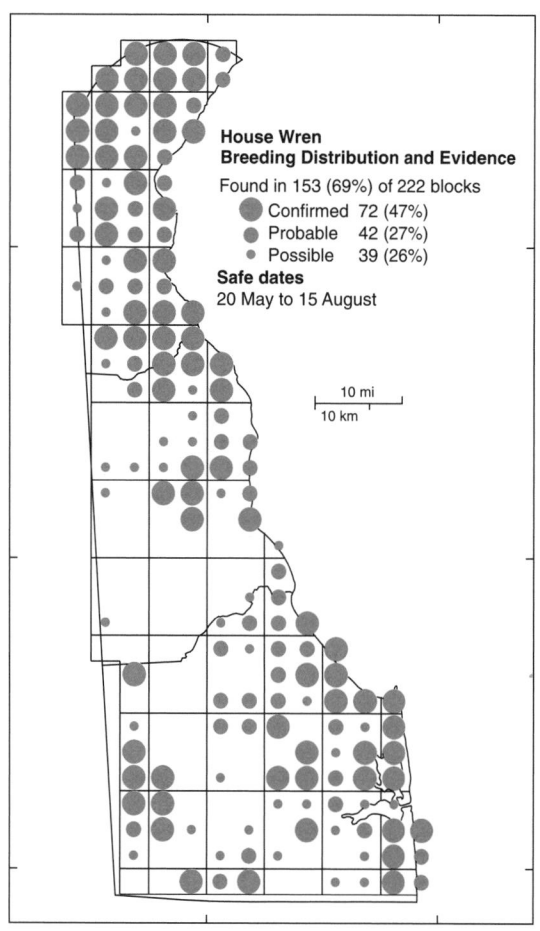

House Wren
Breeding Distribution and Evidence

Found in 153 (69%) of 222 blocks

- ● Confirmed 72 (47%)
- ● Probable 42 (27%)
- • Possible 39 (26%)

Safe dates
20 May to 15 August

10 mi
10 km

House Wren
Relative Abundance

No. of 3-minute stops
(of 15) in June where
at least one was found:
253 of 3240 (7.8%)

10 mi
10 km

1960s to 40 per 100 ha near Heritage Park in the late 1960s to none found in 30% of the 2,500-ha Atlas blocks.

FALL: Beginning in August, House Wrens sing infrequently and become relatively difficult to find. Accordingly, in the August–October 1991 Neotropical migrant study (Mabey et al. 1993) 86% of the House Wrens were identified in the first half of August (*n* = 35). Migration probably begins 1–10 September, peaks in the remainder of the month, and ends 15–30 October. Reports from Dragon Run in 1974 reveal the beginning of migration: 22 on 31 August, and 10 on 8 September. Other high counts are

2 Sep 1974	10	Brandywine Creek SP [Wayn66]
2 Oct 1985	12	Prime Hook NWR [Frec1]

Although some individuals remain into winter, the only ones reported in November are

1 Nov 1974	1 banded	University woodlot [Line4]
3 Nov 1966	1	University woodlot [Long3]
21 Nov 1970	1	Brandywine Creek SP [WarD10]

Reports after mid-October should be carefully documented.

WINTER: A few lingering breeders or late migrants from farther north are reported on CBCs, usually 1 or 2, and rarely 3. The latest are 1 reported on 4 January 1976 on the Middletown CBC, and 1 collected in Sussex County on 10 January 1960 (DMNH 1525).

1966–89 CBC Summary

Christmas Bird Count	Years Found	Range of No. Found	Median
Wilmington	8	1–3	
Middletown	5	1	
Bombay Hook	6	1–2	
Cape Henlopen	6	1–2	
Rehoboth	5	1	
STATEWIDE (high in 1974)	16	1–7	1

SPECIMENS: 14; DMNH, ANSP, UDEL. Egg records: DMNH, WFVZ.

Winter Wren (*Troglodytes troglodytes*)

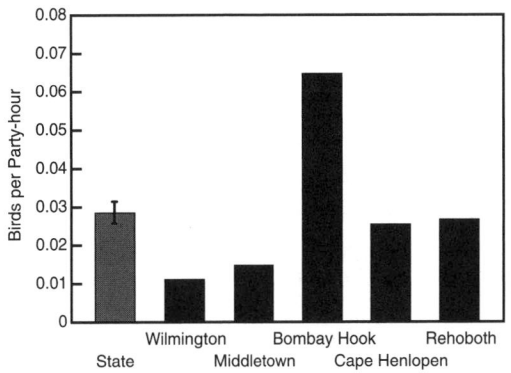

CBC Geographic Distribution

Regular; winter visitor; uncommon. Expected late September to late April. Numbers decreasing.

HABITAT: Floodplain, swamp, and moist upland forests.

SPRING: Most Winter Wrens leave Delaware by the time House Wrens arrive in late April. Migration probably begins during March and ends by 20–30 April. Exceptionally late reports include

8 May 1991	1	near Trap Pond SP [Shor5]
9 May 1981	1	north Delaware [Kell5]
11 May 1971	1	Bombay Hook NWR [Holg53]

Most reports mention 1 or 2 birds, but 3 were present on 12 and 15 April 1965 at Alapocas Woods, Wilmington [West7].

FALL: In late September and early October, during the period House Wrens are departing, Winter Wrens arrive. Migration is from 10–20 September through 15–25 November, peaking 10 October–10 November. The earliest arrival date is 13 September at Assawoman WA in 1969 and 1981 [DuPG14] (Haas 1983) and at Dover in 1977 [Pure10]. Most reports mention 1 or 2 birds. The highest counts reported are

14 Oct 1972	3	Winterthur [Wayn34]
16, 20 Oct 1990	6	Bombay Hook NWR [Holg96]
2 Nov 1974	3	Dragon Run [Edni47]
17 Nov 1973	3	Dragon Run [Beac8]

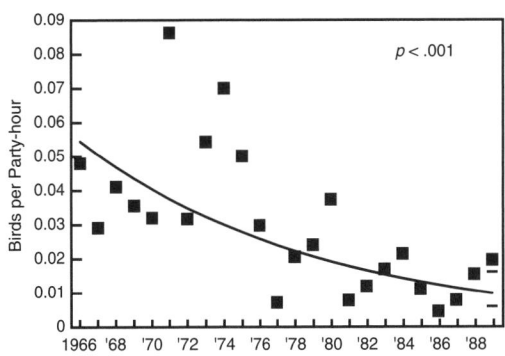

CBC Trend; Decreasing at 7% per Year

WINTER: This species has declined on Delaware CBCs an average of about 7% per year, related in part to the severe winters of 1976–77 and 1977–78. Robbins et al. (1986) report that "The Winter Wren was one of the species most vulnerable to the severe winter weather of 1976–77 and 1977–78," further stating that it "was increasing in the Eastern region, . . . but the drop in the following 2 years that resulted from two severe winters actually reversed the trend in the Eastern region." It is most often reported on the Bombay Hook and Seaford CBCs.

SPECIMENS: 7; DMNH, UDEL.

1966–89 CBC Summary

Christmas Bird Count	Years Found	Range of No. Found	Median
Wilmington	14	1–7	1
Middletown	14	1–4	1
Bombay Hook	24	1–18	2
Cape Henlopen	17	1–7	1
Rehoboth	19	1–8	2
STATEWIDE	24	1–31	11

(decreasing; low in 1971, 1981, and 1986; high in 1974)

Sedge Wren *(Cistothorus platensis)*

Regular; summer resident; rare, local. To be looked for from May through September and occasionally into winter near the Delaware River and Bay marshes. Seriously declining though never common.

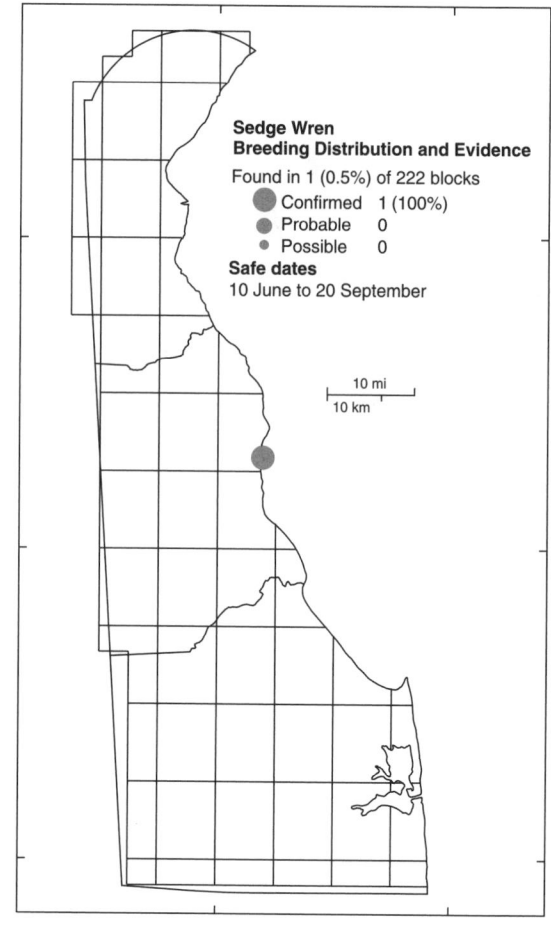

Sedge Wren
Breeding Distribution and Evidence
Found in 1 (0.5%) of 222 blocks
● Confirmed   1 (100%)
● Probable   0
· Possible   0
Safe dates
10 June to 20 September

10 mi
10 km

HABITAT: Wet meadows, marshes. Found in the highest parts of the Delaware River marshes, away from regular tidal action.

SPRING: Most records are from May, when this wren is singing, and include only 1 or a few birds. A March report is too vague and unusual to be trusted as published (DuMont and DuMont 1973). A few April reports suggest early arrival in some years:

7 Apr 1972	>1	Broadkill Beach [Barn52]
18 Apr 1992	2	Bombay Hook NWR [Litt1]
28 Apr 1972	2	Little Creek WA [MiJC1]

Some reports imply noteworthy migration:

5 May 1974	12	Gordon Pond WA [DuPG26]
10 May 1975	13	Sussex County [Stri6]
14 May 1967	15–20	Broadkill Beach [Carr16]
24 May 1953	15	Bethany Beach [Davi4]

The 1 spring specimen is from New Castle on 6 May 1911 (ANSP 80234).

BREEDING: In the last 30 years, breeding or summer occurrences have been confined to a few tidal marshes from Bombay Hook NWR south to Broadkill Beach.

Recent breeding sites. The most persistent colony in the state was discovered along Broadkill Beach Rd. on 14 May 1967 by Merritt and Carrick, who found 15–20 birds [MerJ1]. The birds stayed, and the next year Carrick reported 20 pairs there on 30 May [Carr10]. They returned for at least 15 years but in decreasing numbers. Six were recorded on 25 May and a few on 15 June 1975 [West8; Barn29]. No wrens were reported there during the Atlas period, but reports from the site have been made as recently as 30–31 July 1989 [Frec1; Perr6].

The colony near the entrance to Little Creek WA on Pickering Beach Rd. was reported on 9 May 1964, remained throughout the spring season [Cutl29], and flourished again in 1965 [Armi7]. Two were reported there on 8 May 1971 [John4; Falk1], and Wayne (notes) recorded the species during the last week of July 1971. The most recent reports there include a probable migrant seen on 10–15 May 1989 [Perr2; Cutl31] and present during the summer of 1990, [Edni70].

The Sedge Wren has been reported from the Little Creek WA dikes infrequently: 1 August 1964 (Stickley 1967), 4 times from 11 July to 4 August 1984 [Rufe1], 25 July 1986 [Barn1], and the summer of 1990 [Edni70].

Birds that could have been migrants were reported on Port Mahon Rd. on 23 May 1975 [Lehm1] and 22 May 1976 [Barn31]. A small colony was noted there again on 13 August 1988 [Perr5], and birds were still singing there in May and June 1992 (Maier 1993).

Sedge Wrens were seen in Bombay Hook NWR on 30 July 1966 [PetA1] and summered there intermittently through 1981, when at least 3 pairs were noted on 4 July. These were described as "the sole remnant of the once common and widespread coastal population in the region" [Cutl5]. They were noted again at Bombay Hook NWR on 10–14 May 1990 [Shoc5], summer 1990 [Edni70], 18 August 1991 [Hess1], and spring 1991 [anon2].

Summer reports from the BBSs at Slaughter Beach on 3 June 1973 and along Rt. 9 on 25 June 1975 show that it was more prevalent at that time than generally recognized [Line5]. Probable migrants were reported on Bennetts Pier Rd. on 31 May 1986 [Litt6] and again on 14 May 1990 [Shoc5]. They were also present at 1 or 2 other sites south of Little Creek during 1991 and 1992 (D. Rothstein, DNHI, pers. comm.).

Nesting. The known nesting records include a nest with 3 fresh eggs on 11 June, a nest with 3 fresh eggs on 10 July (see "History"), and a nest with young near the pumping station at Little Creek WA in July [Rufe1].

A Minnesota study revealed that males defended 0.275-ha territories (based on 12 males in 3.3 ha); about one-third of the males were polygynous. Females were frequently double-brooded. The first clutch usually consisted of 7 eggs, the second 4–7 (Burns 1982). Time of arrival at breeding sites may vary considerably from one year to another. Birds present in May sometimes disappear by July, whereas first arrivals at a breeding site may appear as late as mid-July (Meanley 1952). In short, Sedge Wrens are characterized by high mobility during the breeding season and low site tenacity between seasons (Burns 1982). This is also true of this species in Delaware.

History. A specimen in Bush's collection was probably taken in Delaware in 1878 [Penn1]. A nest with 3 eggs was taken at Newport on 11 June 1886 by Pennock (Rhoads and Pennock 1905; WFVZ egg data). Three eggs were collected on 10 July 1904 3 mi east of Odessa by Pennock (WFVZ egg data).

Specimens were secured at New Castle on 6 May 1911 and at Newport on 14 October 1911. Four were seen at Lewes by Potter and the DVOC on 29 May 1927 [Penn1]. Barry (1939) listed it as "migrant, rare summer resident [in] lower part of state," perhaps based on this report but changed the status (in 1942) to "summer resident and migrant, nesting only in New Castle [County]." The latter statement is appropriate based on the only 2 nest records. The most recent record we have for New Castle County is 7 November 1959 (DMNH 1365). Hanson searched the Christiana area by canoe in 1928 and 1929 and found only Marsh Wrens. He never recorded Sedge Wrens in the state; thus the species' abundance and distribution at that time remain enigmatic.

Since Pennock's and Hanson's field work 12 were found on a 17 August 1941 trip to the Delaware coast [Kram5]. Wayne (notes) found it on 11 trips down Rt. 9 taken about 1 May in 1950–52, 1956, 1958, and 1962–67.

Breeding population. Its breeding population is less than 10 pairs, and in some years none may breed. It was probably always uncommon and local near tidal waters. An exceptional 40 estimated to be present along Broadkill Beach Rd. on 30 May 1967 may have included late migrants [Carr10]. Linehan and Jones (1971) noted there were no recent breeding records.

Conservation. This species is under evaluation for listing by the USFWS. It has appeared on the Blue List and is listed by many northeastern states; it is listed as Endangered in New Jersey, Threatened in Pennsylvania, and a Species of Special Concern in Maryland. It has declined in the northeastern United States on the BBS during 1966–90 (Gibbs and Melvin 1992d) and declined steeply in Delaware according to the May Count results during 1969–91.

FALL: This species is most often found in September when, presumably, it is migrating, but August reports may refer to birds about to nest (Gibbs and Melvin 1992d). The few October and November records include

14 Oct 1911	1	Newport marshes (ANSP 80235)
1 Nov 1952	4	Bethany Beach [Davi2]
7 Nov 1959	1	Newport marshes (DMNH 1365)
18 Nov 1953	3	Bombay Hook NWR [Spri1]

1966–89 CBC Summary

Christmas Bird Count	Years Found	Range of No. Found	Median
Wilmington			
Middletown			
Bombay Hook	13	1–2	1
Cape Henlopen	6	1–3	
Rehoboth	9	1–4	
STATEWIDE (high in 1972)	15	1–7	1

WINTER: A few may winter, but its status during this season is poorly known. One or 2 individuals were consistently found on the 1959 through 1981 CBCs at Bombay Hook, Cape Henlopen, or Rehoboth. The remaining winter records include

12 Dec 1987	2	Gordon Pond WA [Holg26]
23 Dec 1969	1	Pickering Beach [Gord5]
16 Jan 1988	1	Gordon Pond WA [Holg1]

It has not been reported after mid-January until its return in late April.

SPECIMENS: ANSP 80234, New Castle, 6 May 1911; ANSP 80235, Newport, 14 October 1911; DMNH 1365, Newport, 7 November 1959. Egg records: WFVZ.

Marsh Wren (*Cistothorus palustris*)

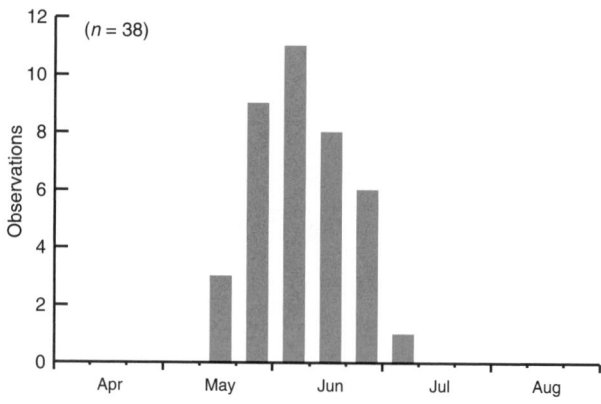

Estimated Clutch-Completion Dates

Regular; summer resident; fairly common along the Delaware River and Bay tidal marshes; less common around the Inland Bays or in fresh cattail marshes.

| J | F | M | A | M | J | J | A | S | O | N | D |

HABITAT: Estuarine emergent brackish or saltmarshes with tall cordgrass, cattail, phragmites, needlerush, or other tall grasses, or impounded marshes with similar vegetation. Less commonly in palustrine emergent cattail marsh.

SPRING: In some years a few arrive in April (e.g., at Dragon Run in 1973–74 [DOS1]), but usually Marsh Wrens are not numerous until 5–10 May. Migration peaks 10–20 May and ends by 20–25 May. A 2-year survey in Bombay Hook NWR resulted in 2 early records, 3 on 20 March 1983 [Hess14] and 1 on 17 April 1983 [Boll4]. Some high counts are

5 May 1984	23	Cape Henlopen SP and Indian River Inlet [Edni34].
8 May 1982	150	Bombay Hook NWR [Line18]
19 May 1974	66	Dragon Run [BroW22]

BREEDING: Its strongholds are the brackish and saltmarshes distributed from Newport south to Gordon Pond WA and it is found in phragmites marshes along the Chesapeake and Delaware Canal. A few inhabit Inland Bays but in such reduced numbers that the species was not registered on the relative abundance study. It is common in some impounded tidal marshes, such as those at Dragon Run, but rare at nontidal freshwater sites—the small population in the common cattail marsh at Brandywine Creek SP [Wayn30] being the only known site.

Atlas. During the Atlas project the Marsh Wren was much more common along Delaware Bay and River than along Chesapeake Bay in Maryland (Robbins 1996). The most common method of confirmation was by finding an occupied nest, but caution was necessary because males build a number of nests before females arrive (Metz 1991). Two reported from the Nanticoke drainage in Delaware were not believed to be breeding.

Nesting. Hanson (notes) in 1923 described nests located at Kitts Hummock in a large bed of cattail flags about 3 ft from the head of the marsh. They were woven of the wide leaves of wild meadow grasses, 6 in. in diameter and oblong in shape, and with a round entrance hole 1 in. in diameter and a little above the center on one side. A nest with 5 eggs was lined with very fine vegetable fibers and a few small dark feathers. It was about 18 in. from the ground and supported by both green and dead cattail flags. Other nest substrate described in Delaware includes saltmarsh cordgrass, marsh elder, groundsel bush, and phragmites, the last rather commonly. Clutches range from 3 to 5, with 5 the most common.

The Delaware estimated clutch-completion dates depict a considerably shorter breeding period than the egg dates of 3 May–17 August given for Maryland (Robbins 1996). The earliest egg date in Delaware is 25 May [MerW1], the latest 11 July. The large number of nests with eggs found by Hanson and Buckalew on 11 July may have been from second nestings.

In a Georgia saltmarsh about 5% of males were bigamous, 4% of the males that established territories remained unmated, and 20% of nestings were second-brood attempts by females, 1 of which unsuccessfully attempted a third brood (Kale 1965).

Standing water was an important factor in nest-site selection in a Washington study (Verner and Engelsen 1970). Deeper water and denser vegetation were preferred and produced more young at 2 Ontario sites, even though the preferred site contained some phragmites (Leonard and Picman 1987).

Trends. Stone (1937) pointed out that no other summer resident land bird suffered such habitat depletion as this wren did

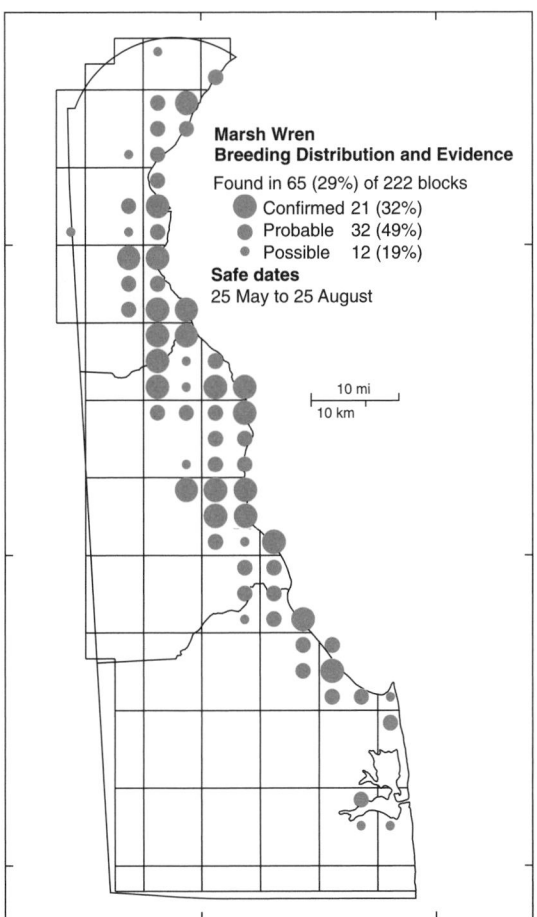

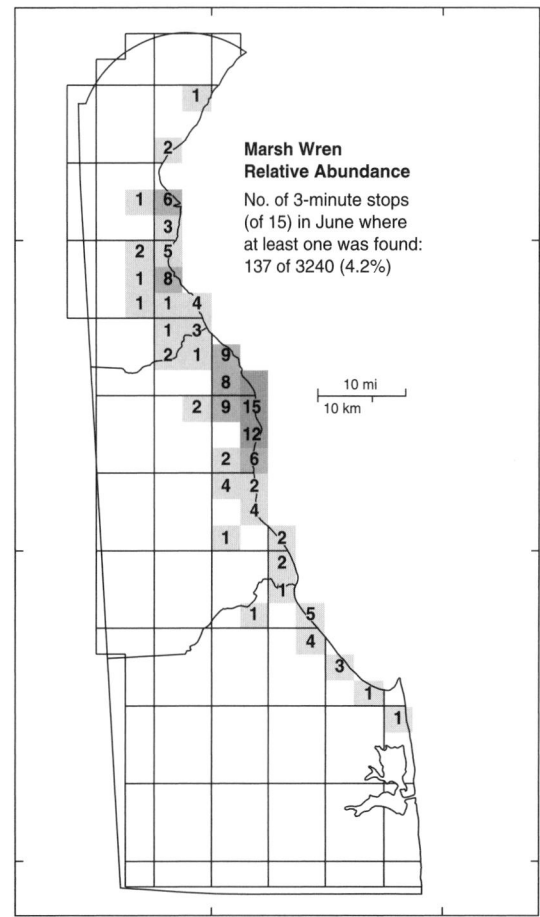

by the draining and filling of the marshes at Cape May in the early twentieth century. The marshes have been changed more recently by the invasion of phragmites, but this plant has served the wren as a nest support. No good method of measuring or monitoring the Marsh Wren's population has been developed. Its numbers have increased on the May Count (peak of 392 in 1986), but assessment of the effort spent in the marshes looking for this species is not possible. The BBS in Delaware provides no significant trend information, but the Marsh Wren has declined at an average annual rate of 3% per year during 1966–90 in the Upper Coastal Plain, which includes Delaware [Usfw3].

Breeding population. High breeding season counts include 200 from the dikes of Bombay Hook NWR on 29 May 1982 [Rufe5] and 66 in Dragon Run on 9 June 1974 [West2]. A study of the effects of phragmites control in Kent County showed that the Marsh Wren population in phragmites was about 150 pairs per 100 ha, and that the density decreased to zero in treated plots except those where some phragmites remained (Moore 1989). Delaware high counts of Marsh Wrens obtained from canoes in the relative abundance study reflect this species' acceptance of cordgrass marsh along tidal guts (West pers. obs.). A Black Rail survey found Marsh Wrens extremely com-

mon along the inland edges of tidal marshes, with 5–15 singing birds audible at many stops (Maier 1993). Only 2 were found on a BBC in Assawoman WA, where saltmarsh and cattail marsh were a small part of the habitat studied (McLaughlin 1968).

In a study in a Georgia estuarine marsh, breeding Marsh Wrens were confined to cordgrass exceeding 1 m in height. Cordgrass of this height is limited to streamsides and levee marshes. The wrens' preference resulted in a linear arrangement of territories in the tallest grass along tidal streams. The density of breeding pairs per total marsh area was 50 pairs per 100 ha, but if only the tall cordgrass area was counted, the density increased to 5,000 pairs per 100 ha, that is, 456–568 pairs in 10.1 ha of tall cordgrass (Kale 1965). Mean tidal change in the Delaware River is 87% of that at the Georgia site, so tidal constraints on nesting location may be similar, but slightly less restrictive, in Delaware. A breeding density of 260 territories per 100 ha (23.2 territories per 22.25 acres) was found in a Maryland needlerush marsh in Somerset County (Springer and Stewart 1948a).

FALL: A decrease in the number of reports begins during 10–20 August and may result from decreased singing. Migration probably begins during 20–25 August, with most leaving by 30 September. Occasional stragglers remain thereafter.

Except for 6 found on 24 October 1985 at Port Mahon [Wayn2], only 1–3 birds were reported on trips made after 1 October. Some high counts are

22 Aug 1981	14	Bombay Hook NWR [Wayn62]
6 Sep 1981	33	Bombay Hook NWR [Bayn4]
8 Sep 1974	45	Dragon Run [John8]
22 Sep 1973	9	Dragon Run [SpSB40]

1966–89 CBC Summary

Christmas Bird Count	Years Found	Range of No. Found	Median
Wilmington	1	1	
Middletown	6	1–9	
Bombay Hook	18	1–45	2
Cape Henlopen	8	1–8	
Rehoboth	14	1–7	1
STATEWIDE *(low in 1966, 1977, and 1983; high in 1984)*	24	1–45	7

WINTER: The CBC trend analysis shows a low but stable winter population. Few CBC reports exceed 6–8 birds, but 2 high counts are 12 in 1981 and a remarkable 45 in 1984, both on the Bombay Hook CBC. The dot in the seasonal graph at the beginning of January represents a few Marsh Wrens that have occurred on CBCs that week. Other January records include

8 Jan 1991	1	Broadkill Beach [Edni29]
26 Jan 1974	4	Cape Henlopen SP [Lehm22]
30 Jan 1965	1	Little Creek WA [McLP5]

This last bird was "so benumbed by the cold that it could be picked up."

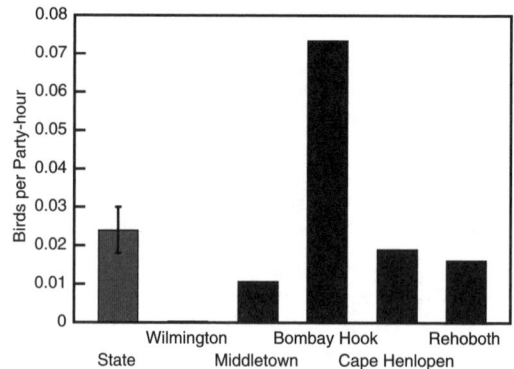

CBC Geographic Distribution

REMARKS: Most Delaware Marsh Wrens are found in tidal habitat typical of *C. p. palustris*, which breeds along the Atlantic coast from Rhode Island to Virginia. The colony in Brandy-wine Creek SP is in fresh marsh habitat typical of an inland form, *C. p. iliacus*, which has a buffy chin, throat, and belly.

SPECIMENS: DMNH 65651 and DMNH 65652, Delaware City, 30 May 1979; DMNH 51755, Bethany Beach, 20 September 1948; DMNH 51756, Bethany Beach, 22 September 1948; DMNH 73422, Newport, 2 October 1982. Egg records: DMNH, WFVZ.

Golden-crowned Kinglet *(Regulus satrapa)*

Regular; winter visitor; uncommon to fairly common. Expected late September to late April. Occasional late spring appearance in evergreen groves suggestive of nesting attempts.

J F M A M J J A S O N D

HABITAT: Coniferous or mixed forest. Also deciduous forests and wooded suburbs during migration. Preferred winter habitat (warm, moist coniferous and, to a lesser extent, hardwood forests), such as found in the Pacific Northwest and the southeastern Coastal Plain, is similar to their breeding habitat (dense, substantial conifer forest) (Lepthien and Bock 1976).

SPRING: Migration begins during March and peaks during 1–15 April. High counts include

9 Apr 1972	22	Winterthur [WarD6]
18 Apr 1975	40	White Clay Creek [Lehm5]
27 Apr 1992	11	Burrows Run [Wayn64]

Late reports are

30 Apr 1972	1	Winterthur [BroW8]
9 May 1975	1	White Clay Creek [Lehm1]
20 May 1976	1	Winterthur (see "Summer," Niles 1977)

The latter 2 constitute the only May records other than reports from 5 May Counts on dates from 8 to 14 May during 1971–88. Although some of these reports are probably correct, no notes or observer's names have been preserved, and it is likely that some of the reporters did not recognize the rarity of this species in May.

SUMMER: Niles (1977) reported a probable breeding attempt in a half-acre spruce grove at Winterthur: copulation was observed on 23 April 1976, and the male was singing on 20 May and driving a House Finch from a spruce tree. It was not observed subsequently, however.

This species has dramatically expanded its breeding range southward by exploiting Norway spruce plantations (Mulvihill 1992b). It has been confirmed breeding as close as southern Berks County, Pennsylvania, during July 1988 [Kell2]. Fledged young were found during July 1983 in Carroll County, Maryland, and 40 were counted there and in adjacent Pennsylvania on 10 July 1985 in large tracts of spruce (Blom in Robbins 1996) [Blom1].

FALL: First arrivals usually appear during 20–30 September, and peak numbers of migrants occur in October. Two birds reported at Hoopes Reservoir in early August 1971 were too early to be regarded as migrants. Other early reports are

| 19 Sep 1981 | 1 | Cape Henlopen SP [Frec32] |
| 20 Sep 1981 | 1 | Lewes [Frec1] |

High counts include

4 Oct 1981	27	Brandywine Creek SP [West2]
29 Oct 1990	89	Mt. Cuba [Wayn25]
2 Nov 1988	24	Cape Henlopen SP [Frec1]

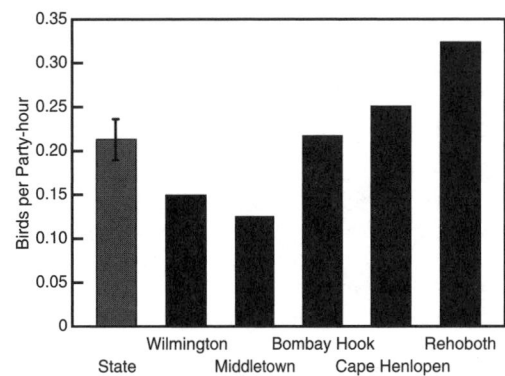

CBC Geographic Distribution

1966–89 CBC Summary

Christmas Bird Count	Years Found	Range of No. Found	Median
Wilmington	23	1–72	17
Middletown	23	1–29	9
Bombay Hook	24	1–47	13
Cape Henlopen	23	1–61	14
Rehoboth	24	2–116	24
STATEWIDE (low in 1976, high in 1975)	24	21–233	99

WINTER: Typical reports mention fewer than 4–5 birds. It is progressively more common southward on Delaware CBCs. The Seaford CBC has reported high numbers since its inception in 1983, averaging 65 during 1990–92. Its numbers on CBCs have varied widely without showing a long-term trend. Its population dropped sharply following the severe winters of 1976 and 1977, but it appears to have since recovered.

SPECIMENS: 22; DMNH, ANSP, UDEL.

Ruby-crowned Kinglet (*Regulus calendula*)

Regular; winter visitor; uncommon. Expected mid-September to early winter, sporadically through the winter, and early April to early May.

HABITAT: Brushy deciduous and mixed forests. Generally breeds and winters in open or edge habitats. Prefers wintering sites that are warm; precipitation level does not affect winter range or density (Lepthien and Bock 1976).

SPRING: The onset of northward migration is obscured by a few wintering individuals, but perhaps begins 1 April, with most migration taking place from 10 April to 5 May and the last migrants recorded 13 May. Two reports of stragglers have been received (no field notes):

| 27 May 1973 | 1 | Dragon Run [BroW1] |
| 11 Jun 1977 | 1 | White Clay Creek [Wayn33]. |

High counts are

13 Apr 1974	22	Dragon Run [Phal9]
18 Apr 1975	40	White Clay Creek [Lehm5]
3 May 1975	35	Wilmington [Cutl3]

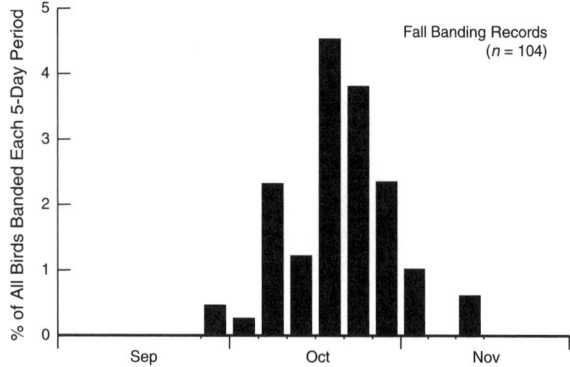

Fall Migration Activity

FALL: Migration typically occurs from 15 September to 1 November, with peak migration occurring 5–25 October. Peak banding occurs in mid-October. First arrivals some years appear by the end of August (excluding reports of earlier arrivals in 1964, 1977, and 1979):

29 Aug 1970	1	Brandywine Creek SP [Wayn63]
29 Aug 1971	1	Little Creek WA [John6]
31 Aug 1991	2	Burrows Run [Wayn36]

The earliest verified arrival is a bird banded on 18 Septem-

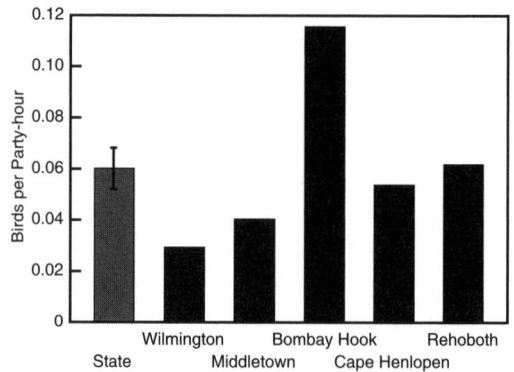

CBC Geographic Distribution

ber 1966 near Rehoboth Beach [RusW1], so care should be taken in identifying kinglets before then. In the August–October 1991 Neotropical migrant study (Mabey et al. 1993) 94% of the Ruby-crowned Kinglets were reported after 20 September ($n = 236$); 4% were reported in the first third of August.

1966–89 CBC Summary

Christmas Bird Count	Years Found	Range of No. Found	Median
Wilmington	22	1–10	3
Middletown	19	1–11	2
Bombay Hook	23	1–34	6
Cape Henlopen	21	1–21	2
Rehoboth	21	1–41	4
STATEWIDE *(low in 1985, high in 1975)*	24	4–74	24

WINTER: The Ruby-crowned Kinglet is usually absent, or present in extremely low numbers, once cold weather arrives.

SPECIMENS: 11; DMNH, UDEL.

Blue-gray Gnatcatcher (*Polioptila caerulea*)

Regular; summer resident; fairly common. Expected early April to early September, sporadically to mid-October, and occasionally into winter.

HABITAT: Wet or damp forests with brushy areas.

SPRING: First arrival is usually during 1–10 April, with peak numbers occurring from 10 April to 5 May. March reports include

22 Mar 1975	1	Pickering Beach Rd. [Phal1]
31 Mar 1979	1	Ashland [BroH9]
31 Mar 1991	1	Trap Pond SP [Camp16]

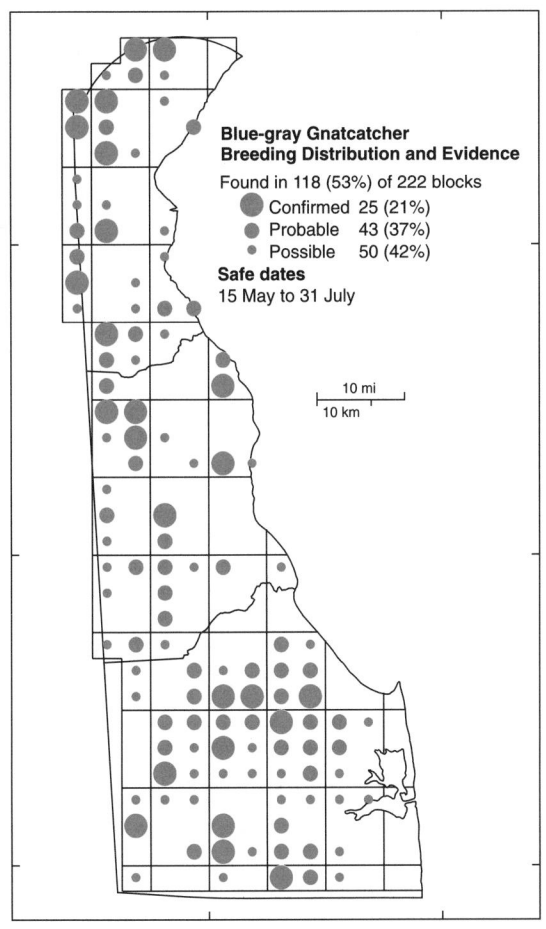

Blue-gray Gnatcatcher Breeding Distribution and Evidence

Found in 118 (53%) of 222 blocks

● Confirmed 25 (21%)
● Probable 43 (37%)
· Possible 50 (42%)

Safe dates
15 May to 31 July

10 mi
10 km

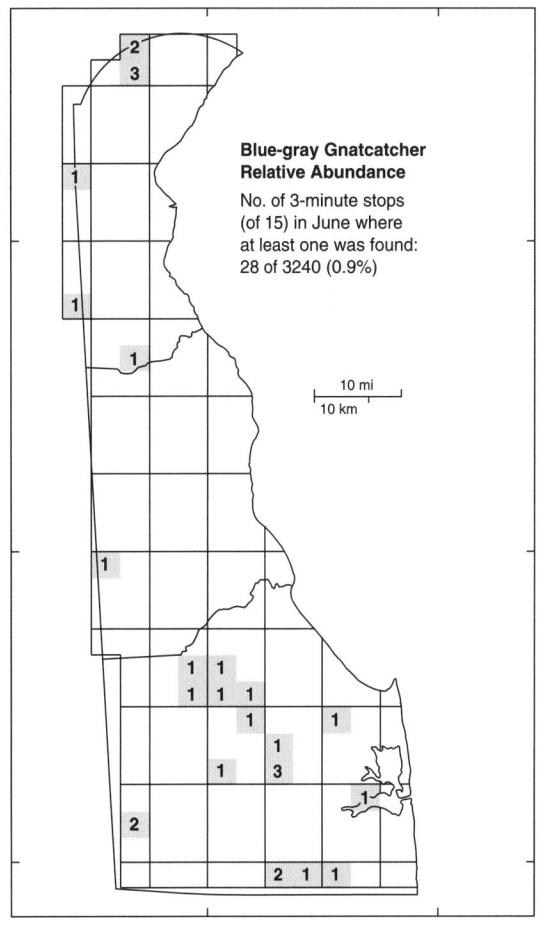

Blue-gray Gnatcatcher Relative Abundance

No. of 3-minute stops (of 15) in June where at least one was found: 28 of 3240 (0.9%)

10 mi
10 km

High counts, all from a DOS survey conducted along White Clay Creek, are

24 Apr 1976	45	White Clay Creek [SpSB21]
29 Apr 1978	35	White Clay Creek [SpSB18]
30 Apr 1977	43	White Clay Creek [SpSB18]

Late April is still during the migration period, and local breeders are conspicuously building nests.

BREEDING: The relative abundance study results suggest that the gnatcatcher is more common in forested parts of the

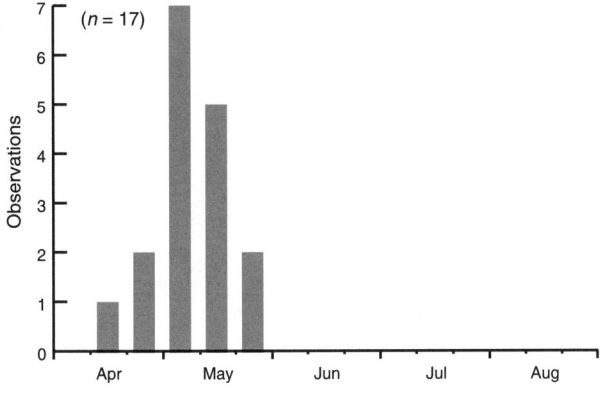

Estimated Clutch-Completion Dates

Piedmont and Sussex County than elsewhere, but it has such a quiet voice that this technique did not produce a very good map.

Atlas. Away from the tidal marshes the gnatcatcher is widespread in wooded habitat. The irregular pattern of its distribution suggests it may have been missed in some blocks, probably because it is inconspicuous, particularly following territory establishment and nest building (Root 1969; Nice 1932). The 2 most common confirmation methods were nest building, when it is active and calling, and attending its vocal young.

Nesting. Hanson (notes) described a nest built on 8 June 1928 as 3 in. high and 2.5 in. wide. It was saddled on a small branch of a young apple tree in a neglected orchard in west Dover. It was fashioned of very fine grasses and plant down, mostly willow, and decorated on the outside with bits of gray and green lichens. These birds were the only gnatcatchers Hanson reported; thus his record may indicate the northern limit of their breeding range at that time. Of 17 clutch-completion dates estimated, 9 were from 8 to 12 May. The only egg dates recorded are 7 May in Kent County and 15 May in Choptank Swamp (DMNH mount). In Sussex County Ednie [Edni4] observed an almost completed nest being decorated with lichens on 13 April, suggesting an early egg date. Maryland egg dates extend from 11 April to 10 June (Robbins 1996).

History. This species was formerly confined to Sussex County. Rhoads and Pennock (1905) described the gnatcatcher as common in summer throughout Sussex County, and Pennock (notes) observed it only in Sussex County. Stone (1919) listed the gnatcatcher as a southern bird that might be found in Delaware in the river bottoms of the Chesapeake drainage. Carter (notes, DMNH) collected a nest with 4 eggs on 15 May 1926 in the Choptank Swamp, the site of the first Delaware report (Rhoads 1903b); the nest was placed 40 ft above ground in a sweetgum covered with poison ivy. Barry (1939) listed its summer range as Sussex County. It occurred in New Castle County at least by 1956, when found at Rockford Park on 5 May [Wayn1]. By the 1960s or early 1970s it had established a statewide summer distribution, as shown by the May Count, weekly surveys, BBS, and BBC.

Even though Wilson (1808–14) first described this species in the early nineteenth century from a Pennsylvania specimen, Warren (1890) and Stone (1894) stated that it was rare in Pennsylvania and did not breed there. Its expansion north of the Mason-Dixon line as a regular breeding bird has been accomplished mainly during the twentieth century (Grube 1957; Meade 1988a; Leberman 1992a).

Trends. The May Count shows it has increased since 1969 at about 3% per year, but the BBS, which does not survey the Piedmont portion of Delaware, shows no trend [Usfw3].

Breeding population. One measure of the gnatcatcher's abundance is the May Count average of 90 per year, with a maximum of 164 recorded on 5 May 1984. Approximately 80% as many Blue-gray Gnatcatchers as Carolina Wrens are reported on the May Count, though gnatcatchers are usually much less conspicuous. They were one-sixth as common as Carolina Wrens on BBCs in 18 wooded sites, but most of those sites

were woodlots smaller than 10 ha that would not be expected to support gnatcatchers, a forest interior species (Robbins et al. 1989a). At two Delaware sites (White Clay Creek and Assawoman WA) this species bred at densities of 8 and 10 males per 100 ha, in Maryland at 15–18 territorial males per 100 ha (Stewart and Robbins 1958), and in West Virginia averaged 32 males per 100 ha (Hall 1983). Its Delaware density is about 10–20% of the density it attains in Coastal Plain states farther south (Robbins et al. 1986).

FALL: The decline in numbers of birds reported after July may in part reflect cessation of calling by adults and of begging by young birds. Migration begins in early August, with few records occurring after the first week of September. High counts are

14 Aug 1976	8	White Clay Creek [West16]
27 Aug 1977	5	White Clay Creek [Rufe10]
28 Aug 1987	6	east of Georgetown [Frec1]
3 Sep 1977	4	White Clay Creek [Barn20]

The latest departure date is obscured by an occasional individual remaining into winter. The last record of more than 1 occurred on 14 October 1972 when 2 were found at Winterthur [Beac5]. In the August–October 1991 Neotropical migrant study (Mabey et al. 1993) 8 gnatcatchers were reported in August ($n = 9$) and 1 on 29 September [Bart1].

WINTER: Single individuals of this species were recorded on the 1971 Wilmington CBC and the 1972 Bombay Hook CBC. A specimen from Wilmington dated 16 January 1985 (DMNH 76045) and a record of 1 found dead near Townsend, New Castle County, on 5 January 1981 [Hess5] confirm its occasional winter occurrence.

SPECIMENS: 10; DMNH, ANSP, UWBM. Egg records: WFVZ.

[Northern Wheatear *(Oenanthe oenanthe)*]

Accidental.

DOCUMENTATION: Adequate published notes.

REMARKS: A single bird has occurred, 1 seen on 21–22 September 1957 (Dyke 1958) [Cove1] near Indian River Inlet. The bird was seen perching on a low telephone line and flying frequently to a "sparsely grass-covered flat." The notes mention but do not describe the white pattern of tail and rump, and the white eye line and dark ear patch are noted. These marks would establish the identification of the bird as a wheatear, although the unlikely Isabelline Wheatear is not excluded.

Northern Wheatears breed in the North American Arctic and normally migrate to Europe, but there is a pattern of fall records along the U. S. Atlantic coast.

Eastern Bluebird (*Sialia sialis*)

Resident; uncommon to fairly common. Migrates February–April and October–November; winter numbers increasing at 17% per year.

HABITAT: Edges and fencerows in agricultural and residential settings with adjacent open areas.

SPRING: A modest migration, not apparent on the seasonal graph, occurs from 5–15 February to 10–20 April, with a peak throughout March. High counts are

25 Feb 1984	16	Sussex County [Hess20]
12 Mar 1988	20	along the coast [Wayn25]
30 Mar 1986	10	Cape Henlopen SP [Frec1]

BREEDING: The relative abundance study and Atlas project show its distinct preference for Sussex County, western Kent County, and those portions of New Castle County near the Pennsylvania border, all predominantly forested areas. Perhaps forest edges are its favored habitat, with the forest providing shelter and forage for those that remain during winter.

Atlas. This species was confirmed frequently because it uses nest boxes and is not secretive when entering natural cavities. One-third of the confirmed records resulted from sightings of fledged young, which are easily distinguished by their spotted breasts. In some instances young were found far from nest boxes and human habitation, suggesting they were raised in natural cavities.

Nesting. Most reported nests are in boxes; natural cavities used include old woodpecker holes, cavities in rotten wood, and even in a "crevice between two cedar trees" [Bush1]. The nest is a cup often composed of grass or pine needles (nest records); feathers are used as lining material (Darlington, WFVZ egg data).

The bluebird is double-brooded, as shown by the clutch-

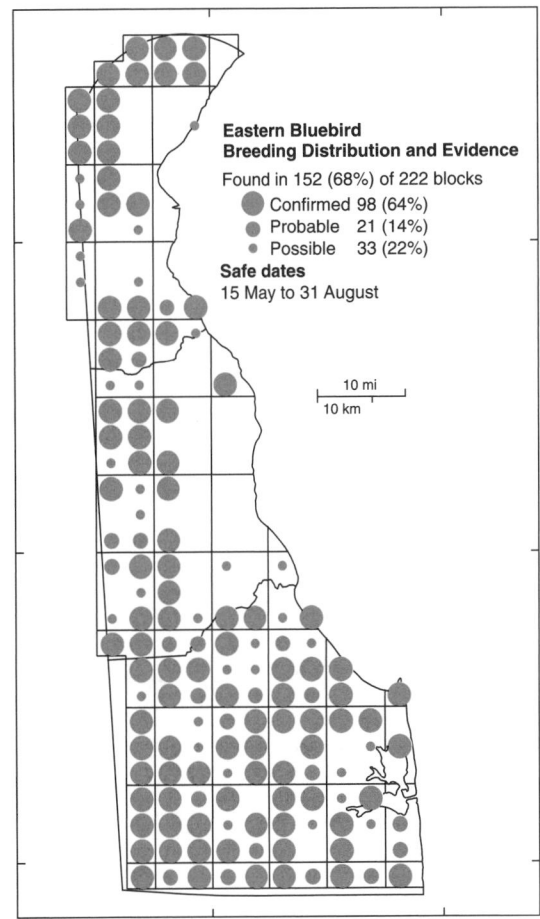

Eastern Bluebird
Breeding Distribution and Evidence
Found in 152 (68%) of 222 blocks
⬤ Confirmed 98 (64%)
● Probable 21 (14%)
• Possible 33 (22%)
Safe dates
15 May to 31 August

10 mi
10 km

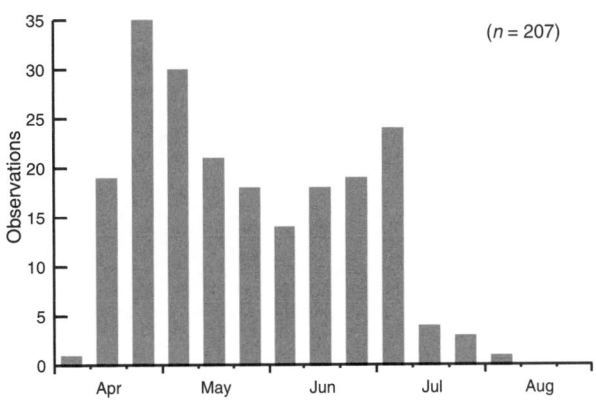

Estimated Clutch-Completion Dates

completion dates. Even though extreme egg dates—4 April to 17 August [Jahn1]—in Delaware denote a long breeding season, the Maryland extreme egg dates—12 March to 5 September—suggest still earlier and later breeding may take place (Robbins and Bystrak 1977). Extreme nestling dates for Delaware are 28 April and 25 August [Jahn1]. Clutch size ranges from 3 to 6, usually 4 or 5 (Peakall 1970).

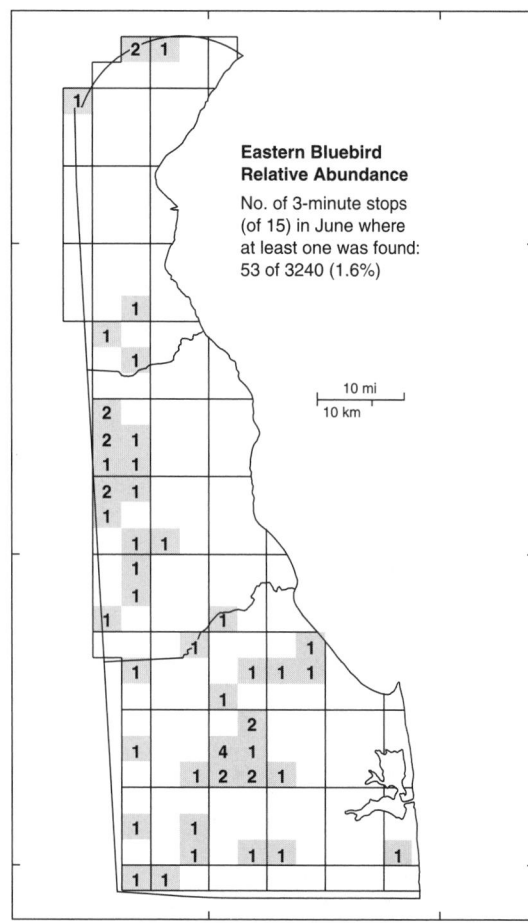

**Eastern Bluebird
Relative Abundance**

No. of 3-minute stops
(of 15) in June where
at least one was found:
53 of 3240 (1.6%)

10 mi
10 km

1 Oct 1989	35	west of Lewes [Frec1]
2 Nov 1991	126	Burrows Run [SpeE17]
3 Nov 1972	46	Brandywine Creek SP [Phal4]
12 Nov 1984	20	near Centerville [SpSB24]

Eastern Bluebird 1966–89 CBC Summary

Christmas Bird Count	Years Found	Range of No. Found	Median
Wilmington	23	2–192	34
Middletown	7	1–13	
Bombay Hook	4	1–4	
Cape Henlopen	11	1–33	
Rehoboth	18	3–89	11
STATEWIDE	24	6–275	45

(increasing; low in 1971, high in 1983)

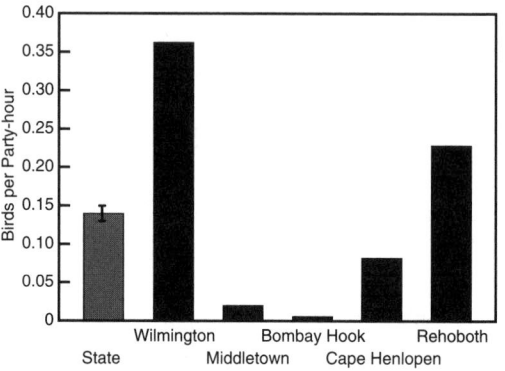

CBC Geographic Distribution

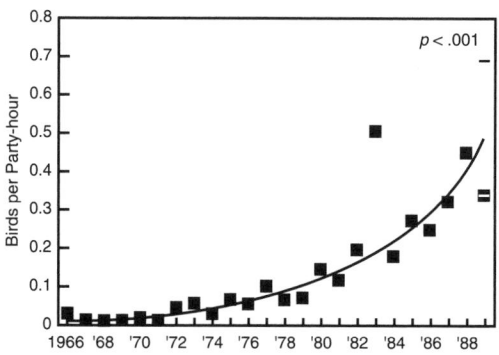

CBC Trend; Increasing at 17% per Year

History. Bush writes of bluebirds in nesting boxes in the Wilmington of 1879. Since then the town has become a city, its open spaces are gone, and House Sparrows and starlings have arrived to compete with bluebirds for cavities. Added to these restrictions on its population are occasional decimations caused by severe cold during late winter in the Southeast (James 1962) where many bluebirds winter.

Trends. BBS results show a decline of 5% per year in the bluebird's breeding population in the East during 1966–78, when a period of several consecutive cold winters ended. From 1978 to 1987 its population in the East increased by an average of 8% per year and in Delaware by a remarkable 23% per year (Sauer and Droege 1990) [Usfw1]. Mild late-winter weather and nest box programs by the Sussex Bird Club, the Delaware Audubon Society, and others have helped this increase.

Breeding population. The total Eastern Bluebird population is difficult to estimate because it changes markedly as winter weather conditions change. It averaged 0.85 bird per BBS route on 6 routes during 1981–90 while achieving a 13-fold increase. The highest May Count result is only 73 found in 1989.

FALL: Although the seasonal bar graph does not depict a migration period, a modest peak in bluebird numbers from 1 October to 15 November indicates migrational activity. High counts are

WINTER: This species has increased significantly in winter paralleling the increase detected for the breeding season. The highest numbers are recorded on the Wilmington and Seaford CBCs. Some high counts are

7 Dec 1985	30	Laurel [Frec1]
7 Jan 1983	24	Prime Hook NWR [Frec39]
1 Feb 1984	10	Brandywine Creek SP [Batt1]

Some of the population may be resident (adults as well as young), a supposition suggested by the winter occurrence of bluebirds at sites where bluebirds also breed; Hanson (notes), for example, reported birds throughout the winter of 1924–25 at a Dover breeding location. One strategy bluebirds use in winter is for several to bundle into 1 cavity or nest box in cold weather (Speck 1966; Frazier and Nolan 1959). In Maryland a banded female and her entire second brood were recaptured in a nest box in winter (C. S. Robbins, pers. comm.).

BANDING: The only recovery of a bluebird banded in Delaware resulted from a young bird that dispersed 7 mi (11 km) north into Pennsylvania.

SPECIMENS: 7; DMNH, ANSP, UDEL. Egg records: DMNH, WFVZ.

Veery (*Catharus fuscescens*)

Regular; summer resident; fairly common. Expected early May to late September.

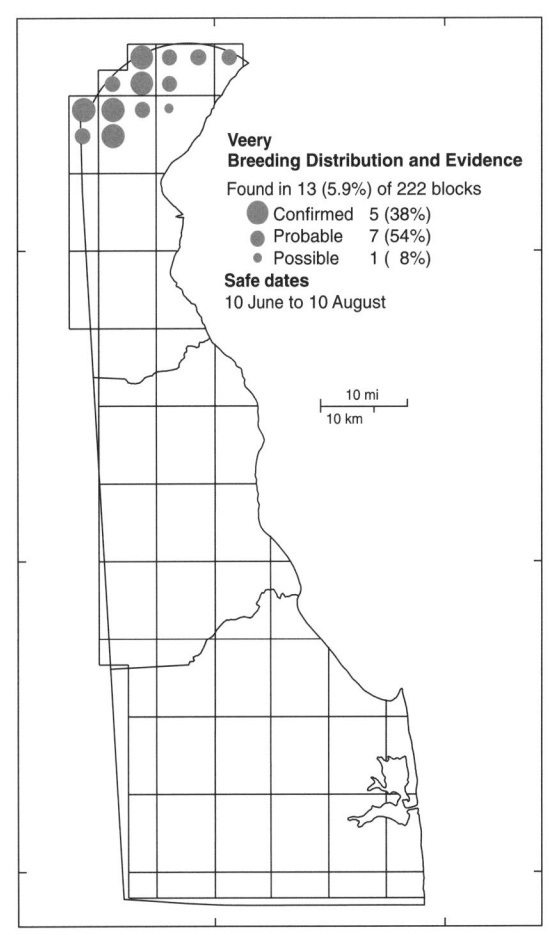

HABITAT: Moist upland forest and floodplain forest. Requires moist woods, typically in a moist hollow or on a north-facing slope, or thickets or early successional woods (Bertin 1977). In Delaware, thickets on wooded north-facing slopes, with mountain laurel present at some locations.

SPRING: First acceptable arrival reports may be as early as 25–30 April in some years, but first arrival of this thrush is not expected until 1–7 May. The earliest specimen is 5 May 1983 near Centerville. The earliest banding record is during the first 5-day period in May 1970 near Newark. The earliest acceptable sight records probably begin in late April:

25 Apr 1990	1	Greenville [Dyer6]
26 Apr 1964	1	Hoopes Reservoir [Klab4]
29 Apr 1973	1	Centerville [Wayn18]

Evaluation of sight records remains a problem because confusion may occur with some races of the Hermit Thrush in poor light. The end of the migration is not apparent; Stewart and Robbins (1958) give the end dates as 15–25 May in Maryland. Reports occur occasionally in late May from Kent and Sussex counties (DOS notes), where it is not expected to breed,

and unexpectedly in June (see "Breeding"). High counts include

7 May 1977	9	White Clay Creek [Dyer7]
14 May 1977	23	White Clay Creek [Jahn11]
15 May 1976	26	White Clay Creek [Patt6]
23 May 1964	20	Hoopes Reservoir [Klab3]

The highest May Count is 80 reported on 5 May 1984.

BREEDING: As a breeding bird this species is probably restricted to Piedmont Delaware and possibly nearby coastal areas.

Atlas. The 5 confirmations shown on the map all involved young birds rather than location of nests. No nest was discovered during the Atlas period. During the Atlas project Veery records were also received from the Coastal Plain. However, these are not included on the map out of caution, because no nest has ever been reported on the Coastal Plain in Delaware, Virginia, Maryland, or New Jersey, and the habitat where they were found is different from the north-facing hillsides where they breed on the Delaware Piedmont. The evidence for breeding in the Coastal Plain follows: Veeries were observed at 2 sites of young deciduous swampy forest in the Sawmill Branch drainage between Taylors Bridge and Smyrna [SpeE12]. One was observed feeding a fledgling near Rd. 465 on 2 July 1984. One was seen again near Rd. 466 on 26 July. Also on 2 July 1984 a Veery was seen feeding a fledgling about 1.5 mi (2 km) away near Rds. 51 and 45. In both cases of attending young the birds were observed on the forest floor at 3–6 m for 5 min.

Further supporting these records of Coastal Plain breeding are the observation of a singing Veery on 9 June 1984 on Primehook Neck [Patt10] and the observation of 1 seen carrying nest material on 7 June 1981 at Bombay Hook [Citr2]. Summering Veeries have been reported from central and southern New Jersey and it may be a scarce breeder there (Leck 1984).

Other Coastal Plain reports in Delaware include

8 Jun 1980	2	Churchmans Marsh [Kell6]
14 Jun 1975	1	near Dover [Pure6]
15 Jun 1974	1	Dragon Run [Broo21]
26 Jun 1965	2	Churchmans Marsh [WarM3]

Veeries occur at sites with high moisture and a cool microclimate in early successional and disturbed woodland, as well as in mature woods (Bertin 1977), and sites close to the Delaware River and Bay would tend to be cooler in early summer than inland sites. Occasional Coastal Plain instances of its breeding in thick, moist woods might be expected, since breeding has expanded in the twentieth century to the glaciated Coastal Plain of Long Island, New York (Bonney 1988b).

Nesting. Nest records of adult on nest on 21 May [Jahn1] and carrying food to the nest site on 16 June [SpeE3] suggest clutch completion occurs in the last half of May. The nest is a stout cup, often with a base of dead leaves and often placed on or near the ground; usually 4 eggs are laid (Harrison 1978). Pairs may be double-brooded in New Hampshire (Harding in Bent 1949) and may be so in Delaware.

History. The Veery may be a recent arrival as a Delaware breeding bird. Rhoads and Pennock (1905) classified it as a migrant but also cited 1 heard in a deep ravine near Greenville on 8 July 1903. This remained the only published summer record until 1964, when it was regularly reported on the Hoopes Reservoir survey. It had not summered there during the 1943–45 survey [Hoff4]. After 1964 it was reported during summer on all other Piedmont weekly surveys, as well as on BBCs at Heritage Park (1968), White Clay Creek (1970), and the University of Delaware woodlot (1970).

Trends. BBS data indicate a 2% average annual decline in its population in the East over the past 10 years, more than offsetting the slight gain posted during the previous 15 years.

Breeding population. Probably at least 50, but not over 500, pairs breed in the state (average of 5–45 pairs per block where detected). Some indication of its population in favored locations is reflected by peak counts on the weekly surveys:

13 Jun 1964	13	Hoopes Reservoir [Nixd1]
3 Jul 1971	8	Brandywine Creek SP [BroW7]
19 Jun 1976	15	White Clay Creek [Wayn33]
7 Jul 1979	6	Ashland Nature Center [SpSB10]

Conservation. Because it has a definite preference for larger tracts of forest (Robbins et al. 1989a), it will probably decline in Delaware unless substantial Piedmont forested tracts can be maintained in the face of increasing human population pressure.

FALL: Migration begins 20–25 August and usually ends by 20–25 September. The peak banding period is 15–20 September [Usfw3]. Late reports include

4 Oct 1974	1	1 mi south of Arden (DMNH 52563)
6 Oct 1975	1 banded	University of Delaware woodlot [Line4]
7 Oct 1973	1	near Wilmington [Hubb3]
11 Oct 1985	1	north of Wilmington (DMNH 77479)

High counts are

28 Aug 1976	10	White Clay Creek [Litt7]
10 Sep 1977	21	White Clay Creek [BroW12]
6 Sep 1981	10	Bombay Hook NWR [Bayn1]

Veeries are not detected in fall as frequently as in spring, with most fall reports consisting of 1–3 birds.

SPECIMENS: 39; DMNH, UDEL. Egg records: WFVZ.

Gray-cheeked Thrush (*Catharus minimus*)

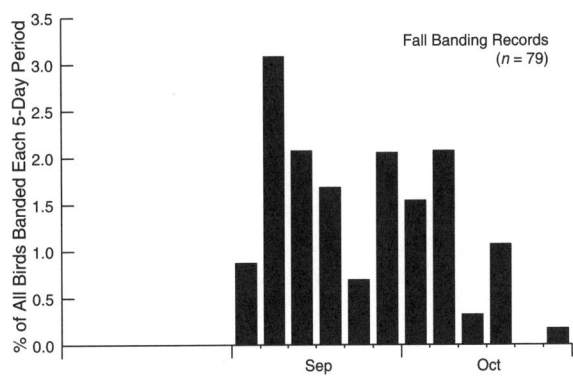

Fall Migration Activity

Regular; migrant; uncommon. Rare in spring. Expected mid- to late May and mid-September to mid-October.

HABITAT: Wet or damp forest or floodplain forest with brushy understory.

SPRING: First arrival may be as early as 5 May. The main migration occurs 10–25 May, with only a few remaining later. Early reports include

5 May 1979	1	Ashland [Patt9]
7 May 1977	1	White Clay Creek [Dyer10]
9 May 1984	2	Centerville [SpeE6]
9 May 1984	1	Rd. 290 [Frec1]

A 19 April 1877 specimen from Wimington (UDEL 346-68) is very early; it predates W. D. Bush's collecting notes by a year, so the date cannot be corroborated from that source, but Rhoads and Pennock (1905) give as the only Delaware record "One from near Wilmington in Bush collection taken Sept., 1877." Late reports include

26 May 1973	1 banded	near Claymont [Conw3]
26 May 1985	4	Prime Hook NWR [Frec1]
29 May 1978	present	Assawoman WA [DuPG30]

Typically only single birds are found, but these high counts were reported:

16 May 1964	5	Hoopes Reservoir [Hoff4]
20 May 1984	6	near Lewes [Frec1]

Banding data from Montgomery County, Maryland, give a migration range of 2–31 May, median of 21 May, with 80% of the migration taking place in the second half of the month (Mehlman 1990). This thrush is not usually a coastal migrant, especially in the spring (Sibley 1993) [Frec1].

FALL: First arrival may be as early as late August, but the typical migration period is from 10 September to 5 October. Banding records show a similar pattern. Early records are

21 Aug 1976	1	White Clay Creek [Dyer7]
1 Sep 1970	2 banded	University of Delaware woodlot [Jone2]
4 Sep 1964	1 banded	6 mi east of Red Lion [Line4]

Late banding and sight reports are

16 Oct 1970	1 banded	Newark [Jone2]
19 Oct 1973	1 banded	Newark [Line4]
21 Oct 1978	1	Ashland [Broo18]
26 Oct 1969	1	Brandywine Creek SP [SpSB1]
28 Oct 1989	1 banded	Prime Hook NWR [Thor1]

A report of 1 banded in November (Stickley 1965) could not be corroborated in the USFWS banding records. All reports are of 1–3 birds. Banding data from Montgomery County, Maryland, give a migration range of 19 August–26 October, median of 30 September, with 90% of the migration taking place from 18 September to 11 October (*n* = 738) (Mehlman 1990). This suggests that the Delaware early and late records (mentioned earlier) are unusually early or late and should be accepted with caution.

SPECIMENS: 16; DMNH, ANSP, UDEL, USNM, UWBM.

Bicknell's Thrush (*Catharus bicknelli*)

Migrant; frequency and abundance unknown but, perhaps, regular, rare.

REMARKS: An adult female Bicknell's Thrush was collected near Ellendale on 15 September 1948 (USNM 422403). Buckalew (1950) stated it was the first recorded specimen for the state and none has been reported since. Ouellet (1993) listed New Jersey, Maryland, and Virginia among the states from which specimens of migrants had been obtained. It "migrates mainly through eastern North America east of the Appalachi-ans from southern Quebec to Florida" (AOU 1995), as does a much larger population of Gray-cheeked Thrushes. Bicknell's and Gray-cheeked thrushes sing distinctive songs, so some spring migrants can be distinguished in the field. Bicknell's Thrushes breed in southern Quebec, Nova Scotia, and southward in the mountains through New England and New York; its range has been decreasing (Ouellet 1993).

SPECIMEN: USNM 422403, Ellendale, 15 September 1948.

Swainson's Thrush (*Catharus ustulatus*)

Regular; migrant; uncommon. Expected mid- to late May and early September to mid-October.

J F M A M J J A S O N D

HABITAT: Wet or damp forest or floodplain forest with brushy understory.

SPRING: Although first arrival has occurred as early as April, it is not expected before 5–10 May. It arrives about the same time as the Gray-cheeked Thrush but some stay about a week longer. The number of reports peaks during 10–25 May. The peak banding period is 20–25 May [Usfw2]. The earliest banding report refers to 1 at the University of Delaware woodlot on 8 May 1970 [Jone2]. Early sight reports are

13 Apr 1974	1	White Clay Creek [WilC2]
16 Apr 1977	2	White Clay Creek [Conw11]
17, 20 Apr 1965	1	Redden SF [Broo6]
22 Apr 1973	1	Dragon Run [BroW11]

Virtually all have passed through by the end of May. The latest departures are

2 Jun 1973	1	Dragon Run [Beac6]
9 Jun 1988	1	University of Delaware woodlot (DMNH 77473)

High counts include

13 May 1972	11	Winterthur [Falk9]
15 May 1976	6	White Clay Creek [Patt6]
22 May 1983	6	Bombay Hook NWR [Bayn4]

Banding data from Montgomery County, Maryland, give a migration range of 25 April–1 June, median of 18 May, with 90% of the migration taking place during 5–25 May ($n = 1,077$) (Mehlman 1990). This thrush is not usually a coastal migrant, especially in the spring (Sibley 1993).

FALL: The Swainson's Thrush usually arrives about a week earlier than the Gray-cheeked Thrush, and some may linger. First arrival is usually 1–10 September. Peak migration lasts from about 15 September to 15 October. The peak banding period is 25–30 September. Early arrivals are

20 Aug 1972	1	Wilmington (DMNH 22078)
26 Aug 1973	1	Prime Hook NWR [DuPG3]

The following record is probably the latest acceptable one, but even identification in hand is tricky for some races:

26 Oct 1976	1 banded	University of Delaware woodlot [Line4]

Typical counts involve 1–3 birds. High counts are

12 Sep 1971	8	Brandywine Creek SP [BroW1]
1 Oct 1974	6	near Dover [Lehm1]

Delaware banding data show a peak 26–30 September and continue to the end of October ($n = 190$). Similarly banding data from Montgomery County, Maryland, give a migration range of 17 August–29 October, median of 25 September, with 90% of the migration taking place from 10 September to 10 October ($n = 738$) (Mehlman 1990). This suggests that Del-

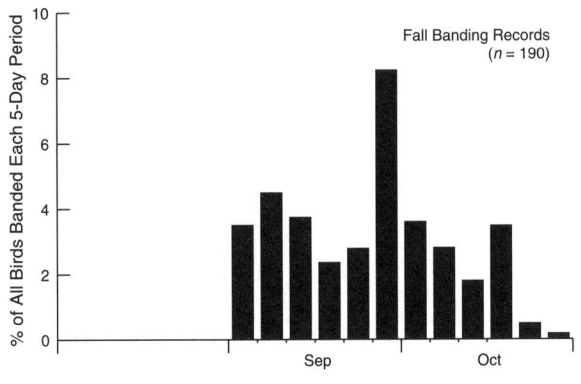

Fall Banding Records
(n = 190)

Fall Migration Activity

aware reports for November 1964, 1965, and 1978 and CBC records in 1964 and 1965 are unusually late and should not be accepted as published. Stragglers are always possible and should be carefully observed and documented to establish their presence. No one in Delaware has yet had the skill to identify a large nocturnal migration by call notes and report the hundreds that may be flying over the state (C. S. Robbins, pers. comm.).

WINTER: No acceptable reports for Delaware.

SPECIMENS: 44; DMNH, UDEL.

Hermit Thrush *(Catharus guttatus)*

Regular; migrant and winter visitor; uncommon. Expected early October to late April, sporadic February through mid-March. Early winter numbers apparently increasing.

HABITAT: Wet or damp forest or floodplain forest with brushy understory.

SPRING: Migration begins 15–20 March and peaks during 1–20 April. Most leave by 30 April–5 May. Late records are

12 May 1966	1 banded	University of Delaware woodlot [Line4]
13 May 1972	1	Winterthur [Falk9]
14 May 1981	1	west of Laurel (DMNH 71589)

High counts are

2 Apr 1988	12	Prime Hook NWR [Frec1]
14 Apr 1965	12	Iron Hill, Newark [Faus5]
23 Apr 1965	15	Bellevue, Wilmington [Jone3]

It has been found on the May Count in all but 3 years, with highest counts of 8 (10 May 1975) and 6 (3 May 1980 and 4 May 1985).

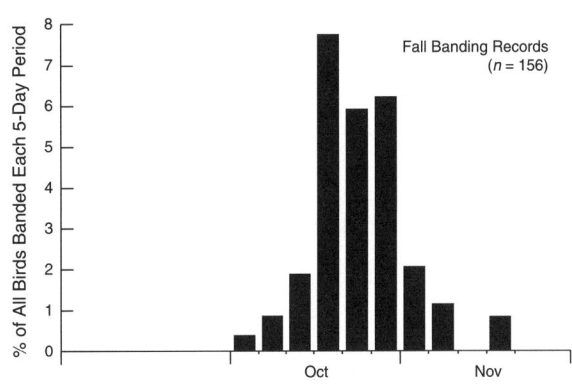

Fall Banding Records
(n = 156)

Fall Migration Activity

FALL: Although a few sometimes arrive in September, Hermit Thrushes are not expected before 1–10 October. Peak migration occurs during 15–30 October, and the peak banding period is 15–30 October. The earliest reports include some unprecedented early sight records that may stem from misidentification of other migrating *Catharus* thrushes more common in September:

3 Sep 1972	1	Winterthur [Broo20]
8 Sep 1979	1	Ashland [Rufe7]
13 Sep 1975	2	Dragon Run [John1]
15 Sep 1967	1 banded	University of Delaware woodlot [Jone2]

The earliest Delaware specimen is dated 8 October 1973 from Wilmington (DMNH 37651). Because Hermit Thrushes are unexpected in September, observations should be carefully made and corroborated. High counts are

| 13 Oct 1973 | 8 | Brandywine Creek SP [Edni37] |
| 20 Oct 1974 | 10 | Brandywine Creek SP [Walt3] |

1966–89 CBC Summary

Christmas Bird Count	Years Found	Range of No. Found	Median
Wilmington	22	1–42	9
Middletown	21	1–13	4
Bombay Hook	24	1–24	5
Cape Henlopen	24	1–26	6
Rehoboth	24	2–62	15
STATEWIDE (low in 1968, high in 1975)	24	6–128	46

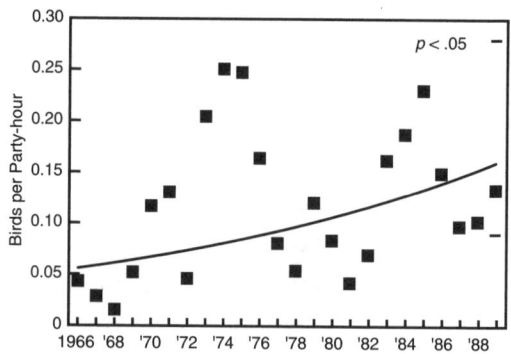

CBC Trend; Autocorrelation may Invalidate the Significance Test

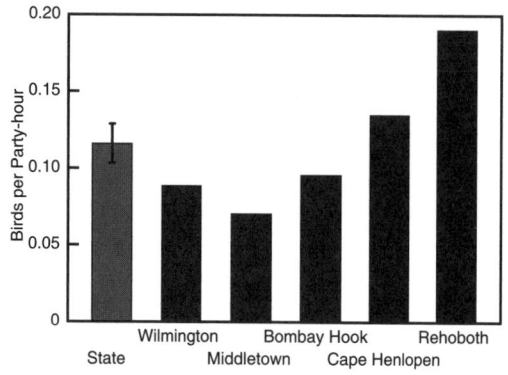

CBC Geographic Distribution

WINTER: Most reports are of 1–2 birds during early winter (November–January). There are only 8 reports between 31 January and 15 March, most of 1–3 birds. The maximum CBC count is 72, recorded on the 1989 Seaford CBC.

CBC data show a significant increase in Hermit Thrushes, but this increase could easily be an artifact of increased tape recorder use, since this species responds well to recordings of screech-owls in winter. Possibly more significant is a sharp reduction shown in the CBC trend graph in 1977 paralleling the sharp reduction in Carolina Wren numbers following the severe winter of 1976–77.

SPECIMENS: 50; DMNH, ANSP, UDEL.

Wood Thrush *(Hylocichla mustelina)*

Regular; summer resident; fairly common. Expected late April to mid-October.

HABITAT: Wet, shaded areas, moderate understory vegetation, and tall trees (Roth and Johnson 1993), such as found in floodplain forest or moist mature deciduous forest. Less sensitive to forest fragmentation than most Neotropical migrants.

SPRING: First arrival is 20–25 April, with the peak occurring 10–20 May; migration ends 20–25 May. The earliest report, of 2, comes from Brandywine Creek SP on 18 April 1965 [Hoff1]. Some high counts are

17 May 1975	48	Dragon Run [Rich1]
20 May 1978	48	White Clay Creek [Falk11]
25 May 1981	73	Prime Hook NWR [Frec1]

BREEDING: The Wood Thrush is widespread and fairly common in Delaware woodlands.

Atlas. It was recorded in almost every block but confirmed in only 31%, disappointingly low for a species whose nest should be relatively easy to locate. Nests were reported only 19 times. Despite the low confirmation rate it was frequently reported as a probable breeder based on persistent singing. It is, of course, absent from urban Wilmington and open marshy and coastal areas, but the relative abundance study suggests it is

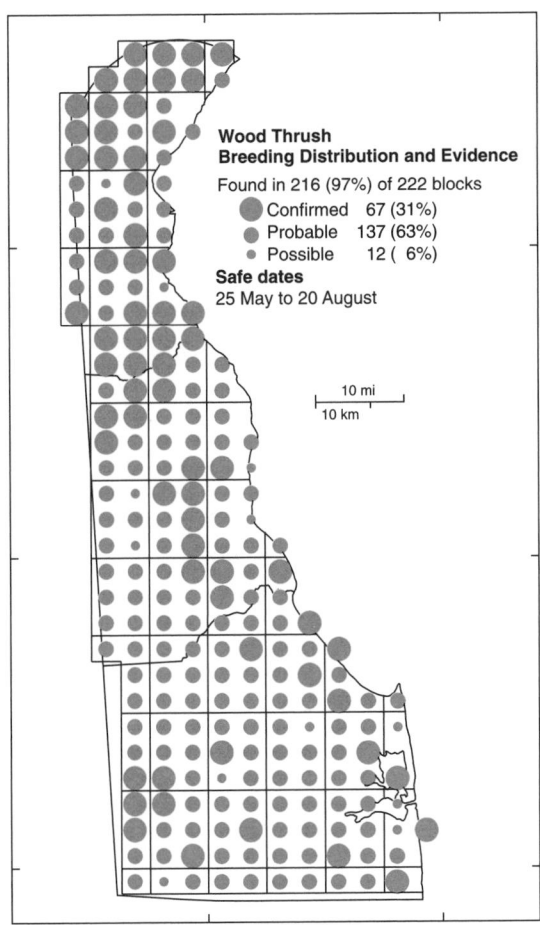

**Wood Thrush
Breeding Distribution and Evidence**

Found in 216 (97%) of 222 blocks

● Confirmed 67 (31%)
● Probable 137 (63%)
• Possible 12 (6%)

Safe dates
25 May to 20 August

10 mi
10 km

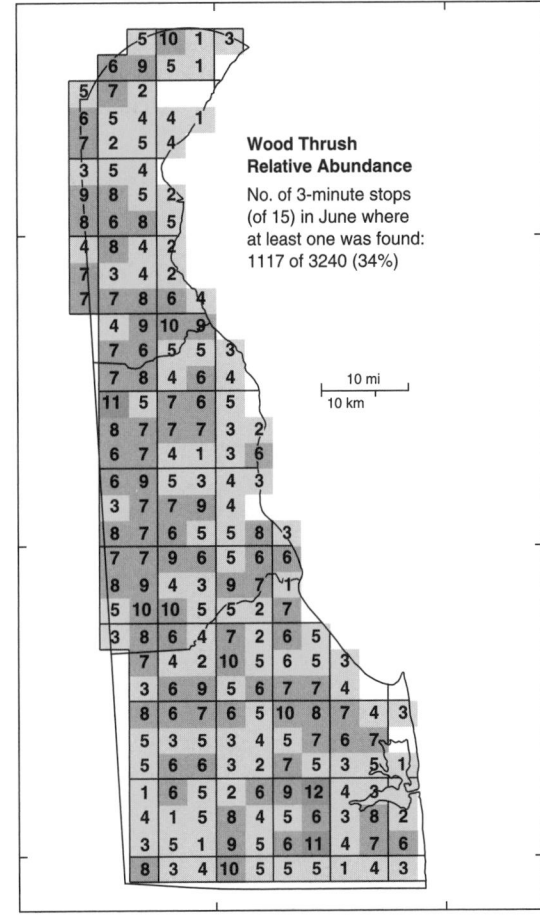

**Wood Thrush
Relative Abundance**

No. of 3-minute stops
(of 15) in June where
at least one was found:
1117 of 3240 (34%)

10 mi
10 km

otherwise about equally common throughout the state. It does not show an increased population density in the large expanse of forest in Sussex County, possibly because the open pine habitat there does not favor its nesting. Its abundance in otherwise open farming and marshy areas of southern New Castle and eastern Kent counties, areas avoided, for example, by Ovenbirds, suggests that it uses small woodlots and streamside wood strips in those areas.

Nesting. A Wood Thrush nest found by Hanson (notes) on 10 May in a swamp near Camden was described as "seven feet from the ground in a thicket of [American] elder bushes. It was 5 inches in diameter outside and 3 ¹/₂ inches deep. Inside it was 3 ¹/₄ inches in diameter and 2 ¹/₄ inches deep. The outside was of dried wild grass leaves with a layer of grass stems next to a wall of swamp mud. It was lined with rootlets, mostly black, but with a few reddish ones." R. Roth (pers. comm.) points out that the base of the nest often contains bleached leaves, paper, or plastic.

The clutch-completion graph does not clearly show a second peak for the second broods of this species, but does show its long breeding season. Year-to-year shifts in the onset of breeding, and production of replacement clutches after failure, tend to spread out the time second clutches are started after a first successful one is completed. Second nests are often diffi-

cult to find, being placed at greater heights than early ones (R. Roth, pers. comm.). In Delaware replacement clutches may be started as early as mid-May [Roth1]. The early egg date is 5 May [Roth1]. The latest clutch-completion date is 29 July, estimated from the hatching of the last egg on 10 or 11 August [Roth2]. First clutch size is typically 4, occasionally 5, later clutches usually 3 or 2 (R. Roth, pers. comm.).

Trends. May Count data indicate a general decrease in the early 1980s and an increase during 1989–91. Studies in the Uni-

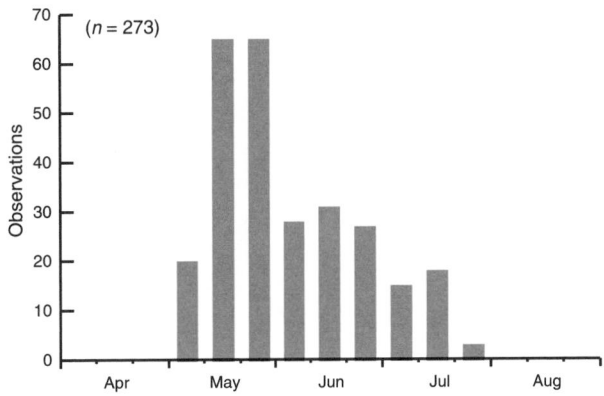

Estimated Clutch-Completion Dates

versity of Delaware woodlot generally parallel this pattern (Roth and Johnson 1993). The recent increase may partially mask a long-term downward trend. A longer perspective is provided by BBS data, which show the Wood Thrush and many other Neotropical migrants increasing across the continent during 1966–78 but then declining during 1978–87 (Robbins et al. 1989b), a decline also reflected in Delaware BBS data [Usfw3].

Breeding population. Indications of the Wood Thrush's abundance are provided by 171 registered on 10 state BBSs in 1976 and by 459 noted on the May Count of 13 May 1989. The 15-ha University of Delaware woodlot (high-quality thrush habitat) averaged about 18 pairs during 1982–87 when Wood Thrush numbers were at their nadir; the average for better years is about 26 pairs (Roth and Johnson 1993).

Conservation. The Wood Thrush is somewhat sensitive to forest fragmentation and occurs with reduced probability in smaller fragments (Robbins et al. 1989a); yet this species also has been described as a familiar resident of gardens and shrubbery about houses (Forbush and May 1939). Roth (1987) described a breeding population, in a Newark residential subdivision, whose members were most likely to be productive and return the next year if the lots had areas with at least 70% canopy cover and natural shrub cover, leaf litter, and moist soil. This finding can serve as a guide to communities that wish to attract this species.

The clearing of North American woodlands and of Central American forests should have reduced the Wood Thrush's population in proportion to the amount of habitat lost, possibly more, if habitat fragmentation has also had an effect. This species heavily uses primary tropical forests in winter (Powell et al. 1992; Petit et al. 1992; Blake and Loiselle 1992) and is at risk if tropical deforestation continues unabated for another half century, leading to a landscape of fields and little acreage of secondary growth in its wintering range.

FALL: A noticeable decline in the numbers of birds reported begins during 10–15 August. The August–October 1991 Neotropical migrant study (Mabey et al. 1993), counting both migrants and residents before they depart, recorded 68% of the Wood Thrushes in August, 29% in September, and 3% in October ($n = 72$); over half were recorded before 15 August. Stewart and Robbins (1958) give 20–30 August as the beginning of migration in Maryland, and Dwight (1900) notes molt occurs during July and August.

A modest increase in birds banded occurs during 5–20 September, a pronounced increase from 25 September to 10 October. Migration, then, begins in August, is fully underway throughout September and early October, and is essentially finished by mid-October. Late specimens are

| 20 Oct 1973 | | Wilmington (DMNH 37303) |
| 24 Oct 1967 | | Arden (UDEL 158-68). |

The latest reports include

29 Oct 1989	1	Port Penn [Jano4]
16 Nov 1986	4	Lewes [Frec1]
27 Nov 1964	1	Hoopes Reservoir [Klab3]

Some high counts are

28 Aug 1976	17	White Clay Creek [Litt7]
10 Sep 1977	19	White Clay Creek [BroW12]
26 Sep 1970	14	Brandywine Creek SP [SpSB39]
14 Oct 1967	8	Avon woodlot near Newark [Wayn2]

SPECIMENS: 79; DMNH, UDEL, UWBM. Egg records: DMNH, WFVZ.

Fieldfare *(Turdus pilaris)*

Casual, 1 record.

DOCUMENTATION: Convincing published notes.

REMARKS: An individual of this European species was present at Bombay Hook NWR from 30 March to 4 April 1969 (Holgersen 1970) [Hol108]. The published notes are detailed and completely convincing. Mentioned are the posture and foraging behavior, the gray head and rump, rusty back, black tail, white wing linings, and dark legs. The buffy breast, the white belly, and the streaking on the underparts are well described. No other species from Europe or the Western Hemisphere fits the description.

Fieldfares, although primarily European, breed in southern Greenland. Eight records, including this one, are mentioned for eastern North America in the AOU Check-list (AOU 1983).

American Robin *(Turdus migratorius)*

Resident; fairly common to common. Migration occurs February through April and September through November.

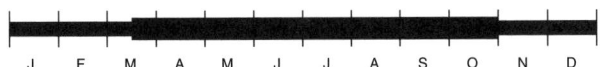

HABITAT: Breeding robins occur in residential and agricultural areas with short grass and nearby wood edges or small woodlots. Transient and wintering robins occur in various edge and forest habitats.

SPRING: Migration begins during 1–10 February and continues to 20–30 April, with peak numbers occurring in March. An exceptional migration report estimated 10,000 robins from the District of Columbia to Bombay Hook NWR to Ocean City, Maryland, on 15–16 March 1958 [Davi10]. Somewhat less unusual were 1,000 recorded on 6 March 1978 in the Lewes area [Frec1], and reports of several hundred are not uncommon during March and April.

BREEDING: The common American Robin has benefited from changes to its habitat following European settlement, since it nests less commonly in open forests than in suburban

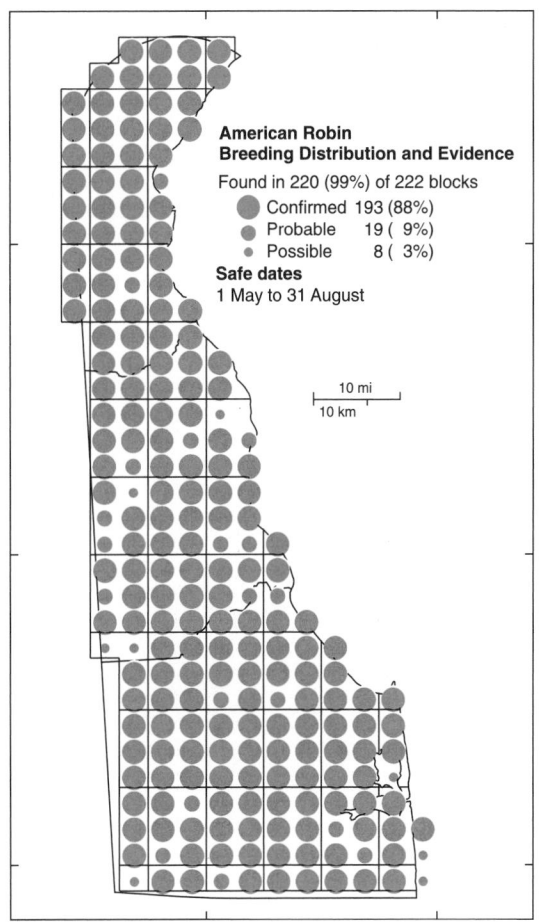

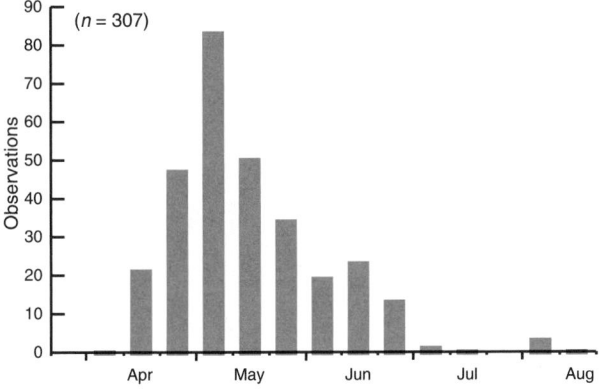

Estimated Clutch-Completion Dates

yards (Kibbe 1985a). The relative abundance study shows it to be common throughout the state and abundant in suburban areas from Wilmington, Newark, and New Castle south to Seaford, Laurel, and Delmar.

Atlas. This species ranked behind only the European Starling and the Common Grackle as the most widely confirmed species of the Atlas project. One of the first confirmations came from an active nest on a parked railroad car at Montchanin. One-quarter of the confirmations involved fledged young.

Nesting. Experienced male robins begin taking up territories in suburbia by late February, returning at night to local roosts (Eiserer 1976). By March robins sing regularly on territory and begin building mud-reinforced straw nests. The first nests, built before deciduous leaves appear, are frequently concealed in pines or ornamental evergreens.

The clutch-completion dates extend from early April to August. The secondary peak in mid-June, 6 weeks after the main peak in early May, is evidence of second broods. August clutches may represent third broods or persistent renesting after failure. The August data are probably incomplete because searches for nests diminish in August (see Mourning Dove

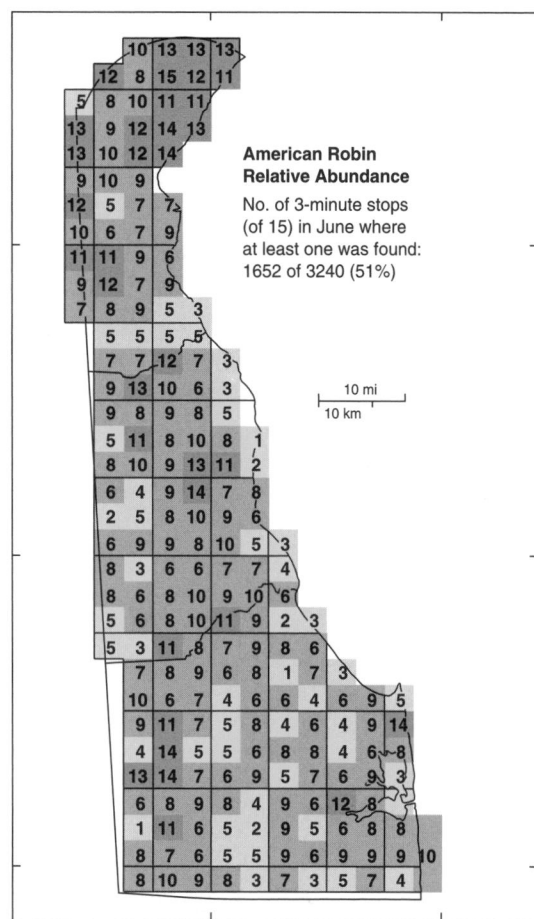

**American Robin
Relative Abundance**

No. of 3-minute stops
(of 15) in June where
at least one was found:
1652 of 3240 (51%)

10 mi
10 km

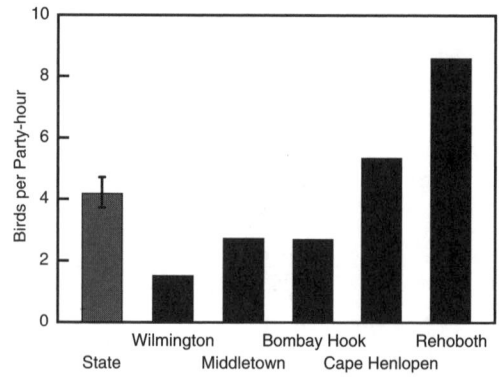

CBC Geographic Distribution

ha (250 acres) for open rural Maryland (Stewart and Robbins 1958).

FALL: Migration probably begins 10–20 September and continues through 10–20 November, with a peak during October. The high estimates are

28 Oct 1967	22,000 (roost)	near Newark [Faus8]
2 Oct 1974	1,500	near Newark [Edni1]
5 Nov 1977	1,300	White Clay Creek [Lehm28]

1966–89 CBC Summary

Christmas Bird Count	Years Found	Range of No. Found	Median
Wilmington	24	14–854	179
Middletown	24	8–2135	101
Bombay Hook	24	25–1108	155
Cape Henlopen	24	18–988	239
Rehoboth	24	68–2502	573
STATEWIDE (low in 1978, high in 1979)	24	278–5367	1591

account). The earliest egg date is 16 April [Hans1] and the latest 5 August, from a clutch that hatched on 14 August [Nile2]. The earliest nestling date is 17 April, implying clutch completion on about 1 April [Hubb1]; the latest is 4 September (TSBR 87-1130). Clutch size is usually 4 or 3, with 2 records of 5 (n = 128).

History. The robin's range expansion and population increase in the East in previous centuries probably paralleled its twentieth-century expansion in the West and North, where its appearance soon followed the conversion of prairie, desert, and forest to lawns and orchards (Stone 1937; Bent 1949). More recently, it has extended its range southward into Florida and other states (James and Shugart 1974), where it now nests near open lawns in larger towns. It was welcome wherever it appeared since it was formerly hunted for the pot (Stone 1919; Eiserer 1976).

Trends. The robin's increase has continued as shown by the 1% annual increase on May Counts since 1969 and the 4% annual increase on the Delaware BBS routes during 1966–90. These increases parallel a 1% annual increase in the East on the BBS [Usfw3]. The increase in the 1960s may have been partly recovery from past use of DDT (Robbins et al. 1986), but continued establishment of suburbs and vacation homes has increased its preferred habitat.

Breeding population. Densities of 111 pairs per 100 ha are reported for open suburban Maryland and 18–60 pairs per 100

WINTER: No CBC significant long-term trend is apparent for the state because of a high amount of variation, but the Rehoboth CBCs in the 1960s averaged about 13 birds per hour, in the 1970s about 11 birds per hour, and in the 1980s about 5 birds per hour. The high count on the Rehoboth CBC was 140 birds per hour obtained in 1959. The reduction since then may result from a change in location of roost sites to an area outside the count circle. Because wintering birds require forests for food and cover, replacement of forests with open spaces and summer homes in the Rehoboth CBC area would be expected to result in a decrease in the wintering population even though it provides additional habitat for breeding birds.

The American Robin is increasingly abundant on CBCs southward through the state. The Seaford CBC for 1983–89 reported an average of 13 robins per party-hour, noticeably more than reported on the coastal CBCs.

BANDING: Five American Robins banded in summer in Delaware have been found in winter from North Carolina south to Florida [Usfw3].

SPECIMENS: 143; DMNH, ANSP, UDEL, USNM. Egg records: DMNH, WFVZ.

Varied Thrush (*Ixoreus naevius*)

Accidental (1995).

DOCUMENTATION: Photograph (A. P. Ednie, NASFN 50: 152).

REMARKS: An individual of this species was discovered at a feeder in Wilmington on 20 December 1995 and photographed by Ednie on 9 January 1996 [Edni33]. It was seen sporadically through the rest of the winter.

The Varied Thrush occurs casually in central and northeastern North America and in Atlantic coastal states from Maryland to Florida (AOU 1983). Hence its occurrence in Delaware is not unexpected.

Gray Catbird (*Dumetella carolinensis*)

Regular; summer resident; fairly common in New Castle County and near Delaware Bay and the ocean but uncommon in parts of western Kent and Sussex counties. Expected late April, occasionally earlier, through October. Winter numbers sporadic but increasing at 7% per year.

HABITAT: Dense shrub, forest edges, wooded suburbs, often near wet or swampy areas.

SPRING: First individuals arrive sometimes as early as 9 April, although these may have wintered nearby. The first report clearly signaling the migration is of 7 on 27 April 1991 at Burrows Run [SpeE1]. Migration probably ends by 15–25 May. Some high counts, all from Bombay Hook NWR, are

8 May 1982	109	[Boll4]
15 May 1982	75	[Kell4]
22 May 1983	68	[Bayn1]

Reports of 30–40 birds are not uncommon. The highest May Count is 808 (13 May 1989), the lowest 236 (8 May 1971, the third year of the count).

BREEDING: Catbirds are fairly common in suburban Wilmington in backyards and wet thickets but quite scarce in parts of rural Sussex County. On the distribution map this is shown

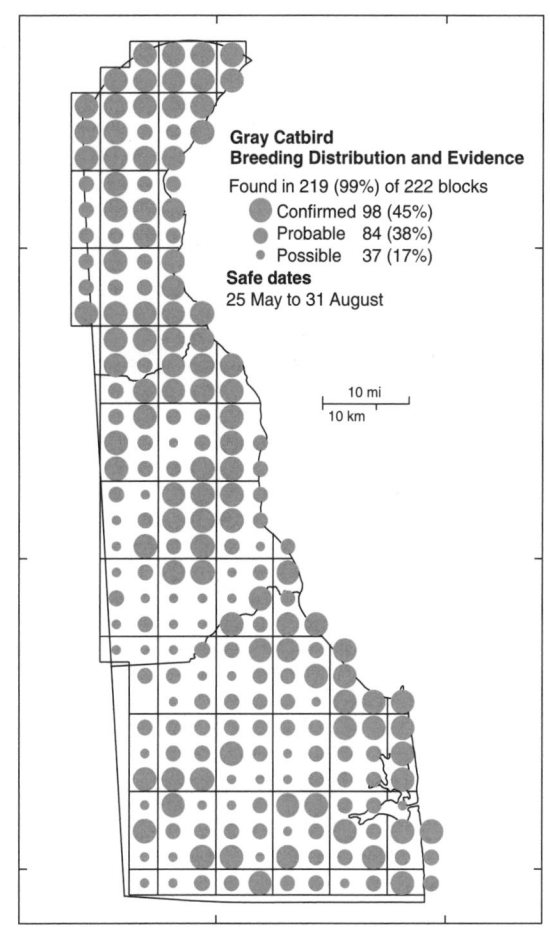

Gray Catbird
Breeding Distribution and Evidence
Found in 219 (99%) of 222 blocks
Confirmed 98 (45%)
Probable 84 (38%)
Possible 37 (17%)
Safe dates
25 May to 31 August

10 mi
10 km

only as a single missed block in western Sussex County, but it is obvious from the relative abundance map. This reduction in density signals the beginning of its decrease on the Coastal Plain, a decrease that continues southward until catbirds are absent in parts of South Carolina, southern Georgia, and Florida (Robbins et al. 1986, map). The demarcation falls not at the Piedmont edge but near the Chesapeake and Delaware Canal and away from the cooler coastal woods. The catbird is twice as abundant in New Castle County as in the southern counties.

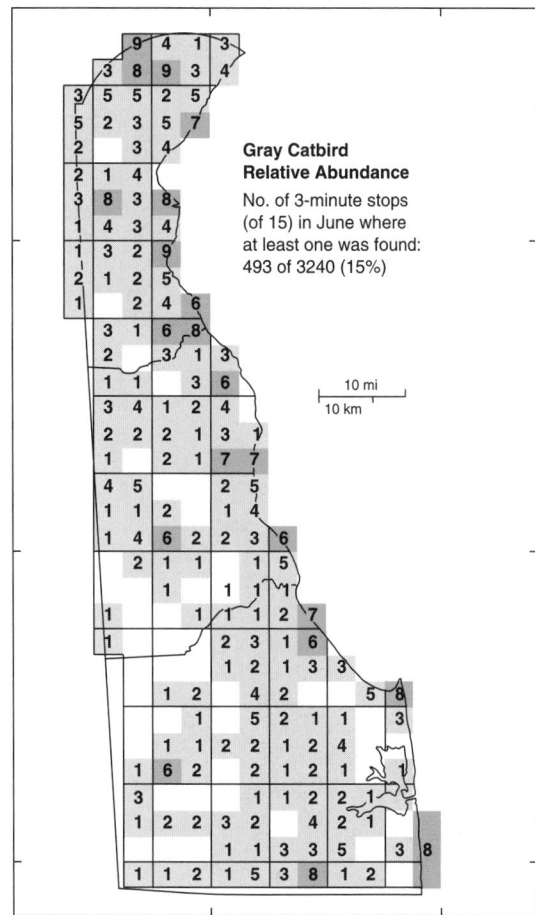

Gray Catbird
Relative Abundance

No. of 3-minute stops
(of 15) in June where
at least one was found:
493 of 3240 (15%)

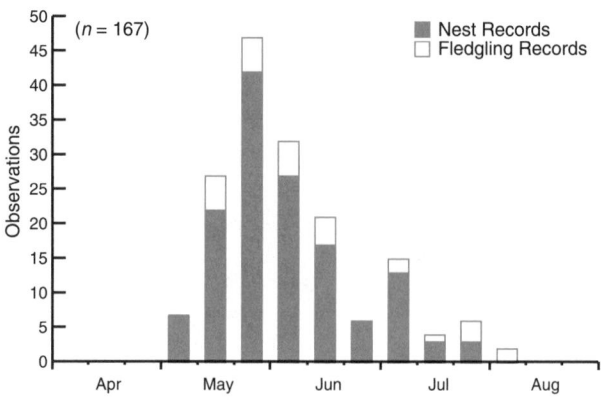

Estimated Clutch-Completion Dates

Atlas. Attending young (usually carrying food) provided 40% of confirmations during the Atlas project; active nests accounted for an additional 35%.

Nesting. A nest with 3 eggs found on 9 May on the St. Jones River in Dover was described by Hanson (notes): "It was about 5 feet above ground in a tangle of greenbrier and honeysuckle. It was about 5 inches across and 4 inches deep outside, and about 3 inches across and 2 inches deep inside. It was built of dried meadow grasses, fibrous bark, and small stems, lined with fine brown roots. On the tenth there were 4 eggs."

It is usually double-brooded in Michigan (Zimmerman 1963; Nickell 1965); Hanson (notes) reported a second nest with 3 eggs on 17 July in the same territory that had a brood in June. The second clutch-completion peak in early July reflects second broods. The earliest egg date is 9 May [Hans1] and the earliest date for nestlings is 20 May near Lewes [Frec2]. The latest are eggs on 25 July that hatched about 2 August in the University of Delaware woodlot [DavV1]. The latest clutches are 1 that produced a 23-g nestling found on 27 August and 1 that produced a 29-g nestling found on 30 August, both in New Castle County (TSBR 91-1445 and TSBR 91-1467); these clutches were probably completed in early August. Three clutches of 5 eggs have been reported; those of 3 outnumber those of 4 by 50% (*n* = 97).

History. The Gray Catbird undoubtedly has greatly increased in numbers as human populations have expanded into many areas formerly unsuitable for its needs. Yards, gardens, parks, and cemeteries are accepted as nest sites and feeding areas. All sorts of dense edges created by fields and openings provide suitable nest sites (Nickell 1965).

Trends. The Gray Catbird population on the May Count and BBS has shown no significant long-term change during 1966–91, but during the 1981–90 decade it declined significantly on the Delaware BBS [Usfw3] in sharp contrast to the small but apparently growing winter population described later.

Breeding population. It is difficult to estimate the catbird population because its density varies from high in edge habitat, such as along Piedmont streams, to low in forest interiors, such as are found in Sussex County (Robbins et al. 1989a). Catbirds reach breeding densities of about 100 pairs per 100 ha in Assawoman WA and 120–250 pairs per 100 ha in the Piedmont (BBC data). These densities are similar to those given for Maryland (Stewart and Robbins 1958).

FALL: The beginning of fall migration is not apparent from the observational reports but is clearly evident from banding data. The numbers of Gray Catbirds banded begins to increase during 25–30 August and peaks from 15 September to 15 October. By the end of October few catbirds are banded. The latest banding record is 1 at the University of Delaware woodlot on 4 November 1975 [Line4], and the latest specimen is from Wilmington on 16 November 1974 (DMNH 44380). The observational data show a decline in numbers the first week of October. In the August–October 1991 Neotropical migrant study (Mabey et al. 1993), only 6% of the catbirds were recorded as late as October (*n* = 244), with the last on 19 October. Most high counts (30–60 birds) occur in September. Some high counts are

2 Sep 1979	60	Cape Henlopen SP [Frec1]
10 Sep 1977	112	White Clay Creek [BroW9]
7 Oct 1973	125	Dragon Run [John13]

WINTER: The AOU Check-list (1983) states that the winter range includes the Atlantic coastal lowlands from Long Island south. Our records indicate that from November through early April the number of catbirds steadily declines in Delaware, and none have been recorded in the first week of April—just before the first migrants arrive. Only in 1978 do we have a suggestion

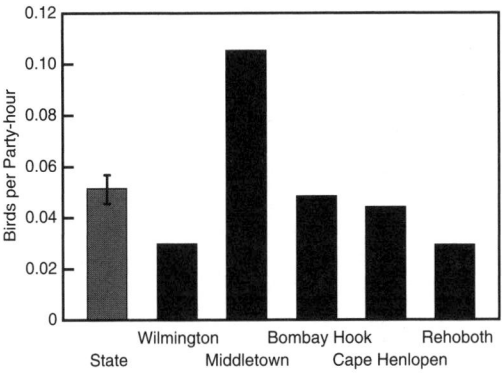

CBC Geographic Distribution

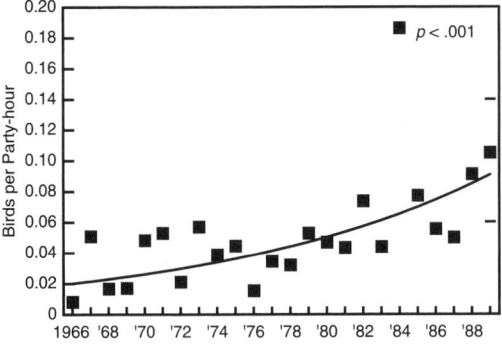

CBC Trend; Increasing at 7% per Year

of successful wintering—in a brushy stream flowing into White Clay Creek. That year 1 or more were found fairly regularly with a gap only between 25 March and 8 April. It may have some sensitivity to severe winter weather (Robbins et al. 1986), though such sensitivity was not evident in 1989, when November and December were the coldest on record, yet catbirds were still found on the CBCs. Perhaps cold and ice in late winter, when food is scarcest, are greater limiting factors. The catbird is most abundant on the Middletown CBC.

1966–89 CBC Summary

Christmas Bird Count	Years Found	Range of No. Found	Median
Wilmington	19	1–25	3
Middletown	21	1–24	4
Bombay Hook	21	1–17	2
Cape Henlopen	22	1–9	3
Rehoboth	22	1–7	2
STATEWIDE (increasing; low in 1966, high in 1984)	24	3–72	19

BANDING:	BANDING RECOVERIES:
banded 7 May 1948, Delaware	recovered Jun 1949, Connecticut
banded 15 Jul 1948, Delaware	recovered 18 Mar 1954, Florida
banded 14 Mar 1973, Florida	recovered 30 Jun 1974, Delaware

SPECIMENS: 81; DMNH, ANSP, UDEL, USNM, UWBM. Egg records: DMNH, WFVZ.

Northern Mockingbird (*Mimus polyglottos*)

Nancy C. Willis

Resident; common. In winter most common in New Castle and Kent counties. Winter numbers increasing after a low in the 1970s.

HABITAT: Often associated with residential areas having scattered trees and shrubs and with hedgerows in agricultural areas.

HISTORY: Stone (1937) explained the early status of this species as follows: "Alexander Wilson, writing in 1810 says 'the eagerness with which the nest of the Mockingbird is sought after in the neighborhood of Philadelphia has rendered the bird extremely scarce for an extent of several miles around the city. In the country around Wilmington and New Castle, they are very numerous, from whence they are brought here for sale. The usual price for a singing bird is from seven to fifteen and

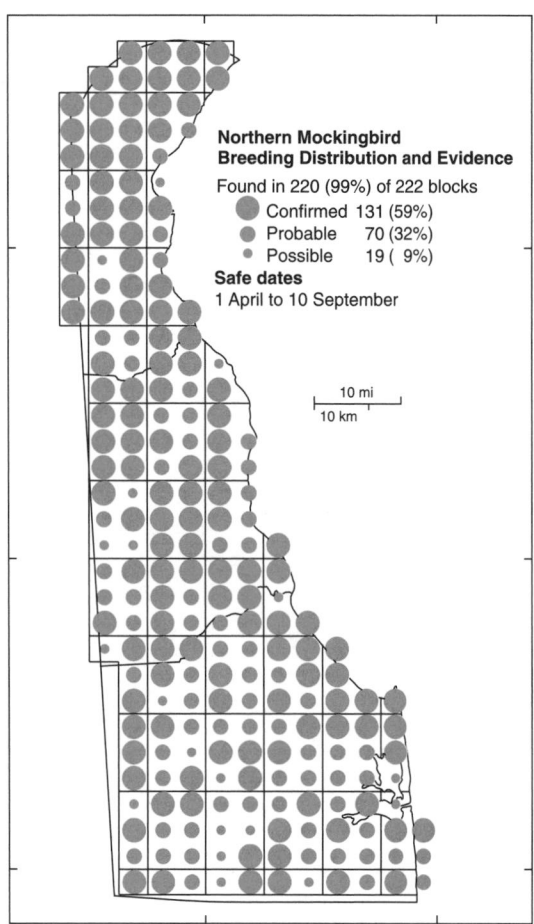

Northern Mockingbird
Breeding Distribution and Evidence
Found in 220 (99%) of 222 blocks
● Confirmed 131 (59%)
● Probable 70 (32%)
● Possible 19 (9%)
Safe dates
1 April to 10 September

10 mi
10 km

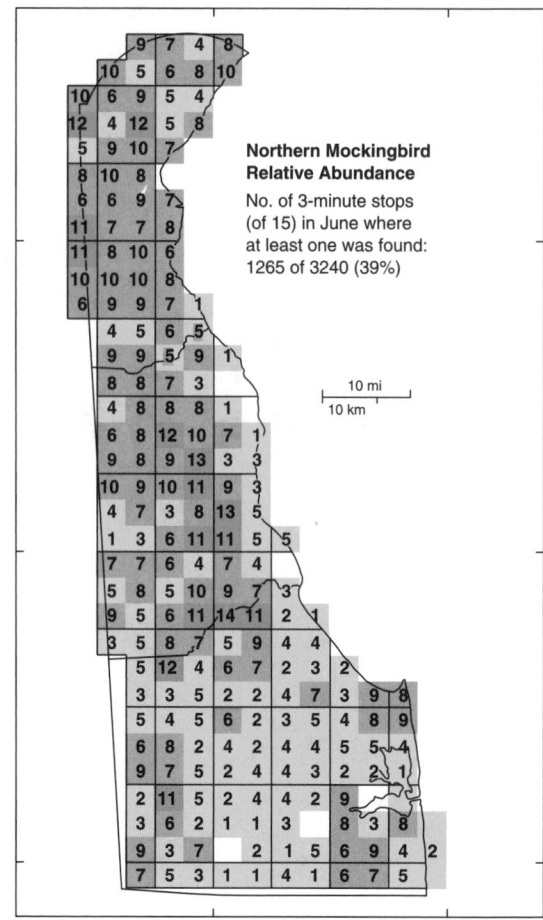

Northern Mockingbird
Relative Abundance
No. of 3-minute stops
(of 15) in June where
at least one was found:
1265 of 3240 (39%)

10 mi
10 km

even twenty dollars.' In William Bartram's manuscript diary, 1802–1820, he mentions occurrences of single birds in his garden at Philadelphia but all in winter with the exception of one April and one October record."

In Delaware in the nineteenth and early twentieth centuries Northern Mockingbirds were generally scarce and local and probably more frequent in winter. Elizabeth Montgomery reminisced in 1851 about earlier days when "mocking birds build their nests" (in Findlay 1938). Turnbull (1869) called it rare in southern Pennsylvania, but "it appears to have been plentiful in former years." Krider (1879, 39) reported "[I] found this bird very plenty in Virginia, and have shot it in . . . Delaware." Pennock reported "a single Mockingbird" on a May 1905 trip to Millsboro, where he had also reported 1 in October 1903, his only sightings in 5 trips south. In spite of this scarcity he reported at the 19 May 1904 DVOC meeting as "inclined to think that the Mockingbird was on the increase in the upper part of [Delaware]" (Anon. 1905). Rhoads and Pennock (1905) listed it as "Locally abundant as far north as the C[hesapeake] & D[elaware] Canal," based on 6 reports from Odessa southward [Penn1]. Reports from north of the Chesapeake and Delaware Canal come from Stanton in 1907 [Hens1], Delaware City on 2 May 1911, and Red Lion on 31 March 1912 [Penn1]. A bird census in Lincoln Delaware found 2 pairs breeding in 170 acres in May 1915 [Tran1]. Stone wrote in 1919 that traffic in caged mockingbirds had been stopped by law and that the mockingbird was spreading over the state from southern Delaware where it was "always a resident." The next reports we have are of 2 on 10 April 1925 [Pott3] at Delaware City, which became a New Castle County birding hot spot; 1 on 26 December 1927 [Doak1]; 12 on 5 April 1932 [Emle3]; 1 on 20 April, and 5 on 12 November 1933 (*Cassinia,* DVOC minutes); and "8 flushed from one tree" on 9 September 1938 [Moor1]. Hanson (notes) first reported a mockingbird in the Dover area in January 1926, when 1 was coming to a feeder for apple pieces. Nesting was reported starting in 1929 at Silver Lake, Dover, but most reports were winter records until 1933, when Hanson found his first nest with eggs on 7 May at Kitts Hummock and a second 1 at Little Creek on 22 May. One was first reported in Rehoboth Beach on 28 November 1931 [Hans1], and 90 were found there on the 1 January 1958 CBC. Two were on the first Bombay Hook CBC on 20 December 1939, 13 there in 1940, 19 in 1947, and 99 in 1957. Barry (1939) described its status as "abundant from Delaware City southward," but it has surely become even more common since then. Neither Bush's (1878–81) Wilmington diary nor Rumford's (1914–24) banding notebooks list the mockingbird, though both include the catbird and thrasher, and we have no reports from the Piedmont

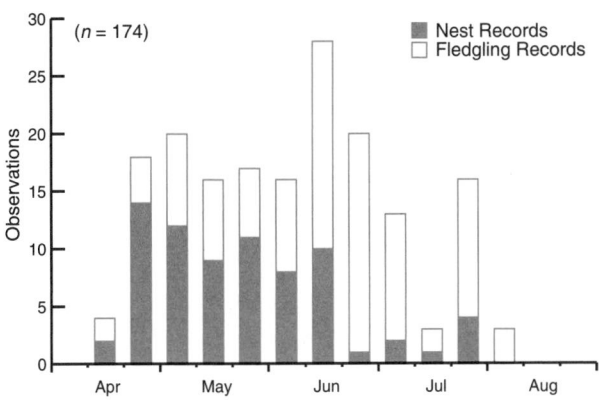

Estimated Clutch-Completion Dates

until 1943, when up to 4 were found on the Hoopes Reservoir survey each year during 1943–45 [Hoff4].

BREEDING: The Northern Mockingbird is about a third less common in Sussex County as in the northern two counties according to the relative abundance study, a status supported by CBC results. The highest counts are not concentrated in the suburbs as they are for the American Robin, but rather in open country, including the open agricultural lands in southern New Castle County.

Atlas. In the Atlas project two-thirds of the confirmations were of fledged young, which are easy to find because they call and beg in open areas.

Nesting. Hanson (notes) described the nest with 5 eggs he collected on 7 May 1933 as being placed 3 ft above ground in an osage orange. It was made of weed and grass stems, small sticks, and roots, and lined with fine rootlets and horse hair. It measured 5 in. across and 3 in. deep outside, 3 in. across and 1 1/2 in. deep inside.

The clutch-completion graph shows an extended season from mid-April through early August. The irregular abundances and particularly the late July peak reflect its double-broodedness; it is sometimes triple-brooded and was once recorded as quadruple-brooded in Tennessee (Laskey 1962). The earliest egg date is 22 April in Claymont [Edni4], the latest 5 August [O'Sh2]. The earliest nestling is 6 May in Newark, the latest 14 August [both Nile2]. The latest clutch is 1 that produced a 27-g nestling found in New Castle County on 24 August (TSBR 87-1090); its clutch was probably completed in early August. Clutch size in Delaware is usually 4 or 3. The only clutch of 5 reported in Delaware is described earlier (*n* = 18).

The pattern of clutch-completion dates shown by the nest records is similar to that found in Tennessee, with peak egg-laying early in the season (Lasky 1962). The TSBR nestling data give a different picture, with most nestlings found from nests started in mid- to late June.

Trends. The mockingbird is expanding its range northward as a permanent resident. Suburban expansion, complete with berry bushes and warm chimneys, provides a means of sur-

vival in severe winter weather. These factors, together with the relatively mild climate of the twentieth century, have allowed continued range expansion, shown by increased numbers on the BBS in New York, Connecticut, and Massachusetts (Beddall 1963; Robbins et al. 1986). Mockingbirds appear to have increased in Delaware at about 1.6% a year during 1969–91 according to May Count data, for a total increase of 40%, but this trend is not reflected in Delaware BBS data except for the 1981–90 decade [Usfw3]. The increase may represent the effect of improved habitat resulting from suburbanization combined with the long-term cyclic effect discussed under "Winter."

Breeding population. Little information is available on breeding densities of the mockingbird. In Maryland its density in a residential suburb was 40 pairs per 100 ha (Stewart and Robbins 1958), and Florida suburbs densities ranged from 60 to 100 pairs per 100 ha (Woolfenden and Rohwer 1969).

FALL: A study with marked birds shows that young, after they become independent, disperse from the nest site as early as June to areas of good food supply, traveling up to 12 mi (20 km), possibly farther (Kale and Jennings 1966). Considerable movement occurs from August to October. By the end of October older residents have set up winter territories, forcing young birds to move to unoccupied areas to establish territories based on availability of winter food, often to areas with multiflora rose. This dispersal is probably the source of the winter mockingbirds found in the early records for Delaware. A second movement in spring occurs as breeding territories are reclaimed and first-year birds seek nest sites and mates. Seasonal movement is more evident in Illinois (Graber et al. 1970) and westward than in Delaware.

1966–89 CBC Summary

Christmas Bird Count	Years Found	Range of No. Found	Median
Wilmington	24	106–270	154
Middletown	24	34–145	67
Bombay Hook	24	11–185	87
Cape Henlopen	24	18–95	51
Rehoboth	24	22–115	68
STATEWIDE (low in 1978, high in 1976)	24	293–625	450

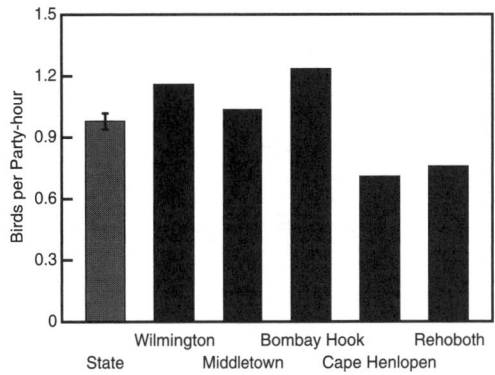

CBC Geographic Distribution

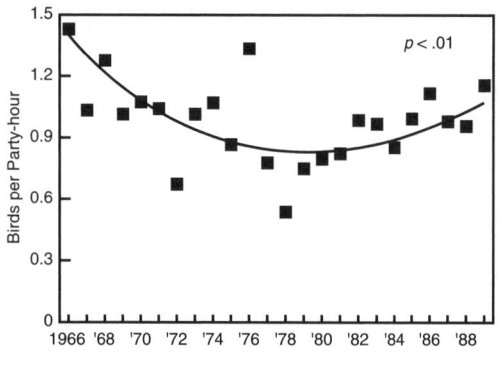

CBC Trend

inversely with severe winter weather. The reductions in 1977 and 1978 of CBC numbers correspond to similar reductions on the BBS and have been attributed to severe winter weather (Robbins et al. 1986). The high count is 270 on the 1986 Wilmington CBC. Mockingbirds are about equally common on all CBCs.

SPECIMENS: 39; DMNH, ANSP. Egg records: DMNH.

Sage Thrasher *(Oreoscoptes montanus)*

Accidental (1985).

DOCUMENTATION: Convincing notes.

REMARKS: This western thrasher occurs regularly no further east than central Texas. It is casual in the East, having occurred "from Massachusetts south to North Carolina" (AOU 1987), and there is a record on 24 October 1971 from Assateague Island, Maryland [Rowl11]. The only recorded occurrence in Delaware comes from Bombay Hook NWR on 29 October 1985 (Wilson 1986) [Wils1]. The published notes,

written in the field before the observer consulted field guides, are admirably detailed, completely eliminating other species and beautifully evoking the field appearance of this slightly atypical thrasher. All relevant marks and the overall appearance of the species are perfectly conveyed. After later examining 2 skins of Sage Thrashers at San Jose State University, the observer compared their appearance to the appearance of the Bombay Hook NWR bird in the published notes. The record is completely convincing.

Brown Thrasher *(Toxostoma rufum)*

Regular; summer resident; uncommon. Sporadic in winter; expected early April to mid-October.

HABITAT: Hedgerows, wood margins, gardens, and shrubby areas.

SPRING: First arrival is usually during 25–30 March, though in some years a few hardy individuals are present earlier. Migration probably ends by 1–10 May in Maryland (Stewart and Robbins 1958). The earliest banding record is 1 at the University of

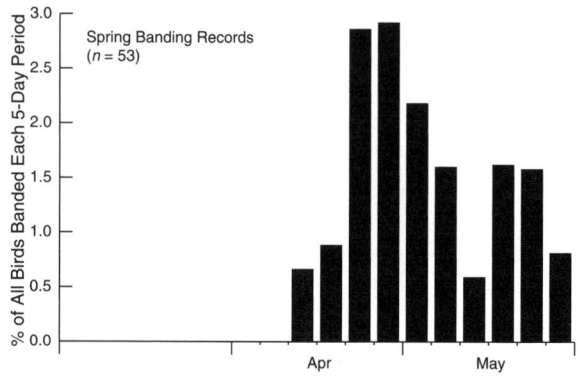

Spring Banding Records
(n = 53)

Spring Migration Activity

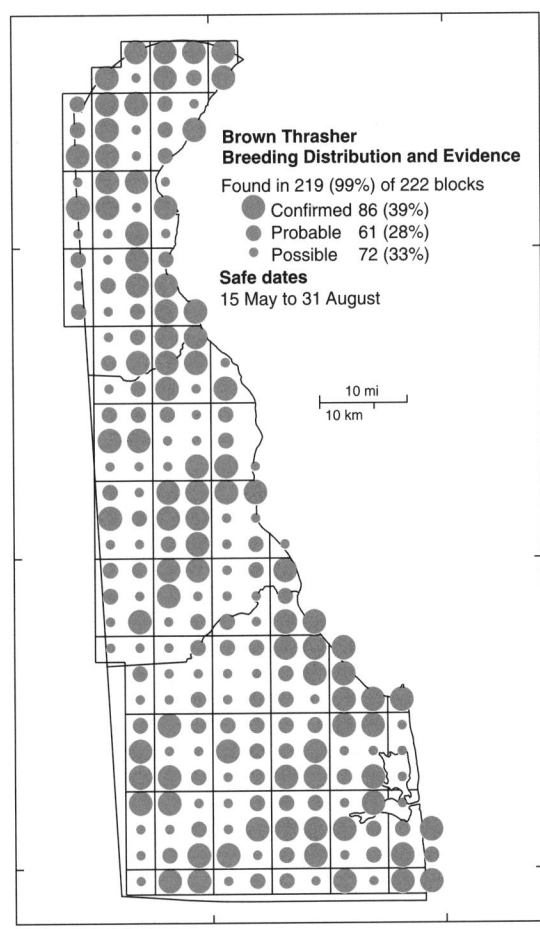

Brown Thrasher
Breeding Distribution and Evidence

Found in 219 (99%) of 222 blocks

● Confirmed 86 (39%)
● Probable 61 (28%)
· Possible 72 (33%)

Safe dates
15 May to 31 August

10 mi
10 km

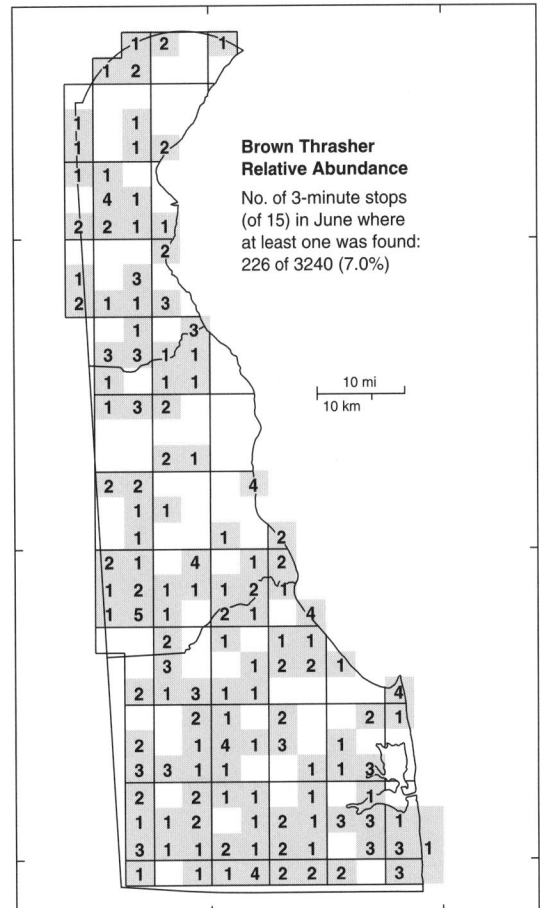

Brown Thrasher
Relative Abundance

No. of 3-minute stops
(of 15) in June where
at least one was found:
226 of 3240 (7.0%)

10 mi
10 km

Delaware woodlot on 17 March 1971 [Jone2]. Peak numbers are banded in late April and early May; high counts are

25 Apr 1970	10	Brandywine Creek SP [BroH10]
26 Apr 1964	12	Hoopes Reservoir [Klab4]
3 May 1969	11	Brandywine Creek SP [SpSB13]

The highest May Count is 150 (13 May 1989), the lowest 48 (12 May 1990), and the average 93 (1971–90).

BREEDING: It is about 50% more common in Sussex County than in the northern counties, just the opposite of the mockingbird's population density pattern.

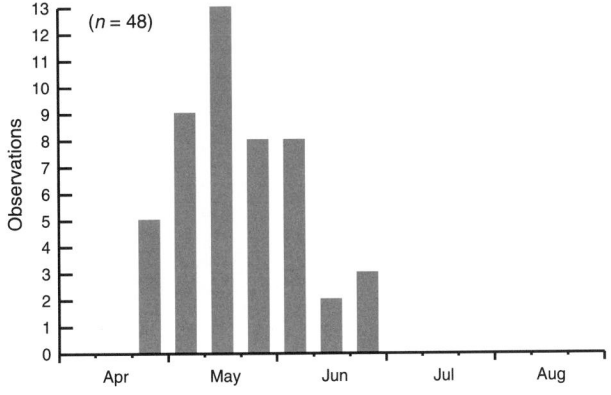

Estimated Clutch-Completion Dates

Atlas. During the Atlas project 40% of confirmations involved carrying food and another 30% were of fledged young; active nests were reported only 20% of the time.

Nesting. Hanson (notes) described a nest collected on 14 May from 4 ft up in a bush. It was the usual bulky affair, having a groundwork of coarse sticks and being composed of roots, dried grass, and leaves. The nest proper was 5½ inches in diameter and 4 inches high outside, 3 inches in diameter and 2 inches deep inside. Hanson also described nests found on the ground.

The clutch-completion graph is probably incomplete for lack of July data, but in Illinois most egg-laying ends by the last week of June (Graber et al. 1970). Egg dates extend through 30 July in Maryland (Robbins and Bystrak 1977) as would be expected, since most females attempt a second brood (Murphy and Fleischer 1986). The earliest Delaware egg date is 7 May [Hans1], the latest 28 June [HalK1]. The earliest nestling date is 24 May [West3], and the latest hatchling date is 12 July [Hans1]. Clutch size varies from 2 to 5, with 1 record of 6 (*n* = 27), most common is 4.

History and trends. The Brown Thrasher was probably less common in Delaware before the land was cleared for agriculture than now, since clearing increased the amount of early successional habitat and woodland edges that this thrasher prefers (Kibbe 1985b). During 1969–91, the summer population has sharply declined at 4% a year on the May Count, twice as fast as the 2% per year shown on the BBS in the East. Delaware BBS data do not show a 24-year change, although thrasher numbers have shown a decreasing tendency during the past 10 years.

Breeding population. Since the Brown Thrasher is an inconspicuous species found in edges and forest openings, its population may easily be underestimated.

FALL: The beginning of the migration period is not apparent, but in most years the bulk of the thrasher population leaves by 15–20 October. In the August–October 1991 Neotropical migrant study (Mabey et al. 1993), only 50% of the thrashers were recorded during the first half of August ($n = 30$) before the residents departed; migrants and stragglers were reported through 12 October. Stewart and Robbins (1958) give 5–15 September to 5–15 October as the migration period in Maryland. Peak numbers of Brown Thrashers are banded in September. The latest banding records are individuals banded on 20 October 1969 and 1971 at the University of Delaware woodlot [Line4], and on 28 October 1989 at Prime Hook NWR headquarters [Thor1]. High counts are

6 Sep 1980	14	Churchmans Marsh [Dyer9]
12 Sep 1971	17	Brandywine Creek SP [BroW17]
18 Sep 1965	20	Churchmans Marsh [Klab2]

1966–89 CBC Summary

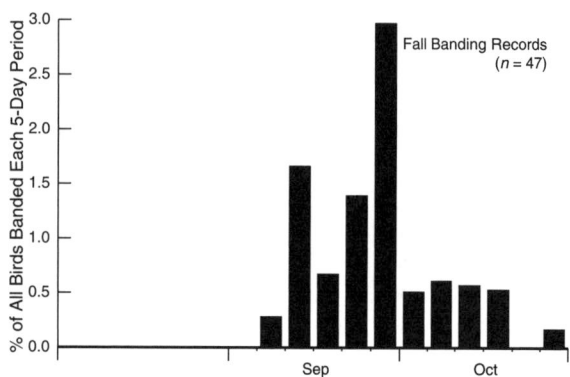

Fall Migration Activity

Christmas Bird Count	Years Found	Range of No. Found	Median
Wilmington	19	1–4	1
Middletown	15	1–5	1
Bombay Hook	23	1–19	2
Cape Henlopen	20	1–23	3
Rehoboth	22	1–15	4
STATEWIDE	24	4–54	13
(decreasing; low in 1982, 1986, and 1988; high in 1970)			

WINTER: Brown Thrashers become increasingly rare during the winter through early March. However, they are more likely to be reported only until the end of the CBC period, after which most depart or succumb to cold conditions. Banding records include

2 Dec 1962	1	near Hockessin [Know3]
7 Dec 1969	1	near Wilmington [Farr1]
8 Jan 1972	1	Wilmington [Hubb2]
11 Jan 1971	2	University of Delaware woodlot [Jone2]

The Brown Thrasher has shown a decline in CBC numbers. The drop in CBC numbers in 1972 is reflected by a similar decrease in the spring data. The severe winters in the mid-1970s also caused a noticeable decrease in numbers, from which this species has not recovered. It is most common on the southern 3 CBCs.

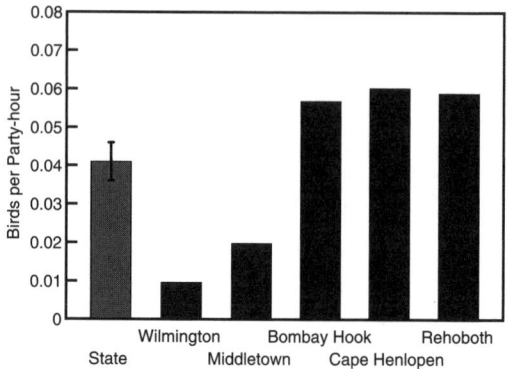

CBC Geographic Distribution

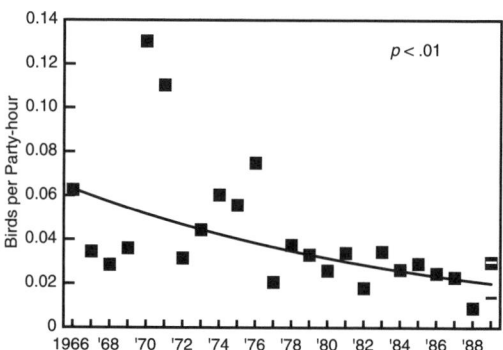

CBC Trend; Decreasing at 5% per Year

BANDING: BANDING RECOVERIES:

banded 18 Apr 1945   recovered 16 May 1945, NE New Jersey
banded 21 Sep 1961   recovered 4 Aug 1962, New York

SPECIMENS: 24; DMNH, UDEL. Egg records: DMNH.

European Starling (*Sturnus vulgaris*)

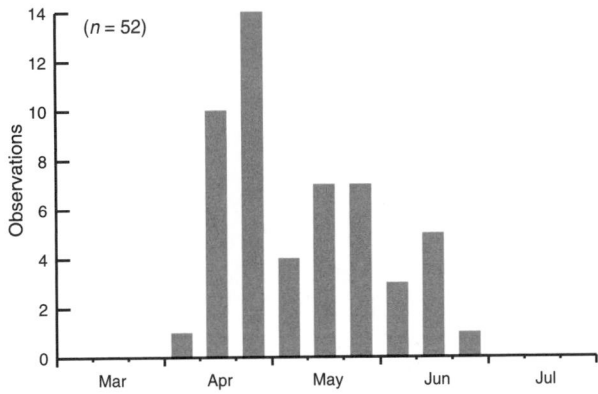

Estimated Clutch-Completion Dates

Introduced resident; common. Most numerous in cities, towns, and around farmsteads. Population about 30% lower in 1991 than in 1966.

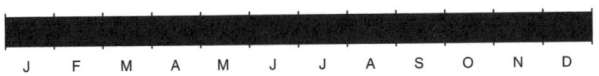

HABITAT: Open country, particularly in winter. Around people, fields, and dumps. Almost any cavity for breeding, though rarely in interior woodland.

BREEDING: The relative abundance study shows the starling's considerable compatibility with the high human population of northern New Castle County. Starlings eat almost anything, including garbage. Small openings in buildings provide favored nest sites. Southern New Castle County, in contrast, has less favorable habitat than elsewhere, because neither marshes nor open horse farm country provides nest sites. Lower densities also prevail in heavily forested areas of Sussex County.

Atlas. It was confirmed in 210 blocks, more than any other species, but only 1 nest with eggs was reported [O'Sh1]. Adults carrying food to young accounted for 35% of confirmations.

Nesting. The first nest recorded in Delaware (see "History") was 15 ft above ground in a hollow limb of an old apple tree in an orchard; the nest was of straw, lined with grass and feathers (DMNH 23635). Many nests are placed in outbuildings or in nooks around houses. Starlings are aggressive and usually successful in competing for woodpecker holes and natural cavities.

Clutch-completion dates extend over 3 months; because starlings are double-brooded (Feare 1984) the late May and June dates may represent either second broods or renestings after failure. Egg dates extend only from 26 April (DMNH 23365) to 24 May [Broo3]; nestling dates range from 28 April [West3] to 20 July [Jesc1]. By comparison, a New Jersey study found that most first clutches were completed between about 19 April and 2 May, and second clutches between 4 June and 15 June; only 44% of females attempted second broods (Stouffer

1991). Average clutch size in New Jersey is 5; Delaware clutches are 3–5 eggs (*n* = 4).

History. The starling typically establishes breeding in new areas after dispersing into them during winter. Pennock (1908b) reported that a male starling was shot near Odessa, about 1901, from a flock that was seen several times. This seems to be the first report for the region; Cooke (1925) reported that wandering flocks had reached Philadelphia by 1904. It was not until 1910 that they started wintering regularly, when Garrett McConnell saw 1 on his farm 1 mi south of Delaware City. They reappeared in 1911 and McConnell shot 8 on 8 December, and Pennock shot 1 the next day [Penn1]. They were reported in New Castle in the 18 January 1912 *Every Evening* newspaper, and the local attitude toward these new birds was revealed in a letter published there on 29 January: "more than two dozen English starlings were found last week. Some of these have been stuffed, while others are to be treated and will be seen on spring bonnets or headgear. One person has a live bird in a cage." On 31 December 1912 a flock of 12 was found near Rehoboth Bay by Trotter and Pennock (notes).

Isolated breeding began in Trevose, just north of Philadelphia, in 1904, and it was an established breeder in Philadelphia by 1910 (Cooke 1925). The first breeding record for Delaware describes a nest with 5 eggs collected on 26 April 1919 from the Keen farm on Rockland Rd. near Wilmington (DMNH 23635). Hanson, who came to Dover in 1920, noted that the first starlings he ever saw were 6 in a garden in Dover on 5 February 1922. They were quite common there the following winter, and he found a nest with young in a cornice of the State Laboratory Building on 1 May 1923. A nest with large young was found in a telephone pole in Little Creek on 9 July 1923. A pair was seen between Bear and Glasgow, and several pairs were between Middletown and Smyrna on 16 July 1923. It was commonly found in flocks up to several dozen that October and November in Dover [Hans1].

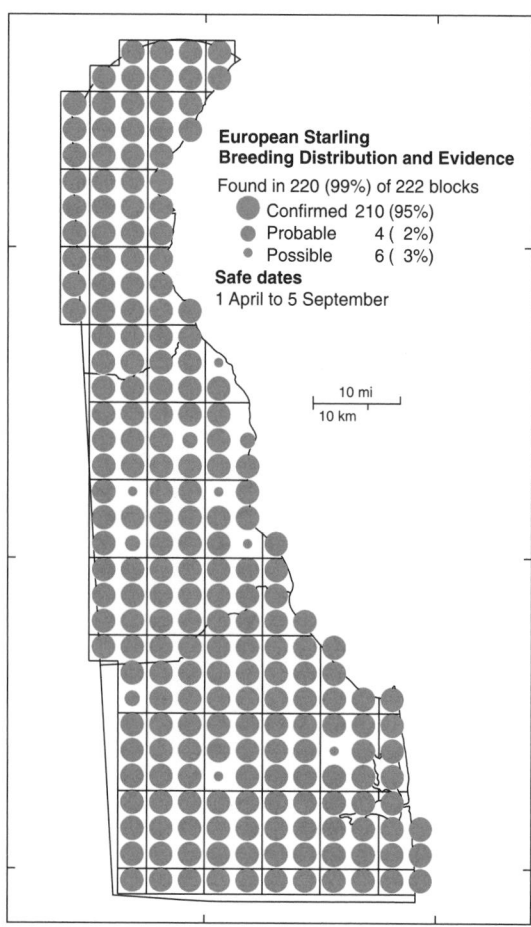

European Starling
Breeding Distribution and Evidence

Found in 220 (99%) of 222 blocks

● Confirmed 210 (95%)
● Probable 4 (2%)
· Possible 6 (3%)

Safe dates
1 April to 5 September

10 mi
10 km

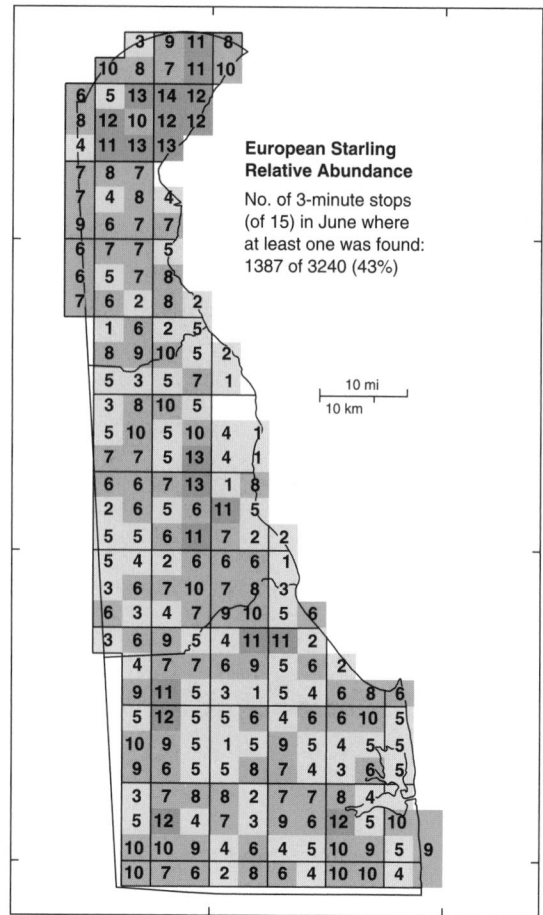

European Starling
Relative Abundance

No. of 3-minute stops
(of 15) in June where
at least one was found:
1387 of 3240 (43%)

10 mi
10 km

Barry's 1938 compilation classified it as an abundant resident throughout the state less than 28 years from the first breeding in Philadelphia and less than 16 years from the first report from Dover.

Trends. BBS data indicate that the starling's population declined in the East an average of 1.3% a year during 1966–90, an overall reduction of almost 30% [Usfw3]. Delaware BBS and May Count data also suggest a slight decline. Severe late winter weather in 1977 and 1978 caused widespread decreases (Robbins et al. 1986).

Breeding population. Starlings were registered at 1,387 stops on the relative abundance study, and the Delaware BBS recorded an average of 6.5 birds per stop where found [Usfw3], extrapolating to an minimum of 30,000 pairs; the actual population is undoubtedly larger.

1966–89 CBC Summary

Christmas Bird Count	Years Found	Range of No. Found	Median
Wilmington	24	2,686–103,335	8,305
Middletown	24	1,482–127,717	3,433
Bombay Hook	24	1,069–15,425	3,079
Cape Henlopen	24	808–901,925	4,509
Rehoboth	24	746–253,000	5,512
STATEWIDE *(low in 1989, high in 1982)*	24	11,658–919,226	108,591

WINTER: The maximum CBC report is 901,925 on the 1982 Cape Henlopen count. High counts in 1982 and 1983 obscure what otherwise appears to be a 4–5% annual decrease in the CBC population during 1966–89. The starling is reported most abundantly on the Cape Henlopen CBC, reflecting a large local blackbird roost.

BANDING: The banding map depicts the distribution of 116 birds banded in Delaware and later shot or found dead. Of 35 out-of-state recoveries, 24 (69%) came from adjacent states, suggesting that short-distance movements predominate. Only part of the population disperses or migrates, mainly hatching-year and yearling birds, but some birds that winter in Delaware breed to the north (Kessel 1953; Suthers 1978) [Usfw2].

REMARKS: Chapman (1895) describes the introduction of the European Starling into North America as follows: "This Old-World species has been introduced in eastern North America on several occasions, but only the last importation appears to have been successful. The birds included in this lot, about 60 in number, were released in Central Park, New York City, [on 6 March] 1890, under the direction of Mr. Eugene Schieffelin. They seem to have left the park and have established themselves in various favorable places in the upper part of the city. They have bred for three successive years in the roof of the

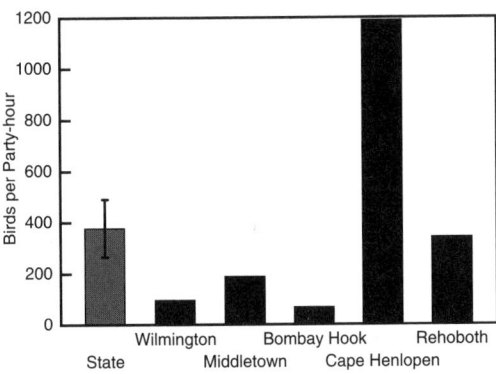

CBC Geographic Distribution

Museum of Natural History and at other points in the vicinity. In the suburbs about the northern end of the city they are frequently observed in flocks containing as many as fifty individuals. These birds are resident throughout the year, and as they have already endured our most severe winters, we may doubtless regard the species as thoroughly naturalized." The spread from the New York area was initially slow, but within 80 years of its introduction the starling had become one of the most numerous birds in North America. It inflicts economic damage particularly on wheat, cattle food, and cherries. Attempts to control its population have included dynamiting roosts, spraying birds at roosts with poisons or detergents, and using poisoned bait or antifertility chemicals. Repeated mass killings

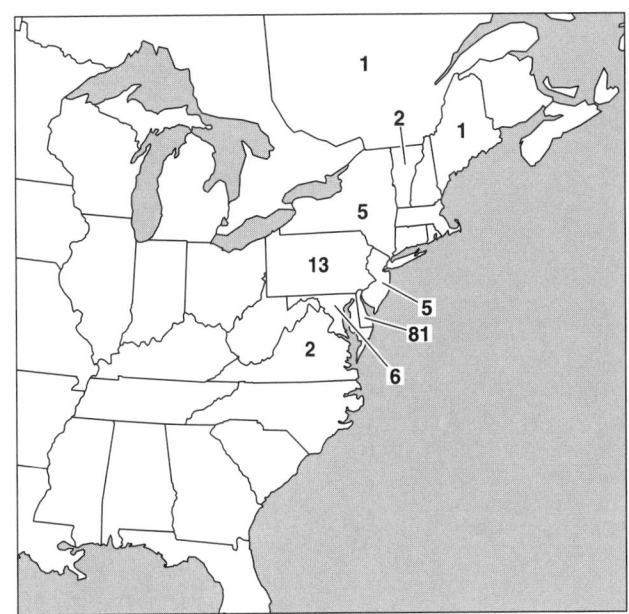

Total European Starlings Banded in Delaware and Recovered Dead or Shot in Each State.

having had no effect, efforts to reduce its population in the United States have stopped (Feare 1984; Dolbeer et al. 1978).

SPECIMENS: 81; DMNH, ANSP, UDEL. Egg records: DMNH.

American Pipit (*Anthus rubescens*)

Regular; winter visitor; fairly common when present. Expected mid-October to early April, occasionally six weeks earlier or later. Infrequently encountered, usually in flocks.

DOCUMENTATION: Multiple sight reports.

HABITAT: Cultivated fields, short grass fields.

REMARKS: Pipits can occur in flocks of hundreds or as single individuals. Comparatively few reports exist for this species, particularly from the migration periods, and more reports are needed to better determine migration periods and abundances in Delaware.

SPRING: The onset of migration remains obscure because the number of reports gradually decrease from midwinter through April. Stewart and Robbins (1958) give the period as 25 March–5 April to 1–10 May in Maryland. The latest Delaware records are

22 Apr 1972	75	various fields in state [Barn51]
26 Apr 1975	60	Bombay Hook NWR [Lehm1]
30 Apr 1967	flock	near Redden [Wayn71]
12, 14 May 1967	present	Cape Henlopen SP [Armi5]

FALL: Usual first arrival starts 15–20 October, but sometimes a few are present as much as 6 weeks earlier. Early reports include

| 3 Sep 1973 | 5 | Bombay Hook NWR [Lehm14] |
| 9 Sep 1973 | 3 | Dragon Run [SpSB13] |

| 18 Sep 1989 | 35 | Five Points [Frec1] |
| 3 Oct 1982 | 1 | Bombay Hook NWR [RusJ6] |

For Maryland, Stewart and Robbins (1958) give 20–30 September to 25 November–5 December as the migration period, with the peak from 10 October to 5 November. Large flocks reported in Delaware include

3 Nov 1974	250	Bombay Hook NWR [JohR1]
16 Nov 1974	208	by Dover AFB [Lehm26]
26 Nov 1979	250	Lewes [Frec59]

1966–89 CBC Summary

Christmas Bird Count	Years Found	Range of No. Found	Median
Wilmington	3	2–25	
Middletown	4	1–100	
Bombay Hook	21	1–315	18
Cape Henlopen	5	2–98	
Rehoboth	5	1–60	
STATEWIDE	22	4–317	28
(zero in 1981 and 1989, high in 1973)			

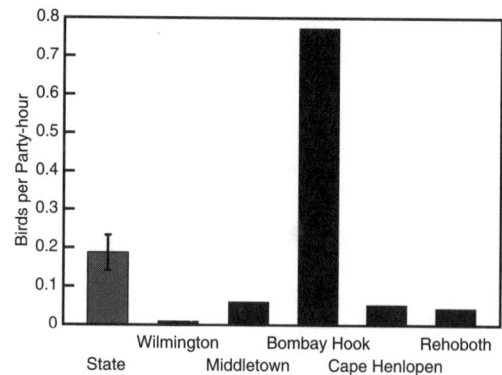

CBC Geographic Distribution

WINTER: American Pipits are reported most commonly on the Bombay Hook CBC. Half of the pipit reports come from CBCs, probably because that is when observers check fields most carefully for this bird.

[Sprague's Pipit *(Anthus spragueii)*]

Accidental (1954).

DOCUMENTATION: Published notes.

REMARKS: There is a plausible Delaware record of a Sprague's Pipit seen with American Pipits on 3 April 1954 near Bombay Hook NWR (Price 1955). The notes mention "general straw color, yellowish legs, and streaked back." The separation of Sprague's Pipit from American Pipit is not entirely routine, so more detail, such as the distances at which the birds were observed, would have been desirable. Meadow Pipit *(Anthus pratensis),* which breeds in Greenland, and other Eurasian pipits, whose occurrence in Delaware are improbable but not impossible, are not excluded by the description.

A report of 1 from Bombay Hook NWR on 31 July 1991, with a description that "went beyond the pink legs, to note other features, such as pale coloration and eye ring" [MerJ2], is a noteworthy record. Again, Meadow Pipit is not clearly excluded.

Sprague's Pipit breeds in the northern plains and winters in the south-central United States and in Mexico. Casual observations of the species also come from the south Atlantic coast north to Virginia.

[Bohemian Waxwing *(Bombycilla garrulus)*]

One report.

DOCUMENTATION: None.

REMARKS: One report ("a flock" noted during April 1962) has not been documented.

Cedar Waxwing *(Bombycilla cedrorum)*

Occurs all year; fairly common to common. Most numerous late October to early May. Spring, summer, and winter populations increasing. Wanders in flocks, so can be either common or absent on any day.

| J | F | M | A | M | J | J | A | S | O | N | D |

HABITAT: Open or brushy wooded areas, parks, orchards, gardens, wood edges in residential or agricultural areas.

SPRING: Migration is underway by 20–30 April and continues through 25 May–10 June. Some high counts are

16 Apr 1972	100	Newark [MiPD5]
3 May 1985	125	Rehoboth Beach [Edni57]
5 May 1985	150	Goslee Pond [Frec1]

Although migration takes place during May and the numbers of individuals reported on the May Count vary noticeably from year to year, the Cedar Waxwing shows an annual increase of 9% a year during 1969–91.

BREEDING: Numbers of Cedar Waxwings are erratic from year to year, so the recent increase may be only temporary. Nonbreeding flocks occur into June.

Atlas. Safe dates for this late breeding species were set to start 20 June so that records of late flocks of nonbreeders would not confuse the Atlas results. The late breeding date probably resulted in its being missed in many blocks where insufficient field work was done after early June. It was found in 42 Atlas blocks before 20 June in addition to those shown. Fledged young was the confirmation code most frequently used; only 5 nests were found during the Atlas project.

Nesting. Hanson (notes) described the nest he found in 1933 as situated on a horizontal branch 15 ft up in a pear tree. Outside it was 5 in. across and 3 in. deep, and inside 2 1/2 in. across and 1 1/2 in. deep. It was made of small sticks, grass stems, and

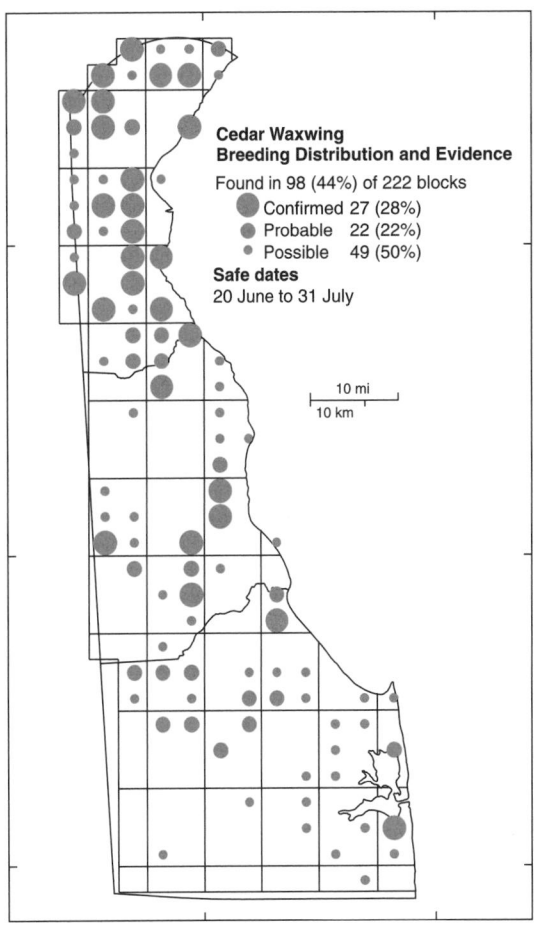

**Cedar Waxwing
Breeding Distribution and Evidence**

Found in 98 (44%) of 222 blocks

● Confirmed 27 (28%)
● Probable 22 (22%)
· Possible 49 (50%)

Safe dates
20 June to 31 July

10 mi
10 km

vine tendrils, rather closely packed and woven, and lined with finer dry grass, a few horse hairs, and a little plant down.

Estimated clutch-completion dates based on 11 Delaware records extend from 22 May to 21 June, unexpectedly early and brief, but corresponding roughly to the period for first clutches. In Ohio some are double-brooded, and breeding extends through August (Putnam 1949). Egg dates extend from 3 June [Jahn1] to 24 June [Hans3]; nestling dates from 13 June [Zeit2] to 19 July [West3]. The only clutch size reported in Delaware was 4 [Hans1]; Leck and Cantor (1979) give typically 3–5 from North American Nest Record Cards.

History. The habits of this beautiful bird are suited to some changes wrought by civilization, and it appears to have increased in population during the twentieth century. It prefers the early succession and open areas brought about by clearing the forest for agriculture, and it eats the berries of ornamental plantings. It was listed as a resident in 1905 (Rhoads and Pennock) but was not mentioned in any of Pennock's published accounts of Delaware trips. Hanson (notes) provided the first records, all from summer, and classified it as a summer resident. He found a nest that had young several days old in Silver

Lake Park, Dover, 8 July 1924. In 6 of the next 10 years he encountered waxwings from 29 May to 26 July, including a pair collecting string on the latter date. On 8 July 1930 he and Dicky found a nest with 2 young probably at least a week old in a pear orchard north of Little Creek. On 24 June 1933 they found 2 nests, both in pear trees in a Dover orchard, 1 with 1 egg and 1 young several days old, the other with 4 fresh eggs. The next possible breeding records were 3 and 5 individuals recorded on 2 and 30 July 1944 on the Hoopes Reservoir survey [Hoff4]. After that there are no late June or July records until 1973:

21 June 1973	3	Prime Hook NWR [Holg40]
23 June 1973	1	Cape Henlopen SP [Wayn1]
20 July 1973	2	nest building, White Clay Creek [Lehm13]

The first occupied nest reported since 1933 was found on 12 June 1974 at White Clay Creek [Jahn1].

Trends. This species increased on BBSs in the East at an average annual rate of 3% during 1966–90. In Delaware it has also increased over the long term, but most strongly during 1981–90 [Usfw1].

Breeding population. If each block where this species was found contained an average of only 10 pairs, the population in the mid-1980s would have been about 1,000 pairs, a substantial increase over the 1950s and 1960s when its breeding population was much lower.

FALL: The first increase in numbers begins in early August but possibly represents only local dispersal. Migration is underway by late August and continues at least to the end of October, when the winter abundance level is reached. Some high counts are

| 16 Sep 1979 | 95 | Ashland [Falk14] |
| 26 Oct 1980 | 300 | Brandywine Creek SP [RusR1] |

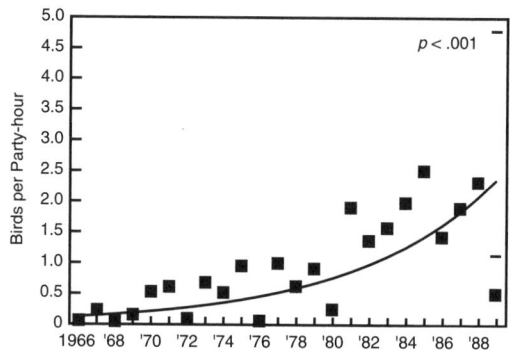

CBC Trend; Increasing at 13% per Year

WINTER: This species has shown a strong increase in CBC numbers during 1966–89. It is most numerous on the Bombay Hook CBC. On 1 January 1978 500 were found at Cape Henlopen SP, and on 2 March 1986 500 were at Lewes Beach [Frec1].

Barry (1939), using Natural History Society bird records, properly recorded its status as "resident, more common in winter." The first published winter records are

19 Dec 1939	10	Rehoboth CBC
24 Oct 1943	48	Hoopes Reservoir [Hoff4]
29 Dec 1944	11	Middletown CBC
21 Dec 1947	6	Bombay Hook CBC

SPECIMENS: 46; DMNH, ANSP, UDEL, USNM.

1966–89 CBC Summary

Christmas Bird Count	Years Found	Range of No. Found	Median
Wilmington	23	7–352	97
Middletown	18	1–299	11
Bombay Hook	22	2–486	66
Cape Henlopen	19	2–244	28
Rehoboth	23	1–414	40
STATEWIDE (increasing; low in 1966, high in 1985)	24	25–1,073	332

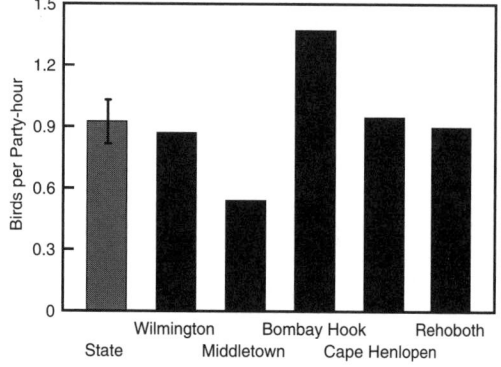

CBC Geographic Distribution

Forest Fragmentation and Forest Birds

Roland R. Roth

Eighty acres of forest turn into five acres surrounded by asphalt, lawns, or cropland. A right-of-way splits a forest into two remnants and creates two warmer, brighter, and drier edges where once cool, shaded, moist interior conditions had prevailed. This is fragmentation—the division and reduction of a habitat type into ever smaller and more isolated remnants. In this case, the habitat is forests, the dominant primeval ecosystem of Delaware.

No data on fragmentation per se exist for Delaware. Neither the average size of forests nor the average distance between them is known. Estimates of total acreage provide some perspective on changes in forest cover. Unfortunately, the U.S. Forest Service uses such a broad definition of forest that its periodic surveys of forest acreage do not provide ecologically meaningful estimates of the changes. However, John MacKenzie (1989) recently calculated from aerial photographs changes in actual forest cover between 1974 and 1984. He estimated declines from the 1974 base of 3.6% for deciduous forest, 7.1% for mixed forest, and 15.4% for coniferous forest. Proportions and actual acres lost were highest in Sussex County, where forest acreage is greatest. Deciduous and mixed forests, key avian habitats, had the following losses, by county: New Castle, 1,075 acres; Kent, 1,860 acres; and Sussex, 12,180 acres. As economic growth boomed during the late 1980s and into the 1990s, fragmentation and reduction of forests also continued in Delaware.

Although forest loss is obvious to most observers, its effects on birds go largely unnoticed and unlamented. Cameras cannot record birds killed by habitat loss. The negative consequences of fragmentation are subtle and affect species usually seen only by bird enthusiasts, while species familiar to the general public thrive. But the phenomenon is real and will simplify Delaware's avifauna greatly in the coming decades.

For forest birds, fragmentation means less living space and less diversity of microhabitats, resulting in fewer breeding pairs and less variety of species. Fragmentation also increases the influence of the edge. As the size of a forest remnant decreases, the edge's environmental conditions reach closer to the center. At some limit, this "edge effect" encompasses the entire remnant, virtually eliminating typical interior conditions.

Many studies have demonstrated consequences of forest fragmentation and increased edge. First, the variety of breeding species declines as area decreases. The reduced variety is biased heavily in favor of common generalists that tolerate edge habitats—the Northern Cardinal, Tufted Titmouse, Blue Jay, and Gray Catbird, for example. Some species are predictably rare or absent in forest fragments of fewer than 100 acres. Typically they spend the winter in tropical America and are small and unfamiliar to the general public. Various warblers, vireos, and flycatchers are examples. However, three Delaware nonmigrants—the Pileated Woodpecker, Hairy Woodpecker, and White-breasted Nuthatch—are affected in the same way.

A second major consequence is also an edge effect. Several predators of nests (Blue Jay, Common Grackle, American Crow, raccoon, and opossum) and a brood parasite (Brown-headed Cowbird) thrive in edge-type habitats and so are favored by fragmentation. Some studies show predation and parasitism rates to be highest near edges and in fragments. For species trying to nest in fragments dominated by edge conditions, the consequence may be reduced reproductive success.

The unavoidable conclusion is that forest fragmentation seriously threatens interior-dwelling species. With fewer places to nest, perhaps under exceptional pressure from predation or parasitism, productivity of interior-dwelling species may be reduced below the level needed to sustain a local population. Some of these species may persist in smaller fragments only in small numbers and only through immigration of surplus individuals from larger, more productive sites.

Data in this book show that fragmentation is taking its toll in Delaware. For example, 11 species identified by Maryland researchers as upland forest interior specialists occurred at "possible" or higher levels in far fewer of the 220 Delaware Breeding Bird Atlas blocks (average is 52 blocks) than did 15 interior-edge species (average is 213 blocks). (See the accompanying table listing species used in the analysis of the distribution.) Four other interior species—the Hairy Woodpecker, Acadian Flycatcher, Ovenbird, and Scarlet Tanager—occurred more widely (avg. = 181) but still at notably lower levels than the interior-edge species. Interior species were often scarce where they did occur, so an occupied block could have represented only one pair.

Large forests with favorable interior conditions are especially vital to forest birds, but 5- to 50-acre forests are also worth saving. They serve as stopover places for transients and may provide tolerable, although suboptimal, conditions for breeding attempts by some interior species. They may also serve as anchors for additional lands secured over time or as seed sources for forest succession on adjacent lands.

At the University of Delaware in the 1960s, Jack Linehan, Bob Jones, and Jerry Longcore recognized the value of remnants in urban environments and were among the first to study bird populations in urban woodlands. Although harboring mostly generalists, these remnants contribute to urban environmental quality. These habitats and the birds they harbor foster an interest in nature among urban dwellers that can lead to a deeper concern for birds and conservation.

List of Species Used in Analysis of Distribution

Interior	Interior-edge
Pileated Woodpecker	Yellow-billed Cuckoo
White-breasted Nuthatch	Red-bellied Woodpecker
Veery	Northern Flicker
Yellow-throated Warbler	Downy Woodpecker
Cerulean Warbler	Great Crested Flycatcher
Black-and-white Warbler	Blue Jay
American Redstart	Carolina Chickadee
Worm-eating Warbler	Tufted Titmouse
Louisiana Waterthrush	Carolina Wren
Kentucky Warbler	Gray Catbird
Hooded Warbler	Wood Thrush
	White-eyed Vireo
	Red-eyed Vireo
	Northern Cardinal
	Eastern Towhee

Note: Group assignments follow Whitcomb et al. (1981).

Delaware, like the rest of eastern North America, has a vital place in the perpetuation of migrant, forest-dwelling birds in the Western Hemisphere. As the Breeding Bird Atlas shows, the state still has some nesting habitat for many of these species. Even if all the present wintering habitat in tropical America were to survive, bird populations will decline further unless Delaware and its neighboring states preserve these nesting habitats.

Atlas maps for the forest interior species show how patchily distributed, and thus vulnerable, these birds are in Delaware. The distributions identify areas that are critical because of their extent and quality. The major areas recurring in the Atlas maps are the White Clay, Red Clay, and Brandywine valleys; the three state forests—Blackbird, Redden, and Ellendale; and the Great Cypress Swamp. On a broader scale the forests of Sussex County and to a lesser extent western Kent County also have frequent records of forest interior species. The biological integrity of all these areas must be defended.

One may be tempted to dismiss the spotty distributions shown by the Atlas maps in this book as a Delaware phenomenon, thus assuming that the species are abundant elsewhere or in toto over the continent. Yet, many other places in the deciduous forest biome are at least as susceptible. The process of becoming rare or extirpated everywhere may begin when a species gradually becomes scarce locally—without exceptional mortality, but simply through reduced reproductive success. Local extirpations eventually add up—to extinction.

Perpetuation of breeding populations of Delaware's forest birds requires immediate attention. Sizable forests must be kept intact, and neighboring fragments must be linked. Failure to do so will greatly simplify Delaware's avifauna and result in an homogenized "McFauna" instead of a rich, varied avian menu.

Blue-winged Warbler (*Vermivora pinus*)

Regular; migrant and summer resident; uncommon. Expected late April to mid-September. Breeding, reestablished in 1971, mostly confined to the Piedmont.

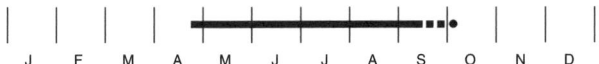

HABITAT: Wet or moist brushy, cut-over second-growth areas with saplings; also interior floodplain woods with closed canopy.

SPRING: Normally, first arrival occurs 25 April–1 May; migration peaks 5–15 May and concludes 20–25 May. Early reports include

20 Apr 1965	1	Lewes area [Stri3]
22 Apr 1985	1	New Castle (DMNH 76235).

High counts along White Clay Creek (where they breed) include

7 May 1977	18	[Dyer7]
20 May 1978	19	[Falk11]
28 May 1977	21	[MiDP12]

The May Count usually totals 20–40 birds; the highest counts are 77 on 8 May 1981 and 64 on 9 May 1982.

BREEDING: Most evidence for this species' breeding in Delaware is limited to 2 periods in the Piedmont—clutches collected in 1894 and 1905 by Norris (WFVZ egg data) and adults feeding young at several sites from 1970 through 1989. Additionally a single nest was collected in Sussex County on 25 May 1957 (DMNH 9268), and few scattered records of singing males in the Coastal Plain have accumulated.

Atlas. The Atlas data show that the Blue-winged Warbler frequents Piedmont creek valleys, particularly where farmland is reverting to woods. Although 3 Coastal Plain Atlas possible reports fell within the safe dates, none of those observations was upgraded, so they should be interpreted cautiously. Further observations are needed from southern Delaware to better define the Blue-winged's status there.

Nesting. J. R. Norris described the first Delaware nest: "on ground under a small bush near edge of wood, made of leaves and lined inside with stripped bark and horse hair." The nest was "4 inches high in a grass clump, a cup of grass and fibers."

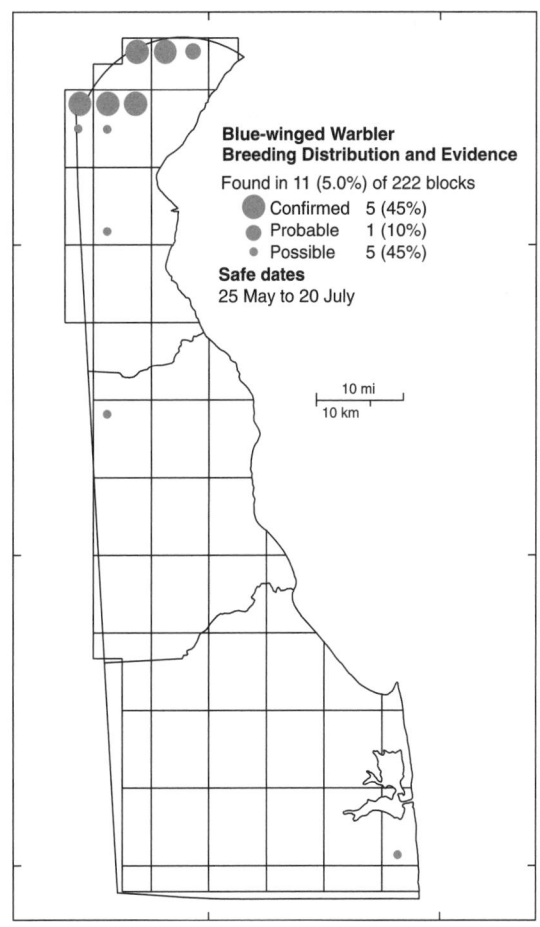

Blue-winged Warbler
Breeding Distribution and Evidence

Found in 11 (5.0%) of 222 blocks

Confirmed 5 (45%)
Probable 1 (10%)
Possible 5 (45%)

Safe dates
25 May to 20 July

10 mi
10 km

Estimated clutch-completion dates fall between 21 May and 1 June (*n* = 6). Clutch size is 4 or 5.

History. The Blue-winged Warbler was present during the late nineteenth century as described by Gill (1980): "Historically Blue-wings occurred west of the Appalachians (Cooke 1904; Short 1963). Exactly when populations of this species became established in the Delaware Valley . . . is not clear, but by the late 1800s they were well known and were isolated from the main western populations." Turnbull (1869) classified this warbler as somewhat rare in east Pennsylvania. Bush indicated several (which he called "blue eyed yellow warblers") present in Wilmington as migrants in the week preceding 8 May 1880. Three early clutches were found in New Castle County—26 May 1894 (5 eggs), 6 June 1894 (4), and 30 May 1905 (4) (WFVZ egg data). A male was singing near Porter on 6 June 1908 [Penn1]. With 2 exceptions little information exists for the period between 1908 and 1970:

1. Barry (1939; 1942) listed the Blue-wing as a "summer resident," a designation probably borrowed from Rhoads and Pennock (1905).

2. A nest found in Sussex County on 25 May 1957 (DMNH 9268) is the only one yet discovered south of the Piedmont.

The Blue-winged Warbler, included neither on 1967 or 1971 lists of Delaware breeding birds (both Linehan) nor on Stickley's 1963 White Clay Creek list, must have been absent or scarce during most of the twentieth century (see Gill 1980).

Reestablishment. Linehan suspected breeding after finding Blue-winged Warblers in early July 1968 in the White Clay Creek valley [Line1], and West reported the species on a BBC there in 1970. Two were feeding young in the nest on 12 June 1971 at Brandywine Creek SP [Wayn8], and it has since been a regular summer resident in the valley. Blue-wings have also been fairly regular breeders along White Clay Creek: adults were feeding fledglings near there on the Louviers property on 13 June 1974 [Jahn1]; nest building was reported on 21 May 1978; adults were carrying food on 19 June 1982 [Hess4]; and adults were feeding young on 22 June 1983 [Jahn1].

Trends. May Count data display an almost significant ($p < .1$) 3% average annual increase in Blue-winged Warblers since 1969, probably reflecting the species' general eastward expansion and its increased breeding in Delaware. BBS data reflect a continent-wide increase during 1965–79 as well as an increase in the Northeast over the same period (Robbins et al. 1986). It is not effectively monitored by the BBS in Delaware, because the BBS does not adequately sample the Piedmont. Blue-wings were recorded on the BBS from the Coastal Plain on 2 June 1973 in Kent County [Line5] and on 15 June 1980 in Sussex County [Edni5].

Breeding population. Based on Atlas results, the Bluewing's breeding population is probably between 10 and 100 pairs, most residing in the Piedmont.

Conservation. Without habitat management designed for its maintenance, this species will probably be extirpated for the second time because there is little chance of additional Piedmont fields going through the early successional stages of reversion to forest in northern Delaware.

FALL: Fall migration, not as evident as spring migration, probably begins in late July or early August. Most birds depart by 10–15 September, the latest report mentioning 1 at White Clay Creek on 2 October 1977 [Rufe6]. Usually 1 or 2 birds per sighting are reported in contrast to 4 or 5 in spring. Consequently, there is no discernible migration peak, though the number of reports drops noticeably following 5 September— only 12 reports existing thereafter. High counts include

19 Aug 1973	10	Brandywine Creek SP [Phal6]
27 Aug 1977	7	White Clay Creek [Rufe6]

REMARKS: The Blue-winged Warbler hybridizes regularly and extensively with the Golden-winged Warbler (Gill 1980). Hybrids are variable in plumage and song type (Parkes 1951; Short 1963; Gill and Murray 1972). "Brewster's" Warbler and "Lawrence's" Warbler, 2 recognizable extreme types, are occasionally found in Delaware; for example, a "Lawrence's" was seen on 6 May 1932 near Montchanin (Brown 1934b); a "Brewster's" paired with a Blue-wing and summered near Pyles Ford Rd. in 1987 [SpeE3].

SPECIMENS: 7; DMNH, UDEL. Egg records: DMNH, WFVZ.

Golden-winged Warbler *(Vermivora chrysoptera)*

Occasional (16 years, 1911–87), perhaps regular, but on the basis of its decreasing range in the Northeast, expected less often; migrant; rare. Present May and mid-August to mid-September.

J F M A M J J A S O N D

HABITAT: Various open woodland habitats.

MIGRATION: Reports are few and include about a dozen from spring, during 1–22 May, and a similar number from fall, from 14 August to 8 September. A male taken on 13 May 1900 was in the collection of E. M. Lyman, Newport [Penn1]. Pennock collected the only extant specimen near New Castle on 6 May 1911 (ANSP 65471); the only bird banded was netted at the University of Delaware woodlot on 7 September 1967 [Line4]. A published October report (Ednie 1985) does not appear in the original observer's field notes.

REMARKS: See Blue-winged Warbler.

SPECIMEN: ANSP 65471, details earlier.

Tennessee Warbler *(Vermivora peregrina)*

HABITAT: Deciduous forest.

SPRING: All spring migration records fall between 3 and 24 May, with the majority of reports coming from the middle 2 weeks of May. Usually only a few birds are found. The high count is 12 from White Clay Creek on 13 May 1984 [Hess15]. The May Count usually totals 10–12 birds, the highest count being 22 on 10 May 1975.

FALL: Usual first arrival is 1–10 September. Early reports include

| 17 Aug 1963 | 1 | Thompsons Bridge, Brandywine Creek [Tala1] |
| 27 Aug 1988 | 1 | near Lewes [Frec1] |

Departure usually ends by 5–10 October, but later sightings are

| 14 Oct 1972 | 1 | Winterthur [Wayn31] |
| 16 Oct 1977 | 1 | Newark [Barn7] |

The high report consists of 4 in Newark on 12 September 1982 [Litt3].

SPECIMEN: DMNH 77075, Newark, 1 October 1981.

Regular; migrant; uncommon. Expected May and early September to mid-October.

Orange-crowned Warbler *(Vermivora celata)*

DOCUMENTATION: Multiple sight reports.

HABITAT: In migration hedgerows, or other wood edge habitat; in winter evergreen broadleaf bushes or trees.

MIGRATION: Migration primarily takes place west of the Appalachians, rarely in the eastern states (AOU 1983). When located, only 1 or 2 birds are present. Fall reports generally occur from 15 September to 7 October, with scattered reports to the end of the month. Given the CBC reports, the lack of November reports is surprising. It is rarely found in spring.

WINTER: The winter range extends north to South Carolina and only casually to the northern United States (AOU 1983). Thus there are expectedly few winter sightings. Delaware reports of wintering come from the Wilmington area, where single birds regularly visited suet feeders, the first during the winter of 1962 [Broo8] and the second during the winter of 1967 [WarM2]. In addition, individuals were reported on CBCs in 1939, 1954, 1955, 1966, 1972, 1977, and 1982.

REMARKS: All reports should be documented.

Occasional (19 years, 1939–89), perhaps regular during migration, sporadic in winter; migrant; rare. Very rare in spring; in fall to be looked for mid-September to early October.

Nashville Warbler (*Vermivora ruficapilla*)

Regular; migrant; uncommon. Expected late April to mid-May and late August to mid-October.

| J | F | M | A | M | J | J | A | S | O | N | D |

HABITAT: Wood edges, open stands of wet or moist forests.

SPRING: Spring migration is inconspicuous. Of approximately 2 dozen reports, most involve 1 or 2 birds found from 30 April to 20 May. Extreme dates of reports include

| 23 Apr 1961 | 1 | Assawoman WA [Davi18] |
| 22 May 1983 | 1 | Bombay Hook NWR [Bayn5] |

The highest number reported is 3 at Winterthur on 21 May 1972 [Broo13]. The May Count usually totals 1–3 birds, but 10, 8, and 9 were recorded on 10 May 1975, 7 May 1977, and 5 May 1981, respectively.

FALL: First arrival is 20–25 August, the migration peaks during September, and the last migrants depart by 10–15 October. Typical reports, as in the spring, feature 1 or 2 individuals. A high report is of 5 at Winterthur Museum on 23 September 1972 [West14]. A report of 9 found along White Clay Creek on 11 September 1976 [Boll5] is erroneous, since the original data sheets list 2 birds.

SPECIMENS: DMNH 72304, Centerville, 3 May 1982; UDEL 94-66, Newark, 12 May 1966; DMNH 71151, Centerville, 27 August 1980; DMNH 77362, Wilmington, 15 September 1988; DMNH 63238, Greenville, 23 September 1977.

Northern Parula (*Parula americana*)

Regular; migrant; uncommon; rare summer resident; expected late April to mid-October. Nest records only from the White Clay Creek valley since the 1930s.

| J | F | M | A | M | J | J | A | S | O | N | D |

HABITAT: Floodplain or swamp forest; rich, moist upland forest.

SPRING: The first arrival usually appears 20–25 April, the migration peaks 30 April–20 May, and most depart by 25–30 May. Earliest reports include

| 16 April 1977 | 3 | White Clay Creek [Samp6] |
| 17 April 1976 | 5 | White Clay Creek [Conw11] |

High counts include

24 Apr 1976	11	White Clay Creek [Jahn14]
9 May 1970	22	Brandywine Creek SP [Broo15]
13 May 1984	15	White Clay Creek [Hess12]
22 May 1976	12	White Clay Creek [BroH12]

The highest May Count is 172 (10 May 1986), the lowest is 12 (5 May 1973). This species is reported up until 2 June in places where it not known to breed: Dragon Run [Beac6], Brandywine Creek SP [Edni51], Ashland Nature Center [SpSB9], and the BBS in southern New Castle County [Line5].

BREEDING: In Pennsylvania, Poole (1964) labeled this warbler "a strangely erratic and local summer resident," and so it is in Delaware.

Atlas. Parulas were reported in 14 blocks during the Atlas project. Although there were no confirmations, the 7 probable reports are a reassuring sign of the species' continued presence. The possible report near Rehoboth Beach was based on a male singing at Welchs Pond, a Delmarva bay, on 20 June 1986 [West3]. Parulas should also be sought in the Pocomoke and Nanticoke drainages where the species was not reported,

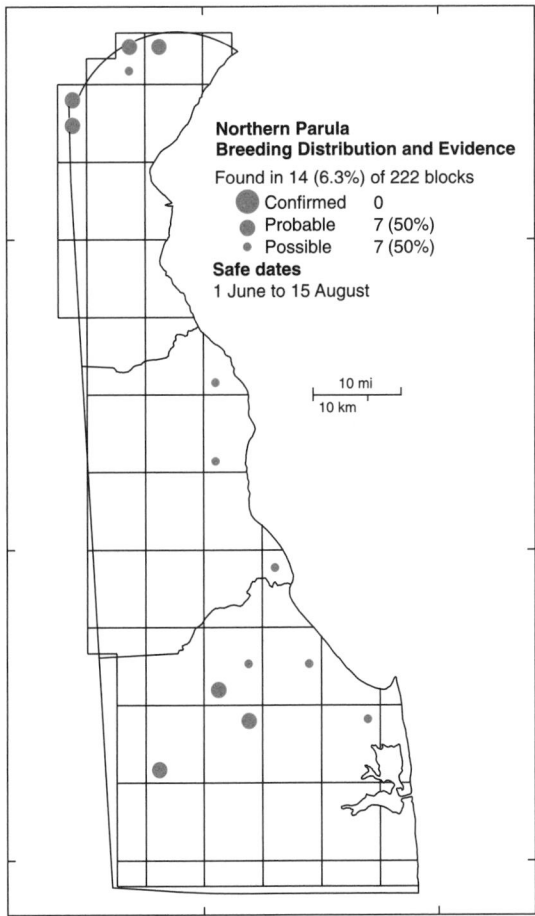

Northern Parula
Breeding Distribution and Evidence

Found in 14 (6.3%) of 222 blocks

● Confirmed   0
● Probable   7 (50%)
• Possible   7 (50%)

Safe dates
1 June to 15 August

10 mi
10 km

begins in early May, but some migrants remain through 2 June and then disappear.

History. The Northern Parula was listed as a summer resident by Rhoads and Pennock (1905), based on Rhoads finding it abundant at Rehoboth Beach on 22 June 1903 and nesting at Seaford on 18 June 1903. W. D. Miller, American Museum, also found it breeding about Seaford in June 1908 [MiWD1]. In Dover Hanson found it only during fall migration in the 1920s and 1930s. Barry's 1939 summary remains fairly accurate: "breeding in Sussex County but rare." The first documented summer observation for New Castle County is on 10 June 1944 at Hoopes Reservoir [Hoff4]. Of all the Piedmont areas where DOS has run weekly summer surveys, White Clay Creek is the only area where the Northern Parula has been found, having been reported there regularly since at least 1963 (Stickley 1963). Summer records in southern New Castle County include appearances on a 9 June 1979 BBS [Line5] and at Bombay Hook NWR on 20 June 1982 [Knar1]. Neither the BBS nor the May Count indicates a significant change in its population in the past 25 years, but it was probably severely reduced in the first half of the twentieth century to the same degree as the population in New York (Bull 1974).

Breeding population. It is difficult to estimate the breeding population of such an erratic species using little but the absence of reports. High summer counts on the weekly surveys in the White Clay Creek valley are 11 each on 12 June 1976 and 2 July 1977 [Boll8; Boll7]. Perhaps its breeding population is 5–50 pairs, a range consistent with 14 reports during 5 years of Atlas work and the species' general scarcity. The parula's breeding range may be limited because it usually relies on old man's beard to support and to hide its nest in the part of its range north of Spanish moss occurrence (Bent 1953; Chapman 1917). Morse (1989) disagrees, citing several nests described in Bent (1953) that contain neither of these materials.

In summary, breeding Northern Parulas should be watched for in moist forests anywhere in the state, but they appear unable to maintain a vigorous population in the absence of verdant growth of old man's beard. Intriguingly, 100 mi to the west in the mid-1940s, 40 were found in 85 acres (116 per 100 ha) on the Patuxent NWR (Stewart and Robbins 1958).

FALL: Normally, migration starts 10–15 September and runs until 5–10 October, with the peak falling 15–25 September. Late reports include

16 Oct 1965	1	Assawoman WA [Carl7]
24 Oct 1984	1	Cape Henlopen SP [Pulc2]
31 Oct 1971	1	Assawoman WA [DuPA4]

Typically, only a few birds are reported. High counts include

15 Sep 1974	13	Dragon Run [WarD13]
26 Sep 1970	24	Brandywine Creek SP [SpSB39]
28 Sep 1989	12	around Lewes [Frec1]

In the 1991 Neotropical migrant study (Mabey et al. 1993) about 90% of the Northern Parulas were reported during 7–29 September (*n* = 73).

SPECIMENS: 13; DMNH, ANSP, CM, UDEL.

although it was found just over the state line (Robbins 1986). A 1966 BBC report of a territorial male in Assawoman WA [Line17] should not be interpreted as definitely breeding because most of the field work for that study was conducted in May, before migration is complete.

Nesting. There are few nest records:

late May 1939	eggs	Choptank River [Cutl30]
5 Jun 1939	3 eggs	Bombay Hook NWR [Cutl30]
24 Jun 1973	carrying food	White Clay Creek (E. Dyer, D.P. Miller, pers. comm.)

On 26 Jun 1976 an adult was feeding a fledgling in a Norway spruce near White Clay Creek [MiDP3]; this observation corroborates reports of this species' breeding in evergreens in areas where Spanish moss or old man's beard is not available as nesting substrate (Bent 1953). Nest building was observed during 2–11 May 1989 near White Clay Creek about 11 ft up in a honeysuckle tangle on a large grapevine, though the nest was abandoned after 11 May [MiDP3]; placement of the nest in a tangle is also consistent with nest-site selection when old man's beard is unavailable (Petrides 1942). A similar nest was found a mile north in Pennsylvania on 6 June 1992 (D. P. Miller, pers. comm.).

Clutch completion occurs in late May and early June (*n* = 5). Egg dates in Maryland are 7 April–14 June (Robbins 1996). Clutch size is usually 4–5 (Ehrlich et al. 1988). Nest building

Yellow Warbler *(Dendroica petechia)*

Regular; migrant and summer resident; fairly common. Expected late April to mid-September and sporadically through October. Breeds much less commonly in interior Sussex and Kent counties than along the tidal marsh edge and on the Piedmont.

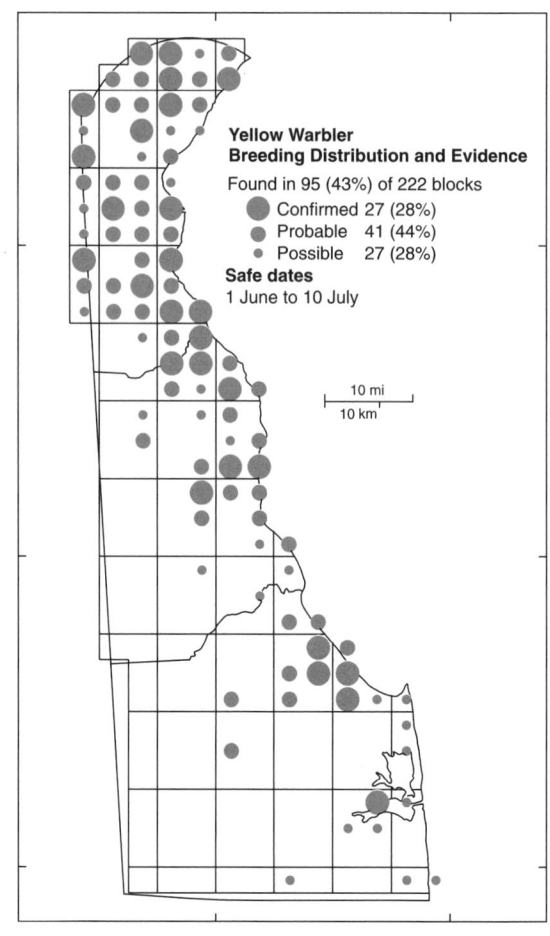

Yellow Warbler
Breeding Distribution and Evidence
Found in 95 (43%) of 222 blocks

- Confirmed 27 (28%)
- Probable 41 (44%)
- Possible 27 (28%)

Safe dates
1 June to 10 July

10 mi
10 km

HABITAT: Breeding—open growth of willow and other shrubs and small trees on wet or moist areas, especially edges of tidal marshes. Migration—any wet area with open growth.

SPRING: Migration usually begins 20–25 April, peaks 1–25 May, and ends 25–30 May. Early reports include

14 Apr 1973	1	Dragon Run [BroW7]
16 Apr 1976	1	near Dover [Pure7]
17 Apr 1966	1	near Centerville [WarD2]

High counts, all from Bombay Hook NWR, are 88 on 8 May 1982, 60 on 15 May 1982, and 58 on 22 May 1983 [Boll4, Kell4, Bayn1]. The May Count usually totals 150–200 birds; highest counts are 353 (3 May 1980) and 314 (14 May 1988); lowest counts 59 (10 May 1969, the first survey year), 65 (8 May 1971), and 49 (5 May 1973).

BREEDING: The Yellow Warbler prefers open country, a preference that makes it one of the best known and easiest to see of the "wood warblers." Most common in shrubby growth at the edge of marshes, it is also commonly found in open shrubby successional or disturbed habitats such as along the Chesapeake and Delaware Canal. The distribution map shows a clear reduction in its occurrence in the interior of the Delmarva Peninsula, indicating the expected reduced abundance near its southern limit on the Coastal Plain.

Atlas. Only 27 confirmations occurred; 13 were based on locating an active nest or nest building. The nests, often placed in isolated bushes along edges, are relatively easy to find and the adults easy to observe.

Nesting. Hanson (notes) described a streamside nest located 5 ft up in a tangle of honeysuckle, greenbrier, and bushes; it contained 4 eggs on 25 May. The nest was 3 in. deep and 3 in. wide outside, and $1^1/2$ in. deep and $1^3/4$ in. wide inside, "very skillfully made and very beautiful, constructed of plant fibers and down."

The estimated clutch-completion dates show an abrupt peak of breeding in mid-May. About 80% of clutches are completed during 15–29 May, overlapping the end of migration. Lack of clutches earlier in May is consistent with data from New Jersey where egg dates ($n = 32$) start on 15 May (Bent 1953). Maryland's begin on 6 May (Robbins 1996), and there is an egg date of 7 May for the District of Columbia (Stewart and Robbins 1958). The earliest Delaware egg date, 21 May, has occurred several times, including at Lums Pond SP where 5 eggs were present in a nest that had been completed on the eleventh [Line3]. The earliest young were found on 1 June [Buck1], the latest on 22 June [BrRF1]. This warbler's nest is subject to cowbird parasitism—8% reported in Delaware, 12%

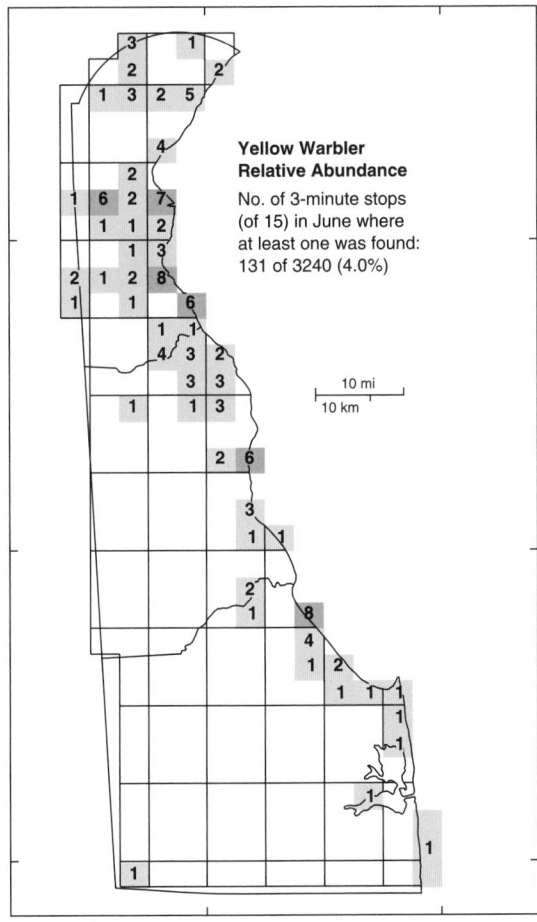

**Yellow Warbler
Relative Abundance**

No. of 3-minute stops
(of 15) in June where
at least one was found:
131 of 3240 (4.0%)

10 mi
10 km

Trends. BBS data indicate it has increased in the East at about 2% per year. Delaware BBS data also show a strong increase since 1979, partly offsetting declines during the preceding 15 years [Usfw3]. The May Count, which surveys migrants as well as residents, reflects an increase since 1969. Local changes in abundance are probably tied to changes in the amount of habitat in the successional stage attractive to this species. For example, most farmland in northern New Castle County has been taken out of production, and some of it has been allowed to revert to old fields with scattered trees, creating suitable habitat for this species.

Breeding population. Because the Yellow Warbler's population is concentrated along often inaccessible marsh edges, estimates are subject to substantial error. High summer counts on the weekly surveys include

7 June 1975	33	Dragon Run [Wayn25]
19 June 1976	19	White Clay Creek [Wayn57]
9 June 1979	15	Ashland [Ross3]
20 June 1982	65	Bombay Hook NWR [Bayn6]

FALL: The migration probably begins in July and ends by 10–15 September; no peak is discernible. Stewart and Robbins (1958) give the period for Maryland as 15–25 July to 20–30 September, with the peak from 25 July to 1 September. Late records include

16 Sep 1966	3 banded	near Rehoboth Beach [RusW1]
4 Oct 1966	1 banded	near Rehoboth Beach [Armi2]
6 Oct 1974	1	Dragon Run [BroW7]
12 Oct 1974	1	Delaware City [Lehm36]

Typically, only a few birds are reported. The high count is 15 at Jimtown, west of Lewes, on 9 August 1988 [Frec1]. According to original field reports, the following published reports of high numbers or late dates refer to Yellow-rumped Warbler rather than Yellow Warbler: Ashland in September 1979 (Speck 1980), Churchmans Marsh twice in October 1965 (West and Klabunde 1977).

WINTER: The report of 1 found on the 1987 Bombay Hook CBC was supported by good details [Ring2].

SPECIMENS: 17; DMNH, ANSP, UDEL. Egg records: DMNH, WFVZ.

in Maryland (Robbins 1996), 42% in Michigan, and 22% of those listed in the Cornell files (Friedmann et al. 1977)—but it is not a good host, frequently rebuilding its nest on top of the parasitized one, thus burying its own eggs along with those of the cowbird (Harrison 1984).

History. The Yellow Warbler has probably benefited from habitat changes accompanying European settlement and from protection of Delaware's saltmarshes.

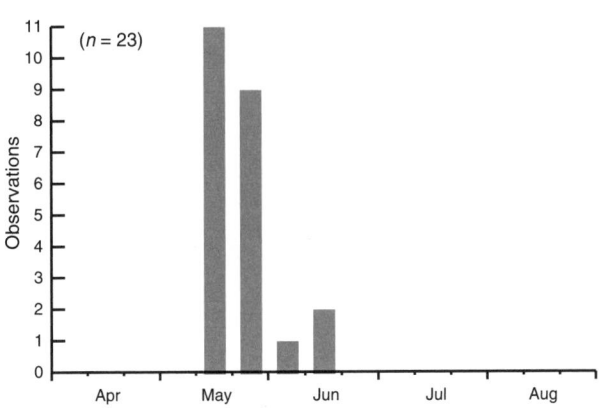

Estimated Clutch-Completion Dates

Chestnut-sided Warbler (*Dendroica pensylvanica*)

Regular; migrant; uncommon. Expected May and late August to early October. Rare intermittent summer resident in northern Delaware since 1966.

HABITAT: Young deciduous succession. Brushy areas surrounding a small pocket of field adjacent to deciduous woods [SpeE3].

SPRING: In most years first arrival is 1–5 May. The migration peaks 10–20 May and ends by 25 May–1 June. The earliest report refers to 1 along White Clay Creek on 30 April 1989 [RusJ1]. This warbler is seldom present past the first week of June. Typical counts include 1 or 2 birds. High counts are

9 May 1970	8	Brandywine Creek SP [Broo15]
13 May 1984	6	White Clay Creek [Hess12]
17 May 1975	6	Dragon Run [Rich1]

The May Count usually totals 10–15 birds; highest counts are 36 (11 May 1974), 31 (14 May 1988), and 19 (5 May 1984 and 13 May 1989).

BREEDING: The Chestnut-sided Warbler is a rare and intermittent breeder in Delaware. The first breeding report describes a female flushed from the nest it was building on 24 May 1966 in the University of Delaware woodlot. Four eggs were present on 31 May, 3 on 1 June, and none 7 June. The nest was 2 ft above ground in a bush in deciduous woods [Long4]. In 1968 an individual was found in early July in the White Clay Creek valley [Line1]. In the summer of 1969 the species was observed 7 July at Brandywine Creek SP [SpSB30], and 2 years later 2 were there through the breeding season: 31 May, 12 and 26 June [WarD7]. A singing male was observed on 12 June 1988 along White Clay Creek (D. P. Miller, pers. comm.).

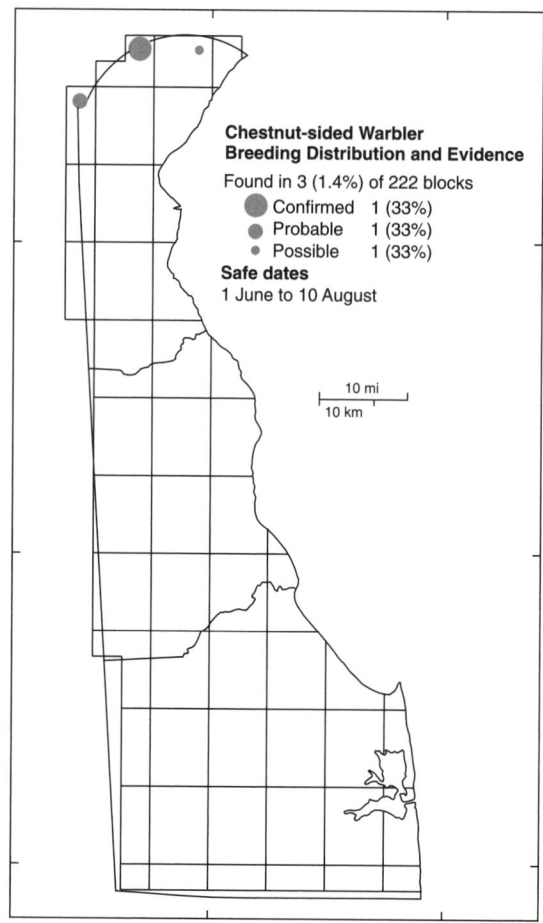

Chestnut-sided Warbler
Breeding Distribution and Evidence
Found in 3 (1.4%) of 222 blocks
● Confirmed 1 (33%)
● Probable 1 (33%)
• Possible 1 (33%)
Safe dates
1 June to 10 August

10 mi
10 km

Atlas. The most frequent Atlas observations were made in the White Clay Creek valley. R.W. Russell noted 2 on 2 June 1983, and D. P. Miller found 1 singing on 30 June 1983; both were near the monument on Hopkins Rd. D. P. Miller observed 1 there again on 5 and 14 June 1984, but did not confirm breeding. H. P. Brokaw noted a singing male near Woodlawn Rd. on 23 June 1984 but could not relocate it during 4 later trips to that site [BroH2]. Beginning 10 May 1987, E. B. Speck observed 2 or 3 pairs in a woodland adjoining an overgrown field, and followed 1 pair twice weekly until it was feeding young on 27 June and 1–2 July, establishing the second breeding record for the state and the only confirmation for the Atlas project. The nest was about 2 ft up in brushy understory. The species probably does not breed south of the Piedmont, but a report of 1 at Dragon Run 1 June 1975 is noteworthy [BroW16].

Nesting. Harrison (1978) describes its nest as a compact cup of fine grasses, bark fibers, shredded weed stems, and plant down, lined with fine grasses and hair. Placement is in a sapling, shrub, thicket, or vine tangle, usually 1–3 ft high. Clutch size is usually 4.

The clutches of the 2 Delaware breeding records were completed between 25 May and 3 June. Egg dates in Maryland are 28 May–26 June (Robbins and Bystrak 1977).

History and trends. Forbush and May (1939) wrote of the Chestnut-sided Warbler: "Audubon met with it but once; Wilson saw little of it; Nuttall . . . saw very few. Since his time, however, its numbers have increased until it has become one of the commonest of eastern warblers. Its increase was favored by the destruction of the primeval forest . . . and later by the increase of neglected fields and pastures with their growths of bushes and brambles, for it is not a frequenter of deep woods, nor yet of well-kept gardens, orchards or farmyards. . . . So we may find it . . . in low roadside and brookside thickets. . . . As the coppice grows up [Chestnut-sided Warblers abandon it]."

This species has extended its breeding range so that Piedmont Delaware is just on the southern edge. It was found in about 20 blocks in Chester and Delaware counties during the Pennsylvania Atlas project (Schwalbe 1992a). It is too scarce in Delaware to monitor using BBS data, but its numbers appear stable in the East since 1966 [Usfw3].

Breeding population. Based on the few preceding reports, the breeding population has probably not exceeded 10 pairs; perhaps none breed during most years.

Conservation. Its success as a breeding bird will depend on the availability of brushy fields in the Piedmont.

FALL: First arrival is 20–25 August, the migration peak is 1–15 September, and migration is over by 25 September–5 October. The latest reports refer to

10 Oct 1976	1	White Clay Creek [Edni38]
14 Oct 1975	1 banded	University of Delaware woodlot [Line4]
19 Oct 1969	1	Assawoman WA [DuPG14]

Typical counts, as in the spring, involve 1 or 2 birds. The high count is 6 at Brandywine Creek SP on 12 September 1970 [BroH10].

SPECIMENS: DMNH 63332 and DMNH 63335, Wilmington, May 1878; UDEL 331-68, Wilmington, May 1878; UDEL 88-66, Newark, 5 May 1966; ANSP 65535, Yorklyn, 15 May 1909.

Magnolia Warbler (*Dendroica magnolia*)

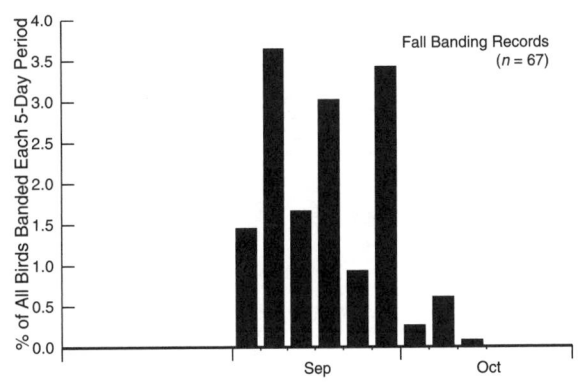

Fall Banding Records (*n* = 67)

Fall Migration Activity

Regular; migrant; uncommon. Expected mid- to late May and late August to early October.

J F M A M J J A S O N D

HABITAT: Deciduous woods with an understory of shrubs.

SPRING: Magnolia Warblers arrive slightly later than many other warblers. First arrivals typically appear 5–10 May, peak passage occurs 10–25 May, and migration ends by 25–30 May. Early records include

1 May 1991	1	Hockessin [Maie2]
3 May 1965	1	Iron Hill, Newark [Faus3]

The only June report refers to 1 bird at Dragon Run on 1 June 1975 [BroW16]. The high count is 8 at Little Creek WA on 18 May 1968 [Adki1]. May Count totals range from 0 (8 May 1982) to 65 (14 May 1988), with no apparent relation to whether the survey was conducted in early or mid-May.

FALL: First arrival is usually 25 August–1 September. The migration peaks 5–30 September and ends by 1–10 October. Peak banding occurs from 6–10 September to 26–30 September. The earliest reports are

22 Aug 1971	3	Brandywine Creek SP [Falk2]
23 Aug 1969	1	Brandywine Creek SP [SpeE11]

In the 1991 Neotropical migrant study (Mabey et al. 1993) 80% of the Magnolia Warblers were reported from 31 August to 22 September ($n = 46$). Typical counts total 3 or 4 birds. Two high counts from Brandywine Creek SP are 20 on 19 September 1970 and 18 on 26 September 1970 [Beac6, SpSB13], respectively. The latest banding record and 2 straggler reports are

13 Oct 1966	1 banded	near Rehoboth Beach [RusW1]
23 Oct 1973	1	Centerville [Edni13]
24 Oct 1964	1	Cape Henlopen [McLP3]

SPECIMENS: 23; DMNH, UDEL, UWBM.

Cape May Warbler *(Dendroica tigrina)*

on 13 October 1966 [RusW1] and 1 at the University of Delaware woodlot on 24 October 1979 [Line4]. The November straggler reports include

2 Nov 1971	1	near Wilmington [MiHM1]
2 Nov 1979	1	Bellevue SP, Wilmington [ConJ1]
9 Nov 1977	1	Cape Henlopen SP [Frec1]
28 Nov 1954	1	Bombay Hook NWR [Cutl38]

A high of 3 birds occurred at Cape Henlopen SP on 10 and 18 September 1980, 12 September 1988 [Frec1], and 6 October 1985 [Edni34].

SPECIMENS: DMNH 820, Sussex Co., 24 May 1958; DMNH 76425, Newark, 28 September 1986; ANSP 65504, Rehoboth Beach, 29 September 1908.

Regular; migrant; uncommon. Expected early to mid-May and early September to mid-October.

HABITAT: Various forest types, especially oaks; forages high in tall trees.

SPRING: This warbler passes through rather quickly, usually arriving 1–7 May, peaking 10–15 May, and leaving by 15–20 May. Rarely is it recorded before 1 May. Late reports are

24 May 1981	1	Assawoman WA [Barn23]
29 May 1982	1	Camp Arrowhead, Angola Neck [Frec1]
30 May 1969	1	Brandywine Creek SP [BroW1]

The high count is 3 at Trap Pond SP on 10 May 1975 [Edni1]. The May Count usually reports 1–5 birds; the highest counts are 11 (13 May 1972) and 19 (10 May 1975), the lowest count 0 (5 May 1973 and 9 May 1981).

FALL: Although Cape May Warblers may sometimes occur as early as late August, first arrival is usually 1–10 September. The migration peaks 15 September–5 October and ends by 10–15 October. Early reports include 2 at Prime Hook NWR on 26 August 1972 [DuPG7] and 1 in Lewes on 30 August 1982 [Frec1]. The late banding records are 2 near Rehoboth Beach

Black-throated Blue Warbler *(Dendroica caerulescens)*

Regular; migrant; uncommon. Expected late April to mid-May and early September to mid-October.

HABITAT: Various kinds of deciduous forests with shrubby undergrowth, low shrubs and trees.

SPRING: First arrival is usually 25–30 April; migration peaks 1–15 May and ends by 15–20 May. Extensive notes support the sight record of a late migrant at the Van Dyke Tract of Blackbird SF, southwest of Townsend, on 7 June 1981 [Hess7]. High counts are

2 May 1982	8	Prime Hook NWR [Frec1]
11 May 1974	10	Dragon Run [Conw10]
20 May 1967	8	near Newark [Wayn2]

The May Count usually reports 20–40 birds; the highest counts are 94 (11 May 1974) and 89 (10 May 1975).

FALL: First arrival is usually 1–10 September. The migration peaks 15 September–1 October and ceases by 5–10 October. Early arrivals include

16 Aug 1969	1	Brandywine Creek SP [West13]
20 Aug 1972	1	Winterthur [Beac7]
27 Aug 1970	1 banded	University of Delaware woodlot [Jone2]

Usually 1–4 birds are reported, and the high count is 8 at Brandywine Creek SP on 24 September 1980 [Edni42]. Late fall reports are few, ending with a cluster in late November:

26 Nov 1967	1	Assawoman WA [Lake5]
27 Nov 1966	2	Redden SF [PetA2]
29 Nov 1928	male and female	Christiana [Dick1]

In the 1991 Neotropical migrant study (Mabey et al. 1993) 70% of the Black-throated Blue Warblers were reported during 7–29 September (*n* = 118), the last on 13 October.

WINTER: Notably, a Black-throated Blue Warbler arrived at a suet feeder in Newark on 29 November 1988 and successfully wintered, being observed at the site until at least 1 March 1989 [RusJ2].

SPECIMENS: 22; DMNH, UDEL.

Yellow-rumped Warbler *(Dendroica coronata)*

Regular; winter resident; fairly common. Expected mid-September to mid-May and sporadically into June.

HABITAT: Wet or damp forests, brushy areas.

SPRING: This winter resident is fairly common into spring. The migration begins 1–5 April, peaks 15 April–15 May, and concludes by 15–20 May. Late reports are

2 Jun 1973	2	Dragon Run [Beac10]
6 Jun 1987	1	Red Mill Pond [Fint11]
13 Jun 1985	male	Red Mill Pond [Fint14]

A published report for White Clay Creek on 19 June 1976 is not corroborated by the original field report [RusJ7]. High counts are

20 Apr 1974	95	Dragon Run [Wayn49]
1 May 1988	200	around Lewes [Frec1]
10 May 1980	100	Churchmans Marsh [Palm4]

The May Count usually reports 200–300 birds. The highest counts are 598, 680, and 922, on the earliest May Counts (3 May 1980, 5 May 1984, and 4 May 1985, respectively).

FALL: Yellow-rumped Warblers seldom arrive before 10–20

September. The migration peaks 5 October–1 November and ceases by 20–30 November. Banding data corroborate the observed peak [Usfw2]. Early records include 1 at Assawoman WA on 20 August 1984 [Edni20] and 1 at Bombay Hook NWR on 22 August 1954 [Kerr1]. A published report of 2 along White Clay Creek on 21 August 1976 [Dyer7] does not appear on the original field report. High counts of about 1,000 were obtained at Cape Henlopen SP on 15 October 1980 [Frec1] and at Assawoman WA on 16 October 1971 [Gail1].

1966–89 CBC Summary

Christmas Bird Count	Years Found	Range of No. Found	Median
Wilmington	19	1–53	4
Middletown	24	6–182	37
Bombay Hook	24	19–422	102
Cape Henlopen	24	28–1,170	383
Rehoboth	24	163–1,279	534
STATEWIDE (low in 1989, high in 1974)	24	426–2,787	1,327

WINTER: This is the most common of the few warblers that winter in our area. No CBC trend is apparent, because the numbers present vary too much from winter to winter. The

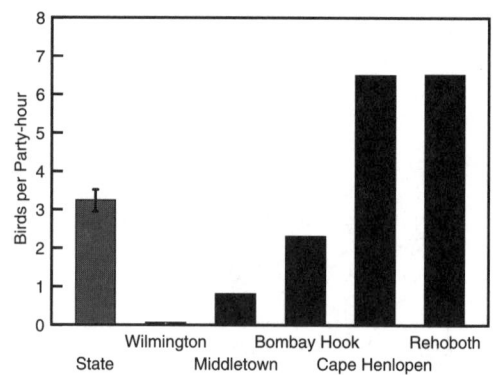

CBC Geographic Distribution

high CBC count was obtained on the 1959 Rehoboth CBC, and the high non-CBC count is 1,000 at Prime Hook NWR on 19 December 1982 [Frec1]. This warbler is progressively more common southward on CBCs.

SPECIMENS: 28; DMNH, ANSP, UDEL. We are not aware of any Audubon's Warbler (*Dendroica coronata* [*auduboni* group]) specimens.

[Black-throated Gray Warbler *(Dendroica nigrescens)*]

DOCUMENTATION: None.

REMARKS: An individual of this species was reported at

Cape Henlopen SP on 9 October 1994 (Boyle et al. 1995). No notes or photographs are available.

Black-throated Green Warbler *(Dendroica virens)*

Regular; migrant; uncommon. Expected late April to late May and early September to mid-October.

HABITAT: Deciduous forests.

SPRING: Black-throated Green Warblers arrive earlier than many other warblers, 25 April–1 May. The migration peaks 5–20 May and concludes 20–30 May. The earliest arrival was seen at White Clay Creek on 11 April 1972 [Barn2]. The latest spring migrant was found in the Wilmington area on 2 June 1973 [Falk6]. Highest counts include

11 May 1974	5	Dragon Run [Conw10]
15 May 1984	6	west of Lewes [Frec1]

The May Count usually reports 15–50, though an extraordinary high of 138 was recorded on 5 May 1984.

FALL: First arrival is usually 25 August–1 September. The

main passage is from 5 September to 10 October, and migration ends by 15–20 October. Extreme dates of migration are

23 Aug 1980	1	Churchmans Marsh [Kell8]
24 Aug 1969	1	Brandywine Creek SP [Wayn68]
25 Aug 1984	1	Assawoman WA [RusJ10]
31 Oct 1971	1	Assawoman WA [DuPA4]
1 Nov 1981	1	Winterthur [RusR11]
2 Nov 1980	1	Wilmington [Homs1]

The high counts are 22 at Winterthur on 23 September 1972 [West19] and 15 at Brandywine Creek SP on 24 September 1980 [Edni42]. In the 1991 Neotropical migrant study (Mabey et al. 1993) Black-throated Green Warblers were reported from 31 August to 6 October ($n = 58$), 60% of them from 28 September to 6 October.

SPECIMENS: 8; DMNH, ANSP, UDEL, UWBM.

[Hermit Warbler *(Dendroica occidentalis)*]

One report (1981).

DOCUMENTATION: Unpublished notes.

REMARKS: The sighting took place at White Clay Creek on 25 September 1981 [Jahn9]. The crucial point in the notes is "absolute yellow head and face." The back was described as "grey and olive color mixed." The description is correct for a Hermit Warbler and appears to exclude other species. However, the Hermit Warbler is sufficiently unlikely that a more detailed description or some additional confirmation is required. The record must be regarded as uncorroborated.

The Hermit Warbler, which breeds in coniferous forest from the Sierra Nevada west and has been reported as a vagrant in Nova Scotia, Massachusetts, and Connecticut (AOU 1983), closely resembles the Black-throated Green and Townsend's warblers.

Blackburnian Warbler *(Dendroica fusca)*

Regular; migrant; uncommon. Expected May and late August to late September.

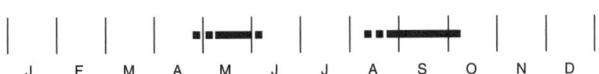

HABITAT: Various forest types.

SPRING: First arrivals usually appear 5–10 May. The migration peaks 10–20 May and concludes by 25–30 May. About a half-dozen reports before the second week of May have accumulated, the earliest and latest are

28 Apr 1989	1	Alapocas Woods [Zeit1]
29 Apr 1989	2	Lums Pond SP [Litt5]
30 Apr 1974	1	west Wilmington [Nile1]
3 Jun 1984	1	Lewes area [Frec1]

Most reports total 1–4 birds, and the May Count usually totals 1–10, with highest counts of 15 and 29 (11 May 1974 and 14 May 1988).

FALL: First arrival is usually 20–30 August. The migration peaks during 1–20 September and ends by 25 September–1 October. Early and late reports include

8 Aug 1988	1	Middle Run, north of Newark [Edni69]
15 Aug 1964	1	Hoopes Reservoir [SpSB12]
15 Aug 1970	1	Brandywine Creek SP [WarD4]
4 Oct 1981	1	Bombay Hook NWR [Hess2]
4 Oct 1984	1	west of Lewes [Frec1]

Most reports total only a few birds, but as many as 10 have been recorded, once on 13 September 1964 at Hoopes Reservoir [FalD2] and again on 12 September 1971 at Brandywine Creek SP [BroW17].

SPECIMENS: 6; DMNH, UDEL.

Yellow-throated Warbler *(Dendroica dominica)*

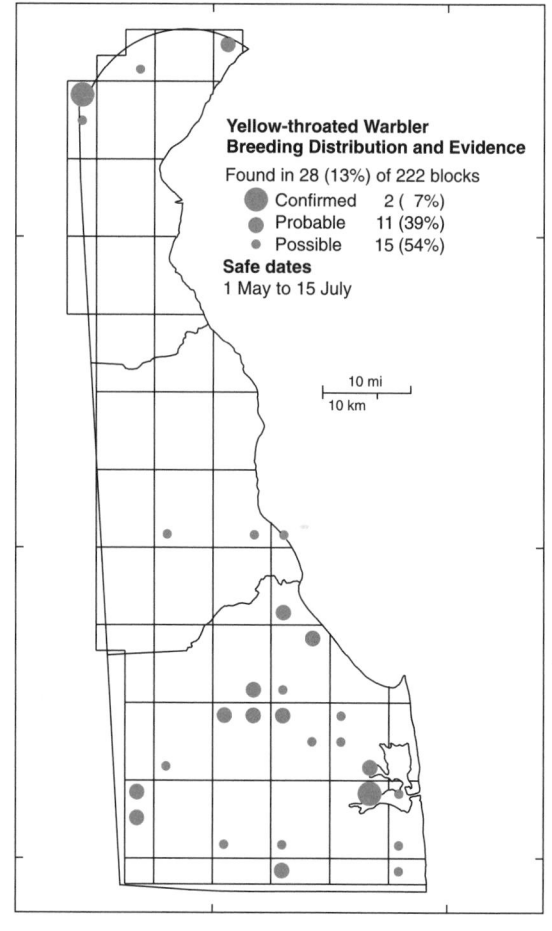

**Yellow-throated Warbler
Breeding Distribution and Evidence**
Found in 28 (13%) of 222 blocks
● Confirmed   2 (7%)
● Probable   11 (39%)
● Possible   15 (54%)
Safe dates
1 May to 15 July

10 mi
10 km

Regular; summer resident; uncommon, rare in the north, and absent between the Piedmont and Milford Neck. Rarely seen as a migrant away from its breeding locations. Expected mid-April to early September. The birds breeding in northern and southern Delaware may be different subspecies.

J F M A M J J A S O N D

HABITAT: Deciduous forests, especially with streamside sycamores, in northern Delaware. Open pine and mixed forests, preferably near water courses, in southern Delaware.

SPRING: Typical first arrivals appear 10–15 April with the earliest reports involving

29 Mar 1989	1	Bombay Hook NWR [Vand1]
31 Mar 1991	1	Trap Pond SP [Camp8]
2 Apr 1987	1	White Clay Creek [MiDP8]

The May Count, run about 9 May, records about 2 dozen birds in an average year. Unexpectedly, the May Count also reflects a 6% decrease in numbers, with each day later (during 3–14 May) that the survey is run. This corresponds to a 50% decrease in numbers with increasing date in May. Since a migration peak is not expected in Delaware, so close to the species' northern breeding limit, this decrease with increasing date may reflect withdrawal of some migrants that have overflown their destinations, or it may indicate that the species just becomes less conspicuous as May progresses.

BREEDING: Most Yellow-throated Warblers breed in the pines of southern Delaware, with Assawoman WA, Prime Hook NWR, Milford Neck, Redden SF, Cypress Swamp, and Nanticoke WA being typical breeding sites. However, a small population inhabits sycamore stands in northern Delaware.

Atlas. In southern Delaware a bird carrying nesting material was observed at Prime Hook NWR on 8 May 1985 [Frec1] and feeding young on 30 June 1987 on Long Neck [Brig1]. In northern Delaware nest building was observed in sycamores along White Clay Creek on 15 May 1984 [Line21]; that site remains the best to observe this species in the north. Other Atlas obser-

vations in northern Delaware include 1 singing throughout the 1984 season in Nottingham Green, Newark [Wels1], 2 in the Atlas block west of Hoopes Reservoir in June 1987 [Maie1], and 1 present in the summers of 1986 and 1987 near Arden [Quin1].

Nesting. No Delaware nests have been described, but the nest elsewhere is usually 15–60 ft up on a horizontal branch; it is a cup constructed of fine grasses and fibrous materials, lined with plant down; usually containing 4 eggs (Harrison 1978).

Nest building has been reported on 8, 15, 22, and 30 May, and feeding young on 30 June. Maryland egg dates begin on 16 May (Robbins and Bystrak 1977).

History. The southern and northern populations seem to be distinct (see "Remarks"), so their histories are treated separately.

This species was first found in Delaware at Seaford on 19 June 1903 and Frankford on 21 June 1903 (Rhoads and Pennock 1905), and a specimen was secured near Seaford on 7 May 1909 (ANSP 65476). The swamps of southwestern Delaware became known as the northern limit of its range (Stone 1919), and southern Delaware was still given as its range in 1939 (Barry) and 1957 (AOU). Reports from other locations trickled in: at

Smyrna on 26 and 27 May 1928 [Wcbc1], a nest with 4 young on 30 May 1936 near Millsboro [Buck9]; and near the coast on 17 Aug 1941 [Kram5].

The first northern Delaware sighting was made on 14 May 1966 at White Clay Creek [RusW4]. Nest building was observed there on 22 May 1971 (D. P. Miller with Dawson, pers. comm.), and a singing bird was present through 17 July.

Trends. BBS data suggest that its population has been fairly stable in the East for the past 25 years. It is regaining territory in the Central states (Evers, in Brewer et al. 1991) and expanding its range in the East in Pennsylvania and, in 1984, into New York (Carroll 1988b).

Breeding population. Breeding population density in good habitat in Maryland (territorial males per 100 ha):

70 (6 in 21 acres) in immature loblolly–shortleaf pine in Worcester County (Springer and Stewart 1948b)

FALL: This species slips by almost without notice during fall migration, which may begin in late July or in August. The latest date on record is 23 September 1972 at Winterthur [SpSB15]. Stewart and Robbins (1958) also lacked information and gave 10–20 September as the end of the normal period of occurrence and 27 September as the extreme departure date for Maryland. Seldom is more than 1 bird reported.

REMARKS: Yellow-throated Warblers of the Delmarva population are characterized by longer bills than those in nearby mainland areas. At Shad Landing, Maryland, on the Delmarva Peninsula, this species is confined to pine forest where it competes with its congener, the Pine Warbler. Ficken et al. (1968) observed that the Yellow-throated Warblers there were probing deeply into pine cones while feeding, a food location the Pine Warbler could not reach; as a result, competition was avoided. Presumably, southern Delaware birds are also of this same long-billed population. Pennock's specimen, collected near Seaford, is consistent with Ficken's description (ANSP 65476).

The Yellow-throated population in New Castle County is strongly associated with sycamores, not pines as in Sussex County. It also appears to arrive later—only 1 record before 17 April; additionally, the song of 1 on the Brandywine Creek during May 1991 was different, somewhat resembling a Yellow-rumped Warbler song (West pers. obs.). This suggests that Piedmont Yellow-throated Warblers may be part of an eastwardly expanding population of the midwestern *albilora* race (which commonly breeds in sycamores). If so, then these are comparable to 2 collected 80 mi to the north near the Delaware River, Hunterdon County, New Jersey, in June 1955 (DMNH 49393 and DMNH 49394).

These separate breeding populations may represent the northern limit, in Sussex County, of the southeastern race *(D. d. dominica)* and in New Castle County an eastern extension of the midwestern race *(D. d. albilora)*. A similar distributional pattern exists in New Jersey (Leck 1984). Mengel (1965), examining Kentucky specimens, found long-billed, white-lored individuals, and short-billed, yellow-lored ones, but he was reluctant to refer to any Kentucky population as *dominica* without a longer series of specimens. Perhaps we should refer to Delaware populations simply as pine-dwelling and sycamore-dwelling until more is known.

SPECIMEN: ANSP 65476, Sussex Co., Concord, 7 May 1909.

Pine Warbler *(Dendroica pinus)*

Occurs all year; summer resident; uncommon to fairly common in southern Kent and Sussex counties. Rare local summer resident in pine plantings in New Castle County. Rare in late winter.

| J | F | M | A | M | J | J | A | S | O | N | D |

HABITAT: Pine forest, including planted pines that have reached the pole timber size; lower densities in mixed pine–hardwoods.

SPRING: Numbers of reports increase beginning 1–10 March. Migration may conclude by 15–20 April, but this is not entirely clear from the Delaware data. More observations are needed from Sussex County from March through May to establish satisfactorily the migration and peak migration periods. Stewart and Robbins (1958) report 10–20 March to 20–30 April as the normal period, with the peak during 20 March–20 April, in Maryland. High counts are 24 at Prime Hook NWR on 28

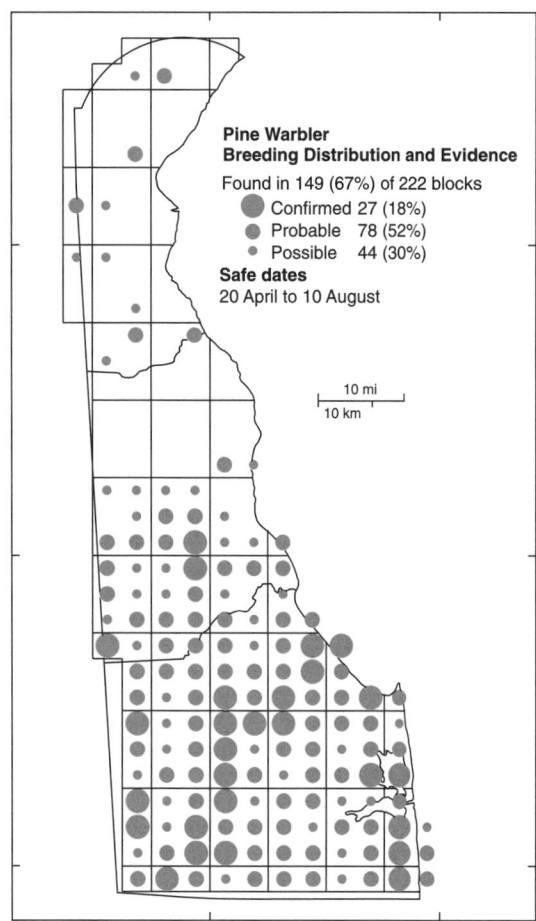

**Pine Warbler
Breeding Distribution and Evidence**

Found in 149 (67%) of 222 blocks

● Confirmed 27 (18%)
● Probable 78 (52%)
· Possible 44 (30%)

Safe dates
20 April to 10 August

10 mi
10 km

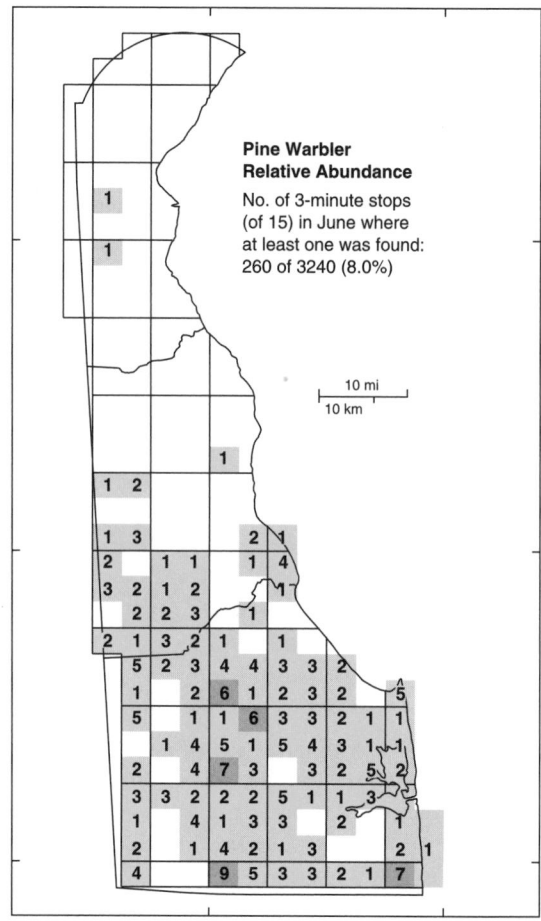

**Pine Warbler
Relative Abundance**

No. of 3-minute stops
(of 15) in June where
at least one was found:
260 of 3240 (8.0%)

10 mi
10 km

April 1985 and 35 west of Lewes on 5 May 1985 [both Frec1]. The May Count usually totals 90–115 birds; the highest counts are 148 and 136 (14 May 1988 and 13 May 1989), the lowest 52 (7 May 1977, following 2 severe winters; Robbins et al. [1986] report a reduction the same year on the BBS).

BREEDING: The Pine Warbler's range coincides with pine forests, which it requires for breeding. Highest concentrations occur around the Redden area, around Trap Pond SP, and near Assawoman Bay. The northernmost locations are in Valley Garden Park (near Hoopes Reservoir) and just to the west in planted pines.

Atlas. Confirmation occurred in only 18% of blocks. Two-thirds of the confirmations were the result of attending young and fledged young. Young out of the nest are exceptionally vocal as they follow adults for food, and the begging call led to many confirmations. Pine Warblers may have been overlooked in some northern locations where the species is much less common than in the south and its song mistaken at a distance for that of a Chipping Sparrow. Since the conclusion of the Atlas project, this species has been reported in Carpenter SP on 16 and 24 June 1990 [MiDP1], near where it was reported on 13 May 1973 [HalD2]. It was found near Greenville on 29 April 1975 (Niles notes) but was not reported there during the Atlas project.

Nesting. The first published nest record involved a nest with 3 eggs and a cowbird egg near Lincoln on 12 May 1935 [Buck10]. Three other nests have been reported. On 2 June 1957 in Sussex County a nest with 2 eggs was found 30 ft above ground in a pine; the cup was constructed of needles and twigs and lined with feathers (DMNH 9331). An early occupied nest was reported on 21 April 1985 near Ellendale [Litt6]. On 22 June 1986 in extreme southwestern Kent County, a nest with young was located 30 ft up in the crotch of a pine bough. Young were being fed once per minute and brooded 15 seconds at each feeding but did not appear over the edge of the cup [West3]. Atlas reports also included rather late dates of carrying food on 16 July 1984 [Wees2] and fledged dependent young on 11 August 1983 [Atch2].

Most clutches are completed in mid- to late May, but the extended season suggests some double-broodedness. Harrison (1984) suggested that this species has a long enough breeding season to produce 3 broods, but he did not establish double-broodedness.

The Pine Warbler is infrequently reported being parasitized by cowbirds (Friedmann et al. 1977); 2 of 17 nests were reported parasitized in Maryland (Robbins 1996). A male was observed feeding a begging cowbird fledgling at Trap Pond SP on 24 June 1983 [Edni4].

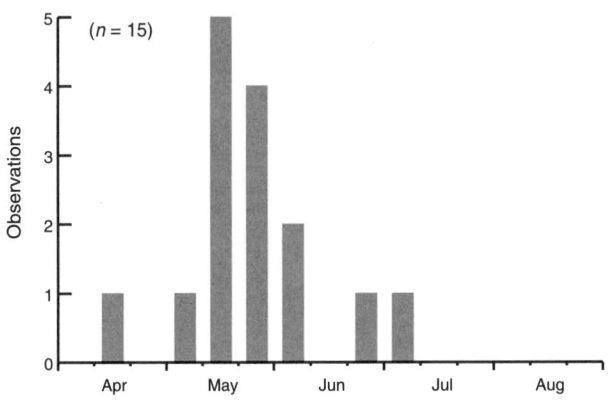

Estimated Clutch-Completion Dates

Trends. BBS data show it has increased in the East at an average of 2% per year since 1966 and at an average of 5% since 1981. BBS data have also shown a sharp increase in Delaware since 1981 but not a long-term increase [Usfw3].

Breeding population. Breeding population density in good habitat (males per 100 ha):

50 (average of 3.5 per 24 acres in 1966 and 6 per 24 in 1967) in coastal lowland mixed woods at Assawoman WA (Ward et al. 1966; Linehan 1965a)

Outside of Delaware:

190 (16 in 21 acres) in immature loblolly–shortleaf pine stand in Worcester County, Maryland (Springer and Stewart 1948b)

50 (6.4 in 32.2 acres) in pine–oak forest in Prince George's County, Maryland, in 1944 (Stewart and Robbins 1958)

Mixed pines appear to support fewer pairs than pure pines, and pine plantations at the pole timber size can support high populations.

FALL: Numbers of reports are high from 1 September to 5 October. Peak passage is probably during that period, though migration probably begins some time in August. The few reports from November presumably reflect a lack of observer effort in proper habitat. As in spring, more reports are needed from Sussex County to establish the precise migration periods. In the 1991 Neotropical migrant study (Mabey et al. 1993), the mid-70% of the Pine Warblers were reported from 31 August through 29 September ($n = 278$), the last on 20 October. High counts are 40 on 7 September 1974 [DuPG33], 75 on 24 September 1988, and 25 on 10 October 1987 [Frec1], all at Cape Henlopen SP.

1966–89 CBC Summary

Christmas Bird Count	Years Found	Range of No. Found	Median
Wilmington	1	1	
Middletown			
Bombay Hook	4	1–3	
Cape Henlopen	4	1	
Rehoboth	19	1–14	2
STATEWIDE	21	1–17	2
(zero in 1966, 1983, and 1985; high in 1977)			

WINTER: This is one of the few warbler species to attempt to winter, although in small numbers, in Delaware. Although November reports are few, the Pine Warbler is present regularly through early winter, as reflected in CBC reports. Reports are few between mid-January and mid-March, since the last of the birds disappear during the coldest part of winter. The high winter report is of 16 from the 1986 Seaford CBC. The few non-CBC reports involve 1–3 birds.

SPECIMENS: 15; ANSP, CM, DMNH, UWBM. Egg records: DMNH.

Prairie Warbler *(Dendroica discolor)*

Regular; summer resident; fairly common. Expected mid-April–mid-September. Although fairly common in Sussex County, it is uncommon in New Castle County and absent in much of Kent County.

HABITAT: Open abandoned fields with young growth of pines or other open brushy or scrubby second growth. Typically, old fields in New Castle County and cut-over forest or young pine plantations in Sussex County; still breeds in small numbers in scrub along the shore.

SPRING: First arrival is usually 15–25 April. The migration peaks 5–20 May and ends by 20–25 May. The earliest migrant

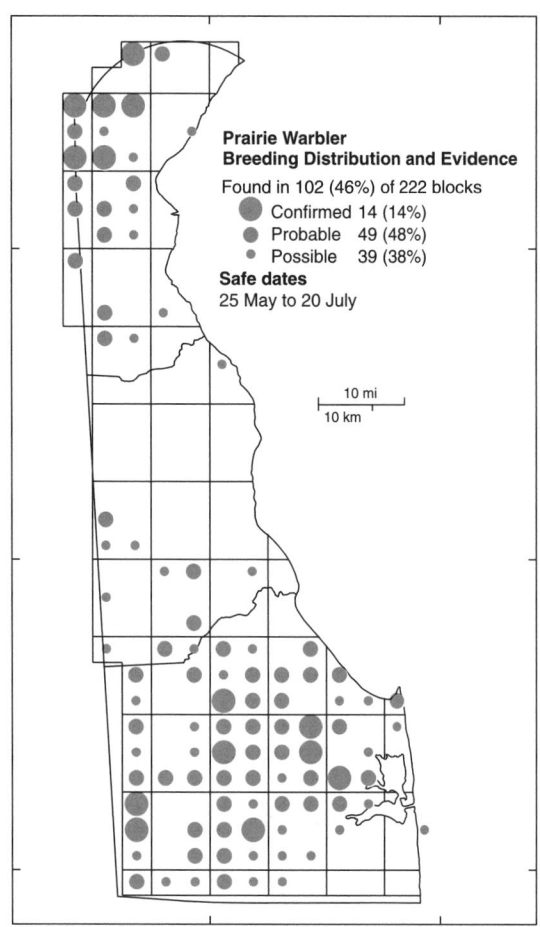

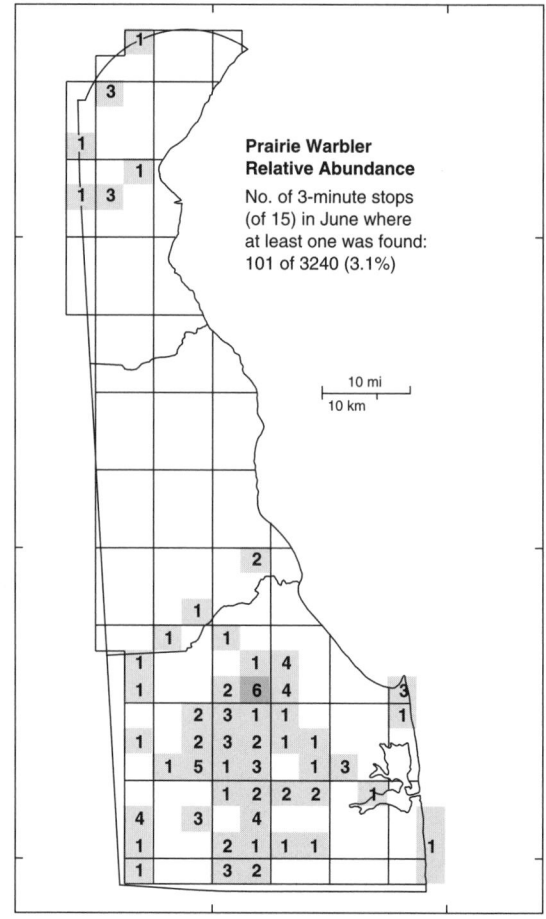

reported was at Prime Hook NWR on 14 April 1978 [Frec22]. Some high counts are

23 Apr 1977	9	White Clay Creek [Lehm23]
4 May 1974	10	Redden SF [Edni1]
20 May 1978	12	White Clay Creek [Falk11]

The highest May Count is 98 (7 May 1983), the lowest 31 (10 May 1969 and 12 May 1990).

BREEDING: Prairie Warblers are most frequently found in Sussex County, which has an active forest industry. Reverting farmland in New Castle County provides habitat for smaller numbers. Kent County harbors the fewest Prairie Warblers, since it has the least suitable habitat.

Nesting. The first nest described in our files was "6 inches above ground in a thick sheath of fresh shoots 15 inches high, well hidden by the thick foliage in a dry hardwood [shrub];" the clutch of 4 was collected on 25 May 1903 at Newport (R.F. Miller, LSU egg data). A nest made of leaves lined with grass and containing 4 eggs was found 8 ft up in a bush in Sussex County on 2 June 1957 (DMNH 9342). More recently, on 19 May 1972, a nest with 2 eggs (4 later) was found on a brushy hillside near Appleton Rd., Newark, about 30 in. above ground in a tangle of honeysuckle and sumac [Jahn12]. A nest, placed 4 ft up in an autumn olive shrub in the White Clay Creek valley, was found with 4 young on 30 May 1976 [Jahn1].

Based on these 4 records, estimated clutch-completion dates are 14–30 May. Breeding extends much later in Indiana; 15–18% of females successfully fledge a brood in early June and attempt a second (Nolan 1978, 430, 530). Nolan (1978, 188) found the average date for the last clutch completed was 14 July. Egg dates extend through 11 July in Maryland (Robbins and Bystrak 1977). Late breeding and some second broods should be expected in Delaware.

History. Before European settlement, this warbler typically would have bred behind the dunes at Cape Henlopen, along the Delaware Bay shore, or in early successional growth following hot forest fires. With forest clearing it has spread inland throughout a large part of eastern North America (Nolan 1978, 8).

Trends. BBS data indicate an average annual decrease of 3–4% in the Prairie Warbler population in the East but do not show a trend for Delaware [Usfw3]. The May Count shows an increase from 1969 through about 1983, and thereafter a decrease. Coincidentally, brushland in Delaware increased by 50% from 1974 to 1984 to 37,000 acres (Mackenzie 1989), but this scrub may since have grown too tall (over 13–20 ft or 4–6 m) to support Prairie Warblers.

Breeding population. Prairie Warbler territories averaged about 1.6 ha (4 acres) in Indiana study plots, but suboptimal sites had territories up to 4 ha (Nolan 1978, 332). A densely occupied BBC study site in Maryland had territories averaging 0.4 ha (1 acre) (Robbins et al. 1947). High summer counts on the weekly surveys include

4 Jun 1977	14	White Clay Creek [Barn62]
12 Jun 1971	11	Brandywine Creek SP [Beac6]
13 Jun 1964	13	Hoopes Reservoir [SpSB12]

Conservation. Its future abundance will depend on the amount of early successional habitat produced as a result of disturbance of the land.

FALL: Prairie Warblers move through without attracting attention. The migration begins 15–20 August, peaks 20 August–20 September, and ceases 25 September–1 October.

Late banding records mention 1 on 4 October 1966 [Armi2] and another on 8 October 1966 near Rehoboth Beach [RusW1]. Stragglers include

11 Oct 1981	1	near Wilmington [Boll3]
20 Dec 1969	1	Rehoboth CBC [Line22]
1 Jan 1971	1	Cape Henlopen CBC [John2]

Usual reports mention only 1 or 2 individuals. High counts include

9 Aug 1987	8	west of Lewes [Frec1]
11 Sep 1976	7	White Clay Creek [Boll5]
17 Sep 1979	6	Cape Henlopen SP [Frec1]

SPECIMENS: 7; DMNH, ANSP, UDEL. Egg records: DMNH, LSU.

Palm Warbler *(Dendroica palmarum)*

Regular; migrant; uncommon. Expected early April to early May and mid-September to late October, sporadic in early winter.

HABITAT: Wood edges, hedgerows, roadsides, and other edge habitats; open areas.

SPRING: One of the earliest warblers, the Palm first appears 1–5 April, peaks 10–25 April, and has pushed through by 30 April–5 May. Extreme dates for spring migrants are

3 Apr 1965	1	Churchmans Marsh [Stri3]
3 Apr 1971	2	Brandywine Creek SP [Broo2]
14 May 1975	2	Dover [Pure1]
14 May 1988	1	Cape Henlopen SP [Gord14]
21 May 1982	1	Centerville (DMNH 72297)
24 May 1982	1	Centerville (DMNH 72300)

Peak reports include

13 Apr 1969	15	Brandywine Creek SP [SpSB1]
16 Apr 1989	15	Brandywine Creek SP [Zeit1]
20 Apr 1974	18	Dragon Run [Wayn9]

It has been tallied on about half the May Counts.

FALL: The first arrival is usually 15–20 September, and the normal last departure 20–30 October. Its passage peaks from about 20 September to 15 October. The early dates are

| 8 Sep 1979 | 1 | Ashland [Rufe7] |
| 13 Sep 1982 | 2 | Assawoman WA [Frec1] |

High counts are 15 on 9 October 1988 and 8 on 13 October 1989, both west of Lewes [Frec1].

1966–89 CBC Summary

Christmas Bird Count	Years Found	Range of No. Found	Median
Wilmington	1	1	
Middletown	1	1	
Bombay Hook	11	1–7	
Cape Henlopen	11	1–10	
Rehoboth	14	1–16	1
STATEWIDE	21	1–16	4
(zero in 1968, 1986, and 1989; high in 1972)			

WINTER: This warbler is very rare in November and December. Most December reports are from CBCs and involve 1–5 birds, but 22 were recorded on the 1984 Seaford CBC. Late winter records are

24 Jan 1988	1	Cape Henlopen SP [Holg1]
28 Jan 1981	2	Indian River Inlet [Nile15]
27 Feb 1988	1	Cape Henlopen SP [Holg1]

No March records exist.

SPECIMENS: 10; DMNH, ANSP, UDEL.

Bay-breasted Warbler *(Dendroica castanea)*

Regular; migrant; uncommon. Expected May and early September to early October.

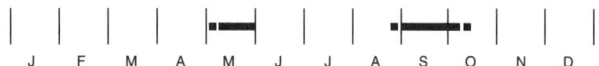

J F M A M J J A S O N D

HABITAT: Various forest types.

SPRING: Migration takes place entirely during May, beginning 7–12 May, peaking 15–20 May, and concluding by 20–30 May. Records from the first week of May include

| 2 May 1981 | 1 | Lewes area [Frec1] |
| 3 May 1984 | 1 | Lewes area [Frec1] |

The latest records involve

| 26 May 1985 | 1 | Sussex County coast [Barn45] |
| 27 May 1973 | 2 | Dragon Run [BroW11] |

Most reports total 1–3 birds, and the high count is 10 along White Clay Creek on 20 May 1978 [RusJ7]. This species has been recorded on about two-thirds of the May Counts (1969-1990). Numbers reported were usually fewer than 5, although 10 were tallied on 14 May 1988.

FALL: First arrival is 1–10 September; migration peaks 10–25 September and ends by 1–5 October. Early records involve

| 27 Aug 1977 | 2 | White Clay Creek [SpSB16] |
| 30 Aug 1969 | 1 | Brandywine Creek SP [Wayn25] |

A bird found on 10 October 1976 along White Clay Creek [BroW24] is the latest recorded. Most reports total 1 or 2 birds; the high count is 6 at Dragon Run on 15 September 1974 [WarD13].

SPECIMENS: DMNH 63336, Wilmington, May 1878; UDEL 176-68, Wilmington, May 1878; UDEL 97-66, Newark, 17 May 1966; DMNH 75579, Greenville, 21 May 1984; DMNH 77618, Newark, 6 September 1988.

Blackpoll Warbler *(Dendroica striata)*

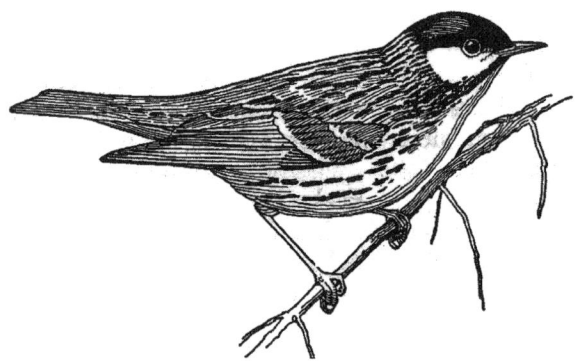

Regular; migrant; uncommon to fairly common. Expected May and September.

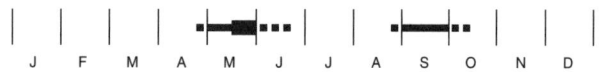

J F M A M J J A S O N D

HABITAT: Various kinds of forest.

SPRING: First arrivals appear 1–5 May. The migration peaks 10–25 May and concludes by 25–30 May. The early record involves a single bird at Dublin Hill, Sussex County, on 29 April 1984 [West11]. Late reports include

11 Jun 1987	1	east of Milford [RusR2]
14 Jun 1981	1	Prime Hook NWR [Frec1]
21 Jun 1976	1	Wilmington area [Conw5]

Typical counts total 10–15 birds. Some high counts are

21 May 1972	25	Winterthur [Broo16]
22 May 1983	24	Bombay Hook NWR [Bayn4]
24 May 1969	21	Brandywine Creek SP [Wayn25]

The May Count usually totals 20–30, but a remarkable 191 were recorded on 12 May 1979.

FALL: Migration begins 1–7 September, peaks 15–25 September, and ceases by 25–30 September. The earliest records mention

| 27 Aug 1977 | 1 | White Clay Creek [Rufe6] |
| 29 Aug 1979 | 12 | Assawoman WA [Frec1] |

Late records include

9 Oct 1965	1	Churchmans Marsh [Klab11]
9 Oct 1971	1	Brandywine Creek SP [Wayn25]
11 Oct 1980	1	Lewes [Frec1]

Most reports record 1 or 2 birds, but 1 high count mentions 10 at Hoopes Reservoir on 4 October 1964 [Falk12].

SPECIMENS: 10; DMNH, UDEL.

Cerulean Warbler (*Dendroica cerulea*)

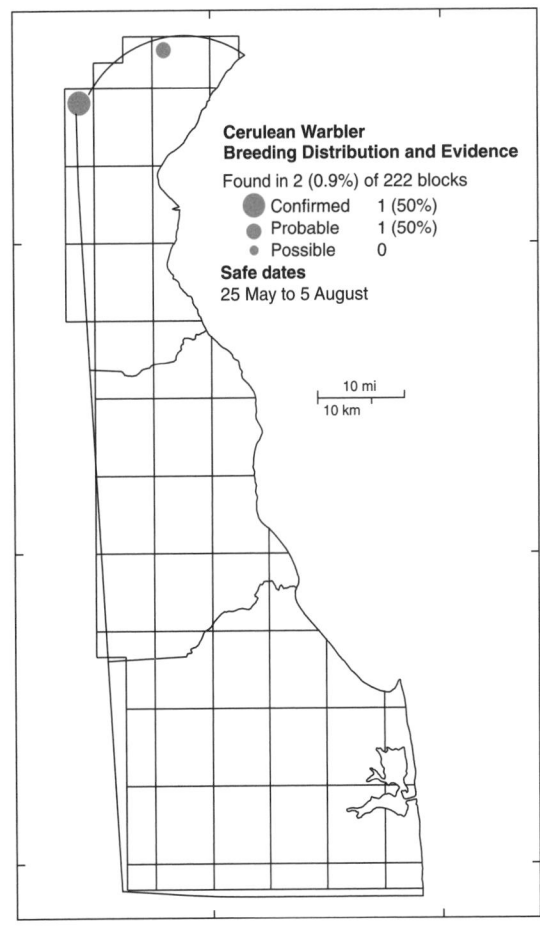

Cerulean Warbler
Breeding Distribution and Evidence

Found in 2 (0.9%) of 222 blocks
- ● Confirmed   1 (50%)
- ● Probable   1 (50%)
- ● Possible   0

Safe dates
25 May to 5 August

Regular; summer resident; uncommon and local in the Piedmont. Expected early May to mid-July, sporadically in August. Reestablished as a summer resident in the 1960s. Rare spring migrant away from breeding habitat.

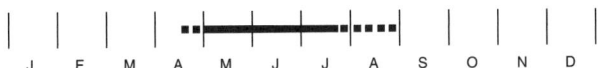

J F M A M J J A S O N D

HABITAT: Mature floodplain forests with sycamore and green ash in North Carolina (Lynch 1981, in Robbins et al. 1992). Large tracts (preferably > 1,750 acres or 700 ha) of mature, semi-open deciduous forest.

SPRING: First arrival is usually 25 April–5 May; migration ends 15–20 May. Early reports pertain to

18 Apr 1930	1	Milford [Buck3]
18 or 19 Apr 1976	1 or 2	Brandywine Creek SP [Niel1]
24 Apr 1972	1	Assawoman WA [Holg19]

In northern Delaware most reports involve 1–3 pairs. The May Count usually reports 4–10 birds, but the highest counts are 20 (9 May 1981), 17 (7 May 1983), and 14 (14 May 1988).

BREEDING: This species' arrival in the White Clay Creek valley in the 1960s was good news, especially since it established a breeding population.

Cerulean Warblers were first noted singing in breeding habitat along White Clay Creek on 17 June 1961 by A. R. Stickley [Broo1], in late May 1963 by F. H. Lesser (Linehan 1973), on 26 April 1964 [Broo28], and more than 1 in late May 1964 just north of the state line along White Clay Creek [Line11], where it successfully bred that year (West Chester Bird Club 1979). Thereafter they became increasingly regular, but the first Delaware nest was not located until 13 May 1972 (Linehan 1973). It was 40 ft up in a small crotch of a white ash, which grew in a field overgrown with sumac, blackberry, and black gum, a short distance from White Clay Creek. A cowbird was investigating the site on 17 May, the female was on the nest on 31 May, young were being fed on 7 June, and fledging started on 12 June when 1 of the 2 young hopped to a branch about a foot away from the nest after being fed. The second nest was located by C. Conway on 15 July 1972 when the 3 nestlings were being fed. The nest was unusually low in an osage orange, 17 ft above the parking area at Thompsons Bridge and about 20 yd from White Clay Creek. The nestlings fledged on 19 or 20 July (Linehan 1973; D. P. Miller, in Dyer et al. 1973).

Atlas. White Clay Creek remained the best place to find this warbler during the Atlas project, but records from the Brandywine Creek valley in 1986 and 1987 (Atlas notes) suggest it was expanding its breeding range. This treetop specialist's nest is difficult to locate, and the only breeding confirmed during the Atlas project resulted from seeing a bird carrying nest material.

Nesting. Its nest is often placed well out on a branch from 15 to 100 ft up in a fork. It is constructed of bark fibers, fine grass, lichen, and moss; bound with spiders' webs; and lined with hair and fruiting moss stems. Usually 4, occasionally 3 or 5, eggs are laid (Harrison 1978).

History. Though the Cerulean Warbler is primarily a bird of the Mississippi drainage, it was first discovered by Wilson in the early 1800s along Pennsylvania's Schuylkill River. He noted it as a rare summer bird in Pennsylvania (Wilson and Bonaparte 1859–60). It was originally part of the Delaware breeding avifauna too, but it disappeared when the deep woods that harbored it were cut down. Rhoads (Rhoads and Pennock 1905) reported finding Ceruleans in Delaware on 3–6 June 1903: "My surprise was great to hear the song of this bird mingling with that of the Prothonotary in the heavily timbered bottoms below the dam, and on down the river—Choptank. They were quite frequently seen, and kept to the higher treetops, where their actions showed clearly they were nesting. Two specimens were taken to make sure of the identification. They did not go into the highland woods adjoining the river bottom." Rhoads also reported them from Seaford on 18–20 June 1903, and Pennock from the Choptank bottomlands on 29 May 1904, when the female of a pair was observed collecting nest material (Pennock 1908). This record was cited as the northernmost location for this species on the East Coast by Stone (1919). Pennock (1935) and Barry (1939) gave the Rehoboth Beach area as another summer locality, but this was based on a possibly migrating pair seen on 14 May 1905 [Penn1].

This species is fairly common in the Mississippi Valley and recently has been expanding in the East. Delaware birds are part of a small Eastern population that expanded north to Connecticut by 1972 [CarP1] and Vermont by 1977 (Ellison 1985b). Poole described it in 1964 as breeding locally in the valleys of the Susquehanna and Delaware Rivers in Pennsylvania, but it is known to have become more widespread in eastern Pennsylvania (Ickes 1992a). It has been breeding in the Hudson Valley at least since 1922 (Connor 1988b) and first began breeding in New Jersey in 1947 (Leck 1984).

Trends. During 1966–87 Cerulean Warblers experienced an average decline on the BBS of 3.4% per year in the East (Robbins et al. 1992). This trend appears to run counter to the breeding-range expansion taking place.

Breeding population. About 12 pairs resided along the Delaware portion of White Clay Creek in 1984 [MiDP6]. The state population has probably been in the range of 2–20 pairs during most years since the 1960s.

Conservation. The Cerulean Warbler is thought to be one of the Neotropical migrants most sensitive to forest fragmentation in its breeding range, since it usually requires extensive tracts of mature deciduous forest (Robbins et al. 1989a). Preservation of woods in creek corridors may help retain the small breeding population in Delaware. It is on the USFWS list of migratory nongame species of management concern for the Northeast and North Central regions (Hamel 1992).

FALL: Cerulean Warblers are early migrants, often arriving on the Gulf Coast in mid- to late July (Bent 1953; Chapman 1907). Therefore, its sporadic occurrence in August—only 8 records—and the lack of reports thereafter are not unexpected; most probably migrate before August. Linehan banded 1 on 11 August 1969 at the University of Delaware woodlot [Usfw2]. The remaining August records were obtained on the 1976–78 White Clay Creek survey: 2 on 6 August, 1 on 13 August, 2 on 21 August, 1 on 27 August, and 1 on 28 August.

SPECIMENS: ANSP 48008 and ANSP 48009, Kent Co., Choptank Mills, 29 May 1904; ANSP 47780 (no locality given) 1903; ANSP 47779 (no date or locality given).

Black-and-white Warbler (*Mniotilta varia*)

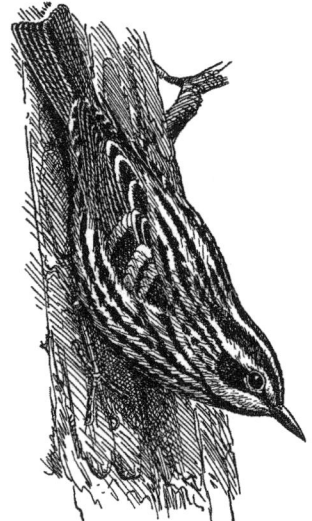

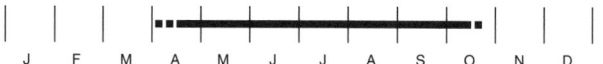

| | | | | | | | | | | | |
|J|F|M|A|M|J|J|A|S|O|N|D|

HABITAT: Various types of forests, especially mature moist deciduous woods; some breed in dense stands of young trees. Often seen in migration on trunks and limbs of large trees.

SPRING: Typical first arrival is 15–20 April. Migration peaks 25 April–10 May and ends by 15–25 May. A high of 37 was recorded at Dragon Run on 11 May 1974 [Conw10]. The highest May Counts are 310 (11 May 1974) and 146 (4 May 1985), the lowest 44 (10 May 1969, the first year of the survey). Typically, 60–120 birds are reported on the May Count.

BREEDING: This species is closely associated with remnants of moist inland forest such as are still present in Sussex County. Its probable decline since European settlement is undoubtedly related to clearing the forest.

Atlas. The Black-and-white Warbler is considered one of the Neotropical migrants sensitive to forest fragmentation in its breeding range (Robbins et al. 1989a). Other recent studies

Regular; migrant; uncommon; summer resident. Expected mid-April to early October. Increasingly rare breeder toward the northern part of the state.

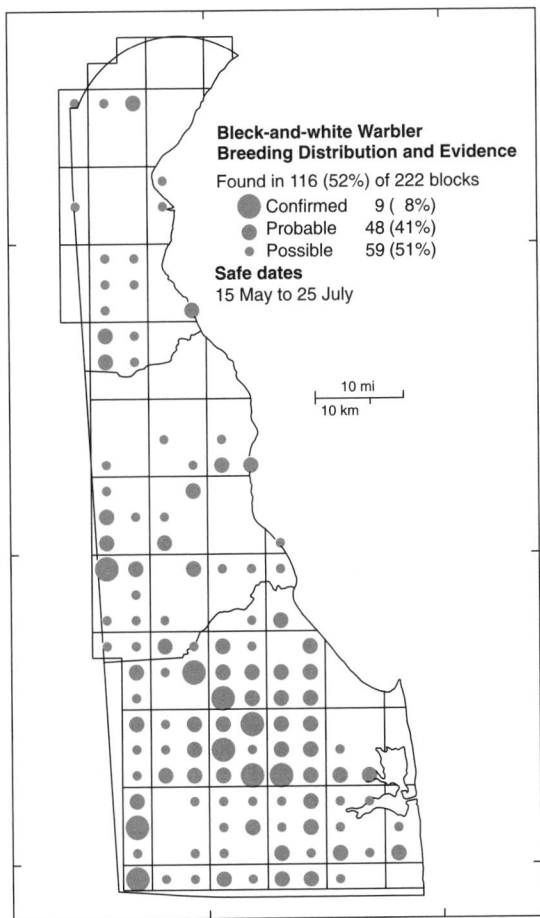

Bleck-and-white Warbler
Breeding Distribution and Evidence

Found in 116 (52%) of 222 blocks

- Confirmed 9 (8%)
- Probable 48 (41%)
- Possible 59 (51%)

Safe dates
15 May to 25 July

10 mi
10 km

Black-and-white Warbler
Relative Abundance

No. of 3-minute stops
(of 15) in June where
at least one was found:
35 of 3240 (1.1%)

10 mi
10 km

have also characterized it as intolerant of forest fragmentation in New Jersey (Galli et al. 1976) and in Maryland (Whitcomb et al. 1981). Despite these findings, its range in Delaware extends unexpectedly into Kent and southern New Castle counties in areas with very little forest cover. Comparison of the relative abundance and distribution maps with maps of forest cover and types, however, shows that it is most common in central Sussex County in areas such as Redden SF and parts of the Broad Creek and Pocomoke River drainages where there are substantial stands of moist woods. Although it can also be found in less wooded regions, its population there is much reduced and may not be self-sustaining. It was not reported from Brandywine Creek SP, Ashland, or Churchmans Marsh, all locations where it had been found in earlier studies, and its disappearance from those locations may have been the result of encroaching urbanization. Its ragged distribution suggests that this inconspicuous species may have been overlooked in some blocks, such as the Assawoman WA, where Dyke reported nests in the past [Dyke14].

Nesting. The first and only nest reported with details was found by Hanson at Moores Mill Pond in 1929. It was finished on 7 May, there was 1 egg on 11 May, and the bird was sitting on 2 eggs and a cowbird egg on 17 May and again on 21 May when the nest was taken. It was built with leaves as a foundation, of coarse plant fibers such as cedar bark, and lined with pine nee-

dles. It was 2 in. across and 1½ in. deep on the inside and situated in a bunch of leaves on the ground, partly sheltered by a laurel branch. No nest was found during the Atlas project; the few confirmations were made mainly by finding recently fledged young.

Egg dates in Maryland are 12 May–19 June (Robbins 1996), and clutch size is usually 4–5 (Bent 1953).

Trend. BBS data for Delaware show that the Black-and-white Warbler declined an average of about 4% a year during 1966–90 (a 37% decline). This downward trend is not shown either by the BBS results for the East or by the May Count in Delaware (both of which survey birds not breeding in Delaware), suggesting that it is declining in Delaware but not in other parts of its range. In 1905 Rhoads and Pennock described it as an abundant breeder throughout the state.

Breeding population. The only BBC on which it occurred in signficant numbers was the Avon woodlot (Linehan and Burr 1967), which was characterized as the youngest of a set of woodlots studied and as containing a permanent stream. In 1967 there were 3.5 Black-and-white Warbler territories per 27 acres (32 per 100 ha) at Avon; it was listed as a visitor there in 1966 and with less than a half territory in 1968. Six Maryland BBCs with good populations had densities ranging from 50 to 10 males per 100 ha (Stewart and Robbins 1958).

FALL: Migration probably begins 20–25 August, peaks 1–25

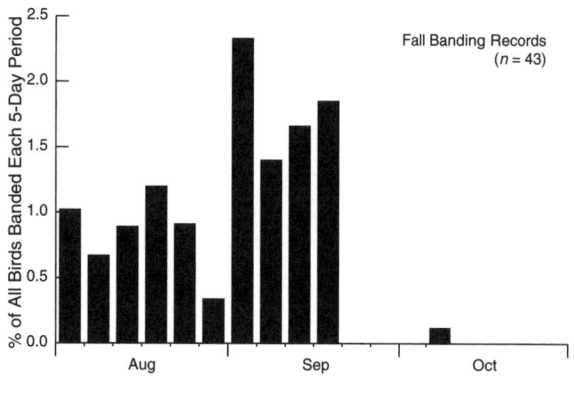

Fall Migration Activity

September, and ceases 10–15 October. Peak banding occurs 1–20 September. Late reports include

20 Oct 1984	1	Prime Hook NWR [Frec1]
20 Oct 1991	3	Eastern Kent County [Leit1]
21 Oct 1980	1	Cape Henlopen SP [Frec1]

High counts include

27 Aug 1977	17	White Clay Creek [Rufe9]
12 Sep 1971	15	Brandywine Creek SP [BroW17]
21 Sep 1974	13	Dragon Run [Falk13]

In the 1991 Neotropical migrant study (Mabey et al. 1993) 90% of the Black-and-white Warblers were reported during 17 August–29 September, 50% during 31 August–15 September (*n* = 579); the last 1% on 19–20 October.

SPECIMENS: 39; DMNH, ANSP, UDEL, UWBM.

American Redstart *(Setophaga ruticilla)*

Regular; migrant; fairly common; rare summer resident. Expected late April to early October. Extends spring migration into June, making interpretation of breeding data difficult.

HABITAT: "Second-growth river swamps and flood-plain forests." (Stewart and Robbins 1958).

SPRING: First arrival is usually from 25 April to 1 May. Migration peaks 10–30 May and ends 1–5 June. The earliest arrivals include

| 18 Apr 1974 | 1 | Cypress Swamp, Sussex County [Wees1] |
| 20 Apr 1984 | 1 | Cypress Swamp, Sussex County [Frec1] |

Extreme and average arrival dates given by Gross (1953) for southern Delaware are early by more than a month and cannot be supported by more recent data taken mainly in northern Delaware. Some high counts are

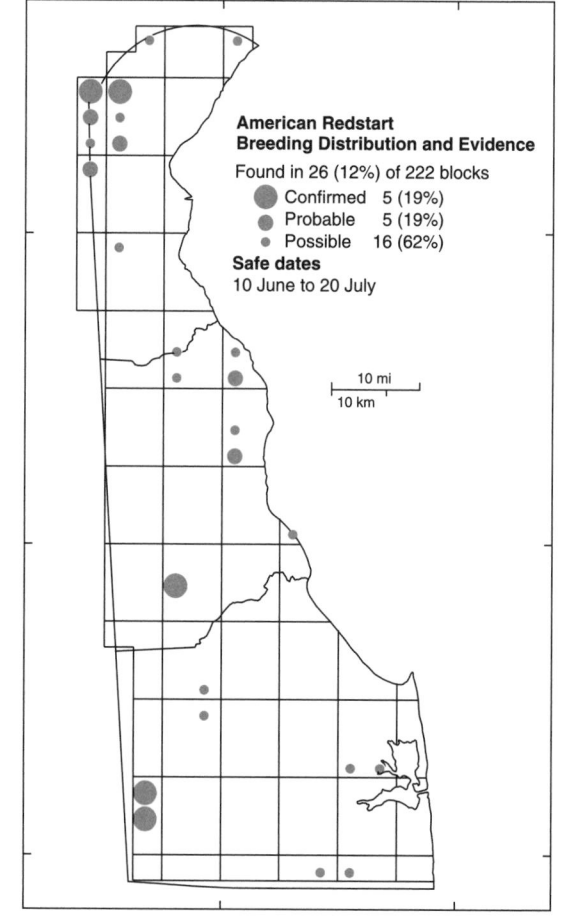

American Redstart
Breeding Distribution and Evidence
Found in 26 (12%) of 222 blocks
● Confirmed 5 (19%)
● Probable 5 (19%)
· Possible 16 (62%)
Safe dates
10 June to 20 July

10 mi
10 km

20 May 1978	42	White Clay Creek [Falk17]
22 May 1983	49	Bombay Hook NWR [Bayn4]
28 May 1977	33	White Clay Creek [MiPD15]

The highest May Count is 162 (14 May 1988), the lowest 20 (5 May 1973).

BREEDING: The redstart is a fairly common spring migrant with a prolonged migration period, thereby giving the impression of being a more common breeding bird than is actually the case. Breeding redstarts are uncommon on the Delmarva Peninsula except in the Pocomoke drainage south of Delaware (Robbins 1996; Ridd 1989).

Atlas. During the Atlas project no nests were found, but fledged young were reported 5 times from 18 June [RusR2] to 9 July [Pfef1]. Its greatest abundance appears to be in the well-studied northwestern corner of the state, especially the White Clay Creek valley. It may have been missed in some blocks because in order to avoid registrations of late migrants the safe dates start on 10 June, about 4 weeks after nest building begins. Atlas notes indicate that redstarts were found early in the breeding season in 45 blocks (20% of the state's area) where they were not found after 10 June (and in which they were not recorded on the distribution map). The bird remains vocally and visually conspicuous throughout the summer (Ficken 1962), so it should have been detected wherever it remained to breed. It has been reported from the following locations between 10 June and 20 July prior to the Atlas project but was not located in them during the project: Brandywine Creek SP; Dragon Run; Little Creek WA; and Sussex County near Lewes, Cape Henlopen SP, along Oyster Rocks Rd., and near Guinea Creek.

Nesting. Delaware nests have been reported at 40 ft (exceptionally high) in an ash, 20 ft above the ground on a sycamore branch, 20 ft above a stream in honeysuckle, 20 ft up in a walnut, 15 ft up in a catalpa, and 3 times at 20 ft up in crotches of slender hickory saplings. Typical nests are compact cups of grasses, fibers, rootlets, or tendrils, bound with spider web; ornamented with lichen flakes or other bits; and lined with fine grasses, fibers, and often hair. There are usually 4 eggs, sometimes 3 or 5 (Harrison 1978).

In Delaware most clutches are completed during the last third of May or in early June (*n* = 14). Egg dates for Maryland range from an exceptionally early 25 April to 20 June (Robbins 1996), showing how much the breeding and migration periods overlap.

History. A nest with 4 fresh eggs was found near Wilmington on 18 June 1871 (C.F. Phillips, *Forest and Stream* 6:67, 1876). Rhoads and Pennock (1905) each found redstarts breeding along the Choptank but supplied no details beyond "June 1903" and "May 30, 1904," respectively. Hanson reported a nest with 4 eggs along Red Clay Creek at Stanton on 1 June 1933. Three nests were being built on 11–12 May 1953 in the University of Delaware woodlot (Harmic 1953). Sitting females have been observed in the White Clay Creek valley on 28 May 1972 [MiDP16], 23 May 1976 [BroH3], and 7 June 1977 [Lehm3].

Breeding population. Because redstarts were reported from 26 blocks, it probably has a breeding population of over 100 pairs, but less than 1,000. High summer counts on the weekly surveys include

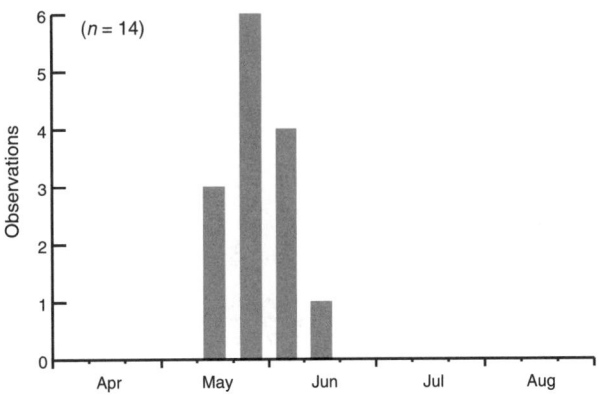

Estimated Clutch-Completion Dates

| 19 Jun 1976 | 33 | White Clay Creek [RusJ13] |
| 25 Jun 1977 | 11 | White Clay Creek [MiDP17] |

It was reported on a 1966 BBC where 3 males' territories were plotted on 20 acres in Assawoman WA (Linehan 1966). However, the field work for that study was completed by 5 June, probably too early to obtain reliable data on breeding redstarts. Its population appears to be stable in the East, as indicated by BBS. Its small population is not monitored effectively by the Delaware BBS, however, which detected 27 redstarts in the first 24 years, but only 5 after 10 June including:

14 Jun 1981	1	east of Milford [Patt2]
14 Jun 1975	1	Choptank Mills [Line5]
15 Jun 1975	3	Gumboro [Lehm4]

Trend and conservation. This species declined in the East during 1966–90 on significantly more BBS routes than those on which it increased. It may be declining in Delaware, where it is near the southern edge of its range. Its status in Delaware should be further studied to determine if redstarts are declining in the state as a breeding bird and to devise management strategies to prevent a decline should it exist.

FALL: Migration begins 15–20 August, peaks 1–25 September, and ceases by 1–15 October. Peak numbers of redstarts are banded in September. Late specimens and bandings include

14 Oct 1966	1 banded	near Rehoboth Beach [RusW1]
16 Oct 1975	1	Wilmington (DMNH 54669)
16 Oct 1932	1	Cape Henlopen [Buck12]
24 Oct 1975	1 banded	University of Delaware woodlot [Line4]

The latest sight records are

18 Oct 1975	2	Dragon Ru [WarD1]
21, 26 Oct 1953	1 immature male	Bombay Hook NWR [Spri1]
15 Dec 1973	2	Bombay Hook NWR [Holg23]

Some high counts are

28 Aug 1976	59	White Clay Creek [Wayn50]
8 Sep 1974	64	Dragon Run [John7]
12 Sep 1971	75	Brandywine Creek SP [BroW17]

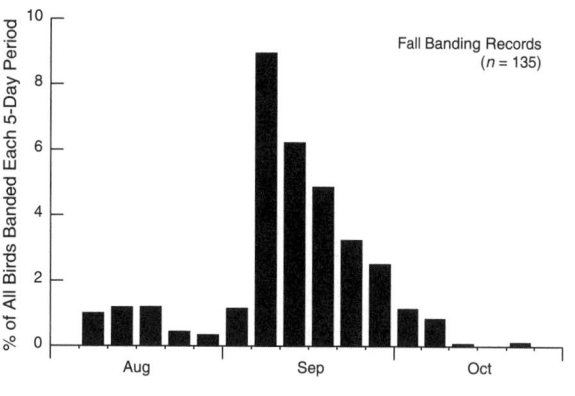

Fall Migration Activity

REMARKS: First-year male redstarts have plumage similar to that of females, though usually males display a few black throat feathers and also sing. Field workers in Delaware should distinguish older from first-year males in their reports. Ficken (1962) describes a number of behavioral differences characterizing first-year males. For example, the last of the older males arrive a week before the first-year males in Ithaca, New York. Consequently, younger males are left with less desirable territories and have less success in attracting females. They may cease defending territories after 2 weeks if they have not attracted a female and are more likely to become part of a "floater" population. Thus, in Delaware, an older male in late May is probably part of the breeding population, but in the absence of definitive breeding evidence a first-year male should be regarded as nonbreeding.

SPECIMENS: 34; DMNH, ANSP, UDEL, UWBM.

Prothonotary Warbler *(Protonotaria citrea)*

Regular; summer resident; uncommon. Expected early May to mid-August.

| | | | | | | | | | | | |
|J|F|M|A|M|J|J|A|S|O|N|D|

HABITAT: Swampy forest, wooded floodplains, brushy edges of mill ponds.

SPRING: Although this warbler is occasionally found as early as mid-April, it is not expected until 1–5 May. Migration peaks 10–15 May and probably ends 20–25 May. The high count involves 12 found on 28 May 1978 in the Pocomoke Swamp [Frec1]. The highest May Count is 61 (14 May 1988), the lowest 9 (10 May 1969 and 5 May 1973).

BREEDING: Prothonotary Warblers breed primarily in central and western Sussex County and in lesser numbers north to New Castle County.

Atlas. During the Atlas project the Specks and Wayne located the northernmost Prothonotary Warbler near Smalleys Pond on 25 June 1987 [SpeE18]. The next 3 Atlas records south along the western edge of the state are from the upper Chesapeake drainage (Bohemia River and Back Creek) and could have been in Maryland, since the Atlas protocol called for studying full blocks there regardless of the state line. The next 2 records to the south, still in New Castle County in the vicinity of Blackbird SF, were at the northern limit of its breeding range known before the Atlas project (Atlas notes).

Nesting. Rhoads described the nest he found in 1914 as constructed of "moss and dried grass in hole of stub 5 ft above ground, in swampy woods near river bank," a typical nest and site (WFVZ egg data). Not typical was a 1986 nest with eggs in a hunting coat pocket inside a garage near Seaford [MiDR1]. Other nests were in woodpecker and other natural cavities 3–6 ft high, and one in a nest box 4.5 ft above the ground [Hess4].

Clutch-completion dates extend from the first third of May through mid-June and peak in the last third of May (n = 12); clutch size is 2–6, usually 4 or 5 (n = 6). On the James River, Virginia, clutch completions were strongly bimodal, extending from about the first week in May to the first week in July, with peaks during 5–10 May and 10–15 June; 40% of the nests were late (n = 266). First and second clutches were typically 5 and 4 eggs (Blem and Blem 1992). It is double-brooded in Michigan (Walkinshaw 1941), but Blem and Blem do not have direct evidence for this in Virginia.

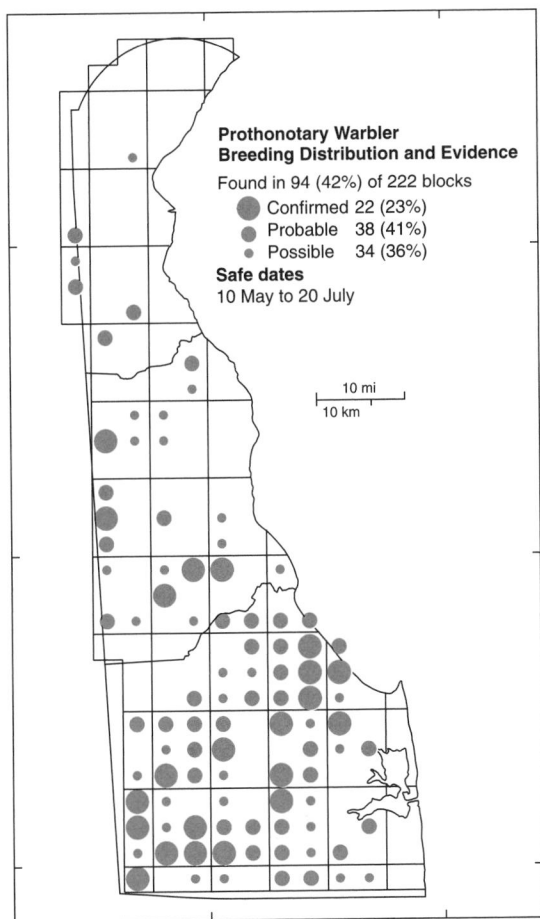

Prothonotary Warbler
Breeding Distribution and Evidence

Found in 94 (42%) of 222 blocks
● Confirmed 22 (23%)
● Probable 38 (41%)
· Possible 34 (36%)
Safe dates
10 May to 20 July

10 mi
10 km

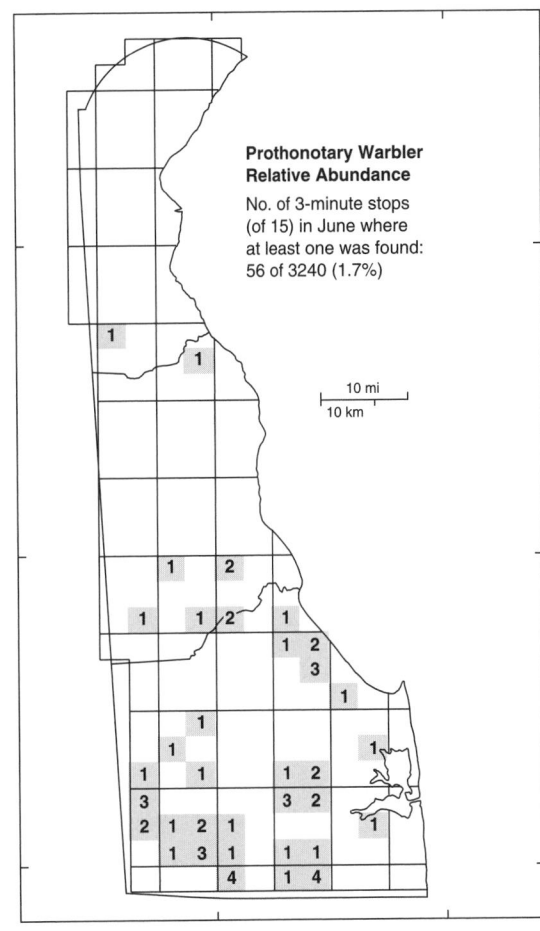

Prothonotary Warbler
Relative Abundance

No. of 3-minute stops
(of 15) in June where
at least one was found:
56 of 3240 (1.7%)

10 mi
10 km

History. Prothonotary Warblers may have become more common in New Castle County during the twentieth century, but the draining of forested wetlands surely reduced its presence in Kent and Sussex counties. The formation of millponds flooded other prime habitat, but the periphery of some millponds harbors some of the remaining breeding populations. The discovery of breeding Prothonotary Warblers in the Marydel area should be credited to I. N. DeHaven, Ardmore, Pennsylvania, who collected a Prothonotary Warbler on 13 July 1898 and saw 2 others at the head of the Choptank River (W.G. Smith 1899) [Penn1]. This record was considerably north of its known breeding range at that time and the first for Delaware. Rhoads found them abundant in the bottomlands of the Choptank below Marydel, where he found a nest on 3–6 June 1903, and he also found them at Seaford on 18–19 June 1903 (Rhoads and Pennock 1905) [Penn1]. Carter and Evans found a nest with 3 young on 3 July 1904 [Penn1]. The first specimen evidence of breeding is a clutch collected on 7 June 1914 by Rhoads and another collected on 19 June 1915 (both WFVZ egg data). The swamps of southwestern Delaware still remained the northern edge of its known eastern range in 1919 (Stone 1919; AOU 1910). A nest with eggs was found in the Choptank Swamp on 27 May 1928 (J. D. and J. H. Carter, DMNH mount). Hanson reported seeing a Prothonotary Warbler in the late 1920s near

Dover at Moores Mill Creek and Jones Creek; he reported another in shrubbery at 37 N. Bradford Street, Dover, on 11 May 1933. By the 1960s Redden SF and the Pocomoke Swamp were the most visited sites by observers seeking Prothonotary Warblers, and Bombay Hook NWR was known as the northernmost site. Hess added New Castle County to the breeding range when he found nestlings being fed on 7 July 1981 2 mi west of Townsend in habitat associated with a Delmarva bay [Hess 4]. The following New Castle County spring records should be ascribed to lone migrant or vagrant birds rather than breeders: shot near Wilmington by John Cassin (Turnbull 1869), near Stanton on 23 April 1927 [DicC1], Wilmington on 24 April 1972 [Nile16], White Clay Creek on 14 May 1976 (Speck and Brokaw 1979), and possibly the one at St. Georges on 17 May 1924 [Cart4]. A Prothonotary Warbler heard singing 2 mornings in May 1968 on a BBC along White Clay Creek near Windy Hills (Burr and Jones 1968) is suggestive of breeding and may have represented the northernmost breeding record in Delaware had further observations been made.

Trends. Both the Delaware BBS and the May Count indicate its population may have increased in Delaware since the 1960s, but the BBS data also indicate that, if changing at all, it is generally decreasing in the East [Usfw3]. The Delaware increase may reflect an extension of its range in Kent and New Castle counties where almost a third of the blocks with Atlas records lie, even though Sussex County harbors about 90% of the population.

Breeding population. Its density in good habitat can be quite high, 100 per 100 ha, in "second-growth river swamp" in Worcester County, Maryland (Springer and Stewart 1948c). Counting Prothonotaries from roadsides may lead to underestimation of its numbers since much of its habitat is not sampled by that method.

Conservation. Comparison of its range with the relative abundance map for the House Wren suggests that the Prothonotary does not commonly breed in areas of high wren abundance in eastern Delaware, Assawoman WA being a good example. House Wrens significantly compete for nest sites and destroy Prothonotary nests in Michigan (Walkinshaw 1941)

and Ohio (K.E. Petit 1988 in L. Petit 1989). In the Michigan study House Wrens and other predators destroyed over 100 eggs of 413 laid. Wasps (Blem and Blem 1991) are competitors for cavities in Virginia. In spite of such competitive pressures, the Prothonotary is expanding its range in the Northeast through New Jersey, Pennsylvania, and into New York (Eaton 1988d).

FALL: Lack of reports makes determining the onset of migration difficult. The latest reports include

| 12 Sep 1982 | 1 | White Clay Creek [Litt3] |
| 14 Sep 1986 | 1 | Red Mill Pond [Frec1] |

One to three birds are usually reported.

SPECIMENS: 16; DMNH, ANSP, UWBM. Egg records: DMNH, WFVZ.

Worm-eating Warbler *(Helmitheros vermivorus)*

Regular; summer resident; uncommon. Expected early May to late August.

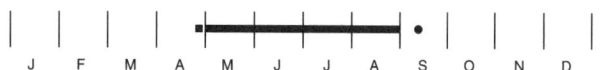

HABITAT: Dry upland deciduous forest with an understory of shrubs; prefers steep hillsides.

SPRING: First arrivals appear 1–5 May; migration concludes by 10–15 May. Although most reports mention only 1 or 2 birds, greater numbers can be counted by those with knowledge of the Worm-eating Warbler's habitat and song. Individual high counts are 10 on 3 May 1980 [Barn38] and 8 on 9 May 1981 [Barn54], both the result of all-day efforts in Sussex County. The highest May Count is 42 (12 May 1990), the lowest 4 (5 May 1984).

BREEDING: Breeds uncommonly in northern New Castle County and in greater numbers in southern Delaware.

Atlas. Although found in only 2 blocks in northern Delaware during the Atlas project, the Worm-eating Warbler is to be expected in the White Clay Creek valley. Roth's students have encountered it in the late 1980s in several wooded areas near Newark during studies of the Wood Thrush (pers. comm.). It is found in Sussex County in extensive pine–oak woods in the Pocomoke and Nanticoke drainages that have slight sandy ridges of well-drained soil in generally swampy woods. The May Count and the BBSs in Delaware and the East [Usfw3] suggest that its population has not changed much since 1966. Its relative abundance on the Delaware BBS ranks eighth among 21 states where this species is regularly recorded; its population is more concentrated to the west in Virginia, West Virginia, and Tennessee [Usfw3].

Nesting. The only breeding details we have for Worm-eating Warblers are observations made in the Oak Hill tract of Blackbird SF on 30 June 1986. An adult was observed in underbrush catching insect larva that it subsequently brought to a fledgling with short tails and stubby wings. The habitat consisted of mesophytic hardwoods of oak, maple, and sweet gum with an understory of blueberry and greenbrier [Edni4]. Other confirmations were for

6 Jun 1986	attending young	southwest of Towns end [Hess3]
24 Jun 1985	attending young	south of Trap Pond SP [West3]
24 Jun 1985	recently fledged young	northwest of Trap Pond SP [RusR2]
25 Jun 1983	attending young	Trap Pond SP [Nile10]

Apparently the last week in June is the time of loudest begging by recently fledged young.

This species nests on the ground, usually concealing its nest

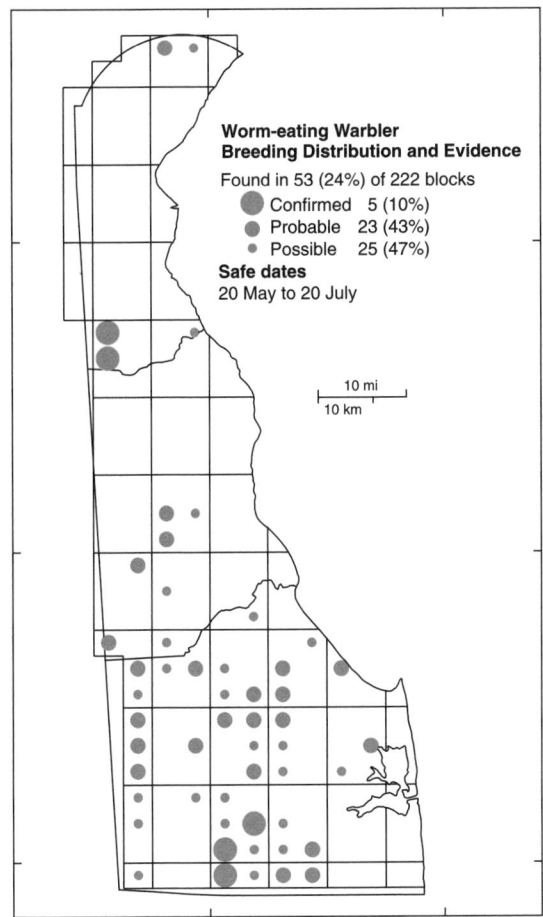

**Worm-eating Warbler
Breeding Distribution and Evidence**

Found in 53 (24%) of 222 blocks
● Confirmed 5 (10%)
● Probable 23 (43%)
• Possible 25 (47%)
Safe dates
20 May to 20 July

10 mi
10 km

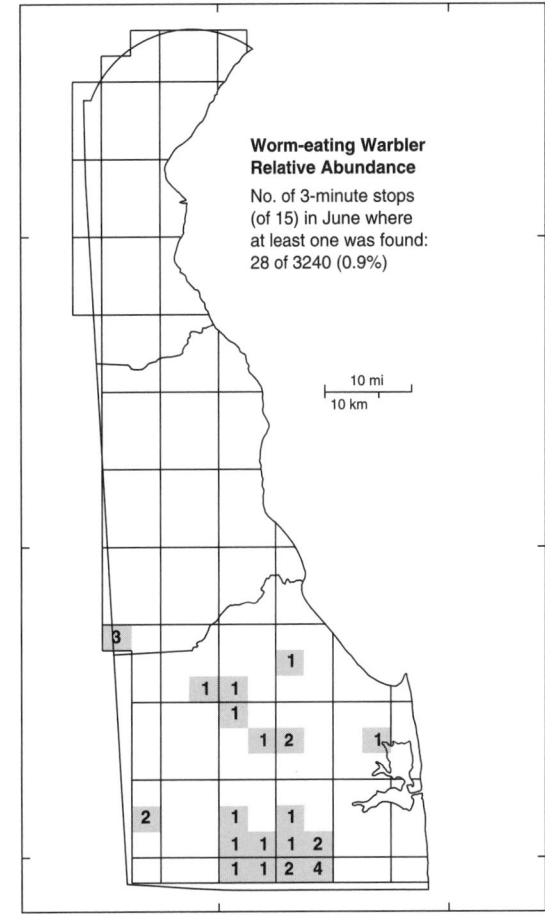

**Worm-eating Warbler
Relative Abundance**

No. of 3-minute stops
(of 15) in June where
at least one was found:
28 of 3240 (0.9%)

10 mi
10 km

in leaf litter on a slope at the base of a shrub or in a slight cavity; clutch size is usually 4–5 eggs (Harrison 1978). Egg dates for Maryland are 29 May–5 June (Robbins and Bystrak 1977); for Pennsylvania 15 May–30 June (Bent 1953). In southern Delaware steep wooded hillsides are nonexistent, and the species breeds in sites only vaguely resembling a hillside. Hess (pers. obs.) located a pair at the edge of a fairly deep Delmarva bay on the steepest slope in the area. West (pers. obs.) saw a nest in Maryland about a mile south of Delaware in the Pocomoke Swamp. It was at the base of a shrub growing on a sandy "dune" that sloped sharply down about 2 ft to the road.

History. The first record we have for this species involves 1 collected by Bush in New Castle County in May 1882. Rhoads reported 3 or 4 pairs feeding young along Brandywine Creek near Wilmington on 14 July 1903 (Rhoads and Pennock 1905). Barry, in 1939, reported "many records" in Delaware. More recently, in contrast, this forest interior specialist was not found in any of the small Piedmont woodlots censused in the 1960s (Linehan et al., 1967a) and only occurred on a BBC along White Clay Creek where the site was part of a large wooded tract (West 1970). In a Maryland study it was more frequently found in forest tracts larger than 50 acres (20 ha) (Robbins et al. 1989a). This factor seems to be the key to its almost complete disappearance from northern New Castle County during the

twentieth century as wooded tracts have yielded to suburban development. It has been reported in the Piedmont only 6 times during summer on the many weekly surveys since 1964, 3 times each at White Clay Creek and Brandywine Creek SP. It is more common in nearby southern Pennsylvania (Santner 1992b). Its presence in summer south of the Chesapeake and Delaware Canal went largely unpublished, though Carter mentioned it in an article on nest hunting in the Choptank Bottoms (1929); its occurrence at Pocomoke, Trap Pond SP, and Redden SF was apparently well known (Barry 1939) [Wayn1] and was suggested from the map in Stewart and Robbins (1958).

Breeding population. It is extremely difficult to survey for this species when the more common Pine Warbler and Chipping Sparrow are also present. Distance can distort the similar songs of these species, while road noise or nearby mockingbirds can make it difficult to decide during a 3-min stop which species is singing. Thus the Worm-eating Warbler may often be overlooked on such surveys. Although it should be easiest to detect in northern Delaware, its population there is so low that it is rarely encountered. The breeding density of Worm-eating Warblers on a hillside 6 mi (10 km) southeast of Frederick, Maryland, in chestnut oak woods was 100–150 pairs per 100 ha (Greenberg 1987). Its density in Delaware woods is considerably less, but no studies have been conducted.

FALL: Virtually no fall reports are available. The latest records include

4 Sep 1971	1 banded	University of Delaware woodlot [Line4]
8 Sep 1979	1	near Wilmington [Nile14]
9 Sep 1990	1	Middle Run [Barn42]
10 Sep 1894	1	Wilmington (DMNH 8198)
2 Oct 1962	1	St. Georges (UF 19218)

In the 1991 Neotropical migrant study (Mabey et al. 1993) 85% of the Worm-eating Warblers were reported from 17

August to 1 September ($n = 12$). Stewart and Robbins (1958), writing about Maryland, report migration extends from 10–20 August to 10–20 September, with the peak 20 August–10 September.

SPECIMENS: DMNH 63343, Wilmington, May 1882; DMNH 76476, Wilmington, 8 May 1987; UDEL 84-66, Newark, 11 May 1966; UDEL 85-66, Newark, 12 May 1966; DMNH 8198, Wilmington, 10 September 1894; UF 19218, St. Georges, 2 October 1962.

Swainson's Warbler (*Limnothlypis swainsonii*)

Casual (1949, 1957, 1988); local.

HABITAT: "River and stream swamps, being most numerous in the drier portions with partially opened canopy, and with dense understory brush composed of greenbrier, sweet pepperbush, and other shrubs" (Stewart and Robbins 1950).

REMARKS: Since there is hope of finding the Swainson's Warbler breeding again in Delaware, because they still breed in the nearby Pocomoke drainage of Maryland, additional notes on habitat for the Delmarva Peninsula are included. Preferred nesting habitat is a sweet pepperbush and greenbrier thicket in the higher portion of a swamp that is otherwise constantly boggy, where the swamp is in a stage of secondary succession after being cut over to the extent that only second growth remains. In the drier portions of the Pocomoke Swamp, near the Delaware line, a heavy growth of laurel is found in which an occasional Swainson's Warbler is singing. Although this bird occasionally occurs where the ground is swampy or boggy, deep shade, moderately dense undergrowth, and dry land are generally characteristic of most of its breeding habitat. A rather sparse undergrowth and ground cover would seem to fit its quick feeding motion on the ground. A thin or rather flat

leaf litter also seems to suit it. In some habitats—for example, the cypress bay—the general aspect or structure of the area may be extremely dense. However, its niche is usually where the shrubs are the least dense and in small openings between clumps of greenbrier or other undergrowth (from Meanley 1950, 1966, for the Delmarva peninsula). It prefers seasonally wet swamp, composed of shrubs, reeds, and small trees (du Pont 1973).

BREEDING: Although the AOU Check-list (AOU 1983) includes southern Delaware in this species' breeding range, there is only 1 valid breeding record and 2 other reliable reports. The breeding record is represented by a clutch of 4 (DMNH 9266) obtained "about 2 miles west of Bethany Beach" on 25 May 1957. The following observations are regarded as having been obtained in Delaware: 1 on 14 May 1988 at Cedar Swamp, near Gumboro [SpSB27], and another on 30 May 1949 at Pocomoke Swamp (Meanley 1950). Reports from 1971 and 1973 are believed to refer to birds located in Maryland. A September 1966 report of an individual singing north of Rehoboth Beach is not acceptable as published. The May Count report from 1978 is insufficiently documented.

Nesting. The only nest reported was made of grass and reeds and situated 18 in. up in reeds (du Pont 1973). The nest is larger and bulkier than those of most warblers; clutch size is usually 3. Earliest nest building reported for the Dismal Swamp, Virginia, is on 23 April; 2 others were under construction there on 1 May. In the Pocomoke Swamp, Maryland, on 15 May a bird was captured with an egg in the oviduct ready to be laid; on 13 July newly hatched young were observed; and on 20 June adults were observed feeding young out of the nest. Perhaps the latest nest involves one with eggs reported by Perry on 13 July 1886 at Savannah, Georgia (Meanley 1971).

Conservation. The Swainson's Warbler is listed as a Species of Special Concern in Maryland. If breeding is rediscovered in Delaware (Shoch 1991), measures to protect the birds must be put into effect quickly.

SPECIMEN: Egg record: DMNH 9266, details in preceding.

Ovenbird *(Seiurus aurocapillus)*

Regular; summer resident; fairly common. Expected mid-April to late September, sporadically into October.

HABITAT: Well-drained upland, deciduous canopied forest.

SPRING: Migration begins 20–25 April, peaks 1–20 May, and concludes 25–30 May. The earliest records are

7 Apr 1991	1	Middle Run, Newark [Barn54]
11 Apr 1960	1	Millsboro [Davi14]
12 Apr 1992	1	Assawoman WA [Atch1]

The average and extreme arrival dates given by Gross (in Bent 1953, 474) for southern Delaware cannot be supported by data taken mainly in northern Delaware and are early by about a week. High counts are

15 May 1976	30	White Clay Creek [Broo25]
23 May 1988	28	Middle Run, Newark [Edni3]

The highest May Count is 400 (7 May 1983), the lowest 132 (10 May 1969, the first year of the count).

BREEDING: Its loud voice and terrestrial habits cause this warbler to be heard long before it is seen. The areas where it was not found in southwestern New Castle and eastern Kent counties have little suitable breeding habitat, the woods there being reduced to narrow strips along stream corridors.

Atlas. During the Atlas project migrants may have been reported from some blocks because data were accepted starting 20 May. Late migration was not fully appreciated when the safe dates were chosen, and some migration may still be in progress after that date. This problem is probably minor, however, since the Ovenbird is common and most areas that would attract migrants would also attract a breeding population. Of the 40 confirmed reports, 27 involved fledged young or attending young. Active nests were reported from only 7 blocks; nest building was reported in 2 other blocks. The Ovenbird's distraction display was reported 3 times.

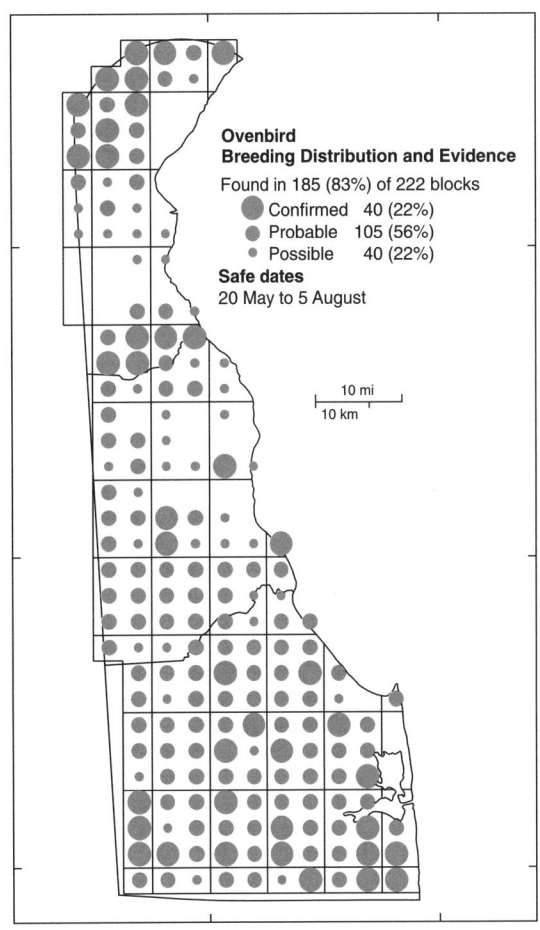

Ovenbird
Breeding Distribution and Evidence
Found in 185 (83%) of 222 blocks
- Confirmed 40 (22%)
- Probable 105 (56%)
- Possible 40 (22%)

Safe dates
20 May to 5 August

10 mi
10 km

Nesting. Hanson described a nest found west of Dover on 17 June 1924: "The nest was typical, roofed over, with the entrance on the south side. It was in the dry leaves of the rather open woods, about 6 inches high, 6 inches across from side to side, and 4 inches from front to back. Inside the opening was about 2.5 inches in diameter. It was rather loosely constructed of grass mixed with a few leaves, lined with finer grass and a few horse hairs." It contained 3 Ovenbird eggs and 2 cowbird eggs.

Clutch completion clearly peaks in late May. The June dates, after a gap, may be second clutches or renestings after failure. Second broods are reported rarely in Michigan (Hann 1937) but frequently in Ohio (Peterjohn and Rice 1991.)

The earliest egg date reported in Delaware is 5 May—3 eggs plus 2 cowbird eggs in Sussex County [Nile12]. Four nestlings were found on 16 May [Buck1]. Extreme fledgling dates are 28 May and 2 August [Lehm3, SpeE3]. Of 8 Delaware clutches reported, 5 had 3 eggs, 2 had 4 eggs, and 1 had 5 eggs. Hann (1937) reports 3–6 eggs, usually 4 or 5.

Trends. The BBS has generally detected a variable population with no long-term trend, but for the period 1980–89

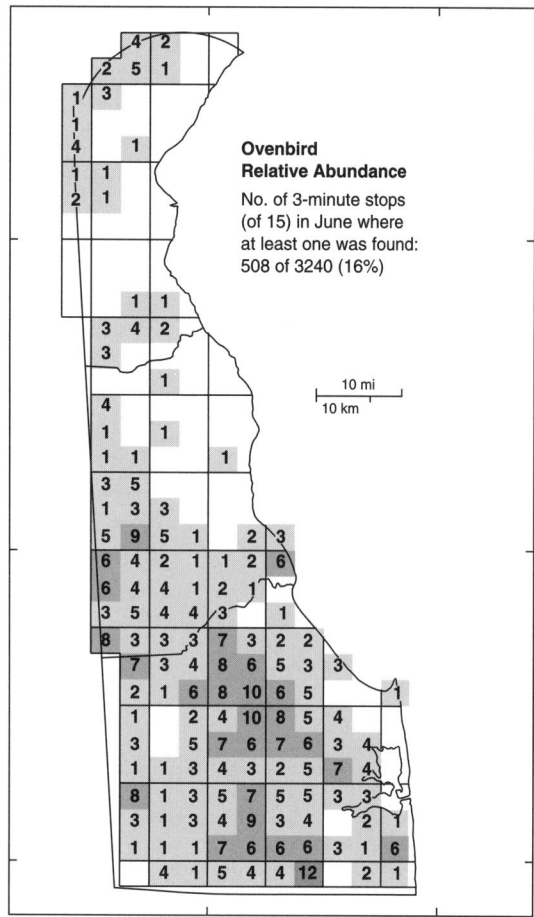

Ovenbird
Relative Abundance

No. of 3-minute stops
(of 15) in June where
at least one was found:
508 of 3240 (16%)

10 mi
10 km

| 21 June 1964 | 12 | Hoopes Reservoir [SpSB12] |
| 23 June 1979 | 9 | Ashland [Conw14] |

In the isolated Piedmont woodlots studied, its population was usually much reduced (Linehan, Jones, and Longcore 1967), from none to about 25 pairs per 100 ha; the Tulip Tree Woods at Brandywine Creek SP had 50–100 pairs per 100 ha (West et al. 1966; West 1967), but this woods is joined with others by a wide corridor. In Assawoman WA the average density for 2 sites was 37 per 100 ha (Linehan 1965a; Ward et al. 1966; Linehan 1969a; McLaughlin 1968). It is surprising to find a higher density in Sussex County in the mixed woods than in the Piedmont, where the rolling deciduous woodland appears ideal for the Ovenbird. Outside of Delaware it shows increasing abundance toward the north, becoming about 5 times more abundant in Ontario as in Delaware (Robbins et al. 1986).

Conservation. The Ovenbird is a forest interior species subject to the effects of forest fragmentation (Robbins et al. 1989a). Its population in northern Delaware is particularly at risk.

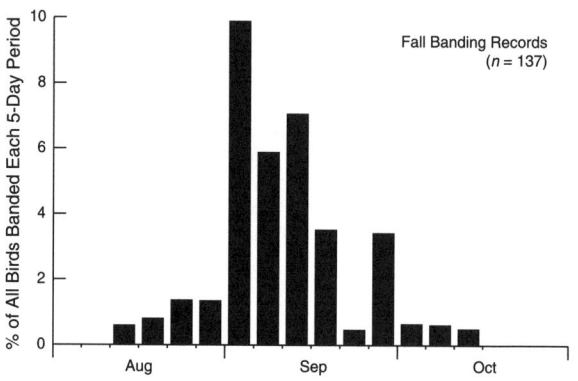

Fall Banding Records
(*n* = 137)

Fall Migration Activity

FALL: An increase in the number of reports beginning 20–30 August marks the onset of fall migration. Peak migration is from 1–15 September. Banding data extend the peak another 5 days. Most leave by the end of the month, but birds occasionally linger to 15 October. Four late specimens were taken on 1–6 October, all from Wilmington (DMNH 44130, DMNH 44374, DMNH 52274, DMNH 63262). Eleven birds were banded during 6–15 October [Usfw2]. Late migrants include

13 Oct 1967	2 banded	Newark [Line16]
15 Oct 1988	1	Middle Run, Newark [Call1]
17 Oct 1971	1	Brandywine Creek SP [SpSB13]

A late October 1965 report (West and Klabunde 1977) is not supported by the original field data sheet. Most reports mention 1–4 birds, although 9 were found at Dragon Run on 21 September 1974 [Falk13].

SPECIMENS: 82; DMNH, UDEL. Egg records: DMNH.

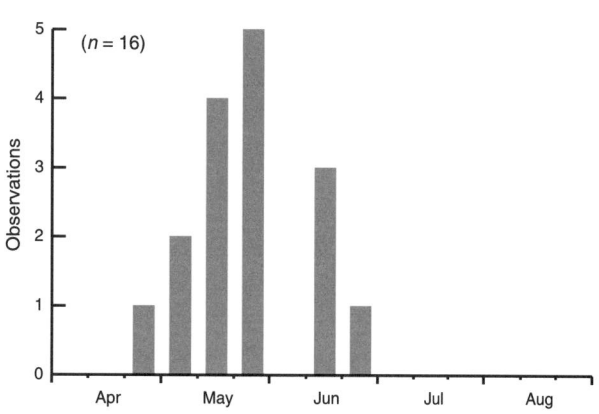

(*n* = 16)

Estimated Clutch-Completion Dates

reports declined sharply, and Robbins et al. (1989) reported a small, but significant, reduction throughout its range for a similar interval. May Count data, taken during migration, also suggest its population peaked around 1980.

Breeding population. Ovenbirds were detected at 508 of 3,240 stops in the relative abundance study, making it the second most frequently detected warbler. High summer counts on the weekly surveys include

| 3 June 1978 | 33 | White Clay Creek [MiDP12] |
| 5 June 1971 | 14 | Brandywine Creek SP [Wayn39] |

Northern Waterthrush (*Seiurus noveboracensis*)

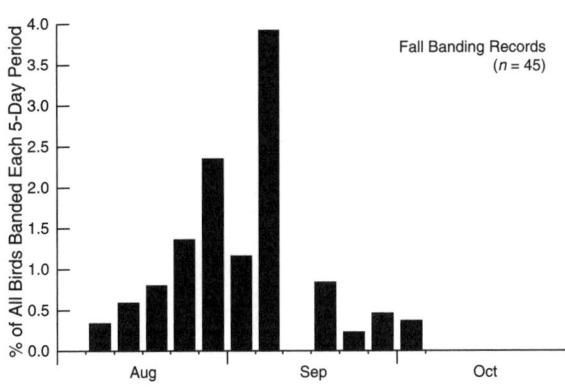

Fall Migration Activity

Regular; migrant; uncommon. Expected late April to late May and mid-August to late September.

HABITAT: Wooded stream banks.

SPRING: First arrival is usually 25 April–5 May. Migration peaks 5–20 May and ends 20–30 May. Early reports include

15 Apr 1978	1	White Clay Creek [Boll5]
17 Apr 1976	2	White Clay Creek [Conw11]
19 Apr 1980	2	Redden SF [Barn13]

The latest reports are

26 May 1911	1	Choptank Mills, Kent County (ANSP 80222)
29 May 1965	1 banded	Gordon Pond WA [Line4]
31 May 1965	1	Churchmans Marsh [Klab9]
31 May 1975	1	Dragon Run [Lehm32]

Most reports total 1–3 birds. The highest May Count is 31 (13 May 1972), the lowest 1 (8 May 1971).

FALL: First arrival is 10–20 August. Migration peaks 1–20 September and ceases 25–30 September. The numbers of birds banded increase steadily from early August to mid-September and diminish rapidly thereafter. The earliest fall reports include

30 Jul 1971	1 banded	University of Delaware woodlot [Line4]
5 Aug 1983	1	Killens Pond SP [Wees1]
7 Aug 1975	1	Dragon Run [Mars3]

Late records include

5 Oct 1984	1	Cape Henlopen SP [Frec1]
5 Oct 1963	1 banded	Red Lion [Line4]
6 Oct 1963	1 banded	Red Lion [Line4]
7 Oct 1963	2 banded	Red Lion [Line4]
15 Nov 1969	1	Bombay Hook NWR [Rich3]

Rather more unusual is a report of 1 at Prime Hook NWR on 1 January 1980 [Weir1]. The *American Birds* account simply states that "The bird was well observed and its characteristic pumping action noted." It was found during a winter when many vagrant warblers were reported. Most reports of the Northern Waterthrush include single birds.

SPECIMENS: 24; DMNH, ANSP, UWBM.

Louisiana Waterthrush *(Seiurus motacilla)*

Regular; summer resident; uncommon. Expected early April to early September.

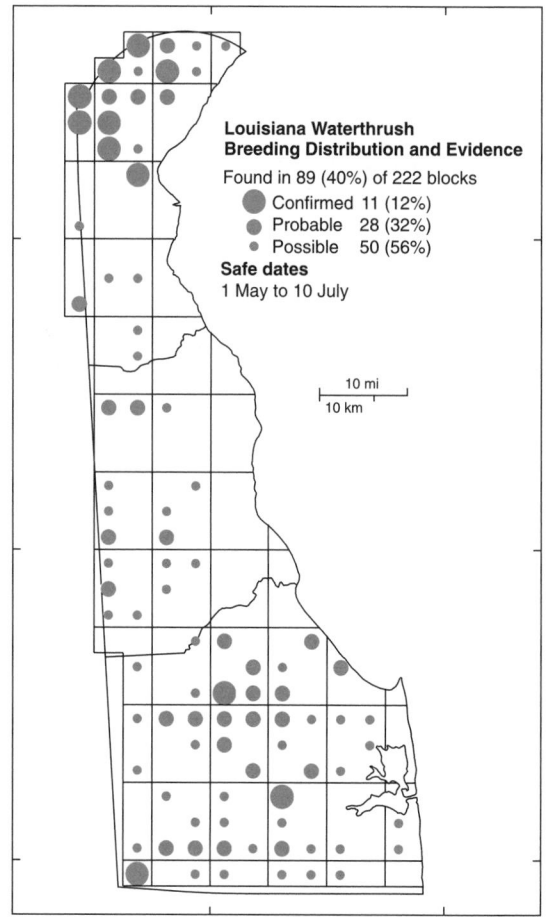

**Louisiana Waterthrush
Breeding Distribution and Evidence**
Found in 89 (40%) of 222 blocks
● Confirmed 11 (12%)
● Probable 28 (32%)
● Possible 50 (56%)
Safe dates
1 May to 10 July

10 mi
10 km

HABITAT: "Flood-plain and swamp forests" (Stewart and Robbins 1958); small streams through forests especially in the Piedmont. Wet woods, like those in our state forests and in the Pocomoke drainage, usually near a small flowing streamlet or overgrown drainage ditch.

SPRING: First arrival is 1–10 April; Bent (1953) gave 1 April and 10 April (average for 16 years) for Kent and Sussex counties as early and average arrival dates, respectively. Migration peaks 15–30 April. The 2 March reports are

29 March 1987	1	near Delmar [West2]
31 March 1986	2	Blackiston WA [Edni62]

Usually 1–5 birds are reported. The highest May Count is 30 (11 May 1990), the lowest 7 (7 May 1977 and 5 May 1984).

BREEDING: This stream-haunting warbler is a loud but sporadic singer after the female arrives in April (Eaton 1958), so it is infrequently recorded during roadside surveys in June. Favored places to find it are along feeder streams flowing into White Clay Creek, in Alapocas Woods, and downstate in Redden SF and the Pocomoke Swamp. It is regular, but perhaps becoming less common, along Piedmont streams. It was apparently more common in northern Delaware in the 1980s than it was at the turn of the twentieth century, because Rhoads and Pennock (1905) commented it was common along the Choptank and had been seen at Seaford and Frankford. Likewise, Stone (1919) mentioned it as a southern species that could be heard singing from the swamps of southwestern Delaware. Had it been easily found in northern Delaware, they would not have named places to find it in southern Delaware.

Atlas. The Atlas technique was the most successful way of finding the Louisiana Waterthrush, which is widespread within the wooded parts of Delaware. Nest building was observed 3 times, but no occupied nest was located. Other confirmations were for attending young or fledged young.

Nesting. Hanson (notes) described a nest he found along a ditch in a deep woods west of Dover. It was in an almost perpendicular bank about 5 ft high and 2 ft above the water in the ditch. It was placed in a depression, sheltered by a slight overhang of the bank, formed of mud and leaves, and lined with dark-colored roots. A nest found in New Castle County was situated at the base of a stump by a stream; it was constructed of leaves, lined with grass and hair, and contained 5 eggs (DMNH 9368).

Peak clutch completion occurs about the first of May. Egg dates range from 5 May (DMNH mount collection 527) to 2 June (DMNH 9368), but earlier and later dates are to be expected. Clutch size is 5 or 4, but 6 is also reported in other states (Bull 1974). The 2 June egg date probably represents a renesting after failure, since 2 broods are not expected (Eaton 1958). This species molts early, sometimes beginning in June (Mengel 1965), and is an early southward migrant, as if its breeding were timed to coincide with active flow in little streams and to be completed before the streams dry up in summer.

Trends. BBS data suggest a nonsignificant decrease, but the numbers of birds recorded on the BBS, totaled by 5-year peri-

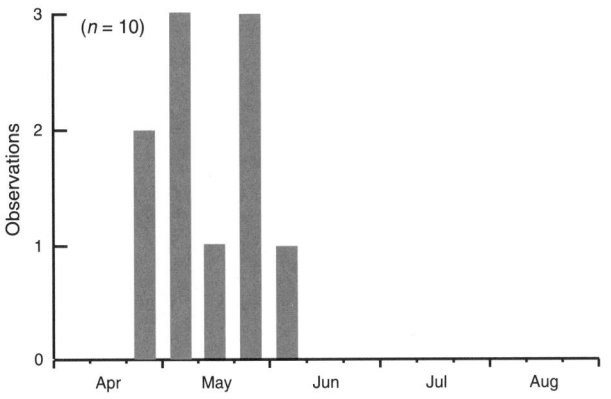

Estimated Clutch-Completion Dates

ods since 1966, present an ominous trend: 14, 10, 6, 5, and 0 (1966–90). May Count data, taken during the first half of May, show a strong and significant increase in the numbers reported for later dates during the period 3–14 May, suggesting a continued influx of birds or an increased obviousness (more singing) of those present. This finding appears to contradict Eaton's New York study (1958), which found few arrivals in May and reported reduced singing after pair formation.

Breeding population. This waterthrush was found in 89 blocks, so its population is surely over 100 pairs. Because of the limited amount of streamside or swampy habitat, however, its breeding population is less than 1,000 pairs. A BBC along White Clay Creek adjacent to Pennsylvania registered 2 pairs in 25 acres (20 per 100 ha) on territories along streamlets feeding into the creek (West 1970). Twice that abundance was reported for one Maryland section of the Pocomoke Swamp (Springer and Stewart 1948c). Territories follow streams for about a quarter mile (400 m) in New York (Eaton 1958). High summer counts on the weekly surveys include 2 at Brandywine Creek SP on 21 June 1969 [WarD1] and 8 at White Clay Creek on 18 June 1977 [Dyer11].

Conservation. Efforts to protect stream corridors should benefit this scarce species.

FALL: The onset of fall migration is difficult to discern, but migration is probably underway by the second week of August and finishes by the first week of September. Any observations after then should be treated with caution and supported with notes. Bent (1953) gives 28 September and 15 September as late and average departure dates for Kent and Sussex counties, but our records do not support such late dates. Nearly all reports mention 1 bird.

SPECIMENS: DMNH 72310 and DMNH 72311, Centerville, 4 May 1982; DMNH 71585, Laurel, 14 May 1981; DMNH 72301, Centerville, 24 May 1982; ANSP 47784, Medford Mills, 1903. Egg records: DMNH.

Kentucky Warbler *(Oporornis formosus)*

Regular; summer resident; uncommon. Expected early May to early September. Less common within 5 mi of the Delaware River or the ocean. Declining.

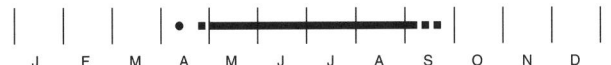

HABITAT: "Swamp and flood-plain forests, and rich, moist deciduous forests on the upland" (Stewart and Robbins 1958). Sensitive to forest fragmentation (Robbins et al. 1989a). In Delaware will accept early successional situations in which the woods are not completely canopied but have moist scrubby thickets. Occurs in small numbers in southern New Castle County west of Odessa where the Ovenbird is absent and where the woods are fragmented and mostly in strips along streams.

SPRING: Typical first arrival is 1–7 May. Migration peaks 10–20 May and ends by 25–30 May. The earliest records are

14 Apr 1987	1	Rittenhouse Park, Newark [MiDP1]
17 Apr 1991	1	White Clay Creek [MiDP10]

Extreme and average arrival dates given in Bent (1953, 512) for southern Delaware are early by 2 or 3 weeks and cannot be supported by data taken mainly in northern Delaware. Observations at White Clay Creek were consistently the highest reported: 8 on 8 May 1976, 12 on 21 May 1977, and 13 on 29 May 1976 [Dyer7; RusJ7; Falk11] respectively. The highest May Count is 45 (13 May 1989), the lowest 15 (5 May 1984).

BREEDING: This species is widespread yet uncommon. The

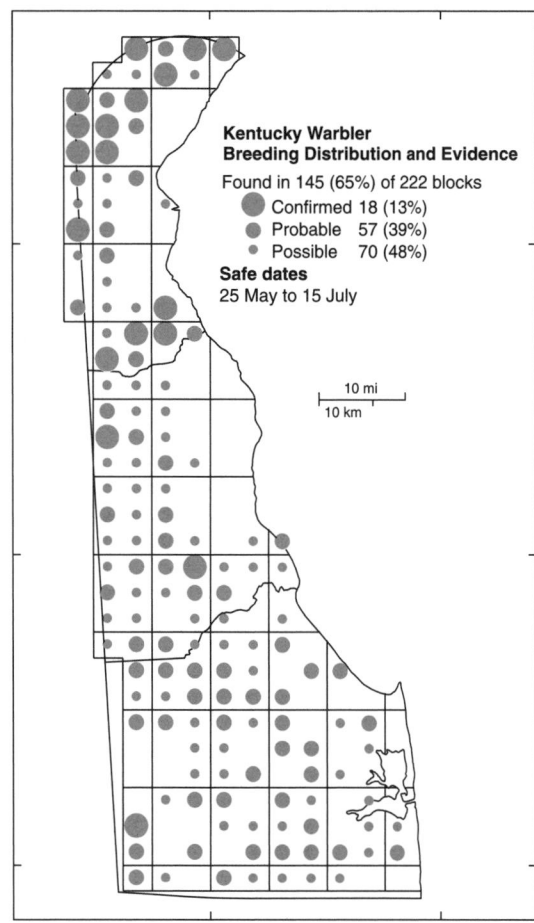

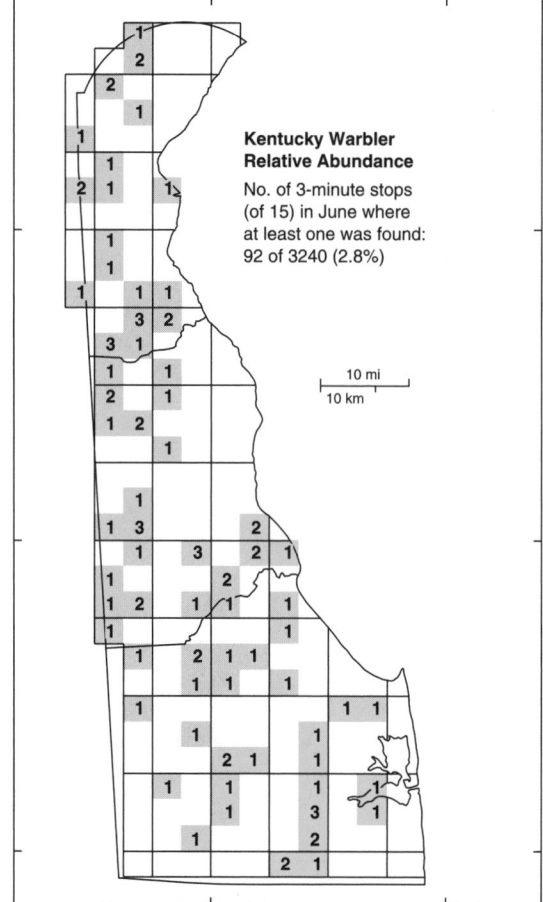

relative abundance map shows that its range closely coincides with forested areas. The most reliable places for finding it are in the White Clay Creek valley and in the mesic state forests and the Pocomoke Swamp.

Atlas. The distribution map's spottiness suggests that the Kentucky Warbler may have been missed in some Sussex County areas, but it occurs in such low numbers that it is difficult to find. Three confirmations resulted from finding a nest, and nest building was observed once.

Nesting. Hanson (notes) described a nest found under a bush

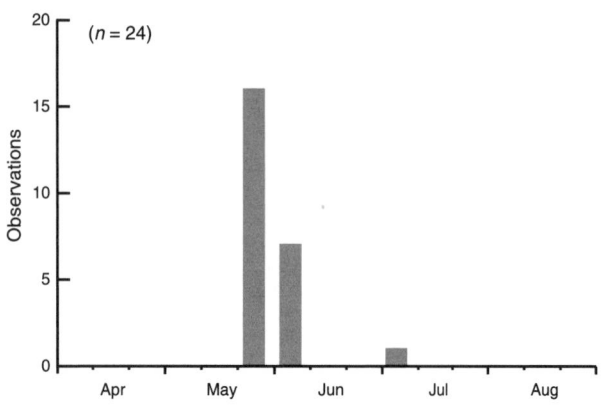

Estimated Clutch-Completion Dates

near Asbury Church, Dover, on 11 May 1929. The structure of small twigs, stems, and grass, with a thin lining of black horsehair and dark rootlets, was placed on a foundation of a dry leaf pile. The nest measured 2 ¼ in. across inside and 2 in. deep. Outside it was about 3 ½ in. across. The nest site was a rather low place in hardwoods.

Estimated clutch-completion dates peak strongly in late May, and the earliest estimated date is 21 May (clutch of 4 collected, in which incubation had commenced, on 26 May) (WFVZ egg data). Adults were bringing food to the site of an unusually late nest on 25 July where fledglings were observed on 31 July (SpeE3]. This single late breeding record may reflect a second brood. The latest egg date reported involves a nest with 4 eggs and a cowbird egg found on 12 June near Newark; the cowbird hatched on 13 June, but no Kentucky Warblers hatched through 21 June [Hudy1]. Second broods have been suggested for Ohio on meager evidence (Peterjohn and Rice 1991) and in Maryland (Whitcomb et al. 1981), the latter apparently based on the extended egg dates—16 May–31 July (Robbins and Bystrak 1977). Published Delaware clutch-completion dates for this species should be disregarded because of a clerical error in their estimation (Baer 1989). Clutch size reported in Delaware is usually 4 or 5 eggs.

History and trends. It may have once been considerably more common, since one observer ranked it earlier in the twentieth century among "Delaware's most common breeders," though surely with some exaggeration (Kenworthy 1917). Another oologist wrote of finding a number of nests near Wilmington early in the twentieth century, adding it was "always to be found around here in the nesting season, a pair generally in every low woods" (Darlington 1912b). The BBS and May Count results suggest its population declined slightly during 1966–90 [Usfw1], possibly related to loss of habitat.

Breeding population. High summer counts on the weekly surveys include

19 Jun 1976	12	White Clay Creek [RusJ12]
1 Jun 1980	4	Churchmans Marsh [Kell12]
21 Jun 1969	2	Brandywine Creek SP [WarD1]

Maximum population densities reported on BBCs range from 40 males per 100 ha in the Avon woodlot (Linehan and Burr 1967) to 25 per 100 ha along White Clay Creek at the state line (West 1970). For Maryland, Stewart and Robbins (1958) report about the same density in the Pocomoke Swamp and twice that density in some Piedmont areas.

FALL: The data do not clearly reveal the beginning of migration, but presumably migration occurs mostly during August; few reports later than 7 September are available. The latest records are

| 18 Sep 1976 | 1 | White Clay Creek [Falk11] |
| 19 Sep 1971 | 1 | Brandywine Creek SP [Edni1] |

Bent (1953) gives a late date of 18 September and average (for 19 years) late date of 5 September for Kent and Sussex counties. Most reports mention single birds.

SPECIMENS: 12; DMNH, ANSP, UDEL, UWBM. Egg records: DMNH, WFVZ.

Connecticut Warbler *(Oporornis agilis)*

Presumably regular in fall, but only occasionally reported (15 years, 1963–89); migrant; rare. Most likely in September.

HABITAT: "Wood margins and other brushy areas in moist situations" (Stewart and Robbins 1958).

SPRING: Connecticut Warblers occur on the Atlantic coast primarily in fall (AOU 1983). In Maryland, Stewart and Robbins (1958) report only 11 spring records. In New Jersey, Stone (1937) cites only 1 spring record, and Leck (1984) notes it is "extremely rare in spring." In Pennsylvania, Poole (1964) calls it "A very rare transient in spring," and in nearby Lancaster County it is "More common in fall than spring" (Lancaster County Bird Club, 1984). Thus, the fact that there is only 1 spring report in Delaware [BeaJ1] is not unexpected. Any spring report should be carefully documented.

FALL: Although there are quite a few records, Connecticut Warblers are tricky to identify in fall. Except for the specimen records, the following summary should be viewed with caution.

Specimens were collected on 12 September 1980 near Centerville (DMNH 71228) and 22 September 1986 near Hockessin (DMNH 76362). All but 2 sight records are in September, most from 12–24 September, the 2 specimen records thereby supporting the range of dates of the majority of sight records. Early records include

3 Sep 1906	1	west of Delaware City [Penn1]
7 Sep 1986	1	west of Lewes [Frec1]
9 Sep 1984	1	west of Lewes [Frec1]

The late dates are

24 Sep 1905	1	near Hockessin [Penn1]
30 Sep 1909	1	near Hockessin [Penn1]
30 Sep 1967	1 banded	University of Delaware woodlot [Line15]
1 Oct 1977	1	White Clay Creek [West20]
4 Oct 1912	1	New Castle Co. [WriM1]
24 Oct 1979	1	Rehoboth Beach [Frec27]

The 22 banding records span the period 6–10 September to 6–10 October [Usfw2]. Banding data from Montgomery County, Maryland, give a migration range of 25 August–21 October (*n* = 134), median of 21 September, with 90% of the migration taking place from 6 September to 11 October (Mehlman 1990). Usually only 1 bird is reported, but occasionally as many as 3 are found.

SPECIMENS: DMNH 71228 and DMNH 76362 details above; UDEL 139-67, Newark, no date.

Mourning Warbler (*Oporornis philadelphia*)

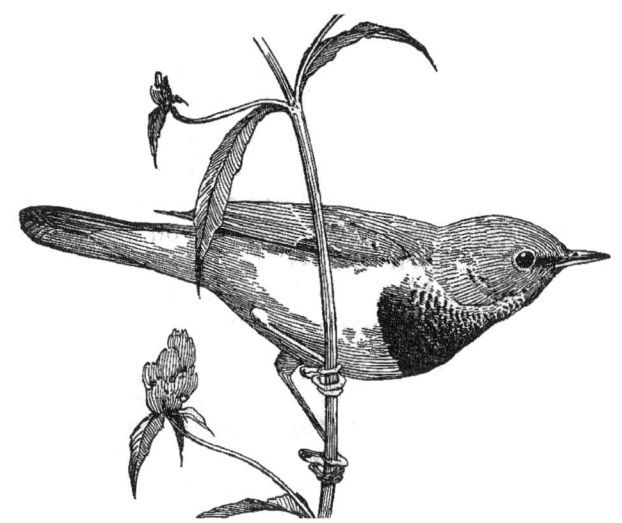

Regular; migrant; rare. Expected late May and to be looked for during September.

J F M A M J J A S O N D

HABITAT: Wood margins and moist, brushy cut-over areas.

SPRING: This elusive warbler is seldom reported in Delaware. Most reports (9 of 13) are clustered in the week of 23–31 May. Two very early but undocumented reports are

| 5 May 1974 | 1 | Assawoman WA [DuPG27] |
| 8 May 1965 | 1 | Camp Rodney [Broo30] |

Late reports are

| 2 Jun 1985 | 1 | Prime Hook NWR [Frec1] |
| 3 Jun 1978 | 1 | White Clay Creek [SpSB16] |

Specimens were taken on 24 May 1878 in Shellpot Woods, Wilmington (DMNH 63334), and on 25 May 1983 in Nanticoke WA, near Laurel (UWBM 36709). Banding data from Montgomery County, Maryland, give a migration range of 11 May–1 June (*n* = 102), median of 24 May, with 90% of the migration taking place in the second half of the month (Mehlman 1990). Usually only 1 bird is reported.

FALL: Specimens were taken on 30 August 1985 in Wilmington (DMNH 76621) and on 19 September 1981 in Newark (DMNH 71875). The 5 banding records are evenly distributed throughout the period 1–5 September to 11–15 October [Usfw2]. The 5 fall sight records are evenly distributed in the period 2 September–1 October; note the possibility of confusion with Connecticut Warbler in this season. Banding data from Montgomery County, Maryland, give a migration range of 15 August–10 October, median of 8 September, with two-thirds of the migration taking place from 27 August to 24 September (Mehlman 1990).

REMARKS: Krider (1879, 27) writes that he "found it from Delaware to New York, but have never found it breeding."

SPECIMENS: DMNH 63334, DMNH 71875, DMNH 76621, UWBM 36709, details above.

Common Yellowthroat (*Geothlypis trichas*)

Regular; summer resident; common. Expected mid-April to mid-October, sporadically into early winter.

J F M A M J J A S O N D

HABITAT: Wet, swampy, brushy areas.

SPRING: First arrival is usually 15–20 April. Migration peaks 20 April–5 May and ceases 15–25 May. The earliest records refer to

7 Apr 1982	1	Centerville (DMNH 72332)
7 Apr 1989	1 banded	Fowler Beach area of Prime Hook NWR [Thor1]
7 Apr 1973	11	Dragon Run [Beac2]

Extreme and average arrival dates given by Gross (1953) for southern Delaware are early by about a month and cannot be

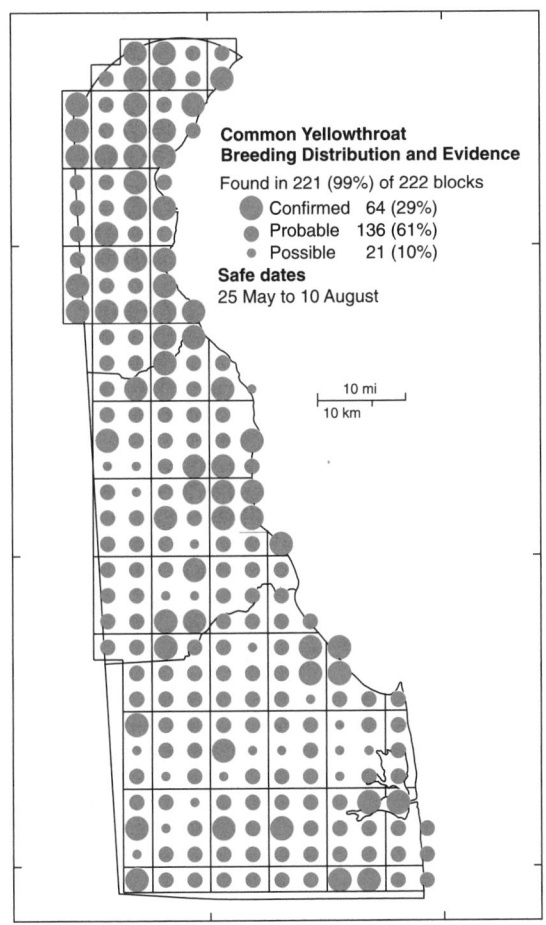

**Common Yellowthroat
Breeding Distribution and Evidence**

Found in 221 (99%) of 222 blocks

● Confirmed   64 (29%)
● Probable   136 (61%)
● Possible   21 (10%)

Safe dates
25 May to 10 August

10 mi
10 km

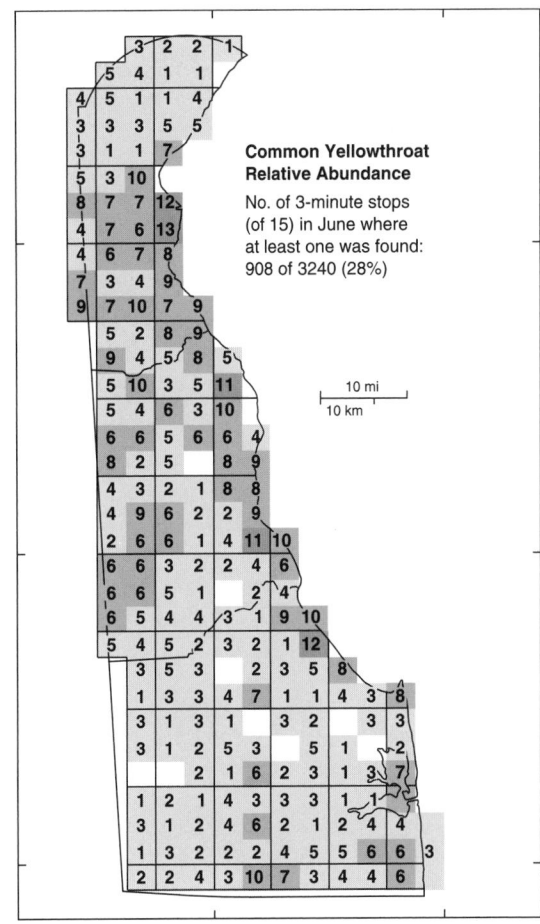

**Common Yellowthroat
Relative Abundance**

No. of 3-minute stops
(of 15) in June where
at least one was found:
908 of 3240 (28%)

10 mi
10 km

supported by data taken mainly in northern Delaware. Banding data from Montgomery County, Maryland, give a migration range of 15 April–31 May, with 90% of the migration taking place during 29 April–24 May (Mehlman 1990). A high count of 143 was tallied on 8 May 1982 at Bombay Hook NWR [Boll4]; the following week (15 May) 80 were recorded [Kell11]. The highest May Count is 1,031 (3 May 1980), the lowest 256 (10 May 1969, the first year of the survey).

BREEDING: Common Yellowthroat is the most common and widespread warbler in Delaware and in much of the East. The relative abundance study shows that it was most frequently recorded near river and bay marshes. It is less common but still widespread in northern New Castle County and around Dover and Seaford, since it will breed in a spot of rank vegetation in neglected areas amidst suburban sprawl.

Atlas. During the Atlas project the yellowthroat was easily found by its song and easily observed because of its bold nature and preference for open habitat. Its nest, however, is difficult to find, and it was confirmed only 10 times by locating an active nest. Most (46) of the confirmations were for attending young or fledged young.

Nesting. Hanson described a nest found in a swamp just west of Dover on 22 May 1926: "It was in a tussock of weeds and grass down as far as it could be built and was made of dry leaves and coarse grass, lined with finer grass. Outside it was 3 inches deep and 4 inches across and inside it was 1 3/4 inches deep and 1 1/2 inches across. It contained 3 fresh eggs."

Estimated clutch-completion dates peak in late May. The July completion dates probably represent second broods; Stewart (1953) observed in Michigan that each female that succeeded in raising young attempted a second brood. Extreme egg dates reported are 18 May [Hans1] and 26 July [Long1], but the Maryland data give an even longer egg season—4 May–4 August (Robbins and Bystrak 1977).

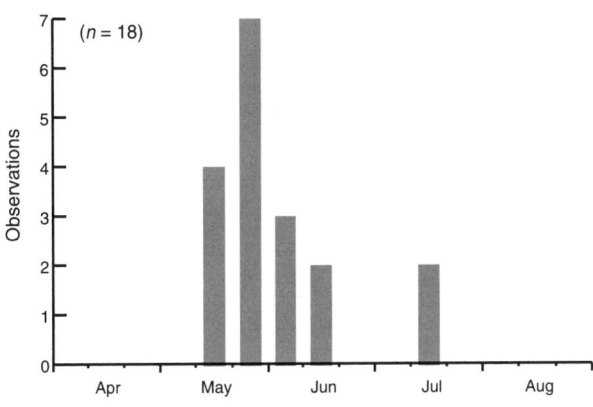

Estimated Clutch-Completion Dates

History and trends. Because of its abundance and acceptance of a modest piece of moist scrub for breeding, it is impossible to determine any change in the Common Yellowthroat population since European settlement. Generally speaking, however, clearing the forests for farming has provided an increase in suitable edge habitat, while progressive draining of wetlands and channeling of streams has had the opposite effect. BBS data show that it has had a significant population decline in the Upper Coastal Plain (1966–90) and recently in the East (1981–90), but these declines are not reflected in the Delaware BBS data [Usfw3] and only weakly so in the May Count data.

Breeding population. High breeding season counts on the DOS weekly surveys were

2 Jun 1973	45	Dragon Run [Beac6]
7 Jun 1969	35	Brandywine Creek SP [Broo15]
13 Jun 1981	47	Bombay Hook NWR [Gord12]
26 Jun 1976	55	White Clay Creek [Conw16]

The highest densities of yellowthroats found on Delaware BBCs (pairs per 100 ha) are

160 (13 in 20 acres) saltmarsh edge in Assawoman WA(Linehan 1965b, 1966c)

100 (11 in 27 acres) uneven-aged red maple–tulip poplar forest (Avon woodlot, Linehan 1968c)

75 (11 in 14.3 ha) brackish tidal marsh, Prime Hook NWR (West 1993)

70–100 (11–16 in 16 ha)phragmites-infested impounded brackish marsh east of Dover (Moore 1989:23)

40 (5 in 12 ha, 2 in 4.8 ha)impounded brackish marsh east of Dover with new vegetation 2 years after herbicide treatment and burning (Moore 1989:23)

In a Michigan study Stewart (1953) calculated its average defended territory size as 0.5 ha (1.25 acres). One of its habitats, nonforested wetland, amounts to 37,000 acres (15,000 ha) in Delaware (Mackenzie 1989).

FALL: Migration begins 15–25 August, peaks 10–30 September, and ends by 15–30 October. After that time only stragglers

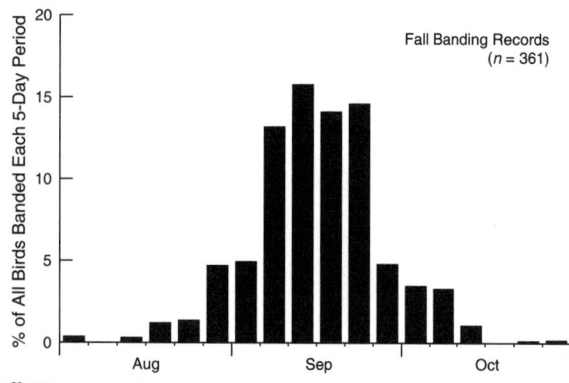

Fall Migration Activities

are present through early winter. The latest specimen was collected in Wilmington on 30 October 1976 (DMNH 59621), and the latest banding record involves 1 on 28 October 1989 at the Prime Hook NWR headquarters [Thor1]. Peak numbers of

Common Yellowthroats are banded in mid-September. High counts are 74 on 31 August 1974 and 60 on 15 September 1974, both at Dragon Run [Wayn25; WarD4] respectively.

1966–89 CBC Summary

Christmas Bird Count	Years Found	Range of No. Found	Median
Wilmington	9	1–3	
Middletown	12	1–10	
Bombay Hook	21	1–19	1
Cape Henlopen	14	1–9	1
Rehoboth	13	1–5	1
STATEWIDE *(zero in 1989, high in 1984)*	23	1–21	6

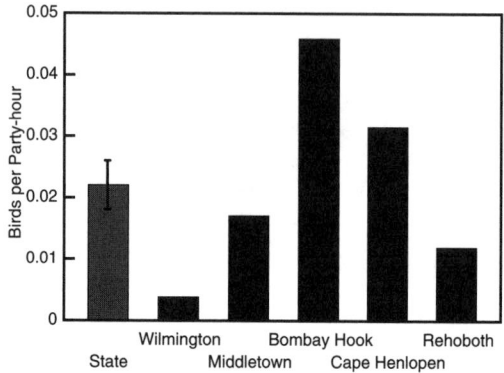

CBC Geographic Distribution

WINTER: Nearly all December and early January records are from CBCs. Unusually late records include

19 Jan 1980	1	Bombay Hook NWR [Barn38]
23 Jan 1989	1	Middle Run, Newark [Call1]
26 Jan 1974	1	Cape Henlopen SP [Barn18]
22 Feb 1975	1	Dragon Run [SpSB39]

SPECIMENS: 65; DMNH, ANSP, CM, UDEL, USNM. Egg records: DMNH, WFVZ.

Hooded Warbler (*Wilsonia citrina*)

Regular; summer resident; rare. Expected early May to mid-September.

HABITAT: Swamp forest or rich, moist upland forest with a dense shrub layer.

SPRING: First arrival is 1–10 May and sometimes earlier. April records include

26 Apr 1991	1	White Clay Creek [MiDP1]
27 Apr 1985	1	Prime Hook NWR [Frec1]
30 Apr 1989	1	White Clay Creek [RusJ1]

Extreme and average arrival dates given by Bent (1953, 625) for southern Delaware are early by 2 weeks and cannot be supported by data taken mainly in northern Delaware. The lack of reports makes it impossible to determine when migration ends; Stone saw a late migrant at Cape Henlopen on 30 May 1927 [Penn1]. Stewart and Robbins (1958) give an end period of 20–30 May and a peak from 1–15 May for Maryland. Most reports total 1 or 2 birds. The highest May Count is 18 (11 May 1990), the lowest 0 (9 May 1981).

BREEDING: Breeding Hooded Warblers frequent heavily wooded slopes with spots of dense understory in the Piedmont, such as the White Clay Creek location, and also on the Coastal Plain east of the headquarters at Redden SF, and along Rd. 418 leading south into the Pocomoke Swamp.

Atlas. Miller provided the first Atlas confirmation on 29 June 1985, with a report of a brood out of the nest with the male feeding 1 of the young along the White Pine Trail at Carpenter SP. She observed another brood farther up the trail on 28 July 1985 [MiDP2]. The Specks observed a pair on territory beginning on 10 May 1987, found the nest, and saw 3 fledglings on 1

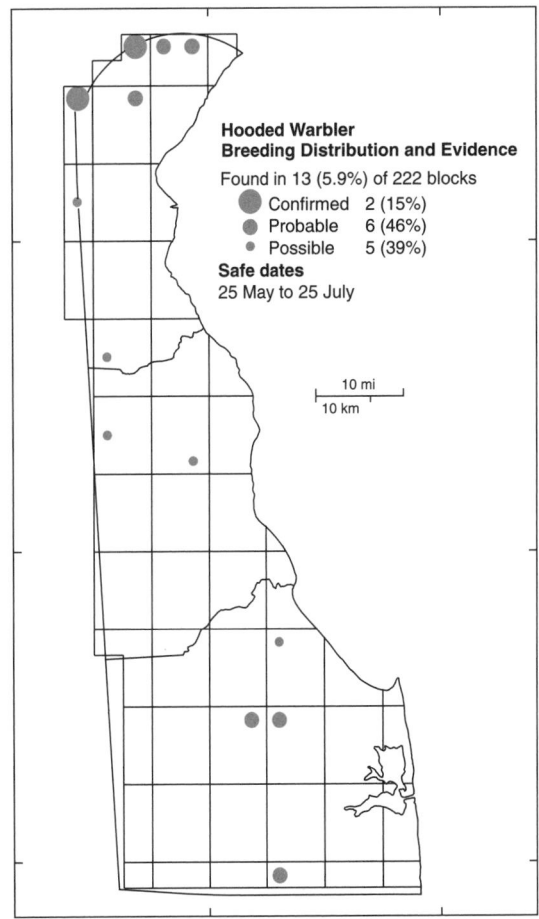

Hooded Warbler
Breeding Distribution and Evidence
Found in 13 (5.9%) of 222 blocks
● Confirmed 2 (15%)
● Probable   6 (46%)
● Possible   5 (39%)
Safe dates
25 May to 25 July

10 mi
10 km

July at a site located half a mile up an abandoned dirt road between Rt. 82 and Pyles Ford [SpeE13]. This warbler was probably missed in some blocks, but its sporadic distribution and low numbers made it hard to locate.

Nesting. The nest is often about 2 ft above ground in shrubby growth or thick undergrowth in moist woodlands—the only Delaware nest reported was about 4 ft up in a similar situation [SpeE3]. It is a compact cup with a loose outer layer of dead leaves, a main cup of bark strips, weed stems, and various plant fibers, lined with finer fibers such as rootlets and moss fibers. Usually 3–4 eggs, rarely 5, are laid (Bent 1953).

Our scant Delaware data indicate clutch completion 3 times in the first third of June and once in the first third of July. Extreme egg dates in Maryland are 21 May–30 July (Robbins and Bystrak 1977); in New Jersey the height of the egg reports occurs during 27–31 May (Bent 1953).

History. The Hooded Warbler was placed on the list of Delaware's breeding birds relatively recently. It was first listed as a summer resident by Barry (1942). Buckalew, through correspondence in 1953 to Cutler (1969), reported a pair carrying nesting material on 1 June 1938 at Bombay Hook NWR, thus providing the first breeding record. Linehan and Miller (in Dyer et al. 1973) observed a male feeding a young cowbird on 11 July 1970 in the White Clay Creek valley north of Wedgewood Rd.

Trends. The Hooded Warbler has been detected in Delaware on the BBS infrequently, e.g., on 26 June 1966 near Gumboro [DeGa1] and on 26 June 1984 west of Lums Pond SP [West5]. BBS data indicate that it has increased in the East at an average annual rate of 3% for 25 years, but most of this gain came during the first 15 years [Usfw3].

Breeding population. Finding 10 established pairs in the state during a single year would be difficult. However, because the Hooded Warbler was reported from 15 blocks, the population is over 10 pairs, though surely fewer than 100.

Conservation. Powell and Rappole (1986), in a conservation review of the Hooded Warbler, pointed out that the forested area in the Mid-Atlantic states had fallen in the late nineteenth century to half its present level, and much more of the woodland was then in farm woodlots. On that basis the small numbers now breeding in Delaware may reflect a resurgence in response to twentieth-century reforestation. Current threats include increased forest fragmentation in North America and deforestation in the Hooded Warbler's winter range, principally in southern Mexico.

FALL: Reports number 6—3 for August, 2 for September, and 1 for October. Holgersen found an individual at Broadkill Beach on 30 October 1972 [Holg77]. Stewart and Robbins (1958) give the migration period as 25 July–5 August to 20–30 September, with the peak from 15 August to 10 September for Maryland.

SPECIMENS: UDEL 100-66, Newark, 5 May 1966; ANSP 65594, no locality or date.

Wilson's Warbler *(Wilsonia pusilla)*

NCW

Regular; migrant; uncommon. Expected May and late August to late September.

J F M A M J J A S O N D

HABITAT: Wood edges, hedgerows, or other brushy habitats, often associated with moist sites.

SPRING: First arrival is usually 8–12 May. Two-thirds of all reports occur during 10–25 May, and most pass through by 31 May. A very early individual was found along Dutch Neck Rd. on 24 April 1927 [Hans1]. A little north of there at Dragon Run 1 appeared on the late date of 2 June 1973 [Beac6]. Most reports involve 1 or 2 birds. A report of 22 along White Clay Creek on 28 May 1977 (Speck and Brokaw 1979) should have referred to the Yellow-breasted Chat. The highest May Count is 13 (11 May 1974), the lowest 0 (1971, 1973, 1983, and 1984—mostly years when the survey was conducted early).

FALL: Migration lasts from 25 August–30 September, with a peak 5–15 September. The early date is 23 August 1980 at Churchmans Marsh [Falk10]. The late fall reports include

13 Oct 1966	1 banded	near Rehoboth Beach [RusW1]
21 Oct 1973	1	Dragon Run [Mars4]
25 Nov 1973	1	Greenville [Cado2]

Almost all reports mention 1 bird, but 4 were found at Kitts Hummock on 16 September 1983 [SpSB32].

WINTER: There are a number of winter reports, including

18 Dec 1973	1	Hockessin [McCH1]
22 Dec 1930	1	Clayton [Hans1]
23 Dec 1979	1	Bombay Hook CBC [Citr3]
29, 30 Dec 1983	1	Middletown [Edni71]

SPECIMENS: DMNH 49836, Wilmington, 14 May 1975; DMNH 73789, Centerville, 22 May 1983; CM 86259, Ocean View, 1 September 1922 (extant?); DMNH 68133 and DMNH 68134, Wilmington, 1975

Canada Warbler *(Wilsonia canadensis)*

Regular; migrant; uncommon. Expected May and late August to mid-September.

J F M A M J J A S O N D

HABITAT: Wet or moist forest.

SPRING: Typical first arrival is 8–12 May, peak migration is 16–23 May, and usual last departure is 25–30 May. Early reports include

30 Apr 1970	1 banded	University of Delaware woodlot [Jone2]
2 May 1970	1	Brandywine Creek SP [SpSB13]

June reports include

2 Jun 1973	3	Dragon Run [Beac6]
4 Jun 1971	1	Bombay Hook NWR [Holg10]
4 Jun 1983	1	Wilmington (DMNH 74087)
5 Jun 1976	1	White Clay Creek [West18]
9 Jun 1986	1	north of Millville [BroW1]
20 Jun 1967	1	Brandywine Creek SP [West17]

High counts are

20 May 1978	13	White Clay Creek [Falk17]
22 May 1971	18	Brandywine Creek SP [Wayn25]
22 May 1983	18	Bombay Hook NWR [Bayn4]

The highest May Count is 25 (14 May 1988), the lowest 0 (1979, 1980, 1983, and 1985, mostly years when the count was conducted early).

FALL: Arrivals appear 15–20 August; most depart by 20–25 September, with peak numbers occurring from about 25 August to about 10 September. Early reports include

17 Jul 1977	1	White Clay Creek [Jahn11]
6 Aug 1970	1 banded	Newark [Jone2]
9 Aug 1969	1 banded	University of Delaware woodlot [Line4]

Late reports include

28 Sep 1981	1	Centerville (DMNH 72188)
1 Oct 1972	4	Winterthur [Broo16]
11 Oct 1964	1	Hoopes Reservoir [Falk12]

Highest counts are

22 Aug 1982	8	Phillips Park, Newark [Litt1]
29 Aug 1970	13	Brandywine Creek SP [McCT1]

Typical reports involve up to 4 or 5 birds.

SPECIMENS: 25; DMNH, ANSP, UDEL.

Yellow-breasted Chat *(Icteria virens)*

Regular; summer resident; fairly common. Expected early May to mid-September, sporadic into early winter.

J F M A M J J A S O N D

HABITAT: Hedgerows and other brushy second-growth areas.

SPRING: First arrival is usually 1–7 May, with peak numbers being reached within a week. The end of migration is obscure but is probably in late May. Early arrivals include

4 Apr 1975	4	Dragon Run [Gran1]
18 Apr 1981	1	Little Creek WA [Pure12]

Three reports are dated 29 April. The extreme and average arrival dates given in Bent (1953, 597) for southern Delaware are early by 1–3 weeks and cannot be supported by data taken mainly in northern Delaware. Some high counts at White Clay

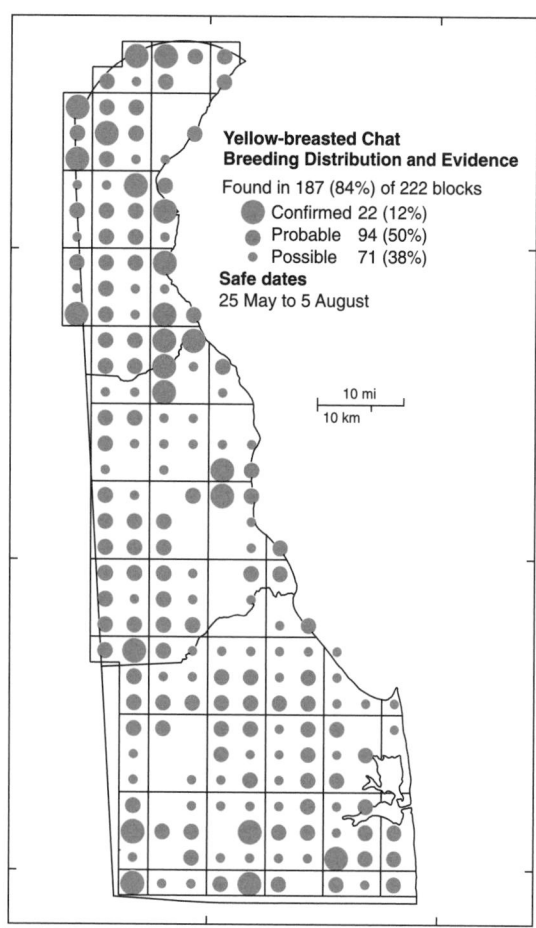

**Yellow-breasted Chat
Breeding Distribution and Evidence**

Found in 187 (84%) of 222 blocks

- Confirmed 22 (12%)
- Probable 94 (50%)
- Possible 71 (38%)

Safe dates
25 May to 5 August

10 mi
10 km

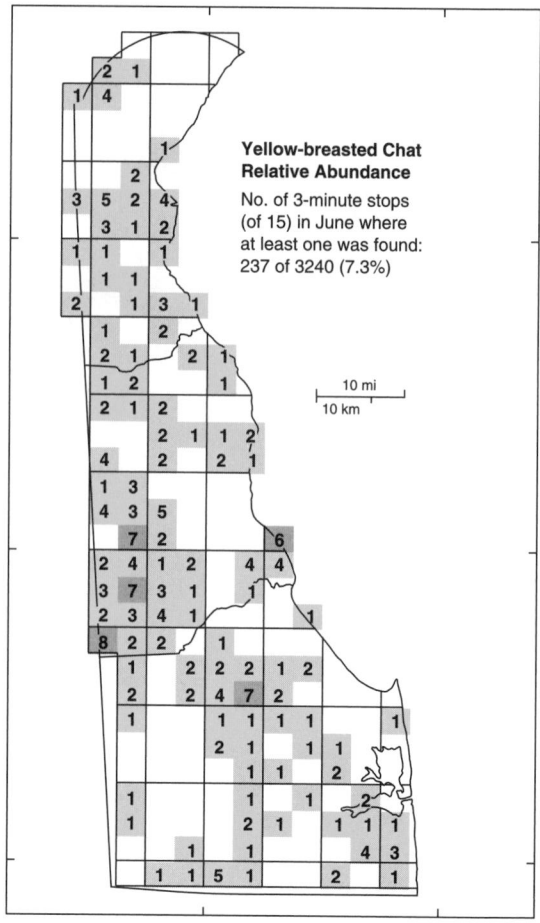

**Yellow-breasted Chat
Relative Abundance**

No. of 3-minute stops
(of 15) in June where
at least one was found:
237 of 3240 (7.3%)

10 mi
10 km

Creek include

7 May 1977	16	[Dyer7]
22 May 1976	17	[Jaco3]
28 May 1977	22	[MiDP14]

The highest May Count is 92 (12 May 1979), the lowest 14 (8 May 1971).

BREEDING: Areas where the chat is most common are characterized by fields or cutovers reverting to forest but still at the scrub stage. These patchy areas are scattered over the state and not shown on available habitat maps for comparison with the

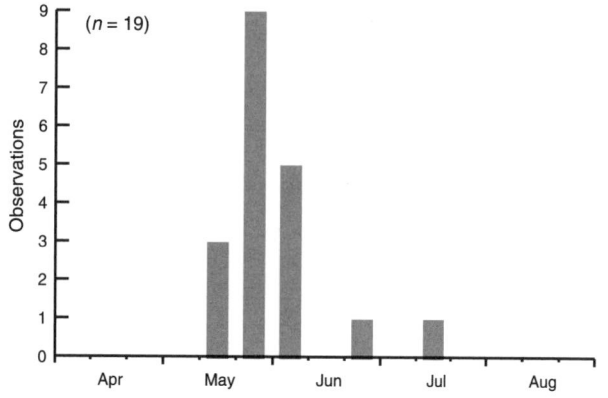

Estimated Clutch-Completion Dates

relative abundance map. Although it breeds over most of northern Delaware in small numbers, not much habitat remains in suburban areas, and many unattended fields have passed the scrub stage.

Atlas. Chats were difficult to confirm during the Atlas project; of 22 confirmed reports, only 6 were for occupied nests, and none described nest contents.

Nesting. Hanson described a nest found in Ellendale Swamp on 26 May 1925. It was about 3 ft up in a tangle of vines near a brook. The nest was constructed of vines, stems, and leaves and was 3 in. deep and 5 in. across outside, and 2¼ in. deep and 2¾ in. across inside. Other Delaware nests had grapevine bark as a common component.

Clutch completion peaks strongly in the last week in May. Egg date extremes are 3 fresh eggs found on 20 May (DMNH 14457) and 3 fresh eggs on 24 July (Bush notes). Clutch size in Delaware is usually 4 early in the season, 3 later (*n* = 16). The July clutch may be a second brood; Peterjohn and Rice (1991) report that second broods are fairly frequent in Ohio.

Trends. Delaware BBS data alone show no significant population trend, but chats are declining on a significant number of routes in the East [Usfw3]. This decline may reflect a decrease in habitat—perhaps fewer roadside clearcuts reverting to scrub. The chat is listed as Endangered in Rhode Island—a clear indication of what soon can be expected in northern Delaware.

The Prairie Warbler, which uses this early successional habitat, is also declining in Delaware.

Breeding population. It is difficult to estimate its population, which is tied closely to successional growth stages and forestry practices. The method used in the relative abundance study provided the best way to locate this species in its successional habitat, as it was found at 237 stops.

It was most commonly found on the Delaware BBCs in Assawoman WA, where densities of 15 and 14 per 100 acres (37–35 per 100 ha) were reported in coastal lowland mixed woods (Linehan 1965a; McLaughlin 1968). Stewart and Robbins (1958) report densities of 15–36 pairs per 100 acres (36–90 per 100 ha) in shrubby fields and burned-over forests; the same densities may be expected in Delaware (see also Thompson 1977) where Mackenzie (1989) reported 37,000 acres of brushland in 1984.

High summer counts on the weekly surveys include

12, 26 Jun 1971	16	Brandywine Creek SP 1971 [both Beac6]
23 Jun 1979	11	Ashland [Conw14]
3 Jul 1976	23	White Clay Creek [Jahn14]
7 Jul 1973	27	Dragon Run [BroW7]

FALL: The beginning of fall migration cannot be determined from available data but probably begins in mid-August. Migration usually ends 25–30 September. The average late date of 30 August reported in Bent (1953, 598) is clearly based on less information than we now have. After September some single birds occur, including 3 sight records and 6 banding records for October, and 2 banding records for November. High counts of 21 and 10 were reported on 22 and 29 September 1973, respectively, at Dragon Run [SpSB13; RobT3] respectively.

1966–89 CBC Summary

Christmas Bird Count	Years Found	Range of No. Found
Wilmington	1	1
Middletown	1	1
Bombay Hook	5	1
Cape Henlopen	1	1
Rehoboth	4	1
STATEWIDE (two in 1967, 1971, and 1978)	9	1–2

WINTER: The pattern of fall stragglers continues into early winter, although there are more winter than late fall reports, probably the result of increased observer effort during the CBC period. There are 9 non-CBC reports and 17 CBC reports, all but 1 involving single birds, the other involving 2 birds. Most unusual is a report of 1 feeding on honeysuckle on 9 February 1981 at Cape Henlopen SP [Frec8].

SPECIMENS: 15; DMNH, ANSP, UDEL. Egg records: DMNH, LSU, WFVZ.

Summer Tanager *(Piranga rubra)*

Regular; summer resident; uncommon migrant. Expected early May to mid-September. Uncommon to rare breeding species, usually confined to Sussex and southwestern Kent counties.

HABITAT: Loblolly and Virginia (scrub) pine, including pine plantations and rural yards, oak–hickory forest. Overlaps with breeding Scarlet Tanagers, but generally prefers a more open, drier, and scrubbier habitat; thus more likely to select an edge situation or enter suburban areas.

SPRING: First arrival is usually 25 April–1 May. The end of migration cannot be determined from available data, but Stewart and Robbins (1958) give 20–25 May for Maryland. Early arrivals include

26 Apr 1960	1	Millsboro [Davi15]
27 Apr 1986	1	Red Mill Pond [Frec1]
28 Apr 1951	2	Ellendale [MiJC1]

High counts, all obtained in Sussex County, are

3 May 1980	10	[Barn38]
7 May 1983	8	[Barn13]
13 May 1989	9	[Edni1]

The highest May Count is 39 (1979), the lowest 2 (1981). This species is underreported because birders stop looking for it as soon as they find 1 or 2 birds. Summer Tanagers are sometimes found north of their normal breeding range in spring as if they had overflown their destination, as exemplified by these records for the Brandywine Valley: present on 6 May 1945

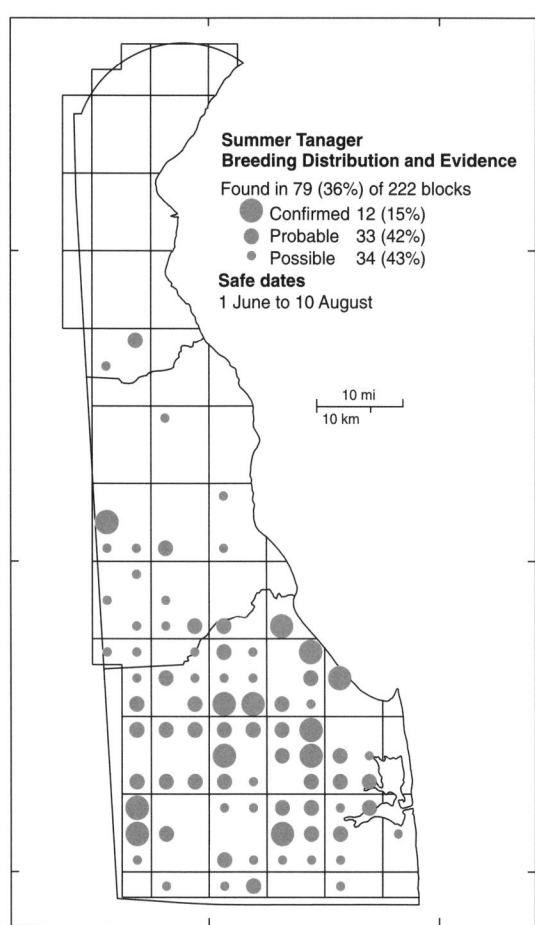

**Summer Tanager
Breeding Distribution and Evidence**

Found in 79 (36%) of 222 blocks
● Confirmed 12 (15%)
● Probable 33 (42%)
• Possible 34 (43%)
Safe dates
1 June to 10 August

10 mi
10 km

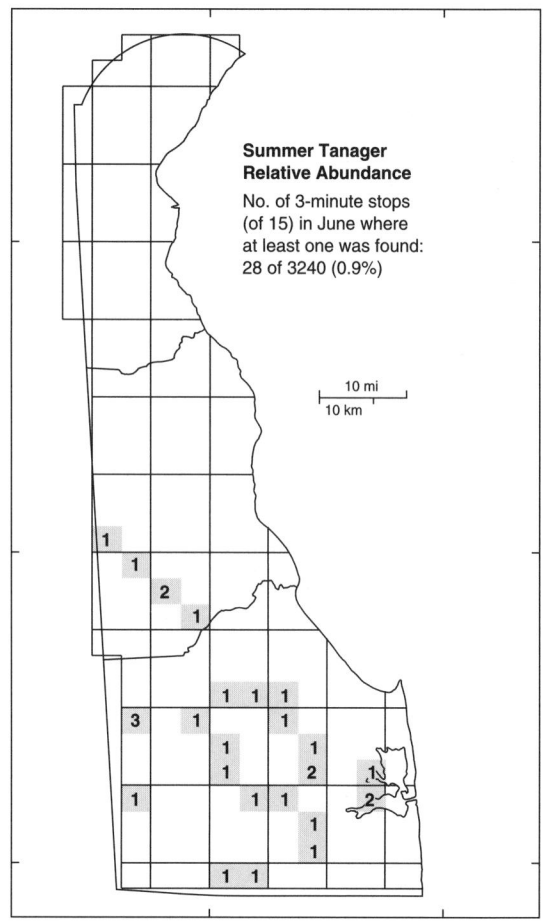

**Summer Tanager
Relative Abundance**

No. of 3-minute stops
(of 15) in June where
at least one was found:
28 of 3240 (0.9%)

10 mi
10 km

[Kram1], 3 on 15 May 1978 [BroH6], and present on 19 May 1974 [Phal1]. One reported on 3 June 1991 at Bombay Hook NWR (D. Rothstein, DNHI, pers. comm.) had probably overflown its normal range and still not reached suitable habitat by that date.

BREEDING: The relative abundance study shows how infrequently this species is found, as would be expected for a species near the northern limit of its range. This study, more than the Atlas project, shows its relative aversion for the coast and bay shore, where little habitat exists.

Atlas. During the Atlas project it was located in a higher than expected number of blocks, showing for the first time its widespread, if thin, distribution. In retrospect, additional field-work might have filled in some of the blank areas depicted on the map. On the distribution map the northernmost 3 points and a number of the others may represent temporary locations that did not have an established pair for the breeding season. The most often used confirmation method for this species was observing nest building. It is easily located by its distinctive call note and song.

Nesting. The first Delaware nest was not reported until 30 May 1965 on Long Neck [Broo10]. Others reported are eggs in a nest 8 ft up at the edge of oak–pine forest at Trap Pond on 22 May [Frec3], nest building 40 ft up in an oak in Nanticoke WA

on 24 May, a bird on nest 15 ft up in deciduous woods in river bottom 1 mi south of Choptank Mills on 21 June [both Hess4], a nest with eggs west of Seaford on 27 May 1983 [MiDR1], and a nest with young in Cape Henlopen SP pine barrens on 16 August 1990 (D. Rothstein, DNHI, pers. comm.).

Nests are usually located on a branch's flimsy end at least 6 ft from the ground; 1 nest was constructed of fine grass fibers and dried mosses (D. Rothstein, DNHI, pers. comm.). Clutches usually include 4 eggs (Harrison 1978). Mengel (1965) suggests that some pairs may raise 2 broods in Kentucky, based on the length of the season and other evidence, and the late nest found by Rothstein suggests this for Delaware.

History. Witmer Stone described the Summer Tanager as a native of "Dixie" that pushes up as far as southern Delaware and no farther (1919); he later traced its near extirpation in New Jersey (1937). Rhoads described it as a common breeder in lower Sussex County (Rhoads and Pennock 1905). Pennock found it near Millsboro on 15 May 1905 (Pennock 1908a) and passed on a report that it was believed to be nesting near Stanton in 1908 [Penn6]. Birds near their present northern limit were found by Dicky at Odessa on 8 June 1925 and Hanson near Camden on 10 June 1929 [both Hans1]. Barry (1939) summarized Natural History Society notes with "summer resident, rare north of Dover," a summary that remains true.

Trends. The May Count and BBS data suggest that its population has remained fairly stable in Delaware, though it has decreased in the East during the past decade, 1981–90 [Usfw3].

Breeding population. One estimate of its population density on the Delmarva Peninsula, based on BBC data collected in Worcester County, Maryland, is 25 pairs per 100 ha (2 in 21 acres) of loblolly and shortleaf pines (Springer and Stewart 1948b). D. Rothstein (pers. comm.) estimated the population in Cape Henlopen SP pine barrens at 37 pairs per 100 ha (4–5 in 30 acres). In most cases breeding pairs are isolated, so the species' occurrence during 0.9% of stops of the relative abundance study and its presence in 36% of Atlas blocks are the best indicators of its abundance.

FALL: A lack of late summer and fall reports prevents determination of the beginning of migration. Summer Tanagers seen along White Clay Creek on 11 July 1979 [Barn9] and on 14 July 1974 [Lehm1] represent unexpectedly early postseason movement, perhaps after breeding failure. Stewart and Robbins (1958) give 15–25 August as the onset of the normal migration period in Maryland. Migration normally ends by 20–25 September. Late records involve

25 Sep 1987	3	Rds. 257 and 260, Sussex Co. [Frec1]
28 Sep 1989	1	along Rt. 260, Sussex Co. [Frec1]
5 Oct 1946	1	Dover [Hans1]

Usually only 1 or 2 birds are reported. More late summer and fall reports are needed.

SPECIMENS: 8; ANSP, DMNH, UWBM.

Scarlet Tanager *(Piranga olivacea)*

Regular; summer resident; fairly common, especially in forested areas of Sussex and western Kent counties. Expected late April to early October.

HABITAT: Larger tracts of deciduous and mixed forest, especially forested wetlands; also wooded parks with large trees.

SPRING: First arrival is 25–30 April and last departure 25–30 May. Peak numbers occur 10–25 May. The earliest report describes 1 on 17 April 1984 at Gordon Pond WA [Frec1]. High counts involve

15 May 1984	10	Goslee Mill Pond [Frec1]
20 May 1978	33	White Clay Creek [Falk11]
21 May 1972	15	Winterthur [Broo16]

The highest May Count is 143 (1988), the lowest 28 (1971).

BREEDING: Although this tanager is one of Delaware's

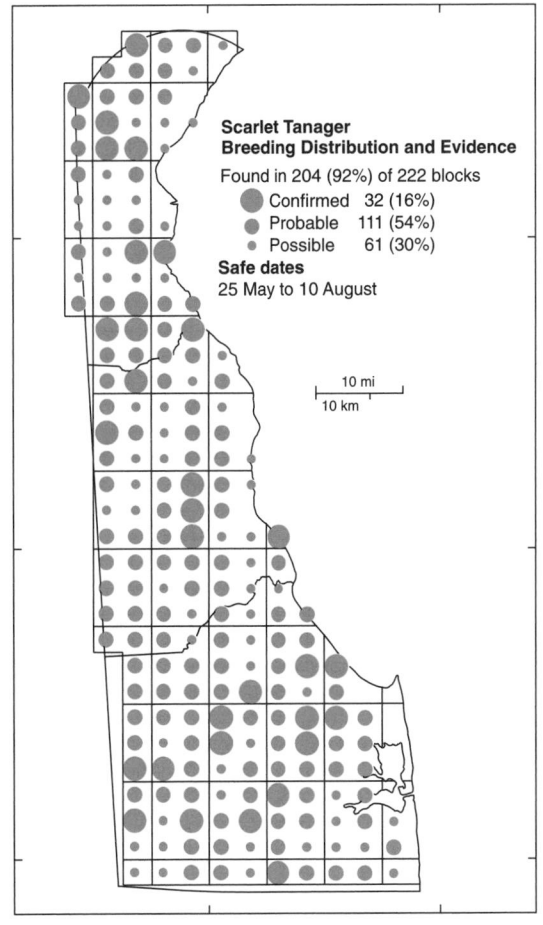

Scarlet Tanager
Breeding Distribution and Evidence
Found in 204 (92%) of 222 blocks
Confirmed   32 (16%)
Probable   111 (54%)
Possible   61 (30%)
Safe dates
25 May to 10 August

10 mi
10 km

most striking birds, it is often overlooked because it usually remains at treetop level in larger tracts of woods. It is sensitive to forest fragmentation and is 5–10 times more likely to be found in forest tracts over 2,500 acres (1,000 ha) as in woodlots of 2.5 acres (Robbins et al. 1989a). The relative abundance

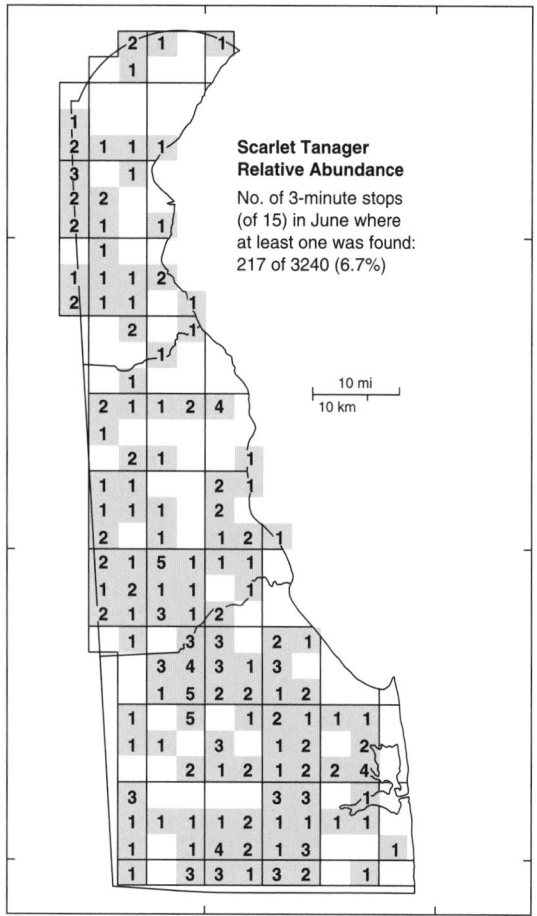

Scarlet Tanager
Relative Abundance

No. of 3-minute stops
(of 15) in June where
at least one was found:
217 of 3240 (6.7%)

10 mi
10 km

small twigs. It was 5 in. across and 2½ in. deep outside and 2¼ in. across and 1¼ in. deep inside. It was constructed of small, gray, dead tendrils and lined with finer brown tendrils. It was rather loosely constructed and could easily escape detection. The general requirements for the nest are that it be shaded by leaves, be placed out on a horizontal branch, have a clear view of the ground, and have clear flyways to adjacent trees (Prescott 1965).

Estimated clutch-completion dates, based on only 7 records, extend from mid-May to the first of July, with a peak in early June. Egg date extremes are 24 May in Bethel [Edni4] and 19 June in Wilmington (Darlington 1914), but a late nesting or replacement clutch can extend the nestling season into early August as shown for Maryland (Stewart and Robbins 1958). Clutch size is 3–4. Two of 4 nests reported in Delaware were parasitized by cowbirds.

Trends. Its population may have increased in parts of the state where deciduous and mixed forests have regrown and matured during the twentieth century, but it decreased regionally during 1966–90 in the Upper Coastal Plain of New Jersey south through Virginia (Robbins et al. 1989b) [Usfw1].

Breeding population. High BBC densities recorded in Delaware are 24 males per 100 ha (3.5 in 36 acres) at the University of Delaware woodlot (Longcore et al. 1966), and 20 males per 100 ha (2 in 25 acres) along White Clay Creek (West 1970), but usual density in northern Delaware is fewer than 10 per 100 ha, if the species is present at all. Ideal habitat in Kent and Sussex counties has not been surveyed by this technique.

FALL: Migration begins 15–20 August, last departure 1–7 October. Late records include

17 Oct 1969	1 banded	University of Delaware woodlot [Line4]
19 Oct 1972	1	Wilmington (DMNH 27905)
19 Oct 1973	1	Greenville (DMNH 37710)
15 Nov 1973	1 banded	Newark [Line6]
23 Nov 1985	1	Cape Henlopen SP [MurW1]

The last, a sight record, was reported as a male "in basic (winter) plumage . . . impeccably described." High counts involve

| 11 Sep 1976 | 15 | Wilmington [Edni16] |
| 21 Sep 1985 | 8 | west of Lewes [Frec1] |

SPECIMENS: 25; DMNH, ANSP, UDEL, UWBM. Egg records: DMNH.

study showed a decided decrease in abundance in northern Delaware, the result of habitat loss and fragmentation of the woods that remain. Both tanagers occur most often in the heavily wooded areas of western Kent and Sussex counties. There is no hint that the Scarlet is being displaced by the Summer in southern Delaware.

Atlas. The Scarlet Tanager can be found throughout suburban areas (distribution map) despite its preference for larger forest tracts, though it avoids the outermost woods along the ocean. During the Atlas project the most common means of confirming this species was by observing nest building; only 3 active nests were reported, 2 of which held young.

Nesting. A nest described by Hanson (notes) was found on 4 June 1929 in deciduous woods near Asbury Church, Dover, 30 ft up in a white oak and 10 ft out on a horizontal limb in the

[Western Tanager *(Piranga ludoviciana)*]

Two undocumented sight reports.

DOCUMENTATION: None.

REMARKS: There are reports from 2 different May Counts, one of which was published with a very brief comment (Scott

and Cutler 1973b). However, neither observation adequately excluded the possibility of an aberrant Scarlet or Summer tanager.

Green-tailed Towhee (Pipilo chlorurus)

Casual (1964).

DOCUMENTATION: Photograph (A. E. Conway, DMNH 465).

REMARKS: This western species, which rather frequently strays eastward (AOU 1983), has been recorded once in Delaware. A single bird was banded and photographed on 28–29 February 1964 at Bellevue Manor, north of Wilmington [WilD1]. It was reported to be present there from early February until early April. The photograph clearly establishes the occurrence of the species in Delaware.

Eastern Towhee (Pipilo erythrophthalmus)

Occurs all year; uncommon in winter to fairly common in summer. Decreasing at 5% per year on CBCs and in summer.

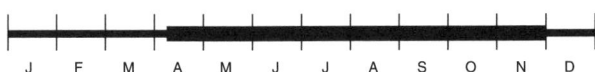

HABITAT: Brushy second-growth fields, brushy upland forests, hedgerows; coastal scrub.

SPRING: Migration begins 15–30 March, peaks 15 April–10 May, and ceases 15–25 May. Peak banding occurs during the last third of April. High counts involve

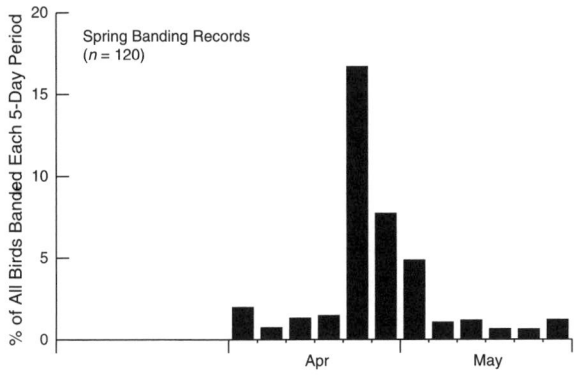

Spring Migration Activity

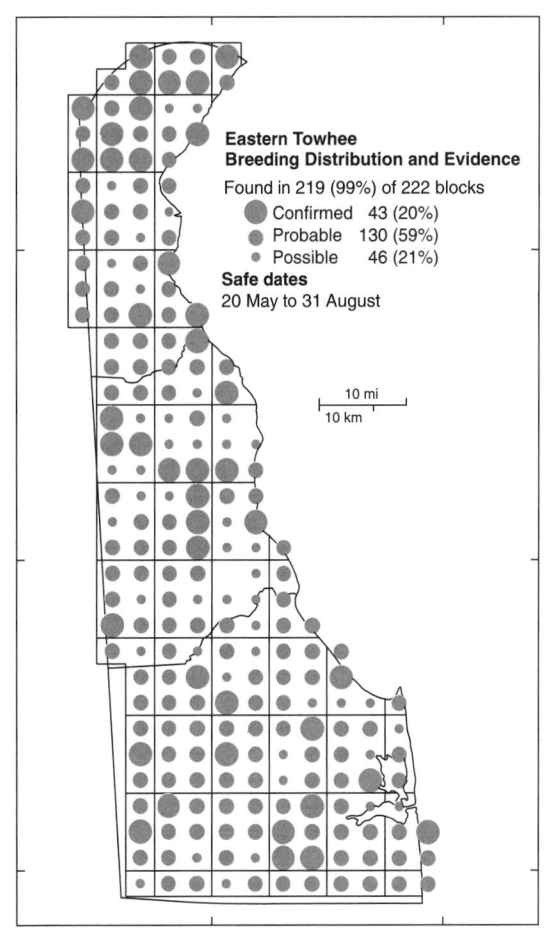

19 April 1975	42	Dragon Run [BroH1]
26 April 1964	40	Hoopes Reservoir [Klab4]
30 April 1972	32	Winterthur [BroW14]

The highest May Count is 378 (1971), the lowest 183 (1986).

BREEDING: The relative abundance map shows it to be less common in Kent County, where decreased woodland and extensive cropland and marshes are factors, than in the rest of the state. The high numbers found at Cape Henlopen correspond to high numbers noted in coastal scrub on Long Island, New York (Bull 1974).

Atlas. This species was easily recorded in most blocks,

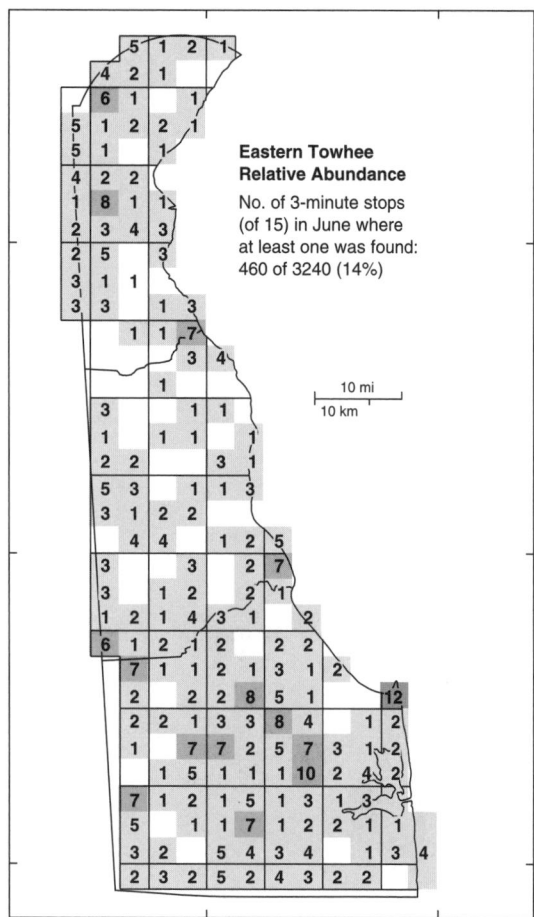

Eastern Towhee
Relative Abundance

No. of 3-minute stops
(of 15) in June where
at least one was found:
460 of 3240 (14%)

10 mi
10 km

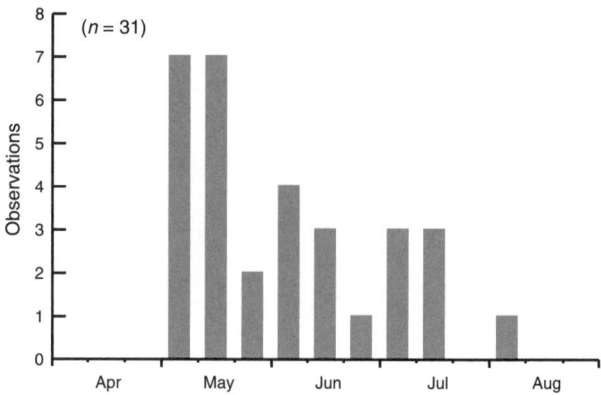

Estimated Clutch-Completion Dates

though finding it in the few blocks where it was initially missed often proved difficult. It was confirmed in most blocks when fledged young became active in following adults, but 10 active nests were found, and nest building was observed in 5 blocks.

Nesting. Of 22 nests described, 15 were on the ground in situations such as at the base of a grass clump or bush, under Japanese honeysuckle or greenbriar, or among dense stands of small bushes or other cover; 7 were 1–3 ft above ground in a vine tangle or bush. As also noted in Ohio (Peterjohn and Rice 1991), nests completed in May were usually on the ground (10 versus 2 above ground), but not later nests (5 versus 5 above ground). Harmic (1953) reported a nest at the University of Delaware woodlot concealed in a dense stand of lily-of-the-valley; it was constructed of grass and tendrils, and lined with moss sporophytes.

Estimated clutch-completion dates extend from early May to the end of July, with half completed in May. Extreme egg dates are 5 May (Harmic 1953) to 9 August [Long1], but a longer season in Delaware is suggested by the Maryland egg dates of 22 April–22 August, peaking 22 May–14 June (Dickinson 1968). Delaware May clutches usually contain 4 eggs, and summer clutches contain 3 (*n* = 15). One nest contained 7 eggs on 12 May (Harmic 1953); the "excess" eggs were likely similar cowbird eggs, since about 10% of towhee nests are parasitized

by cowbirds (*n* = 30). A New Jersey study revealed that the towhee is often double-brooded, clutch completion into the first third of July is routine, and earlier and larger clutches could be related to an early supply of invertebrate food such as found in mesic forest (Greenlaw 1978).

Trends. This species is so common at times that it is hard to believe that its population has been decreasing, yet the May Count data show a 4–5% per year reduction in the towhee population, about 60% over 21 years. BBS data show a similar 60% reduction (1966–90) for the East, and the less precise Delaware BBS data also suggest a decline [Usfw3].

Breeding population. High population densities were found on BBCs at Assawoman WA (50–90 males per 100 ha) and in northern Delaware woodlots (75–120 males per 100 ha). A similar density of 110 territories per 100 ha (9.5 in 21 acres) was reported for an immature loblolly–shortleaf pine stand in the Maryland county just south of Delaware (Springer and Stewart 1948b).

FALL: Numbers of towhees begin to decline about 20 August and continue declining to about 30 September, perhaps representing the departure of most of the breeding population. From 1–20 October numbers reported are similar to summer numbers and may reflect the passage of more northerly breeders. From 20 October–1 December numbers slowly decline to the winter level. This pattern of a possible bimodal migration is reflected in the banding data. High counts are

6 Oct 1974	42	Dragon Run [BroW1]
9 Oct 1971	60	Brandywine Creek SP [Wayn2]
11 Oct 1964	41	Hoopes Reservoir [Falk12]

1966–89 CBC Summary

Christmas Bird Count	Years Found	Range of No. Found	Median
Wilmington	24	3–73	30
Middletown	24	3–39	19
Bombay Hook	24	7–230	27
Cape Henlopen	24	1–270	14
Rehoboth	24	5–201	35
STATEWIDE	24	47–767	124

(decreasing; low in 1980, high in 1970)

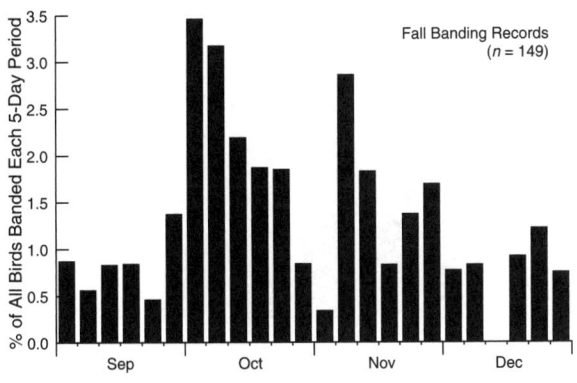

Fall Migration Activity

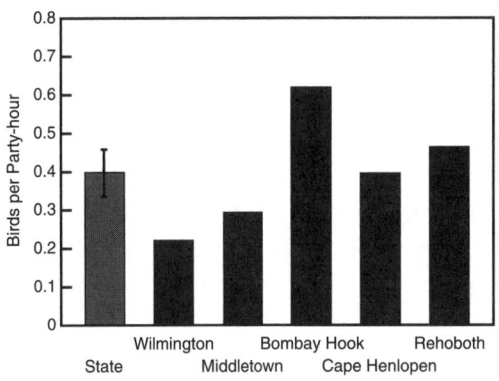

CBC Geographic Distribution

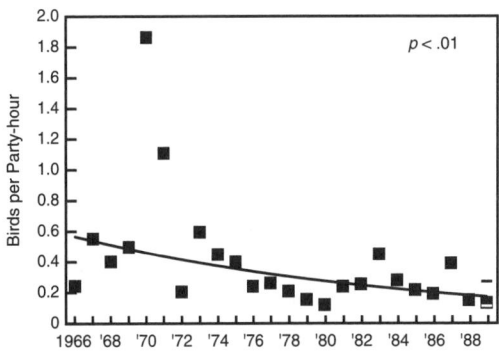

CBC Trend; Decreasing at 5% per Year

WINTER: This woods-dwelling bird has decreased significantly on CBCs. BBS data also revealed a decrease in the East (Robbins et al. 1986). Although much smaller numbers are involved, the CBC decrease is proportionate to the decline shown on the BBS and May Counts. The 1970 and 1971 CBCs resulted in unusually high counts, with 3 of 5 CBCs reporting more than 200 birds (> 2 birds per hour) in 1970 and 3 of 5 reporting more than 100 (> 1 birds per hour) in 1971. Typically, only a few birds are reported in non-CBC tallies. High counts are

3 Dec 1971	11	Brandywine Creek SP [Beac2]
3 Dec 1977	19	White Clay Creek [Falk21]
7 Jan 1978	10	White Clay Creek [Edni72]

SPECIMENS: 25; DMNH, ANSP, UDEL, UWBM.

American Tree Sparrow *(Spizella arborea)*

Regular; winter visitor; fairly common. Expected early November to late March and sporadically into April. Most abundant in New Castle and Kent counties. Has declined notably on CBCs.

HABITAT: Hedgerows, woods edges, second growth or abandoned fields.

SPRING: Migration probably begins in late February or early March and ends by 31 March. Numbers quickly decline after about 15 March. The latest specimen and late sight records are

29 Mar 1911	1	Newport (ANSP 80058)
11 Apr 1970	1	Brandywine Creek SP [Wayn25]
16 Apr 1974	1	Walnut Ridge [SpSB1]
25 Apr 1971	2	Brandywine Creek SP [Broo12]
8 May 1971	2	Brandywine Creek SP [Broo12]

High counts are

19 Feb 1978	100	Broadkill Beach [Frec1]
21 Feb 1970	90	Cape Henlopen SP [DuPA8]
6 Mar 1978	200	Cape Henlopen SP [Frec1]

FALL: First arrival is 5–10 November. Early reports include

8 Oct 1972	30	Winterthur [BroW8]
19 Oct 1931	250	Montchanin [BrJW2]
7 Nov 1964	1 banded	near Hockessin [Know3]
8 Nov 1979	2	Delaware City (DMNH 68052, DMNH 68053)

Peak numbers usually occur from 15 November to 5 December. High counts are

15 Nov 1970	49	Brandywine Creek SP [SpSB1]
21 Nov 1970	35	Brandywine Creek SP [WarD1]
21 Nov 1965	40	Little Creek WA [Long2]

1966–89 CBC Summary

Christmas Bird Count	Years Found	Range of No. Found	Median
Wilmington	24	17–899	95
Middletown	23	1–497	55
Bombay Hook	24	7–711	67
Cape Henlopen	22	1–129	14
Rehoboth	17	1–58	3
STATEWIDE	24	60–1,912	277
(decreasing; low in 1978, high in 1968)			

WINTER: This species has declined significantly on CBCs, a trend observed as early as the late 1970s when Speck (1978) commented on the species' local scarcity. Typical reports involve 10-15 birds. High counts in the 1970s are

5 Dec 1970	83	Brandywine Creek SP [BroW1]
10 Feb 1974	100	Dragon Run [Phal1]
21 Feb 1970	90	Cape Henlopen SP [DuPA8]
19 Feb 1978	100	Broadkill Beach [Frec1]

High counts in the 1980s are

| 23 Jan 1983 | 40 | Bombay Hook NWR [RusR17] |
| 12 Feb 1989 | 25 | Broadkill Beach [Frec1] |

SPECIMENS: 46; DMNH, ANSP, UDEL, USNM.

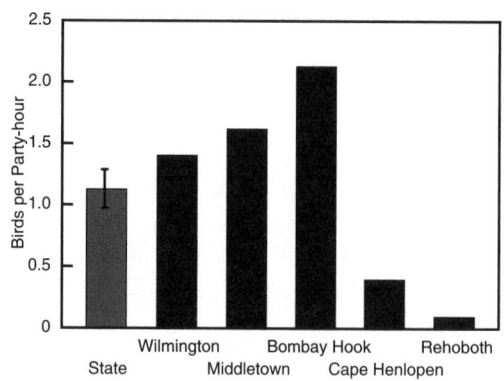

CBC Geographic Distribution

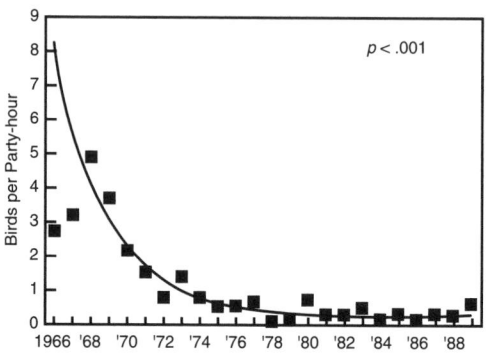

CBC Trend; Decreasing at 11% per year

Chipping Sparrow (*Spizella passerina*)

Regular; summer resident; fairly common. Expected early April to mid-November and sporadically into early winter.

HABITAT: Edges and areas with scattered trees or shrubs with nearby areas of short grass or open ground. Open pine forests in southern Delaware. Frequently found in red cedars, planted evergreens, or deciduous vegetation in open areas or edges.

SPRING: First arrival is 25 March–1 April. Migration peaks 10–30 April and concludes by 1–10 May. Early reports, perhaps wintering birds, include

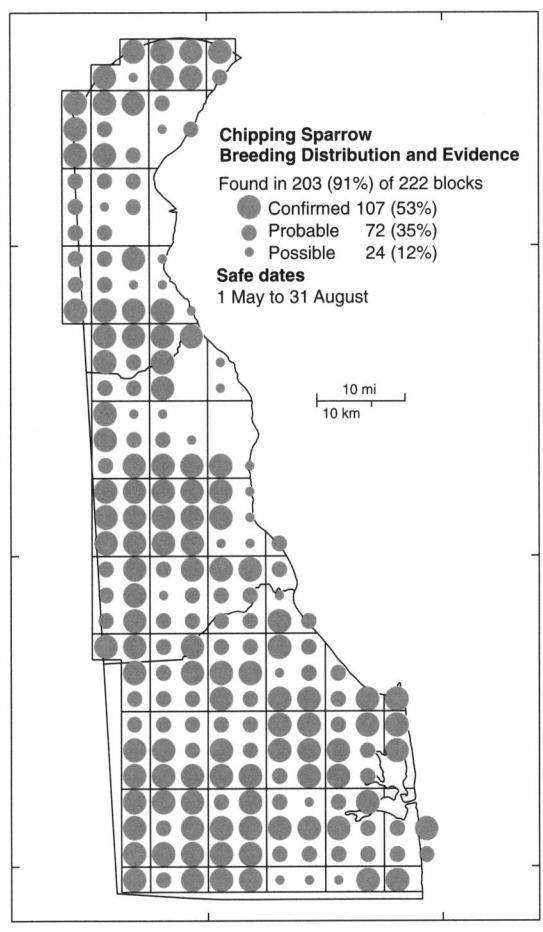

Chipping Sparrow
Breeding Distribution and Evidence

Found in 203 (91%) of 222 blocks
● Confirmed 107 (53%)
● Probable 72 (35%)
• Possible 24 (12%)

Safe dates
1 May to 31 August

10 mi
10 km

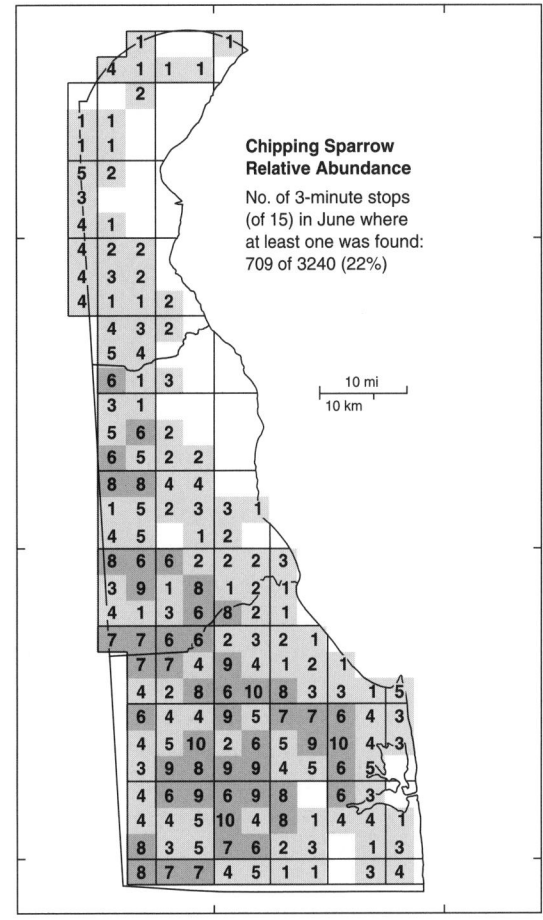

Chipping Sparrow
Relative Abundance

No. of 3-minute stops
(of 15) in June where
at least one was found:
709 of 3240 (22%)

10 mi
10 km

27 Feb 1974	1	Dover [Pure4]
6 Mar 1985	12	Five Points [Frec1]
10 Mar 1982	2	Cape Henlopen SP [Frec1]
11 Mar 1988	1	South Bethany [Jano1]

Early reports from the Piedmont, where fewer winter, include

20 Mar 1991	1	Sherwood Park [Samp5]
29 Mar 1978	2	Newark [Jahn4]
31 Mar 1978	1 banded	Claymont [Conw3]

High counts at Cape Henlopen SP are 35 on 14 April 1981 and 75 on 24 April 1982 [Frec1]; at Winterthur 26 were present on 30 April 1972 [BroW8].

BREEDING: The relative abundance map shows that Sussex County is its stronghold, whereas it avoids a wide strip along the Delaware River and Bay where it is difficult to find on the upland necks.

Atlas. Since it is easily detected from roadsides by its frequent song, those blocks lacking reports probably had few, if any, pairs. It was confirmed in over half the blocks, frequently by observers alerted by the loud begging chips of fledged young. In addition, active nests were located in 24 blocks.

Nesting. Its typical nesting situation is near the end of a branch in a pine at the edge of a woods. Outside of the pine forest, a typical situation is exemplified by a nest in a "lone ornamental blue spruce in rural yard" [Gord2]. It also builds its nests in rose bushes, forsythia, osage orange, and apples, the common factor being a tree or shrub in an open area; the required area is generally larger than the plots typical of modern subdivisions (Arbib 1988a). Hanson (notes) described a nest, 30 in above the ground in an osage orange, made of small grass stems and vine twigs, and lined with fine rootlets and horse hair [the usual substitute for horse hair is fine plant fibers]. It was 3 in. across and 2 in. deep outside; 1¾ in. across and 1¼ in. deep inside. Nest heights reported in Delaware range from 2½ ft to 15 ft, median is 6 ft ($n = 26$), but can range from ground level to 50 ft (Stull 1968).

Extrapolated clutch-completion dates extend from about 25 April to 29 July, with a strong peak in mid-May. Extreme egg dates are 30 April [Jahn1] and 6 August [Jone1]. The bimodal curve is strongly suggestive of some second broods. Three studies at more northern latitudes did not detect double broods but found frequent renestings after failure (Reynolds and Knapton 1984; Buech 1982; Walkinshaw 1944). Mengel (1965) suspected double broods by many pairs based on the long season in Kentucky even though his clutch data were not bimodal. Others, for example, Peterjohn and Rice (1991) in Ohio, suggest regular double broods. Clutch size is usually 3 or 4, less commonly 2, and once 5 ($n = 39$).

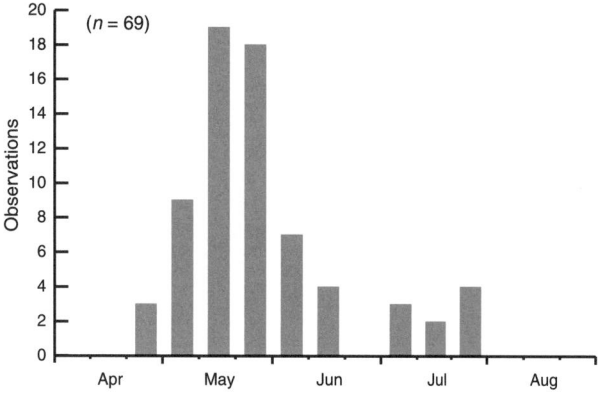

(n = 69)

Estimated Clutch-Completion Dates

History and trends. The Chipping Sparrow's primeval habitat probably consisted of open pine forests such as those formerly found in Sussex County. As Native Americans and then Europeans created openings, the sparrows quickly occupied these additional open areas so that its population greatly increased (Stull 1968). There have probably been fluctuations related to the harvesting of the forests and reforestation, changes in agricultural practices, and local conversion of countryside to suburbia. Its population has shown no long-term trend during the past 21 years on the Delaware May Count, but the Delaware BBS indicates a significant decline over the 25 years since 1966, partly offset by a more recent recovery. Its population has remained fairly stable in the East for this period [Usfw1].

Breeding population. Territory size varies but averages 1 acre (Stull 1968). Chipping Sparrows occurred only sporadically at BBC sites in northern Delaware woods, but from one Assawoman WA site of coastal lowland mixed woods a density of 90 males per 100 ha (7.5 in 21 acres) was reported (McLaugh-

lin 1966). Stewart and Robbins (1958) report densities of 100–130 males per 100 ha in Worcester County, Maryland, apple orchards, and similar densities may occur in Sussex County. The May Count, which occurs after the migration peak, usually reports 100–200 birds. The highest total (266) was reported in 1989.

FALL: Migration begins 5–15 September, peaks 20 September–15 October, and ends 5–15 November. High counts are

21 Sep 1985	50	west of Lewes [Frec1]
18 Oct 1970	150	Cape Henlopen SP [DuPG20]
24 Oct 1984	25	Brandywine Creek SP [Edni21]

1966–89 CBC Summary

Christmas Bird Count	Years Found	Range of No. Found	Median
Wilmington	6	1–5	
Middleton	5	1–2	
Bombay Hook	5	1–4	
Cape Henlopen	4	1–38	
Rehoboth	14	3–63	4
STATEWIDE (high in 1984)	19	1–66	5

WINTER: After mid-November, vagrants occur in some years. Most (that is, about two-thirds) lingering birds are found on CBCs rather than by casual birding efforts. Five reports are clustered during 17–25 January from Bombay Hook NWR and Lewes [Frec1; Palm3]. Winter banding records include

24 Dec 1963	2	Bellevue Manor [Conw3]
1 Jan 1961	1	near Wilmington [Farr1]
17 Feb 1971	1	University of Delaware woodlot [Jone2]

SPECIMENS: 18; DMNH, ANSP. Egg records: DMNH.

Clay-colored Sparrow *(Spizella pallida)*

Occasional (8 years, 1966–93); mostly occurring in fall but records in winter and spring.

REMARKS: The Clay-colored Sparrow is principally a western species that occurs regularly in fall and less frequently in winter along the Atlantic Coast (AOU 1983). Delaware records fit this pattern of occurrence, ranging from 31 August 1988 [Frec1] to 1 March 1982 [Wayn21]. There are 4 September records, 1 each in August, October, November, and March, and 2 in December. In addition, Barnhill (notes) observed a bird at his feeder during winter and early spring 1981. A March 1967 specimen of a bird present since January or February (UDEL 126-67) was identified by Laybourne (1968). The detailed notes on a bird seen on 30 September 1966 (Carlson 1967) at Cape Henlopen are published.

Clay-colored Sparrows are extending their breeding grounds eastward (Peterson 1980, map 375). The species now breeds in Ontario and New York and was registered as possibly breeding in 3 blocks of the Pennsylvania Breeding Bird Atlas (Ickes 1992b). This eastward extension could bring more to Delaware.

SPECIMEN: UDEL 126-67, Centerville, Walnut Ridge, March 1967.

Field Sparrow (*Spizella pusilla*)

Resident; fairly common inland and away from suburbs. Migrates early March to early May and late September through November. Summer and winter populations declining.

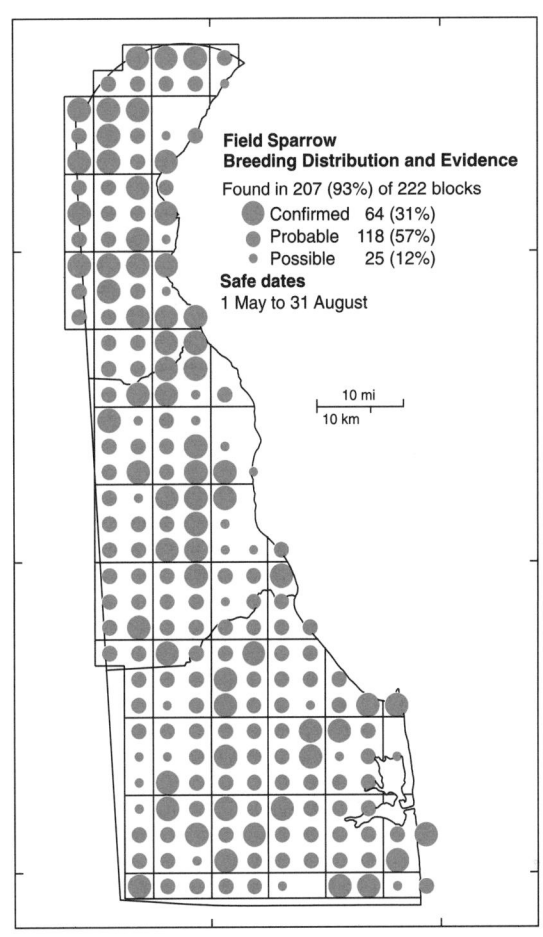

Field Sparrow
Breeding Distribution and Evidence
Found in 207 (93%) of 222 blocks
- Confirmed 64 (31%)
- Probable 118 (57%)
- Possible 25 (12%)
Safe dates
1 May to 31 August

10 mi
10 km

HABITAT: Old fields, overgrown pastures with scattered trees or shrubs, edge.

SPRING: Migration begins 5–10 March and continues to 30 April–5 May, peaking in April. High counts are

4 April 1970	51	Brandywine Creek SP [Beac12]
14 April 1973	57	Dragon Run [HalA2]
25 April 1970	53	Brandywine Creek SP [BroH10]

BREEDING: This species surely increased as a result of clearing the forest for agriculture; however, the shrubby edges of fallow fields, rather than tilled ones, are its habitat.

Atlas. It was found in almost every block that contained fields, showing it is adaptable to the habitat Delaware offers, but it does not colonize suburbs as readily as does the Chipping Sparrow, a circumstance made more obvious by the relative abundance map than by the distribution map. The blank area in northern Delaware will probably grow larger as more fields there are converted to housing developments. The relative abundance study also shows that the Field Sparrow is less common in prime agricultural areas, which probably have fewer old fields. It was not frequently confirmed: active nests were reported in only 12 blocks, nest building in only 7.

Nesting. Delaware nests have ranged from on the ground to 4 ft above ground in a pine sapling in an old field [Nile2], but they are rarely placed over 2 ft above ground. Hanson (notes) described a nest that was constructed of fine roots, weed stems, and vine twigs, and lined with horse hair.

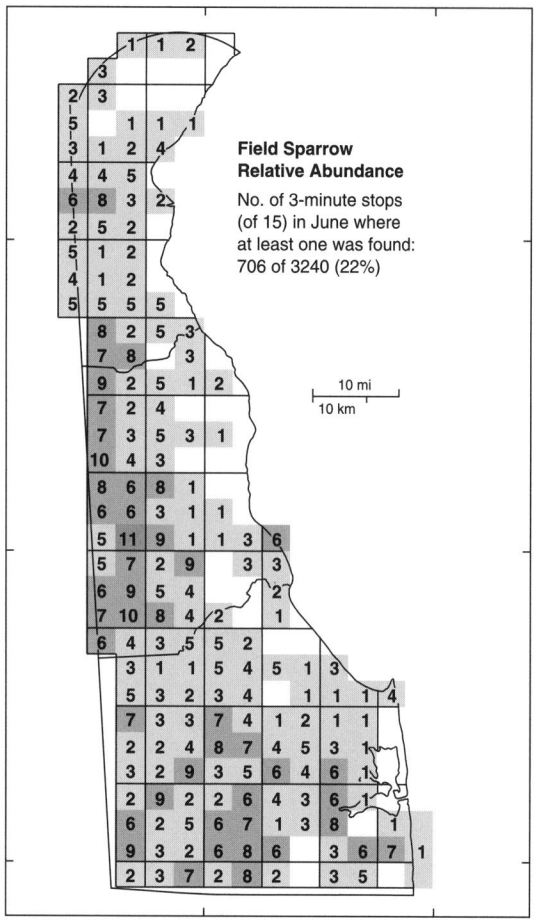

Field Sparrow Relative Abundance

No. of 3-minute stops (of 15) in June where at least one was found: 706 of 3240 (22%)

10 mi
10 km

would be triple-brooded in Michigan if left undisturbed, but frequent failure leads instead to renesting, with the first egg usually laid on the fifth day after a nest is lost. Nest success in the Michigan study was about 35%, clutch size usually 4, sometimes fewer.

Trends. This species' population level has been falling for 21 years, declining about 60% overall according to May Count data. Similar long-term reductions have been registered on the BBS in Delaware and in the Eastern and Central regions [Usfw3]; the severe winters of 1976–77 and 1977–78 contributed to its decline, but the decline began before those winters (Robbins et al. 1986). Some selective pressure seems to be affecting it more than the Chipping Sparrow. It is more dependent on successional habitat (like the Prairie Warbler) and on open fields in the early stages of reversion, and the extent of these habitats is declining. The Field Sparrow also is less tolerant of suburban development and more likely to depend on caterpillars—the supply of which would be disrupted by the use of insecticides—from agricultural fields for its young. This difference could affect its population on a continental scale. Another grassland species, the Eastern Meadowlark, is also declining.

Breeding population. Territories average about 3 acres (1.2 ha) in good habitat (Walkinshaw 1968), and high BBC results are 15–200 territories per 100 ha in various open and mixed habitats in Maryland (Stewart and Robbins 1958). The May Count, which takes place after the migration peak, registered its highest total (173) in 1983 and its lowest (67) in 1977, noticeably fewer than the equivalent numbers the Chipping Sparrow.

Extrapolated clutch-completion dates extend from about 8 May to mid-August. The latter date is suggested by a still-dependent young bird found on 19 September at Brandywine Creek SP; it was starting postjuvenal molt on its crown [Nile2]. Extreme egg dates in Delaware are 13 May [Penn1] and only 28 June [Hans1]. However, extreme egg dates observed in Maryland are 21 April and 25 August and peak 10 May–8 June, showing potential for a longer breeding season at the latitude of Delaware (Walkinshaw 1968). Walkinshaw indicates that most

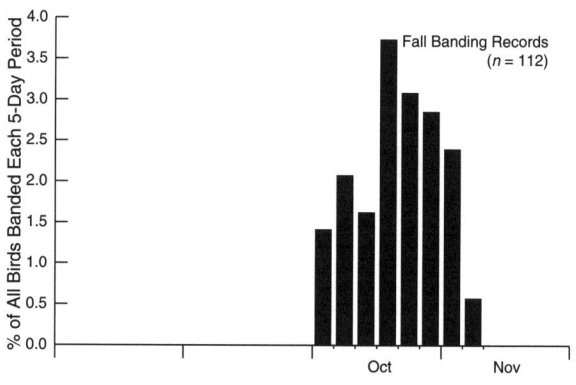

Fall Banding Records
(*n* = 112)

Fall Migration Activity

FALL: Migration is not readily determined from available data. Stewart and Robbins (1958) give 20–30 September to 1–10 December as the normal period, with the peak occurring 10 October–1 November in Maryland. Peak banding occurs during the last half of October. High counts are 53 on 12 September 1971 and 59 on 7 November 1970, both at Brandywine Creek SP [BroW1; Wayn2] respectively, and a remarkable 400 at Cape Henlopen SP on 18 October 1970 [DuPG20].

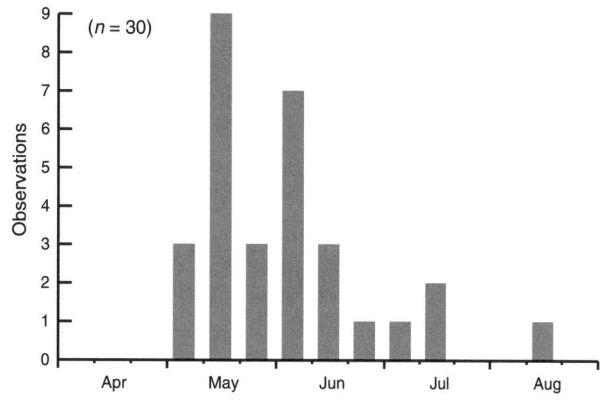

(*n* = 30)

Estimated Clutch-Completion Dates

1966–89 CBC Summary

Christmas Bird Count	Years Found	Range of No. Found	Median
Wilmington	24	37–310	135
Middletown	24	4–93	38
Bombay Hook	24	10–207	47
Cape Henlopen	24	6–197	49
Rehoboth	24	12–460	86
STATEWIDE	24	156–1,012	346

(decreasing; low in 1989, high in 1967)

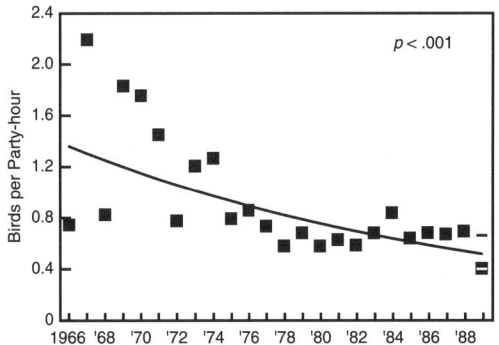

$p < .001$

CBC Trend; Decreasing at 4% per Year

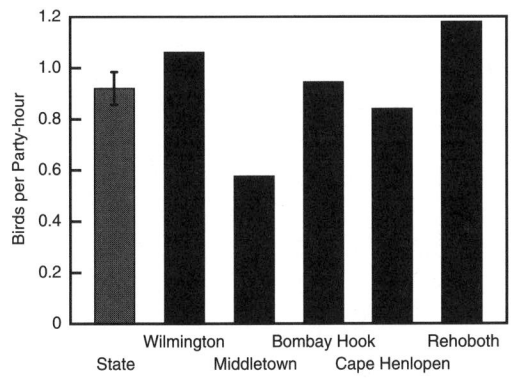

CBC Geographic Distribution

WINTER: This species' winter population has declined significantly, corroborating summer declines registered by the BBS. The Field Sparrow is found about equally on all CBCs. Typical reports mention 10–20 birds, while some high counts total

1 Dec 1991	100	Cape Henlopen SP (D. Rothstein, DNHI, pers. comm.)
5 Dec 1970	73	Brandywine Creek SP [BroW1]
14 Dec 1969	98	Brandywine Creek SP [BroW1]
12 Feb 1978	50	Broadkill Beach [Frec1]
13 Feb 1978	50	Cape Henlopen SP [Frec1]

SPECIMENS: 37; DMNH, ANSP. Egg records: DMNH, WFVZ.

Vesper Sparrow *(Pooecetes gramineus)*

Regular; summer resident; uncommon. Expected early April to late October and sporadically into early winter. The remnant population in southern Delaware seriously declining; no longer breeds in northern Delaware.

HABITAT: Breeds primarily in plowed fields with well-drained sandy soil, usually corn or soybeans in Delaware. Winters along edges of short-growth or sparsely vegetated fallow fields.

SPRING: This underreported species first arrives 5–15 April. The end of migration is not apparent from available data, but Stewart and Robbins (1958) give 1–10 May as the end of migration in Maryland. The early records are

1 Apr 1928	several	Dover [Hans1]
2 Apr 1980	1	Lewes [Frec1]
3 Apr 1908	1 specimen	Lewes (ANSP 80061)

The high count is 12 at Dragon Run on 7 April 1973 [Beac2]. Typical reports mention 1–3 birds. The May Count usually totals 1–5 and its highest was 8 in 1980.

BREEDING: A small population breeds in Kent and Sussex counties, and a few breed in western New Castle County.

Atlas. It was most often found during the Atlas project by hearing its song during the 3-min stops of the relative abundance study. If not found then, additional short stops were made by large fields. Its persistent singing often allowed upgrading to probable by Atlas workers who returned to the same site a week later. Typical breeding locations were large

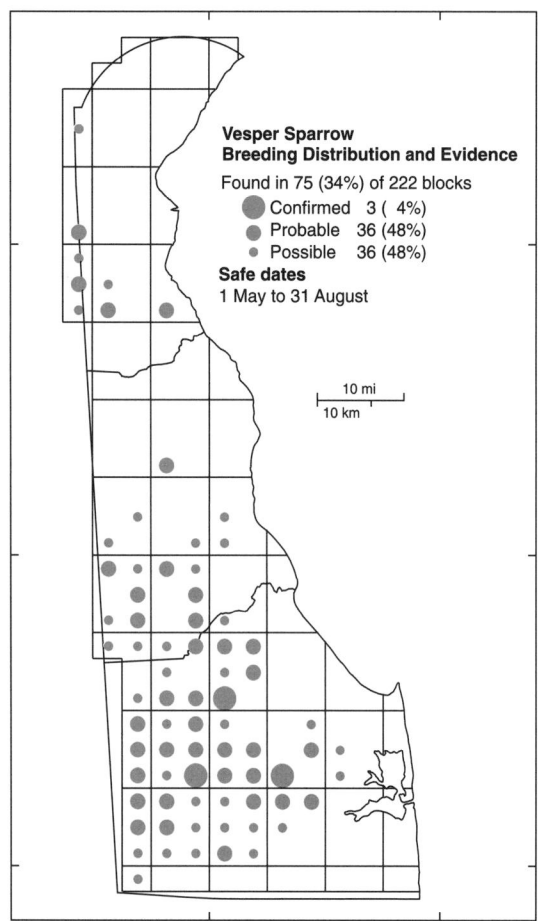

Vesper Sparrow
Breeding Distribution and Evidence

Found in 75 (34%) of 222 blocks
- Confirmed 3 (4%)
- Probable 36 (48%)
- Possible 36 (48%)

Safe dates
1 May to 31 August

10 mi
10 km

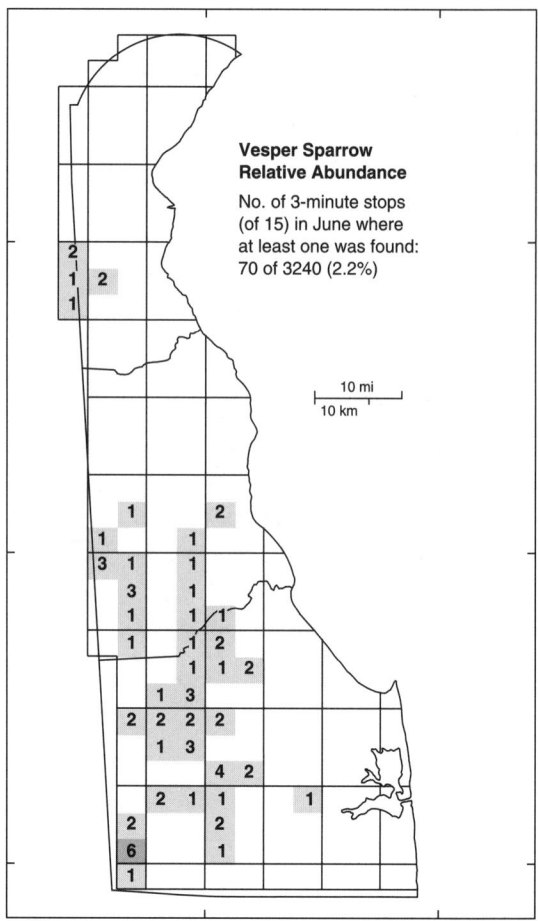

Vesper Sparrow
Relative Abundance

No. of 3-minute stops
(of 15) in June where
at least one was found:
70 of 3240 (2.2%)

10 mi
10 km

soybean or corn fields with dry light-colored soil in which the sparrows regularly take dust baths (Berger 1968). Confirmations include nest building southwest of Ellendale on 5 June 1985, an adult carrying food into a corn field near Georgetown on 4 July 1985, and fledged young in a soybean field near Concord Pond on 24 June 1985 [Litt6; Hess3; RusR2], respectively.

Nesting. The nest is a loose cup of grass, stems, and rootlets lined with finer grasses, rootlets and hair, and placed in a small depression excavated by the bird in a dry field (Harrison 1976).

The 5 breeding records indicate a fairly long season: from nest building near Asbury Church, Dover, on 2 April [Hans1] to carrying food near Georgetown on 4 July [Hess4]. In Maryland egg dates are reported as late as 1 August (Robbins and Bystrak 1977). F. C. Evans (in Berger 1968) noted in a Michigan study that the male apparently takes over most of the feeding of the first brood while the female starts a second brood. Evans found the clutch size was usually 4, sometimes fewer, especially after May.

History. Breeding Vesper Sparrows in southern Delaware did not attract attention earlier in the twentieth century because the species was then breeding in and around Philadelphia: "common and partial to truck farms, where it nests amongst the vegetables" (Miller 1933). It also bred in northern Del-

aware. Rhoads and Pennock listed it as "Rare in the lower part of the state and on the Choptank. Common in more northern sections." Southern Delaware and the Delmarva Peninsula provided its southern limit in the Coastal Plain, still the case.

Since Pennock's days, the tide of progress has almost pushed it out of northern New Castle County. It may have increased in Sussex and western Kent counties, where clearing and ditching have provided wide fields with dry, sandy soil, its preferred habitat. It is still found a few miles back in the country from Millsboro, possibly just where Pennock (1908a) saw 3 on 15 May 1905. It is found in fields not far from Camden, possibly where Hanson (notes) found a nest with 3 young on 10 June 1925 along a cross road between Dover and Camden. It is also found in fields along the road to Oak Orchard near where he found several on 23 May 1925. None were reported as close to Dover as back of the high school, where Hanson noted 1 on 1 April 1928, but it is still present west of there where he observed nest building on 2 May 1928.

Trends. Prospects for the future look dim. According to the BBS this species has been declining for 24 years, by about 50% in the East and more than 70% in Delaware during 1966–90. The May Count data corroborate the Delaware BBS data. The Delmarva population is a noncontiguous remnant at the southern extreme of its Coastal Plain range. This species is a member of the guild of grassland species that have been declining in the East (Droege and Sauer 1990).

Breeding population. The best indicators of the population of this widely distributed species are its appearance on 70 stops during the relative abundance study and in 75 blocks during the Atlas project. It was spread so thinly through these blocks that its population probably does not exceed 1,000 pairs.

Conservation. An Iowa study found that a favored territory contained a vegetated fencerow with an elevated song perch between a soybean and corn field. The nest was placed on the ground in the field. If nesting was disrupted on one side by tilling, renesting could take place in the other crop without leaving the territory. Frequent agricultural disruption and predation led to a low nest success rate of only 13%. Most successes came late in the season from nests placed in washes that sustained low vegetation. Productivity in cropland may be insufficient to offset adult mortality (Best and Rodenhouse 1984). Such a pattern of reproductive insufficiency on the Delmarva Peninsula, with very similar agriculture, could quickly lead to extirpation, since there is little potential for recruitment from adjacent populations. It is already listed as Endangered in Rhode Island and New Jersey and as a Species of Special Concern in New York. Maryland has a western population and has, possibly, given insufficient attention to the Delmarva population.

FALL: Migration usually ceases by the end of October. After that vagrants are found into early winter (only 6 reports for November). The only banding record involves 1 near Rehoboth Beach on 14 October 1966 [RusW1]. The last fall specimen came from Wilmington on 29 October 1910 (ANSP 81568). High counts are

4 Sep 1965	12	Churchmans Marsh [SpSB20]
8 Sep 1983	6	west of Lewes [Frec1]
18 Oct 1970	6	Cape Henlopen SP [DuPG20]

1966–89 CBC Summary

Christmas Bird Count	Years Found	Range of No. Found
Wilmington	4	1–6
Middletown	2	1
Bombay Hook	4	1–3
Cape Henlopen	1	2
Rehoboth	4	1
STATEWIDE (high in 1970)	9	1–7

WINTER: All but 3 of the 42 winter reports derive from CBCs. The numbers of birds reported on CBCs range up to 7, with 1–3 most frequent. The non-CBC reports involve

20 Dec 1958	2	Sussex County (DMNH 1523, DMNH 1524)
1 Jan 1924	several	northern Delaware [Dick1]
10 Jan 1932	2	Claymont [Gill3]

Vesper Sparrows were strikingly less common in the 1970s and 1980s than in the 1940s and 1950s. Analysis of 186 CBCs taken in Delaware from 1940 to 1989 shows that Vesper Sparrows have declined for 50 years at an average annual rate of about 6%, falling 96% during the 50 years. Analysis over the 24 years using CBC trends is not feasible because there is too little data. Delaware is near the northern edge of the Vesper Sparrow's present wintering range (Root 1988), so the low number of reports is expected.

SPECIMENS: 11; DMNH, ANSP, CM, UDEL, USNM.

Lark Sparrow *(Chondestes grammacus)*

DOCUMENTATION: Published and unpublished notes.

REMARKS: The Lark Sparrow is a bird of the western and central United States; it formerly bred almost to the East coast and currently winters regularly along the Southeast coast. With a complicated head pattern and white corners on its tail, it is distinctive and easy to identify. There are at least 16 published Delaware records, but, oddly, no specimens or photographs. Published notes (Barnhill 1974) of 1 at Bombay Hook NWR on 26 August 1973 cover the required points. Unpublished notes describing 4 additional birds are also extant [DuPG1; Frec1]. Although a photograph is clearly desirable, the published notes, the 2 sets of additional unpublished notes, and the fairly large number of other records affirm the place of Lark Sparrow on the Delaware list.

Occasional (14 years, 1941–91); fall migrant; rare. Casual in winter and spring.

Lark Bunting (*Calamospiza melanocorys*)

Casual (6 years, 1965–89), spring and fall.

DOCUMENTATION: Convincing notes.

REMARKS: The Lark Bunting is a western plains species recorded casually along the entire Atlantic coast (AOU 1983). Of 5 Delaware records, the best documented describes 1 at Indian River Inlet on 4 May 1981 [Jaco2; Wayn1]. Wayne's notes describe an adult male in alternate plumage, mentioning the size, chunkiness, white shoulders, and white edging in the secondaries. Other records are

19 Mar 1989	Lewes Beach [Frec1]
14 Sep 1970	Broadkill Beach [Holg51]
13 May 1971	Bombay Hook NWR [Lieh1]
20 Oct–30 Nov 1965	Bombay Hook NWR [Hard3; Hard4]

In view of the number of records and the available description, the occurrence of Lark Bunting in Delaware is established.

Savannah Sparrow (*Passerculus sandwichensis*)

Regular; winter visitor; fairly common. Expected mid-September to early May; breeding population extirpated.

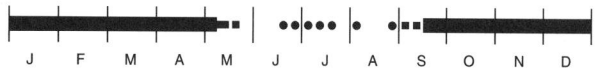

HABITAT: Barrier beaches with American beach grass, marsh meadows, grassy dikes, weedy fields.

SPRING: Migration begins 10–15 March, peaks 1–20 April, and ends 10–15 May. High counts are

4 Apr 1964	43	Little Creek WA [LesC5]
18 Apr 1964	110	Little Creek WA [LesC6]
5 May 1988	75	Prime Hook NWR [Frec1]

The highest May Count is 61 (1971), the lowest 3 (1978).

BREEDING: There are 15 summer records, but most probably involve nonbreeding birds. The dates range from 19 June to 25 August, though the latter date may represent early migrants rather than wandering individuals. Specimen records are 2, a young bird (ANSP 65620) in juvenal plumage and an adult male (ANSP 65618) in very worn plumage, both collected by Pennock at Delaware City on 24 June 1911. Two were banded during summer, 1 on 29 June 1961 near Wilmington [Know3] and 1 on 21 July 1963 near Downes Chapel, Clayton [Pepp1].

Atlas. There was 1 Atlas record—a singing male, present northeast of Bridgeville on 19, 23, and 29 June 1985, but not located thereafter [West3]. This probable breeding record, in the absence of recent breeding, does not warrant a distribution map.

Nesting. Nest records were provided by Buckalew, who wrote the following account: "June 6, 1936. Two nests found near Indian River Inlet, Delaware, were each located near the base of a small sand dune, in the base of a clump of sedge. The nests were in slight hollows, the rim almost even with the sand, and were constructed of fine dead marsh grass, lined with what appeared to be very fine marsh hay *(Spartina patens)"* (Baird 1968, 680).

Conservation. This species once bred on the Delmarva Peninsula from Indian River Inlet south through Assateague Island (Stewart and Robbins 1958), which constituted the southern limit of its range in the Coastal Plain. This population has been extirpated. It is listed as Threatened in New Jersey.

FALL: First arrival is 1–15 September. Migration peaks 1–25 October and ceases 1–10 November. The earliest probable migrant was reported on 25 August 1983 west of Lewes [Frec1], which is followed by a half a dozen reports from 6 to 9 September. One was banded on 13 September 1956 near Red Lion [Mitc1]. High counts are

28 Sep 1980	200	Broadkill Beach [Frec1]
3 Oct 1982	250	Broadkill Beach [Frec1]
9 Oct 1987	100	Prime Hook NWR [Frec1]
11 Oct 1987	150	Prime Hook NWR [Frec1]

1966–89 CBC Summary

Christmas Bird Count	Years Found	Range of No. Found	Median
Wilmington	22	1–54	4
Middletown	23	2–87	17
Bombay Hook	24	12–81	37
Cape Henlopen	24	3–116	35
Rehoboth	24	1–152	32
STATEWIDE (low in 1982, high in 1970)	24	39–365	144

WINTER: Although there is not a significant CBC trend, the analysis revealed a downward aspect. The BBS data show generally stable populations but reflect local declines in Massachu-

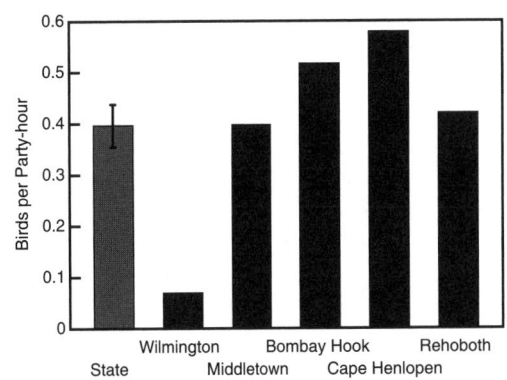

CBC Geographic Distribution

setts and New Brunswick through 1979 (Robbins et al. 1986); it has since declined in the East [Usfw3]. It should continue to be monitored. Typically, fewer than 10 are reported. High counts are

3 Dec 1984	35	west of Lewes (Frech notes)
16 Dec 1977	25	Sandy Landing on Pepper Creek [Frec1]
25 Dec 1968	25	Cape Henlopen SP [Mess1]

REMARKS: The Ipswich Sparrow is a distinctive race *(P. s. princeps)* that winters along the Atlantic coast in barrier beach dunes. It apparently arrives late October to early November, departs in late March to early April, and is reported in numbers ranging from a few to 10–20. It is frequently found wintering on Cape Henlopen. Dwight (1885) recorded it from Rehoboth on 22 November 1884 and Burleigh (1935) recorded it on 4 and 5 January 1935.

SPECIMENS: 64; ANSP, DMNH, USNM.

Grasshopper Sparrow *(Ammodramus savannarum)*

Regular; summer resident; uncommon but more frequent in the western part of state. Expected early May to mid-September. Declining from habitat loss.

HABITAT: Overgrown pastures, hayfields, weedy fields. Neglected wet portions of fields and field margins with higher grass.

SPRING: First arrival is 25 April–5 May, migration concludes 20–25 May, but no peak is evident. Early records include

22 Apr 1964	1	near Newark [LesC1]
23 Apr 1941	1	near Newark [MayR1]
30 Apr 1967	1	near Newark (UDEL 125-67)

Typical reports total only a few birds. High counts at

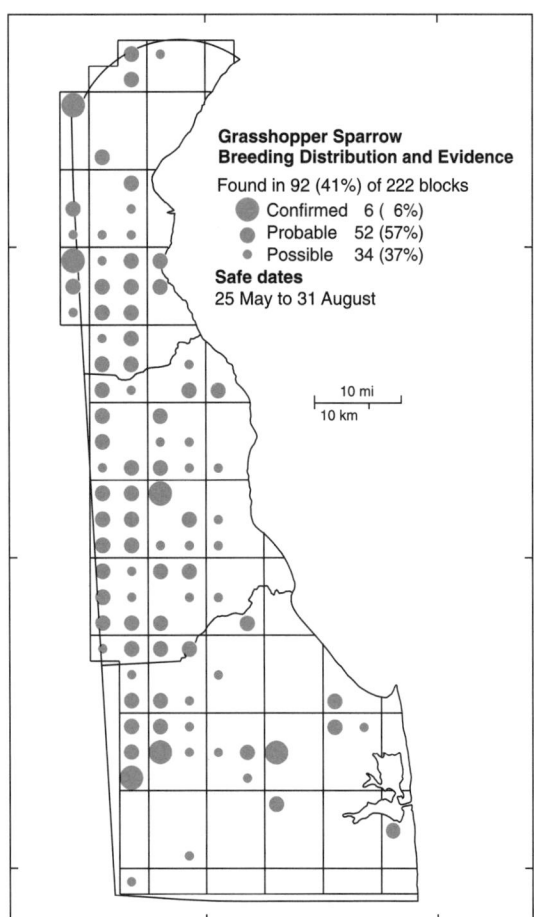

**Grasshopper Sparrow
Breeding Distribution and Evidence**

Found in 92 (41%) of 222 blocks

● Confirmed 6 (6%)
● Probable 52 (57%)
· Possible 34 (37%)

Safe dates
25 May to 31 August

10 mi
10 km

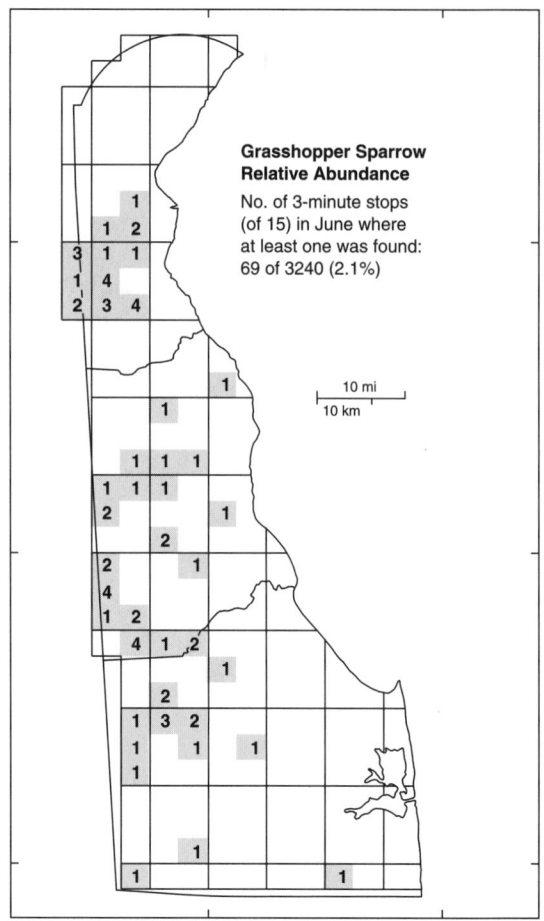

**Grasshopper Sparrow
Relative Abundance**

No. of 3-minute stops
(of 15) in June where
at least one was found:
69 of 3240 (2.1%)

10 mi
10 km

Brandywine Creek SP are 12 on 2 May 1970 and 10 on 23 May 1970 [SpSB13; BroW7], respectively, and 50 were reported in Sussex County on 11 May 1968 [Carr11]. The highest May Count is 21 (1979), the lowest 1 (1976).

BREEDING: This inconspicuous species is little known but easy to recognize by its insect-like voice. Although it is still widespread on the Delmarva Peninsula and into Virginia, Delaware is near the southeastern corner of its range. Most were located in the western part of the state, but Rothstein (DNHI, pers. comm.) reports a number breed amid sedges in dry places in the saltmarshes along Delaware Bay, especially at Great Marsh. There was once a breeding colony in similar habitat at Bombay Hook NWR (West pers. obs.).

Atlas. During the Atlas project it was most widely found in Kent County, but the relative abundance study revealed a noticeable concentration in southern New Castle County near Middletown. This latter area has a low abundance of Eastern Meadowlark and Killdeer. Since Grasshopper Sparrows sing at night, some were first located during the Atlas project while searches were conducted for owls and Whip-poor-wills.

Nesting. There are few Delaware nest records. From Hanson's notes we learn that "Knight in 'Birds of Maine' describes a clutch of five eggs taken by a collector at Newport, Del., May 25, 1894. 'The nest was on the ground in a small bunch of grass in a grass field.'" Darlington (1902) reported from Wilmington

that he had found nests with young on 9 July 1899, with 5 young in late May 1900, and with 5 eggs on 30 May 1902. All were constructed in depressions in the ground, and 1 was arched over. The Atlas project yielded 3 nest records:

19 June 1983	6 eggs	White Clay Creek [Jahn1]
11 July 1986	young	west of Seaford [MiDR1]
11 July 1987	young	west of Glasgow [BroH2]

The last nests are late enough to represent second broods, and immatures were seen in the area of the Seaford nest.

Clutch completion extends from about mid-May to late June. Egg dates in Maryland extend from 15 May to 19 August, suggesting a longer potential season in Delaware. They are triple-brooded in Florida (Nicholson, in Smith 1968), double-brooded in Pennsylvania (Smith 1963), and probably so in Delaware, but late renestings cannot be ruled out as a cause for the extended season.

History. In the forested regions of the East it was originally restricted to extensive natural clearings and sparsely wooded areas. Clearing the land for agriculture permitted it to spread far beyond these limits. We have no reason to believe it was anything but common earlier in the twentieth century. Agricultural practices emphasizing grassland farming appeared to favor an increase in its population (Smith 1963). More recently agricultural grasslands have been disappearing, and this species has been very quietly disappearing, too.

Trends. According to BBS data this species' population declined in the East at an average annual rate of about 5% during 1966–90 (by over two-thirds in 25 years) and by almost that much in Delaware [Usfw3]. May Count data corroborate the Delaware BBS trend. Continued decline at the current rate will lead to range contraction and likely extirpation in Delaware.

Breeding population. It was found on 69 stops during the relative abundance study, it frequently forms small colonies in Delaware, averaging 2 or 3 pairs, and it cannot be heard from a great distance, so its population probably still exceeds 1,000 pairs.

Conservation. It is another member of the guild of grassland species that have been declining in the East (Droege and Sauer 1990). It is listed as Endangered in Maine, Threatened in Rhode Island and New Jersey, and a Species of Special Concern in Massachusetts and New York. It has become progressively difficult to find in northern Delaware, where it was formerly common. Management of public open areas such as parkland (Brandywine Creek SP, Delcastle Recreation Area, and Carpen-ter SP) and golf course rough should provide for inclusion of weed patches maintained for this species. Loss of habitat from changes in land use and altered farming practices are probable causes for some of its 5% annual decline rate, but the decline seems more precipitous than the loss rate for grassy fields.

FALL: We lack data for fall migration. After 31 July there are only 10 August records, 3 September records, and 1 October record in addition to the following records. Thus departure may begin in August and migration continues through October. Migration records include

23 Sep 1988	1	Oyster Rocks Rd [Frec1]
26 Sep 1965	1 banded	Cape Henlopen SP [PylR1]
28 Sep 1962	1 banded	Fenwick Island [Fisk1]
25 Oct 1979	1	Rehoboth [Frec27]

Stewart and Robbins (1958) give a departure period of 20–30 October in Maryland.

SPECIMEN: UDEL 125-67, details earlier; ANSP 65626, Delaware City, 24 June 1911.

Henslow's Sparrow *(Ammodramus henslowii)*

Extirpated as a breeding bird. Formerly regular; summer resident; rare, local.

HABITAT: Chiefly upland edges by tidal marshes; broomsedge fields and weedy sedge meadows.

REMARKS: Until 1954 Henslow's Sparrow was regularly present from late April until early August and was a scarce breeder. Additionally, it was probably present as a migrant through October and may have been a scarce early winter visitor, leaving by the end of December. There are no January or February reports and only 1 from March.

History. This species' status has changed dramatically in the mid-twentieth century. It was first reported in the state in 1903 when Rhoads noted it at Delaware City and collected a nesting pair at Medford Mills on 3–6 June in lower Sussex County (ANSP 47782, ANSP 47783, Hyde 1939, 17). Pennock observed 2 at his Odessa farm on 10 July 1904 (Rhoads and Pennock 1905). Pennock collected 1 of 3 singing on 13 May 1905 on a marsh east of Millsboro (Pennock 1908a). Pennock (notes) lists 10 locations where it was found in 1902–13. One was collected at Bethany Beach on 14 September 1922 (CM 86289, not extant). Scoville reported a Henslow's Sparrow "nest completed" on 28 May 1921 near Smyrna [Scov1]. May (notes), an observer from Maryland, found it on 10 Delaware trips spanning 18 April 1940 to 18 August 1941. The next published report was on 17 August 1941 when 3 were found along the coast [Kram5]; two were also reported on the Bombay Hook CBC that year (unusually late for the latitude). During 1943 and 1945 it was located 4 times each year from 10 June to 14 August, as well as once in May and twice in October on the weekly Hoopes Reservoir survey; most reports involved 1–3 birds, but 8 were found on 9 October 1943 (Falk 1971). On 16 and 23 May and 6 and 27 June 1948 1 was singing near Rt. 9 and Woodland Beach [Pres1]. A specimen was collected at Bethany Beach on 24 September 1948 (DMNH 51065). During 1950–54 the Prests had at least 1 bird singing from late April to early August near their home at Porter [Pres1]. Additionally, they found 1 singing south of Redden SF on 1 May 1949, 1 near Pocomoke Swamp on 4 May 1949, and 1 near Bombay Hook

NWR on 25 June and 7 August 1949. They also recorded singing individuals at 3 different locations between Wilmington and Smyrna on 31 May 1953 [Pres1]. The only other reports we have seen from this period include Miller's observations at Bombay Hook NWR—2 on 21 April 1951 and 2 on 30 May 1956 [MiJC1]—and the collection of a specimen at Bethany Beach on 7 November 1957 (DMNH 1370).

Trends. Since 1954 the situation has changed for the worse. Despite much interest in locating this sparrow, there have been only 25 reports (the last in 1981), none confirming its presence for an entire season. In 1955, 1956, 1959, 1960, and 1962 single birds were present near Porter—in what had apparently been acceptable habitat—for only 1 day, usually in late April, during each year; no records since then have occurred at the site [Pres1]. During the period 1955–81 there were 10 years with no reports, 10 years with 1 report, 6 years with 2 reports, and 1 year with 3 reports. It was found twice on the 1965 trial BBS in Delaware, but only 3 times on a BBS since then [Line5; Boon1], with none since 1978. Since 1967 most reports have been from Broadkill Beach or elsewhere in coastal Sussex County. Thus since 1954 there has been a significant decline in the species' presence and a reduction in localities where it has been found; apparently, it no longer lingers or attempts to breed in Delaware. It was last reported in Delaware on the 9 May 1981 May Count [Barn54].

BBS data reflect an average annual decline of 5% in the East in 1966–90, resulting in a 70% reduction during that period [Usfw3].

Along the Atlantic coast, the species probably bred on the edges of saltmarshes before the arrival of Europeans (Smith 1992). Its historical Atlantic coast distribution is mapped by Hyde (1939, 23). Its Atlantic coast population has now all but disappeared (map, in Smith 1992), so even migrants are no longer expected in Delaware.

Conservation. Henslow's Sparrow was placed on the Blue List in 1974–86 and considered a species of special concern in 1982–86 (Tate 1986). It is regarded as a migratory bird of management concern in the Northeast (USFWS 1987). More recently, the USFWS petitioned to make the species a candidate for listing as a federally Endangered or Threatened species (USFWS 1991). It is listed as Endangered in New Hampshire, Vermont, Massachusetts, and New Jersey, and as a Species of Special Concern in New York and Maryland. The Henslow's Sparrow and its habitat should be regarded as requiring special attention in Delaware. Smith (1992) recommended that habitat management regimes be established to maintain plots of at least 30 acres in areas with suitable vegetation.

SPECIMENS: 6; ANSP, CM, DMNH.

Le Conte's Sparrow *(Ammodramus leconteii)*

Casual (1974 and 1991).

DOCUMENTATION: Photograph (J. F. White, DMNH 411).

REMARKS: The Le Conte's Sparrow breeds in the Northwest, coming closest to Delaware on a regular basis in northeastern Wisconsin and northern Michigan (AOU 1983). It occurs in migration "casually to the east coast from Maine south to southern Florida" (AOU 1983). The first Delaware report of this elusive sparrow involves a "quite probable" bird observed at Indian River Inlet at the end of November 1974 [AbbD1]. A reported resighting of this bird the following January [Lehm10] actually refers to a bird in Maryland (J. G. Lehman, pers. comm.).

A Le Conte's Sparrow reported at Cape Henlopen SP, photographed on 9 February 1992 [Whit2], and seen again briefly on the twelfth, is the first verified record.

Nelson's Sharp-tailed Sparrow *(Ammodramus nelsoni)*

Occasional; rare and secretive migrant; winter status unknown.

REMARKS: Nelson's Sharp-tailed Sparrows migrate, in part, along the Atlantic coast; they winter, in part, along the Atlantic coast from Massachusetts (rare) south to Florida (Rising 1996). Specimens of 3 immature birds were obtained on 23 September 1948 at Indian River Inlet. Sharp-tailed sparrows reported on 5 October 1980 in Churchmans Marsh [Kell3] and in a cattail swamp on 6 October 1971 at Winterthur [Gran2], nonbreeding sites, might suggest the presence of this species. The CBC results for sharp-tailed sparrows tabulated in the Saltmarsh Sharp-tailed Sparrow account may include individuals of this species.

SPECIMENS: 3; DMNH 51016, DMNH 51017, DMNH 51019, details earlier.

Saltmarsh Sharp-tailed Sparrow (*Ammodramus caudacutus*)

Regular; summer resident; uncommon, local. Expected early May, probably earlier, to early January, but may occur all year. Appears to be seriously declining.

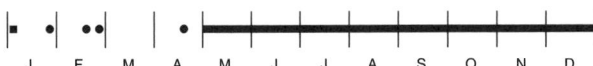

HABITAT: Saltmarsh dominated by saltmarsh cordgrass, occasionally in salt hay. Selects wetter marsh than that selected by Seaside Sparrow.

BREEDING: It is a scarce breeder in cordgrass saltmarshes from northern Kent County to Assawoman WA and is sometimes found in small colonies.

Atlas. The distribution map probably does not display the full extent of the Saltmarsh Sharp-tailed Sparrow's present range, or, if it does, the range has seriously contracted. It was not reported from Milford Neck where Buckalew found a nest in the 1930s and where suitable habitat remains. It was not reported near Indian River Inlet where West (pers. obs.) and others found sharp-tails regularly in the 1970s. It was not reported from the upper reaches of Indian River Bay, where it was reported during an environmental survey near the Indian River power plant (Burkholder 1976). However, the extent of the range from the marshes at Assawoman WA north to northern Kent County is probably correct. There are no New Castle County summer records.

Nesting. We have few breeding records. A nest with 4 eggs was reported at Big Stone Beach on 27 May 1935 [Buck10]. Nests with eggs were reported at Bombay Hook NWR, including 1 with 4 eggs on 2 June, 2 with 2 and 4 eggs, respectively, on 3 June, and 2 nests with eggs on 18 June [Peli1]; another nest with eggs was noted at Prime Hook NWR on 10 June [O'Sh1]. A nest 2 mi south of Ocean View had young ready to fledge on

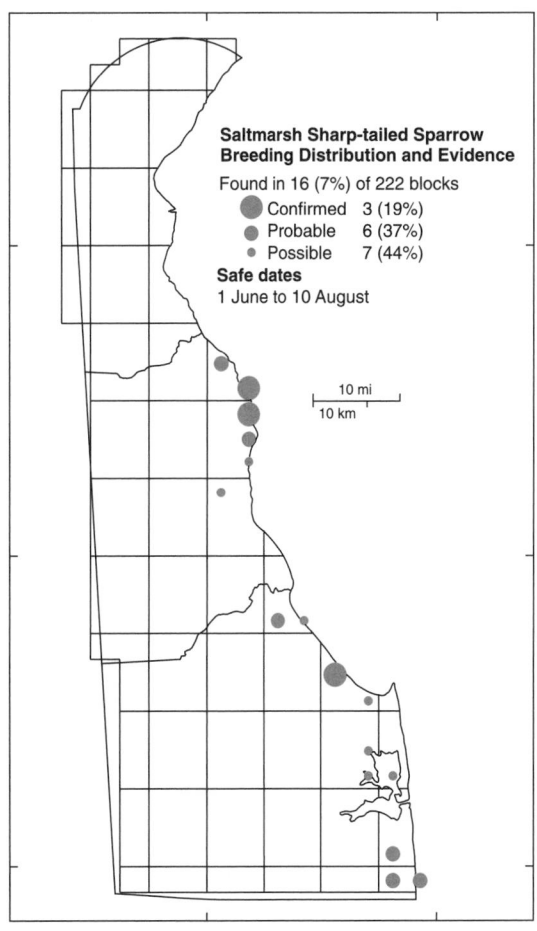

Saltmarsh Sharp-tailed Sparrow Breeding Distribution and Evidence

Found in 16 (7%) of 222 blocks

●	Confirmed	3 (19%)
●	Probable	6 (37%)
●	Possible	7 (44%)

Safe dates
1 June to 10 August

10 mi
10 km

25 August [Jesc2]. It was recorded nesting in saltmarsh cordgrass, usually mixed with salt meadow cordgrass. The nest is placed low, woven in grass stems. Sharp-tails are colonial and promiscuous. The male does not maintain a traditional territory (Woolfenden 1956), but this should not prevent use of the "T" code in the Atlas sense.

Estimated clutch-completion dates extend from about 27 May to 5 August. Egg dates extend from 14 May to 21 August in Maryland (Robbins and Bystrak 1977) and from 22 May to 21 August—peak is 30 May–22 June—in New Jersey. It raises 2 broods in New Jersey but only 1 in New England (Hill 1968a). The Delaware population has a breeding season long enough to raise 2 broods.

History. The first record we have of this species is 1 shot by Pennock at Lewes on 8 June 1898; he speculated correctly that it was probably not rare in suitable localities (Rhoads and Pennock 1905). On 20 May 1907 at Indian River Inlet he found it was about equal in number with the Seaside Sparrow in a marsh close to the ocean, but much the less common of the two back in the bay coves (Pennock 1908a).

Trends. The May Count, which is taken during migration,

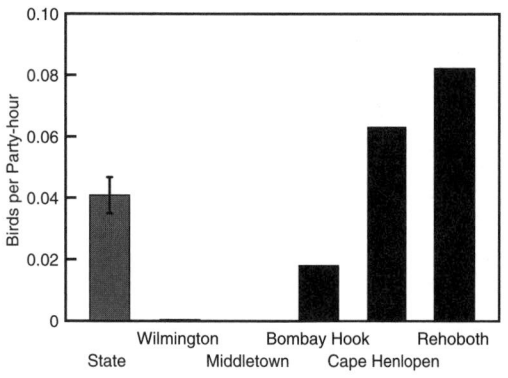

CBC Geographic Distribution; Average of 4 Count Areas

totaled its highest (60, an outlier) in 1975 and its lowest (3) in 1987. The sharp-tail's trend on the May Count is down about 5% per year 1969–91, concurring with its winter trend. BBS data for Delaware and the Upper Coastal Plain, a broader measure of its Mid-Atlantic population, suggest a downward trend based on meager data, but the species appears to be increasing farther to the north [Usfw1].

Breeding population. Its population may be in the range of 100–1,000 breeding females. It was found in 14 blocks and probably occurs in some of the other 24 blocks where the Seaside Sparrow was located. Much saltmarsh remote from roads was never inventoried. On the other hand, great effort was required to locate the ones that were registered, and no large colonies were reported, so it is difficult to support an estimate of more than 1,000. In the spring and summer it is typically reported in small numbers—up to 5 or 6.

Conservation. Alteration (e.g., ditching or other management programs) of marshes should be avoided unless known not to adversely affect this species. Phragmites control does not adversely effect it since it does not use this habitat, but follow-up establishment of vegetation and drainage should be carefully evaluated for effect on it.

NONBREEDING: This elusive marsh sparrow may be present all winter in low numbers, but after the CBC period and before the first week of May there are only a few reports, as depicted on the seasonal graph. One was collected on 21 February 1975 near Dewey Beach (DMNH 44703). The April dot represents a focused collection effort from 12 to 19 April (DMNH specimens). Several factors contribute to the low number of mid- and late-winter reports. First, and perhaps most important, few observers want to tramp over cold, wet, soggy, ditched, windy saltmarshes during some of the worst weather to find a bird that prefers to run mouselike through the grass, with which it blends perfectly, rather than to fly. Even those inclined to marsh-tramping quickly discover that "Sharp-tailed Sparrows are rather difficult birds to observe, especially if they are vigorously followed, as they then lie close, and when flushed, soon drop into the grass and instantly conceal themselves" (Townsend 1905, in Hill 1968a, 803). Next, it undergoes "a

complete molt prior to migration in March and April" (Hill 1968a, 803), perhaps thus causing it to be even more secretive. Lastly, it may completely vacate Delaware when the marshes are likely to be frozen in January, February, and early March. Consequently, its status at this time of year remains enigmatic. After the mid-April records, the next reports are

| 28 Apr 1991 | 1 | Little Creek WA [Barn45] |
| 4 May 1981 | 1 | Savages Ditch [Frec1] |

Beginning with the preceding May report it is recorded regularly through the end of August—it acquires winter plumage "by complete molts before migration in late August and September" (Hill 1968a, 804)—and sparingly through fall and early winter. It is usually found on 1 or more CBCs each year.

Although the CBC data do not show a trend, they do have a downward aspect due in part perhaps to the manner in which the species is sought on these counts. Typically, observers tromp through a saltmarsh counting Song and Seaside sparrows until finding 1, or at most 2, sharp-tailed sparrows, unless they get cold, wet, or tired first. Sharp-tails are most common on the Cape Henlopen and Rehoboth CBCs.

1966–89 CBC Summary

Christmas Bird Count	Years Found	Range of No. Found	Median
Wilmington	1	1	
Middletown			
Bombay Hook	16	1–5	1
Cape Henlopen	15	1–26	2
Rehoboth	21	1–30	6
STATEWIDE	22	1–40	13
(zero in 1986 and 1989, high in 1978)			

REMARKS: Of the several populations of sharp-tailed sparrows, the population breeding in Delaware is *A. c. diversa,* which ranges from Tuckerton, New Jersey, south to Chincoteague Island, Virginia. It winters mainly from Charleston, South Carolina, to Titusville, Florida, and along the Gulf Coast from Tarpon Springs to Wakulla County, Florida (Hill 1968b). The northern populations migrate through our region.

Greenlaw (1993) concluded that there were 2 distinct populations of the sharp-taile1d sparrow complex, which he divides into 2, closely-related species, a northern and interior population *A. nelsoni,* Nelson's Sparrow, and a southern population south from Maine along the Atlantic seaboard for which he retains *A. caudacutus,* Sharp-tailed or Salt-marsh Sparrow. The latter, found in Delaware, is characterized by a longer, softer, and more variable song, a bill averaging a millimeter longer, and more distinct, darker streaking on the back (see Rising 1996).

SPECIMENS: 23; DMNH, ANSP, USNM.

Seaside Sparrow *(Ammodramus maritimus)*

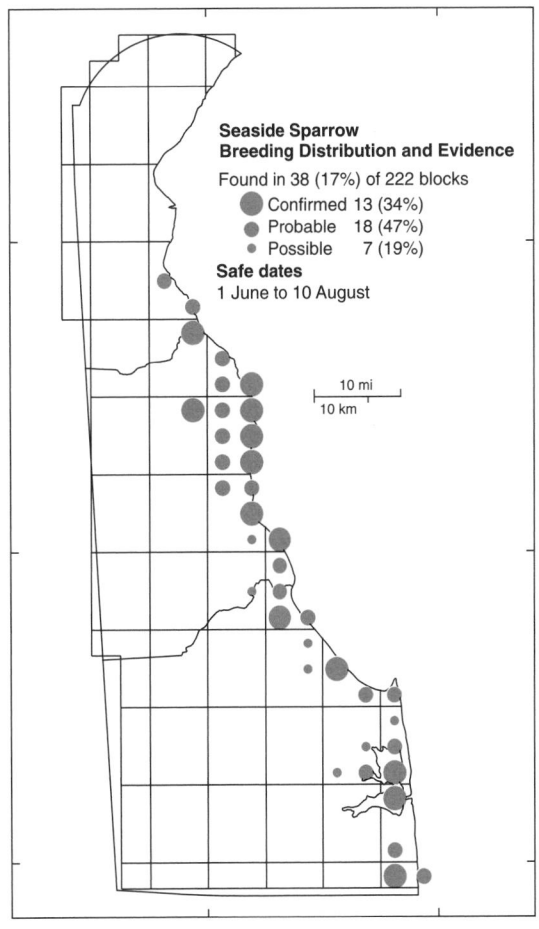

Seaside Sparrow Breeding Distribution and Evidence
Found in 38 (17%) of 222 blocks
● Confirmed 13 (34%)
● Probable 18 (47%)
· Possible 7 (19%)
Safe dates
1 June to 10 August

10 mi
10 km

Regular; summer resident; fairly common. Expected late April to late September. Late fall and early winter status uncertain. Numbers sharply reduced by ditching of saltmarshes. Overall numbers possibly increasing after a decline in the 1970s.

HABITAT: Saltmarshes with "salt-water cordgrass and salt-water meadow grass types that contain scattered shrubs of marsh elder and sea myrtle" (Stewart and Robbins 1958). This same description is applicable to Delaware BBC sites where this species was found, but its northernmost site found during the Atlas project was dominated by needlerush.

SPRING: First arrival is about 25 April to 5 May, and the end of migration is probably 20 May–1 June. The first April report results from focused collecting efforts (DMNH specimens) near Dewey Beach during 13–16 April (1974–76). On 14 April 1976 Niles (notes) observed several singing birds south of Dewey Beach. It is possible that by mid-April the Seaside Sparrow has arrived and some may be on territory. Other early reports are

17 Apr 1983	2	Bombay Hook NWR [RusR20]
19 Apr 1980	several	Little Creek WA [Barn13]
21 Apr 1991	1	Indian River Inlet [Hess13]

Beginning 1–10 May its numbers quickly build and by 15 May reach summer levels. Cruickshank (1942), reporting for the New York City region, noted that "while there is sometimes a light flight in mid-April, the first widespread movement seldom comes before the initial week of May. A spring peak is reached during the third week of this month." The May Count usually reports 100–140 birds, but a high of 361 was reported in 1975.

BREEDING: The distribution map of this sparrow reiterates the distribution of saltmarsh in Delaware. The relative abun-

dance study shows that Seaside Sparrows are much less common in Sussex County than elsewhere in the state.

Atlas. The Atlas project produced the first New Castle County records for this species in 75 years, the northernmost represented by a bird singing from a small patch of needlerush on the north side of Blackbird Creek on 25 June 1983 [West3]. The spotty distribution in Sussex County suggests its population is sharply down. It was found, for example, in 1975 near the Indian River power plant (Burkholder 1976) but was not detected in that block during the Atlas period. Five of the confirmed records entailed location of a nest, and 8 represented fledged young or attending young.

Nesting. The first breeding record comes from Pennock (1908a), who observed nest building on 20 May 1907 at Indian River Inlet. Nests reported in Delaware have been about 6 in. off the ground in salt hay and spike grass, but Woolfenden (1968) reports them also nesting in needlerush and low in marsh elder in a New Jersey study area.

Clutch completion extends from about 11 May to 27 June. From the data, it appears to be single-brooded in Delaware, but 2 broods are fledged successfully by some pairs in New York,

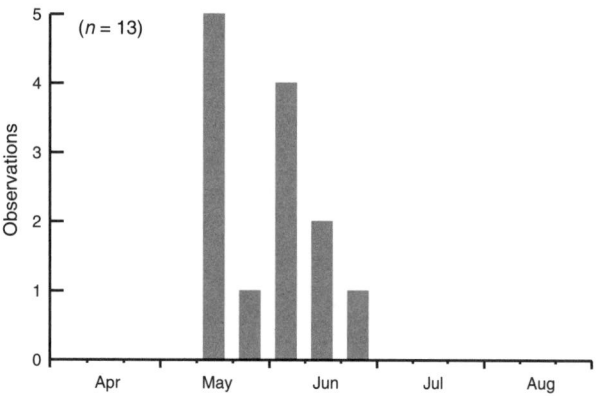

Estimated Clutch-Completion Dates

where the interval from fledging to initiation of a new clutch was 17.5 days (Greenlaw and Post 1992). Egg dates extend from 21 May [Nile2] to 3 July [Line3], both at Little Creek WA.

History and trends. Pennock found several pairs of this sparrow on 7 July 1902 on River Farm just above Appoquinimink Creek, the farthest up the Delaware it has been recorded. He found it common at Indian River Inlet in 1907, and it has remained relatively common in some of our marshes, although it has suffered setbacks resulting from marsh destruction and ditching. It appears to have held its own as a breeding species in Delaware during 1966–90 (i.e., it did not decline further) by some measures, but data are too meager to be conclusive. It is probably holding steady on the May Count. It appears to be increasing on the BBS in Delaware and significantly increasing an average of 2% per year in the Maryland to New Jersey Upper Coastal Plain [Usfw1].

Breeding population. Reports of more than a few birds are rarely submitted, but Rowlett's report of 165 at Port Mahon on 21 July 1974 [Rowl4] is quite believable if he went out into the marsh; however, shortly after his visit this marsh was reditched and its complement of sparrows plummeted. Breeding densities on Long Island were 809 pairs per 100 acres (2,000 pairs per 100 ha) for unditched saltmarsh and 26 per 100 acres (60 per 100 ha) for ditched saltmarsh (Post 1970a,b). A study at Assawoman WA (ditched) averaged 50 pairs per 100 ha (4.25 in 20 acres) for 2 years (Linehan 1965a; Ward et al. 1966). A BBC in a Prime Hook NWR saltmarsh revealed 30 territories per 100 ha (4 in 35.3 acres) (West 1993).

Conservation. The USFWS listed Seaside Sparrow as a nongame bird of management concern in 1987. Its primary threat is habitat loss, as happened at Cape May (Stone 1937) and as could happen in Delaware if the coastal zone and wetlands laws do not remain intact. Its population has been reduced in the past by manipulating tidal wetlands for waterfowl and muskrat enhancement and mosquito control; the invasion of phragmites into these marshes has also adversely affected this species' population.

Essentially all Delaware's marshes have been ditched at one time or another, but when the ditches silt in, the habitat gradu-

ally reverts to the undisturbed state. In drained marshes small populations of sparrows remain at the moisture gradient that was once representative of the entire marsh before ditching. Greenlaw and Post (1992) recommend a statewide survey to determine the current abundance and distribution of this species beyond the information the Atlas study provides. They specifically call for research in Delaware to ascertain the effect that current and planned marsh alteration programs are having on this species, which at one time probably maintained a state population exceeding 1 million pairs.

SUMMER: Migration probably begins about mid-August, and by 20 August the numbers of sparrows reported decrease noticeably. Few reports occur after 25 September, but a few sparrows remain throughout the fall and early winter as evidenced by CBC reports. Cruickshank (1942), referring to the New York area, notes that "With the first light frost in September a definite southward movement sets in. It reaches a peak during the middle of October and is virtually concluded by the middle of November." It remains for future observers to find evidence of the peak fall migration in Delaware.

1966–89 CBC Summary

Christmas Bird Count	Years Found	Range of No. Found	Median
Wilmington			
Middletown	1	1	
Bombay Hook	21	1–22	1
Cape Henlopen	9	1–10	
Rehoboth	24	1–52	5
STATEWIDE	24	2–62	11
(low in 1980 and 1983, high in 1966)			

WINTER: The Seaside Sparrow is seldom reported between the CBC period and late April for the same reasons that few sharp-tailed sparrows are noted then (see Saltmarsh Sharp-tailed Sparrow account). Winter records, all of single birds,

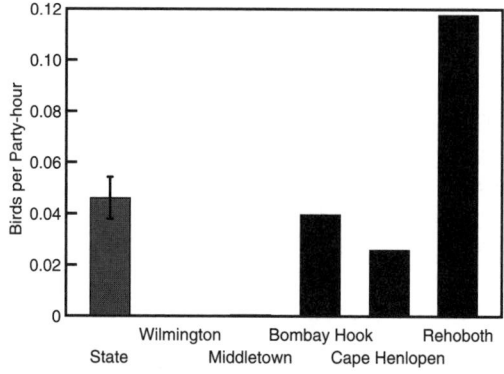

CBC Geographic Distribution; Average of 4 Count Areas

include 29 January 1983 at Burton Island, 12 February 1978 at Broadkill Beach [Frec1], 18 February 1984 along the coast, and 24 February 1980 at Indian River Inlet [Barn13]. On 30 March 1991 Speck and Wayne in good weather spent an entire day in an attempt to locate this and a few other species but failed to do so [SpSB39]. Based on these observations, admittedly few, it is

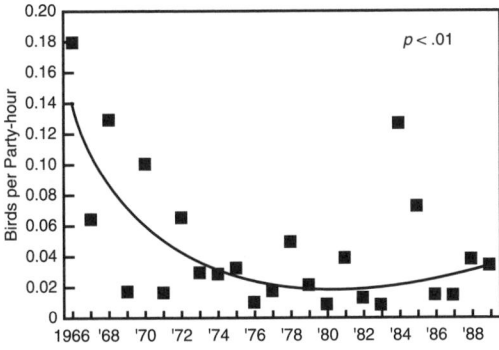

CBC Trend; May be Autocorrelated

likely Seaside Sparrow is not present in most years and, when present, occurs in low numbers. Additionally, Woolfenden (1968, 820) notes that "Though a few individuals winter fairly regularly throughout its breeding range, the northern seaside sparrow population is essentially migratory, and most individuals winter to the southward." The AOU Check-list gives the winter range of the northern Seaside Sparrow as extending from the Virginia coastal marshes south to northeastern Florida and only occasionally north of Virginia (AOU 1957).

Numbers of this species on CBCs have shown a significant decline. It is most abundant on the Rehoboth CBC.

SPECIMENS: 22; DMNH, CM, USNM.

Fox Sparrow (*Passerella iliaca*)

Regular; winter visitor; uncommon to fairly common. Expected late October to mid-April.

HABITAT: "Wood margins, hedgerows, and brushy cutover areas of swamp, flood-plain, and moist upland forest" (Stewart and Robbins 1958).

SPRING: Fox Sparrows migrate early. Beginning 15–25 February the number of reports increases; migration continues throughout March, but by 1–15 April virtually all have departed. Late reports include 1 at Woodland Beach WA on 9 May 1987 [Samp8] and 1 at Cape Henlopen SP on 16 May 1970 [DuPG16]. High counts involve

11 March 1968	30	near Newark [McCT2]
13 March 1971	50	Brandywine Creek SP [Edni1]
22 March 1968	20	northwest New Castle County [Crum3]

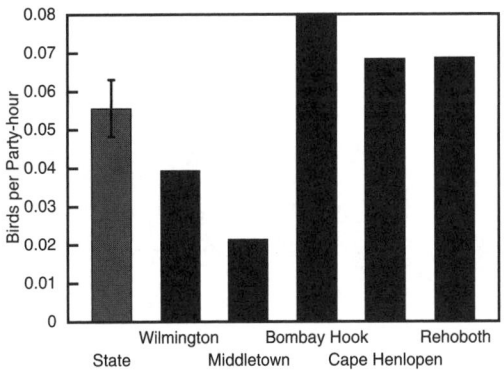

CBC Geographic Distribution

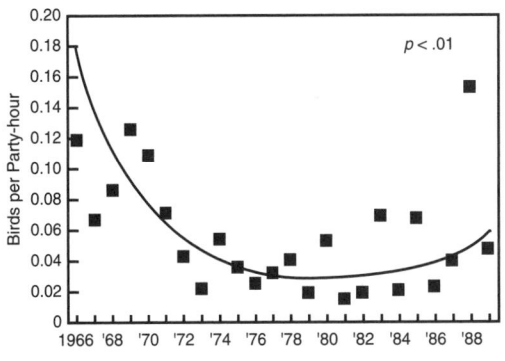

CBC Trend; May be Autocorrelated

FALL: The Fox Sparrow is a late migrant, with first arrival usually occurring 20 October–1 November. Migration peaks 5–25 November and probably ends 25 November–10 December. Early reports are

4 October 1964	2	Hoopes Reservoir [Falk12]
7 October 1973	1	Dragon Run [John1]
15 October 1989	1 banded	Prime Hook NWR [Thor1]

High counts are

Date	No.	Location
6 November 1976	25	White Clay Creek [BroW6]
9 November 1969	27	Brandywine Creek SP [Falk24]
13 November 1971	33	Brandywine Creek SP [Falk8; WarD4]

1966–89 CBC Summary

Christmas Bird Count	Years Found	Range of No. Found	Median
Wilmington	23	1–14	4
Middletown	16	1–6	1
Bombay Hook	24	1–24	4
Cape Henlopen	20	1–33	3
Rehoboth	22	1–37	4
STATEWIDE	24	7–56	20
(low in 1981 and 1982, high in 1970)			

WINTER: This species has shown a significant decline in CBC numbers. The severe winters of 1976–77 and 1977–78 may have contributed to its decline, but those winters were preceded by 4 years (1970–73) of falling numbers. Because Fox Sparrows nest north of the road systems, the BBS is unable to determine a trend in the East (Robbins et al. 1986). Typical reports involve 1 or 2 birds. High counts are

Date	No.	Location
3 Dec 1977	4	White Clay Creek [Falk21]
4 Dec 1982	12	Trap Pond SP [Frec1]
8 Dec 1984	4	Nanticoke WA [Frec1]

SPECIMENS: 6; DMNH, ANSP.

Song Sparrow (*Melospiza melodia*)

Resident; common. Migrates late February to mid-April and late September to late November. CBC numbers increasing after a low in the 1970s.

Spring Migration Activity

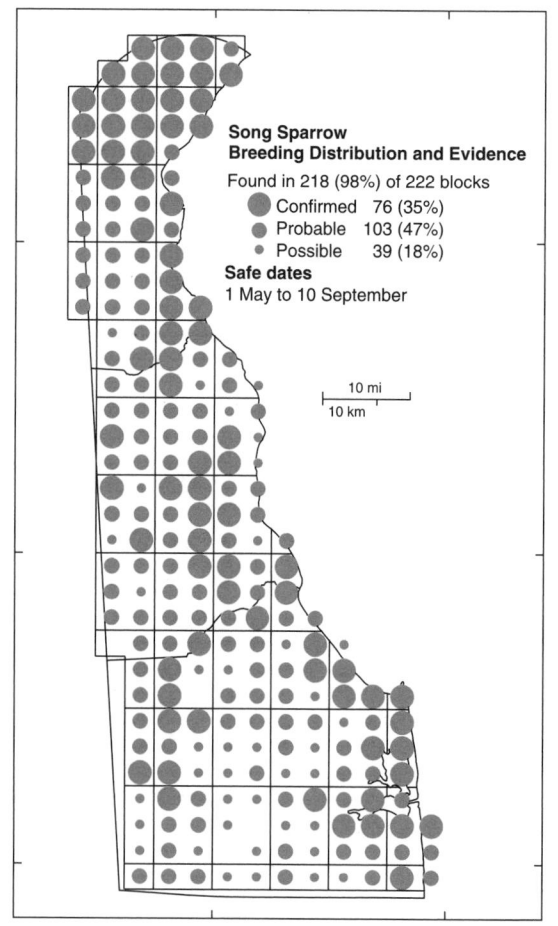

**Song Sparrow
Breeding Distribution and Evidence**
Found in 218 (98%) of 222 blocks
● Confirmed   76 (35%)
● Probable   103 (47%)
· Possible   39 (18%)
Safe dates
1 May to 10 September

10 mi
10 km

HABITAT: Agricultural areas with hedgerows, wood margins, urban areas with shrubs and small trees, marshes and meadows with shrubs or small trees; also saltmarshes.

SPRING: DOS survey data indicate a migration period from

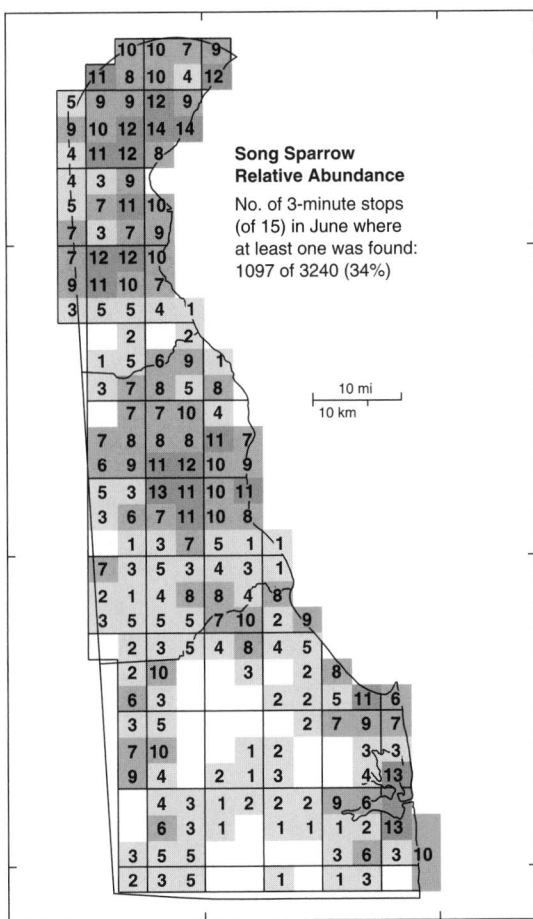

Song Sparrow
Relative Abundance

No. of 3-minute stops
(of 15) in June where
at least one was found:
1097 of 3240 (34%)

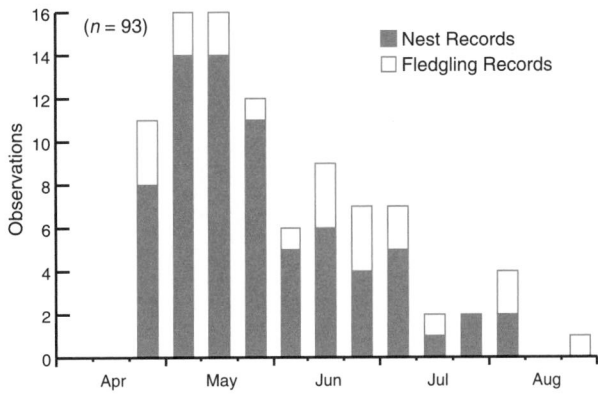

Estimated Clutch-Completion Dates

about 25 February to about 20 April with a peak from 10 March to 1 April. Banding data support the peak. A high of 305 was recorded at Dragon Run on 11 March 1973 [Conw1]. Typical reports are of 10–20 birds. The highest May Count, which occurs after migration is complete, is 463 (1984), and the lowest 158 (1990). A Baltimore study, dealing with a subspecies presumed to breed in Delaware (see "Remarks"), found that the breeding population consists of both migratory and sedentary individuals (Brackbill 1953).

BREEDING: It is difficult to imagine that this familiar sparrow is scarce in some parts of Delaware. These areas of scarcity are not reflected on the distribution map, which shows it present in all but 4 blocks, but the relative abundance map tells an entirely different story. The Song Sparrow is quite common in towns and suburbs and common in some coastal areas. It decreases southward and toward the interior, which should be viewed as a tapering off of numbers toward the southern breeding range limit of the more upland *M. m. melodia* subspecies (see "Remarks"). Lower numbers are to be expected in the more forested areas of Sussex County, but it is scarce there even around houses.

Atlas. The only way the Song Sparrow was found in some blocks was by looking for an old farmstead with brushy areas nearby, since such sites seem to meet it needs. Twenty confir-

mations represent active nests, and nest building was reported from another 12 blocks.

Nesting. Hanson (notes) described 1 Song Sparrow nest as follows: "The nest was found in a bush about 3 ft from the ground and covered with honeysuckle vines in a thicket on St. Jones Creek May 9, 1923. It was 5 in. across and 4 in. deep outside, inside it was 2¼ in. across and 4 in. deep. It was constructed of the dried wide leaves of meadow grasses outside, and dried grass stalks inside, lined with horse hair." Song Sparrow nests are sometimes placed on the ground, such as 1 found directly on the sand under the grass [Hans1]. Of 43 nests with heights given, 8 were on the ground, and the others ranged up to 7 ft, except for 1 that was 20 ft up in a red cedar [Samp2]. Median height of those off the ground was 3 ft. Substrates were variable, with grass, evergreens, Japanese honeysuckle, and ornamental bushes being most frequent.

Estimated clutch-completion dates extend from about 21 April to 27 August. Extreme egg dates extend from 29 April in Dover [Hans1] to 14 August in Fairfax [Till1]. Extreme dates for nestlings extend from 5 feathered young found on 12 May [SpeE3] to a 15-g fledgling (about 8 days old) brought to Tri-State Bird Rescue on 17 September (TSBR 87-1161), both in New Castle County. A nest found by Bray on 19 April [Bray2] represents an early record but may refer to one before egg-laying. Second and third broods are produced regularly. Fourth broods probably occur occasionally as far north as Massachusetts (Nolan 1968); four successful broods were raised in British Columbia at monthly intervals (Smith 1982). This is consistent with the Delaware clutch-completion graph; the open portion of the bars is based on data from nestlings brought to Tri-State Bird Rescue; the fledgling data do not show a strong peak in May that is evident from the combined data. Clutch sizes were 3 eggs (6), 4 eggs (26), and 5 eggs (8); 4 clutches of 2 may have been incomplete.

Trends. It is declining at about 2% per year in Delaware according to May Count data. BBS data suggest a slight decline in the East, but Delaware and regional data are inconclusive. For this species to be declining even slightly is unexpected and cause for concern, since it benefits from forest fragmentation and suburban sprawl.

Breeding population. Population estimates of edge species are difficult to make. The Song Sparrow's territory size in favorable habitat is less than an acre (Nolan 1968). The BBS and the relative abundance study probably sample Song Sparrow populations best but may exaggerate its numbers. The highest population of Song Sparrows reported on a Delaware BBC was at two suburban woodlots, which held an average of 44 pairs per 100 acres (110 per 100 ha) for two lots over 2 years (Jones and Burr 1967, 1968); these were wooded strips behind a suburb. Other woodlots averaged about 20 pairs per 100 acre (50 per 100 ha), and there were fewer where the woods were more extensive. It was also common at a marsh edge in Assawoman WA, where it averaged 36 pairs per 100 acres (90 per 100 ha) (Linehan 1965a; Ward et al. 1966).

FALL: Based on DOS survey data, the migration period is 20–30 September to 10–25 November, with the peak from 5 October to 10 November. Banding data reveal two peaks, one in late August and early September and one in the first half of October. A high of 1,100 was recorded at Gordon Pond WA, Cape Henlopen SP, on 18 October 1970 [DuPG20]. Less spectacular high counts include

9 Oct 1971	136	Brandywine Creek SP [Wayn25]
24 Oct 1970	179	Brandywine Creek SP [Wayn25]
19 Oct 1974	102	Dragon Run [Falk8]
30 Oct 1976	112	White Clay Creek [John12]

Typical reports total 15–25 birds.

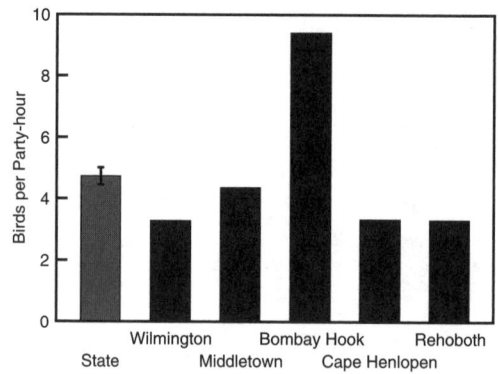

CBC Geographic Distribution

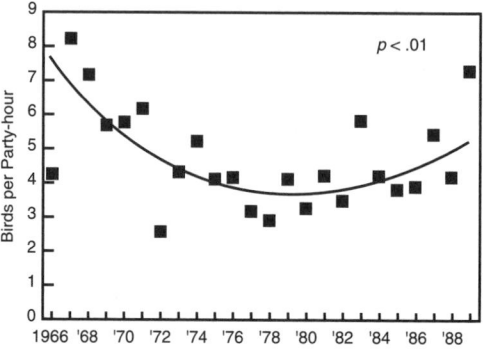

CBC Trend

WINTER: This species has shown a significant decrease in CBC numbers but appears to be recovering. The severe winters of 1976–77 and 1977–78 contributed to the decline, which was reflected in BBS data (Robbins et al. 1986). Except for the Bombay Hook CBC it is about equally common on all CBCs. Typical reports are of 15–25 birds. High counts are

18 Dec 1976	109	White Clay Creek [Boll5]
10 Feb 1974	200	Dragon Run [Phal9]
12, 19 Feb 1978	100	Broadkill Beach [Frec1]

REMARKS: Two subspecies of Song Sparrow may breed in Delaware as they do at Cape May (Stone 1937). *M. m. atlantica* breeds in tidelands along the Atlantic coast from Long Island south to North Carolina, including the lower Chesapeake Bay (AOU 1957) and parts of the Delaware tidelands at least in Sussex County and winters north to Kitts Hummock. *M. m. melodia* breeds from southwestern Newfoundland south through eastern New York, Pennsylvania (including Philadelphia) to central Virginia (AOU 1957) and throughout Delaware away from tidal areas.

SPECIMENS: 244; DMNH, ANSP, USNM, UWBM. Egg records: DMNH, WFVZ.

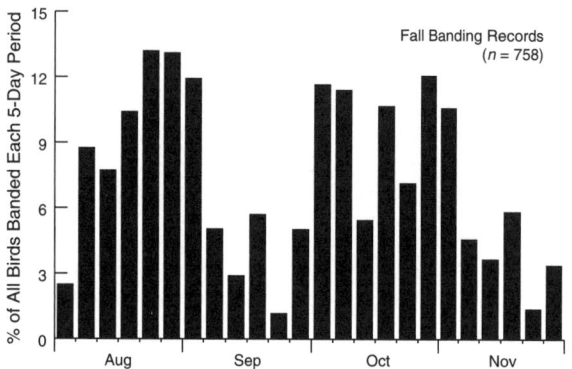

Fall Migration Activity

1966–89 CBC Summary

Christmas Bird Count	Years Found	Range of No. Found	Median
Wilmington	24	237–641	486
Middletown	24	147–597	255
Bombay Hook	24	154–1,213	626
Cape Henlopen	24	51–655	231
Rehoboth	24	133–789	318
STATEWIDE	24	1,164–3,319	1,981
(increasing; low in 1972, high in 1967)			

Lincoln's Sparrow *(Melospiza lincolnii)*

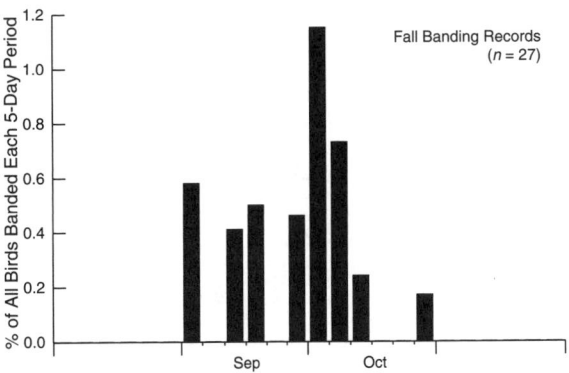

Fall Migration Activity

report involves 12 at Churchmans Marsh on 30 October 1965 [SpSB38].

SPECIMENS: DMNH 75294, Newark, 24 September 1983; DMNH 37698, Wilmington, 6 October 1973; DMNH 43345, Wilmington, 20 October 1974.

Regular; migrant; rare. Very rare spring migrant; expected late September through October.

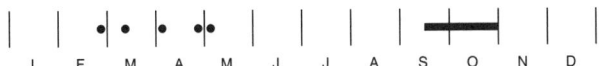

HABITAT: Moist, brushy woods. Also "hedgerows, wood margins, and brushy marsh-meadows" (Stewart and Robbins 1958).

SPRING: Our scant records cover the period 27 February–7 May. The records all involve 1 bird:

27 Feb 1974	near Dover [Pure4]
2 Apr 1989	Middle Run, near Newark [Edni25]
26 Apr 1975	Redden SF [BroW4]
3 May 1982	southwest of Wilmington [Batt3]
7 May 1972	banded near Centerville [Conw3]

Based on reports from other eastern states (Speirs and Speirs 1968), any occurring before late April should be carefully documented.

FALL: The early banding records include 2 at the University of Delaware woodlot on 3 September 1970 [Jone2] and 1 east of Red Lion on 15 September 1964 [Line4]; the latest was banded during the last 5 days of October [Line4]. It is banded most commonly from 26–30 September through 11–15 October. The few fall sight records, mostly of single birds, span the period from 17 September to 30 October—the period of greatest frequency is from 26 September to 18 October. A remarkable

Swamp Sparrow *(Melospiza georgiana)*

Resident; fairly common. Breeding population present from mid-May to about mid-September, perhaps departing earlier. Nonbreeding population present from about mid-September to mid-May.

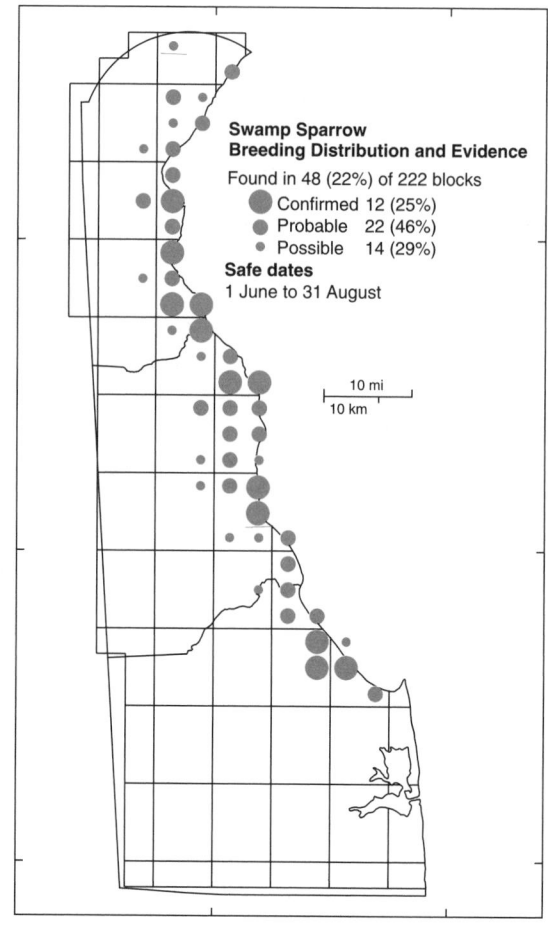

Swamp Sparrow
Breeding Distribution and Evidence
Found in 48 (22%) of 222 blocks
● Confirmed 12 (25%)
● Probable 22 (46%)
● Possible 14 (29%)
Safe dates
1 June to 31 August

10 mi
10 km

HABITAT: Breeding—brackish to nearly fresh tidal wetlands; winter—marshes; wet or moist wood edges, hedgerows, or other brushy situations.

OCCURRENCE: Throughout most of the year Swamp Sparrows from the northern and western populations *(M. g. georgiana* and *M. g. ericrypta)* are present in Delaware. During the breeding season a third, darker population *(M. g. nigrescens)* is present. When *nigrescens* was first described (Bond and Stewart 1951), it was believed to be resident in the marshes of the Nanticoke River, eastern Maryland, and along Delaware Bay (AOU 1957). More recently Greenberg and Droege (1990) have shown that all 3 subspecies are migrants in Delaware and elsewhere in the breeding range of *nigrescens.* Their study indicates that from September or October to about early May *ericrypta* and *georgiana,* but not *nigrescens,* are present in Delaware. Between about 15 May and about 25 May the 3 overlap in the coastal marshes. The 2 nonbreeding populations are widely distributed in the state (including in tidal marshes), whereas the breeding population is limited to brackish and tidal marshes. There are 6 specimens in the USNM identified as *nigrescens* from Delaware City and Bombay Hook with dates from 25 June to 7 August. Additionally, there are 2 specimens from the Delaware City area in the DMNH that, although not subspecifically identified, were in breeding condition on 3 June 1982 and probably represent *nigrescens.* The USNM holds 4 specimens, of nonbreeding birds, from Fowler Beach and Bombay Hook, taken on dates ranging from 13 December to 13 May; 3 were identified as *ericrypta* and 1 as *georgiana.*

An examination of Delaware data with the foregoing in mind reveals that at nontidal locations the usual first fall arrival

of inland Swamp Sparrows is about 18 September—earliest being 1 at Brandywine Creek SP on 2 September 1974 [Wayn66]—and that the first occurrence of more than 10 is 1–10 October. The fall banding data do not provide subspecies information, but a plot of those data shows 2 peaks, 1 that ends 6–10 September and 1 beginning 25–30 September. Some August records are from inland locations, indicating arrival of migrating or wintering birds that presumably are not *nigrescens.*

In spring the usual last departure at inland locations is about 15 May. The latest occurrence was 1 at White Clay Creek on 18 June 1977 [Samp6]. There are only 6 inland reports from 15 May to 18 June.

BREEDING: It is found along ditches in some fields on the freshwater side of marshes but not far from the tidal area. Some such situations appear to be definitely on the freshwater side of brackish, particularly north of Wilmington along the Delaware River. Additional work to find out its ecological limits inland along tidal streams would be useful in defining its needs.

Atlas. The Swamp Sparrow was registered in and next to tidal marshes from Lewes to Edgemoor; however, south of Cape Henlopen it is absent. Its absence from tidal marshes of

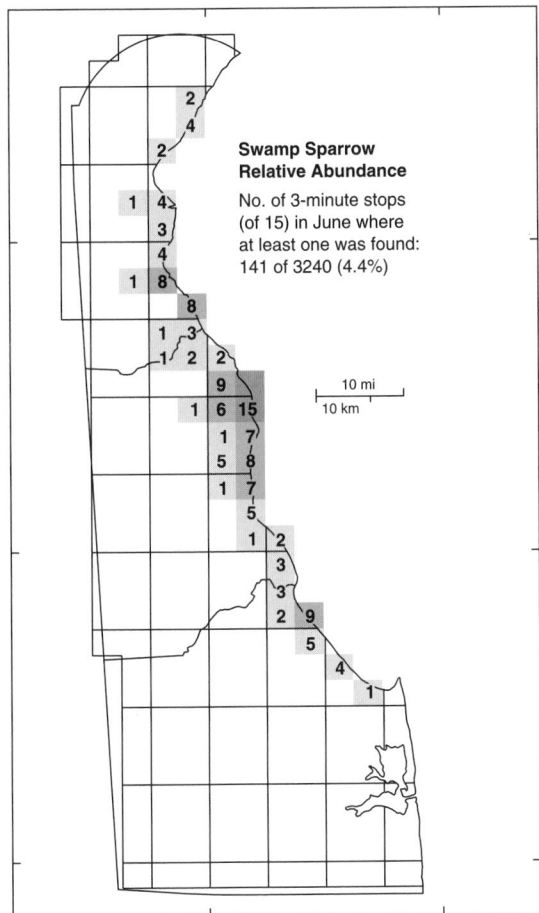

Swamp Sparrow
Relative Abundance

No. of 3-minute stops
(of 15) in June where
at least one was found:
141 of 3240 (4.4%)

10 mi
10 km

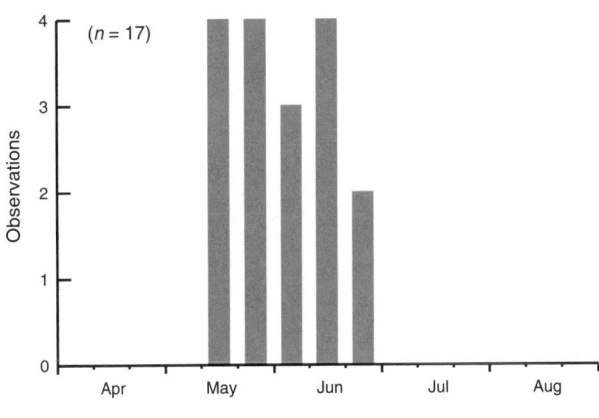

Estimated Clutch-Completion Dates

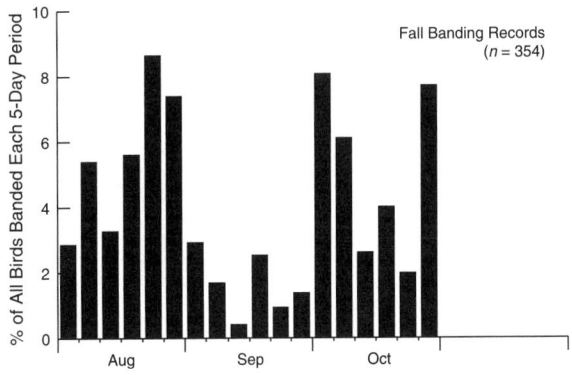

Fall Migration Activity

high salinity was noted by Greenberg and Droege (1990), who also noted that migratory Swamp Sparrows of interior populations vigorously defended saltmarsh territories in May before migrating. Thus the BBC report of its presence on an Assawoman study site may represent a misinterpretation of lingering migrants, since the field work was conducted during 22–31 May (Linehan 1965a).

An Atlas report of a male singing about 1 July 1983 at Brandywine Creek SP [BroH2] stands out because this area does not provide the expected habitat for our saltmarsh population. However, the observation is somewhat supported by a clutch collected on 30 May 1915, ambiguously reported from "a marsh along Brandywine Creek" (Kenworthy, WFVZ egg data), and by breeding records from Chester County, Pennsylvania (West Chester Bird Club 1979). These are seemingly attributable to the more northern population *(georgiana)* that does not usually summer in Delaware. Active nests were reported from 5 of the blocks that confirmed the species.

Nesting. Hanson (notes) recorded these comments about a Swamp Sparrow nest: "On June 15, 1929, a nest was found in a wet field by the side of a little run containing water near New-port Marsh. The nest was in a clump of weeds raised from the ground 6 inches and built of dry grass stems entirely. There was first a rather loose foundation and framework of coarse grass and inside and on top of this a compact and well-built main structure. Outside the nest is about 6 inches across and 3½ inches deep; inside 2 inches across and 1½ inches deep." The 4 eggs in the nest were well advanced in incubation, and just outside the nest was a spoiled egg. Other sites given for nests are 8 in. above ground in fine grass, and 7, 10, and 12 in. above ground in. small marsh elders in brackish marshes [Schw1]. Of 7 other nests at grassy sites, 3 were in the base of a grass tussock with no height given, and 4 others were atop the base of a grass clump at 8–18 in. above ground. Six others were in small shrubs, frequently marsh elder, at heights of 5–12 in., averaging 9 in.

Estimated clutch-completion dates for Delaware range from 16 May to 25 June. Extreme egg dates for 12 clutches are 22 May to 8 July [both Nile2]. Egg data (DMNH) for 26 clutches taken from along the Delaware River in Philadelphia County, Pennsylvania, give dates from 22 May, incubation started, to 13 July, one-third incubated [both MiRF1]. Clutch sizes were 3 egss (4), 4 eggs (16), and 5 eggs (6). Nests for Miller's clutches varied from 2 to 15 in. above ground, averaging 7 in., and were usually concealed in a grassy tussock or goldenrod clump.

Trends. BBS data for our region suggest that the Swamp Sparrow is declining on significantly more routes than increasing. The meager Delaware data do not suggest a decline.

Breeding population. If its population size is to be estimated, it must be from meager data. Moore (1989) found it common in impounded saltmarshes dominated by phragmites and in those that had been sprayed and burned, with abundances generally about 90 and 80 males per 100 ha in untreated and sprayed stands. West (1993) found a density of 150 territories per 100 ha (18 in 35.3 acres) in a Prime Hook NWR saltmarsh in 1975. Those portions of relative abundance studies done by canoe registered Swamp Sparrows at least along the channels.

1966–89 CBC Summary

Christmas Bird Count	Years Found	Range of No. Found	Median
Wilmington	24	6–80	39
Middletown	24	18–549	43
Bombay Hook	24	27–555	147
Cape Henlopen	24	9–234	38
Rehoboth	24	14–257	61
STATEWIDE (low in 1977, high in 1986)	24	146–943	394

WINTER: It is reported most abundantly on the Bombay Hook CBC. Although analysis did not reveal a CBC trend, a sharp reduction in numbers resulted from the severe winters in the mid-1970s, with steady recovery since then, including

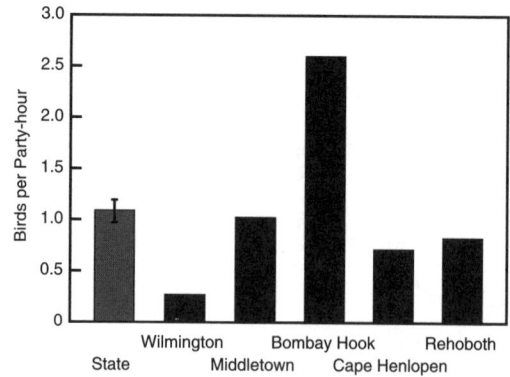

CBC Geographic Distribution

exceptionally high numbers in 1986. Typical reports involve 5–6 birds. High counts are

6 Dec 1975	23	Dragon Run [BeaF1]
14 Dec 1975	32	Dragon Run [Dyer1]
9 Jan 1977	23	White Clay Creek [BroH11]
25 Jan 1982	24	Broadkill Beach [Frec1]

SPECIMENS: 45; DMNH, ANSP, UDEL, USNM, UWBM. Egg records: WFVZ.

White-throated Sparrow (*Zonotrichia albicollis*)

Regular; winter visitor; common. Expected late September to mid-May.

HABITAT: Hedgerows, wood edges, brushy cutover areas, suburbs.

SPRING: The onset of the northward migration is difficult to determine but probably begins in late March and certainly continues through 15 May. Banding data reveal 40–70 birds banded each 5-day period, 16 March–5 May, followed by 10 or fewer banded in each of the 2 subsequent periods [Usfw2]. In some years the White-throat can be found after 15 May but is

quite scarce, with these the only reports of more than 1:

19 May 1965	2	Iron Hill, Newark (Faust 1965)
19 May 1974	2	Dragon Run [BroW20]
19 May 1984	2	Delaware Seashore SP [Frec1]
20 May 1978	4	White Clay Creek [RusJ8]

Occasional stragglers remain through May and into summer.

Highest counts include

11 Mar 1973	297	Dragon Run [Conw10]
22 Apr 1978	124	White Clay Creek [Jahn13]
22 Apr 1965	60	Iron Hill, Newark (Faust 1965).

The highest May Count is 485 (3 May 1980), the lowest 5 (12 May 1979).

SUMMER: These summer records probably refer to non-breeding birds:

5 Jun 1987		near Seaford High School [Rigb1]
17 Jun 1992	1 singing	Dover yard (D. Rothstein, DNHI, pers. comm.)
3, 10, 11 Jul 1986	1 singing	University of Delaware woodlot [Roth2]
14 Jul 1970	1 singing	Prime Hook NWR [Holg62]
Aug 1980	1	SW of Townsend (DMNH 71203, Hess 1980a)

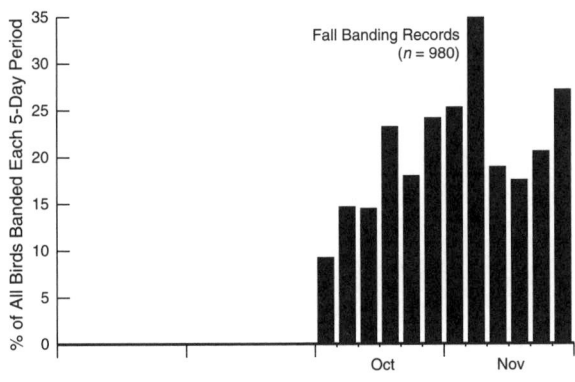

Fall Migration Activity

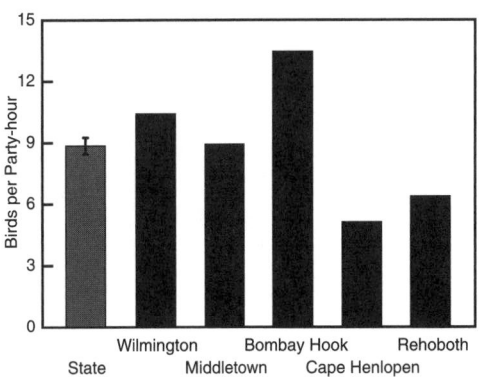

CBC Geographic Distribution

The nearest regular breeding location for this species is the Pocono Mountains, but they frequently summer south of their breeding range (Gross 1992).

FALL: First arrival is 20–25 September. Earlier reports are

18 Sep 1977	4	White Clay Creek [Broo17]
18 Sep 1982	1	White Clay Creek [Hess2]
19 Sep 1964	1	Hoopes Reservoir [Matl1]

Migration probably continues into late November as illustrated by weekly DOS surveys averaging over 100 birds from 15 October to 30 November before declining to 80–90 birds. The banding data follow a similar pattern. There are 6 reports of more than 500 (503–795) birds on a DOS survey, 5 from White Clay Creek (Speck and Brokaw 1979), and 1 from Dragon Run [Falk20]. The dates of those records range from 16 October to 3 December.

1966–89 CBC Summary

Christmas Bird Count	Years Found	Range of No. Found	Median
Wilmington	24	294–2,418	1,355
Middletown	24	234–901	629
Bombay Hook	24	376–2,020	891
Cape Henlopen	24	92–895	359
Rehoboth	24	210–1,555	544
STATEWIDE (low in 1966, high in 1977)	24	1,952–5,942	4,116

WINTER: White-throated Sparrows are reported in similar numbers on all CBCs. Early winter numbers are only slightly lower than those for fall, suggesting some continued migration; however, from January through April DOS survey numbers average 30–40 birds.

SPECIMENS: 156; DMNH, ANSP, UDEL.

Harris's Sparrow *(Zonotrichia querula)*

Occasional (8 years, 1963–88); winter visitor; rare.
DOCUMENTATION: Photograph (W. A. Fintel, DMNH 331).

REMARKS: Harris's Sparrow breeds in the Subarctic west of Hudson Bay. It winters primarily in the central plains and casually along the East coast (AOU 1983). Harris's Sparrow is a large sparrow and is distinctive owing to its dark breast band, which in alternate plumage extends to the entire throat and crown. There are published reports of 4 birds in Delaware, ranging from 24 October 1965 [LewC1] to 1 that wintered and remained at a feeding station until 4 May 1986 [Frec14]. An identifiable photograph was taken of the 1986 bird, and notes were published on an occurrence in Smyrna on 11 November 1973 (Holgersen 1974d). Holgersen's notes are convincing, describing a bird with extensive black on the throat, forehead, and crown. The bird recorded on the Wilmington CBC by Wayne at Buena Vista on 23 December 1977 [Wayn10] was subsequently observed by many on 7 January 1978 [Kell1].

The first record for the state is apparently an unpublished observation in Newark during the spring of 1963 [Well1].

There is an additional unpublished winter record of 2 birds at Red Mill Pond near Lewes on 10 February 1988 [Frec1].

These Delaware records fit the general pattern of winter occurrence of the Harris's Sparrow outside its usual wintering range of the south-central United States west of the ninety-eighth meridian (AOU 1983; Root 1988). In addition, an "immature male," stated to have been "closely observed," was reported at Broadkill Beach on 31 July 1971 [Conw17], but not supported by a photograph or sufficient details for such an unexpected date.

White-crowned Sparrow *(Zonotrichia leucophrys)*

Regular; winter visitor; uncommon. Expected early October to mid-May. Decreasing on CBCs at 6% per year.

HABITAT: "Hedgerows and wood margins in agricultural areas" (Stewart and Robbins 1958); also residential areas with ornamental shrubs, overgrown farmsteads, multiflora rose.

SPRING: The presence of wintering birds obscures the beginning of migration. Migration ends about mid-May, and peak numbers of reports occur 5–15 May. The latest spring reports include

18 May 1965	1	Iron Hill, Newark (Faust 1965)
20 May 1984	2	Dover [Wees1]
24 May 1981	1	Assawoman WA [Barn54]

The highest May Count is 32 (1977); none were found in 1972, 1979, or 1985.

FALL: First arrival is usually 1–10 October. The end of migration is not discernible but probably occurs in late October or early November when migrating White-crowns are no longer found at Cape Henlopen SP. Although several earlier records have been published, the earliest credible arrivals include

25 Sep 1976	1	White Clay Creek [Samp6]
27 Sep 1981	1	Prime Hook NWR [Frec33]
29 Sep 1979	1	Assawoman WA [Frec1]

A 9 September report (Speck 1980) should refer to Field Sparrow. Six banding records occurred during 1–5 October and 36 during October, but none occurred in September [Usfw2]. Typically only 1–3 are found, but 8 have been reported several times:

19 Oct 1972	8	Broadkill Beach [Holg77]
30 Oct 1980	8	Cape Henlopen SP [Frec1]
1 Nov 1988	8	Lewes [Frec49]

Reports of higher numbers should have corroboration because mixed flocks may prompt estimates that are too high.

1966–89 CBC Summary

Christmas Bird Count	Years Found	Range of No. Found	Median
Wilmington	17	1–47	8
Middletown	23	1–129	6
Bombay Hook	20	1–40	3
Cape Henlopen	15	1–33	2
Rehoboth	14	1–26	2
STATEWIDE	24	6–161	30

(decreasing; low in 1979 and 1987; high in 1974)

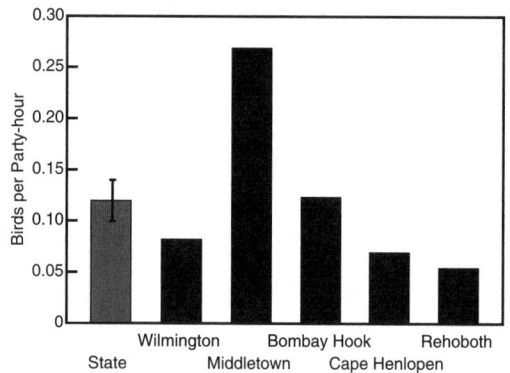

CBC Geographic Distribution

WINTER: This species has shown a significant decrease in CBC numbers. The BBS does not sample White-crowned Sparrow breeding grounds (mainly in northern Canada) sufficiently to determine a trend in its breeding population (Robbins et al. 1986). Perhaps loss of fields with hedgerows is contributing to

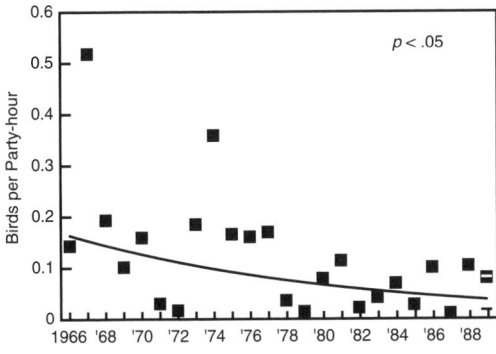

CBC Trend; Decreasing at 6% per Year

its decline in winter in Delaware. Typical reports are of 2 or 3 birds. The highest counts reported include

19 Dec 1981	14	Dagsboro [Frec37]
20 Feb 1974	12	Centerville [Wayn2]
Winter 1988–89	8	near Port Penn [Jano3]

SPECIMENS: DMNH 43343, Wilmington, 5 October 1974; ANSP 65651, Hockessin, 8 October 1904; DMNH 43344, Wilmington, 20 October 1974; DMNH 1369, 7 November 1957, Sussex Co.; DMNH 46721, Wilmington, 17 November 1974.

Dark-eyed Junco (*Junco hyemalis*)

Regular; winter visitor; common. Expected late September to late April.

HABITAT: Hedgerows, wood edges, brushy cutover areas, residential areas with shrubs.

SPRING: The migration probably begins in early March, peaks 20 March to 15 April, and usually ends 25–30 April. Thereafter, 1 or a few are occasionally found. The only reports after 8 May are

9–13 May	1–4	on each of 7 May Counts (these sightings were not treated as unusual, but should have been)
19 May 1965	1	Iron Hill (Faust 1965)
27 May 1981	2	Cape Henlopen SP [Frec1]
5 Jun 1976	1	White Clay Creek [MiDP12]
20 Jun 1982	1	Bombay Hook NWR [Knar1]
23 Jul 1993	1	near Greenville (H.P. Brokaw, pers. comm.)

The highest counts are

6 Mar 1978	200	Cape Henlopen SP [Frec1]
21 Mar 1981	500	around Lewes [Frec1]
14 Apr 1973	85	Dragon Run [HalA2]

A report of 200 at Winterthur on 26 March 1972 [Falk25], should be changed to 41. It has been recorded on about half of May Counts in numbers ranging from 1 to 5.

FALL: First arrival is usually 25–30 September; migration concludes 15–30 November. Early reports include

8 Sep 1985	4	Pyles Ford Rd. [SpeE8]
17 Sep 1985	2	Brandywine Creek SP [Nile7]
19 Sep 1982	1	Bombay Hook NWR [Hess12]

The numbers of birds reported increase rapidly after 1 October, with the peak from 1 November to 1 December. The banding data show a similar pattern. High counts include

18 Oct 1970	250	Gordon Pond WA [DuPG20]
30 Oct 1976	174	White Clay Creek [RusJ7]
12 Nov 1977	153	White Clay Creek [Jahn11]
28 Nov 1976	138	White Clay Creek [SpSB16]

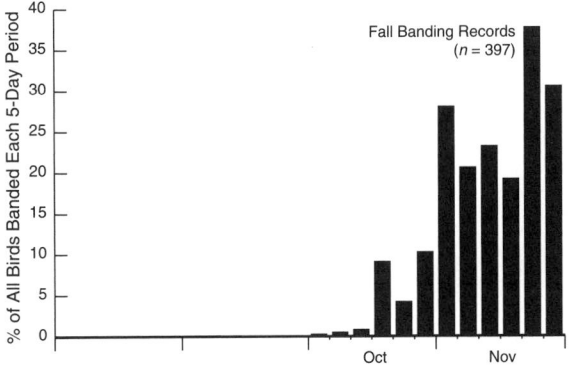

Fall Migration Activity

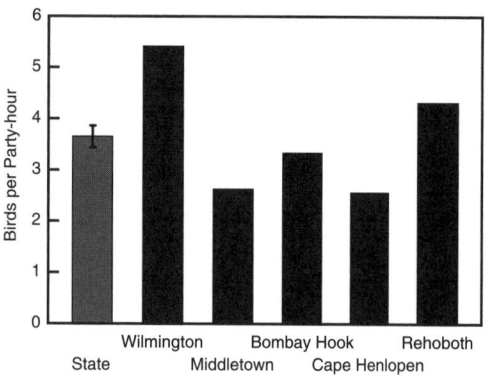

CBC Geographic Distribution

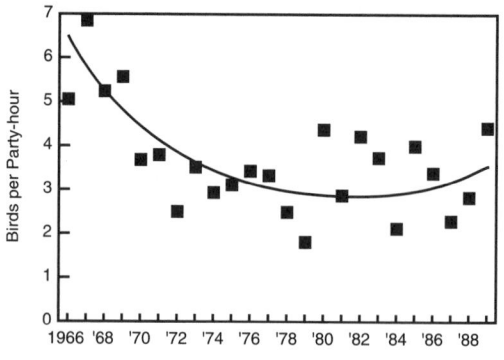

CBC Trend

1966–89 CBC Summary

Christmas Bird Count	Years Found	Range of No. Found	Median
Wilmington	24	302–1,450	708
Middletown	24	52–544	162
Bombay Hook	24	54–607	179
Cape Henlopen	24	48–434	167
Rehoboth	24	115–1,944	349
STATEWIDE (low in 1979, high in 1967)	24	1,046–3,579	1,727

WINTER: This species has shown a significant decline in CBC numbers. It is unclear if a recent population recovery is underway: a curved trend line suggests the beginning of a recovery, but a declining linear trend at 2% per year also fits the data. The severe winters of the mid-1970s may have contributed to the decline, but this species was decreasing before the mid-1970s. The BBS reports significant decreases in breeding numbers in the East, particularly in New Brunswick, New Hampshire, and New York (Robbins et al. 1986). Typical reports total about 25 birds. High counts are

13 Dec 1981	150	Prime Hook NWR [Frec1]
15 Jan 1972	120	Winterthur [BroW18]
3 Feb 1978	125	Cape Henlopen SP [Frec1]

SPECIMENS: 109; DMNH, UDEL.

Lapland Longspur (*Calcarius lapponicus*)

Regular; winter visitor; rare. Expected early November to mid-March.

| J | F | M | A | M | J | J | A | S | O | N | D |

HABITAT: Open agricultural fields, road edges.

OCCURRENCE: This late-arriving and early-departing winter visitor, occurring in all but 4 years during 1959–91, is usually not reported before November or after March. Extreme dates are

23 Oct 1991	3	near Bombay Hook NWR [MagJ1]
1 Nov 1969	2	Cape Henlopen SP [Carl5]
6 Nov 1990	1	Bombay Hook NWR [Holg1]
10 Nov 1974	2	Cape Henlopen SP [WilV1]
17 Mar 1973	1	Cape Henlopen SP [WilC3]
6 Apr 1991	1	Bombay Hook NWR [Holg1]
15 Apr 1990	6	Rt. 12 [Edni1]

Some spring males attain alternate (breeding) plumage before departing Delaware; 2 males found on 14 March 1990 are the earliest reported in alternate plumage [Edni1]. In some years this species may be reported only once. Most records are concentrated in the last 2 weeks of December and are therefore probably an artifact of the effort on CBCs where it has been found 17 times (1966–89). Except for that, the records are fairly evenly distributed from November to March. It is usually found in 1s and 2s, but these high counts have been reported:

14 Nov 1990	11	near Bombay Hook NWR [Holg97]	
25 Nov 1989	8	near Bombay Hook NWR [Holg30]	
18 Mar 1990	12	near Bombay Hook NWR [Camp6]	

1966–89 CBC Summary

Christmas Bird Count	Years Found	Range of No. Found	Median
Wilmington			
Middletown	2	1–2	
Bombay Hook	13	1–5	1
Cape Henlopen	1	1	
Rehoboth	1	1	
STATEWIDE (high in 1977)	15	1–5	1

Longspurs are most easily located by searching along the gravel or sand edge of a freshly plowed road after a snowstorm, by inspecting flocks of Snow Buntings, or by hearing the buzzy longspur call note overhead; favored spots are in fields near Bombay Hook NWR and in Cape Henlopen SP. This species is sufficiently rare that it had not been reported in Delaware until 3 were found near Delaware City on 3 December 1910 by Pennock and Trotter (Pennock 1911); he collected additional specimens there on 19 December 1910 and 12 February 1912 (Pennock 1912) [Penn5].

SPECIMENS: 8; ANSP, DMNH.

Snow Bunting *(Plectrophenax nivalis)*

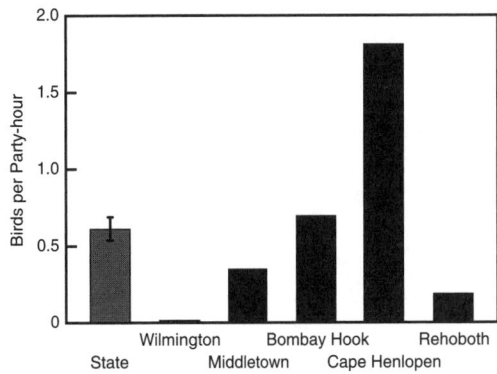

CBC Geographic Distribution

1966–89 CBC Summary

Christmas Bird Count	Years Found	Range of No. Found	Median
Wilmington	6	1–33	
Middletown	8	2–250	
Bombay Hook	21	1–390	10
Cape Henlopen	22	20–351	142
Rehoboth	14	1–103	1
STATEWIDE (low in 1968, high in 1980)	24	24–505	205

Regular; winter visitor; fairly common. Expected early November to early March.

J F M A M J J A S O N D

HABITAT: Coastal beaches, large open fields.

OCCURRENCE: Like the Lapland Longspur, this species arrives late and departs early, often being present from 1 November to 1 March. Extreme credible dates are

17 Oct 1982	1	Delaware Seashore SP [Wees4]
18 Oct 1978	20	Gordon Pond WA [DuPG21]
19 Oct 1968	3	Cape Henlopen SP [Carl3]
9 Mar 1988	1	Indian River Inlet [Frec1]
10 Mar 1973	24	Cape Henlopen SP [Wayn2]
16 Mar 1970	10	Little Creek WA [DuPG16]

Stragglers are occasionally reported on the East Coast in April and May. The Snow Bunting most often occurs in flocks, ranging in size from 10–50 to 200–500 birds, and are prone to wandering over a large area. Although most often reported from Cape Henlopen SP and Bombay Hook NWR, it should be looked for in any large open area, particularly near the bayshore. Pennock (1904) first reported this species in Delaware on flats between Lewes and the lighthouse; A. D. Poole found 1 dead at the Wilmington reservoir on 25 November 1910.

SPECIMENS: 6; DMNH, ANSP.

Northern Cardinal (*Cardinalis cardinalis*)

Resident; common. Numbers recovering from a low in the late 1970s.

J F M A M J J A S O N D

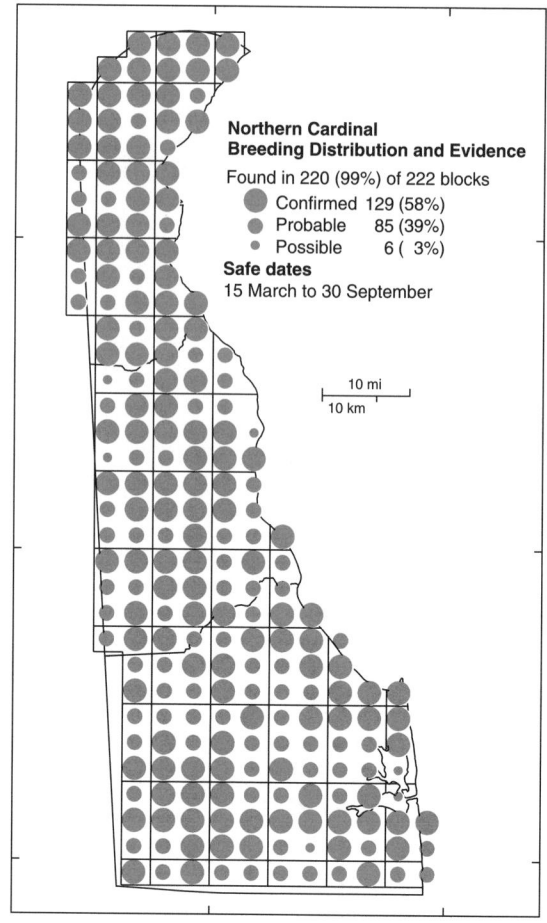

**Northern Cardinal
Breeding Distribution and Evidence**

Found in 220 (99%) of 222 blocks

● Confirmed 129 (58%)
● Probable 85 (39%)
· Possible 6 (3%)

Safe dates
15 March to 30 September

10 mi
10 km

HABITAT: Various edge or margin habitats, residential areas, brushy wet or moist forest.

BREEDING: The distribution map and the relative abundance study show the cardinal is common and widespread. It will accept almost any habitat in Delaware with shrubby growth except saltmarsh, and even within the marsh it can sometimes be found on small wooded islands.

Atlas. It was most frequently confirmed by observation of fledged young, which can be detected by their chattering food call beginning the seventh day following hatching and by their dark mandibles. Some young are fed by the male for more than a month (Laskey 1944). Active nests were reported in 38 blocks, nest building in another 10.

Nesting. Hanson (notes) described a cardinal nest found near Dover in a bush covered with Japanese honeysuckle, well concealed, about 3 ft above ground, as follows: "It was 5 inches across and 4 inches deep outside, and 2½ inches across and 2 inches deep inside. It was made of threads of vine (honeysuckle), meadow grass, corn husks, leaves, and paper, and lined with fine threads of vine."

Extreme egg dates are 19 April [Nile17] and 19 July [Long5]. Clutches continue to mid-August based on a 28-g fledgling brought to Tri-State Bird Rescue on 5 September (TSBR 91-1491) and a report of eggs just hatching in September [Buck3]. Some cardinals are triple-brooded in Delaware based on the length of the season and the secondary peak in mid-June. Shaver and Roberts report, in Tennessee, that a pair may build as many as 5 nests, but usually no more than 4 broods are raised successfully (in Laskey 1944), and triple broods have been validated with banded birds in Tennessee and New York (Bull 1974). Rumford banded a third brood from the same nest on 2 August 1922 in Bringhurst Woods, Wilmington [Rumf1].

Fifty clutches of 3, and 25 of 2, were reported, the latter probably often not representing full clutches.

History. Since the 1940s the Northern Cardinal has expanded its range and numbers in Pennsylvania, New Jersey, and southern New England (Beddall 1963; Robbins et al. 1986). It has long been present in Delaware. Wilson found it resident in the lower part of Pennsylvania, Nuttall gave its range as north to

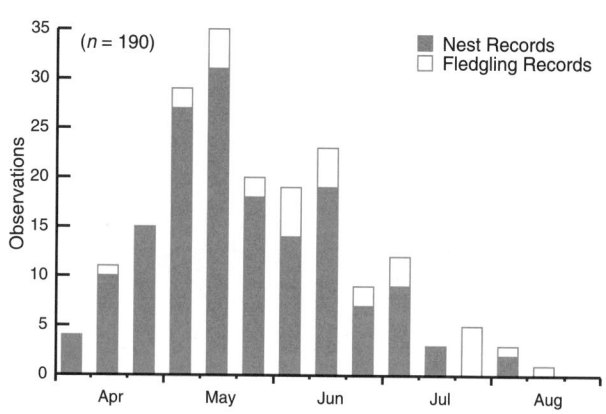

Estimated Clutch-Completion Dates

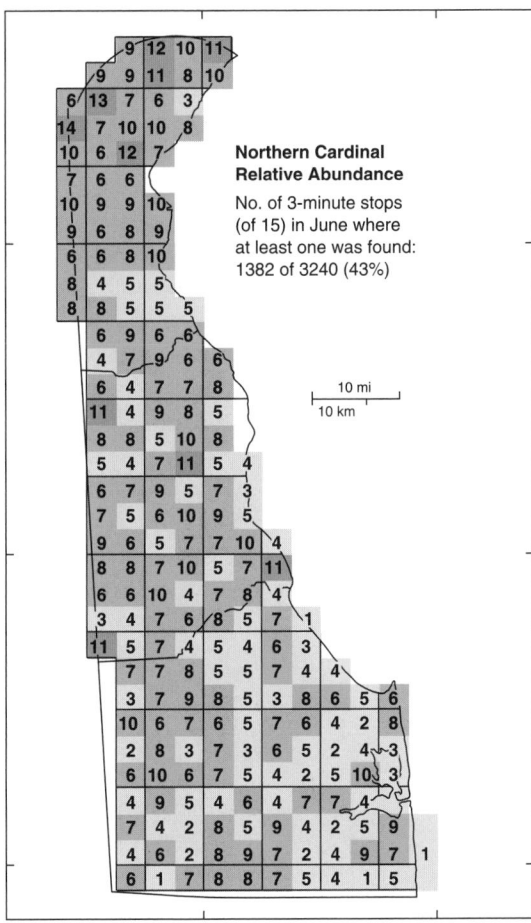

**Northern Cardinal
Relative Abundance**

No. of 3-minute stops
(of 15) in June where
at least one was found:
1382 of 3240 (43%)

10 mi
10 km

although less frequently than the male (Ritchison 1986), possibly leading to registration of unwarranted territories in studies like the BBC.

1966–89 CBC Summary

Christmas Bird Count	Years Found	Range of No. Found	Median
Wilmington	24	210–636	446
Middletown	24	81–339	169
Bombay Hook	24	114–436	226
Cape Henlopen	24	46–243	98
Rehoboth	24	79–363	158
STATEWIDE (low in 1985, high in 1970)	24	805–1,411	1,113

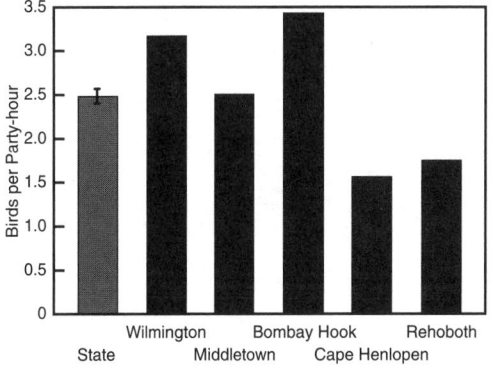

CBC Geographic Distribution

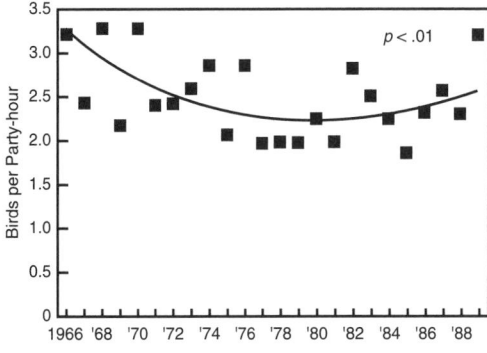

CBC Trend; May be Autocorrelated

New York, and Bush found it in Wilmington in the 1880s. The relative abundance map reflects that it is most common near suburban development, and Wilson found it more numerous in the neighborhood of settlements. Clearing the forest provided the open edge habitat it requires. Thus its numbers have increased in Delaware as a result of habitat alteration since European settlement. Feeders also appear to have been a factor, since cardinals seemed to be located first near feeders as they expanded northward, and such feeder-supported populations may serve as a nucleus for repopulation in the event of severe winter casualties (Bull 1974).

Trends. The BBS for the East, as well as the CBC and May Count, suggests that its abundance has decreased at an insignificant 0.6% per year during 1966–90, which means its population is relatively stable. The Delaware BBS, based on less data, indicates a much sharper 4% decline for the same period.

Breeding population. The May Count usually totals 300–500 birds; the highest was 588 recorded in 1989. The 6 CBCs, sampling about 40% of the land area of the state, reported a high of 1,350 cardinals (in 426 party-hours) in 1989. Its average density calculated from data collected on Delaware BBCs is about 64 territories per 100 ha, but this figure is strongly influenced by the studies conducted in northern Delaware woodlots that contain a high proportion of edge habitat. The female sings,

WINTER: Numbers of this species have changed significantly on CBCs. It was adversely affected by severe winters in the mid–70s. The BBS reflected a decline in the eastern region during the same period it was declining on Delaware CBCs (Robbins et al. 1986). It appears to be recovering from those lows. Typical non-CBC reports involve 10–20 birds. A high of 53 was reported on 7 January 1978 at White Clay Creek [Edni72].

SPECIMENS: 156; DMNH, ANSP, UDEL, USNM. Egg records: DMNH, WFVZ.

Rose-breasted Grosbeak *(Pheucticus ludovicianus)*

Regular; migrant; uncommon. Expected May and early September to mid-October, sporadically both earlier and later in the fall.

HABITAT: Various mature deciduous forest types, also more scrubby areas during migration.

SPRING: Migration usually takes place entirely during May and peaks 5–20 May. Early arrivals are most likely 27–30 April. One arrived very early on 17 April 1983 near Centerville (DMNH 75496). The last migrants usually leave by the end of May. One late migrating male was at Little Creek WA on 21 June 1970 [DuPG17]. Rather more unusual is a report of 2 on 1 July 1973 at Dragon Run [SpSB1]. Both of these could represent the wanderings of unmated birds. High counts are

| 9 May 1964 | 12 | Little Creek WA [anon15] |
| 10 May 1980 | 8 | Churchmans Marsh [Ross4] |

The highest May Count is 53 (1990), the lowest 3 (1976).

BREEDING: This species bred in Delaware in 1988.

Atlas. One was heard singing in the University of Delaware woodlot on 13 June 1987 [Roth2], but this report did not qualify as an Atlas observation, since the species was not known to breed in Delaware at that time.

Nesting. A pair was observed 27 May–3 June 1988 at the previously cited location following the conclusion of the Atlas project. A nest, containing a young cowbird, was found on 17 June, and a female was observed bringing food to it. The cowbird fledged on 20 or 21 June. No young grosbeaks were observed. The nest, a very flimsy platform with spaces that could be seen through, was 18 ft up in a dogwood in mesic deciduous woods (Roth, in Hess 1989b).

Clutch completion was about 29 May for this nest. Egg dates recorded in Maryland are 27 May–13 June (Robbins and Bystrak 1977). The Rose-breasted Grosbeak usually lays 4 eggs and is double-brooded (Harrison 1978).

Trends. This species has expanded its breeding range southward in Ohio (Peterjohn 1989) and increased its population in southeastern Pennsylvania in the twentieth century (Leberman 1992b). Leberman observed it was found much less frequently in areas in which mean maximum July temperature exceeds 86°F (30°C), suggesting it will never be common in Delaware.

FALL: Usually first arrival is 1–10 September and last departure 10–15 October. Peak numbers often occur 15–25 September. Early reports are

7 Aug 1975	1	Dragon Run [Mars1]
14 Aug 1965	1	Churchmans Marsh [Stri7]
18 Aug 1979	1	Ashland [Wayn59]

Late reports refer to

| 27 Oct 1974 | 1 | Dragon Run [HalD1] |
| 14 Nov 1976 | 1 | White Clay Creek [MiDP12] |

High counts involve

| 12 Sep 1971 | 23 | Brandywine Creek SP [BroW1] |
| 19 Sep 1970 | 25 | Brandywine Creek SP [Beac2] |

SPECIMENS: 25; DMNH, ANSP, UDEL.

Black-headed Grosbeak (*Pheucticus melanocephalus*)

Casual (1978 and 1985).

DOCUMENTATION: Photograph (S. B. Speck, AB 40:451).

REMARKS: The Black-headed Grosbeak is a western species closely allied to the Rose-breasted Grosbeak. The adult male is distinctive, but the female and immature closely resemble the female and immature Rose-breasted Grosbeak, providing significant field identification problems. Delaware has 2 records, both convincingly documented. The first record involved a bird at a feeder in Dover, first seen on 4 March [Wola2]. We have 2 unpublished sets of notes [Wola1; Wees1], both mentioning the yellow breast, with the breast unstreaked and the flanks slightly speckled. The second record involved an immature male at a feeder near Wilmington from 5 December 1985 to 21 March 1986 [SpSB25]. The published notes mention the buffy cinnamon underparts of the immature male Black-headed, along with the yellow wing-linings that eliminate the immature male Rose-breasted Grosbeak. Over the course of the spring the bird acquired the black head of the adult male. A photograph of this bird was published (Speck 1986). These notes, aided by the photograph, firmly establish the occurrence of the species in Delaware. A report of 1 in September 1991 was not documented (Ednie 1992).

Blue Grosbeak (*Guiraca caerulea*)

Regular; summer resident; fairly common south of the Chesapeake

J F M A M J J A S O N D

and Delaware Canal. Expected late April to early October.

HABITAT: Wood edges, hedgerows, old fields, open agricultural areas with some remnant vegetation (see James 1971 for general description).

SPRING: First arrival is 25 April–1 May. Migration peaks 10–20 May and probably ends 20–25 May. The early arrivals are

20 Apr 1976	1	Dover [Pure7]
25 Apr 1982	1	Lewes [Frec1]

High counts are

11 May 1985	12	Nanticoke WA [Frec1]
30 May 1980	10	Prime Hook NWR [Frec1]

The highest May Count is 131 (1989), the lowest 7 (1971).

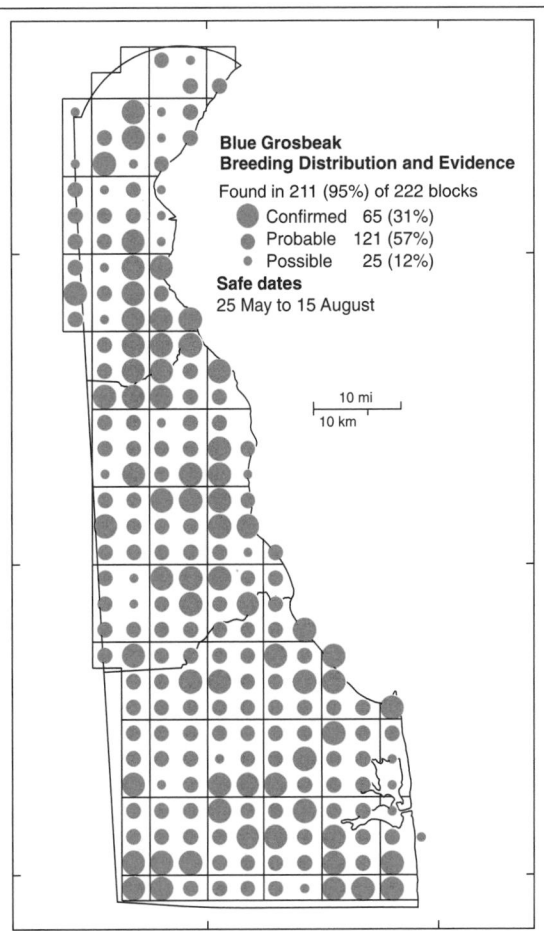

Blue Grosbeak
Breeding Distribution and Evidence
Found in 211 (95%) of 222 blocks
● Confirmed 65 (31%)
● Probable 121 (57%)
· Possible 25 (12%)
Safe dates
25 May to 15 August

10 mi
10 km

BREEDING: There is 1 chance in 3 of being within earshot of this large bunting along roadsides south of the Chesapeake and Delaware Canal on a June morning, according to data collected on the relative abundance study. North of the canal its abundance decreases in Delaware, and it reaches its northeastern

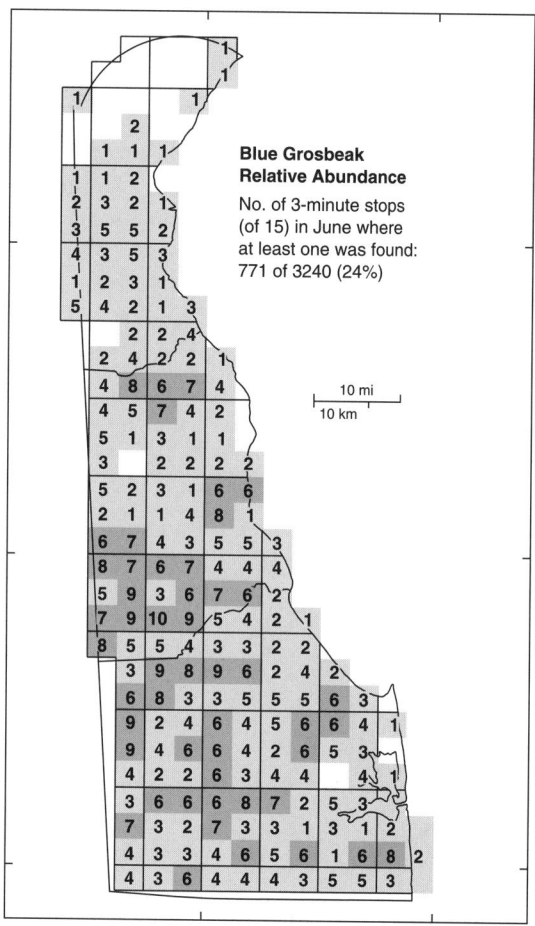

Blue Grosbeak
Relative Abundance

No. of 3-minute stops
(of 15) in June where
at least one was found:
771 of 3240 (24%)

10 mi
10 km

limit in southeastern Pennsylvania and central New Jersey (Ingold 1993).

Atlas. The northern New Castle County sites of Blue Grosbeak occurrence during the Atlas project include Fox Point SP [Frey1], Cherry Island [West3], Blueball [Zeit2], and Brandywine Creek SP [Atla1]. Of these sites the first is probably the most regular. The grosbeak was confirmed most frequently by observation of adults attending young or fledged young, but 11 active nests and 9 instances of nest building were also reported.

Nesting. The following are nest situations described in nest records: 3 ft above ground in a small sumac in reverting pasture [Pres2], 2 ft above ground in 5-ft sumac among weed and vine stems [West4], 4 ft off ground in kudzu vine in brushy field [Edni4], 7 ft up in sassafras sapling in hedgerow by corn field [Hess4], and 5 ft up in center top of azalea in suburban yard [Atch3].

Scant Delaware egg dates run from 11 June [Edni4] to 3 July [West4], but young out of nest on 21 June and young fledging on 1 August [both Pres1] suggest clutch completion occurs 29 May–8 July. Maryland egg dates extend from 5 May to 30 August (Robbins and Bystrak 1977). The Blue Grosbeak usually lays 4 eggs and is double-brooded in the southern part of its range (Harrison 1978, Ingold 1993). The long Maryland breeding season suggests it may be double-brooded in Delaware. The eastern Blue Grosbeak population was found to be para-

sitized at a 17% rate by the Brown-headed Cowbird (Friedmann et al. 1977), but no Delaware example has been reported.

History. A century ago Krider (1879, 50) wrote that "It is very rare. I have never found it except in Delaware, and there it was not plenty." Pennock (1908b) thought it was more common: "I saw a male by the roadside near Lewes on May 7, 1906, and I believe they are not rare in the lower end of the State." He also reported that a male from a group of 3 or 4 was shot near Delaware City several years before 1907. Stone (1937) was more cautious in his assessment: "It is of casual occurrence in Delaware and doubtless breeds in that state. Charles Pennock and Samuel Rhoads recorded a specimen taken near Dover in 1882, and John Emlen and Benjamin Hiatt saw one at Rehoboth Beach on May 12 and 13, 1928. On the Choptank River near the Delaware–Maryland line it is known to breed. John Carter found a male, female, and young there on July 3, 1904, and Clifford Marburger saw one in full song on July 26, 1932." Hanson (notes) reported finding it 5 times between 1929 and 1937 in areas between Stanton and Leipsic; he found no nests but twice recorded males carrying food. By 1949 the Prests (notes) were able to find grosbeaks in 3 locations in southern Delaware and found them regularly after that near Porter on their farm that was reverting to woods. The DOS weekly surveys reported 1 at Hoopes Reservoir on 5 May 1965, establishing the first Piedmont record, and it was subsequently found in small numbers on most of these surveys in northern Delaware.

Trends. According to May Count data it has increased about 6% per year during the 21 years since 1969; the Delaware BBS data support this sharp increase. In the East the increase has taken place at a much more sedate average of 2% per year [Usfw1]. No reason has been offered to explain this change, but an increase of this magnitude must be related to modification of agricultural practices here or in its wintering range.

Breeding population. It is infrequently found on BBCs, but a report of 2.5 territories on 20 acres (30 per 100 ha) of open, lightly grazed woodlot in Virginia (Murray 1951) may be comparable with the densities achieved in the best Sussex County areas.

FALL: The beginning of migration is probably 15–20 August. It peaks 1–15 September and usually ceases by 1–10 October. Late dates include

14 Oct 1956	6	Bombay Hook NWR [MiJC1]
18 Oct 1975	1	Dragon Run [WarD1]
18 Oct 1958	4	Porter [Pres1]

High counts refer to

7 Sep 1986	35	Cape Henlopen SP [Frec1]
9 Sep 1985	30	Assawoman WA [Frec1]
21 Sep 1985	25	west of Lewes [Frec1]

SPECIMENS: DMNH 76467, Seaford, 2 June 1986; DMNH 72758, Delaware City, 3 June 1982; DMNH 75748, New Castle, 8 June 1984; DMNH 77455, Rd. 47, SW Townsend, 13 June 1989; DMNH 76437, 5 mi (8 km) W Dover, 1 July 1986.

Indigo Bunting *(Passerina cyanea)*

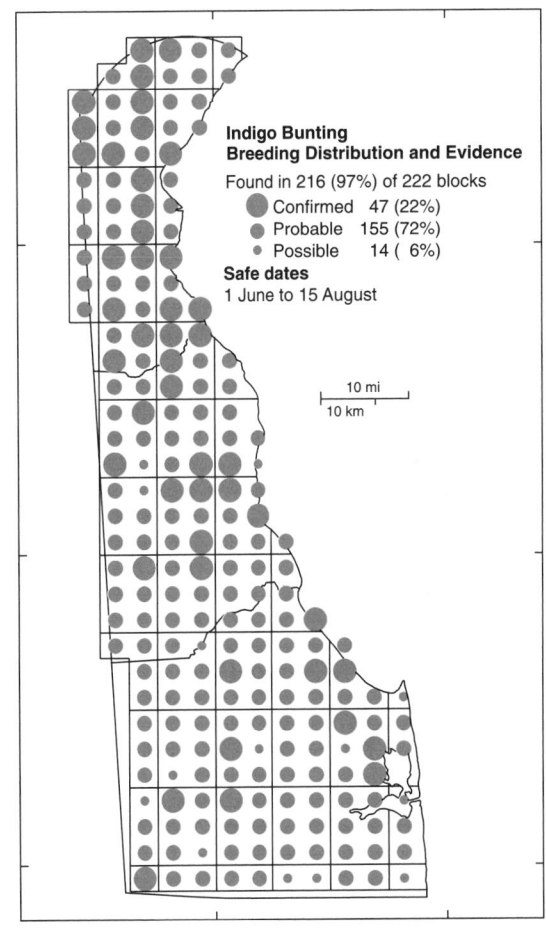

**Indigo Bunting
Breeding Distribution and Evidence**

Found in 216 (97%) of 222 blocks

- Confirmed   47 (22%)
- Probable   155 (72%)
- Possible   14 (6%)

Safe dates
1 June to 15 August

10 mi
10 km

Regular; summer resident; common over most of Delaware, fairly common near the Delaware River and ocean, and in northern Delaware. Expected late April to early October. Increasing population.

J F M A M J J A S O N D

HABITAT: Rich moist or wet wood edges, or brushy cutover areas. Reaches its highest density in agricultural areas, particularly in fields that have reverted to scrubland, and along hedgerows and edges. Found in openings but not dense woodland.

SPRING: First arrival is usually 25 April–5 May. Migration often ends by 25 May–5 June. Peak numbers usually occur after about 10 May. Early dates include

8 Apr 1971	2 banded	University of Delaware woodlot [Line4]
11 Apr 1984	1	Lewes [Frec1]
14 Apr 1984	1	Woodland Beach WA [SpeE7]
17 Apr 1987	1	Rehoboth Beach [Frec1]

High counts along White Clay Creek in 1976 and 1977 are

21 May 1977	40	[RusJ4]
22 May 1976	39	[BroH7]
28 May 1977	50	[HalA1]

The highest May Count is 231 (1979), the lowest 13 (1973).

BREEDING: The distribution and relative abundance maps indicate how widespread and common buntings are across the state.

History and trends. An open country, seed-eating bird such as the Indigo Bunting surely benefited from the clearing of forests that followed European settlement; it probably also benefits to

some extent from tropical deforestation. It has long been common in Delaware and, therefore, little mentioned, but Krider (1879, 50) wrote it was "very plenty in Delaware." It became even more common during 1966–90 based on BBS data, increasing at an average rate of 2 or 3% per year, generally consistent with its gradual increase in the East [Usfw3]. Its population increase will cease if land-use patterns change toward either more and larger tilled fields or larger forests.

Atlas. Active nests were found 8 times, but the contents were reported only once. Most confirmations involved attending young or fledged young. For the Atlas, persistently singing males were presumed to represent probable breeding pairs, but this assumption is not always true. A series of studies shows that many singing males are unmated, and furthermore that 10–15% of males that are mated are polygynous. Males choose between providing parental care and seeking extra-pair copulations. Males infrequently help with fledgling care, but when they do the female can start a second brood sooner (Carey and Nolan 1979; Westneat 1988; Payne 1989).

Nesting. Hanson (notes) described a nest found near Blackbird as follows: "It was [29 inches from the ground] in a large

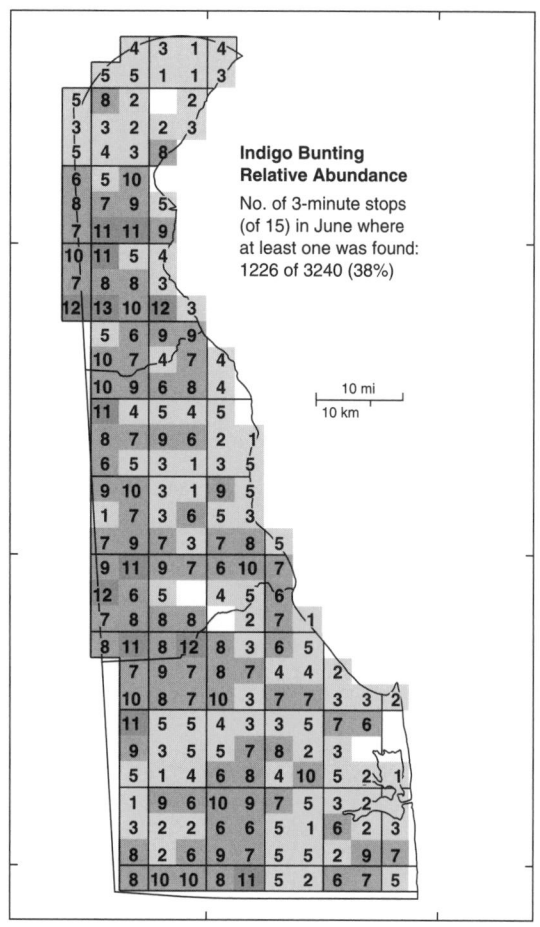

Indigo Bunting Relative Abundance

No. of 3-minute stops (of 15) in June where at least one was found: 1226 of 3240 (38%)

10 mi
10 km

decumbent blackberry bush in a sumac thicket. The nest is a very compact and finely woven structure measuring 4 inches across and 3 inches deep outside and 2 inches across and 1¾ inches deep inside. It is made of dead leaves, grape vine fibers, and fine grass stems, the lining being of the latter. The outside was decorated with the dead flowering tops of a small compositae, dead leaves and spiders' web." The nest is usually constructed in a twig crotch 2–15 ft above ground (Harrison 1978; Peck and James 1987).

Egg dates extend from 12 June to 6 July (*n* = 4); 3–4 eggs are laid. Clutches are completed as late as early August based on a young with half-grown tail netted on 1 September 1973 (DMNH 35766). Maryland egg dates extend from 24 May to 16 August and peak 3–23 June (Tabor and Johnson 1968). Many pairs are double-brooded in Michigan (Payne 1991) and probably are in Delaware.

Breeding population. The bunting was found regularly on the edges of the woodlots that were part of BBCs in northern Delaware, but it only achieved a high density in the less mature woods of the Avon woodlot, where it averaged 50 territories per 100 ha for 4 years with a high of 80 per 100 ha (9 in 27 acres) (Jones et al. 1966). Payne (1991), using color-banded birds, found the density of breeding Indigo Buntings was 15 pairs per 100 ha in a Michigan county that had a bunting population density comparable (based on BBS data) to Delaware's. Graber and Graber (1963) calculated it reached densities in Illinois of 100–150 pairs per 100 acres (250–370 pairs per 100 ha) in edge shrubs, along drainage ditches, and in hedgerows (calculated as strips 30 yd wide, and so about 160 yd long per acre).

FALL: Migration begins 15–20 August and continues to 1–10 October. Peak numbers of Indigo Buntings are banded late August through September. Four reports for 11 October are the latest on record: 1 near Newark in 1967 [Line16], 2 at Brandywine Creek SP in 1969 [SpSB1], 1 at Little Creek WA in 1984 [Edni55], and 1 at Prime Hook NWR [Frec1].

High counts along White Clay Creek in 1976 and 1977 include

28 Aug 1976	29	[Wayn19]
24 Sep 1977	21	[SpSB8]
2 Oct 1976	12	[Dyer4]

SPECIMENS: 17; DMNH, UDEL, UWBM.

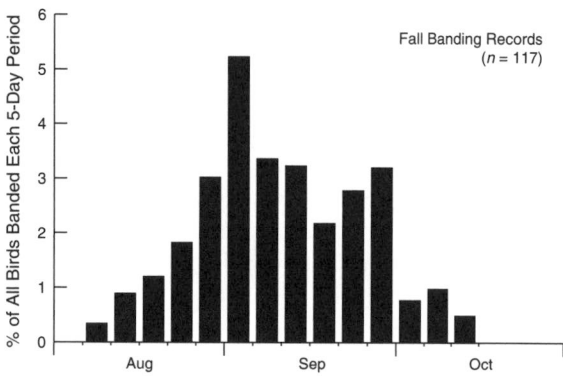

Fall Migration Activity

Painted Bunting (*Passerina ciris*)

NCW

Casual (6 years, 1968–92).

DOCUMENTATION: Photograph (R. B. Supernaw DMNH 466, 467).

REMARKS: Two documented records involve adult males photographed at feeders. The first frequented the feeder of R. B. Supernaw in Oceanview during the late winter of 1987 (pho-

tographed 14 March, DMNH 466-467). The distinctive colors of the Painted Bunting are clearly visible. The second attended the feeder of C. R. Peck near Millville on 3 December 1989 to 5 January 1990 [m.ob3]. It was seen by several observers, and a photograph is on file (DMNH, print collection).

Another adult male was seen by Shoch, Barnhill, and many others at Bombay Hook NWR during 19–24 August 1989 (Shoch 1990b) [Shoc4]. Again the bird was a distinctive male— red below, yellow-green on the back, and blue on the head. The next year a female was seen by Frech near Lewes on 19 May 1990 (Shoch 1990b). Another female was noted in Leipsic on 22 December 1968 by Barnhill (notes). This bird was slim and plain greenish overall, with an inconspicuous eye ring. An immature male at Bombay Hook NWR was observed by many during 4–9 August 1991 [HilA3]. An adult male was observed by many during 2–11 February 1992 from a kitchen window in Rehoboth Beach [Frec21].

The Painted Bunting is a southern species that sometimes strays northward. The Delaware records fit this pattern, and the photographic evidence firmly establishes its occurrence in the state.

Dickcissel (*Spiza americana*)

Occasional (24 years, 1934–89).

```
|• • |•• |   |   • |   |•• |•• |   |   • |   |•• • |
  J   F   M   A   M   J   J   A   S   O   N   D
```

HABITAT: Weedy or agricultural fields.

OCCURRENCE: About 3 dozen reports from throughout the year exist. Most involve 1 bird, but a remarkable occurrence of

14 along the coast during September 1966 was reported [RusW2]. An adult male was banded on 13 November 1965 near Hockessin [Know3], and 1 was found dead on 22 November 1981 near Porter (DMNH 75068).

This species' former eastern breeding range included the Atlantic lowlands from Massachusetts south to North Carolina, where it has become a sporadic and irregular breeder (AOU 1983). It was a regular breeding bird in the Atlantic coastal states, including nearby Chester and Delaware counties, Pennsylvania, from the time of Wilson until its rather sudden disappearance about 1850–80 (Hurley and Franks 1976; Rhoads 1903a). Rhoads and Pennock (1905) and Pennock (1908b) do not mention it in their lists of Delaware birds, but Pennock thought it must have been regular, perhaps common, prior to 1870 [Penn1].

We know of no Delaware breeding record, but several suggestive reports exist. Victor Debes found 3 Dickcissels singing near Mt. Pleasant on 23 June 1934, and a single bird was singing at the same site on 19 May 1935 (Stone 1937) [Debe2]. Ward tape recorded 1 singing from a field near Corner Ketch in 1967; Wayne and Speck subsequently heard it singing there on 8 July [Wayn58]. In 1983 Frech located 1 singing from a wire by an alfalfa field southeast of Milton on 11 and 12 June; on 13 June the field was mowed, and the bird disappeared [Frec40]. In 1985 in a field near Concord Pond 1 was heard overhead on 20 June, and a male was singing on 14 July [RusR15].

Although the Dickcissel winters mainly south of the United States, its North American winter range includes coastal lowlands from southern New England south to Florida and west to southern Texas, where it occurs locally in small numbers (AOU 1983).

SPECIMEN: DMNH 75068, details earlier.

Bobolink *(Dolichonyx oryzivorus)*

Regular; migrant; common. Expected during May and late July to late September.

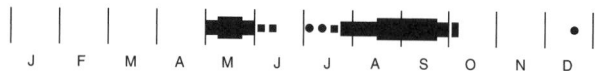

HABITAT: Weedy overgrown fields, hayfields, marshes. Spring flocks closely tied to ripening alfalfa with attendant weevils and other insects. Formerly, it used wild rice areas during fall migration, but few remnant wild rice stands remain. Accepts fallow fields and marsh edges where wild rice is unavailable (Linehan 1994).

SPRING: The Bobolink's spring migration takes place almost entirely in May, with the first arrival usually occurring during 1–5 May, peak numbers in the middle 2 weeks of May, and the last departure during 20–30 May. Flocks reported on 9 and 12 April 1972 (Wayne and Roberts 1973) probably referred to observations made on those dates in May. J. H. Buckalew reported a very early arrival date of 13 April (Bent 1958, 50). Recent early reports include

24 Apr 1992	6	Bombay Hook NWR [Anth1]
27 Apr 1991	1	Burrows Run [Wayn64]
1 May 1989	1	Rd. 261 [Frec1]

Late reports include

4 Jun 1969	1	Brandywine Creek SP [Falk8]
5 Jun 1971	2	Brandywine Creek SP [Wayn39]
15 Jun 1974	2	Dragon Run [Broo21]

High counts involve

10 May 1933	several hundred	Slaughter Beach [Hans1]
10 May 1980	250	Prime Hook NWR [Frec7]
20 May 1984	150	Cape Henlopen SP [Frec1]

The highest May Count is 661 (8 May 1982); none were found in 1973 and 1985.

SUMMER: Bobolinks breed in Pennsylvania close to the Delaware border (Reid 1992a). The June reports in Delaware may suggest breeding attempts. Breeding evidence should be sought, especially in hay fields in the northern part of the state.

FALL: Occasionally, a few birds arrive during early or mid-July; however, the first flocks are usually noted between 25 July and 1 August. Early arrivals include

1 Jul 1990	20	Woodland Beach [Edni28]
7 Jul 1979	2	Ashland [SpSB17]
12 Jul 1959	6	Fenwick Island [Dyke10]

Although Bobolinks are seldom present after 25–30 September, late reports include

1 Oct 1972	4	Winterthur [Broo16]
8 Oct 1989	4	Bombay Hook NWR [Camp21]
20 Dec 1981	1	Cape Henlopen CBC [Barn41]

The latter report, well documented with many observers, was unexpected, because Bobolinks winter in southern South America. Peak numbers occur from about 20 August to 20 September. High counts are

1 Sep 1964	2,000	Woodland Beach WA [Mean1]
2 Sep 1987	3,000	Bombay Hook NWR [Wayn2]

Even more remarkable is a report of an estimated 100,000 at Wilmington on 2 September 1948 [Morg1]; the editors noted that "Perhaps the outstanding feature of the land bird migration in the northern part of the region was the enormous number of bobolinks observed" (Potter and Murray 1949). Bobolinks (rice birds) were formerly hunted over wild rice marshes during fall migration. A brief report is in Pennock's notes for 9–10 September 1903: "Abundant on marshes about Odessa and River Farm. Gunners shooting them—many crippled."

SPECIMENS: DMNH 63812, Greenville, 13 May 1978; ANSP 65974, Odessa, 7 September 1907; DMNH 74121, Bombay Hook, autumn 1970s.

Blackbird Roosts in Delaware

John T. Linehan

"This is a maelstrom!" "It's like being inside a washing machine!" These were the exclamations of ornithology students standing on the dike at Dragon Run while a myriad of blackbirds sped by with a train-like *swoosh* as they dived into the adjacent phragmites. The stern rejoinder was "Just keep counting!"

And keep counting we did—through evening flights into the roosts and through morning flights out of the roosts, both during the fall migrations and during the smaller spring migrations. We counted the birds close to their roosts up and down the lower Delaware River marshes, and we counted flight lines 10 and 20 miles distant from the roosts. We counted easily discernible blocks of 20, 50, or 100 birds flying in regular lines passing high overhead on a steady tailwind, and we counted broad fronts of scrambling masses of birds close to the ground as they bucked a headwind.

These counts were made—over the 25-year period ending in 1981—because of the importance of the lower Delaware valley as a staging area for blackbird migration. The marshes along the river and bay are visited in spring or fall by most of the northeastern North American population of Red-winged Blackbirds, Brown-headed Cowbirds, and Common Grackles. Altogether an estimated 500–900 million blackbirds and starlings visit the state of Delaware yearly, with Red-winged Blackbirds accounting for about 60% of the total.

Over the 25-year period the information and experience gained from counting blackbirds in large flocks were used to develop a system that yields dependable counts (see, for example, Alexander 1969). Dependability was confirmed by the consistency among counts by different people who used the system. Four teams, standing about 50 yards apart, each counted the same flight line. During eight five-minute intervals before dusk, blocks of birds passing over were counted for three minutes, one minute was spent noting the species composition, and one minute was spent recording the data. Each group then calculated the total number of birds passing overhead. The totals varied by an average of only 7–8% for observers with as little as one evening's experience (Jumars 1969).

In addition to detailed counts on selected flight lines, surveys were made to count, map, and classify the flight lines across upper New Castle County, along Route 9 parallel to the Delaware River, and in Kent and Sussex counties in Delaware and in Salem and Cumberland counties in New Jersey. These surveys were carried out during the fall roosting period of some five weeks starting in early November and the spring roosting period of three weeks in March.

The total number of blackbirds passing through Delaware varies from year to year, as does the tempo at which they migrate; during some years most birds appear to stop only briefly, but in other years they accumulate. A few stay all winter. In one exceptional year, 1964, the approximately 1,230 flight lines, multiplied by that year's average of 355,000 birds per line, produced an estimate for the night of 28 November of 437 million blackbirds.

In the fall blackbirds are generally present in greatest numbers from about 10 November to 6 December. During most years the peak number on a single night approaches 70 million birds. For every 100 birds present on the peak date, 50 birds are to be expected 12 days earlier and 6 days later. The species composition changes as the migration progresses, with the following median peak dates:

21 November	female and immature male redwings
22 November	cowbirds
27 November	adult male redwings
29 November	grackles

A January thaw may bring in a million or more blackbirds from the south, but northward winter movements stop when another freeze sets in. The major movement north in Delaware, perhaps a third the size of the southward migration in fall, begins in March, and again the composition of the flocks changes as the migration proceeds. In 1968, for example, the species composition changed from about 95% redwings in February to less than 50% redwings in mid-April (Jumars 1969).

There may be several reasons why these blackbirds aggregate into such vast flocks, but it is generally agreed that information exchange is an important function of the roost; the eager birds leaving in the predawn light are the ones returning to a good feeding place. For a successful day, others can follow them on their flights, which may be as long as 55 miles. The various species usually segregate into their own feeding flocks—the grackles to oak woods, the cowbirds to short seedy grass, and the redwings to corn stubble or wild rice in season.

After a day's foraging, birds return to their roosting area over an 80-minute period. Early arrivals fly nervously about the roost and nearby assembly areas; the last birds arrive in darkness. A "blackbird avalanche" occurs during the 9-minute period from 20 to 11 minutes before darkness, when almost two-thirds of the birds fly in. This remarkable synchronization is accomplished by four different species of birds flying to roosts in unfamiliar country from feeding areas averaging 20–40 miles away.

The tasks of enumeration were lightened by the sheer awe

these birds inspired by the incredible discipline of high-speed maneuvers performed in near perfect unison. The amazement expressed by conservationist Maurice Broun as he watched the smokelike, wavering line of blackbirds snaking across the Delaware River was but one of the many deeply emotional expressions I've heard from people exposed to this scene. The Delaware River blackbird roost flights are surely well up on the list of the world's natural wonders.

A banding program that began in 1954 aimed to discover the breeding and wintering areas of the Delaware visitors. A key to this program was the development of two methods of capturing large numbers of icterids. One scheme, capitalizing on the sociability of blackbirds, resulted in catches of up to 900 birds per day in a decoy trap. The other method, exploiting a blackbird reaction to head-lamps that I had observed, frequently resulted in nightly catches exceeding 10,000 birds in a floodlight trap specially designed for the purpose. We thus obtained information not available from previous techniques, which had produced a meager dozen birds per trap-day.

In total we captured approximately one-third of a million blackbirds in Delaware, mostly in traps operated year-round at the University of Delaware Experimental Farm in Newark, and we banded 79,000 of them. Recoveries were made in 29 states (25 east of the Mississippi River), five eastern Canadian provinces, and five countries in Latin America and the West Indies. The distribution of recoveries made more than 40 miles from the banding site is shown in the accompanying table.

Despite thousands of hours of sloshing through insect-ridden marshes, counting ticks in birds' ears, and measuring bird activity in hot cornfields—despite it all—this research ecologist knows with certainty that the blackbirds of Delaware have provided the most stimulating experiences of his life.

Recovery Locations of Banded Blackbirds
(recovered more than 40 miles from Delaware banding site)

Location of Recovery	Percentage of Recoveries			Number of Recoveries
	Cowbirds	Redwings	Grackles	
Quebec and Maritime Prov.	16	17	13	244
New England	17	9	11	235
N.Y., N.J., Pa.	26	21	33	405
Va., N.C., S.C.	21	24	19	327
Other	20	29	24	337
TOTAL NO. RECOVERED	1,140 (100%)	210 (100%)	198 (100%)	1,548

Red-winged Blackbird *(Agelaius phoeniceus)*

Resident; common to abundant. Migrates mostly in March and April and late July to early December. Breeds most commonly along the Delaware River and ocean. Forms roosts, which increase to enormous numbers in late November.

J F M A M J J A S O N D	

HABITAT: Breeds most densely in the saltmarsh transition zone containing hightide bush and groundsel bush, whether or not invaded by phragmites, and in rank vegetation along wet ditches, ponds, and other wet sites; found year-round gleaning agricultural fields, preferring wetter areas. Roosts in dense young woods and in phragmites and other marsh vegetation. Feeds in late summer and fall on wild rice when available and can greatly damage ripening corn. Spring flocks forage in open thawing fields for soil organisms (Linehan 1994).

SPRING: Migration usually takes place about 1 March to 5 May, but Linehan (1961) reported that large flocks of adult male Red-winged Blackbirds arrived on 18 February in 1961; the arrival was more abrupt than in previous years and coincided with the melting of accumulated snow. Estimates of several thousand birds are not unusual, particularly when made shortly after sunrise while the birds are dispersing from roosts. The following reports undoubtedly sampled a small portion of enormous flocks wintering and moving through Delaware (see "Blackbird Roosts in Delaware" essay):

3 March 1979	5,600	Ashland [Dyer8]
18 March 1978	20,800	White Clay Creek [Boll5]
25 March 1978	17,000	White Clay Creek [RusJ7]

On 10 March 1962 Linehan (1962) witnessed the greatest concentration of blackbirds he had noted that spring or any previous spring. A complete "umbrella" of blackbirds was overhead continuously from 5:45 to 6:20 P.M. at Bear, not heavy but so complete that no gaps in the flight were evident. He surmised that this flock contained the bulk of the Atlantic Flyway birds. The highest May Count, taken after the roosts have broken up, is 5,326 (1982), the lowest 1,382 (1972).

BREEDING: This species breeds all over the state, but the relative abundance study shows it to be most common along the Delaware River and coast and less common in central Sussex County. It was encountered with considerable frequency in northern Delaware in spite of intense suburban development there.

Atlas. The Red-winged Blackbird is the only species registered in all 222 blocks, though several trips were required to locate it in some inland blocks, such as the one that includes Trap Pond SP. It was confirmed in almost 60% of the blocks, most commonly by seeing the adults carrying food for the young. Active nests were found in 42 blocks. The fledged young code, a risky code for Atlas data because birds of the year leave their territory as soon as they can fly and begin flocking in early July, was used infrequently. Year-old male red-wings do not breed, and their presence may have led to some false possible codes because Atlas observers were not forewarned of this trait. However, only 8% of blocks remained at the possible level, so the degree of error introduced in this way must be small.

Nesting. Hanson (notes) described nests as 4–5 in. wide and deep, woven of coarse meadow grasses, and lined with somewhat finer grass. The substrate mentioned in Delaware nest records includes groundsel bush (15 times), unspecified shrub (10), cattail (10), and phragmites (5). Nest heights were usually from 1 to 8 ft.

Extreme egg dates are 5 May 1983 at Trussum Pond SP [Edni4] to 10 July near Ocean View [Jesc2]. The bimodal clutch-completion graph suggests redwings are partially double-brooded in Delaware; studies in other states indicate second clutches may be laid following successful first broods about 10% of the time (Dolbeer 1976; Case and Hewitt 1963; Fankhauser 1964). Two clutches of 5 were reported from egg collections (DMNH), but most were 3 (36), 4 (16), or 2 (6—possibly incomplete clutches).

Trends. BBS results indicate Red-winged Blackbirds decreased in the East and the Upper Coastal Plain at an average of 2% per year during 1966–90, whereas May Count and BBS data suggest lesser rates of decline in Delaware [Usfw3].

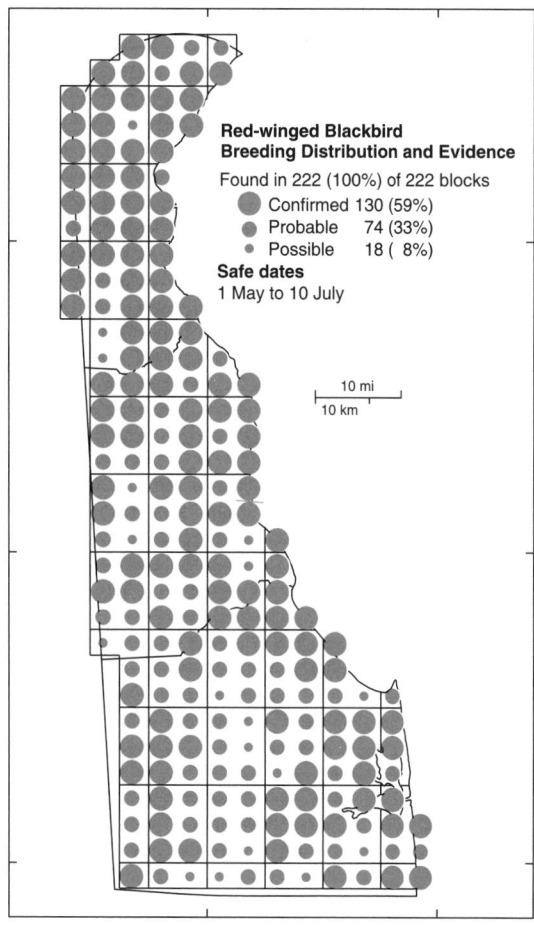

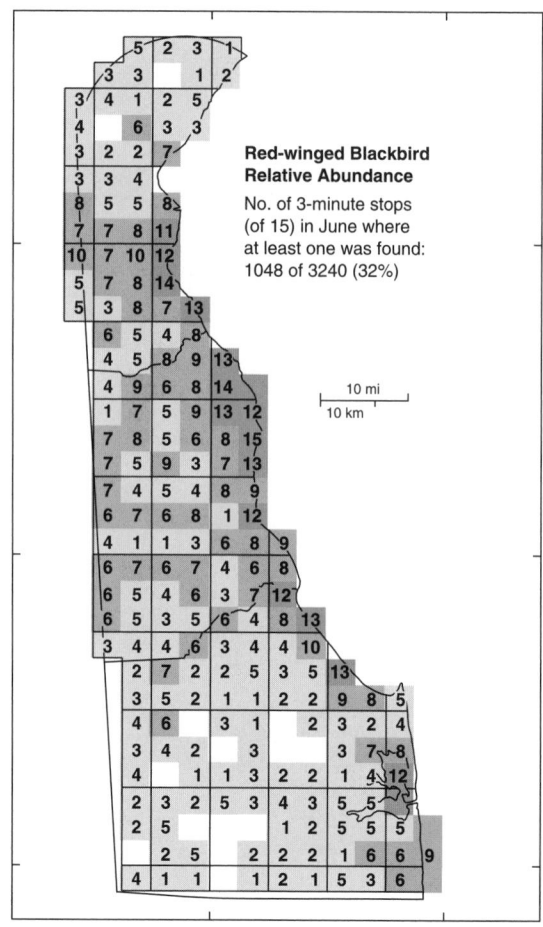

High numbers of blackbirds are not a new phenomenon; Wilson and Audubon noted them in the early nineteenth century though redwings were probably common in Delaware only in the tidal marshes before European settlement. Bush noted large flocks, and Pennock (notes) reported immense flocks on 9–10 September 1903 at Odessa and River Farm that were damaging sugar corn. Twentieth century reports of Red-winged Blackbirds nesting in habitats other than marshes have become common; the widespread use of such upland habitat

seems associated with a population increase (Case and Hewitt 1963).

Breeding population. This species is a colonial or clumped nester much of the time, with nesting density varying from 2 to 40 per acre (4 to 100 nests per ha) in New Jersey (Caccamise 1976). BBCs in Delaware have revealed Red-winged Blackbird densities of 130 male territories per 100 ha (average of 3 plots, 3 years) in impounded saltmarsh in Kent County (Moore 1989), 100 per 100 ha in a Prime Hook NWR marsh (West 1992), and 100 per 100 ha (three-year average of 9.7 per 24 acres) in an Assawoman WA marsh (Linehan 1969a). Red-wings infrequently bred in northern Delaware woodlots but did so at a density of 27 territories per 100 ha (4-year average of 2.8 per 27 acres) in a woodlot that had a permanent stream, dense understory, and much edge (Linehan et al. 1967a). A correlation was developed between BBS counts and census results in an agricultural area of Quebec (Clark et al. 1983), which, when applied in Delaware, suggests a density of 7.8 males per 100 ha along Delaware BBS routes. These routes do not adequately sample the Delaware marshes where breeding is probably more dense. Generally, more than 1 female nests on a male's territory (Dolbeer 1976).

FALL: Seasonal movement away from breeding territories starts 20–30 July when small flocks, composed of local breeders and birds of the year, begin to form. Packard (1936) noted that

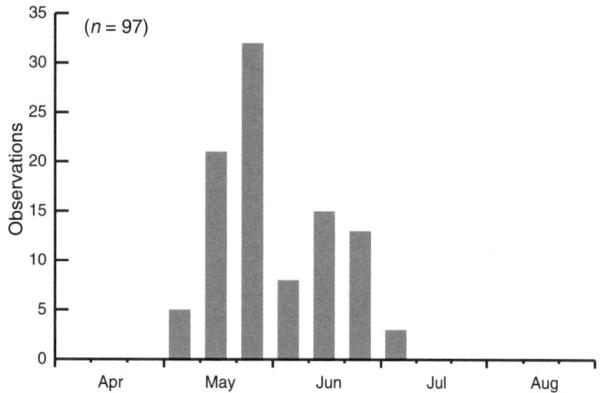

Estimated Clutch-Completion Dates

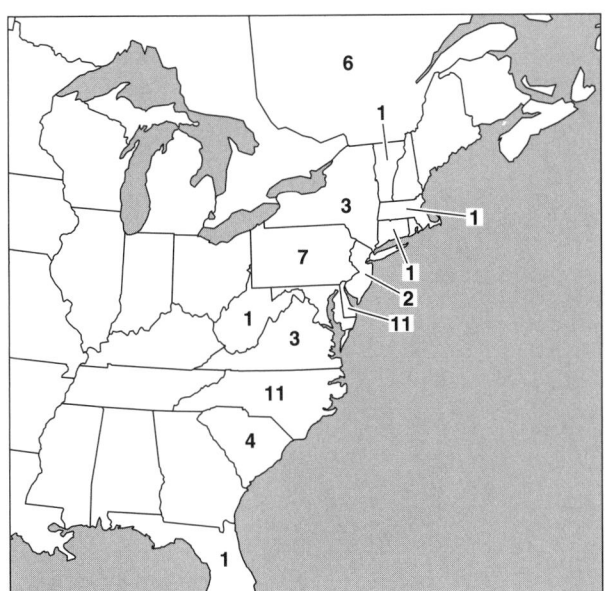

Total Red-winged Blackbirds Banded in Delaware and Recovered Dead or Shot in Each State

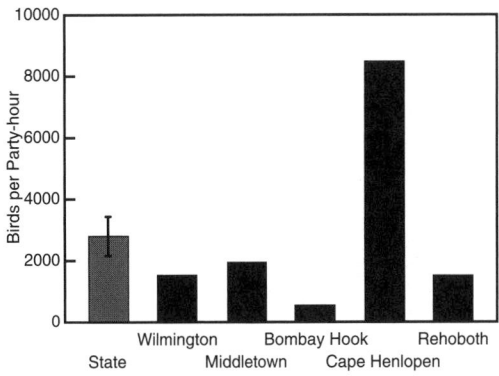

CBC Geographic Distribution

Blackbirds are usually faithful to 1 winter roost, but they do not necessarily return to that roost in subsequent years (Dolbeer 1978).

BANDING: The banding map depicts the distribution of birds banded in Delaware and later shot or found dead. Thus results from large banding operations in other states do not bias these data. The map shows that most of the migratory birds from Delaware go south to the Carolinas and come from as far north as Quebec. There is little crossover to the Mississippi Flyway; for example, the large winter roosts in Tennessee and other central states do not involve Delaware birds to any considerable extent.

SPECIMENS: 69; DMNH, ANSP, UDEL, USNM. Egg records: DMNH, WFVZ.

some New England birds apparently begin southward movements in late summer. In Delaware reports of several thousand birds begin to occur regularly about 15 October and continue into late fall and early winter as roosts grow larger.

1966–89 CBC Summary

Christmas Bird Count	Years Found	Range of No. Found	Median
Wilmington	24	642–3,073,418	14,301
Middletown	24	1,360–636,000	11,095
Bombay Hook	24	2,868–235,385	20,412
Cape Henlopen	24	651–4,840,950	111,066
Rehoboth	24	1,036–1,002,700	21,452
STATEWIDE (low in 1989, high in 1981)	24	13,997–5,084,601	825,473

WINTER: A sunrise drive along Delaware Rt. 9 or U.S. Rt. 13 will greatly impress the observer not familiar with winter blackbird roosting behavior. Mixed roosts, often exceeding 1 million redwings, grackles, cowbirds, starlings, and other species, are formed in a number of localities in the United States, including the marshes of the Delaware River and Bay. Meanley and Webb (1961) estimated that a roost on the Delaware River held 2.5 million birds. Twenty years later almost 9.5 million blackbirds (including 4.8 million redwings) were observed on the 20 December 1981 Cape Henlopen CBC.

It is abundant on all CBCs but especially so on the Cape Henlopen count. In most years the Delaware valley roosts break up in late December. Many redwings spend mid-winter in Virginia and the Carolinas; comparatively few remain in Delaware. These birds come from widely divergent breeding populations (Dolbeer 1978). In a given winter Red-winged

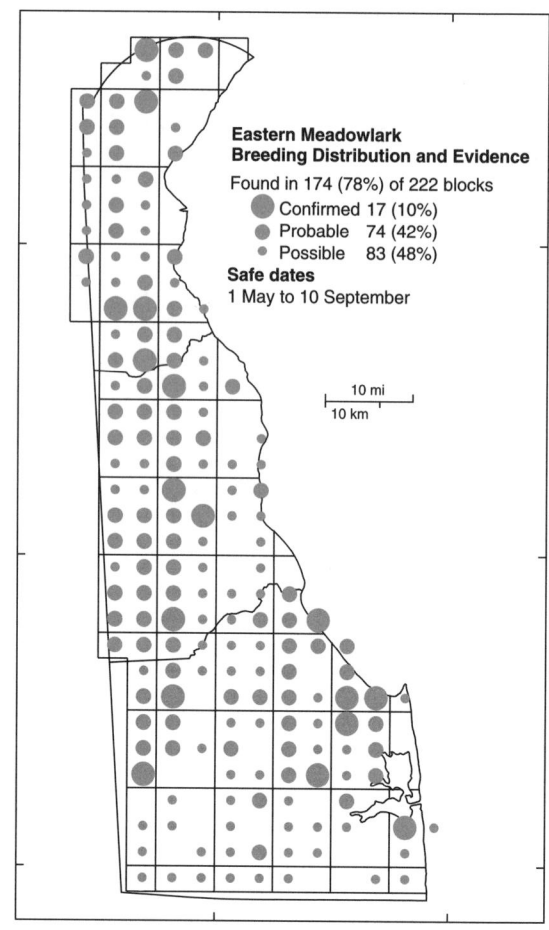

**Eastern Meadowlark
Breeding Distribution and Evidence**
Found in 174 (78%) of 222 blocks
● Confirmed 17 (10%)
● Probable 74 (42%)
· Possible 83 (48%)
Safe dates
1 May to 10 September

10 mi
10 km

Resident; fairly common. Migration probably during March–April and October–November. Decreasing sharply on BBSs, May Counts, and CBCs. Breeds most commonly in western Kent County.

J F M A M J J A S O N D

HABITAT: Large grass or hay fields, pastures. Grassy, coastal succession. Higher parts of tidal marshes with a meadow structure.

SPRING: The Delaware data do not reveal the migration pattern, but Stewart and Robbins (1958) give the normal period in Maryland as 5–15 March to 25 April–5 May with the peak 25 March–20 April.

BREEDING: The Eastern Meadowlark breeds most commonly in the grassy fields of western Kent County farmlands and in adjacent portions of Sussex and New Castle counties. A remnant population breeds in Piedmont New Castle County. Meadowlarks also breed in smaller numbers near the coast.

Atlas. Atlas results reflect its presence in many blocks. Blocks where it was not recorded are spotty, suggesting that additional fieldwork might reveal meadowlarks breeding in some of them. Particularly unexpected was its absence in the block west of Townsend in country where horses are raised. This block also lacked Killdeer, suggesting a singular lack of food in otherwise suitable habitat. Meadowlarks were found in increased numbers near the ocean and lower Delaware Bay in grassy areas. They are increasingly difficult to find in northern Delaware as fields give way to suburban development. Of 17 confirmations, only 3 mentioned location of a nest. Most confirmations involved an adult carrying food or feeding fledged young.

Nesting. Hanson (notes) described a nest placed in grass on the roadside and so well concealed that it was found only when the female flushed. Made of grass, it was 6 in. across, roofed over, and 4 in. high. Inside it was 4 in. across and 2½ in. high.

Extrapolated clutch-completion dates extend from 5 May to 25 June (*n* = 9). Extreme egg dates are 18 May at Newark [Jahn2] to 2 July at Trussum Pond SP [Edni4]. Four early nestlings were found on 25 May near Smyrna [West3]. The breeding season probably extends beyond 2 July in Delaware, because Maryland egg dates extend from 4 May to 9 August (Robbins 1996). Clutches include 4 eggs (3), 5 (2), and 6 (1, DMNH 7373). In Minnesota Lanyon (1957) found that females that were successful in their first nesting always attempted a second brood.

Trends. This species surely increased greatly in Delaware when the forests were cleared for fields and pastures. Just as surely it has decreased in the twentieth century as numbers of grazing farm animals have decreased. The Amish manner of farming in western Kent County still provides good meadowlark habitat, or the species would probably have declined more than it has. BBS data show that the meadowlark has been

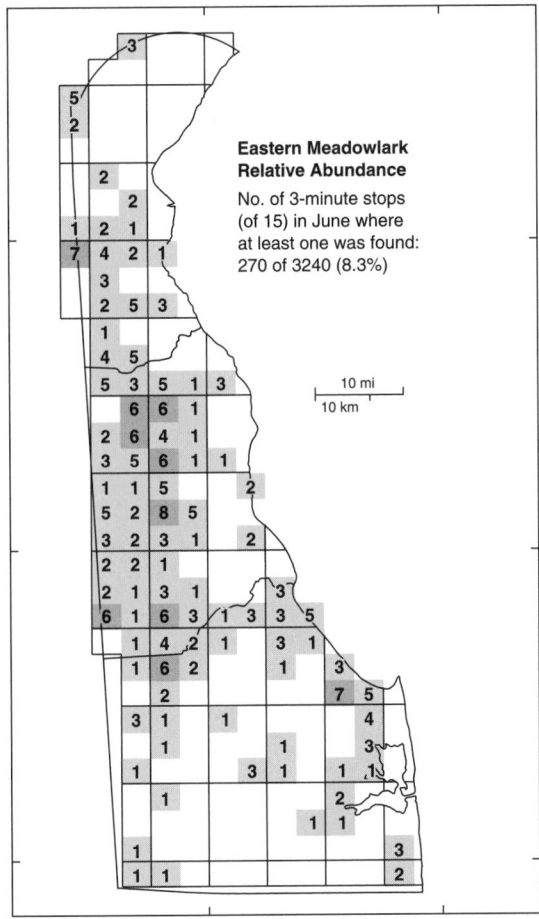

**Eastern Meadowlark
Relative Abundance**

No. of 3-minute stops
(of 15) in June where
at least one was found:
270 of 3240 (8.3%)

The species has been Blue Listed since 1980 and was listed as a species of special concern in 1986 (Tate 1986). Because it is quite common over large parts of its range and because it is still fairly common in Delaware, little effort will probably be made in its behalf in the near term. Its sharp reduction in numbers, however, is an inescapable environmental signal.

FALL: As in the spring, migration is not discernible in the Delaware data. Stewart and Robbins (1958) give the normal period in Maryland as 1–10 October through 25 November–5 December with the peak from 15 October to 15 November. Typically 5–10 birds are seen in a day. High reports are

18 Oct 1981	34	Bombay Hook NWR [RusR16]
8 Nov 1981	45	Bombay Hook NWR [Bayn4]
6 Sep 1987	50	Prime Hook NWR [Frec1]
25 Oct 1977	50	Cape Henlopen SP [Frec1]

1966–89 CBC Summary

Christmas Bird Count	Years Found	Range of No. Found	Median
Wilmington	18	1–387	8
Middletown	24	3–170	68
Bombay Hook	24	20–1,034	182
Cape Henlopen	24	12–475	137
Rehoboth	24	2–748	108
STATEWIDE	24	48–1,878	605
(decreasing; low in 1988, high in 1966)			

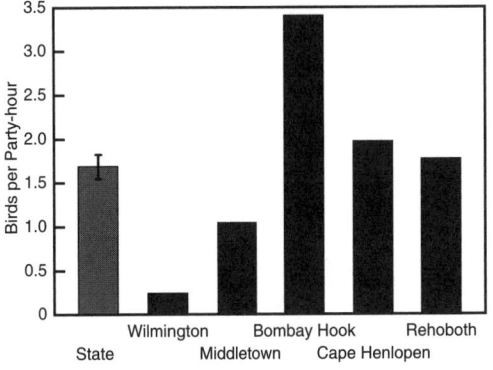

CBC Geographic Distribution

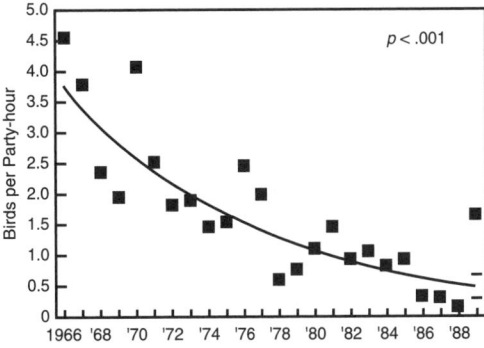

CBC Trend; Decreasing at 9% per Year

declining during 1966–90 at an average annual rate of 4.5% in Delaware and 3.5% in the East. An even sharper 7% annual decline was registered on Delaware May Counts, 1969–91. It is one of a guild of grassland species showing a continuing decline (Droege and Sauer 1989).

Breeding population. Good meadowlark habitat in pastures has not been studied in Delaware, though the meadowlark was present in saltmarsh edge in studies at Prime Hook NWR (West 1993) and Assawoman WA (Linehan 1965c). In Maryland it was recorded at a density of 16–19 males per 100 ha in marsh meadows and mixed hayfields and pastures (Stewart and Robbins 1958) and presumably would reach that density in comparable Delaware habitat. In southern Illinois a density of 250 nests per 100 ha (40 in 40 acres) was found in an ungrazed pasture, but the next highest density was 40 nests per 100 ha (Roseberry and Klimstra 1970). The highest May count for this species is 125 (10 May 1975), and a recent high count is 49 (1989); its habitat is not extensively sampled on May Counts. An average of 7 birds per BBS route was reported in 1989, also a recent high.

Conservation. Little can be done to counter the loss of meadows on farmland, but public grassland should be managed to attract meadowlarks and other declining grassland species by selecting favorable mowing regimes. Invasion of higher marshes by phragmites eliminates nesting meadowlarks.

WINTER: This species has shown a sharp decrease averaging 9% annually during 1966–89. This 90% decline in winter numbers since 1966 is more severe than the reduction indicated by the BBS in the eastern region (Robbins et al. 1986). The sharp decline in 1978 undoubtedly resulted from the severe weather of the previous winter, and this decline is also shown by reduced numbers on the 1978 and 1979 May Counts. Typical winter reports total 10–15 birds. High reports, all from Sussex County, include

20 Dec 1981	75	Clarkesville [Frec1]
20 Dec 1981	60	Love Creek [Frec1]
21 Dec 1980	100	Prime Hook NWR [Frec1]

SPECIMENS: 15; ANSP, DMNH.

Yellow-headed Blackbird *(Xanthocephalus xanthocephalus)*

DOCUMENTATION: Three sets of unpublished notes, numerous sight records, banding record.

HABITAT: Agricultural fields, urban lawns; often associated with flocks of other blackbirds.

OCCURRENCE: This distinctive western blackbird is casual in winter in eastern North America (AOU 1983). It has been recorded in Delaware in 22 years during the 1964–93 period. Males [Lehm1] and females [Nile1] have been recorded. Typically, only 1 or 2 are present. This species has occurred in all months, but two-thirds of the birds occurred from late December to early April. One was banded on 9 November 1964 on the University of Delaware farm, Newark [Line4]. In winter months it associates with other blackbirds and may be seen foraging with them at bird feeders or in cornfields.

Occasional (22 years, 1964–93); mostly winter visitor; rare. To be looked for from late December to early April.

Rusty Blackbird *(Euphagus carolinus)*

Regular; winter visitor; fairly common. Expected late October (perhaps earlier) to mid-April. Decreasing at 8% per year on CBCs.

HABITAT: Wet or moist deciduous woods, occasionally at urban feeders.

SPRING: Migration probably begins in late February or early March, since the available data show a slight increase in numbers from about 20 February to about 5 March. Migration usually ends by about 15 April. The latest stragglers reported include

21 Apr 1973	1	Bombay Hook NWR [John11]
28, 30 Apr 1975	1	Greenville [Nile1]
13 May 1991	1	Trap Pond SP [Edni66]

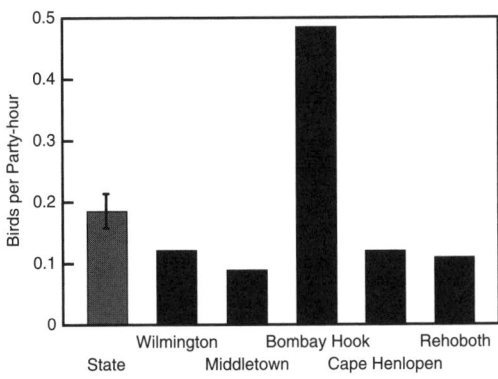

CBC Geographic Distribution

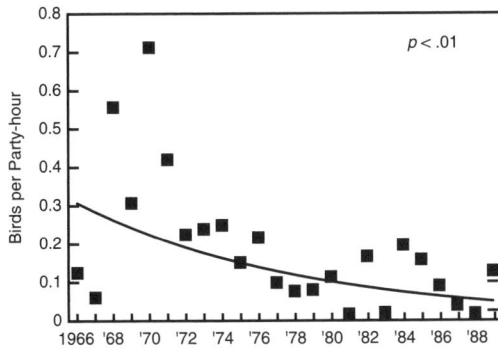

CBC Trend; Decreasing at 8% per Year

The highest count is 75 at Dragon Run on 22 February 1975 [SpSB13]. Spring numbers are noticeably lower than those for fall.

FALL: Although occasional arrivals are reported in the first 3 weeks of October, first arrival is frequently not reported until the last week of October. The earliest reports mention

22 Sep 1973	3	Dragon Run [SpSB13]
9 Oct 1971	1	Brandywine Creek SP [Wayn25]
11 Oct 1975	11	Dragon Run [Barn2]

The earliest specimen was taken at Newport on 14 October 1911 (ANSP 79988). Peak numbers usually occur from 25 October through 25 November. High counts are

7 November 1965	300	Churchmans Marsh [Broo14]
10 November 1974	110	Dragon Run [John7]
6 December 1970	100	Lewes [Carl11]

1966–89 CBC Summary

Christmas Bird Count	Years Found	Range of No. Found	Median
Wilmington	22	1–46	13
Middletown	16	1–24	3
Bombay Hook	24	1–137	19
Cape Henlopen	15	1–43	3
Rehoboth	16	1–82	2
STATEWIDE	24	5–280	60

(decreasing; low in 1988, high in 1970)

WINTER: This species has shown a significant decline in CBC numbers. It was apparently affected adversely by the severe winters of the mid-1970s and has not fully recovered. Winter numbers typically range up to 15–20 birds.

SPECIMENS: 6; DMNH, ANSP, UDEL.

Brewer's Blackbird *(Euphagus cyanocephalus)*

Occasional (34 years, 1951–93); winter visitor; usually uncommon when present.

DOCUMENTATION: Published and unpublished notes.

HABITAT: Feed lots, crop fields, and adjacent roadsides.

OCCURRENCE: This western species regularly winters as close as western South Carolina and occurs casually in the Northeast during migration and winter (AOU 1983). It was first reported in Delaware on 10 February 1951 near Bombay Hook NWR [Sutt1], when it was noted as the "First local report in several years," indicating prior reports unknown to us. The next record, providing the first available description, occurred in October 1953 (Cutler 1955a). From then through 1993 the Brewer's Blackbird has been found in 34 different years. Most reports occur during the CBC period, when observer effort increases, and in late February and early March, when the birds may be migrating and present in larger numbers. It is most commonly reported in the Bombay Hook NWR–Little Creek WA region where much observer effort is focused, but it occurs elsewhere. Its numbers usually range from a few to 20–30; the highest numbers reported are 223 on the 27 December 1992 Bombay Hook CBC and 180 at Bombay Hook NWR on 22 December 1956 [Cutl32]. A typical example of wintering involved 3–20 near Bombay Hook NWR from 23 January 1976 [Barn6] to 17 April 1976 [Lehm20]. Extreme published dates are

5 Oct 1953	5	Bombay Hook NWR [Cutl36]
22 Oct 1954	12	Bombay Hook NWR [Cutl18]
3 Nov 1951	3	Bombay Hook NWR [Lamp2]
17 Apr 1976	3	near Bombay Hook NWR [Lehm20]
22 Apr 1955	2	Bombay Hook NWR [Lamp2]
26 Apr 1975	3	near Bombay Hook NWR [Stod2]

Since 1978 the status has changed again: there have been no reports before 15 December or after 27 February, and the number of reports has decreased.

REMARKS: The occurrence of the Brewer's Blackbird in Delaware is probably associated with 2 other phenomena. First, the 700-mi eastward expansion of its breeding range this century reaching Indiana, Michigan, and Ontario by the 1970s (Bent 1958, 302; Stepney and Power 1973; Gordon 1987; Granlund 1991) probably contributed to a real increase of its wintering in the East (Stepney 1975). Second, the large blackbird roosts in Delaware probably attract some individuals of this species (compare Mengel 1965, 449).

The extension into Delaware of its wintering range was observed as follows: "There have been so many recent records of the Brewer's Blackbird in eastern Pennsylvania and Delaware that the highlights of the history should be reviewed here. First appearances were of a single bird at Lake Ontelanee near Reading, Pa., on Oct. 15, 1951, and 3 at Bombay Hook, Del., on Nov. 3, 1951. . . . In 1952 none were seen. In 1953 five were seen at Bombay Hook on Oct. 5. . . . Since then these birds have been regular winter residents at Bombay Hook, Oct. 10 to April 11" (Potter and Murray 1955). P. B. Street wrote that it now appears to be a regular winter visitor to Delaware (in Walkinshaw and Zimmerman 1961).

1966–89 CBC Summary

Christmas Bird Count	Years Found	Range of No. Found	Median
Wilmington	1	2	
Middletown	1	1	
Bombay Hook	12	1–35	
Cape Henlopen	3	2–51	
Rehoboth	4	1–4	
STATEWIDE (high in 1966)	15	1–53	6

After 1975 populations of the Brewer's Blackbird dropped sharply in Ontario (Gordon 1987) and so did the winter reports of it in Delaware.

Common Grackle *(Quiscalus quiscula)*

Resident; common to abundant. Migrates mid-February through April and August to early December. Breeds commonly throughout the state.

J   F   M   A   M   J   J   A   S   O   N   D

HABITAT: Wet areas in agricultural fields; field edges, farmyards, urban and suburban areas; marshes, open woods. Early season colonial nesting sites require heavy cover before most deciduous trees have leafed out. These sites include stands of Norway spruce or loblolly pine, or scrubby growth of swamp maple or willow overgrown with Japanese honeysuckle or other vines. It gleans corn stubble in winter and spring, and eats planted corn just as the seed germinates. Feeds in the duff of open woods on acorns and insects (Linehan 1994).

SPRING: Migration probably begins 15–20 February and continues through 1–5 May. During this period typical numbers seen flying over and in fields range from several thousand during the peak of migration to 30–50 at the end; numbers at roosts are much higher (see "Blackbird Roosts in Delaware" essay).

BREEDING: Breeding commonly throughout the state, this grackle was detected more frequently than any other species on the BBS and relative abundance study. The latter shows possible lower numbers in the Piedmont and in the forested part of central Sussex County. These slightly lower counts may simply result from the presence of more trees at stops in these areas and thus reduced opportunity to observe flying grackles.

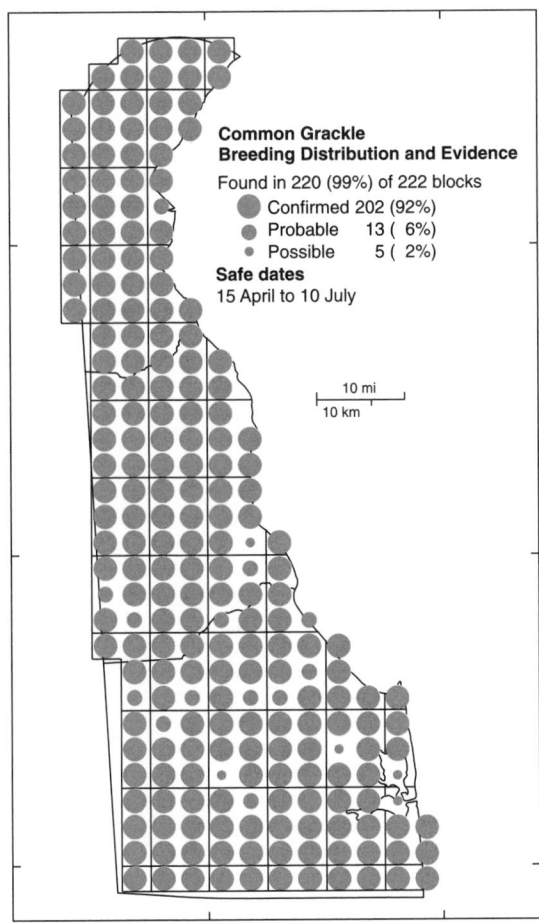

Common Grackle
Breeding Distribution and Evidence

Found in 220 (99%) of 222 blocks

● Confirmed 202 (92%)
● Probable 13 (6%)
• Possible 5 (2%)

Safe dates
15 April to 10 July

10 mi
10 km

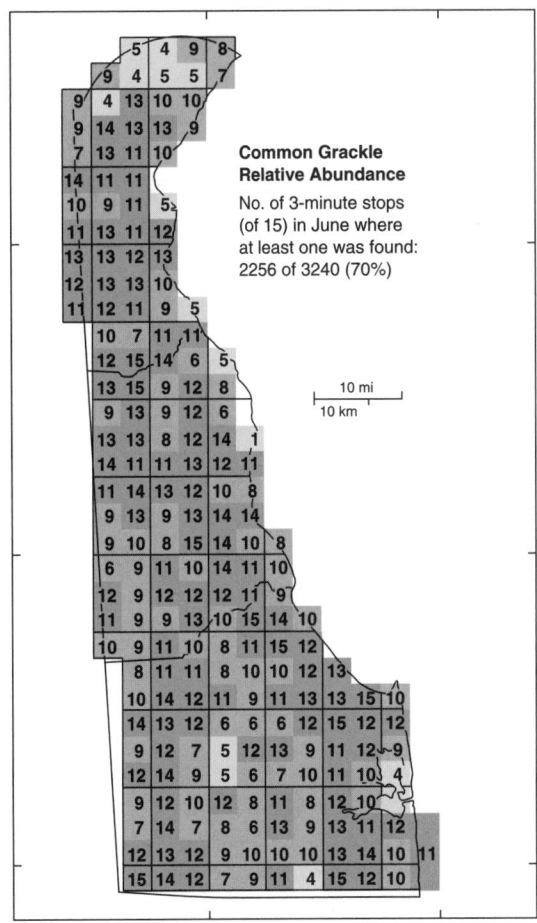

Common Grackle
Relative Abundance

No. of 3-minute stops
(of 15) in June where
at least one was found:
2256 of 3240 (70%)

10 mi
10 km

Atlas. It was found in every block except 2, which were in the outer marshes of Bombay Hook NWR where there are no trees suitable for nesting. It was confirmed more than any other species, but only 29 confirmations involved finding an active nest. Most confirmations were made by seeing females carrying food (typically with male following) or recently fledged, nonflying young (often begging noisily on a limb). These 2 methods allowed confirmation to be attained quickly without the need to find a nest.

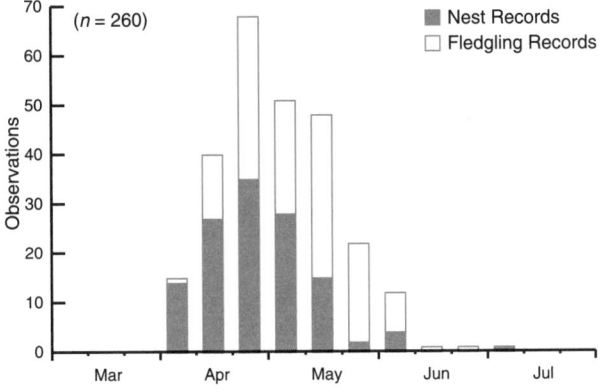

Estimated Clutch-Completion Dates

Nesting. Hanson (notes) described a nest taken from an orchard near Dover: "The nest was saddled on a limb and well fastened. It was 10 inches across and 6 inches high, and the inside measured 4 inches across and 3½ inches deep. It was built of roots, vines, straw, and hay, and was lined with fine hay. Just under the lining was a layer of mud much like the construction of a robin's nest. Several pieces of string were woven in." Nests reported in the nest records were mainly between 6 and 25 ft above the ground, but 1 nest 50 ft up was reported. Various trees and thick or viney bushes are used, with pines most frequently reported. Evergreens are probably preferred because breeding activity starts before deciduous trees are fully leafed out.

Clutch-completion dates in a colony often fall within a short period of time, since females seem to synchronize egg-laying. For example, Burr and Stevens (1969) reported that most eggs in a large colony hatched within a 10-day period, and 90% of the eggs within sections of the colony hatched during a 2-day period. Variations between sites and years widen the spread of nesting dates.

The clutch-completion data from nest records and from TSBR fledglings show remarkable concordance. Many of the nest records come from systematic work done by people associated with the University of Delaware; the TSBR data come

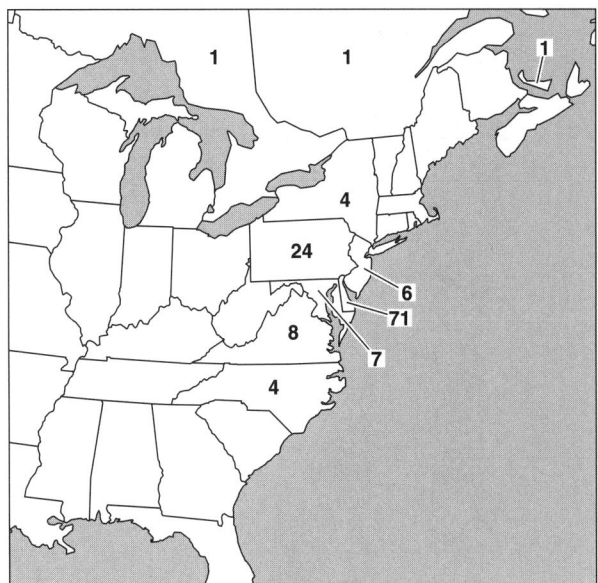

Total Common Grackles Banded in Delaware and Recovered Dead or Shot in Each State.

FALL: Migration begins about the first week of August and continues through early December. Early in the migration period, numbers range up to about 100. As the season progresses, numbers increase rapidly until about mid-October when reports of 1,000 or so are common; by the beginning of November reports of 3,000–5,000 are common at locations away from their large roosts.

1966–89 CBC Summary

Christmas Bird Count	Years Found	Range of No. Found	Median
Wilmington	24	28–947,124	3,068
Middletown	24	49–612,224	4,682
Bombay Hook	24	54–305,000	1,033
Cape Henlopen	24	203–9,700,000	107,869
Rehoboth	24	71–723,950	20,122
STATEWIDE (low in 1989, high in 1969)	24	14,474–9,772,402	344,584

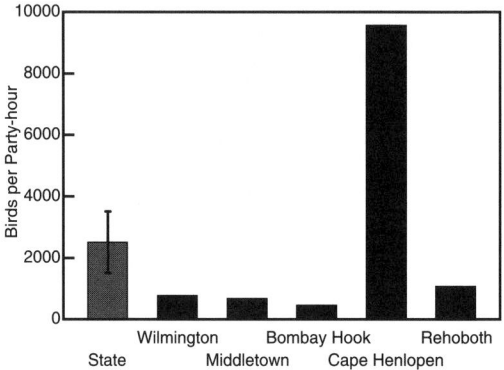

CBC Geographic Distribution

from young birds brought in for care. Extreme egg dates are 9 April at Newark [Burr1] and 15 June at Bombay Hook NWR [Brit1]. An early nestling date is 16 April (Burr and Stevens 1969); the latest date, of a newly fledged young being fed on 15 August at Bellevue [Conw2], is late enough to be a second brood. Bendire (1895) and Harrison (1978) indicate that the Common Grackle is sometimes double-brooded, but neither source cites any studies. If it is double-brooded in Delaware, second broods are not frequent enough to have much effect on the clutch-completion graph.

One Delaware colony had an average clutch size of 4.5 eggs (range = 1–6, mode = 5, *n* = 43). Only 1 clutch of 6 was reported, and all 6 eggs hatched between 26 and 28 April [Stev1]. In that study most clutches were completed in mid-April (Burr and Stevens 1969).

Trends. This versatile species was probably common in Delaware before European settlement, but it must have become even more so because of its ability to exploit agricultural habitat. Mechanical harvesting of corn, with increased spillage, led to further population increases during the twentieth century. Recently it has increased in Delaware at an average annual rate of 2% according to May Count data (1969–91), and it appears to have similarly increased according to Delaware BBS data, although the latter increase is not statistically significant. The Delaware trend contrasts with an average annual 2% decline for the East [Usfw1].

Breeding population. Totals exceeding 4,000 have been reported 3 times on May Counts, but this figure is just a fraction of the number breeding. Robbins and Dowell (1986), in describing a possible method for estimating populations, estimated Delaware's June Common Grackle population at 332,000 males.

WINTER: At this time tens of thousands of birds roost in the Delaware River and Bay marshes. The 1969 Cape Henlopen CBC recorded 9.7 million Common Grackles, a figure obtained by counting birds flying to and from a roost. See the "Winter" section in the Red-winged Blackbird account and "Blackbird Roosts in Delaware" essay for a general discussion of winter blackbird roosts.

BANDING: The banding map depicts the distribution of birds banded in Delaware and later shot or found dead.

SPECIMENS: 133; DMNH, ANSP, CM, UDEL, USNM. Egg records: DMNH, LSU.

Boat-tailed Grackle (*Quiscalus major*)

Resident; fairly common, but local, in Kent and Sussex counties. Colonial breeder; forms flocks in winter.

J F M A M J J A S O N D

HABITAT: Saltmarshes, brackish impoundments, and nearby bordering areas; barrier dunes and beaches. Penetrates inland near towns, such as Five Points inland from Lewes.

BREEDING: This species breeds in small colonies in and near the saltmarshes of Kent and, primarily, Sussex counties, as well as in bushes on Cape Henlopen.

Atlas. The most frequent confirmation method was observing adults carrying food for young, but nests and nest building were observed 8 times. The high number of confirmations and the extensive range reported in Sussex County were the result of searches by Russell, who was interested in defining its inland limits [RusR2]. The northernmost confirmation was in Kent County, where a small colony was located in the northern part of Woodland Beach WA [BrRF1]. The northernmost observation was near the mouth of Blackbird Creek, New Castle County, on 22 May 1987 [West3].

Nesting. Buckalew (1934) recorded the first nest found, which was constructed about 12 ft up in a cedar. It was built of coarse marsh grasses lined with finer grass, 9 by 7 in. with the

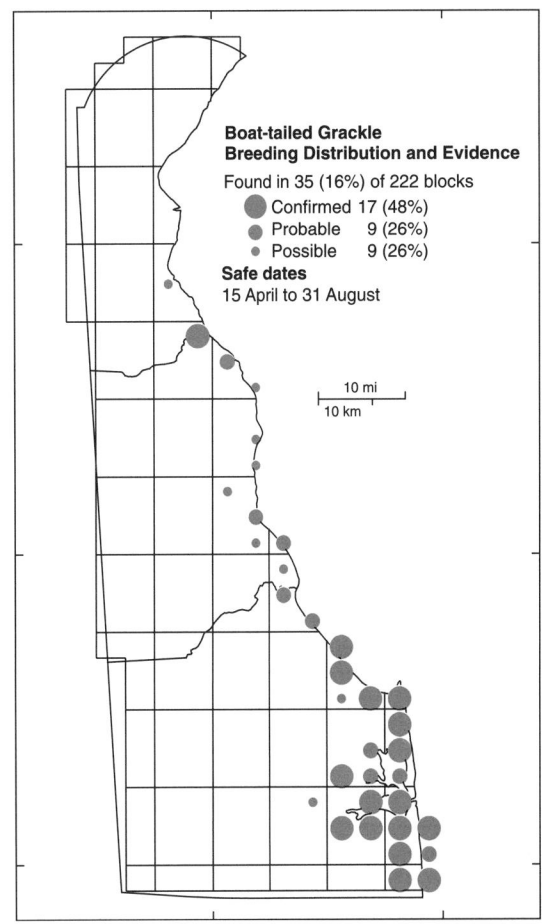

Boat-tailed Grackle
Breeding Distribution and Evidence

Found in 35 (16%) of 222 blocks
- Confirmed 17 (48%)
- Probable   9 (26%)
- Possible   9 (26%)

Safe dates
15 April to 31 August

10 mi
10 km

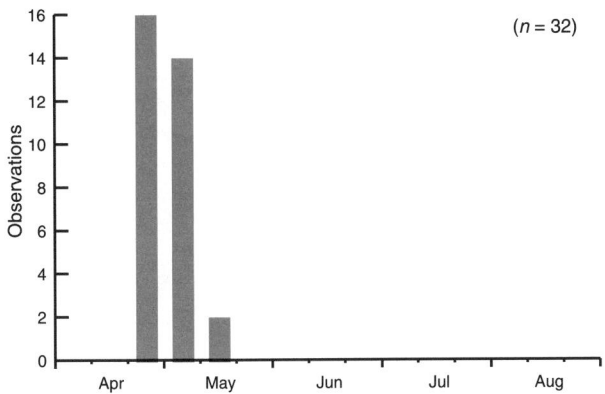

Estimated Clutch-Completion Dates

(n = 32)

cup 4 by 5½ in. All nests found in Delaware have been constructed in trees or bushes, but the species also breeds in phragmites stands, a Delaware habitat amply available. Boat-tailed Grackles often breed in colonies.

The clutch-completion graph is based on data from 32 nests—an inadequate sample because the nests in the few colonies visited were in about the same stage of breeding development. Egg dates begin on 24 April and extend only to 8 May. In Maryland egg dates extend to 7 July (Robbins 1996), suggesting that later breeding can be expected in Delaware. Clutch sizes were 3 (17 nests), 4 (6), and 2 (6). Sprunt (1958), who is cited by most references, wrote that 2 and sometimes 3 broods are raised, but there is no evidence for multiple broods in Delaware. In a Florida study, Bancroft (1986, 1987) found no evidence of multiple broods but gave evidence for low nest success and for 3 renesting attempts during 1 season.

History. Boat-tails have extended their range northward along the Atlantic coast in the twentieth century (Sprunt 1958), and this extension has continued beyond Delaware. It was first found breeding in New Jersey in 1952 and on Long Island in 1981 (Leck 1984; Connor 1988). The first Delaware records

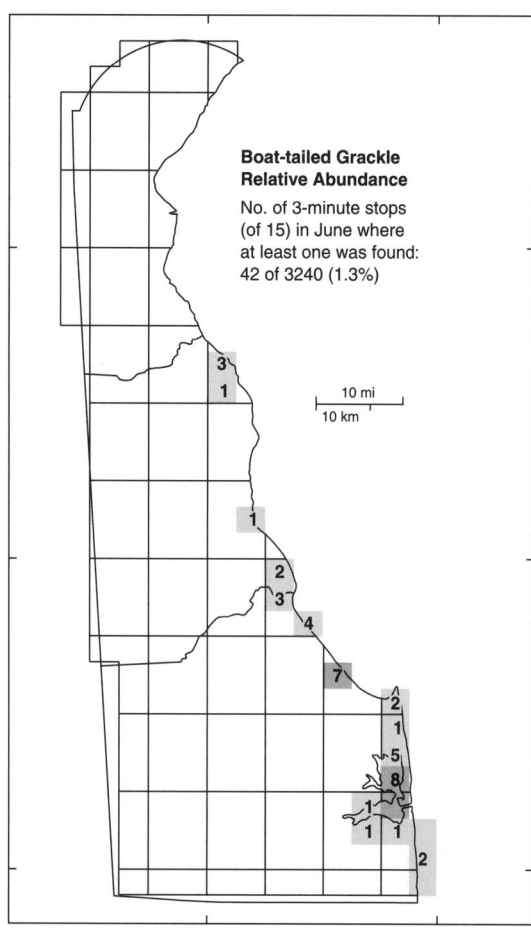

**Boat-tailed Grackle
Relative Abundance**

No. of 3-minute stops
(of 15) in June where
at least one was found:
42 of 3240 (1.3%)

10 mi
10 km

Trends. This species, being close to its northern limit in Delaware, occurs irregularly, most often in small flocks. The BBS data for Delaware and the Upper Coastal Plain suggest an increase (1966–91), which is not supported by CBC data.

Breeding population. The highest May Count is 856 (1981), the lowest 24 (1969). The Cape Henlopen colony had 16 nests on 8 May 1981 [Nile2].

1966–89 CBC Summary

Christmas Bird Count	Years Found	Range of No. Found	Median
Wilmington	1	2	
Middletown			
Bombay Hook	21	1–3,005	5
Cape Henlopen	18	3–805	120
Rehoboth	24	1–376	49
STATEWIDE (low in 1988, high in 1976)	24	4–3,015	346

WINTER: High reports are

23 Dec 1965	400	Lewes [Cutl21]
16 Dec 1979	300	Lewes [Frec1]
20 Feb 1982	300	Lewes [Frec1]
13 Jan 1985	300	Rehoboth Beach [Edni57]

SPECIMENS: 7; DMNH, UDEL, USNM. Egg records: DMNH.

come from a 1930 sighting at Cedar Beach by Buckalew (Stone 1937, 869) and a specimen taken by him before April 1933 near Slaughter Beach (Buckalew 1934).

The first breeding records involved a nest with 3 eggs on 5 May 1933 (Stone 1937, 869) and a nest with 3 eggs found by Buckalew on 10 May 1935 [Hans1]. He later reported seeing a fledgling on 18 June [Buck5]. Other breeding sites recorded prior to the Atlas project were at Indian River Inlet in 1937 [Hans1] and at Cape Henlopen since 1978, where beach plum and bayberry are used as substrate [FreL1].

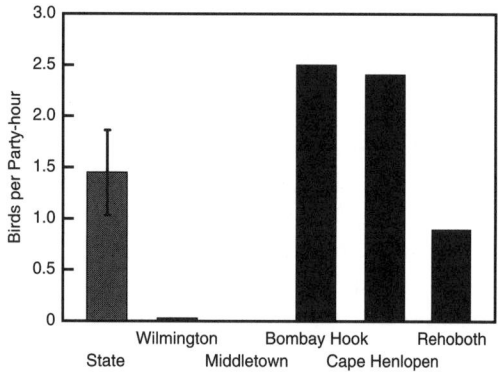

CBC Geographic Distribution; Average of 4 Count Areas

Brown-headed Cowbird *(Molothrus ater)*

Resident; fairly common to common. Migrates from late February to mid-April and late July to early December.

| J | F | M | A | M | J | J | A | S | O | N | D |

HABITAT: Agricultural areas with waste grain, weed seeds, and insects. During the breeding season seeks host species in a variety of field habitats and woodlands adjacent to fields. Roosts in fall and winter in phragmites with other blackbirds, tending to concentrate at the upland edges (Linehan 1994).

SPRING: First departure is 20–25 February. A noticeable decrease in numbers occurs in mid-March, and migration is usually finished 15–20 April. High reports are

| 26 Feb 1977 | 2,000 | White Clay Creek [Dyer7] |
| 15 Mar 1975 | 1,450 | Dragon Run [Citr4] |

BREEDING: Songbirds are nowhere safe from cowbird parasitism in Delaware except, perhaps, in the saltmarshes. The relative abundance study detected the cowbird slightly more frequently in Sussex and western Kent counties, areas with high populations of songbird hosts, especially warblers and vireos.

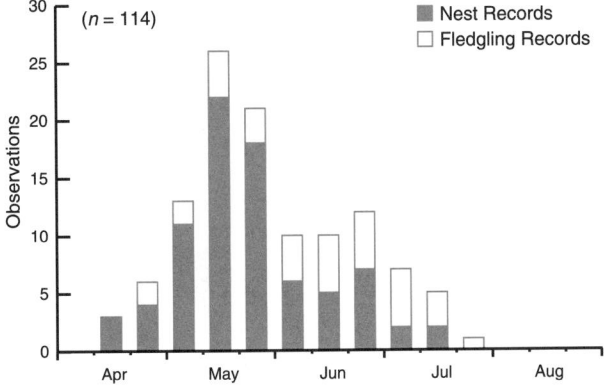

Estimated Clutch-Completion Dates

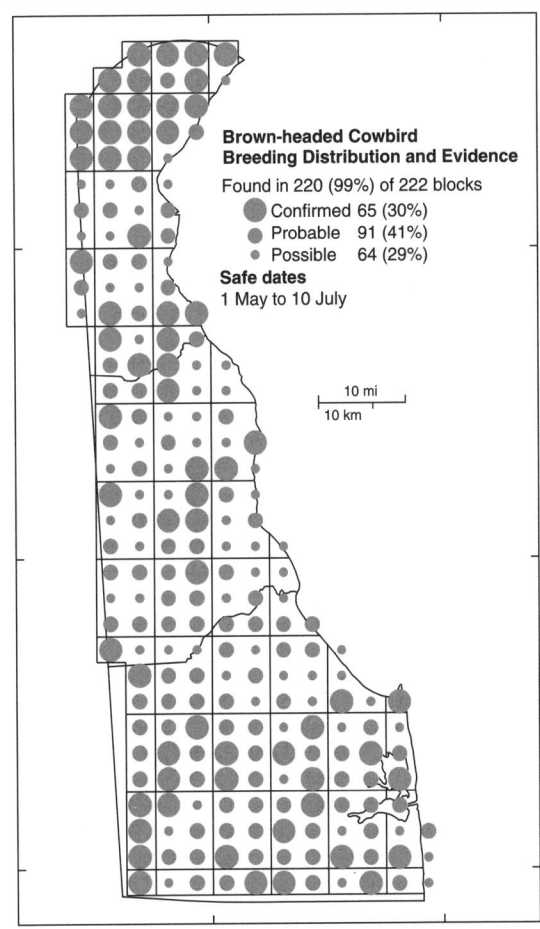

Brown-headed Cowbird Breeding Distribution and Evidence
Found in 220 (99%) of 222 blocks
● Confirmed 65 (30%)
● Probable 91 (41%)
· Possible 64 (29%)
Safe dates
1 May to 10 July

Atlas. Cowbirds were found in all but 2 Atlas blocks, in part because a special effort was made during the fifth year of the project to locate them in blocks where they had not been registered during the first 4 years. Finding highly vocal fledglings accounted for 74% of confirmations. Twelve nests with eggs and 5 nests with young were reported.

Nesting. Cowbirds do not build nests or raise young, but instead lay their eggs in the nests of other species, leaving the foster parents to raise the young cowbirds. Occasionally, however, they may feed young (Bent 1958, 441), not necessarily their own.

Clutch-completion dates estimated from field reports of cowbird eggs, nestlings, or fledglings (solid bars) suggest a strong peak in eggs laid in May, but this peak may be the incidental result of more fieldwork being conducted in May. The clutch-completion dates estimated from TSBR fledgling data (open bars) may better represent the situation of steady brood parasitism pressure exerted by cowbirds from May into July. Egg dates extend from 20 April to 26 July. Some species can start a late, more successful, clutch after cowbird pressure lessens, but delay is not possible for most long-distance

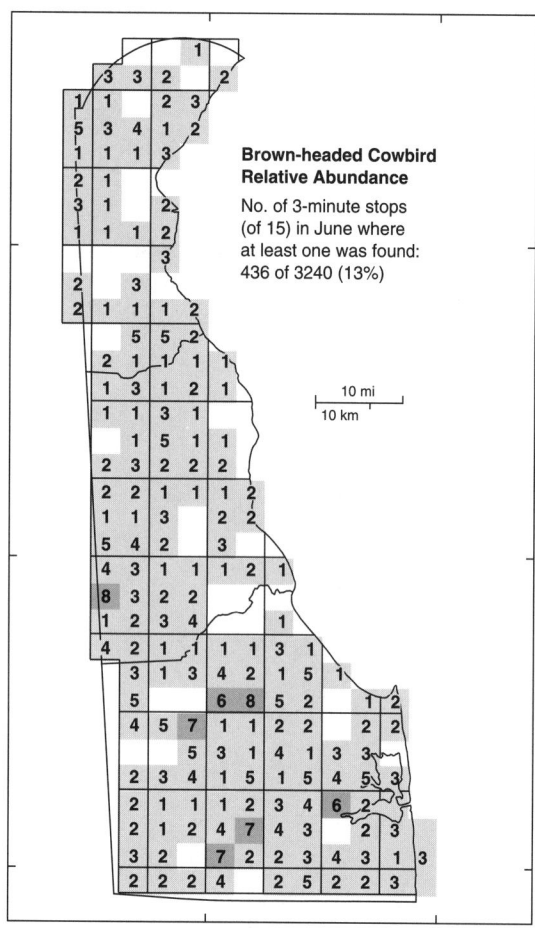

**Brown-headed Cowbird
Relative Abundance**

No. of 3-minute stops
(of 15) in June where
at least one was found:
436 of 3240 (13%)

10 mi
10 km

description on the first list of Delaware birds: "Resident. Rare in winter" (Rhoads and Pennock 1905). It is no longer rare in winter. Its overall trend in the East is downward (1966–90), but Delaware data show an anomalous sharp increase for 1981–90 [Usfw1], an increase not corroborated by May Count results.

Breeding population. The highest cowbird numbers reported on May Counts are 398 (1973) and 353 (1984); this ubiquitous bird is inconspicuous and dispersed during its breeding season. For the period 1966–79 Delaware had an average BBS density of 3.9 birds per route, similar to the 3.1 birds per route reported in New Jersey but only one-third the density reported in Pennsylvania and Maryland (Robbins et al. 1986). Three BBCs conducted near the Assawoman WA marshes averaged densities of 20 females per 100 ha. The average density reported for the University of Delaware woodlot during 5 years was 25 females per 100 ha (Jones 1970); for Brandywine Creek SP during 2 years, 30 per 100 ha (West 1967); and for 2 small woodlots at Windy Hills, Newark, during 2 years, 65 per 100 ha (Burr and Jones 1968).

FALL: Migration probably begins about 25 July to 1 August and continues through early December. Peak numbers are reached 15–20 October to 30 November. High reports are

5 Nov 1980	10,000	Cape Henlopen SP [Frec1]
16 Nov 1974	10,000	Dragon Run [Phal9]
24 Nov 1974	50,000	Dragon Run [Phal9]

A blackbird roost was near Dragon Run in 1974, and estimates of birds flying over Dragon Run from the roost were made during DOS weekly surveys there.

1966–89 CBC Summary

Christmas Bird Count	Years Found	Range of No. Found	Median
Wilmington	24	22–303,027	574
Middletown	24	17–125,611	298
Bombay Hook	24	65–6,100	444
Cape Henlopen	24	11–1,602,789	11,571
Rehoboth	24	7–102,900	766
STATEWIDE (low in 1985, high in 1981)	24	1,759–1,632,544	61,860

migrants, which must molt after nesting and before flying south. The high incidence of parasitism reported early in the season represents, to some extent, the greater number of nests reported during this period. Eighteen host species have been identified in Delaware (Baer 1989), a small percentage of those known to be subject to parasitism. Ten of the 18 are Neotropical migrants that construct open cup nests. The following species have been reported parasitized more than 3 times in Delaware—of these Scarlet Tanager and Red-eyed Vireo seem to be suffering the greatest percentage of parasitism in relation to the total numbers of their nests reported:

Host Species	Percentage Parasitized
Red-eyed Vireo	42 (11 nests of 26 reported)
Scarlet Tanager	37 (3 nests of 8)
Wood Thrush	8 (31 nests of 373)
Song Sparrow	6 (4 nests of 72)
Mourning Dove	5 (4 nests of 85)

These percentages are not as high as those reported in numerous studies in other states.

History and trends. Cowbirds, once birds of the Great Plains, increased in the East once land was cleared for agriculture. No early trend information for Delaware is available beyond the

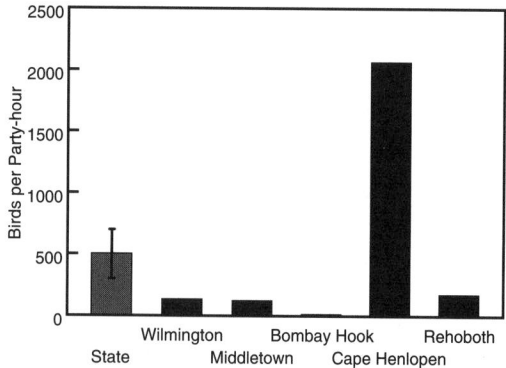

CBC Geographic Distribution

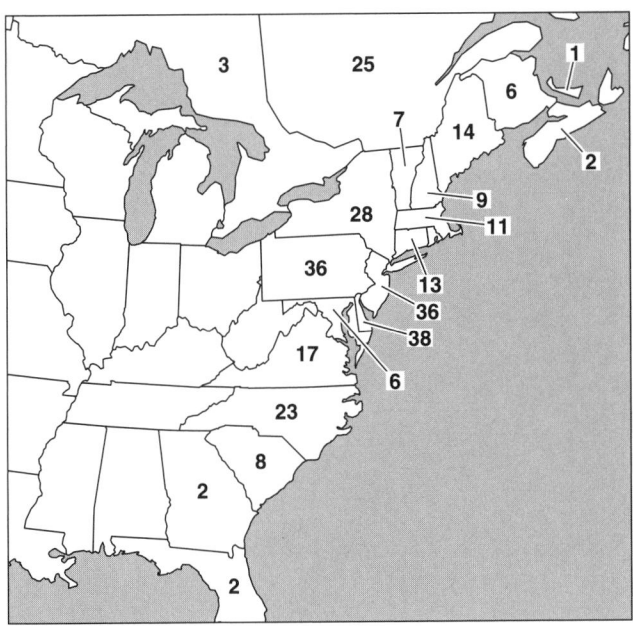

Total Brown-headed Cowbirds Banded in Delaware and Recovered Dead or Shot in Each State.

WINTER: The 1981 Cape Henlopen CBC recorded a high of 1.6 million birds, a figure obtained by counting birds flying to and from a roost. See "Winter" in the Red-winged Blackbird account and "Blackbird Roosts in Delaware" essay for a general discussion of blackbird roosts.

BANDING: The banding map depicts the distribution of birds banded in Delaware and later shot or found dead, thus preventing results from large banding operations in other states from biasing the information shown.

SPECIMENS: 52; DMNH, UDEL. Egg records: DMNH.

Orchard Oriole (*Icterus spurius*)

Regular; summer resident; uncommon but widespread in rural Delaware. Expected late April to mid-August.

HABITAT: Rural yards, farmsteads, estates, and open suburbs and towns with widely spaced shade trees. Trees in fencerows, out from woods edges, or in open areas along marshes and creeks. Nests primarily in deciduous trees, occasionally ornamental conifers.

SPRING: First arrival is usually 25–30 April. The earliest arrivals, all reported from Sussex County, involve

21 Apr 1991	1	Assawoman WA [Edni1]
23 Apr 1983	2	Lewes [Frec1]
24 Apr 1988	1	female Trap Pond SP [Barn54]

Although no peak is discernible, the following high counts may be representative:

8 May 1982	14	coastal Sussex County [Frec1]
11 May 1985	15	Nanticoke WA [Frec1]
17 May 1988	17	Brandywine Creek SP [MurW3]

The highest May Count is 93 (1986), the lowest 9 (1971).

BREEDING: This species is most easily found south of the Chesapeake and Delaware Canal in farming areas where a large deciduous tree is located on the farmstead. It is not abundant anywhere although widely distributed near rural houses and edges.

Atlas. For most people living in northern Delaware, the Atlas results showing the extensive Orchard Oriole distribution throughout much of the state must come as a surprise, because this species is not found with regularity in northern Delaware, near the marshes along Rt. 9, or along the coastal strip. The 2 locations along Delaware Bay where it was found at 6 stops in the relative abundance study are on Milford Neck and near Woodland Beach WA. These locations have a mixture of large

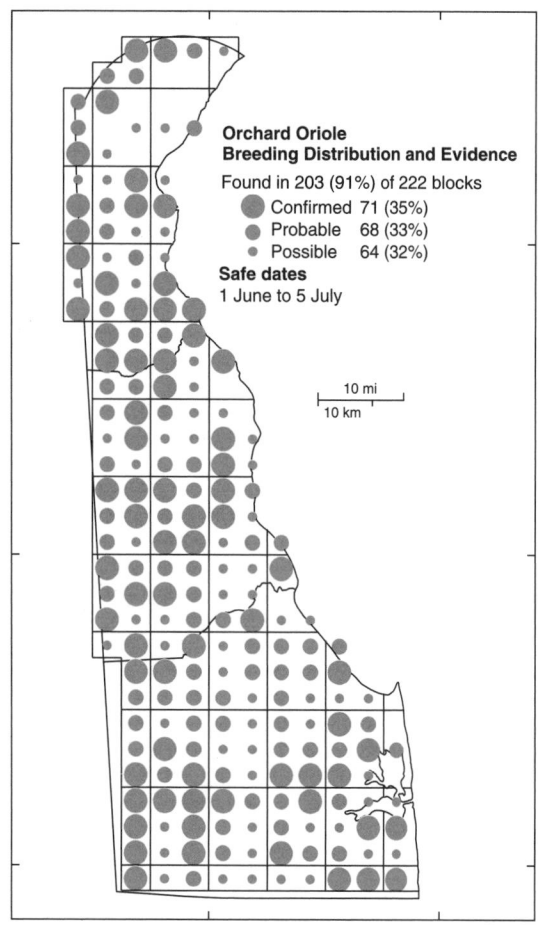

Orchard Oriole
Breeding Distribution and Evidence

Found in 203 (91%) of 222 blocks
● Confirmed 71 (35%)
● Probable   68 (33%)
· Possible   64 (32%)

Safe dates
1 June to 5 July

10 mi
10 km

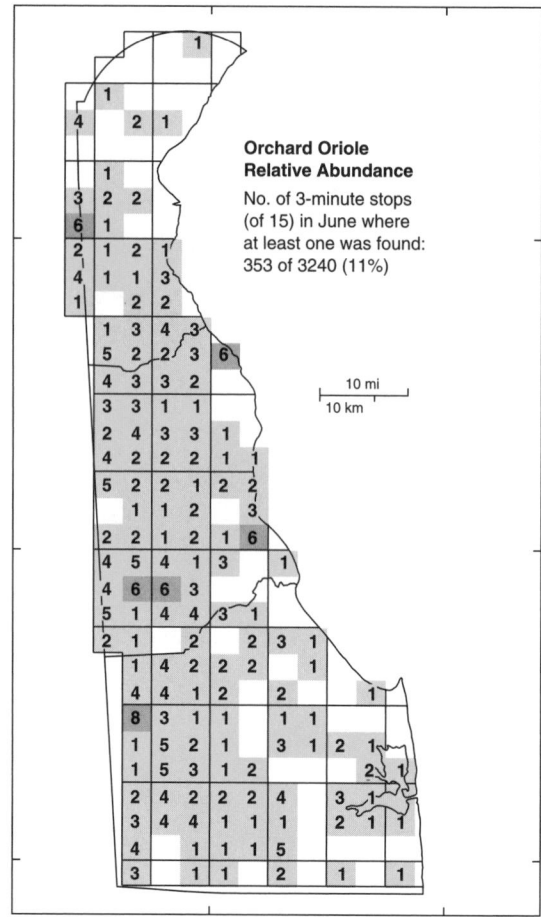

Orchard Oriole
Relative Abundance

No. of 3-minute stops
(of 15) in June where
at least one was found:
353 of 3240 (11%)

10 mi
10 km

deciduous trees and open areas. The most frequent method of confirmation was seeing adults carrying food, but observing the nest and nest building were reported 28 times. The young, before and after they fledge, are quite vocal, simplifying confirmation.

Nesting. Hanson (notes) described a nest that was a cup 3¼ in. deep and 4 in. across outside and 2½ in. deep and 3 in. across inside. The top was constructed so that it was only 2 in. across. It was made of blades of tough narrow grass, some of them

green, with a thick soft bed and lining of cinnamon fern down. Most nests are placed in deciduous trees, but 2 (of 21) were in conifers, 1 in a farmyard evergreen [Pres3] and another in a spruce in a rural yard [Patt1].

Extreme egg dates are 30 May (DMNH 28763) to 14 June [Hans1]. The earliest nest is implied from young fledging on 13 June and the latest from young fledging on 13 July, both near Bear [Pres3]. Clutch size is usually 4. Orchard Orioles are single-brooded, clearly indicated by the short span of clutch-completion dates.

Trends. This species has benefited by the modification of the eastern forests for farming. In the early part of the twentieth century its stronghold was in old orchards [Hans1], but as these were cut down, the species declined. It was put on the Blue List as a species of special concern in the Delaware–Hudson Valley and other regions for 1982–86. The BBS has produced encouraging results: it did not decrease in the East during 1966–90; rather, it has increased on a significant number of routes [Usfw3]. Both BBS and May Count data indicate it has increased in Delaware during this period at a 3–6% average annual rate.

Breeding population. During 1966–79 Delaware had fewer Orchard Orioles per BBS route than Maryland, but considerably more than New Jersey or Pennsylvania (Robbins et al.

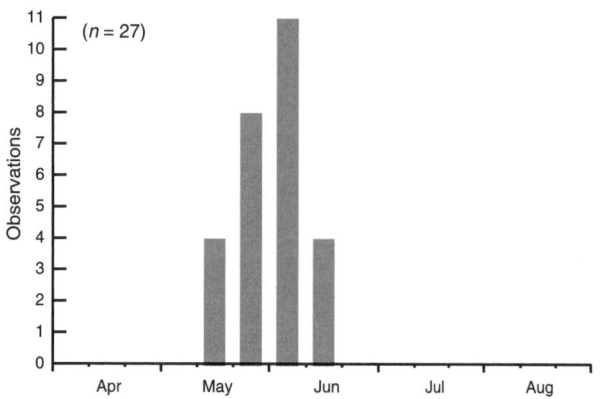

Estimated Clutch-Completion Dates

1986). Roadside counts, such as the BBS, could lead to overestimation of the number of orioles because they prefer roadside habitat.

FALL: A sharp decline in reports after the first week of July marks the onset of migration, which usually ends by mid-August. A series of observations in Sussex County by Frech may indicate the peak migration period: 20 on 6 August 1979, 12 on 8 August 1988, 12 on 10 August 1979, and 12 on 11 August 1987 [Frec1]. Because Orchard Orioles are infrequently reported in August, it is not known whether his reports are representative. Late records, both from Brandywine Creek SP, extend only into the first half of September, 1 on 5 September 1970 [Wayn25] and another on 12 September 1970 [BroH10].

SPECIMENS: 8; DMNH, ANSP, UDEL, USNM. Egg records: DMNH.

Baltimore Oriole *(Icterus galbula)*

Regular; summer resident; fairly common in the Piedmont, becoming uncommon southward, particularly in Sussex County; fairly common during migration. Expected late April to late September.

HABITAT: Large deciduous trees in open woods, parks, and suburbs; generally in larger trees, and more wooded situations, than the Orchard Oriole; particularly found along Piedmont creeks in sycamores. Below the fall line found sparingly in tulip-trees, willows, and even pines where insect larvae are available.

SPRING: First arrival is usually 25–30 April. Migration continues through 25–30 May. Early reports, partly obscured by the presence of wintering birds, include

20 Apr 1981	1	Angola, Sussex County (Haas 1983)
23 Apr 1978	1	Lewes [Frec23]
23 Apr 1991	1	Burrows Run [Wayn64]
24 Apr 1976	2	White Clay Creek [Barn20]

Peak numbers probably occur during mid-May. The highest reports are

14 May 1977	28	White Clay Creek [Jahn11]
16 May 1970	24	Brandywine Creek SP [WarD4]
22 May 1971	38	Brandywine Creek SP [Wayn25]

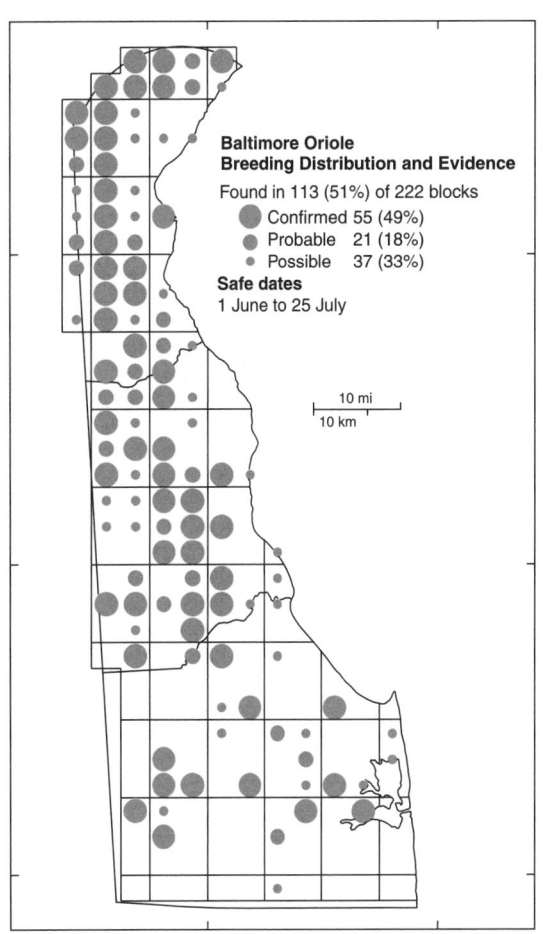

Baltimore Oriole
Breeding Distribution and Evidence
Found in 113 (51%) of 222 blocks
● Confirmed 55 (49%)
● Probable 21 (18%)
· Possible 37 (33%)
Safe dates
1 June to 25 July

10 mi
10 km

The highest May Count is 132 (1989), the lowest 19 (1973).

BREEDING: This oriole is primarily a resident of Piedmont deciduous woodland; it becomes less common southward.

Atlas. Its characteristic pendant nest is fairly conspicuous; consequently, it was confirmed in half the blocks where it was detected. The most frequent confirmation code was occupied nest. Observing adults building nests and adults carrying food for young were also frequent means of confirmation. The somewhat irregular pattern of its distribution suggests that it was probably present in some blocks where it was not regis-

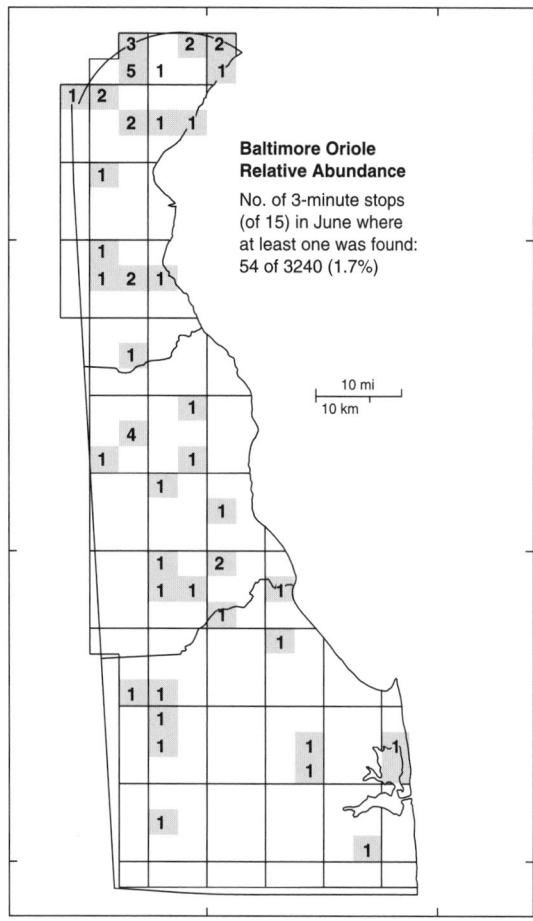

**Baltimore Oriole
Relative Abundance**

No. of 3-minute stops
(of 15) in June where
at least one was found:
54 of 3240 (1.7%)

10 mi
10 km

deciduous tree, drawn close at the top, and lined with hair or soft plant fibers.

Only 1 nest with eggs has been reported, 6 eggs on 5 June 1934 in a nest 30 ft up in an elm at Silver Lake Park, Dover [Hans1]. The earliest young in the nest were heard on 4 June [West4], the latest on 10 July [Phal2]. Estimated clutch-completion dates extend from mid-May through mid-June. It is single-brooded.

Trends. Baltimore Orioles have been relatively stable in Delaware and the East over the 25-year period of 1966–90, but the species declined sharply in the East during the 1980s [Usfw1].

Breeding population. This species was found only 15% as often on the relative abundance study as the Orchard Oriole; the difference in abundance of these congeners is probably less than that because the Baltimore Oriole prefers more wooded situations and may be harder to locate during a roadside count. It was frequently encountered on BBCs in Piedmont woodlots. High densities reported were 45 territories per 100 ha (3 in 17 acres) in mixed deciduous floodplain woodlots (Burr and Jones 1968) and 30 territories per 100 ha (3 in 25 acres) in mixed mesophytic forest (West 1970), both along White Clay Creek.

FALL: Baltimore Orioles begin migration 1–5 August, a month later than Orchard Orioles. Migration usually concludes by 25–30 September. Latest fall reports involve

11 Oct 1977	2	Cape Henlopen SP [Frec1]
11 Oct 1984	1	Cape Henlopen SP [Frec1]
30 Oct 1971	1	Brandywine Creek SP [BroH10]
30 Nov 1957	1 banded	near Kirkwood, New Castle County [Pres4]

High counts are

7 Aug 1971	33	Brandywine Creek SP [Wayn25]
16 Aug 1969	23	Brandywine Creek SP [West13]
30 Aug 1964	27	Hoopes Reservoir [Hoff4]

WINTER: Baltimore Orioles winter "regularly in small numbers in the Atlantic states north to Virginia" (AOU 1983); thus its presence in Delaware during winter is not completely unexpected. Most Delaware reports occurred during a few years in the 1970s. It is most often found attending feeders. Among the numerous observations, those by Prest were the first—a female on 2–4 January 1955 at a feeder near Bear, and a male there 4 and 10 December 1957 [Pres1]; Roberts' sighting included complete notes—a female Baltimore Oriole 12 December 1971 to 1 February 1972 at Arundel, Pike Creek Valley (Roberts 1972).

REMARKS: The western Bullock's Oriole *(I. bullockii),* is casual in migration in northeastern North America south to New Jersey and winters in small numbers in the Gulf Coast region east to Florida and south Georgia (AOU 1983). In winter most female and immature Baltimore and Bullock's orioles cannot be distinguished with confidence in the field (Hubbard 1972). Bullock's Orioles reported in Delaware have not been substantiated (Brinkley et al. 1994).

SPECIMENS: 15; DMNH, ANSP, UDEL.

tered. Furthermore, the relatively short period of safe dates prevented its being accepted in some blocks where it might have bred; it was reported from 15 blocks outside the safe dates period. Most rural people proudly told Atlas workers if they had nesting orioles and where they nested, making it possible to confirm this species in some Sussex County blocks where it was very scarce and would otherwise have been missed.

Nesting. Its familiar nest is a deep pouch so well constructed of grape vine and other plant fibers (and frequently string) that it lasts through the winter. It is hung high from a fork of a

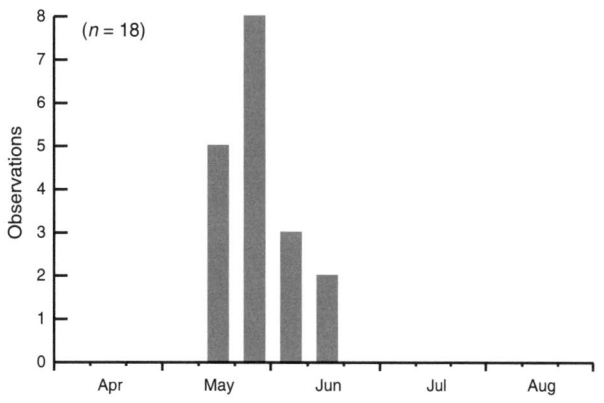

(n = 18)

Estimated Clutch-Completion Dates

Irruptive Northern Visitors to Delaware

Gregory A. Inskip

Almost by definition, the class of irruptive northern visitors resists any generalizations. This is particularly true from the perspective of Delaware, a small state that is altogether south of the wanderings of some species, such as Great Gray Owl, and that sees relatively low numbers of others. However, CBCs and other data show that from the early 1960s through the mid-1980s, most winter finches, Black-capped Chickadees, and Red-breasted Nuthatches fluctuated according to a two- or three-year cycle, which has been related by other authors to seed crop failure of northern trees. These short-term fluctuations occurred against the backdrop of a longer-term rise and fall, during three or four decades, for some of the same species. The small numbers of Northern Goshawks that visit Delaware may peak every nine or ten years, but lately this species is being seen every winter. Another rare raptor, the Snowy Owl, likewise appears to be visiting the state as often as it ever did.

Long-Term Trends of Winter Finches and Black-capped Chickadee

The Pine Siskin, Purple Finch, and Evening Grosbeak are our three most common winter finches. They are closely similar in historical abundance, as shown by the combined 1966–93 totals of the five Delaware CBCs conducted continuously since 1966 (Bombay Hook, Cape Henlopen–Prime Hook, Middletown, Rehoboth, and Wilmington) and a sixth (Seaford–Nanticoke) since 1983: Pine Siskin, 2,963; Purple Finch, 2,957; Evening Grosbeak, 2,832.

Compared with the period 1968–82, all three species show a declining trend in CBCs after 1983. The decline followed an increase in earlier years, as illustrated by the graphs in the Evening Grosbeak and Purple Finch species accounts, and by a rough running average of Pine Siskins seen during 1953–92 by the two oldest continuously run CBCs (Bombay Hook and Rehoboth), as shown in table 1.

Table 1. Pine Siskin Trends—Bombay Hook and Rehoboth CBCs

Decade	Pine Siskins per Year
1953–62	5.6
1958–67	59.7
1963–72	172.3
1968–77	177.6
1973–82	73.6
1978–87	14.0
1983–92	2.5

The combined Pine Siskin count in 1993 for all Delaware CBCs was 64 (mostly Wilmington), the highest since 1985.

The sparser records of Red Crossbills and Common Redpolls display similar trends. Red Crossbills were recorded on Delaware CBCs in 1963, 1969, 1971, 1972, and 1973, but not thereafter. On the May Count, Red Crossbills were seen in 1964, 1970, 1974, and 1976 (Rufe 1987, 39, 44) but not thereafter until 1992, when two were seen (Janowski and Kelly 1993, 26). Common Redpolls were absent from CBCs after 1977, but this species often arrives too late to be seen on CBCs. It was sighted in January 1994 (many observers) and in the winters of 1971–72, 1973–74, and 1986–87 (see Common Redpoll species account; Scott and Cutler 1972, 588; Boyle, Paxton, and Cutler 1987, 263). The Black-capped Chickadee invaded Delaware every few years from 1963 to 1983, but only an occasional few have since been reported on CBCs.[1]

Incursions of Pine Siskins, Black-capped Chickadees, and Red-breasted Nuthatches

In the period since 1962 (except for several recent years of low counts), Pine Siskin totals on Delaware CBCs have varied erratically on a two- or three-year cycle, in which one or two "off" years were followed by one to three "on" years. The totals are shown in table 2.[2]

Table 2. Pine Siskins Reported on Delaware CBCs

"On" Years (more than 10)		"Off" Years (10 or fewer)	
Year	No.	Year	No.
		1962	0
1963	74		
		1964	2
1965	568		
		1966	1
		1967	0
1968	99		
1969	1135		
		1970	10
1971	157		
1972	95		
1973	612		
		1974	5
1975	94		
		1976	0
1977	316		
		1978	1
		1979	8
1980	153		
		1981	2
		1982	7
1983	20		
		1984	0
1985	96		
1986	12		
1987	21		
		1988	0
		1989	10
		1990	8
		1991	2
		1992	0
1993	64		

During the period 1962–70, Pine Siskins invaded Delaware in the same years (1963, 1965, 1968, 1969) that brought widespread invasions of Black-capped Chickadees and Red-breasted Nuthatches (Bagg 1969, 8–9, and 1970, 5; Bock and Lepthien 1972). The authors cited showed that the chickadee and nuthatch incursions coincided precisely with seed-crop failures of conifers and other trees recorded by Alma Chapman in 1957, 1959, 1961, 1963, 1965, and 1968 in Penobscot County in Maine. The results are believed by Bock and Lepthien to exemplify "widespread, synchronous cone-crop failures in northern forests."[3]

For the years 1970–85, Pine Siskin incursions in Delaware coincide closely with fall banding records of Black-capped Chickadee at Manomet Observatory in Massachusetts, which varied from a low of 58 birds in 1984 to a high of 4,499 in 1971 (Lloyd-Evans, pers. comm.). Manomet banded more than 900 chickadees per year in *1971, 1973, 1975, 1980*, 1981, *1983*, and *1985* (italics indicates years in which Pine Siskin irruptions occurred in Delaware).

In Delaware, the Black-capped Chickadee is an irruptive winter visitor, reported less frequently than the Pine Siskin. The Red-breasted Nuthatch is seen every winter in Delaware, but its numbers vary widely. Table 3 shows the years between 1964 and 1994 when Delaware CBCs had high counts for either the Black-capped Chickadee (> 100) or the Red-breasted Nuthatch (> 50) or both;

Table 3. Delaware CBC High Counts of Black-capped Chickadees and Red-breasted Nuthatches

	1965[a]	1968[a]	1969[a]	1970	1975[a]	1980[a]	1981	1983[a]
Black-capped Chickadee (1966–92 mean 40.2)	225	118	139	131	291	113	6	100
Red-breasted Nuthatch (1966–82 mean 28.6; 1983–92 mean [with Seaford-Nanticoke CBC data] 26.4)	19	23	84	1	102	22	80	54

a. Year in which Pine Siskin irruption occurred in Delaware.

Black-capped Chickadees also invaded Delaware in the winter of 1963–64 (Knowles 1965, 26). With the exception of 1970, the Black-capped Chickadee incursions identified by Delaware CBCs coincide both with Pine Siskin incursions in Delaware and with large chickadee irruptions observed elsewhere in the Northeast (Bagg 1969, 1970; Scott and Cutler 1976, 167; Manomet data). The odd year, 1970, was low at Manomet, but New York CBCs saw almost as many Black-caps per party-hour as in the preceding high year, 1969 (Yunick 1984, 32). In general, Delaware CBC participants distinguish resident Carolina Chickadees from invading Black-caps in the field.

Table 3, based on absolute numbers seen by Delaware CBCs, suggests that there is a 75% chance that exceptional numbers of Red-breasted Nuthatches in Delaware will be accompanied by incursions of Pine Siskins and Black-capped Chickadees. The coincidence may actually be greater. A state-by-state analysis of Red-breasted Nuthatches per CBC party-hour reveals invasions in 1963, 1965, 1968, and 1969 over much of the continent, including Delaware (Bock and Lepthien 1972); an independent study identified the same invasion years in neighboring Pennsylvania (Davis and Morrison 1987, 1343). Collectively, the data show simultaneous Delaware incursions of Pine Siskins, Black-capped Chickadees, and Red-breasted Nuthatches in 1963, 1965, 1968, 1969, 1975, and 1983—six years out of the eight when Black-capped Chickadees invaded and six of the seven Red-breasted Nuthatch invasions.[4]

Yunick (1984) analyzed Boreal Chickadee reports in New York from 1950 to 1982 and described a series of irruptions that substantially coincides with the Black-capped Chickadee and Red-breasted Nuthatch irruptions reflected in the Delaware data and in earlier data presented by Bagg (1969, 1970) and Bock and Lepthien (1972). Delaware's two Boreal Chickadee records, in November 1954 and April 1982 (see species accounts), both occurred in incursion years (1954–55 and 1981–82) identified by Yunick.[5]

Incursions of Other Winter Finches

When other winter finches have invaded Delaware in large numbers, it almost always has been an irruption year for Pine Siskins in the state. Table 4 was prepared by listing all winter finches seen by the earlier five Delaware CBCs in each of twelve years, selected as follows: (1) of the span when all five CBCs have been held (1966–93), the top five years for Purple Finch and Evening Grosbeak, plus (2) any additional years (in that span or earlier) in which Pine Grosbeak, Common Redpoll, or more than one crossbill of either species was recorded. The twelve years selected in this way turn out to include all eleven of the Pine Siskin irruption years from 1963 to 1983, as shown in table 4.

All of the CBC records of the Pine Grosbeak, Common Redpoll, and Red Crossbill occurred in a Pine Siskin irruption year.[6] Of two White-winged Crossbill records, the large count of 20 occurred in a Pine Siskin year (1963), and one was seen in an "off" year (1966), as was a single unidentified crossbill (1964). The largest Evening Grosbeak years (1968, 1969, 1971, 1972, 1973, and 1983) also occurred in "on" years for Pine Siskins. Although these two species share irruption years, their relative abundance in any given year varies. The year 1965 was big for Pine Siskins (568) but mediocre for Evening Grosbeaks (16); 1983 was big for Evening Grosbeaks (180) but mediocre for Pine Siskins (20).

Table 4 suggests a strong coincidence between incursions of the Evening Grosbeak and Red Crossbill. The first of five Red Crossbill years, 1963, also had the highest Evening Grosbeak CBC in more than a decade. The remaining CBCs in which Red Crossbills were recorded (1969, 1971, 1972, and 1973) were four of the six highest Evening Grosbeak years ever.

From the (perhaps too narrow) perspective of Delaware

Table 4. Delaware CBC Years with High Counts of One or More Species of Winter Finches

	1963[a]	1965[a]	1968[a]	1969[a]	1971[a]	1972[a]	1973[a]	1975[a]	1977[a]	1980[a]	1982	1983[a]
Evening Grosbeak	51[b]	16	387	568	757	403	115	43	73	46	6	180
Purple Finch	7	166	127	67	215	399	93	50	330	212	348	78
Pine Grosbeak		1										
Common Redpoll		4		2				1	119			
Pine Siskin	74[b]	568	99	1135	157	95	612	94	316	153	7	20
Red Crossbill	46[c]			332[c]	3	12	68[c]					
White-winged Crossbill	20											

a. Year in which Pine Siskin irruption occurred in Delaware.

b. Only two CBCs (Bombay Hook and Rehoboth) were conducted in 1963. The 51 Evening Grosbeaks recorded that year were more than were compiled in any of the preceding 10 years, 1953–62 (range 0–41, mean 4.6). The same is true of the 74 Pine Siskins in 1963 (compared with a range of 0–30 and a mean of 5.6 for the preceding 10 years).

c. Indicates that Red Crossbills also were recorded on the May Count following this CBC (Rufe 1987, 39, 44).

CBCs, Red Crossbill counts fluctuate independently of counts of Common Redpolls. Whenever either of these species invades Delaware, however, Pine Siskin counts are likely to be high. At least 74 Pine Siskins (as compared to an off-year mean of fewer than 4) have been seen by Delaware CBCs in each year when either Red Crossbills or Common Redpolls were observed (1963, 1965, 1969, 1971, 1972, 1973, 1975, and 1977).[7] In 1969, when Red Crossbills were here in force and Common Redpolls were present too, the Pine Siskin count was huge (1,135).

The Purple Finch marches to its own drummer. It is more regular than any other winter finch, having been recorded on at least one Delaware CBC from 1955 to 1993. The substantial fluctuations in its occurrence—from almost none to almost 400—coincide with the fluctuations of other finches in some years, but not all. The Purple Finch count may be low when Pine Siskins and Evening Grosbeaks are high (1963, 1969, 1973), and one year it was very high when both of the others were very low (1982). On the other hand, four of the five highest Purple Finch CBCs occurred in "on" years for Pine Siskins (1971, 1972, 1977, 1980). High counts of Purple Finches do not appear to coincide with Black-capped Chickadee incursions in Delaware.

Northern Predatory Birds

Northern Goshawk

Table 5 summarizes reports of Northern Goshawks in Delaware for the last three decades, from November through March, as noted in CBCs, *Delmarva Ornithologist, American Birds,* and the species account in this book.[8] An attempt was made to avoid double-counting individuals seen more than once at the same place.

Some of Delaware's reports of Northern Goshawks (1963–64, 1972–73, 1973–74, and 1982–83) fall within the schedule compiled by Palmer (1988, 4:365–66) of major continental incursions "about once a decade" and tending "to last at least 2 years." Viewed by themselves, the Delaware data suggest a slightly different nine- or ten-year periodicity, marked by the earlier mentioned years but especially by the multiple

goshawks seen in 1981–82 (a year ahead of Palmer's schedule), 1990–91 and 1991–92. Two goshawks seen on the Rehoboth CBC in 1981 were the most ever seen on any one Delmarva Peninsula CBC during 1907–85 (Falk 1987, 68). The two highest counts in Delaware (1981–82, 1991–92) coincide with high counts of goshawks at hawk watches on the eastern Great Lakes.[9]

Table 5. Delaware Reports of Northern Goshawks, 1963–93

Winter	Number Seen	Reference
1963–64	1	Linehan 1964, 3
1964–65	1	Linehan 1965, 23
1972–73	2	Scott and Cutler 1973, 144
1973–74	2	1973 CBC; species account
1975–76	1	species account
1978–79	1	Niles 1979, 16
1980–81	1	Barnhill 1983, 35
1981–82	7	1981 CBC; species account; Hess 1984, 34
1982–83	2	Boyle, Paxton, and Cutler 1983, 284
1987–88	2	1987 CBC; Hess 1989, 51
1988–89	1	Ednie 1989, 2–3
1989–90	1	Ednie 1990, 25
1990–91	3	Hess, 1991, 57
1991–92	4	1991 CBC; Ednie 1991, 66; Hess 1993, 51
1992–93	2	Campbell and Potrafke 1993, 29; Esther B. Speck, pers. comm.
1993–94	2	1993 CBC; Esther B. Speck, pers. comm.

Fluctuations aside, one or two Northern Goshawks are now being reported annually in Delaware, which is not surprising given the state's proximity to regular goshawk migration routes along the Appalachian ridges in Pennsylvania and past Cape May, New Jersey. Like the other accipiters, goshawks have learned to exploit bird feeders and may return to them in successive winters. Stanley and Esther Speck have observed an adult visiting their bird feeding area in the winters of 1990–91, 1991–92, 1992–93, and 1993–94 (Esther B. Speck, pers. comm.; Hess 1991, 57, and 1993, 51).

Rough-legged Hawk

The Rough-legged Hawk is a regular migrant that vacates its Arctic and Subarctic breeding range every fall (Palmer 1988, 5:177). However, CBCs and older data from other states indicate that wintering populations fluctuate on a roughly four-year cycle, similar to the cycles sometimes described for Snowy Owl and Northern Shrike (Garrison 1993,572; Newton 1979, 185–86, 364). A four-year cycle is not obvious in the fluctuating numbers seen on Delaware CBCs since 1966 (see seasonal bar graph in species account). Since then, the rough-leg has been a regular, but uncommon and declining, winter visitor in this state.

Snowy Owl

The species account cites several records (November 1926, 1930, December 1934, 1954, 1964, and 1981–82) that coincide with Snowy Owl invasion years that have been compiled (collectively, from the nineteenth century through 1981) by Gross (1947), Davis (1974), Newton (1979, 364), Kerlinger et al. (1985), and others. Other Delaware records are out of step. The early record in October 1897 was a year "late" for the irruption in 1896. Delaware recorded Snowy Owls in January 1940 and December 1942, but the main irruption in New England was in the intervening winter of 1941–42 (Davis 1974). Delaware's owls in 1965 and 1979 occurred at low points in eastern fluctuations (Kerlinger et al. 1985). Snowy Owls occurred in Delaware for three winters in a row: one near Lewes in March 1992 (see species account); one near Smyrna in December 1992 (Bombay Hook CBC and many observers), and as many as four at Cape Henlopen in December 1993 (many observers; 1993 CBC).[10] Kerlinger et al. (1985) conclude that the Snowy Owl is a regular migrant to the northern Great Plains, where it is usually more abundant than elsewhere in its winter range.

Northern Shrike

When the three earliest of six Northern Shrike records (see species account) are compared with Newton's (1979, 364) table of Snowy Owl incursions through 1966, they coincide two-thirds of the time (i.e., the shrikes in January 1931 and 1954). Delaware's first Northern Shrike record, in March 1909, preceded a Snowy Owl incursion at the end of that year.

Elsewhere in eastern North America, Northern Shrike and Snowy Owl irruptions usually coincided in the late nineteenth and early twentieth centuries, but the coincidence became less marked as the twentieth century wore on (Davis, 1974). Snowy Owls declined after invasions of both species in the winters of 1953–54 and 1954–55, but Northern Shrikes continued to come south for two more winters (Davis, 1974), bringing Delaware its fourth record in January 1956. From 1965 through 1979, no synchrony was evident between fluctuations of the Northern Shrike and the Snowy Owl in eastern North America (Davis and Morrison 1987; Davis 1974).

Origin of Our Visitors

Banding recoveries show that Sharp-shinned Hawks migrating southward past Cape May in the fall (most of them crossing the Delaware River–Bay estuary to Delaware) return to summer in New York, New England, the Maritime Provinces and Quebec (Clark 1985, 140, 143). The limited information available suggests that most of our irruptive visitors originate in this large area as well.[11]

As noted earlier, Delaware's two biggest Northern Goshawk winters coincide with high counts of southbound goshawks diverted west around Lake Erie in the fall (1981 and 1991) and highs for northbound goshawks diverted east and west around Lake Ontario in the spring (1982). The Delaware birds and these eastern Great Lakes birds may be neighbors, experiencing the same food supply fluctuations in a region of boreal forest somewhere in Quebec.

At least some of our wintering Pine Siskins hail from Quebec as well. Conway (1978, 3) reported that Pine Siskins banded at Bellevue Manor on 7 February and 3 March 1978 were retrapped on 27 April and 2 May 1978, at Hellertown, Pennsylvania, and Schenectady, New York, respectively. These birds were migrating on a north-northeasterly bearing toward the Adirondacks or beyond into south-central Quebec.

A Black-capped Chickadee recovered north of Wilmington on 12 January 1964, had been banded at Chamberlain, Maine, on 20 September 1963 (Bagg 1969, 12). Chamberlain is on a peninsula on Maine's southeast coast; the chickadee doubtless already had migrated some distance before being captured there.

Northern Shrikes wintering in the northeastern United States belong to the population that breeds in the spruce taiga–tundra ecotone (the Hudsonian Zone) east of Hudson Bay in Quebec and Labrador (Cade 1967, 65; Davis 1974, 823).

The population of Snowy Owls wintering in the Mid-Atlantic region fluctuates synchronously with those wintering north into Quebec and west to the western Great Lakes, but not with populations wintering on the Great Plains and farther west (Kerlinger et al. 1985). Our Snowy Owls presumably migrate south from breeding areas east of Hudson Bay, including the Ungava Peninsula, Labrador, and southeastern Baffin Island.

The Long View

Charles J. Pennock's Delaware bird notes (on file at the Historical Society of Delaware) suggest that the status of northern visitors was not appreciably different a century ago than it is now. For the period 1879–1910, Pennock recorded the Purple Finch five times. He described the Red-breasted Nuthatch as a migrant and winter visitor. He recorded the Rough-legged Hawk three times, the Pine Siskin and the Red Crossbill twice, and the Common Redpoll, Northern Shrike, and Snowy Owl only once. The Northern Goshawk, Boreal Chickadee, Pine Grosbeak, White-winged Crossbill, and Evening Grosbeak were not recorded at all. Pennock regarded the Black-capped Chickadee as "hypothetical." In all likelihood, if Pennock had been able to rely on as many observer hours as this project did, his list would have been similar to our own, with one exception. The big news since Pennock's time is the invasion of eastern North America (and the Delaware bird list) by the Evening Grosbeak.

Notes

1. At Manomet Observatory in Massachusetts, there have been no large fall movements of this species since 1985 (Trevor Lloyd-Evans, pers. comm.). Spring population indices at Manomet from 1970 to 1992 (based on chickadees banded per netting effort) show a decline in this species, though with considerable year-to-year variation.

2. Includes Bombay Hook and Rehoboth from 1962 forward, joined by Wilmington and Cape Henlopen–Prime Hook from 1964 forward and Middletown from 1966 forward.

3. In a later paper, the same authors found that CBCs and other data from 1948 to 1971 suggest that passerine irruptions in North America and Eurasia are linked to "a circumboreally synchronized pattern of seed crop fluctuations in certain high-latitude tree species," notably spruce *(Picea)*, fir *(Abies)*, and birch *(Betula)* (Bock and Lepthien 1976, 569). In the Spanish Pyrenees, where pine trees produce cones every year, Red Crossbills are sedentary from year to year (Senar et al. 1993).

4. The 1981 Red-breasted Nuthatch incursion was seen in neighboring states (Paxton, Boyle, and Cutler 1982, 279) and at Manomet Observatory in Massachusetts, where the nuthatches were accompanied by a modest incursion of Black-capped Chickadees (Lloyd-Evans, pers. comm.). Manomet itself has not seen a significant correlation between numbers of the two species banded each fall from 1970 to 1985.

5. The Delaware CBCs that were run in 1954 (Bombay Hook, Middletown, and Rehoboth) counted 23 Black-capped Chickadees, 10 Red-breasted Nuthatches, and 19 Pine Siskins. In 1954 there appears to have been an irruption when compared with the totals counted by the same three CBCs in 1953 (only one Black-capped Chickadee), and 1955 (3 Black-capped Chickadees, 2 Red-breasted Nuthatches, and 6 Pine Siskins). The Red-breasted Nuthatch was the only irruptive passerine that made a big showing on the 1981 Delaware CBCs, although later in the winter there was "a great winter finch invasion" of the region, including both crossbills in Delaware (Paxton, Boyle, and Cutler 1982, 279; species account for White-winged Crossbill).

6. There are three Pine Grosbeak records for the state (see species account). Two (December 1965, November 1983) coincided with Pine Siskin irruptions; one (November 1974) did not.

7. The 1985 and 1986 CBCs are not shown in table 4, but Pine Siskins invaded the state each winter, as did Evening Grosbeaks and a few Red Crossbills in 1985–86, and Common Redpolls in 1986–87 (Ednie 1987, 20; Boyle, Paxton, and Cutler 1986, 264, and 1987, 263). The winter of 1993–94 brought a Common Redpoll invasion (missed by the CBCs) and the highest CBC of Pine Siskins (64) in eight years.

8. Most of these Delaware records coincide with reports of a significant fall migration or winter holdover of goshawks in surrounding states. See Heintzelman 1986, 282; Scott and Cutler 1973, 144, and 1974, 623; Smith, Paxton, and Cutler 1979, 268; Paxton, Boyle, and Cutler 1982, 278, and 1992, 68; Boyle, Paxton, and Cutler 1983, 284; 1988, 241; 1989, 291, and 1991, 255.

9. In the fall of 1981, Ontario hawk watches on the north shore of Lake Erie recorded a major invasion of goshawks (Kleiman 1982, 28), while Mid-Atlantic hawk watches saw a good but not record fall flight (Paxton, Boyle, and Cutler 1982, 278). The 1982 spring migration on the south shore of Lake Ontario was "spectacular" (Klabunde 1983, 17). The fall of 1991 was once again "exceptional" for goshawks on the north shore of Lake Erie (Benoit 1992, 58). In the Mid-Atlantic region, "Northern Goshawks staged a mini-invasion along the coast," with "an exceptional number of adults" and Cape May's second highest count of the species (Paxton, Boyle, and Cutler 1992, 68). Elsewhere in the region, totals were only a little above average (Paxton, Boyle, and Cutler 1992, 68).

10. From 1907 through 1985, all CBCs on the Delmarva Peninsula recorded the Snowy Owl only once (one bird, Lower Kent County, Maryland, 1978) and the Northern Goshawk in only six years (twelve birds total; Falk 1987, 68, 70). Since 1985, Snowy Owls have been seen on two Delaware CBCs (1992 and 1993), and Northern Goshawks have been seen on three Delaware CBCs (1987, 1991, and 1993).

11. This is the geographically obvious hypothesis, assuming that fall migrants from this area proceed south unless diverted in a southwesterly direction by the Atlantic coast.

Pine Grosbeak *(Pinicola enucleator)*

DOCUMENTATION: Published notes.

REMARKS: The Pine Grosbeak, a bird of northern forests, irrupts to as far south as Virginia and North Carolina (AOU 1983), but only 4 records from Delaware exist, perhaps reflecting a preference of the species for moving south along montane corridors. Published notes of an observation of an immature male near Newark on 18 November 1983 (Ross 1984) imply a size near that of a robin and mention the reddish rump and head and the 2 white wingbars. We consider this observation satisfactory. The other sightings include

4 Jan 1930	7	Wilmington [Bick1]
31 Dec 1965	1	Rehoboth CBC [McLP2]
18 Nov 1974	1	Wilmington [Walt1]

The 18 November sighting was also very well described. For completeness, we add that documentation of a 1970 May Count sight record is insufficient to overcome a date later than any reported for the eastern United States (Bent 1968) and more than 2 months later than the latest given for Maryland (Robbins and Bystrak 1977).

Casual (1930, 1965, 1974, 1983) in winter.

Purple Finch *(Carpodacus purpureus)*

sunflower seeds at feeders (Linehan, pers. comm., 1992).

SPRING: Spring migration begins 10–15 March and ceases by 30 April–5 May. Late departures include

11 May 1978	1	Greenville [Nile4]
15 May 1986	2	White Clay Creek [Barn14]
26 May 1984	present	Cypress Swamp, near Frankfort [DOS2]

In 1984 Purple Finches also stayed late at White Clay Creek [RusJ1]. Typical reports involve fewer than 10 birds. High reports are

| 11 Mar 1978 | 24 | White Clay Creek [Broo17] |
| 28 Apr 1984 | 30 | Goslee Mill, west of Rehoboth Beach [Frec1] |

This species was found on 17 of 22 May Counts; the highest count was 57 (5 May 1973).

FALL: First arrival is usually 1–10 October. The earliest banding report is 1 on 29 September 1967 at the University of Delaware woodlot [Line4]. Earlier sight reports include

31 Aug 1974	1	Dragon Run [Wayn25]
31 Aug 1990	1 male	Walnut Ridge [SpSB11]
12 Sep 1973	1	Brandywine Creek SP [Lehm15]

As in spring, typical counts involve fewer than 10 birds. High reports are

Regular; winter visitor; fairly common; expected early October to early May.

HABITAT: Various deciduous woods and suburban areas, feeding in treetops on sweetgum and tuliptree seeds, and on

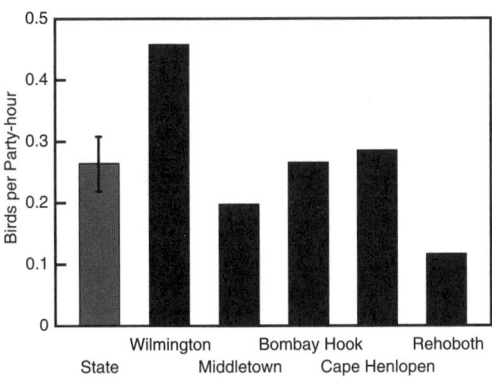

CBC Geographic Distribution

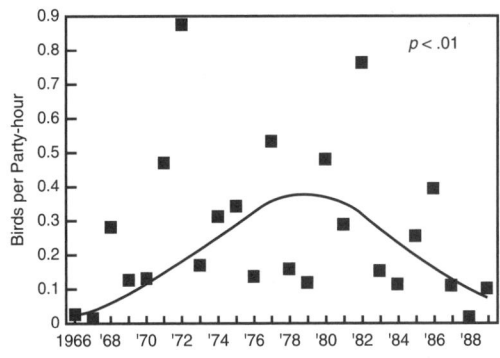

p < .01

CBC Trend

14 Oct 1972	90	Winterthur [Beac4]
29 Oct 1977	113	White Clay Creek [Dyer12]
22 Nov 1970	60	Lewes [MatD1]

1966–89 CBC Summary

Christmas Bird Count	Years Found	Range of No. Found	Median
Wilmington	24	4–212	50
Middletown	20	1–68	8
Bombay Hook	22	1–129	10
Cape Henlopen	23	1–87	12
Rehoboth	17	1–105	3
STATEWIDE (low in 1967, high in 1972)	24	7–399	83

WINTER: This winter visitor frequents feeders and is also readily detected flying overhead by its distinctive *pick-pick* call note. High counts are 212 on the 1975 Wilmington CBC and 160 at Brandywine Creek SP on 2 February 1969 [Serr1].

SPECIMENS: 63; DMNH, ANSP, UDEL.

House Finch *(Carpodacus mexicanus)*

Resident; fairly common, especially in urban and suburban areas. A western North American species introduced into the East. Has increased at 10–20% per year and may still be increasing and expanding its range.

HABITAT: Urban and suburban areas. Open grassy areas with ornamental evergreen plantings around suburbs, rural homes, schools, and cemeteries. Attracted to winter feeders; will stay to breed.

HISTORY: The House Finch is a native resident of western North America. In 1940 many were released in New York City by 1 or several bird dealers (Elliott and Arbib 1953). House Finches were first noticed in Delaware on 7 March 1962 by C. Stevenson (Niles and Conway 1976), but the first breeding season record was not until 1967 (see "Breeding"). By 1972 it was considered a common year-round resident but was "only irregularly and uncommonly reported on the Delmarva Peninsula away from the immediate vicinity of the Delaware bayshore and the Atlantic coast as well as away from Wilmington and its suburbs" (Niles and Conway 1976). By the 1980s it was found throughout New Castle and Kent counties and mainly near the coast in Sussex County.

DISPERSAL: Grinnell and Miller (1944), writing about California birds, state that the House Finch "Wanders to some degree, especially in late summer, but definite migratory patterns not apparent." It rapidly expanded its Eastern range since its New York introduction (Bull 1974; Cohen and Cohen 1971; Paxton 1974; Woods 1968). Mundinger and Hope (1982) postulate that 2 dispersal mechanisms were involved: diffusion (i.e., gradual dispersion from a central area) and jump-dispersal (i.e., movement over area not occupied by House Finches). Their maps, using CBC data, clearly show an initial radiation following the coast and major river valleys and toward the southwest;

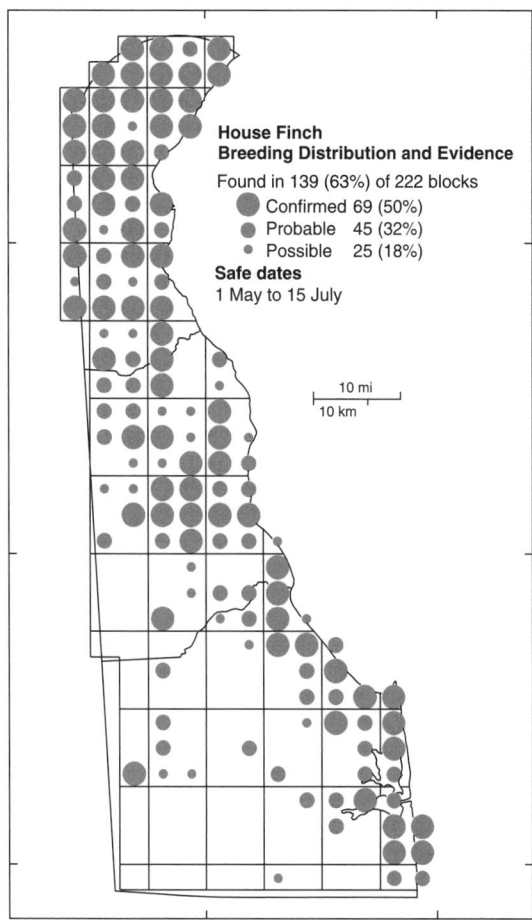

House Finch
Breeding Distribution and Evidence

Found in 139 (63%) of 222 blocks

● Confirmed 69 (50%)
● Probable   45 (32%)
· Possible   25 (18%)

Safe dates
1 May to 15 July

10 mi
10 km

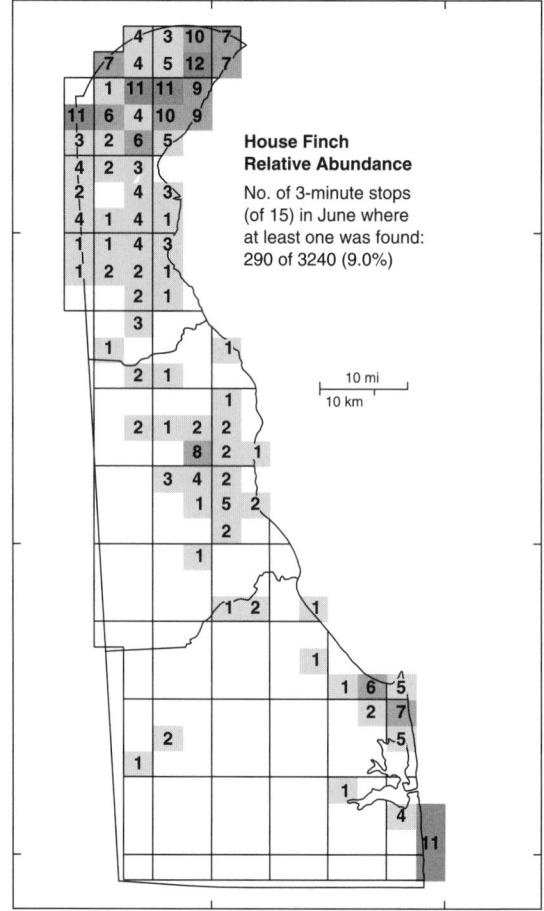

House Finch
Relative Abundance

No. of 3-minute stops
(of 15) in June where
at least one was found:
290 of 3240 (9.0%)

10 mi
10 km

also, isolated clusters formed away from major concentrations (representing jump-dispersals). Eventually these satellite areas merged with the core areas.

In some instances this dispersal had a migratory component. In Delaware the first observations of wintering birds were 2 years before the first breeding season observations (1962–64). Breeding evidence was not reported until 1967, and this species was found in much higher numbers in winter for a number of years. In Tennessee banders recovered many birds

banded in the Northeast; some banded in Tennessee were caught weeks, even days, later 180–300 mi (300–500 km) northeast (S. J. Stedman, pers. comm.).

Although House Finch winter numbers have increased at the same time Purple Finch winter numbers have declined, and food is probably the resource most in common between the species, Bosakowski (1986) suggests competition may be minimal due to differences in habitat selection, with House Finches finding a greater proportion of their food at feeders and ornamental plantings in suburban and urban areas.

BREEDING: It mainly breeds in towns and around suburban and rural homes south to Dover and farther south along the coast. In southwestern Delaware it is confined mainly to larger towns. Heavily urbanized northern Delaware is its stronghold.

Atlas. The House Finch may breed in Sussex County more extensively than the Atlas results reflect as it has continued to consolidate its range in eastern North America. During each year of the Atlas project it was found breeding in additional towns in southern and western Delaware where it was not reported before. In late July and early August large flocks were observed feeding in weedy fields where they had not been present previously, reason enough for the safe dates to end on 15 July. Active nests were reported in 22 blocks and nest building in 16 others, but attending young (carrying food) was the most frequently used confirmation code.

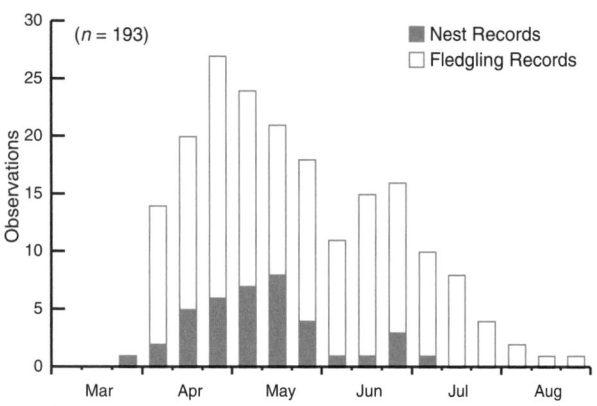

Estimated Clutch-Completion Dates

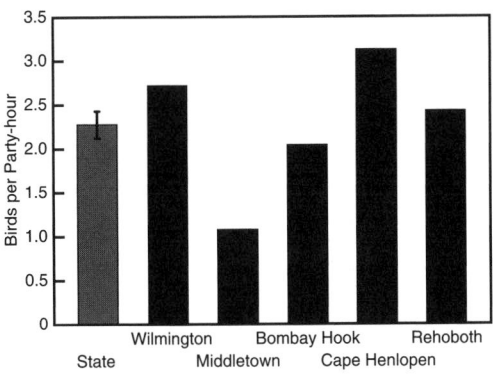

CBC Geographic Distribution

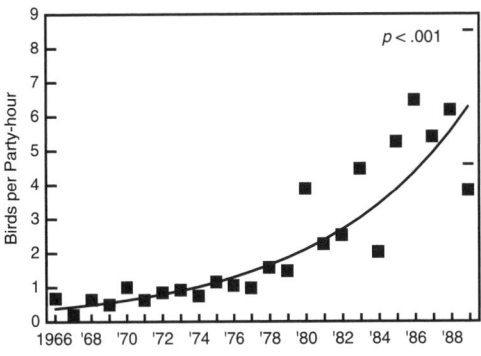

CBC Trend; Increasing at 13% per Year

Nesting. This species was first reported summering in 1964 in the Speck's yard near Hoopes Reservoir [SpSB3]. The first breeding report came from Strickland, who saw 2 adults with young at his feeder near Elsmere during 1967 [Carr18], but H. and C. Stevenson had noted adults feeding young "before 1967" at Blue Rock Manor (Niles and Conway 1976). Three young House Finches, with "eyebrows" still sporting natal down, showed up at the W. A. Brokaw feeder in Chatham on 9 June 1971. The Conways banded 32 birds of the year at Belleview Manor in 1972 (Niles and Conway 1972). Young were heard in a nest about 20 ft up in a Colorado blue spruce on 14 June 1973 in Newark [Lehm18]. The first nest in which young were actually seen in Delaware was found on 20 June 1974 [Cado1]. It was situated in ivy on a wall at Hagley Museum and held 2 young.

The nest is most often constructed in a conifer, but ivy on a wall and honeysuckle tangles have been used. Indoor sites are also selected—a pillar on a church porch, a garage rafter, a flower pot, and even a high shelf in a university lab. The nest is a cup woven of sticks and grass [Edni4].

Although its estimated clutch-completion dates extend 5 months, from March to August, dates of observed eggs extend only from 12 April [Nile2] to 22 June [Jesc1]. Use of nestling data to supplement nest records makes a distinct difference in our view of its breeding season. The earliest clutch-completion date—for a fledgling being fed out of the nest, possessing a two-thirds grown tail, and showing natal down on its head on 24 April [Nile2]—is about 21 March; the latest clutch-completion date—derived from a 12-g, 8-day-old fledgling found on 11 September (TSBR 87-1146)—is about 21 August. In 1 instance 2 broods were fledged from the same nest on 28 May and 11 July, a 44-day interval [Gree1]. Females have ample time to complete 3 successful broods during the breeding period. Clutch size is 4 or 5 ($n = 7$).

Trends. BBS data indicate the House Finch has increased in the East at an average annual rate of 20% during 1966–90 [Usfw3]. The Delaware BBS, the May Count, and the CBC show a rapid increase, probably at an average annual rate of 10–20%.

Breeding population. We have few indicators of its breeding abundance. It is found at the rate of 9 birds per 50-stop BBS route, but the routes do not adequately sample Wilmington or Brandywine Hundred, where it is most common. The highest May Count is 372 (1989).

1966–89 CBC Summary

Christmas Bird Count	Years Found	Range of No. Found	Median
Wilmington	24	73–1,403	295
Middletown	16	1–504	9
Bombay Hook	24	7–679	91
Cape Henlopen	22	30–605	176
Rehoboth	22	8–728	166
STATEWIDE	24	120–2,909	711
(increasing; low in 1967, high in 1988)			

WINTER: This species has shown a significant increase in CBC numbers. Bock and Lepthien (1976b) have documented its rapid increase east of the Mississippi River. The CBC graph shows a nearly exponential increase. This increase may have stopped in 1989, but it will take several years to determine the new trend. Postbreeding dispersal and a tendency to winter along the coast may account for the greater numbers observed in winter and its presence in areas where it does not breed.

SPECIMENS: 115; DMNH, UDEL.

Red Crossbill *(Loxia curvirostra)*

being noted variously from late October to early June. Three were observed at Lewes on 10 May 1894 [Hugh1]. The only 3 specimens were taken in pines near Rehoboth Beach on 15 and 18 May 1908 [Penn1]. Extreme dates of occurrence are

30 Oct 1973	1	Lewes [LewA1]
3 Nov 1972	6	Felton [Holg15]
18 Nov 1981	1	Cape Henlopen SP [Frec58]
30 May 1974	"a few"	Pocomoke Swamp [Dyke15]
30 May 1970	10	Henlopen Acres [PylR5]
6 Jun 1976	4	White Clay Creek [West2]

The length of crossbill visits varies from 1 day to 2–3 months; crossbills are prone to wandering in search of food (Griscom 1937). About half of reports involve 10 or fewer birds, and most of the rest involve fewer than 35 birds. The winter of 1969 produced 2 high counts: 233 on the Rehoboth CBC and 99 on the Cape Henlopen CBC. The invasion in the winter of 1975–76 was long enough that Red Crossbills had opportunity to breed, but breeding was not observed. However, 25 were observed on 30 May of that spring at Henlopen Acres [Line8]. Peck and James (1987) note that this species can nest almost any time of year when the food supply is plentiful, and Peterson (1988d) quotes Merriam reporting that Red Crossbills can breed in February and March with several feet of snow on the ground.

SPECIMENS: ANSP 65713, Rehoboth Beach, 15 May 1908; ANSP 65706 and ANSP 65714, Rehoboth Beach, 18 May 1908.

Occasional (18 years, 1960–92); winter visitor; fairly common. To be looked for from late October to June.

HABITAT: Conifer stands; hemlocks in northern Delaware and loblolly pine and bald cypress in southern Delaware (Linehan, pers. comm., 1992).

OCCURRENCE: Red Crossbill is an irregular, irruptive species. It has occurred during 18 years from 1960 to 1992,

White-winged Crossbill *(Loxia leucoptera)*

Occasional (13 years, 1963–88); winter visitor; uncommon. To be looked for November–March.

DOCUMENTATION: Multiple sight records.

HABITAT: Conifer stands.

OCCURRENCE: Like the Red Crossbill, this species is irregular and irruptive in occurrence. It may be present any time from late October through March. The occurrence of a flock of 20–40 in the Greenville–Centerville area during February 1982 [m.ob7] is indicated by the February peak shown in the seasonal bar graph. Extreme dates of occurrence are

27 Oct 1973	1	Hockessin [McCT3]
2 Nov 1965	2	Marshallton [Carr12]
16 Nov 1963	20–30	Hoopes Dam [Peop1]
22 Feb 1982	35	near Greenville [Wayn20]
7 Mar 1978	2	Claymont [Nacz1]
14 May 1972	1	Rehoboth Beach [Armi6]

Common Redpoll *(Carduelis flammea)*

Occasional (15 years, 1962–89); winter visitor; uncommon to fairly common. To be looked for from late December to early April.

OCCURRENCE: This winter finch is yet another irregular, irruptive visitor. In some years (1970, 1972, 1974, and 1987) it was present at feeders for up to a month. Although most redpolls are noted in February and March, they may occur from late December to mid-April. The extreme reports include

26 Nov 1969	5	Gordon Pond WA [Unge1]
19 Dec 1989	1	Lewes [Frec20]
20 Dec 1975	1	Rehoboth CBC [John10]
7 Apr 1974	1	Greenville [Walt2]
10 Apr 1982	5	Dragon Run [Barn13]
11 Apr 1971	4	Wilmington [BroW2]

Typically, reports total fewer than 10 birds, but in February and March 1972 more than 30 were present at 3 different feeders in northern New Castle County [m.ob6]. When away from feeders, redpolls use various habitats from willow bottoms to pine-covered sand dunes, where they feed on cones and weed seeds (Linehan, pers comm., 1992).

SPECIMENS: 9; DMNH, UDEL.

[Hoary Redpoll *(Carduelis hornemanni)*]

One sight report.

DOCUMENTATION: Unpublished notes.

REMARKS: There is a single report (Brinkley et al. 1991) of a bird seen 26 February 1994 in a group of Common Redpolls at a feeder by 2 observers who had previously seen both species. The description mentions the paleness of the bird and the presence of an unstriped, white rump. No additional observers are known to have seen the individual.

Pine Siskin *(Carduelis pinus)*

Regular; winter visitor; fairly common to common. Expected mid-December to mid-April, sporadically earlier and later.

HABITAT: "Pine stands and flood-plain and swamp deciduous forests; also in hedgerows and wood margins" (Stewart and Robbins 1958). Regularly visits thistle seed feeders.

SPRING: Last departure is 15–20 April, although in some years lingering or late birds may be found into June. The latest reports include

30 May 1988	1	near Greenville [SpSB28]
2 Jun 1981	3	Newark [Jahn8]
4–10 June 1973	1	near Newark [KelJ1]

FALL: First arrival is usually about 15 December but in

some years may be as early as 15 October. Earliest arrivals include

22 Sep 1984	1	Milton [Frec44]
14 Oct 1987	15	Walnut Ridge [SpeE1]
16 Oct 1973	40	Wilmington [Phal7]

Numbers range up to as many as the 200 found at Cape Henlopen SP on 30 October 1980 [Frec35].

1966–89 CBC Summary

Christmas Bird Count	Years Found	Range of No. Found	Median
Wilmington	17	1–137	5
Middletown	10	1–78	
Bombay Hook	16	1–142	2
Cape Henlopen	11	1–114	
Rehoboth	10	1–876	
STATEWIDE (high in 1969)	20	1–1,135	11

WINTER: Like other winter finches, it is prone to wandering and is seldom at any one site long. It is attracted to feeders with thistle seed. Numbers range from a few to flocks up to about 100.

REMARKS: A specimen taken by W. T. Woods in October

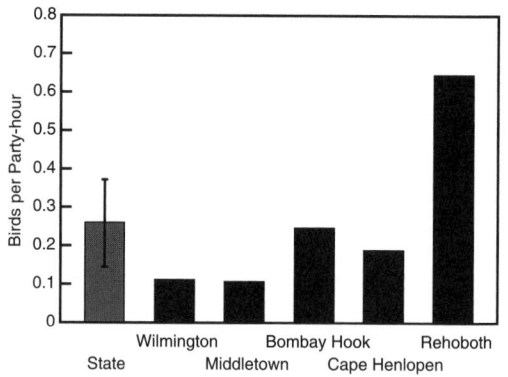

CBC Geographic Distribution

1878 (in Delaware, no location given) was in Bush's collection [Penn1]. Another was shot on 22 December 1907 from a flock of goldfinches at the edge of the woods west of Henlopen lighthouse, and a flock of others was seen [Penn1]. Other early records include

| 3 Nov 1916 | 1 | New Castle County [WriM1] |
| 1 Nov 1936 | 15 | Drawyers Creek [Pell1] |

SPECIMENS: 15; DMNH, USNM.

American Goldfinch *(Carduelis tristis)*

Resident; common but declining, less common southward and inland. Migrates late March to early June and late September to late November. Decreasing at about 5% per year in spring, summer, and winter.

J F M A M J J A S O N D

HABITAT: Weedy fields, various deciduous forest types, shrubby second-growth areas, especially feeding on thistle,

sweetgum, ragweed, and shepherd's purse (Linehan, pers. comm., 1992).

SPRING: The migration period cannot be determined from Delaware data. Stewart and Robbins (1958) give the normal period in Maryland as 20–30 March to 1–10 June, with the peak 5 April–15 May. High counts, all at White Clay Creek, are

23 Apr 1977	136	[Patt6]
1 May 1976	144	[Lehm37]
7 May 1977	101	[Dyer7]

The highest May Count is 1,459 (1969), the lowest 266 (1980).

BREEDING: Found throughout the state in June, it is more common in northern New Castle County and along the coastline than in the hotter interior of the peninsula.

Atlas. It was difficult to do justice to this species because it breeds so late compared with other passerines. Safe dates start late—10 June, a couple of months before it lays eggs—but still after enthusiasm for fieldwork is beginning to wane. Consequently, most Atlas workers were satisfied by just observing the species in the block. It was confirmed 9 times by finding recently fledged young and 8 times by observing nest building. Only 2 nests were reported, both with young. It probably could be found in summer in most of the blocks where it was missed.

Nesting. Hanson (notes) wrote that a nest Buckalew brought

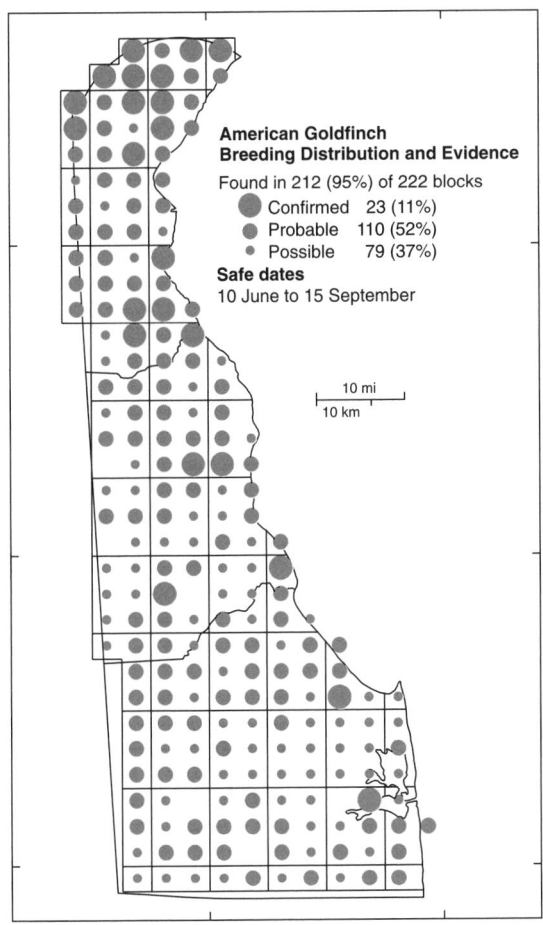

American Goldfinch
Breeding Distribution and Evidence

Found in 212 (95%) of 222 blocks
- ⬤ Confirmed 23 (11%)
- ● Probable 110 (52%)
- · Possible 79 (37%)

Safe dates
10 June to 15 September

10 mi
10 km

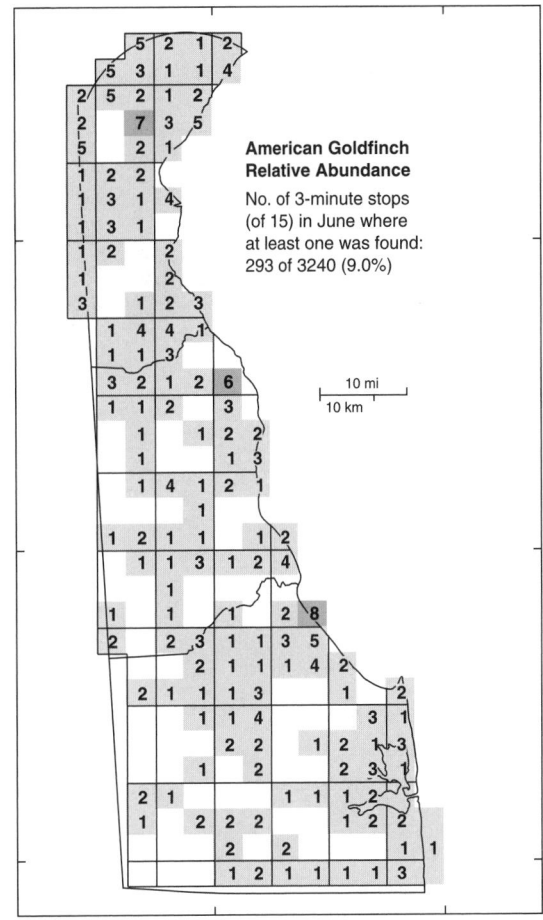

American Goldfinch
Relative Abundance

No. of 3-minute stops
(of 15) in June where
at least one was found:
293 of 3240 (9.0%)

10 mi
10 km

him was found in the crotch of a small limb growing horizontally out from the trunk of a sweet gum about 15 ft above ground. Prest found 1 16 ft up in a sassafras [Pres3]. Moorhouse and Ednie [MooJ3] found 1 10 ft up in a 15-foot silver maple. The nest is a neat, compact cup of plant fibers, strips of bark, and plant down, lined with down and strengthened with spider silk, usually 3–10 ft above ground (Harrison 1978).

Estimated clutch-completion dates extend from 15 July to 1

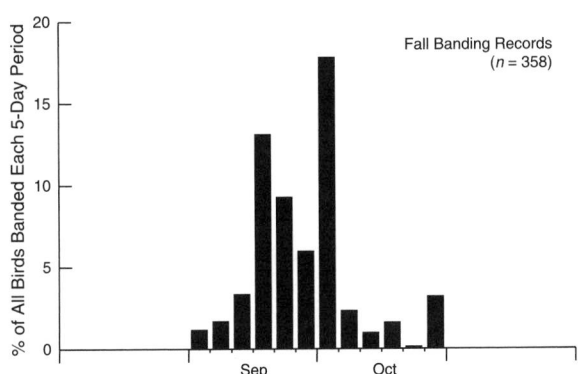

Fall Migration Activity

September (*n* = 9). The earliest nest with eggs was found near Bear on 16 July [Pres3], the latest on 26 August [Buck10]. Maryland egg dates extend to 21 September (Robbins and Bystrak 1977), suggesting that later nests may occur in Delaware also.

Trends. Since the 1960s this species has been declining in Delaware at an average annual rate of about 5% a year by every measure we have: the May Count, the Delaware BBS, and the CBC. It is declining generally in the East at a lower average annual rate [Usfw1].

Breeding population. The average number found on a 50-stop Delaware BBS route is 3.7 birds, about the same as New Jersey but only half the average for Maryland and a third the average for Pennsylvania (Robbins et al. 1986).

FALL: The migration period cannot be determined from Delaware data, although peak banding occurs from mid-September through early October. Stewart and Robbins (1958) give the normal period in Maryland as 20–30 September to 20–30 November, with the peak 15 October–15 November. High reports include

12 Sep 1971	264	Brandywine Creek SP [BroW17]
24 Oct 1970	139	Brandywine Creek SP [Wayn25]
30 Oct 1965	160	Churchmans Marsh [SpSB37]

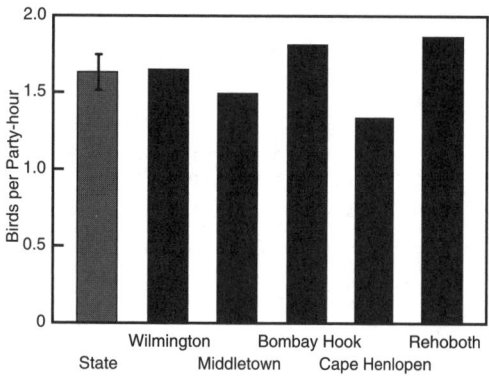

CBC Geographic Distribution

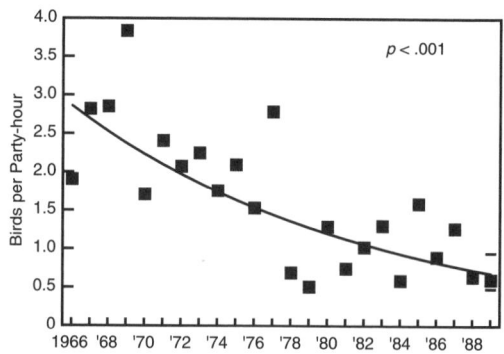

CBC Trend; Decreasing at 6% per Year

1966–89 CBC Summary

Christmas Bird Count	Years Found	Range of No. Found	Median
Wilmington	24	80–566	189
Middletown	24	26–265	94
Bombay Hook	24	28–537	114
Cape Henlopen	24	4–373	61
Rehoboth	24	23–597	133
STATEWIDE	24	245–1,690	714
(decreasing; low in 1989, high in 1969)			

WINTER: This species has shown a significant decline in CBC numbers. A small decline occurred before the severe winters of the mid-1970s, but after that numbers decreased precipitously and do not appear to be recovering. Typically, 5–15 birds are reported. Reports of 76 at White Clay Creek on 12 December 1976 and 83 there on 1 January 1977 are the result of transcribing errors (Speck and Brokaw 1979). One high report involves 200 in eastern Sussex County on 1 January 1988 [Frec1].

SPECIMENS: 43; DMNH, ANSP, UDEL. Egg records: WFVZ.

Evening Grosbeak (*Coccothraustes vespertinus*)

Regular (1963–90); winter visitor; fairly common. Present sporadically mid-October to mid-May.

HABITAT: Suburbs, towns, parks, and forests, but particularly in the vicinity of feeders with sunflower seeds; partial to box elder seeds (Godfrey 1986). Also feeds on maples, hawthorn, tuliptree, chokecherry, and most conifers.

HISTORY: Formerly a western species, the Evening Grosbeak has rapidly expanded its breeding range eastward during the twentieth century. It first bred in western Ontario in 1920 and has since expanded its breeding range east to Nova Scotia (Godfrey 1986). The first big invasion in the East was recorded during the winter of 1889–90 in New York. Its status changed from occasional winter visitor in the early part of the twentieth century to a somewhat regular, locally common, migrant, and winter visitor (Bull 1974). Breeding has also moved southward into New York (Peterson 1988b).

It was first recorded in Delaware on 2 March 1942 at Middletown [BraE1]. A flock was seen in Dover on several occasions at the R. C. Wilson feeder beginning 11 February 1946 and at other places in Dover later that month. Hanson counted 10 on 10 February, and Wilson reported 12 or 15 on 23 February, the last day they were seen [Hans1]. Winter invasions increased in frequency and magnitude since then.

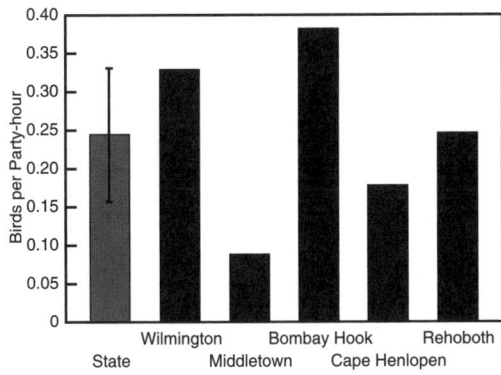

CBC Geographic Distribution

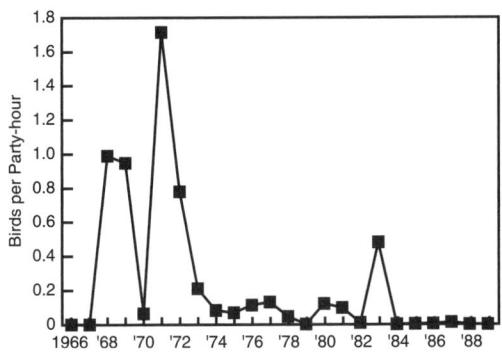

Christmas Bird Count Data

SPRING: Migration takes place from 20–25 March to 5–10 May. Virtually all leave by 15 May. Late reports include

| 15 May 1984 | 1 | Five Points [Frec1] |
| 24 May 1984 | 4 | Centerville [SpeE7] |

High reports are

| 29 Mar 1975 | 50 | Viola [Pure1] |
| 14 Apr 1984 | 50 | Five Points [Frec1] |

The highest May Count was 92 (5 May 1973), and none was found in nine years during the 1969–90 period.

FALL: First arrival in years when it comes is about 20 October to 1 November. Early reports include

2 Oct 1974	15	Milltown Rd., southwest of Wilmington [Jaco1]
22 Oct 1972	43	Winterthur [Falk22]
23 Oct 1977	44	White Clay Creek [Conw16]

Reports are of either a few birds or flocks up to 20–40 birds. Occasionally larger flocks are encountered, such as

| 9 Nov 1980 | 100 | Arundel, SW of Wilmington [RusR14] |
| 19 Nov 1972 | 104 | Winterthur [Falk15] |

1966–89 CBC Summary

Christmas Bird Count	Years Found	Range of No. Found	Median
Wilmington	15	1–487	7
Middletown	12	1–54	
Bombay Hook	13	2–287	3
Cape Henlopen	10	1–122	
Rehoboth	11	1–193	
STATEWIDE *(decreasing; high in 1971)*	19	1–757	31

WINTER: This is another irruptive winter visitor. See the "Irruptive Northern Visitors to Delaware" essay for a discussion of irruptive species. Typically, either a few are reported or flocks of up to 10–20. Wandering Evening Grosbeaks often come to feeders. They may visit for only a few minutes or may stay a few days or a week. The CBC data indicates a decline in population. However, because Evening Grosbeaks are irruptive, this result is difficult to interpret, and the decline may be part of a larger cyclic population fluctuation.

SPECIMENS: 10; DMNH, UDEL.

House Sparrow *(Passer domesticus)*

Introduced. Resident; common in cities, towns, and farming districts. Declining at about 5% per year.

HABITAT: Cities, towns, barnyards; around feedlots and open dumpsters. Suburbs where food is available; requires a supply of grains and weed seeds. Nests in buildings and ornamental shrubbery.

HISTORY: "The multiple introductions of *Passer domesticus* into North America are a classic example of how man, with utter disregard for the long-term effects of his irresponsible acts, has permanently altered the ecology of an entire nation and almost an entire continent." So begins Robbins (1973) in summarizing the introduction and expansion of the House Sparrow in North America. The following history is taken from his work. Two reasons are often given for the introduction of House Sparrows: European immigrants longed for familiar birds, and they believed the introduced birds would be useful in controlling insect pests. Eight pairs were first brought to this country in 1850 and released the following spring in Brooklyn, New York. They did not prosper. In 1852 about 100 more were imported. Half were released immediately, the rest the following spring. At first the rate of spread was minimal. After 5 years sparrows could be found within a radius of 25 mi, after 10 years 50 mi, and after 15 years 100 or more mi. It was introduced into Philadelphia in 1869. Sometime between then and 1886 it invaded Delaware. Indeed, Delaware, Florida, West Virginia, and New Hampshire are the only eastern states lacking evidence of deliberate introduction.

BREEDING: This species is found throughout the state but is not evenly distributed. It is most common in Wilmington and other towns, as well as in farming districts. It concentrates in small colonies around food sources.

Atlas. The House Sparrow could usually be confirmed while Atlas workers drove around looking for a Purple Martin house and was often easier to find than martins. If it was not con-

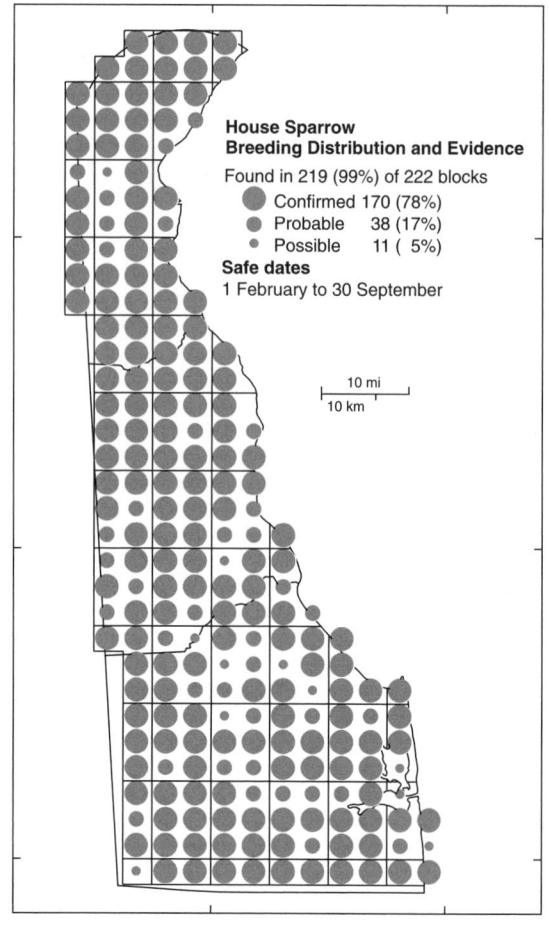

House Sparrow
Breeding Distribution and Evidence
Found in 219 (99%) of 222 blocks
- Confirmed 170 (78%)
- Probable 38 (17%)
- Possible 11 (5%)
Safe dates
1 February to 30 September

firmed immediately, a query at local farms would often lead to a confirmation even if there was no active nest at the time. The most common confirmation method was finding an occupied nest, though seeing nest building and carrying food were also frequent.

Nesting. Its nest is often an untidy clutter of straw, weeds, and rubbish in a domed structure, lined with feathers, tissue paper, and whatever is available. If the nest is in a cavity, enough nest material is brought to entirely fill the cavity. House Sparrows frequently nest in martin houses, bluebird boxes, or in crannies in buildings; they also nest in thick bushes and trees.

The earliest clutch-completion date involves a bird that fledged on 30 April 1923, indicating clutch completion in early April [Hans1]. Extreme egg dates are 19 April [Jahn1] to 10 July [Nile2]. Fledgling data from Tri-State Bird Rescue show that its breeding season extends into August. About 50% of the clutches contained 4 eggs, but single clutches of 5, 6, and 7 also occurred (*n* = 18). The last of these was in a bluebird box on 22 April [Jahn1] and may have been laid by more than 1 female.

Trends. House Sparrow populations have decreased in the

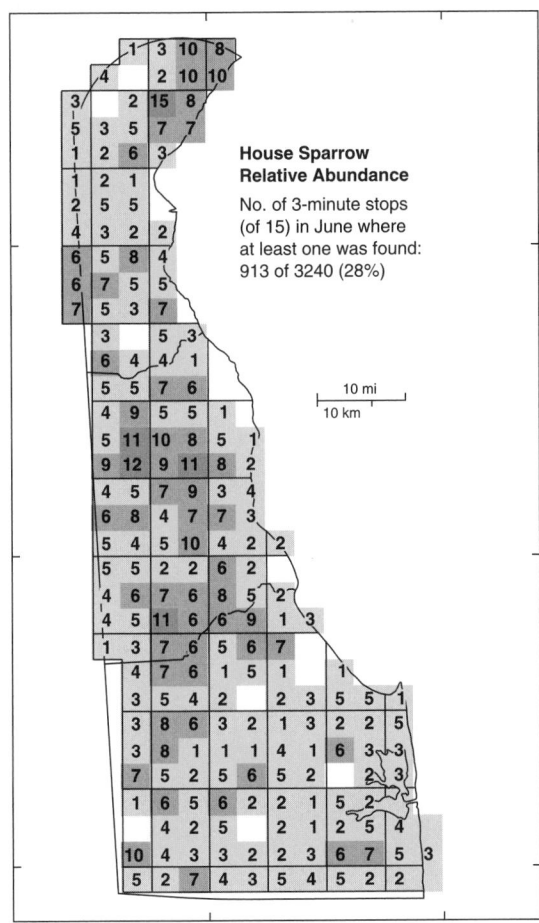

House Sparrow
Relative Abundance

No. of 3-minute stops
(of 15) in June where
at least one was found:
913 of 3240 (28%)

10 mi
10 km

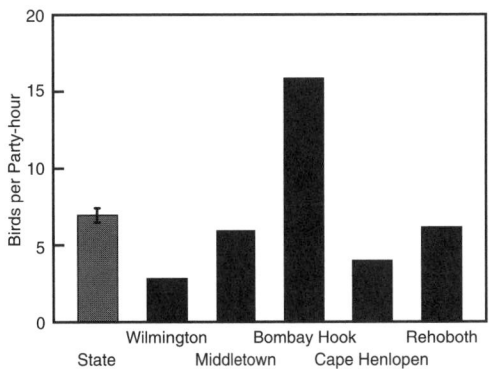

CBC Geographic Distribution

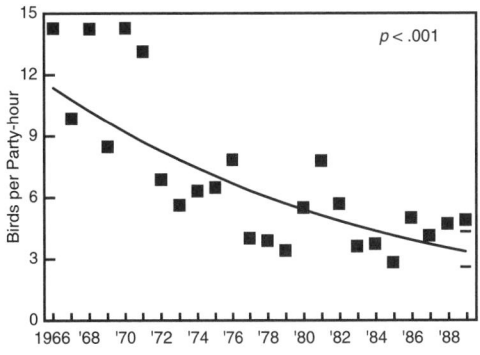

$p < .001$

CBC Trend; May be Autocorrelated

twentieth century. Since the 1960s it has decreased at an aver-age annual rate of about 5% in Delaware [Usfw1], a trend sup-ported by May Count and CBC data.

Breeding population. Its abundance of 96 birds per BBS route is about the same as found in Maryland but almost double the numbers found in New Jersey and Pennsylvania.

WINTER: House Sparrows have shown a significant decline in numbers on CBCs. Additional analysis suggests the decline is over or nearly so. Robbins (1973) commented that some observers believed that it peaked about 1890 in the East, and numbers have declined since that time. Forbush and May (1939) comment that "In recent years, however, they have decreased in numbers in the cities at least, especially in the northern parts of the country, where their chief food supply in winter formerly was found in the street droppings. With the invention of the automobile and its introduction in place of other vehicles, horses began gradually to disappear from city life, and as motorcars increased, Sparrows starved in winter." Robbins et al. (1986) comment that improved sanitation on dairy farms and improvements in other farming practices are probably largely responsible for the continued decline.

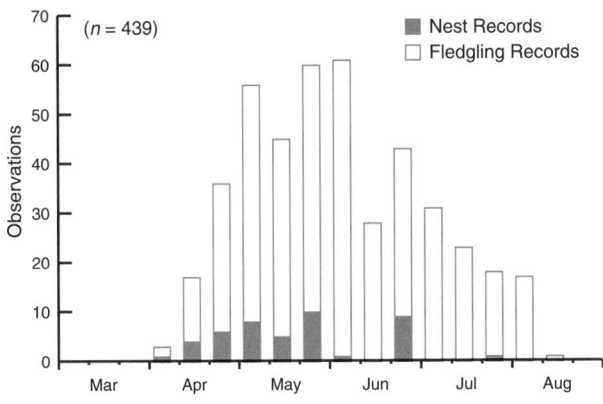

Estimated Clutch-Completion Dates

1966–89 CBC Summary

Christmas Bird Count	Years Found	Range of No. Found	Median
Wilmington	24	147–1,134	300
Middletown	24	140–1,171	326
Bombay Hook	24	380–2,490	877
Cape Henlopen	24	79–990	236
Rehoboth	24	95–1679	480
STATEWIDE	24	1,074–5,869	2,428
(decreasing; low in 1985, high in 1966)			

SPECIMENS: 57; DMNH, UDEL. Egg records: DMNH, WFVZ.

Appendices

Observers and Sources

Literature Cited

Sources of Illustrations

Addendum

Index

Common and Scientific Names of Animals and Plants

Table A.1. Names of Animals

Common Name	Scientific Name
American tent caterpillar	*Malacosoma americanum*
Baltic clam	*Macoma balthica*
Clamworm	*Nereis* sp.
Deerfly	*Chrysops vittatus*
Earthworm	*Lumbricus terrestris*
Fiddler crab	*Uca* sp.
Forest tent caterpillar	*Malacosoma disstria*
Gypsy moth	*Lymantira dispard*
Horseshoe crab	*Limulus polyphemus*
Mummichog	*Fundulus heteroclitus*
Nematode	*Eustrongylides ignotus*
Rabbit (eastern cottontail)	*Sylvilagus floridanus*
Raccoon	*Procyon lotor*
Red-jointed fiddler crab	*Uca minax*
Saltmarsh mosquito	*Aedes solicitans*

Sources: Gosner 1979; Merritt 1987; L. and M. Milne 1980; Raasch and Altemus 1991.

Table A.2. Names of Plants

Common Name	Scientific Name
Alder	*Alnus* sp.
Alfalfa	*Medicago sativa*
American beach grass	*Ammophila breviligulata*
American beech	*Fagus grandifolia*
American elm	*Ulmus americana*
American holly	*Ilex opaca*
American white birch	*Betula papyrifera*
Apple	*Malus* sp.
Arrow-arum	*Peltandra virginica*
Arrowhead	*Sagittaria* sp.
Atlantic white cedar	*Chamaecyparis thyoides*
Autumn olive	*Elaeagnus umbellata*
Azalea	*Rhododendron* sp.
Bald cypress	*Taxodium distichum*
Bayberry	*Myrica pensylvanica*
Beach heather	*Hudsonia tomentosa*
Beach plum	*Prunus maritima*
Beggar ticks	*Bidens* sp.
Big cordgrass	*Spartina cynosuroides*
Birch	*Betula* sp.
Black ash	*Fraxinus nigra*
Black gum, or sour gum	*Nyssa sylvatica*
Black locust	*Robinia pseudoacacia*
Black oak	*Quercus velutina*
Black willow	*Salix nigra*
Black walnut	*Juglans nigra*
Blackberry	*Rubus* sp.
Blackjack oak	*Quercus marilandica*
Bladderwort	*Utricularia* sp.
Box elder	*Acer negundo*
Broomsedge	*Andropogon virginicus*

Table A.2. Names of Plants *(continued)*

Common Name	Scientific Name
Buckwheat	*Fagopyrum esculentum*
Burreed	*Sparganium* sp.
Bush blackberry	*Rubus pensylvanicus*
Buttonbush	*Cephalanthus occidentalis*
Canada thistle	*Cirsium arvense*
Catalpa, common	*Catalpa bignonioides*
Cattail	*Typha* sp.
Cattail, common	*Typha latifolia*
Cattail, narrow-leaved	*Typha angustifolia*
Cedar	*Juniperus* sp.
Cherrybark oak	*Quercus falcata* var. *pagodaefolia*
Chestnut oak	*Quercus prinus*
Cinnamon fern	*Osmunda cinnamomea*
Clover	*Trifolium* sp.
Cocklebur	*Xanthium* sp.
Colorado blue spruce	*Picea pungens*
Common reed, giant reed grass, or phragmites	*Phragmites australis*
Coontail	*Ceratophyllum demersum*
Corn	*Zea mays*
Cranberry	*Vaccinium macrocarpon*
Deerberry	*Vaccinium stamineum*
Dogwood	*Cornus* sp.
Duckweed	*Lemna* sp.
Eastern red cedar	*Juniperus virginiana*
Eel grass	*Zostera marina*
Elderberry, common; American elder	*Sambucus canadensis*
Elm	*Ulmus* sp.
Evergreen bayberry	*Myrica heterophylla*
Floating-heart	*Nymphoides cordata*
Flowering dogwood	*Cornus florida*
Forsythia	*Forsythia* sp.
Fragrant water lily	*Nymphaea odorata*
Giant reed grass, or phragmites	*Phragmites australis*
Goldenrod	*Solidago* sp.
Grape	*Vitis* sp.
Green ash	*Fraxinus pennsylvanica*
Greenbrier, or catbrier	*Smilax* sp.
Greenbrier, common	*Smilax rotundifolia*
Groundsel bush, groundsel tree or sea myrtle	*Baccharis halimifolia*
Gum	*Nyssa* sp.
Hazel alder	*Alnus serrulata*
Hemlock, Canadian or eastern	*Tsuga canadensis*
Hickory	*Carya* sp.
High tide bush, or marsh elder	*Iva frutescens*
Highbush black blueberry	*Vaccinium atrococcum*
Highbush blueberry	*Vaccinium corymbosum*
Honeysuckle	*Lonicera* sp.
Hydrilla	*Hydrilla verticillata*
Ivy (English)	*Hedera helix*
Japanese honeysuckle	*Lonicera japonica*
Juniper	*Juniperus* sp.
Kudzu vine	*Pueraria thunbergiana*

Common Name	Scientific Name
Lily-of-the-valley	*Convallaria majalis*
Loblolly pine	*Pinus taeda*
Maple	*Acer* sp.
Marsh elder, or high tide bush	*Iva frutescens*
Marsh hay, salt hay, or saltmeadow cordgrass	*Spartina patens*
Mimosa	*Albizia julibrissin*
Mockernut hickory	*Carya tomentosa*
Mountain laurel	*Kalmia latifolia*
Multiflora rose	*Rosa multiflora*
Naiad	*Najas* sp.
Narrow-leaved cattail	*Typha angustifolia*
Needlerush	*Juncus* sp.
Northern red oak	*Quercus rubra*
Norway spruce	*Picea abies*
Nuttall oak	*Quercus nuttallii*
Oak	*Quercus* sp.
Old man's beard (lichen)	*Usnea* sp.
Olney three-square	*Scirpus americanus (S. olneyi)*
Osage orange	*Maclura pomifera*
Pear, common	*Pyrus communis*
Phragmites	*Phragmites australis*
Pickerel weed	*Pontedaria cordata*
Pignut hickory	*Carya glabra*
Pine	*Pinus* sp.
Pipewort	*Eriocaulon* sp.
Pitch pine	*Pinus rigida*
Pitcher plant	*Sarracenia purpurea*
Poison ivy	*Toxicodendron radicans* or *Rhus radicans*
Pond pine	*Pinus serotina*
Ponderosa pine	*Pinus ponderosa*
Pondweed	*Potamogeton* sp.
Post oak	*Quercus stellata*
Ragweed, common	*Ambrosia artemisiifolia*
Red birch, or river birch	*Betula nigra*
Red cedar, eastern	*Juniperus virginiana*
Red maple, or swamp maple	*Acer rubrum*
Rose	*Rosa* sp.
Rose mallow, or marsh mallow	*Hibiscus palustris,* or *H. moscheutos*
Rush	*Juncus* sp.
Rye	*Secale cereale*
Salt hay, salt hay grass, or saltmeadow cordgrass	*Spartina patens*
Salt marsh bulrush	*Scirpus robustus*
Salt marsh cordgrass, or salt-water cordgrass	*Spartina alterniflora*
Sand blackberry	*Rubus cuneifolius*
Sargassum	*Sargassum* sp.
Sassafras	*Sassafras albidum*
Scarlet oak	*Quercus coccinea*
Scrub pine, or Virginia pine	*Pinus virginiana*
Sea lettuce	*Ulva lactuca*
Sea myrtle, groundsel bush, or groundsel tree	*Baccharis halimifolia*
Sea oats	*Uniola paniculata*
Sea rocket	*Cakile edentula*
Seaside alder	*Alnus maritima*
Seaside beardgrass	*Andropogon scoparius* var. *littoralis*
Seaside goldenrod	*Solidago sempervirens*
Shepherd's purse	*Capsella bursa-pastoris*
Shortleaf pine	*Pinus echinata*
Silky dogwood	*Cornus amomum*
Silver maple	*Acer saccharinum*

Common Name	Scientific Name
Smartweed	*Polygonum* sp.
Sourgum, or black gum	*Nyssa sylvatica*
Southern arrowwood	*Viburnum dentatum*
Southern red oak	*Quercus falcata*
Spanish moss	*Tillandsia usneoides*
Spatterdock	*Nuphar advena*
Spike grass	*Distichlis spicata*
Spruce	*Picea* sp.
Sugar maple	*Acer saccharum*
Sumac	*Rhus* sp.
Swamp black gum, water tupelo, or swamp tupelo	*Nyssa aquatica*
Swamp chestnut oak, or basket oak	*Quercus michauxii*
Swamp maple	*Acer rubrum*
Swamp pink	*Helonias bullata*
Swamp white oak	*Quercus bicolor*
Sweet pepperbush	*Clethra alnifolia*
Sweetbay magnolia	*Magnolia virginiana*
Sweetgum	*Liquidambar styraciflua*
Switchgrass	*Panicum virgatum*
Sycamore	*Platanus occidentalis*
Three-square	*Scirpus* sp.
Three-square, Olney	*Scirpus americanus (S. olneyi)*
Thistle	*Cirsium* sp.
Tide marsh water hemp	*Acnida cannabina*
Trumpet creeper	*Campsis radicans*
Tuliptree, or tulip poplar	*Liriodendron tulipifera*
Viburnum	*Viburnum* sp.
Virginia pine, or scrub pine	*Pinus virginiana*
Water lily	*Nymphaea* sp.
Water milfoil	*Myriophyllum* sp.
Water starwort	*Callitriche heterophylla*
Water tupelo	*Nyssa aquatica*
Water willow	*Decodon verticillatus*
Watershield	*Brasenia schreiberi*
Wax myrtle	*Myrica cerifera*
Wheat	*Triticum aestivum*
White oak	*Quercus alba*
White pine	*Pinus strobus*
White ash	*Fraxinus americana*
Wild black cherry	*Prunus serotina*
Wild celery	*Vallisneria americana*
Wild rice	*Zizania aquatica*
Willow	*Salix* sp.
Willow oak	*Quercus phellos*
Winged sumac	*Rhus coppalina*
Winterberry	*Ilex verticillata*
Yellow birch	*Betula allegheniensis*
Yellow-poplar, or tuliptree	*Lirodendron tulipifera*

Sources: Daiber et al. 1976; Gleason 1952; Petrides 1988; Phillips 1974; Tiner 1987.

The Breeding Bird Atlas and Relative Abundance Study Grid

The area of an average Delaware study block (one-sixth the area of a 7.5 minute U.S. Geological Survey map) is 9.64 square miles (6,170 acres), equivalent to 25 square kilometers. A total of 222 blocks were designated part of the Delaware Breeding Bird Atlas Project (map 4.1).

The 41 fractional blocks contiguous with Maryland were included as entire blocks in either the Maryland or the Delaware study by prior agreement with the Maryland Breeding Bird Atlas Project.

Four of the eight blocks shared with Pennsylvania were included in the Delaware study, though most of the area was in Delaware and therefore included fieldwork in small portions of Pennsylvania. The Pennsylvania Atlas did not do field work in Delaware. Another four shared blocks fell mainly in Pennsylvania and were not included in the Delaware study. The biggest unstudied Delaware area is 1 square mile north of Hockessin.

New Jersey territory was excluded from the two shared blocks that were part of this study.

Fifteen fractional blocks along the Delaware River and the coast were omitted as analytic units, but some of them were covered by fieldwork, as indicated on map B.1 and table B.1. Similarly, six Atlas blocks have no relative abundance data (map B.1 and table B.2).

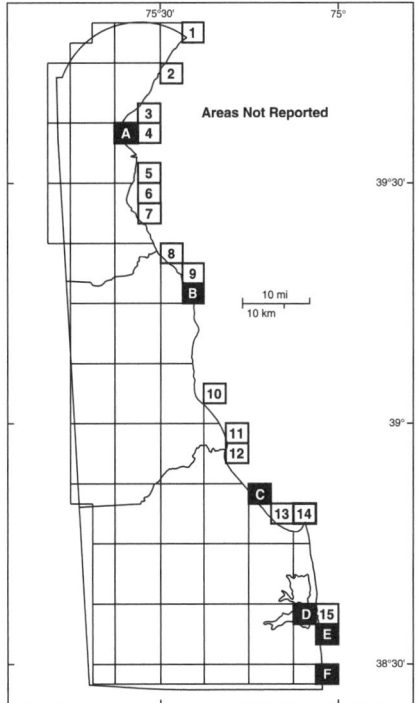

Map B.1. Portions of Delaware Not Separately Reported in the Atlas Project (white) or in the Relative Abundance Study (black)

Table B.1. Portions of Eastern Delaware Not Separately Reported in the Breeding Bird Atlas Project

1. Marcus Hook EC (east central): 0.3 sq mi. Industrial site (not studied).
2. Penns Grove NW: 0.09 sq mi. Industrial site (not studied).
3. Wilmington South SE: 0.1 sq mi. + 0.05 sq mi. Portion of town of New Castle (included in block to north), and portion of Killcohook NWR (included in block to west).
4. Delaware City NE: 0.3 sq mi. Portion of Killcohook NWR (included in block to west).
5. Delaware City SE: 0.02 + 0.02 sq mi. Portion of Reedy Island and tip of Artificial Island (not studied).
6. Taylors Bridge NE: 0.05 sq mi. Slice of Artificial Island (not studied).
7. Taylors Bridge EC: 0.8 sq mi. Marsh land north of Liston Point (not studied).
8. Bombay Hook NW: 0.5 sq mi. Marsh land north of Woodland Beach, including Persimmon Hummock and Bakeoven Point (not studied).
9. Bombay Hook EC: 0.4 sq mi. Bombay Hook Point (included in block to west).
10. Bennetts Pier WC (west central): 0.04 sq mi. Sandy Point, south of South Bowers Beach (not studied).
11. Mispillion River NE: 0.03 sq mi. Section of beach north of Mispillion Lighthouse (not studied).
12. Mispillion River EC: 0.02 sq mi. Mainly islands along Mispillion Jetty (included in block to west).
13. Lewes EC: 0.6 sq mi. Beach Plum Island and portion of Great Marsh (included in block to west; Least Tern on island included in block to south).
14. Cape Henlopen WC: 0.2 sq mi. Tip of Cape Henlopen (included in block to south).

Table B.1. Portions of Eastern Delaware . . .   (continued)

15. Bethany Beach NE: 0.3 sq mi. Beach south of Indian River Inlet (included in block to west).

Note: Numbers correspond to those in Map B.1.

Table B.2. Atlas Blocks Not Separately Reported in the Relative Abundance Study

A. Delaware City NW: This block contains an industrial site and Pea Patch Island. There was too little land area, not suitable for a 15-stop route; not included in the study.
B. Bombay Hook SE: This block is a treeless tidal marsh. It was combined with (and reported in) the block to the south with similar habitat. Roughly half of the area of each block lies in the Delaware River. The survey route was run by canoe with five stops in the two blocks (multiplied by three for the report).
C. Lewes NW: This almost roadless block contains insufficient land for a survey route; not included in the study.
D. Bethany Beach NE: This block, which contains Indian River Bay, has insufficient land area for a 15-stop route. It was combined with (and reported in) the block to the north, which contains Rehoboth Bay and is insufficient by itself for a route.
E. and F. Bethany Beach SE and Assawoman Bay NE: These blocks were reported as part of the block between them. The survey route comprised five stops in each block. None could support a route by itself.

Note: Letters correspond to those shown on Map B.1.

A relative abundance study was conducted during 1985–87, the last three years of the Delaware Breeding Bird Atlas project, using a miniroute technique based on the BBS point counts. The technique, developed by Bystrak (1980), was applied to the Howard County, Maryland, breeding bird atlas in 1973 (Klimkiewicz and Solem 1974), and evaluated in Maryland by Robbins and Dowell (1986). A route of 15 three-minute point counts spaced about 0.5 miles apart was run in each Atlas block. In blocks where the possible number of roadside stops fell short of 15, supplementary stops were made on foot or by canoe. When an Atlas partial block contained insufficient land area, two or three blocks were combined, providing a grid of 216 blocks for the relative abundance study (see appendix B). Lists of species identified (but not numbers) were recorded, and the results for each block were stated as the number of stops, 15 or fewer, at which a species was identified—yielding a frequency index rather than total numbers found. Most stops were made during the two and a half hours after sunup, between 25 May and 5 July. Care was taken to minimize bias in selection of stops, times, and personnel.

The relative abundance study recorded on a gridded map the number of stops at which a species was detected. The term "relative abundance" in fact denotes relative frequency of detection, which is obviously correlated with abundance. Chi-square tests ($p < .05$) were used to determine significant differences in population among the counties or among other groups of blocks where differences in habitat persisted. Since only a single sample of 15 stops was made in each block, differences between individual blocks should not be emphasized; groups of 4 blocks (60 stops) or 9 blocks (135 stops) give more reliable comparisons. The raw data could have been smoothed by computer, but for the limited number of 216 blocks, smoothing by eye is more informative. A map of the total number of species found in each block indicates species richness by block (map 4.5, in chapter 4).

Because effectiveness of detection by this technique varies greatly among the various species, the technique is not a basis for comparisons among species; it indicates only differences in the occurrence of a single species among different parts of the state. For example, Ovenbirds and Common Grackles are much more easily detected than Blue-gray Gnatcatchers and Ruby-throated Hummingbirds. Nocturnal birds, vultures and hawks, and ducks are not easily monitored by this technique.

Eighty-eight of the most meaningful relative abundance maps are presented in the species accounts along with the breeding distribution maps provided by the Atlas study. These give added information about differences in populations.

Breeding Dates and Clutch Sizes

Estimated Clutch-completion Dates

We describe the breeding season for 80 species for which we had ten or more dated breeding records by displaying bar graphs of estimated clutch-completion dates derived from these records. These clutch-completion bar graphs direct attention to the ten-day periods of high breeding activity. This approach has the advantage of focusing on a specific biological event, whose date is estimated from data for nests containing eggs or young or for recently fledged young. Clutch-completion dates can be estimated within several days if the degree of incubation is given by the egg collector, or if observations from more than one nest visit are recorded on a nest card, or if the development stage or weight of the nestling is reported. If the degree of incubation or development is not reported, the observation is assumed to be made half-way through either the incubation or nestling period, respectively (Johnston 1964, Peakall 1970). This assumption leads to an uncertainty of half a period, or about plus or minus one week for many passerines. This variance, which is usually canceled out by the number of observations grouped around the peak nesting period, has a side effect of sometimes extending the ends of the clutch-completion bar graphs beyond the extremes of actual observations of clutches. These bar graphs show the peak of initial breeding fairly accurately, but the shapes may be biased by our sources of data.

Egg collectors and other nest hunters before the mid-twentieth century undoubtedly prized large clutches of fresh eggs. The best of them followed the progress of a nest until no more eggs were laid, and then collected the eggs. This assured them a full clutch of fresh eggs. Since first clutches tended to be larger, and competition was inevitable, they tended to collect early in the season, beating others to the best clutches.

Nest record programs began to proliferate in the United States in the 1960s, Cornell's in 1963 (Peakall 1964, 1969). Delaware's program began in 1964 (Stickley 1964; Jones 1967; Hubbard 1974) and was summarized by Niles (1980) and Baer (1989). These programs solicited adventitious nest records and encouraged multiple nest visits and habitat documentation. Such records are likely biased toward the earlier part of the breeding season when enthusiasm is higher, the promise of results greater, and the weather cooler. Overwhelming bias arose from visits to colonies, such as when over 100 tern nests were found in one day, or from intensive efforts such as the U.S. Fish and Wildlife Service one-day nest box check for Wood Ducks; records from these sources were not used for the clutch-completion bar graphs.

Breeding Bird Atlas records are concentrated in the perceived middle of the breeding season, away from migration and dispersal periods, as set forth by the safe dates for Atlas field work. Consequently most Atlas observations were made in June.

All three of the preceding sources seem to be biased in favor of early or first nestings, a bias that becomes especially apparent for species with extended breeding seasons. For example, these sources indicate that Mourning Dove breeding in Delaware tapers off in July, a finding inconsistent with information from other states, which record breeding into September (Swank 1955; Robbins and Bystrak 1977). The records of Tri-State Bird Rescue and Research (TSBR) were examined for fledgling Mourning Doves brought in for rehabilitation; TSBR routinely records the date each bird was found and the weight and condition of the bird on its arrival. The weights of the young doves can be related to age (Nice 1922) and thus to clutch-completion dates. These data, although biased toward suburban habitats, should not have a strong seasonal bias. In fact, they show that Mourning Dove breeding continues strongly throughout July and August and into September (Baer 1992). (See clutch-completion bar graph in Mourning Dove species account.) This is consistent with the findings of others and tends to validate this source of information, so we also used similar nestling data for other species.

TSBR data on the weights of young birds, mostly premature fledglings, brought in for care (1983–92) were combined with the other data to give a broader view of the breeding season for 17 species. Since the fledgling data come from an untested source, they are denoted by open bars in the clutch-completion graphs in the species accounts; solid bars denote nest record data.

Clutch-Completion Dates and Multibroods

Interpretation of clutch-completion bar graphs led to discussion of whether or not various species are multibrooded, that is, lay additional clutches after successfully fledging at least one young.

Some species were shown to be double-brooded by clearly separated peaks of clutch completion for the first and second broods (e.g., Eastern Bluebird). In other instances separate peaks were less obvious or not present because the breeding rhythm was obscured by (1) renestings after failure at various points in the breeding cycle (e.g., Wood Thrush), (2) variation in onset of breeding caused by variations in weather conditions or food supply (especially cuckoos), (3) variation in onset time based on age (e.g., Purple Martin), or (4) second broods so infrequent that they do not register as a distinct peak. When two or more peaks are not shown on the clutch-completion bar graph, the length of the breeding season and the shape of the bar graph, especially the relative number of clutches reported a month or more after the peak of initial clutches, give some indication of the frequency of second broods. Also late clutches frequently result from renestings after one or more failures.

The ornithological literature is often vague on evidence for double-broodedness, sometimes citing merely a late nest or instances of a second brood in the same territory where breeding has been observed earlier in the breeding season. Better studies use color-marked females. Rarely is the extent of double-broodedness known.

Some exemplary studies have been conducted, providing a model of information that can be obtained. Nolan (1978) determined that 78% of the female Prairie Warblers that successfully fledged a first brood at his Indiana study site attempted a second brood on the same territory, and that if the first brood succeeded by 10 June, 73% of the females did so. In this benchmark study Nolan was not able to determine how many females attempted a second brood away from his study area, but he thought it likely that nearly all females that produced fledglings by 10 June nested again, either on or off the study area.

Discussions presented in the species accounts attempt to shed some light on the existence and importance of second broods for various species in Delaware.

Clutch Size

The distribution of clutch sizes is summarized from sizes reported in Delaware, information sometimes derived from single observations of nests. Clutch sizes based only on repeated observations, which would detect incomplete clutches and egg losses, would average higher values. Clutch distribution is presented in various ways in the text—lists, tables, middle 50%, or average, range and mode—using whatever means seemed best to communicate our data without introducing errors from possibly incomplete clutches. The number of observations in which a summary is based is indicated, for example, $n = 20$. Reference is made to Harrison (1978) or information from nearby states when Delaware data are insufficient.

Breeding Bird Survey

The ten Delaware Breeding Bird Survey (BBS) routes are covered by volunteers; the methods and analysis are provided by the U.S. Fish and Wildlife Service. Each route, comprising 50 three-minute stops made at 0.5-mile intervals, is covered once between 25 May and 30 June via roadside routes set up to randomly sample Delaware birdlife (see maps 4.2a, b, and c). Species and numbers seen or heard at each stop are recorded. An average of eight of the ten routes per year have been run since 1965.

Trend Calculation

The description here is condensed from Robbins et al. (1986, 177). The average annual trend for a species is calculated by a route regression method. A trend is first calculated for each route using linear regression to estimate the slope of the logarithmic transformed counts. These route estimates are combined to estimate the population trends, by species, for physiographic strata, states, or regions. In combining the route trends, they are weighted for (1) relative area represented by each route, (2) abundance of the species on each route, and (3) number of years' data for each route. The weighted estimates for each physiographic strata, state, or region are back-transformed from the logarithmic scale to the original scale to produce the average annual rate of change. Variances are calculated using the jackknife method.

Results

The 1965–79 results have been published with discussions of the trends for many species from a continental and a regional perspective in Robbins et al. 1986. For purposes of this book, unpublished summary calculations were provided by S. J. Droege and B. G. Peterjohn of the Office of Migratory Bird Management, U.S. Geological Survey, Biological Resources Division. They include 25- and 10-year summaries (1966–90 and 1981–90) for Delaware and the East and 1966–90 summaries for the Upper Coastal Plain.

BBS data for the East (see map 5.1) are robust because many routes are included. They give a good indication of what species are increasing or decreasing but little specific information for Delaware; they serve as a means of comparison when more specific information is not available. The BBS trends for Delaware and the East are listed in appendix I and compared with Spring Count and CBC trends for Delaware.

The Upper Coastal Plain encompasses the Delmarva Peninsula, the Coastal Plain of New Jersey and Maryland, and most of Virginia's Coastal Plain; it continues as an interior strip that extends to Texas (see map 5.1). Trends for the Upper Coastal Plain are particularly useful to us for about 30 species whose ranges in this physiographic region are restricted to the Coastal Plain near the Delmarva Peninsula, for example, the Glossy Ibis, Osprey, Bald Eagle, Northern Harrier, Willet, Least Tern, Black Skimmer, Cedar Waxwing, Vesper Sparrow, Seaside Sparrow, and Swamp Sparrow.

Advantages and Limitations

The BBS, designed to provide comparative data on a random sample from year to year, yields reliable results from a small amount of data. Careful analysis by U.S. Fish and Wildlife Service statisticians gives a solid basis for management decisions. However, the BBS does not satisfactorily sample nocturnal species, marsh species, raptors, or particularly those species already rare. Delaware is transected by only ten routes, the minimum for sound statistical analysis. If a species is rare, or does not range statewide, it may not be recorded on some routes or may be found too seldom for reliable analysis.

APPENDIX F *Breeding Bird Census*

A total of 26 Breeding Bird Censuses (BBCs) in Delaware have been reported in *Audubon Field Notes*, 1965–70. (See "Breeding Bird Census" in chapter 5 for a description of this technique.) The BBCs concentrated on eight urban woodlots on or near the Piedmont in northern Delaware, but they also included two sites at the marsh edge in Assawoman Wildlife Area. The list of Delaware BBCs in table F.1 includes sources for BBC studies of an additional seven sites. The most useful of these sources compiles seven woodlot censuses, 1965–72, discussed by Martin (1976).

Table F.1. List of Delaware Breeding Bird Census Sites

Coastal Plain

1. Coastal Lowland Mixed Woods [Assawoman WA] (Linehan 1965a; Ward et al. 1966; Linehan 1969b)
2. Saltmarsh Edge [Assawoman WA] (Linehan 1965c, 1966b)
3. Coastal Lowland Mixed Woods, Strawberry Landing [Assawoman WA] (McLaughlin 1966)
4. Phragmites Brackish Marshes [Ted Harvey CA] (Moore 1989)
5. Saltmarsh [Prime Hook NWR] (West 1993)

Piedmont Woodlots

6. Uneven-aged Mixed Hardwood Forest (Urban Woodlot) [University Woodlot] (Longcore et al. 1966; Linehan et al. 1967b; Jones and Steiner 1968; Jones 1969c, 1970; Martin, 1976)
7. Mature Tulip Poplar Forest (Suburban Woodlot) [Brandywine Creek SP] (West et al. 1966; West 1967)
8. Uneven-aged Sweet Gum–Red Maple–Beech Forest (Urban woodlot) [Weldin Road woodlot] (Longcore and Jones 1966; Jones 1967b)
9. Uneven-aged Red Maple–Tulip Poplar Forest (Urban Woodlot) [Avon Woodlot] (Jones et al. 1966; Linehan and Burr 1967a; Linehan 1968c, Linehan and Jones 1969)
10. Uneven-aged Sweet Gum–Red Maple Forest (Urban Woodlot) [Heritage Park Woodlot] (Jones and Longcore 1966; Jones and Faust 1967; Faust and Jones 1968; Martin 1976)
11. Mixed Deciduous Floodplain Woodlot (Urban Woodlot) I and II [Windy Hills Woodlots] (Jones and Burr 1967; Burr and Jones 1968; Jones and Burr 1968; Martin 1976)
12. Second Growth Tulip Poplar–Red Oak woods (Urban Woodlot), Beech–Oak Woodlot (Urban Woodlot) [SE & SW Cloverleaves of Interstate 95 and Delaware 896] (Jones 1967a, 1968, 1969b)
13. Beech–Maple Woodland Nature Center (Urban Woodlot) [Maclary Elementary School and Nature Center] (Jones 1969a)
14. Mixed Mesophytic Forest [White Clay Creek] (West 1970)
15. Urban Woodlands [Banning Park] (Martin 1976)
16. Urban Woodlands [Rittenhouse Park] (Martin 1976)
17. Urban Woodlands [Pike Creek Valley] (Martin 1976)

Note: Some student BBCs were not analyzed (DO 6:25-29).

The woodlot censuses conducted in 1966–67, discussed by Linehan et al. (1967), are unique in two ways. First, the standard census trips were strongly supplemented by nest searching and, in some instances, by netting and banding. Second, they were conducted and calculated to cover entire woodlots, including the edges. The results were population densities for some species of about 50% higher than given by standard techniques. For a woods interior species such as the Wood Thrush, the Linehan results are consistent with work later done by Roth, if one accepts that there was an intervening population drop of about 30% (Roth, pers. comm.). The results show that a given acreage of woodlot can support a high concentration of breeding birds, but the extent of the use of open area adjacent to the breeding territories is difficult to assess. For example, 6 pairs of Great Crested Flycatchers were reported from a 27-acre woodlot (22 pairs per 40 ha). It seems unlikely that 6 pairs would be compressed into contiguous 4.5-acre territories if there were no added open areas on the edges for their feeding forays. The highest Great Crested Flycatcher density for interior woods reported for Maryland by Stewart and Robbins (1958) was 8 per 40 ha. The Linehan study demonstrates the ability of the species to utilize edges of woodlots.

May Counts (Delaware Spring Roundup)

We analyzed the May Counts for the period 1969–91 in such a way as to get an average annual rate of change that could be compared with the results of the Breeding Bird Survey (West 1992). The state was divided into six areas (Rufe 1985), and a count of individuals and species was conducted in each area on a Saturday between 3 and 14 May. The leader for each area recruited as many people as possible and sent the team into known good-birding spots to maximize the area's count of species. Double coverage of areas was avoided. The result was quasi-annual coverage of a wide variety of habitats throughout the state and regular annual coverage of the most important ones—the shoreline, national wildlife refuges, and many of the state parks, state forests, and wildlife management areas.

Indexing

Party-hours were not recorded for every year, and even when such records were kept, the hours spent in owling, sea watching, and counting shorebirds were not separated from those spent in upland habitats. For trend analysis, an "index of effective effort" was devised by selecting for reference ten widespread upland birds that appeared to have stable populations in the East, according to the BBC (table G.1). For each of the ten species, the count for each year was divided by the species' average annual count for the 1969–91 period. The results for each year for all ten species were averaged to obtain the mean quotient, or yearly index, which ranged from 0.68 to 1.35. The year's totals for each species were then divided by the index figure for that year (instead of by party-hours) to compensate for varying effort from year to year:

(Number recorded) / (Effort index) = "Count"

Table G.1. Species Selected for Indexing

Species	% Change on BBS in East
Red-bellied Woodpecker	0
Downy Woodpecker	0
American Crow	1
Carolina Chickadee	0
Tufted Titmouse	0
House Wren	0
American Robin	1
Northern Mockingbird	−1
European Starling	−1
Northern Cardinal	0
TOTAL CHANGE (1969–90)	0

The index and the number of party-hours increase in parallel, though not exactly, at about 3% per year (fig. G.1). The net result of indexing is to adjust the number of upland birds seen to reflect what would have been seen on a May Count with average party-hours (about 270 hours). All species that appeared on the May Count in at least half the years and that averaged at least one per year during 1969–91 were analyzed with the regression: $\ln(\text{Count}) = A + B\ln(\text{Year})$. Out of 222 species, 13 (owls, shorebirds, and pelagics) were dropped from this study because the indexing method was obviously not applicable. The population changes of resident species revealed by the May Count analysis are quite similar to those derived from BBSs or CBCs (figs. G.2 and G.3).

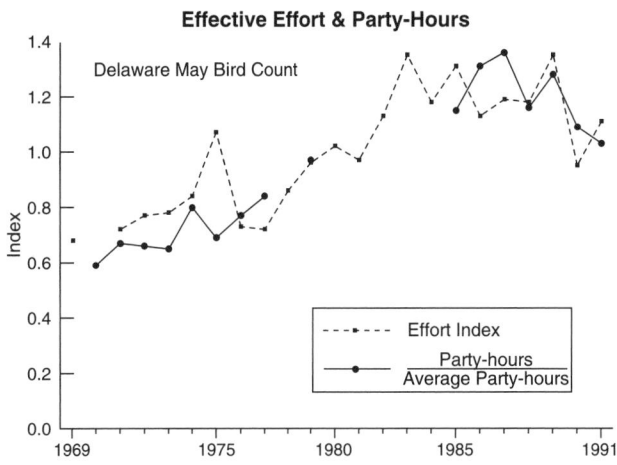

Figure G.1 Effective Effort and Party-Hours

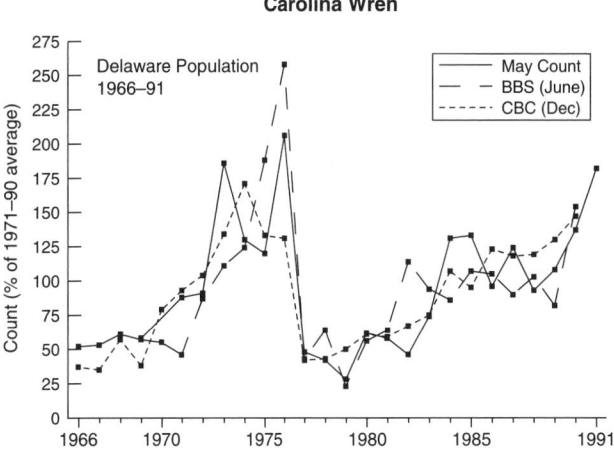

Figure G.2 Carolina Wren Populations by Three Methods

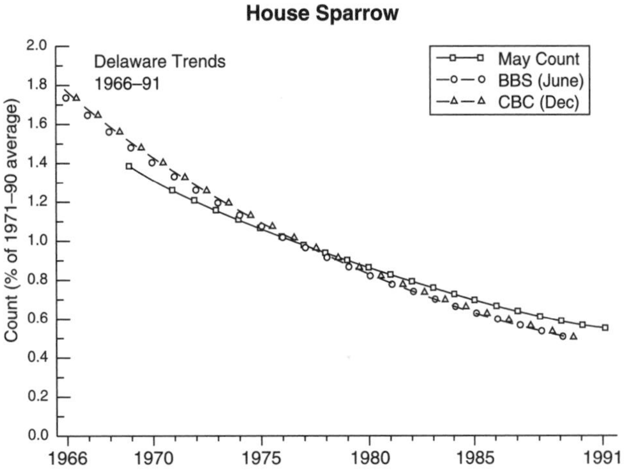

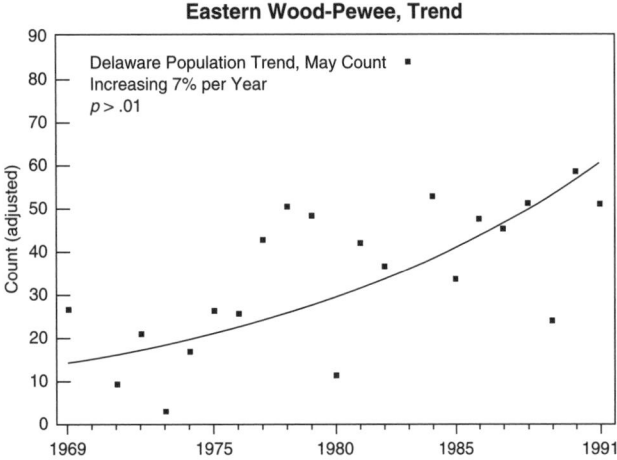

House Sparrow

Delaware Trends
1966–91

Legend:
- May Count
- BBS (June)
- CBC (Dec)

Y-axis: Count (% of 1971–90 average)

Figure G.3 House Sparrow Trends by Three Methods

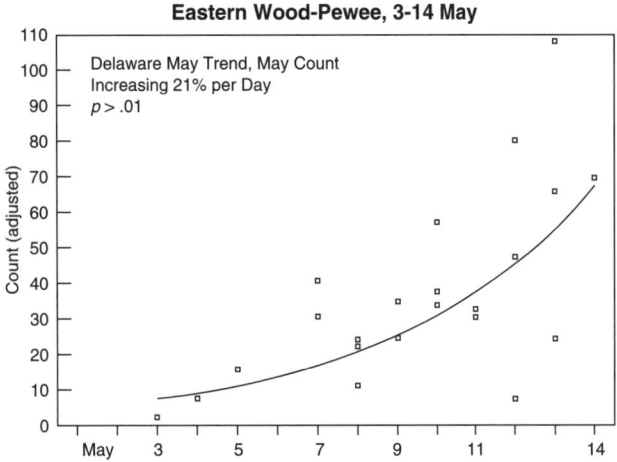

Eastern Wood-Pewee, Trend

Delaware Population Trend, May Count ■
Increasing 7% per Year
$p > .01$

Y-axis: Count (adjusted)

Figure G.4 Eastern Wood-Pewee, Annual Trend

Eastern Wood-Pewee, 3-14 May

Delaware May Trend, May Count
Increasing 21% per Day
$p > .01$

Y-axis: Count (adjusted)

Figure G.5 Eastern Wood-Pewee, May Trend

Adjustment for May Date

The date of the count varied from 3 May to 14 May, introducing a large source of variation in the numbers of migrating species. Migratory species were thus examined by multiple regression, with year and day as variables: $\ln(\text{Count}) = A + B\ln(\text{Year}) + C\ln(\text{Date})$. The results revealed both annual and daily trends. For example, the Eastern Wood-Pewee was found to be increasing ($p < .001$) at an average annual rate of about 7% for 1969–91 (fig. G.4), and increasing ($p < .001$) at an average daily rate of 21% for the period 3–14 May consistent with its migration dates (fig. G.5).

Of the 209 species analyzed, 71 showed an annual trend ($p < .05$), and 18 had a possible trend ($p < .10$). There was no aggregate trend for Delaware; the decreases of some species canceled the increases of others.

Advantages and Limitations

This method counts a large number of birds and includes migrants not sampled by the BBS or CBC. Its weakness is the lack of control over the participants, many of whom make the count simply for the fun of it. Several persist in not keeping numbers. Annual coverage of specialized habitats such as cordgrass marshes or pine forests may not be consistent.

The trend results are tabulated in appendix I.

CBC Circles

The Wilmington count, started in 1962, was moved 3 miles west in 1965 to its present location centered on Newport Gap Pike near the southwest corner of Brandywine Springs Recreation Area: 39°44'32"N, 75°38'29"W.

The Middletown Count, run intermittently since 1931, was started again in 1966 and moved 2.25 miles west in 1968 to its present location, reducing its extension into New Jersey. Its western edge is tangent with the state line, the center is 2 miles from Odessa at 60 degrees: 38°48'32"N, 75°11'12"W.

The Bombay Hook Count, started in 1939, was moved 2 miles southeast in 1954 to its present location centered 2 miles south of the old Bombay Hook NWR headquarters: 39°13'N, 75°27'W.

The Cape Henlopen–Prime Hook Count, started in 1964, was moved 2 miles southeast in 1966 to its present location centered in Delaware Bay: 38°48'32"N, 75°11'12"W.

The Rehoboth Count, started in 1953, was moved 6.5 miles southeast in 1956 close to its present location centered in Indian River Bay. In the early 1970s the center was shifted somewhat west and south: 38°36'N, 75°5.7'W.

The Seaford–Nanticoke Count, started in 1983, is centered at the intersection of state roads 468 and 470: 38°35'5"N, 74°33'41"W.

Fifteen-mile diameter circles, constructed by our cartographer on the previously mentioned centers and shown on the road maps (figs. 4.2a, b, and c, in chapter 4), correspond closely to the maps used by the CBC participants.

CBC Analysis for Long-Term Trends

The five Delaware CBCs run with constant participation since 1966 are ideal for analysis for long-term trends. Each circle was subdivided permanently into territories to be covered by a party. CBC trend graphs in this book show the average of the number of birds found per party-hour (which is the "Count") for these five Delaware CBCs plotted against the years of the counts.

The CBC population trend for each species for 1966–89 was calculated by regressing the linear equation: $\ln(\text{Count}) = A + B(\text{Year})$. The slope term, B, of this equation is used to calculate the average rate of change, or trend (Robbins et al. 1986; Geisler and Sauer 1990):

Average rate of change = $1 - \text{antiln}[B - 1/2(\text{variance of } B)]$

The significance of the trend was evaluated using the F-test, and the probability given is that the trend was the result of chance alone: $p < .05$ (Sokal and Rohlf 1981).

Those species that showed a significant trend were examined for autocorrelation using the Durbin-Watson test (Netter et al. 1989). Eight species showing autocorrelation by this test are noted, and less importance can be attached to their trend.

The plots of some species, showing a definite peak or minimum, were regressed using the nonlinear equation: $\ln(\text{Count}) = A + B(\text{Year}) + C(\text{Year})^2$. Seventeen species that had not fit the linear regression showed significant fits to this curve. From this curve one can see the approximate time of peak or minimum numbers and the current direction of the trend. Other species were irruptive, flocking, scarce, or otherwise unsuitable for these trend analyses.

We present figures for the species that seem to have significant CBC trends, but we must emphasize that, since field work was not rigorously controlled, the statistical results are merely suggestions of trends and not reliable proofs of them. The CBC trend results are tabulated in appendix I.

Zeros in the CBC Calculations

Reports of no birds in a given year for a species being analyzed required special handling. In the CBC tables, years with zero counts are not included when giving the range of numbers reported. Zero years are included in calculating the median count. In the CBC bar graphs, the state averages do not include CBC circles that never reported the species during the 24-year analysis period. In calculating long-term trends, 0.1 bird is added to the counts of all species each year so as to avoid taking the log of zero birds in a year when none of a species was reported.

Table I.1 presents long-term trends of bird populations in Delaware as determined by three different studies. The methods of collecting and analyzing the data are discussed in chapter 5 and appendices E, G, and H.

The bird populations analyzed in the three different seasons—winter, spring, migration, and breeding—are frequently not the same. For example, far fewer Brown Thrashers winter in Delaware than breed here, and additional transients pass through in May. Wintering Canada Geese overwhelm the much smaller number of semidomestic ones that breed here. Yet Bobwhite, Rock Doves, Tufted Titmice, Cardinals, and a number of other species are sedentary, and their numbers should exhibit similar changes in each seasonal analysis (see figs. G.2 and G.3). Population trends calculated for the East do not always agree with the Delaware trends, because of special factors affecting Delaware birds and because some of the Delaware calculations are based on few data.

The data gathered by each study are biased. The CBCs are set in national wildlife refuges and other "good" birding areas. On the Spring Counts, birders out for fun try to see how many different species they can find, and only as an aside count numbers and report party-hours. The BBS is limited to roadsides, where real estate development proceeds at its most rapid pace.

Our analysis periods for the three counts begin in the 1960s when insectivore and raptor populations were probably still depressed from the impact of widespread DDT use. Using tape recorders as a birding tool became popular, causing a bias in counts of owls and other species that respond to recordings of their vocalizations. As development occurs and removes one marsh or patch of woods as habitat, another patch is substituted, so that habitat loss is not fully reflected in the trends.

The population changes over 25 years that have been documented by these studies are large enough to be apparent, even though the field methods were not rigorous. Population changes of less than ±1.5% annually are tabulated as zero change unless the trend is statistically significant; these seemingly small rates, compounded over 24 years, amount to a range from +43% to –30%.

Some statistical rigor was maintained in the analysis of these data. The U.S. Fish and Wildlife Service developed a route regression method that compensated for some of the problems with the data collection and calculated the median trend and statistical significance using a bootstrapping technique (Robbins et al. 1986). The CBC and Spring Count used similar regression equations, but trend and significance are derived from the regression calculation. Some numbers displayed have little calculated statistical significance; those accompanied by an asterisk have a probability of less than .05 that there is no trend (see the footnote to the table). The annual change given is not to be taken as more than an estimate; a plus or minus alone indicates only a possiblity of a change

Long-term trends may obscure other population changes. In some cases the direction of trends has changed in the past ten years; some populations changes are cyclical or affected by weather or food availability. A lack of fit to a long-term trend model may simply mean that the wrong model was used.

Table I.1. Avian Population Trends in Delaware, 1966–91

Species Name	Christmas Count 1966–89		May Count 1969–91		Breeding Bird Survey 1966–89 Delaware			East
	Rate	Median	Rate	Avg	Rate	No. of Rts	Avg	Rate
Red-throated Loon	–	101	–	5				
Common Loon	+	14	4%	9				2%*
Pied-billed Grebe	–6%**	33	–7%**	5				0
Horned Grebe	–6%*	98	–	2				
Double-crested Cormorant	11%**	24	11%**	727	+	4	2	8%**
American Bittern	–5%**	4	3%	2	–	2	0.2	1%
Least Bittern			–6%*	5				0
Great Blue Heron	inc**	188	5%**	103	4%**	10	9	3%**
Great Egret		3	0	131	+	7	5	–
Snowy Egret			2%	172	+	5	6	+
Little Blue Heron			+	17	–	4	0.4	– –
Tricolored Heron			–	3				– –
Cattle Egret			–5%**	428	13%*	9	27	+ +
Green Heron			–2%*	65	–	10	9	–
Black-crowned Night-Heron	dec**	13	–	37	+	5	1	+

Table I.1. Avian Population Trends in Delaware, 1966–91 (continued)

Species Name	Christmas Count 1966–89 Rate	Median	May Count 1969–91 Rate	Avg	Breeding Bird Survey 1966–89 Delaware Rate	No. of Rts	Avg	East Rate
Glossy Ibis			4%*	199	+	6	13	+
Black Vulture	8%**	24	12%**	12	+	7	1	+
Turkey Vulture	0	459	2%*	249	−	10	43	2% +
Snow Goose	33%**	10449						
Canada Goose	dec**	56022	−4%**	349	+	7	5	10%**
Brant	−	2122						
Mute Swan	irr		12 −11%**	11				14%**
Tundra Swan	dec**	239						
Wood Duck	+	6	2%*	70	−2%*	8	2	3%**
Gadwall	0	190	−5%*	79				0
American Wigeon	dec**	188	−14%**	5				7%**
Am. Black Duck	−4%**	6301	0	151	+	8	4	−
Mallard	−	5211	3%**	228	6%*	9	12	4%**
Blue-winged Teal			−8%**	72	4%**	3	1	+
Shoveller	−8%	211						1%**
Northern Pintail	dec**	1182						+
Green-winged Teal	+	395	+	41				1%
Canvasback	−4%*	915	0	2				
Redhead	−	5						
Ring-necked Duck	−7%**	16						0
Greater Scaup	−11%**	1244						
Lesser Scaup	0	147	0	1				1%
Surf Scoter	−	144						
White-winged Scoter	−	51						
Black Scoter	−	135	0	6				
Oldsquaw	0	109						
Bufflehead	0	907	0	5				
Common Goldeneye	−5%*	249						−2%
Hooded Merganser	3%	38						−1%
Common Merganser	dec**	141	5%*	1				+ +
Red-breasted Merganser	−7%**	187	+	10				−
Ruddy Duck	irr	759	−14%**	35				
Osprey			7%**	53	−	6	8	4%**
Bald Eagle	inc**	4	7%**	3				3%**
Northern Harrier	0	165	4%**	10		2	0.2	2%*
Sharp-shinned Hawk	11%*	23				2	0.1	0
Cooper's Hawk	6%*	5				2	0.1	1% +
Red-shouldered Hawk	0	7	0	5	0	3	1	0 +
Broad-winged Hawk			−3%	5	−2%	4	0.2	+
Red-tailed Hawk	2%**	158	5%**	28	2%	9	3	2%**
Rough-legged Hawk	−3%*	23						
American Kestrel	−2%**	194	−4%**	22	−	8	4	+
Merlin			+	1				+
Rg-necked Pheasant	−8%**	42	−6%**	48	−7%	8	4	−3%*
Northern Bobwhite	−7%**	225	−3%**	123	−	10	333	−3%**
Clapper Rail	irr	9			+	5	4	+
King Rail		1	−5%	6				−3%*
Sora			0	3				0
Common Moorhen			0	16				0
American Coot	−18%*	335						−2%**
Blk-bellied Plover	+	15						
Piping Plover			−5%	4				
Killdeer	−	103	+	52	−	10	30	1% +
American Oystercatcher			10 **	7				8%**
Black-necked Stilt			+	25				0
Greater Yellowlegs	7%*	5						
Lesser Yellowlegs	4%irr	5						
Willet			4%**	518	8%	5	68	2%
Spotted Sandpiper			0	66	−	2	0.1	−1%

Table I.1. Avian Population Trends in Delaware, 1966–91 (continued)

Species Name	Christmas Count 1966–89		May Count 1969–91		Breeding Bird Survey 1966–89 Delaware			East
	Rate	Median	Rate	Avg	Rate	No. of Rts	Avg	Rate
Ruddy Turnstone	irr	56						
Sanderling	inc	380						
Purple Sandpiper	–	23						
Dunlin	4%irr	1161						
Common Snipe	–	33	–6%	7				0
American Woodcock	–	6	–6%*	16	–3%*	4	0.2	–
Laughing Gull			4%	6887	–1%	8	283	7%**
Bonaparte's Gull	–	303	–	32				+
Ring-billed Gull	5%**	6046	5%	1300	–	7	24	10%**
Herring Gull	–5%**	6286	0	916	2%	8	36	–
Great Black-backed Gull	2%*	552	+	205	–	5	7	–
Common Tern			–9%**	198	–6%**	4	29	–5%**
Forster's Tern	+	4	13%**	49	+	5	1	16%**
Least Tern			+	154	+	5	30	–
Black Skimmer			–	82	–11%**	4	10	–
Rock Dove	2%*	1301	0	220	–	10	72	+ +
Mourning Dove	2%*	1873	+	315	3%*	10	152	+ +
Black-billed Cuckoo			0	5	–	9	2	+
Yellow-billed Cuckoo			+	32	6%**	10	23	–2%**
Barn Owl	dec**	9						0
Eastern Screech-Owl	dec**	71			+	4	0.2	0
Great Horned Owl	2%	100			0	7	2	+ +
Barred Owl	–	4			–3%	5	0.6	+ +
Short-eared Owl	–	12						–
Common Nighthawk			+	6	–10%*	4	8	–2%*
Chuck-will's-widow			+	17	3%	5	2	–2%*
Whip-poor-will			0	31	–6%**	7	6	–1%–
Chimney Swift			–	248	–8%*	10	77	–1%*
Ruby-throated Hummingbird			+	22	–	9	2	+
Belted Kingfisher	0	79	0	18	0	9	2	–1%*
Red-headed Woodpecker		1	0	2	0	2	0.1	–2%**
Red-bellied Woodpecker	0	198	1%*	142	+	10	47	0 +
Yellow-bellied Sapsucker	3%	9						–2%
Downy Woodpecker	0	315	0	67	+	10	14	0
Hairy Woodpecker	–1%*	45	0	13	0	9	2	1%*
Northern Flicker	0	253	–2%**	145	–	10	30	–3%**
Pileated Woodpecker			6%**	6	–	4	0.4	2%**
Eastern Wood-Pewee			7%**	44	0	10	30	–1%*
Acadian Flycatcher			0	41	–	9	13	0
Willow Flycatcher					2%**	3	0.2	7%**
Least Flycatcher			–7%*	2				–2%*
Eastern Phoebe		1	3%**	35	0	10	10	0
Great Crested Flycatcher			0	97	–8%**	10	21	0
Eastern Kingbird			2%*	161	–2%*	10	22	0 –
White-eyed Vireo			2%*	222	2%	10	36	0
Yellow-throated Vireo			0	22	2%	10	3	0 +
Blue-headed Vireo0			–	4				4%**
Warbling Vireo			–	6	–	7	1	0
Red-eyed Vireo			+	299	3%*	10	75	2%**
Blue Jay	0	1017	–	607	0	10	98	–2%**
American Crow	dec*	1873	0	353	0	10	201	1% +
Fish Crow	dec**	319	3%*	160	+	10	39	3%*
Horned Lark	–10%**	352	0	29	0	10	42	0 –
Purple Martin			7%**	248	8%*	10	72	0
Tree Swallow		6	–	2758	0	9	6	1% +
Northern Rough-winged Swallow			+	49	3%**	10	8	2%*
Bank Swallow			0	87	–	5	2	0 –
Cliff Swallow			–	1				0
Barn Swallow			–	1719	+	10	188	0
Carolina Chickadee	0	846	0	214	0	10	31	0

Table I.1. *Avian Population Trends in Delaware, 1966–91* (continued)

Species Name	Christmas Count 1966–89		May Count 1969–91		Breeding Bird Survey 1966–89 Delaware			East
	Rate	Median	Rate	Avg	Rate	No. of Rts	Avg	Rate
Tufted Titmouse	0	353	–1%*	184	– –	10	66	0 +
Red-breasted Nuthatch	+	22	–	2				3%**
White-breasted Nuthatch	0	109	–	9	0	3	0.1	2%**
Brown-headed Nuthatch	–8%**	18	–5%**	7	–5%**	2	0.2	0
Brown Creeper	0	41	–	1				0 +
Carolina Wren	+	233	+	107	–	10	52	0 +
House Wren		1	–1%	116	–4%	10	16	1% +
Winter Wren	–	11						+ +
Sedge Wren		1	–7%*	2	0	2	0.1	+ –
Marsh Wren		7	7%**	204	0	5	8	0
Golden-crowned Kinglet	0	100						6%*
Ruby-crowned Kinglet	–4%	25	–	11				–2%*
Blue-gray Gnatcatcher			3%**	84	0	9	2	0
Eastern Bluebird	17%**	45	10%**	24	0	6	4	1%*
Veery			0	44				–1% –
Gray-cheeked Thrush			–8%**	1				+
Swainson's Thrush			–	9				0
Hermit Thrush	+	47	–	2				2% +
Wood Thrush			0	332	7%**	10	108	–2%**
American Robin	–3%	1591	1%*	872	4%**	10	325	1%**
Gray Catbird	7%**	20	0	515	0	10	57	0 –
No Mockingbird	inc**	450	2%**	174	0	10	190	–1%*
Brown Thrasher	–5%**	13	–4%**	91	0	10	23	–2%**
European Starling	–	108591	0	1634	0	10	1062	–1%**
American Pipit	–10%	29	–2%	5				
Cedar Waxwing	13%**	333	9%	98	1%	7	3	3%**
Blue-winged Warbler			3%	34				0
Tennessee Warbler			–	6				+
Nashville Warbler			0	3				+
Northern Parula			0	85				1%*
Yellow Warbler			4%**	201	0	10	7	2%**
Chestnut-sided Warbler			0	11				0
Magnolia Warbler			+	13				3%**
Cape May Warbler			0	4				+ +
Black-throated Blue Warbler			–	30				0
Yellow-rumped Warbler	0	1328	–3%	309				2%**
Black-throated Green Warbler			+	24				0
Blackburnian Warbler			0	6				0
Yellow-throated Warbler			–	24	–	4	1	0 +
Pine Warbler		2	0	97	0	9	17	2%**
Prairie Warbler			–2%*	59	0	10	8	–2%**
Palm Warbler		4	–	2				+
Bay-breasted Warbler			0	2				0
Blackpoll Warbler			–5%	36				+ –
Cerulean Warbler			3%	9				–3%**
Black-and-white Warbler			0	100	–4%**	8	4	0
American Redstart			0	75	–4%**	6	1	0 –
Prothonotary Warbler			3%	32	7%*	7	4	0
Worm-eating Warbler			0	17	0	5	2	0
Ovenbird			0	234	2%	10	41	0 +
Northern Waterthrush			–	9				0
Louisiana Waterthrush			0	17	–	7	1	0
Kentucky Warbler			–2%	25	0	10	8	0
Common Yellowthroat	–	6	0	472	2%	10	106	0
Hooded Warbler			0	6	0	4	0.4	3%**
Wilson's Warbler			0	3				+
Canada Warbler			0	5				0
Yellow-breasted Chat			0	45	–	10	19	–1% –
Summer Tanager			+	13	+	5	1	0
Scarlet Tanager			0	97	0	10	17	0 +
Eastern Towhee	–5%**	124	–5%**	289	–3%	10	84	–3%**

Table I.1. *Avian Population Trends in Delaware, 1966–91* (continued)

Species Name	Christmas Count 1966–89		May Count 1969–91		Breeding Bird Survey 1966–89 Delaware			East
	Rate	Median	Rate	Avg	Rate	No. of Rts	Avg	Rate
Am Tree Sparrow	–11%**	277						
Chipping Sparrow		5	0	166	–5%**	10	111	0 +
Field Sparrow	+4%**	347	–3%**	104	–6%**	10	81	–3%**
Vesper Sparrow			6%*	3	–	10	6	–3%**
Savannah Sparrow	–3%	145	–4%	23				–2%**
Grasshopper Sparrow			–2%	9	–4%*	10	12	–5%**
Henslow's Sparrow							0.2	–5%**
"Sharp-tailed" Sparrow	–	13	–5%**	12	–5%**	3	0.6	+
Seaside Sparrow	inc*	11	0	99	+	5	5	4%**
Fox Sparrow	inc*	21						4%*
Song Sparrow	inc**	1982	–2%**	265	+	10	121	–1%
Swamp Sparrow	0	395	0	104	+	8	6	0 +
White-crowned Sparrow	–6%*	31	0	5				–7%**
White-throated Sparrow	0	4116	–6%*	140				–1% –
Dark-eyed Junco	inc	1727	–	1				–
Snow Bunting		206						
Northern Cardinal	inc**	1114	–1%	445	–4%**	10	143	0 +
Rose-breasted Grosbeak			0	22				0 +
Blue Grosbeak			6%**	47	12%**	10	51	2%**
Indigo Bunting			+	87	3%**	10	136	0
Bobolink			0	178				0 –
Red-winged Blackbird	–	825474	0	2920	0	10	476	–2%**
Eastern Meadowlark	–9%**	606	–7%**	60	–5%*	10	51	–3%**
Rusty Blackbird	–8%**	61	0	6				– –
Common Grackle	–	344585	2%*	2657	+	10	1473	–2%**
Boat-tailed Grackle	–	346	+	211	+	5	58	+ +
Brown-headed Cowbird	–	61861	–2%	220	+	10	37	–2%**
Orchard Oriole			6%**	38	+	10	12	0 +
Baltimore Oriole			0	74	0	10	9	0
Purple Finch	dec	83	–8%	8				0
House Finch	13%**	711	28%**	96	5%**	8	31	20%**
Pine Siskin	–	11	–	7				2%
American Goldfinch	–6%**	715	–4%**	490	–8%**	10	30	–1%*
Evening Grosbeak	–14%**	32	–10%*	8				–
House Sparrow	–5%**	2428	–4%**	393	–5%**	10	670	–2%**

Sources: BBS data are unpublished U.S. Fish and Wildlife Service data. The spring trends are from West 1992.

Note: Extreme caution must be exercised in using this table, because trend direction may be affected by biases in the study, and trend magnitudes are inexact. The following comments apply to the mathematical analysis, and assume the field work is unbiased:

** = Direction of trend highly significant ($p < .01$); magnitude has some significance.

* = Direction of trend significant ($p < .05$), but magnitude of trend not well known.

No asterisk, but number given = Direction of trend not statistically significant ($p < .1$) but may be used to support other information. Magnitude of trend even less reliable than preceding.

0 = No statistical evidence for a population trend ($p > .05$ and annual trend = –1.5% to +1.5%); may be caused by consistent data and no trend or by data not explained by the trend curve.

+ or – in the rate column instead of a number = Direction of trend not significant, but magnitude of suggested trend > ± 1.5% per year.

+ or – in place of an asterisk (for the BBS trends) = The route regression does not give a statistically significant trend, but gives a statistically significant number of routes with increasing or decreasing numbers.

inc or dec (for the CBC trends) = a curve fitted to the trend showing an increase after a minimum or a decrease after a maximum, respectively.

irr = irregular

Rates = annual rates of change, and, like compound interest, long-term trends must be compounded. For example, a 5% rate decrease for 24 years equals a 71% decline, and a 5% increase amounts to more than tripling the population.

Median = The median number of each species counted annually on the five CBCs combined. Avg = the average number of each species reported on the May Count or the combined BBSs. Trends based on low numbers are less reliable, but the BBS is the most efficient at extracting a trend from few data. When the number of BBS routes on which a species is reported falls below ten (as is frequently the case for Delaware) the trend becomes less reliable.

Estimates of State Populations of Breeding Birds

Populations of most terrestrial birds cannot be measured accurately on a statewide basis, but broad estimates may be possible. In Europe, the major breeding bird atlases provide estimates of populations of birds (Robbins 1981)—for Britain and Ireland see Sharrock (1976) and Gibbons et al. (1993). Following Britain's lead, the breeding bird atlases of Ontario (Cadman et al. 1987) and the Maritime Provinces (Erskine 1992) provided population estimates.

After completing the Delaware Breeding Bird Atlas and the associated relative abundance study, and after compiling the information for this book, we have a fairly good basis for making estimates within an order of magnitude for many species breeding in Delaware during the 1983–87 period. Indicators of abundance of each species are given in the species accounts, including the number of blocks where found by the Breeding Bird Atlas project and the number of stops where found in the relative abundance study. We used these indicators to develop statewide estimates as follows:

1. Direct estimates are published or in Delaware Department of Natural Resources and Environmental Control files for a number of species such as the Bald Eagle, Osprey, colonial species, beach nesters, and some game birds. Direct estimates can be made for other species that breed locally (e.g., the Cerulean Warbler) or in very low numbers (e.g., the Sedge Wren, Northern Harrier). High counts during breeding season serve as a guide to minimum populations.

2. Estimates that have some numerical basis are extrapolated using assumptions sometimes supported only by field experience. These estimates consider all sources of numerical data, and the extrapolations were judged for their reliability.

a. Pairs per 100 acres from the Breeding Bird Census and other studies were multiplied by hundreds of acres of suitable habitat. Assumptions are made about suitability of habitat and about its availability in the state.

b. Published population estimates from Illinois, North Dakota, or Ontario were adjusted by the BBS relative abundance ratio and ratio of state areas to approximate a Delaware population (Robbins et al. 1986; Robbins and Dowell 1986, Cadman et al. 1987). Corrections for long-term population trends were made if needed using data from appendix I.

c. The number of a species counted on an average three-minute BBS stop and the number of encounters with a species in the 3,240 three-minute stops of the relative abundance study were adjusted to state populations using an assumed detection efficiency in a 0.25 mile radius circle of detection. Robbins and Dowell (1986) used an efficiency of

0.1 for some illustrative obvious species, and Whitcomb et al. (1981) published maximum distances for hearing some common songbirds.

d. The number of Atlas blocks in which a species is found was multiplied by an estimated average number of pairs in the blocks where found. This technique was used in Britain, where an abundance of background data is available from other sources (Sharrock 1976; Gibbons et al. 1993).

3. Special studies yielded useful information such as the relative abundance of vultures derived from a hawk survey (Hess 1987), the estimate of Mourning Doves in New York (Decker 1985), and a correlation between BBS counts and census results for Red-winged Blackbirds in farmland (Clark 1983).

The population estimates of birds breeding in Delaware, given in table J.1, are only to be taken as a starting point from which others can improve. Their absolute values should not be used to estimate population trends, since there are better methods for doing that.

Table J.1. Species Breeding in Delaware, 1983–87, and their Estimated Populations

Species	Estimated Population (stated as pairs)[1]
Pied-billed Grebe	10–100
American Bittern	5–50
Least Bittern	100–1,000
Great Blue Heron	400–800
Great Egret	about 200
Snowy Egret	about 400
Little Blue Heron	about 500
Tricolored Heron	5–50
Cattle Egret	4,000–5,000
Green Heron	200–2,000
Black-crowned Night-Heron	about 50
Yellow-crowned Night-Heron	4–40
Glossy Ibis	100–500
Black Vulture	20–200
Turkey Vulture	500–5,000
Canada Goose	100–1,000[2]
Mute Swan	1–5
Wood Duck	1,000–5,000
Gadwall	50–500
American Black Duck	300–3,000
Mallard	1,000–10,000
Blue-winged Teal	2–20
Green-winged Teal	0–10
Hooded Merganser	0–5
Red-breasted Merganser	0–5
Osprey	about 80
Bald Eagle	about 5
Northern Harrier	2–20
Cooper's Hawk	3–30
Red-shouldered Hawk	30–300
Broad-winged Hawk	5–50

Species	Estimated Population (stated as pairs)[1]
Red-tailed Hawk	100–1,000
American Kestrel	200–2,000
Peregrine Falcon	0–4
Ring-necked Pheasant	500–5,000
Wild Turkey	20–200
Northern Bobwhite	8,000–40,000
Black Rail	10–100
Clapper Rail	1,000–10,000
King Rail	10–100
Virginia Rail	100–1,000
Common Moorhen	5–50
American Coot	0–5
Piping Plover	1–5
Killdeer	3,000–30,000
American Oystercatcher	5–20[3]
Black-necked Stilt	20–30
Willet	300–3,000
Spotted Sandpiper	0–10
Upland Sandpiper	0–10
American Woodcock	1,000–10,000
Laughing Gull	2,000–10,000
Herring Gull	2–20
Great Black-backed Gull	0–10
Common Tern	100–500
Forster's Tern	5–200
Least Tern	800–1,000
Black Skimmer	40–200
Rock Dove	10,000–100,000
Mourning Dove	50,000–500,000
Black-billed Cuckoo	0–10
Yellow-billed Cuckoo	4,000–40,000
Barn Owl	50–500
Eastern Screech-Owl	1,000–10,000
Great Horned Owl	1,000–10,000
Barred Owl	100–1,000
Short-eared Owl	0–10
Common Nighthawk	20–200
Chuck-will's-widow	200–2,000
Whip-poor-will	2,000–20,000
Chimney Swift	1,000–10,000
Ruby-throated Hummingbird	2,000–20,000
Belted Kingfisher	10–100
Red-headed Woodpecker	3–30
Red-bellied Woodpecker	5,000–50,000
Downy Woodpecker	3,000–30,000
Hairy Woodpecker	600–6,000
Northern Flicker	3,000–30,000
Pileated Woodpecker	60–600
Eastern Wood-Pewee	5,000–50,000
Acadian Flycatcher	2,000–20,000
Willow Flycatcher	200–2,000
Eastern Phoebe	300–3,000
Great Crested Flycatcher	4,000–40,000
Eastern Kingbird	2,000–10,000
Loggerhead Shrike	0–10
White-eyed Vireo	10,000–100,000
Yellow-throated Vireo	1,000–10,000
Warbling Vireo	20–200
Red-eyed Vireo	20,000–200,000
Blue Jay	10,000–100,000
American Crow	2,000–10,000
Fish Crow	500–5,000

Species	Estimated Population (stated as pairs)[1]
Horned Lark	4,000–20,000
Purple Martin	10,000–100,000
Tree Swallow	300–3,000
Northern Rough-winged Swallow	300–3,000
Bank Swallow	100–1,000
Barn Swallow	10,000–100,000
Carolina Chickadee	20,000–50,000
Tufted Titmouse	10,000–50,000
White-breasted Nuthatch	100–1,000
Brown-headed Nuthatch	40–200
Brown Creeper	0–10
Carolina Wren	2,000–20,000
House Wren	2,000–10,000
Sedge Wren	1–10
Marsh Wren	10,000–50,000
Blue-gray Gnatcatcher	5,000–50,000
Eastern Bluebird	1,000–5,000
Veery	50–500
Wood Thrush	20,000–200,000
American Robin	50,000–500,000
Gray Catbird	3,000–30,000
Northern Mockingbird	5,000–50,000
Brown Thrasher	1,000–10,000
European Starling	30,000–300,000
Cedar Waxwing	500–5,000
Blue-winged Warbler	10–100
Northern Parula	5–50
Yellow Warbler	2,000–20,000
Chestnut-sided Warbler	0–10
Yellow-throated Warbler	100–1,000
Pine Warbler	3,000–30,000
Prairie Warbler	1,000–10,000
Cerulean Warbler	2–20
Black-and-white Warbler	1,000–10,000
American Redstart	100–1,000
Prothonotary Warbler	1,000–10,000
Worm-eating Warbler	1,000–10,000
Ovenbird	5,000–50,000
Louisiana Waterthrush	100–1,000
Kentucky Warbler	1,000–10,000
Common Yellowthroat	20,000–200,000
Hooded Warbler	10–100
Yellow-breasted Chat	1,000–10,000
Summer Tanager	250–2500
Scarlet Tanager	1,000–20,000
Eastern Towhee	7,000–70,000
Chipping Sparrow	6,000–60,000
Field Sparrow	5,000–50,000
Vesper Sparrow	200–2,000
Grasshopper Sparrow	1,000–10,000
Saltmarsh Sharp-tailed Sparrow	200–2,000
Seaside Sparrow	5,000–50,000
Song Sparrow	8,000–80,000
Swamp Sparrow	5,000–50,000
Northern Cardinal	20,000–200,000
Blue Grosbeak	2,500–25,000
Indigo Bunting	15,000–150,000
Red-winged Blackbird	30,000–300,000
Eastern Meadowlark	5,000–50,000
Common Grackle	100,000–1,000,000
Boat-tailed Grackle	200–2,000
Brown-headed Cowbird	20,000–200,000

Table J.1. Species Breeding in Delaware, 1983–87,
and their Estimated Populations   *(continued)*

Species	Estimated Population (stated as pairs)[1]
Orchard Oriole	10,000–100,000
Baltimore Oriole	5,000–50,000
House Finch	10,000–100,000
American Goldfinch	10,000–100,000
House Sparrow	10,000–100,000

1. Population is given as "number of pairs," even if the starting data are in terms of breeding females, territorial males, family groups, or individuals counted. The ranges given are intuitive, not confidence intervals.
2. Breeding pairs.
3. Includes paired nonbreeders.

Observers and Sources

We give reference here to the sources of the many observations cited in the text. In citing the observers directly, we have omitted the names of the editors and compilers of seasonal reports. The efforts of these people were essential to the writing of this book. We gratefully acknowledge their work in evaluating and publishing the many reports that form the basis of much of what we know about birds in Delaware. The observations came from unpublished materials, collected seasonal observations such as in *American Birds,* and to incidental observations scattered in the literature. A characteristic of these observations is that little information is available other than the observed presence of the birds. The observations cited come from a much larger data set of about a million bird observations in Delaware that we have examined.

The following abbreviations are used in this section:

anon.	anonymous
AB	*American Birds*
AFN	*Audubon Field Notes*
AN	*Atlantic Naturalist*
DNREC	Department of Natural Resources and Environmental Control
DO	*Delmarva Ornithologist*
DOS	Delmarva Ornithological Society
NASFN	*National Audubon Society Field Notes*
SNHD	Society of Natural History of Delaware
TSBR	Tri-State Bird Rescue and Research, Inc.
USFWS	United States Fish and Wildlife Service

AbbD1	Abbott, D. F. AN 30:189
AbbF1	Abbott, F. AB 32:1142
Abbo2	Abbott, J. M. Cornell nest record
Abbo3	Abbott, J. M. AB 26:586
Abbo4	Abbott, J. M. AB 28:786
Abbo5	Abbott, J. M. AB 33:849
Abbo6	Abbott, J. M. AFN 11:331
Abbo7	Abbott, J. M. AFN 21:492
Abbo8	Abbott, J. M. AN 10:216
Abbo9	Abbott, J. M. AN 20:146
Abbo10	Abbott, J. M. AN 24:216
Abbo11	Abbott, J. M. AN 25:138
Abbo12	Abbott, J. M. AN 25:139
Abbo13	Abbott, J. M. AN 25:139
Abbo14	Abbott, J. M. AN 26:44
Abbo15	Abbott, J. M. DO 6:1
Abbo16	Abbott, J. M., and D. F. Abbott. AB 28:786
Abbo17	Abbott, J. M., C. W. Carlson, and R. Augustine. AB 36:158, DO 16:38

Abbo18	Abbott, J. M., and W. McDowell. AB 26:42
Abbo19	Abbott, J. M., and R. M. Schutsky. AB 31:1118
Adam1	Adams, C. Nest record, photograph
Adki1	Adkisson, K. AN 23:156
Aker1	Akers, B. and T. F. Wiebolt. AN 31:31
Alex1	Alexander, H. G. AB 28:34
Anne1	Annett. Bird-Lore 42:301
anon1	anon. [H. and D. Blades] AFN 22:427
anon2	anon. AB 45:423
anon3	anon. AN 8:147
anon4	anon. AN 9:36
anon5	anon. AN 9:145
anon6	anon. AN 12:132
anon7	anon. AN 13:260
anon8	anon. AN 14:275
anon9	anon. AN 15:269
anon10	anon. AN 17:131
anon11	anon. AN 18:35
anon12	anon. AN 18:36
anon13	anon. AN 18:180
anon14	anon. AN 26:44
anon15	anon. DO 1:5
anon16	anon. DO 4:32
anon17	anon. DO 4:34
anon18	anon. Cassinia 1:12
anon19	anon. Cassinia 30:22
Anth1	Anthony, M. A. DOS notes
Armi1	Armistead, H. T. Letter, 7 Feb 1994
Armi2	Armistead, H. T. USFWS unpublished banding data
Armi3	Armistead, H. T. AFN 20:491
Armi4	Armistead, H. T. AFN 20:559
Armi5	Armistead, H. T. AN 22:180
Armi6	Armistead, H. T. AN 27:193
Armi7	Armistead, H. T. DO 3:6
Armi8	Armistead, H. T., et al. AFN 21:492
Atch1	Atchison, M. L. DOS notes
Atch2	Atchison, M. L. Atlas notes
Atch3	Atchison, M. L. Nest record
Atch4	Atchison, M. L. DNREC shorebird survey
Atch5	Atchison, M. L. NOAA unpublished data, Mabey et al. 1993
Atch6	Atchison, M. L. AB 38:299
Atki1	Atkinson, C. U. AFN 24:28
Atla1	Atlas notes
Augu1	Augustine, R. AB 36:158
Aull1	Aull, J., G. F. O'Shea, and A. P. Ednie. AB 43:1296
Bake1	Baker, S. S. AN 23:41

Bake2   Baker, S. S., and C. W. Carlson. AN 18:179

Bald1   Baldwin, E. G., et al. AN 6:123

BarT1   Barnekov, T., and Barnekov, C. AB 47:400

BarI1   Barnes, I. R., et al. Wood Thrush 3:20

BarI2   Barnes, I. R., et al. Wood Thrush 2:54

BarI3   Barnes, I. R., et al. Wood Thrush 4:38

Barn1   Barnhill, M. V. Notes

Barn2   Barnhill, M. V. DOS notes

Barn3   Barnhill, M. V. Colonial Waterbird Registry

Barn4   Barnhill, M. V. AB 38:300

Barn5   Barnhill, M. V. DO 7(2):24

Barn6   Barnhill, M. V. DO 11:47

Barn7   Barnhill, M. V. DO 13:24

Barn8   Barnhill, M. V. DO 14:37

Barn9   Barnhill, M. V. DO 15:50

Barn10   Barnhill, M. V. DO 17:41

Barn11   Barnhill, M. V. DO 20:23

Barn12   Barnhill, M. V. DO 25:36

Barn13   Barnhill, M. V., et al. Barnhill notes

Barn14   Barnhill, M. V., et al. DOS notes

Barn15   Barnhill, M. V., et al. AB 36:959

Barn16   Barnhill, M. V., et al. AB 40:448

Barn17   Barnhill, M. V., et al. AB 46:71, DOS notes

Barn18   Barnhill, M. V., et al. DO 9:67

Barn19   Barnhill, M. V., et al. DO 12:52

Barn20   Barnhill, M. V., et al. DO 14:37

Barn21   Barnhill, M. V., et al. DO 21:10

Barn22   Barnhill, M. V., m.obs. DO 24:55, DOS notes

Barn23   Barnhill, M. V., and DOS. Barnhill notes

Barn24   Barnhill, M. V., and DOS. Nest record

Barn25   Barnhill, M. V., and DOS. DO 11:53

Barn26   Barnhill, M. V., and DOS. DO 12:7

Barn27   Barnhill, M. V., P. G. DuMont, H. Morrin, et al. AB 27:36

Barn28   Barnhill, M. V., and A. P. Ednie. DO 9:61

Barn29   Barnhill, M. V., and A. P. Ednie DO 11:9

Barn30   Barnhill, M. V., and A. P. Ednie. DO 11:10

Barn31   Barnhill, M. V., A. P. Ednie, and D. N. Niles. DO 23:21

Barn32   Barnhill, M. V., W. A. Fintel, et al. Atlas notes

Barn33   Barnhill, M. V., W. A. Fintel, and W. W. Frech. DO 11:12

Barn34   Barnhill, M. V., and W. W. Frech. DO 17:41

Barn35   Barnhill, M. V., and W. W. Frech. DO 19:33, notes

Barn37   Barnhill, M. V., W. W. Frech and W. A. Fintel. DO 17:42

Barn38   Barnhill, M. V., and J. A. Gordon. Barnhill notes, DO 25:62

Barn39   Barnhill, M. V., and J. A. Gordon. AB 35:806

Barn40   Barnhill, M. V., and J. A. Gordon. DO 16:36

Barn41   Barnhill, M. V., J. A. Gordon, et al. AB 36:280, 383, 504

Barn42   Barnhill, M. V., and G. K. Hess. Barnhill notes

Barn43   Barnhill, M. V., and G. K. Hess. Notes

Barn44   Barnhill, M. V., and G. K. Hess. Hess notes

Barn45   Barnhill, M. V., G. K. Hess, et al. Barnhill notes

Barn46   Barnhill, M. V., and D. W. Holmes. DO 17:39

Barn47   Barnhill, M. V., J. G. Lehman, and J. T. Linehan. AB 33:269, 438

Barn48   Barnhill, M. V., and S. J. McCandless. Barnhill notes

Barn49   Barnhill, M. V., S. J. McCandless, et al. Barnhill notes

Barn50   Barnhill, M. V., and H. Morrin. DO 7(2):25

Barn51   Barnhill, M. V., and H. Morrin. DO 8:15

Barn52   Barnhill, M. V., H. Morrin, et al. DO 8:15

Barn53   Barnhill, M. V., and D. N. Phalen. DOS notes

Barn54   Barnhill, M. V., and J. W. Russell. Barnhill notes

Barn55   Barnhill, M. V., and J. W. Russell. Notes

Barn56   Barnhill, M. V., and J. W. Russell. AB 35:807

Barn57   Barnhill, M. V., and J. W. Russell. DO 25:36

Barn58   Barnhill, M. V., J. W. Russell, and G. K. Hess. DO 21:10

Barn59   Barnhill, M. V., J. W. Russell, and S. J. McCandless. DO 17:33

Barn60   Barnhill, M. V., and D. T. Shoch. Barnhill notes

Barn61   Barnhill, M. V., D. T. Shoch, et al. Barnhill notes

Barn62   Barnhill, M. V., R. L. West, et al. DO 14:37

Bart1   Bartlett, C. R. NOAA unpublished data, Mabey et al. 1993

Batt1   Batt, D. G. Notes

Batt2   Batt, D. G. Nest record

Batt3   Batt, D. G. DO 8:16

Batt4   Batt, D. G. DO 18:51

Batt5   Batt, D. G., and K. M. Batt. DO 18:56

Batt6   Batt, D. G., and K. M. Batt, et al. AB 38:890

Bayn1   Bayne, G. H, et al. DOS notes

Bayn2   Bayne, G. H., A. P. Ednie, et al. DOS notes

Bayn3   Bayne, G. H., and H. Fogleman. DOS notes

Bayn4   Bayne, G. H., H. Fogleman, et al. DOS notes

Bayn5   Bayne, G., and D. Knarr. DOS notes

Bayn6   Bayne, G., D. Knarr, et al. DOS notes

Bays1   Baysinger, E. B. USFWS unpublished banding data

Bazu1   Bazuin, J. AB 36:158

BeaF1   Beach, F. H. DOS notes

BeaJ1   Beach, J. E. DO 8:15

Beac2   Beach, P. E. DOS notes

Beac3   Beach, P. E. DO 8:17

Beac4   Beach, P. E. DO 8:52

Beac5   Beach, P. E. DO 12:17

Beac6   Beach, P. E., et al. DOS notes

Beac7   Beach, P. E., et al. DO 12:17

Beac8   Beach, P. E., and J. Grantham. DOS notes

Beac9   Beach, P. E., and J. F. Kelley. AB 27:256

Beac10   Beach, P. E., J. W. Patterson, et al. DOS notes

Beac11   Beach, P. E., and P. E. Strickland. AB 27:855

Beac12   Beach, P. E., and W. J. Wayne. DOS notes

Beac13   Beach, P. E., R. L. West, et al. DOS notes

Benn1	Bennett, J. C. Atlas notes
Beza1	Bezark, P. AB 36:960
Bick1	Bicking, C. A. SNHD notes
Blad1	Blades, Y. Atlas notes
Blad2	Blades, Y. Nest record
Blod1	Blodget, Brad. fide AB 42:1269
Blom1	Blom, E. AB 39:898
Bloo1	Bloor, E. D., and J. K. Meritt. AFN 23:647
Boll1	Boller, D. J. Atlas notes
Boll2	Boller, D. J. Nest record
Boll3	Boller, D. J. DO 16:41
Boll4	Boller, D. J., et al. DOS notes
Boll5	Boller, D. J., et al. DO 14:37
Boll6	Boller, D. J., H. T. Keller, et al. DOS notes
Boll7	Boller, D. J., and J. G. Lehman. DO 14:37
Boll8	Boller, D. J., and M. A. Rubin. DO 14:37
Bomb1	Bombay Hook NWR staff. Atlas notes
Bomb2	Bombay Hook NWR staff. Nest record
Bomb3	Bombay Hook NWR staff. USFWS unpublished banding data
Bonh1	Bonham, L. D., N. E. Holgersen, respectively. AN 28:28
Boon1	Boone. USFWS unpublished data
Bord1	Borden, W. H. AFN 24:491
Bowl1	Bowlen. AN 28:128
BraA1	Brady, A. DOS notes
BraE1	Brady, E. Audubon Mag. 44 [supp. to 3]:5
Bray1	Bray, D. F. Cornell nest record
Bray2	Bray, D. F. DO 2:47
Bray3	Bray, D. F. DO 5:30
Brez1	Brezina, D. W. AN 23:154
Brez2	Brezina, D. W. AN 26:175
Brez3	Brezina, D. W., and G. Lowe. AN 25:181
Brig1	Brighton, E. D. Atlas notes
Brit1	Britton, E. Nest record
BroH1	Brokaw, H. P. DOS notes
BroH2	Brokaw, H. P. Atlas notes
BroH3	Brokaw, H. P. Nest record
BroH4	Brokaw, H. P. AB 26:254, 585
BroH5	Brokaw, H. P. DO 7(1):6
BroH6	Brokaw, H. P. DO 14:10
BroH7	Brokaw, H. P. DO 14:37
BroH8	Brokaw, H. P., et al. DO 14:37
BroH9	Brokaw, H. P., et al. DO 15:28
BroH10	Brokaw, H. P., et al. DOS notes
BroH11	Brokaw, H. P., E. Dyer, et al. DO 14:37
BroH12	Brokaw, H. P., L. S. Jaco, et al. DO 14:37
BroH13	Brokaw, H. P., W. J. Wayne, et al. DOS notes
BroW1	Brokaw, W. A. DOS notes
BroW1	Brokaw, W. A. Atlas notes
BroW2	Brokaw, W. A. AN 27:193
BroW3	Brokaw, W. A. AN 30:183
BroW4	Brokaw, W. A. DO 10:38
BroW5	Brokaw, W. A. DO 11:12

BroW6	Brokaw, W. A. DO 14:37
BroW7	Brokaw, W. A., et al., both DOS notes
BroW8	Brokaw, W. A., et al. DO 12:17
BroW9	Brokaw, W. A., et al. DO 14:37
BroW10	Brokaw, W. A., and DOS. DO 11:12
BroW11	Brokaw, W. A., E. Dyer, et al. DOS notes
BroW12	Brokaw, W. A., E. Dyer, et al. DO 14:37
BroW13	Brokaw, W. A. and L. L. Falk. DO 12:17
BroW14	Brokaw, W. A., L. L. Falk, et al. DO 12:17
BroW15	Brokaw, W. A., and C. O. Johnson. DOS notes
BroW16	Brokaw, W. A., and B. M. Marshall. DOS notes
BroW17	Brokaw, W. A., and D. N. Phalen. DOS notes
BroW18	Brokaw, W. A., and T. S. Roberts. DO 12:17
BroW19	Brokaw, W. A., T. S. Roberts, et al. DOS notes
BroW20	Brokaw, W. A., and P. M. Walters. DOS notes
BroW21	Brokaw, W. A., and W. J. Wayne. DOS notes
BroW22	Brokaw, W. A., W. J. Wayne, et al. DOS notes
BroW22	Brokaw, W. A., W. J. Wayne, et al. DOS notes
BroW23	Brokaw, W. A., and R. L. West. DO 14:37
BroW24	Brokaw, W. A. AN 28:172
Broo1	Brooks, S. T. Notes
Broo2	Brooks, S. T. DOS notes
Broo3	Brooks, S. T. Cornell nest record
Broo4	Brooks, S. T. AFN 16:17
Broo5	Brooks, S. T. AFN 16:394
Broo6	Brooks, S. T. AFN 19:459, DO 2:38
Broo7	Brooks, S. T. AFN 21:493
Broo8	Brooks, S. T. Cassinia 47:44
Broo9	Brooks, S. T. Cassinia 52:30
Broo10	Brooks, S. T. DO 3:24
Broo11	Brooks, S. T. DO 4:31
Broo12	Brooks, S. T. DO 7(1):4
Broo13	Brooks, S. T. DO 12:17
Broo14	Brooks, S. T. DO 12:56
Broo15	Brooks, S. T., et al. DOS notes
Broo16	Brooks, S. T., et al. DO 12:17
Broo17	Brooks, S. T., et al. DO 14:37
Broo18	Brooks, S. T., et al. DO 15:28
Broo19	Brooks, S. T., et al. DO 2:38
Broo20	Brooks, S. T., and W. A. Brokaw. DO 12:17
Broo21	Brooks, S. T., and A. P. Ednie. DOS notes
Broo22	Brooks, S. T., and H. T. Keller. DOS notes
Broo23	Brooks, S. T., and P. P. McLaughlin. AFN 20:172
Broo24	Brooks, S. T., and F. Murphy. DO 4:32
Broo25	Brooks, S. T., J. W. Patterson, et al. DO 14:37
Broo26	Brooks, S. T., and A. R. Stickley. DO 2:14
Broo27	Brooks, S. T., and S. B. Speck. DO 12:66
Broo28	Brooks, S. T., and T. T. Talarowski. DO 1:5
Broo29	Brooks, S. T., and T. T. Talarowski. DO 2:22
Broo30	Brooks, S. T., and T. T. Talarowski. DO 2:38
Broo31	Brooks, S. T., and W. J. Wayne. DOS notes
BrMa1	Broun, M. AB 25:560
BroC1	Brown, C., et al. AFN 2:200
BrJW1	Brown, J. W. Bird-Lore 33:128

BrJW2	Brown, J. W. Bird-Lore 34:12
BrRF1	Brown, R. F. Atlas notes
BrRF2	Brown, R. F. DO 18:49
Buck1	Buckalew, J. H. notes
Buck2	Buckalew, J. H. Refuge Reports, in Patuxent Bird Distribution and Migration Files
Buck3	Buckalew, J. H. Hanson notes
Buck4	Buckalew, J. H. AB 25:718
Buck5	Buckalew, J. H. Bird-Lore 35:271
Buck6	Buckalew, J. H. Cassinia 30:26
Buck7	Buckalew, J. H. DO 4:47
Buck8	Buckalew, J. H. DO 5:35, notes
Buck9	Buckalew, J. H. DO 5:36, notes not building nest, J. K. Potter, Bird-Lore 38:30
Buck10	Buckalew, J. H. DO 5:36, notes
Buck11	Buckalew, J. H. Post 1960
Buck12	Buckalew, J. H. Gross 1955, notes, collected 16 October 1932
Buck13	Buckalew, J. H. Notes, 1 egg
BucF1	Buckley, F. G., and P. A. Buckley. AFN 22:594
BucP2	Buckley, P. A. AFN 21:554, Erwin 1979, Andrews 1990
BucP3	Buckley, P. A., et al. AFN 21:554
BucP1	Buckley, P. A. AB 25:716
Buda1	Buday, J., and P. J. Vanderhorst. AB 42:241
Buhl1	Buhl, F. C., and DOS. DO 23:19
Buhl2	Buhl, F. C., and R. G. Rufe. DOS notes
Burn1	Burns, P. F. Notes
Burr1	Burr, R. M. Cornell nest record
Bush1	Bush, W. D. notes
Bush2	Bush, W. D. Letter to Pennock, Pennock notes
Byrd1	Byrd, M. A. Colonial Waterbirdbird Registry
Byrd2	Byrd, M. A., G. Seek, and B. Smith. Raven 42:68
Cadb1	Cadbury, J. Bird Lore 41:253
Cadb2	Cadbury, J. Cassinia 32:45
Cadb3	Cadbury, J. Cassinia 36:6
Cado1	Cadot, A. A. Nest record
Cado2	Cadot, A. A. DO 9:66
CadH1	Cadot, H. M. DOS notes
Call1	Callahan, J. M., TSBR notes
Camp1	Campbell, C. D. DOS notes
Camp2	Campbell, C. D. Letter, 16 June 1991
Camp3	Campbell, C. D. Nest record
Camp4	Campbell, C. D. DO 23:27
Camp5	Campbell, C. D. DO 24:62
Camp6	Campbell, C. D. DO 25:38
Camp7	Campbell, C. D. DO 25:48
Camp8	Campbell, C. D. DO 25:49
Camp9	Campbell, C. D., et al. AB 47:245
Camp10	Campbell, C. D., B. Cooper, et al. DO 24:62, DOS notes
Camp11	Campbell, C. D., N. E. Holgersen and M. V. Barnhill. DOS notes
Camp12	Campbell, C. D., B. J. Lantz, and E. S. Short. DOS notes
Camp13	Campbell, C. D., M. C. Little, and E. S. Short. DNREC shorebird survey
Camp14	Campbell, C. D., O'Brian, et al. AB 45:1098
Camp15	Campbell, C. D., and E. S. Short. DOS notes
Camp16	Campbell, C. D., and E. S. Short. Cassinia 64:9-20
Camp17	Campbell, C. D., and E. S. Short. DO 25:46
Camp18	Campbell, C. D., and E. S. Short. DO 25:48
Camp19	Campbell, C. D., E. S. Short, and E. Potrafke. DOS notes
Camp20	Campbell, C. D., E. S. Short, and E. Potrafke. DO 24:59
Camp21	Campbell, C. D., and J. F. Swertinski. DO 23:29
Carl1	Carlson, C. W. AB 25:37
Carl2	Carlson, C. W. AB 25:842
Carl3	Carlson, C. W. AFN 23:32
Carl4	Carlson, C. W. AFN 23:648
Carl5	Carlson, C. W. AFN 24:30
Carl6	Carlson, C. W. AN 21:41
Carl7	Carlson, C. W. AN 21:42
Carl8	Carlson, C. W. AN 24:171
Carl9	Carlson, C. W. AN 25:47
Carl10	Carlson, C. W. AN 25:91
Carl11	Carlson, C. W. AN 26:90
Carl12	Carlson, C. W. AN 26:130
Carl13	Carlson, C. W. AN 26:41
Carl14	Carlson, C. W. AN 26:87
Carl15	Carlson, C. W., and P. G. DuMont. AN 26:44
Carr1	Carrick, B. D. DOS notes
Carr2	Carrick, B. D. AFN 18:21, DOS notes
Carr3	Carrick, B. D. AFN 19:459
Carr4	Carrick, B. D. AFN 20:24
Carr5	Carrick, B. D. AFN 20:491
Carr6	Carrick, B. D. AFN 20:492
Carr7	Carrick, B. D. AFN 21:402
Carr8	Carrick, B. D. AFN 22:426
Carr9	Carrick, B. D. AFN 22:512
Carr10	Carrick, B. D. AFN 22:513
Carr11	Carrick, B. D. AFN 22:514
Carr12	Carrick, B. D. DO 3:12
Carr13	Carrick, B. D. DO 4:21
Carr14	Carrick, B. D. DO 5:5
Carr15	Carrick, B. D. DO 6:1
Carr16	Carrick, B. D., and J. K. Merritt. AFN 21:493
Carr17	Carrick, B. D., and E. B. Nixdorf. DO 12:56
Carr18	Carrick, B. D., and P. E. Strickland. AFN 21:555
Carr19	Carrick, B. D., and P. E. Strickland. DO 5:10, AFN 21:402
CarP1	Carrier, P., and W. Williams. AB 26:836
Cart1	Carter, J. D. Letter to Pennock, Pennock notes
Cart2	Carter, J. D. Westtown School collection, DMNH
Cart3	Carter, J. D. Cassinia 25:47

Cart4   Carter, J. D. Cassinia 25:49

Char1   Charles, G. AB 40:236

Citr1   Citron, J. D. DOS notes

Citr2   Citron, J. D. Nest record

Citr3   Citron, J. D., et al. AB 34:439

Citr4   Citron, J. D., et al. DOS notes

Citr5   Citron, J. D., and L. L. Falk. DOS notes

Citr6   Citron, J. D., D. J. Hallenbeck, and Ann Hallenbeck. DOS notes

Citr7   Citron, J. D., and Keck. NOAA unpublished data, Mabey et al. 1993

Citr8   Citron, J. D. and W. J. Wayne. DOS notes

Clar1   Clark, W. S. USFWS unpublished banding data

Clat1   Clattenburg. Bird-Lore 31:341

Coff1   Coffer, H. AFN 22:19, DO 5:11, AN 23:40

Cole1   Coleman, J. Nest record

Conw1   Conway, A. E. DOS notes

Conw2   Conway, A. E. Nest record

Conw3   Conway, A. E. USFWS unpublished banding data

Conw4   Conway, A. E. AB 28:786, fide

Conw5   Conway, A. E. AB 30:937

Conw6   Conway, A. E. AN 28:33

Conw7   Conway, A. E. DO 2:14

Conw8   Conway, A. E. DO 8:17

Conw9   Conway, A. E. DO 15:53

Conw10   Conway, A. E., et al. DOS notes

Conw11   Conway, et al. DO 14:37

Conw12   Conway, A. E. and C. Conway. AB 26:44

Conw13   Conway, A. E., P. A. DuMont, Rowlett, and Vaughn. AB 26:585

Conw14   Conway, A. E., E. Dyer, et al. DO 15:28

Conw16   Conway, A. E., C. Sample, et al. DO 14:37

Conw17   Conway, A. E., and S. B. Speck. AB 25:843, DO 7(1):6, Conway 1972

ConJ1   Conway, J. R. DO 15:51

Coop1   Cooper, B., et al. AB 44:1118

Coop2   Cooper, B., P. G. DuMont, et al. AB 38:1003, notes

Coop3   Cooper, B., and H. Feddern. AN 31:33

Cove1   Coven, G. E. and S. H. Dyke. AFN 12:18

Crea1   Creameans, C. D. AN 26:133

Crum1   Crumb, D. DO 4:23

Crum2   Crumb, D. DO 6:2

Crum3   Crumb, D. DO 6:3

Cutl1   Cutler, D. A. AB 25:718

Cutl2   Cutler, D. A. AB 26:746

Cutl3   Cutler, D. A. AB 29:836

Cutl4   Cutler, D. A. AB 35:164

Cutl5   Cutler, D. A. AB 35:925

Cutl6   Cutler, D. A. AB 36:277

Cutl7   Cutler, D. A. AB 37:852

Cutl8   Cutler, D. A. AB 37:853

Cutl9   Cutler, D. A. AB 38:890

Cutl10   Cutler, D. A. AB 38:891

Cutl11   Cutler, D. A. AB 38:892

Cutl12   Cutler, D. A. AB 39:278, DO 19:18

Cutl13   Cutler, D. A. AB 42:415

Cutl14   Cutler, D. A. AB 45:1097

Cutl15   Cutler, D. A. AB 47:397

Cutl16   Cutler, D. A. AB 47:1092

Cutl17   Cutler, D. A. AFN 8:10, 98

Cutl18   Cutler, D. A. AFN 9:16

Cutl19   Cutler, D. A. AFN 12:114

Cutl20   Cutler, D. A. AFN 14:137

Cutl21   Cutler, D. A. AFN 20:408

Cutl22   Cutler, D. A. AFN 21:493

Cutl23   Cutler, D. A. AFN 22:20

Cutl24   Cutler, D. A. AFN 24:586

Cutl25   Cutler, D. A. Audubon Magazine 43:567

Cutl26   Cutler, D. A. Audubon Magazine 45[sup.4]:5

Cutl27   Cutler, D. A. Audubon Magazine 48:46

Cutl28   Cutler, D. A. Cassinia 41:82, Cassinia 46:24

Cutl29   Cutler, D. A. DO 1:5

Cutl30   Cutler, D. A. DO 6:45

Cutl31   Cutler, D. A. DO 23:21

Cutl32   Cutler, D. A., and M. Broun. AFN 11:254

Cutl33   Cutler, D. A., and H. S. Cutler. AFN 18:501

Cutl34   Cutler, D. A., and H. S. Cutler. AFN 20:491

Cutl35   Cutler, D. A., and Frech. AB 36:961

Cutl36   Cutler, D. A., and W. Jay. AFN 9:248

Cutl37   Cutler, D. A., and R. J. Newman. DO 6:45

Cutl38   Cutler, D. A., and E. J. Reimann. Cassinia 41:83

Cutl39   Cutler, D. A., and R. L. West. West notes

CutH1   Cutler, H. S. Cassinia 49:29

CutH2   Cutler, H. S. and B. Cutler. AB 40:262

Czap1   Czaplak, D. S., R. Anderson, and K. H. Bass. AB 37:977

Czap2   Czaplak, D. S., and M. A. Todd. DOS notes

Czap3   Czaplak, D. S., M. A. Todd, and A. E. Hill. DO 25:57

DNRE1   DNREC, unpublished Great Marsh study

DNRE2   DNREC, unpublished 1992 shorebird survey

DNRE3   DNREC, unpublished 1993 shorebird survey

DOS1   DOS notes

DOS2   DO 18:60, DOS Rendezvous

DVOC1   DVOC, J. K. Merritt, ed. Cassinia 52:43

DVOC2   DVOC, H. W. Todd, comp. Cassinia 53:33

Davi1   Davis, E. G. AN 7:194

Davi2   Davis, E. G., ed. AN 8:148

Davi3   Davis, E. G., ed. AN 8:203

Davi4   Davis, E. G., ed. AN 9:37

Davi5   Davis, E. G., ed. AN 9:145

Davi6   Davis, E. G., ed. AN 9:257

Davi7   Davis, E. G., ed. AN 11:234

Davi8   Davis, E. G., ed. AN 12:36

Davi9   Davis, E. G., ed. AN 12:131

Davi10   Davis, E. G., ed. AN 13:187

Davi11   Davis, E. G., ed. AN 13:261

Davi12   Davis, E. G., ed. AN 14:276

Davi13   Davis, E. G., ed. AN 15:131

Davi14   Davis, E. G., ed. AN 15:203

Davi15   Davis, E. G., ed. AN 15:204

Davi16   Davis, E. G., ed. AN 15:269

Davi17   Davis, E. G., ed. AN 16:50

Davi18   Davis, E. G., ed. AN 16:194

Davi19   Davis, E. G., ed. AN 17:50

Davi20   Davis, E. G., ed. AN 18:35

Davi21   Davis, E. G., ed. AN 18:179

Davi22   Davis, E. G., ed. AN 18:180

Davi23   Davis, E. G., and R. L. Pyle. AB 25:560

Davi24   Davis, E. G., and J. E. Willoughby. Wood Thrush 3:59

DavT1   Davis, T. H. AB 29:830

DavV1   Davis, V. E. Cornell nest record

Debe1   Debes, V. A. Cassinia 29:47

Debe2   Debes, V. A. Cassinia 30:20; Stone 1937

DeCh1   DeChene, M. P. Atlas notes

DeGa1   DeGarmo, W. R. USFWS unpublished data

DeGa2   DeGarmo, W. R. AFN 20:491

DeGa3   DeGarmo, W. R. DO 4:52

Dos1   Delmarva Ornithological Society notes

DicC1   Dickey, Mrs C. P. in Hanson notes

Dick1   Dickey, R. E. Hanson notes

Doak1   Doak, W. C. and C. B. Doak Bird-Lore 30:44

Dode1   Dodey, C. AB 47:71

DuPA1   DuMont, P. A. AN 9:92

DuPA2   DuMont, P. A. AN 22:130

DuPA3   DuMont, P. A. AN 23:154

DuPA4   DuMont, P. A. AN 27:45

DuPA5   DuMont, P. A. AN 30:32

DuPA6   DuMont, P. A. DO 6:2

DuPA7   DuMont, P. A. DO 7(2):23

DuPA8   DuMont, P. A., and P. G. DuMont. AN 25:96

DuPA9   DuMont, P. A., and P. G. DuMont. AN 30:79

DuPG1   DuMont, P. G. Notes

DuPG2   DuMont, P. G. AB 27:754

DuPG3   DuMont, P. G. AB 28:36

DuPG4   DuMont, P. G. AB 28:786

DuPG5   DuMont, P. G. AB 30:43

DuPG6   DuMont, P. G. AB 38:890

DuPG7   DuMont, P. G. AFN 27:39

DuPG8   DuMont, P. G. AFN 28:786

DuPG9   DuMont, P. G. AFN 30:43

DuPG10   DuMont, P. G. AN 22:43

DuPG11   DuMont, P. G. AN 22:139

DuPG12   DuMont, P. G. AN 25:32

DuPG13   DuMont, P. G. AN 25:46

DuPG14   DuMont, P. G. AN 25:50

DuPG15   DuMont, P. G. AN 25:136

DuPG16   DuMont, P. G. AN 25:142

DuPG17   DuMont, P. G. AN 25:186

DuPG18   DuMont, P. G. AN 26:42

DuPG19   DuMont, P. G. AN 26:46

DuPG20   DuMont, P. G. AN 26:48

DuPG21   DuMont, P. G. AN 26:49

DuPG22   DuMont, P. G. AN 26:134

DuPG23   DuMont, P. G. AN 26:135

DuPG24   DuMont, P. G. AN 30:29

DuPG25   DuMont, P. G. AN 30:31

DuPG26   DuMont, P. G. AN 30:32

DuPG27   DuMont, P. G. AN 30:33

DuPG28   DuMont, P. G. AN 30:185

DuPG29   DuMont, P. G. DO 11:49

DuPG30   DuMont, P. G. DO 14:9

DuPG31   DuMont, P. G., et al. AN 25:136

DuPG32   DuMont, P. G., et al. AN 25:181

DuPG33   DuMont, P. G., et al. AN 30:137

DuPG34   DuMont, P. G., and C. W. Carlson. AN 26:177

DuPG35   DuMont, P. G., and R. Hahn. AB 26:842

DuPG36   DuMont, P. G., and R. L. Pyle. AN 30:129

DuMP1   DuMont, P. [sic]. AN 22:180

Dyer1   Dyer, E. DOS notes

Dyer2   Dyer, E. Atlas notes

Dyer3   Dyer, E. DO 11:56

Dyer4   Dyer, E. DO 14:37

Dyer5   Dyer, E. DO 15:28

Dyer6   Dyer, E. DO 25:37

Dyer7   Dyer, E., et al. DO 14:37

Dyer8   Dyer, E., et al. DO 15:28

Dyer9   Dyer, E., et al. DO 16:53

Dyer10   Dyer, E., P. E. Beach, et al. DO 14:37

Dyer11   Dyer, E., C. E. Sample, et al. DO 14:37

Dyer12   Dyer, E., W. J. Wayne, et al. DO 14:37

Dyke1   Dyke, S. H. In Brooks notes

Dyke2   Dyke, S. H. AFN 13:359

Dyke3   Dyke, S. H. AFN 15:456

Dyke4   Dyke, S. H. AFN 17:315

Dyke5   Dyke, S. H. AFN 18:21

Dyke6   Dyke, S. H. AFN 18:501

Dyke7   Dyke, S. H. AFN 20:407

Dyke8   Dyke, S. H. AFN 49:31

Dyke9   Dyke, S. H. AN 14:275

Dyke10   Dyke, S. H. AN 14:277

Dyke11   Dyke, S. H. AN 15:203, 270

Dyke12   Dyke, S. H. DO 2:14

Dyke13   Dyke, S. H. DO 5:35

Dyke14   Dyke, S. H. DO 5:36

Dyke15   Dyke, S. H., F. G. Scheider, et al. AFN 18:442

Edni1   Ednie, A. P. DOS notes

Edni2   Ednie, A. P. Atlas notes

Edni3   Ednie, A. P. TSBR notes

Edni4   Ednie, A. P. Nest record

Edni5   Ednie, A. P. USFWS unpublished BBS data

Edni6   Ednie, A. P. AB 34:259, fide

Edni7	Ednie, A. P. AB 39:277
Edni8	Ednie, A. P. AB 42:51
Edni9	Ednie, A. P. AB 43:1296
Edni10	Ednie, A. P. AB 44:1116, fide
Edni11	Ednie, A. P. AB 45:1098
Edni12	Ednie, A. P. AFN 48:186
Edni13	Ednie, A. P. DO 9:66
Edni14	Ednie, A. P. DO 11:53
Edni15	Ednie, A. P. DO 12:8
Edni16	Ednie, A. P. DO 12:50
Edni17	Ednie, A. P. DO 14:37
Edni18	Ednie, A. P. DO 18:51
Edni19	Ednie, A. P. DO 19:27
Edni20	Ednie, A. P. DO 19:28
Edni21	Ednie, A. P. DO 19:29
Edni22	Ednie, A. P. DO 19:34
Edni23	Ednie, A. P. DO 20:20
Edni24	Ednie, A. P. DO 20:27
Edni25	Ednie, A. P. DO 23:21
Edni26	Ednie, A. P. DO 23:26
Edni27	Ednie, A. P. DO 24:54
Edni28	Ednie, A. P. DO 24:55
Edni29	Ednie, A. P. DO 24:59
Edni30	Ednie, A. P. DO 24:62
Edni31	Ednie, A. P. DO 25:36
Edni32	Ednie, A. P. NASFN 49:231
Edni33	Ednie, A. P. NASFN 50:152
Edni34	Ednie, A. P., et al. DOS notes
Edni35	Ednie, A. P., et al. AB 40:89
Edni37	Ednie, A. P., et al. DO 9:65
Edni38	Ednie, A. P., et al. DO 12:7
Edni39	Ednie, A. P., et al. DO 17:29
Edni40	Ednie, A. P., et al. DO 18:58
Edni41	Ednie, A. P., and J. D. Citron. AB 35:925
Edni42	Ednie, A. P., and J. Coveney. DOS notes
Edni43	Ednie, A. P., D. A. Cutler, and K. C. Liehr. AB 38:181
Edni44	Ednie, A. P., and DOS, DOS notes
Edni45	Ednie, A. P., L. L. Falk, et al. DOS notes
Edni46	Ednie, A. P., and W. W. Frech. DO 17:31
Edni47	Ednie, A. P., A. Hallenbeck, et al. DOS notes
Edni48	Ednie, A. P., and G. K. Hess. DOS notes
Edni49	Ednie, A. P., and G. K. Hess. DNREC shorebird survey
Edni50	Ednie, A. P., and H. T. Keller. DOS notes
Edni51	Ednie, A. P., and T. J. Marshall. DOS notes
Edni52	Ednie, A. P., and J. H. Moorhouse
Edni53	Ednie, A. P., and D. M. Niles. DO 18:51
Edni54	Ednie, A. P., and D. M. Niles. DO 18:53
Edni55	Ednie, A. P., and D. M. Niles. DO 19:28
Edni56	Ednie, A. P., and J. L. Skolnicki. DOS notes
Edni58	Ednie, A. P., and J. L. Skolnicki. Nest record
Edni59	Ednie, A. P., and J. L. Skolnicki. AB 37:286
Edni60	Ednie, A. P., and J. L. Skolnicki. DO 18:38
Edni61	Ednie, A. P., and J. L. Skolnicki. DO 20:24
Edni62	Ednie, A. P., and J. L. Skolnicki. DO 20:25
Edni63	Ednie, A. P., and J. L. Skolnicki. DO 23:15
Edni64	Ednie, A. P., S. B. Speck, and E. B. Speck. DO 18:53
Edni65	Ednie, A. P., and J. F. Swertinski. DOS notes
Edni66	Ednie, A. P., and J. F. Swertinski. AB 45:424
Edni67	Ednie, A. P., and J. F. Swertinski. DO 19:34
Edni68	Ednie, A. P., and J. F. Swertinski. DO 19:35
Edni69	Ednie, A. P., and A. J. Travis. TSBR notes
Edni70	Ednie, A. P., and P. J. Vanderhorst. AB 44:1119
Edni71	Ednie, A. P., and W. J. Wayne. AB 38:301
Edni72	Ednie, A. P., and R. L. West. DO 14:37
Emle1	Emlen, J. T. Bird-Lore 28:206
Emle2	Emlen, J. T. Bird-Lore 30:195
Emle3	Emlen, J. T. Bird-Lore 34:207
Ersk1	Erskine. Cassinia 30:15
Even1	Evenden, F. G. AFN 23:29
Even2	Evenden, F. G. AN 30:132
Ever1	Evered, D. AB 39:32
Ever2	Evered, D. AB 39:32, pers. comm.
Fage1	Fager, S. Atlas notes
FalD1	Falk, D. F, et al. Falk 1971
FalD2	Falk, D. F., L. L. Falk, et al. DO 2:18
Falk1	Falk, L. L. Notes
Falk2	Falk, L. L. DOS notes
Falk3	Falk, L. L. Nest record
Falk4	Falk, L. L. NOAA unpublished data, Mabey et al. 1993
Falk5	Falk, L. L. AB 26:41
Falk6	Falk, L. L. DO 9:19
Falk7	Falk, L. L. DO 14:37
Falk8	Falk, L. L., et al. DOS notes
Falk9	Falk, L. L., et al. DO 12:17
Falk10	Falk, L. L., et al. DO 12:56
Falk11	Falk, L. L., et al. DO 14:37
Falk12	Falk, L. L., et al. Falk 1971
Falk13	Falk, L. L., M. V. Barnhill, et al. DOS notes
Falk14	Falk, L. L., H. P. Brokaw, et al. DO 15:28
Falk15	Falk, L. L., and J. Grantham. DO 8:52
Falk16	Falk, L. L., and C. M. Hoff. DO 2:17
Falk17	Falk, L. L., J. W. Russell, et al. DO 14:37
Falk18	Falk, L. L., and S. B. Speck. AB 38:890
Falk19	Falk, L. L., S. B Speck, et al. Falk 1971
Falk20	Falk, L. L., and P. M. Walters. DOS notes
Falk21	Falk, L. L., and R. L. West. DO 14:37
Falk22	Falk, L. L., R. L. West, et al. DO 12:17
Falk23	Falk, L. L., K. I. Zeitler, et al. Atlas notes
Falk24	Falk, L. L., D. A. Ward, and R. Ward. Atlas notes
Falk25	Falk, L. L., and W. A. Brokaw. Atlas notes
Farr1	Farrand, H. F. USFWS unpublished banding data
Faus1	Faust, W. AFN 19:458
Faus3	Faust, W. DO 2:33
Faus4	Faust, W. DO 6:2

Faus5	Faust, W., et al. DO 2:33
Faus6	Faust, W., et al. DO 12:56
Faus7	Faust, W., and K. Light. DO 2:17
Faus8	Faust, W., and J. T. Linehan. AFN 22:20, DO 5:24
Faus9	Faust, W., and A. R. Stickley. AFN 19:459
Finc1	Finch, D. W., et al. AB 30:819
FinS1	Fintel, S. W. DOS notes
FinS2	Fintel, S. W. AB 38:1003
Fint1	Fintel, W. A. DOS notes
Fint2	Fintel, W. A. Frech notes
Fint3	Fintel, W. A. AB 38:891
Fint4	Fintel, W. A. AB 39:893, Fintel notes
Fint5	Fintel, W. A. AB 44:62
Fint6	Fintel, W. A. AB 45:62
Fint7	Fintel, W. A. DO 17:36; not 28 Dec, AB 36:279
Fint8	Fintel, W. A. DO 18:47
Fint9	Fintel, W. A. DO 18:50
Fint10	Fintel, W. A. DO 23:12
Fint11	Fintel, W. A., and S. W. Fintel. AB 41:1417
Fint12	Fintel, W. A., S. W. Fintel, and W. W. Frech. Frech notes
Fint13	Fintel, W. A., S. W. Fintel, and G. F. O'Shea. AB 40:449
Fint14	Fintel, W. A., S. W. Fintel, and R. L. West. Atlas notes
Fint15	Fintel, W. A., W. W. Frech, and G. Huyzers. AB 44:65
Fint16	Fintel, W. A., S. A. Fintel, and G. F. O'Shea. AB 46:69
Fisk1	Fisk, E. J. USFWS unpublished banding data
Flin1	Flint, P. DOS notes
Flor1	Florio, A. Cornell nest record
Fogl1	Fogelman, H., Sr. DO 18:50
Fogl2	Fogleman, H., Sr., et al. DOS notes
Fogl3	Fogleman, H., Sr., and G. Bayne. DOS notes
Frec1	Frech, W. W. Notes
Frec2	Frech, W. W. Atlas notes
Frec3	Frech, W. W. Nest record
Frec4	Frech, W. W. AB 33:755
Frec5	Frech, W. W. AB 33:756
Frec6	Frech, W. W. AB 34:256
Frec7	Frech, W. W. AB 34:761
Frec8	Frech, W. W. AB 35:285, DO 16:35
Frec9	Frech, W. W. AB 36:835, notes
Frec10	Frech, W. W. AB 37:284
Frec11	Frech, W. W. AB 37:286
Frec12	Frech, W. W. AB 37:853, notes
Frec13	Frech, W. W. AB 39:151
Frec14	Frech, W. W. AB 40:451
Frec15	Frech, W. W. AB 42:1275
Frec16	Frech, W. W. AB 43:74
Frec17	Frech, W. W. AB 43:1298, notes
Frec18	Frech, W. W. AB 44:241
Frec19	Frech, W. W. AB 44:243
Frec20	Frech, W. W. AB 44:245
Frec21	Frech, W. W. AB 46:243
Frec22	Frech, W. W. DO 14:9
Frec23	Frech, W. W. DO 14:10
Frec24	Frech, W. W. DO 14:15, notes
Frec25	Frech, W. W. DO 15:49, notes
Frec26	Frech, W. W. DO 15:51
Frec27	Frech, W. W. DO 15:54, picked up dead
Frec28	Frech, W. W. DO 15:58
Frec29	Frech, W. W. DO 16:34
Frec30	Frech, W. W. DO 16:39, specimen not preserved
Frec31	Frech, W. W. DO 16:40
Frec32	Frech, W. W. DO 16:41
Frec33	Frech, W. W. DO 16:42
Frec34	Frech, W. W. DO 17:30
Frec35	Frech, W. W. DO 17:32
Frec36	Frech, W. W. DO 17:34
Frec37	Frech, W. W. DO 17:37
Frec38	Frech, W. W. DO 17:38
Frec39	Frech, W. W. DO 18:45
Frec40	Frech, W. W. DO 18:50
Frec41	Frech, W. W. DO 18:51
Frec42	Frech, W. W. DO 18:53
Frec43	Frech, W. W. DO 18:56, notes
Frec44	Frech, W. W. DO 19:29
Frec45	Frech, W. W. DO 20:17
Frec46	Frech, W. W. DO 20:21
Frec47	Frech, W. W. DO 20:26, notes
Frec48	Frech, W. W. DO 21:7
Frec49	Frech, W. W. DO 23:16
Frec50	Frech, W. W., and J. Aull. Frech notes
Frec51	Frech, W. W., M. V. Barnhill, and W. A. Fintel. Nest record
Frec52	Frech, W. W., and A. P. Ednie. DO 17:31
Frec53	Frech, W. W., and W. A. Fintel. AB 37:853
Frec54	Frech, W. W., W. A. Fintell, and J. Aull. DO 21:3
Frec55	Frech, W. W., and D. Gardner. AB 47:69
Frec56	Frech, W. W., and D. Gardner. DO 24:67
Frec57	Frech, W. W., C. McIntyre, and Gert Huyzers. AB 36:834
Frec58	Frech, W. W., T. Projector, and D. Projector. DO 16:42
Frec59	Frech, W. W. DO 15:54
Free1	Freeland, L. T., and C. D. Lewis. DO 2:16
Frey1	Frey, E. Atlas notes
FreL1	Frey, L. T. Cornell Nest records
Frin1	Frink, J. DNREC 1986 shorebird survey in Thomas 1986
Gail1	Gailey, J. DO 7(2):23
Gamb1	Gambill, C. H. AB 38:1002
Gano1	Gano, Rob. Atlas notes
Gard1	Gardner, A. C. Nest record

GarR1   Gardner, R. DO 17:41

GarM1   Garner, M., Jr. AB 33:849

Gelv1   Gelvin-Innvaar, L. A B 47:397

Gilb1   Gilbert, H., and M. Teele. AN 26:46

Gill1   Gill, F. B., M. O'Brian. AB 45:421

Gill1   Gillespie, J. A. Bird-Lore 29:272

Gill2   Gillespie, J. A. Bird-Lore 34:339

Gill3   Gillespie, J. A. Cassinia 29:52

Gill4   Gillespie, J. A., and C. E. Underdown. Bird-Lore 32:430

Gilr1   Gilroy, M. AB 40:1183

Gith1   Githeus, C. DOS notes

GolT1   Goldsmith, T., and M. H. Martin. AN 7:194

Gold1   Goldstein, R. T. Brooke, Jr., and J. R. Lamplugh. Cassinia 40:35

Gord1   Gorden, J. A. DOS notes

Gord2   Gordon, J. A. Nest record

Gord3   Gordon, J. A. BHNWR notes

Gord4   Gordon, J. A. AB 34:258

Gord5   Gordon, J. A. AB 34:259

Gord6   Gordon, J. A. AB 34:760

Gord7   Gordon, J. A. AB 34:878

Gord8   Gordon, J. A. AB 36:835

Gord9   Gordon, J. A. DO 15:49

Gord10   Gordon, J. A. DO 15:51

Gord11   Gordon, J. A. DO 15:55

Gord12   Gordon, J. A., R. D. Ross, et al. DOS notes

Gord13   Gordon, J. A., and B. Stocku. AB 37:161

Gord14   Gordon, J. A., and J. F. Swertinski. DOS notes

Gran1   Grantham, J. DOS notes

Gran2   Grantham, J. DO 7(2):23

Gran3   Grantham, J., et al. DO 12:17

Gran4   Grantham, J., and P. Beach. DOS notes

Gree1   Greenewalt, C. H. Nest records

Grim1   Grim, K. A. AB 35:925

Grim2   Grim, K. A. DO 16:35

Gros1   Grosz, K. DOS notes

Guar1   Guarente, A. AB 29:37

Gust1   Gustafson, M. E., and B. G. Peterjohn. AB 46:240

Gust2   Gustafson, M. E., and B. G. Peterjohn. AB 46:399

Gust3   Gustafson, M. E., and B. G. Peterjohn. AB 47:399

Gust4   Gustafson, M. E., B. G. Peterjohn, Dunn. AB 46:240

HaaB1   Haas, B., and Haas, F. C. DOS notes

Haas1   Haas, F. C. DO 16:24

Haas2   Haas, F. C. DO 16:26

Haas3   Haas, F. C., and Haas, B. DO 16:24

Hahn1   Hahn, R. AN 25:138

Hale1   Haley, S.; photograph R. Prescott. AB 45:415

HalK1   Hall, K. Atlas notes

HalA1   Hallenbeck, A. DO 14:37

HalA2   Hallenbech, A., C. O. Johnson, et al. DOS notes

HalD1   Hallenbeck, D. J. DOS notes

HalD2   Hallenbeck, D. J. DO 9:16

Hals1   Halstead, R. O. USFWS unpublished data

Hann1   Hannay, E. and I. AN 26:133

Hann2   Hannay, E. and I. AN 28:172

Hans1   Hanson, H. H. Notes

Hans2   Hanson, H. H. Notes; Griffith 1946

Hans3   Hanson, H. H., and R. E. Dickey. Hanson notes

Hard1   Hardy, C. M. AFN 17:452

Hard2   Hardy, C. M. AFN 18:344

Hard3   Hardy, C. M. AFN 20:26

Hard4   Hardy, C. M. DO 3:8, photograph reported

Hard5   Hardy, C. M. AFN 20:407

Hard6   Hardy, C. M. Cassinia 49:36

Hard7   Hardy, C. M. DO 2:14

Hard8   Hardy, C. M. DO 3:4

Hard9   Hardy, C. M., et al. DO 3:4

Heac1   Heacock and P. F. Springer. AFN 8:304

Hens1   Hensel, G. Pennock notes, fide C. J. Pennock

Herb1   Herbert, K. DO 3:5

Herh1   Herholdt, J. F. Letter, 8 July 1938

Herh2   Herholdt, J. F. Hanson notes

Herh3   Herholdt, J. F. Bird-Lore 41:52; AN 12:128

Hess1   Hess, G. K. Notes

Hess2   Hess, G. K. DOS notes

Hess3   Hess, G. K. Atlas notes

Hess4   Hess, G. K. Nest record

Hess5   Hess, G. K. AB 35:285

Hess6   Hess, G. K. AB 35:924, 36:962

Hess7   Hess, G. K. DO 16:36

Hess8   Hess, G. K. DO 18:40

Hess9   Hess, G. K. DO 18:51

Hess10   Hess, G. K. DO 19:34

Hess11   Hess, G. K. DO 20:26

Hess12   Hess, G. K., et al. DOS notes

Hess13   Hess, G. K., and M. V. Barnhill. Hess notes

Hess14   Hess, G. K., D. G. Batt, and K. Batt. DOS notes

Hess15   Hess, G. K. and DOS. DO 18:60

Hess16   Hess, G. K., and A. P. Ednie. Hess notes

Hess17   Hess, G. K., A. P. Ednie, et al. DOS notes

Hess18   Hess, G. K., K. A. Hess, et al. DOS notes

Hess19   Hess, G. K., and J. P. Janowski. DOS notes

Hess20   Hess, G. K., and A. Mack. DO 18:57

Hess21   Hess, G. K., and R. D. Ross. DOS notes

Hess22   Hess, G. K., and R. L. West. DO 20:27

Hewi1   Hewitt, M. W. AN 10:34

Hiat1   Hiatt, B. C. Bird-Lore 30:195

Hiat2   Hiatt, B. C. Bird-Lore 39:315

Hiat3   Hiatt, B. C. Cassinia 27:34

Higm1   Higman, J., D. R. Simonson, and C. B. Swift. AFN 22:19

HilA1   Hill, A. E. DOS notes

HilA2   Hill, A. E. AB 42:414

HilA3   Hill, A. E. AB 46:72

HilA4	Hill, A. E. AB 47:398
HilA5	Hill, A. E. DOS 25:47
HilJ1	Hill, J. W. AB 26:745
HilJ2	Hill, J. W. Cassinia 31:44
HilJ3	Hill, J. W., and R. F. Miller. Bird-Lore 42:381
HilC1	Hills, C. F. AB 26:746
Hilt1	Hilton, Robert, W. S. Clark, Daphne Gemmill. AB 43:1296
Hoff1	Hoff, C. M. DO 2:38
Hoff2	Hoff, C. M. DO 3:53
Hoff3	Hoff, C. M. DO 5:22
Hoff4	Hoff, C. M. Falk 1971
Hold1	Holden, E. K. DOS notes
Holg1	Holgersen, N. E. DOS notes
Holg2	Holgersen, N. E. Refuge notes
Holg3	Holgersen, N. E. Cornell nest record
Holg4	Holgersen, N. E. AB 25:36
Holg5	Holgersen, N. E. AB 25:37
Holg6	Holgersen, N. E. AB 25:38
Holg7	Holgersen, N. E. AB 25:717
Holg8	Holgersen, N. E. AB 25:841
Holg9	Holgersen, N. E. AB 25:842
Holg10	Holgersen, N. E. AB 25:843
Holg11	Holgersen, N. E. AB 26:42
Holg12	Holgersen, N. E. AB 26:585
Holg13	Holgersen, N. E. AB 27:37
Holg14	Holgersen, N. E. AB 44:62
Holg15	Holgersen, N. E. AB 27:39
Holg16	Holgersen, N. E. AB 27:596
Holg17	Holgersen, N. E. AB 27:597
Holg18	Holgersen, N. E. AB 27:598
Holg19	Holgersen, N. E. AB 27:747
Holg20	Holgersen, N. E. AB 27:854
Holg21	Holgersen, N. E. AB 28:33
Holg22	Holgersen, N. E. AB 28:623
Holg23	Holgersen, N. E. AB 28:625, DO 9:67, no notes now available
Holg24	Holgersen, N. E. AB 41:1416
Holg25	Holgersen, N. E. AB 42:49
Holg26	Holgersen, N. E. AB 42:51, 241; DOS notes
Holg27	Holgersen, N. E. AB 43:290-91
Holg28	Holgersen, N. E. AB 44:62; DO 23:21, 24
Holg29	Holgersen, N. E. AB 44:65
Holg30	Holgersen, N. E. AB 44:66
Holg31	Holgersen, N. E. AB 44:242
Holg32	Holgersen, N. E. AFN 22:512
Holg33	Holgersen, N. E. AFN 23:29
Holg34	Holgersen, N. E. AFN 23:30
Holg35	Holgersen, N. E. AFN 23:31
Holg36	Holgersen, N. E. AFN 23:464
Holg37	Holgersen, N. E. AFN 24:28
Holg38	Holgersen, N. E. AFN 24:587
Holg39	Holgersen, N. E. AFN 24:669
Holg40	Holgersen, N. E. AFN 27:855
Holg41	Holgersen, N. E. AN 17:50
Holg42	Holgersen, N. E. AN 25:47
Holg43	Holgersen, N. E. AN 25:49
Holg44	Holgersen, N. E. AN 25:92
Holg45	Holgersen, N. E. AN 25:136
Holg46	Holgersen, N. E. AN 25:139
Holg48	Holgersen, N. E. AN 25:181
Holg49	Holgersen, N. E. AN 25:184
Holg50	Holgersen, N. E. AN 26:44
Holg51	Holgersen, N. E. AN 26:48
Holg52	Holgersen, N. E. AN 26:131
Holg53	Holgersen, N. E. AN 26:136
Holg54	Holgersen, N. E. AN 27:40
Holg55	Holgersen, N. E. AN 27:191
Holg56	Holgersen, N. E. AN 28:28
Holg57	Holgersen, N. E. AN 29:124
Holg58	Holgersen, N. E. AN 29:125
Holg59	Holgersen, N. E. AN 29:129
Holg60	Holgersen, N. E. AN 29:174
Holg61	Holgersen, N. E. Cassinia 52:27
Holg62	Holgersen, N. E. Cassinia 53:55
Holg63	Holgersen, N. E. Cassinia 53:57
Holg64	Holgersen, N. E. DO 7(1):3
Holg65	Holgersen, N. E. DO 7(1):5
Holg66	Holgersen, N. E. DO 7(2):14
Holg67	Holgersen, N. E. DO 7(2):21
Holg68	Holgersen, N. E. DO 7(2):22
Holg69	Holgersen, N. E. DO 7(2):23
Holg70	Holgersen, N. E. DO 7(2):24
Holg71	Holgersen, N. E. DO 7(2):25
Holg72	Holgersen, N. E. DO 8:15
Holg73	Holgersen, N. E. DO 8:16
Holg74	Holgersen, N. E. DO 8:17
Holg75	Holgersen, N. E. DO 8:50, AB 27:37
Holg76	Holgersen, N. E. DO 8:51
Holg77	Holgersen, N. E. DO 8:52
Holg78	Holgersen, N. E. DO 8:59
Holg79	Holgersen, N. E. DO 8:60
Holg80	Holgersen, N. E. DO 9:16
Holg81	Holgersen, N. E. DO 9:17
Holg82	Holgersen, N. E. DO 9:18
Holg83	Holgersen, N. E. DO 9:57
Holg84	Holgersen, N. E. DO 9:58
Holg85	Holgersen, N. E. DO 9:61
Holg86	Holgersen, N. E. DO 9:64
Holg87	Holgersen, N. E. DO 23:14
Holg88	Holgersen, N. E. DO 23:15
Holg89	Holgersen, N. E. DO 23:25
Holg90	Holgersen, N. E. DO 23:27
Holg91	Holgersen, N. E. DO 24:53
Holg92	Holgersen, N. E. DO 24:63
Holg93	Holgersen, N. E. DO 25:35

Holg94	Holgersen, N. E. DO 25:41	Jann1	Janni, O. DO 26:11
Holg95	Holgersen, N. E. DO 25:42	Jano1	Janowski, J. P. DOS notes
Holg96	Holgersen, N. E. DO 25:43	Jano2	Janowski, J. P. Nest record
Holg97	Holgersen, N. E. DO 25:44	Jano3	Janowski, J. P. DO 23:19
Holg98	Holgersen, N. E. DO 25:47	Jano4	Janowski, J. P. DO 23:28
Holg99	Holgersen, N. E., et al. AB 27:755	Jano5	Janowski, J. P. DO 25:44
Hol100	Holgersen, N. E., et al. AB 28:34	Jano6	Janowski, J. P., and R. G. Rufe. AB 44:401
Hol101	Holgersen, N. E., et al. AB 28:622	Jesc1	Jeschke, C. F. Atlas notes
Hol102	Holgersen, N. E., et al. AFN 24:28, 490; AN 25:137	Jesc2	Jeschke, C. F. Cornell nest record
Hol103	Holgersen, N. E., and C. Bode. AN 26:84	JohA1	Johnson, A. M. DO 3:11
Hol104	Holgersen, N. E., C. D. Campbell, et al. DO 24:53, DOS notes	John1	Johnson, C. O. DOS notes
		John2	Johnson, C. O. AB 25:239
Hol105	Holgersen, N. E., A. P. Ednie, and J. F. Swertinski. DO 25:41	John3	Johnson, C. O. DO 7(1):2
		John4	Johnson, C. O. DO 7(1):3
Hol106	Holgersen, N. E., W. W. Frech, et al. AB 28:785	John5	Johnson, C. O. DO 7(2):22
Hol107	Holgersen, N. E., and N. J. Scarpulla. DOS notes, DO 24:63	John6	Johnson, C. O. DO 7(2):23
		John7	Johnson, C. O., et al. DOS notes
Hol108	Holgersen, N. E., R. P. Teale, and D. A. Ward. AFN 23:465, DO 6:44; Holgersen et al. Cassinia 52:31	John8	Johnson, C. O., and W. A. Brokaw. DOS notes
		John9	Johnson, C. O., and H. E. Johnson. DO 8:60
Hol109	Holgersen, N. E., and R. W. Thomen. DO 7(2):14	John10	Johnson, C. O., B. M. Marshall, and D. T. Weesner. AB 30:300
Holm1	Holmes, V. Atlas notes		
Homs1	Homsey, S. P. DOS notes	John11	Johnson, C. O., and K. C. Richards. DOS notes
Howk1	Howk, B. W., and S. B. Speck. DO 2:17	John12	Johnson, C. O., J. W. Russell, et al. DO 14:37
Hubb1	Hubbard, J. P. Nest record	John13	Johnson, C. O., S. B. Speck, et al. DOS notes
Hubb2	Hubbard, J. P. USFWS unpublished banding data	JohH1	Johnson, H. M. AFN 20:23
Hubb3	Hubbard, J. P. DO 9:65	JohR1	Johnson, R., and D. N. Phalen. DOS notes
Hudy1	Hudy, R. Cornell nest record	Jone1	Jones, R. E. Cornell nest record
Hugh1	Hughes, W. E., Brown, and W. A. Shyrock. Cassinia 4:6	Jone2	Jones, R. E. USFWS unpublished banding data
		Jone3	Jones, R. E., and J. R. Longcore. DO 2:38
HurB1	Hurlock, B., and P. L. Hurlock. AFN 13:359	JonW1	Jones, W. R. AFN 14:439
Hurl1	Hurlock, P. L. AB 31:156	Kane1	Kane, Rich. AB 35:923
Hurl2	Hurlock, P. L. AB 44:1118	Keel1	Keelan, B., F. Day, and T. Wilson. AB 34:758
Insk1	Inskip, G. A. AB 40:87, DO 20:18	Keit1	Keith, A. AB 27:37
Insk2	Inskip, G. A. DO 16:38	Kell1	Keller, H. T. DOS Notes
Jaco1	Jaco, L. S. DOS notes	Kell2	Keller, H. T. AB 42:1276
Jaco2	Jaco, L. S. AB 35:808	Kell3	Keller, H. T. DO 16:53
Jaco3	Jaco, L. S., et al. DO 14:37	Kell4	Keller, H. T., et al. DOS notes
Jahn1	Jahn, M. G. Nest record	Kell5	Keller, H. T., et al. DO 16:51
Jahn2	Jahn, M. G. Cornell nest record	Kell6	Keller, H. T., et al. DO 16:53
Jahn3	Jahn, M. G. Colonial Waterbird Registry	Kell7	Keller, H. T., and C. A. Butler. DOS notes
Jahn4	Jahn, M. G. DO 14:10	Kell8	Keller, H. T., L. L. Falk, et al. DO 16:86
Jahn5	Jahn, M. G. DO 14:37	Kell9	Keller, H. T., S. Keller, and H. Griffith. DOS notes
Jahn6	Jahn, M. G. DO 15:49	Kell10	Keller, H. T., J. A. Pie, et al. DOS notes
Jahn7	Jahn, M. G. DO 15:50	Kell11	Keller, H. T., R. D. Ross, et al. DOS notes
Jahn8	Jahn, M. G. DO 16:37	Kell12	Keller, H. T., S. B. Speck, et al. DO 16:53
Jahn9	Jahn, M. G. DO 16:41	KelJ1	Kelley, J. F. DO 9:19; DOS notes
Jahn10	Jahn, M. G. DO 16:42	Kenn1	Kennedy, C., and R. Naczi. Nest record
Jahn11	Jahn, M. G., et al. DO 14:37	Kerr1	Kerr, R. R. AN 10:95
Jahn12	Jahn, M. G., and D. P. Miller. DO 8:28	King1	King, J. E., and E. R. Greene. Atlantic Naturalist 20:146
Jahn13	Jahn, M. G., Sample, et al. DO 14:37		
Jahn14	Jahn, M. G., S. B. Speck, et al. DO 14:37	Klab1	Klabunde, P. K. AFN 19:366
Jalo1	Jalot, F. Atlas notes	Klab2	Klabunde, P. K. DO 12:56
Jame1	James, H. F. Cornell nest record	Klab3	Klabunde, P. K. Falk 1971

Klab4   Klabunde, P. K., et al. Falk 1971
Klab5   Klabunde, P. K., and S. T. Brooks. DO 12:56
Klab6   Klabunde, P. K., B. D. Carrick, et al. DO 12:66
Klab7   Klabunde, P. K., B. D. Carrick, and R. L. West. DO
    2:37
Klab8   Klabunde, P. K., and G. L. New. Falk 1971
Klab9   Klabunde, P. K., and T. T. Talarowski. DO 12:56
Klab10   Klabunde, P. K., and W. J. Wayne. DOS notes
Klab11   Klabunde, P. K., and R. L. West. DO 12:56
Knar1   Knarr, D., and S. Lewis. DOS notes
Know1   Knowles, R. N. Nest record
Know2   Knowles, R. N. Cornell nest record
Know3   Knowles, R. N. USFWS unpublished banding data
Know4   Knowles, R. N. DO 3:47
Kofe1   Kofer, H. AFN 16:464
KraE1   Kramer, Mrs. E. Y. AFN 2:171
Kram1   Kramer, Q. Audubon Magazine supp. 47:32
Kram2   Kramer, Q. Cassinia 31:46
Kram3   Kramer, Q. Cassinia 31:47
Kram4   Kramer, Q. DO 3:11
Kram5   Kramer, Q., et al. Audubon Magazine 43:566
Kram6   Kramer, Q., and C. Price. AFN 3:203
Kron1   Kronschnarbel, A. AB 25:560
Kunk1   Kunkle, D., and G. Regensburg. AB 31:1119
Lake1   Lakeman, M. AB 25:560
Lake2   Lakeman, M. AFN 19: 531
Lake3   Lakeman, M. AN 20:216
Lake4   Lakeman, M. AN 21:40
Lake5   Lakeman, M., and M. Nelson. AFN 22:21
Lake6   Lakeman, M., and M. Nelson. AN 19:242
Lake7   Lakeman, M., and M. Nelson. DO 4:22, AFN 21:17
Lake8   Lakeman, M. DO 4:20, AN 22:43
Lamp1   Lamplugh, J. R. AFN 9:324
Lamp2   Lamplugh, J. R., and R. T. Brooke, Jr. AFN 9:248
Lawr1   Lawrence, S. R. AB 22:427
Lawr2   Lawrence, S. R. AB 25:841
Lawr3   Lawrence, S. R. AB 28:36
Lawr4   Lawrence, S. R. AB 33:849
Lawr5   Lawrence, S. R. AFN 18:502
Lawr6   Lawrence, S. R. AFN 23:578
Lehm1   Lehman, J. G. DOS notes
Lehm2   Lehman, J. G. Atlas notes
Lehm3   Lehman, J. G. Nest record
Lehm4   Lehman, J. G. USFWS unpublished data
Lehm5   Lehman, J. G. AB 29:836
Lehm6   Lehman, J. G. AB 31:985
Lehm7   Lehman, J. G. AFN 22:596
Lehm8   Lehman, J. G. AN 30:80
Lehm9   Lehman, J. G. AN 30:81
Lehm10   Lehman, J. G. AN 30:189
Lehm11   Lehman, J. G. AN 31:31
Lehm12   Lehman, J. G. DO 9:18, AB 27:855
Lehm13   Lehman, J. G. DO 9:19
Lehm14   Lehman, J. G. DO 9:65

Lehm15   Lehman, J. G. DO 9:68
Lehm16   Lehman, J. G. DO 11:9
Lehm17   Lehman, J. G. DO 11:10
Lehm18   Lehman, J. G. DO 11:44
Lehm19   Lehman, J. G. DO 11:53
Lehm20   Lehman, J. G. DO 11:56
Lehm21   Lehman, J. G. DO 12:53
Lehm22   Lehman, J. G., et al. DOS notes
Lehm23   Lehman, J. G., et al. DO 14:37; mistakenly published
    as 10
Lehm24   Lehman, J. G., and M. V. Barnhill. Barnhill notes
Lehm25   Lehman, J. G., and M. V. Barnhill. DOS notes
Lehm26   Lehman, J. G., and M. V. Barnhill. AN 30:135
Lehm27   Lehman, J. G., and M. V. Barnhill. DO 11:53
Lehm28   Lehman, J. G., and M. V. Barnhill, et al. DO 14:37
Lehm29   Lehman, J. G., and W. A. Brokaw. DO 14:37
Lehm30   Lehman, J. G., and P. G. DuMont. AB 31:980
Lehm31   Lehman, J. G., D. N. Phalen, C. A. Sample, and D. J.
    Boller. DO 12:4, 14:47
Lehm32   Lehman, J. G., and W. J. Wayne. DOS notes
Lehm33   Lehman, J. G., and W. J. Wayne. AN 31:33, DOS
    nest record card
Lehm34   Lehman, J. G., and W. J. Wayne. DO 14:37
Lehm35   Lehman, J. G., W. J. Wayne, et al. DO 14:63
Lehm36   Lehman, J. G., R. L. West, and M. V. Barnhill. AN
    30:137
Lehm37   Lehman, J. G., et al. DO 14:37
Leit1   Leitzinger, W. A. NOAA unpublished data. Mabey
    et al. 1993
LesC1   Lesser, C. A. DO 1:6
LesC2   Lesser, C. A. DO 2:15
LesC3   Lesser, C. A., and J. R. Longcore. Nest record
LesC4   Lesser, C. A., F. Murphy, E. K. Pennypacker, and
    R. L. West. DO 4:31
LesC5   Lesser, C. A., F. Murphy, E. K. Pennypacker, and
    R. L. West. DO 4:34
LesC6   Lesser, C. A., and R. L. West. DO 2:5
LesC7   Lesser, C. A., and R. L. West. DO 4:31
Less8   Lesser, F. H. AN 18:35
Less9   Lesser, F. H. AFN 15:456
Less10   Lesser, F. H. AFN 16:16
Less11   Lesser, F. H. AFN 16:316
Less12   Lesser, F. H. AFN 16:464
Less13   Lesser, F. H. AFN 16:465
Less14   Lesser, F. H. AFN 17:20
Less15   Lesser, F. H. Cassinia 46:34
Less16   Lesser, F. H. Cassinia 46:35
Less17   Lesser, F. H. Cassinia 47:41
Less18   Lesser, F. H., and A. R. Stickley. AFN 16:16, Cassinia
    46:28
Less19   Lesser, F. H., and A. R. Stickley. AFN 18:441
Levy1   Levy, M., and K. T. Mullen. AN 23:108, DO 6:1
LewA1   Lewis, A. R. DO 9:68
LewC1   Lewis, C., and B. D. Carrick. AFN 20:27

Lieh1	Liehr, K. C. AB 25:719	Maie2	Maier, L. DO 25:49
Lieh2	Liehr, K. C. AB 28:624	Mann1	Manners, E. Cassinia 37:27
Lieh3	Liehr, K. C. DO 9:60	Mann2	Manners, E., et al. Cassinia 37:27
Lieh4	Liehr, K. C. DO 9:64	Mars1	Marshall, B. R. DOS notes
Ligh1	Light, K., and W. Faust. AFN 19:459	Mars2	Marshall, B. R. DO 10:7
Line1	Linehan, J. T. Notes	Mars3	Marshall, B. R., et al. DOS notes
Line2	Linehan, J. T. DOS notes	Mars4	Marshall, B. R., and D. N. Phalen. DOS notes
Line3	Linehan, J. T. Cornell nest record	Marv1	Marvel, C. S., et al. AFN 21:491
Line4	Linehan, J. T. USFWS unpublished banding data	Marv2	Marvel, C. S., et al. DO 9:63
Line5	Linehan, J. T. USFWS unpublished data	Marv3	Marvel, C. S., H. L. Rice, et al. DO 1:1, Wayne notes
Line6	Linehan, J. T. AB 28:36	Marv4	Marvel, C. S., R. A. Rowlett, and W. J. Wayne. AB
Line7	Linehan, J. T. AB 29:833		28:889
Line8	Linehan, J. T. AB 30:822	Matl1	Matlack, A. S., W. J. Wayne, et al. Falk 1971
Line9	Linehan, J. T. AB 32:1143	MatD1	Matthews, D. AN 26:48
Line10	Linehan, J. T. AFN 21:17	MatH1	Matthews, H. AFN 8:304
Line11	Linehan, J. T. DO 1:5	Maur1	Maurer, R. AB 36:834
Line12	Linehan, J. T. DO 4:33	MayR1	May, R. M. Notes, DMNH
Line13	Linehan, J. T. DO 5:20	McCH1	McClure, H. AB 28:625
Line14	Linehan, J. T. DO 5:5	McCT1	McClure, T. R. DOS notes
Line15	Linehan, J. T. DO 6:23	McCT2	McClure, T. R. DO 6:3
Line16	Linehan, J. T., et al. DO 1:5,	McCT3	McClure, T. R. DO 9:68
Line17	Linehan, J. T., et al. AFN 20:628	McDo1	McDonald, N. Bird-Lore 29:424
Line18	Linehan, J. T., D. J. Boller, et al. DOS notes	McLa1	McLaughlin, F. AFN 3:8
Line19	Linehan, J. T., and H. T. Keller. DOS notes	McLP1	McLaughlin, P. P. USFWS unpublished BBS data
Line20	Linehan, J. T., and H. T. Keller. DO 15:29	McLP2	McLaughlin, P. P. AFN 20:173, 409 and 21:19
Line21	Linehan, J. T., and D. P. Miller. Atlas notes	McLP3	McLaughlin, P. P. DO 2:17
Line22	Linehan, J. T., and P. E. Strickland. AFN 24:202	McLP4	McLaughlin, P. P. DO 4:6
Litt1	Little, M. C. DOS notes	McLP5	McLaughlin, P. P., and A. R. Stickley. DO 2:24
Litt2	Little, M. C. DO 18:40	McMu1	McMullin. Bird-Lore 36:243
Litt3	Little, M. C. DO 18:41	McNe1	McNeill, J. T. AB 26:745
Litt4	Little, M. C. DO 25:46	McWh1	McWhorter, R. L., and D. L. Smathers. AB 41:408
Litt5	Little, M. C., and DOS. DOS notes	Mean1	Meanley, B. DO 2:18
Litt6	Little, M. C., and R. Miller. Atlas notes	MerW1	Meridith, W. Atlas notes
Litt7	Little, M. C., W. J. Wayne, et al. DO 14:37	MerW2	Meridith, W. Atlas notes; letter, 1981
Livi1	Livingston, P. A. Bird-Lore 30:336	MerW2	Meridith, W. Atlas notes; letter, 1981
Livi2	Livingston, P. A. Bird-Lore 36:243	MerJ1	Meritt, J. K., and B. D. Carrick. AFN 21:493
Long1	Longcore, J. R. Cornell nest record	MerJ2	Meritt, J. K., and J. D. Danzenbaker. AB 45:1100
Long2	Longcore, J. R. DO 3:8	Mess1	Messersmith, D. H., and C. S. Robbins. AN 24:104
Long3	Longcore, J. R. DO 4:23	Mich1	Michael, T. R. Cornell nest record
Long4	Longcore, J. R. AFN 20:645, Cornell nest record	MiDP1	Miller, D. P. DOS notes
Long5	Longcore, J. R. Cornell nest record, probably	MiDP2	Miller, D. P. Atlas notes
	hatched the next day	MiDP3	Miller, D. P. Nest record
Lope1	Loper, G. Atlas notes	MiDP4	Miller, D. P. Cornell nest record
Lowe1	Lowe, S. H. Wood Thrush 3:66	MiDP5	Miller, D. P. DO 8:15
Lyma1	Lyman, E. Letter, Pennock notes	MiDP6	Miller, D. P. DO 19:25
Lyma2	Lyman, E. Hanson notes	MiDP7	Miller, D. P. DO 21:8
Mack1	Mack, H. Hanson notes, no site given	MiDP8	Miller, D. P. DO 21:10
MacG1	Mackiernen, G., and B. Cooper. DOS notes	MiDP9	Miller, D. P. DO 24:54
MacT1	MacTavish, B. AB 42:408, 43:56	MiDP10	Miller, D. P. DO 25:49
MagJ1	Magnan, J., and J. Danzenbacker. DO 24:70	MiDP11	Miller, D. P., et al. DOS notes
MagR1	Magnan, R. E. DO 18:47	MiDP12	Miller, D. P., et al. DO 14:37
MagR2	Magnan, R. E. NOAA unpublished data, Mabey	MiDP13	Miller, D. P., and D. J. Boller. DO 14:37
	et al. 1993	MiDP14	Miller, D. P., A. Hallenbeck, et al. DOS notes
Maie1	Maier, L. Atlas notes	MiDP15	Miller, D. P., A. Hallenbeck, et al. DO 14:37

MiDP16	Miller, D. P., and M. G. Jahn. Nest record
MiDP17	Miller, D. P., and J. W. Russell. DO 14:37
MiDP18	Miller, D. P., J. Patterson, et al. DO 14:37
MiDR1	Miller, D. R. Atlas notes
MiDR2	Miller, D. R., F. Jalot, and J. Coleman. Nest record
MiDR3	Miller, D. R., and R. J. Keene. Atlas notes
MiJC1	Miller, J. C. Notes
MiJC2	Miller, J. C. DOS notes
MiJC3	Miller, J. C. Cornell Nest record
MiJC4	Miller, J. C., and W. Stocku, Pennsylvania Birds 3:79
MiJC5	Miller, J. C. Cassinia 29:48
MiJC6	Miller, J. C. Cassinia 41:80
MiJC7	Miller, J. C. USFWS unpublished data
MiJC8	Miller, J. C. Pair with young, notes
MiRF1	Miller, R. F. DMNH egg data
MiWD1	Miller, W. D. Letter, C. J. Pennock notes
MiHM1	Milliken, H. M. DO 7(2):23
Mitc1	Mitchell, R. USFWS unpublished banding data
m.ob1	m.obs. DOS notes
m.ob2	m.obs. AB 41:1416
m.ob3	m.obs. AB 44:244
m.ob4	m.obs. AN 26:45
m.ob5	m.obs. Cassinia 37:26
m.ob6	m.obs. DO 7(2):25; DOS notes
m.ob7	m.obs. DO 17:37
Mohr1	Mohr, C. E. DO 4:22, 45
Moor1	Moore. Bird-Lore 40:460
MooJ1	Moorhouse, J. H. Nest record
MooJ2	Moorhouse, J. H. DO 12:54
MooJ3	Moorhouse, J. H., and A. P. Ednie. Nest record
Morg1	Morgan and Reid. AFN 3:9
Moun1	Mount, E. AN 24:35
Mudd1	Mudd, S. H. AN 28:66
Mulh1	Mulholland, J. AN 20:216
Murd1	Murdoch, F., and A. Brady. AB 32:1144
MurF1	Murphy, F., fide. DO 3:46
MurW1	Murphy, W. AB 40:90
MurW2	Murphy, W., and N. Murphy. DNREC shorebird survey
MurW3	Murphy, W., and N. Murphy. AB 42:415
MurW3	Murphy, W., and N. Murphy. AB 42:416
MurW4	Murphy, W., N. Murphy, and Jon Dunn. AB 46:71
Nacz1	Naczi, R. DO 14:10
Niel1	Nielson, T. AB 30:822. DO 11:50
Nile1	Niles, D. M. Notes
Nile2	Niles, D. M. Nest record
Nile3	Niles, D. M. DO 11:53
Nile4	Niles, D. M. DO 14:10
Nile5	Niles, D. M. DO 18:49
Nile6	Niles, D. M. DO 20:19
Nile7	Niles, D. M. DO 20:20
Nile8	Niles, D. M. DO 21:5
Nile9	Niles, D. M. DO 21:6

Nile10	Niles, D. M. and A. P. Ednie. Atlas notes
Nile11	Niles, D. M. and A. P. Ednie. DO 20:19
Nile12	Niles, D. M. and S. P. Homsey. Nest record
Nile13	Niles, D. M. and S. P. Homsey. DO 14:12
Nile14	Niles, D. M. and S. P. Homsey. DO 15:54
Nile15	Niles, D. M. and S. P. Homsey. DO 16:35
Nile16	Niles, D. M. and S. P. Homsey. DO 16:36
Nile17	Niles, D. M. Nest record, 2 warm eggs
Nixd1	Nixdorf, E. B., S. B. Speck, and G. W. Whitman. Falk 1971
Nixd2	Nixdorf, E. B., and P. E. Strickland. DO 2:16
O'BJ1	O'Brien, J. AB 48:93
O'BM1	O'Brien, M. DOS notes
O'BM2	O'Brian, M. AB 36:960
O'BM3	O'Brian, M. AB 45:1098
Oliv1	Oliver, J. Notes
Orin1	Oring, L. W. AN 13:38
O'Sh1	O'Shea, G. F. Atlas notes
O'Sh2	O'Shea, G. F. Nest record
O'Sh3	O'Shea, G. F. AB 37:286
O'Sh4	O'Shea, G. F. DO 18:48
Palm1	Palmer, A. B. DO 18:38
Palm2	Palmer, A. B. DO 20:31, Atlas notes
Palm3	Palmer, A. B., et al. DOS notes
Palm4	Palmer, A. B., et al. DO 16:53
Park1	Parker, T. AB 25:38
Patt1	Patterson, J. W. Nest record
Patt2	Patterson, J. W. USFWS unpublished data
Patt3	Patterson, J. W. DO 12:54
Patt4	Patterson, J. W. DO 14:8
Patt5	Patterson, J. W. DO 14:37
Patt6	Patterson, J. W., et al. DO 14:37
Patt7	Patterson, J. W., et al. DOS notes
Patt8	Patterson, J. W., and N. Lloyd. DOS notes
Patt9	Patterson, J. W., S. B. Speck, et al. DO 15:28
Patt10	Patterson, J. W. USFWS unpublished data and DOS notes
Patt11	Patterson, J. W. Atlas notes
Paul1	Paul, R. T., J. F. Alcock, and John Alcock. AFN 20:23
Pede1	Pederson, C., R. Hilton, and A. P. Ednie. AB 40:1184
Peli1	Pelizza, C. Nest record
Pell1	Pell, W., 2nd. SNHD notes
Pell2	Pell, W., 2nd. AFN 7:207
Penn1	Pennock, C. J. Notes
Penn2	Pennock, C. J. Hanson notes
Penn3	Pennock, C. J. Cassinia 5:52
Penn4	Pennock, C. J. Cassinia 11:37
Penn5	Pennock, C. J. Cassinia 16:33, Pennock notes
Penn6	Pennock, C. J. Proceedings of the D.O.V.C. 1908
Penn7	Pennock, C. J., and S. Trotter. Bird-Lore 10:32
Peop1	Peoples, B., and D. Peoples. DO 1:2, AFN 18:23
Pepp1	Pepper, Mrs. E. J. USFWS unpublished banding data
Pepp1	Pepper, Mrs. E. J. USFWS unpublished banding data
Perk1	Perkins, S. AB 42:1269, fide

Pero1	Peron, L., M. V. Barnhill, and J. A. Gordon. AB 34:258
Perr1	Perry, C. AB 41:407
Perr2	Perry, C., and H. T. Armistead. AB 43:493
Perr3	Perry, C., H. T. Armistead, and J. W. Sparks. AB 42:414
Perr4	Perry, C., R. Mitchell, et al. AB 42:1276
Perr5	Perry, C., and D. T. Shoch. AB 42:1276
Perr6	Perry, C., and D. T. Shoch. AB 42:1298
PerD1	Perry, D. B. AFN 19:365, 368
PeBG1	Peterjohn, B. G. AB 47:398, 1095
PeBG2	Peterjohn, B. G., et al. DO 24:65
PeBG3	Peterjohn, B. G., and M. E. Gustafson. AB 46:399
PeHS1	Peters, H. S. Letter, 13 April 1963, to Seal Brooks
PetA1	Peterson, A. DO 4:8
PetA2	Peterson, A. DO 4:24
PetB1	Peterson, B. AB 33:756
Pfef1	Pfeffer, J., and M. A. Rubin. Atlas notes
Phal1	Phalen, D. N. DOS notes
Phal2	Phalen, D. N. Nest record
Phal3	Phalen, D. N. DO 8:50
Phal4	Phalen, D. N. DO 8:52
Phal5	Phalen, D. N. DO 9:64
Phal6	Phalen, D. N. DO 9:66
Phal7	Phalen, D. N. DO 9:68
Phal8	Phalen, D. N., et al. AB 39:151
Phal9	Phalen, D. N., et al. DOS notes
Phal10	Phalen, D. N., and B. R. Marshall. DOS notes
PiéJ1	Pié, J. A. DOS notes
PiéJ2	Pié, J. A., et al. DOS notes
PiéJ3	Pié, J. A., W. J. Wayne, et al. DOS notes
PooA1	Poole, A. D. Pennock notes
PooE1	Poole, E., and C. F. Poole. DOS notes
PooC1	Poole, C. F., and H. L. Rice. Falk 1971
Port1	Portnoy, J. W. Colonial Waterbird Registry
Pott1	Potter, J. K., ed. AFN 1:4
Pott2	Potter, J. K., ed. Bird-Lore 25:258
Pott3	Potter, J. K., ed. Bird-Lore 27:186
Pott4	Potter, J. K., ed. Bird-Lore 31:198
Pott5	Potter, J. K., ed. Bird-Lore 35:212, Cassinia 30:11
Pott6	Potter, J. K. Stone 1937
Preb1	Preble, E. A. Patuxent Bird Distribution and Migration Files, fide C. S. Robbins
Pres1	Prest, G. A. Notes
Pres2	Prest, G. A. Nest record
Pres3	Prest, G. A. Cornell nest record
Pres4	Prest, G. A. USFWS unpublished data
Pres5	Prest, G. A. AN 21:186
Pres6	Prest, G. A. DO 5:18
Pres6	Prest, G. A. DO 5:18
Prim1	Prime Hook NWR. Notes
Pulc1	Pulcinella, N. J. AB 47:399
Pulc2	Pulcinella, N. J. DO 19:28
Pulc3	Pulcinella, N. J. DO 24:67

Pulc4	Pulcinella, N. J., and P. Bacinski. DO 24:67, AB 46:69
Pure1	Purey, L. J. DOS notes
Pure2	Purey, L. J. AB 34:258
Pure3	Purey, L. J. DO 8:59
Pure4	Purey, L. J. DO 9:69
Pure6	Purey, L. J. DO 11:9
Pure7	Purey, L. J. DO 11:54
Pure8	Purey, L. J. DO 12:53
Pure9	Purey, L. J. DO 13:22
Pure10	Purey, L. J. DO 13:23
Pure11	Purey, L. J. DO 15:49
Pure12	Purey, L. J. DO 16:36
Pure13	Purey, L. J., and N. Irish AB 34:146, 259, 439; DO 15:57
Pure14	Purey, L. J., and D. T. Weesner. DO 14:12
Pure15	Purey, L. J. DO 9:57
PylP1	Pyle, P. AB 28:623
PylR1	Pyle, R. L. USFWS unpublished banding data
PylR2	Pyle, R. L. AFN 18:21
PylR4	Pyle, R. L. AFN 19:22
PylR5	Pyle, R. L. AFN 24:588, AN 25:141
PylR6	Pyle, R. L. AN 20:216
PylR7	Pyle, R. L. DO 3:4
PylR8	Pyle, R. L., et al. DO 2:15
PylR9	Pyle, R. L., and C. W. Carlson. AFN 19:23
PylR10	Pyle, R. L., and P. G. DuMont. AN 30:133
Quan1	Quantrille, T. DO 3:4
Quic1	Quickmire, J. S. AFN 6:189
Quin1	Quinn, D. Atlas notes
Quin2	Quinn, D. DOS notes
Rals1	Ralston, J. G., Jr. AB 29:36
Rals2	Ralston, J. G., Jr. AFN 11:332
Rals3	Ralston, J. G., Jr., and D. M. Niles. Nest record
Reim1	Reimann, E. J. AFN 27:598
Reim2	Reimann, E. J., and W. Carr. AB 37:851
Reyb1	Reybold, U. U. Manuscript notes, 19 November 1925, in Patuxent Bird Distribution and Migration Files
Rich1	Richards, K. C. DOS notes
Rich2	Richards, K. C. AB 26:746
Rich3	Richards, K. C. AFN 24:30
Rich4	Richards, K. C. DO 9:15
Rigb1	Rigby, J. Atlas notes
Rigb2	Rigby, J. AFN 5:10
Rigb3	Rigby, J. Cassinia 31:48
Ring1	Ringler, R. F. AB 36:277
Ring2	Ringler, R. F., ed. AB 42:727
Robb1	Robbins, C. S., compiler. Wood Thrush 4:200
Robb2	Robbins, C. S., et al. AFN 23:578
Robe1	Roberge, J. Cassinia 36:33
RobT1	Roberts, T. E. DOS notes
RobT2	Roberts, T. E. DO 9:60
RobT3	Roberts, T. E., et al. DOS notes

RobT4   Roberts, T. E., H. P. Brokaw, et al. DO 12:17
Rosc1   Rosche, R. C. Cornell nest record
Rosc2   Rosche, R. C. AFN 16:464
Rose1   Rose, B. J. AB 47:1094
Ross1   Ross, R. D., and C. Richter. DOS notes
Ross2   Ross, R. D., D. Beatty, and D. J. Boller. DO 15:28
Ross3   Ross, R. D., et al. DO 15:28
Ross4   Ross, R. D., et al. DO 16:53
Roth1   Roth, R. R. Unpublished data
Roth2   Roth, R. R. Atlas notes
Rowl1   Rowlett, R. A. AB 26:44
Rowl2   Rowlett, R. A. AB 26:585
Rowl3   Rowlett, R. A. AB 27:854
Rowl4   Rowlett, R. A. AB 28:889
Rowl5   Rowlett, R. A. AB 30:39
Rowl6   Rowlett, R. A. AB 33:848
Rowl7   Rowlett, R. A. AB 34:758
Rowl8   Rowlett, R. A. AB 30:820
Rowl9   Rowlett, R. A. AN 26:133
Rowl10   Rowlett, R. A. AN 27:43, 137
Rowl11   Rowlett, R. A. AN 27:85
Rowl12   Rowlett, R. A. AN 28:66
Rowl13   Rowlett, R. A. AN 28:173
Rowl14   Rowlett, R. A. AN 30:78
Rowl15   Rowlett, R. A. AN 30:186; DO 11:45, 53; AB 30:39
Rowl16   Rowlett, R. A. DO 11:46
Rowl17   Rowlett, R. A. DO 11:53, 11:45; AB 30:39
Rowl18   Rowlett, R. A. DO 11:53
Rowl19   Rowlett, R. A. DO 15:49
Rowl20   Rowlett, R. A., and C. P. Wilds. Photo of 16, AB 28:785
Rowl21   Rowlett, R. A., et al. AB 30:42
Rubi1   Rubin, M. A., and J. Pfeffer. Atlas notes
Rufe1   Rufe, R. G. Atlas notes, fide
Rufe2   Rufe, R. G. DNREC 1986 shorebird survey in Thomas 1986
Rufe3   Rufe, R. G. AB 43:1296
Rufe4   Rufe, R. G. DO 23:23
Rufe5   Rufe, R. G., et al. DOS notes
Rufe6   Rufe, R. G., et al. DO 14:37
Rufe7   Rufe, R. G., et al. DO 15:28
Rufe8   Rufe, R. G., et al. DO 20:23
Rufe9   Rufe, R. G., Speck, et al. DO 14:37
Rufe10   Rufe, R. G., Speck, et al. DO 14:37
Rumf1   Rumford, L. Notes, band # 40477, DMNH
RusJ1   Russell, J. W. DOS notes
RusJ2   Russell, J. W. AB 43:292, DOS notes
RusJ3   Russell, J. W. DO 14:11
RusJ4   Russell, J. W. DO 14:37
RusJ5   Russell, J. W. DO 26:11
RusJ6   Russell, J. W., et al. DOS notes
RusJ7   Russell, J. W., et al. DO 14:37
RusJ8   Russell, J. W., L. L. Falk, et al. DO 14:37

RusJ9   Russell, J. W., W. W. Frech, H. Cutler. DO 19:33; AB 39:278 in error, Frech notes
RusJ10   Russell, J. W., R. Kabis. DOS notes
RusJ11   Russell, J. W., S. B. Speck, et al. DOS notes
RusJ12   Russell, J. W., W. J. Wayne, et al. DO 14:37
RusJ13   Russell, J. W., W. J. Wayne. DO 14:37
RusK1   Russell, K., D. and B. Cadbury, and T. Serrano. AB 41:262
RusR1   Russell, R. W. DOS notes
RusR2   Russell, R. W. Atlas notes
RusR3   Russell, R. W. Cornell nest record
RusR4   Russell, R. W. AB 35:282
RusR5   Russell, R. W. AB 35:806
RusR6   Russell, R. W. AB 36:834
RusR7   Russell, R. W. DO 15:51
RusR8   Russell, R. W. DO 15:53
RusR9   Russell, R. W. DO 15:55
RusR10   Russell, R. W. DO 16:40
RusR11   Russell, R. W. DO 16:41
RusR12   Russell, R. W. DO 17:30
RusR13   Russell, R. W. DO 17:31
RusR14   Russell, R. W. DO 17:32
RusR15   Russell, R. W. DO 19:34. Atlas notes
RusR16   Russell, R. W., and J. D. Citron. DOS notes
RusR17   Russell, R. W., and A. P. Ednie. DOS notes
RusR18   Russell, R. W., and R. L. West. DOS notes
RusR19   Russell, R. W., and R. L. West. DO 17:38
RusR20   Russell, R. W., and S. McCandless. DOS notes
RusW1   Russell, W. C. USFWS unpublished banding data
RusW2   Russell, W. C. AN 22:45
RusW3   Russell, W. C. DO 3:46
RusW4   Russell, W. C. DO 3:53
RusW5   Russell, W. C. DO 4:7
RusW6   Russell, W. C. DO 4:8
RusW7   Russell, W. C. DO 5:10
RusW8   Russell, W. C., D. A. Cutler, et al. AB 43:456 and DOS notes
Rydg1   Rydgren, A. Nest record
SPCA1   SPCA. Dover, thence to TSBR, 1983
Samp1   Sample, C. E. DOS notes
Samp2   Sample, C. E. Nest record
Samp3   Sample, C. E. DNREC shorebird survey
Samp4   Sample, C. E. DO 21:8
Samp5   Sample, C. E. DO 25:49
Samp6   Sample, C. E., et al. DO 14:37
Samp7   Sample, C. E., et al. DO 16:53
Samp8   Sample, C. E., and N. Sample. DOS notes
Scar1   Scarpulla, N. J., and P. G. DuMont. AB 47:1094
SchH1   Schall, H. AFN 20:25
SchE1   Scharr, E. AB 36:959
Sche1   Scheider, F., et al. AN 18:35
Sche2   Scheider, F., et al. AN 18:36
Schm1   Schmid. Cassinia 31:45

Schw1	Schwalbe, P. W. Cornell nest record
Schw2	Schwalbe, P. W. Cassinia 46:34
Schw3	Schwalbe, P. W. S. T. Brooks notes
Scov1	Scoville. Cassinia 24:46
Serr1	Serridge, et al. DOS notes
Shoc1	Shoch, D. T. DOS notes
Shoc2	Shoch, D. T. AB 42:414
Shoc3	Shoch, D. T. AB 43:1295
Shoc4	Shoch, D. T. AB 44:66, DOS notes
Shoc5	Shoch, D. T. AB 44:404
Shoc6	Shoch, D. T. DO 23:23
Shoc7	Shoch, D. T., et al. AB 43:1294, DOS notes
Shoc8	Shoch, D. T., and M. V. Barnhill. DO 23:22, AB 43:97
Shor1	Short, E. S. AB 47:244
Shor2	Short, E. S., and C. D. Campbell. DO 25:47
Shor3	Short, E. S., A. P. Ednie, C. D. Campbell, J. F. Swertinski, G. K. Hess, R. L. West, and C. M. Ostapchenko DOS notes
Shor4	Short, E. S., and B. Lantz. DOS notes
Shor5	Short, E. S., M. C. Little, et al. DO 25:46
Shor6	Short, E. S., J. F. Swertinski, W. W. Frech, et al. AB 47:244
Smit1	Smith, E. F. Nest record
Smit2	Smith, E. F. Bombay Hook NWR notes
SmiP1	Smith, P. W., et al. AB 37:284
SpeE1	Speck, E. B. DOS notes
SpeE2	Speck, E. B. Atlas notes
SpeE3	Speck, E. B. Nest record
SpeE4	Speck, E. B. DO 17:34
SpeE5	Speck, E. B. DO 18:49
SpeE6	Speck, E. B. DO 18:55
SpeE7	Speck, E. B. DO 18:60
SpeE8	Speck, E. B. DO 20:20
SpeE9	Speck, E. B. DO 23:20
SpeE10	Speck, E. B., and A. P. Ednie. AB 38:890
SpeE11	Speck, E. B., and S. B. Speck. DOS notes
SpeE12	Speck, E. B., and S. B. Speck. DOS and Atlas notes, DO 19:25
SpeE13	Speck, E. B., and S. B. Speck. Nest record
SpeE14	Speck, E. B., and S. B. Speck. DO 20:20
SpeE15	Speck, E. B., and S. B. Speck. DO 20:21
SpeE16	Speck, E. B., and S. B. Speck. AB 47:398
SpeE17	Speck, E. B., S. B. Speck, and W. J. Wayne. DOS notes
SpeE18	Speck, E. B., S. B. Speck, and W. J. Wayne. Atlas notes
SpeS1	Speck, Sharon. Nest record
SpSB1	Speck, S. B. DOS notes
SpSB2	Speck, S. B. Cornell nest record
SpSB3	Speck, S. B. AFN 19:24
SpSB4	Speck, S. B. DO 1:3
SpSB5	Speck, S. B. DO 3:6
SpSB6	Speck, S. B. DO 12:56
SpSB7	Speck, S. B. DO 12:56
SpSB8	Speck, S. B. DO 14:37
SpSB9	Speck, S. B. DO 15:28
SpSB10	Speck, S. B. DO 15:28
SpSB11	Speck, S. B. DO 25:45
SpSB12	Speck, S. B. Falk 1971
SpSB13	Speck, S. B., et al. DOS notes
SpSB14	Speck, S. B., et al. DO 7(2):24
SpSB15	Speck, S. B., et al. DO 12:17
SpSB16	Speck, S. B., et al. DO 14:37
SpSB17	Speck, S. B., et al. DO 15:28
SpSB18	Speck, S. B., M. V. Barnhill, et al. DO 14:37
SpSB19	Speck, S. B., P. E. Beach, et al. DOS notes
SpSB20	Speck, S. B., and S. T. Brooks. DO 12:56
SpSB21	Speck, S. B., M. G. Jahn, et al. DO 14:37
SpSB22	Speck, S. B., C. O. Johnson, et al. DOS notes
SpSB23	Speck, S. B., and J. G. Lehman. DOS notes
SpSB24	Speck, S. B., and E. B. Speck. DOS notes
SpSB25	Speck, S. B., and E. B. Speck. AB 40:451
SpSB26	Speck, S. B., and E. B. Speck. AB 40:1184
SpSB27	Speck, S. B., and E. B. Speck. AB 42:415
SpSB28	Speck, S. B., and E. B. Speck. AB 42:416
SpSB29	Speck, S. B., and E. B. Speck. DO 20:2
SpSB30	Speck, S. B., E. B. Speck, et al. DOS notes
SpSB31	Speck, S. B., E. B. Speck, et al. DNREC shorebird survey
SpSB32	Speck, S. B., E. B. Speck, and A. P. Ednie. DO 18:54
SpSB33	Speck, S. B., E. B. Speck, and L. L. Falk. DO 18:54
SpSB34	Speck, S. B., E. B. Speck, and C. O. Johnson. DOS notes
SpSB35	Speck, S. B., E. B. Speck, and D. P. Miller. DO 14:37
SpSB36	Speck, S. B., E. B. Speck, and D. A. Ward. DO 14:37
SpSB37	Speck, S. B., and M. L. Ward. DO 12:56
SpSB38	Speck, S. B., and M. L. Ward. DO 12:62
SpSB39	Speck, S. B., and W. J. Wayne. DOS notes
SpSB40	Speck, S. B., W. J. Wayne, et al. DOS notes
SpSB41	Speck, S. B., R. L. West, et al. DOS notes
SpSB42	Speck, S. B., C. O. Johnson, and A. Conway. AB 28:784
SpSB43	Speck, S. B., P. M. Walters. DOS notes
Spen1	Spence, L. Atlas notes
Spen2	Spence, L. DNREC 1986 Shorebird survey
Sper1	Sperling, B. AN 28:72
Spri1	Springer, P. F. Patuxent Bird Distribution and Migration Files
Spri2	Springer, P. F. AFN 7:302
Spri3	Springer, P. F. AFN 8:304
Spri4	Springer, P. F. AFN 16:464
Stev1	Stevens, D. Cornell nest record
StiA1	Stickley, A. R. AFN 15:457
StiA2	Stickley, A. R. DO 1:5,
StiA3	Stickley, A. R. DO 2:15,
StiA4	Stickley, A. R., compiler. DO 4:31
StiA5	Stickley, A. R., compiler. DO 4:33

StiA6 Stickley, A. R., and J. T. Linehan. DO 2:17, 29

StiA7 Stickley, A. R., T. T. Talarowski, and R. L. West. DO 2:14

Stoc1 Stock, T., et al. AB 40:1184

Stod1 Stoddard, P. AB 29:38

Stod2 Stoddard, P. AN 31:36

Stri1 Strickland, P. E. DOS notes

Stri2 Strickland, P. E. AB 35:974

Stri3 Strickland, P. E. DO 2:38

Stri4 Strickland, P. E. DO 20:55

Stri5 Strickland, P. E., et al. DOS notes

Stri6 Strickland, P. E., et al. DO 11:19

Stri7 Strickland, P. E., and A. S. Matlack. DO 12:56

SutC1 Sutton, C. AB 36:158

Sutt1 Sutton, H. A., I. R. Barnes, K. Trever, S. A. Briggs. AN 6:5

Sutt2 Sutton, H. A., et al. AN 11:137

Swer1 Swertinski, J. F. DOS notes

Swer2 Swertinski, J. F. DO 20:19

Swer3 Swertinski, J. F., and A. P. Ednie. DO 20:24

Sysa1 Sysak, M. DO 18:59

Tala1 Talarowski, T. T. DO 1:2

Teel1 Teele, Mr. and Mrs. R. AFN 18:344

Terb1 Terborgh, J. AN 10:94

ThoJ1 Thomas, J. Atlas notes

ThoJ2 Thomas, J. Nest record

ThoJ3 Thomas, J. AB 42:241

ThoR1 Thomen, R. W. AB 25:38

ThoR2 Thomen, R. W. Cassinia 53:52

ThoR3 Thomen, R. W. , and L. L. Falk. DO 12:17

Thor1 Thor, A. USFWS unpublished banding data

Till1 Tillmanns, E.-J. Nest record

Todd1 Todd, M. R. Cornell nest record

Tous1 Tousey, R. Wood Thrush 2:29

Tran1 Transue, W. R., Patuxent Bird Distribution and Migration Files

Twin1 Twining, R. D. Cassinia 30:minutes

Usda1 US Agricultural Report, 1853, cited in C. J. Pennock notes

Usfw1 USFWS unpublished BBS data

Usfw2 USFWS unpublished banding data

Usfw3 USFWS unpublished data

Usfw4 USFWS unpublished data; Robbins et al. 1986

Usfw5 USFWS midwinter waterfowl survey. AB 37:284

Ulme1 Ulmer, F. AFN 8:243

Unge1 Unger, E., and O. McCourt. AN 25:46

Vand1 Vanderhorst, P. J. DOS notes

Vand2 Vanderhorst, P. J. DO 24:59

Vand3 Vanderhorst, P. J., et al. DOS notes

Vaug1 Vaughn, C. R. AB 28:885

Vaug2 Vaughn, C. R. AB 43:1303

Voel1 Voelker. Cassinia 1:12

WalS1 Walter, S., B. Kurtz, et al.; M. and R. Moloughney

Walt1 Walters, P. M. DOS notes

Walt2 Walters, P. M. AB 28:788

Walt3 Walters, P. M., and W. A. Brokaw. DOS notes

WarD1 Ward, D. A. DOS notes

WarD2 Ward, D. A. DO 3:53

WarD3 Ward, D. A. DO 11:45

WarD4 Ward, D. A., et al. DOS notes

WarD6 Ward, D. A., et al. DO 12:17

WarD7 Ward, D. A., P. E. Beach, et al. DOS notes

WarD8 Ward, D. A., and D. Sibley. AB 38:183

WarD9 Ward, D. A., and E. B. Speck. DOS notes

WarD10 Ward, D. A., and R. Ward. DOS notes

WarD12 Ward, D. A., R. Ward, and G. E. Suskeep. AFN 22:513

WarD13 Ward, D. A., W. J. Wayne, et al. DOS notes

WarM1 Ward, M. L. DO 5:23,36

WarM2 Ward, M. L. DO 6:3

WarM3 Ward, M. L., and G. M. Whitman. DO 12:60

WarM4 Ward, M. L., and G. M. Whitman. DO 12:56

Wayn1 Wayne, W. J. Notes

Wayn2 Wayne, W. J. DOS notes

Wayn3 Wayne, W. J. Atlas notes

Wayn4 Wayne, W. J. Nest record

Wayn5 Wayne, W. J. Cornell nest record

Wayn6 Wayne, W. J. 1993 DNREC shorebird survey

Wayn7 Wayne, W. J. AB 25:38

Wayn8 Wayne, W. J. AB 25:843, fide, DOS notes

Wayn9 Wayne, W. J. AB 28:786

Wayn10 Wayne, W. J. AB 32:564

Wayn11 Wayne, W. J. AB 37:852

Wayn12 Wayne, W. J. AB 40:262

Wayn13 Wayne, W. J. AFN 22:20

Wayn14 Wayne, W. J. AFN 24:27

Wayn15 Wayne, W. J. Cassinia 53:54

Wayn16 Wayne, W. J. DO 3:6

Wayn17 Wayne, W. J. DO 3:50

Wayn18 Wayne, W. J. DO 9:16

Wayn19 Wayne, W. J. DO 14:37

Wayn20 Wayne, W. J. DO 17:37, DOS notes

Wayn21 Wayne, W. J. DO 17:40

Wayn22 Wayne, W. J. DO 18:50, fide, DOS notes

Wayn23 Wayne, W. J. DO 19:34

Wayn24 Wayne, W. J. DO 20:22

Wayn25 Wayne, W. J., et al. DOS notes

Wayn26 Wayne, W. J., et al. AB 27:855

Wayn27 Wayne, W. J., et al. AFN 22:595

Wayn28 Wayne, W. J., et al. DO 2:29, 45

Wayn29 Wayne, W. J., et al. DO 2:45

Wayn30 Wayne, W. J., et al. DO 7(1):6

Wayn31 Wayne, W. J., et al. DO 12:17

Wayn32 Wayne, W. J., et al. DO 13:30

Wayn33 Wayne, W. J., et al. DO 14:37

Wayn34 Wayne, W. J., P. E. Beach, et al. DO 12:17

Wayn35 Wayne, W. J., P. E. Beach, et al. DO 12:31

Wayn36 Wayne, W. J., and H. P. Brokaw. DOS notes

Wayn37	Wayne, W. J., H. P. Brokaw, and D. Brokaw. DO 15:59
Wayn38	Wayne, W. J., and W. A. Brokaw. DOS notes
Wayn39	Wayne, W. J., and S. T. Brooks. DOS notes
Wayn40	Wayne, W. J., S. T. Brooks, et al. DOS notes
Wayn41	Wayne, W. J., and C. A. Butler. DOS notes
Wayn42	Wayne, W. J., A. P. Ednie, and T. E. Roberts. DOS notes
Wayn43	Wayne, W. J., L. L. Falk, et al. DOS notes
Wayn44	Wayne, W. J., G. K. Hess, et al. DOS notes
Wayn45	Wayne, W. J., and H. T. Keller. DOS notes
Wayn46	Wayne, W. J., and J. G. Lehman. DOS notes
Wayn47	Wayne, W. J., and J. G. Lehman. AB 28:886
Wayn48	Wayne, W. J., and J. G. Lehman. AN 31:35
Wayn49	Wayne, W. J., J. G. Lehman, et al. DOS notes
Wayn50	Wayne, W. J., M. C. Little, et al. DO 14:37
Wayn51	Wayne, W. J., and J. D. Metzger. Winter bird census in DOS notes
Wayn52	Wayne, W. J., D. N. Phalen, et al. DOS notes
Wayn53	Wayne, W. J., and J. A. Pie. DOS notes
Wayn54	Wayne, W. J. AB 36:160
Wayn55	Wayne, W. J., and T. E. Roberts. DOS notes
Wayn56	Wayne, W. J., R. G. Rufe, et al. DO 15:28
Wayn57	Wayne, W. J., J. W. Russell, et al. DO 14:37
Wayn58	Wayne, W. J., and S. B. Speck. DOS notes
Wayn59	Wayne, W. J., and S. B. Speck. DO 15:28
Wayn60	Wayne, W. J., and S. B. Speck. DO 20:19
Wayn61	Wayne, W. J., and S. B. Speck. DO 21:8
Wayn62	Wayne, W. J., S. B. Speck, et al. DOS notes
Wayn63	Wayne, W. J., S. B. Speck, and W. A. Brokaw. DOS notes
Wayn64	Wayne, W. J., S. B. Speck, and E. B. Speck. DOS notes
Wayn65	Wayne, W. J., S. B. Speck, and E. B. Speck. DO 25:49
Wayn66	Wayne, W. J., and P. M. Walters. DOS notes
Wayn67	Wayne, W. J., R. Ward, and D. A. Ward. DOS notes
Wayn68	Wayne, W. J., and K. Weber. DOS notes
Wayn69	Wayne, W. J., and R. L. West. AFN 23:29
Wayn70	Wayne, W. J., R. L. West, et al. DOS notes
Wayn71	Wayne, W. J., R. L. West, et al. AN 22:180, Wayne notes
Wayn72	Wayne, W. J., R. L. West, H. P. Brokaw, and D. Brokaw. DOS notes
Wayn73	Wayne, W. J., R. L. West, and P. M. Walters. AB 28:786, DOS notes
Wees1	Weesner, D. T. DOS notes
Wees2	Weesner, D. T. Atlas notes
Wees3	Weesner, D. T. DO 18:40
Wees4	Weesner, D. T. DO 18:42
Wees5	Weesner, D. T. DO 18:55
Wees6	Weesner, D. T. DO 21:4
Wees7	Weesner, D. T. DO 21:5
Wees8	Weesner, D. T. DO 23:18
Wees9	Weesner, D. T., et al. DOS notes
Weggl1	Weggel, V. AN 28:176
Weir1	Weirick, P. AB 34:259
Weir2	Weirick, P. and D. L. Yoder. Cassinia 41:82, AFN 8:99
Weis1	Weissmann, B. AB 41:66
Well1	Wells, L. A. West notes, fide R. L. West
Well2	Wells, L. A., and J. W. Zerbe. DO 8:14
Wels1	Welsheimer, T. Atlas notes
Wert1	Wertz, D. W. AB 27:37
Wcbc1	West Chester Bird Club. Cassinia 27:37
West1	West, R. L. Notes
West2	West, R. L. DOS notes
West3	West, R. L. Atlas notes
West4	West, R. L. Nest record
West5	West, R. L. USFWS unpublished BBS data
West6	West, R. L. AB 37:854
West7	West, R. L. DO 2:37
West8	West, R. L. DO 11:13
West9	West, R. L. DO 14:37
West10	West, R. L. DO 18:49
West11	West, R. L. DO 18:59
West12	West, R. L. DO 19:35
West13	West, R. L., et al. DOS notes
West14	West, R. L., et al. DO 12:17
West15	West, R. L., et al. DO 14:37
West16	West, R. L., E. Dyer, et al. DO 14:37
West17	West, R. L., and P. K. Klabunde. West notes
West18	West, R. L., and J. W. Patterson. DO 14:37
West19	West, R. L., and T. E. Roberts. DO 12:17
West20	West, R. L., and R. G. Rufe. DOS notes, not 2 Oct 1976, DO 14:45
West21	West, R. L., and S. B. Speck. DOS notes
West22	West, R. L., W. J. Wayne, and H. P. Brokaw. DOS notes
West23	West, R. L., W. J. Wayne, and T. E. Roberts. AFN 21:554, DOS notes
West24	West, R. L., and K. I. Zeitler. DO 20:2
West25	West, R. L., K. I. Zeitler, and J. W. Patterson. DO 18:59
West26	West, R. L., and W. J. Wayne. DO 7(2):22
Weyl1	Weyl, E. S. Bird-Lore 31:198
Weyl2	Weyl, E. S., et al. Bird-Lore 32:206
Whit1	White, J. F. DOS notes
Whit2	White, J. F. AB 46:243, 330
Whit3	White, J. F. DO 23:17
Whit4	White, J. F. DO 23:28
Whit5	White, J. F., and R. Lego. DO 25: 51
Whit6	White, J. F., M. V. Barnhill, et al. AB 42:414
Whit7	White, T., et al. AB 40:263, 451
Wild1	Wilde. Proc. DVOC 3:2, fide
WilN1	Wilder, N. G. Nest record
WilC1	Wilds, C. P. AB 32:985, DO 14:9
WilC2	Wilds, C. P. AN 30:32

WilC3   Wilds, C. P., I. Hannay, and H. Hannay. AN28:177

WilV1   Willet, V. AN 30:139

WilB1   Williams, B. Colonial Waterbirdbird Registry

WilD1   Williams, Mrs. D. H., and A. E. Conway. AFN 18:345; USFWS unpublished data

Wils1   Wilson, E. AB 40:90

Wola1   Wolanski, D. DOS notes

Wola2   Wolanski, D. AB 32:987

Wort1   Worth, C. B. Bird-Lore 31:270

WriJ1   Wright, J. K. AN 9:36

WriJ2   Wright, J. K., and C. L. Clagett. AN 9:145

WriM1   Wright, M. B., SNHD notes

Zeit1   Zeitler, K. I. DOS notes

Zeit2   Zeitler, K. I. Atlas notes

Zaru1   Zarudsky, J., M. Gochfeld, and J. Burger. AB 35:924

Literature Cited

Abbott, J. M. 1959. Traill's Flycatcher breeding in the District of Columbia. *Atlantic Naturalist* 14:272.

Abbott, J. M. 1978. Chesapeake Bay Bald Eagles. *Delaware Conservationist* 22 (2):3–9.

Abbott, J. M. 1982. Status of the Bald Eagle—Chesapeake Bay region, 1981. *Delaware Conservationist* 25 (1):8–11.

Abbott, J. M. 1985. 1985 breeding success of Chesapeake Bay Bald Eagles. Unpublished manuscript, copy in Delaware Museum of Natural History, Greenville, Del.

Adamus, P. R. 1988. *Atlas of breeding birds in Maine, 1978–1983.* Augusta, Maine: Maine Department of Inland Fisheries and Wildlife.

Addy, C. E., and J. D. Heyland. 1968. Canada Goose management in eastern Canada and the Atlantic Flyway. In *Canada Goose management,* edited by R. L. Hine and C. Schoenfeld, pp. 10–23. Madison, Wisc.: Dembar Educational Research Service.

Aldrich, J. W. 1953. Habits and habitat differences in two races of Traill's Flycatcher. *Wilson Bulletin* 65:8–10.

Aldrich, J. W. 1963. Geographic orientation of American Tetraonidae. *Journal of Wildlife Management* 27:529–45.

Alexander, H. L. 1969. Roost-flight patterns used by Delaware blackbirds. *Delmarva Ornithologist* 6:10–13.

Alexander, H. L. 1989. Executive summary—Canada Goose management in Delaware. May 15. DNREC document.

Allen, R. P. 1952. *The Whooping Crane.* National Audubon Society Research Report, no. 3. New York.

Allen, R. P. 1962a. Wood Stork: Migration. In *Handbook of North American birds.* Vol. 1, *Loons through flamingos,* edited by R. S. Palmer, pp. 511–13. New Haven, Conn.: Yale University Press.

Allen, R. P. 1962b. Yellow-crowned Night-Heron: Habits. In *Handbook of North American birds.* Vol. 1, *Loons through flamingos,* edited by R. S. Palmer. New Haven, Conn.: Yale University Press.

Allen, R. P., and R. T. Peterson. 1936. The hawk migrations at Cape May Point, New Jersey. *Auk* 53:393–404.

Ambuel, B., and S. A. Temple. 1982. Songbird populations in southern Wisconsin forests: 1954 and 1979. *Journal of Field Ornithology* 53:149–58.

American Ornithologists' Union. 1885. *The A.O.U. code of nomenclature and check list of North American birds.* Cambridge: Cambridge University Press.

American Ornithologists' Union. 1910. *Check-list of North American birds.* 3rd ed. New York.

American Ornithologists' Union. 1957. *Check-list of North American birds.* 5th ed. Baltimore, Md.: Lord Baltimore Press.

American Ornithologists' Union. 1973. Thirty-second supplement to the American Ornithologists' Union check-list of North American birds. *Auk* 90:411–19.

American Ornithologists' Union. 1983. *Check-list of North American birds.* 6th ed. Lawrence, Kans.: Allen Press

American Ornithologists' Union. 1985. Thirty-fifth supplement to the American Ornithologists' Union check-list of North American birds. *Auk* 102:680–86.

American Ornithologists' Union. 1993. Thirty-ninth supplement to the American Ornithologists' Union check-list of North American birds. *Auk* 110:675–82.

American Ornithologists' Union. 1995. Fortieth supplement to the American Ornithologists' Union check-list of North American birds. *Auk* 112:819–30.

American Ornithologists' Union. 1997. Forty-first supplement to the American Ornithologists' Union check-list of North American birds. *Auk* 114:542–52.

American Ornithologists' Union. 1998. *Check-List of North American Birds.* 7th ed. Washington, D.C.: American Ornithologists' Union.

Anderson, B. 1991. Epibenthic invertebrate survey of Little Assawoman Bay. In *A day in the life of Delaware's forgotten bay: A scientific survey of Little Assawoman Bay,* edited by W. Ullman, pp. 23–24. Dover, Del.: Scientific and Technical Advisory Committee, Inland Bays Estuary Program, DNREC.

Anderson, J. B. 1977. Yellow Rail *(Coturnicops noveboracensis).* In *Management of migratory shore and upland game birds in North America,* edited by G. C. Sanderson. Washington, D.C.: International Association of Fish and Wildlife Agencies. Reprint, Lincoln: University of Nebraska Press, 1980, pp. 66–70.

Andrews, R., comp. 1990. *Coastal waterbird colonies: Maine to Virginia, 1984–85.* Newton Corner, Mass: U.S. Fish and Wildlife Service.

Andrle, R. F., and J. R. Carroll, eds. 1988. *The atlas of breeding birds in New York State.* Ithaca, N.Y.: Cornell University Press.

anon. 1900a. Bird slaughter in Delaware. *Bird-Lore* 2:60.

anon. 1900b. The bird protection fund. *Bird-Lore* 2:60, 90.

anon. 1905. Abstracts of the minutes of the D.V.O.C. for 1904. *Cassinia* 8:68.

Arbib, R. S., Jr. 1988a. Chipping Sparrow. In *The atlas of breeding birds in New York State,* edited by R. F. Andrle and J. R. Carroll. Ithaca, N.Y.: Cornell University Press.

Arbib, R. S., Jr. 1988b. Double-crested Cormorant. In *The atlas of breeding birds in New York State,* edited by R. F. Andrle and J. R. Carroll. Ithaca, N.Y.: Cornell University Press.

Arbib, R. S., Jr., ed. 1971. Announcing—the Blue List: An "early warning system" for birds. *American Birds* 25:948–49.

Armisted, H. T. 1991. The summer season: Middle Atlantic Coast region. *American Birds* 45:1101–6.

Armstrong, E. R., and D. L. G. Nokes. 1983. Wintering biology of Mourning Doves, *Zenaida macroura,* in Ontario. *Canadian Field-Naturalist* 97:434–38.

Armstrong, J. T. 1965. Breeding home range in the Nighthawk and other birds: Its evolutionary and ecological significance. *Ecology* 46:619–29.

Arnett, J. H., Jr. 1955. Other records. *Cassinia* 40:34.

Artmann, J. W. 1977. *Woodcock status report, 1975.* U.S. Fish and Wildlife Service Special Scientific Report, Wildlife, no. 201. Washington, D.C.

Audubon, J. J. 1831–39. *Ornithological biography.* 5 vols. Edinburgh: Adam and Charles Black.

Audubon, J. J. 1839–44. *Birds of America.* 7 vols. New York: J. J. Audubon; Philadelphia, Pa.: J. B. Chevalier.

Austin, D. V. 1975. Bird flowers in the eastern United States. *Florida Scientist* 38:1–12.

Austin, O. L., Jr., ed. 1968. *Life histories of North American cardinals, grosbeaks, buntings, towhees, finches, sparrows, and allies.* 3 parts. U.S. National Museum Bulletin, no. 237. Washington, D.C.

Austing, G. R., and J. B. Holt. 1966. *The world of the Great Horned Owl.* Philadelphia, Pa.: Lippincott.

Avise, J. C., and R. M. Zink. 1988. Molecular genetic divergence between avian sibling species: King and Clapper rails, Long-billed and Short-billed dowitchers, Boat-tailed and Great-tailed grackles, and Tufted and Black-tailed titmice. *Auk* 105:516–28.

Baer, D. R. 1989. Delaware birds—Nest records and egg-laying dates. *Delmarva Ornithologist* 22:4–35.

Baer, D. R. 1991. Nesting of Mourning Doves. Delmarva Ornithologist 24:16–18.

Bagg, A. M. 1967. Factors affecting the occurrence of the Eurasian Lapwing in eastern North America. *Living Bird* 6:87–122.

Bagg, A. M. 1969. The changing seasons. *Audubon Field Notes* 23:4–12.

Bagg, A. M. 1970. A summary of the 1969 fall migration season. *Audubon Field Notes* 24:4–13.

Bailey, W. L. 1900. The Kingfisher's home life. *Bird-Lore* 2:76–80.

Bailey, W. L. 1927. Glossy Ibis in Delaware. *Auk* 44:417.

Baillie, J. L., Jr. 1963. Three bird immigrants from the Old World. *Transactions of the Royal Canadian Institute* (Part 2) 34:95–105. [Not examined.] Cited in S. R. Johnson and W. J. Adams. 1977. The Little Gull (*Larus minutus*) in Arctic North America, *Canadian Field-Naturalist* 91: 294–96.

Baird, J. 1968. Eastern Savannah Sparrow. In *Life histories of North American cardinals, grosbeaks, buntings, towhees, finches, sparrows, and allies,* edited by O. L. Austin, Jr. Pt. 2, pp. 678–96. U.S. National Museum Bulletin, no. 237. Washington, D.C.

Baird, S. F., T. M. Brewer, and R. Ridgway. 1884. *The water birds of North America.* Vol. 1. Boston, Mass.: Little, Brown.

Bancroft, G. T. 1986. Nesting success and mortality of the Boat-tailed Grackle. *Auk* 103:86–99.

Bancroft, G. T. 1987. Mating system and nesting phenology of the Boat-tailed Grackle in central Florida. *Florida Field Naturalist* 15:1–18.

Banko, W. E. 1960. *The Trumpeter Swan.* North American Fauna, no. 63. Washington, D.C.: U.S. Fish and Wildlife Service.

Barber, R. D. 1987. Wilson's Storm-Petrel in New Jersey. *Records of New Jersey Birds* 13:20.

Barnhill, M. V., III. 1974. A Lark Sparrow at Bombay Hook. *Delmarva Ornithologist* 9:6.

Barnhill III, M. V., ed. 1975. Delaware Spring Roundup, May 11, 1974. *Delmarva Ornithologist* 10:12–15.

Barnhill III, M. V., ed. 1977. The Passing Scene: September through November 1976. *Delmarva Ornithologist* 12:4–8.

Barnhill III, M. V., ed. 1979. The Passing Scene: March through May 1978. *Delmarva Ornithologist* 14:8–10.

Barnhill III, M. V., ed. 1980. The Passing Scene: June through Agust 1979. *Delmarva Ornithologist* 15:49–61.

Barnhill, M. V., III. 1983. The passing scene, March–May 1981. *Delmarva Ornithologist* 16:35–37.

Barnhill, M. V., III, and P. G. DuMont. 1973. Observation of a White-faced Storm Petrel off Delaware. *American Birds* 27:17.

Barnhill, M. V., III, and J. Gordon. 1979. Barnacle Goose at Bombay Hook. *Delmarva Ornithologist* 14:7.

Barry, E. M. 1939. Our animals, fish, and birds of Delaware. Dover, Del.: Board of Game and Fish Commissioners, Division of Education. Mimeographed booklet.

Barry, E. M. 1942. Status of Delaware wildlife. Delaware natural history notes: Birds, App., pt. 6, pp. 28–34. Pittman-Robertson Report, no. 4. Dover, Del.: Board of Game and Fish Commissioners. Mimeographed.

Bartgis, R. 1992. Loggerhead Shrike. In *Migratory nongame birds of management concern in the Northeast,* edited by K. J. Schneider and D. M. Pence. Newton Corner, Mass.: U.S. Fish and Wildlife Service.

Baumgartner, F. M. 1939. Territory and population in the Great Horned Owl. *Auk* 56:274–82.

Beal, F. E. L. 1918. *Food habits of the swallows, a family of valuable native birds.* U.S. Department of Agriculture Bulletin, no. 169. Washington, D.C.

Beason, R. C., and E. C. Franks. 1974. Breeding behavior of the Horned Lark. *Auk* 91:65–74.

Beck, R. 1988. Where did the geese go? *The Island Paper,* January, pp. 4–5. Hancocks Bridge, N.J.: Public Service Electric and Gas. Copy in Delaware Museum of Natural History, Greenville, Del.

Beddall, B. G. 1963. Range expansion of the Cardinal and other birds in the northeastern states. *Wilson Bulletin* 75:140–58.

Bednarz, J. C., and T. Kimmel. 1992. Northern Goshawk. In *Atlas of breeding birds in Pennsylvania,* edited by D. W. Brauning. Pittsburgh, Pa.: University of Pittsburgh Press.

Bednarz, J. C., D. Klem, Jr., L. J. Goodrich, and S. E. Senner. 1990. Migration counts of raptors at Hawk Mountain, Pennsylvania, as indicators of population trends, 1934–1986. *Auk* 107:96–109.

Belant, J. L., and R. A. Dolbeer. 1993a. Migration and dispersal of Laughing Gulls in the United States. *Journal of Field Ornithology* 64:557–65.

Belant, J. L., and R. A. Dolbeer. 1993b. Population status of nesting Laughing Gulls in the United States: 1977–1991. *American Birds* 47:220–24.

Belles-Isles, J.-C., and J. Picman. 1986. House Wren nest-destroying behavior. *Condor* 88:190–93.

Bellrose, F. C. 1976. *Ducks, geese, and swans of North America.* 2nd ed. Wildlife Management Institute. Harrisburg, Pa: Stackpole Books.

Belthoff, J. R. 1987. Post-fledging behavior of the Eastern Screech-Owl. M.Sc. thesis abstract. *Raptor Research* 21:80–81.

Bender, R. O. 1930. Golden Plover (*Pluvialis dominica*) near Dover, Delaware. *Auk* 47:80. [Correction: 1931, *Auk* 48:416.]

Bendire, C. E. 1895. *Life histories of North American birds.* U.S. National Museum Special Bulletin, no. 3. Washington, D.C.

Bennett, G. 1987. Great Crested Flycatcher. In *Atlas of the breeding birds of Ontario,* edited by M. D. Cadman, P. F. J. Eagles, and F. M. Helleiner. Don Mills, Ontario: University of Waterloo Press.

Benoit, D. 1992. Fall records, 1991: Eastern Great Lakes region. *Journal of the Hawk Migration Association of North America* 17 (3):57–59.

Bent, A. C. 1907. Report on conditions of bird colonies on Cobb's Island, Virginia, 1907. *Bird-Lore* 9:316–18.

Bent, A. C. 1921. *Life histories of North American gulls and terns.* U.S. National Museum Bulletin, no. 113. Washington, D.C.

Bent, A. C. 1923. *Life histories of North American wild fowl, pt. 1.* U.S. National Museum Bulletin, no. 126. Washington, D.C.

Bent, A. C. 1926. *Life histories of North American marsh birds.* U.S. National Museum Bulletin, no. 135. Washington, D.C.

Bent, A. C. 1927. *Life histories of North American shore birds.* Pt. 1. U.S. National Museum Bulletin, no. 142. Washington, D.C.

Bent, A. C. 1929. *Life histories of North American shore birds.* Pt. 2. U.S. National Museum Bulletin, no. 146. Washington, D.C.

Bent, A. C. 1932. *Life histories of North American gallinaceous birds.* U.S. National Museum Bulletin, no. 162. Washington, D.C.

Bent, A. C. 1939. *Life histories of North American woodpeckers.* U.S. National Museum Bulletin, no. 174. Washington, D.C.

Bent, A. C. 1940. *Life histories of North American cuckoos, goatsuckers, hummingbirds, and their allies, pt 1.* U.S. National Museum Bulletin, no. 176. Washington, D.C.

Bent, A. C. 1942. *Life histories of North American flycatchers, larks, swallows, and their allies.* U.S. National Museum Bulletin, no. 179. Washington, D.C.

Bent, A. C. 1946. *Life histories of North American jays, crows, and titmice.* U.S. National Museum Bulletin, no. 191. Washington, D.C.

Bent, A. C. 1948. *Life histories of North American nuthatches, wrens, thrashers, and their allies.* U.S. National Museum Bulletin, no. 195. Washington, D.C.

Bent, A. C. 1949. *Life histories of North American thrushes, kinglets, and their allies.* U.S. National Museum Bulletin, no. 196. Washington, D.C.

Bent, A. C. 1950. *Life histories of North American wagtails, shrikes, vireos, and their allies.* U.S. National Museum Bulletin, no. 197. Washington, D.C.

Bent, A. C. 1953. *Life histories of North American warblers.* U.S. National Museum Bulletin, no. 203. Washington, D.C.

Bent, A. C. 1958. *Life histories of North American blackbirds, orioles, tanagers, and their allies.* U.S. National Museum Bulletin, no. 211. Washington, D.C.

Berger, A. J. 1968. Eastern Vesper Sparrow. In *Life histories of North American cardinals, grosbeaks, buntings, towhees, finches, sparrows, and allies,* edited by O. L. Austin, Jr. Pt. 2, pp. 868–82. U.S. National Museum Bulletin, no. 237. Washington, D.C.

Bertin, R. I. 1977. Breeding habitats of the Wood Thrush and Veery. *Condor* 79:303–11.

Best, L. B., and N. L. Rodenhouse. 1984. Territory preference of Vesper Sparrows in cropland. *Wilson Bulletin* 96:72–82.

Biggs, R. B., and T. M. Church. 1983. Bottom sediments. In *The Delaware estuary: Research as background for estuarine management and development,* a report to the Delaware River and Bay Authority, edited by J. H. Sharp, pp. 95–106. University of Delaware College of Marine Studies and New Jersey Marine Sciences Consortium, Lewes, Del.

Bildstein, K. L. 1988. Northern Harrier: Migration. In *Handbook of North American birds.* Vol. 4, pt. 1, *Diurnal raptors,* edited by R. S. Palmer. New Haven, Conn.: Yale University Press.

Bird, D. M. 1988. American Kestrel: Habitat, migration, reproduction. In *Handbook of North American birds.* Vol. 5, pt. 2, *Diurnal raptors,* edited by R. S. Palmer, pp. 253–90. New Haven, Conn.: Yale University Press.

Blake, J. G., and B. A. Loiselle. 1992. Habitat use by Neotropical migrants at La Selva Biological Station and Braulio Carrillo National Park, Costa Rica. In *Ecology and conservation of Neotropical migrant landbirds,* edited by J. Hagan and D. W. Johnston, pp. 257–72. Washington, D.C.: Smithsonian Institution Press.

Blancher, P. J., and R. J. Robertson. 1982. A double-brooded Eastern Kingbird. *Wilson Bulletin* 94:212–13.

Blandin, W. W. 1963. Renesting and multiple brooding studies of marked Clapper Rails. *Proceedings of the 17th Annual Conference of the Southeastern Association of Game and Fish Commissioners* 17:60–68.

Blem, C. R., and L. M. Blem. 1991. Nest box selection by Prothonotary Warblers. *Journal of Field Ornithology* 62:299–307.

Blem, C. R., and L. M. Blem. 1992. Prothonotary Warblers nesting in nest boxes: Clutch size and timing in Virginia. *Raven* 63:15–20.

Blodgett, K. D., and R. M. Zammuto. 1979. Chimney Swift nest found in hollow tree. *Wilson Bulletin* 91:154.

Blokpoel, H., and G. D. Tessier. 1986. *The Ring-billed Gull in Ontario: A review of a new problem species.* Canadian Wildlife Service Occasional Paper 57. Ottawa, Ontario.

Blokpoel, H., P. J. Blancher, and P. M. Fetterolf. 1985. On the plumage of nesting Ring-billed Gulls of different ages. *Journal of Field Ornithology* 56:113–24.

Blokpoel, H., L-G. Naranjo, and G. D. Tessier. 1984. Immature Little Gull in South America. *American Birds* 38:372–74.

Bock, C. E., and L. W. Lepthien. 1972. Winter eruptions of Red-breasted Nuthatches in North America, 1959–1970. *American Birds* 26:558–61.

Bock, C. E., and L. W. Lepthien. 1976a. Changing winter distribution and abundance of the Blue Jay, 1962–1971. *American Midland Naturalist* 96:232–36.

Bock, C. E., and L. W. Lepthien. 1976b. Growth in the eastern House Finch population, 1962–1971. *American Birds* 30:791–92.

Bock, C. E., and L. W. Lepthien. 1976c. Synchronous eruptions of boreal seed-eating birds. *American Naturalist* 110:559–71.

Bombay Hook NWR. 1938–91. Narrative reports. U.S. Fish and Wildlife Service.

Bombay Hook NWR. 1966. Birds of Bombay Hook NWR. RL-131-R-4, rev. 12/66. U.S. Fish and Wildlife Service.

Bond, G., and R. E. Stewart. 1951. A new Swamp Sparrow from the Maryland Coastal Plain. *Wilson Bulletin* 63:38–40.

Bonney, R. E., Jr. 1988a. Fish Crow. In *The atlas of breeding birds in New York State,* edited by R. F. Andrle and J. R. Carroll. Ithaca, N.Y.: Cornell University Press.

Bonney, R. E., Jr. 1988b. Veery. In *The atlas of breeding birds in New York State,* edited by R. F. Andrle and J. R. Carroll. Ithaca, N.Y.: Cornell University Press.

Bonney, R. E., Jr., and J. L. Burrill. 1988. Willow Flycatcher. In *The atlas of breeding birds in New York State,* edited by R. F. Andrle and J. R. Carroll. Ithaca, N.Y.: Cornell University Press.

Booth, W. 1958. Nesting Cliff Swallows in the Washington area. *Atlantic Naturalist* 13:258.

Bortner, J. B. 1989. *American Woodcock harvest and breeding population status, 1989.* U.S. Fish and Wildlife Service Report. Washington, D.C.

Bosakowski, T. 1986. Winter population trends of the House Finch and ecologically similar species in northeastern New Jersey. *American Birds* 40:1105–10.

Botton, M. L., and R. E. Loveland. 1993. Predation by Herring Gulls and Great Black-backed Gulls on horseshoe crabs. *Wilson Bulletin* 105:518–21.

Bouton, J. J. 1987. Sandy Hook hawk watch—Spring 1987. *Peregrine Observer* (Cape May Bird Observatory) 10 (2):3–5.

Boyle, W. J., Jr., R. O. Paxton, and D. A. Cutler, eds. 1980. The nesting season: Hudson-Delaware region. *American Birds* 34:878–82.

Boyle, W. J., Jr., R. O. Paxton, and D. A. Cutler, eds. 1983. The winter season: Hudson-Delaware region. *American Birds* 37:283–87.

Boyle, W. J., Jr., R. O. Paxton, and D. A. Cutler, eds. 1986. The winter season: Hudson-Delaware region. *American Birds* 40:261–65.

Boyle, W. J., Jr., R. O. Paxton, and D. A. Cutler, eds. 1987. The winter season: Hudson-Delaware region. *American Birds* 41:260–63.

Boyle, W. J., Jr., R. O. Paxton, and D. A. Cutler, eds. 1988. The winter season: Hudson-Delaware region. *American Birds* 42:240–43.

Boyle, W. J., Jr., R. O. Paxton, and D. A. Cutler, eds. 1989. The winter season: Hudson-Delaware region. *American Birds* 43:289–93.

Boyle, W. J., Jr., R. O. Paxton, and D. A. Cutler, eds. 1991. The winter season: Hudson-Delaware region. *American Birds* 45:253–57.

Boyle, Jr., W. J., R. O. Paxton, and D. A Cutler, ed. 1983. The spring migration: Hudson-Delaware Region. *American Birds* 37:850–55.

Boyle, Jr., W. J., R. O. Paxton, and D. A Cutler, ed. 1987. The spring migration: Hudson-Delaware Region. *American Birds* 41:407–11.

Boyle, Jr., W. J., R. O. Paxton, and D. A Cutler, ed. 1995. Hudson-Delaware Region. *National Audubon Society Field Notes* 49:25–30.

Brackbill, H. 1953. Migratory status of Song Sparrows at Baltimore, Maryland. *Bird-Banding* 24:68.

Brackbill, H. 1970. Tufted Titmouse breeding behavior. *Auk* 87:522–36.

Brackbill, H. 1987. Duration of Tufted Titmouse, Carolina Chickadee pairings (breeding). *North American Bird Bander* 12:146–47.

Brady, E. M. 1930. Evening Grosbeak in Delaware. *Auk* 47:420.

Brauning, D. W. 1992a. Peregrine Falcon. In *Atlas of breeding birds in Pennsylvania,* edited by D. W. Brauning. Pittsburgh, Pa.: University of Pittsburgh Press.

Brauning, D. W., ed. 1992. *Atlas of breeding birds in Pennsylvania.* Pittsburgh, Pa.: University of Pittsburgh Press.

Brewer, R. 1955. Size of home range in eight bird species in a southern Illinois swamp-thicket. *Wilson Bulletin* 67:140–41.

Brewer, R. 1961. Comparative notes on the life history of the Carolina Chickadee. *Wilson Bulletin* 73:348–73.

Brewer, R. 1963. Ecological and reproductive relationships of Black-capped and Carolina chickadees. *Auk* 80:9–47.

Brewer, R., G. A. McPeek, and R. J. Adams, Jr. 1991. *The atlas of breeding birds of Michigan.* East Lansing: Michigan State University Press.

Brinkley, E. S., W. J. Boyle, Jr., R. O. Paxton, and D. A. Cutler. 1994. Hudson-Delaware Region. *National Audubon Society Field Notes* 48:185–92.

Brinton, D. G., and A. S. Anthony. 1888. *A Lenape English dictionary.* Philadelphia, Pa.: Historical Society of Philadelphia.

British Museum. 1874. *Catalogue of the birds in the British Museum,* vol. 1, p. 198.

Brokaw, H. P., and W. J. Wayne. 1985. Wilson's Plover—First Delaware state record. *Delmarva Ornithologist* 18:32.

Brokaw, W. A. 1975. Sightings of Purple Gallinules in Dragon Run Marsh. *Delmarva Ornithologist* 10:2.

Broley, C. L. 1947. Migration and nesting of Florida Bald Eagles. *Wilson Bulletin* 59:3–20.

Broley, C. L. 1958. The plight of the Florida Bald Eagle. *Audubon* 60:162–63.

Brooks, J. 1992. Preserving Delaware's farmland. *Wilmington News Journal,* May 17, sec. E, p. 1.

Brooks, S. T. 1957. Churchman's Marsh Wildlife Refuge. Wilmington: Society of Natural History of Delaware. Copy in Delaware Museum of Natural History, Greenville, Del.

Brooks, S. T. 1965. The numbers game. *Delmarva Ornithologist* 2:40.

Brooks, S. T. 1972. Reports of parrots in the Atlantic Coastal region. *Delmarva Ornithologist* 7 (2):2–8.

Brooks, S. T. 1973. Formation of the Delmarva Ornithological Society. *Delmarva Ornithologist* 8:45–47.

[Brooks, S. T., D. B. Palmer, et al.]. 1955. Lattoniken Newsletter. Wilmington, Del.: private issue. Copy in Delaware Museum of Natural History, Greenville, Del.

Broun, M. 1953. Fulmar in Delaware. *Cassinia* 39:24.

Brown, J. W. 1934a. First record of Ring-necked Duck in Delaware. *Auk* 51:227–28.

Brown, J. W. 1934b. Lawrence's Warbler in Delaware. *Auk* 51:242–43.

Brown, L., and D. Amadon. 1968. *Buteo lineatus.* In *Eagles, hawks, and falcons of the world.* Vol. 2, pp. 576–81. New York: McGraw-Hill, Country Life Books.

Bryant, T. L., and J. R. Pennock, eds. 1988. *The Delaware estuary: Rediscovering a forgotten resource.* Newark: University of Delaware Sea Grant College Program.

Buckalew, [J.] H. 1933. American Egret nesting in Delaware. *Auk* 50:206.

Buckalew, [J.] H. 1934. Nesting of Boat-tailed Grackle and Blue-winged Teal in Delaware. *Auk* 51:384.

Buckalew, J. H. 1949. The eastern Glossy Ibis in Delaware. *Auk* 66:196–97.

Buckalew, J. H. 1950. Records from the Del-Mar-Va Peninsula. *Auk* 67:250–52.

Buckley, F. G., and P. A. Buckley. 1972. Breeding ecology of Royal Terns, *Sterna (Thalasseus) maxima maxima. Ibis* 114:344–66.

Buech, R. R. 1982. Nesting ecology and cowbird parasitism of Clay-colored, Chipping, and Field sparrows in a Christmas tree plantation. *Journal of Field Ornithology* 53:363–69.

Bull, E. L. 1987. Ecology of the Pileated Woodpecker in northeastern Oregon. *Journal of Wildlife Management* 51:472–81.

Bull, J. 1964. *Birds of the New York area.* New York: Harper and Row.

Bull, J. 1974. *Birds of New York State.* Garden City, N.Y.: Doubleday, Natural History Press.

Bunn, D. S., A. B. Warburton, and R. D. S. Wilson. 1982. *The Barn Owl.* Vermillion, S. Dak.: Buteo Books.

Burger, J. 1986. The effect of human activity on shorebirds in two coastal bays in northeastern United States. *Environmental Conservation* 13 (2):123–30.

Burger, J., and J. Shisler. 1978. Nest-site selection of Willets in a New Jersey salt marsh. *Wilson Bulletin* 90:599–607.

Burkholder, J. C. [1976]. A terrestrial baseline census at the Indian River power plant, property, Millsboro, Delaware, and the adjacent area. Chapter 9. Unpublished draft. Ecological Analysts, Inc. Baltimore, Md. Copy in Delaware Museum of Natural History, Greenville, Del.

Burleigh, T. D. 1935. Notes on the winter bird life of the Delaware coast. *Auk* 52:317–18.

Burley, N. 1980. Clutch overlap and clutch size: Alternative and complementary tactics. *American Naturalist* 115:223–46.

Burns, F. L. 1911. A monograph of the Broad-winged Hawk *(Buteo platypterus). Wilson Bulletin* 23:143–320.

Burns, F. L. 1919. *The ornithology of Chester County, Pennsylvania.* Boston, Mass.: Gorham Press.

Burns, J. T. 1982. Nests, territories, and reproduction of Sedge Wrens *(Cistothorus platensis). Wilson Bulletin* 94:338–49.

Burns, P. F. 1982. Peregrines. *Delaware Conservationist* 25 (1):26–28.

Burns, P. F., and A. L. Zayatz. [1981]. Unpublished data sheets of raptor observations at Cape Henlopen. Courtesy of P. F Burns, DNREC. Delaware Museum of Natural History, Greenville, Del.

Burr, R. M., and R. E. Jones, comp. 1968. Mixed deciduous floodplain woodlot (urban woodlot). *Audubon Field Notes* 22:688.

Burr, R. M., and J. T. Linehan, comp. 1967a. Uneven-aged red maple-tulip poplar forest (urban woodlot). *Audubon Field Notes* 21:639.

Burr, R. M., and J. T. Linehan, comp. 1967b. Uneven-aged sweet gum-red maple-beech forest (urban woodlot). *Audubon Field Notes* 21:639.

Burr, R. M., and D. Stevens. 1969. Nesting activities of the Common Grackle. *Delmarva Ornithologist* 6:5–7.

Burr, R. M., J. T. Linehan, and G. Prest. 1968. Observations in an article titled The nesting season: Middle Atlantic Coast region, edited by F. R. Scott and D. A. Cutler. *Audubon Field Notes* 22:594–97.

Burtt, E. H., Jr. 1989. Personal communication. In *Swallows and martins,* by A. Turner and C. Rose, p. 99. Boston, Mass.: Houghton Mifflin.

Bush, W. D. 1878–81. Diary of birdwatching, bound with Delaware State Poultry Society Records, 1870–81. Manuscript 45:30 Societies D in the collection of the Historical Society of Delaware, Wilmington, Del. Typescript of the diary was donated to T. S. Palmer, in care of the Department of Agriculture, Biological Survey, Washington, D.C., on 5 April 1905, by J. Danforth Bush, and is on file with the Lighthouse Section of Biological Survey papers at Patuxent Wildlife Research Center, Laurel, Md., 1 November 1990.

Butler, R. W. 1992. *Great Blue Heron.* The Birds of North America, edited by A. Poole, P. Stettenheim, and F. Gill, no. 25. Philadelphia, Pa.: Academy of Natural Sciences; Washington, D.C.: American Ornithologists' Union.

Bystrak, D. 1980. Application of Miniroutes to bird population studies. *Maryland Birdlife* 36:131–38.

[Bystrak, D., and K. Klimkiewicz]. 1982. Safe dates. Maryland and D.C. breeding bird atlas project handbook. *Maryland Birdlife* 38 (supplement):15–18.

Cabot, Samuel, Jr. 1855. [Distribution of Grouse in New England.] *Proceedings of the Boston Society of Natural History,* 5, 154.

Caccamise, D. F. 1976. Nesting mortality in the Red-winged Blackbird. *Auk* 93:517–34.

Cade, T. J. 1967. Ecological and behavioral aspects of predation by the Northern Shrike. *Living Bird* 6:43–86.

Cade, T. J. 1982. *The falcons of the world.* Ithaca, N.Y.: Cornell University Press.

Cade, T. J., J. H. Enderson, C. G. Thelander, and C. M. White, eds. 1988. *Peregrine Falcon populations: Their management and recovery.* Boise, Idaho: Peregrine Fund.

Cadman, M. D. 1987. Loggerhead Shrike. In *Atlas of the breeding birds of Ontario,* edited by M. D. Cadman, P. F. J. Eagles, and F. M. Helleiner. Don Mills, Ontario: University of Waterloo Press.

Cadman, M. D., P. F. J. Eagles, and F. M. Helleiner. 1987. *Atlas of the breeding birds of Ontario,* edited by M. D. Cadman, P. F. J. Eagles, and F. M. Helleiner. Don Mills, Ontario: University of Waterloo Press.

Cairns, W. E., and I. A. McLaren. 1980. Status of the Piping Plover on the east coast of North America. *American Birds* 34:206–8.

Campanius Holm, T. 1702. *Kort Beskrifning om Provincien Nya Suerige uti America. . . .* Stockholm: Tryct ut Kongl.

Campanius Holm, T. 1834. A short description of the province of New Sweden. Translated by P. Du Ponceau. *The Memoirs of the Historical Society of Pennsylvania.* Vol. 3. Philadelphia, Pa.

Campbell, C. D. 1991a. Great Skuas in Delaware waters. *Delmarva Ornithologist* 24:10.

Campbell, C. D. 1991b. Little Creek's Reddish Egret. *Delmarva Ornithologist* 24:2–3.

Campbell, C. D. 1992. The Delaware 300. *Cassinia* 64:9–20.

Campbell, C. D. 1993. Summer firsts in the First State. *Philadelphia Larus* 20 (1):1, 3.

Campbell, C. D. 1994. Suddenly last summer. *Delmarva Ornithologist* 26:5–9.

Campbell, C. D., and E. Potrafke. 1993. DOS bird alert—A summary. *Delmarva Ornithologist* 25:27–33.

Cannings, R. J. 1993. *Northern Saw-whet Owl.* The Birds of North America, edited by A. Poole and F. Gill, no. 42. Philadelphia, Pa.: Academy of Natural Sciences; Washington, D.C.: American Ornithologists' Union.

Cantwell, R. 1961. *Alexander Wilson, naturalist and pioneer.* Philadelphia, Pa.: Lippencott.

Carey, H. R. 1926. Hawk extermination. *Auk* 43:275–76.

Carey, M., and V. Nolan, Jr. 1979. Population dynamics of Indigo Buntings and the evolution of avian polygyny. *Evolution* 33:1180–92.

Carlson, C. W. 1967. Clay-colored Sparrow at Cape Henlopen. *Atlantic Naturalist* 22:41.

Carney, S. M. 1964. *Preliminary keys to waterfowl age and sex identification by means of wing plumage.* U.S. Fish and Wildlife Service Special Scientific Report, Wildlife, no. 82. Washington, D.C. [Cited in Bellrose 1964, p. 421; not examined.]

Carney, S. M., M. F. Sorensen, and E. M. Martin. 1983. *Distribution of waterfowl harvested in states and counties during 197–1980 hunting seasons.* U.S. Fish and Wildlife Service Special Scientific Report, Wildlife, no. 254. Washington, D.C.

Carroll, J. R. 1988a. Black Rail. In *The atlas of breeding birds in New York State,* edited by R. F. Andrle and J. R. Carroll. Ithaca, N.Y.: Cornell University Press.

Carroll, J. R. 1988b. Yellow-throated Warbler. In *The atlas of breeding birds in New York State,* edited by R. F. Andrle and J. R. Carroll. Ithaca, N.Y.: Cornell University Press.

Carter, J. D. 1929. Delaware as a hunting ground. *Cassinia* 27:8–11.

Carter, J. W. 1992. Upland Sandpiper. In *Migratory nongame birds of management concern in the Northeast,* edited by K. J. Schneider and D. M. Pence. Newton Corner, Mass.: U.S. Fish and Wildlife Service.

Case, N. A., and O. H. Hewitt. 1963. Nesting and productivity of the Red-winged Blackbird in relation to habitat. *Living Bird* 2:7–20.

Castro, G., and J. P. Myers. 1993. Shorebird predation on eggs of horseshoe crabs during spring stopover on Delaware Bay. *Auk* 110:927–30.

Castro, G., J. P. Myers, and A. R. Place. 1989. Assimilation efficiency of Sanderlings *(Calidris alba)* feeding on horseshoe crab *(Limulus polyphemus)* eggs. *Physiological Zoology* 62:716–31.

Ceglia, P. 1956. *Estuarine Studies.* Vol. 1, no. 6. Newark: University of Delaware, Marine Biology Laboratory.

Chabreck, R. H. 1963. Breeding habits of the Pied-billed Grebe in an impounded coastal marsh in Louisiana. *Auk* 80:447–52.

Chamberlain, E. B., and A. J. Florio. 1958. Woodcock singing-ground count. Pittman-Robertson Report, W-16-R-7. Dover, Del.: Game and Fish Commission.

Chapman, F. M. 1895. *Handbook of birds of eastern North America.* New York: D. Appleton.

Chapman, F. M. 1899. The passing of the tern. *Bird-Lore* 1:205–6.

Chapman, F. M. 1907. *The warblers of North America.* New York: D. Appleton. 3rd ed., 1917. Reprint, New York: Dover Publications, 1968.

Clark, K. E. 1991. *Delaware Bay shorebird project, 1990.* Endangered and Nongame Species Program; Division of Fish, Game, and Wildlife; New Jersey Department of Environmental Protection. Trenton, N.J.

Clark, R. G., P. J. Weatherhead, and R. D. Titman. 1983. On the relationship between breeding bird survey counts and estimates of male density in the Red-winged Blackbird. *Wilson Bulletin* 95:453–59.

Clark, R. J. 1975. A field study of the Short-eared Owl *Otus flammeus* (Pontopidan) in North America. *Wildlife Monographs* 47:1–67.

Clark, W. S. 1985a. Migration of the Merlin along the New Jersey coast. *Raptor Research* 19:85–93.

Clark, W. S. 1985b. The migrating Sharp-shinned Hawk at Cape May Point: Banding and recovery results. In *Proceedings of Hawk Migration Conference IV,* edited by M. Harwood, pp. 137–48. Rochester, N.Y.: Hawk Migration Association of North America.

Coggins, H. L. 1903. Crow roosts and flight lines in southern Pennsylvania and New Jersey. *Cassinia* 7:29–42.

Cohen, J. R., and S. Cohen. 1971. Sight record in North Carolina of House Finch banded in New York. *Bird-Banding* 42:50.

Coleman, J. S., and J. D. Fraser. 1989. Habitat use and home ranges of

Black and Turkey vultures. *Journal of Wildlife Management* 53:782–92.

Colvin, B. A. 1984. Barn Owl foraging behavior and secondary poisoning hazard from rodenticide use on farms. Ph.D. dissertation, Bowling Green State University, Ky.

Colvin, B. A. 1985a. Common Barn-Owl population decline in Ohio and the relationship to agricultural trends. *Journal of Field Ornithology* 56:224–35.

Colvin, B. A. 1985b. A comprehensive research effort on the Common Barn-Owl. Abstract from symposium on the management of birds of prey. Raptor Research Foundation International Meeting, 1–11 September 1985, Sacramento, Calif.

Conner, R. N., and C. S. Adkisson. 1975. Effects of clearcutting on the diversity of breeding birds. *Journal of Forestry* 73:781–85.

Conner, R. N., and C. S. Adkisson. 1977. Principal component analysis of woodpecker nesting habitat. *Wilson Bulletin* 89:122–29.

Connor, P. F. 1988a. Boat-tailed Grackle. In *The atlas of breeding birds in New York State,* edited by R. F. Andrle and J. R. Carroll. Ithaca, N.Y.: Cornell University Press.

Connor, P. F. 1988b. Cerulean Warbler. In *The atlas of breeding birds in New York State,* edited by R. F. Andrle and J. R. Carroll. Ithaca, N.Y.: Cornell University Press.

Connor, P. F. 1988c. Forster's Tern. In *The atlas of breeding birds in New York State,* edited by R. F. Andrle and J. R. Carroll. Ithaca, N.Y.: Cornell University Press.

Conway, A. E. 1943. *A check-list of the birds of Chester County, Pennsylvania.* Philadelphia, Pa.: Academy of Natural Sciences.

Conway, A. E. 1972a. Charles John Pennock, 1857–1935. *Delmarva Ornithologist* 7 (1):14–17.

Conway, A. E. 1972b. Summer record of Harris' Sparrow in Delaware. *Cassinia* 53:49.

Conway, A. E. 1974a. Hypothetical records of Northern Three-toed Woodpeckers in Delaware and southeastern Pennsylvania. *Delmarva Ornithologist* 9:76–78.

Conway, A. E. 1974b. Lincoln's Sparrow in Delaware. *Delmarva Ornithologist* 9:78–79.

Conway, A. E. 1976a. A Clapper Rail record from Brandywine hundred. *Delmarva Ornithologist* 11:39.

Conway, A. E. 1976b. Sandhill Cranes in Delaware and New Jersey. *Delmarva Ornithologist* 11:63.

Conway, A. E. 1978a. The Common Redpoll invasion of 1977–78 in Delaware. *Delmarva Ornithologist* 13:2–5.

Conway, A. E. 1978b. Rufous Hummingbird: A new species for Delaware. *Delmarva Ornithologist* 13:26.

Conway, A. E., and S. R. Drennan. 1979. Rufous Hummingbirds in eastern United States. *American Birds* 33:130–32.

Cook, F. W. 1946. Occurrence of the Hudsonian Curlew on national wildlife refuges along the Atlantic coast. *Auk* 63:90–92.

Cooke, M. T. 1925. *Spread of the European Starling in North America.* U.S. Department of Agriculture Circular 336. Washington, D.C.

Cooke, W. W. 1904. *The distribution and migration of North American warblers.* U.S. Department of Agriculture, Biological Survey Bulletin, no. 18.

Cooke, W. W. 1906. *Distribution and migration of North American ducks, geese, and swans.* U.S. Department of Agriculture, Biological Survey Bulletin, no. 26.

Cooke, W. W. 1914. *Distribution and migration of North American rails and their allies.* U.S. Department of Agriculture Bulletin, no. 128. Washington D.C.

Cooper, B. E. 1991. Rufous-necked Stint in Delaware. *Delmarva Ornithologist* 24:4–5.

Cooper, R. J. 1981. Relative abundance of Georgia Caprimulgids based on call-counts. *Wilson Bulletin* 93:363–71.

Cornell Laboratory of Ornithology. 1985. Colonial bird register. Cooperative research program, Ithaca, N.Y. Computer printout in Delaware Museum of Natural History, Greenville, Del.

Cottam, C. 1934. Possible extension of regular winter range of the Great Black-backed Gull. *Auk* 51:376.

Cottam, C. 1935. Blue and Snow geese in eastern United States in the winter of 1934–35—with notes on their food habits. *Auk* 52:432.

Cottam, C. 1937. American Egret and Black-bellied Plover in Delaware in winter. *Auk* 54:382.

Cottam, C. 1945. American Eider in Delaware. *Auk* 62:634.

Coues, E. 1903. *Key to North American birds.* 5th ed. Vol. 1. Boston, Mass.: Dana Estes.

Craighead, J. J., and F. C. Craighead. 1956. *Hawks, owls, and wildlife.* Harrisburg, Pa.: Stackpole and Wildlife Management Institute. Reprint, New York: Dover Publications, 1969, p. 225.

Cramp, S., ed. 1985. *Handbook of the birds of Europe, the Middle East, and North Africa: The birds of the western Palearctic.* Vol. 4, Terns to woodpeckers. Oxford: Oxford University Press.

Cramp, S., and K. E. L. Simmons, eds. 1977. *Handbook of the birds of Europe, the Middle East, and North Africa: The birds of the western Palearctic.* Vol. 1, Ostrich to ducks. Oxford: Oxford University Press.

Cramp, S., and K. E. L. Simmons, eds. 1983. *Handbook of the birds of Europe, the Middle East, and North Africa: The birds of the western Palearctic.* Vol. 3, Waders to gulls. Oxford: Oxford University Press.

Crosby, G. T. 1972. Spread of the Cattle Egret in the Western Hemisphere. *Bird-Banding* 43:205–12.

Cruickshank, A. D. 1942. *Birds around New York City.* New York: American Museum of Natural History.

Cutler, D. A. 1955a. Brewer's Blackbird at Bombay Hook, Delaware. *Cassinia* 40:34–35.

Cutler, D. A. 1955b. Pink-footed Goose at Bombay Hook, Delaware. *Cassinia* 40:33.

Cutler, D. A. 1964. Observations in an article titled The nesting season: Middle Atlantic Coast region, edited by F. R. Scott and D. A. Cutler. *Audubon Field Notes* 18:500–3.

Cutler, D. A. 1969. Delaware breeding records, addenda (letter). *Delmarva Ornithologist* 6:45.

Cutler, H. S. 1965. Two new Delaware breeding records. *Cassinia* 48:41.

Daiber, F. C., L. L. Thornton, K. A. Bolster, T. G. Campbell, O. W. Crichton, G. L. Esposito, D. R. Jones, and J. M. Tyrawski. 1976. *An atlas of Delaware's wetlands and estuarine resources.* Delaware State Planning Office Technical Report no. 2. Dover, Del.

Darlington, E. J. 1902. Grasshopper Sparrow. *Oologist* 19:164–65.

Darlington, E. J. 1912. Kentucky Warblers. *Oologist* 29:303–4.

Darlington, E. J. 1914. Scarlet Tanager. *Oologist* 31:89–90.

Davis, C. M. 1978. A nesting study of the Brown Creeper. *Living Bird* 17:237–63.

Davis, D. E. 1974. Emigrations of Northern Shrikes, 1959–70. *Auk* 91:821–25.

Davis, D. E., and M. L. Morrison. 1987. Changes in cyclic patterns of abundance in four avian species. *American Birds* 41:1341–47.

Davis, E. G. 1969. Ivory Gull at Cape Henlopen, Delaware. *Atlantic Naturalist* 24:215.

Davis, W. J. 1982. Territory size in *Megaceryle alcyon* along a stream habitat. *Auk* 99:353–62.

Decker, D. J. 1985. More Mourning Doves in New York? *New York Conservationist* 39 (4):34–38.

Delacour, J. 1964. *The waterfowl of the world.* Vol. 4. London: Country Life.

Delaware Department of Agriculture. 1989. Delaware forest types. Unpublished report, Forestry Section, Delaware Department of Agriculture, Dover, Del.

Dennis, J. V. 1969. Yellow-shafted Flicker on Nantucket Island, Massachusetts. *Bird-Banding* 40:290–308.

Dexter, R. W. 1969. Banding and nesting studies of the Chimney Swift, 1944–1968. *Ohio Journal of Science* 69:193–213.

Dexter, R. W. 1981. Nesting success of Chimney Swifts related to age and number of adults at the nest, and the subsequent fate of the visitors. *Journal of Field Ornithology* 52:228–32.

Dickinson, J. C., Jr. 1968. Rufous-sided Towhee. In *Life histories of North American cardinals, grosbeaks, buntings, towhees, finches, sparrows, and allies,* edited by O. L. Austin, Jr. Pt. 1, pp. 562–97. U.S. National Museum Bulletin, no. 237. Washington, D.C.

Dixon, K. L. 1963. Some aspects of social organization in the Carolina Chickadee. In *Proceedings of the 13th International Ornithological Congress,* pp. 240–58. Lawrence, Kans.: AOU.

DNREC. 1974–93. Aerial waterfowl count summaries. Division of Fish and Wildlife, DNREC, Dover, Del.

DNREC. 1976. 1975 special pheasant season. Federal Aid in Wildlife Restoration, W-16-R-25. Dover, Del.: DNREC.

DNREC. 1983. Investigation of the release of exotic pheasants in Delaware. Federal Aid in Wildlife Restoration, W-16-R-32. Dover, Del.: DNREC.

DNREC. 1986. Introduction of Peregrine Falcons to Delaware. Federal Aid for Endangered Species, E-1-8, II-5. Dover, Del.: DNREC.

DNREC. 1987, rev. 1988. Proposal to develop an estuarine conservation and management plan for Delaware's Inland Bays. DNREC, Division of Water Resources; New Jersey Department of Environmental Protection; and Pennsylvania Department of Environmental Resources; Dover, Del.

DNREC. 1988. Table 7. Resident and nonresident (combined) harvest expansions, 1975–1986. Federal Aid in Wildlife Restoration, W-16-R, I-4. Dover, Del.: DNREC.

DNREC. 1991. Unpublished heronry data. Division of Fish and Wildlife, DNREC, Dover, Del.

DNREC. 1993. *Delaware hunting and trapping guide.* Division of Fish and Wildlife. Dover, Del.: DNREC.

DNREC, NJDEP, and PADER. 1988. Delaware estuary nomination package for the National Estuary Program. DNREC, New Jersey Department of Environmental Protection, and Pennsylvania Department of Environmental Resources, Dover, Del.

Dolbeer, R. A. 1976. Reproductive rate and temporal spacing of nesting of Red-winged Blackbirds in upland habitat. *Auk* 93:343–55.

Dolbeer, R. A. 1978. Movement and migration patterns of Red-winged Blackbirds: A continental overview. *Bird-Banding* 49:17–34.

Dolbeer, R. A., P. P. Woronecki, A. R. Stickley, Jr., and S. B. White. 1978. Agricultural impact of a winter population of blackbirds and Starlings. *Wilson Bulletin* 90:31–44.

Dolton, D. D. 1986. *Mourning Dove: 1986 breeding population status.* Administrative report, Office of Migratory Management, U.S. Fish and Wildlife Service, Laurel, Md.

Drennan, M. P., and R. S. Bowman. 1993. Ground-nesting Snowy Egrets in Maine—A new northernmost-breeding record. *American Birds* 47:376–77.

Drilling, N. E., and C. F. Thompson. 1991. Mate switching in multibrooded House Wrens. *Auk* 108:60–70.

Droege, S. J. 1988. Communication to researchers on interpreting some statistical tables, 24 August 1988. Office of Migratory Bird Management, U.S. Fish and Wildlife Service, Laurel, Md.

Droege, S. J., and J. R. Sauer. 1990. *North American breeding bird summary, 1989.* U.S. Fish and Wildlife Service Biological Report, vol. 90, no. 8. Washington, D.C.

Duffy, K., and P. Kerlinger. 1992. Autumn owl migration at Cape May Point, New Jersey. *Wilson Bulletin* 104:312–20.

DuMont, P. A. 1957. Avocets on national wildlife refuges along the Atlantic coast. *Atlantic Naturalist* 12:128.

DuMont, P. G. 1975. White-winged Black Terns in Virginia and Delaware. *Atlantic Naturalist* 30:85–86.

DuMont, P. G., and DuMont, P. A., eds., 1970a. Birds of the Season. *Atlantic Naturalist* 25:45–51.

DuMont, P. G., and DuMont, P. A., eds., 1970b. Birds of the Season. *Atlantic Naturalist* 25:181–86.

DuMont, P. G., and DuMont, P. A., eds., 1971a. Birds of the Season. *Atlantic Naturalist* 26:41–49.

DuMont, P. G., and DuMont, P. A., eds., 1971b. Birds of the Season. *Atlantic Naturalist* 26:174–80.

DuMont, P. G., and DuMont, P. A., eds., 1972a. Birds of the Season. *Atlantic Naturalist* 27:133–40.

DuMont, P. G., and DuMont, P. A., eds., 1972b. Birds of the Season. *Atlantic Naturalist* 27:186–94.

DuMont, P. G., and DuMont, P. A., eds., 1973. Birds of the Season. *Atlantic Naturalist* 28:169–78.

DuMont, P. G., and DuMont, P. A., eds., 1975a. Birds of the Season. *Atlantic Naturalist* 30:27–34.

DuMont, P. G., and DuMont, P. A., eds., 1975c. Birds of the Season. *Atlantic Naturalist* 30:128–39.

Dunmore, R., and D. E. Davis. 1963. Reproductive condition of feral pigeons in winter. *Auk* 80:374.

Dunne, P. 1984. Northern Harrier breeding survey in coastal New Jersey. *Records of New Jersey Birds* 10:2–5.

Dunne, P., D. Sibley, C. Sutton, and W. Wander. 1982. 1982 aerial shorebird survey of Delaware Bay. *Records of New Jersey Birds* 8:68–75.

du Pont, J. E. 1973. Swainson's Warbler breeding in Delaware. *Delmarva Ornithologist* 8:13.

du Pont, W. K. 1963. Delaware's resident geese. *Delaware Conservationist* 7 (4):3–7.

Dutcher, W. 1888. Bird notes from Long Island, N.Y. *Auk* 5:169–83.

Dutcher, W. 1893. Notes on some rare birds in the collection of the Long Island Historical Society. *Auk* 10:267–80.

DVOC. 1900. Meeting of 17 February 1898. Abstracts of the *Proceedings of the Delaware Valley Ornithological Club of Philadelphia* 3:2.

Dwight, J. 1885. Ipswich Sparrow. *Auk* 2:105.

Dwight, J., Jr. 1900. The sequence of plumages and moults of the passerine birds of New York. *Annals of the New York Academy of Science* 13:73–360.

Dwyer, T. J., G. F. Sepik, E. L. Derleth, and D. G. McAuley. 1988. *Demographic characteristics of a Maine Woodcock population and effects of habitat management.* U.S. Fish and Wildlife Service Research Report, no. 4. Washington, D.C.

Dyer, E., M. Jahn, and D. P. Miller. 1973. Birds of the White Clay Creek valley. *Delmarva Ornithologist* 8:24–30.

Dyke, S. 1958. A Greenland Wheatear. *Atlantic Naturalist* 13:36.

Eastman, A. B. 1915. The Wood Duck. *Oologist* 32:95.

Eaton, E. H. 1910. *Birds of New York.* Pt. 1. Albany: State University of New York.

Eaton, E. H. 1914. *Birds of New York.* Pt. 2. Albany: State University of New York.

Eaton, S. W. 1958. A life history study of the Louisiana Waterthrush. *Wilson Bulletin* 70:211–36.

Eaton, S. W. 1988a. Eastern Phoebe. In *The atlas of breeding birds in New York State,* edited by R. F. Andrle and J. R. Carroll. Ithaca, N.Y.: Cornell University Press.

Eaton, S. W. 1988b. Mourning Dove. In *The atlas of breeding birds in New York State,* edited by R. F. Andrle and J. R. Carroll. Ithaca, N.Y.: Cornell University Press.

Eaton, S. W. 1988c. Northern Pintail. In *The atlas of breeding birds in New York State,* edited by R. F. Andrle and J. R. Carroll. Ithaca, N.Y.: Cornell University Press.

Eaton, S. W. 1988d. Prothonotary Warbler. In *The atlas of breeding birds in New York State,* edited by R. F. Andrle and J. R. Carroll. Ithaca, N.Y.: Cornell University Press.

Ebbers, B. C. 1991. Barred Owl. In *The atlas of breeding birds of Michigan,* edited by R. Brewer, G. A. McPeek, and R. J. Adams, Jr. East Lansing: Michigan State University Press.

Ebeling, C. D. 1883. *Geography and history of America.* Originally published in 1799 by C. E. Bohn, Hamburg. 1883 translation of Delaware material. Historical Society of Delaware, Wilmington.

Ednie, A. P. 1977. Sooty Tern and Swallow-tailed Kite—New birds for Delaware. *Delmarva Ornithologist* 12:2.

Ednie, A. P. 1984. Observations of a probable Pileated Woodpecker roosting cavity, with comments on the species distribution in Delaware. *Delmarva Ornithologist* 17:27–28.

Ednie, A. P. 1987. The passing scene, August–November 1985. *Delmarva Ornithologist* 20:17–20.

Ednie, A. P. 1989. Goshawk at Middle Run Wildlife Area, Newark, Delaware. *Delmarva Ornithologist* 22:2–3.

Ednie, A. P. 1990. The passing scene, August–November 1989. *Delmarva Ornithologist* 23:23–29.

Ednie, A. P. 1991. The passing scene, 1 August–30 November 1991. *Delmarva Ornithologist* 24:64–70.

Ednie, A. P., ed., 1985. The Passing Scene: August through November 1982. *Delmarva Ornithologist* 18:37–42.

Ednie, A. P., ed., 1991. The Passing Scene: August through November 1991. *Delmarva Ornithologist* 24:64–70.

Ednie, A. P., ed., 1993. The Passing Scene: August through November 1990. *Delmarva Ornithologist* 25:38–45.

Ednie, A. P. 1994. Delaware's first successful nesting of Cliff Swallow. *Delmarva Ornithologist* 26:3–4.

Ehrlich, P. R., D. S. Dobkin, and D. Wheye. 1988. *The birder's handbook: A field guide to the natural history of North American birds.* New York: Simon and Schuster.

Eiserer, L. A. 1976. *The American Robin: A backyard institution.* Chicago, Ill.: Nelson Hall.

Elder, W. H. 1985. Survivorship in the Tufted Titmouse. *Wilson Bulletin* 97:517–24.

Elliott, J. J., and R. S. Arbib, Jr. 1953. Origin and status of the House Finch in the eastern United States. *Auk* 70:31–37.

Ellis, E., and Ellison, W. G. 1985. Northern Pintail. In *The atlas of breeding birds of Vermont,* edited by S. B. Laughlin and D. P. Kibbe. Hanover, N.H.: University Press of New England.

Ellison, W. G. 1985a. Brown Creeper. In *The atlas of breeding birds of Vermont,* edited by S. B. Laughlin and D. P. Kibbe. Hanover, N.H.: University Press of New England.

Ellison, W. G. 1985b. Cerulean Warbler. In *The atlas of breeding birds of Vermont,* edited by S. B. Laughlin and D. P. Kibbe. Hanover, N.H.: University Press of New England.

England, M. E. 1985. 1985 Northern Harrier productivity, Long Island, New York. Report to NYSDEC, New York State Department of Environmental Control, Delmar, N.Y. Mimeographed.

English, P. F. 1950–56. *Woodcock singing-ground counts.* U.S. Fish and Wildlife Service Special Scientific Reports, Wildlife, nos. 8, 14, 18, 24, 28, and 31. Washington, D.C.

Enser, R. W. 1992. *The atlas of breeding birds in Rhode Island.* Rhode Island Department of Environmental Management. Providence, R. I.

Epstein, M. B., and R. L. Joyner. 1987. Use of managed and open tidal marsh by waterbirds and alligators: Project perspectives. In *Waterfowl and Wetlands Symposium: Proceedings of a symposium on waterfowl and wetlands management in the coastal zone of the Atlantic Flyway,* edited by W. R. Whitman and W. H. Meredith, pp. 46–49. Dover, Del.: Delaware Coastal Management Program, DNREC.

Eriksson, K. 1970. Ecology of the irruption and wintering of Fennoscandian Redpolls (*Carduelis flammea* coll.). *Annales Zoologici Fennici* 7:273–82.

Erskine, A. J. 1979. Man's influence on potential nesting sites and populations of swallows in Canada. *Canadian Field-Naturalist* 93:371–77.

Erskine, A. J. 1992. *Atlas of breeding birds of the Maritime Provinces.* Halifax, Nova Scotia: Nova Scotia Museum.

Erwin, R. M. 1979. *Coastal waterbird colonies: Cape Elizabeth, Maine to Virginia.* U.S. Fish and Wildlife Service, Biological Services Program, FWS/OBS-79/10.

Erwin, R. M., and C. E. Korschgen. 1979. *Coastal waterbird colonies: Maine to Virginia, 1977. An atlas showing colony locations and species compositions.* U.S. Fish and Wildlife Service, FWS/79/08.

Evans, K. E., and R. N. Conner. 1979. Snag management. In *Management of North Central and Northeastern forests for nongame birds,* compiled by R. M. D. Graaf and K. E. Evans. U.S. Department of Agriculture, Forest Service General Technical Report NC-51. St. Paul, Minn.

Every Evening Newspaper. 1894. *History of Wilmington.* F. T. Smiley and Co., Wilmington, Del.

Falk, L. L. 1971. *Bird census surveys of the Hoopes Reservoir area.* Delmarva Ornithological Society, Monograph no. 1. Wilmington, Del.

Falk, L. L. 1972a. Christmas bird counts of Delaware. *Delmarva Ornithologist* 7 (2):30.

Falk, L. L. 1972b. Skylarks—In Delaware??? *Delmarva Ornithologist* 7 (1):7–8.

Falk, L. L. 1975. Loons on Middle Atlantic region Christmas counts. *Delmarva Ornithologist* 10:9–11.

Falk, L. L. 1977. Bird censuses of the Winterthur Museum estate. *Delmarva Ornithologist* 12:17–35.

Falk, L. L. 1978. Woodpeckers on Middle Atlantic region Christmas counts. *Delmarva Ornithologist* 13:33.

Falk, L. L. 1984. Vultures on Middle Atlantic region Christmas counts. *Delmarva Ornithologist* 17:44–55.

Falk, L. L. 1987. Christmas bird counts of the Delmarva Peninsula. *Delmarva Ornithologist* 20:56–81.

Falk, L. L. 1988. Upland Sandpiper at Wilmington, Delaware, Airport, 1986–1988. *Delmarva Ornithologist* 21:26–34.

Fankhauser, D. P. 1964. Renesting and second nesting of individually marked Red-winged Blackbirds. *Bird-Banding* 35:119–21.

Faust, W. R. 1965. Spring on Iron Hill. *Delmarva Ornithologist* 2:33–35.

Faust, W. R., ed., 1968a. The Passing Scene. *Delmarva Ornithologist* 5:5–7.

Faust, W. R. 1968b. A Delaware Bank swallow colony. *Delmarva Ornithologist* 5:7.

Faust, W. R., and R. E. Jones, comp. 1968. Uneven-aged sweet gum–red maple forest (urban woodlot). *Audubon Field Notes* 22:688.

Feare, C. 1984. *The Starling.* New York: Oxford University Press.

Ficken, M. S. 1962. Agonistic behavior and territory in the American Redstart. *Auk* 79:607–32.

Ficken, R. W., M. S. Ficken, and D. H. Morse. 1968. Competition and character displacement in two sympatric pine-dwelling warblers (*Dendroica,* Parulidae). *Evolution* 22:307–14.

Finch, D. M. 1990. Effects of predation and competitor interference on nesting success of House Wrens and Tree Swallows. *Condor* 92:674–87.

Findlay, V. F. [1938]. Our Delaware today—Wild life and its protection. In *Delaware then and now: 1638 to 1938.* Wilmington Public Schools. Historical Society of Delaware, Wilmington. Pamphlet.

Fingerhood, E. D. 1992a. History of Pennsylvania ornithology. In *Atlas of breeding birds in Pennsylvania,* edited by D. W. Brauning, pp. 35–39. Pittsburgh, Pa.: University of Pittsburgh Press.

Fingerhood, E. D. 1992b. Pintail. In *Atlas of breeding birds in Pennsylvania,* edited by D. W. Brauning. Pittsburgh, Pa.: University of Pittsburgh Press.

Fintel, W. A. 1984. American Swallow-tailed Kite over Delaware Bay, DE / NJ. *Delmarva Ornithologist* 17:6.

Fintel, W. A. 1985. Summary report to the shorebird committee (Division of Natural Resources and Environmental Control) of 1982–1985 surveys of Rehoboth Bay, 15 September 1985.

Fintel, W. A., and S. W. Fintel. 1986. Rufous Hummingbird at Lewis, Delaware. *Delmarva Ornithologist* 19:13.

Fisher, A. K. 1901. Two vanishing game birds: The Woodcock and the Wood Duck. In *Yearbook of the U.S. Department of Agriculture for 1901.* USDA, Washington, D.C.

Fisher, R. B. 1958. *Breeding biology of the Chimney Swift,* Chaetura pelagica *(Linnaeus).* New York State Museum Bulletin, no. 368. Albany, N.Y.

Fleming, L. M. 1978. *Delaware's outstanding natural areas and their preservation.* Hockessin, Del.: Delaware Nature Education Society.

Forbush, E. H. 1925. *Birds of Massachusetts and other New England states.* Norwood, Mass: Norwood Press.

Forbush, E. H., and J. B. May. 1939. *A natural history of American birds of eastern and central North America.* Rev. ed. Boston, Mass.: Houghton Mifflin. Edition used, New York: Bramhall House, [*ca.* 1960].

Ford, R. P. 1987. Summary of recent Brown Creeper observations in west Tennessee. *Migrant* 58:50–51.

Forshaw, J. M. 1973. *Parrots of the world.* Garden City, N.Y.: Doubleday.

Fraser, J. D., and D. R. Luukkonen. 1986. The Loggerhead Shrike. In *Audubon Wildlife Report 1986,* edited by R. L. Di Silvestro, pp. 933–41. New York: National Audubon Society.

Frazier, A., and V. Nolan, Jr. 1959. Communal roosting by the Eastern Bluebird in winter. *Bird-Banding* 30:219–25.

Frech, W. W. 1984. Sabine's Gull at Cape Henlopen, Delaware. *Delmarva Ornithologist* 17:13.

Frederick, P. C., N. Dwyer, S. Fitzgerald, and R. E. Bennetts. 1990. Relative abundance and habitat preferences of Least Bitterns (*Ixobrychus exilis*) in the Everglades. *Florida Field Naturalist* 18:1–20.

Fredrickson, L. H. 1977. American Coot. In *Management of migratory shore and upland game birds in North America,* edited by G. C. Sanderson. Washington, D.C.: International Association of Fish and Wildlife Agencies. Reprint, Lincoln: University of Nebraska Press, 1980, pp. 122–47.

Fredrickson, L. H., and F. A. Reid. 1986. Wetland and riparian habitats: A non-game management overview. In *Management of nongame wildlife in the Midwest: A developing art,* edited by J. B. Hale, L. B. Best, and R. L. Clawson, pp. 59–96. Proceedings of the Symposium of the 47th Midwest Fish and Wildlife Conference, Grand Rapids, Mich.

Friedmann, H. 1950. *The birds of North and Middle America.* Pt. 11. U.S. National Museum Bulletin, no. 50. Washington, D.C.

Friedmann, H., L. F. Kiff, and S. I. Rothstein. 1977. *A further contribution to knowledge of the host relations of the parasitic cowbirds.* Smithsonian Contributions to Zoology, no. 235. Washington, D.C.

Frieswyk, T. S., and D. M. DiGiovanni. 1989. *Forest statistics for Delaware—1972 and 1986.* U.S. Department of Agriculture, Northeastern Forest Experimental Station, Resource Bulletin NE-109. Broomall, Pa.

Fuller, M. D., D. Bystrak, C. S. Robbins, and R. M. Patterson. 1987. Trends in American Kestrel counts from the North American Breeding Bird Survey. *Raptor Research Reports* 6:22–27.

Galli, A. E., C. F. Leck, and R. T. T. Forman. 1976. Avian distribution patterns in forest islands of different size in central New Jersey. *Auk* 93:356–64.

Game and Fish Commission. 1954. Pheasant range determination, pp. 19–21. Pittman-Robertson Report, W-16-R-3. Dover, Del.: Game and Fish Commission.

Gardner, A. C. 1921. Hooded Warbler in Delaware. *Auk* 38:463.

Garrison, B. A. 1993. Distribution and trends in abundance of Rough-legged Hawks wintering in California. *Journal of Field Ornithology* 64:566–74.

Gaston, A. J., and R. Decker. 1985. Interbreeding of Thayer's Gull, *Larus thayeri,* and Kumlien's Gull, *Larus glaucoides kumlieni,* on Southampton Island, Northwest Territories. *Canadian Field-Naturalist* 99:257–59.

Gehlbach, F.R. 1995. Eastern Screech Owl *(Otus asio).* In *Birds of North America, No. 165,* A. Poole and F. Gill, eds. Academy of Natural Sciences, Philadelphia, and American Ornithologists' Union, Washington.

Gelvin-Innvaer, L. A. 1990–95. Migratory shorebird annual project report. Dover, Del.: DNREC.

Gelvin-Innvaer, L. A. 1992a. Reproduction and survival of the Osprey in Delaware lower bays. Federal Aid in Wildlife Restoration, W-16-R. Dover, Del.: DNREC.

Gelvin-Innvaer, L. A. 1992b. Studies of the nesting biology of Bald Eagles. Federal Aid for Endangered Species, E-1-14. Dover, Del.: DNREC.

Gelvin-Innvaer, L. A. 1992c. Studies of the nesting biology of Piping Plovers. Federal Aid for Endangered Species Research and Management, E-1-15. Dover, Del.: DNREC.

Gelvin-Innvaer, L. A. 1993. A report from the Non-Game and Endangered Species Program. *Delmarva Ornithologist* 25:12–17.

Gentry, T. G. 1876–77. *Life histories of birds of Eastern Pennsylvania.* Vol. 1, Philadelphia, Pa.: published by the author, 1876. Vol. 2, Salem, Mass.: Naturalists' Agency, 1877. [Not examined.] Cited in B. H. Warren, *Report on the birds of Pennsylvania,* 2nd ed. (Harrisburg, Pa.: State Board of Agriculture, 1890), p. 167.

Gibbs, J. P. 1991. Spacial relationship between nesting colonies and foraging areas of Great Blue Herons. *Auk* 108:764–70.

Gibbs, J. P., and S. M. Melvin. 1992a. American Bittern. In *Migratory nongame birds of management concern in the Northeast,* edited by K. J. Schneider and D. M. Pence. Newton Corner, Mass.: U.S. Fish and Wildlife Service.

Gibbs, J. P., and S. M. Melvin. 1992b. Least Bittern. In *Migratory nongame birds of management concern in the Northeast,* edited by K. J.

Schneider and D. M. Pence. Newton Corner, Mass.: U.S. Fish and Wildlife Service.

Gibbs, J. P., and S. M. Melvin. 1992c. Pied-billed Grebe. In *Migratory nongame birds of management concern in the Northeast,* edited by K. J. Schneider and D. M. Pence. Newton Corner, Mass.: U.S. Fish and Wildlife Service.

Gibbs, J. P., and S. M. Melvin. 1992d. Sedge Wren. In *Migratory nongame birds of management concern in the Northeast,* edited by K. J. Schneider and D. M. Pence. Newton Corner, Mass.: U.S. Fish and Wildlife Service.

Gibbs, J. P., S. M. Melvin, and F. A. Reid. 1992. *American Bittern.* The Birds of North America, edited by A. Poole, P. Stettenheim, and F. Gill, no. 18. Philadelphia, Pa.: Academy of Natural Sciences; Washington, D.C.: American Ornithologists' Union.

Gibbs, J. P., F. A. Reid, and S. M. Melvin. 1992. *Least Bittern.* The Birds of North America, edited by A. Poole, P. Stettenheim, and F. Gill, no. 17. Philadelphia, Pa.: Academy of Natural Sciences; Washington, D.C.: American Ornithologists' Union.

Gibson, C. D. 1883. Pigeon Hawk. *Ornithologist and Oologist* 8:72, 80.

Gibson, D. D. 1987. Hammond's Flycatcher *(Empidonax hammondii)* new to Maryland and the Atlantic coast. *Wilson Bulletin* 99:500.

Gill, F. B. 1980. Historical aspects of hybridization between Blue-winged and Golden-winged warblers. *Auk* 97:1–18.

Gill, F. B. 1992. Carolina Chickadee. In *Atlas of breeding birds in Pennsylvania,* edited by D. W. Brauning. Pittsburgh, Pa.: University of Pittsburgh Press.

Gill, F. B., and B. G. Murray, Jr. 1972. Song variation in sympatric Blue-winged and Golden-winged warblers. *Auk* 89:625–43.

Giraud, J. P. 1844. *Birds of Long Island.* New York: Wiley and Putnam. [Not examined.] Cited in J. Bull, *Birds of the New York area* (New York: Harper and Row, 1964).

Gleason, H. A. 1952. *The new Britton and Brown illustrated flora of the northeastern United States and adjacent Canada.* 3 vols. New York: New York Botanical Garden.

Godfrey, W. E. 1962. Common Loon: Habits. In *Handbook of North American birds.* Vol. 1, *Loons through flamingos,* edited by R. S. Palmer, pp. 33–35. New Haven, Conn.: Yale University Press.

Godfrey, W. E. 1986. *Birds of Canada.* Rev. ed. Ottawa, Ontario: National Museums of Canada.

Goodwin, D. 1976. *Crows of the world.* London: British Museum (Natural History).

Goodwin, D. 1983. *Doves and pigeons of the world.* 3rd ed. Ithaca, N.Y.: Cornell University Press.

Gordon, A. C. 1987. Brewer's Blackbird. In *Atlas of the breeding birds of Ontario,* edited by M. D. Cadman, P. F. J. Eagles, and F. M. Helleiner. Don Mills, Ontario: University of Waterloo Press.

Gosner, K. L. 1979. *A field guide to the Atlantic seashore.* Boston, Mass.: Houghton Mifflin.

Graber, J. W., R. R. Graber, and E. L. Kirk. 1977. *Illinois birds: Picidae.* Illinois Natural History Survey Biological Notes, no. 102. Department of Registration and Education.

Graber, J. W., R. R. Graber, and E. L. Kirk. 1985. *Illinois birds: Vireos.* Illinois Natural History Survey Biological Notes, no. 124. Department of Registration and Education.

Graber, J. W., R. R. Graber, and E. L. Kirk. 1987. *Illinois birds: Corvidae.* Illinois Natural History Survey Biological Notes, no. 126. Department of Registration and Education.

Graber, R. R., and J. W. Graber. 1963. *A comparative study of bird populations in Illinois, 1906–1909 and 1956–1958,* pp. 379–528. Illinois Natural History Survey Bulletin, vol. 28, no. 3. Ill.: Department of Registration and Education.

Graber, R. R., J. W. Graber, and E. L. Kirk. 1970. *Illinois birds: Mimidae.* Illinois Natural History Survey Biological Notes, no. 68. Department of Registration and Education.

Graham, D. S. 1988. Responses of five host species to cowbird parasitism. *Condor* 90:588–91.

Granlund, J. G. 1991. Brewer's Blackbird. In *The atlas of breeding birds of Michigan,* edited by R. Brewer, G. A. McPeek, and R. J. Adams, Jr. East Lansing: Michigan State University Press.

Grantham, J. 1977. Gannet(s) in Delaware and Chester Counties, Pennsylvania, and New Castle County, Delaware. *Cassinia* 56:27.

Greenberg, R. 1987. Seasonal foraging specialization in the Worm-eating Warbler. *Condor* 89:158–68.

Greenberg, R., and S. J. Droege. 1990. Adaptations to tidal marshes in breeding populations of the Swamp Sparrow. *Condor* 92:393–404.

Greenlaw, J. S. 1978. The relation of breeding schedule and clutch size to food supply in the Rufous-sided Towhee. *Condor* 80:24–33.

Greenlaw, J. S. 1993. Behavioral and morphological diversification in Sharp-tailed Sparrows *(Ammodramus caudacutus)* of the Atlantic coast. *Auk* 110:286–302.

Greenlaw, J. S., and C. W. Post. 1992. Seaside Sparrow. In *Migratory nongame birds of management concern in the Northeast,* edited by K. J. Schneider and D. M. Pence. Newton Corner, Mass.: U.S. Fish and Wildlife Service.

Greenway, J. C., Jr. 1967. *Extinct and vanishing birds of the world.* 2nd rev. ed. New York: Dover Publications.

Griffith, R. E. 1946. Nesting of Gadwall and Shoveller on the Middle Atlantic Coast. *Auk* 63:436–38.

Grinnell, G. B. 1910. *American game-bird shooting.* New York: Field and Stream Publishing. [Not examined.] Cited in R. E. Stewart and C. S. Robbins, *Birds of Maryland and the District of Columbia,* North American Fauna, no. 62 (Washington, D.C.: U.S. Fish and Wildlife Service, 1958).

Grinnell, J., and A. H. Miller. 1944. *The distribution of the birds of California.* Pacific Coast Avifauna, no. 27.

Griscom, L. 1937. A monographic study of the Red Crossbill. *Proceedings of the Boston Society of Natural History* 41:77–210.

Groskin, H. 1945. Chimney Swifts roosting at Ardmore, Pennsylvania. *Auk* 62:361–70.

Gross, A. O. 1942. Northern Cliff Swallow. In *Life histories of North American flycatchers, larks, swallows, and their allies,* edited by A. C. Bent, pp. 463–84. U.S. National Museum Bulletin, no. 179. Washington, D.C.

Gross, A. O. 1947. Cyclic invasions of the Snowy Owl and the migration of 1945–46. *Auk* 64:584–601.

Gross, A. O. 1953a. Eastern Ovenbird. In *Life histories of North American warblers,* edited by A. C. Bent, pp. 457–76. U.S. National Museum Bulletin, no. 203. Washington, D.C.

Gross, A. O. 1953b. Northern and Maryland Yellowthroats. In *Life histories of North American warblers,* edited by A. C. Bent, pp. 542–65. U.S. National Museum Bulletin, no. 203. Washington, D.C.

Gross, A. O. 1953c. Southern American Redstart. In *Life histories of North American warblers,* edited by A. C. Bent, pp. 656–81. U.S. National Museum Bulletin, no. 203. Washington, D.C.

Gross, D. A. 1992. White-throated Sparrow. In *Atlas of breeding birds in Pennsylvania,* edited by D. W. Brauning. Pittsburgh, Pa.: University of Pittsburgh Press.

Grosz, K., and G. K. Hess. 1987. Thick-billed Murre in Delaware. *Delmarva Ornithologist* 20:29.

Grube, G. E. 1957. Observations on gnatcatcher range extension. *Auk* 74:494–96.

Guilday, J. E., P. W. Parmalee, and D. P. Turner. 1962. Aboriginal butchering techniques at the Eschleman site (36 LA 12). *Lancaster County, Pennsylvania Archaeologist* 32 (2):59–83.

Haas, B., and F. Haas. 1983. Our big year in Delaware. *Delmarva Ornithologist* 16:19–27.

Hagan, J. M., III, and D. W. Johnston, eds. 1992. *Ecology and conservation of Neotropical migrant landbirds.* Washington, D.C: Smithsonian Institution Press.

Hagar, J. A. 1988. Broad-winged Hawk: Migration. In *Handbook of North American birds.* Vol. 5, pt. 2, *Diurnal raptors,* edited by R. S. Palmer. New Haven, Conn.: Yale University Press.

Hager, D. C., Jr. 1957. Nesting populations of Red-tailed Hawks and Horned Owls in central New York State. *Wilson Bulletin* 69:263–72.

Hake, T. R. 1949. Western Grebe reported. *Wood Thrush* 4:105.

Hall, G. A. 1983. *West Virginia birds: Distribution and ecology.* Carnegie Museum of Natural History, Special Publication no. 7. Pittsburgh, Pa.

Hamas, M. J. 1974. Human incursion and nesting sites of the Belted Kingfisher. *Auk* 91:835–36.

Hamel, P. B. 1992. Cerulean Warbler. In *Migratory nongame birds of management concern in the Northeast,* edited by K. J. Schneider and D. M. Pence. Newton Corner, Mass.: U.S. Fish and Wildlife Service.

Hamel, P. B., H. E. LeGrand, Jr., M. R. Lennartz, and S. A. Gauthreaux, Jr. 1982. *Bird-habitat relationships in southeastern forest lands.* U.S. Forest Service General Technical Report SE-22. Washington, D.C

Hamerstrom, F., F. N. Hamerstrom, and J. Hunt. 1973. Nest boxes: An effective management tool for Kestrels. *Journal of Wildlife Management* 37:400–403.

Hamilton, F. 1990. Small wonders. *Wilmington News Journal,* February 20.

Hamilton, W. J., III, and M. E. Hamilton. 1965. Breeding characteristics of Yellow-billed Cuckoos in Arizona. *Proceedings California Academy of Science* (4th series) 32:405–32.

Haney, J. C. 1985. Band-rumped Storm-Petrels occurrences in relation to upwelling off the coast of southeastern United States. *Wilson Bulletin* 97:543–47.

Haney, J. C. 1990. Winter habitat of Common Loons on the continental shelf of the southeastern United States. *Wilson Bulletin* 102:253–63.

Hann, H. W. 1937. Life history of the Oven-bird in southern Michigan. *Wilson Bulletin* 49:146–237.

Hanson, H. H. [1920–48]. Birds in Delaware. Manuscript notebook of observations in Delaware Museum of Natural History, Greenville, Del.

Hanson, H. H. 1932. List of birds occurring in Delaware. Untitled manuscript list dated 17 March 1932, in Delaware Museum of Natural History, Greenville, Del.

Hardin, D. L. 1987. An evaluation of impoundments and ponds created for waterfowl in Delaware tidal marshes. In *Waterfowl and Wetlands Symposium: Proceedings of a symposium on waterfowl and wetlands management in the coastal zone of the Atlantic Flyway,* edited by W. R. Whitman and W. H. Meredith, pp. 120–26. Dover, Del.: Delaware Coastal Management Program, DNREC.

Hardy, J. W. 1961. Studies in behavior and phylogeny of certain New World jays (Garrulinae). *University of Kansas Science Bulletin* 42:13–149.

Harmic, J. L. 1953. Notes on the vertical and horizonal distribution of birds in the university woodlot, submitted as a report on laboratory work in animal ecology. Copy with S. T. Brooks' notes in Delaware Museum of Natural History, Greenville, Del.

Harrington, B. A. 1982. Untying the enigma of the Red Knot. *Living Bird Quarterly* (2):4–7.

Harrington, B. A. 1983. The migration of the Red Knot. *Oceanus* 26:44–48.

Harrington, B. A. 1986. Red Knot. In *Audubon Wildlife Report 1986,* edited by R. L. Di Silvestro, pp. 871–85. New York: National Audubon Society.

Harrington, B. A., and R. I. G. Morrison. 1979. Semipalmated Sandpiper migration in North America. *Studies in Avian Biology* 2:83–100.

Harrington, B. A., J. P. Myers, and J. S. Grear. 1989. Coastal refueling sites for global bird migrants. In *Proceedings of the 6th Symposium on Coastal and Ocean Management,* edited by O. T. Magoon, H. Converse, D. Miner, L. T. Tobin, and D. Clark, pp. 4293–307. Charleston, S.C. American Society of Civil Engineers, New York, NY 1989.

Harrison, C. 1978. *Field guide to the nests, eggs, and nestlings of North American birds.* New York: Collins.

Harrison, H. H. 1975. *A field guide to birds' nests in the United States east of the Mississippi.* Boston, Mass.: Houghton Mifflin.

Harrison, H. H. 1984. *Wood Warbler's world.* New York: Simon and Schuster.

Hartman, F. E. 1992. American Black Duck. In *Atlas of breeding birds in Pennsylvania,* edited by D. W. Brauning. Pittsburgh, Pa.: University of Pittsburgh Press.

Hasbrouck, E. M. 1891. The Carolina Paroquet *(Conurus carolinensis). Auk* 8:369–79.

Hayes, J. 1984. Ruff migration in eastern North America. *Records of New Jersey Birds* 10:9.

Hayman, P., J. Marchant, and T. Prater. 1986. *Shorebirds: An identification guide to waders of the world.* Boston, Mass.: Houghton Mifflin.

Hegdal, P. A., and B. A. Colvin. 1988. Potential hazard to Eastern Screech-Owls and other raptors of Brodifacoum bait used for vole control in orchards. *Experimental Toxicology and Chemistry* 7:245–60.

Heintzelman, D. S. 1968. *Empidonax hammondii* in Pennsylvania. *Auk* 85:512.

Heintzelman, D. S. 1986. *The migrations of hawks.* Bloomington: Indiana University Press.

Heintzelman, D. S., and A. C. Nagy. 1968. Clutch size, hatchability rates, and sex ratios of Sparrow Hawks in eastern Pennsylvania. *Wilson Bulletin* 80:306–11.

Hennessey, T. E., and L. Van Camp. 1963. Wintering Mourning Doves in northern Ohio. *Journal of Wildlife Management* 27:367–73.

Henny, C. J., and N. E. Holgersen. 1974. Range expansion and population increase of the Gadwall in eastern North America. *Wildlife* 25:95–101.

Herman, B. L. 1992. *The stolen house.* Charlottesville: University Press of Virginia.

Hespenheide, H. A. 1971. Flycatcher habitat selection on the eastern deciduous forest. *Auk* 88:61–74.

Hess, G. K. 1980a. Early arrival of White-throated Sparrow in Delaware. *Delmarva Ornithologist* 15:9.

Hess, G. K. 1980b. Summary of the status of shrikes in Delaware. *Delmarva Ornithologist* 15:8–9.

Hess, G. K. 1983. Churchman's Marsh bird censuses, 1980. *Delmarva Ornithologist* 16:53–91.

Hess, G. K. 1984a. Possible Cliff Swallow nest in Delaware. *Delmarva Ornithologist* 17:2–3.

Hess, G. K. 1984b. The passing scene, December 1981–February 1982. *Delmarva Ornithologist* 17:33–37.

Hess, G. K. 1986. American White Pelican in Delaware. *Delmarva Ornithologist* 19:12.

Hess, G. K. 1987. Delaware hawk censuses, 1983–1986. *Delmarva Ornithologist* 20:2–16.

Hess, G. K. 1989a. Hypothetical record of Clark's Grebe in Delaware. *Delmarva Ornithologist* 22:55–56.

Hess, G. K. 1989b. Rose-breasted Grosbeak breeding in Delaware. *Delmarva Ornithologist* 22:62–63.

Hess, G. K. 1989c. The passing scene, December 1987–February 1988. *Delmarva Ornithologist* 22:50–53.

Hess, G. K. 1991. The passing scene, December 1990–February 1991. *Delmarva Ornithologist* 24:55–61.

Hess, G. K. 1993. The passing scene, December 1991–February 1992 and March–May 1992. *Delmarva Ornithologist* 25:50–56.

Hesselius, A. 1947. Journal of Andreas Hesselius, 1711–1724. Translated by Amandus Johnson. *Delaware History* 2:69–118. Historical Society of Delaware.

Hiatt, B. C., and J. T. Emlen, Jr. 1927. Glossy Ibis at Wilmington, Delaware. *Auk* 44:417–18.

Hickey, M. B., and M. C. Brittingham. 1991. Population dynamics of Blue Jays at a bird feeder. *Wilson Bulletin* 103:401–14.

Hill, J. R., III. 1988. The breeding distribution and relative abundance of the Purple Martin in North America. *Purple Martin Update* 1:8–10.

Hill, N. P. 1968a. Eastern Sharp-tailed Sparrow. In *Life histories of North American cardinals, grosbeaks, buntings, towhees, finches, sparrows, and allies,* edited by O. L. Austin, Jr. Pt. 2, pp. 795–812. U.S. National Museum Bulletin, no. 237. Washington, D.C.

Hill, N. P. 1968b. Southern Sharp-tailed Sparrow. In *Life histories of North American cardinals, grosbeaks, buntings, towhees, finches, sparrows, and allies,* edited by O. L. Austin, Jr. Pt. 2, pp. 812–14. U.S. National Museum Bulletin, no. 237. Washington, D.C.

[Hilles, Mrs. W. S.]. 1900. Reports of societies, Delaware Society. *Bird-Lore* 2:95–96.

Hindman, L. J. 1985. The trumpeter swan blasts back. *American Birds* 39:260.

Hoff, C. M. 1973. Recollections. *Delmarva Ornithologist* 8:6–12.

Hoffman, W., A. Sprunt IV, P. Kalla, and M. Robson. 1993. Bridled Tern breeding record in the United States. *American Birds* 47:379–81.

Holgersen, N. E. 1970. Fieldfare in Delaware. *Atlantic Naturalist* 25:176–77.

Holgersen, N. E. 1970. Sandwich Tern in Delaware. *Cassinia* 52:33.

Holgersen, N. E. 1971a. Black-necked Stilt nesting in Delaware. *Wilson Bulletin* 83:100.

Holgersen, N. E. 1971b. Yellow Rail at Bombay Hook Refuge. *Atlantic Naturalist* 26:168.

Holgersen, N. E. 1972. Avocets at Bombay Hook. *Delmarva Ornithologist* 7 (2):14–15.

Holgersen, N. E. 1974a. Barnacle Goose at Bombay Hook Refuge. *Atlantic Naturalist* 29:133.

Holgersen, N. E. 1974b. A Harris' Sparrow near Smyrna. *Delmarva Ornithologist* 9:79.

Holgersen, N. E. 1974c. Sora breeding at Bombay Hook Refuge. *Atlantic Naturalist* 29:73.

[Holgersen, N. E.]. [1974d]. Accidental birds of the Bombay Hook National Wildlife Refuge. Copy in Delaware Museum of Natural History, Greenville, Del. Typescript.

Holliman, D. C. 1977. Purple Gallinule. In *Management of migratory shore and upland game birds in North America,* edited by G. C. Sanderson. Washington, D.C.: International Association of Fish and Wildlife Agencies. Reprint, Lincoln: University of Nebraska Press, 1980, pp. 105–9.

Holroyd, G. L., and J. G. Woods. 1975. Migration of the Saw-whet Owl in eastern North America. *Bird-Banding* 46:101–5.

Holt, J. B., Jr., and R. Frock, Jr. 1980. Twenty years of raptor banding on the Kittatinny Ridge. *Hawk Mountain News* 54:8–32.

Holthuijzen, A. M. A., and L. Oosterhuis. 1985. Implications for migration counts from telemetry studies of Sharp-shinned Hawks (*Accipiter striatus*) at Cape May Point, New Jersey. In *Proceedings of Hawk Migration Conference IV,* edited by M. Harwood, pp. 305–12. Rochester, N.Y.: Hawk Migration Association of North America.

Howe, A. H., P. H. Geissler, and B. A. Harrington. 1989. Population trends of North American shorebirds based on the International Shorebird Survey. *Biological Conservation* 49:185–99.

Howe, M. A. 1982. Social organization in a nesting population of Eastern Willets. *Auk* 99:88–102.

Howe, R. H., Jr., and E. Sturtevant. 1899. *The birds of Rhode Island.* [Cambridge.] [Not examined.] Cited in J. C. Phillips. 1923. *A natural history of the ducks.* Vol. 2. Boston, Mass.: Houghton Mifflin.

Hoyt, S. F. 1953. Incubation and nesting behavior of the Chuck-will's-widow. *Wilson Bulletin* 65:204–5.

Hoyt, S. F. 1957. The ecology of the Pileated Woodpecker. *Ecology* 38:246–56.

Hubbard, J. P. 1972. Identification of wintering orioles in the Northeast. *Delmarva Ornithologist* 7 (2):10–12.

Hubbard, J. P. 1973. Identification of parakeets in Delaware. *Delmarva Ornithologist* 8:22–23.

Hubbard, J. P. 1974a. Nesting birds in Delaware: The record and the future. *Delmarva Ornithologist* 9:27–30.

Hubbard, J. P. 1974b. Another Psittacine in Delaware—The Rose-ringed Parakeet. *Delmarva Ornithologist* 9:73–74.

Hull, C. N. 1991. Red-eyed Vireo. In *The atlas of breeding birds of Michigan,* edited by R. Brewer, G. A. McPeek, and R. J. Adams, Jr. East Lansing: Michigan State University Press.

Hunt, W. G., and F. P. Ward. 1988. Habitat selection by spring migrant Peregrines at Padre Island, Texas. In *Peregrine Falcon populations: Their management and recovery,* edited by T. J. Cade et al., pp. 527–35. Boise, Idaho: Peregrine Fund.

Hurley, R. J., and E. C. Franks. 1976. Changes in the breeding ranges of two grassland birds. *Auk* 93:108–15.

Hussell, D. J. T. 1980. The timing of fall migration and molt in Least Flycatchers. *Journal of Field Ornithology* 51:65–71.

Hussell, D. J. T. 1991. Fall migrations of Alder and Willow flycatchers in southern Ontario. *Journal of Field Ornithology* 62:260–70.

Hyde, A. S. 1939. *The life history of Henslow's Sparrow,* Passerherbulus henslowi (*Audubon*). University of Michigan Museum of Zoology, Miscellaneous Publication no. 41, Ann Arbor.

Ickes, R. 1992a. Cerulean Warbler. In *Atlas of breeding birds in Pennsylvania,* edited by D. W. Brauning. Pittsburgh, Pa.: University of Pittsburgh Press.

Ickes, R. 1992b. Clay-colored Sparrow. In *Atlas of breeding birds in Pennsylvania,* edited by D. W. Brauning. Pittsburgh, Pa.: University of Pittsburgh Press.

Ingold, D. J. 1989. Nesting phenology and competition for nest sites among Red-headed and Red-bellied woodpeckers and European Starlings. *Auk* 106:209–17.

Ingold, D. J. 1991. Nest-site fidelity in Red-headed and Red-bellied woodpeckers. *Wilson Bulletin* 103:118–22.

Ingold, J. L. 1993. *Blue Grosbeak.* The Birds of North America, edited by A. Poole and F. Gill, no. 79. Philadelphia, Pa.: Academy of Natural Sciences; Washington, D.C.: American Ornithologists' Union.

Ireland, W., Jr., and E. D. Matthews. 1974. *Soil survey of Sussex County, Delaware.* Washington, D.C.: Soil Conservation Service, U.S. Department of Agriculture in cooperation with the Delaware Agricultural Experimental Station.

Jackson, J. A. 1988. Turkey Vulture: Migration. In *Handbook of North American birds.* Vol. 4, pt. 1, *Diurnal raptors,* edited by R. S. Palmer, pp. 31–33. New Haven, Conn.: Yale University Press.

Jackson, J. A., and J. Tate, Jr. 1974. An analysis of nest box use by Purple Martins, House Sparrows, and Starlings in eastern North America. *Wilson Bulletin* 86:435–49.

Jackson, J. B. 1967. The wildlife found in the Delaware basin by the earliest explorers, traders, and settlers. *Delaware Conservationist* 11 (4):3–6.

James, D. 1962. Winter 1961–62: Dominated by movements of boreal birds and marked by still low numbers of Eastern Bluebirds. *Audubon Field Notes* 16:306–11.

James, F. C. 1971. Ordinations of habitat relationships among breeding birds. *Wilson Bulletin* 83:215–36.

James, F. C., and H. H. Shugart, Jr. 1974. The phenology of the nesting season of the American Robin *(Turdus migratorius)* in the United States. *Condor* 76:159–68.

James, R. D. 1976. Foraging behavior and habitat selection of three species of vireos in southern Ontario. *Wilson Bulletin* 88:62–75.

James, R. D. 1984. Structure, frequency of usage, and apparent learning in the primary song of the Yellow-throated Vireo, with comparative notes on Solitary Vireos. *Canadian Journal of Zoology* 62:468–72.

Jameson, J. F. 1909. *Narratives of New Netherland, 1609–1664.* New York: Charles Scribner's Sons.

Janowski, J. P., and R. E. Kelly. 1993. Delaware spring roundup—9 May 1992. *Delmarva Ornithologist* 25:23–26.

Jehl, J. R., Jr. 1963. An investigation of fall-migrating dowitchers in New Jersey. *Wilson Bulletin* 75:250–61.

Johnsgard, P. A. 1973a. Bobwhite. In *Grouse and quails of North America,* pp. 408–30. Lincoln: University of Nebraska Press.

Johnsgard, P. A. 1973b. Pinnated Grouse. In *Grouse and quails of North America,* pp. 274–99. Lincoln: University of Nebraska Press.

Johnsgard, P. A. 1975. Pheasant. In *North American game birds,* pp. 103–7. Lincoln: University of Nebraska Press.

Johnsgard, P. A. 1979. Order Anseriformes. In *Check-list of Birds of the World,* 2nd ed., edited by E. Mayr and G. W. Cottrell. Vol. 1, pp. 425–506. Cambridge, Mass.: Museum of Comparative Zoology.

Johnsgard, P. A. 1981. *The plovers, sandpipers, and snipes of the world.* Lincoln: University of Nebraska Press.

Johnsgard, P. A. 1983. *The hummingbirds of North America.* Washington, D.C.: Smithsonian Institution Press.

Johnson, A. 1911. *The Swedish settlements on the Delaware, 1638–1664.* Philadelphia, Pa.: Swedish Colonial Society.

Johnson, A. 1917. The Indians and their culture as described in Swedish and Dutch records from 1614 to 1664. *International Congress of Americanists* 19:277–82.

Johnson, S. R., and W. J. Adams. 1977. The Little Gull *(Larus minutus)* in Arctic North America. *Canadian Field-Naturalist* 91:294–96.

Johnston, D. W. 1971a. Ecological aspects of hybridizing chickadees *(Parus)* in Virginia. *American Midland Naturalist* 85:124–34.

Johnston, D. W. 1971b. Niche relationships among some deciduous forest flycatchers. *Auk* 88:796–804.

Johnston, R. F. 1964. *Breeding birds of Kansas.* University of Kansas Publications, Museum of Natural History 12[14]:588, 601.

Johnston, R. F. 1992. *Rock Dove.* The Birds of North America, edited by A. Poole, P. Stettenheim, and F. Gill, no. 13. Philadelphia, Pa.: Academy of Natural Sciences; Washington, D.C.: American Ornithologists' Union.

Jones, F. M. 1950. Reminiscences of a Delaware naturalist. *Delaware Notes* 23:13–35.

Jones, J. 1949. Description of the cypress swamps in Delaware and Maryland states, edited by F. M. Jones. *Delaware History* 3 (3):123–37.

Jones, R. E. 1967a. Second-growth tulip poplar–red oak woods (urban woodlot); Beech–oak woodlot (urban woodlot). *Audubon Field Notes* 21:648.

Jones, R. E. 1967b. Delaware summary of nest record cards. *Delmarva Ornithologist* 4:35–38.

Jones, R. E. 1968. Second-growth tulip poplar–red oak woods (urban woodlot); Beech–oak woodlot (urban woodlot). *Audubon Field Notes* 22:689–90.

Jones, R. E. 1969a. Beech–maple woodland nature center (urban woodlot). *Audubon Field Notes* 23:726.

Jones, R. E. 1969b. Second-growth tulip poplar–red oak woods (urban woodlot); Beech–oak woodlot (urban woodlot). *Audubon Field Notes* 23:726–27.

Jones, R. E. 1969c. Uneven-aged mixed hardwood forest (urban woodlot). *Audubon Field Notes* 23:727.

Jones, R. E. 1970. Uneven-aged mixed hardwood forest (urban woodlot). *Audubon Field Notes* 24:776.

Jones, R. E., comp. 1967b. Uneven-aged sweet gum–red maple–beech forest (urban woodlot). *Audubon Field Notes* 21:640.

Jones, R. E., and R. M. Burr, comp. 1967. Mixed deciduous floodplain woodlot (urban woodlot)—I and II. *Audubon Field Notes* 21:646–47.

Jones, R. E., and R. M. Burr, comp. 1968. Mixed deciduous floodplain woodlot (urban woodlot)—II. *Audubon Field Notes* 22:688.

Jones, R. E., and J. R. Longcore, comp. 1966. Uneven-aged sweet gum–red maple forest (urban woodlot). *Audubon Field Notes* 20:647.

Jones, R. E., comp., and W. R. Faust. 1967. Uneven-aged sweet gum–red maple forest (urban woodlot). *Audubon Field Notes* 21:646.

Jones, R. E., comp., and F. M. Steiner, Jr. 1968. Uneven-aged mixed hardwood forest (urban woodlot). *Audubon Field Notes* 22:689.

Jones, R. E., J. R. Longcore, and J. T. Linehan, comp. 1966. Uneven-aged red maple–tulip poplar forest (urban woodlot) (Avon Woodlot). *Audubon Field Notes* 20:647.

Jordan, T. G. and M. Kaups. 1989. *The American backwoods frontier—An ethnic and ecological interpretation.* Baltimore, Md.: Johns Hopkins University Press.

Jumars, P. 1969. Studies on the roosting flights of blackbirds in New Castle County, Delaware. *Delmarva Ornithologist* 6:14–17.

Kain, T., ed. 1987. *Virginia's birdlife: An annotated checklist.* Virginia Avifauna, no. 3. Virginia Society of Ornithology.

Kale, H. W., II. 1965. *Ecology and bioenergetics of the Long-billed Marsh Wren in Georgia salt marshes.* Publications of the Nuttall Ornithological Club, no. 5. Cambridge, Mass.

Kale, H. W., II. 1968. Relationship of Purple Martins to mosquito control. *Auk* 85:654–61.

Kale, H. W., II, and W. L. Jennings. 1966. Movements of immature Mockingbirds between swamp and residential areas of Pinellas County, Florida. *Bird-Banding* 37:113–20.

Kalm, P. 1937 [1753–61]. *Peter Kalm's travels in North America.* Edited by A. B. Benson. 2 vols. New York: Wilson-Erickson.

Kalmbach, E. R. 1915. Winter crow roosts. In *Yearbook of Department* of Agriculture for 1915, pp. 83–100. USDA, Washington, D.C.

Kalmbach, E. R. 1918. *The crow and its relation to man.* U.S. Department of Agriculture Bulletin, no. 621. Washington, D.C.

Kalmbach, E. R. 1939. *The crow and its relation to agriculture.* U.S. Department of Agriculture Bulletin, no. 1102. Washington, D.C.

Karalus, K. E., and A. W. Eckert. 1974. *The Owls of North America (north of Mexico).* Garden City, N.Y.: Doubleday.

Katholi, K., and J. T. Linehan. 1969. Cape Henlopen tern census. *Delmarva Ornithologist* 6:34–36.

Kaufman, K. 1990. *Advanced birding.* Boston, Mass.: Houghton Mifflin.

Keeler, J. E. 1977. Mourning Dove. In *Management of migratory shore and upland game birds in North America,* edited by G. C. Sanderson. Washington, D.C.: International Association of Fish and Wildlife Agencies. Reprint, Lincoln: University of Nebraska Press, 1980, pp. 274–98.

Kelley, A. H. 1978. *Birds of southeastern Michigan and southwestern Ontario.* Bloomfield Hills, Mich.: Cranebrook Institute of Science.

Kendeigh, S. C. 1941. *Territorial and mating behavior of the House Wren,* pp. 1–120. Illinois Biological Monographs, vol. 18, no. 3. Urbana, Ill.: University of Illinois.

Kendeigh, S. C. 1944. *Measurement of bird populations,* pp. 67–106. Ecological Monographs, no. 14.

Kennard, J. H. 1976. A biennial rhythm in the winter distribution of the Common Redpoll. *Bird-Banding* 47:231–37.

Kennard, J. H. 1977. A biennial rhythm in Purple Finch migration. *Bird-Banding* 48:155–57.

Kennedy, R. S. 1973. Notes on the migration of juvenile Ospreys from Maryland and Virginia. *Bird-Banding* 44:180–86.

Kenworthy, E. M. 1914. A find. *Oologist* 31:103.

Kenworthy, E. M. 1917. Breeding of the Kentucky Warbler in Delaware. *Oologist* 34:104,106.

Kerlinger, P. 1981. Delaware Bay: An obstacle to hawk migration? *Peregrine Observer* (Cape May Bird Observatory) 4 (1):7–8.

Kerlinger, P. 1982. The migration of Common Loons through eastern New York. *Condor* 84:97-100.

Kerlinger, P. 1989. *Flight strategies of migrating hawks.* Chicago, Ill.: University of Chicago Press.

Kerlinger, P., and S. A. Gauthreaux, Jr. 1984. Flight behavior of Sharp-shinned Hawks during migration. I: Over land. *Animal Behavior* 32:1021–28.

Kerlinger, P., and M. R. Lein. 1988. Population ecology of Snowy Owls during winter on the Great Plains of North America. *Condor* 90:866–74.

Kerlinger, P., M. R. Lein, and B. J. Sevick. 1985. Distribution and population fluctuations of wintering Snowy Owls (*Nyctea scandiaca*) in North America. *Canadian Journal of Zoology* 63:1829–34.

Kessel, B. 1953. Distribution and migration of the European Starling in North America. *Condor* 55:49–67.

Kibbe, D. P. 1985a. American Robin. In *The atlas of breeding birds of Vermont,* edited by S. B. Laughlin and D. P. Kibbe. Hanover, N.H.: University Press of New England.

Kibbe, D. P. 1985b. Brown Thrasher. In *The atlas of breeding birds of Vermont,* edited by S. B. Laughlin and D. P. Kibbe. Hanover, N.H.: University Press of New England.

Kilham, L. 1961. Reproductive behavior of Red-bellied Woodpeckers. *Wilson Bulletin* 73:237–54.

Kilham, L. 1972. Reproductive Behavior of White-breasted Nuthatches. II. Courtship. *Auk* 89:115–29.

Kilham, L. 1981. Agonistic behavior of the White-breasted Nuthatch. *Wilson Bulletin* 93:271–74.

Kilham, L. 1983. *Life history studies of woodpeckers of eastern North America.* Publications of the Nuttall Ornithological Club, no. 20. Cambridge, Mass.

Kinsley, K. R. 1982. Changes in habitat structure on Woodcock singing grounds in central Pennsylvania. In *Woodcock ecology and management,* edited by T. G. Dwyer and G. L. Storm. 7th Woodcock Symposium, 1980, Pennsylvania State University. U.S. Fish and Wildlife Service Wildlife Research Report, no. 14. Washington, D.C.

Kirby, R. E. 1988. *American Black Duck breeding habitat enhancement in northeastern United States: A review and synthesis.* U.S. Fish and Wildlife Service Biological Report, vol. 88, no. 4.

Klaas, E. E. 1975. *Cowbird parasitism and nesting success in the Eastern Phoebe,* pp. 1–18. Occasional Papers of the University of Kansas Museum of Natural History, no. 41. Lawrence, Kans.

Klabunde, W. 1983. Spring records, 1982: Eastern Great Lakes. *Newsletter of the Hawk Migration Association of North America* 8 (1):16–17.

Kleiman, J. P. 1982. Fall records, 1981: Eastern Great Lakes. *Newsletter of the Hawk Migration Association of North America* 7 (2):27–29.

Knowles, R. N. 1965. Chickadee: Carolina or Black-capped? *Delmarva Ornithologist* 2:26.

Kochenberger, R. 1983. Survey of shorebird concentrations along the Delaware bayshore, spring 1983. *Peregrine Observer* (Cape May Bird Observatory) 6 (2):3–4.

Kortwright, F. H. 1942. *Ducks, geese, and swans of North America.* Harrisburg, Pa.: Stackpole.

Kraft, J. C. 1971. *A guide to the ecology of Delaware's coastal environments.* Newark: College of Marine Studies, University of Delaware.

Kraft, J. C. 1988. Geology. In *The Delaware estuary,* edited by T. L. Bryant and J. R. Pennock, pp. 31–41. Newark: University of Delaware, Delaware Sea Grant Program.

Kraft, J. C., and R. L. Caulk. 1973. The evolution of Lewes Harbor. *Transactions of the Delaware Academy of Science (Newark)* 1 and 2:79–125.

Kramer, E. Y. 1948. Oystercatcher breeding in New Jersey. *Auk* 65:460.

Krider, J. 1879. *Forty years' notes of a field ornithologist.* Philadelphia, Pa.: personally published, press of Joseph H. Weston.

Lack, D. 1954. *The natural regulation of animal numbers.* Clarendon: Oxford University Press.

Lancaster County Bird Club. 1984. *A guide to the birds of Lancaster County, Pennsylvania.* Lancaster County Bird Club.

Lantz, B. J. 1994. Red-necked Grebes in Delaware. *Delmarva Ornithologist* 26:10–13.

Lanyon, W. E. 1957. *Comparative biology of the meadowlarks in Wisconsin.* Publications of the Nuttall Ornithological Club, no. 1. Cambridge, Mass.

Laskey, A. R. 1944. A study of the Cardinal in Tennessee. *Wilson Bulletin* 56:27–44.

Laskey, A. R. 1958. Blue Jays at Nashville, Tennessee—Movements, nesting, age. *Bird-Banding* 29:211–18.

Laskey, A. R. 1962. Breeding biology of Mockingbirds. *Auk* 79:596–606.

Latham, R. M. 1956. Mid-winter courtship flights of Woodcock in Delaware. *Journal of Wildlife Management* 20:209.

Laughlin, S. B. 1985. Common Tern. In *The atlas of breeding birds of Vermont,* edited by S. B. Laughlin and D. P. Kibbe. Hanover, N.H.: University Press of New England.

Laughlin, S. B., and D. P. Kibbe. 1985. *The atlas of breeding birds of Vermont.* Hanover, N.H.: University Press of New England.

Lawrence, L. de K. 1953. Nesting life and behavior of the Red-eyed Vireo. *Canadian Field-Naturalist* 67:47–87.

Lawrence, L. de K. 1967. *A comparative life-history study of four species of woodpeckers.* American Ornithologists' Union, Ornithological Monographs, no. 5. Lawrence, Kans.: Allen Press.

Lawson, J. 1967. *A new voyage to Carolina.* Edited by H. T. Lefler. Chapel Hill: University of North Carolina Press.

Laybourne, R. C. 1968. Letter quoted in *Delmarva Ornithologist* 5:31.

Leberman, R. C. 1992a. Blue-gray Gnatcatcher. In *Atlas of breeding birds in Pennsylvania,* edited by D. W. Brauning. Pittsburgh, Pa.: University of Pittsburgh Press.

Leberman, R. C. 1992b. Rose-breasted Grosbeak. In *Atlas of breeding birds in Pennsylvania,* edited by D. W. Brauning. Pittsburgh, Pa.: University of Pittsburgh Press.

Leck, C. F. 1984. *The status and distribution of New Jersey's birds.* New Brunswick, N.J.: Rutgers University Press.

Leck, C. F., and F. L. Cantor. 1979. Seasonality, clutch size, and hatching success in the Cedar Waxwing. *Auk* 96:196–98.

Lee, D. S. 1988. The Little Shearwater (*Puffinus assimilis*) in the western North Atlantic. *American Birds* 42:213–20.

LeGrand, H. E., Jr. 1987. The nesting season: Southern Atlantic Coast region. *American Birds* 41:1422–25.

Lehman, J. G. 1975. Summer Glaucous Gull and problems in identification. *Delmarva Ornithologist* 10:16–17.

Lent, R. A. 1988. American Oystercatcher. In *The atlas of breeding birds in New York State,* edited by R. F. Andrle and J. R. Carroll. Ithaca, N.Y.: Cornell University Press.

Leonard, M. L., and J. Picman. 1987. Nesting mortality and habitat selection by Marsh Wrens. *Auk* 104:491–95.

Lepthien, L. W., and C. E. Bock. 1976. Winter abundance patterns of North American kinglets. *Wilson Bulletin* 88:483–85.

Lesser, F. H. 1964. Waterbirds of Little Creek. *Cassinia* 47:22–32.

Lesser, F. H. 1965. Some environmental considerations of impounded tidal marshes on mosquito and waterbird prevalence, Little Creek Wildlife Area, Delaware. Master's thesis, University of Delaware.

Lester, R. T., and J. P. Myers. 1990. Global warming, climate disruption, and biological diversity. In *Audubon Wildlife Report 1989/1990,* edited by W. J. Chandler, pp. 177–202. New York: National Audubon Society.

Levine, E. 1988. Brown Creeper. In *The atlas of breeding birds in New York State,* edited by R. F. Andrle and J. R. Carroll. Ithaca, N.Y.: Cornell University Press.

Lindestrom, Peter. 1925. *Geographia Americae (with an account of the Delaware Indians).* Translated and edited by A. Johnson. Philadelphia, Pa.: Swedish Colonial Society.

Linehan, J. T. 1961. Monthly activities report for February dated 27 February 1961. U.S. Fish and Wildlife Service, Newark, Del.

Linehan, J. T. 1962. Narrative report for February and March dated 11 April 1962. U.S. Fish and Wildlife Service, Newark, Del.

Linehan, J. T. 1964a. Operation Recovery in Delaware. *Delaware Ornithologist* 1:11–12.

Linehan, J. T. 1964b. The passing scene. *Delaware Ornithologist* 1:1–6.

Linehan, J. T. 1965a. Coastal lowland mixed woods. *Audubon Field Notes* 19:601.

Linehan, J. T. 1965b. Operation Recovery: Two hundred hours vs. one recovery. *Delmarva Ornithologist* 2:48–50.

Linehan, J. T. 1965c. Salt marsh edge. *Audubon Field Notes* 19:619.

Linehan, J. T. 1966a. Audubon's friend, Thomas Bewick. *Delmarva Ornithologist* 3:45.

Linehan, J. T. 1966b. Salt marsh edge. *Audubon Field Notes* 20:664.

Linehan, J. T. 1967. Delaware breeding records. *Delmarva Ornithologist* 4:12–15.

Linehan, J. T. 1967b. Operation Recovery, 1966. *Delmarva Ornithologist* 4:39–42.

Linehan, J. T. 1967c. The passing scene (summer). *Delmarva Ornithologist* 4:6–8.

Linehan, J. T. 1968a. A Cape Henlopen nesting tern survey. *Delmarva Ornithologist* 5:27–28.

Linehan, J. T. 1968b. Delaware breeding records: Update. *Delmarva Ornithologist* 5:34–37.

Linehan, J. T. 1968c. Uneven-aged red maple–tulip poplar forest (urban woodlot). *Audubon Field Notes* 22:689.

Linehan, J. T., comp. 1969a. Coastal lowland mixed woods. *Audubon Field Notes* 23:719–20.

Linehan J. T. 1969b. A new shorebird. *Delmarva Ornithologist* 6:41.

Linehan, J. T. 1969c. Operation Recovery, 1967. *Delmarva Ornithologist* 6:22–24.

Linehan, J. T. 1973. Nest records of Cerulean Warbler in Delaware. *Wilson Bulletin* 85:482–83.

Linehan, J. T. 1974. Unpublished statement regarding the proposed channel construction near Pea Patch Island, Delaware. [Not examined.] Cited in J. H. Wiese, *Study of reproductive biology of herons, egrets, and ibis nesting on Pea Patch Island, Delaware* (interpretive report for the period March through September 1975 for Delmarva Power and Light Company, Manomet Bird Observatory, Manomet, Mass., 1976).

Linehan, J. T. 1994. Blackbird habitats in Delaware. *Delmarva Ornithologist* 26:14–18.

Linehan, J. T., and R. E. Jones. 1971. *Delaware bird list.* Wilmington: Society of Natural History of Delaware.

Linehan, J. T., comp., and R. E. Jones. 1969. Uneven-aged red maple-tulip poplar forest (urban woodlot). *Audubon Field Notes* 23:727–28.

Linehan, J. T., R. E. Jones, and J. R. Longcore. 1967a. Breeding bird populations in Delaware's urban woodlots. *Audubon Field Notes* 21:641–46.

Linehan, J. T., R. E. Jones, comp., and C. Strehl. 1967b. Uneven-aged mixed hardwood forest (urban woodlot). *Audubon Field Notes* 21:639.

Lock, A. R. 1988. Recent increases in the breeding population of Ring-billed Gulls, *Larus delawarensis,* in Atlantic Canada. *Canadian Field-Naturalist* 102:627–33.

Long, J. L. 1981. *Introduced birds of the world.* New York: Universe Books.

Longcore, J. R., comp., and R. E. Jones. 1966. Uneven-aged sweet gum-red maple-beech forest (urban woodlot). *Audubon Field Notes* 20:646.

Longcore, J. R., comp., R. E. Jones, and J. T. Linehan. 1966. Uneven-aged mixed hardwood forest (urban woodlot). *Audubon Field Notes* 20:643.

Lord, J., and D. J. Munns. 1970. *The atlas of breeding birds of the West Midlands.* London: Collins.

Lowery, G. H., Jr. 1974. *Louisiana birds.* 3rd ed. Baton Rouge: Louisiana State University Press for the Louisiana Wild Life and Fisheries Commission.

Ludwig, J. P. 1965. Biology and structure of the Caspian Tern (*Hydroprogne caspia*) population of the Great Lakes from 1896 to 1964. *Bird-Banding* 36:217–33.

Ludwig, J. P. 1974. Recent changes in the Ring-billed Gull population and biology in the Laurentian Great Lakes. *Auk* 91:575–94.

Lumsden, H. G. 1987. American Woodcock. In *Atlas of the breeding birds of Ontario,* edited by M. D. Cadman, P. F. J. Eagles, and F. M. Helleiner. Don Mills, Ontario: University of Waterloo Press.

Lumsden, H. G. 1991. The Ontario trumpeter swan restoration program. *Ontario Birds* 9:89.

Lunk, W. A. 1962. *The Rough-winged Swallow* (Stelgidopteryx serripennis): *A study based on its breeding biology in Michigan.* Publications of the Nuttall Ornithological Club, no. 4. Cambridge, Mass.

Lynch, J. M. 1981. Status of the Cerulean Warbler in the Roanoke River basin of North Carolina. *Chat* 45 (2):29–35.

Mabey, S. E., J. McCann, L. J. Niles, C. Bartlett, and P. Kerlinger. 1993. *The Neotropical migratory songbird coastal corridor study: Final report.* Virginia Department of Environmental Quality report to the National Oceanic and Atmospheric Administration, Award no. NA90AA-H-CZ839.

Mace, T. R. 1978. Killdeer breeding densities. *Wilson Bulletin* 90:442–43.

Mackenzie, J. 1989. *Land use transitions in Delaware, 1974–1989.* University of Delaware, Agricultural Experimental Station Bulletin, no. 483. Washington, D.C.

Macoun, J., and J. M. Macoun. 1909. *Catalogue of Canadian birds.* Pt. 1. Geological Survey of Canada, Department of Mines. Ottawa: Government Printing Bureau. [Not examined.] Quoted in P. A. Woodliffe, Red-bellied Woodpecker, in *Atlas of the breeding birds of Ontario,* edited by M. D. Cadman, P. F. J. Eagles, and F. M. Helleiner (Don Mills, Ontario: University of Waterloo Press, 1987).

MacRae, D. 1985. Over-water migration of raptors: A review of the literature. In *Proceedings of Hawk Migration Conference IV,* edited by M. Harwood, pp. 75–98. Rochester, N.Y.: Hawk Migration Association of North America.

Maier, C. 1993. On the trail of the rail: A north Delaware survey of Black Rails *(Laterallus jamaicensis)* and other marsh birds. *Delmarva Ornithologist* 25:2–10.

Mangold, R. E. 1977. Clapper Rail. In *Management of migratory shore and upland game birds in North America,* edited by G. C. Sanderson. Washington, D.C.: International Association of Fish and Wildlife Agencies. Reprint, Lincoln: University of Nebraska Press, 1980, pp. 84–109.

Marino, G. R., J. L. DiLorenzo, H. S. Litwack, T. O. Najarian, and M. L. Thatcher. 1991. General water quality assessment and trend analysis of the Delaware estuary, pt. 1: *Status and trends.* Report submitted to Delaware Estuary Program. Najarian Associates, Eatontown, N.J.

Marti, C. D. 1992. *Barn Owl.* The Birds of North America, edited by A. Poole, P. Stettenheim, and F. Gill, no. 1. Philadelphia, Pa.: Academy of Natural Sciences; Washington, D.C.: American Ornithologists' Union.

Martin, C. C. 1974. A biological, chemical, and physical survey of Delaware's tidal streams, pp. 1–47. Federal Aid Project F-22-R. Dover, Del.: DNREC.

Martin, C. C., and R. W. Miller., rev. ed. 1986. *Delaware's public ponds.* Dover, Del.: DNREC.

Martin, E. M. 1979. *Hunting and harvest trends for migratory game birds other than waterfowl in 1964–1976.* U.S. Fish and Wildlife Service Special Scientific Report, no. 218.

Martin, P. S. 1976. Avian density and vegetation structure in seven urban Delaware woodlots. App. 2, pp. 47–49. Master's thesis, University of Delaware, Newark.

Matthews, E. D., and W. Ireland, Jr. 1971. *Soil survey of Kent County, Delaware.* Washington, D.C.: Soil Conservation Service, U.S. Department of Agriculture in cooperation with the Delaware Agricultural Experimental Station.

Matthews, E. D., and O. L. Lavoie. 1970. *Soil survey of New Castle County, Delaware.* Washington, D.C.: Soil Conservation Service, U.S. Department of Agriculture in cooperation with the Delaware Agricultural Experimental Station.

Mayfield, H. 1964. Yearly fluctuations in a population of Purple Martins. *Auk* 81:274–80.

Mayr, E., and L. L. Short. 1970. *Species taxa of North American birds.* Publications of the Nuttall Ornithological Club, no. 9. Cambridge, Mass.

McCann, J., S. E. Mabey, L. J. Niles, C. Bartlett, and P. Kerlinger. 1993. A regional study of coastal migratory stopover habitat for Neotropical migrant songbirds: Land management implications. *Transactions of the North American Wildlife and Natural Resources Conference* 58:398–407.

McCartney, R. B. 1963. The Fulvous Tree Duck in Louisiana. Master's thesis, Louisiana State University, Baton Rouge.

McClanahan, R. C. 1938. Double-crested Cormorant in Delaware. *Auk* 55:271.

McDaniel, J. W. 1973. Vagrant albatrosses in the western North Atlantic and Gulf of Mexico. *American Birds* 27:563–65.

McDowell, M. 1989. Cypress, sea rockets, and Nuttall's trip to Delaware. *Delaware Conservationist* 32 (3):4–7.

McGarigal, K., and J. D. Fraser. 1985. Barred Owl responses to recorded vocalizations. *Condor* 87:552–53.

McGinnes, B. S. 1956. *Upland game investigations in Delaware, 1949–55.* Dover, Del.: Game and Fish Commission.

McKinley, D. 1979. History of the Carolina Parakeet in Pennsylvania, New Jersey, Delaware, Maryland, and the District of Columbia. *Maryland Birdlife* 35:1–10.

McLaughlin, P. P. 1968. Coastal lowland mixed woods: Strawberry Landing. *Delmarva Ornithologist* 5:8–9.

McNair, D. B. 1984. Clutch-size and nest placement in the Brown-headed Nuthatch. *Wilson Bulletin* 96:296–301.

Meade, G. M. 1988a. Blue-gray Gnatcatcher. In *The atlas of breeding birds in New York State,* edited by R. F. Andrle and J. R. Carroll. Ithaca, N.Y.: Cornell University Press.

Meade, G. M. 1988b. Breeding season table. In *The atlas of breeding birds in New York State,* edited by R. F. Andrle and J. R. Carroll. Ithaca, N.Y.: Cornell University Press.

Meade, G. M. 1988c. Tufted Titmouse. In *The atlas of breeding birds in New York State,* edited by R. F. Andrle and J. R. Carroll. Ithaca, N.Y.: Cornell University Press.

Meanley, B. 1943. Red-cockaded Woodpecker breeding in Maryland. *Auk* 60:105.

Meanley, B. 1950. Swainson's Warbler on the coastal plain of Maryland. *Wilson Bulletin* 62:93–94.

Meanley, B. 1952. Notes on the ecology of the Short-billed Marsh Wren in the lower Arkansas rice fields. *Wilson Bulletin* 64:22–25.

Meanley, B. 1965. King and Clapper rails of Broadway Meadows. *Delaware Conservationist* 9 (1):3–7.

Meanley, B. 1966. Some observations on the habitats of the Swainson's Warbler. *Living Bird* 5:151–65.

Meanley, B. 1969. *Natural history of the King Rail.* North American Fauna, no. 67. Washington, D.C.: U.S. Fish and Wildlife Service.

Meanley, B. 1971. *Natural history of the Swainson's Warbler.* North American Fauna, no. 69. Washington, D.C.: U.S. Fish and Wildlife Service.

Meanley, B. 1975. *Birds and marshes of the Chesapeake Bay country.* Cambridge, Md.: Tidewater Publishers.

Meanley, B. 1978. *Blackwater.* Cambridge, Md.: Tidewater Publishers.

Meanley, B. 1981. Nesting of the Fish Crow in the Shenandoah Valley, Virginia. *Raven* 52:45–46.

Meanley, B. 1985. *The marsh hen: A natural history of the Clapper Rail of the Atlantic coast salt marsh.* Centreville, Md.: Tidewater Publishers.

Meanley, B. 1992. *King Rail.* Birds of North America, no. 3, edited by A. Poole, P. Stettenheim, and F. Gill. Philadelphia, Pa.: Academy of Natural Sciences; Washington, D.C.: American Ornithologists' Union.

Meanley, B., and J. S. Webb. 1961. Distribution of winter Red-winged Blackbird populations on the Atlantic coast. *Bird-Banding* 32:94–97.

Meanley, B., and D. K. Wetherby. 1962. Ecological notes on mixed populations of King Rails and Clapper Rails in Delaware Bay marshes. *Auk* 79:453–57.

Mehlman, D. W. 1990. Migration timing of four uncommon species in Montgomery County. *Maryland Birdlife* 46:79–82.

Mendall, H. L. 1976. Ring-necked Duck: Migration. In *Handbook of North American birds.* Vol. 3, pt. 2, *Waterfowl,* edited by R. S. Palmer, pp. 194–96. New Haven, Conn.: Yale University Press.

Mendall, H. L., and C. A. Aldous. 1943. *The ecology and management of American Woodcock.* Orono, Maine: Maine Cooperative Wildlife Research Unit.

Mengel, R. M. 1952. Certain molts and plumages of Acadian and Yellow-bellied flycatchers. *Auk* 69:273–83.

Mengel, R. M. 1965. *Birds of Kentucky.* American Ornithologists' Union, Ornithological Monographs, no. 3. Lawrence, Kans.: Allen Press.

Mengel, R. M., and M. A. Jenkenson. 1971. Vocalizations of the Chuck-will's-widow and some related behavior. *Living Bird* 10:171–84.

Merritt, J. F. 1987. *Guide to mammals of Pennsylvania.* Pittsburgh, Pa.: University of Pittsburgh Press.

Meritt, J. K. 1969. Magnificent Frigate-bird in Delaware. *Cassinia* 51:59–60.

Metz, K. J. 1991. The enigma of multiple nest building by male Marsh Wrens. *Auk* 108:170–73.

Middleton, R. J. 1949. Tufted Titmouse nesting seven years. *Bird-Banding* 20:151–52.

Miller, R. F. 1933. The breeding birds of Philadelphia, Pennsylvania. *Oologist* 50:86–95.

Miller, R. F. 1942. The Pied-billed Grebe: A breeding bird of the Philadelphia region. *Cassinia* 32:22–34.

Miller, R. F. 1943. The Great Blue Heron: Breeding birds of the Philadelphia region, pt. 2. *Cassinia* 33:1–23.

Miller, R. F. 1946. The Florida Gallinule: Breeding birds of the Philadelphia region, pt. 3. *Cassinia* 36:1–16.

Miller, R. F. 1949. The Killdeer: Breeding birds of the Philadelphia region, pt. 4. *Cassinia* 37:1–8.

Mills, A. 1987a. Chuck-will's-widow. In *Atlas of the breeding birds of Ontario,* edited by M. D. Cadman, P. F. J. Eagles, and F. M. Helleiner. Don Mills, Ontario: University of Waterloo Press.

Mills, A. 1987b. White-breasted Nuthatch. In *Atlas of the breeding birds of Ontario,* edited by M. D. Cadman, P. F. J. Eagles, and F. M. Helleiner. Don Mills, Ontario: University of Waterloo Press.

Mills, A. M. 1986. The influence of moonlight on the behavior of goatsuckers (Caprimulgidae). *Auk* 103:370–78.

Millsap, B. A., and S. L. Vana. 1984. Distribution of wintering Golden Eagles in the United States. *Wilson Bulletin* 96:692–701.

Milne, L. and M. 1980. *The Audubon Society field guide to North American insects and spiders.* New York: Alfred A. Knopf.

Mindell, D. P. 1988. Rough-legged Hawk: Habitat, migration. In *Handbook of North American birds.* Vol. 5, pt. 2, *Diurnal raptors,* edited by R. S. Palmer. New Haven, Conn.: Yale University Press.

Minor, W. F., M. Minor, and M. F. Ingraldi. 1993. Nesting of Red-tailed Hawks and Great Horned Owls in a central New York urban/suburban area. *Journal of Field Ornithology* 64:433–39.

Monroe, B. L., Jr., and A. Barron. 1980. The Forked-tailed Flycatcher in North America. *American Birds* 34:842–45.

Montague, C. L., A. V. Zale, and H. F. Percival. 1987. Ecological effects of coastal marsh impoundments: A review. *Environmental Management* 11 (6):743–56.

Montevecchi, W. A., M. Impekoven, A. Serge-Terkel, and C. G. Beer. 1979. The seasonal timing and dispersion of egg-laying among Laughing Gulls *(Larus atricilla). Ibis* 121:337–44.

Montgomery, E. 1851. Reminiscences of Wilmington. Cited in V. F. Findlay, Delaware then and now: 1638 to 1938. Wilmington Public Schools. Historical Society of Delaware, Wilmington. Mimeographed.

Moore, E. G. 1989. Effect of phragmites control on use of salt marsh impoundments by breeding birds. Master's thesis, University of Delaware.

Moore, G. C., and A. M. Pearson. 1941. *The Mourning Dove in Alabama.* Alabama Department of Conservation Bulletin. Montgomery, Ala.

Moore, W. S. 1995. *Northern Flicker.* Birds of North America, A. Poole and F. Gill, eds. Philadelphia, Pa.: Academy of Natural Sciences, no. 166; Washington, D.C.: American Ornithologists' Union.

Morehouse, E. L., and R. Brewer. 1968. Feeding of nestling and fledgling Eastern Kingbirds. *Auk* 85:44–54.

Morrison, R. I. G., and B. A. Harrington. 1992. The migration system of the Red Knot *(Calidris canutus)* in the New World. In *The migration of Knots,* edited by T. Piersma and N. Davidson, pp. 71–84. Wader Study Group Bulletin 64 Supplement.

Morse, D. H. 1989. *American Warblers: An ecological and behavioral perspective.* Cambridge, Mass.: Harvard University Press.

Morton, E. S., L. Forman, and M. Braun. 1990. Extrapair fertilizations and the evolution of colonial breeding in Purple Martins. *Auk* 107:275–83.

Mosher, J. A. 1988. Broad-winged Hawk: Habitat. In *Handbook of North American birds.* Vol. 5, pt. 2, *Diurnal raptors,* edited by R. S. Palmer. New Haven, Conn.: Yale University Press.

Mosher, J. A., and C. J. Henny. 1976. Thermal adaptiveness of plumage color in Screech Owls. *Auk* 93:614–19.

Mosher, J. A., and R. S. Palmer. 1988. Broad-winged Hawk: Habits. In *Handbook of North American birds.* Vol. 5, pt. 2, *Diurnal raptors,* edited by R. S. Palmer. New Haven, Conn.: Yale University Press.

Mueller, H. C., and D. D. Berger. 1967. Wind drift, leading lines, and diurnal migration. *Wilson Bulletin* 79:50–63.

Mueller, H. C., D. D. Berger, and G. Allez. 1977. The periodic invasions of Goshawks. *Auk* 94:652–63.

Mulvihill, R. S. 1992a. Common Raven. In *Atlas of breeding birds in Pennsylvania,* edited by D. W. Brauning. Pittsburgh, Pa.: University of Pittsburgh Press.

Mulvihill, R. S. 1992b. Golden-crowned Kinglet. In *Atlas of breeding birds in Pennsylvania,* edited by D. W. Brauning. Pittsburgh, Pa.: University of Pittsburgh Press.

Mulvihill, R. S. 1992c. Least Flycatcher. In *Atlas of breeding birds in Pennsylvania,* edited by D. W. Brauning. Pittsburgh, Pa.: University of Pittsburgh Press.

Mumford, R. E. 1964. *The breeding biology of the Acadian Flycatcher.* University of Michigan Museum of Zoology, Miscellaneous Publication no. 125. Ann Arbor, Mich.

Mundinger, P. C., and S. Hope. 1982. Expansion of the winter range of the House Finch: 1947–79. *American Birds* 36:347–53.

Murphy, M. T., and R. C. Fleischer. 1986. Body size, nest predation, and reproductive patterns in Brown Thrashers and other mimids. *Condor* 88:446–55.

Murphy, R. C., and W. Vogt. 1933. The Dovekie influx of 1932. *Auk* 50:325–49.

Murphy, W. L. 1982. The Ash-throated Flycatcher in the East: An overview. *American Birds* 36:241–47.

Murray, B. G., Jr. 1964. A review of Sharp-shinned Hawk migration along the northeastern coast of the United States. *Wilson Bulletin* 76:257–64.

Murray, J. J. 1951. Open mixed hardwoods with grassy clearings. *Audubon Field Notes* 5:330.

Myers, A. C., ed. 1912. *Narratives of early Pennsylvania, west New Jersey, and Delaware, 1630–1707.* New York: Charles Scribner's Sons. Reprint, Barnes and Noble, 1959.

Myers, J. P. 1989a. Delaware Bay: A spectacle of spring passage. *Nature Conservancy News* 39 (2):14–18.

Myers, J. P. 1989b. The Sanderling. In *Audubon Wildlife Report, 1988/1989,* edited by W. J. Chandler, pp. 651–66. New York: National Audubon Society.

National Geographic Society. 1983. *Field guide to the birds of North America.* Washington, D.C.: National Geographic Society.

Nelson, J. B. 1978. *The Sulidae: Gannets and boobies.* Oxford: Oxford University Press.

Neter, J., W. Wasserman, and M. H. Kutner. 1989. *Applied linear regression models,* 2nd ed. Boston: Richard D. Irwin, Inc.

Newton, I. 1979. *Population ecology of raptors.* Vermillion, S. Dak.:Buteo Books.

Nice, M. M. 1922. Nest of Mourning Doves. *Auk* 39:457–74.

Nice, M. M. 1932. Observations on the nesting of the Blue-gray Gnatcatcher. *Condor* 34:18–22.

Nichols, B. H. 1990. Trumpeter. *Michigan Natural Resources Magazine* 59:12–17.

Nickell, W. P. 1948. Alternate care of two nests by a Ruby-throated Hummingbird. *Wilson Bulletin* 60:242–43.

Nickell, W. P. 1965. Habitats, territory, and nesting of the Catbird. *American Midland Naturalist* 73:433–78.

Nikula, B. 1993. The winter season: New England region. *American Birds* 47:239–42.

Niles, D. M. 1977. Probable attempted breeding by Golden-crowned Kinglets in Delaware. *Delmarva Ornithologist* 12:14–15.

Niles, D. M. 1979. The passing scene, December 1978–February 1979. *Delmarva Ornithologist* 14:15–16.

Niles, D. M., and A. E. Conway. 1976. House Finches on the Delmarva Peninsula: An historical summary. *Delmarva Ornithologist* 11:40–44.

NOAA. 1990. *Estuaries of the United States: Vital statistics of a national resource base.* Rockville, Md.: National Oceanic and Atmospheric Administration.

Nol, E., and A. Lambert. 1984. Comparison of Killdeers (*Charadrius vociferus*) breeding in mainland and peninsula sites in southern Ontario. *Canadian Field-Naturalist* 98:7–11.

Nolan, V., Jr. 1968. Eastern Song Sparrow. In *Life histories of North American cardinals, grosbeaks, buntings, towhees, finches, sparrows, and allies,* edited by O. L. Austin, Jr. Pt. 3, pp. 1492–512. U.S. National Museum Bulletin, no. 237. Washington, D.C.

Nolan, V., Jr. 1978. *The ecology and behavior of the Prairie Warbler (Dendroica discolor).* American Ornithologists' Union, Ornithological Monographs, no. 26. Lawrence, Kans.: Allen Press.

Nolan, V., Jr., and C. F. Thompson. 1975. The occurrence and significance of anomalous reproductive activities in two North American non-parasitic cuckoos *Coccyzus* spp. *Ibis* 117:496–503.

Northeast Nongame Technical Committee. 1991. Legal categories of rare species in the northeastern states. July 6 and 7.

Novak, P. G. 1992. Black Tern. In *Migratory nongame birds of management concern in the Northeast,* edited by K. J. Schneider and D. M. Pence. Newton Corner, Mass.: U.S. Fish and Wildlife Service.

Nuttall, T. 1832–34. *A manual of the ornithology of the United States and Canada.* Vols. 1 and 2. Cambridge: Hilliard and Brown. (*A popular handbook of the birds of the United Stated and Canada.* New revised and annotated edition, edited by M. Chamberlain. Boston, Mass.: Little, Brown. 1916.)

O'Brien, M., and R. A. Askins. 1985. The effects of Mute Swans on native waterfowl. *Connecticut Warbler* 5:27–31.

O'Halloran, K. A., and R. N. Conner. 1987. Habitat used by Brown-headed Nuthatches. *Bulletin of the Texas Ornithological Society* 20:7–13.

Oliver, J. K. [1978–84]. Unpublished data sheets of raptor observations at Carpenter State Park. Courtesy of J. K. Oliver, University of Delaware. Delaware Museum of Natural History.

Oring, L. W. 1958. Shorebird and waterbird observations in Delaware. *Atlantic Naturalist* 13:38–39.

Ouellet, H. 1993. Bicknell's Thrush: Taxonomic status and distribution. *Wilson Bulletin* 105:545–72.

Owen, D. F. 1963. Polymorphism in the Screech Owl in eastern North America. *Wilson Bulletin* 75:183–90.

Owen, R. B., Jr. 1977. American Woodcock. In *Management of migratory shore and upland game birds in North America,* edited by G. C. Sanderson. Washington, D.C.: International Association of Fish and Wildlife Agencies. Reprint, Lincoln: University of Nebraska Press, 1980, pp. 148–86.

Packard, F. M. 1936. An analysis of some banding records of the eastern Red-wing. *Bird-Banding* 7:28–37.

Palmer, R. S. 1967. Species accounts. In *The shorebirds of North America,* edited by G. D. Stout. New York: Viking Press.

Palmer, R. S., ed. 1962. *Handbook of North American birds.* Vol. 1, *Loons through flamingos.* New Haven, Conn.: Yale University Press.

Palmer, R. S., ed. 1976. *Handbook of North American birds.* Vols. 2 and 3, *Waterfowl.* New Haven, Conn.: Yale University Press.

Palmer, R. S., ed. 1988. *Handbook of North American birds.* Vols. 4 and 5, *Diurnal raptors.* New Haven, Conn.: Yale University Press.

Palmer, T. S., and others. 1954. *Biographies of members of the American Ornithologists' Union.* Washington, D.C.: American Ornithologists' Union.

Parkes, K. C. 1951. The genetics of the Golden-winged x Blue-winged warbler complex. *Wilson Bulletin* 63:5–15.

Parkes, K. C. 1966. *The Carolina Chickadee in the Pennsylvania mountains—newly arrived or overlooked?* Powdermill Nature Reserve Educational Release, no. 69. Pittsburgh, Pa.: Carnegie Institute.

Parkes, K. C. 1987. Sorting out the chickadees in southwestern Pennsylvania. *Pennsylvania Birds* 1:105–6.

Parmalee, D. F. 1992. *Snowy Owl.* The Birds of North America, edited by A. Poole, P. Stettenheim, and F. Gill, no. 10. Philadelphia, Pa.: Academy of Natural Sciences; Washington, D.C.: American Ornithologists' Union.

Parnell, J. F. 1967. Nesting season: Southern Atlantic Coast region. *Audubon Field Notes* 21:555–58.

Parsons, K. C. 1993. The Pea Patch Island wader colony: A proactive plan for natural resource protection and management. Unpublished report, Manomet Bird Observatory, Manomet, Mass., and DNREC, Dover, Del.

Parsons, K. C., and A. C. McColpin. [1994.] Great Blue Heron reproductive success in upper Delaware Bay. Unpublished Manomet Observatory report to DNREC.

Paulson, R. W., E. B. Chase, R. S. Roberts, and D. W. Moody, comp. 1991. Delaware floods and droughts. In *National water summary 1988–89—hydrologic events and floods and droughts*, pp. 223–30. U.S. Geological Survey Water-Supply Paper 2375. Denver, Colo.: Government Printing Office.

Paxton, R. O. 1974. The changing seasons. *American Birds* 28:604–9.

Paxton, R. O., W. J. Boyle, Jr., and D. A. Cutler. 1982. The winter season: Hudson-Delaware region. *American Birds* 36:278–80.

Paxton, R. O., W. J. Boyle, Jr., and D. A. Cutler. 1986. The autumn migration: Hudson-Delaware region. *American Birds* 40:86–91.

Paxton, R. O., W. J. Boyle, Jr., and D. A. Cutler. 1988. The autumn migration: Hudson-Delaware region. *American Birds* 42:47–52.

Paxton, R. O., W. J. Boyle, Jr., and D. A. Cutler. 1992. The fall season: Hudson-Delaware region. *American Birds* 46:68.

Paxton, R. O., W. J. Boyle, Jr., and D. A. Cutler. 1993. The summer season: Hudson-Delaware Region. *American Birds* 47:1092–95.

Paxton, R. O., K. C. Richards, and D. A. Cutler. 1980. The autumn migration: Hudson-Delaware region. *American Birds* 34:143–47.

Paxton, R. O., P. W. Smith, and D. A. Cutler. 1979. The Autumn Migration: Hudson-Delaware Region. *American Birds* 33:159–63.

Payne, R. B. 1989. Indigo Bunting. In *Lifetime reproduction in birds,* edited by I. Newton, pp. 152–73. London: Academic Press.

Payne, R. B. 1991. Indigo Bunting. In *The atlas of breeding birds of Michigan,* edited by R. Brewer, G. A. McPeek, and R. J. Adams, Jr. East Lansing: Michigan State University Press.

Peakall, D. B. 1964. Nest record card programs of North America. *Audubon Field Notes* 18:35–38.

Peakall, D. B. 1969. Nest record card programs: A progress report. *Audubon Field Notes* 23:59–63.

Peakall, D. B. 1970. Eastern Bluebird: Its breeding season, clutch size and nesting success. *Living Bird* 9:239–55.

Peck, G. K., and R. D. James. 1983. *Breeding birds of Ontario: Nidiology and distribution.* Vol. 1, *Non-passerines.* Toronto, Ontario: Royal Ontario Museum.

Peck, G. K., and R. D. James. 1987. *Breeding birds of Ontario: Nidiology and distribution.* Vol. 2, *Passerines.* Toronto, Ontario: Royal Ontario Museum.

Penn, W. 1683. Letter to Society of Traders. In *Narratives of early Pennsylvania, west New Jersey, and Delaware, 1630–1707,* edited by A. C. Myers. New York: Charles Scribner's Sons. Reprint, Barnes and Noble, 1959.

Pennock, C. J. 1878–1933. Two notebooks on Delaware birds. Manuscript ms 66.10, Personal P. Notes consulted comprise a ledger, "Delaware Birds," providing a page per bird for notes. Entries start about 1900, with notes on earlier reports included. Entries regular through about 1910, less through 1920, and a few notes added through 1931. Tucked in this ledger are a few loose notes, lists, slips, and letters. Historical Society of Delaware, Wilmington.

Pennock, C. J. 1887. Birds of Chester County, Penn. *Oologist* 4:1–10.

Pennock, C. J. 1904a. Delaware bird notes. *Auk* 21:286.

Pennock, C. J. 1904b. *Some of our useful birds.* State Board of Agriculture, Dover, Delaware, Bulletin no. 5.

Pennock, C. J. 1905. A glimpse of winter bird life in Delaware. *Cassinia* 8:142–45.

Pennock, C. J. 1908a. Bird life of the Indian River country of Delaware. *Cassinia* 11:29–44.

Pennock, C. J. 1908b. Birds of Delaware—Additional notes. *Auk* 25:282–88.

Pennock, C. J. 1908c. *Rallus virginianus* breeding in the Delaware Valley. *Auk* 25:219.

Pennock, C. J. 1911. Lapland Longspur and other birds in Delaware. *Auk* 28:114.

Pennock, C. J. 1912. Lapland Longspur in Delaware. *Auk* 29:246–47.

Pennock, C. J. 1914. A census of the Turkey Vulture in Delaware. *Cassinia* 17:30–34.

Pennock, C. J. 1930. Little Blue Heron breeding in Delaware. *Auk* 47:555–56.

Pennock, C. J. [ca. 1935]. Two hundred seventy-five birds seen at Rehoboth Beach, Delaware. Sent by W. S. Corkran to H. H. Hanson, spring 1935. Delaware Museum of Natural History, Wilmington, Del.

Perring, F. H., and S. M. Walters, eds. 1962. *Atlas of the British flora.* New York: T. Nelson.

Perry, C. 1988. Some observations of Ross' Geese at Kitt's Hummock, Delaware. *Cassinia* 62:37–43.

Peterjohn, B. G. 1988. S.A.: Fish Crows are expanding their breeding range up river valleys, including the Ohio river to Kentucky and Indiana. *American Birds* 42:1297.

Peterjohn, B. G. 1989. *The birds of Ohio.* Bloomington, Ind.: Indiana University Press.

Peterjohn, B. G., and D. L. Rice. 1991. *The Ohio breeding bird atlas.* Columbus: Ohio Department of Natural Resources.

Peterson, A. T. 1986. Rock Dove nesting in trees. *Wilson Bulletin* 98:168–69.

Peterson, D. M. 1988a. Common Tern. In *The atlas of breeding birds in New York State,* edited by R. F. Andrle and J. R. Carroll. Ithaca, N.Y.: Cornell University Press.

Peterson, D. M. 1988b. Roseate Tern. In *The atlas of breeding birds in New York State,* edited by R. F. Andrle and J. R. Carroll. Ithaca, N.Y.: Cornell University Press.

Peterson, D. M. 1988c. Willet. In *The atlas of breeding birds in New York State,* edited by R. F. Andrle and J. R. Carroll. Ithaca, N.Y.: Cornell University Press.

Peterson, J. M. C. 1988a. Caspian Tern. In *The atlas of breeding birds in New York State,* edited by R. F. Andrle and J. R. Carroll. Ithaca, N.Y.: Cornell University Press.

Peterson, J. M. C. 1988b. Evening Grosbeak. In *The atlas of breeding birds in New York State,* edited by R. F. Andrle and J. R. Carroll. Ithaca, N.Y.: Cornell University Press.

Peterson, J. M. C. 1988c. Herring Gull. In *The atlas of breeding birds in New York State,* edited by R. F. Andrle and J. R. Carroll. Ithaca, N.Y.: Cornell University Press.

Peterson, J. M. C. 1988d. Red Crossbill. In *The atlas of breeding birds in New York State,* edited by R. F. Andrle and J. R. Carroll. Ithaca, N.Y.: Cornell University Press.

Peterson, J. M. C. 1988e. Three-toed Woodpecker. In *The atlas of breeding birds in New York State,* edited by R. F. Andrle and J. M. Carroll. Ithaca, N.Y.: Cornell University Press.

Peterson, J. M. C., and S. T. Crocoll. 1992. Red-shouldered Hawk. In *Migratory nongame birds of management concern in the Northeast,* edited by K. J. Schneider and D. M. Pence. Newton Corner, Mass.: U.S. Fish and Wildlife Service.

Peterson, R. T. 1980. *Field guide to the birds of eastern and central North America.* Boston, Mass.: Houghton Mifflin.

Peterson, V. M. 1980. Maps in *Field guide to the birds of eastern and central North America,* by R. T. Peterson. Boston, Mass.: Houghton Mifflin.

Petit, D. R., L. J. Petit, and K. G. Smith. 1992. Habitat associations of migratory birds overwintering in Belize, Central America. In *Ecology and conservation of Neotropical migrant landbirds,* edited by J. Hagan and D. W. Johnston. Washington, D.C.: Smithsonian Institution Press.

Petit, K. E. 1988. Milk carton nest box use by Prothonotary Warblers. *Ohio Department of Natural Resources Nongame Quarterly* 3:5.

Petit, L. J. 1989. Breeding biology of Prothonotary Warbler in riverine habitat in Tennessee. *Wilson Bulletin* 101:51–61.

Petrides, G. A. 1942. Variable nesting habits of the Parula Warbler. *Wilson Bulletin* 54:252–53.

Petrides, G. A. 1988. *A field guide to eastern trees: Eastern United States and Canada.* The Peterson Field Guide Series. Boston, Mass.: Houghton Mifflin.

Pettingill, O. S., Jr. 1936. *The American Woodcock (Philohela minor* Gmelin), pp. 169–391. Memoirs of the Boston Society Natural History, no. 9, 169–391.

Phillips, A. R. 1975. Semipalmated Sandpiper: Identification, migrations, summer and winter ranges. *American Birds* 29:799–806.

Phillips, C. E. 1974. *Woody vines, shrubs, and trees of Delaware and the Eastern Shore: A guide to their identification in summer.* Society of Natural History of Delaware, Newark, Del.

Phillips, J. C. 1923. *A natural history of the ducks.* Vol. 2. Boston, Mass.: Houghton Mifflin.

Phillips, J. C. 1926. *A natural history of the ducks.* Vol. 4. Boston, Mass.: Houghton Mifflin.

Pickens, A. L. 1944. Seasonal territory studies of rubythroats. *Auk* 61:88–92.

Pickett, T. E. 1976. *Generalized geologic map of Delaware.* Revised from N. Spoljaric and R. R. Jordan, 1966. Delaware Geological Survey. Newark: University of Delaware.

Pickwell, G. B. 1931. *The Prairie Horned Lark.* Transactions of the Academy of Science of St. Louis, no. 27.

Pitelka, F. A. 1942. Territoriality and related problems in North American hummingbirds. *Condor* 44:189–204.

Pitelka, F. A. 1950. *Geographic variation and the species problem in the shorebird genus* Limnodromus. University of California Publications in Zoology no. 50, 1–108.

Poole, A. F., and B. Alger. 1987. Recoveries of Ospreys banded in the United States. *Journal of Wildlife Management* 51:148–55.

Poole, E. L. 1964. *Pennsylvania birds: An annotated list.* Narbeth, Pa.: Livingston Publishing for the Delaware Valley Ornithological Club.

Post, P. W. 1960. First specimens of Sooty Shearwater for Delaware. *Auk* 77:82.

Post, P. W. 1967. Manx, Audubon's, and Little shearwaters in the northwestern North Atlantic. *Bird-Banding* 38:278–303.

Post, P. W. 1970a. Ditched salt marsh. *Audubon Field Notes* 24:772–74.

Post, P. W. 1970b. Salt marsh. *Audubon Field Notes* 24:771–72.

Post, P. W., and G. S. Raynor. 1964. Recent range expansion of the American Oystercatcher into New York. *Wilson Bulletin* 76:339–46.

Potter, E. F. 1980. Notes on nesting Yellow-billed Cuckoos. *Journal of Field Ornithology* 51:17–29.

Potter, J. K. 1926. Yellow-crowned Night Heron in New Jersey in June. *Auk* 43:538.

Potter, J. K. 1938. The season, 15 April to 15 June 1938: Philadelphia region. *Bird-Lore* 40:286.

Potter, J. K. 1939. The season, 15 April to 15 June 1939: Philadelphia region. *Bird-Lore* 41:253–54.

Potter, J. K. 1940. The season, 15 April to 15 June 1940: Philadelphia region. *Bird-Lore* 42 (supplement):380.

Potter, J. K. 1941. The season, 1 April to 1 June 1941: Philadelphia region. *Audubon Magazine* 43 (supplement no. 4):388–89.

Potter, J. K. 1947. Fall migration: Philadelphia region. *Audubon Field Notes* 1:4.

Potter, J. K., and J. J. Murray, eds. 1949. Middle Atlantic coast region. *Audubon Field Notes* 3:8–10.

Potter, J. K., and J. J. Murray. 1955. Winter season: Middle Atlantic Coast region. *Audubon Field Notes* 9:246–48.

Powell, G. V. N., and J. H. Rappole. 1986. The Hooded Warbler. In *Audubon Wildlife Report, 1986,* edited by R. L. DiSilvestro, pp. 827–53. New York: National Audubon Society.

Powell, G. V. N., J. H. Rappole, and S. A. Sader. 1992. Neotropical migrant landbird use of lowland Atlantic habitats in Costa Rica: A test of remote sensing for identification of habitat. In *Ecology and conservation of Neotropical migrant landbirds,* edited by J. Hagan and D. W. Johnston, pp. 287–98. Washington, D.C.: Smithsonian Institution Press.

Powers, K. D. 1983. *Pelagic distributions of marine birds off the northeastern United States.* NOAA Technical Memorandum NMFS-F/NEC-27. Rockville, Md.

Powers, K. D., and J. Cherry. 1983. Loon migrations off the coast of the northeastern United States. *Wilson Bulletin* 95:125–32.

Preble, D., and F. Heppner. 1981. Breeding success in an isolated population of Rock Doves. *Wilson Bulletin* 93:357–62.

Prescott, D. R. C. 1986. Polygyny in the Willow Flycatcher. *Condor* 88:385–86.

Prescott, K. W. 1965. *The Scarlet Tanager: Studies in the life history of the Scarlet Tanager.* New Jersey State Museum, Investigations, no. 2.

Price, C. A., Jr., J. C. Miller, and J. H. Arnett, Jr. 1955. European Lapwing in Delaware and New Jersey. *Cassinia* 40:33–34.

Price, C. E., Jr. 1955. Sprague's Pipit in Delaware. *Cassinia* 41:79.

Price, I. M., and D. V. Weseloh. 1986. Increased numbers and productivity of Double-crested Cormorants *(Phalacrocorax auritus)* on Lake Ontario. *Canadian Field-Naturalist* 100:474–82.

Price, J., S. Droege, and A. Price. 1995. *The summer atlas of North American birds.* New York: Academic Press.

Prime Hook NWR. 1970–90. Narrative reports. U.S. Fish and Wildlife Service. Washington, D.C.

Putnam, L. S. 1949. The life history of the Cedar Waxwing. *Wilson Bulletin* 61:141–82.

Putman, S. H. 1977. Probable breeding record for Purple Gallinule in Bombay Hook National Wildlife Refuge. *Cassinia* 56:28–29.

Pyle, R. L., ed., 1965. Birds of the Season. *Atlantic Naturalist* 20:215–19.

Raasch, M. S. and V. L. Altemus, Sr. 1991. *Delaware's freshwater and brackish water fishes.* Dover: Delaware State College Center for the Study of Del-Mar-Va Habitats and Society of Natural History of Delaware.

Ralston, J. G., Jr. 1975. White-phase Gyrfalcon observation in Delaware. *Delmarva Ornithologist* 10:34.

Reese, J. G. 1975. Productivity and management of feral Mute Swans in Chesapeake Bay. *Journal of Wildlife Management* 39:280–86.

Reid, W. 1992a. Bobolink. In *Atlas of breeding birds in Pennsylvania,* edited by D. W. Brauning. Pittsburgh, Pa.: University of Pittsburgh Press.

Reid, W. 1992b. Sora. In *Atlas of breeding birds in Pennsylvania,* edited by D. W. Brauning. Pittsburgh, Pa.: University of Pittsburgh Press.

Reinoehl, J. 1991. Yellow-throated Vireo. In *The atlas of breeding birds of Michigan,* edited by R. Brewer, G. A. McPeek, and R. J. Adams, Jr. East Lansing: Michigan State University Press.

Rendell, W. B., and R. J. Robertson. 1990. Influence of forest edge on nest-site selection by Tree Swallows. *Wilson Bulletin* 102:634–44.

Renken, R. B., and E. P. Wiggers. 1989. Forest characteristics related to Pileated Woodpecker territory size in Missouri. *Condor* 91:642–52.

Reynolds, J. D., and R. W. Knapton. 1984. Nest-site selection and breeding biology of the Chipping Sparrow. *Wilson Bulletin* 96:488–93.

Reynolds, K. M. 1984, 1987. Introduction and evaluation of the Wild Turkey in Delaware. Federal Aid in Wildlife Restoration, W-16-R, IX. Dover, Del.: DNREC.

Reynolds, K. M. 1988. Return of the native. *Delaware Conservationist* 31 (3):4–7.

Reynolds, K. M. 1992a. Yelp, yelp: Gobble, gobble. *Outdoor Delaware* 1 (2):12–15.

Reynolds, K. M. 1992b. Hunting outlook '92. *Outdoor Delaware* 1 (fall):14–17.

Rhoads, S. N. 1903a. Exit the Dickcissel—A remarkable case of local extinction. *Cassinia* 7:17–28.

Rhoads, S. N. 1903b. In minutes of the DVOC meeting, 1 October 1903. *Cassinia* 7:75–76.

Rhoads, S. N., and C. J. Pennock. 1905. Birds of Delaware: A preliminary list. *Auk* 22:194–205.

Rhoads, S. W. 1886. Crow roosts and roosting crows. *American Naturalist* 20:691–701.

Richards, K. C. 1975. Spring record of Baird's Sandpiper in Delaware. *Delmarva Ornithologist* 10:31.

Ricklefs, R. E. 1972. Latitudinal variation in breeding productivity of the Rough-winged Swallow. *Auk* 89:826–36.

Ridd, S. E., ed. 1989. *Virginia's breeding birds: An atlas workbook.* Richmond: William Byrd Press for Virginia Society of Ornithology.

Ringler, R. F., and C. P. Wilds. 1985. The eighty-fifth Christmas bird count: Delaware, Maryland, D.C., Virginia. *American Birds* 39:402.

Ripley, S. D. 1977. *Rails of the world.* Boston, Mass.: David Godine.

Rising, J. D. 1968. A multivariate assessment of interbreeding between the chickadees *Parus atricapillus* and *P. carolinensis. Systematic Zoology* 17:160–69.

Rising, J. D. 1987. Eastern Wood-Pewee. In *Atlas of the breeding birds of Ontario,* edited by M. D. Cadman, P. F. J. Eagles, and F. M. Helleiner. Don Mills, Ontario: University of Waterloo Press.

Rising, J. D. 1996. *A guide to the identification and natural history of the sparrows of the United States and Canada.* New York: Academic Press.

Ritchison, G. 1986. The singing behavior of female northern Cardinals. *Condor* 88:156–59.

Robbins, C. S. 1973. Introduction, spread, and present abundance of the House Sparrow in North America. In *A symposium on the House Sparrow* (Passer domesticus) *and European Tree Sparrow* (P. montanus) *in North America, S. C. Kendeigh, chairman.* American Ornithologists' Union, Ornithological Monographs, no. 14. Lawrence, Kans.: Allen Press.

Robbins, C. S. 1981. Numerical Estimates. In *Proceedings of the Northeastern Breeding Bird Atlas Conference,* ed. S. B. Laughlin, pp. 74–75. Woodstock, Vt.: Vermont Institute of Natural Science.

Robbins, C. S., Sr., ed. 1996. *Atlas of the breeding birds of Maryland and the District of Columbia.* Pittsburgh: University of Pittsburgh Press.

Robbins, C. S., and D. Bystrak. 1977. *Field list of the birds of Maryland.* 2nd ed. Maryland Avifauna, no. 2. Baltimore: Maryland Ornithological Society.

Robbins, C. S., and B. A. Dowell. 1986. Use of miniroutes and breeding bird survey data to estimate abundance. In *Proceedings of the 2nd Northeastern Breeding Bird Atlas Conference,* compiled by S. M. Sutcliffe, R. E. Bonney, Jr., and J. D. Lowe. Ithaca, N.Y.: Cornell Laboratory of Ornithology.

Robbins, C. S., D. Bystrak, and P. A. Geissler. 1986. *The breeding bird survey: Its first fifteen years, 1965–1979.* U.S. Fish and Wildlife Service Resource Publication, no. 157.

Robbins, C. S., D. K. Dawson, and B. A. Dowell. 1989a. Habitat area requirements of breeding forest birds of the Middle Atlantic states. *Wildlife Monographs* 103:1–34.

Robbins, C. S., J. W. Fitzpatrick, and P. B. Hamel. 1992. A warbler in trouble: *Dendroica cerulea.* In *Ecology and conservation of Neotropical migrant landbirds,* edited by J. M. Hagan III and D. W. Johnston, pp. 549–62. Washington, D.C.: Smithsonian Institution Press.

Robbins, C. S., R. E. Stewart, and M. Karplus. 1947. Dry deciduous scrub. *Audubon Field Notes* 1:200–201.

Robbins, C. S., J. R. Sauer, R. S. Greenberg, and S. Droege. 1989b. Population declines in North American birds that migrate to the Neotropics. *Proceedings of the National Academy of Science* 86:7658–62.

Robbins, M. B. 1989. What's your name, my little chickadee? *Birding* 21:205–7.

Robbins, M. B., and D. A. Easterla. 1991. *Birds of Missouri: Their distribution and abundance.* Columbia: University of Missouri Press.

Robbins, M. B., M. J. Braun, and E. A. Tobey. 1986. Morphological and vocal variation across a contact zone between the chickadees *Parus atricapillus* and *P. carolinensis. Auk* 103:655–66.

Roberts, T. E. 1972. Wintering orioles. *Delmarva Ornithologist* 7 (2):13–14.

Robertson, R. J., and H. L. Gibbs. 1982. Superterritoriality in Tree Swallows: A reexamination. *Condor* 84:313–16.

Rogers, J. P., and J. L. Hansen. 1967. Second broods in the Wood Duck. *Bird-Banding* 38:234–35.

Rohwer, S. A. 1971. Molt and annual cycle of the Chuck-will's-widow. *Auk* 88:485–519.

Root, R. B. 1969. The behavior and reproductive success of the Blue-gray Gnatcatcher. *Condor* 71:16–31.

Root, T. 1988. *Atlas of wintering North American birds.* Chicago, Ill.: University of Chicago Press.

Rosene, W. 1969. *The Bobwhite Quail: Its life and management.* New Brunswick, N.J.: Rutgers University Press.

Rosenfield, R. N. 1988. Cooper's Hawk: Migration. In *Handbook of North American birds.* Vol. 4, *Diurnal raptors,* edited by R. S. Palmer, p. 331. New Haven, Conn.: Yale University Press.

Ross, V. I. 1984. A Delaware record for Pine Grosbeak. *Delmarva Ornithologist* 17:3.

Roth, R. R. 1987. Assessment of habitat quality for Wood Thrush in a residential area. In *Proceedings of the National Symposium on Urban Wildlife,* edited by L. W. Adams and D. L. Leedy. Columbia, Md.: National Institute for Urban Wildlife.

Roth, R. R., and R. K. Johnson. 1993. Long-term dynamics of a Wood Thrush population breeding in a forest fragment. *Auk* 110:37–48.

Rothfels, M., and M. R. Lein. 1983. Territoriality in sympatric populations of Red-tailed and Swainson's hawks. *Canadian Journal of Zoology* 61:60–64.

Rothstein, D. S. 1991a. Northern Harrier breeding territories for Delaware. Delaware Natural Heritage Inventory, draft of unpublished report, DNREC, Dover, Del.

Rothstein, D. S. 1991b. Habitat use of rails in coastal southern Delaware. Delaware Natural Heritage Inventory, draft of unpublished report, DNREC, Dover, Del.

Rothstein, D. S., and L. A. Gelvin-Innvaer. 1992. Heronries in Sussex County. Delaware Natural Heritage Inventory, draft of unpublished report, DNREC, Dover, Del.

Rous, J. L., comp. 1974. *Mourning Dove status report 1973.* U.S. Fish and Wildlife Service Special Scientific Report, Wildlife, no. 186.

Rowlett, R. A. 1980a. Little Stint *(Calidris minuta)* in Delaware. *American Birds* 34:850–51.

Rowlett, R. A. 1980b. *Observations of marine birds and mammals in the northern Chesapeake Bight.* U.S. Fish and Wildlife Service, Biological Services Program, FWS/OBS-80/04.

Rowley, G. D. 1877. *Somateria labradoria* (J. F. Gmelin): The Pied Duck. In *Ornithological miscellany,* edited by G. D. Rowley. Vol. 2, pt. 4, pp. 205–23. London: Trubner.

Rufe, R. G. 1987. Summary of spring roundups held in Delaware from 1969 to 1986. *Delmarva Ornithologist* 20:38–54.

Rufe, R. G., comp. 1980. Delaware spring roundups, 1979 and 1980. *Delmarva Ornithologist* 15:19–27.

Rufe, R. G., comp. 1985. Delaware Spring Roundup, May 1984. *Delmarva Ornithologist* 18:20–29.

Rufe, R. G., comp. 1988. Delaware spring roundup—9 May 1987 and 14 May 1988. *Delmarva Ornithologist* 21:12–25.

Russell, K. 1988. Hammond's Flycatcher in Kent County, Delaware. *Cassinia* 62: 64–65.

Russell, R. W. 1983. Delaware's first White-faced Ibis. *Delmarva Ornithologist* 16:17–18.

Russell, R. W., P. Dunne, C. Sutton, and P. Kerlinger. 1991. A visual study of migrating owls at Cape May Point, New Jersey. *Condor* 93:55–61.

Ryan, R. H. 1976. Escapes, exotics, and accidentals. *Birding* 8:223–28.

Salzman, E. 1985. A ground nesting mixed heronry in Suffolk County. *Kingbird* 35:253–54.

Samson, F. B., and J. R. Longcore. 1971. Stilts nest at Little Creek. *Atlantic Naturalist* 26:37–38.

Sanderson, G. C., ed. 1977. *Management of migratory shore and upland game birds in North America.* Washington, D.C.: International Association of Fish and Wildlife Agencies. Reprint, Lincoln: University of Nebraska Press, 1980.

Santner, S. J. 1992a. Red-breasted Nuthatch. In *Atlas of breeding birds in Pennsylvania,* edited by D. W. Brauning. Pittsburgh, Pa.: University of Pittsburgh Press.

Santner, S. J. 1992b. Worm-eating Warbler. In *Atlas of breeding birds in Pennsylvania,* edited by D. W. Brauning. Pittsburgh, Pa.: University of Pittsburgh Press.

Santner, S. J., D. W. Brauning, G. Schwalbe, and P. W. Schwalbe. 1992. *Annotated list of the birds of Pennsylvania.* Pennsylvania Biological Survey Contribution, no. 4.

Sauer, J. R., and S. J. Droege. 1990. Recent population trends of the Eastern Bluebird. *Wilson Bulletin* 102:239–52.

Schein, M. W. 1954. Survival records of young feral pigeons. *Auk* 71:318–20.

Schmidt, F. V., and P. A. McLain. 1951. The Clapper Rail in New Jersey. In *Proceedings of the 7th Annual Northeastern Fish and Wildlife Conference.* Wilmington, Del. [Not examined.] Cited in B. Meanley, *The marsh hen: A natural history of the Clapper Rail of the Atlantic coast salt marsh* (Centreville, Md.: Tidewater Publishers, 1985).

Schneider, K. J., and D. M. Pence, eds. 1992. *Migratory nongame birds of management concern in the Northeast.* Newton Corner, Mass.: U.S. Fish and Wildlife Service.

Schorger, A. W. 1952. Introduction of the domestic pigeon. *Auk* 69:462–63.

Schorger, A. W. 1955. *The Passenger Pigeon.* Madison, Wisc.: University of Wisconsin Press.

Schorger, A. W. 1966. *The Wild Turkey: Its history and domestication.* Norman: University of Oklahoma Press.

Schutsky, R. M. 1992. Yellow-crowned Night-Heron. In *Atlas of breeding birds in Pennsylvania,* edited by D. W. Brauning. Pittsburgh, Pa.: University of Pittsburgh Press.

Schwalbe, P. W. 1992a. Chestnut-sided Warbler. In *Atlas of breeding birds in Pennsylvania,* edited by D. W. Brauning. Pittsburgh, Pa.: University of Pittsburgh Press.

Schwalbe, P. W. 1992b. Cliff Swallow. In *Atlas of breeding birds in Pennsylvania,* edited by D. W. Brauning. Pittsburgh, Pa.: University of Pittsburgh Press.

Scott, F. R. 1954. The 1953 summer season in Virginia. *Raven* 25:97–98.

Scott, F. R., and D. A. Cutler, ed. 1963. The spring migration: Middle Atlantic Coast Region. *Audubon Field Notes* 17:395–97.

Scott, F. R., and D. A. Cutler, ed. 1966. The fall migration: Middle Atlantic Coast Region. *Audubon Field Notes* 20:22–27.

Scott, F. R., and D. A. Cutler, ed. 1970. The fall migration: Middle Atlantic Coast Region. *Audubon Field Notes* 24:26–31.

Scott, F. R., and D. A. Cutler, ed. 1971. The spring migration: Middle Atlantic Coast Region. *American Birds* 25:840–43.

Scott, F. R., and D. A. Cutler. 1972. The winter season: Middle Atlantic Coast region. *American Birds* 26:588.

Scott, F. R., and D. A. Cutler. 1973a. The winter season: Middle Atlantic Coast region. *American Birds* 27:144.

Scott, F. R., and D. A. Cutler, ed. 1973b. The spring migration: Middle Atlantic Coast Region. *American Birds* 27:754–57.

Scott, F. R., and D. A. Cutler. 1974a. The winter season: Middle Atlantic Coast region. *American Birds* 28:623.

Scott, F. R., and D. A. Cutler, ed. 1974b. The spring migration: Middle Atlantic Coast Region. *American Birds* 28:784–88.

Scott, F. R., and D. A. Cutler. 1976. The winter season: Middle Atlantic Coast region. *American Birds* 30:167.

Scott, F. R., and J. K. Potter. 1959. Nesting season: Middle Atlantic Coast region. *Audubon Field Notes* 13:422–24.

Scott, G. A. 1963. First nesting of the Little Gull *(Larus minutus)* in Ontario and in the New World. *Auk* 80:548–49.

Scott, J. 1807. *Geographical description of the states of Maryland and Delaware.* Philadelphia, Pa.: Kimper Conrad.

Sealy, S. G. 1978. Possible influence of food on egg-laying and clutch size in the Black-billed Cuckoo. *Condor* 80:103–4

Sealy, S. G. 1985. Erect posture of the young Black-billed Cuckoo: An adaptation for early mobility in a nomadic species. *Auk* 102:889–92.

Semenchuk, G. P., ed. 1992. *The atlas of breeding birds of Alberta.* Edmonton, Alberta: Federation of Alberta Naturalists.

Senar, J. C., A. Borras, T. Cabrera, and J. Cabrera. 1993. Testing for the relationship between coniferous crop stability and Common Crossbill residence. *Journal of Field Ornithology* 64:464–69.

Serrentino, P. 1992. Northern Harrier. In *Migratory nongame birds of management concern in the Northeast,* edited by K. J. Schneider and D. M. Pence. Newton Corner, Mass.: U.S. Fish and Wildlife Service.

Seutin, G. 1991. Morphometric identification of Traill's Flycatchers: An assessment of Stein's formula. *Journal of Field Ornithology* 62:308–13.

Sharrock, J. T. R. 1976. *The atlas of breeding birds in Britain and Ireland.* Thetford, Staffordshire, U.K.: British Trust for Ornithology (T. and A. D. Poyser).

Shaver, J. M., and M. B. Roberts. 1930. Some nesting habits of the Cardinal. *Journal of the Tennessee Academy of Science* 5:157–70.

Sheldon, W. G. 1967. *The book of the American Woodcock.* Amherst: University of Massachusetts Press.

Shoch, D. T. 1989. Rare gulls at Cherry Island, Wilmington, Delaware. *Delmarva Ornithologist* 22:41–42.

Shoch, D. T. 1990a. Spring migration of the Yellow Rail in Delaware. *Delmarva Ornithologist* 23:42–43.

Shoch, D. T. 1990b. Painted Bunting at Bombay Hook. *Delmarva Ornithologist* 23:48.

Shoch, D. T. 1991. Are there Swainson's Warblers in Delaware's Pocomoke Swamp? *Delmarva Ornithologist* 24:11–15.

Short, L. L. 1963. Hybridization in the wood warblers *Vermivora pinus* and *V. chrysoptera.* In *Proceedings of the 13th International Ornithological Congress,* pp. 147–60. Lawrence, Kans.: The Allen Press.

Short, L. L. 1982. *Woodpeckers of the world.* Delaware Museum of Natural History Monograph Series, no. 4. Greenville, Del.

Shuster, C. N., Jr., and M. L. Botton. 1985. A contribution to the population biology of horseshoe crabs (*Limulus polyphemus* L.) in Delaware Bay. *Estuaries* 8:363–72.

Sibley, D. 1993. *Birds of Cape May.* Cape May Point, N.J.: Cape May Bird Observatory.

Sibley, S. C. 1988a. Common Nighthawk. In *The atlas of breeding birds in New York State,* edited by R. F. Andrle and J. R. Carroll. Ithaca, N.Y.: Cornell University Press.

Sibley, S. C. 1988b. Red-breasted Merganser. In *The atlas of breeding birds in New York State,* edited by R. F. Andrle and J. R. Carroll. Ithaca, N.Y.: Cornell University Press.

Sibley, S. C. 1988c. Ruby-throated Hummingbird. In *The atlas of breeding birds in New York State,* ed. R. F. Andrle and J. R. Carroll. Ithaca: Cornell University Press.

Smith, C. R. 1988. Yellow-throated Vireo. In *The atlas of breeding birds in New York State,* edited by R. F. Andrle and J. R. Carroll. Ithaca, N.Y.: Cornell University Press.

Smith, C. R. 1992. Henslow's Sparrow. In *Migratory nongame birds of management concern in the Northeast,* edited by K. J. Schneider and D. M. Pence. Newton Corner, Mass.: U.S. Fish and Wildlife Service.

Smith, D. G., and R. Gilbert. 1984. Eastern Screech Owl home range and use of suburban habitats in southern Connecticut. *Journal of Field Ornithology* 55:322–29.

Smith, D. G., A. Devine, and R. Gilbert. 1987. Screech owl roost site selection. *Birding* 19:6–15.

Smith, D. G., A. Devine, and D. Walsh. 1987. Censusing Screech Owls in Southern Connecticut. In *Biology and conservation of northern forest owls: Symposium proceedings.* U.S. Department of Agriculture, Forest Service General Technical Report RM-142. Washington, D.C.

Smith, J. 1907. *The general historie of Virginia, New England, and the Summer Isles.* 2 vols. Glasgow, Scotland: James Maclehose and Sons, Publishers to the University of Glasgow; New York: Macmillan.

Smith, J. N. M. 1982. Song Sparrow pair raise four broods in one year. *Wilson Bulletin* 94:584–85.

Smith, P. W. 1987. The Eurasian Collared-Dove arrives in the Americas. *American Birds* 41:1371–79.

Smith, P. W., R. O. Paxton, and D. A. Cutler. 1979. The winter season: Hudson-Delaware region. *American Birds* 33:268.

Smith, R. L. 1963. Some ecological notes on the Grasshopper Sparrow. *Wilson Bulletin* 75:159–65.

Smith, R. L. 1968. Grasshopper Sparrow. In *Life histories of North American cardinals, grosbeaks, buntings, towhees, finches, sparrows, and allies,* edited by O. L. Austin, Jr. Pt. 2, pp. 725–44. U.S. National Museum Bulletin, no. 237. Washington, D.C.

Smith, W. G. 1900. Meeting of January 1899. *Abstracts of the Proceedings of the Delaware Valley Ornithological Club of Philadelphia* 3:9.

Snell, R. R. 1989. Status of *Larus* Gulls at Home Bay, Baffin Island. *Colonial Waterbirds* 12:12–23.

Sokal, R. R., and F. J. Rohlf. 1981. *Biometry,* 2nd ed. New York: W. H. Freeman and Company.

Soucy, L. J. 1980. Three long distance recoveries of banded New Jersey owls. *North American Bird Bander* 5:97.

Southern, W. E. 1958. Nesting of the Red-eyed Vireo in the Douglas Lake region, Michigan. *Jack-Pine Warbler* 36:103–30, 185–207.

Southern, W. E. 1967. Colony selection, longevity, and Ring-billed Gull populations: Preliminary discussion. *Bird-Banding* 38:52–60.

Southern, W. E. 1974. Florida distribution of Ring-billed Gulls from the Great Lakes Region. *Bird-Banding* 45:341–52.

Sowls, L. K. 1976. Northern Shoveler: Reproduction. In *Handbook of North American birds.* Vol. 2, pt. 1, *Waterfowl,* edited by R. S. Palmer. New Haven, Conn.: Yale University Press.

Speck, E. B. 1986. Black-headed Grosbeak—A special winter visitor in Walnut Ridge. *Delmarva Ornithologist* 19:2.

Speck, F. G. 1927. *The Nanticoke and Conoy Indians.* Papers of the Historical Society of Delaware, New Series I. Wilmington, Del.

Speck, S. B. 1980. Bird censuses of the Ashland Nature Center area. *Delmarva Ornithologist* 15:28–45.

Speck, S. B. 1966. Bundling—Bluebird style. *Delmarva Ornithologist* 3:2.

Speck, S. B. 1978. What has befallen the Tree Sparrow? *Delmarva Ornithologist* 13:20–21.

Speck, S. B. 1980. Bird Censuses of the Ashland Nature Center Area. *Delmarva Ornithologist* 15:28–45.

Speck, S. B., and W. A. Brokaw. 1979. Bird censuses of the White Clay Creek area. *Delmarva Ornithologist* 14:37–85.

Speirs, J. M. 1985. *Birds of Ontario.* Vol. 2. Natural Heritage, Toronto, Ontario.

Speirs, J. M., and D. H. Speirs. 1968. Lincoln's Sparrow. In *Life histories of North American cardinals, grosbeaks, buntings, towhees, finches, sparrows, and allies,* edited by O. L. Austin, Jr. Pt. 3, pp. 1434–67. U.S. National Museum Bulletin, no. 237. Washington, D.C.

Speiser, R., and T. Bosakowski. 1984. History, status, and future management of Goshawk nesting in New Jersey. *Records of New Jersey Birds* 10:28–33.

Spencer, O. R. 1943. Nesting habits of the Black-billed Cuckoo. *Wilson Bulletin* 55:11–22.

Springer, P. F., and R. E. Stewart. 1948a. Tidal marshes. *Audubon Field Notes* 2:223–26.

Springer, P. F., and R. E. Stewart. 1948b. Immature loblolly-shortleaf pine stand. *Audubon Field Notes* 2:239.

Springer, P. F., and R. E. Stewart. 1948c. Second-growth river swamp. *Audubon Field Notes* 2:240–41.

Sprunt, A., Jr. 1940. Chuck-will's-widow. In *Life histories of North American cuckoos, goatsuckers, hummingbirds, and their allies,* edited by A. C. Bent. U.S. National Museum Bulletin, no. 176. Washington, D.C.

Sprunt, A., Jr. 1954. *Florida bird life.* New York: Coward-McCann and National Audubon Society.

Sprunt, A., Jr. 1958. Eastern Boat-tailed Grackle. In *Life histories of North American blackbirds, orioles, tanagers, and allies,* edited by A. C. Bent. U.S. National Museum Bulletin, no. 211. Washington, D.C.

Sprunt, A., Jr., and E. B. Chamberlain. 1970. *South Carolina bird life.*

Rev. ed. With a supplement by E. M. Burton. Columbia: University of South Carolina Press.

Stauffer, D. F., and L. B. Best. 1982. Nest-site selection by cavity-nesting birds of riparian habitats in Iowa. *Wilson Bulletin* 94:329–37.

Stein, M., M. Docherty, R. Jung, and J. P. Myers. 1988. Migratory shorebirds. In *The Delaware estuary*, edited by T. L. Bryant and J. R. Pennock, pp. 115–22. Newark: University of Delaware.

Stein, R. C. 1958. *The behavioral, ecological, and morphological characteristics of two populations of the Alder Flycatcher,* Empidonax traillii *(Audubon)*. New York State Museum Bulletin, no. 371. Albany, N.Y.

Stein, R. C. 1963. Isolating mechanisms between populations of Traill's Flycatchers. *Proceedings of the American Philosophical Society* 107:25–27.

Stepney, P. H. R. 1975. Wintering distribution of Brewer's Blackbird: Historical aspects, recent changes, and fluctuations. *Bird-Banding* 46:106–25.

Stepney, P. H. R., and D. M.Power. 1973. Analysis of the eastward breeding expansion of Brewer's Blackbird plus general aspects of avian expansion. *Wilson Bulletin* 85:452–64.

Stevens, G. L. 1890. Capture of a Trumpeter Swan. *Oologist* 7:15–16.

Stewart, P. A. 1952. Dispersal, breeding behavior, and longevity of banded Barn Owls in North America. *Auk* 69:227–45.

Stewart, P. A. 1969. Movements, population fluctuations, and mortality among Great Horned Owls. *Wilson Bulletin* 81:155–62.

Stewart, P. A. 1980. Population trends of Barn Owls in North America. *American Birds* 34:698–700.

Stewart, R. E. 1949. Ecology of a nesting Red-shouldered Hawk population. *Wilson Bulletin* 61:26–35.

Stewart, R. E. 1953. A life history study of the Yellowthroat. *Wilson Bulletin* 65:99–115.

Stewart, R. E. 1962. *Waterfowl populations in the Upper Chesapeake Region*. U.S. Fish and Wildlife Service Special Scientific Report, no. 65.

Stewart, R. E., and J. W. Aldrich. 1956. Distinction of maritime and prairie populations of Blue-winged Teal. *Proceedings of the Biological Society of Washington* 69:29–36.

Stewart, R. E., and C. S. Robbins. 1958. *Birds of Maryland and the District of Columbia*. North American Fauna, no. 62. Washington, D.C.: U.S. Fish and Wildlife Service.

Stewart, R. E., J. B. Cope, C. S. Robbins, and J. W. Brainerd. 1946. Effects of DDT on birds at the Patuxent Research Refuge. *Journal of Wildlife Management* 10:195–201.

Stickley, A. R. [1963]. Birds of the White Clay Creek valley. Typescript, 2 pp. in S. T. Brooks' notes in Delaware Museum of Natural History, Greenville, Del.

Stickley, A. R. 1964. Breeding records. *Delaware Ornithologist* 1:12–13.

Stickley, A. R. 1965. The passing scene. *Delmarva Ornithologist* 2:22–25.

Stickley, A. R. 1967. The Little Creek census, 1967. *Delmarva Ornithologist* 4:29–34.

Stocek, R. F. 1970. Observations on the breeding biology of the Tree Swallow. *Cassinia* 52:3–20.

Stoddard, H. L., Sr. 1969. *Memoirs of a naturalist*. Norman: University of Oklahoma Press.

Stokes, D. W., and L. Q. Stokes. 1983. *A guide to bird behavior.* Vol. 2. Boston, Mass.: Little, Brown.

Stone, W. 1919. Wild bird life of Delaware. *Delaware Magazine* 1 (June):48–51, 72.

Stone, W. 1928. Dickcissel *(Spiza americana)* in Delaware County, Pennsylvania. *Auk* 45:507–8.

Stone, W. 1937. *Bird studies at Old Cape May.* 2 vols. Philadelphia, Pa.: Delaware Valley Ornithological Club.

Stone, W., and R. Erskine. 1927. The Glossy Ibis in Delaware. *Auk* 44:416–17.

Stouffer, P. C. 1991. Intraseasonal costs of reproduction in Starlings. *Condor* 93:683–93.

Stouffer, P. C., and D. F. Caccamise. 1991. Roosting and diurnal movements of radio-tagged American Crows. *Wilson Bulletin* 103:387–400.

Strickland, P. E. 1987. Pelagic bird trips, 1967–1973. *Delmarva Ornithologist* 20:55.

Stull, W. DeM. 1968. Eastern and Canadian Chipping Sparrows. In *Life histories of North American cardinals, grosbeaks, buntings, towhees, finches, sparrows, and allies,* edited by O. L. Austin, Jr. Pt. 3, pp. 1166–84. U.S. National Museum Bulletin, no. 237. Washington, D.C.

Stutchbury, B. J. 1991. Coloniality and breeding biology of Purple Martins *(Progne subis hesperia)* in saguaro cacti. *Condor* 93: 666–75.

Sullivan, J. K., R. Holderman, and M. Southerland. 1991. *Habitat status and trends in the Delaware estuary.* Report prepared for the Delaware Estuary Program. Dynamac Corporation, Rockville, Md.

Sundell, R. 1968. Letter reporting sighting of Black Rail by F. G. Everton, J. V. Hoeman, and G. Monson. *Delmarva Ornithologist* 5:32.

Sutherland, D. E. 1971. *A 1965 waterfowl population model.* Bureau of Sport Fisheries and Wildlife, Flyway Habitat Management Unit, Project Report 4.

Suthers, H. B. 1978. Analysis of a resident flock of Starlings. *Bird-Banding* 49:35–46.

Sutton, C. C. 1988. Barred Owl Survey in South Jersey. *Records of New Jersey Birds.* 14:2–5.

Sutton, C. C., and P. Sutton. 1986. The status and distribution of Barred Owl and Red-shouldered Hawk in southern New Jersey. *Cassinia* 61:20–29.

Swales, B. H. 1922. Prairie Horned Lark *(Otocoris alpestris praticola)* in Maryland in summer. *Auk* 39:568–69.

Swank, W. G. 1955. Nesting and production of the Mourning Dove in Texas. *Ecology* 36:495–505.

Swift, B. L., S. R. Orman, and J. W. Ozard. 1988. Response of Least Bitterns to tape-recorded calls. *Wilson Bulletin* 100:496–99.

Sykes, P. W. 1976. Cliff Swallow breeding in south-central Florida. *Wilson Bulletin* 88:671.

Tabb, E. C. 1973. A study of wintering Broad-winged Hawks in southeastern Florida, 1968–1973. *EBBA News* (supplement) 36:11–29.

Taber, W., and D. W. Johnston. 1968. Indigo Bunting. In *Life histories of North American cardinals, grosbeaks, buntings, towhees, finches, sparrows, and allies,* edited by O. L. Austin, Jr. Pt. 1, pp. 80–111. U.S. National Museum Bulletin, no. 237. Washington, D.C.

Talley, J. H., comp. 1989. Monthly report on water conditions in Delaware for August and September 1989. Delaware Geological Survey, University of Delaware, Newark.

Tate, G. R. 1992. Short-eared Owl. In *Migratory nongame birds of management concern in the Northeast,* edited by K. J. Schneider and D. M. Pence. Newton Corner, Mass.: U.S. Fish and Wildlife Service.

Tate, J., Jr. 1981. The blue list for 1981. *American Birds* 35:3–10.

Tate, J., Jr. 1986. The blue list for 1986. *American Birds* 40:227–36.

Tatum, J. W. 1934. Brown Pelican in Delaware. *Auk* 51:508.

Taylor, D. M., and C. D. Littlefield. 1986. Willow Flycatcher and Yellow Warbler response to cattle grazing. *American Birds* 40:1169–73.

Terborgh, J. 1989. *Where have all the birds gone?* Princeton, N.J.: Princeton University Press.

Terres, J. K. 1980. *The Audubon Society encyclopedia of North American birds.* New York: Knopf.

Teulings, R. P. 1970. The nesting season: Southern Atlantic Coast region. *American Birds* 24:670–73.

Teulings, R. P. 1972. The nesting season: Southern Atlantic Coast region. *American Birds* 26:844–47.

Teulings, R. P. 1974. The nesting season: Southern Atlantic Coast region. *American Birds* 28:889–92.

Thayer, A. H., and seven others. 1900. An appeal to bird lovers. *Bird-Lore* 2:33.

Thomas, J. E. 1986, 1987a, 1988a, 1989a. Shorebird migration reports, DNREC, Dover, Del.

Thomas, J. E. 1987b. Northern Harrier nest in Delaware. *Delmarva Ornithologist* 20:16.

Thomas, J. E. 1988b. Delaware. *The Eyas* 11 (1):11.

Thomas, J. E. 1988c. 1988 Beachnester final report (incorporating Delaware Audubon Society data). Presented October 20 at the Shorebird Meeting. DNREC. Mimeographed.

Thomas, J. E. [1989b]. Pea Patch heronry, 1985–1989. Table in the Non-Game Wildlife Section of DNREC unpublished data. Personal communication to G. K. Hess, 8 June 1989.

Thomas, J. E. [1989c]. Shorebird projects updated in an undated form letter, May 1989. DNREC, Dover, Del.

Thomas, J. E. 1989d. Studies of the nesting biology of Bald Eagles. Federal Aid for Endangered Species, E-1-11. Dover, Del.: DNREC.

Thompson, A. M. 1976. A summary of the geology of the Piedmont in Delaware. *Transactions of the Delaware Academy of Science* 7:115–34. Reprint, Delaware Geological Survey Special Publication no. 10, Newark, 1980.

Thompson, C. F. 1977. Experimental removal and replacement of territorial male Yellow-breasted Chats. *Auk* 94:107–13.

Tinbergen, N. 1960. *The Herring Gull's world.* Rev. ed., p. 60. New York: Basic Books. 1961.

Tindall, E. E. 1961. A two-year study of mosquito breeding and wildlife usage in Little Creek impounded salt marsh, Little Creek Wildlife Area, 1959–1960. *Proceedings N.J. Mosquito Ext. Association* 48:100–105.

Tiner, R. W., Jr. 1985. *Wetlands of Delaware.* Newton Corner, Mass.: U.S. Fish and Wildlife Service; Dover, Del.: Division of Environmental Control, DNREC.

Tiner, R. W., Jr. 1987a. *A field guide to coastal wetland plants of the northeastern United States.* Amherst: University of Massachusetts Press.

Tiner, R. W., Jr. 1987b. *Mid-Atlantic wetlands, a disappearing natural treasure.* U.S. Fish and Wildlife Service, Fish and Wildlife Enhancement, National Wetlands Inventory Project, Region 5, Newton Corner, Mass.; and U.S. EPA, Region 3, Philadelphia, Pa.

Tiner, R. W., Jr., and J. T. Finn. 1986. *Status and recent trends of wetlands in five Mid-Atlantic states: Delaware, Maryland, Pennsylvania, Virginia, and West Virginia.* Technical report submitted to U.S. Environmental Protection Agency, Region 3, Philadelphia, Pa.; and U.S. Fish and Wildlife Service, Fish and Wildlife Enhancement, National Wetlands Inventory Project, Region 5, Newton Corner, Mass.

Tinsman, J. 1991. Preliminary hard clam and macrobenthic algae survey of Little Assawoman Bay. In *A day in the life of Delaware's forgotten bay: A scientific survey of Little Assawoman Bay,* edited by W. Ullman, pp. 25–26. Dover, Del.: Scientific and Technical Advisory Committee, Inland Bays Estuary Program, DNREC.

Todd, R. L. 1977. Black Rail. In *Management of migratory shore and upland game birds in North America,* edited by G. C. Sanderson. Washington, D.C.: International Association of Fish and Wildlife Agencies. Reprint, Lincoln: University of Nebraska Press, 1980, pp. 71–83.

Todd, W. E. C. 1963. *Birds of the Labrador Peninsula and adjacent areas.* Toronto, Ontario: University of Toronto Press.

Toland, B. R. 1985. Double-brooding by American Kestrels in central Missouri. *Condor* 87:434–36.

Tompkins, I. R. 1965. The Willets of Georgia and South Carolina. *Wilson Bulletin* 77:151–67.

Townsend, C. W. 1905. *The birds of Essex County, Massachusetts.* Memoirs, Nuttall Ornithological Club, no. 3. Cambridge, Mass.

Townsend, C. W. 1926. Virginia Rail. In *Life histories of North American marsh birds,* edited by A. C. Bent, pp. 292–301. U.S. National Museum Bulletin, no. 135. Washington, D.C.

Tuck, L. M. 1972. *The snipes: A study of the genus* Capella. Canadian Wildlife Service, Monograph Series, no. 5. Ottawa, Ontario.

Turnbull, W. P. 1869. *Birds of East Pennsylvania and New Jersey.* [Philadelphia, Pa.: Henry Grambo.] Glasgow, Scotland: printed for private circulation.

Turner, A., and C. Rose. 1989. *Swallows and martins: An identification guide and handbook.* Boston, Mass.: Houghton Mifflin.

Turner, C., J. Hill, and D. W. Johnston. 1984. Chimney Swift nesting in a hollow tree. *Raven* 55:12.

Tyler, W. M. 1929. Piping Plover. In *Life histories of North American shore birds,* edited by A. C. Bent. Pt. 2. U.S. National Museum Bulletin, no. 142. Washington, D.C.

Tyler, W. M. 1940. Chimney Swift. In *Life histories of North American cuckoos, goatsuckers, hummingbirds, and their allies,* edited by A. C. Bent, pp. 271–93. U.S. National Museum Bulletin, no. 176. Washington, D.C.

Tyler, W. M. 1942. Eastern Phoebe. In *Life histories of North American flycatchers, larks, swallows, and their allies,* edited by A. C. Bent, pp. 140–53. U.S. National Museum Bulletin, no. 179. Washington, D.C.

Tyrrell, W. B. 1936. Unpublished report of eagle survey. Copy in Delaware Museum of Natural History, Greenville, Del.

Urner, C.A., and R. W. Storer. 1949. The distribution and abundance of shorebirds on the north and central New Jersey coast, 1928–1938. *Auk* 66:177–94.

U.S. Bureau of the Census. 1989. *Census of agriculture: Geographic area series—Delaware.* U.S. Department of Commerce, Washington, D.C.

U.S. Fish and Wildlife Service. 1990. Unpublished banding data. Patuxent Wildlife Research Center, Laurel, Md.

U.S. Fish and Wildlife Service. 1991. Endangered and threatened animals and plants; animal candidate review for listing as endangered or threatened species, proposed rule. *Federal Register* 56 (225):58804–36.

U.S. Fish and Wildlife Service. 1993. Endangered and threatened wildlife and plants. 50 *CFR* 17.11 and 17.12 (23 August 1993).

U.S. Fish and Wildlife Service. 1993. *Waterfowl status and fall flight forecast, 1993.* Laurel, Md.

U.S. Fish and Wildlife Service, Office of Migratory Bird Management. 1987. *Migratory nongame birds of management concern in the United States: The 1987 list.* Washington, D.C.

U.S. Fish and Wildlife Service, Office of Migratory Bird Management. 1990. Breeding bird survey trends in the East, Delaware, and Upper Coastal Plain, 1966–1990; East, Delaware, 1981–1990. Unpublished data and computations. Patuxent Wildlife Research Center, Laurel, Md.

U.S. Soil Conservation Service. 1973. General soil map, Delaware. First State Resources, Conservation, and Development Project in cooperation with Delaware Agricultural Experimental Station.

Hyattsville, Md.: U.S. Department of Agriculture, Soil Conservation Service.

Van Camp, L., and C. J. Henny. 1975. *The Screech Owl: Its life history and population ecology in northwestern Ohio.* North American Fauna, no. 71. Washington, D.C.: U.S. Fish and Wildlife Service.

Van Velzen, W. T. 1967. First observed Brown Creeper nest in Maryland. *Maryland Birdlife* 23:68–69.

Veit, R. R., and L. Jonsson. 1984. Field identification of smaller sandpipers within the genus *Calidris. American Birds* 38:853–76.

Veit, R. R., and W. R. Petersen. 1993. *Birds of Massachusetts.* Massachusetts Audubon Society.

Vermeer, K., and L. Rankin. 1984. Population trends in nesting Double-crested and Pelagic cormorants in British Columbia. *Murrelet* 65:1–9.

Verner, J., and G. H. Engelsen. 1970. Territories, multiple nest building, and polygyny in the Long-billed Marsh Wren. *Auk* 87:557–67.

Via, J., and D. C. Duffy. 1992. Gull-billed Tern. In *Migratory nongame birds of management concern in the Northeast,* edited by K. J. Schneider and D. M. Pence. Newton Corner, Mass.: U.S. Fish and Wildlife Service.

Vickers, C. R. 1987. Delaware's rare plants: An invitation to protection. *Transactions of the Delaware Academy of Science* 16:3–6.

Voelzer, J. F., E. Q. Lauxen, S. L. Rhodes, and K. N. Norman. 1982. *Waterfowl status report, 1979.* U.S. Fish and Wildlife Service Special Scientific Report, Wildlife, no. 246.

Walkinshaw, L. H. 1941. The Prothonotary Warbler: A comparison of nesting conditions in Tennessee and Michigan. *Wilson Bulletin* 53:3–21.

Walkinshaw, L. H. 1944. The Eastern Chipping Sparrow in Michigan. *Wilson Bulletin* 56:193–205.

Walkinshaw, L. H. 1966a. Studies of the Acadian Flycatcher in Michigan. *Bird-Banding* 37:227–57.

Walkinshaw, L. H. 1966b. Summer biology of Traill's Flycatcher. *Wilson Bulletin* 78:31–46.

Walkinshaw, L. H. 1968. Eastern Field Sparrow. In *Life histories of North American cardinals, grosbeaks, buntings, towhees, finches, sparrows, and allies,* edited by O. L. Austin, Jr. Pt. 2, pp. 1217–35. U.S. National Museum Bulletin, no. 237. Washington, D.C.

Walkinshaw, L. H., and D. A. Zimmerman. 1961. Range expansion of the Brewer's Blackbird in eastern North America. *Condor* 63:162–77.

Wander, W., and S. A. Brady. 1984. Probable Hammond's Flycatcher in New Jersey. *Records of New Jersey Birds* 10:27–28.

Ward, D. A., R. Ward, and J. T. Linehan, comp. 1966. Coastal lowland mixed woods. *Audubon Field Notes* 20:628.

Ward, F. P., K. Titus, W. S. Seegar, M. A. Yates, and M. R. Fuller. 1988. Autumn migrations of Peregrine Falcons at Assateague Island, Maryland/Virginia, 1970–1984. In *Peregrine Falcon populations: Their management and recovery,* edited by T. J. Cade, J. H. Enderson, C. G. Thelander, and C. M. White, pp. 485–95. Boise, Idaho: Peregrine Fund.

Ward, R. 1966. Regional variation in the song of the Carolina Chickadee. *Living Bird* 5:127–50.

Ward, R., and D. A. Ward. 1974. Songs in contiguous populations of Black-capped and Carolina chickadees in Pennsylvania. *Wilson Bulletin* 86:344–56.

Warren, B. H. 1890. *Report on the birds of Pennsylvania.* 2nd ed. Harrisburg, Pa.: State Board of Agriculture.

Watson, G. E. 1977. A second specimen of Red Phalarope from Delaware. *Delmarva Ornithologist* 12:49.

Wayne, W. J. 1965. Walk gingerly at Cape Henlopen. *Delmarva Ornithologist* 2:29.

Wayne, W. J. 1966. More nests on Cape Henlopen. *Delmarva Ornithologist* 3:50.

Wayne, W. J. 1967. A Canada Jay; Or how to spoil our fun. *Delmarva Ornithologist* 4:44.

Wayne, W. J. 1975. White-winged Black Tern in Delaware. *Delmarva Ornithologist* 10:4–5.

Wayne, W. J. 1983. The Delmarva Ornithological Society's first twenty years. *Delmarva Ornithologist* 16:3–6.

Wayne, W. J. 1989. Yellow-nosed Albatross off Cape Henlopen, Delaware, 1989. *Delmarva Ornithologist* 22:54–55.

Wayne, W. J., and Roberts, T. E., eds. 1973. The Passing Scene. *Delmarva Ornithologist* 8:14–17.

Weber, J. W. 1981. The *Larus* gulls of the Pacific Northwest's interior, with taxonomic comments on several forms. Pt 1. *Continental Birdlife* 2:1–10.

Weeks, H. P., Jr. 1978. Clutch size variation in the Eastern Phoebe in southern Indiana. *Auk* 95:656–66.

Weeks, H. P., Jr. 1979. Nesting ecology of the Eastern Phoebe in southern Indiana. *Wilson Bulletin* 91:441–54.

Weir, R. D. 1987. Barred Owl. In *Atlas of the breeding birds of Ontario,* edited by M. D. Cadman, P. F. J. Eagles, and F. M. Helleiner. Don Mills, Ontario: University of Waterloo Press.

Weller, M. W. 1958. Observations on the incubation behavior of the Common Nighthawk. *Auk* 75:48–59.

Weller, M. W. 1961. Breeding biology of the Least Bittern. *Wilson Bulletin* 73:11–35.

Weller, M. W. 1965. Bursa regression, gonad cycle, and molt of the Great-horned Owl. *Bird-Banding* 36:102–12.

West Chester Bird Club. 1979. *Annotated list of Chester County birds.* 3rd ed. Westtown, Pa.: West Chester Bird Club.

West, R. L. 1967. Mature tulip poplar forest (suburban woodlot). *Audubon Field Notes* 21:640.

West, R. L. [1970]. Nesting bird census, White Clay Creek (mixed mesophytic forest). In *Observations on the ecology of the White Clay Creek valley with particular reference to the effects of a proposed dam,* a report prepared for the New Castle County government. Ashland, Del.: Delaware Nature Education Center.

West, R. L. 1991. Trend analysis of Delaware spring bird counts. *Delmarva Ornithologist* 24:19–38.

West, R. L. 1993. Breeding bird census from a Prime Hook NWR marsh: Salt marsh. *Delmarva Ornithologist* 25:11–12.

West, R. L., and P. K. Klabunde. 1977. Bird censuses of the Churchman's Marsh area. *Delmarva Ornithologist* 12:56.

West, R. L., R. E. Jones, J. R. Longcore, and J. T. Linehan. 1966. Mature tulip poplar forest (suburban woodlot). *Audubon Field Notes* 20:645–46.

Westmoreland, D., L. B. Best, and D. E. Blockstein. 1986. Multiple brooding as a reproductive strategy: Time-conserving adaptations in Mourning Doves. *Auk* 103:196–203.

Westneat, D. F. 1988. The relationships among polygyny, male parental care, and female breeding success in the Indigo Bunting. *Auk* 105:372–73.

Weston, F. M., and E. A. Williams. 1965. Recent records of the Eskimo Curlew. *Auk* 82:493–96.

Whitcomb, R. F., C. S. Robbins, J. F. Lynch, B. L. Whitcomb, M. K. Klimkiewicz, and D. Bystrak. 1981. Effects of forest fragmentation on avifauna of the eastern deciduous forest. In *Forest island dynamics in man-dominated landscapes,* edited by R. L. Burgess and D. M. Sharpe, pp. 125–205. New York: Springer-Verlag.

White, C. M. 1988. Peregrine. In *Handbook of North American birds.* Vol. 5, *Diurnal raptors,* edited by R. S. Palmer. New Haven, Conn.: Yale University Press.

White, H. C. 1953. *The Eastern Belted Kingfisher in the Maritime Provinces.* Fisheries Research Board of Canada Bulletin, no. 97.

White, J. F. 1987. Amphibians of Delaware. *Transactions of the Delaware Academy of Science* 16:17–22.

Whiting, R. M., Jr., and T. G. Boggus. 1982. Breeding biology of American Woodcock in eastern Texas. In *Woodcock ecology and management,* edited by T. G. Dwyer and G. L. Storm. 7th Woodcock Symposium, 1980, Pennsylvania State University. U.S. Fish and Wildlife Service Wildlife Research Report, no. 14. Washington, D.C.

Whitman, W. R., and R. V. Cole. 1986. Ecological conditions and implications for waterfowl management in selected coastal impoundments of Delaware. In *Waterfowl and Wetlands Symposium: Proceedings of a symposium on waterfowl and wetlands management in the coastal zone of the Atlantic Flyway,* edited by W. R. Whitman and W. H. Meredith, pp. 99–119. Dover, Del.: Delaware Coastal Management Program, DNREC.

Whittendale T. W., Jr. 1975. Evaluation of introduced Ruffed Grouse in Delaware. Federal Aid in Wildlife Restoration, W-16-R-24, III-1. Dover, Del.: DNREC.

Whittendale, T. W., Jr. 1976. Pheasants in green. *Delaware Conservationist* 20 (4):4–6.

Whittendale, T. W., Jr. 1983, 1984. *Reproduction and survival of the Osprey in Delaware's lower bays.* Federal Aid in Wildlife Restoration, W-16-R, VIII-1. Dover, Del.: DNREC.

Wiedenfeld, D. A., L. R. Messick, and F. C. James. 1992. Population trends in 65 species of North American birds: 1966–1990. Final report to National Fish and Wildlife Foundation, U.S. Fish and Wildlife Service, and U.S. Forest Service. Contract no. 91-017. Coastal Plains Institute, Tallahassee, Fla.

Wiemeyer, S. N. 1977. Unpublished letters to R. R. Perkutchin, manager, Bombay Hook NWR, June 10 and August 10. Copy in Delaware Museum of Natural History, Greenville, Del.

Wiese, J. H. 1976. *Study of reproductive biology of herons, egrets, and ibis nesting on Pea Patch Island, Delaware.* Interpretive report for the period March through September 1975 for Delmarva Power and Light Company. Manomet Bird Observatory, Manomet, Mass.

Wiese, J. H. 1977. *Study of reproductive biology of herons, egrets, and ibis nesting on Pea Patch Island, Delaware.* Interpretive report for the period March through September 1976 for Delmarva Power and Light Company. Manomet Bird Observatory, Manomet, Mass.

Wiese, J. H. 1978. *Study of reproductive biology of herons, egrets, and ibis nesting on Pea Patch Island, Delaware.* Interpretive report for the period March through September 1977 for Delmarva Power and Light Company. Manomet Bird Observatory, Manomet, Mass.

Wiese, J. H. 1979. *Study of reproductive biology of herons, egrets, and ibis nesting on Pea Patch Island, Delaware.* Final interpretive report for Delmarva Power and Light Company. Manomet Bird Observatory, Manomet, Mass.

Wilcove, D. S. 1988. Changes in the avifauna of the Great Smoky Mountains, 1947–1983. *Wilson Bulletin* 100:256–71.

Wilcox, Le Roy. 1959. A twenty-year banding study of the Piping Plover. *Auk* 76:129–52.

Wilds, C. P. 1972. Western Grebe at Cape Henlopen. *Atlantic Naturalist* 27:130.

Wilds, C. P. [1990]. Shorebirds at Chincoteague: Patterns of migration on the Virginia coast. Draft typescript mailed March 1990, copy in Delaware Museum of Natural History, Greenville, Del.

Wilds, C. P. 1991. The status and identification of Western Sandpipers in Virginia in spring migration. *Raven* 62:3–6.

Wilds, C. P., and M. Newlon. 1983. The identification of dowitchers. *Birding* 15:151–66.

Wiley, J. P., Jr. 1992. Phenomena, comments, and notes. *Smithsonian* 23 (2):24.

Williams, L. E., Jr., D. H. Austin, T. E. Peoples, and R. W. Phillips. 1971. Laying data and nesting behavior of Wild Turkeys. *Proceedings of the 25th Annual Conference of the Southeastern Association of Game and Fish Commissioners* 25:90–106.

Willis, N. M. 1988. *An analysis of selected Delaware bottomland forests.* U.S. Forest Service, Northeastern Area State and Private Forestry, and Delaware Department of Agriculture, Forestry Section. Dover, Del.

Wilson, A. 1808–14. *American ornithology, or the natural history of the birds of the United States.* 9 vols. Philadelphia, Pa.: Bradford and Inskeep.

Wilson, A., and C. L. Bonaparte. [1859–60]. *American ornithology.* Willis P. Hazard Edition. Philadelphia, Pa.: Porter and Coates.

Wilson, E. M. 1986. Sage Thrasher—First record for Delaware. *Delmarva Ornithologist* 19:6–9.

Wilson, G. 1950. Bird changes in Mammoth Cave National Park 1938–1949. *Kentucky Warbler* 26 (2):17–24.

Winters, C. L. 1995. Northern Saw-whet Owl sightings in New Castle County. *Delmarva Ornithologist* 27:3–5.

Woodliffe, P. A. 1987. Red-bellied Woodpecker. In *Atlas of the breeding birds of Ontario,* edited by M. D. Cadman, P. F. J. Eagles, and F. M. Helleiner. Don Mills, Ontario: University of Waterloo Press.

Woods, R. S. 1968. House Finch. In *Life histories of North American cardinals, grosbeaks, buntings, towhees, finches, sparrows, and allies,* edited by O. L. Austin, Jr. Pt. 1, pp. 290–314. U.S. National Museum Bulletin, no. 237. Washington, D.C.

Woolfenden, G. E. 1956. *Comparative breeding behavior of Ammospiza caudacuta and A. maritima,* pp. 45–75. University of Kansas Publications, Museum of Natural History, no. 10. Larence, Kans.

Woolfenden, G. E. 1968. Northern Seaside Sparrow. In *Life histories of North American cardinals, grosbeaks, buntings, towhees, finches, sparrows, and allies,* edited by O. L. Austin, Jr. Pt. 2, pp. 819–31. U.S. National Museum Bulletin, no. 237. Washington, D.C.

Woolfenden, G. E., and S. A. Rohwer. 1969. *Breeding birds in a Florida suburb,* pp. 1–83. Florida State Museum Biological Sciences Bulletin, vol. 13, no. 1.

Wright, A. H. 1911. Other early records of Passenger Pigeon: Pennsylvania, New Jersey, and Delaware. *Auk* 28:427–49.

Wright, G. A., and D. W. Speake. 1975. Compatibility of the eastern Wild Turkey with recreational activities at Land between the Lakes, Kentucky. *Proceedings of the 29th Annual Conference of the Southeastern Association of Game and Fish Commissioners* 29:578–84.

Yunick, R. P. 1984. An assessment of the irruptive status of the Boreal Chickadee in New York State. *Journal of Field Ornithology* 55:31–37.

Zerbe, J. W. 1986. A Fork-tailed Flycatcher in Delaware. *Delmarva Ornithologist* 19:39.

Zimmerman, J. L. 1963. A nesting study of the Catbird in southern Michigan. *Jack-Pine Warbler* 41:142–60.

Zimmerman, J. L. 1977. Virginia Rail. In *Management of migratory shore and upland game birds in North America,* edited by G. C. Sanderson. Washington, D.C.: International Association of Fish and Wildlife Agencies. Reprint, Lincoln: University of Nebraska Press, 1980, pp. 46–56.

Sources of Illustrations

Courtesy of Margaretta Bredin Brokaw and reprinted with permission from the Academy of Natural Sciences, Philadelphia, pages 72, 108, 110, 159b, 303, 398, 412.

Courtesy of Joan Stark, pages 236–38.

Rob Stine, pages 46, 50b, 54, 55a, 55b, 56, 60, 88–89, 91, 93, 151a, 191, 200, 202–04, 212, 218, 223b, 240, 242b, 246a, 247b, 249a, 254b, 255a, 258b, 259a, 265b, 269, 272b, 275, 280, 315, 340, 346, 357a, 357b, 379, 386, 410, 422, 429, 435a, 435b, 436a, 445, 456, 458, 465, 469, 470b, 486, 505, 512, 525, 530b, 541.

Elizabeth Traynor, pages 76, 80, 82, 166, 178, 196, 245, 261, 276, 300, 306, 355b, 390, 395, 433, 441, 444, 453, 467, 483, 489, 506, 548b, 553b.

Nancy C. Willis, pages 97, 169, 184, 187, 256, 281b, 286, 288, 294, 298, 302, 313, 317, 322, 325, 328, 332b, 335, 337, 342, 351, 353, 355a, 360, 374–75, 377–78, 400–01, 405, 407, 415, 419, 425, 436b, 460, 462, 463, 466, 474, 477, 479, 484, 492a, 501, 510–11, 513–14, 517, 519, 521a, 528, 530a, 531, 532, 548a, 549, 552a, 552b, 553a, 558.

Reprinted with permission from the State Library of Massachusetts. E. H. Forbush. *Birds of Massachusetts and Other New England States, Vol. 1.* Boston: Massachusetts Department of Agriculture, 1925. Artists E. H. Forbush and others. Pages 213, 262, 272a, 273, 278.

Reprinted with permission from the Wildlife Management Institute. F. H. Kortwright. *The Ducks, Geese, and Swans of North America.* Washington, D.C.: The American Wildlife Institute, 1943. Artist, T. M. Shortt. Pages 95–6, 102a, 113, 116a, 118, 121, 124, 128, 139, 141–42, 143a, 144–47, 152–53, 155.

Reprinted with permission from Oxford University Press. O. S. Pettingill Jr. *A Guide to Bird Finding East of the Mississippi.* New York: Oxford University Press, 1951. Artist G. M. Sutton. Pages 75, 102b, 107, 143b, 151b, 171, 182, 190, 207, 209, 211, 217, 281a, 285, 307, 310, 320, 332a, 367, 387, 392, 402, 409, 443a, 446, 452a, 452b, 470b, 475a, 475b, 491, 492b, 497, 508–09, 516, 521b, 522, 535.

Reprinted with permission from Oxford University Press. O. S. Pettingill Jr. *A Guide to Bird Finding West of the Mississippi.* New York : Oxford University Press, 1953. Artist G.M. Sutton. Pages 51, 126, 179, 227, 330.

Reprinted with permission from Oxford University Press. O. S. Pettingill Jr. *A Guide to Bird Finding East of the Mississippi,* 2nd Ed. New York: Oxford University Press, 1977. N.Y. Artist G.M. Sutton. Pages 61–2, 229, 250.

Reprinted with permission from Oxford University Press. O. S. Pettingill Jr. *A Guide to Bird Finding West of the Mississippi,* 2nd Ed. New York: Oxford University Press, 1981. Artist G. M. Sutton. Pages 64, 159a, 258a, 493

Reprinted with permission from Delaware Valley Ornithological Club. E. L. Poole. *Pennsylvania Birds.* Narbeth, Pa: Livingston Publishing Co. 1964. Artist E.L. Poole. Pages, 59, 156, 158, 174, 183, 189, 220, 243, 305, 319, 434, 440, 556.

Reprinted with permission from Delaware Valley Ornithological Club and Dover Publications. W. Stone. 1937. *Bird Studies at Old Cape May,* Vols. 1 and 2. Philadelphia, Pa.: Delaware Valley Ornithological Club. Artists R. E. Bishop, H. Brown, E. L. Poole, C. Roland, and J. F. Street. Pages 45, 47, 49, 50a, 57–8, 63, 65, 67, 78, 83, 85, 87, 111, 116b, 130, 136, 138, 148, 149, 150, 168, 172, 176, 180, 193–94, 198, 206, 210, 215, 221–22, 223a, 226, 230, 231a, 231b, 239, 241, 242a, 244, 246b, 247a, 248, 249b, 253a, 253b, 254a, 255b, 259b, 265a, 266a, 266b, 268, 270–71, 283, 284a, 284b, 292, 296, 308, 311, 323, 344, 351a, 351b, 362, 365, 368, 370, 372, 383, 385, 389, 393, 396, 411, 417, 427, 438, 442, 443b, 447, 449, 451, 454, 473, 481, 487, 495, 499, 502, 537, 539, 554.

Cover and title page art by Nancy C. Willis.

Addendum

These reports, among those received during the final preparation of this volume, were selected from *Delmarva Ornithologist,* volume 30, 1998, the 1997 and 1998 reports of the Delaware Records Committee, and recent additions to the collections of the Delaware Museum of Natural History. The authors did not review these reports.

Wood Stork (*Mycteria americana*); 19 August 1997; Bombay Hook NWR; K.C. Liehr, photograph A. P. Ednie, many others; second state report.

Northern Lapwing (*Vanellus vanellus*); 6 and 7 July 1996; Bombay Hook NWR; photograph B. Peterjohn, M. Gustafson; second state report, first photographic documentation.

California Gull (*Larus californicus*); 24 June 1995; Indian River Inlet; photograph M. Gustafson, B. Peterjohn; first state record.

Ross's Gull (*Rhodostethia rosea*); 16–30 Jan 1997; Indian River Inlet; B. Peterjohn, photograph J. White and others, many observers; first state record.

Bridled Tern (*Sterna anaethtus*); 6 Sep 1997; 43 mi E Cape Henlopen; photographs J. Kinney, M. Gustafson; second state documentation.

Atlantic Puffin (*Fratercula arctica*); 16 Feb 1997; east of Cape Henlopen, 38° 28'N 73° 47'E; F. Rohrbacher; photographs, C. Campbell, F. Rohrbacher; first state documentation.

Chuck-will's-widow (*Caprimulgus carolinensis*); 16 Oct 1998; Rehoboth Beach; TSBR 98–126; extends documented late date by 81 days.

Rufous Hummingbird (*Selasphorus rufus*); 18 Dec 1996; Wilmington; photograph of hand-held bird, C. Campbell; second state documentation.

Allen's Hummingbird (*Selasphorus sasin*); 18 Nov 1997–12 Feb 1998; Wilmington; photograph 14 Jan of hand-held bird, M. Gustafson; first state record.

Orange-crowned Warbler (*Vermivora celata*); 4 Feb–17 Mar 1997; Rehoboth Beach; photographs Liz Dumont, B. Lantz; first state documentation of this perhaps regular migrant.

Index

References to the species accounts appear in boldface

Accipiter cooperii 10, 12, 22, 35, 162, 165, 168, **169–70**, 175, 176
  gentilis 162, **171**, 543, 545–47
  striatus 162–65, **168–69**, 170, 173, 546
Actitis macularia 7, 12, 19, 20, 33, 34, 35, **226–27**
Aechmophorus clarkii 51
  occidentalis 51
Aegolius acadicus **307–08**
Agelaius phoeniceus 6, 22, 23, 32, 200, 364, 523, 524, **525–27**
Aix sponsa 6, 7, 35, **111–13**, 135
Aluada arvensis 367
Albatross, Black-browed 54
  Yellow-nosed 54
Alca torda 52, **284–85**
Alle alle 52, **283**
Ammodramus caudacutus 5, 13, 16, 496, **497–98**, 500
  henslowii 5, 12, 16, 19, 35, **495–96**
  leconteii 197, **496**
  maritima 5, 497, 498, **499–501**
  nelsoni **496**, 498
  savannarum 11, 13, 14, **493–95**
Anas acuta 5, 7, 13, 35, **128–29**
  americana 12, 13, 22, 34, 35, **116–18**
  bahamensis 127
  clypeata 7, 12, 13, 34, 35, **126–27**
  crecca 7, 12, 22, 34, **130–32**
  cyanoptera **126**, 200
  discors 5, 7, 13, 35, **124–26**, 135, 200
  penelope **116**
  platyrhynchos 7, 13, 35, 120, **121–23**, 135
  querquedula **130**
  rubripes 5, 6, 8, 12, 21, **118–20**, 121, 123, 135, 186
  strepera 5, 7, 12, 13, 35, **113–15**, 135
Anhinga **64**
Anhinga anhinga **64**
Anser albifrons **96**
  brachyrhynchus **95**
  erythropus **96**
Anthus rubescens 11, **427–28**
  pratensis **428**
  spragueii **428**
Aquila chrysaetos 162, **179**
Archilochus colubris 6, 10, 11, 22, 32, **315–16**
Ardea alba 5, 13, 35, 69–70, 73, **75–76**, 77, 78
  herodias 5, 13, 21, 69–70, **72–74**, 78, 208, 301
Arenaria interpres 6, 23, 134, 233, 234, **236**
Asio flammeus 5, 12, 16, 19, 33, 34, **306–07**
  otus 10, 12, 35, **305**
Avocet, American 7, 35, 134, **220**
Aythya affinis 7, 8, 141, **142**
  americana 8, **138–39**
  collaris 7, 13, 18, **139–40**
  marila 8, 13, 18, **141**, 142
  valisineria 7, 8, 13, 18, **136–37**

Baeolophus bicolor 10, 32, **383–84**, 431
Bartramia longicauda 11, 12, 34, 35, **227–28**
Bittern, American 5, 12, 16, 33, **65–66**, 67, 135
  Least 5, 12, **67–68**, 135
Blackbird, Brewer's 11, **531–32**
  Red-winged 6, 22, 23, 32, 200, 364, 523, 524, **525–27**

  Rusty 10, **530–31**
  Yellow-headed 11, **530**
Bluebird, Eastern 10, 11, 14, 23, 372, **405–07**, 558
Bobolink **522**
Bobwhite, Northern 11, 13, 14, 15, 21, 22, 23, 32, 189, **191–93**
Bombycilla cedrorum 9, 10, 30, **429–30**
  garrulus **428**
Bonasa umbellus 12, 22, 23, 35, **189**
Botaurus lentiginosus 5, 12, 16, 33, **65–66**, 67, 135
Brant 8, 21, **107**
Branta bernicla 8, 21, **107**
  canadensis 7, 11, 13, 15, 21, 35, 97, 100, **102–04**, 105–06, 135
  leucopsis **108**
Bubo virginianus 10, 23, 32, 70, 77, 173, 214, **300–02**, 303, 304
Bubulcus ibis 5, 9, 11, 13, 35, 69–70, **82–83**
Bucephala albeola 7, **149**
  clangula 7, 8, 13, **150**, 151
  islandica **151**
Bufflehead 7, **149**
Bunting, Indigo 11, 14, 32, **519–20**
  Lark **492**
  Painted **521**
  Snow 8, 11, 23, **513**
Buteo jamaicensis 10, 11, 13, 35, 162–65, 173, 174, **176–78**, 181, 301
  lagopus 5, 162, **178–79**, 545–46
  lineatus 6, 10, 13, 16, 162–65, **172–74**, 175
  platypterus 6, 10, 12, 35, 162–64, **174–75**
Butorides virescens 13, **83–84**

Calamospiza melanocorys **492**
Calcarius lapponicus 11, **512–13**
Calidris acuminata **244**
  alba 6, 8, 22, 134, 233, 234, **238**
  alpina 6, 8, 134, 233, **245**
  bairdii **242–43**
  canutus 6, 134, 233, 234, **237**
  ferruginea **246**
  fuscicollis 6, **242**
  himantopus **246–47**
  maritima 8, **244**
  mauri 6, 239, **240**
  melanotos 6, **243**
  minuta **241**
  minutilla **241**
  pusilla 6, 233, **239**, 240
  ruficollis **240**
Calonectris diomedea 22, 25, 52, **55**
Camptorhynchus labradorius **144–45**
Canvasback 7, 8, 13, 18, **136–37**
Caprimulgus carolinensis 10, 13, 35, **310–11**, 312, [Addendum]
  vociferus 6, 10, 13, 15, 23, 310, **311–12**
Cardinal, Northern 9, 10, 23, 32, 36, 41, 431, **514–15**
Cardinalis cardinalis 9, 10, 23, 32, 36, 41, 431, **514–15**
Carduelis flammea 543–46, **553**
  hornemanni **553**
  pinus 10, 11, 22, 40, 543–47, **553–54**
  tristis 9, 10, 13, 22, 32, 338, **554–56**

Carpodacus mexicanus 11, 36, **549–51**
  purpureus 10, 11, 543–46, **548–49**, 550
Casmerodious
  see *Ardea*
Catbird, Gray 9, 10, 32, 295, **417–19**, 431
Catharacta maccormicki **254–55**
  skua **254–55**
Cathartes aura 11, 22, 28, 92, **93–94**, 162–65
Catharus bicknelli **410**
  fuscescens 6, 10, 13, 36, **407–08**
  guttatus 6, **411–12**
  minimus 6, **409**, 410
  ustulatus 6, **410–11**
Catoptrophorus semipalmatus 5, 6, 13, 22, 32, 35, 135, **223–25**, 257
Certhia americana 10, 12, 34, 36, **389–90**
Ceryle alcyon 7, 135, **317–18**
Chaetura pelagica 11, 13, 32, 35, **313–14**
Charadrius melodus 8, 12, 16, 17, 19, 35, 41, 186, **213–14**, 274, 278
  semipalmatus 6, **212**, 214
  vociferus 10, 11 32, 35, 135, **215–16**, 227, 228, 494, 528
  wilsonia 35, **211**
Chat, Yellow-breasted 9, 23, 474, **475–77**
Chen caerulescens 5, 7, 8, 11, 15, 21, 23, **97–98**, 99–101, 102, 135, 200
  rossii 101, **102**, 200
Chickadee, Black-capped 11, 380, **381–82**, 543–47
  Boreal, **382**, 544, 546
  Carolina 10, 32, **379–81**, 382, 384, 544
Chicken
  see Prairie-Chicken
Chlidonias hybridus **280**
  leucopterus **280**
  niger 8, 35, **281**
Chondestes grammacus **491**
Chordeiles minor 8, 13, 16, 17, 162, **308–10**
Chuck-will's-widow 10, 13, 35, **310–11**, 312, [Addendum]
Circus cyaneus 3, 5, 12, 16, 162–65, **166–67**
Cistothorus palustris 6, 397, **398–400**
  platensis 5, 12, 16, 36, 135, **396–97**
Clangula hyemalis 8, **148**
Coccothraustes vespertinus 11, 543–47, **556–57**
Coccyzus americanus 6, 10, 13, 23, 292, 293, **294–95**
  erythropthalmus 9, **292–93**, 294, 295
Colaptes auratus 10, 13, 32, 324, **328–30**
Colinus virginianus 11, 13, 14, 15, 21, 22, 23, 32, 189, **191–93**
Collared-Dove, African 288
Columba livia 10, 32, 35, **286–87**
Columbina passerina **291**
Contopus cooperi **332**
  virens 10, 11, 32, **332–34**
Conuropsis carolinensis 22, 35, **291**
Coot, American 5, 13, 33, **206–07**
Coragyps atratus 11, 13, 35, **91–92**, 94, 162
Cormorant, Double-crested 8, 12, 13, 18, 34, 35, **63–64**
  Great 62
Corvus brachyrhynchos 10, 22, 23, 25, 32, 70, 305, **362–64**, 365, 431

corax 22, **367**
  ossifragus 5, 10, 14, 25, 70, 77, 214, 363, **365–66**
Coturnicops noveboracensis **193**
Cowbird, Brown-headed 10, 15, 23, 28, 32, 333,
  342, 352, 354, 358, 359, 364, 431, 438–39, 448,
  455, 463, 468, 474, 482, 516, 518, 523, 524, 527,
  537–39
Crane, Sandhill 21, 22, 99, **207–08**
  Whooping **208**
Creeper, Brown 10, 12, 34, 36, **389–90**
Crossbill, Red 10, 543–47, **552**
  White-winged 544, 546, 547, **552**
Crow, American 10, 22, 23, 25, 32, 70, 305, **362–64**,
  365, 431
  Fish 5, 10, 14, 25, 70, 77, 214, 363, **365–66**
Cuckoo, Black-billed 9, **292–93**, 294, 295
  Yellow-billed 6, 10, 13, 23, 292, 293, **294–95**
Curlew, Eskimo **229**
  Long-billed 22, **230**
Cyanocitta cristata 10, 32, **360–62**, 431
Cygnus buccinator **109**
  columbianus 7, 11, **110–11**
  olor 7, 12, 35, **108–09**

Dendrocygna bicolor **95**
Dendroica caerulescens 10, **443**
  castanea 10, **452**
  cerulea 6, 12, 15, 36, 42, **453–54**
  coronata 6, 9, 200, 439, **443–44**, 447
  discolor 10, 14, **449–51**, 477, 488
  dominica 6, 12, **446–47**
  fusca 10, 41, **445**
  magnolia **441–42**
  nigrescens **444**
  occidentalis **445**
  palmarum 11, **451**
  pensylvanica 12, 36, **440–41**
  petechia 6, 14, 134, 338, **438–39**
  pinus 10, **447–49**, 461
  striata 10, **452**
  tigrina 10, **442**
  virens 10, **444–45**
Dickcissel 19, 35, **521–22**
Diomedea
  see *Thalassarche*
Dolichonyx oryzivorus **522**
Dove, Mourning 10, 15, 22, 32, 35, **288–90**, 538
  Rock 10, 32, 35, **286–87**
  see Ground-Dove
  see Turtle-Dove
Dovekie 52, **283**
Dowitcher, Long-billed 248, **249**
  Short-billed 6, 233, **248**, 249
Dryocopus pileatus 10, 13, 36, **330–31**, 431
Duck, American Black 5, 6, 8, 12, 21, **118–20**, 121,
  123, 135, 186
  Harlequin **144**
  Labrador **144–145**
  Ring-necked 7, 13, 18, **139–40**
  Ruddy 8, 12, 13, 18, 34, 35, **155–56**
  Wood 6, 7, 35, **111–13**, 135
  see Whistling-Duck
Dumetella carolinensis 9, 10, 32, 295, **417–19**, 431
Dunlin 6, 8, 134, 233, **245**

Eagle, Bald 12, 17, 18, 22, 35, 41, **159–61**, 162, 173,
  185, 186
  Golden 162, **179**
Ectopistes migratorius 22, 23, 228, **290–91**
Egret, Cattle 5, 9, 11, 13, 35, 69–70, **82–83**, [Adden-
  dum]
  Great 5, 13, 35, 69–70, 73, **75–76**, 77, 78
  Reddish **81**
  Snowy 5, 9, 13, 35, 69–70, **76–77**

Egretta caerulea 5, 9, 69–70, **78–79**, 85
  rufescens **81**
  thula 5, 9, 13, 35, 69–70, **76–77**
  tricolor 5, 12, 35, 69–70, **80–81**
Eider, Common 8, **143–44**
  King 8, **143**, 144
Elanoides forficatus **158**
Empidonax alnorum 337, 338, 339
  flaviventris **334**
  hammondii **341**
  minimus 10, 12, 35, **340–41**
  traillii 6, 36, 335, **337–39**
  virescens 6, 13, 334, **335–36**, 337, 431
  wrightii **341**
Eremophila alpestris 11, 13, 23, 36, 228, **368–70**
Eudocimus albus **88**
Euphagus carolinus 10, **530–31**
  cyanocephalus 11, **531–32**

Falco columbarius 162, 164–65, **182**
  peregrinus 12, 33, 35, 162, 164, **183–84**, 185, 186
  rusticolus **184**
  sparverius 10, 11, 13, 14, 18, 162–65, **180–81**
Falcon, Peregrine 12, 33, 35, 162, 164, **183–84**, 185,
  186
Fieldfare **414**
Finch, House 11, 36, **549–51**
  Purple 10, 11, 543–46, **548–49**, 550
Flicker, Northern 10, 13, 32, 324, **328–30**
Flycatcher, Acadian 6, 13, 334, **335–36**, 337, 431
  Alder **337**, 338, 339
  Ash-throated 346
  Fork-tailed **349**
  Gray **341**
  Great Crested 10, 11, 32, **344–46**, 347
  Hammond's **341**
  Least 10, 12, 35, **340–41**
  Olive-sided **332**
  Scissor-tailed **348**
  Traill's 338, 339
  Vermilion **344**
  Willow 6, 36, 335, **337–39**
  Yellow-bellied **334**
Fratercula arctica 52, **285**, [Addendum]
Fregata magnificens **64**
Frigatebird, Magnificent **64**
Fulica americana 5, 13, 33, **206–07**
Fulmar, Northern 52, **54**
Fulmarus glacialis 52, **54**

Gadwall 5, 7, 12, 13, 35, **113–15**, 135
Gallinago gallinago 5, 11, **249–50**, 257
Gallinula chloropus 21, 22, 135, **204–05**
Gallinule, Purple 12, 35, **203**
Gannet, Northern 23, 53, **60**, 277
Garganey **130**
Gavia immer 7, 8, 45, **46**
  stellata 8, **45**, 46
Geothlypis trichas 6, 32, 134, **470–72**
Gnatcatcher, Blue-gray 6, 10, 14, **402–04**
Godwit, Black-tailed **230**
  Hudsonian 6, **231**, 234
  Marbled 6, **231–32**
Golden-Plover, American 11, **210–11**, 234
  European **210**
  Pacific 210
Goldeneye, Barrow's **151**
  Common 7, 8, 13, 18, **150**, 151
Goldfinch, American 9, 10, 13, 22, 32, 338,
  554–56
Goose, Barnacle **108**
  Canada 7, 11, 13, 15, 21, 35, 97, 100, **102–04**,
  105–06, 135
  Greater White-fronted **96**

Lesser White-fronted **96**
Pink-footed **95**
Ross' 101, **102**, 200
Snow 5, 7, 8, 11, 15, 21, 23, **97–98**, 99–101, 102,
  135, 200
Goshawk, Northern 162, **171**, 543, 545–47
Grackle, Boat-tailed 5, 13, 36, **535–36**
  Common 11, 22, 23, 32, 214, 364, 415, 431, 523,
  524, 527, **532–34**
Grebe, Clark's **51**
  Eared **50–51**
  Horned 8, **49**
  Pied-billed 7, 12, 16, **47–48**, 135
  Red-necked **50**
  Western **51**
Grosbeak, Black-headed **517**
  Blue 11, 14, 32, 36, **517–18**
  Evening 11, 543–47, **556–57**
  Pine 544, 546, 547, **548**
  Rose-breasted 10, 12, 34, 36, **516**, 517
Ground-Dove, Common **291**
Grouse, Ruffed 12, 22, 23, 35, **189**
Grus americana **208**
Grus canadensis 21, 22, 99, **207–208**
Guiraca caerulea 11, 14, 32, 36, **517–18**
Gull, Black-headed **259**
  Bonaparte's 8, 258, **259–60**
  California [Addendum]
  Common 260
  Franklin's **258**
  Glaucous **266**
  Great Black-backed 8, 12, 13, 34, 35, **266–67**
  Herring 5, 7, 8, 12, 13, 18, 35, **262–64**, 267
  Iceland 264, **265**
  Ivory **268**
  Laughing 5, 8, 11, 13, 35, 233, **256–57**, 258, 262,
  275
  Lesser Black-backed **265**
  Little **258**
  Mew **260**
  Ring-billed 7, 8, 18, 260, **261–62**, 267
  Ross' [Addendum]
  Sabine's **268**
  Thayer's **264**
Gyrfalcon **184**

Haematopus palliatus 8, 13, 35, **217–18**
Haliaeetus leucocephalus 12, 17, 18, 22, 35, 41,
  159–61, 162, 173, 185, 186
Harrier, Northern 3, 5, 12, 16, 162–65, **166–67**
Hawk, Broad-winged 6, 10, 12, 35, 162–64,
  174–75
  Cooper's 10, 12, 22, 35, 162, 165, 168, **169–70**,
  175, 176
  Red-shouldered 6, 10, 13, 16, 162–65, **172–74**,
  175
  Red-tailed 10, 11, 13, 35, 162–65, 173, 174,
  176–78, 181, 301
  Rough-legged 5, 162, **178–79**, 545–46
  Sharp-shinned 162–65, **168–69**, 170, 173, 546
Helmitheros vermivorus 10, **460–62**
Hen, Heath
  see Prairie-Chicken
Heron, Great Blue 5, 13, 21, 69–70, **72–74**, 78, 208,
  301
  Green 13, **83–84**
  Little Blue 5, 9, 69–70, **78–79**, 85
  Tricolored 5, 12, 35, 69–70, **80–81**
  see Night-Heron
Himantopus mexicanus 7, 13, 35, 135, **218–19**
Hirundo rustica 11, 32, 36, 342, **378–79**
  see *Petrochelidon*
Histrionicus histrionicus **144**
Hummingbird, Allen's 317, [Addendum]

Ruby-throated 6, 10, 11, 22, 32, **315–16**
Rufous **317**
Hylocichla mustelina 10, 11, 14, 32, **412–14**, 538

Ibis, Glossy 5, 9, 13, 35, 69–70, 88, **89–90**, 134, 135
  White **88**
  White-faced **90**
Icteria virens 9, 23, 474, **475–77**
Icterus bullockii 542
  galbula 10, 11, **541–42**
  spurius 11, 14, 32, **539–41**, 542
Ictinia mississippiensis 159
Ixobrychus exilis 5, 12, **67–68**, 135
Ixoreus naevius 417

Jaeger, Long-tailed 255
  Parasitic 52, **255**
  Pomarine 52, **255**
Jay, Blue 10, 32, **360–62**, 431
  Gray 359
Junco, Dark-eyed 9, 11, 41, **511–12**
Junco hyemalis 9, 11, 41, **511–12**

Kestrel, American 10, 11, 13, 14, 18, 162–65,
  180–81
Killdeer 10, 11 32, 35, 135, **215–16**, 227, 228, 494,
  528
Kingbird, Eastern 5, 11, 32, **346–48**
  Gray 348
  Western 346
Kingfisher, Belted 7, 135, **317–18**
Kinglet, Golden-crowned 35, **400–01**
  Ruby-crowned 10, **401–02**
Kite, Mississippi 159
  Swallow-tailed 158
Kittiwake, Black-legged 268
Knot, Red 6, 134, 233, 234, **237**

Lanius excubitor 351, 546
  ludovicianus 11, 12, 19, 23, 33, 34, 36, **349–350**
Lapwing, Northern **208**, [Addendum]
Lark, Horned 11, 13, 23, 36, 228, **368–70**
  Sky 367
Larus argentatus 5, 7, 8, 12, 13, 18, 35, **262–64**, 267
  atricilla 5, 8, 11, 13, 35, 233, **256–57**, 258, 262,
    275
  californicus [Addendum]
  canus 260
  delawarensis 7, 8, 18, 260, **261–62**, 267
  fuscus 265
  glaucoides 264, **265**
  hyperboreus 266
  marinus 8, 12, 13, 34, 35, **266–67**
  minutus 258
  philadelphia 8, 258, **259–60**
  pipixcan 258
  ridibundus 259
  thayeri 264
Laterallus jamaicensis 5, 13, 16, 33, **194–95**
Limnodromus griseus 6, 233, **248**, 249
  scolopaceus 248, **249**
Limnothlypis swainsonii 12, 19, 35, **462**
Limosa fedoa 6, **231–32**
  haemastica 6, **231**, 234
  limosa 230
Longspur, Lapland 11, **512–13**
Loon, Common 7, 8, 45, 46
  Red-throated 8, **45**, 46
Lophodytes cucullatus 7, 12, 35, **151–52**
Loxia curvirostra 10, 543–47, **552**
  leucoptera 544, 546, 547, **552**

Magpie, Black-billed 362
Mallard 7, 13, 35, 120, **121–23**, 135

Martin, Purple 11, 13, 36, **370–72**, 558
Meadowlark, Eastern 11, 13, 14, 23, 227, 488, 494,
  528–30
Melanerpes carolinus 10, 13, 32, 36, 40, 319, **320–22**,
  324, 325
  erythrocephalus 10, 15, 23, 35, **319–20**, 324
Melanitta fusca 8, 146
  nigra 8, 13, 18, 145, **147**
  perspicillata 8, 13, 18, **145**, 146
Meleagris gallopavo 11, 12, 13, 22, 34, 185, **190–91**
Melospiza georgiana 3, 5, 9, **506–08**
  lincolnii 505
  melodia 10, 32, 134, 497, **502–04**, 538
Merganser, Common 7, 13, 18, **152–53**
  Hooded 7, 12, 35, **151–52**
  Red-breasted 8, 13, 18, 34, 35, **153–54**
Mergus merganser 7, 13, 18, **152–53**
  serrator 8, 13, 18, 34, 35, **153–54**
Merlin 162, 164–65, **182**
Mimus polyglottos 10, 14, 22, 23, 32, 36, **419–22**, 461
Mniotilta varia 10, 13, 15, **454–56**
Mockingbird, Northern 10, 14, 22, 23, 32, 36,
  419–22, 461
Molothrus ater 10, 15, 23, 28, 32, 333, 342, 352, 354,
  358, 359, 364, 431, 438–39, 448, 455, 463, 468,
  474, 482, 516, 518, 523, 524, 527, **537–39**
Moorhen, Common 21, 22, 135, **204–05**
Morus bassanus 23, 53, **60**, 277
Murre, Common 52, **284**
  Thick-billed 52, 284, 285
Mycteria americana **90**, [Addendum]
Myiarchus crinitus 10, 11, 32, **344–46**, 347
  cinerascens 346
Myiopsitta monachus 291

Night-Heron, Black-crowned 18, 69–70, 78–79,
  85–86, 87
  Yellow-crowned 12, 35, 69–70, **87–88**
Nighthawk, Common 8, 13, 16, 17, 162, **308–10**
Numenius americanus 22, **230**
  borealis 229
  phaeopus 6, 22, **229–30**
Nuthatch, Brown-headed 3, 10, 13, 15, **387–88**
  Red-breasted 10, 35, **385**, 543, 544, 546
  White-breasted 10, **386–87**, 431
Nyctanassa violacea 12, 35, 69–70, **87–88**
Nyctea scandiaca **302–03**, 543, 546, 547
Nycticorax nycticorax 18, 69–70, 78–79, **85–86**, 87

Oceanites oceanicus 22, 25, 52, 55, **58**, 59
Oceanodroma castro 52–53, **59**
  leucorhoa 52, **59**
Oenanthe oenanthe **404**
Oldsquaw 8, **148**
Oporornis agilis 6, **469**, 470
  formosus 6, 10, **467–69**
  philadelphia 470
Oreoscoptes montanus 422
Oriole, Baltimore 10, 11, **541–42**
  Bullock's 542
  Orchard 11, 14, 32, **539–41**, 542
Osprey 5, 8, 13, 17, 18, 135, **156–58**, 162–65, 173,
  185, 301
Otus asio 10, 32, **298–300**, 303, 304, 306
Ovenbird 10, 413, 431, **463–64**, 467
Owl, Barn 10, 11, 13, **296–97**
  Barred 6, 13, 16, **303–04**
  Great Horned 10, 23, 32, 70, 77, 173, 214,
    300–02, 303, 304
  Long-eared 10, 12, 35, **305**
  Northern Saw-whet **307–08**
  Short-eared 5, 12, 16, 19, 33, 34, **306–07**
  Snowy **302–03**, 543, 546, 547
  see Screech-Owl

Oxyura jamaicensis 8, 12, 13, 18, 34, 35, **155–56**
Oystercatcher, American 8, 13, 35, **217–18**

Pagophila eburnea 268
Pandion haliaetus 5, 8, 13, 17, 18, 135, **156–58**,
  162–65, 173, 185, 301
Parakeet, Carolina 22, 35, **291**
  Monk **291**
Parula americana 6, 13, 33, 36, **436–37**
Parula, Northern 6, 13, 33, 36, **436–37**
Passer domesticus 11, 13, 32, 36, 371, 406, **558–59**
Passerculus sandwichensis 5, 8, 12, 35, 36, **492–93**
Passerella iliaca 9, 11, **501–02**
Passerina ciris 521
  cyanea 11, 14, 32, **519–20**
Pelagodroma marina 53, **58**
Pelecanus erythrorhynchos 61
  occidentalis 19, **61**
Pelican, American White **61**
  Brown 19, **61**
Perisoreus canadensis 359
Petrel, Black-capped 53
  see Storm-Petrel
Petrochelidon pyrrhonota 12, 34, 36, **377**
Pewee
  see Wood-Pewee
Phalacrocorax auritus 8, 12, 13, 18, 34, 35, **63–64**,
  carbo 62
Phalarope,
  Red 254
  Red-necked **253–54**
  Wilson's 6, **253**, 254
Phalaropus fulicaria 254
  lobatus **253–54**
  tricolor 6, **253**, 254
Phasianus colchicus 5, 11, 13, 35, **187–88**, 189
Pheasant, Green 188
  Ring-necked 5, 11, 13, 35, **187–88**, 189
Pheucticus ludovicianus 10, 12, 34, 36, **516**, 517
  melanocephalus 517
Philomachus pugnax 41, **247–48**
Phoebe, Eastern 10, 11, 13, 22, 36, 332, 334,
  342–44
Pica pica 362
Picoides arcticus 328
  borealis 35, **327**
  pubescens 10, 32, **323–25**, 326
  tridactylus **327–28**
  villosus 10, 323, **325–27**, 431
Pigeon, Passenger 22, 23, 228, **290–91**
Pinicola enucleator 544, 546, 547, **548**
Pintail, Northern 5, 7, 13, 35, **128–29**
  White-cheeked 127
Pipilo chlorurus 481
  erythrophthalmus 9, 11, 13 14, 15, 32, **481–83**
Pipit, American 11, **427–28**
  Meadow 428
  Sprague's 428
Piranga ludoviciana 480
  olivacea 10, 32, 41, 431, **479–80**, 538
  rubra 3, 10, 36, **477–79**, 480
Plectrophenax nivalis 8, 11, 23, **513**
Plegadis chihi 90
  falcinellus 5, 9, 13, 35, 69–70, 88, **89–90**, 134, 135
Plover, Black-bellied 6, 11, **209**
  Piping 8, 12, 16, 17, 19, 35, 41, 186, **213–214**, 274,
    278
  Semipalmated 6, **212**, 214
  Wilson's 35, **211**
  see Golden-Plover
Pluvialis apricaria 210
  dominica 11, **210–11**, 234
  fulva 210
  squatarola 6, 11, **209**

Podiceps auritus 8, **49**
   grisegena **50**
   nigricollis **50–51**
Podilymbus podiceps 7, 12, 16, **47–48**, 135
Poecile atricapillus 11, 380, **381–82**, 543–547
   carolinensis 10, 32, **379–81**, 382, 384, 544
   hudsonicus **382**, 544, 546
Polioptila caerulea 6, 10, 14, **402–04**
Pooecetes gramineus 3, 13, 14, **489–91**
Porphyrula martinica 12, 35, **203**
Porzana carolina 5, 12, 13, 34, 199, 201, **202**
Prairie-Chicken, Greater 22, 35, **189–90**
Progne subis 11, 13, 36, **370–72**, 558
Protonotaria citrea 6, 23, **458–60**
Pterodroma hasiatata 53
Puffin, Atlantic 52, **285**, [Addendum]
Puffinus gravis 22, 25, 52, **55**
   griseus 22, 25, 52, 55, **56**
   lherminieri 52, 53, **57**
   puffinus 52, **57**
Pyrocephalus rubinus 344

Quiscalus major 5, 13, 36, 135, **535–36**
   quiscula 11, 22, 23, 32, 214, 364, 415, 431, 523,
      524, 527, **532–34**

Rail, Black 5, 13, 16, 33, **194–95**, Black 5, 13, 16, 33,
      194-95, Black 5, 13, 16, 33, **194-95**
   Clapper 5, **196–98**, 199, 200
   King 5, 13, 16, 135, 196, **198–200**
   Virginia 5, 16, 135, **200–01**
   Yellow **193**
Rallus elegans 5, 13, 16, 135, 196, **198–200**
   limicola 5, 16, 135, **200–01**
   longirostris 5, **196–98**, 199, 200
Raven, Common 22, **367**
Razorbill **284–85**
Recurvirostra americana 7, 35, 134, **220**
Redhead 8, **138–39**
Redpoll, Common 543–46, **553**
   Hoary **553**
Redstart, American 6, 13, **456–58**
Regulus calendula 10, **401–02**
   satrapa 35, **400–01**
Rhodostethia rosea [Addendum]
Riparia riparia 28, 36, **375–76**
Rissa tridactyla **268**
Robin, American 10, 14, 23, 32, **415–16**, 421
Ruff 41, **247–48**41, **247–48**41, **247-48**
Rynchops niger 8, 12, 16, 17, 35, 135, **281–83**

Sanderling 6, 8, 22, 134, 233, 234, **238**
Sandpiper, Baird's **242–43**
   Buff-breasted **247**
   Curlew **246**
   Least **241**
   Pectoral 6, **243**
   Purple 8, **244**
   Semipalmated 6, 233, **239**, 240
   Sharp-tailed **244**
   Solitary 7, **223**
   Spotted 7, 12, 19, 20, 33, 34, 35, **226–27**
   Stilt **246–47**
   Upland 11, 12, 34, 35, **227–28**
   Western 6, 239, **240**
   White-rumped 6, **242**
Sapsucker, Yellow-bellied 10, **322–23**
Sayornis phoebe 10, 11, 13, 22, 36, 332, 334,
      342–44
Scaup, Greater 8, 13, 18, **141**, 142
   Lesser 7, 8, 141, **142**
Scolopax minor 6, 9, 13, 16, 23, 35, **250–52**
Scoter, Black 8, 13, 18, 145, **147**
   Surf 8, 13, 18, **145**, 146

White-winged 8, **146**
Screech-Owl, Eastern 10, 32, **298–300**, 303, 304,
      306
Seiurus aurocapillus 10, 413, 431, **463–64**, 467
   motacilla 6, **466–67**
   noveboracensis **465**
Selasphorus rufus 317
   sasin 317, [Addendum]
Setophaga ruticilla 6, 13, **456–58**
Shearwater, Audubon's 52, 53, **57**
   Cory's 22, 25, 52, **55**
   Greater 22, 25, 52, **55**
   Manx 52, **57**
   Sooty 22, 25, 52, 55, **56**
Shoveler, Northern 7, 12, 13, 34, 35, **126–27**
Shrike, Loggerhead 11, 12, 19, 23, 33, 34, 36,
      349–350
   Northern 349, 546
Sialia sialis 10, 11, 14, 23, 372, **405–07**, 558
Siskin, Pine 10, 11, 22, 40, 543–47, **553–54**
Sitta canadensis 10, 35, **385**, 543, 544, 546, 547
   carolinensis 10, **386–87**, 431
   pusilla 3, 10, 13, 15, **387–88**
Skimmer, Black 8, 12, 16, 17, 35, 135, **281–83**
Skua, Great **254–55**
   South Polar **254–55**
Skylark
   see Lark
Snipe, Common 5, 11, **249–50**, 257
Somateria mollissima 8, **143–44**
   spectabilis 8, **143**, 144
Sora 5, 12, 13, 34, 199, 201, **202**
Sparrow, American Tree 9, 11, **483–84**
   Chipping 9, 10, 32, 448, 461, **484–86**, 487, 488
   Clay-colored **486–87**
   Field 11, 13, 14, 32, **487–89**
   Fox 9, 11, **501–02**
   Grasshopper 11, 13, 14, **493–95**
   Harris's **509–10**
   Henslow's 5, 12, 16, 19, 35, **495–96**
   House 11, 13, 32, 36, 371, 406, **558–59**
   Ipswich 493
   Lark **491**
   Le Conte's 197, **496**
   Lincoln's **505**
   Nelson's Sharp-tailed 496, 498
   Saltmarsh Sharp-tailed 5, 13, 16, 496, **497–98**,
      500
   Savannah 5, 8, 12, 35, 36, **492–93**
   Seaside 5, 497, 498, **499–501**
   Song 10, 32, 134, 497, **502–04**, 538
   Swamp 3, 5, 9, **506–08**
   Vesper 3, 13, 14, **489–91**
   White-crowned 11, **510–11**
   White-throated 11, **508–09**
Sphyrapicus varius 10, **322–23**
Spiza americana 19, 35, **521–22**
Spizella arborea 9, 11, **483–84**
   pallida **486–87**
   passerina 9, 10, 32, 448, 461, **484–86**, 487, 488
   pusilla 11, 13, 14, 32, **487–89**
Starling, European 10, 15, 32, 36, 38, 319, 329, 345,
      346, 364, 371, 406, 415, **425–27**, 523, 527
Stelgidopteryx serripennis 7, 13, **374–75**
Stercorarius longicaudus 255
   parasiticus 52, **255**
   pomarinus 52, **255**
Sterna anaethetus 53, **279**, [Addendum]
   antillarum 8, 13, 16, 17, 23, 28, 35, 41, 213, 257,
      274, **278–79**, 282
   caspia 8, 19, **270**, 271
   dougallii **272–73**, 275
   forsteri 8, 13, 19, 33, 35, 273, 274, **276–77**
   fuscata 279

   hirundo 8, 13, 16, 17, 19, 35, 269, 272, **273–75**,
      276, 277
   maxima 8, 35, **271**, 272, 275
   nilotica 8, 12, 35, **269**
   paradisaea 275
   sandvicensis 8, **272**
Stilt, Black-necked 7, 13, 35, 135, **218–19**
Stint, Little **241**
   Red-necked **240**
Stork, Wood 90, [Addendum]
Storm-Petrel, Band-rumped 52–53, **59**
   Leach's 52, **59**
   White-faced 53, **58**
   Wilson's 22, 25, 52, 55, **58**, 59
Streptopelia 'risoria' **288**
   roseogrisea 288
Strix varia 6, 13, 16, **303–04**
Sturnella magna 11, 13, 14, 23, 227, 488, 494,
      528–30
Sturnus vulgaris 10, 15, 32, 36, 38, 319, 329, 345,
      346, 364, 371, 406, 415, **425–27**, 523, 527
Swallow, Bank 28, 36, **375–76**
   Barn 11, 32, 36, 342, **378–79**
   Cliff 12, 34, 36, **377**
   Northern Rough-winged 7, 13, **374–75**
   Tree 11, 36, **372–73**, 375
Swan, Mute 7, 12, 35, **108–09**
   Trumpeter **109**
   Tundra 7, 11, **110–11**
Swift, Chimney 11, 13, 32, 35, **313–14**

Tachycineta bicolor 11, 36, **372–73**, 375
Tanager, Scarlet 10, 32, 41, 431, **479–80**, 538
   Summer 3, 10, 36, **477–79**, 480
   Western **480**
Teal, Blue-winged 5, 7, 13, 35, **124–26**, 135, 200
   Cinnamon **126**, 200
   Green-winged 7, 12, 22, 34, **130–32**
Tern, Arctic 275
   Black 8, 35, **281**
   Bridled 53, **279**, [Addendum]
   Caspian 8, 19, **270**, 271
   Common 8, 13, 16, 17, 19, 35, 269, 272, **273–75**,
      276, 277
   Forster's 8, 13, 19, 33, 35, 273, 274, **276–77**
   Gull-billed 8, 12, 35, **269**
   Least 8, 13, 16, 17, 23, 28, 35, 41, 213, 257, 274,
      278–79, 282
   Roseate **272-73**, 275
   Royal 8, 35, **271**, 272, 275
   Sandwich 8, **272**
   Sooty **279**
   Whiskered **280**
   White-winged **280**
Thalassarche chlororhynchos 54
   melanophris 54
Thrasher, Brown 9, 11, 13, 32, **422–24**
   Sage **422**
Thrush, Bicknell's **410**
   Gray-cheeked 6, **409**, 410
   Hermit 6, **411–12**
   Swainson's 6, **410–11**
   Varied **417**
   Wood 10, 11, 14, 32, **412–14**, 538
Thryomanes bewickii 392
Thryothorus ludovicianus 9, 10, 32, **390–92**, 393,
      404
Titmouse, Tufted 10, 32, **383–84**, 431
Towhee, Eastern 9, 11, 13 14, 15, 32, **481–83**
   Green-tailed 481
Toxostoma rufum 9, 11, 13, 32, **422–24**
Tringa flavipes 7, 11, 41, **222**
   melanoleuca 7, **221**, 222
   solitaria 7, **223**

Troglodytes aedon 10, 11, 372, 373, **393–94**, 460
   troglodytes 6, **395**
Tryngites subruficollis 247
Turdus migratorius 10, 14, 23, 32, **415–16,** 421
   pilaris 414
Turkey, Wild 11, 12, 13, 22, 34, 185, **190–91**
Turnstone, Ruddy 6, 23, 134, 233, 234, **236**
Turtle-Dove, Ringed **288**
Tympanuchus cupido 22, 35, **189–90**
Tyrannus dominicensis 348
   forficatus 348
   savana 349
   tyrannus 5, 11, 32, **346–48**
   verticalis 346
Tyto alba 10, 11, 13, **296–97**

Uria aalge 52, **284**
   lomvia 52, **284**, 285

Vanellus vanellus **208**, [Addendum]
Veery 6, 10, 13, 36, **407–086**
Vermivora celata **435**, [Addendum]
   chrysoptera 434
   peregrina 10, 356, **435**
   pinus 13, 36, **433–34**
   ruficapilla 6, **436**
Vireo flavifrons 6, 13, **353–54**
   gilvus 6, 11, **355–56**
   griseus 9, 11, 32, **351–53**
   olivaceus 10, 13, 32, 353, **357–59**, 538
   philadelphicus 10, **357**
   solitarius 10, **355**
Vireo, Blue-headed 10, **355**
   Philadelphia 10, **357**
   Red-eyed 10, 13, 32, 353, **357–59**, 538
   Warbling 6, 11, **355–56**
   White-eyed 9, 11, 32, **351–53**
   Yellow-throated 6, 13, **353–54**
Vulture, Black 11, 13, 35, **91–92**, 94, 162
   Turkey 11, 22, 28, 92, **93–94**, 162–65

Warbler, Audubon's 444
   Bay-breasted 10, **452**
   Black-and-white 10, 13, 15, **454–56**
   Black-throated Blue 10, **443**
   Black-throated Gray **444**
   Black-throated Green 10, **444–45**
   Blackburnian 10, 41, **445**
   Blackpoll 10, **452**
   Blue-winged 13, 36, **433–34**
   "Brewster's" 434
   Canada 6, 11, **475**
   Cape May 10, **442**
   Cerulean 6, 12, 15, 36, 42, **453–54**
   Chestnut-sided 12, 36, **440–41**
   Connecticut 6, **469**, 470
   Golden-winged 434
   Hermit **445**
   Hooded 10, 12, 36, **473–74**
   Kentucky 6, 10, **467–69**
   "Lawrence's" 434
   Magnolia **441–42**
   Mourning **470**
   Nashville 6, **436**
   Orange-crowned **435**, [Addendum]
   Palm 11, **451**
   Pine 10, **447–49**, 461
   Prairie 10, 14, **449–51**, 477, 488
   Prothonotary 6, 23, **458–60**
   Swainson's 12, 19, 35, **462**
   Tennessee 10, 356, **435**
   Wilson's **474**
   Worm-eating 10, **460–62**
   Yellow 6, 14, 134, 338, **438–39**
   Yellow-rumped 6, 9, 200, 439, **443–44**, 447
   Yellow-throated 6, 12, **446–47**
Waterthrush, Louisiana 6, **466–67**
   Northern **465**
Waxwing, Bohemian **428**
   Cedar 9, 10, 30, **429–30**
Wheatear, Northern **404**

Whimbrel 6, 22, **229–30**
Whip-poor-will 6, 10, 13, 15, 23, 310, **311–12**
Whistling-Duck, Fulvous **95**
Wigeon, American 12, 13, 22, 34, 35, **116–18**
   Eurasian 116
Willet 5, 6, 13, 22, 32, 35, 135, **223–25**, 257
Wilsonia canadensis 6, 11, **475**
   citrina 10, 12, 36, **473–74**
   pusilla 474
Wood-Pewee, Eastern 10, 11, 13, 32, **332–34**
Woodcock, American 6, 9, 13, 16, 23, 35, **250–52**
Woodpecker, Black-backed **328**
   Downy 10, 32, **323–25**, 326
   Hairy 10, 323, **325–27**, 431
   Pileated 10, 13, 36, **330–31**, 431
   Red-bellied 10, 13, 32, 36, 40, 319, **320–22**, 324, 325
   Red-cockaded 35, **327**
   Red-headed 10, 15, 23, 35, **319–20**, 324
   Three-toed **327–28**
Wren, Bewick's 392
   Carolina 9, 10, 32, **390–92**, 393, 404
   House 10, 11, 372, 373, **393–94**, 460
   Marsh 6, 397, **398–400**
   Sedge 5, 12, 16, 36, 135, **396–97**
   Winter 6, **395**

Xanthocephalus xanthocephalus 11, **530**
Xema sabini 268

Yellowlegs, Greater 7, **221**, 222
   Lesser 7, 11, 41, **222**
Yellowthroat, Common 6, 32, 134, **470–72**

Zenaida macroura 10, 15, 22, 32, 35, **288–90**, 538
Zonotrichia albicollis 11, **508–09**
   leucophrys 11, **510–11**
   querula 509–10